Anacalypsis
VOL 2

By: Godfrey Higgins

ISBN: 978-1-63923-082-2

All Rights reserved. No part of this book maybe reproduced without written permission from the publishers, except by a reviewer who may quote brief passages in a review to be printed in a newspaper or magazine.

Printed August, 2021

Cover Art By: Paul Amid

Published and Distributed By:

Lushena Books

607 Country Club Drive, Unit E

Bensenville, IL 60106

www.lushenabks.com

ISBN: 978-1-63923-082-2

PREFACE.

THE *first* volume of this work was finished in June, 1833, although the Title, for the sake of uniformity, bears the date of 1836. The *second* volume was commenced; and it was the Author's intention to have proceeded to its completion. But, having attended *The British Association for the Advancement of Science*, held that year at Cambridge, he wrote thence to his printer, stating, that he was labouring under severe bodily affliction; that he should endeavour to reach home as speedily as possible; and adding, as it were prophetically, that he should *never leave it again, till he was conveyed to* his *grave*. So deeply interested, however, did Mr. Higgins feel in the completion of his work, that he wrote frequently—alternately expressing hope and doubt of his recovery. Having made what he deemed necessary arrangements for placing the manuscript in the hands of his appointed editor, he continued to devote his attention to it, till a few days previous to his decease. This occurred on the 9th of August, 1833.

After Mr. Higgins's interment, his only Son and Executor wrote to say he was directed to forward the copy, that the printing might be proceeded with, and expressing his desire to carry his Father's wishes fully into effect. Here it may suitably be stated, that, at the sole expense of Godfrey Higgins, his son, this posthumous volume of the Author's is published.

The Friends and the Literary and Scientific Associates of the Author may have felt surprised that this publication has been so long delayed. The delay has been unavoidable: for, although Mr. Higgins had made preparations for the progress of the work, had his life been spared, yet when the manuscript was placed in the hands of another, many parts of it appeared to require curtailment, or omission, to avoid repetitions. The doubts of the Editor might have been removed immediately had he been able to submit them to the Author.—As numerous quotations had been made, it was necessary for the Editor frequently to go to the British Museum to collate them with the originals. His distance from the Museum, the number of books often required for a single sheet, and the time unavoidably consumed in finding them, sometimes occupied the greater part of a day, without the object being fully accomplished; for it sometimes happened, that quotations had been made from works which could not be found even in that great establishment: and, at certain periods of each month, the Editor's attention was fully occupied by the incidental duties of his profession. During those periods, the work was delayed, as no part of the manuscript was placed in the hands of the compositor till it had been carefully examined, in order to supply references to the *first* volume, or to preceding sheets of the *second*—some of which had not been, and many of which could not be, supplied by the Author. Delays have also occasionally arisen from the Editor's inability to attend to the work in consequence of indisposition. Suffice it to say, that the publication of the volume has not been retarded by Mr. Higgins, who has uniformly evinced an anxiety to see his Father's wishes realized.

In supplying references to the *first* volume, it was sometimes found, that the Index, though copious, was not so specific as was desirable, as subjects alluded to under a given name, could be found only by referring to many pages appended to that name. To obviate this inconvenience, a more detailed Index is given with this volume; and it is hoped, that nearly every subject or opinion contained in it may be found by seeking it under its appropriate head.

The reader may possibly feel somewhat disappointed, if he peruse the entire volume carefully, that the promise made (in p. 145) by the Author, that he would "exhibit, in a future book, the Christianity of Jesus Christ, from his own mouth," has not been fulfilled so amply as he anticipated. The probability is, that had the Author's life been spared, he would have left no pledge unredeemed. He may, however, have thought, that what is contained in the concluding page was sufficient. At all events, neither the Author's Son nor the Editor felt justified in attempting to supply what may, perhaps, be regarded as an omission. They esteemed it their duty to allow the Author alone to speak for himself. His views respecting Jesus Christ and his religion are stated explicitly in various parts of the volume. These views will doubtless excite astonishment in some, and displeasure in those who, while they deny *infallibility* to the Pope, write, and speak, and act, as if they possessed that attribute. To the honest and intelligent inquirer after truth, there can be nothing really offensive in the statement of opinions directly opposed to his own, if those opinions are honestly propounded. If the Author's statements respecting many of the rites and doctrines of the endowed and unendowed sects of Christendom can be shewn to be groundless, numerous advocates of those rites and doctrines will, without doubt, speedily appear in their defence. Truth can lose nothing by fair discussion.

The Author having given, in the Preface to the first volume, what he designates a Portrait of himself, it is deemed unnecessary to enter into any further particulars. The following obituary notice may, however, appropriately be added, as an unbiassed testimony to the Author's worth, and as expressive of the opinion entertained of him by his fellow-countrymen in the neighbourhood of his residence.

" Friday morning, August 16, 1833, the late Mr. Higgins.—It has been our painful
" duty to announce, in our obituary of this week, the death of a much esteemed and re-
" spected gentleman, Godfrey Higgins, Esq., of Skellow Grange. As journalists, we
" feel that Mr. Higgins has long occupied too large a space in the public eye to be per-
" mitted to slide silently into the grave; while we are, at the same time, conscious of
" our inability to do justice to the claims of the neighbour we have lost. Mr. Higgins
" was, in early life, an assiduous and able magistrate; quick to discover the right, and
" firm and fearless to promote and to maintain it; and his indefatigable exertions in the
" detection and correction of the great abuses then existing in the management of the
" York Lunatic Asylum, and the formation of another and very extensive establishment
" for the care and protection of pauper lunatics at Wakefield, will be monuments of his
" public spirit, and perseverance, and philanthropy, which many, once visited by the
" privation of human reason (that severest of human afflictions,) will have reason to be
" grateful for long after the present generation shall have passed away. Retiring from
" a regular attention to magisterial duty, Mr. Higgins, for some years preceding his
" death, had devoted a considerable portion of his leisure to antiquarian research—
" travelling much in the pursuit and cultivation of his favourite study; and publishing
" from time to time, his discoveries and constructions in works interesting to the man
" of science, and of value to the public; while, as a moral and political writer, his pro-
" ductions were numerous and important; possessing much of originality and inde-
" pendent feeling, and always having the increasing happiness and improved condition
" of his fellow-creatures for their object. Being accustomed to think for himself—
" (taking what he considered reason and good sense, more than the rules of the schools,
" for his guide)—and to write and to speak what he thought, his sentiments and opi-
" nions have by many been admired and adopted; whilst by others—perhaps less candid
" and liberal than he was—they have been impugned and assailed with acrimony. Yet
" were their motives never called in question. They were admitted by all to have their
" fountain in a manly, honest heart; nor could they fail to be acceptable in the sight of
" that Being whose eye expands itself over all the thoughts and transactions of man-
" kind; and appreciates, and registers, and will reward them, not according to conse-
" quence, but intention. Be the sentiments and opinions we allude to founded in truth
" or in error, they at least united in the instance before us, to form the honourable, the
" punctual, the hospitable, the cheerful, and kind-hearted gentleman; and it will be
" long, very long, ere it can be the province of the *Doncaster Gazette* to report the
" decease of a neighbour more deservedly and deeply respected and regretted."

ADVERTISEMENT.

The Author lived to revise only the first *four* sheets of this volume. Apprehending that his life was drawing to a close, he wrote to his printer, expressing a wish that he would edit the remainder of the work. From so responsible an office the printer would have shrunk, had not the Author informed him that the manuscript was so far arranged, that, with proper attention, he would be able to complete the volume. Whether Mr. Higgins's confidence was well-founded, must be left to the judgment of the reader.

Two injunctions were laid on the appointed Editor,—that he should *not* send out the proof sheets to any literary friend; and that, in any instance of a difference of opinion, he should append *Editor* to the note. The *first* injunction is respectfully urged on the kind and candid consideration of the reader, in excuse for the *errata*, which, it is lamented, are numerous. On the *second* injunction, the Editor begs to remark, that he has scrupulously endeavoured to leave every opinion of the Author's as he found it; and that, sustaining the twofold office of Printer and Editor, he has reluctantly expressed any dissent from the views of the Author. One note, especially, the Editor wishes he had not inserted—that in p. 122, as it was written in ignorance of the Author's opinion, subsequently expressed (pp. 131, 132), respecting the book of The Acts. It will be obvious from other notes, that the Editor views the character and doctrines of Paul in a different light from that in which the Author regarded them. It will, therefore, it is hoped, not offend or shock the philosophical reader, when he finds it added, that the Editor avows his firm conviction of the divine mission, the death (by crucifixion), the resurrection, and the ascension to a state of immortality, of JESUS *of Nazareth.*

The respected Author, could he speak from the grave, would not, the Editor is confident, disapprove of this frank and conscientious avowal. Mr. Higgins was, indeed, as he claimed to be considered, *a philalethean*; and he was too liberal and too generous to deny to his Editor the right of expressing his love of that which *he* regards as *the truth*. By the great majority of Christians the Author's opinions will doubtless be considered as very remote from "the truth as it is in *Jesus*;" but when HE shall return to judge the word in righteousness (an event which the Editor gratefully anticipates), HE will determine who most inadequately appreciated his nature and office—those who believed him *a good man*, but not a divinely commissioned prophet; or those who endeavoured to invest him with the attributes, and to place him on the throne, of his eternal and ever-merciful FATHER.

THE EDITOR.

Homerton, June 4, 1836.

CONTENTS.

ANACALYPSIS.

BOOK I. CHAPTER I.
Page
SACA.—Saxons 1

CHAPTER II.
Georgius.—Scala 5

CHAPTER III.
Judæan Mythos in Egypt.—Menes. Noah.—Ceres.—Abraham Tulis.—Joseph.—Grecian History a Travesty.—Language of Egypt.—Deisul Voyage of Salvation 10

CHAPTER IV.
Lord Kingsborough on Mexico.—Malcolme.—Mexican Mythos the same as that of the Old World.—Humboldt and Spineto.—Chronology and Cyclic Periods.—Towers of Mexico and Babel.—Jewish Language and Mexican Rites.—Cross and Crucifixes.—Immaculate Conception. Female Principle.—Humboldt.—Bochica, Peruvian Rites, &c.—The Ass and Horse. Races of Men.—China. Tibet. Spanish Policy.—Laws of the Mexicans.—Easter Island.—Last Avatar expected.—Tod on Tibet. Island sunk. Jewish Mythos.—General Observations 21

BOOK II. CHAPTER I.
Christian Religion not New.—The Carmelites Pythagoreans.—Pontifex Maximus.—Seven Sacraments. Eucharist.—Baptism.—Christening.—Confirmation.—Baptism of Bells.—Ordination.—Marriage.—Extreme Unction—Purgatory.—Auricular Confession 42

CHAPTER II.
Revenues.—Monks and Nuns.—Mitre.—Zone.—Cassock—Praying Standing.—White Surplice Tithes paid. Tonsure practised. Crosier, &c.—Candles, Incense.—Processions. Images. St. Abraham.—Festivals.—Epiphany. St. Denis, &c.—Bambino at Rome. Dedicating Churches, &c., &c.—Bulla. Agnus Dei. Angels. Dæmons.—Sunday, Dies Solis. Various Customs 76

CHAPTER III.
Bethlehem, Birth of Jesus Christ.—Birth, Death, and Resurrection of all the Gods.—Passover.—Lamb of God.—Gentile Crucifixion.—Jesus Christ was not Crucified.—Jewish Incarnation.—Pythagoras.—Observations - 95

BOOK III. CHAPTER I.
LETTERS.

Origin of Letters.—Moon's Period.—Names of Letters.—Boucher.—Dr. Wait on Sanscrit.—Cycle of Fourteen.—Thoth.—Om. Homer.—Targums.—Dr. Young. Sol.—Joseph, Proteus. Stalls.—Solomon. Sindi. Peter.—Cryptography, Indian.—Vowel Points.—Acrostic. Anagram.—Metathesis. The Number Nine.—Arabic Letters.—The God Xangti.—'Εις, μιᾶ, ἓν.—Signets.—Sigma Tau.—Adam. Genesis 147

CHAPTER II.

Dis Mariebus.—Systems of Letters.—Last Avatars. Mohamed, &c.—Names of the Gods of the Week.—Chinese Writing.—Abacus and Nabathean Alphabet.—Java.—Northmore's System.—Von Hammer's Book. Saxons.—Bacchus. Janus. Ogham.—Rhyme. Bards. Fates. Veds.—Chinese.—Immaculate Conception of Saca.—Pallium.—Apocrypha.—Deisul.—Hammer's Arabic Book — — — — — — — — — 203

CHAPTER III.

Roma. Flora. Pushto.—Allegory of the Flower continued.—General Observations.—Allegories.—Allegories continued.—Retrospect — — — — — — — — — — — — — — — 238

BOOK IV.

FEODAL OR FEUDAL TENURE.

Universal Pontifical Government.—Religion of Tibet.—Chartres' Stone.—The Linga.—Island of Iona.—Feodal or Feudal Tenure.—Gavel-kind.—Frank-al-Moign.— Lands in Demesne.— Burgage Tenure. — Tenure by Knights' Service.—Origin of Monks and Nuns.—Land Tax of India.—The Scythians.—The Arabians.—Mythic Divisions of Countries, with their Officers.—Trade, Craft, Ras or Caste.—Cathedrals, &c., were Druidical, then Roman, Temples.—Inga Lands.—Allodial Lands.—History of the Island of Ii, or Iona, or Icolmkill.—Ceylon.—Cal.—Vitrified Forts of Scotland.—Mystery, Wittenagemote.—The Scandinavians.—German Rosicrucians.—Di-Om, D'Om, Domus, Om.—Ceres, Bethlehem.—Chivalry.—Sea Kings, Runes.—Golden Age — 254

BOOK V. CHAPTER I.

Object of the Mythos.—Book of Enoch on the Earth's Axis.—Noah and Ships of the Ancients.—Cause and Extent of the Flood.—Change of the Earth's Axis.—Flood of Ogyges.—Inachus.—Comets held to be Planets.—Seven-Day Cycle and Length of Year.—Whiston on Year of 360 Days.—Whiston on Length of Antediluvian Year.—Whiston on Comet of 1680.—Comet of 575½ Years' Period the Cause of the Flood.—Periods of Comets.—Encke's Comet.—Drs. Gregory and Halley on Whiston's Theory.—Dr. Keill on Whiston's Theory.—Comet of 575½ Years continued.—M. Arago on Comets.—Lexel's Comet.—Genesis, in Substance, found in many Countries.—Agency of Comets.—Digression on Gas, Spirit, Inspiration, the Soul.—Comet and Flood resumed.—The World's History renewed.—Early History a Mythos.—Barasit and Mercavah — — — 309

CHAPTER II.

Cæsar.—Alexander.—Gengis Khan.—Akbar.—Napoleon.—Supreme Pontiff.—Races of Man. Black Gods.—Trinitarian Doctrine of Genesis. Jewish Polity. Priesthood.—Supreme Priesthood — — — — 343

CHAPTER III.

Niebuhr on Pontifical Government in Italy.—Patriarchal Government in China.—Mohamed.—Pontifical Government.—The Assassins.—Niebuhr on Landed Tenures renewed.—Confederated States under Pontifical Government. Letters and Population — — — — — — — — — — — — 371

CHAPTER IV.

Microcosm.—Atoms.—Chinese Microcosm.—The World, &c., divided into Three.—Sacred Numbers.—Mercavah and Caaba.—Measures of the Ancients.—Etruscan Agrimensores. Templum. Mount Gargarus. Cor. Cardo. Agrimensores. Termini.— The Britons. — The Saxons.—Tithes resumed. —The Athenians.—Division into Castes, into Three, &c.—Archierarch, Sanhedrim, Amphictyons.—Religious Dances. Poetry. Music — 397

CHAPTER V.

Microcosm continued. Vedanta and Nyaya Philosophy or Doctrines.—Nature of the Microcosm.—Pythagoras on Numbers. Cycles.—Mythology. Patron and Client. Colonies. Isopolity. Numa Pompilius.—Symbolic and Alphabetic Writing.—Adoration of Animals. The Onion. Crest.—The Ancile of Numa. Cyclic Mythos. Clemens Alexandrinus. Ancient Mysteries. Baptism, the Eucharist, &c. Doctrine of the Ancient and Modern Χρσ.—Bailly, Buffon, &c., on Birth-place of Mankind. Former Heat at the Poles. The Mythic-Cyclic-Microsmic System. What has happened may happen again. Illusion — — — — — — — 427

CONCLUSION — — — — — — — — — — — — — — — — — — 446

(xi)

ERRATA et CORRIGENDA.

Page 3, line 1, for 'Scythim,' read *Scythæ*.
    line 3, for 'que,' read *quæ*.
    line 24, for 'la même,' read *le même*.
    line 25, for 'ils en suivra,' read *il s'en suivra*.
    line 26, between 'n'ont eu' and 'la philosophie,' insert *pour*.
    line 29, for 'sufferait,' read *suffirait*.
65, line 24, for 'sacres,' read *sacrées*.
75, line 29, for 'accurrit,' read *occurrit*.
102, line 22, for 'Zelmissus,' read *Telmissus*.
107, line 22, for 'deficire,' read *deficere*.
108, line 25, for 'religione,' read *religioni*.
109, line 4 from the bottom, for 'grounds,' read *crowns*.
122, omit Editor's note, and see bottom of p. 131 and top of p. 132, for the Author's opinion of the *The Acts*, and reference to Evanson's *Dissonance*.
127, line 5, for 'constantialia,' read *substantialia*.
135, line 8, dele 'the,' before holy Call.
136, line 8, for 'κυκλοντς,' read *κυκλωντες*.
138, lines 8, 9, for '5 × 10 = 60, and 60 × 10 = 360,' read 5 × 12 = 60, and 60 × 5 = 300.
144, line 13, for 'accomd,' read *second*.
164, line 14, insert *ce* between 'C'est que.'
169, line 33, for 'Fostia,' read *Fortia*.
170, lines 10, 11, for 'Αυκυρδη and ΓΑΡΨΑΣ,' read Αυκυρδε and ΓΡΑΨΑΣ.
172, line 29, for 'Pope,' read *Pape*.
    line 32, for 'veillés' and 'rassemble,' read *veilléss* and *rassemble*.
196, line 3 of note, for 'Fostia,' read *Fortia*.
220, line 11, for 'had been,' read *has been*.
259, line 32, for 'des ses,' read *de ses*.
    line 7 from bottom, for 'imprembrent,' read *imprimèrent*.
273, line 8, for 'Sotland,' read *Scotland*.
277, line 18, for 'in preces,' read *in pieces*.
287, line 31, for 'which resc.' read *which rose*.
301, line 18, for 'coavert,' read *convent*.
309, line 7 of contents, for 'Lexall's,' read *Lexel's*.
309, lines 2 and 3, } for 'Floods of Ogyges and Inachus, read *Flood of Ogyges. Inachus.*
314, line 1,
311, line 5 from the bottom, for 'sains,' read *signs*.
333, line 37, for '2920,' read 2926.
336, line 23, for 'coporeal,' read *corporeal*.
345, lines 5 and 4 from the bottom, for 'Rammensium' and 'Rammenses,' read *Ramnensium* and *Ramnenses*.
350, line 24, for 'crées,' read *créées*.
352, first note, for 'Axsiat.' read *Asiat*.
366, last line, for 'henious,' read *heinous*.
371, in note 4, for '2 Kings xxiii., &c., &c.,' read 2 *Kings xxiii. 6, &c.*
372, line 6 of note 2, for 'de Saques,' read *des Saques*.
385, line 7, for 'de saintes' read *des saintes*.
386, line 4 from the bottom, for 'Egypté,' read *Egypte*.
391, line 3, for 'passé, read *passée*.
400, line 21, for 'three son,' read *three sons*.
406, line 4, for 'furnish,' read *furnishes*.
411, line 38, for 'Godyean,' read *Gordyean*.
426, line 25, for 'corda,' read *cordes*.
437, last line of text, for 'οψις,' read *οψ*.

ANACALYPSIS.

BOOK I.

CHAPTER I.

SACÆ.—SAXONS.

I SHALL in this Chapter submit to my reader some observations relating to the ancient Sacæ of Tartary or North India. These observations will be of importance in the discussion of the Origin of Letters, which will be contained in a future Book; and also of the first importance in the two following Books, the object of which will be to shew, that a real, not a poetical, age of gold—an age of learning, peace, and civilization—once existed; and that this was under the rule of a sacerdotal caste or order which governed the whole world, and which originated the feudal system. I shall also shew, that all the sacred numbers and cycles were intimately connected with, and indeed partly arose out of, a microcosmic theory, named by Plato in his Timæus, which was a part of the secret doctrine of Genesis; and the whole of this I shall also shew was intimately connected with the feudal system. I fear the extracts from Georgius will be found by many of my readers tedious; but as proofs of my system, from an unwilling witness, they are of the first importance, and cannot be dispensed with.

We have seen, (Vol. I. p. 153,) that one of the most common names of Buddha was Sacya (the name of the Lama of Tibet) and Saca, and Saca-sa. From this name of Buddha it was that the tribes who inhabited an extensive country east of the Caspian Sea and north of Tibet, were called Sacæ. (Vide Ptolemy.) This was the hive whose castes are yet found in the West, called Saxons, having, as Dr. Geddes says, the Hebrew language.[1] They were the Belgic Suessones of Gaul;

---

[1] From Dr. Wait I learn that there are an IMMENSE number of Chaldee roots to be found in the Sanscrit lists of Dhatoos. (See Class. Journal, Vol. XVI. p 213.) These Chaldee roots are Hebrew roots also, and are, I have no doubt, in a very considerable degree, the origin or base whereon the Sanscrit was built. We shall see in a future Book that they were of the old Tamul language, or at least the vernacular tongue of great numbers of people occupying the country of the Tamuls at this day, and are called by them Pushto, the same as the language of Western Syria: indeed, a close attention to what has been said in Vol. I. Book X. respecting St. Thomas and the Tamuls, must have shewn a high probability of this already. But I shall return to this in my book on the Origin of Letters.

The Sanscrit Dhatoos are *data*—things given or granted or assumed, on which other things are built—the roots of the language. The word is what I call Sanscrit Latin.

one of their capitals was Soissons:[1] they were called Sausen by the Welsh, Sacon by the Scotch, and Sasenach or Saxsenach by the Irish. They are the people said by Herodotus to be the same as the Scythians.[2]

Dr. Scheller maintains the whole of Europe to have been occupied by the Saxons before the arrival of the Celts.[3] But they were, in fact, both tribes of the same people. Scythians, Celts, Saxons, were successive castes or swarms from the same hive. If there were any difference, it was merely in the time of their arrival in the West. But it is probable that they were only different names for the same people; as the Britons are called English, Scotch, Welsh, Albanians, Caledonians, Cambrians, &c. The difference in their dialects is only what would naturally arise in unwritten languages, in the space of four or five hundred years.

They were castes or swarms sent out in succession, from a great and excessively populous hive in Tartary or North India—the country of the thousand cities of Strabo. They were exactly like the tribes sent out from Britain in modern times—at one time to America, at another time to Africa, at another time to Australia. They were the subjects of the only civilized nation on the earth. They took with them every where their manners, government, language, religion, and allegiance to their supreme head, as our colonies all retain their allegiance to the mother country. They at first nowhere found any of their own high caste, none in fact but such persons as we found in America—Aborigines, as we call them. They met with no resistance; but, by degrees, as the world became peopled with the successors of previous tribes of their own countrymen, and land scarce, wars for possession began to arise. This I shall discuss, however, in my next Book.

The word Saca is the same as the Hebrew word שכה *ske*, imagiuari, and scio, *to contemplate*,[4] and the Greek γινωσκω—in short, *mind*, constantly confounded with wisdom. The Sciakam of Georgius is probably Sa-ca-akim. The root is שכ *sk*, whence came שכל *skl*, wisdom,[5] and our skill. Saca is sax; and sakl or skl, or skill or cunning or knowledge or *scientia* or wisdom, in any art, is X or Xaca, KL, which means the cal or wisdom of X; and KL is X=600, L=50,=650: and the KL-di is the origin, in its most remote degree, of the Calidei or Chaldeans. I promised this explanation in Book XI. Chap. I. Sect. 1; Callidè (wisely), cunning, king, incarnation of wisdom or cunning. The origin of the root sk and kl, I shall shew when I treat of the Origin of Letters. I have no doubt that this root is, in fact, the same as the שג *sg*, whence come שגה *sgh* and the Latin *sagio*,[6] and saga *a witch*, and sagacitas, præsagio—English, sage, sagacious, presage;[7] and the Roman officer called *sagart*, who was the sacrificer, and the Hebrew *sagan*, the assistant or adviser of the high priest. From this came the word שלט *slt*, Scalit, the name given to Joseph in Egypt, and the meaning of which, I apprehend, was *wise man*.[8] Joseph was called a saviour; and this word is the same as *salus, salutis*. (Vide Book X. Chap. V. Sect. 6.) The barbarian who marched from the North and plundered Jerusalem, was a Scythian, or Tat-ar or Tartar; he was called Shesach.[9] This is nothing but Saxon or Sasenach. Tat is a name of Buddha.

Mohamed was called a Saca or Saceswara, as well as a Vicramaditya. These are all merely descriptive epithets. And from the fact named above we find the reason why the Mohamedans spared the statues of Buddha in India. It strongly confirms the doctrine of the secret religion of the Mohamedans. Mohamed was thought to be a renewed incarnation of divine wisdom, and of course of Buddha, in his tenth avatar.

---

[1] Probably town of the *Saxones*, softened to Soissons.
[2] Foreign Quart. Rev., July 1831, p. 224; and Vallancey, Coll Hib. Vol. V. pp. 12, 23, 34, 49, 181, 182.
[4] Parkhurst, p. 733; vide Littleton's Dict.
[5] See Cicero, de Divinat. Lib i. Cap. xxxi.
[6] Vide Guerin de Rocher, Vol. I. p. 119.
[3] Guerin de Rocher, Vol. I. p. 152.
[8] Parkhurst, p. 734.
[7] Vide Parkhurst in voce.
[9] Shishak, 2 Chron. xii. 7—9.

Abrah. Ortelius en ses Synonymes et Thrésors Géographiques Scythiæ, a Persis Sagæ, ut Mela habet, vel Acæ ut Plinius, Solinus, et Eustathius scribunt Scythia Saga est in originibus Catonis, quæ circumferuntur.¹

In the time of the Pharaohs the Egyptians had a class of persons called Sages or *wise men*.²

Considering that Saca means Buddha the God of Wisdom, I cannot much doubt that the Irish Sagan, a priest, the Scandanavian Saga, the Hebrew סגן *sgn*, *noble* or *great man*, are all the same. "The heathen Irish had their Sagan, like the Tyrians and Chaldæans........Berosus gives the "epithet of Sagan Ogygisan to Noah. The Sagan Cohenia was the Aristites Sacerdotum, i. e. "primarius Sacerdotum post summum.³ Sagan Babyloniorum sive Chaldæorum vox, a quibus "ad Hebræos transivit."⁴ The Cohenia is the Hebrew word for a priest—a Cohen; and it is not unlikely that the Chaons, who are said by the Indians and Persians to have erected the Druidical circles, had their names from this word. I think it probable, also, that the Cohen had a near relation to the *Kan*.

Vallancey says, from some author whose name he does not give, but I suspect from Georgius, " In Indiis Xacæ religio per omnes fere earum regionum populos latissimè funditur : tempus quo " Xaca vixerit, incertum est, plures sunt ex Europæis scriptoribus, qui floruisse velint Salomone " in Judæa regnante : non idem est et Xaca novus, i. e. Apollonius Tyaneus, qui floruit A. D. 60. " (T. 161.) Xacam eundem esse ac Buddum, La Crosius aliique non dubitant Xacæ nominis " origo à *Saca* Babiloniorum et Persarum numine repetendo. Tibetanorum litera scribitur " Sachia, quod idem est cum Sechia Sinensium (T. 21). Les Japonois se disent originaire du pais, " ou il est adoré sous le nom de Budhu, et de Sommona-cadam."⁵ Bailly, p. 200, says, " Le " Xaca des Japonais, le Sommona-chutana, du Pegu, le Sommona-kodam de Siam, le Butta des " Indiens, ne sont qu'un seul et même personage, regardé ici comme un Dieu, là comme un " législateur—si j'ai bien prouvé que Butta, Thoth et Mercure ne sont également que la même " inventeur des sciences et des arts : ils en suivra que toutes les nations de l'Asie, anciennes et " modernes, n'ont eu la philosophie et pour la religion, qu'un seul et même législateur placé à leur " origine. Alors je dirai que ce législateur unique n'a pu aller partout dans l'Asie, ni en même " tems parceque, sans doute, il n'avait pas d'ailes : ni successivement parceque la vie d'un " homme ne sufferait pas aux voyages. L'existence de ce peuple antérieur est prouvée par le " tableau qui n'offre que des débris, astronomie obliée, philosophie mêlée à des absurdités, " physique dégénérée en fables, religion épurée, mais cachée sous un idolatrie grossière." From what my reader has seen in the tenth Book, I think he can have little or no doubt that the débris here alluded to, refers to the refined and beautiful system of Wisdom there developed.

There is scarcely a corner of the globe where the doctrines of Wisdom may not, as a mythos, be found. My learned friend Eusèbe de Salverte⁶ has clearly proved that, by the Sagas of the Scandinavians, the books of Wisdom are meant—the word Saga being the same as the French *sagesse* and the Latin *sagax*.

From the same author, p. 395, it appears that the Razanæ or Razanui can be nothing but children of Ras or Wisdom.⁷ Thus it is evident, that to speak of the Sacæ or Saxons was the same as to speak of the Buddhists. It was the general name, as we call many sects of Catholics

---

¹ Claude Duret, Hist. des Lang. p. 513. ² Abbé de Rocher, Vol. V. p. 173. ³ Jer. xx. 1.
⁴ Buxtorf; Vall. Coll. Hib.   ⁵ Vall. Coll. Hib. Vol. IV. Part I. p. 162.
⁶ Essai sur les Noms, Vol. II. pp. 373, 375, 381, 385.
⁷ In the list of names given in p. 408, most of them are in reality Hebrew; for instance, Aretia for *earth* is Arets, Arsa, the Sun, ארס *Ars*, &c.

or Protestants *Christians*. From this their sacred books were called Sacas or Sagas, as we call the books of the Indians Vedas or Bedas, or, in fact, Buddhas or books of wisdom. This all agrees very well with the learned language of Cashi-Mere or Cashmere having been Chaldee; and it accounts for Dr. Geddes' having found their language to be Hebrew. The Norwegian kings were called *Haquin*. This is but Hakim or הכם *hkm*; and the substitute for the Jewish high priest was a Sagan. Closely allied to these is the Hebrew root כשף *ksp* an enchanter.[1] כשף *ksp* is literally two words, and means שף *sp, wise*, and כ *k* as, that is, *as* a wise person. Refer to Vol. I. pp. 733, 734, to my explanation of Lokman.

Anciently all priests were physicians, and were called Hakim: (as physicians are yet called in the East:) but this word always conveyed with it a sacredness of character. This is all in keeping with their Gods—Odin, Woden, Thor; with the Budwas Trigeranos in Wales, and the Old Man Budda in Scotland; all these came with the first or the second tribe of Saxons to the north of Germany and to Britain.

Strabo says,[2] " ALL the tribes eastward of the Caspian Sea are called Scythic: the Dasæ next "the sea, and the Sacæ more eastward: but every tribe has *a particular name;* all are nomadic." It is inattention to this which causes all our confusion. We have here the Clans of Scotland, and the Tribes of Bedoween Arabs. The Sacæ, pronounced in Sanscrit like our Sak-hæ,[3] have made in Asia irruptions similar to those of the Cimmerians: thus they possessed themselves of Bactria, and the district of Armenia, called after them Sacasena. This word, I believe, is only Sacas-ana, *country of Sacas*. I have no doubt that when nomade tribes were driven out of the lands which they loosely settled, they passed, like the Israelites from Egypt, through countries occupied by other tribes, in search of new habitations, till they could go no farther; then a desperate struggle took place for the possession of the extreme country: thus Saxons arrived in Germany and Britain, from countries the most remote.

It appears from a note of Dr. Geddes's on the word *create* in the first verse of Genesis, to be seen in his Critical Remarks on that passage, that my view of this subject is supported by the book of Wisdom, Justin Martyr, and Origen. He also shews that a passage in the book of Maccabees, which has been supposed to oppose my doctrine, has been wrongly translated. He also shews that in the Scoto-Saxon dialect the word ברא *bra* still retains its original signification; and, in a note, he says, he hopes he shall one day be able to prove that almost all our genuine Saxon words are either Hebrew, Chaldee, Arabic, or Persic. I am very sorry the Doctor did not live to carry his intention into effect, which I am sure he could have done. I shall return to the Saxons again in a future Book, and give their history, which will be found to be of the very first importance.

---

[1] See Frey's Hebrew Lex.   [2] Lib. xi.   [3] Tod's Hist. Raj. 59.

CHAPTER II.

GEORGIUS.—SCALA.

1. In the extracts which I shall now give from Georgius will be found much useful information, which I think will not be thought long or unnecessary by those who read for information and not merely for amusement. The following passage justifies what I have said: " Gjam-phel sapiens " mirificus, quasi חכם (hkm), Syr. Kam, פלא (plaí) Peli, vel Giam פלא (pla) Pele, SAPIENTIÆ " miraculum, aut etiam Arcanum."[1] Here we have in the Gjam the Iao, the Wisdom, and the Pala, or the Pallium, or Pallas, or Minerva, all united. A little before he says, " A Syris, Chaldæis ea vox " Gnos derivari potuit. Syris enim Ganes idem est ac ostendit et demonstravit. Hinc Indorum " Ganessa SAPIENTIÆ Deus. In Sota vero, teste Castello גניסי gnisi, γνωσις, " notitia."[2] Again he says, " Profecto Gnios cum superaddito nota ܢ, quæ est indicium magni " alicujus arcani, eadem ipsa est Græca vox γνωσις, gnosis, agnitio."[3] IE, in Syriac Io, was the God of Wisdom or Knowledge. In Hebrew letters Io was written יו io; this, as the Hebrew letter o was corrupted into ng, was the origin of the gnios. The God of Wisdom was the spiritual fire. He was Agni. Write this in the Syriac or Pushto dialect, but the Chaldee letter, and we have יוא ioa, the last letter being emphatic, the Io.

Georgius says,[4] " Pho-tha Sinica voce dictus Budda." (This Pho-tha is evidently the Phtha or Thas of Egypt.[5]) " Jah, quod additur, JAO interpretor, magnum scilicet, et ineffabile illud Dei " nomen JEHOVA à Gnosticis et Basilidianis corruptum, et in Jao improbo ingenio mutatum. Si " cognita fuissent Tyrboni nomina magica, quæ Budda præceptor Manetis invocare solebat, inter " ea fortasse reperiretur JAO. Nam et apud Paganos nomen hoc Dei sanctissimum erat. Quod " quidem eruditis omnibus compertum est. Fewardentius et Galassius animadvers. in S. Irenæi " libros factum putant ex Hebr. יה Ja cum addito o, JAO. Samaritani, teste Theodoreto et adno- " tatore Grabio in eundem Irenæum, Jabe (here we have the Jave or Jove) illud appellasse dicun- " tur, Judæi vero Aīa Aja, quod est Hebraicè יה ie Jah, Tibeticè pariter Jah. In his igitur voci- " bus PHOTA-JAH, nominatus cernitur XACHA tamquam magnus ille Lhamarum, et Bonsiorum " DEUS BUDDA."[6] In the Aja here named may be the origin of the Aje-mere treated of in Vol. I. pp. 405, 407, 408, &c., and in the whole passage there is a confirmation of several other suggestions of mine in the former part of this work.

Georgius,[7] without having the slightest suspicion of the nature of my theory, states his opinion that the Kam-deva is derived from, or is the same as, the חכם hkm or wisdom of the Chaldee. It is very certain that, if my theory be right, every deity resolves into the Sun; each one of their names, either directly or indirectly, ought to have the meaning of wisdom.[8] Kam פלא pla, sapientia.

Was not Ερως often used as the name of Venus as well as Cupid? In like manner Kanyā, the name of Cristna, was also the name of the Zodiacal sign Virgo.[9] Ερως read anagrammatically is

---

[1] Georgius, Alph. Tib. p. 750. [2] P. 749. [3] P. 748. [4] P. 745.
[5] Vide p. 747. [6] Ibid. p. 746. [7] Ibid. III. p. 728.
[8] See also ibid. 750. [9] Bentley, p. 202.

nothing but *rose*, from which Jesus was called the Rose—the rose of Sharon—of Is-uren. And from this came the Rossi-crusians.

The Cabalistic Jews often insert the *jod* or prefix it to words, as they say, for the sake of a mystery; but in reality for the same reason that the Irish Bishop writes his name X Doyle. This practice admitted, I believe that C-ama was both Cupid and Venus, Cama and Cama-deva, כמה *kme*, desiderare, amare,[1] and was in fact C or X-ama. See pp. 760, 761, and Appendix to the first volume. Cuma was the same, as was also Kumari or Komari on Cape Comarin, near which ruled the Xamorin or Zamorin, or Semiramis. Was Comarin the Coma-Marina? I believe that Cæsar was X-æsar—Tzar, whence the female Tzarina. I believe that ΠΧΘΥΣ, as I have formerly said (Vol. I. p. 636), is I-IXΘΥΣ: and that in like manner also Mama is M-ama; that Momptha is M-Omptha; that Mia is M-ia or M-ie. I is the tenth letter of the new alphabet, and M is the tenth letter of the sixteen-letter alphabet. Then י *i* in the Hebrew notation answers to the X in the Etruscan, Oscan, or Latin, which we have seen stands both for 10 and 600. This is like the Samech, which is the Mem final. As the Samech it is 60; as Mem final, 600. The Ξ called Xi, is 60, X *Chi*, 600. The Hebrew שש *ss* is six—Greek ΕΞ ·εξ six; the aspirant breathing, as in other cases,[2] being substituted for the sibillant letter, which, however, is found in the Latin, Saxon, and English, *six*.

Iodia is Ayoudia. I suspect that the Ad of Rajahpoutana and Western Syria, and Hadad, is Iad, or I-hadad; that IE is Io יי *io* of Syria; that God, Chod, is Od, Hod.[3] In all the cases above, the I, the X, and the M, are monograms prefixed for the sake of mystery, as we constantly see the X prefixed to sentences when not used as a letter, in our religious books of the middle ages; and as Romish priests still use it.

The Jod is a point, the Centre is a point, every thing tends to the Centre.

The word Saca. I believe is found in the Hindoo word *Para-sachti*. The Tibetian language has no B. Para is ברא *bra*, creator. *Sach* is, in the Egyptian language, *flamma*, and Ti is Di, *sacred, holy.* Georgius[4] says, Para-sachti is " excellentissima virtus, &c., primam emanationem " Dei; Flammam fluentem a Deo." But I do not doubt that it was also *akme* or *hkm*. In fine, it is *divine* WISDOM.[5]

Parasakti, Adisakti, Devaki, and Parakta, have all the same meaning. Para or Ad, and Devaki, mean the Deity, and sakti *a flame*.[6] These are also the same as Bayani and Mama-ja. Sometimes Parasakti is masculine, sometimes feminine. Sakti is also the same as *verbum* and *sapientia*.[7] Chati, I am persuaded, is the same as Sacti, and is the Hebrew חתה *hte*, and in English means *heat*. Substituting, as Parkhurst says was very common in the Hebrew, the ש *s*, the sibillant letter for the aspirate ה *h*, the word would become sati. I am quite satisfied we have here, or in the word just now named, Sci-akham, the meaning of the Saca or Xaca, and that it means the Logos, the Sapientia, the Ras.

Parasakti, like Semele, the mother of Bacchus, was combustam in æthereo igne.[8] She was consumed in the flames of her son. This is the assumption of the blessed virgin, which took place in the autumn, when the constellation of Virgo disappears, and is rendered invisible by the solar rays.[9] But Para-sacti was Lachmi, and Lachmi was nothing but L'hkm, *the wise*.

" Ex his, quæ mecum inter viam communicarunt laudati PP. Cappucini e Tibetanis Missioni-" bus reduces, protinus intellexi tam arcto et inseparabili vinculo apud eas gentes duo hæc, *litteras*

---

[1] Georg p. 728.   [2] Parkhurst, p. 776.
[3] But Georgius (Alp. Tib. p. 685) has shewn, Ad or Adad or Hadad, in Syria, to be Buddha.
[4] P. 97.   [5] Ib. p. 98.   [6] Ib.   [7] Ib.   [8] Ib. p. 102.   [9] Vide Dupuis.

" et *superstitionem,* inter se cohærescere, ut alterum sine altero nec pertractari, nec cogitari
" queat. Ut enim video, quem admodum defluunt radii à natura solis, sic litteras ab ipsa Dei
" substantia defluxisse concipiunt. Simile quiddam de Vedam Brambœ, deque *Atzala Isureni*
" libro, opinantur Indi."[1] The truth of the observation respecting the close connexion between
letters and superstition cannot be denied, and thus this beautiful invention, which ought to have
been the greatest blessing to mankind, has been, till lately, its greatest curse. But if at first it
forged the chain, it will break it at last.

On the Tibetian alphabet Georgius says, " Aliud quid longe majus atque præstantius de litte-
" rarum suarum natura, ac dignitate Tibetani opinantur. Istas uti prodigiosa quædam munera e
" cœlo demissa venerantur: Deoque *Sapientiæ Giam-Jang* tanquam auctori, et artifici principi
" referunt acceptas." When I consider the *Deoque Sapientiæ,* the name of the country Áchim,
the Pushto in North and South India, the evident Judæan mythos in both, I cannot help suspecting that the Deus Giam-Jang is the God or Iao of Siam or Sion, in the country of Judia, adjoining
to the present Nepaul and Tibet. The close connexion between letters and superstition, noticed
by Georgius, tends materially to support my opinion, that letters were at first mythical and magical, and we know that they were every where supposed to emanate from the Deity. Georgius
explains the word Tangut to mean *Dominus Cœli* et Terræ. If the *T* be a nominal prefix, the
a=א, ng=ע, u=ו, thus *Aou*. Tangut is the name of God in Peru. Georgius then goes on to explain
that Ti-bet is *Ti-bot,* or *Ti-bout,* or Ti-Boutta, or Di-Buddha.[2] He adds, " Hoc vero recta oritur
" à gentili *Pot-Jid,* quo certo nomine non ante famosi Buttæ tempora insigniri ea natio cœpit."[3]
Tibet is called Potyid by Sir W. Jones.[4] He makes an important observation on the nature of the
Tibetian language,[5] which appears to be in a great measure Monosyllabic, and thus tends to
prove its antiquity. He then goes on to state, that *Jid* is a cognomen of Buddha, and means
Unicus or Unigenitus;[6] and that it is the " *Jehid* Phœnicium, aut Ihido Syrum." (It is, in fact,
Ii-di.) He confirms almost all which I have before given from Creuzer respecting Buddha. On
the name of Xaca, he says it is called, in the Tibetian language, *Sciakham.* That is, I suppose,
the *Sci-akham* or *Hakim,* just now treated of.

I suspect that the Phœnician Jehid or Iid, is nothing but the Chaldee II of the Targums, with
an abbreviation of the Deus, Dis, Deva, and means the God Ii.

The Deity Isan and Isuren of India was the Isis of Egypt. The name came from the Hebrew
יסע *iso,* with the Tamul termination in *en,* Isur-en. This deity is the same as Mahdeus and
Mahadeva. It has generally four arms, and is often seated on the Lotus. Fire is its peculiar
emblem. It has three eyes. It is also often carried on a BULL. One of its epithets is Hydropism.[7] This is the Greek ὕδωρ and Ἶσις, and connects it with the refined doctrine of water,
which approaches to something very near to the spiritual fire and the hydrogen of the moderns.
It is adored under the form of the Linga, or Priapus. It is Pluto, the Egyptian Amenti and the
Giam Indicus. It is Brahma and Tchiven. " *Dominus humidæ naturæ* et origo sacrorum flumi-
" num," the Giam Indicus—judex universorum. From the word Giam comes, I suspect, the Ganga
or Janga. Finally, Georgius says, " Sol est Isuren, qualis erat Osiris apud Egyptios."[8]

It is said of Mani that he left a book of paintings. In one of the apocryphal Gospels Jesus is
said to have been the son of a Dyer or a Painter, another of a Potter, in *the four* of a Carpenter,
and in all of an Artificer. Georgius says, " Verum non opus est multis, ut ostendam orientales

---

[1] Georg. Alph. Tib. præf. p. ix. [2] Alph. Tib. p. 16. [3] Præf. p. 10.
[4] Asiat Res. Vol. III. p. 10. [5] P. 11. [6] Ib. p. xi. [7] Georg. Alph. Tib. p. 156.
[8] P. 155.

" omnes uno· eodemque nomine *Pictorem, Tinctoremque* vocare. Vide Castellum in צבע *(zko)*.
" Quum vero *Arteng* dicimus, eoque designamus *Librum* picturarum Mani, (quia, ut inquit
" Renaudotius, figuris peregrinis, et ignotis refertus erat,) intellegere *debemus Librum eo sensu,*
" *quo intelligunt Brammhanes Vedam, et Tibetani Ciò sive Cioch.* Nempe, ut *Vedam* est Bramha,
" et ciò Xaca, ita *Arteng* est ipse Mani, *virtus, emanatio Patris luminum, ejusque Filius,* et *anima*
" dans et accipiens formas, ac figuras omnes in eo portentoso mysteriorum libro contentas."[1]
Here we find Brahma and Buddha both having the meaning of the word *Book.* Here is confirmed what I have before said that *Veda* is *Beda* or *Buddha.* The book of the Manichæans was called *the treasure,* and being a Veda would be *a treasure of Wisdom.* Bacchus is called Liber, בבא *bka* and תות *tut,* which in Chaldee mean *Morus,* the name of the *Morea* of Greece.[2] The Morus or Mulberry-tree is a very mystical plant; it is said to be *sapientissima arbor.* It was probably thus designated because it had the same name as the God of Wisdom. Brahma is the same as Brahaspati, who is worshiped the same day as Suarasuoti, (Sara-iswati,) the *Dea scientiarum:* from this, Georgius says, he thinks the word Brahma came to mean Scientia. The truth is, wherever Scientia is found, Sapientia may be written.[3]

We have seen, in p. 320, that the natives of Siam call their God Iach Iach, the Greek Iacchè. Now, is it not possible that in the Tibetian language this may be the Siakhim, the aspirated הכם *hkm*—and this Siak and Iacch the same? Parkhurst says, the aspirate breathing is constantly substituted for the sibillant letter.[4] This would make Saca Iaca. The festivals of Bacchus in Greece were called Iacæa.[5]

" At Typhon ab eodem Plutarcho ex Phrygiis literis dicitur filius Isaacci Ισαακε τυ Ἡρακλεως
" ὁ Τυφων, Isaacci, quem genuit Hercules, filius fuit Typhon."[6] May Isaac, the son of Hercules, who was Cristna, who was Samson, have come from ישע *iso, to save,* and Xaca, or from I and Xaca, or from ישע *iso* and הכם *hkm?* Either of these etymons is strictly in keeping with the remainder of the mythos.

Brahma is said to have been the inventor of Hymns and Verses, and the Brahmins are not permitted to *recite* but only to *sing* the Vedas. To account for this they have a story of Brahma, like Jupiter for the love of Leda, being turned into a swan. When he was about to be killed by Iswara, he sung hymns and verses to her praise, to pacify her. From this came the story of the musical singing of swans when they are about to die.[7]

Brahma carries a book as an emblem. This was because he was the first emanation or divine Wisdom, and the Wisdom contained in the Veda or book of Wisdom came from him. Hence, in Greece, Bacchus or Brahme was called Liber.[8]

I think, from a passage in Georgius, the real origin of the meaning of the term Judah or Juda,— the religion or the name of the tribe may be discovered,—of the tribe or religion which Eusebius said existed before the time of Abraham. He observes, that Buddha is called Jid, which is the same as Ieoud, who was the son of Saturn, and that it is merely an epithet, meaning ·Unigenitum. Hebræis est יחיד *(ihid)* Iehid Isaacci epithetum.[9] Gen. xxii. 2.[10] Now I think this shews that the tribe were followers of the Unigenitum, in short, of the Logos or Buddha, who was the only-begotten of his Father.

---

[1] Tib. Alph. [2] Vall. Coll. Hib. Vol. IV. Part i. p. 265. [3] Georg. p. 114.
[4] In voce שש *ss,* II p. 776. [5] Vide Hermes Scythicus, p. 136. [6] Georgius Alph. Tib. p. 26.
[7] Vide Georg. Alph. Tib. p. 110. [8] Ib. p. 114. [9] Bocharto.
[10] Georg. Alph. Tib. Sect. xi.

Again Georgius says,[1] "Brevi, Xaca *Jehid, Ihido,* and *Ihid,* (quod est insigne cognomentum et "attributum *Buddæ, Butæ,* sive *Boto* in vernaculâ voce *Tibeti Pot-Tit,*) *Poto* scilicet, seu *Boutta* "Unigenitus aut Primogenitus." He had before shewn that Jehid was Juda; hence we come to the fact, that the tribe of Isaac, Ihid, or Judah, was a tribe of Buddhists.

2. The Scala or ladder, formerly alluded to in Vol. I. p. 413, I believe signified a chain or ladder of transmigration, by which the soul climbed up to heaven,[2] and that Scala or Sacala is Xaca-clo, and came to mean a ladder, or the ladder of the Mount of Solyma, or Peace or Salvation, from the ladder of metamorphoses or regenerations. The system of regeneration is exactly that of a ladder. The dream of Jacob, with the seventy-two angels ascending and descending, the mysticism of which no one will deny, alludes to this: the Xaca-clo is the series of ten regenerations, which the Brahmins taught that every human being passed through. In the names of Sicily we have, first, Siculia, as it is called by Virgil, which is Xaca-clo-ia; this was Buddhist. The next was, Trina-cria or Trina-crios—the Triune Aries; this was Crestism.[3] In Vol. I. pp. 813—816, I represented the double trinity and the system of emanations to form a chain; the last link of the first forming the first link of the second; and thus the whole system, beginning at the Το Ον, formed a chain or a ladder from the highest to the lowest.

Is it possible that the veneration for Apes may have taken its rise from a word of the ancient language—the Chaldean misunderstood? Georgius says,[4] "Simia Arabicè בראם *bram,* Boram, "Africanis ברם *brm.*" It is well known to all Indian scholars, that Cristna is said to have invaded Ceylon, accompanied by an army of Monkeys, by whose means he conquered it; and we are told that this is the belief of the country. The simple fact was, that the sectaries of the Crest, the Brahmins, invaded it, and the whole arises from the identity in the Indian language of the words for Brahmin and Ape or Monkey. In this manner numbers of little mythoses have arisen in all parts of the world. In a similar manner arose the mythos of Bacchus's *grapes.* The word for *grape* in Greek is Βοτρυς, this is a corruption of Buddha, and Bacchus was Buddha, and Buddha was Wisdom; whence the grape in Latin is called *race-mus*—evidently the Hebrew Ras, *wisdom,* and the 'Ραξ, *the stone of the grape.*

Salivahana is also called Saca.[5] In Bali they have a period called the year of Saca.[6] The God in the temple on the mountain of Lawuh, in Java, is called Sukuh.[7] This is the mountain of L'Awu or THE Ieo, and his name Saca.

The large temples in Java are built without cement in the joints, in the Cyclopæan order of architecture—all the stones mortised together.[8]

We are constantly told by all travellers, that the Lama of Tibet is adored as God. But in this I do not doubt that our travellers permit their prejudice and bigotry to blind them. If he be considered to be the Supreme Being, how came the Tibetians to have a *most magnificent* temple to Buddha, at Lassa, the place of the Lama's residence? of which a ground-plan is given in Georgius.[9] The fact is, the followers of the Lamb at Rome elect their Vicramaditya or Grand Vicar from themselves, generally choosing the most imbecile of the college for the God upon earth, as he does call, or used to call, himself. The followers of the Lamb in Tibet have found it better to select an

---

[1] Sect. cxxiii.
[2] Vide Georgius Alph. Tib. Ap. iii. p. 678.
[3] From this idea the division of any given space into equal parts, and probably from the decimal notation, *ten* parts, was called a Scala or Scale.
[4] Alph. Tib. p. 28.
[5] Crawfurd, Hist. Ind. Arch. Vol. I. p. 300.
[6] Ibid.
[7] Ib. Vol. II. pl. 18.
[8] Ib. p. 199.
[9] Sect. cxliii. p. 406.

July 28, 1833.

infant, whom they educate. The same reason operates in both conclaves. In each, a similar cause produces a similar effect,—an imbecile Lama.

The whole of what we have seen respecting Saca and the Saxons, must be considered as a preparation for an inquiry into a Pontifical government, (to be developed in the future books,) which was brought with the feudal system to England and Europe, long before the time of Cæsar. It will be found useful also in considering the origin of letters.

CHAPTER III.

JUDÆAN MYTHOS IN EGYPT.—MENES. NOAH.—CHERES.—ABRAHAM TULIS.—JOSEPH.—GRECIAN HISTORY A TRAVESTY.—LANGUAGE OF EGYPT.—DEISUL VOYAGE OF SALVATION.

I now beg my reader to recall to his recollection the multitude of fragments of the Christian and Jewish mythos which, in his reading, he must have found scattered about Upper Egypt. I beg him to look at and read the accounts of my Figures 27 B and 35. These things are all disguised or instantly put out of sight by the assertion, that they are the remains of the Gnostic or Nestorian (that is, as the learned Nimrod says, the Buddhists) Christians. The existence of the mythos, which I shall now exhibit, in Egypt, easily accounts for and explains all these hitherto inexplicable remains of the Jewish and Christian mythos, on the ancient temples in Upper Egypt and in Nubia. As might be expected, the prejudices of education have operated on the learned German Heeren, to blind him to the Jewish and Christian mythos; but yet, in one instance, the truth involuntarily creeps out. He says, "Another field opens itself here for divines, if they would like "to compare the religious notions of ancient Thebes with the descriptions given by the Jews of "their sanctuaries, the tabernacle, the temple, and the sacred utensils.

"This is not the place for a comparison of this kind: but how many things described in the "Scriptures do we find in these engravings! the ark of the covenant (here carried in procession), "the cherubim with their extended wings, the holy candlesticks, the shew bread, and many parts "of the sacrifices! In the architecture itself a certain similarity is instantly recognised, although "among the Jews every thing was on a smaller scale."[1] In his maps the temples of Meroe, in several instances, appear built in the exact cross-form of our churches.

The observation of Heeren, I shall now shew, has been confirmed by a very learned Frenchman, the Abbé Guerin de Rocher. But my reader will be kind enough to observe, that although the similitudes pointed out by Heeren, amount to almost a proof of my theory, they, in a similar manner, amount almost to a proof of the falsity of the Abbé's theory, which will now be explained.

After finding the Judæan mythos, the mythos which Eusebius asserts existed before Abraham, in North and South India, in Syria, and in China, it would have been very singular if it had not been found in Egypt. This singularity has been proved not to exist by the Abbé Guerin de

---

[1] Heeren, on Egypt, Vol. II. p. 297

Rocher, who has undertaken to shew, in his work called *Histoire des Temps Fabuleux*, that the history of Egypt, detailed by Herodotus, Diodorus, Suidas, Manetho, &c., is not a true history of Egypt, but a mere travesty of the history of the Jews; and however much I may differ from him, both generally and in many particulars, yet I think he has proved his case, so far as to shew, that the two were, in many instances, substantially the same, as they ought to be, if they were nothing but a repetition of the same mythos; but which they could not possibly be, and be at the same time both true histories of countries, as he very justly observes. All this tends strongly to prove that Herodotus was really the father of history, the first real historian: all the works before his, being mere mythoses, founded on the traditionary, unwritten stories of each country, detailed by the priests for the purpose of religion, not of history.

It is necessary to observe, that the Abbé does not pretend to shew merely that parts of the Egyptian history agree with and dovetail into such parts of the history of the Jews as relate to respective periods, but that the Egyptians have taken the Jewish history, and have travestied it (to use his word) to form a n*ew* history. Between these two my reader must perceive that there is a mighty difference. Had he shewn the former, he would indeed have greatly strengthened the Jewish history as a history, but the latter is another matter.

The Abbé has exhibited so much skill and ingenuity in discovering the meaning of several parables called parts of the Egyptian history, that I have no doubt whatever, if he had been unfettered by religious prejudice, he would have made out the whole mythos. The discoveries he has made did not arise from his abstract love of truth, but merely from a belief that it would enable him the better to defend his own religion and the interests of his order.

He supposes that the history of Egypt was completely lost by the natives, in the course of the period when the Persians possessed it, after the conquest of it by Cambyses. Nothing but the excess of religious prejudice could have induced any one to believe, that, in the short time during which the Persians possessed Egypt, all knowledge of their ancient history, and of their history at that time not properly ancient to them, should be completely lost by the natives, and also that they should all of them have been so totally devoid of understanding, as that they could not make up a story of their own to pass off as a history of their country, but that they should be obliged to go to the little distant mountain tribe which Herodotus could not discover, said to have been driven out of their country several hundred years before, to borrow their history, by a travesty or transfer of which they made up a history for themselves [1] —not using the names of their own kings, but actually names out of the history of the distinct mountain tribe just alluded to? The Abbé has been attacked in no very measured or very fair terms by several of the philosophers, on account of his etymologies and other little matters; but he has been very ably and successfully defended. His opponents do not appear to have touched upon the absurdity of the theory to account for these travesties, or historic parables. As all party writers do, they laid hold of exceptions—they seized on and exposed particular points, but the general whole, which they ought to have attacked, they left untouched. In fact, the Abbé overthrew all their previous doctrines, and not having the least idea of any universal mythos, or other cause, to account for the undeniable effect pointed out by him, they could give him no reasonable answer, though the general absurdity of the cause which he assigned, or the way in which he accounted for the effect, was evident enough. They ought candidly to have admitted the fact of the identity of the histories of Genesis and of Egypt, and have said, "We admit the identity you contend for; we cannot

---

[1] Why did they not go to their obelisks, which M. Champollion has found covered with their histories? Why? but because M. Champollion has discovered nothing!

" deny it; but the reason which you assign for the identity appears to us absurd, and we cannot admit it: there must be some other reason for it, which is yet unknown." This would have been candid; but instead of this, as defeated parties usually act, they had recourse to ridicule, misrepresentation, and clamour, and endeavoured to poh-poh him down.

The Abbé says, " Je commence par les temps fabuleux des Egyptiens, depuis Ménès, leur premier roi, suivant tous leurs historiens, jusqu' au temps où l'Egypte soumise aux Perses, devint une province de leur empire. On verra, par un rapprochement soutenu de toute la suite des règnes, et des faits de chaque règne, que cette histoire répond à l'histoire sainte, depuis Noé, le père de tous les hommes d'après le déluge, jusqu' à la fin de la captivité des Juifs à Babylone: et que ce n'est même qu'un extrait suivi, quoique défiguré, de ce que l'Ecriture elle-même nous apprend de l'Egypte dans cet intervalle; en un mot, que tout ce qu' Hérodote, Manéthon, Eratosthène et Diodore de Sicile nous racontent de l'Egypte jusqu' à cette époque, n'est, aux descriptions près, qu'une traduction, à la vérité, pleine d'erreurs et de fautes grossières, que les Egyptiens s'étoient faite ou procurée des endroits de l'Ecriture qui les regardent, et dont ils s'étoient composé une histoire; c'est le sujet de trois premiers volumes que je présente au public."[1] This is a very different matter from having taken parts of the Jewish history, to fill up the lacunæ in the corresponding parts of their own history.

The Abbé's assertion that, in the time of Menes, the first king, whose name was, in fact, the same as that of Noah, Egypt was a marsh, with the exception alone of the district of Thebes, which comprised all Upper Egypt, that is, that it was covered with water, is in exact accordance with what I have said in Vol. I. pp. 291, &c., and 336. He afterward shews that the history of Thebes is a travesty of the history of the flood of Noah and of the Ark. That the same particulars are in both the histories,—that from Thebes the doves went out,—that the name Thebes for that city and the ark are the same,—that at Thebes an immense ship was built, and that the first men and animals of the present world came out from Thebes, &c., &c. But I will now give to my reader, an extract from the work of Mons. Bonnaud,[2] one of the Abbé's defenders, in which, abstracted from the Abbé's book, he places by the side of each other the History of Herodotus and of Genesis, which will serve to give a general idea of the nature of the Abbé's work better than any description which I can write.

Debutons par l'arche de Noé, laquelle s'appelle en Hébreu THBE, que les Egyptiens ont prise pour le ville de *Thèbes;* nous verrons en suite l'histoire de Jacob travestie par eux en celle de Sésostris, roi conquérant. Tenons-nous-en pour le moment à ces deux morceaux que l'auteur de l'*histoire véritable* a dévoilés.

HISTOIRE D' EGYPTE.	HISTOIRE SAINTE.
1. Ménès est celui qui regna le premier des hommes.	1. Noé, dont le nom en Hébreu est Né ou Mnée, son dérivé, qui signifie *répos*,[3] est le père commun de tous les peuples : c'est dans l'Ecriture le premier homme qui règne dans un sens après le déluge : puis qu'il se trouve le chef et le souverain naturel de tout le genre humain réduit alors à sa famille.

---

[1] P. xliii.

[2] Vol. V. p. 6. Histoire Des Temps Fabuleux, Tome V. 8vo. à Paris. Par L'Abbé Guérin de Rocher. Chez Gautier et Frères, et Co. 1824.

[3] M, en Hébreu est une lettre servile au commencement du mot. J'ai cru que, pour me mettre plus à portée des lecteurs qui ignorent les langues anciennes, il convenoit d'écrire en lettres ordinaires les mots Hébreux dont il m'a fallu faire un fréquent usage, vu la nature de l'objet que je me propose de discuter. Ceux qui seroient curieux de vérifier ces mots de la langue Hébraïque, peuvent recourir à l'*histoire véritable des temps fabuleux.*

BOOK II. CHAPTER III. SECTION 3.

2. Du tems de *Ménès* toute l'Egypte n'étoit qu'un marais à l'exception du seul *nome* ou canton de *Thèbes*, c'est-à-dire, qu'elle était tout inondée.

3. Les habitans de *Thèbes* se disoient les plus anciens des hommes.

4. À *Thèbes* fut construit un grand navire de près de trois cents coudées de long.

5. Hérodote dit que deux columbes s' étoient envolées de *Thèbes* en différentes contrées.

6. Les animaux, suivant les Egyptiens, furent formés d'abord dans le pays de *Thèbes*.

7. Ménès apprit aux peuples à honorer les Dieux et à leur faire des sacrifices.

8. Ménès fut le premier à introduire le luxe de la table.

9. Les habitans de *Thèbes* se vantoient d'avoir été les premiers à connoître la vigne.

2. Du temps de Noé, non seulement l'Egypte, mais la terre entière fut inondée par le déluge, et ce nome de *Thèbes*, qui seul ne l'étoit pas, c'est *l'arche* qui se sauva du déluge. THBE ou comme on prononce THEBAH, est le mot constamment employé dans le texte Hébreu pour signifier *arche*.

3. *Thbe* ou *Thebah* (l'arche de Noé) renferma en effet dans son sein les pères de tous les hommes, et par conséquent les plus anciens de tous, à dater du déluge qui fut comme un renouvellement du genre humain.

4. La *Thbe* ou la *Thebah*, l'arche de Noé, avoit *trois cents coudées* de *longueur*.

5. Noé fait envoler une columbe par *deux fois* de sa Thbe ou de son *arche*, pour s'assurer, avant que d'en sortir, que la terre a été desséchée.

6. L'Ecriture dit que *tous les animaux* furent renfermés dans l'arche, et en sortirent, *Thbe* en Hébreu signifiant l'arche, voilà comme tous les animaux sont sortis de *Thèbes*.

7. Mnée autrement Noé au sortir de l'arche *éleva un autel au Seigneur*, dit l'Ecriture ······*et offrit des holocaustes sur cet autel*, par conséquent, *des sacrifices*

8. Noé après le déluge eut la permission expresse de se nourrir de la chair des animaux.

9. Noé en sortant de l'arche *(Thbe)* fut le premier qui planta la vigne.

That the two stories are closely connected no one can doubt: but the Abbé's theory, that the Egyptian is a travesty of that of the Jews, to which the Egyptians had recourse in consequence of the destruction, by Cambyses, of all their records, receives a terrible blow from an observation which he makes in the next page—that the same history is told of the Grecian Thebes as is told of the Thebes of Egypt. The consequence of this the Abbé does not perceive, viz. that it is totally incredible that they should both be the same, without a common cause, and this could not be the conquest by Cambyses, because he never conquered the Grecian Thebes. In fact, it overthrows the Abbé's whole system; but it confirms mine beautifully, viz. that the stories are all one common mythos, in all countries disguised in the dress of history. Accident could not possibly be the cause.

The Abbé's observation, that the word used for the name of Thebes is exactly the same word as that used to describe the ark of Noah, again overthrows the whole of his system: for the ancient city of Thebes destroyed by Cambyses, and sung of by Homer, under *the name of Thebes*, could not have had its name given by the priests about the time of Herodotus, which is what the Abbé's system requires. The very great antiquity of the names of the cities of Thebes in Egypt and Greece, as proved by Homer, takes from under the edifice erected by the Abbé every part of its foundation. It is not credible that one or both these cities should have this name given as a substitute for the real history lost in Cambyses' conquest, though there can be no doubt that the history of Genesis and of Herodotus are the same.

3. I have observed, Vol. I. p. 602, that the kings of Egypt, whose names ended in *cheres*, were renewed incarnations of the Χρης, *mitis*. On these kings the Abbé says, "Mycérinus, successeur de Chéphren ou Chabryis, appellé par Diodore, Menchérinus ou Chérinus; par Eratosthène,

Caras ou Ocaras; par Manéthon, Men-cheres, et de quantité d'autres noms terminés en ce rès ou cherès, sans compter ceux qui ne le sont pas; roi plein de douceur, de religion et d'équité, qui rend au peuple opprimé la liberté de sacrifier, qui le soulage dans ses maux, qui se rend recommendable par son extrême exactitude à rendre la justice: qui va jusqu'-à satisfaire à ses dépens, ceux qui se plaignent de ses jugements : qui est condamné par l'oracle à *mourir avant le temps ;* qui prend le parti d'errer dans des lieux solitaires, où il se fait éclairer la nuit, comme le soleil l'éclaire durant le jour" [1] ...... I think few persons will fail to see in this early chres or Χρης, the prototype of a later one. The same mythos is here, and this cannot be disputed. We have here in the *mourir avant le temps,* the person crucified in Egypt of the Apocalypse. The Abbé after this proceeds to shew, that the Cheres was Moses, but this only tends to strengthen the proof that Moses was an Avatar,[2] a Messiah, a divine incarnation, saving his people, in fact a Χρης. Amidst the blunders and confusion of the different historians of Egypt, it is easy to see here, the *Christian* mythos; even the name Χρης is found in the word *Chœres,*[3] one name of what is called by Manetho the second dynasty, consisting of three kings, *Ilas,* Sethenès, Chœres,[4] evidently the mistaken Tripety. And we must not forget the infant Orus, and the Virgo paritura.

4. The Abbé finds Abraham in Binothris, whom he asserts to be *Bn-Thré* בן-תרח *bn tre,* or Ben-Therah, son of Terah. This Binothris he shews was said by Manetho to be succeeded by a king called Tulis. Binothris is said to have established the first queen in Egypt, or to have first given to females the honours of Royalty. This queen was Sarah, whose name when changed from *Sarai* meant, instead of *a* queen or princess, *the* queen. After Binothris, Manetho puts Ilas or Tulis; but this person the Jews and Arabs make to be the ravisher of Sarah. The different historians, all ignorant of the true state of the case, confound the parties; but they are all evidently here. The word Tulis means *ravisher* in the Hebrew and Arabic.[5] Thus Tulis or Ilas was the stealer or ravisher of Sarah, the sister of Abraham. The history of this Tulis, as given by Suidas, is very remarkable.[6] He says, "Thulis reigned over all Egypt, and his empire "extended even over the ocean. He gave his name to one of its isles (Ultima Thule). Puffed "up with success, he went to consult the oracle of Serapis; and, after having offered his sacrifice, "he addressed to him these words: 'Tell me, Oh, master of Fire, the true, the happy par excel- "'lence, who rulest the course of the stars,—tell me if ever there was before one greater than I, "'or will ever be one greater after me.' The oracle answered him in these words: 'First God, "'afterward the Word, and with them the Holy Spirit:'[7] all three are of the same nature, and "'make but one whole, of which the power is eternal; go away quickly, mortal, thou who hast "'but an uncertain life.' Going out from the temple he was put to death by his own countrymen "in the country of the Africans." (Αφρων.)[8] But the most remarkable part of this story is, that the word Tulis means *crucified,* תלה *tle,* suspendit: תלוי *tlui,* suspensus, crucifixus. Here in the country of the Africans—in Egypt we have again *the crucified* of the Apocalypse. Thlui is the name given by the Jews to Jesus Christ,[9] meaning *the crucified.* Serapis, the God consulted, was regarded as the Saviour of Egypt.[10] I have little doubt that Serapis was put to death as well as Osiris, but that he was crucified. It was under his temple at Alexandria that the cross

---

[1] Histoire Des Tems Fabuleux. Tome V. p. 136.
[2] The word Avatar is probably *abba-tur,* a renewal of father, Tur.
[3] P. 300.   [4] P. 297.   [5] Ib. p. 298.
[6] See, for the answer of the Oracle to Sesostris, Vol. I. p. 805.
[7] Πρωτα Θεος, μετεπειτα Λογος, και Πνευμα συν αυτοις.   [8] Ib. p. 403.   [9] Ib. p. 306.   [10] Ib. p. 309.

was found when it was destroyed by one of the Roman Emperors. We cannot forget that Serapis was considered by Hadrian and the Gentiles to be the peculiar God of the Christians.

The Egyptian history is evidently a garbled, and, in many respects, a confused misrepresentation of the same history or mythos as that of the Jews; the Abbé attributes this misrepresentation to the ignorance of the Egyptians in the Jewish language, but who, on the contrary, must have been well acquainted with it, as appears from their names of men and places, which are almost all Hebrew. It is much more probably attributable to the ignorance of the four Greek authors, who evidently betray their ignorance in a variety of ways, and indeed confess it. But the fact that they are, at the bottom, the same mythoses or histories cannot be doubted. Here, then, we find the reason why the Jewish prophet, Isaiah xix. 18, says, that the true God *should* be adored, or *was*[1] adored at five temples in the land of Egypt; and here we find the reason of the pictures of the Judæan mythos in Egypt in several of my groups of figures, and of the Judæan names of towns, mountains and districts, which I have before pointed out, and here we find the meaning of the expression in the Apocalypse, the *Lord crucified in Egypt*.[2]

But it is a very important observation which I have to make in addition to this, viz. that the text (Isa. xix. 18) does not only say, as our Bible renders it, that one shall be called the city of destruction; but it also says, that one shall be called the city of the Ers, יאשר לאחת ההרס *e-ers*, or THE SUN,[3] or the Saviour—according to the Arabic جسم *to save*. Here we have proof of several of my theories. Here we have the Χρης, the Chres, the Ceres, the Ερος, the Eri, and Heri, and Hari of Arabia, all identified with the Sun, and with the Preserver and Destroyer. And here we have the Hebrew הרים *ers*, the origin of the Sanscrit, Eri or Heri, *Saviour*.

Of late I have never closely examined a text of the Bible which has not brought to my mind an assertion of the Tamuls, that their ancient sixteen-letter sacred book had five meanings. I am quite certain that I shall be able to shew—to prove—that every letter of the Hebrew had four, and I think probably five, meanings. I request my reader to consider well the different meanings of this word, הרים *ers*, as an example. I have lately begun to have some suspicion, that it was with a reference to this mystery, that several of the Hebrew letters were what we call similars, but that they were originally identicals. This will be scouted,—poh-pohed down, by every Christian and Jewish Hebraist with whom I am acquainted, for I do not know one who is not afraid of too much being discovered. I never speak to any one of them upon these subjects, without finding all their eloquence instantly in requisition, either to shew that I have made no discovery, or to shew that it is quite out of the question that any should be made; but never do I find them take the other side, and endeavour to clear up doubts or remove difficulties.

To return to my subject: although there are many things in which I cannot agree with the learned Abbé Guerin de Rocher, I maintain that he has made out his case, that the history of Genesis, from Noah to the captivity, is to be found substantially in the history of Egypt, which he calls travestied, or, as he says, one taken from the other. Then here we have to all appearance a history in the time of Herodotus, which is, in fact, no history at all; for if it is merely a copy or travesty of the history of the people of Syria, it cannot be a history of the people of Egypt. Here, then, we have a most striking fact to support my doctrine, that we have really nothing of the nature of a true history before the time of Herodotus. And here we have Herodotus searching for history in Egypt, deceived by a mythos, the same as a mythos in Syria: and, if it were not a

---

[1] Here is a double reading יהיו *ieiu* and יהי *ici*, so it may be either, There shall be, or There have been. See Pagninus.

[2] See Vol. I., p. 694, note 3, where, for Rev. ii. 8, read Rev. xi. 8.   [3] Vide Gessenius in voce.

mythos, what could induce the priests of Egypt to have given Herodotus a story in which Abraham, Sarah, and the other persons, in the Syrian history, were actors, as Egyptian history? Why did they not give the history, or the greatest part of it, correctly, as we have it in Genesis, instead of travestying it? Of course, the Abbé takes as much of the histories as is enough for his purpose, omitting all the remainder; but we can have no difficulty in finding the remainder of the mythos of North and South India, in the death and resurrection of Orus and Osiris. The Abbé observes,[1] that the different histories are confused, but that certain of the kings are but repetitions of Moses; that is, reincarnations of the Saviour. They are merely renewed incarnations—of course as we have found them in India—all having a family likeness.[2]

I have often suspected that our LXX is not the work which Ptolemy caused to be made from the Hebrew or the Samaritan, but is a translation from the sacred books of the five temples of Egypt referred to by Isaiah. Now if we suppose the sacred books of the Jews to refer, and to have been admitted by them to refer, to an *Eastern Ayoudia* in their secret doctrines, they would not permit this to be publicly known. Of course, when the writings became public, they would be believed, generally, to refer to no other place or places than those in Western Syria; and immediately all persons answering to the description of the Jews, of any of the temples scattered about the world, would be believed to belong to the religion of Western Syria. I am now calculating upon these secret books being kept secret at all the other temples of Solumi. (At Telmessus, for example.) Of course, if they had sacred books containing this mythos, I suppose in every case they would be accommodated to the respective localities, as we have found them in India, near Cape Comorin, and as they were in Western Judæa, and as by and by we shall find the Χρης-ian mythos was in vast numbers of places, all over the world.

The reason why I have suspected our LXX, is to be found in the excessively great variation which may be perceived between it and the Hebrew—much too great, I think, to be accounted for, by the unintentional corruptions of Origen, with his obelisks and asteriks. May not the sole difference at last, between the Jews at the respective temples of Solomon and other Gentiles, be found in the Jews being a sect of iconoclasts, and keeping to this dogma or doctrine, when it was lost sight of by other nations; in consequence of which their religion ran into all kinds of absurdities, from which that of these temples continued free? I think this is worthy of consideration. Since I wrote the above I have been told by a learned Jew, that my suspicion respecting the LXX has been proved to be well founded, by an author of the name of De Rossi, who is noticed in Louth's Preface to his Translation of Isaiah.

5. The Abbé de Rocher shews that several kings are copies of Abraham, several of Joseph, several of Moses, &c., and that Joseph was the Proteus of the Egyptians and Greeks. He observes that Joseph was called a saviour, and this, from the peculiarity of his story, would be of no consequence; but the Abbé artlessly observes, which is indeed of great consequence, that St. Jerom calls Joseph *Redemptor Mundi*—here evidently letting the secret of the mythos escape him. The Abbé was not aware of the consequence of shewing that Moses and Joseph are repeatedly described, by different persons, particularly the latter, as a saviour. He had no knowledge of the new incarnations. Both Moses and Joseph are appellative terms, made into proper names. This raises a probability that the same history was told to the people every 600 years; and if the art of writing were not known by them, it is not surprising that they should have believed it.

---

[1] P. 138.

[2] In Egypt there was a Cashmouric district, that is, District of Cashmere.—Spineto's Lectures on Hieroglyphics, p. 87.

BOOK I. CHAPTER III. SECTION 6.

Eutychius says,[1] that the first city built by Noah was Thebes, which he called Thamanim. This is strongly confirmatory of the theory of the Abbé de Rocher, and of my system, that the whole mythic history has been in Egypt; but, as we might expect, accommodated to its local and other circumstances.

I beg my reader to look back into our own history for six hundred years, and consider what we should know of it, if we had not possessed the art of writing.

There have been a hundred and seventeen different theories, to account for the difficulties in the Egyptian history.[2]

Speaking of the Egyptians, it is said by another learned Abbé, the Abbé Bazin,[3] that the words *I am that I am*, were on the front of the temple of Isis at Sais, and that the name esteemed the most sacred by the Egyptians was that which the Hebrews adopted, Y-HA-HO. He says, it is variously pronounced: but Clement, of Alexandria, assures us, in his *Stromatis*, that all those who entered into the temple of Serapis, were obliged to wear on their persons, in a conspicuous situation, the name of *I-ha-h* , or I-ha-hou, which signifies *the God eternal.* From this, I think, we may fairly infer, that the Egyptians were of the same religion, in its fundamentals, as the Jews. An attentive consideration of the passage of the book of Esther, where the Persian idolaters are described as being put to death, will, I think, justify me in saying, that it affords grounds for the opinion, that they were the same. The book of Esther appears to have been part of the chronicles of the kings of Persia, adopted by the Jews into their canon, evidently to account for their feast of Purim.

Herodotus was in Egypt about four hundred and fifty years before Christ, and Alexander conquered it about three hundred and fifty years before Christ, which was the time when the Greeks first began to have any influence there. After their conquest of it nearly the same thing happened to it which happened to Carthage, after it was conquered by the Romans. Its history was lost, except the tradition that it had been previously conquered by the Persians: the reason of this was, because there was no history, the art of writing history had not been invented. But there was this difference between Carthage and Egypt,—the latter continued a nation, the former did not. These circumstances account for the loss of the particulars of the Egyptian history, but not for the loss of general great events, easily transmissive by memory.

My reader must recollect, that the example which I have given him of Thebes and Noah, constitutes but a very small part of the *rapprochements* (as the Abbé calls them) which, in fact, relating to Egypt alone, fill three volumes. It is selected as an example, not because it is the most striking, but because it happens to be the first, and one of the shortest.

6. But the Abbé Guerin de Rocher is not content with shewing that the Egyptian only travestied the Holy Scripture; he goes much further. He says,[4] "Je crois pouvoir, en effet, montrer assez clairement, et par la signification des noms, et par les principaux traits des caractères, et par la suite des faits, quoique souvent altérés, que ces premiers personnages de l'histoire sainte sont devenus autant de rois ou de héros, dans les temps fabuleux de l'histoire profane, et surtout dans les poëtes de la Grèce, et de là vient que les héros d'Homère, malgré les altérations du paganisme, conservent encore une si grande simplicité."

Again, speaking of the comparison between the history of the Architect of Rhamsinites and the testament of Jacob, he says,[5] "On ne me croiroit pas sans doute, vu le peu de ressemblance, si je

---

[1] See Vol. I. p. 755.   [3] Guerin de Rocher, Vol. I. p. 167.
[2] Translation from his MS. by Henry Wood Gandell, printed for North, Paternoster Row, 1829, p 130.
[4] Vol. II. p. 15.   [5] Vol. II. p. 379.

ne faisois un rapprochement assez sensible pour opérer la conviction. Je ne ferois pas ce devoilement, si je ne le regardois comme une preuve décisive, que les Egyptiens, pour composer leur histoire, ont réellement traduit, et très-mal traduit, les endroits de l'Ecriture qui ont quelque rapport à l'Egypte: cela servira du moins à constater de plus en plus sa véritable antiquité : ce sera en même temps un example frappant de la manière pitoyable dont l'ignorance et l'aveuglement des païens, et du peuple même réputé le plus sage parmi les païens, ont altéré ce qu'il y a de plus respectable et de plus sacré, car c'est un des chapitres les plus intéressants qui se trouvent dans l'histoire sainte.

" Ce travestissement une fois constaté, nous servira encore à en rendre d'autres moins incroyables: car les mêmes personnages dont il s'agit dans ce chapitre, se trouvent aussi travestis dans l'histoire fabuleuse de la Grèce, où ils sont devenus les principaux héros de la guerre de Troie, sous les mêmes noms traduits en Grec, avec les mêmes traits distinctifs de leurs caractères, et le même fond des principaux faits, comme je le ferai voir dans la mythologie Greque, ou je montrerai en même temps quelle est la guerre de l'histoire sainte, entreprise pour une femme, qui est devenue pour les Grecs la guerre de Troie: et quel est le morceau poëtique de l'Ecriture qui a servi de germe à l'Iliade d'Homère, comme les Grecs eux-mêmes l'ont equivalemment reconnu avant moi, sous des noms traduits dans leur langue."

Speaking of the Greeks he observes, that the meaning of the word Noé נח nuh in Hebrew is *quies* and *requies*, (vide Gen. v. 29,) and that " Le nom de Deucalion se forme naturellement en Grec du mot Δευκος, suavitas, dulcedo, qui signifie douceur: comme le nom de Sigalion, Dieu du Silence, se forme de Σιγη, silentium, que signifie silence. Δευκος *Deucos* a pu avoir ses dérivés comme Σιγη a les siens — Σιγηλος, Σιγαλεος, &c. Voilà donc Deucalion qui, par son nom même, se retrouve être Noé."[1] He shews that the story of the stones, by which Deucalion and Pyrrha repeopled the earth, is only a mistake arising from the Hebrew word בנים *bnim*, filii, having been confounded with the word אבנים *abnim*, lapides.[2] He then shews, that Noé is found in a similar manner in the Nannacus of the Phrygians, who is said, by Suidas, to have *foreseen* the flood, and in consequence to have collected and saved his people in a sacred asylum. This reminds me that one of the Sibyls placed Ararat in Phrygia: that is, placed a mount of il-avarata, of God the Creator, in Phrygia. All this tends to shew the mythos to be universally spread over the world. Nannacus foreseeing the flood, reminds me also that Enoch says, that Noé foresaw it —learnt from the moons or planets, that the earth would become inclined, and that destruction would take place. But this I shall discuss hereafter.

Again, Mons. Bonnaud says, " Mais si chaque trait de ses dévoilemens aura de quoi surprendre, que sera-ce, quand l'auteur de l'histoire véritable entreprendra d'expliquer comment les Grecs ayant imaginé leurs temps héroiques d'après nos livres saints, en ont emprunté ces noms illustres par les deux plus grands poëtes qui aient jamais existé, les noms d'Ajax, d'Enée, de Diomède, d'Agamemnon, de Ménélas? L'on verra que ces noms ne sont tous que les traductions de ceux des enfans de Jacob, Ruben, Siméon, Lévi, Juda, Dan, Issacar, Zabulon, &c., que les Grecs ont rendus dans leur langue, tantôt avec une exactitude litérale, et tantôt avec des altérations grossières, découverte assurément très-heureuse et si singulière, quelle paroîtra un paradoxe incroyable : découverte féconde, elle nous révélera un mystère que jusqu'ici l'esprit humain n'avoit pas même soupçonné. En effet, quelle sera la surprise de toutes les nations cultivées par le goût de la belle littérature, quand, par une suite de dévoilemens des héros de la Grèce, copiés sur les noms

---

[1] Vol. I. p 174.
[2] Ib. p. 175. The Abbé says, that Jameson, in his Spicelegia, has proved all the Egyptian proper names Hebrew.

des chefs des douze tribus d'Israël, M. l'Abbé de Rocher fera voir que la guerre de Troie, cette guerre, dont le fracas a retenti jusqu'au bout de l'univers: cette guerre, dont la célébrité propagée d'age en age, et perpétuée de bouche en bouche depuis tant de siècles, a fait placer cet évènement mémorable au rang des grands époques de l'histoire: cette guerre de Troie, chantée par un Homère et un Virgile, n'est dans le fond que la guerre des onze tribus d'Israël, contre celle de Benjamin, pour venger la femme d'un Lévite, victime de l'incontinence des habitans de la ville de Gabaa;[1] qui fut prise par les autres tribus confédérées, à l'aide d'une ruse de guerre, et qui fut à la fin livrée aux flammes par les vainqueurs."[2]

I confess I should have liked very much to see the Abbé attempt the Grecian history, as he has done that of Egypt. The striking marks of resemblance between parts of the Iliad, and of the names in it, and the fabulous history of Greece, to names and to parts of the Sacred Writings, has been observed thousands of times, and for this no reason has yet been assigned, having even the slightest degree of probability—unless the doctrine of a common and universal mythos in an universal language, as proposed to be proved in this work, be considered to possess such probability.

I think it expedient here to add some observations from another learned Abbé respecting the Grecian Bacchus. In Bacchus we evidently have Moses. Herodotus says he was an Egyptian, brought up in Arabia Felix. The Orphic verses relate that he was preserved from the waters, in a little box or chest, that he was called *Misem* in commemoration of this event; that he was instructed in all the secrets of the Gods; and that he had a rod, which he changed into a serpent at his pleasure; that he passed through the Red Sea dry-shod, *as Hercules subsequently did*, in his goblet, through the Straits of Abila and Calpe; and that when he went into India, he and his army enjoyed the light of the Sun during the night: moreover, it is said, that he touched with his magic rod the waters of the great rivers Orontes and Hydaspes; upon which those waters flowed back and left him a free passage. It is even said that he arrested the course of the sun and moon. He wrote his laws on two tables of stone. He was anciently represented with horns or rays on his head.[3]

We see Bacchus, who in so many other particulars is the same as Moses, is called Misem, in commemoration of his being saved from the water. Gessenius, in his explanation of the word Moses, says it is formed of μω *water* and υσης *delivered*. I can find no Greek μω for water in my Lexicons. But *Misem* may be the Saviour—yw *iso*, the Saviour ם m. And when I recollect all that I have said in Vol. I. pp. 530, 531, respecting the sacredness of water, and what Mr. Payne Knight has said of the derivation of the word Ice, and that Bacchus was Isis and Omadios, I cannot help suspecting that there is another mystery under this name, which I cannot fully explain.

We have found the Mosaic mythos in China, in North India, and it was found in South India by the Jesuits: then, according to the Abbé, Genesis must have been travestied in all these places, as well as in Egypt and Greece. This circumstance raises another insurmountable objection to the Abbé's theory, but it supports mine.

---

[1] "Il est remarquable, en effet, qu' en Hebreu le mot Gabaa, qui veut dire un lieu élévé, a le même sens que Pergama, en Grec, qui est aussi le nom qu'on donne à Troie."

[2] "Mons. l'Abbé dit, que la guerre de Troie est prise de *la guerre des Tribus*, racontée *à la fin du Livre des Juges*. Ce morceau de l'Ecriture est le dix-neuvième et le vingtième chapitre du Livre des Juges."

[3] Abbé Bazin, by Wood Gandell, p. 158. This ought to have come in another part of the work, but like many other passages it was not copied till the other parts were printed.

My reader will probably recollect that I have formerly shewn that the Rev. Dr. Joshua Barnes published a work to prove that Solomon was the author of the Iliad.[1]

The idle pretence that because the Egyptians had lost their own history they had recourse to that of the Jews, is at once done away with by the Abbé's observation respecting Thebes, and that all the same history is to be found among the Greeks as among the Egyptians. I feel little doubt that it was the discovery by the priests that this fact overthrew the Abbé's theory, and led to consequences of a very different nature, which prevented him from keeping his promise, to shew, in a future work, that the Greek and Latin history was the same as the Egyptian, and not the dispersion of his papers in the Revolution: but this I most exceedingly regret. His success in the case of Deucalion and Nannacus makes it probable that he could have performed his promise if he had thought proper.

7. The learned writer, in the Edinburgh Encyclopædia, whom I have several times before quoted, says,[2] "By the description above translated, (the passage of Clemens relating to hiero-"glyphics,) it plainly appears that the sacred character of the Egyptians was entirely different "from the hieroglyphic: and by this consideration we are in a good measure justified in sup-"posing, as we have done all along, that the sacred letters of the Egyptians were actually the "Chaldaic. The inscriptions on the obelisks, mentioned by Cassiodorus, so often quoted, were "certainly engraved in the sacred character; and the character in which they were drawn was "that above-mentioned. If the sacred letters were Chaldaic, the sacred language was probably "the same."

It is a very remarkable circumstance that we should here find the old Hebrew or Chaldee language, for they were both the same, to be the oldest used in Egypt. Did the Egyptians change their language, out of compliment to those pastors or shepherds whom they permitted to reside in a corner of their country, and at last expelled? The fact was, I have no doubt, that the language was the ancient Coptic, which was Hebrew or Chaldee. I do not speak of the forms of the letters used, because these were changed by caprice every day; nor, indeed, of the written language; for it must have been a Masonic secret. I cannot doubt that 1000 years before the captivity, the Chaldee, the Hebrew, the Syriac, and the Coptic, were all the same languages.

The case of the five dialects of the Celtic, namely, the Scotch, the Manks, the Irish, the Welsh, and the Cornish, is exactly similar to that of the Egyptians named above. The natives of these places do not now *generally* understand one another, but yet no one can doubt that they did all understand one another a thousand or twelve hundred years ago, and that they are merely dialects of the same Celtic language.

In the epithet *cheres*, borne by many of the kings, we have clearly the $\chi\rho\eta\varsigma\eta\rho\iota o\nu$ or $\chi-\rho\sigma\tau$ =600; T or X=300 σ=200 ρ=100=600. In the later Ptolemies the Crestologia is shewn in their names—Soter, Philadelphus, &c. $X\rho\eta\varsigma$ was but an epithet, *mitis, benignus,* applied to the divine incarnation—to the person inspired by the Holy Ghost, and possessing the crown by divine right.

8. I beg that my reader would now reconsider the circumstances, that we have found a repetition of the same mythos of Moses, &c., &c., in several countries; *secondly,* that the voyages of salvation or processions about the country, or Deisuls, as they were called in Britain, are found in most countries; and, *thirdly,* that it appears probable, from the practice of the Roman Church in scenically representing all the acts of the Saviour in the course of every year, that these pro-

---

[1] See Vol. I. p. 364. [2] Art. Phil. S. 73.

cessions or relations of the Mosaic history in the different countries, were originally nothing more than the scenical representation of the first mythos, which probably arose originally in Ayoudia, and in process of time come to be believed by the people who performed them. This scenical representation arose before the knowledge of letters, and was invented in order to keep the scheme from being lost; and I think it not at all unlikely, that the whole vulgar mythos of an incarnated person was a parable, invented by the philosophers for the purpose of keeping their refined and beautiful doctrines, and their cycles and astronomy, from being lost. I can imagine nothing so likely to answer this intended end, before letters were invented.

It seems probable that there was the same multiplication of the mythos in Egypt in the different districts, which we have found in Greece and other countries; and, that the reiteration of the different Moseses, Josephs, Chereses, in dynasties, was nothing but the repetition of the different incarnated Saviours for the same sæculum in different parts of the country. They have often been thought to have been contemporaneous sovereigns, by different authors. This exactly suits my theory. We know they had the voyages of salvation the same as in Greece. When Egypt was divided into small states, each would have its Saviour, its voyage of Salvation, or Dei-sul, or holy procession, its Olympus, Meru, &c., and its mythos of an immaculate conception, crucifixion, resurrection, &c., &c.: but when it became united under one head, it would have, as we read, one for the whole country, which annually made a procession the whole length of the Nile.

I now request my reader, before we proceed to any other subject, to reflect well upon what we have found in the Abbé's work. Let him think upon the two cities of Thebes, or the ark from which pigeons were sent out, and from which all animals and men descended, &c. Let him remember Hercules three days in the Dag, and Jonas three days in the Fish. Let him remember Samson's likeness to Hercules. Let him remember Iphigenia and Jephthah's daughter, &c., &c., &c., and then let him account, if he can, for these things, in any other way than that which I have pointed out.

CHAPTER IV.

LORD KINGSBOROUGH ON MEXICO.—MALCOLME.—MEXICAN MYTHOS THE SAME AS THAT OF THE OLD WORLD.—HUMBOLDT AND SPINETO.—CHRONOLOGY AND CYCLIC PERIODS.—TOWERS OF MEXICO AND BABEL.—JEWISH LANGUAGE AND MEXICAN RITES.—CROSS AND CRUCIFIXES.—IMMACULATE CONCEPTION. FEMALE PRINCIPLE.—HUMBOLDT.—BOCHICA, PERUVIAN RITES, &c.—THE ASS AND HORSE. RACES OF MEN.—CHINA. TIBET. SPANISH POLICY.—LAWS OF THE MEXICANS.—EASTER ISLAND.—LAST AVATAR EXPECTED.—TOD ON TIBET. ISLAND SUNK. JEWISH MYTHOS.—GENERAL OBSERVATIONS.

1. I MUST now draw my reader's attention to perhaps the most curious of all the subjects hitherto discussed, and that is, the history of Mexico and Peru. It might be supposed that these, of all nations, were the least likely to afford any useful information respecting the system or mythos which I have been unveiling; but they are, in fact, rich in interesting circumstances, that have

hitherto been totally inexplicable, but which are easily explained on the hypothesis, that there was, in very early times, an universal empire governed by a learned priesthood.

Many months after the Anacalypsis had been in the press, Lord Kingsborough's magnificent work on Mexico made its appearance. This will account for the manner in which I have spoken of Mexican hieroglyphics in the first volume. My reader will readily believe me when I say it was with great pleasure I discovered in every part of that work circumstances which can only be accounted for on the theory laid down by me, and which therefore confirm it in a very remarkable manner. His Lordship's difficulties are very striking: the language of the Jews, their mythos, laws, customs, are every where apparent. This his Lordship accounts for by supposing that in ancient times colonies of Jews went to America from Alexandria. But this by no means accounts for the difficulty, because the Trinity, the Crucifixion, and other doctrines of Christianity, are intermixed with every part of the Jewish rites, which must be accounted for; therefore, to remove this new difficulty, he is obliged to suppose that Christian missionaries, in the early times of the gospel, found their way to America. Now admitting this to have taken place, its insufficiency to account for the various incomprehensible circumstances, if not already, will very shortly be clearly proved. The South Americans had not the knowledge of letters when the Spaniards arrived among them, nor did they know the use of iron. These facts are of themselves almost enough to prove, and really do prove, when combined with other circumstances, that the Jewish customs and doctrines could not have been carried to them from Alexandria, as above suggested, or by modern Christians, who would have instantly set them to digging their mountains;[1] but, on the contrary, these facts prove that the colonization must have taken place previously to the discovery of iron by the natives of the old world, long before Alexandria was built;[2] and this agrees very well with their ignorance of the use of an alphabet. The two facts exhibit the mythos in existence at a period extremely remote indeed. For, the identity of rites, such as circumcision, &c., found in India, Syria, Egypt, and South America, puts the great antiquity and identity of the mythoses out of all doubt.

2. David Malcolme, in his book called Antiquities of Britain, (which is so ingeniously contrived that it cannot be referred to by chapter, number, page, or in any other way,) gives the following passage as an extract from Salmon's Modern History:[3] "St. Austin, speaking of the notion some "entertained of another continent, he says, 'It is not agreeable to reason or good sense to affirm, "that men may pass over so great an ocean as the Atlantic from this continent to a new-found "world, or that there are inhabitants there, all men being descended from the first man Adam." Now this shews that, from the time of Christ to the fourth century, when this African bishop lived, but then resided at Rome, there had been no colonization. It was impossible to have taken place without his knowledge, and this absolutely proves the truth of the existence of the χρης-ian mythos before the time of Christ.

The jealousy of the Pope and the court of Spain, in keeping all strangers away from South America, even to the extreme length, for many years, of excluding their own bishops and secular clergy, and permitting no priests but Dominicans and Franciscans to go thither, is accounted for. The clear and unquestionable doctrines of Judaism and Christianity, which must have existed before the time of Christ, evidently overthrew all their *vulgar esoteric* doctrines, whatever they

---

[1] Mexico is one of the few places where native iron is found, (see Vallancey's Coll. Hib. Vol. VI. p. 422,) and it lies in masses on the sides of their mountains in the greatest abundance.

[2] According to the Arundelian marbles, iron was not found out till 188 years before the war of Troy. Ibid.

[3] Vol. 28th, but the first concerning America, Introd. Part 4th and 5th.

might do with the *esoteric* or those in the conclave. Lord Kingsborough says,[1] "But one solu-"tion offers itself from all the difficulties and mysteries which seem to be inseparable from the "study of the ancient monuments, paintings, and mythology, of the Mexicans; and that is, the "presence of the Jews in the new world." Had his Lordship said the *Judaic mythos*, he would have been right; for nothing can be more clear than that it is all substantially there, and most intimately mixed, actually amalgamated, he might have added, with the Christian.

3. The similarity between the Jews, Christians, and South Americans, is sufficiently striking; but there is yet something to me still more so, which is, that several of the doctrines which I have advocated in this work, unknown to the vulgar Jews and Christians of this day, are to be found in Mexico. Their Triune God, their Creator, is called by the names Yao and Hom. Lord Kingsborough says,[2] "Hom-eyoca, which signifies the place in which exists the Creator of the uni-"verse, or the First Cause, to whom they gave the name of Hom-eteuli, which means the God of "three-fold dignity, or three Gods, the same as Ol-om-ris ....; and by another name, "Hom-cican, that is to say, the place of the Holy Trinity, who, according to the opinion of many "of their old men,' begot, by their WORD, CIPATSNAL, and a woman called X-UMIO."

In the Hom-eyo-ca, *when joined with the other circumstances*, I cannot but recognize the Om and Ai—*w* כזי *om-ia, place of Om*. And again, in Hom-ei-can the Aom-iao-ania, *the place or country of the Self-existent* (יע *ie*) Hom, who is called the Trinity. And what are we to make of the Hom, the Father of the WORD, by the Logos ?

The Father of the American Trinity is called Om-equeturiqui, ou bien Urago-Zoriso; le nom du Fils est Urus-ana, et l'Esprit se homme Urupo.[3] Here the Om of North India, the Urus or Beeve, and the *pi*-ruh, that is, *the* ruh, are very distinct. These have evidently not come from modern Christianity, but from the ancient system in the most ancient of times. Teutle is repeatedly said to mean Θεος or God. Sahagun says the Mexicans had a God, the same as Bacchus, called Ometeuchtli. Here is clearly Bacchus by his name of Oμαδιος,[4] who was called ΤΗΣ =608, which was the name of Jesus Christ, called *the desire of all nations*—the Om-nu-al of Isaiah. Here, in the Teut, we have not only the θεος of the Greeks, but we have the Teut-ates of the British Druids, and the Thoth of Egypt, and the Buddha of India under his name Tat. But it is expressly said, in several other places, that the God was called Yao. How can any one doubt that here are the remains of an ancient system ? How can any one believe that the Jews would carry all these recondite matters to Mexico, even if they did go at any time, and that they would amalgamate them all together as we have them here ?

The Mexican history gives a long account of their arrival in Mexico, from a distant country, far to the West. The stations where the colony rested, from time to time, during its long migration, which took many years, are particularly described, and it is said that ruins of the towns which they occupied are to be seen in several places along the coast. I think it is evident that this migration from the West is merely a mythos; the circumstances are such as to render it totally incredible. In principle it is the same as that of the Jews, but accommodated to the circumstances of the new world.

It really seems impossible to read Lord Kingsborough's notes, in pp. 241 et seq., and not to see, that the mythos of a chosen people, and a God conducting them after long migrations to a promised land, (attributed by the Spanish monks to the contrivance of the Devil,) was common to Jews, Christians, and Mexicans. I think it seems clear, from p. 186, that Mexico or Mesi-co was the Hebrew משיח *msih*; then it would be *the country of the Messiah*: or it might equally be the

---

[1] P. 82.   [2] Pp. 153, 156, 158.   [3] Ibid. p. 410.   [4] Ibid. Vol. VI. p. 197.

country of the leader, whom we call Moses, of the people whom we have found in Western Syria, in South India, and *Cashmere*. His Lordship shews, that the word Mesitli or Mexica is "precisely the same as the Hebrew word משיח *msih* or משה *mse* or anointed," and that one of these Gods should sit on the right hand of the other, p. 82. In the next page he says, "the full accomplishment of the prophecy of a saviour in the person of Quecalcoatle has been acknowledged by the Jews in America." He says, p. 100, "The temptation of Quecalcoatle, the fast of forty days ordained by the Mexican ritual, the cup with which he was presented to drink, the reed which was his sign, the morning star, which he is designated, the *teepatl*, or stone which was laid on his altar, and called *teotecpatl*, or divine stone, which was likewise an object of adoration; all these circumstances, connected with many others relating to Quecalcoatle, which are here omitted, are very curious and mysterious!" *But why are they omitted* by his Lordship? The pious monks accounted for all these things by the agency of the Devil, and burned all the hieroglyphic books containing them, whenever it was in their power.

This migration of the Mexicans from the West,[1] is evidently exactly similar to the *Exodus* of the Israelites from Egypt. The going out with great noise and clamour is a part of the mythos. Nimrod has shewn that it is to be found among the Greeks in their Bacchic festivals, and also among the Romans: see his second volume, article Populi Fugia.[2] The meaning of the mythos I cannot even suspect, and the nonsense of Nimrod about Babel and the horrors of Gynæocracy give no assistance. But the fact of the similarity of the histories proves that it really is a part of the mythos, that is, that a Regifugia and Populifugia is a part of the mythos.[3]

On the religion of the Hindoos the Cambridge Key says,[4] "The pristine religion of the Hindus was, I think, that of the most pure and ancient *Catholic faith*, and the religion of the enlightened few still continues such. They have worshiped a saviour, as the Redeemer of the world, for more that 4800 years. The religion of their forefathers they brought with them from the old world and established it *in the new one*. They believe implicitly in a Redeemer, whom they consider as the spirit that moved on the waters at the creation, the God that existed before all worlds." We shall find this the Mexican faith.

The God who led the Mexicans in their migration, was called *Yao-teotle, God of Armies*—Yao being said to mean army or victory—the very meaning given to it by the Jews; and, Sanscrit scholars tell me, also by the Indians.[5] Teo is said to be Θεο or Deo, and *tle* a mere termination; but, as I have stated in Vol. I. p. 221, the TTL is T=300, T=300, L=50; and TT is, in fact, the Tat or Buddha of India. Teotle is the same as תלת *tlt*, and means 650, which, as emblem of the Trinitarian God, came to mean *three*. I believe also that this has a connexion, in some way, with the תלד *tld*, probably originally תלת *tlt* or תולאד *tulad*, the male organ of generation. I believe that from this comes our word Lad. Teotl is the Supreme and Invisible Being.[6] The Tat is the name of the Tartars, who are as often called Tatars, and I am persuaded that the famous Titans were properly Tat-ans. Many reasons for these matters will be added hereafter.

Gen. Vallancey says, the earliest Irish history begins with Kartuelta,[7] which is the same as the Indo-Scythian Cear-tiutli, that is, Kaesar or Cæsar, grandson of Noah, on the banks of the Cas-

---

[1] Vide Lord Kingsborough, Vol. VI. p. 237.   [2] P. 370.

[3] I much fear I shall greatly offend the very learned person who calls himself Nimrod, of whose honour and sincerity I have no doubt; but I am quite certain, if he would consult a friend or two, he would find that he gives way to superstition in a manner very unworthy of so fine a scholar and so learned a man. His work is called Nimrod, in four volumes, 8vo., and is sold by Priestley, London.

[4] Vol. II. p. 72.   [5] P. 244.   [6] Miss Williams' Humboldt, p. 83.   [7] Coll. Hib. Vol. VI. p. 21.

pian, 300 years after the flood. Here I suspect that we have the Cæsar of Indo-Scythia, or of the Caspian, joined to the Mexican Tiutli or Teotli.[1]

4. In p. 216, Mr. Humboldt treats of a nation called Xochimileks. This must be Xaca-melech, or, I should rather say, (considering all the other circumstances which we have seen relating to the Rajahpoutans and Royal Shepherds,) *Royal Saxons*, for I much suspect they were all the same people. The Marquess Spineto, in his Lectures,[2] has quoted a person called Carli as having deeply studied the origin of nations and languages, and who, he says, has asserted that the Egyptians peopled America. He particularly notices a word as being held sacred among the Egyptians and in the Pacific ocean,—it is *Tabou*. But this is nothing but Bou-ta read anagrammatically, or, in fact, in the old Hebrew fashion. The High Priest of the North American Indians was called Sachem. I think we have here both the Saga and the Akme,[3] and also the Sciakam, which we have before noticed in Tibet. The dignity of sacrificer was supreme and hereditary, like a feudal title. His title was Papa, his dress scarlet, with fringes as a border.[4] This exactly answers to the Sagart and .'ex Sacrificulus of the ancients. The fringes of the Mexicans were fixed to the four quarters of their garments, as a sacred ordinance, precisely like those of the Jews;[5] and it is only fair to suppose, as they were similar in one respect they should be so in another, and have been descriptive of the number 600.

5. Boturini says, "No Pagan nation refers primitive events to fixed dates like the Indians," meaning the Americans. "They recount to us the history of the creation of the world, of the "deluge, of the confusion of tongues at the time of the tower of Babel, of the other epochs and "ages of the world, of their ancestors' long travels in Asia, with the years precisely distinguished "by their corresponding characters. They record, in the year of Seven Rabbits, the great eclipse "which happened at the crucifixion of Christ our Lord; and the first Indians who were converted "to Christianity, who, at that time, were perfectly well acquainted with their own chronology, "and applied themselves with the utmost diligence to ours, have transmitted to us the informa- "tion, that from the creation of the world to the happy nativity of Christ, five thousand, one "hundred and ninety-nine years had elapsed, which is the opinion or computation of the "LXX."[6]

One of their periods is 4008 years B. C.,[7] another 4801.[8] Their fourth age, the editor says, according to the Mexican symbols, lasted 5206 years, and the early Christian converts made it out 5199 years.[9] This was evidently the computation of 5200 years of Eusebius. The period of 4801 is the sum of the eight ages of the correct Neros, $8 \times 600 = 4800$. The Mexicans are said to be great astrologers.

The Mexicans believed that the millenium would commence at the end of some cycle of 52 years—$4 \times 13 = 52$; and they concluded each of these periods with deep lamentations and terrors, and hailed with corresponding joy the moment when the new cycle had commenced, which shewed that they had a new 52 years' lease. This was exactly the case with the lamentations for the death of Osiris, Adonis, &c., and his resurrection from the tomb. The new cycle having commenced, the danger had past. At first, I doubt not, this was only every 600 years; afterward, with the increasing uncertainty of the ends of those periods, and also with the increase of superstition, the festivals of Osiris, &c., came, for the sake of security, to be celebrated every year.

Lord Kingsborough says,[10] "Christians might have feared the return of every period of fifty-

---

[1] See Basnage, for a kingdom of the Jews in the East called *Cosar*, Cæsar, B. vii. ch. i., and B. viii.
[2] Pp. 199, 200. [3] Pownal on Ant. p. 190. [4] Lord Kingsborough's Mex Vol. VI. p. 69.
[5] Ib. p. 77. [6] Ib. p. 176. [7] Ib. p. 174. [8] Ib. p. 175. [9] Ib. p. 176. [10] Ib. p. 5, *note*.

" two years as being nearly the anniversary of the age which Christ had attained when he was cru-
" cified, and of the great eclipse which sacred history records, and which (since profane history is
" silent respecting it) it is very remarkable how the Mexicans should have become acquainted with."

The first pair were called Huehue.[1] Quecalcoatle disappeared at the end of fifty-two years, at the great festival in Cholula.[2] Here is the Aphanasia.

Mr. Humboldt gives nearly the same account. He says, " At the end of the fifty-two years " they had a grand festival, when all lights were extinguished, and after crucifying a man, they " kindled a fire by the friction of the wood of the Ivy on his breast, from which they were all re- " lighted. It was their belief that the world would be destroyed at the end of one of these " cycles, and as soon as this fire was kindled and the critical moment past, which assured them " that a new cycle was to run, they indulged in the greatest joy.". He shews that they new-cleaned and furnished all their houses and temples, precisely as was done by the ancient Egyptians, and, he might have added, as is also done by the Romish church at every jubilee.[3] He shews that the Mexicans had convents of Monks precisely like the Tibetians and the Romish church. After this, Humboldt states, that M. La Place, from a careful examination, had come to the conclusion, that the Mexicans knew the length of the Tropical Year more correctly than Hipparchus, and almost as correctly as Almamon;[4] and he shews, from various astronomical circumstances, that they must have had a close connexion with Eastern Asia and its cycles.

Humboldt says, "This predilection for periodical series, and the existence of a cycle of sixty " years, appear to reveal the Tartarian origin of the nations of the new continent."[5] He then states, that the cycle of sixty years was divided into four parts. "These small cycles represented " the four seasons of the great year. Each of them contained 185 moons, which corresponded " with fifteen Chinese and Tibetian years, and consequently with the real *indictions* observed in the " time of Constantine."[6] Here we see the identity accounted for of the chronological periods stated above by Lord Kingsborough, with those of the old world, as corrected by the two Cæsars with the assistance of the Chaldæans of the East. On this I shall have something very curious in a future book.

Mr. Niebuhr says, " What we call Roman numerals are Etruscan, and frequently seen on their " monuments. But these signs are of the hieroglyphic kind, and belong to an earlier mode of " symbolical writing, *in use before the introduction of alphabetical characters.*[7] They resemble " the Aztekan in this, that they represent objects individually. They were of native origin, at the " time when the West, with all its primitive peculiarities, was utterly unknown to the East,[8] " at the same period when the Turdetani framed their written characters and literature."[9]

" Here also a phenomenon presents itself, which fills us moderns with astonishment, viz. an ex- " ceedingly accurate measurement of time, and even in the cyclical year, *quite, quite in the spirit* " *in which the early Mexican legislators conducted the chronology;* portions of time measured off " from periods of very long duration, determined with astronomical precision, and without regard " to the lunar changes. Besides these, the Etruscans had a civil lunar year, which the cyclical " only served to correct........But there is something remarkable, and not to be lightly disre-

---

[1] Lord Kingsborough's Mex. Vol. VI. p. 198.   [2] Ib. p. 199.
[3] Humboldt Res. Conc. Mexico, Ed. Miss Williams, Vol. I. pp. 226, 380, 382, 384.   [4] Ibid. p. 392.
[5] Ib. Vol. II. p. 128.   [6] Ib. p. 133.
[7] How extraordinary that this author should stop here and not make the least attempt to ascertain what this symbolical writing was! It will be my object, in a future book, to supply the deficiency; but I beg my reader to recollect the admission of this learned man.
[8] What a mistake!   [9] Strabo, III. Cap. ii. p. 371, Ed. Sylb.

" garded, in the affinity between the wisdom of the ancient West and the science, at one time
" perhaps more widely diffused over that hemisphere, *and of which the Mexicans still preserved the*
" *hereditary, though probably useless possession, at the time when their country was destroyed.*
" This deserves more attentive consideration, since the discovery of an analogy between the
" Basque and American languages, by a celebrated scholar, Professor Vater."[1] In these observations we surely have a very extraordinary confirmation of my theory. If the Romans calculated by a period or sæculum of 120 years, they would come to the same conclusions as if they took the 60 or 600, and in this we see why the Mexican and Roman periods agreed in the time of Constantine and Eusebius. They would not have agreed before the time when the solstice was corrected by Sosigenes the CHALDÆAN. They would have varied more than 500 years. This we shall refer to in a future book, when it will be understood, and something exceedingly striking will be unfolded.

Humboldt says, the Mexicans hold that, before the flood, which took place 4800 years after the creation[2] of the world, he earth was inhabited by giants. One of them after the flood, called Xelhua or the architect, built an immense pyramidal tower which was to reach to heaven—but the Gods offended destroyed it with lightning. Here is a complete jumble of the ancient mythology: the 4800 are the eight cycles before Christ. The architect is the Megalistor or the name of God made into the giant, and is X-al-hua, *the self-existent* X. The tower is the exact model of the tower of Babel, as given in our old histories. After its destruction it was dedicated to Quetzalcoatl, *the God of the Air.* This is Saca, or Indra, whom we found crucified in Nepaul. (See Vol. I. p. 230.)[3] The Mexicans chaunted the word Hululaez, *which belonged to no Mexican dialect,* to the honour of their Gods.[4] This is evidently the Allelujah of the Greeks and Hebrews, and the Ullaloo of the Irish.[5]

6. It is said that after the deluge sacrificing commenced. The person who answers to Noah entered an Ark with six others, and that soon after the deluge his descendants built the tower of *Tulan* Cholula, partly to see what was going on in heaven, and partly for fear of another deluge, but it was destroyed by thunder and lightning. The story of sending birds out of the ark, the confusion and dispersion of tribes, is the same in general character with that of the Bible. His Lordship says, " In attempting to explain how the Indians could have become acquainted with
" events of such remote antiquity, coeval with the foundation of the earliest monarchies, it would
" be absurd to suppose that their annals and native traditions extended backwards to a period
" unknown to Egyptian, Persian, Greek, or Sanscrit history."[6] Absurd as it may be to suppose this, their hieroglyphic annals evidently do thus extend backwards.

His Lordship says,[7] " The difficulty of comprehending the plan of the tower of Belus, given
" by Herodotus, vanishes on inspecting the plans of the Mexican temples. The turrets in the
" great temple, described in p. 380, were 360 in number." Up to the temple Cholula were *ciento y veinte gradas.* The brick base of the tower of Chululan, which remains, and was built

---

[1] Niebuhr, Hist. Rome, Vol. I. p. 92, Ed. Walter.

[2] I think when my reader has seen a few of the following pages he will be convinced that there must here be a mistake of the translator, and that the words *after the creation of the world* ought to be *before the Christian æra.* The space 4800 is about the time of the eight cycles from the entrance of the Sun into Taurus, and when (as I shall shew in a future book) a flood probably took place.

[3] Williams, Vol. I. p. 96.   [4] Ibid.

[5] I have no doubt that the Ullaloo of the Irish, with which they wake their dead friends, was originally an invocation to the Deity to be merciful to their souls.

[6] Vol. VI. p. 117.   [7] Ib. p. 279.

in order to escape another flood if it should come, is eighteen hundred feet in circumference. It is said to have been destroyed by a stone from heaven.[1] It is pyramidal. Humbolt says it is hollow.[2] I have little doubt that the word *Chol* has been XL=650—a monogram, which it may be remembered is found in the oldest catacombs at Rome.

Teocalli is the name of the temple of Cholula; this is said to be the house of Teocalli. This is evidently *teo* or God *Cali*. *House of God* is precisely the Hebrew style.

The word Cholula is thought by Lord Kingsborough to be a corruption of the word Jeru-salem. He thinks the same of a place called Churula;[3] but I suspect that they were identical. At Cholula is the very large temple, with the very celebrated pyramid, which is said to be a very close imitation of the temple of Belus or tower of Babel.[4] A room in one of the pyramids of Cholula had its ceiling formed like the temple at Komilmar, of over-hanging stones.[5]

In Volume XXI.[6] of the Classical Journal will be found some interesting remarks of Mr. Faber's on the close similarity between the pyramid on the mountain Cholula of the Mexicans, and the tower of Belus. That one is a copy of the other, or that they are both taken from some common mythos, cannot possibly be doubted. This being premised, I would ask my reader whether he can doubt a moment, that the well-known deity *Omorca* of the Chaldæans[7] is the Hom-eyo-ca of the Mexicans? Thus we have not only the mythos of the Greeks in Bacchus, of Christianity, of Judaism, of Tartary, and of North and South India in Mexico, but we have the very oldest mythos of Babylon. How came this mythos of Babylon in Mexico? Did it go by China? I think my reader, when he considers all these circumstances, must see that my theory of one universal empire and mythos will explain all the difficulties, and that it alone can explain them.

Mr. Humboldt, after shewing that the tower at Cholula was in every respect a *close imitation* of that described by Diodorus and Herodotus at Babylon, both in its form and in the astronomical uses to which it was applied, states, as if it was not doubted, but a settled fact, that it was built after the time of Mohamed.[8] At this time the tower of Belus had for many centuries been in ruins, and its country a perfect desert. This at once shews that no dependence can be placed in Mr. Humboldt's speculation on this subject,—for surely no one will credit the recent date of this work, supposing even that it were built by emigrants from Egypt or from Chinese Tartary. In that age, after the time of Mohamed, what should induce either Jews or Christians to expend an immense sum in money or labour to build a tower of Babel, in Mexico or any where else? After the description of the Mexican pyramidal towers, Mr. Humboldt goes on to state, that there are similar pyramidal towers in Virginia and Canada, containing galleries lined with stone. He states the temple of Xochicalco accurately to face the four cardinal points,[10] to be built of stone beautifully wrought, but without cement—each stone in form of a parallelopiped.

The Mexicans' large temple, placed on a conical hill, called Xochicalco, meant, as they say, *house of flowers*. This is Xaca and Calx, Calyx, which meant Rose.[11] The hill was excavated into large caves,[12] wonderful to behold, when it is considered (as it is there observed), that the Mexicans had no iron. An observation is made by M. Dupaix, that the Mexicans are now quite ignorant of the meaning of their proper names.[13] In p. 71, it appears that the temple at Mexico

---

[1] Vol. VI. p. 196.   [3] Ib. p. 174. This Tower is in Plate XVI. See ib. p. 192.
[2] P. 34.   [4] Vide Class. Journal, Vol. XXI. p. 10.   [5] Williams's Humboldt, p. 91.
[6] Pp. 10, 11.   [7] Named in Class. Jour. Vol. XX. p. 186.   [8] Ib. p. 100.
[9] Ib. 102.   [10] Ib. p. 110.
[11] Lord Kingsborough's Mex. Ant. p. 430.   [12] Ib. p. 431.   [13] Ib. p. 432.

is, in substance and fact, called the temple of Cihnathe, C being pronounced like S, and thus making *the temple of Sin* or *Sion*, which will be explained in the book on letters. Lord Kingsborough calls it Sinai or Sina.

I feel little doubt that one of the first names of God, in the first written language, for reasons which I shall give when I explain the Origin of Letters, in all nations, languages, and times, would be רי *di, divus*, with its variety of forms : the next, perhaps, would be descriptive of 360. This might be described in various ways, as TLI—T=300 L=50 I=10=360. The meaning of these three numbers would be the glorious orb we daily behold, the Sun and God. For reasons which I shall assign, I suppose *Di* was the *first* and the prevailing name of God during many generations. Afterward, when astronomy so much improved that the knowledge of the Neros of 650 was acquired, the name TTL=650 was adopted as his name, and we have it in Mexico, (where *figures* were known, but not *syllabic letters,)* in the name of the Deity *Teotle*. The periods shew how far, at the time in which they branched off from Asia, the knowledge of the system had extended. Their period from the creation to Christ, of 5200 years, embraces the eight ages of their cycle: their *TTL*, T$_{EOTLE}$=650 ×8=5200, corresponding with the period of Eusebius. In India, the name 360 fell into disuse and was lost, and was probably superseded by the words Titlu=666, TTL=650+IU or *i* U=16=666, and, at last, by the number now used, TT=600. I know not how I could have invented any thing more in accordance with my theory than that this Mexican God should have this peculiar, appropriate name, had I set my wits to work for the purpose of invention. " Teotl signifies, in the Mexican language, both the Sun and an Age ; and " the image of the sun, surrounded with rays, was the symbol of the latter." [1]

Mr. Fred. Schlegel has observed,[2] that the word *atl* or *atel* is found in the languages of the East of Europe ; that it means *water*, and that its symbol has found its way into the Greek alphabet in the letter Mem, in the undulating shape by which water is meant—м ; that it is also in the Phœnician and most western nations. It is in the *Estoteland* of Greenland, which is, I suspect, di-ania-estotel ; and I also suspect that it is the symbol of the centre letter and of water, because it is the symbol of fluid of any kind. I think this leads to the meaning of our word Land, L'-ania-di—the holy country.

7 Almost all persons who have written respecting the Mexicans, have observed the similarity of their language to that of the Hebrews. This and many other strange things the monks admit most unwillingly, and attribute to the devil. Las Casas said that the language of Saint Domingo was "corrupt Hebrew."[3] The Caribbees have the word Neketali, meaning *dead*; in Hebrew קטל *qtl*: Hilaali, *he is dead*; in Hebrew חלל *hll*: Kaniche, *a cane* ; (sugar ;) in Hebrew קנה *qne*: Eneka, *a collar*; in Hebrew ענק *ank*.[4]

Las Casas wrote an account of the Mexicans, in which (we are told) he states his belief that they are descended from the Jews.[5] This account, by his desire, was never published. But why should he object to its being known that the Mexicans descended from the Jews? The reason is very evident: it was because he saw it was ridiculous, and he did not believe it himself. This book is in the Academy of History at Madrid. It was examined a few years ago by the Government, but it was not thought proper to publish it.[6]

Lord Kingsborough gives the following passage:[7] "Las Casas' persuasion that the Indians were "descended from the Jews is elsewhere mentioned : but as the words, ' Loquela tua manifestum

---

[1] Mex. Ant. Vol. VI. p. 157.   [2] Notes on Miss Williams's Humboldt, Vol. II. p. 222.
[3] Mex. Ant. Vol. VI. p. 283.   [4] Anc. Univ. Hist. Vol. XX. p. 161.
[5] Mex. Ant. Vol. VI. p. 7.   [6] Ibid.   [7] Ib. p. 7, *note*.

"te facit, were discovered, with some other reasons tending towards the same conclusion, by
"Torquemada, in some private papers containing the will of Las Casas, at the same time that
"great weight must be attached to so solemnly recorded an opinion, it cannot be said that that
"learned prelate was guilty *of any indiscretion* in promulgating it: but the contrary is proved, by
"the proviso which he made respecting the publication of his history,—that it should not be
"printed till fifty years after his death, and then only if it appeared good to the superior of his
"order, and for the benefit of religion; but that in the intermediate time no layman or young
"ecclesiastic was to be permitted to read it. The work has never been published: and Don
"Martin Fernandez de Navarrete says, that when it was referred some years ago to the Academy
"of History at Madrid, to take their decision respecting its publication, they did not think it
"convenient." I now learn that permission has been given to Lord Kingsborough to copy it.
The secreting practice is found to answer no longer. The old proverb applies, "Omne ignotum
"pro magnifico est." I shall be surprised if any thing important be found in it, as much as I
should have been to have heard, that the French found many diamonds at Loretto when they got
there, or secret learning in the Vatican Library when they got to Rome.

David Malcolme, in his Essay on Ant. of Brit., says, "Take it in the sense of Wytfleet, thus,
"p. m. 12, which in substance amounts to this, &c., when the Spaniards were in the magna
"insula Indice Hayti: When the bell rung for evening prayers, the Spaniards, according to
"custom, bowed their knees, and signed themselves with the cross. The Indians did imitate
"them with great reverence, falling down on their knees, and joining their hands together, (rather,
"as I think, for imitation than for any other reason,) though there are several who think, that
"the Indians had the cross in veneration long before the arrival of Columbus. Gomara, Book iii.
"Chap. xxxii. tells, That St. Andrew's Cross, which is the same with that of Burgundy, was in
"very great veneration among the Cumans, and that they fortified themselves with the cross
"against the incursions of evil spirits, and were in use to put them upon new-born infants; which
"thing very justly deserves admiration. Neither can it be conceived how such a rite should
"prevail among savages, unless they have learned this adoration of the cross from mariners or
"strangers, who, being carried thither by the violence of tempests, have died or been buried there,
"which without all doubt would have also happened to that Andalusian pilot who died in the
"house of Columbus, unless he had been very skilful in sea affairs, and so had observed his
"course, when he was hurried away with the force of the storms: it is very credible that many
"of those who are generally reckoned to have been foundered at sea, did really meet with accidents
"of this kind. But the *Accusamilenses* bring another reason of adoring the cross, and which
"seems nearer truth, to wit, That they had received by tradition from their forefathers, that
"formerly a man more glorious than the sun had passed through these countries and suffered on
"a cross." Here we have the mythos clear enough in Hispaniola.

The Rev. Dr. Hyde, speaking of the priests of Peru, takes occasion to say, "Nam populi
"simplicitas et sacerdotum astutia omni ævo *omnique regione* semper notabilis."[1] No wonder
the University of Oxford refused to print any more of his manuscripts. He was speaking of a
virgin of Peru, who was pregnant by the sun. The Reverend Doctors of Oxford did right not
to publish his works while he lived, and to destroy his manuscripts when he died.[2] He ought to
have been burnt himself—*Omnique regione*, indeed!!!

Acosta says, that the Americans adored the sea, under the name Mammacocha. I believe this
was the Marine Venus Mamma בכבא *cochab*.[3]

---

[1] Cap. iv. p. 123. [2] Vide Toland's Nazarenus, Chap. iv., and Bibliog. Brit. [3] Lord Herbert, p. 149.

The Mexicans baptized their children, and the water which they used they called the *water of regeneration*.[1]

The Mexican king danced before the God, and was consecrated and anointed by the high priest with holy unction. On one day of the year all the fires were put out, and lighted again from one sacred fire in the temple;[2] —the practice of the Druids. Lord Kingsborough[3] shews, that the Messiah of the Jews is foretold to have an ugly or a marred countenance, and that the Mexican Quecalcoatle is said to have had the same. At the end of October they had a festival exactly answering to our *All Saints* and *All Souls*.[4] They call it *the festival of advocates*, because each human being had an advocate to plead for him. Thus we have this festival throughout modern Europe, in Tibet, and in the ancient festival of the Druids' Saman in Ireland, and in Mexico. There is the story of the rebellious angels and the war in heaven.[5] This is not from our Pentateuch.

9. The Peruvians had a festival called *the festival of Capacrayme*, in the first month of their year, called Rayme.[6] *Acosta supposes this was contrived by the Devil in imitation of the Passover*. It may be observed, that all the acts of worship are directed avowedly to the Sun. The Mexicans sacrificed human victims, which Lord Kingsborough[7] has shewn was practised by the Jews, who were, according to his Lordship's account, horrible cannibals.

Georgius shews that the God Xaca was constantly called Cio;—this was the Xiuh-tecutli or God of Fire, or God of Years, or the Everlasting One, of the Mexicans.[8] Volney[9] says, the Teleuteans are a Tartar nation.

Buddha was Hermes, and Hermes was Mercury, and Mercury was the God of Merchants, and Buddha was Xaca, and Saca and the Mexican God of Merchants was Yaca-tecutli.

In the history of the Aztecks of Mexico, we find much respecting one Coxcox saved on a raft, in a great flood. Now when I consider that the Mexicans are so closely connected with North India, and that their accounts are all preserved by a mixture of hieroglyphics and unwritten tradition, I cannot help suspecting that this Coxcox ought to be Sasax or Saxas.

Nagualism is a doctrine known in America, (Naga is שרן nhs, softened or corrupted, and the Hag of England,) where the serpent is called *Culebra*; this is Colubra; and the followers of it are called Chivim; these are the Evites, or Hivites, or Ophites. Eve is חוה hvia or חוה hiua.[10]

The Mexicans had a forty-days' fast in memory of one of their sacred persons who was tempted *forty* days on a mountain. He drinks through a reed. He is called the Morning Star, &c., &c. This must be the same person noticed before (p. 24) to have had a reed for an emblem. As Lord Kingsborough says, "These are things which are very curious and mysterious."[11]

The inhabitants of Florida chaunt the word Hosanna in their religious service, and their priests were named Jouanas.[12]

Sina is the ancient name of China. I suspect Sina, and Sian or Siam, are the same word. The God of Hayti was called Jocanna, the c is evidently instead of the aspirate in Johanna.[13]

One of the temples has the name of Çihnateocalli—that is, I suppose, temple of Cali, the God of Sina or Sian.[14]

Lord Kingsborough says,[15] the Mexicans honour the cross. —"They knew them (the Chiribians,

---

[1] Mex. Ant. Vol. VI. p. 114.   [2] Ib. p. 144.   [3] Ib. p. 167, note.   [4] Ib. p. 101.
[5] Ib. p. 401.   [6] Ib. p. 305.   [7] Ib. p. 328.   [8] Ib. p. 392.
[9] Ruins, Notes, p. 198, and Asiat. Res. Vol. III. p. 358.   [10] See Vol. I. p. 523.
[11] Mex. Ant. Vol. VI. p. 100.   [12] Ib. p. 71.   [13] Ib. p. 98.   [14] Ib. p. 71.   [15] Ib. p. 4.

" or Chiribichenses, which name differs from that of Chibirias, the mother of Bacab,) honour the " cross."

The Incas had a cross of very fine marble, or beautiful jasper, highly polished, of one piece, three-fourths of an ell in length, and three fingers in width and thickness. It was kept in a sacred chamber of a palace, and held in great veneration. The Spaniards enriched this cross with gold and jewels, and placed it in the cathedral of Cusco.[1] Mexican temples are in the form of a cross, and face the four cardinal points.

Quecalcoatle is represented in the paintings of the Codex Borgianus nailed to the cross.[2] Sometimes even the two thieves are there crucified with him.[3]

In Vol. II. plate 75, the God is crucified in the Heavens, in a circle of nineteen figures, the number of the Metonic cycle. A serpent is depriving him of the organs of generation. In the Codex Borgianus, (pp. 4, 72, 73, 75,) the Mexican God is represented crucified and nailed to the cross, and in another place hanging to it, with a cross in his hands. And in one instance, where the figure is not merely outlined, the cross is red, the clothes are coloured, and the face and hands quite black. If this was the Christianity of the German Nestorius, how came he to teach that the crucified Saviour was black? The name of the God who was crucified was Quecal-coatle. I suspect this was Saca, or Xaca, or Kaca—the Coatle (or God).[4] The mother of Quecalcoatle is called Sochi-quetzal; may this be mother of Xaca?[5] Sochi, or Suchi-quecal is both *male* and *female*.[6]

In pp. 71, 73, of the Codex Borgianus, the burial, descent into hell, and the resurrection, are represented.[7]

In one of the plates the God is crucified on a mountain. I suspect that this is Prometheus.

10. The Immaculate Conception is described.[8] This is also described in Torquemada's Indian Monarchy. The Mexican word *Dios* meant God, and he was called *ineffable*.[9]

The Immaculate Conception is described in the Codex Vaticanus.[10] The Virgin Chimalman, also called Sochiquetzal or Suchiquecal,[11] was the mother of Quecalcoatle. Sochiquetzal means *the lifting up of Roses*.

Eve is called Ysnextli, and it is said she sinned by plucking *roses*. But in another place these roses are called *Fruta del Arbor*.[12] The Mexicans called the Father Yzona, the Son Bacab, and the Holy Ghost Echvah. This, they say, they received from their ancestors.[13] The Lakchmi of India is called *Chri*. (Lakchmi is L'Achm; Chri is $X\rho\eta\varsigma$.) These are the same as the Mexican Centeotl, i. e. *Cen*-teotl;[14] and Centeotl, is Can or Cun-teotl,—the Cunti, the name of the female generative principle in India.

The Mexican Eve is called Suchiquecal. A messenger from heaven announced to her that she should bear a son, who should bruise the serpent's head. He presents her with a rose. This was the commencement of an Age, which was called the *Age of Roses*. In India this is called the *Age of the Lotus*, the water rose. Upon this it may be observed, that if this had been a

---

[1] Vega, Book ii. Chap. iii.   [2] Mex. Ant. Vol. VI. p. 166.   [3] Ibid.   [4] Ib. p. 173.
[5] Ib. p. 175.   [6] Ib. p. 176.   [7] Ib. VI. p. 166.   [8] Ib. p. 65.
[9] Ib. p. 68.   [10] Ib. pp. 175, 176.
[11] This is really our Sukey, and the Greek ψυχη. It comes from the language of the Tartars, Tatars, the Sacæ or Saxons, the language of Tanga-tanga or Tangut.
[12] Mex. Ant. Vol. VI. p. 120.   [13] Ib. p. 165.   [14] Humboldt, Ed. Miss Williams, Vol. I. p. 221.

N.B. This was the *last* sheet revised by the Author—a short time before he died.

Papist forgery, the *woman* and not the *seed of the woman* would have bruised the head. It may also be observed, that if this had come from the Western part of the old world, since the time of Constantine, it would certainly have had the woman and not the seed of the woman. All this history the Monkish writer is perfectly certain is the invention of the Devil.[1] Torquemada's Indian History was mutilated at Madrid before it was published.[2] Suchiquecal is called the Queen of Heaven. She conceived a son, without connexion with man, who is the God of Air. This is the immaculate conception, and the God Indra, whom we found crucified and raised from the dead in Nepaul. The Mohamedans have a tradition that Christ was conceived by the smelling of a rose.[3] The temples of Quetzalcoatle were round. He was the inventor of temples in this form.

In the thirty-sixth chapter of Marco Paulo, an account is given of the sacrifice, in the province of Tanguth, a little North of Nepaul, of a Ram of a year old, which is said to be offered as a ransom for the Child. The same is practised among the Chinese.[4] Torquemeda says,[5] "Two "things are very remarkable: the first is, that the parents of the children should have sold them, "and given them voluntarily for sacrifice: the second, that the sale itself should have taken place "on the second day of this month, (February,) at the very time that we, who are Christians, "celebrate the festival of the presentation of the Virgin without spot, in the temple of Jerusalem, "holding in her arms her most blessed child, the Son of God, whose life was sold for the sin of "the first woman who existed in the world, carrying him to present and make an offering of him, "manifesting, as it were to God, the sacrifice which was afterwards to be accomplished on the "tree of the cross."[6]

11. Mr. Humboldt has written much respecting the Americans. It is a remarkable circumstance that it should never have occurred to him, that the ignorance in the South Americans of the use of letters and iron, were decisive circumstantial proofs of their very great antiquity, and their very early separation from the stock of the old world; but this great antiquity he considers proved from a variety of other circumstances. He says, "It cannot be doubted, that the greater "part of the nations of America belong to a race of men, who, isolated ever since the infancy of "the world from the rest of mankind, exhibit in the nature and diversity of language, in their "features and the conformation of their skull, incontestable proofs of an early and complete separation."[7] Except in the article language he is quite right.

Malcolme shews that Tautah in the American language means Father; in Irish, Dad; Welsh, Tad or Taduys; Armoric, Tat; Cornish, Tad and Tas; Scotch, Dad; St. Kelda, Tat; and in Guatimala, Tat; in Old Italy, Tata; in Egypt, Dade; in Greek, Tetta; in Old English, Daddy.[8] The American Taut-ah is the Indian Tat.

After shewing at great length that the Mexicans must have had their mythology from Asia, East of the Indus, Mr. Humboldt[9] observes, that he finds among them neither the Linga nor any of those figures with several heads and hands which characterize the paintings and figures of the Hindoos. But he distinctly admits that he finds the doctrine of repeated regenerations in cycles.

---

[1] Ant. of Mex. Vol. VI. p. 177.   [2] Ib. p. 179.

[3] Ib. p. 176. This was the *water rose* or Lotus. He was the Rose of Sharon, that is, he was the Rose of Ishuren, or the God of the country where the language is called that of Posh or Push—*the flower*.

[4] Ib. note, Marsden.   [5] Monarquia Indiana, Vol. II. p. 261.

[6] Ant. of Mex. Vol. VI. p. 201.

[7] Researches in S. America, by Humboldt, Vol. I. pp. 249, 250, ed. Miss Williams.

[8] Dr. Malcolme's Letters.   [9] Humboldt's Res. Vol. II. p. 36, ed. Miss Williams.

Now this again seems to confirm my hypothesis, that they migrated from the old world so early as to be before these corruptions, early as the Linga was. And it has induced me to review the early history of Buddhism, and to make me *suspect* that, in its early works, the Linga is not to be found, and that it only came into use when the division between the followers of the Linga and Ioni began to arise, which caused the horrible civil and religious wars, noticed in my former volume, pp. 332, &c.

12. The founder of the Peruvian nation was called *Bochica*, the son and emblem of the Sun. He was high priest of Soga-Mozo (here we have the Saga).[1] His wife was called *Chia*, (*Chia* is nothing but *Eva* corrupted,) Isis, or the Moon: he was described with three heads. Here, I think, are the Buddha and Trimurti of India. His priests were called Xeques and Zaques.[2] (These are Xacas, or Sagas, or priests of Wisdom.) Humboldt says, " The form of Government " given by Bochica to the inhabitants of Bogota is very remarkable, from its analogy with those " of Japan and Thibet. The Incas of Peru united in their person the temporal and spiritual " powers. The children of the sun were both priests and kings . . . . . . The Pontiffs or Lamas, " the successors of Bochica, were considered as heirs of his virtue and sanctity. The people " flocked in crowds to offer presents to the high priests, visiting those places which were conse- " crated by the miracles of Bochica."[3] In a very particular and pointed manner this Bochica is said to be white or albus. This reminds me that the Sibyl pronounces the *white* sow of Alba to be *black*. Alba means white: was Bochica Alb or LB=L=50, B=2=52? He had a peculiar cycle of 13 years, and another of four thirteens or 52. This looks as if there was some reference to our astrological instrument, called playing cards, which certainly came from North India. This does not seem so wonderful when we consider that we have just found their cycles the same as the indictions of Constantine. What is the Romish Alb?

The Peruvians believed in one Supreme Being, the Creator of Heaven and Earth, called Vira-chocha and Pachacamack,[4] who had *revealed to them his religion*.[5] The Mexicans called their great God Yao INEFFABLE;[6] and represented him by an Eye in a Triangle. The cross was every where adored.[7] The Mexicans expected a Messiah.[8] Their history of the flood is almost a close copy of that of Moses.[9] Their baptism [10] in the presence of witnesses is almost the same as that of the Jews and Persians, and in the same manner they named their children and offered them in the temple. They had the custom of sacrificing the first-born, the same as the Jews, till it was done away by Abraham or Moses. They had also the right of circumcision. (Refer to Vol. I. Book X. Chap. VI. Sect. 13, p. 724.)[11] Their temples were in the form of a cross, and faced the four cardinal points.[12] Their language has many Greek and Hebrew words in it.[13] They practised auricular confession.[14] They have a sacred and select word like the Indian *Om*, which is never spoken; but what it is, I do not find mentioned.

13. The union of the Jewish and the Christian mythos in one system, instead of their division into two systems, at once proves that they cannot have been brought to Mexico at different and distant periods. Had this been the case, there would have been two religions, as in all other cases, in opposition to one another. It is a wonderful circumstance, that the Jews coming from the city of Egypt built by Alexander, should have forgot to bring with them the knowledge of

---

[1] Humboldt's Res. Vol. II. p. 108, ed. Miss Williams.
[2] Ant. of Mex. Vol. VI. p. 164; Lord Kingsborough calls him the Mithra or Osiris of Bogota.
[3] Humboldt's Res. Vol. II. p. 109, ed. Miss Williams. [4] Antiq. of Mex. Vol. VI. p. 365. [5] Ib. p. 128.
[7] [6] Ibid. P. 141. [8] P. 115. [9] P. 117. [10] Pp. 45, 47.
[11] Pp. 67 and 115. [12] P. 96. [13] Pp. 115, 116. [14] P. 115.

letters and iron; and still more wonderful, that the Christian monks coming in a later day should have had equally bad memories. All that was necessary was, for those Jews to have told these skilful smelters of metals, that by melting the lumps of their native iron in a wood fire they would get iron and steel.

The identity of the Mexican and Chinese or North Indian mythoses being unquestionable, attempts have been made, in several periodical publications, to account for their similarity by supposing, that the Mexicans were colonies fleeing from the arms of Mohamedan or Tartarian conquerors. But the writers do not tell us how the Jewish and Christian doctrines came to be found in America, mixed most intimately together, and also with the idolatry of North India and Greece. Other writers contend, that these colonists were Mongol or Tartar conquerors, who, not contented with the conquest of China, conquered America also. But this leaves all the great difficulties I have stated above unremoved. It is a most wonderful thing that these Tartarian heroes did not take with them the knowledge of iron or letters : and that they, being Mohamedans, should convey the Christian religion to the Mexicans instead of that of Mohamed!

It is also wonderful that they should take with them the knowledge of the Horse and the Ass, though they did not take these animals themselves—pictures of them being seen every where mixed with their other hieroglyphics; and, what is still more, as the reader will instantly see, mixed most intimately with the Judæan mythos,—a hero mounted on an ass or a horse, sometimes carrying a *sword*, sometimes a *cross*. It is impossible, on viewing them, not to recollect the procession of Jesus Christ on the ass, into Jerusalem. The mythoses are evidently identical, but their variations shew that they are not copies. Though they have plenty of pictures of the horse, the animal, be it observed, noticed in the Revelation, they have no knowledge of the elephant or camel. But these were not in the Revelation; were no part of the mythos. They have no sheep, but they have an animal like it, which they call Llama or Lamb.[1]

No part of the Mexican hieroglyphics is more striking than the exhibition of the *horse* or *ass*,[2] (for some are doubtful,) animals totally unknown in a state of nature to the Americans. I refer to the plates' figures. Faria y Sousa, the Jesuit, says, that when the Portuguese arrived in the Azores they found the statue, cut on the side of a mountain, of a man on horseback wearing a cloak, his left hand on the horse's main, his right pointing to the West, with an inscription on the lower rock but not understood.[3]

It is necessary to observe here, that tribes, both of Negroes and bearded men, were found in South America.[4]

The Codex Vaticanus, Volume II., is marked 3738. The plates in it are numbered to 146, but the explanation goes only to plate 92, in either English or Spanish. The explanation purports to be in Volume VI. p. 155, of Lord Kingsborough's work. My reader has only to look to the figures of the crucifixes which I have given, Fig. 12—14; and to reflect for one moment upon the admitted anxiety of the Spaniards and the Popes to keep the knowledge of these things from the European world, to see why the explanation of the Codex Vaticanus ends with plate 92. The remainder has, no doubt, been suppressed to avoid the necessity of giving an explanation of the crucifixes.

We every where meet with the Mexican divine names ending in *tle*, as Teotle, that is, Deo or God *tle*. It has been observed by Lord Kingsborough, *as well as by almost all the Spanish authors*, that the Mexican language is so full of Hebrew words as to be almost Hebrew. We have

---
[1] Antiq. of Mexico, Vol. VI. p. 361.
[2] [Is this indisputable? Do not the accompaniments of the *rider* bespeak a Spanish origin? Yet, is not the Author's opinion supported by the testimony of Faria y Sousa? *Editor*.]
[3] Vol. I. p. 19, Eng. Ed.   [4] Antiq. of Mexico, Vol. VI. pp. 290, 291.

seen the God every where crucified and suspended from the Cross. We have found the sacred animal the Llama[1] or sheep. We have found the mythos of the crucified Saviour. We have found every thing at last to centre in the Sun. The word *tle* is confessed not to be understood by the Mexicans, nor by the Spaniards, who call it, for that reason, merely a termination. All these matters considered, I think it may be the same as the word טלה *tle* or טלא *tla*, the Hebrew name of the sign of the Zodiac, *Agnus* or *Aries*.[2] In Hebrew it means, when spelt with the tau, תלה *tle, hanged* or *suspended*. See Fig. 14. I believe it meant *crucified* by *hanging on a cross*. It was originally Buddha, as noticed before in Sect. 3, p. 24. For the same reason that the word meaning 650 was applied to him, it was in succession applied to the God of wisdom, to the Lamb— his second emblem, and to the crucified God Cristna.

14. All the Mosaic history is to be found in China according to Mons. Paravey, in which he only repeats what was before pointed out by Bergeron, De Guines, &c. The Chinese historians relate that one of their ancient despots endeavoured to destroy their old records, but that a copy of their history, called the Chou-king, escaped. That book treats of the terrestrial paradise, its rivers, waters of immortality, its admirable trees, fall of the angels and of man, and the *appearance at that moment of mercy*; also of the sabbath, confusion of tongues, the manna in the Wilderness, the Trinity; and of the Holy One in the West, who was incomprehensible and one with the TIEN. It states that the world cannot know the Tien except by the Holy One, who only can offer a sacrifice acceptable to the CHANG-TI.[3] The nations are waiting for him like plants for a refreshing shower. The Tien is the Holy One invisible, and the Holy One is the Tien made visible and teaching men. All this was taught by Confucius five hundred and fifty years before Christ. Ancient inscriptions state the Jews to have come into China about the time of Confucius. This is probably the arrival of a colony or doctrine of a new incarnation going to them from the Western Ayoudia. The secret doctrine of the renewed incarnations seems, by being misunderstood, to have operated with them precisely as it did with their Indian and Tibetian neighbours, for they are of the Tibetian or Buddhist faith, into which all these doctrines dovetail perfectly. These facts and many more are detailed from different authors by the learned Nimrod, Vol. III. p. 510. All these things good people, like Nimrod, suppose were taught to the Tartars and Chinese by the lost tribes of Samaria. Those tribes are most useful people; they account for every difficulty. In the East, in the West, in the North, in the South, they are always ready at hand. Here is all the Jewish and the *Christian mythos* amalgamated precisely as it is in Mexico, in Tibet, North India, and South India, all carrying with it proofs of its almost universal prevalence or dissemination. But notwithstanding that we find remnants of this mythos every where, the actual character of which cannot be doubted, yet in the respective countries where they are found, the system is obsolete; they are remnants of an almost forgotten system. They every where carry traits of the system of regeneration or of the cycles recorded in the old Druidical circles or Cyclopæan monuments, found along with them, the origin of which is acknowledged to be totally unknown. There cannot be any doubt that they have all flowed from the same fountain; have the same origin; and the only question will be, whether they flowed from the kingdom of the West, which Herodótus could not find, and Alexander thought it not worth his while to notice, or from the kingdom of Ayoudia of India, with its capital probably, as appears from its ruins, once the largest in the world—a city larger than London, the capital of an empire more extensive than Europe. (See Vol. I. p. 488.)

There is scarcely a page of Lord Kingsborough's work which does not exhibit proofs of the

---

[1] Le Lama. [2] Barret on the Zodiacs, p. 10.
[3] In the Chang-ti, *Ch* is the I aspirated; *ang* is a, o, הן co; Ti is Di, the whole, Di Iao.

anxiety of the Spanish government to suppress the information which I have just now detailed, and which does not also shew that it comes to us through the medium of the most unwilling of witnesses.¹ Every contrivance which was possible was resorted to in order to prevent its arrival in Europe; and this accounts for the extraordinary and systematic opposition to the admission of strangers into New Spain. All people likely to be intelligent, such as physicians, persons suspected of heresy, &c., were prohibited from going thither. The reason assigned by the Spanish government was,² that they were prevented going that they might not create disputes and prevent conversions. The author of the notes to Lord Kingsborough's book³ says, that he believes that the Jews colonized America, and held it for one thousand years, and that they introduced (as it must have been along with their own) the Christian rites into the religion of the Mexicans, *who had never heard of Christianity, to shew their hatred of Christianity, and to turn it into ridicule;* and, that it was for this reason that they established the Christian doctrines along with those of the Jews,—such as the resurrection, ascension, &c. The passage is so extraordinary, that I think the writer must have meant i. for a joke.

The close connexion between the Americans and the old world was long ago seen, notwithstanding all the exertions of the Spaniards to keep mankind in the dark, and fruitless endeavours were made by Grotius and others to find a cause for it. An account of them may be seen in Basnage.⁴ It is there observed, that one of the districts has a German name—Estoteland; that the name of a young sheep is Lam; that one of their Gods is called Theut, and one of their kings Theuch, evidently the same name; that their great Creative Principle is called Pachacama; (Piakm-cama, that is, Pi-Acham, *the wisdom of divine Love;*) that they baptize their children in the form of the cross, and have a notion of the Trinity; that they adorn their idols with the cross and mitre; that they have a kind of Eucharist; that virgins, consecrated to the God, make effigies of paste and honey, which they consecrate with much ceremony, and afterward distribute to the people, who believe they eat the body of their God. The people of North America were thought by *Penn* to have an unaccountable likeness to the Jews, and the Massagetæ were thought to be found in Massachusetts.

Tibet is called Tangutia. This is evidently *ia tangut,* the country of Tangut. The close similarity of the Trinitarian and other doctrines of the Tibetians to those of the Romish Christians we have seen. It is surely a very extraordinary thing to find the Peruvian triune God called *Tanga-Tanga*—evidently the same as the God of Tibet, both in name and character.⁵

15. In Vol. VI. p. 79, the Mexican courts are shewn to have had exactly the same number of judges as those of the Jews; that their sacred numbers were exactly the same; and that both nations kept fasts for exactly the same number of days. Lord Kingsborough says, " the common law of every " state in Europe has been confessedly modelled after the Mosaic law."⁶ This is a very important observation, and I think its truth will not be disputed; but I think there is no other way of accounting for it than to go to my primeval nation. The common law in most states is evidently older than Christianity. We are told that St. Augustin brought Christianity into this island in the year 596; but was there no Christianity in the time of Constantine or before? Lord Kingsborough says, " the affinity between the Mexican and the Hebrew laws is greater than between " the latter and those of any nation with which we are acquainted."⁷ They circumcised with a stone knife, the use of which was expressly ordered.⁸ It is remarkable that the circumcision of

---

¹ Antiq. of Mex. Vol. VI. pp. 111. et seq.   ² Ib. p. 268   ³ Ib. p. 283.
⁴ Book vi. Ch. iii.   ⁵ See Parsons' Rem. Jap. pp. 206, 219, 220; also Georgius, Alph. Tib. p. 9.
⁶ Antiq. of Mex. Vol. VI. pp. 271, 272.   ⁷ Ibid. p. 272.
⁸ Ibid. p 273. The Abyssinian Christians practised circumcision and abstained from Pork, ibid. p. 274.

the Jews should have been performed with a knife made of stone, which is emphatically noticed in the Bible.[1]

16. Easter Island is situated in N. L. 27° 5′ W. L. 109° 46′: it may be considered to be a part of America. The most remarkable curiosity in this island is a number of colossal statues. On the East side of the island were seen the ruins of three platforms of stone-work, on each of which had stood four of these large statues; but they were all fallen down from two of them, and one from the third: they were broken or defaced by the fall. One was fifteen feet long and six feet broad over the shoulders: each statue had on its head a large cylindric stone of a red colour, wrought perfectly round. Others measured nearly twenty-seven feet, and upwards of eight feet over the shoulders: and a still larger one was seen standing, the shade of which was sufficient to shelter all the party of Captain Cook, who reports this, from the sun. The workmanship is rude, but not bad, nor are the features of the face ill formed: the ears are long, according to the distortion practised in that island, and the bodies have hardly any thing of a human figure about them. How these islanders, wholly unacquainted with any mechanical power, could raise such stupendous figures, and afterwards place the large cylindric stones upon their heads, is truly wonderful! It is observed that the most probable conjecture is, that the stone is factitious. The island is about ten or twelve leagues in circumference,[2] and must be in the Gulf of California. But see Cook and Forster's Voyage, March, 1774. The Encyclopædia Londinensis says, the names of the two statues left standing are Dago and Taurico. Here we have Dagon and Taurus. Surely nothing can be more curious than these statues. Who placed them here; and when were they set up?

17. Every one must remember the accounts of the perfect horror with which the unhappy Mexicans viewed the first horses, which the Spaniards took over to their country. This I will now account for. It appears from Lord Kingsborough's book, &c., that they had all the mythos which has been so fully explained, of the old world,—the immaculate conception, the crucifixion, the resurrection after three days, the expectation of the return of their crucified Saviour, &c., &c. Every Indian inquirer knows that the last Avatar was always expected by the people of Java to come mounted on a white horse. Now, in several of the Mexican hieroglyphic pictures, though their owners knew nothing of the horse, an animal, which might be either a horse or an ass, is painted. In these same pictures, the other parts of the mythos, the crucifixion, &c., are described. From this it is evident, that although they were not able to convey the horse over the sea, yet they could convey every part of the mythos; the result of this was, that when the Spaniards arrived in flying machines, or machines propelled by the winds,—on the wings of the wind,—across the boundless ocean, or from heaven,—their commander mounted on the unknown animal, described in their ancient pictures to be that on which the promised God was to come;[3] and, carrying in his hand thunder and lightning, with which he destroyed his enemies at miles distant from him, he was believed to be the last Avatar. Lord Kingsborough gives a very interesting account of the effect which this superstition or belief had upon their conduct—taking away from most of them, from devotion, all wish to resist their God, mounted on his horse and surrounded by thunder and lightning—and from others, through fear, all power: thus giving to their cruel enemies an easy victory. I cannot conceive it possible to devise any thing more conclusive of the truth of my whole system than this. All this accounts for numbers of circumstances relating

---

[1] See Exod. iv 25; Josh. v. 3; and Ant. of Mex. Vol. VI. p. 187.   [2] Encyclopædia Brit. art. Easter Island.

[3] The effect which the death of the first horse had on the Mexicans has been thought very extraordinary and unaccountable. It is now easily explained: by the destruction of the immortal, celestial animal they were in part undeceived.

to the conduct of Montezuma and his people, which have hitherto been utterly unintelligible. And I think it seems evident, that if the miscreants from Spain had really understood their own case, they would have had nothing to do but to have quietly taken possession of the whole empire as its last Avatar and newly-arrived God.

Well, indeed, might Peter Martyr, Las Casas, and Torquemada, be puzzled with the horse, the actual horse of the Revelation, in a country where the people had not the knowledge of the animal, or indeed of any animal of the old world. Instead of accepting the possession of the empire peaceably offered to them, by a most absurd and extraordinary mistake, the Spaniards determined to terrify the people by ill usage, the account of which is given in the Antiquities of Mexico.[1]

18. Col. Tod[2] states the mountains above Tibet, the highest ridge of Asia, to be called Andes— these must have been in the countries of Tungusians. It is impossible on reading this not to recollect the Andes and the Tanga-Tanga of Peru; and it is equally impossible to attribute this paranomasia and the other circumstances already described to accident. To account for this I look into ancient histories, and I adopt the first rational and philosophical cause which is recorded, and without difficulty I find it in the communication formed by the island of Atlantis of Plato; for the subsequent submerging of such an island or continent is neither improbable nor irrational, —but, when the attendant circumstances are considered, a dry historical fact, carrying probability on the face of it. It is no more improbable than the effects we see produced by volcanoes every day. It is neither impossible nor improbable that when the Atlantis sunk, something of the same kind should have happened in the Northern Pacific Ocean.

The legend of the sinking of a very large island is now well known in China and Japan, and in both places an annual festival is kept to celebrate the escape of an excellent prince called *Peiruun*.[3] I cannot help suspecting an identity of mythos or an identity of fact. I apprehend, if the whole or a great part of the Polynesian Islands constituted the highest grounds of a large continent which sunk, the effect would be, when the sinking took place, to raise up the waters so as to drown all the inhabitants, and after a short time to subside, and leave the points of the mountains dry as islands. After all, a great difficulty must be allowed to exist, in all speculations on this subject, arising from the fact, that there are none of the animals of one continent found in the other. See Vol. I. pp. 293, 294, for M. Cuvier's opinion on this part of the subject.

The Mexicans, in their histories, as already stated, say they arrived in their present country from the West. They always persist most strenuously that it was from the West they came; and they describe towns on the coast where they remained, for many years, in their progress to their present situation, the ruins of which, they assert, are yet to be seen. They say they came across the sea from another country. Now, was this Atlantis or not? It is very desirable that the remains of the towns should be sought for.

Lord Kingsborough has gone to an enormous length in proving that the Mexican rites, ceremonies, &c., &c., were almost precisely the same as those of the Jews, and that they must consequently have been brought by the Jews to Mexico. But one most important observation offers itself on this: *We* possess what we believe to be the knowledge of all the Jewish rites, history, &c., &c., in Syria; but this is not the way all these things are known by the Americans. All the things said to have taken place in Western Syria, both with Jews and Christians, are said to have been acted in America, and the case, in a great measure, is the same in India and China. There is the same standing still of the sun, the same populifugia, the same deluge and persons saved in a ship, the same immaculate conception, the same crucifixion and resurrection; but they were all in the American country, not in Syria. Now, it is very improbable that if the Jews of Western

---

[1] Vol. VI. p. 343.   [2] Annals and Antiq. of Rajast'han, Vol. I. p. 44.
[3] Kæmpfer's Japan, Vol. II. Append. p. 13; Fab. Orig. Pag. Idol. Vol. II. p. 180.

Judæa or of Moses had gone in a body from their old country, they would ever wish or permit their history to be located in the new one, towers of Babel to be built, waters to be passed, or places to be shewn where the sun stood still. Nothing can account for all this except that, in all countries, including among them Western Judæa, it was the figurative description of the renewed Avatars.

It seems to me that the mythos which I have shewn to have universally prevailed, accounts in a satisfactory manner, with one exception, for all the difficulties. Parts of it we have seen every where; a small part of it in one place, and a small part in another, but all, including the Jewish, the same mythos. The discovery of the same system in America, as that in South India, in North India, in Tibet, in Western Syria, &c., proves that at some extremely remote æra the same mythos must have prevailed; and the variations which we find, whilst at the same time the general character is preserved, are what we may naturally expect would arise as time advanced. What we have now are the débris of the system.

19. We must recollect that the neglect to teach the Mexicans the arts of writing and making iron, cannot be attributed merely to a few stray mariners and fishermen blown across the ocean. The knowledge of the Americans, if carried to them at all in later times, must have been carried by regular colonies from Greece, who taught them the rites and name of Bacchus ; of colonies from Syria, who taught them all the minute parts of the Judæan mythos; of colonies from Tartary and China, who taught them the knowledge of the mythoses of those countries ; of colonies from Europe, who taught them modern but not Papist Christianity.[1] Is there a human being so credulous as to believe that all these colonies or parties of migrators, following one another time after time, should have omitted to convey the knowledge of iron and letters ? I am sure no person will be found to believe this: then what are we to believe, but that one great and learned race held all these doctrines, as taught by me, in a period of the world when the intercourse between the old and new worlds was easy compared with what it is at at this time?

The one exception alluded to above is the difficulty of accounting for means by which the system reached America. To meet this, may we not have recourse to the formerly-named island of Atlantis, of the submersion of which we are informed by Plato, and which, I suppose, almost connected the two worlds ? It was probably so near both, that, in the frail boats of those days, colonies could pass, but in which the large animals could not be conveyed. Of course this submersion must have taken place, and cut off the communication between the two worlds before the knowledge of letters and the use of iron.

It cannot be believed that if ever the Mexicans had been told of the existence and use of iron, *excellent refiners and smelters of metals as they were*, that they would not instantly have obtained it from their mountains, where it is found in its native state. I shall be asked, How they could pass in any great numbers, without the means of conveying the Horse, the Cow, the Sheep ? For, if the two worlds were nearly connected by an intermediate island or islands, the passage of the animals would have taken place. I admit the force of the argument in its fullest extent; as I do the difficulty of accounting for the extraordinary fact, that there were none of the animals of the old world in America. However, at last, an intimate connexion between the two worlds must be admitted to have existed, and to have existed before the knowledge of iron or letters, in the countries the Mexicans came from.

Some persons have thought that the Americans were colonies who passed by the North, where the continents join, or nearly join; and, to the question, why they had not the horse ?—it may be replied, that if the natives of Tartary or China emigrated by the North, in the neighbourhood of

---

[1] The seed bruising the head, not the woman.

the Arctic circle, as it must have been by that route, there is reason to believe that the horse could not have been conveyed through this cold climate, perhaps could not have lived there. It is said that the North-east of Tartary is too cold for this animal; and that there are none there. If we admit this, then we may suppose that the migration took place from China, where the Hebrew language was spoken, and where the Hebrew and Christian system flourished, as it has before been shewn to have done in a very early period.¹ And if the emigrants went from China, we may thus account for their going without taking with them the knowledge of syllabic writing. If we suppose a body of Japanese or Chinese, amounting only to a few thousands on their arrival in Mexico, after journeying for forty or fifty years, we may readily suppose that they would increase to two or three hundred millions in five or six hundred years, in that fine soil and climate. But suppose we account for their ignorance of letters, and the want of horses, cows, &c., in this manner; this will not account for the ignorance of iron, and at the same time for the knowledge of the mythoses of all the nations which I have just now enumerated: and, satisfactorily to account for this, I am convinced we must ultimately go to my hypothesis, which naturally and easily explains the difficulties.

Lord Kingsborough's work is unquestionably the most magnificent ever undertaken by an individual. It is, indeed, an honour to his order and to his country. The bringing together into one view, by means of Lithographic copies, the different manuscripts, from different and distant countries, will prove, indeed has already proved, of the greatest importance to science, and must greatly aid the philosopher in his inquiries.

¹ Sect. 14, p. 36.

BOOK II.

CHAPTER I.

CHRISTIAN RELIGION NOT NEW.—THE CARMELITES PYTHAGOREANS.—PONTIFEX MAXIMUS.—SEVEN SACRAMENTS. EUCHARIST.—BAPTISM.—CHRISTENING.—CONFIRMATION.—BAPTISM OF BELLS.—ORDINATION.—MARRIAGE.—EXTREME UNCTION.—PURGATORY.—AURICULAR CONFESSION.

1. I SHALL now proceed to complete the proof of the truth of the doctrine of Ammonius Saccas, by shewing that every part of the VULGAR Christian religion is the same as that of the vulgar religion of the Gentiles; that there is nothing new in the Roman Catholic religion; that, in short, it is Reformed or Protestant Gentilism.

The reader has now seen that several of the MOST important doctrinal parts of corrupt modern Christianity are nothing more than scraps of the Heathen mythologies of various kinds taught by different nations, long previous to the Christian æra. He has seen the immaculate conception, the incarnation, the trinity, with its various hypostases, and the crucifixion and resurrection, on all of which I have yet much, which is very important, to produce. But, *first*, I think it expedient to shew where a great number of the forms and ceremonies of minor importance came from. It is more than probable that every part has been copied from some former religion; that no part of what has been really the system of the Christian priests was invented originally for their use. To tradition it is indebted for every doctrine and rite which it possesses, though to fraudulent and dishonest practices it is chiefly indebted for their establishment. This will be said to be a severe and unjust sentence against the priests; but I am supported in my charge against them of systematic falsity and fraud, by some of our first divines—Burnet, Mosheim, &c. In the very early ages they not only practised it, but they reduced it to system; (I allude to Origen's Œconomia;) they avowed it; and they justified it, by declaring it to be meritorious if in a good cause. I repeat, it was justified by the highest divines in the church—openly practised—I believe was never disavowed by any Pope, Council, or authorized body; and, as I have proved in this work, is continued by Archbishops to this day, who just practise as much fraud, as the improved state of the human mind will tolerate.

I must say of Christian priests and their histories what Nimrod[1] has said on another class of persons: "It is difficult to estimate facts delivered under circumstances which deprive the testi-"mony of all moral value; where falsehood is not an accident but a property of the speaker's "character, and is not the error of a moment or the crime of an individual, but an organic "system." The system of fraud is yet continued in the Protestant Church of England: for one instance of which, I produce what is called the Apostles' Creed, which purports to be the composition of the Apostles, (as the Nicene Creed purports to be the composition of the Council of Nice, and the Athanasian Creed, the composition of St. Athanasius,) when it is well known to every

---

[1] Vol. II. p. 494.

Bishop on the Bench, that however true it may be, it was not composed or written till long after the death of all the Apostles: by whom, or when, or where, it was written no one knows; but the people are deluded into a belief, that it is not the work of a council or individual, like those of Nice or St. Athanasius, but of the collective body of the elect companions of Jesus Christ.

Now if we reflect upon the contents of the last book, and consider that all the esoteric doctrines of the Orientals and of the tribe of Ioudi or Jews, and of Plato and the Heathens generally, were at the bottom the same; we shall not be surprised at finding the Lama of Rome adopting such of the forms and ceremonies of his Heathen predecessors as he thought consistent with its restoration to what was, in his opinion, its primeval purity—what he considered its corruptions being left out.

The Rev. Robert Taylor, in his Diegesis, has undertaken to shew that what Protestants have maintained to be the corruptions of Christianity were the origination of it; and that the early Christians were nothing but Egyptian Essenes or Monks, and that the Gospel histories were extracts or compilations from the secret writings of these persons. To support this assertion, he has given a translation of the sixteenth chapter of the second book of Eusebius's Ecclesiastical History, in which the early Christians are most clearly proved to have been the Monks called Essenes. That the Gospel histories are not originals, has been admitted by all divines I believe, who have, or who wish to have, any character for learning. Reasoning after the manner of the German divines—Semler, Lessing, Niemeyer, Halfeld, Eichhorn, Michaelis, &c.,—the learned Bishop Marsh has put this out of all doubt. In his Notes on Michaelis, he has discussed it at great length. Whether the Gospel histories were copied from the Essenean Scriptures may yet admit of doubt, but certainly Mr. Taylor has shewn that all the ecclesiastical polity of the Christian is a close copy from that of the Esseneans, or I should say, Carmelites, according to the account in Eusebius, when honestly translated. Their parishes, churches, bishops, priests, deacons, festivals, are all identically the same. They had Apostolic founders; the manners which distinguished the immediate apostles of Christ; Scriptures divinely inspired; the same allegorical mode of interpreting them, which has since obtained among Christians, and the same order of performing public worship. They had missionary stations or colonies of their community established in Rome, Corinth, Galatia, Ephesus, Philippi, Colosse, and Thessalonica, precisely such, and in the same circumstances, as were those to whom St. Paul addressed his letters in those places. Long before Mr. Taylor wrote, I had written my opinion that the Essenes were not Christians, but that the Christians of the Pope were Essenes.[1] All the fine moral doctrines which are attributed to the Samaritan Nazarite, and I doubt not justly attributed to him, are to be found among the doctrines of these ascetics; but they are found unalloyed with the pernicious, demoralising nonsense,[2] which St. Paul and some of the fathers of the Romish Church obtruded into their religion, and into what they were pleased to call, though to miscal *his* religion: and a great part, and the worst part of which, has been retained by Protestants. If the opinion be well founded, that their Scriptures were the originals of the Gospel histories, then it will follow almost certainly, that they must have been the same as the Samaneans or Gymnosophists of Porphyry and Clemens Alexandrinus, and their books, which they were bound by such solemn oaths to keep secret, must have been the Vedas of India; or some Indian books containing the mythoses of Moses and Jesus Christ: and this opinion, the striking similarity between the

---

[1] See Vol. I. pp. 81—84.

[2] May not this harsh opinion have originated in a too vivid recollection of the *doctrines* deduced from the writings of St. Paul, by both ancient and modern polemics? *Editor.*

histories of Buddha, Cristna, and Jesus, seems strongly to support. The Gymnosophists, it may be remembered, we have found in great power in the isle of Meroe, in Upper Egypt, giving laws to the kings.[1] This is the most reasonable scheme which I have been able to devise to account for the identity of the history of Jesus and Cristna: and this seems to be confirmed by Mr. Taylor.

Benj. Constant says,[2] "En général, on n'a pas, à ce qu'il nous parait, assez considéré la ressemblance du clergé Chrétien avec les institutions hiérarchiques des peuples du Nord. Cette ressemblance est si frappante, même dans les détails, que les ordres religieux en ont tiré la conséquence qu'ils descendaient des Druides. Un historien de la communauté des Carmes appelle les Druides *sanctos druides*, Eliæ filios, fratres nostros et prædecessores (Hist. Carmel, Ordin. I. 1, 4). Si vivendi genus et observantias regulares serio discusseris, dit un autre écrivain, reperies veros fuisse (Druidas) Carmelitas."

In the course of my studies I have turned my attention, in a very particular manner, to the Essenes, and it was my intention to have had a much longer chapter than I have given relating to them in this work, but the learned and ingenious Deist, the Rev. Robert Taylor, has superseded me. It is of no use merely to rewrite the substance of what he has written respecting them in his Diegesis, and written better than I could do it. The Romish Church, I believe, maintains that the Essenes and the Carmelites were the same order of men. Of the truth of this I have no doubt. Pythagoras is allowed to have been an Essenean, and he dwelt or was initiated into the order on Carmel. Pope Gregory the Great invited the Carmelites from Syria and Egypt to Rome, and founded two most splendid and beautiful monasteries of the barefoot and the calceated orders; and at that time he abolished their old rule, and gave them a new one. With the assistance of a most respectable friend, an Augustinian monk of the name of Rice, at both the times when I visited Rome, I applied to the librarians at the monasteries, and endeavoured to obtain a sight of their old rule, by which they lived before the time of Gregory, which they acknowledged that they possessed, but of which, after having first promised it, they would not permit me to have the inspection. Within the cupola of St. Peter's is a colossal statue of the prophet Elias, under which is the inscription, Universus Carmelitarum Ordo Fundatori suo S. Eliæ Prophetæ erexit A. MDCCXXVII. I believe if he were not the founder he regulated the order. But its first regulation, I think, may be found in the sixth chapter of Numbers.[3] A slight attention will satisfy any reader that Moses was then regulating an order brought from Egypt, not instituting a new one. They were called Nazarites. Jesus Christ was called a Nazarite, not a Nazarene. It is odd enough that our learned Grecians should not see, that Ναζωραιος does not mean Nazarene, but Nazarite: had it meant Nazarene it would have been Ναζαρηνος. He was a Nazarite of the city of Nazareth or of the city of the Nazarites.[4] At that place was the monastery of Nazarites or Carmelites, where Pythagoras and Elias both dwelt, *under* Carmel the vineyard or Garden of God.

2. But the Romish Christ was something more than this. He was a renewed incarnation of Divine Wisdom. He was the son of Maia or Maria. He was the Rose of Sharon and the Lily of the Valley, which bloweth in the month of his mother Maia. Thus, when the angel Gabriel gives the salutation to the Virgin, (see hundreds of very old pictures in Italy,) he always presents her with the Lotus or Lily. Mr. Parkhurst says of the lily,[5] "Its six-leaved flower contains " within it *seven* apices or chives, i. e. six single-headed ones and one triple-headed one, in the " midst—emblems of the five primary planets and of the moon, and the triple-headed chive or

---

[1] Vol. I. p. 356.   [2] Thèse Théolog. soutenue à Beziers, en 1682; Const. Vol. II. p. 112.
[3] Verses 13—21.   [4] See Vol. I. pp. 540, 656, 657.   [5] In voce ww as, V.

" style in the midst, of the sun in the centre of this system." Here, I think, in this Lily we have a very pretty emblem of the trinitarian sun, the Creator, Preserver, and Destroyer, in the centre of his system. And where did this Lily grow? It was in Carmel, the Garden or Vineyard of God, that this Nazir was found at Nazareth. But Nazir or Natzir means a flower, and that flower the Lotus or Lily; and it grew in the Valley of the Garden of God. My reader may think this very mystical, but let him turn to the Bible and read the account of the Lilies and Pomegranates in the temple of Solomon, on the high-priest's dress, and in the Canticles and works of Solomon, where may be found the loves of Christ and his church, as our Bibles, in the heads of their chapters, call them. I request him also to refer to what I have said in Vol. I. pp. 339, 340, respecting the Lotus or Lily.

The Carmelites are in a *very peculiar manner* attached to the worship of the Virgin Maria, more particularly than any of the other monastic orders. In Egypt they dwelt, as Eusebius says, on the borders of the lake of *Maria*, and in Upper Egypt the Gymnosophists, that is, the Indian philosophers, were found in the island of Meroe. This, in the old language without points, would be the same as Maria. It was near this place that Dr. Wilson found the temple with the history of the flight of Joseph and Mary in it, *depicted with the greatest truth and precision*, noticed before in Vol. I. p. 272. Now this being considered, I think it raises a presumption that there was some foundation for the story of Jesus, or some other person for whom he has been substituted, fleeing from a tyrant who wished to kill him, and who may have been dedicated, as Samuel was by his parents, and who may, therefore, have become an object of jealousy to the tyrant, and of attention to Eastern astrologers, who might know that the period was ending, as Virgil knew it at Rome, and that a new protecting Genius would come to preside over the new age; and in consequence these astrologers, kings, might come to offer him their gifts—kings of the Mithraic order of the Magi, (vide Tertullian,) like our kings at arms of the order of heralds, not kings of nations. In the book of the office of the Carmelites, which I bought at Clarendon Street monastery and chapel in Dublin, Mary is called *Maris Stella, Mother of our Maker*, and the *glorious Virgin of Mount Carmel*. She has forty-three names, the exact number which I counted under her statue at Loretto. The Gospel of the Egyptians in the office is expressly acknowledged in the following words, the heading of a prayer : *The falling down of the Egyptian idols at the approach of the Son of God*. And the Sibyls are quoted. Dr. Walsh, in his lately published Travels, says, that the Greeks call her Dei-para and Panayia. This last word is worthy of observation; it is not unlike the Pandæa, the daughter of Cristna.

Thus far I had written when the fact of the island of Meroe having its name from mount Meru, and also from the name of the Virgin, occurred to me as something singular, and I was for the first time induced to apply to my Hebrew Bible for the mode of spelling Mount Moriah; and there, behold! I find it is Maria—מריה *Mrie*. When formerly I discussed the meaning of the Meru of India, (Vol. I. pp. 355, 356,) I observed, that its meaning was not known; but now I think we have found it, in the name which we found in Siam—Maria—and it is the Mount of Maria, or of Maia—called also, in Western Syria as in Pegu, Zian, and, as Josephus says, converted[1] into Jerusalem, which, he also says, was built by Melchizedek, and that it was before called Salem. All this probably happened after Abraham sanctified it by the Yajna sacrifice of the Lamb.

Mr. Taylor goes so far as to suppose that our Gospel histories are the very Scriptures of the Therapeutæ or Essenes much corrupted : but I think in this he must be mistaken, and that they are what the learned Christians of the Manichæan sect said of them, and what they have every

---

[1] Lib. vi. Cap. x.

appearance of being, viz., a collection of traditions or histories, made by such men as Papias, Hegisippus, &c., in their travels, taken from the Essenean school, which they found among the devotees at the Essenean settlements above named, and to which St. Paul addressed his letters. They were probably part of their Scriptures. Strangers would probably not succeed in obtaining the whole, but only detached parts, which had become known out of the monasteria—out of the crypts. And it seems almost certain from their titles—Gospel according to Matthew, &c., and other circumstances, that they were never originally intended to be the actual writings of the Apostles, but only on account of what it was believed that they had taught respecting Jesus. Thus they are rescued from the charge, otherwise plausibly brought against them, of being forgeries. They are, in fact, what their titles call them, accounts of the doctrines which Matthew or Luke was supposed to have taught respecting Jesus; but anonymously of course. But of this I shall have much to say hereafter. This scheme seems to me to dovetail into all the other historical accounts. We know Pythagoras was one of the Essenes or Therapeutæ, that he got his learning and morality, identically that of Jesus, either in Egypt or on Mount Carmel, where he long resided,[1] or in Babylon, or still more to the East. Indeed, it seems to supply the only connecting link wanting, between the East and the West.

Certainly the fact noticed by Mr. R. Taylor, that Philo described the Essenes before Christ was born, and that Eusebius has shewn that those very Essenes, so described, were Christians, at once proves that the Christians of his sect were not the followers of the man who lived and preached in the time of Tiberius. I do not see how the evidence of Eusebius is to be disputed: besides, his evidence is confirmed by the work of Philo, which we have and can refer to, in its general character and account of the Essenes, and which completely bears out Eusebius.[2] Between the accounts of Philo and Josephus,[3] I think there will not be found a greater variation, than under the circumstances may be expected. The order may have considerably changed between the time of Philo and Eusebius, and as it was his object to shew that they were Christians, we may safely give a man, who had no regard for truth on other occasions, credit for a little freedom of expression, to say the least, on this.

The early Protestants, having taken a dislike to monastic institutions, have exerted all their ingenuity to persuade their followers, that the monastic order did not arise until about the year 300, when they pretend it was instituted by one Antonius. Their object in fixing on so late a date is, by this means, to strengthen their argument that, from the lateness of its origin, it cannot be an uncorrupted Christian institution, but that it was one of the numerous corruptions of *the scarlet whore of Babylon*, as they courteously call the Romish Church.[4] The falsity of this is at once proved by the fact, that Origen, who was born about the year 180, emasculated himself, which shews in what estimation celibacy was held in his time. In order to be a monk, it was not necessary, in his day, to attach himself to any order of monks, because there was then only one order. But the account given of him by the learned Gale is quite enough to shew what he was.

---

[1] Taylor's Translation of Jamblicus, Chap iii.

[2] These Essenean Christians were probably Χρηστιανοι.

[3] In the works of Philo not a word is said about Jesus Christ, nor about his works. (Bryant on the Logos, p. 17.) But he treats at large on the Logos. Philo appears often to have visited Jerusalem. It has been proved, against Mangey and others, that he lived at the time of Christ. When Philo speaks of being old, though he refers to himself at the time of writing, he is describing the embassy to Caligula many years before.

[4] For they never hesitate to employ the weapons of abuse and sarcastic ridicule against their opponents, which if any person retorts upon them he is instantly sent to Newgate or some other prison for three or four years.

" He gave the first lines to all mystic theology, by turning all scriptures, even the most plain,
" into allegories, according to the Platonic mode.—He was the first founder of *monastic life*,
" *abstinences*, and *austerities*. He emasculated himself, that is, extinguished virility, thereby to
" preserve chastity. He understood those precepts of our Lord, against having two coats, shoes,
" and making provision for the morrow, in a literal sense, as belonging to all Christians: and
" thence affected voluntary poverty, as the monks of Egypt, his successors. He abstained from
" necessary food, as the Pythagoreans and Popish monks: whereby he endangered his health.
" He affected superstitious sanctity and severities, abstaining from necessary sleep, lying on the
" ground, &c., as monks." In addition to the above list of errors, Mr. Gale, as descriptive of
another error, adds the following sentence, a lamentable proof of the pernicious effects of what is
called religion, even upon the greatest learning and talent: " *He held human merits, and justifica-
" tion by works, placing man's satisfactions, tears, contrition, and other good works, as the causes
" of remission of sins.*" [1] It is quite shocking to think into what pernicious absurdities the
corrupt or doubtful passages in those books have drawn even both good and learned men, as the
examples of both Origen and Gale prove.

Bochart against *Veron*,[2] says, "That the law or canon of celibacy is the doctrine of devils,
" 1 Tim. iv. 1, 3, which *was well nigh established throughout Paganism*, when Christ came into
" the world. There were some priests who castrated or gelded themselves, as those of Cybele, or
" of Phrygia, who were called Galli and Archigalli: and the Megabyzes or Megalobyzes, priests of
" Diana at Ephesus, and the Therophantes at Athens. *In brief, the celibacy of priests was in such
" esteem among the Pagans, that Æneas, in Virgil, (Æn.* Lib. vi.,) *passing through the Elysian
" fields, which they made to be paradise, saw no other priests there, but such as had passed their life
" in celibacy*. There has been also a number of philosophers who have contributed to this error.
" This was one of the superstitions which Pythagoras brought out of Egypt, whence returning
" unto Greece, he forbade marriage to those of his sect, and constituted a cloister of nuns, over
" which he placed his daughter. Plato held the same opinion, as also Heraclitus, and Demo-
" critus, and Zeno, the prince of the Stoics, who never approached to a woman. By which,"
says Gale, " It is apparent that Antichrist's prohibition of marriage and monastic constitutions
" or canons are but αποκρισις, an imitation of the Pagan celibacy and monastic rules: that the
" Popish nuns are but imitations or apes of the Pythagorean nuns."[3]

The Pythagoreans were divided in their colleges into *novices* and *perfect*. They affected a
superstitious silence; they enjoyed all things in common; they called their college Κοινοβιον,
a community, as the monks and nuns call theirs Coenobium. They had their fasts the same as
the Egyptian priests, and the Carthusians and Præmonstrants. They had the same white garments. They had the same severities or discipline, mortifications, and purifications. They
were divided into contemplative and active, the same as the Egyptian priests and the monks.[4]

The great and striking similarity between the doctrines of the Essenes, of Jesus, and of Pythagoras, amounts almost to proof of the identity of the systems.

Pythagoras maintained the existence of one Supreme God, the immortality of the soul, and a
state of future rewards and punishments. These sentiments were common to him and almost all
the ancient philosophers. He probably believed in the existence of a great number of created

---

[1] Gale's Court of Gent. Vol. III. Book ii. Chap. i. pp. 134, 135.
[2] Part iii. Chap. xxv. S. 4, Art. 1.
[3] Gale's Court of Gent. Vol. III. Book ii. Chap. ii. Sect. 9, p. 212.
[4] See ibid. Sect. I, pp. 150, 151.

beings, superior to man in their natures and attributes, but in every way inferior to God their Creator. Under different names they answer exactly to the angels of the Brahmins, the Magi, the Jews, the Essenes, and the Christians. The morality which he taught was in a very high degree refined and good. In it is to be found, I believe, every doctrine for which the Christian religion has been so much celebrated by its admirers. The truth of this assertion may be seen in almost every page of Jamblicus's Life of Pythagoras. The examples are far too numerous to recite here.

Pythagoras taught, and his followers maintained, the absolute equality of property, all their worldly possessions being brought into a common store. They separated themselves from the rest of mankind, and lived in buildings called monasteria or monasteries, and were themselves called Κοινοβιοι or Cœnobites. By this name of Cœnobites they are said to have been known at Crotona in Italy, which might induce a suspicion that monasteries were founded in Italy much earlier than has been generally supposed.[1] Before proselytes were admitted into the society they were obliged to keep a long silence, and to serve a tedious noviciate; and they took the three celebrated vows, *tria vota substantialia*, taken by all monks, of chastity, poverty, and obedience. His followers ate no flesh meat, nor drank wine, and though he sacrificed to Apollo or the Sun at Delos, it was at the altar where no blood was shed, and with thanksgivings only. He held the doctrine of the Metempsychosis, the same, or nearly the same, as it was held by the Brahmins, the Persians, many of the Greeks, the Manichees, and many of the early orthodox Christian fathers.

His followers were divided into two classes, one called Pythagoreans, the other Pythagorists. The former only had their possessions in common, and are what answer to those amongst the Christians called elect or perfect—who were, in short, the monks and nuns. They rose before daylight, and though strictly worshipers of one God, they always paid a certain adoration to the sun at his rising. Pythagoras, as well as his disciple Plato, considered the soul to be confined in the body as a certain kind of punishment, and that old age was not to be considered with reference to an egress from the present life, but to the beginning of a blessed life in future.[2]

Of all the Greeks, I apprehend Pythagoras was the most learned. It cannot be supposed that he would spend so many years in Egypt, Phœnicia, and Babylon, in study, without knowing the languages of these nations. He is said to have been the person who discovered the demonstration of the forty-seventh proposition of the first book of Euclid, which, if true, was of itself sufficient to immortalize him. But I am rather inclined to think that he discovered it not by meditation, but by travel amongst the nations of the East, who understood and who taught him the true theory of the motions of the earth and planetary bodies, and who, I believe, understood the qualities of the loadstone,[1] the art of making gun-powder, telescopes, &c., &c., and who were far more learned than the Greeks were at any time. I believe the Greeks were as inferior to the oriental nations in real learning, as they were superior to them in poetry and the fine arts.

I beg the reader to look back to what has been said (Vol. I. pp. 150, &c.) respecting the circumstances related of Pythagoras in the early part of his life, to the same also in the life of Cristna, &c, (ibid. pp. 129, et seq.,) and, coolly divesting his mind, as far as possible, from prejudice, and from all angry feeling, caused by his early opinions being rudely assailed, consider whether it be possible that such similarity in two histories could take place by accident. I beg

---

[1] Jamblicus's Life of Pythag. by Taylor, Chap. v. p. 18.   [2] Vide ibid. *passim*.
[3] See Parkhurst's Lexicon, Cooke on Stonehenge, Stukeley's Stonehenge, and Palæographia, and Drummond in the Classical Journal.

him to ask, whether it be possible that the effect could be produced by any cause except that of one copying after the other—that of the later copying after the earlier. Thomas Burnet says,[1] "Refert Alexander de Symbolis Pythagoricis, Γαλατῶν και Βραχμανων ακηκοεναι τον Πυθαγο- "ραν.² Hos igitur Galatarum Philosophos, Druidas, audivit, non docuit, Pythagoras." That Pythagoras was a Carmelite see Mosheim.[3]

Mr. Maurice seems to consider it of great consequence that the immaculate conception of Jesus by his mother, a virgin, is very different from the birth of Cristna, who had seven or eight elder brothers. But he overlooks the fact that Jesus is said to have had almost as many.[4] Now this seems to me of very little consequence. I do not suppose that one story was exactly copied from the other—that at any time a copyist or transcriber went to the Hindoo books and systematically extracted what he thought necessary to form a new religion. No, indeed! I consider the account of the Manichæans to be the truth—that these books were formed from scraps of traditions collected by the early fathers, some here, some there, as they happened to find them in their journeys, which it is well known that they took into the Eastern countries, in search of the true Gospel. Thus some parts would be as we find them—Indian, some Persian, some Egyptian, &c., &c., jumbled together, forming, after undergoing the corrections which I have before described, the mass which we now possess—after all their corrections in a considerable degree confused and irreconcileable. Thus we find that from India came the murder of the innocents, &c., &c.; from all quarters of the Heathen world came the Trinity, the execution of the Saviour, the Lord Sol, the Iao, born at the winter solstice, triumphing over the powers of hell and darkness, and rising to light and immortality at the vernal equinox; from the Egyptian, and perhaps Eleusinian, mysteries, the worship of the Virgin and Child; and, from the history of the Pythagoras, the immaculate conception, and the several particulars which the reader has seen, are common both to him and Jesus, in the early parts of their lives.

That the Christian Hellenistic Jewish fathers should have searched for the origin of their religion in the East, will not surprise any one who observes that the Greeks found in the same quarter all their astronomy and their mythological fables, as may be seen well developed every where in the Hist. Hind. by Mr. Maurice.

On the subject of the Essenes, who were nothing but Pythagoreans, Thomas Burnet says, "Huic dissertationi de Judæis finem imposuero, venit mihi in mentem Essenorum sive Essæorum, "pervetustæ, celebrisque olim sectæ, apud Judæos: qui priscorum Philosophorum speciem præ "se ferebant, ipsosque Brachmanas institutis et vitæ ratione imitari videbantur.⁵ Horum "meminerunt authores varii. Plinius, subridens, ex pœnitentibus et pertæsis humanæ vitæ "cœtum illum compositum ait, neque unquam defecisse per aliquot annorum millia, licet αγυνον "και ασυνουσιαςον. ' Gens sola, inquit, Esseni, et in toto orbe, præter cæteras, mira. Sine "'ullâ fœminâ, omni venere abdicata, sine pecuniâ, sociâ Palmarum. In diem ex æquo conve- "'narum turba renascitur, frequentantibus, quos vitâ fessos, ad mores eorum fortunæ fluctus "'agitat. Ita per sæculorum millia (incredibile dictu) gens æterna est, in quâ nemo nascitur. "'Tam fœcunda illis aliorum vitæ pœnitentia est.' Argutè dictum si minùs verè. Horum phi- "losophorum vivam imaginem depinxit Philo Judæus: vitamque eorum exhibuit, illi simillimam "quam duxerunt olim in Paradiso innocui parentes: et nos iterum ducturi sumus, Deo volente, in "novâ terrâ futurâ. Onerosum esset totum Philonis de hâc re sermonem adducere: sed, quod

---

[1] Arch. Phil. Cap. ii. p. 8, 4to. [2] Clem. Alex. Strom. Vol. I. p. 304.
[3] Hist. Vol. III. Cent. XII. Ch. ii. p. 75. [4] Matt. xiii. 55, 56; Mark vi. 3. [5] Josephus, cont. Ap. Lib. I.

"hoc spectat maximè quid de philosophiâ censerint, ita paucis enarrat. 'Philosophiæ partem
" 'Logicam, ut parandæ virtuti non necessariam, relinquunt verborum captatoribus. Physicam
" 'verò, ut humano captu majorem, rerum sublimium curiosis: eâ parte exceptâ, quæ de exis-
" 'tentiâ Dei, rerumque ortu, philosophatur. In morali autem se strenuè exercent,' &c. Pauca
" habent, ut vides, in philosophiâ naturali, sed gravissima, capita: de Deo nempe, mundique
" ortu. Sed quâ ratione mundi originem exposuerint, aut quatenus à Mose discesserint, non
" indicat Philo. Neque plura suppetunt, quod sciam, apud authores, Essenorum dogmata
" physica: modò ea adjunxeris, quæ, ex illorum mente tradit Josephus, de animarum immorta-
" litate et futuris paradisis. Reliqua in suis libris sacris, quorum ille meminit,[1] occuluerunt:
" et quærenda sunt maximè apud Brachmanas. Apud Brachmanas dico: cùm illorum esse præ-
" paginem Essenos, ex Clearcho notarit Josephus.[2] Ità enim Clearchum intelligo, non Judæos
" in genere, sed scholam Essenicam derivatam esse à Brachmanicâ. Quod ex cognatis moribus et
" institutis non malè arguitur."[3]

This passage of Burnet's suggests several very important observations. I was not a little gratified to find that the close relation between the Hindoos and the most respectable of all the Jewish sects, of which I have not the slightest doubt that Jesus Christ was a member, that of the Essenes, had been observed by this very learned man almost a hundred years ago, before the late blaze of light from the East had shone upon us. What would he have said had he lived till now? I think from the *tria vota substantialia* being common both to the Essenes and the Samaneans of Porphyry, there can be no doubt that the latter were correctly oriental Essenes.—Their history must have been well known in the time of Pliny: and his observation of their continuance *per millia sæculorum* decidedly proves their existence, if proof were wanting, long before the time of Christ; therefore they could not be merely Christian monks. They could be no other than Sophees.

I cannot help entertaining a suspicion that the Samaneans of Porphyry and Clemens Alexandrinus, the Buddhists or Brachmans, as they were called, the Chaldæans, confessed by Burnet to be only a sect,[4] the Essenes, and the Druides, were, in fact, all orders of monks. Perhaps they were originally one order, but in long periods of time split it into separate communities, as we have them in Europe—but all having the same vows of chastity, poverty, and obedience—vows which, in fact, reduce all monks to one order or genus.

" Constat autem apud has gentes (*Celtas*) viguisse ab omni ævo philosophos, sive hominum
" ordinem, nomine, studiis, et vitæ instituto, à vulgo, aliisque distinctum. Dicti sunt ab omnibus
" Druidæ vel Druides: Semnothei etiam; aliisque nominibus, quæ nil faciunt ad rem nostram,
" distingui solent."[5]

Epiphanus says that there were TWENTY *heresies before Christ*. It is curious, and there can be no doubt that there is much truth in the observation, for most of the rites and doctrines of the Christians of all sects existed before the time of Jesus of Nazareth.[6]

It is the policy of the present Christians to reduce the number of heresies as much as possible. But the fact cannot be disputed, that what were called Christian heresies existed in great numbers before the birth of Jesus of Nazareth, as asserted by Epiphanius and Philaster, and quoted generally with approbation by Eusebius: although he differs from them in some points, particularly as to which of the sects preceded Christianity. It seems singular enough, however, that these good people do not perceive that it proves the actual existence of two Christianities.

---

[1] Bel. Jud. Lib. ii. p. 12. [2] Cont. Ap. Lib. i. [3] Arch. Phil. Cap. vii. pp. 69, 70, 4to.
[4] Arch. Phil. Cap. iv. p. 20. [5] Ib. Cap. ii. p. 7. [6] See Lardner's Hist. Her. Book I. Sect. 5.

But I think my reader who recollects what has been said of the youth of Larissa in the first volume,[1] will not be much surprised at this.

The conduct of the first Christian Emperor Constantine, was very singular. He was both Christian and Pagan. He affected to be descended from Helen the female generative principle, he kept the Heathen festivals after he turned Christian, and when he built his new city he placed it on seven hills, making it as near as possible a second Ilium or new Rome, and dedicated its church to the holy Sophia. I have little doubt that if we could get to the bottom of the subject, we should find proof that he affected to be a renewed incarnation, the Paraclete promised by Jesus, the tenth Avatar, and the renewer of the empire of ancient Rome, in the last cycle. But it must be recollected that we are here in the very centre of the era of frauds, of every kind, and that he, that is, his church, was able to destroy, and did destroy, every thing which it did not approve. It could corrupt what it pleased, and we scarcely possess a single writing which it ordered to be destroyed, which is a sufficient proof of its power to effect its wicked designs. Constantine was, in fact, both Pagan and Christian; and his church, as I will now prove, was more an union of the two, than a substitution of one for the other.

3. I shall now proceed to shew, that the remainder of what, in modern times, are called the rites of the church of Jesus of Nazareth have nothing to do with him, and are only figments of the old Gentile religion, and I shall begin at the head, the Pontifex Maximus.

The Roman Pontifex Maximus was called *King of the Age*.[2] This was the same as Cyrus, Αιων των αιωνων. As endowed with a portion of the *holy spirit* he was God. Thus in him resided a portion of the divinity on earth. It was from these mysticisms that the power of both the ancient and modern chief priests was derived. How this Pontifex arose I shall shew in a future page, along with the origin of feudal tenures, and I conceive it will not be the least interesting part of my work.

Tertullian calls the Pontifex Maximus KING OF THE AGE. This is Βασιλευς αιων των αιωνων—King of the Cycles. Dionysius of Halicarnassus assures us, that the Pontifices Maximi had a sovereign authority in the most important affairs, for to them was referred the judgment of all causes which concerned sacred things, as well those in which individuals were concerned, as those of the public. They made new laws on their own authority, as new occasions called for them. They had the care of all sacrifices, and generally of all the ceremonials of religion. They had also the jurisdiction of all the officers employed in the affairs of religion. They were the interpreters of the prophecies, concerning which the people were used to consult them. They had power to punish at their discretion those who failed to execute their commands, according to the exigency of the case; but were themselves subject to no other person, and were not obliged to render an account either to the senate or to the people. When the high priest died his place was filled by the choice of the college, and not by the senate or people.[3] All this is strictly papistical.

Alexander ab Alexandro says,[4] 'That the sovereign Pontiff was elevated in honour above all others. The people had as much veneration for his dignity as for that of the king's. He had his lictors and guards, his peculiar chair and litter, the same as the consuls: he alone had the power of ascending to the capitol in a chariot. He presided and ruled in the sacred college over all the other pontiffs: the augurs, the priests, and the vestal virgins, all obeyed him: he had the power of chastising them at his pleasure. He governed according to his pleasure all sacred things.

---

[1] Pp. 571—573, 582, 583, 786, 787.
[2] Dion. Halicar. Ant. Rom. Lib. ii.; also Livy in his Life of Numa, Lib. i.
[3] Bassage, Book iii. Chap. xxiii.
[4] Genial. Dierum, Lib. ii.

He ordered on what altars, to what Gods, by what hostiæ, victims, on what days and in what temples the sacrifices should be made: he fixed the feasts and the fasts, when it was permitted to the people to work and when it was forbidden. If this be compared with the Papal powers it will be found in every thing to agree. The Canonists maintain that the Pope is not subject to any human law; that he cannot be judged either by the emperor or by the clergy collectively, neither by the kings nor by the people; that it is necessary to salvation to believe, that all creatures are subject to him; that as the Sun is said to be lord of the planets, so the Pope is the father of all dignities.[1]

Innocent the Third called himself Vicarius Jesu Christi, successor Petri Christus domini, Deus Pharaonis, citra Deum, ultra hominem, minor Deo, major homine.[2] Platina, in his Life of Paul the Second, says, "I and others being cited before the Pope appealed to the judges, when "regarding me with furious eyes, he said, 'How dare you speak to me of judges? ' Ne sais-tu "' pas que j'ay tout le droit dans le coffret de ma poitrine? I speak the word and each quits his "' place according to my will. I am Pope: it is permitted to me to chastise or to approve of all "' others according to my will.'" This is confirmed by Baronius in his remonstrance to the city of Venice.[3] "Whence comes it," he says, "that you dare to judge the Judge of all, whom no "council legitimately assembled has dared to judge; him from whom the universal counsels take "their authority, and without whose fiat they cannot be general councils or be legally convoked, "nor the canons which they ordain have any authority?" In short, Baronius shews that the conformity of the modern to the ancient Pontiffs, called kings of the sacred affairs, is as close as possible, even to the most trifling things, such as not being expected to salute any person or to uncover his head, but that he was used to wear the same purple robes as kings, and a crown of gold on his head.

As I have shewn, the Pontiffs had the power of regulating all festivals, and, in short, the whole calendar. Thus Julius Cæsar, in quality of Pontifex Maximus, reformed the calendar, and in the same manner it was reformed again by the Pontifex Maximus—Pope Gregory the Thirteenth.

Cicero, concerning the Pagan Augurs, says, "No order of true religion passes over the law "concerning the description of priests.

"For some have been instituted for the business of pacifying the Gods."

"To preside at sacred ceremonies.

"Others to interpret the predictions of the prophet.

"Not of the many, lest they should be infinite.

"But that none beside the College should understand those predictions which had been publicly "recognized.

"For augury, or the power of foretelling future events, is the greatest and most excellent thing "in the republic, and naturally allied to authority.

"Nor do thus I think, because I am an augur myself; but because it is absolutely necessary for "us to think so.

"For, if the question be of legal right, what is greater than the power to *put away* from the "highest governments *their right of holding counsels* [councils?] *and issuing decrees; or to abolish* "*them when holden?* What more awful, than for any thing undertaken, to be done away, if but "one augur hath said otherwise?

"What more magnificent than to be able to decree, that the supreme governors should resign

---

[1] Extrav. de Concess. III. Præb. C. Sedes Apost. in Glossa Dist. 19, c.

[2] Nimrod, Vol. III. p. 508.   [3] Judicum Universorum.

" their magistracy? What more religious than to give or not to give the right of treating or
" transacting business with the people? *What than to annul a law* if it hath not been duly
" passed,—and for nothing that hath been done by the government, either at home or abroad, to
" be approved by any one, without their authority?"¹

The present Roman hierarchy is an exact copy of the hierarchy of the Gentiles, as it is also given by Plutarch, and I have no doubt it originally came to the Etruscans from the Ombri and the Eastern nations. Gale says, that " The Romans made Romulus a Flamen; which was a " sort of priesthood so excelling in the Roman sacred things, (witness the Apex,) that they had " only three Flamens instituted to the three Gods: the Diale to Jupiter: the Martiale to Mars: " the Quirinale' to Romulus. Ludovicus Vives on this place, explaining what this Flamen " dedicated to Romulus was, tells us, 'That among the orders of priests, Numa Pompilius made " 'some, which he called Flamens: whose chief ensign was a HAT, as the bishops now, wherein " 'there was a thread of white wool: whence they were called Filamines, from fila lanæ.'—This " Apex, the Romans gave to none but their chiefest priests, as now the Mitres. So Lucan, Et " tollens Apicem generoso vertice flamen." Here, as Gale says,² very truly, is the bishop, the proto-flamen, and the mitre is the *apex;* and to complete the parallel, there is the Pontifex Maximus in each case—the Pope assuming to himself that epithet of dignity in his public titles. The hat of the flamen is the hat of the cardinal in his scarlet robes: but I shall say more on this hereafter.

The Pontifex Maximus had under him a regular gradation of priestly officers, precisely like those of the Pontifex Maximus of the moderns—the Pope. He had, in the first place, his college of high-priests, of whom his council was composed, with whom he deliberated concerning important affairs. To answer to this, the Pope has his cardinals. The Pontifex Maximus had also persons called highnesses,³ who answered to the Primates, the Archbishops, and the Bishops: he had also lesser ones, who answered to the Parsons and Curates of the Pope, and were called *Curiones*, whence comes our word *Curate*. He had also a number of Flamens, that is to say, (Prestres,) priests, who assisted in the offices of the church as at this day.⁴ The Abbé Marolles confesses the conformity, including the Vestals, who are the Nuns.

The ancients had an order of priests called Parasiti or Parasites. These answered correctly to our modern chaplains.

At first the Pontifex Maximus did not interfere with secular affairs; this was, I suppose, after the expulsion of the kings who were priests; but, by degrees, he encroached on the secular authority, till, in the time of Cæsar, he had become so formidable that the Dictator found it necessary to take the office himself, and thus he acquired possession, by the union of the secular and ecclesiastical authority, of absolute and legal power; and the emperors, as may be seen from coins, after Cæsar, were both Pontifices Maximi and Emperors.⁵ The popes followed most closely the footsteps of their predecessors. At first, they did not meddle with secular concerns, but acknowledged the supremacy of the Emperors, and themselves as vassals; but after the death of Constantine the First, pleading a gift from him of the kingdom of Italy, they assumed the

---

¹ De Legibus, Lib. ii. 12, apud R. Taylor's Dieg. pp. 140, 141.

² Court of Gent. Vol. III. Bk. ii. Ch. ii. pp. 224, 225.   ³ Blond, Rom. Triumph. Lib. ii. p. 31.   ⁴ Mem. de Mar.

⁵ The early kings of Rome were both kings and priests, and when they were abolished a chief priest was retained with reduced power, but which he was constantly endeavouring by all means to increase. This will be explained in a future page.

crown, which they yet affect to wear, never yielding up their pretension to it; for they hold the same doctrine as the Protestant Church of England—that Nullum Tempus occurrit Ecclesiæ.

The alleged gift of Italy by Constantine, is said by Protestants to be false. I am inclined to believe it true: for nothing could be too bad for such an unprincipled devotee to execute, at the point of death, that he fancied would save his soul from damnation, which he was conscious he deserved. On the Papal authority Innocent III. said, "Ecclesia sponsa non nupsit vacua, sed "dotem mihi tribuit absque pretio preciosam, spiritualium plenitudinem et latitudinem tempora- "lium. In signum spiritualium contulit mihi Mitram. In signum temporalium dedit mihi "Coronam. Mitram pro sacerdotio, Coronam pro regno, illius me constituens vicarium qui habet "in vestimento et femore suo scriptum, Rex Regum et Dominus Dominantium."[1]

The Roman Pontiff had the name of Papa, which is the same as the natives of central Asia gave to their principal God Jupiter, as may be seen in the fourth book of Herodotus. He was also called the Sovereign Pontiff, which was the title that the Pagans gave to their chief priest.

The Popes on ascending the throne always assume a sacred name. This is an exact imitation of antiquity. All kings were anointed, to render them sacred; and on this occasion I believe they always assumed a sacred name, which had generally, perhaps always, an astrological allusion. The high-priests were anointed for the same reason both among the Jews and Heathens. This is the Etruscan baptism with the Holy Ghost. It is expressly declared to be so in the case of priests. Though Octavius dared not to assume the title of king, he, as high-priest, assumed the sacred title of Augustus—an Egyptian title given to the Nile—as his predecessor, Julius, had assumed the title of Cæsar, the name of the God Mars. This is an exact imitation of the practice of the Hindoo kings, and, indeed, of that of all opulent persons in India who take a sacred name from one of their Gods. This is the custom which has destroyed all ancient history by rendering it impossible to know where history ends and where religious fable begins.

Sextus V., in his bull of excommunication of Henry of Navarre, in 1585,[2] claims to possess power as successor of St. Peter from the Eternal, above all the princes of the earth, and to have power to punish them for their breaches of the laws.

The Emperors, as Roman Pagan pontiffs, claimed the same power and exercised it, as delegates of the person described by the ΤΗΣ 608—until the last age should arrive. They established the claim attempted to be set up by Antiochus, by Sylla, and by Scipio Africanus. At last, Nero claimed to be the Tenth Avatar. Infinite have been the pains of the priests to conceal these things, but I flatter myself they have failed.

It is unnecessary to point out to the reader how very near, in the middle ages, the Popes were in succeeding in their claim to the disposal of all kingdoms. This is a fact. We shall see in a future page the foundation on which this claim rested. By skilfully interfering between the Royal brutes and their oppressed subjects, they had very nearly succeeded, with the acclamations of the people, in establishing their power. Then Europe would have been precisely in the situation of Tibet at this moment.

The Roman Emperors and the Pontifices drew imposts from all the nations of the world. The Pope, in like manner, had his Peter's pence, under which name all Europe paid him tribute. It was the policy of the Roman Emperors to make the Latin tongue the common language of all nations; the Popes desired the same thing—which was the secret reason for their wishing the service always to be in Latin, the language of the See.

It was permitted by the Emperors for any one to kill those who were devoted to the infernal

---

[1] De Coronat. Pot. Serm. III.   [2] M. Mezeray reports this bull in the Life of Henry III. p. 367.

Gods; this was exactly imitated by the Popes who granted leave to any person to kill those who were excommunicated. The Emperors and Pagan Pontiffs had habits and shoes of purple; their senators were clothed in the same colour, which they call *trabea*. The Pope has the same habit and the same shoes, as may be seen in the book of sacred ceremonies.[1] The Cardinals, who compose his Senate, and whom Pius II. called Senators of the city of Rome, are also clothed with purple.[2]

When a Pope is crowned, a triumphal procession takes place from the Vatican to the Church of the Lateran, during which the new Pope throws money to the people, precisely as the Emperors of old were accustomed to do in the processions on their coronation. As the Emperors and Pontiffs were accustomed to send to their allies, as an acknowledgment of their good offices, a baton of ivory, a painted robe, or similar trifling presents; so the Popes send to kings and princes sometimes a rose, sometimes gloves, and sometimes a sacred sword, or an Agnus Dei.

The Emperors had the title of God, Deus or Divus. Virgil, in his first Eclogue, so calls Octavius, and Suetonius, in his Life of Domitian, says,[3] he wished when his commands were sent to his lieutenants, that the words, *The Lord our God commands it* should be used. The same, nearly, was attributed to the Pope.[4] " As there is only one God," says he, " in the heavens, " so there ought to be one God only on earth."[5] Du Perron, in his letter of thanks to Pope Clement VIII. for his promotion to the rank of Cardinal says, " *I have always revered your* " *beatitude as God on earth.*"

Aurelius Victor tells us, speaking of Diocletian, that the Roman Emperors and Pontiffs were adored by the people.

The last excess of baseness required by the Emperors Caligula and Heliogabalus was, the kissing of the foot. This every one knows is done continually to the Pope. Their modern followers say, that they do not kiss the *foot* but the *cross*, which is embroidered on the shoe. A mere idle subterfuge. Why is not the cross placed in some more honourable situation? The same reason would excuse them for kissing a place of still less reverence, which might be named; but it would hardly be thought respectful to place the cross there.

But the kissing of the toe was of much older date than the times of Caligula and Heliogabalus; Julius Cæsar, in quality of Pontifex Maximus, held out his foot to Pompeius Pænus to kiss, in a a slipper embroidered with gold, *socculo aurato*.[6] This was the practice of the Arch Druid in Gaul.[7]

As many of the Emperors were models of every virtue, so it cannot be denied that many of the Popes were most excellent men: but that the parallel might be complete, as many of the Emperors were the most detestable of characters, so it cannot be denied that they were fully equalled by some of the Popes in profligacy of every kind.

The title of Pontifex Maximus is strictly *Heathen*. When the Pope is elected, he is borne in great state to the high altar in St. Peter's, on which he is placed, and where he receives the adoration of all the Cardinals.[8] This is a close copy of the same practice of the Heathen to their high-priest.[9] And it appears that Martin IV. was addressed, " *O lamb of God, who takest away the sins of the world, grant us thy peace.*"[10] The very words used in their service by the Carnutes of Gaul, as we shall soon see.

In the ceremonies of initiation into the mysteries of Samothrace and Eleusis, the novice was

---

[1] Lib i. Cap. vi. Sect. 1.   [2] Vide Lips. Lib. iv. Cap. ii. de Admir. seu de Magni. Rom.
[3] Cap. xiii.   [4] See Froissard, Tome IV. Chap. x.   [5] Deor. I. part. Dist. Cap. xcvi. satis evidenter.
[6] Clel. Spec. Etym. Vocab. p. 104.   [7] Ibid.   [8] Vide Eustace's Travels.
[9] Priestley's Hist. Corrup. Christ. Vol. II. pp. 295, 329 ed. 1782.   [10] Ib. 330, 331.

placed on a throne, and the initiated formed a circle and danced round him to a sacred hymn which they sung.[1] In one of the spurious Gospels, as they are called, Jesus and his apostles, are said to have performed a similar ceremony after his last supper. When the Cardinals advance *in a circle* to the adoration of the Pope, placed on the chair of St. Peter, and when again every Sunday they *draw up in a circle* round him, and go down on their knees to him, they do but repeat this ceremony. And, I think, that although the novice, after the performance of this ceremony, was not in reality the Pope, or head of the fraternity, yet for the sake of admitting him to the highest of the mysteries, he was supposed to have filled the office; he was admitted to have filled it for a few minutes—performing some act of authority whilst so elevated. I have reasons for this which I shall not give. In the ancient mysteries this was called θρονωσις or θρονισμος. In imitation of this our bishops are enthroned—the rite is called the enthroning. One of the hymns of Orpheus is called θρονισμοι.

We are in the habit of abusing Octavius and his people for calling him Divus, Augustus, &c. He was not called *father* of his country until late in life. I believe this title of father of his country, or of Αιων των αιωνων, was given to him because he was really thought to be the father of the future age, the Genius of the Ninth Sæculum—the Cyrus of his day. And if we consider the happy state of the world during his long reign, no man ever lived to whom the title could be more plausibly given.

I suppose no person can have paid much attention to the European history of the middle ages without having observed many circumstances relating to its Popes which have not been satisfactorily accounted for. Among them stands pre-eminent the Papal claim of supremacy over the temporal and Germanic imperial authority. The Emperors claimed to be successors of the Roman Emperors, calling themselves kings of the Romans and Cæsars; and if the house of Hapsburg should ever breed a Napoleon, (a thing not much to be feared,) I have no doubt that the claim would be instantly renewed to all the dominion ruled by Augustus. To their claims as Imperator or Embratur,[2] the Roman Pontiff acceded, but to nothing more—only as Imperator or Dictator. To the authority of the Pontifex Maximus of the ancient Romans, the Pope had succeeded; and that power, in the time of Augustus, had obtained, in fact, the sovereign sway. The triple mitre or crown of the Pontiff had, to all intents and purposes, risen above the single crown of the king. Jesus of Bethlehem, who was foretold by all the Prophets, had come, as Buddha and as Cristna had come, and had, through the medium of St. Peter, transmitted his authority to the head of the Catholic or universal church, which was received with dutiful submission by the Great Constantine, its eldest son. In the person of Octavius Cæsar the offices of Pontifex Maximus and Emperor or Dictator were united, therefore he legally possessed all power. In the person of Constantine,[3] by his surrender of part to the Pope, they became divided, and he surrendered that power, which he only held as delegate, into the hand of its rightful owner, the successor of St. Peter, the head fisherman (as the Pope called himself) of Galilee. But he claimed to be Pontifex Maximus, not Pontifex Magnus, which brought the whole world under his sway. The grounds and nature of this claim, and the general character of the mighty empire which flourished beneath it in a former time, will be described at large in a future book. The claim of the Popes to supernatural knowledge, is not in reality so monstrously absurd, as at first it seems to be, if every thing were supposed (as I have no doubt it was) to occur in each cycle, as it had done before. As the Supreme Pontiff knew the

---

[1] Creuzer, Liv. v. Ch. ii. p. 320.   [2] Niebuhr, ed. Walter, Vol. I. p. 64.

[3] Whose grand equestrian statue stands, as it ought to do, in the portico of St. Peter's, guarding the entrance to the temple, but not in the temple—the first servant of the living God within.

history of the cycle, he could tell what would happen in any part of it. This was the theory, and he might easily account for his own ignorance or his knowledge not being equal to that of his predecessors, as saints account for want of power to perform miracles,—his own want of faith or his own or the general decay of piety. Excuses of this kind are never wanting to devotees. The Pontifex Maximus carried the crosier, as may be seen on the medals of the high-priest Julius Cæsar, and by law his person was sacred, and his life could be forfeited by no crime. The assassin's dagger was the only resource.[1] It is perfectly clear that the mitre in ancient Rome had obtained the supreme power. Fortunately the power of the sword saved the Western world from the fate of Tibet. It was before observed (Vol. I. pp. 691, 692), that when the French possessed Italy, they examined the chair of St. Peter, and found upon it signs of the Zodiac. There is also a published account, written by a Roman of eminence before the time of the French invasion, which states, that the same thing was observed, and much discussed, on the chair being formerly taken down to be cleaned. The Zodiac had been forgotten, or the chair would not have been again taken down. This is the ch. ir of St. Peter with its Zodiacal chain, on which the Pope is supposed to sit to rule the empire of his *first* crown, of the planets, which I named in my last book. It must not be forgotten that his triple crown is emblematical of his *three kingdoms*. The illustrious Spaniard did not err far when he said, that the life of Jesus was written in the stars.

Irenæus was Bishop of Lyons. He was one of the first fathers of the church who suffered martyrdom, and generally accounted one of its most eminent and illustrious early writers. He was an Asiatic, but was sent as bishop to Gaul. He founded or built a church in that country. This church is yet remaining at Lyons, though in the course of almost 2000 years no doubt it has undergone many alterations. On the floor, in front of the altar, may be seen a Mosaic pavement of the Zodiac, though a considerable part of it is worn away. This, like the chair of St. Peter, I have partly discussed before—Vol. I. pp. 19, 20, and 690. Persons who do not look deeply into these matters are easily blinded by being told, that it is the remains of an old temple. But Irenæus had no power to get possession of Roman pagan temples. The pretence is totally void of foundation. The style of building, its records, &c., all shew that what its priests say is true, viz. that it was built by Irenæus. On many other churches, which never were Roman temples, both in Britain and elsewhere, similar marks of the esoteric religion, which I have partly unfolded, may be seen. Nothing of this kind is more striking than the Pagan Sibyls seen in many places, particularly surrounding the Casa Santa at Loretto, the most sacred of all the shrines of the *black* God— where, in the affected poverty of a cottage, and amidst gold and diamonds without measure or number, I saw him sitting enthroned.[2]

I entertain a strong suspicion that if we could fairly get at the secret of the Vatican, we should find it held, that, in ancient times, there were several high-priests or vicars of God upon the earth, but that they were all united in the person of Jesus of Bethlehem, who passed down his power by St. Peter to the Popes, who inherited his undivided power over the whole world. From their adoption of the rites of the Roman Pontiff, and of Jesus, of Cyrus and Cristna, and of the Trojan priests, who, in fact, were the predecessors of those of Rome, I think they were disposed to admit several branches, all centering in Jesus, or perhaps in the last and *tenth*, the Popes. This is correctly the doctrine of the Lama of Tibet. Though the human body of the Lama dies, he is be-

---

[1] R. Taylor's Dieg. pp. 141, 142, *note*.

[2] The riches of this temple were carried away and dissipated by the priests to prevent the French from getting possession of them, when they overran Italy in the great revolution war. But since the restoration, *in this age of light*, in proportion to the time, they have increased faster than ever they did in the age of darkness.

lieved to remove to some new body, not to die. It is with a view to this part of the mythos that the pedigrees are so carefully given in the Old and New Testaments, which are called *testaments*, because they are witnesses to the legality of this claim. But all this will be explained in a future book.

4. Having shewn the identity of the *ancient* and *modern* Roman Pontifex, I shall proceed to the celebrated Seven Sacraments of the Romish church, and first to that of the Eucharist.

The first information we have respecting the sacrifice or offering of *bread* and *wine* is in Genesis xiv. 18, 19, "*And Melchizedek, king of Salem, brought forth bread and wine: and he was the priest of the most high God. And he blessed him, and said, Blessed be Abram of* [by] *the most high God, possessor of heaven and earth.*" There seems no doubt that this king and priest was of the religion of the Persians, of Brahma, of Mithra, and of Abram, as professed at that time. The Mithraitic sacrifice and the payment of tithes are strong circumstances in favour of this opinion. It is not improbable, if Abram left his country to avoid the abuses and idolatry then beginning to prevail, that he should have come to dwell where his religion was not yet corrupted. We know that the religion of the Magi did become corrupted; and it was reformed before the time of Cyrus and Daniel by a man called Zoroaster, or Abraham Zoradust. The Rev. Dr. Milner, Bishop and Apostolic Vicar, says, "It was then in offering up a sacrifice of bread and wine, instead of slaughtered animals, that "Melchizedek's sacrifice differed from the generality of those in the old law, and that he prefigured "the sacrifice which Christ was to institute in the new law from the same elements. No other "sense than this can be elicited from the Scripture as to this matter; and accordingly the holy "fathers[1] unanimously adhere to this meaning."[2]

St. Jerom says, "Melchizedek in typo Christi panem et vinum obtulit: et mysterium Christianum in Salvatoris sanguine et corpore dedicavit."[3].

It is no little confirmation of this opinion, that we find Jesus Christ in the New Testament represented as a priest after the order of Melchizedek.[4] To account for this, divines have been much puzzled. If it be admitted, (and I think it will be difficult to be denied,) that the religions of Melchizedek, of Abram, Mithra, and Jesus, were all the same, there will be no difficulty in explaining the passages in the Epistle to the Hebrews respecting Melchizedek. Jesus was correctly a preacher or priest of this order or religion. The early Christians found the ancient legends, traditions, and circumstances; but probably their connexion was as little known to them as to their successors, the Cyprians, Augustins, &c. However, I cannot well be told that this connexion between the bread and wine of Melchizedek and the Christian eucharist is merely the produce of a fertile imagination, as I am supported, according to Dr. Milner, by the ancient fathers of the church *unanimously*.

The temple of Jupiter, without statue, on Mount Carmel, where Pythagoras[5] studied philosophy, was the temple of Melchizedek, as Eupolemus witnesses.[6]

For a long time violent and even bloody feuds took place among the Christians respecting the celebration of what we call Easter,—the festival, in fact, of the goddess Eostre or the Saxon or Sidonian Asteroth or Astarte.[7] In fact, two separate and distinct things as they were then become, even if they were identical in their origin, were confounded together. These were the

---

[1] St. Cypr. Ep. lxiii.; St. August. in Ps. xxxiii.; St. Chrys. Hom. xxxv.; St. Jerom, Ep. cxxvi., &c.
[2] Milner, End Rel. Cont. Let. 40, p. 56.   [3] Bryant on Philo, p. 275.
[4] Heb. vii. 1, 10, 11, 15.   [5] Who was a follower of that religion of which Jesus of Nazareth was.
[6] See Vol. I. p. 39, *note*, pp. 82, 94, 329, 389, 790, 823.   [7] Bower, Hist. Popes, pp. 27—37.

Jewish Passover and the sacrifice of bread and wine of Melchizedek; and, in the early ages of Christianity, they were still observed by the Persians or the followers of Mithra. The ignorant devotees found a tradition of Jesus keeping the Passover on the *fourteenth* day of the moon, of the first month; they also found traditions of Jesus being declared to be a priest of the order of Melchizedek. They also found among them, or at least among such of them as derived their descent from the Gentiles of Mithra, the sacrifice of Bread and Wine or Water. The mystical and figurative expressions attributed to Jesus they construed literally, and thus came the *real presence*. But their hatred of the Jews would not permit them to acknowledge it to be the Jewish Passover, and therefore they changed it from the day on which it ought to have been celebrated—the *fourteenth* —to the day on which, by no possibility, it could have taken place, viz. the Sunday afterward— the supposed day of the resurrection of Jesus. After many centuries, when the Protestants arose, they seem to have been most exceedingly puzzled to know what to do with this rite; but at last they settled it as we have it now, excluding the sacrifice, and construing the words attributed to Jesus litera-figuratively, but keeping it still on the Sunday, the hatred towards the Jews having at that time suffered no abatement. I have used the compound word litera-figuratively to endeavour to express the nonsense of the Protestants, who say, that the words *flesh* and *blood* are figurative, but still that, as flesh and blood, they are *verily and indeed* taken. The straightforward doctrine of the Romish church may be false and shocking, but it is not, like that of the Protestants, mere contradictory nonsense. I beg that I may not be accused of speaking irreverently of the rite itself, for it is, in my opinion, in its primitive simplicity as used by Jesus Christ, without exception the most beautiful religious ceremony ever established in the world.

The whole of the ancient Gentile and Druidical ceremonies of Easter or the Saxon Goddess אשתרת *Ostrt*, or Eostre of the Germans, is yet continued over all the Christian world.[1] This festival began with a week's indulgence in all kinds of sports, called the carne-vale, or the taking *a farewell to animal food*, because it was followed by a fast of forty days. An account of this, of Shrovetide, of Ash Wednesday, &c., &c., may be found in Cleland's Specimens;[2] but his explanation is not very satisfactory, and he is in several instances mistaken. But I suspect in those countries where the God was feigned to be cut in pieces, as Bacchus on Mont Martre, and Osiris in Egypt, and the limbs scattered about, the forty days were the days passed by Isis or the Mænades in mourning for them and in searching after them.[3] Amidst the great mass of other matters in which the identity of the rites and ceremonies of the Gentiles and of the Christians are shewn, the explanation of the origin of this rite is not very material, and I have not taken much pains about it. But its existence over all the North of Europe long before the time of Christ cannot be disputed.

The celebration of the Eucharist by the followers of Mani, and by some other of the early sects, affords a striking trait of identity between the religion or gospel of the Persians or the Magi, and that of Jesus. Certainly, the nonsense which devotees will talk, or which devotees will believe, is almost incredible. But yet it is quite incomprehensible to me how any set of persons or sect (if they were immediate, or in a direct line, descendants from Jesus Christ, and if the account in the gospel histories be true) can admit the institution of the Lord's Supper, and take the cup with water, instead of wine, the nature of the liquid being considered not a trifle or of little consequence,

---

[1] See Bochart, Vol. I. p. 676; Anc. Univers. Hist., Vol. XIX. p. 177; Parkhurst, in voce.   [2] P. 89.

[3] I suspect the first part only of Lent was devoted to mourning, the last three days only being spent in the search, when long processions took place, and ended with finding the whole God on Easter Sunday, or on the fourteenth day. In all the churches in Italy, during these forty days, the Icons of the Virgin are covered with a black crape veil.

but a matter of the first importance. How is it possible for any sophistry about abstemiousness to persuade a person above the rank of an idiot, that after Jesus had taken the cup with wine as described in our gospel histories, the rite ought to be celebrated by his followers, not with *wine*, but with *water*, as was the case with the Manichæans, the Encratites, Nestorians, and others? [1]

The real state of the case I apprehend to be this: Christians in different countries found various accounts and practices with respect to this matter. The Judaizing Christians considering it a species of passover (Christ is called the Passover of the Christians [2]) or paschal supper, naturally described the cup to contain *wine*, after the manner of the Jews in their passover; and we, who adopt their gospels, take it with wine. On the contrary, the Manichæans and many of the other Eastern sects, who, in fact, had their gospel directly and immediately from the Persian Magi, took this rite with water instead of wine. The eucharist of the Lord and Saviour, as the Magi called the Sun, the second person in their Trinity, or their eucharistic sacrifice, was always made exactly and in every respect the same as that of the orthodox Christians, except that the latter use wine instead of water. This bread-and-water sacrifice was offered by the Magi of Persia, by the Essenes or Therapeutæ, by the Gnostics, and, indeed, by almost if not quite all the Eastern Christians, and by Pythagoras in Greece and Numa at Rome.

The Ebionites or Nazarenes were unquestionably the most immediate and direct followers of Jesus. They were resident in Judea; they are acknowledged to have been among the very earliest of the sects of Christians. As uncertain as tradition is, it is difficult to believe that, in less than one hundred years after the death of Christ, they should not have retained a correct tradition of this rite, if they had really received it from him, and if there had been any certainty on the subject. They are described as a very low, poor, ignorant race of people. They are said to have had a written gospel. Some persons have supposed the gospel of Matthew to have been theirs. But I think the very circumstance of their having used *water* instead of *wine* is sufficient to prove that this cannot be true.—All these circumstances afford traces of the existence of this rite among the Persians long before the man Jesus of Judea is said to have lived.—The moderns have not known what to make of the rite. In the service of our Edward the Sixth, water is directed to be mixed with the wine. This is an union of the two; not a half measure, but a double one. If it be correct to take it with *wine*, then they were right; if with *water*, they still were right; as they took both, they could not be wrong. [3]

The Persians had a rite called the festival of Saka, Sakea, or Sakia, which M. Beausobre has shewn was probably the Manichæan Eucharist or Love Feast. He observes, [4] that Cyril in calling it *Ischas* has probably meant to travesty the work Saka. Ischas or Ischa was the name of both Sarah the wife of Abraham and of Jesus. [5] Most likely it merely means *the Saviour*; but it pretty nearly identifies the name of Jesus with that of Buddha. To the word Saka and its origin or corruptions, I shall return by and by.

According to Justin's account, the devils busied themselves much with the Eucharist. After describing in several places that bread and wine and *water* were used in the Christian rite, he says, "And this very solemnity too the evil spirits have introduced into the mysteries of Mithra; for you do or may know, that when any one is initiated into this religion, bread and a cup of water, with a certain form of words, are made use of in the sacrifice." [6]

---

[1] Clemens Alex. and Epiphanius; Dupuis, Vol. III. pp 85, 325, 4to.
[2] 1 Cor. v. 7.
[3] Dr. Grabe's notes upon Irenæus, Lib. v. Cap. ii.
[4] Liv. ix. Ch. viii. p. 729.
[5] See Vol. I pp. 583, 747, 836.
[6] See Reeves's Justin, and notes on Sect. lxxxvi. The followers of Tatian used no wine, only water, in the Eucharist. Mosh. Hist., Cent. 2, Ch. v. 8. ix.; see also Cent. 2, Ch. iv. 8. xii.

Hyde says, " De Tinctione, de oblatione panis, et de imagine resurrectionis, videatur doctiss. de la Cerda ad ea Tertulliani loca ubi de hisce rebus agitur. Gentiles citra Christum, talia celebrabant Mithriaca quæ videbantur cum doctrinâ *eucharistiæ* et *resurrectionis* et aliis ritibus Christianis convenire, quæ fecerunt ex industriâ ad imitationem Christianismi : unde Tert. et Patres aiunt eos talia fecisse, duce diabolo, quo vult esse simia Christi, &c. Volunt itaque eos res suas ita comparâsse, ut *Mithræ mysteria essent eucharistiæ Christianæ imago.* Sic Just. Martyr, p. 98, et Tertullianus et Chrysostomus. In suis etiam sacris habebant Mithriaci lavacra (quasi regenerationis) in quibus tingit et ipse (sc. sacerdos) quosdam utique credentes et fideles suos, et expiatoria delictorum de lavacro repromittit, et sic adhuc initiat Mithræ."[1] From a quotation of Gorius, it seems the *modern* as well as the *ancient* fathers have recourse to the very satisfactory agency of the devil, to account for these things.

Our catechism says, that the sacrament of the Lord's Supper was ordained for the continual remembrance of the SACRIFICE of the death of Christ; and, that the outward part or sign of the Lord's Supper is bread and wine. It then goes on to say, that the inward part or thing signified is *the body and blood* of Christ (thing signified !), which are *verily* and *indeed* taken, and received by the faithful in the Lord's Supper. It then concludes by saying, that the souls of those who partake of this sacrament are to be refreshed by the body and blood of Christ, as their bodies are by the bread and wine.

A very learned and ingenious clergyman of the Church of England, Mr. Glover,[2] has said, " In " the sacrament of the altar is the natural body and blood of Christ verè et realiter, verily and " indeed, if you take these terms for spiritually by grace and efficacy ; but if you mean really and " indeed, so that thereby you would include a lively and moveable body under the form of bread " and wine, then in that sense is not Christ's body in the sacrament really and indeed." And thus he sophistically explains away the two plain words *verè* and *realiter.* How is it possible, without the grossest abuse of language, to make the words *verily* and *indeed* mean spiritually by grace and efficacy ? However, his ingenious sophistry does not affect my argument, as all I undertake is, to shew that this rite is more ancient than Christianity—and this cannot be disputed.

When the reader has duly considered all the other circumstances which I have brought together respecting the religions or doctrines of Mithra, the Esseneans, Pythagoreans, Jesus, &c., he will not deny the strong probability that the sacrifice of the Mass, or of *bread* and *wine*, as is asserted by the Romish Apostolic Vicar,[3] Dr. Milner, has descended even from the remote time of Abraham.

The Mass of the Romish Church is of the very first importance in their religion. The word Mass, it has been said, is taken from the ceremonies of Isis, in which, after the ceremonies and the other mysteries were ended, the people were dismissed, by the Greeks, with the words Λαοις αφσις, which mean, *the people may retire;* that the Romans, in the same ceremonies, used the words *Ite, Missio est;* (see Apuleius de Missio;) and, that the Missio, by corruption, has become Messe or Mass.[4] This is very unsatisfactory. I believe the meaning of the Mess or Mass is nothing but the Latin name for corn or bread, and that to the expression *Ite, Missio est,* a word for *finished* was originally added or is understood, or has been by degrees dropped.[5] Of

---

[1] De Rel. Vet. Pers. Cap. iv. p. 113.   [2] Remarks on Marsh's Comp. View, p. 102.

[3] The Vicars Apostolic, I understand, receive episcopal ordination, but have more power than ordinary bishops. Dr. Alexander Geddes, whom I have often quoted, sustained the same rank.

[4] Apul. Lib. xv., de Asino aureo; Pol. Virg. Cap. xii.

[5] In Yorkshire, on the festival of St, Thomas, wheat is given to the poor, and it is eaten not *ground*, but boiled whole, called *frumenty.* This is the sacrifice of the Messis or Mass.

the descent of the Mass, or the sacrifice of bread and wine, from Melchizedek, I have had frequent opportunities of speaking.[1] And I have shewn that this sacrifice was common to many ancient nations. M. Marolles, in his Memoirs,[2] quotes Tibullus, in the fourth elegy of his third book, where he says that the Pagans appease the Divinity with *holy bread—Farre pio placant;* that Virgil, in the fifth book of the Æneid, says, they rendered honours to Vesta, with *holy bread.*

Vestæ
Farre pio et plenâ supplex veneratur acerrâ.—Lines 744, 745.

He adds, that the words of Horace, *Farre pio et saliente micâ,* relate to the same thing, and that Tibullus, in the panegyric to Messala, wrote that a little cake or a little morsel of bread appeased the Divinities. *Parvaque cœlestes pacavit mica.* As I have before repeatedly observed, the sacrifice without blood was ordered by Numa Pompilius, and practised by Pythagoras. It may be remarked, in passing, that the term to *immolate,* which is used for sacrifice, may come from the Latin word *mola,* which was the name that the Pagans gave to the little round bits of bread which they offered to their Gods in this sacrifice. The Mass is also called the Host. This word means a host, a giver of hospitality, and also an enemy, and the host of heaven, and is the name of the harbour of the city of Saturn-ja or Valencia or Roma, Ostia.

The Romans celebrated, on the 22nd of February, the feast of Charisties or Caristies or Charistia. From the character of this festival, I have a strong suspicion that the name was a corruption of the ancient Chrest, Χρης and Ερως. Creuzer[3] says, " This was a family or domestic feast, " which the Roman religion exhibits in its aspect most moral and amiable. It followed several " days of mourning for departed friends. The oldest of the family, he who first in the order of " nature would go to increase the number of those who were already gone, reunited all its mem- " bers at a feast of love and harmony ; when the object was to reconcile all differences among the " members of it." As M. Creuzer observes, " it shews beautifully that the ancients did not " separate the contemplation of the future from present joys. The day was sacred to Concord " and the Lares, and finished the old and began the new year." And it must be acknowledged that nothing more beautiful could well be imagined.—From this Charisties comes our Charity and Caritas, not exclusively in the sense of giving to the poor, but in that of brotherly love as used by Paul. And here we have among the oldest of the ceremonies of Italy, the Eucharist or ευχαριςια of the Christians.

Valerius Maximus[4] says, "Convivium etiam solenne *majores* instituerant: idque *Charistia* appel- " laverunt, cui præter cognatos et affines, nemo interponebatur : *ut* si qua inter necessarios querela " esset orta, apud *sacra* mensæ, et inter hilaritatem animorum, favoribus concordiæ adhibitis, tolle- " retur."[5] Cleland shews that this festival was in use, as we might expect, among the Celts and Druids.[6]

This festival in Hebrew was called קום *qum,* a feast, communion.[7] From this comes our communion.

Similar to the Italian Charistia was the beautiful and simple rite of the Jews, of breaking bread and drinking with one another at their great festivals, in fact of celebrating the sacrifice of bread

---

[1] See Vol. I. pp. 718, 726, 823.   [2] P. 215.   [3] Livre cinquième, Ch. iii. p. 456.

[4] Lib. ii. Cap. 1. Sect. 8.

[5] That *bloody* sacrifices were not used in the earliest times is an opinion supported by Sophocles ; Pausanias, de Cerere Phrygialeusi ; by Plato, de Legibus, Lib. vi.; and by Empedocles, Lib. de Antiq. Temp.

[6] Spec. Etymol. Vocab. p. 111.   [7] Vall. Coll. Hib. Vol. V. p. 224.

and wine so appropriate to Jesus, the priest of the order of Melchizedek, which was converted in a later day into a horrible mystery. When a Jew has broken the bread and partaken of the cup with his fellow, it is considered that a peculiar and brotherly affection is to subsist between them for the next year; and, if there had been any previous enmity, this ceremony is considered the outward sign (of an inward, spiritual grace), that it no longer exists. In all Jewish families, after their paschal supper, the bread is always broken, and the grace-cup is tasted and sent round by the master of the house. It is described as one of the last actions of Jesus, when he had reason to believe that his enemies would proceed to violence against him, and is in strict keeping with what I am convinced was the beautiful simplicity of every part of his character and life. The reader will please to observe that when I speak thus of Jesus Christ, I give no credit to the improper conduct ascribed to him, or to the fact of his having taught the immoral doctrines ascribed to him in the gospel histories [1] of the different sects of his followers, so inconsistent with his general character.

Jesus is made to say, " ' his is my flesh," "This is my blood." If we take these words to the letter, they were evidently not true. The articles spoken of were neither his flesh nor his blood. Then it is surely only consistent with candour to inquire what meaning could be given *to them*, agreeable to common sense and the meaning of this, at that time, *ancient* ceremony. This, I think, will be found in the fact which we all know, that he abolished among his followers the shocking and disgusting practice, at that time common, of offering sacrifices of flesh and blood, so well described by the Rev. Mr. Faber, and at that time still practised upon grand occasions among the Druids or Chaldees, and Romans, even to the length of offering human victims.—It seems not unlikely that we have only part of the speech of Jesus, that its object was the abolition of that disgusting and atrocious practice, and that his speech had reference to it. *Speaking as he did*, or is said to have done, *always in parables,* he might readily use the figurative expression in reference to something which had passed before against bloody sacrifices: and at that time he might use the words, *This is my body, and this is my blood, which I offer;* i. e. This is *my* offering of body (or flesh) and blood, and no other. It was the offering of Melchizedek and of Pythagoras, his predecessors, and, probably, originally of all nations. The bread was always broken, and is yet broken, in the ceremony, and given as a token of remembrance, precisely as he used it. *Eat this in remembrance of me.* How could any words be more natural? This agrees very well with what he is made to say in the Gospel of the Nazarenes: " I came to abolish sacrifices, and unless ye " cease to offer sacrifices, the wrath of God shall not cease from you." [2]

The whole paschal supper was a festival of joy and gladness, to celebrate the passage of the sun; and, after the family had eaten, the remainder was given to the poor, along with such other matters as the elect or chapter could spare; for I apprehend the χοινωνιοι, or *community of goods*, was confined at first to the lodge, to the seventy-two; and perhaps the Eucharist was at first taken by only the twelve *elect* or *perfect* in the mysteries. The probability of these matters must be left to the reader. The evidence is not very clear, though the probability is strong. This seems to me to be a rational explanation of the words, and is consistent with the general character of Jesus—the character of the priest after the order of Melchizedek. It dovetails well into the historical fact of no sacrifice of animals having ever taken place in his religion, and with the Gentile histories. And when he was founding his religion on the Mosaic system, there does seem

---

[1] Probably some of the *spurious* gospels; for, happily, on the testimony of the *canonical* Gospels—uncontradicted by respectable profane history—even *unbelievers* have concurred with the Author in paying a tribute of respect to " the " beautiful simplicity of every part of the character and life" of Jesus Christ. *Editor.*

[2] J. Jones on Canon, Pt. II. Chap. xxv. Art. 12, p. 275.

to require an explanation of the reason why the *ordained* sacrifices were abolished. Here we see the reason why the Melchizedekian sacrifice was restored, or declared to be enough, without holocausts or even partial *burnt-offerings*.

Besides the Charistia of the Romans, as above described, there must have been some other ceremony very similar, or some sectaries must have held opinions from which the modern Romish priests have copied their Transubstantiation, as we find the doctrine alluded to by Cicero. The Rev. R. Taylor, in his answer to Dr. Pye Smith,[1] says, "There is a passage in Cicero, written "forty years before the birth of Christ, in which he ridicules the doctrine of transubstantiation, "and asks, how a man can be so stupid as to imagine that which he eats to be a God? Ut illud "quo vescatur Deum esse putet?"

The ancients always washed before they sacrificed, says Eustache upon Homer;[2] and Hesiod forbids any wine to be offered to Jupiter with unwashed hands.[3] And Virgil tells us, that Æneas, even though the city was on fire, durst not touch the Gods to save them, till he had first washed his hands. In the ritual of the Romish church it is said, *Sacerdos sanctam eucharistiam administraturus procedat ad altare lotis prius manibus.*

It was the custom of the Pagan priests to confess before they sacrificed, demanding pardon of the Gods and Goddesses.[4] Numa ordered this to be observed by the Romans, not esteeming the sacrifice *good*, unless the priest had first cleared his conscience *by confession*. The Romish priests are expected to do this before they celebrate the Mass.[4]

Numa ordained that the priest who made the sacrifice should be clothed in white, in the habit called an *alba*.[5] This is the alb which *he* carries who celebrates the Mass. Above the alb, Numa ordered the sacrificer to carry a coloured robe, with a pectoral or breast-plate of brass, which is now often changed into gold or silver. This is what is called *chasuble*. The priests use also a veil, with which they cover the head, called *amict*. All these ornaments were introduced by Numa. They are also most of them found among the Jews.

The turnings and genuflexions of the priests, and their circular processions, were all ordered by Numa.[d] The last were also the Deisuls of the Druids. Du Choul has shewn,[7] that the custom of having the Mass in the morning was taken from the Egyptians, who divided the time, like the Romish church, into prime, tierce, and sexte.

The Pagans had music in their temples, as the Romish devotees have in their churches. Galien says, they have no sacrifice without music.[8] I shall add no more on this subject here, but I shall resume it in a future Book. I shall then try to penetrate to the bottom of this, which I am persuaded is one of the most profaned of the mysteries.

5. The next rite which I shall notice is that of Baptism.

That the ceremony of baptism is older than the time of Jesus is evident from the Gospels;[9] but

---

[1] P. 111. [2] In Il. i. [3] Hist. Operum et Dier. [4] Du Choul, p. 270.
[5] Alex. ab Alex. Lib. iv. Cap. xvii. [6] Du Choul, p. 275; and Pol. Virg. Lib. i. 5, Cap. xi. [7] P. 309.
[8] Gal. Lib. xvii. de Off.; Scaliger, Lib. i. Poet. Cap. xliv.; Strabo, Lib. x.; Arnob. Lib vii.

[9] The Author makes no reference in proof of this assertion; and, whatever may have been the practice of the followers of Zoroaster or others, there is no satisfactory evidence deducible from either the Old Testament or the Gospels, that Baptism was practised by the Jews prior to the ministry of *the* Baptist. The Author, however, like many other writers, both Advocates and Opponents of *baptism*, probably overlooked the difference between βαπτισμοι (washings, *auto* or *self*-cleansings) and βαπτισμα, which is never used in the N T. in the *plural*; or, perhaps, he recollected the question of the Priests and Levites to John, "Why baptisest thou then, if," &c.? (John i. 25.) On which it may be remarked, that the pronoun *thou*, which is often regarded as emphatically contrasting John with others who had previously baptized, is not *emphatically* expressed in the original. It is simply, Τι ου βαπτιζεις; not Τι συ βαπτιζεις Συ; *Editor.*

how much older it may be, it is impossible to ascertain. It was a practice of the followers of Zoroaster.[1] Hyde says, " Pro infantibus non utuntur circumcisione, sed tantum baptismo seu " lotione ad animæ purificationem internam. Infantem ad. sacerdotem in ecclesiam adductum " sistunt coram sole et igne, quâ factâ ceremoniâ, eundem sanctiorem existimant. D. Lord dicit " quod aquam ad hoc afferunt in cortice arboris Holm: ea autem arbor revera est Haum Magorum, " cujus mentionem aliâ occasione supra fecimus. Alias, aliquando fit immergendo in magnum vas " aquæ, ut dicit Tavernier. Post talem lotionem seu baptismum, sacerdos imponit nomen à " parentibus inditum." After this Hyde goes on to state, that when he comes to be fifteen years of age he is confirmed by receiving the girdle, and the sudra or cassock.

The Holm or Haum here spoken of by Hyde, is the Phœnix or Phoinix or Palm-tree, called by Burckhardt and Buckingham, in their Travels in Asia, the Dom-tree—*the tree of the sacred* OM.[2]

" De-là vint, que pour devenir capable d'entendre les secrets de la création, révélés dans ces " mêmes mystères, il fallut se faire *régénérer* par *l'initiation*. Cette cérémonie, par laquelle, *on* " *apprenoit les vrais principes de la vie*, s'opéroit par le moyen de *l'eau* qui avoit été celui de la " *régénération* du monde. On conduisoit sur les bords de l'Ilissus le candidat qui devoit être " initié; après l'avoir purifié avec le sel et l'eau de la mer, on répandoit de l'orge sur lui, ou le " couronoit de fleurs, et *l'Hydranos* ou le *Baptiseur* le plongeoit dans le fleuve. L'usage de ce " *Baptême* par immersion, qui subsista dans l'Occident jusqu' au 8e siècle, se maintient encore " dans l'Eglise Greque: c'est celui que Jean le *Précurseur* administra, dans le Jourdain, à Jesus-" Christ même. Il fut pratiqué chez les Juifs,[3] chez les Grecs, et chez presque tous les peuples, " bien des siècles avant l'existence de la religion Chrétienne: c'est encore une de ces anciennes " cérémonies que Dieu sanctifia pour le bien des hommes. On vient de voir qu'elle en fut " l'origine, dans les tems qui précédèrent celui où le Baptême devint un Sacrement. Les Indiens " continuent à se purifier dans les eaux du Gange, qu'ils regardent comme sacres."[4]

M. Beausobre has clearly proved that the Manichæans had the rite of Baptism, both for infants and adults, in the name of the Father, Son, and Holy Ghost. He has satisfactorily proved the falsity of St. Augustine upon this point; but, indeed, nothing which Augustine says against the sect whom he deserted and betrayed, is worthy of any credit whatever. M. Beausobre[5] says, " Mani had more than one reason for administering baptism to infants. This custom not only " served to confirm his opinion, that corruption is in nature, and comes to man by nature, but in " this he conformed to the custom of the Magi, *from which he deviated as little as he possibly could*. " This was the way to give them a taste for his religion. The ancient Persians carried their " infants to the temple a few days after they were born, and presented them to the priest before " the sun, and before the fire, which was his symbol. Then the priest took the child and baptized " it for the purification of the soul. Sometimes he plunged it into a great vase full of water: it " was in the same ceremony that the father gave a name to the child. When the child had arrived " at fifteen years of age, he was presented again to the priest, who confirmed him by giving him " the robe called the Sudra and the Girdle. These were the symbols or the sacraments of the " promises that he made to God to serve him according to the religion of the Persians." The reader sees that Mani is said to have deviated as little as possible from the rites of the Magi. This is true enough. In fact, the Evangelion of Zoroaster, of the Romish Jesus, and of Mani, were all precisely the same in principle, and very nearly the same in all their ceremonies. The

---

[1] Hyde de Rel. Vet. Pers. Cap. xxxiv. p. 406.
[2] See Vol. I. p. 742, *note*.
[3] See Editor's *note* ut sup.
[4] D'Anc. Res. Vol. I. p. 292.
[5] Liv. ix. Ch. vi. Sect. xvi.

variation was not more than might be expected to arise, from distance in situation, in time, and from difference of languages and nations.

Dr. Hyde says,[1] "Et postea anno ætatis xv°, quando incipit induere tunicam, sudra, et cingulum, ut religionem ingrediatur, et ille in articulis fidei versatur, à sacerdote ei datur confirmatio, ut, ab eo tempore, inter numerum fidelium admittatur, et fidelis esse reputetur." If this account of Dr. Hyde's be correct, which I believe no one ever doubted, it is impossible for any person to be so blind as not to see, that these three extremely important and vital ceremonies of the Christian religion—Baptism, Christening, and Confirmation—were nothing but rites of the religion of the Magi, of Mithra, or of the sun.

Upon this subject Justin says,[2] in Section lxxxi., "The devils no sooner heard of this baptism spoken of by the prophet, but they too set up their baptisms, and made such as go to their temples and officiate in their libations and meat offerings, first sprinkle themselves with water by way of lustration; and they have brought it to such a pass, that the worshipers are washed from head to foot before they approach the sacred place where their images are kept." On the above the Rev. Mr. Reeves makes the following note: "That such mock baptisms were set up by the contrivance of the Devil in the Gentile world, we find not only asserted by Justin, but all the primitive writers, and particularly by Tertullian, *de baptismo*. Certe ludis Apollinaribus et Eleusiniis tinguntur, idque se in regenerationem et impunitatem perjuriorum suorum agere præsumunt. Thus were men initiated into the mysteries of Eleusis, and he who initiated them was called Ὑδρανος, *the waterer*, Ὑδρανος ὁ ἁγνιςης των Ελευσινιων.[3] Thus again we learn from Tertullian, that they initiated men into the rites of Isis and Mithra, Nam et sacris quibusdam per lavacrum initiantur Isidis alicujus aut Mithræ,[4] the chief priest of that Goddess, (as Apuleius describes his own initiation,)[5] leading the party to be initiated to the next bath; where, having first delivered him to the usual washing, and asked pardon of the Goddess, he sprinkled him all about, and bringing him back to the temple, after two parts of the day were spent, placed him before the feet of the Goddess."

Mosheim shews, by many sound and ingenious arguments, that the rite of baptism was an old ceremony of the Israelites long before the time of Christ.[6]

After baptism they received the sign of the cross, were anointed, and fed with milk and honey.[7] Dr. Enfield asserts, that baptism was not used by the Jews, but only by the Samaritans.[8] If this be true, (but I know no authority for it,) it instantly makes a Samaritan of Jesus Christ. I do not think the Doctor would have liked this.

John the Baptist was nothing but one of the followers of Mithra, with whom the deserts of Syria and the Thebais of Egypt, abounded, under the name of Essenes. He was a Nazarite; and it is a curious and striking circumstance that the fountain of Ænon, where he baptized,[9] was sacred to the sun. Though he be said to have baptized Jesus, yet it is very remarkable that he established a religion of his own, as is evident from the men who came to Ephesus, and were there converted from his religion to Christianity by St. Paul.[10] This religion is not extinct, but continues in some parts of Asia, as we have formerly noticed, under the names of Mundaites, Nazoreens, Nazoureans, or Christians of St. John.[11]

---

[1] De Rel. Vet. Pers. Cap. xxxiv. p. 406. [2] See his Apology, Sect. lxxxvii. xcvii. xcviii. ci. [3] Hesych.
[4] De Bapt. Cap. v.   [5] Milesi, li. citat. a Seldeno de Success. ad Leg. Hæbr. Cap. xxvi.
[6] Com. Cent. I. Sect. vi. [7] Mosh. Hist. Cent. II. Ch. iv. Sec. 13. See Dupuis, sur tous les Cultes, Vol. III. p. 325.
[8] Hist. Phil. Vol. II. p. 164.   [9] John iii. 23.   [10] Acts xix. 1—7.   [11] Vol. I. pp. 540, 657, 808.

Michaelis[1] states it to be his opinion, that these men, Iohnists as they are now called, were Essenes. In my article on the Essenes this is proved clearly enough. I have no doubt that John was an Essene, as well as Jesus.

Matthew (iii. 11) makes John say, "I, indeed, baptize you with water; he shall baptize you with the Holy Ghost, and with fire."

"I, indeed, have baptized you with water; but he shall baptize you with the Holy Ghost."—Mark i. 8.

"John answered, saying, I, indeed, baptize you with water; but, he shall baptize you with the *Holy Ghost*, and *with fire*."—Luke iii. 16.

In some parts of Scotland it is a custom at the baptism of children to swing them in their clothes over a fire three times, saying, *Now, fire, burn this child or never.*. Here is evidently the baptism by *fire*. When the priest blowed upon the child in baptizing it, in my presence, in the baptistery at Florence, was this to blow away the devils according to the vulgar opinion, or was it the baptism by air—Spiritus Sanctus? Priests profess to communicate the *spiritus sanctus*.[2] The baptism by *fire* and *water* was in use by the Romans. It was performed by jumping three times through the flame of a sacred fire, and being sprinkled with water from a branch of laurel. Ovid says,[3]

> Certe ego transilui positas ter in ordine flammas,
> Virgaque roratas laurea misit aquas.

This is still practised in India.[4] "From old Grecian authorities we learn, that the Massagetæ "worshiped the sun; and the narrative of an embassy from Justin to the Khakan, or Emperor, "who then resided in a fine vale near the source of the Irtish, mentions the Tartarian ceremony "of purifying the Roman ambassadors by conducting them between two fires." Jones on the Language of the Tartars.[5]

The Etruscans baptized with *air*, with *fire*, and with *water;* this is what is alluded to many times in the Gospels.[6] If the words Ghost, *spiritus* in Latin, πνευμα in Greek, and רוח *ruh*, in Hebrew, be examined, they will all at last be found to resolve themselves into the idea of *air* or *breath*—which gave the first idea of the soul of man. Thus we say, the breath departed from a man, or his soul left him—he gave up the ghost, spiritus. This may give a low or mean idea of the state of science; but I have no doubt that in its infancy the breath of man was supposed to be his soul. When it was the breath of God, of course it was the holy ghost or spirit. This is perfectly in keeping with the materialism, the anthropomorphism of the letter of Genesis, of Moses, and of all other nations. When Jesus communicated the Holy Ghost, he breathed on his disciples.

In plates 172, 173, 174, &c., Gorius gives examples of the baptism of the ancient Etruscans, in the rites of Mithra or Isis, by water, air, fire, and blood. The ancient Etruscans were thought by many to be a colony which escaped from Egypt when the shepherd kings conquered that country. The identity of the worship of ancient Etruria and Egypt makes this not unlikely.

6. In Tab. clxxii. Gorius gives two pictures of ancient Etruscan baptisms by water. In the first,

---

[1] Marsh's Mich. Vol. VI. Ch. xv. § iv. pp. 82, 87.

[2] See Protestant Ordination Service, [and the Petition (to the House of Lords, August 5, 1833) of the Rev. Charles N. Wodehouse, Prebendary of Norwich, for an alteration of this and other parts of the Liturgy. *Editor.*]

[3] Fasti, Lib. iv. ver. 727.   [4] Vide Maurice's Ind. Ant. Vol. V. p. 1075.

[5] Asiat. Res. Vol. II. p. 31, 4to.   [6] See the references ut supra.

the youth is held in the arms of one priest and another is pouring water upon his head. In the second, the young person is going through the same ceremony, kneeling on a kind of altar. Gorius says, "Solennem apud Etruscos baptismatis traditionem per manus sacerdotis, aliis sacris ministris adstantibus, additis modulationibus, precibus et carminibus, ceterisque ceremoniis, quas mox indicabo, nemo alius certe, quam diabolus, nequissimus humani generis hostis, excogitavit docuitque: qui, ut insanas gentes, divinæ lucis expertes, in sui servitium et obedientiam miserandum in modum captivaret, lustrandi complura genera, aëre, aquâ, igne, sanguine, aliasque februationes monstravit, ut Deum divinæ legis conditorem sapientissimum æmularetur. Callidissimas ejus artes ita aperit Tertullianus.[1] *Diabolus ipsas quoque res sacramentorum, in idolorum mysteriis æmulatur, tinguit et ipse quosdam, utique credentes et fideles suos, expiationem de* LAVACRO *repromittit, et sic adhuc initiat Mithræ.: signat ille in frontibus milites suos: celebrat et panis oblationem,[2] et imaginem resurrectionis inducit, et sub gladio redimit coronam. Quid? quod et summum pontificem in unis nuptiis statuit? habet et virgines, habet continentes. Ceterum si Numæ Pompilii superstitiones revolvamus, si sacerdotii officia et privilegia, si sacrificalia ministeria et instrumenta et vasa illa sacrificiorum et piaculorum, et votorum curiositates consideremus nonne manifeste Diabolus morositatem legis Mosaicæ imitatus est?* Addo etiam, Etruscos, compluribus seculis ante Numam Pompilium, non solum in usu habuisse BAPTISMA, verum etiam sacram χειροτονιαν, nam Etruscæ Antistitæ manus imponunt iis, quos initiant, ut alibi ostendam, adlato Etruscæ vrnæ anaglypho opere. Constat enim, initiatos complura probationum genera experiri debuisse, antequam sacris Deorum, ac præsertim MITHRÆ, admitterentur quæ mox considerabimus."

The following are copies of the two Etruscan inscriptions on the monuments above alluded to:

JAII∃ƆAƆ. √∃∃· I2∃†I†I†VA
VAIOIϨV.ƎƆ I2∃∃∃†I†∃∃

In the middle of the second, a letter seems to be wanting.

These Etruscan monuments would have been ascribed to the ancient Christians if the Etruscan inscriptions had not rendered this impossible. In this manner I have no doubt whatever, that great numbers of Gentile monuments of antiquity have been adopted by modern Christians.

From these ancient Etruscan monuments it is evident, that the practice of baptism was common long before the birth of John or Jesus, in the ceremonies of Isis, of Mithra, and of the Eleusinian mysteries; and from the passage in Tertullian,[3] it is evident, that it was not merely a similar ceremony of washing. The words regenerationem et impunitatem perjuriorum suorum (the actual word *regeneratio* used in our order of baptism) prove, that the doctrines as well as the outward forms were identically the same. It appears also from the former part of the quotation, that the practice of sprinkling with holy water, both by the Greek and Romish churchs, was used by the Etruscans, and was only a continuation of their ceremony. On the festival of All Souls, at Florence, the monks went round their cloisters and monasteries, in the presence of the author, sprinkling

---

[1] De Præscript. adv. Hæret. Cap. xl.
[2] The ceremony of baptism was mostly accompanied with the sacrifice of *bread* and *wine*.
[3] De Bapt. Cap. v. quoted in p. 66.

the walls, &c., &c., with holy water, as described by Tertullian to be the practice of the ancient followers of Mithra.

Apuleius also shews, as above stated, that baptism was used in the mysteries of Isis. He says, "Sacerdos, stipatum me religiosa cohorte, deducit ad proximas balneas: et prius SUSTO LAVACRO "traditum, præfatus deûm veniam, purissimè CIRCUMRORANS abluit."

Mr. Maurice shews that purgations or lustrations by water, and holy water, were equally used by the Jews, Persians, Hindoos, and Druids of Britain.[1] Potter, in his Antiquities, proves that every ancient temple had a vase, filled with holy water. This was called a Piscina, and was probably the Bowli of India, noticed in my first volume.[2]

The child is taken to the priest, and is named by him and blessed, &c., before the sacred fire, being sprinkled with holy water, which is put into the bark of a sacred tree called *Holme*.[3]

7. The giving of a name to the child (as indicated by the parents to the priest), the marking of him with the *cross as a sign of his being a soldier of Christ*, followed at fifteen years of age by his admission into the mysteries by the ceremony of confirmation, or the sacred χειροτονια, or imposition of hands, the same as in our ceremonies, prove that the two institutions are identical. But the most striking circumstance of all is the regeneration—and consequent forgiveness of sins—the being born again. This shews that our baptism in *doctrine* as well as in *outward ceremony*, was precisely that of the ancient Etruscans. The χειροτονια is evidently the same ceremony as the admission of our priests into orders, as well as the ceremony of confirmation or admission to church membership. In each case, by the χειροτονια, a portion of the Holy Spirit is supposed to be transferred from the priest to the candidate. I beg my reader carefully to read our baptismal service. This χειροτονια is the baptism by the Holy Ghost. Christian Baptism was called Λουτρον παλιγγενεσιας, the laver of regeneration,[4] and Φωτισμον, illumination.

It is a curious circumstance that not one word can be produced from the New Testament in support of *infant baptism*; every thing adduced in its favour from that authority being a violent and forced implication. Bellarmine is obliged to admit, that *infant baptism* is contained in Scripture "*in universali*" though not "*in particulari*."[5] This is an excellent example of a modern tradition—that is, of a tradition set up since the writing of the gospel histories—a doctrine, a sacrament, forgotten by the Evangelists and the authors of the Epistles, but discovered since, by their more enlightened followers!

8. I must now notice a branch of the Christian baptism of exquisite beauty. I must confess that my *favourite Pagans*, as they will be called, can produce nothing equal to it. And this is the baptism of BELLS. It is peculiar to the *Western* part of the world, though somewhere or other, but where I cannot recollect, I have read, that there is a similar ceremony in China.

We are told by Mr. Maurice that bells were sacred utensils of very ancient use in Asia. The dress of the high-priest of the Jews on the most sacred and solemn occasions was trimmed with bells and pomegranates. Calmet[6] tells us, that the kings of Persia, who were both priests and kings, had their robes trimmed with pomegranates and bells. This almost identifies the Jews and Persians. Mr. Maurice states that bells are used in the ceremonials of the pagodas of India to frighten away the evil spirits or dæmons, who are supposed to molest the devotee in his religious exercises, by assuming frightful forms, to distract his mind from the performance of his

---

[1] Maur. Ind. Ant. Vol. VI. p. 216.
[2] Herbert's Travels, p. 58, fol. 1665.
[3] Glover's Answer to Marsh, p. 140.
[4] P. 516, note 2, and pp. 638, 641.
[5] Note to Reeves's Justin Martyr, p. 99.
[6] Dict. word *bell*.

duty. He says, "The vibration of the sacred bell, however, was ever heard with horror by the "malign demons, who fled at the sound, while the air being put in motion by it, became purified "of the infection which their presence imparted. From Asia, it is probable that the bell, with a "thousand concomitant superstitions, was imported into Europe, and mingled with the rites of a "purer religion. Every body knows its importance in the catholic worship; the ceremony of "anathematizing with bell, book, and burning taper: and the thrilling sound of the dreadful "passing bell, which not only warns the devout Christian to pray for the departing soul of his "brother, and to prepare to meet his own doom, but drives away, said the good Catholics of old "time, those evil spirits that hover round the bed of the dying man, eager to seize their prey, or, "at least, to molest and terrify the soul in its passage into eternal rest."[1]

The bell probably not being known to the Lacedemonians, they used instead of it a kettle-drum. This is stated to be used at the death of their king to assist in the emancipation of his soul at the dissolution of his body;[2] evidently our passing bell.

"Pope John XIV., about the year 970, issued a bull for the baptizing of Bells, '*to cleanse the* "'*air of devils.*' The baptizing of Bells was only permitted to the Bishops suffragan, because it "was of a more principal kind than that of *infants:* priests and deacons could baptize them.

"The tongue of the baptized Bell made the ears of the affrighted demons ring with 'Raphael "'Sancta Margareta, ora pro nobis'—these prayers are on bells at St. Margaret's Mount in "Cornwall.

"In Luther's time the princes of Germany complained to the Legate, 'that, at the time of "baptism, godfathers of the richer sort, after the Suffragan, take hold of the rope, sing together, "name the bell, dress it in new clothes, and then have a sumptuous feast."[3]

During the French Revolution, four of the bells of the cathedral of St. Louis, Versailles, were destroyed. On the 6th of January, 1824, four new ones were baptized. The "King and the "Duchess D'Angoulême were sponsors. The inscription varying the name and number on each "is—' Je suis la première de quatre sœurs, qui ont été offertes à Dieu, &c. J'ai été bénite, &c., "'et nommé Marie par sa Majesté Louis XVIII., Roi de France et de Navarre, et par S. A. R. "'Madame, Fille de Louis XVI., Duchesse d' Angoulême,'" &c.

"The four sisters were suspended in the centre of a platform, under a square canopy of crimson "silk, with broad gold fringe, and surmounted with plumes of ostrich feathers. The eldest wore "a superb petticoat of embroidered gold brocade, over another of silver tissue, festooned at the "bottom, and fastened with white satin rosettes, so as to exhibit the end of the clapper, peeping "out beneath. The others were arrayed in plain gold brocade over a silver tissue. During the "ceremony no splendours in the grand ceremonials of the church were omitted. A white satin "ribbon being passed from the iron tongue of each bell to the hand of the sponsors, they gave a "smart pull for each response, and the sisters each time answered, 'Amen.'"[4] *Ah, happy France, which possesses a family so alive to the comforts of our blessed religion!!!* AND STILL HAPPIER BRITAIN, THE SWORD OF WHOSE ENEMY IS WIELDED BY SUCH A FAMILY!!! A. D. 1830.

9. It cannot be shewn, perhaps, that the Persians had the same forms for the ordination of their priests as those now used by the Christians; but they had all the remainder of the hierarchical system, as Dr. Hyde has shewn; whence it is fair to conclude, that they had also the forms of orders, the χειροτονια, though, from the lapse of ages, &c., it cannot be satisfactorily

---

[1] Maur. Ind. Ant. Vol. V. p. 904.
[2] Schol. in Theocrit. Idyll. ii. ver. 36; see Mr. Knight, p. 167.
[3] Gravam. Cent. German. Grav. 51.
[4] Hog's Hist. Cornwall, p. 470.

proved. Had it not been for the casual mention of some other of the Persian customs by the early fathers, we should have known nothing about them. Therefore, it must be left to the reader to judge for himself, when he has considered what Dr. Hyde has said, whether there may not transpire enough to justify him in inferring from the large part of the system which has come down to us, that the remaining small part existed formerly, though the evidence of it be now lost. This must not be considered as a solitary instance taken by itself, for in that case it would certainly amount to nothing; but it must be considered conjointly with all the other circumstances of striking similarity, indeed of absolute identity, of the two religions. The practice of the Χειροτονια, in the case of Confirmation, raises a strong suspicion, that it would not be wanting in the more important matter of Ordination.

Hyde[1] says, "Et quidem eorum sacerdotium ferè coincidebat cum eo Judæorum, in quo erat "unus summus sacerdos, et deinde plurimi sacerdotes atque Levitæ. Hoc autem excedebat "hierarchica Persica, (quanvis Christum præcesserat, magis cum Christianâ coincidens,) in quâ "præter sacristanos,[2] erant sacerdotes, et præsules et archipræsules, qui hodiernis Christianorum "presbyteris, et episcopis, et archiepiscopis correspondent. Adeò ut ecclesiæ Christianæ amicis "pariter et inimicis fortè novum et inopinatum videbitur in Persiâ reperisse constitutionem eccle- "siasticam prope 3000 abhinc annis fundatam, quæ tam pulchrè coinciderit cum subsequente "hierarchiâ Christianâ. Hocque non sine numine factum, sc. Persas olim ordinâsse idem quod "posteà Christus et Apostoli ejus, in plenitudine temporis, tandem novâ sanctione instituerunt "et confirmarunt. Ecclesiæ itaque eorum regimen in primâ ejusdem constitutione fuit benè "fundatum. Eorum synagogæ minores seu indotatæ ecclesiæ parochiales alunt in singulis unum "sacerdotem, eumque ex decimis ac spontaneis contributionibus: nec ignis perpetui expensas "in eis faciunt, nisi per lampades, exceptis magnis quibusdam diebus. At Pyrea, seu templa "cathedralia, ubi sedes episcoporum, amplis terris et reditibus dotata erant, ad parandum sacri- "ficia, et ligna coëmendum, et ad alendum sacerdotium amplissimum."[3]

As with the Jews, the sacred fire was fed with sacred wood, from which the bark was taken. And as now, in Romish countries, "in propriis ædibus plerique habent perpetuo ardentes lam- "pades ab igno sacro accensas."[4] On the great festivals they sent their victuals to a common table, and ate together with the poor, as described by Pliny to be the case with the early Christians of Bithynia.

From the passages here cited it is evident, that the hierarchy of the Christians is a close copy of that of the Persians, and that where the Christian differs from the Jewish it agrees with the Persian, a proof that it is taken from the latter and not from the former. It has been before observed, that Mr. R. Taylor, in his Diegesis, has clearly proved the Christian hierarchy to be the same as that of the Essenes, even to the most minute parts. The similar customs of keeping candles and lamps always burning in their temples is very striking. The larger endowments for the cathedrals bear a marked resemblance to those of ours in this country, many of which were, I have no doubt, the renovated establishments of the ancient Druids.

10. The rite of marriage was, with the ancient Persians, a religious service; and, for its solemnization, they had a long liturgy or form,[5] after the manner of the Greek, the Romish, and the Protestant Christians, and not according to the custom of the Scotch, among whom it is only

---

[1] De Rel. Vet. Pers. Cap. xxviii. p. 349, ed. 1700.

[2] From the ancient Sacristæ of the Persians the Sacristan of the Catholics is taken, and also, by abbreviation, our Saxten and Sexton. Hyde, ut sup. Cap. xxx. p. 368; Dupuis, Vol. III. p. 86.

[3] Hyde, ut sup. Cap. xxviii. p. 351, ed. 1700. [4] Ibid. p. 352, ed. 1700. [5] Ibid. Cap. xxxiv.

a civil contract.[1] The contents of the liturgy are lost, but we know that the use of the ring, on the second finger from the last on the left hand, was practised by almost all the ancients.[2]

11. Every one knows in what high estimation oil was held among the Eastern nations, and he has not read the Old Testament with attention who is not acquainted with the very frequent use of anointing among the Jews. " The practice of anointing was not confined to kings, but was " extended to prophets and others. It was especially practised on a medicinal account, and " administered publicly in the synagogues by the elders on the Sabbath; where the applying of " this remedy to poor sick people, was accompanied by the prayers of the faithful for their " recovery, and the pardon of their sins; or if the persons were in a very weak condition, the " elders came home to them. Lightfoot observes, out of the Jerusalem Talmud,[3] that Rabbi " Simeon, the son of Eleazar, permitted Rabbi Meir to mingle wine with the oil, when he " anointed the sick on the Sabbath: and quotes as a tradition from them, that anointing on the " Sabbath was permitted."[4] The Apostle James therefore, writing to the Jewish Christians, whose synagogues and rites were precisely the same with those of the other Jews, says " Is any " sick among you? let him send for the elders of the church; and let them pray over him, " anointing him with oil in the name of the Lord; and the prayer of faith shall save the sick, and " the Lord shall raise him up; and, if he have committed sins, they shall be forgiven him."[5]

Whether the Persians had the rite of *extreme unction* I do not know; but if they had it not, then the Christians must have borrowed it from the Jews. When all other circumstances are considered, few unprejudiced persons will be found to doubt, that this practice was probably common to the Jews and the Persians.

There is scarcely any doctrine of the Romish Church which has afforded more matter for the use of the weapon of ridicule than that of *purgatory*—that weapon declared by the Protestants to be so unfair, abominable, and blasphemous, when applied against themselves; but considered to be so fair, honourable, and legitimate, when used by them against their Romish enemies.

The doctrines of *Penance* and *Purgatory*, taught by the Catholics and so much calumniated by the Protestants, are exactly the same in principle as the penances and metempsychosis of the Pythagoreans, Platonists, and Indians. The Romish doctrine of penance is precisely that of the Hindoos, and I have no doubt that from the modified *principle* of the metempsychosis the doctrine of purgatory took its rise. After man, reasoning upon the beauty, order, and sublimity, of the creation, arrived at the knowledge of the First Great Cause and ITS[6] attributes of benevolence &c., the belief in man's immortality followed as a necessary consequence. For, if there were not a future state of existence, where the good would be rewarded and the bad punished, how could the Creator be just or benevolent? And again, how could he be either just or benevolent if the existence of man in a future state was not happy or miserable in proportion to his good or bad conduct here? And as man has been created fallible in his nature, and inevitably subject to fall

---

[1] It was the same in England from 1653 to 1660, and is considered to be a civil contract in the United States of North America. *Editor.*

[2] Vide Tert. Apol. Cap. vi. pp. 173, &c.   [3] Harm. N. Test. Works, Vol. I. p. 333.

[4] Toland's Naz. p. 54.   [5] James v. 14, 15; see also Mark vi. 13, xvi. 18.

[6] I say *its*; for how absurd is it to give a *masculine* or *feminine* gender to the Creator! The *only-begotten* Son of God!! What nonsense! The only excuse which can be made for the use of the word *begotten*, is, that those who adopt it apply to it no idea whatever, or some idea which the word does not mean. [The Evangelist *John* alone uses the expression, (ch. i. 14, 18, iii. 16, 18; 1 Eph. iv. 9,) and as he wrote neither his Gospel nor his Epistle till long after the resurrection and ascension of his revered Lord, the sense in which he used the term may probably be gathered from Rev. i. 5—" Jesus Christ the *first-begotten* of the dead." *Editor.*]

into some degree of guilt, it was also thought to follow that his future state of existence could not be eternally miserable. This was the inevitable consequence if the Creator were just; hence arose the doctrine of purgatory—a state of existence in which the soul of man or that part of him that exists after death, and which though invisible must exist, will in future receive the reward of his good or bad conduct.

This was the simple, unadulterated doctrine of the sages of India, Persia, Greece, and Rome: it remained for the brilliant imagination of John Calvin to discover that it was consistent with the attributes of benevolence in an omnipotent Creator to cause a being to exist, who, from *his very nature*, is obliged to sin, and then, for such sin, to condemn him to endless misery. But these doctrines are deduced by learned men of narrow minds from corrupt passages in the Gospels, and still more from the fanatical nonsense of Paul.[1]

The doctrine of *purgatory* or of a future state, in which man was to receive the greater or less reward of his misconduct in this life, like every thing in which priests have any concern, was soon corrupted and converted into an engine to aggrandize their pernicious order, and to enable them to wallow in luxury and sloth upon the hard earnings of their fellow-creatures. Hence they taught their blind and credulous devotees, that by their superior sanctity they could prevail upon God to alleviate or shorten the term of their future punishment, and by aggravating the faults of the miserable and repentant sinner, in the last stage of weakness and disease, and working upon his terrified imagination, they extorted from him his wealth. Hence arose voluntary acts of supererogation and penances, by suffering which in this life the punishment in another was to be mitigated. Hence masses or services for the dead. Hence extreme unction and all the other figments of Papistical foolery among the devotees of Greek, Catholic, or sectarian Christianity.

Protestants may exclaim against these superstitions, as they call them, but they are real *orthodox* Christianity and cannot be got rid of. It is no argument to say, they are absurd or pernicious. They are not more absurd than the doctrine of demoniacs, nor more pernicious than the doctrine of the efficacy of *faith* without *works*. We have already quoted the opinion of the Apostle James on the subject of anointing the sick, p. 72. He adds, (ch. v. 16,) *Confess your faults one to another, and pray one for another, that ye may be healed. The effectual fervent prayer of a righteous man availeth much.*

The doctrine of Purgatory, so offensive to the gloomy fanatics among the Protestants, because it does away with the doctrine of eternal damnation, is, when not abused, one of the most sensible of the miscalled Christian doctrines, because it is not contrary to the moral attributes of God. It was a close copy of the doctrine of the Heathens and of Plato, who, in his Phædon,[2] divides the dead into three sorts—the *good* in a state of bliss; the *very bad* in Tartarus;[3] and the *curable* in an intermediate state, from which, after they have been in it a suitable time, they are released. For these last, the Gentiles were in the habit of offering sacrifices, called τελεται. In his Republic, II., Plato says, "That these τελεται belong only to the dead, and are named from "τελευτησασι, being sacrifices appointed to deliver us from the infernal sufferings; they were "offered chiefly in the night, and called μυστηρια, *mysteries*." The doctrine of Purgatory is found

---

[1] Rather from passages in the Gospels and in Paul's Epistles misunderstood and misrepresented? *Editor.*

[2] P. 113.

[3] I believe Paradise or Tartarus to be in Tartary, the farther side of Meru, the mount on the side of the North, where the Gods assembled in judgment. Though the Europeans made it hot, I have little doubt that the natives of a country under a tropical sun made their hell *cold*. The same reason in part caused the Hindoos to place the mount Meru in a temperate climate, *on the sides of the North*.

in Tertullian.¹ This early date shews them to be coeval or nearly so with Christianity.² The prayers for the dead are evidently the Gentile τελεται, purchased with gifts.

The Jews had the rite of *Confession*.³

On several of the ancient monuments in the Campigdolia at Rome are bas reliefs of the ancient Sibyls, or of females performing penance, which leave no room to doubt that this sacrament was in use by the Romans. They may be seen by any one who will take the trouble to go to look at them. This fact requires no further proof. The Flagellants were exact copiers of the priests of Bellona, and of the priests of Baal.⁴

The hermits of Italy are humble imitators of the Fakirs of India, who were well known in ancient times. St. Austin says,⁵ "They abstain from women, and philosophize naked in the "solitudes of the Indies. From the rising to the setting of the sun they remain with their eyes "steadfastly fixed upon it. Others stand perpetually on one leg. They expose themselves without "complaint to the extremes of cold and hunger."

The doctrine of purgatory and the efficacy of the prayers of the living to relieve the deceased from their sufferings is a correct copy of the doctrine and practice of the Pagans. Ovid says that Æneas was the first person who introduced the doctrine into Italy. In his *Fasti* he says,

> Hunc morem Æneas, pietatis idoneus auctor,
> Attulit in terras, justo Latine, tuas.
> Ille patris Genio solennia dona ferebat;
> Hinc populi ritus edidicere novos [pios?].—Lib. ii. 543—546.

It was the general belief of the Pagans, that the souls of the dead would return, to demand of the living that they should offer sacrifices for the purpose of relieving them from the pains which they endured. The Pagans differ from the Romish priests in this, that they offered up their prayers for the dead on the ninth day, the Romish on the seventh.⁶ This is confirmed by Polydore Virgil.⁷

Lord Kingsborough⁸ states, that the Jews, of later day I suppose he means, were believers in *purgatory*.

The tombs of the pretended Gods were not set up by merely an ignorant populace, but they were encouraged and protected by law. Ludovicus Vives says, "The religion of sepulchres is "most ancient: whereby it was prohibited to any to violate, throw down, or break them: which "law was not only in the twelve tables, and among Solon's, but also in the most ancient laws of "Numa, and of both Latins and Greeks: which seem to belong not so much to the civil law as to "the sacred: because sepulchres were esteemed as temples of their Manes or Dæmons: whence "there was inscribed on them D. M. S. i. e. *Diis Manibus Sacrum*: and the sacreds which were "performed to them were called *Neria*."⁹ Over the tombs of Heathen Gods rose many a church dedicated to the same God, but denominated a Christian saint. Thus the tomb of Bacchus became a church of St. Baccus. Thus again the pretended tomb of the deified Romulus in Rome became the church of St. Theodorus.

13. Of all the weapons or engines ever yet discovered by rogues to enable them to tyrannize

---

¹ De Moneg., and Origen, Lib. III. in Job.   ⁵ Gale's Court of Gent. Vol. III. Book ii. Ch. ii. Sect. 3 and 11.
² Lord Kingsborough's Mexico, Vol. VI. p. 301.   ⁴ Tertul. Apol. Cap. ix. Lib. ad Mart.; 1 Kings xviii. 28.
³ Lib. xv. de Civ. Dei; Plin. Hist. Nat. Lib. vii. Cap. ii.   ⁶ Blondus, Rom. Trium. Lib. ii. p. 44.
⁷ Lib. vi. Cap. x.   ⁸ Antiq. of Mexico, Vol. VI. p. 96.
⁹ Gale's Court Gent. Book ii. Chap. ii. Sect. 3.

over fools, nothing has ever yet been found so efficacious and powerful as *Auricular Confession*. "Confess your faults one to another," says St. James, and this put the most secret affairs and counsels of all the states of Christendom into the hands of the Pope and his priests. This powerful engine was itself alone sufficient, in the skilful hands of the priests, to lay all the riches and good things of this world at the feet of holy mother church—to enable its bloated, pampered hierarchy to ride triumphant over the liberties of mankind, and to reduce the rest of their fellow-creatures to the lowest state of mental debasement and misery. By means of the priests the kings tyrannized over the people, and by means of the slavery of the kings, the priests had at their command the wealth of the whole world.

The observation is as *true* as it is *trite*, that a small drop will wear a hole in a large stone: thus causes apparently small by long continued and unceasing action produce effects which to superficial observation seem out of proportion to their power. Of this nature is the practice of auricular confession in the papal church. To this, in a great measure, may be attributed the victory which it gained over all its competitors. It is almost inconceivable what a vast variety of opportunities of acquiring power and wealth this must have thrown into its hands. It must have been almost equally useful in enabling it to avoid dangers. The church possessed by this means a species of omniscience. It is evident that by means of its corresponding societies of monks it would be timely warned of the approach of every danger. Knowledge has been said to be power; this is very true, and this knowledge, for a space of almost a thousand years, enabled the Papal See to dictate laws to the whole European world; and, if the art of printing had not been discovered, would have reduced it to the situation in which Tibet now is, under its grand Lama. The God in Tibet and the God (as he was actually called) at Rome would have been in every respect similar. Indeed, I should be glad to learn wherein the difference consists between the adoration [1] paid to the Lama, and that paid by the cardinals to the Pope on his first exaltation on the altar after his instalment. Modern sophistry may talk of civil adoration: the understandings of mankind having become too enlightened, the daring violation of religion and decency must be explained away. But the practice is continued: it awaits a restoration, by the holy allies, of the darkness of the tenth century. The papal policy is sometimes suspended—it never dies. In more senses than one, *nullum tempus accurrit ecclesiæ.*

It would be giving the Christian priests too much credit to allow them the merit of inventing these engines of despotism and priestcraft; they were merely imitators, though they may have improved upon the originals which they copied. They removed some absurdities, they added some stimuli; but all the doctrines to which I have just now drawn the attention of the reader, are to be found with very little deviation in the faith of the oriental nations, and from them they passed to the Christians through the medium of the sects of Gnostics and Essenes, both of which existed among the natives of Asia and Africa long before the time allotted for the birth of Christ. Thus I think the *seven* celebrated sacraments of the Romish Christians, in which the two held by the Protestants are included, are proved to be nothing but renewed Gentile ceremonies, that is, integral parts of the usually called pestilent and idolatrous superstition of the Pagans.

---

[1] See Eustace's Classical Tour.

CHAPTER II.

REVENUES.—MONKS AND NUNS.—MITRE.—ZONE.—CASSOCK.—PRAYING STANDING.—WHITE SURPLICE. TITHES PAID. TONSURE PRACTISED. CROSIER, &c.—CANDLES, INCENSE.—PROCESSIONS. IMAGES. ST. ABRAHAM.—FESTIVALS.—EPIPHANY. ST. DENIS, &c.—BAMBINO AT ROME. DEDICATING CHURCHES, &c., &c.—BULLA. AGNUS DEI. ANGELS. DÆMONS.—SUNDAY, DIES SOLIS. VARIOUS CUSTOMS.

1. THE revenues of the Romish priests came from the same sources as those of the sacrificers of the Pagans. They had first the tithes, then offerings, which the devotees presented to the Gods, which they took and applied to their own use. But as the offerings were casual, and not always to be depended on, a provision was made from the public revenue for the different orders, and in general for all those who were employed about the offices of religion. Besides this, many private individuals consecrated their property to the same purpose; so that rich benefices became founded: and these benefices were, as they are with us, some in the presentation of the prince or the college of pontifices, others in that of individuals who had the right of patronage. And as at this day, complaints against pluralities were made.[1] The Pontifex Maximus, also, had the right to the annates, or fruits of the first year, which he might sell or give away. Another source of wealth was found in the legacies left by those who wished prayers to be said for their souls after their deaths, which is proved by the monuments of the ancient idolaters still remaining. Here is the origin of the Romish prayers for the dead.[2] Another source of wealth arose from confiscations of the property of condemned persons. The houses and property of Cicero were confiscated to the sacred college when he was banished, and the revenue ordered to be expended in sacrifices to the Goddess of liberty. By these means the priests, in ancient and modern times, have equally amassed great wealth.

2. The Pagans, besides their pontiffs, their priests, and their curiones, had different convents or orders of religious men and women, who took the epithet of *holy* or *divi*: some called themselves Quirini from Romulus, others Diales from Jupiter, $\alpha\pi o$ τu $\Delta\iota o\varsigma$, others Martiales from Mars. They called themselves brothers, because they were bound to one another by reciprocal charity and alliance,[3] and were all on an equal footing. Thus, at this day, we have Jesuits, Augustinians, Benedictines, &c. The Monks among the Pagans were proprietors of land. T. Livy says,[4] that Numa instituted the Quirinales and the Vestals, and established for them a revenue. Others were Mendicants, as the religious of the Great Mother of the Gods,[5] who answered exactly to the Christian Mendicants begging for the Virgin, the Mother of God. Apuleius, in his Golden Ass, has ridiculed them for their hypocrisy, by which they, under the pretence of poverty, acquired riches. No beggars were allowed in Rome except these. The Romish Mendicants, like those of the Pagans, were the great dealers in saints, in relics, in apostolic letters, indulgences, and other trumpery. They in both cases had particular habits, and long beards. If they had not been

---

[1] Tit. Liv. Lib. ix. et xxx.; Cic. de Leg. Lib. i.; Suet. in Claudio.
[2] Blondus, Rom. Trium. Lib. ii. p. 33.
[3] Alex. ab Alex. Genial. Lib. i. Cap. xxxvi.
[4] Lib. i.
[5] Augustin, de Civit. Dei, Lib. vii. Cap. vi.

particularly dressed they would not have been known from other people, says Bellarmine.[1] Their silence was an exact copy of the silence of Pythagoras; and their vow of poverty was an imitation of that of some of the ancient philosophers, who distributed all their substance to the poor.

The Hierophantes, at Athens, drank of the *Hemlock* to render themselves impotent, that when they came to the Pontificate they might cease to be men. The priests of Egypt never mixed with women, and to extinguish the passion for the female sex they never ate flesh or drank wine.[2] The priests of the Great Mother drank of a certain river of Phrygia, which putting them in a fury they castrated themselves, and thence were called *Semi-viri*. The priests of Egypt had their fast days, when they abstained from flesh and wine. The priests of Eleusis kept strictly the three commandments given by Triptolemus—to honour their father and mother; the second, to reverence the Gods; and the third, to eat no flesh. Numa established fasts, particularly one in honour of Ceres, when the people offered up their prayers for a good harvest.[3] The Pagan fasts were to appease the Gods; thus Horace says, *Mane die quo tu indicis jejunia*. From these examples we see the origin of the Romish fasts.

3. The father Ange de S. Joseph speaks of the ruins of Persepolis in the following terms: "There "are many inscriptions on the marble of the ruins, but in characters unknown to all the universe, "which shews their great antiquity. Many bas reliefs represent the divinities, the sacrifices, the "funeral pomps, processions of men with large vests, long hair, *with bonnets in form of a* "*mitre.*"[4] From this it is evident that the mitre which we see worn by the priests in the Mithraitic mysteries, and which is still worn on grand occasions by the bishops of the Romish and Greek churches, is of very ancient establishment.

4. When young Persians came to be from twelve to fifteen years of age, prayer and ceremonies took place, and they were invested with the girdle.[5] They were then supposed to be capable of understanding the doctrines of the religion. It was, in fact, the ceremony of confirmation.

In the Sadder, the sacred book of Zoroaster, it is written, that God has commanded the girdle as a sign of the obedience which is due to him.[6] It was believed that it rendered the wearer safe from dæmons. All the Christians of the Levant, whether Syrians, Arabians, Egyptians, or Coptes, believe that they commit a sin if they go into a church without their girdle.[7] They found this practice upon Luke xii. 35. The monks use a girdle with twelve knots to shew that they are followers of the twelve apostles: and when one of them is excommunicated they pull off his girdle. When the Mohamedans receive into their communion a proselyte, either from the sect of the Magi or Christians, they cut off his girdle, which he in future disuses. Thus we here see whence the girdle of the monks is taken.[8]

5. From the same place with the girdle came the use of the Cassock or Sudra. From Hyde we learn that Zoroaster is reported to have said that he received it from heaven along with the girdle: Hyde describes it to be the same with that used by our English clergy, and shews that it was from the girdle that we derived the old English proverb—*ungirt unblessed*.[9]

Concerning the Origin of the Zone and Cassock Hyde[10] says, " In ejus imperio venit Zerdusht " propheta, coram Gushtasp prophetiam prætendens, eique dicens: Ego sum propheta quem Deus

---

[1] De Mon. Lib. ii. Cap. xl.; Socrates, Lib. ii. Cap. xxxiii.; Hieron. ad Eustach. Vol. I. pp. 49, 50.
[2] Hieron. Lib. adv. Jovin. [3] Liv. Lib. xxxv. [4] Beaus. Vol. II. Liv. ii. Ch. iv. p. 207.
[5] Beaus. Hist. Man. Vol. I. Liv. ii. Ch. iv. p. 198. [6] Hyde de Rel. Vet. Pers. p. 441.
[7] Assem. Vol. III. Pt. i. p. 359. [8] D'Herbelot, Bib Orien. p. 68; see also the word Zonnar.
[9] Hyde de Rel. Vet. Pers. Cap. xxx. p. 370. [10] Ibid. Cap. xxiv. p. 320, ed. 1700.

"excelsus ad te misit: et istum librum Zend-avestâ è Paradiso attuli: et hanc Sudram et
"Cingulum mihi dedit, inquiens, istam Sudram indue,¹ et istud Cingulum in medium tuum
"cinge, ut anima tua à Gehennâ liberetur et salvationem inveniat; Religionem quoque Dei in
"mundo propagato." "In primo infantum baptismate imponitur nomen: et postea anno
"septimo ut quidem aiunt, vel potius anno decimo quinto (quando censetur intrare in reli-
"gionem,) tum adhibitis precibus à sacerdote datur confirmatio solennis. Et eo anno decimo
"quinto (ut religionis tessera) eis traditur sudra, seu tunica, et cingulum, quibus nunquam, ne
"per unum momentum (nisi in lecto sint) destitui debent."² "Pueri et Puellæ post quindecim
"annorum ætatem (ut supra) cingulum, religionis tesseram, induere incipiunt, et divina præcepta
"ejus instillantur."³ "Tunica cingitur cingulo, secundum sacerdotalem habitum in Angliâ,
"excepto colore."⁴ Hyde states that the stole was used in the rites of Mithra. "Mithra ibi
"est in figurâ regis Persici, uti constat ex Tiarâ directâ et Stolâ, quæ solis regibus competunt."⁵

6. It often happens that trifling circumstances are more striking than those of more consequence. The identity of the two religions being evident, they are less likely to be the produce of
accident. And what I am going to describe are of so out-of-the-way, unexpected a kind, that
there must be some cause for the similarity.

From Hyde we learn that the ancient Persians set apart four days in each month answering to
the Sabbath days of the Jews and to our Sundays, which were festivals. On these days they met
in their churches, and had more solemn service than on other days, reading portions of their sacred
book, and preaching and inculcating morality and purity. "Habent enim suo modo liturgiam
"publicam, quam certo quodam tono, seu *plano cantu*, modulantur et cantillant, sc. certam atque
"præscriptam precum et aliorum rituum formam." He also says, "Ubi post peractam prostra-
"tionem (ut fiebat in templo Hierosolymitano) STANTES ORANT."⁶ It is impossible here not to
be struck with the identity of the Persian and Christian services. The four days of the month, the
reading of portions of the sacred books, the preaching, the liturgia publica, the præscripta forma
rituum et precum, the *tono seu plano cantu* of the Romish, and chaunting of the Protestant cathedrals. But perhaps among these different traits of resemblance there is no one more striking than
that of the praying standing on the four festival days of the month.⁷ The early Christians always
prayed on a Sunday *standing*. Tertullian says, Die dominicâ jejunare nefas ducimus vel *de
geniculis adorare*.⁸ In Canon sixteen,⁹ worshiping on the knees on Sunday is forbidden. It
says, "Porro in sanctis dominicis diebus sacrisque aliis solennitatibus nullæ fiant genuflexiones,
quia tota sancta ecclesia in hisce lætatur et exultat diebus."

7. Silius, speaking of the strange rites used in the Gaditan temple of Hercules, says, the priests
officiated there barefooted, practised chasity, had no statues, used white linen surplices; and it
was a notorious custom with the ancient Phœnicians to pay tithe. The *shaving* of the *head* and
surplices were borrowed from the Egyptian priests, and the *crosier* or pastoral staff was the *lituus*
of the Roman augurs.¹⁰ The tonsure of the priests and monks is an exact imitation of that of
the priests of Isis;¹¹ and St. Epiphanius witnesses also,¹² that the priests of Serapis at Athens

---

¹ "Sudra est Tunica sacerdotalis brevior, Anglicè a Cassock, ad mediam suram pertingens."
² Hyde de Rel. vet Pers. Cap. xxviii. p. 350, ed. 1700.   ³ Ut sup. p. 353.
⁴ Ib Cap xxx p 370.   ⁵ Ib. Cap. iv. p. 119.   ⁶ Ib. Cap. xxxviii. p. 352.
⁷ This beautiful festival our absurd modern devotees, who are as ignorant as they are bigoted, wish to change from
a festival to a day of humiliation. In my Horæ Sabbaticæ, I have discussed this at length.
⁸ Tertul. de Cor. Cap. iii.   ⁹ Conc. Nic. Pap. Silvester I. A. D. 325.
¹⁰ Priestley's Hist. Cor. Vol II. p. 251, ed. 1782.   ¹¹ Apul. Asino Aureo.   ¹² Hær. 64.

had the head shaved. This custom is forbidden in Lev. xxi. 5, and the prohibition is afterwards repeated, in Ezek. xliv. 20; for this is the meaning of the word קרחה *qrts*, as Rabbi Solomon on the report of Buxtorf has noticed.

The habit and the ornaments of the ecclesiastics at this day have been copied from those of the ancient Pagans. The cross of the bishops I need not name again. The Lituus or Crosier was the Hieralpha of the Hindoos, taken from the cave of Bala-rama near Muttra, and seen in a variety of fantastic forms on the ancient Egyptian monuments. It is often united to the cross thus ⚴ ✝ It was the origin of the jawbone of Samson. It was the first rude, ill-formed plough, thus ⟋

The Amicts and Dominos of the bishops came from the same place; for the Pagans never made any sacrifice without having the head covered with an Amict, which they called Orarium, and a Superhumeral. They wore also an Aube, as the priest does when he goes to say mass.[1] And the Flamens were clothed with a robe made with copes, like those which the Romish priests wear in the churches.[2] The Stole is an imitation of that which they put on the back of the victims which they offer on the altar. The Cardinal Baronius[3] has remarked, under the year 44 of our Lord, that the ancient Pagans had the surplice: that they carried the pastoral staff called the lituus or crosier; that they used the episcopal ring and mitre; that the flamen or priest who sacrificed was clothed in a garment of fine linen, called by the Latins Alba Vestis: and Juvenal, in his 6th Satire, says, that the high priest of Anubis, environed with a crowd of other priests clothed in fine linen, with his head shaved, deserves the first rank and supreme honour.

8. The use of *lamps* and *candles*, in the day-time, in the churches, was copied from the Egyptians, who, according to Clemens Alexandrinus, first invented them.[4] No person can look into the ancient temples of India and Egypt and not see that candles, either by day or night, could not be dispensed with. All their ceremonies must have been by candle-light, as the most sacred parts of their temples had no windows or openings to admit light. During the delivery of sermons I have sometimes met with churches, in Italy, from which the sun was entirely excluded.

The use of *incense* was common both to Jews and Gentiles.

> Sæpe Jovem vidi cum jam sua mittere vellet
> Fulmina, thure dato sustinuisse manum.[5]

Alex. ab Alexandro says,[6] that the Egyptians appeased their Gods with *prayers* and *incense*.

9. The *processions* around the streets and towns, in Catholic countries, are exact imitations of those of the Pagans. When the priests of the Mother of the Gods made their processions through the streets, they carried the image of Jupiter, which they placed for a short time in small bowers dressed out for him, precisely as is done in Paris at the Fête Dieu. Virgil, in the first book of his Georgics,[7] recommends the peasants to carry the statue of Ceres round their fields:

> "———— Annus magnæ
> "Sacra refer Cereri," &c.
> "Terque novas circum felix eat hostia fruges."

Further accounts of the Heathen processions may be seen in Apuleius.[8]

---

[1] Plut. in Ant. Fenestrelle, Chap. v. [2] Du Verdier en ses Leçons, Liv. ii. Ch. iv. p. 86.
[3] Noticed by Marolles in his Memoirs. [4] Strom. i. [5] Ovid's Fasti, 5.
[6] Gen. Dierum, Lib. ii. Cap. xxii. [7] Lines 338, 339, 345.
[8] Lib. ii. Metam. p. 200, edit. Plautin. 1587; also Polyd. Virgil, Cap. xi. p. 414.

As the Roman Church has its processions for rain or fair weather, or to avert tempests or famine, &c., so the Pagans had theirs exactly in the same manner; they are copies of one another.

Though it may be unnecessary to point out the identity of the practices of the modern and ancient Romans in the use of images, yet it may not be unnecessary to observe, that precisely the same reasons were given in excuse for the use of them. Gregory I., against Serenus, bishop of Marseilles, says, that what books are to those who can read, pictures and statues are to those who are ignorant of the art. Porphyry, in Eusebius, justifies images on the same ground. He says they are the books of the ignorant. Theodoret on this subject says, that the demon invented images for the use of the ignorant, that by this means he might establish his superstition. There is no person, says Celsus,[1] so foolish and absurd as to believe that these things are really Gods, and not the symbols which we adore in honour of the deity. And in Arnobius,[2] the Pagan says to the Christian, " You deceive yourselves; for we believe not the brass, the gold, and the silver, " which compose the statues, are God: but we serve God in them, and we venerate the Gods as " dwelling in them, by virtue of consecration." Constantine, bishop of Constance, in the second Council of Nice, declared, " For myself I render to images the same worship of honour which is " due to the Holy Trinity: and let him be anathematized as a Marcionite and Manichæan who " shall refuse to do the same."[3]

The Christians have not only copied the practices of bowing down to the idols of their great men deified or elevated to the rank of inferior Gods or heavenly personages, but they have in many cases adopted the very persons adored by the Heathens. They have not only adopted the same practices of the apotheosis, but they have done it with the same rites and ceremonies, and given the same attributes to their deceased great men. The ancients raised such of their great men or kings to the rank of inferior Gods as had been benefactors to mankind, or as they chose to flatter, calling them by the title of *divus*. The souls of their emperors, if deified, were seen to fly away to heaven, in the form of a bird, from the body, when placed on the funeral pile: thus, in a similar manner the soul of St. Polycarp, when he was burnt, was seen in the form of a dove to wing its way to the mansions of the blessed, and he became *divus* Polycarp. Thus like divus Augustus, the apostles all became *divi*; as Divus Paulus, Divus Petrus, &c.

The Roman Divi were considered only as created inferiores divi, and intercessors with the Supreme God, but residents of the heavenly mansions. This is exactly the case with the Christian Divi; they are considered only as intercessors, but residents of the heavenly mansions; while the remainder of mankind are excluded from these abodes till the day of judgment. The relics of the Divi of each also received adoration, and, at times, worked miraculous cures. They both had altars erected to them, with lights constantly burning before them. Their festivals were kept on set days peculiarly dedicated to them, and the images themselves were in many cases considered to be animated, and to possess and exercise a supernatural power. I had in my possession a book, which I have given to the British Museum, published by the authority of Pope Pius the Sixth, in which the miracles performed by a great number of images are described: they opened their eyes, they wept, they spoke, they performed cures. Some of them are considered more powerful than others, and in consequence acquire more votive offerings, which are given to them in some cases, as at Loretto, to an immense amount both in number and value. It cannot be said that these are merely the idle superstitions of the vulgar. The book alluded to was published by the authority of

---

[1] Orig. cont. Cels. Lib. vii. pp. 387 and 285, 292.

[2] Lib. vi. p. 229, ex edit. Frol.; see also Lact. Lib. ii. Cap. ii.   [3] Act 4, a little from the end.

the Pope and Roman Church, the miracles were all proved before a commission of cardinals, at the head of which was Cardinal Somaglia, and the genuineness of the book itself is actually ascertained beyond dispute by the WRITTEN attestation and signature of the register of the Papal chancery.

Enlightened men, both Greeks and Romists, will be offended at hearing the term idolatry applied to the believers in their religions. But there is in reality no difference between the icon worship of the ancients and that of the moderns. The enlightened men of this day are not idolaters, nor were the Ciceros nor Plinys of ancient times, but the rabble, genteel and ungenteel, who believe in the miracles of the images, and honour them with their votive offerings, most certainly are. It is childish to dispute about the mere word or name given to the practice. Whatever the ancients did to their images, the moderns do to theirs; and in whatever light the ancients considered them, and with whatever attributes they endowed them—precisely in the same light and with the same attributes the moderns view and endow them. The demigods of the ancients are correctly the saints of the moderns, and both bear the name of Divi.

The ἁγιολατρεια of the Greek and Roman, as well indeed as that of the Protestant Church, is nothing more than a servile imitation of the Δαιμονολατρεια or Δεισιδαιμονια of the Gentiles; the proof of this may be seen at great length in Gale's Court of the Gentiles.[1]

On the adoration of saints Bochart says, "They have transferred to their saints all the equipage "of the Pagan Gods: to St. Wolfang the hatchet, or hook of Saturn: to Moses the horns of "Jupiter Hammon: to St. Peter the keys of Janus. In brief, they have chased away all the Gods "out of the Pantheon at Rome, to place in their room all the Saints; whose images they worship "with like devotion as those of the Pagan Gods sometimes were. They dress them up in ap-"parel, they crown them with garlands of flowers, they carry them in procession, they bow before "them, they address their prayers to them, they make them descend from heaven, they attribute "to them miraculous virtues."[2] Bochart then, in support of his assertion that the Romish adoration of *saints* is nothing but a renewal of the adoration of the Pagan *dæmons*, observes, that the Canonization of Saints is correctly the *Apotheosis* of the Pagans, and that *Cajetan's Gods by participation* are the very same as Plato's Θεοι γεννητοι, *made Gods*, which is the title he gives to his dæmons. All these saints, when they were determined to be fit objects of canonization, were deemed to have been possessed of divine inspiration or the afflatus, in a fuller degree than common priests, all of whom have a portion of the Holy Ghost or the *afflatus numinis* instilled into them at their ordination by the imposition of the bishops' hands. These inspirations or entrances into the flesh of portions of the *divine spirit* are correctly the minor Incarnations or Avatars of the Hindoos, who say, there have been thousands of incarnations or avatars of the Supreme Being.

Among the saints of the Roman church we have Saint Abraham and Mary his niece. He came from a place called Edessa in Mesopotamia. He was considered as a saint in the Latin, Greek, and Coptic churches.[3] His holiday is the 15th of March. If we make allowance for the *old style*, this brings him to the 25th of March, the Vernal Equinox. We need not repeat what has been proved respecting Maria, the queen of heaven, being the generative power. We here have her identified with Sarah, the wife of the Brahmin, which serves to prove the mythological character of Abraham and Sarah, who are evident enough in these two saints.[4]

10. The Pagans had their *festival days* in honour of their country or local Gods; these were

---

[1] Vol. III. Book ii. Ch. ii. Sect. iii. p. 184.
[2] Bochart against Veron, p. 3, Ch. xxv. p. 888; Gale's Court Gent. Vol. III. Book ii. Ch. ii. Sect. iv.
[3] Butler's Lives of the Saints.   [4] See Vol. I. pp. 98, 162, 305, 387, 391, 646, 647, 697, 698. *Editor.*

exactly imitated by the Christians in their wakes and revels, which were kept in honour of pretended martyrs, the names of many of whom, being the exact names of the heathen Gods, sufficiently explain what they were.

The Goddess Februa, or the Februata Juno, became the Purificata Virgo Maria. The old Romans celebrated this festival in precisely the same way as the moderns—by processions with wax lights, &c., and on the same day, the 2d of February. The author of the Perennial Calendar observes, that it is a remarkable coincidence that the festival of the miraculous conception of Juno Jugalis, the blessed Virgin, the Queen of Heaven, should fall on the very day the modern Romans have fixed the festival of the conception of the blessed Virgin Mary. Being merely a continuation of an ancient festival, there is nothing remarkable in it.

In the autumn a very peculiar festival was celebrated by almost all nations in honour of the dead.

On the 2d of November the *festum Dei Mortis* is annually celebrated. The priest makes a procession round the burial-ground, with his censer and aspersorio, sprinkling holy water and singing a *miserere* as he goes along. This, again, is nothing more than a heathen ceremony.

This festival is yet annually celebrated by the Buddhists of Tibet, by the Papists at Rome, and has yet its service and day in the calendar of the Protestant church of England.[1] Mr. Turner[2] informs us, that on the last days of October and first of November an annual festival is kept, which is sacred to the souls of the dead. All the monasteries are lighted up and great ceremonies take place among the monks. It appears that this festival is kept at the same time in Bengal and Hindostan. It is remarkable that this festival was anciently kept by the Druids in Ireland, and is yet continued there. In Ireland it was called the festival of Samhan, lasted two days, and was begun to be celebrated on the evening preceding the first of November, which evening is yet called *Oidhche Samhna*, or *the night of Samhan*. This solemnity was consecrated by the Druids to the intercession of the living for the souls of those who had died the year preceding that day; for, according to their doctrine, Samhan called before him these souls, and passed them to the mansions of the blessed, or returned them to a re-existence here as a punishment for their crimes.[3] This Samhan was also called *Bal-Sab* or Lord of Death. This is the Beelzebub of the Christians. On this festival all the fires, except the sacred fires of the Druids, were extinguished, and every one was prohibited, under the most terrible penalties, from procuring this indispensable article in any way except from them, for which a stipulated price was paid.[4] This festival is even yet partly continued by the Irish, who light great fires on the tops of their mountains, and pass their children and flocks through them to Beal or Samhan, as described in the Old Testament to Bel or Baal.[5] The Irish call this festival Bealtine, or the feast of the fires of Baal. This solemnity is what we call All-Souls' Day. Gen. Vallancey says,[6] "it was called La Samhna or Hallowmas-Day. "The Druids taught the Pythagorean system of the transmigration of souls, and that Samhan or "Baal Samhan, at this season called the souls to judgment, which according to their merits or "demerits in the life past, were assigned to re-enter the bodies of the human or brute species, "and to be happy or miserable during their next abode on this sublunary globe: hence Samhan

---

[1] All-Saints' Day—united with All Souls'. This festival was also kept by the Mexicans. See p. 31. *Editor*.

[2] In the account of his Journey to Tibet, p. 318.   [3] Celtic Druids, Ch. v. Sect. xvii.

[4] Samhain, All-Saints' Eve, genit Samhna. Oidhche Shamhna, All-Saints' Eve. (O'Brien's Dict.) Samhain, SHAW and LHYD, Arch. Brit., La Samhna, Hallowmas-day, *Macdonald's* Vocab.

[5] Jeremiah xix. 5, xxxii. 35; see also on Molech, Lev. xviii. 21, xx. 2—4; 2 Kings xxiii. 10. *Editor*.

[6] Coll. Hib. Vol. III. p. 444.

"was named [by the Irish] Balsab or Dominus Mortis, for *Bal* is Lord, and *Sab* death. But the "punishment of the wicked they thought might be alleviated by charms and magic art, and by "sacrifices made by their friends to Bal, and presents to the Druids for their intercession."

"It has been the opinion of some learned men, that the Baal-Zebub of the idolatrous Jews was "the God of flies or locusts, as the LXX. have translated it *Deum Muiαν*. muscam, or Μυιαγρον "muscarum averruncum. Basnage is singular in supposing this deity to be Mars, or the God of "Battles and of Arms, because, says he, the Phœnicians might readily convert צבאת *tsabath* into "בוב *Zebub*. The Irish or Iberno-Celtic retains both; for *sab* is death, and also strong, potent, "valiant; so in Hebrew צבא *tsaba* militia; in Arabic, *zab*, repelling by force; *zabin*, a life guard-"man, and *zaaf*, death; but our Hiberno Druids retaining Balsab synonymous to Samhan, it is "evident, Baal-Zebub is Dominus Mortis."[1] The day following is the festival of Samhan, to whom *black sheep* were offered in sacrifice.[2] This festival lasted till the beginning of December, which was named MI NOLAGH, or the month of the *new born*, from the Hebrew word נולה *nule Nolah*, i. e. parire, *to bring forth y ung*; whence the French word NOËL, and the Irish NOLAGH, Christmas-day. This was a month of great rejoicing, as the former was of mourning.[3] The Persians light fires in their temples, &c., on the day answering to the 2d of November, precisely as the Irish did, and yet do.[4]

Dr. Hyde[5] states, that this custom is continued among the fire worshipers or Guebres of Persia at this day: and he observes, that he learns from the Talmud, that this practice was adopted by the Israelites when they were in captivity in that country among the Medes, who are called Persæ. It continues two days, because it begins on the eve, as the Buddhist book of Genesis reckons time. "*and the evening and the morning were the first day;*" not the morning and the evening. The identity of the religious rites in the East and West, I am justified in here reasserting, cannot be doubted. Among the Druids of Ireland, the same doctrines of a Creator, Preserver, and Destroyer, are found, and many of the Gods have the same names:[6] for instance—Samhan, Bud, Chandra, Om, Eswara, Cali, &c.

The Mohamedans have this festival as well as the Hindoos and Christians; but this is not surprising, as they are merely a sect of the latter.

Now I beg my reader to recollect what he has read in the Preliminary Observations respecting the festival of the Vernal Equinox, when the sun was in Taurus.[7] This was evidently the counterpart of it—the festival of the Autumnal Equinox—exactly six months from the former. At the Vernal Equinox began the empire of glory, of happiness, of the good principle, of Oromasdes; at the Autumnal Equinox began the empire of the evil principle, of Arhiman, and Bal-Sab. No one can for a moment doubt the meaning of the festival; and its universal celebration and reception would fully confirm what is said from Mr. Maurice respecting the Tauric festival, in the Preliminary Observations, if confirmation were wanting. The identity of the religious rite, in both East

---

[1] Vall. Col. Hib. Vol. III. pp. 447, 448, &c.   [2] Ibid., and see Virgil's Geor. Lib. iv. 547.
[3] Vall. ut sup, Vide Parkhurst for root ילי and Frey, under word גולד.
[4] Maur. Hist. Hind. Vol. II. p. 89, ed. 4to. For some curious remarks about the Childermas, or the Feast of the Innocents, see Vallancey, ut sup. Vol. III. p. 446. This relates to the *boy bishop* in some of our cathedrals. The month of November is called in Ireland Mi Samhan, month of Samhan, or Mi dubh, month of sorrow or grief. The Welsh call it *y mis du*, the month of grief. For explanation of Sammael and Samhan, (perhaps Esmun?) Beelzeun, Pluto, Asima, see Vall ut sup. pp. 448, &c, and for every thing relating to the first and second of November.
[5] De Religione Vet. Pers.; Vall. Coll. Hib. Vol. IV. p. 346.   [6] Vide Celtic Druids, Ch 9. Sect. xxvii.
[7] Vol. I. pp. 24—26.

and West, is striking, and proves the wide extent of the Buddhist religion; but it is chiefly important in fixing the chronology. It must have taken place by the true Zodiac about 4680 years before Christ.

The priests disguise to their votaries, and perhaps to themselves, the identity of the Christian and Gentile festivals, by pretending that one of the Popes ordered the missionaries to fix the birthdays of the saints to the heathen festivals, to humour the prejudice of the Heathen, and thus, by degrees, to draw them into Christianity. But here is the doctrine of *prayers for the dead* as well as the ceremony on the same day. Besides, the very fact of the Pope ordering it on a certain specified occasion, goes very far to prove that it was not the general practice. So far were the early Christians from adopting Heathen ceremonies, that they would not intentionally even call the months of the year or the days of the week by their usual names, for fear they should pollute their mouths by those names, particularly that of Venus, which is a practice still continued by the society of Quakers. Gregory Thaumaturgus, who lived in the third century, is commended by Gregory Nyssenus, for thus changing the Pagan festivals into Christian holidays.[1]

11. We Protestants keep *The Epiphany*, pretending that it is the manifestation of Christ to the Gentiles. Isaac Casaubon shall tell us what it is.[2] "Baronius errs, in that he judgeth, that the "Epiphany was instituted, in the primitive time, in commemoration of the Magi, their appari- "tion. This opinion is refuted, first by the very appellation of Epiphanies, and thence by the "use of authors and history. The appellation επιφανειων, of Epiphanies, was brought into eccle- "siastic observation from Pagan rites, on a pious account. Greek writers call επιφανειαν, Epipha- "nie, the apparition of a deity, whatever the manner were by which such a deity was supposed to "have given some sign of his presence." Diodorus says, "That Isis was wont to appear by night: "and Dionysius Halicarnassus greatly reprehended such as derided the epiphanies of the Gods "by which they manifest themselves to men. In commemoration of these apparitions the Gre- "cians instituted certain festivals which they called Epiphanies. The Greek church has its "Epiphany on the sixth of January."[3]

At St. Denis, near Paris, the God Bacchus or Διονυσος is worshiped under the name of St. Denis. At Ancona, on the top of the promontory, Bacchus is worshiped under the name of Liber and Liberius.[4]

---

[1] Priestley's Hist. Cor. Vol. I. p. 336. Speaking of the two classes into which society is divided in Tibet, Mr. Turner (Travels, p. 257) says, "Both, united in one common bond of union, the one part to labour, the other to pray, "enjoy in peace and harmony the fruits of their industry; and find it unnecessary to support a single man in arms, "either to defend their territory or maintain their rights." This is as it should be—the Drones and the Bees; idle priests and industrious slaves. Here every one moves in his proper sphere!

[2] Exercit. 2, An. 1, Num. 36.   [3] Gale's Court of Gent. Vol. III. Bk. ii. Ch. ii. Sect. iii. pp. 192, 193.

[4] Several temples have probably stood together which are now all formed into one church of Gothic architecture. In a crypt, on the left side as a person enters, is a magnificent sarcophagus of brass, of modern workmanship, with the words upon it CORPUS SANCTI LIBERY CONF. In the front of it, under the Roman arches, stands an altar, at which a priest was officiating when I was there. On the wall opposite is a MODERN Latin inscription, which informs its reader that St. Liberius was an Armenian: *Liberius ex Armen. Regum stirpe ortus Sæc. VI*. In the word LIBERY the last letter in one place being Y and in another U, the lower part wanting, proves, notwithstanding the care to prevent mistakes displayed by the monks in the modern inscription, that this S. Liberius was no other than Bacchus-Liber. In the crypt on the right side as you enter the church is a very ancient sarcophagus of stone This, I suspect, in former times, has held the body of the God. It has had two inscriptions, one in the stone now erased with a chisel, the other in metal, which has been removed, the marks of the rivets remaining. I suppose the temples under the decrees of Theodosius, &c., were all thrown down, and from their ruins the present church was built; and amongst the ruins were found the fine columns of marble and the sarcophagus with the inscription *Corpus S. Libery*: and, if it had any where upon it, as it probably had, or if there was found any where near it, the cross or the monogram of Bacchus, this would be thought to prove the deceased a Christian confessor. For, as the Christians adopted the

I must draw my reader's attention to the fact, that the ancients had their miracles performed at the shrines of their saints, Divi, just as commonly as the Christians at the shrines of *their* saints.

The identity of some of the Romish Saints and the Heathen Gods, is in no instance more ridiculously exhibited than in that of St. Denis or Dionysus, the ancient Bacchus; even Mr. Faber is obliged to allow it. He says,[1]

" Dionysus is cut in pieces by the Mænades on the top of Mount Parnassus : Denis is put to
" death in the same manner on the summit of Montmartre. Dionysus is placed on a tomb, and
" his death is bewailed by women: the mangled limbs of Denis are collected by holy females,
" who weeping consign him to a tomb, over which is built the abbey church that bears his name.
" Dionysus experiences a wonderful restoration to life, and quits the coffin within which he had
" been confined: Denis rises again from the dead, replaces his severed head to the amazement of
" the spectators, and then deliberately walks away. On the southern gateway of the abbey, the
" whole history of this surprising martyrdom is represented. A sculptured sprig of the vine,
" laden with grapes, is place.l at the feet of the holy man : and in all parts may be seen the same
" tree blended with tigers and associated with a hunting match. Such numerous and close
" coincidences prevent the possibility of doubting the identity of the God Dionysus and the
" monkish saint Dionysius. Were I more conversant in the hagiographa of the Latin church I
" might perhaps be able to produce many other similar instances."

There is no doubt that at the town of St. Denis, the Romans had some kind of a temple to the Divus Dionysus or Bacchus, whence the ignorance and roguery of the priests made a saint, a Divus Denis, with all his traditionary adventures.

Near Naples the *universe* is worshiped under the name of St. Cosmo—Κοσμος.[2]

The custom of putting D. M., for the words Dis Manibus, on monuments and grave-stones, is continued all over Italy. In the church of St. Clement, at Rome, I observed the actual words Dis Manibus upon a grave-stone; the letters had not long been filled up with a hard cement, to disguise them; but they were sufficiently evident. No doubt at every Jubilee, when the churches are repaired, some remnant of Heathenism is erased.

The way in which the Christians have *made their saints* is perfectly laughable. An explanation of them may be seen in Dupuis.[3] He shews how they have made their St. Bacchus and Liber, Dionysius—Eleutherius, Rusticus—marked in the calendar, 7th Oct, fest. S. Bacchi, 8th festum S. Demetri, and the 9th fest. S. S. Dionysii, Eleutherii et Rustici.

In the Dyonysiacs, of Nonnus, the God Bacchus is feigned to have fallen in love with the soft, genial breeze, under the name of Aura Placida. Out of this they have made the saints Aura and Placida. This festival is on the fifth of October, close to the festival of St. Bacchus, and of St. Denis the Areopagite.

---

monogram of Bacchus for their monogram, wherever it was found, the ignorant monks, thousands of whom in ancient times could neither read nor write, immediately determined that it denoted a martyr or confessor of their religion. The monks were not necessarily in the modern Romish orders, and in the early ages of Christianity very few of them were Romish priests. As they found it increased their influence they gradually got into the way of receiving the Romish ordination; and, as the Popes found them a formidable body, after much quarrelling they formed an union with them, if indeed the monks did not actually conquer the Popes, and get possession of the Papacy.

[1] Pag. Idol. Bk. v. Ch. viii.

[2] The particulars of this Saint may be found in a letter published in the Preface to Mr. Payne Knight's book on the Phallic worship. He was adored with the ancient Phallic rites. In the mean time, when Sir W. Hamilton was at Naples, great numbers of ex votos of the parts of generation adorned his shrine, which was much frequented by modern Neapolitan females to procure fecundity, precisely as it had been by the females of antiquity.

[3] Vol. III. p. 151.

The ancients had a form of wishing happiness to others, in which were used the words *perpetuam felicitatem*. Out of these words were made St. Perpetua and St. Felicita. In the same way, from the words Rogare et Donare, they have made St. Rogatien and St. Donatien. These examples of their saints exhibit a very striking proof of what I have said respecting the nature of the Romish tradition—all these histories are traditions. From such traditions the whole fabric was raised. It could not be expected to be otherwise than as we find it. The President Fauchet, in his Life of Clovis,[1] declares ingenuously, that the feasts of the Romish Church were copied from those of the Pagans: and Polydore Virgil regrets that the feasts are more Pagan than Christian.[2]

The festival of Martinmas was an exact imitation of the feast of the Romans and the Greeks called *Pitegie* which signifies the opening of the wine barrels, which at this time is practised by the Christians. Thomas Neagorus[3] calls it the *second bacchanalia*.

Herodotus[4] says, that the Egyptians had a feast in which the ceremony consisted in lighting numbers of candles in their houses during the whole night, called *the feast of lights*. This solemnity, says Baronius,[5] is also observed by us, having been transferred to the ascension.

I suppose I need not point out the absolute identity of the ancient Saturnalia and the modern Carnival; no one who has paid the least attention to these subjects can entertain any doubt respecting them.

As the Christians have a particular saint to whom each day in the year is dedicated, and who has his particular service for that day; so the Persians had an angel for each day, and a particular service containing a compliment to the angel of that day.[6]

12. As I stated before, to account for the Heathen superstitions in Christian churches, it has been said, that Gregory the Great directed, in order that the prejudices of the vulgar might be as little offended as possible by the change, that the missionaries to Britain, &c., should leave the people in the possession and enjoyment of their festivals, provided they did not actually adore the idols. How can this be reconciled with the actual adoration of the *waxen infant*, with the most magnificent ceremonies, in the churches in Rome, on the first hour after midnight, on the morning of the 25th of December? This I have myself witnessed. The priests pass the image in grand procession, each stopping before it, muttering his prayer, going down on his knees, and kissing the toe of the figure. What was this but the ancient worship continued?

When the Pagans proceeded to build a temple they performed on the ground a variety of ceremonies. The head priest presided at the ceremony, and laid the first stone, after a grand procession.[7] Pieces of gold and silver were laid in the foundation, and the Vestal Virgins or Nuns sprinkled the place with holy water. All this is closely imitated by the Romish and Protestant churches, holy water by the latter excepted.

The long pilgrimages of the Christians are exact imitations of those of the Pagans, who were accustomed to frequent the temples of Delphi, Dodona, Diana at Ephesus, Ceres in Sicily,[8] according to vows made by them on emergences.

It is the custom with Christians to make vows on various occasions to build churches. So Romulus, to arrest the flight of his soldiers, vowed a temple to Jupiter Stator. In like manner Appius vowed a temple to Bellona.[9]

Every one is acquainted with the votive offerings of the ancients:

---

[1] P. 124.   [2] Lib. vi. Cap. viii. &c.   [3] De Regno Pont. Lib. iv.   [4] Lib. ii.
[5] In the year 58, s. 28.   [6] Hyde; Dupuis, Vol. III. p. 325, 4to.
[7] Cicero and Tacitus, Lib. iv. on rebuilding the capitol.   [8] Vide Cic. Acti. 6, in Verrem.
[9] T. Livy, Lib. x.

> —— Me tabulâ sacer
> Votivâ paries indicat humida
> Suspendisse potenti
> Vestimenta maris Deo.[1]

Again,

> Nunc Dea, nunc succurre mihi, nam posse mederi
> Picta docet templis multa tabella tuis.[2]

This is exactly imitated in the Romish churches of Italy. Some of the churches in Florence and Rome are actually covered with votive offerings. Sometimes jewels are given, sometimes pictures of the mode in which some favourite saint has effected a cure, or saved the devotee from the effect of an accident; or a model in wax of some limb cured is hung up; and some very curious limbs may occasionally be seen.

Our long prayers and litanies are exact imitations of those of the Pagans, and are directly in defiance of the command of Jesus Christ. "When ye pray," says he, "use not vain repetitions, "as the Heathen do; for they think that they shall be heard for their much speaking." (Matt. vi. 7.) How directly this is against the Romish "Kyrie, Eleeson; Christe, Eleeson; ora pro nobis; "Domine, exaudi nos;" and our "Lord have mercy upon us," in our litany and repetition of creeds, &c.! All this is an exact imitation of the prayers to Baal, described in 1 Kings xviii. 26, *Baal, exaudi nos*, which they cried from morning to noon. Thus the Romish devotees count their *Paters* and the repetition of their *Credo*, and Ave, Maria, &c., exactly like what Tertullian says of the Pagans—that they think to force heaven with their crowd of prayers. Thus again, in the Protestant Litany, the repetition of the prayer to the *Lamb of God* is taken from the service of the ancient Carnutes of Gaul.

13. The ancient Roman children carried around their necks a small ornament in form of a heart, called Bulla. This was imitated by the early Christians. Upon their ancient monuments, in the Vatican, the heart is very common, and it may be seen in numbers of old pictures. After some time it was succeeded by the Agnus Dei, which, like the ancient Bulla, was supposed to avert dangers from the children and the wearers of them. Pope Urban V. sent one to the Emperor of the Greeks with the following *beautiful* verses:

> Balsamus et munda cera cum chrismatis undâ
> Conficiunt agnum quod munus do tibi magnum.
> Fulgura desursum depellit, omne malignum
> Peccatum frangit, ut Christi sanguis et angit.
> Prægnam servatur, simul et partus liberatur.
> Dona defert dignis, virtutem destruet ignis.
> Portatus mundè de fluctibus eripit undæ.

Cardinal Baronius[3] says, that those who have been baptized carry pendant from their neck an Agnus Dei, in imitation of a devotion of the Pagans, who hang to the neck of their children little bottles in form of a heart, which serve as preservatives against charms and enchantments. And as these bottles were made in form of a heart to shew that man could not exist without a heart; so the Christians carry the image of the lamb, to learn from its example to be humble of heart.

This is the heart which the reader has seen in the figures of India, of Greece, and of Rome, noticed in Vol. I. pp. 146, 572. It seems to me, however, that the origins of both the *heart* and the *agnus* were equally unknown to the Cardinal. But he was probably right in supposing them talismans.

---

[1] Horace, Lib. i. Ode v.   [2] Tibull. Lib. i. Eleg. iii.
[3] Ann. Eccles. en l'ann. 58.

For the manufacture or blessing of these Agni Dei a long ceremony is usually performed by the Pope on the day called the Sunday in Albis.[1]

As the supreme God Bramha was surrounded with good and bad angels, or, as they are called in the Brahminical religion, *Dewtahs*, with some of the latter of whom Cristna the saviour made a war; so with the Persians the Supreme God had his good and bad angels, the latter constantly aided by the destroyer Arhiman, at war with the Supreme Being. Here we see the prototype of the Christian doctrine of the devil and his fallen angels at war with God, and working in every way in their power for the destruction of man. The book of Enoch gives the fullest account of the doctrine of angels. As the genuineness of the book is not doubted, that is to say, as it is not doubted to be the real book referred to by St. Jude, and as he was inspired, I do not clearly see how his authority can be denied by Christians. In the Hindoo work called the Mahabarat, a very long account is given of the wars of Cristna with the rebellious Dewtahs and Assoors. The Hindoo and Persian doctrine of angels and devils, is alluded to in the Epistle of Jude, to which I have just referred.

Stanley also shews that the existence of angels, and of good and bad dæmons, was admitted. He shews that dæmons were held to be of many kinds, and to be corporeal: "Those " dæmons are of many kinds, and various sorts, both as to their figures and bodies, insomuch that " the air is full of them, as well that which is above us, as that which is round about us. The " earth likewise is full, and the sea, and the most retired cavities and depths."

Mr. Colebrook says, that the Vedas throughout teem with prayers and incantations to avert and repel the molestation of aerial spirits, mischievous imps, who crowd about the sacrifice and impede the religious rite.[2] This was precisely the doctrine and belief of the early fathers of the Romish Church.

In the first Liturgy of Edward VI. Anno 2, the following form of Exorcism was ordered in baptism: " Then let the priest, looking upon the children, say, I command thee, unclean spirit, in " the name of the Father, of the Son, and of the Holy Ghost, that thou come out and depart from " these infants, whom our Lord Jesus Christ has vouchsafed to call to his holy baptism, to be " made members of his body and of his holy congregation. Therefore remember, thou cursed " spirit, remember thy sentence, remember thy judgment, remember the day to be at hand " wherein thou shalt burn in fire everlasting, prepared for thee and thy angels. And presume not " hereafter to exercise any tyranny towards these infants, whom Christ hath bought with his " precious blood, and by this holy baptism called to be of his flock." This, on the remonstrance of Bucer, was afterwards omitted.[3]

The sign of the cross, though made by a Jew, Infidel, or Pagan, was of force to drive the devil from one.[4] Pope Alexander ordained that holy water should be tempered with salt, and used ad fugandos dæmones, *to drive away devils.* (Platina in vitâ Alexand.)[5]

But the Persians not only had angels and wars of angels against God, similar to those of the Christians, but they actually had the same names, (as I have somewhere read, though at this moment I cannot recollect where,) such as Gabriel, Michael, Uriel, &c.

---

[1] Vide Cerem. Rom. l. Sect. 7; also Hospinian Festa Christianorum, p. 76, A. D. 1612.

[2] Astron. Vol. I. p. 578.

[3] The seventy-second canon of the Church of England thus expresses itself on Exorcism: " No minister shall, " without the licence of the bishop of the diocese, first obtained and had under his hand and seal, attempt, upon any " pretence whatsoever, either of obsession or possession, by fasting and prayer, to cast out any devil or devils, under " pain of the imputation of imposture or cozenage and deposition from the ministry."—Beverley's Book, xxv.

[4] Bellarmin de Imaginibus Sanct, Cap. xxx.; Hog's Hist. of Cornwall, p. 468.   [5] Hog's Hist. ut supra.

The followers of Mithra always turned towards the East, when they worshiped: the same is done by the Brahmins [1] of the East and the Christians of the West. In the ceremony of baptism, the catechumen [2] was placed with his face to the West, the symbolical representation of the prince of darkness, in opposition to the East, and made to spit towards it at the evil one, and renounce his works. [3]

Tertullian [4] says, that Christians were taken for worshipers of the Sun because they prayed towards the East after the manner of those who adored the Sun. He says the same in his book, Ad Nat. Lib. i. Cap. xiii. [5] Mr. Reeves says, the Christians worshiped towards the East because the altar was there: but why was the altar there, but because the East was the symbol of the *good* Deity—in opposition to the West, the symbol of the Evil One?

To this day, in most English Churches, at particular parts of the service, for instance in the repetition of the Creed, those persons who do not happen to have their faces turned towards the altar or the East, always turn to it; of the reason of this they are probably ignorant. [6] The Essenes always turned to the East to pray. Prideaux, in his Life of Mahomet, says, the Jews always turned to Jerusalem to pray [7] wherever they might be. [8]

" Quod attinet supradictos Christianos Armenos ad Solem se flectentes, de ejusmodi Christianis
" etiam suo tempore conquerebatur *Leo Papa* (Serm. VII. de Nativitate Christi) *Priscillianistas*
" arguens de cultu Solis. *Ut sol exurgens—à quibusdam insipientibus de locis eminentioribus*
" *adoretur. Quod nonnulli etiam Christiani adeò se religiosè facere putant, ut priusquam ad D.*
" *Petri Basilicam perveniant, superatis gradibus,—converso corpore, ad nascentem se Solem reflec-*
" *tant, et curvatis cervicibus, in honorem se splendentis orbis inclinent."* [9] This proves the mixed worship of Jesus and the Sun, which Leo was striving to abolish. Hyde, in the preceding page, shews, that the Armenian Christians were also in the habit, while turning to the Sun to offer their prayers, of constantly crossing themselves.

14. It appears that the Christians were accused by the Heathens of being worshipers of the Sun. Tertullian, in reply to an accusation of this kind, tells us, that the Sunday was celebrated by them in opposition to the Jewish Sabbath, and not because it was consecrated to the Sun. This was evidently a contrivance to evade the charge. The reason assigned by Justin Martyr [10] that Sunday was celebrated because it was the day of Christ's resurrection, would not have been deemed satisfactory; for the Heathens would have replied, " Certainly it was on the Sunday, the " day of the Dominus Sol, the Lord's-day, as you call it, because on that day the resurrection of " the Dominus Sol—the Saviour—was always celebrated in the Mithraitic caves."

This contrariety seems to shew that neither Justin nor Tertullian knew any thing about the matter, any more than they did about the statue of Sangus, which they took for a statue of Simon Magus.

In Sect. 9, the day of meeting of the Essenes is stated to be Saturday; but this feast lasted till sun-rising. In Sect. 17 it is also stated, that they worshiped toward the Sun at its rising. It seems the night was spent in singing hymns, &c. As soon as dawn appeared, they retired to their

---

[1] Maur. Ind. Ant. Vol. II. p. 97.   [2] Tertull. p. 221.   [3] Justin; Reeves's Trans. note, Sect. 79, p. 96.
[4] Apol. Cap. xvi.   [5] Clemens Alex. (Strom. 7,) and Origen say the same.
[6] See Parkhurst, pp. 634, 736.   [7] P. 93.
[8] He refers to Daniel vi. 10; Buxtorfii Synagoga Judaica, Cap. x.; Maimonides in Halachoth Tephillah, Cap. i. Sect. 3.
[9] Hyde, de Rel. Cap. iv. p. 107, ed. 1760.   [10] Apol. I. Sect. 89.

cells, after saluting one another. From the account in Pliny it appears the Christians of Bithynia met before it was light, and sung hymns to Christ as to a God. But the words imply, that they met very early in the morning. Surely the circumstances of the two classes of people meeting before day-light is a very remarkable coincidence. It appears that after their service they saluted one another. This custom is continued in our churches to this day. Every person salutes his nearest neighbours, though it would probably be difficult to get a reason from any one for doing it. It is the remnant of the old custom; so is bowing at the name of Christ,[1] and turning the face to the East at particular parts of the service.

Justin no where calls the Sunday the Sabbath-day, but ἡμερα τυ ἡλιυ, *the day of the sun*. And it is very curious that Constantine, after he pretended to be converted to Christianity, ordered the day Domini invicti Solis, to be set apart for the celebration of peculiar mysteries to the honour of the God Sol.

A very long and terrible schism took place in the Christian Church upon the *important* question, as I have remarked in page 59, whether Easter, the day of the resurrection, was to be celebrated on the 14th day of the first month after the Jewish custom, or on the Lord's-day afterward; and it was at last decided in favour of the Lord's-day. But terrible wars took place before this *most important* affair could be settled.

Besides the above almost an infinite number of small coincidences might be pointed out, each trifling and of little or no moment when taken by itself, but which, in the aggregate, is of very considerable importance. The multitude of the inferior Gods of the Heathens are well matched by the Saints of the Christians: they were thought to be endowed with the same limited powers, and to act as mediators between man and the Supreme Deity, and were equally honoured with the epithet *divus*. The Gods of the Heathens were fond of high places, and equally so are the Saints of the Christians; to some one of whom almost every mount and every fountain was dedicated. Each town had its patron and protecting tutelar God, it has now its patron and protecting Saint— to whom, in a peculiar manner, in all moments of distress, of plague, pestilence, or famine, the inhabitants address their prayers. Scarcely a church exists in Italy in which the numerous votive tablets do not bear witness to the active and miraculous interference of the tutelar saint.

The Viales or Compitales fixed at the corners of the streets, to whom the games called Compitalicii were celebrated, yet remain under the name of a Madonna or some favourite saint—as the Madonna Dolerosa, or Divus Petronius, &c.; generally ornamented like the ancient compitales with flowers. In Sicily the Madonna Vialis is seen with a bunch of ears of corn in her hand. By a decree of Augustus the Compitales were ordered to be honoured with garlands of flowers. These are part of the Lares or household Gods, and are to be met with in every house in Italy: and to them, as was customary in ancient times, the Calabrian shepherds come into Rome a few weeks before the winter solstice to play on the pipes.

> Ante Deûm matrem cornu tibicen adunco
> Cum canit, exiguæ quis stipis aera neget?[2]

---

[1] The Christians of Bithynia met, it appears, before it was light, because they were afraid to hold their religious assemblies in open day, lest their enemies should assault or seize them. Their salutation at parting was probably that which Paul (Rom xvi. 16) recommended—their mutual danger increasing their mutual attachment. Salutations were frequently, as they still are, expressed by writing or orally. Such are those to our neighbours and friends—expressive of courtesy or of regard. " Bowing *at* the name of *Jesus*" appears to have been introduced from a belief in his Deity, and from its being supposed to be required, by what St. Paul says to the Philippians, (ii. 10,) where *ιν* would, perhaps, be more correctly rendered by *in* than by *at*.—*Editor*.

[2] Ovid's Epist. i. *l*. 11.

> When to the mighty Mother pipes the swain,
> Grudge not a trifle for his pious strain.

No person can have spent a winter in Rome without having been often awakened before daybreak, by the beautiful and plaintive airs of these simple shepherds on their bagpipes.[1]

A remnant of the Eleusinian mysteries of Ceres is still retained in the festival of St. Agatha in Sicily. The same horse-races are continued, the same processions made by friendly societies, (the sodalitates of antiquity,) in which the image of the saint, on a triumphal car, and the sacred relics, are borne about with wax lights of an enormous size, precisely as was usual in the processions in honour of Ceres. The procession takes place on the fourth day of the festival of the saint, as it did on the fourth day of the festival of Ceres. At the conclusion of the festival in each case, the sacred relics, which were only shewn on those occasions, were offered to the people to kiss; and, finally, as the Eleusinian mysteries were celebrated twice a year, in spring and in autumn, so are the festivals of St. Agatha.

The numerous names of the Gods of the Heathens are closely copied by the Christians. The ancient Romans had the Jupiter Tonans, Jupiter Sponsor, Jupiter Capitolinus, &c., &c.; then Venus Calva, Venus Verticordia, Venus Capitolina, &c., &c. The modern Romans have their St. Pietro in Vaticano; St. Pietro in Vinculo; St. Pietro in Carcere, &c., &c.; Sa. Maria degli Angeli; Sa. Maria della Consolazione; Sa. Maria dell' Anima, &c., &c., to the number, as stated under her image at Loretto, of upwards of forty names: and in the same manner as the temples were sometimes dedicated to several ancient Divi or Gods, so the churches are sometimes dedicated to several modern Divi or Saints. The temple of *Vesta* is now the church of the *Madonna of the Sun*, fire being the prevailing idea in both appellations. That of Romulus and Remus is now the church of Cosmo and Damien—twin brothers. The temple of Bacchus or the St. Liber, on the promontory of Ancona, is now the church of the Holy Liberius descended ex stirpe regum Armeniorum. The church of St. Denis, near Paris, has succeeded to the temple of Dionusos. The Romans had a tradition, that Anna Perenna, the sister of Dido, was cast ashore near the Numicus, in which she ultimately drowned herself, and of which she became the protecting nymph. She is succeeded by Sa. Anna, the sister of the Virgin, to whose name the epithet Petronilla is added, for some unknown reason.

The Heathens constantly erected temples as votive offerings to their Gods, as was the case with the temple of Jupiter Tonans, erected by Augustus, out of gratitude for his escape from lightning which killed several of his attendants; and so are Christian churches: for instance, the church Della Salute, erected in memory of the deliverance of Venice from plague in 1586. The ancient temples and modern churches are equally built to record certain events or to receive certain sacred deposits. Their walls, in ancient as in modern times, were ornamented with pictures.[2] The images in each case were equally loaded with finery, jewels, paint, &c., and kept in sacred recesses with curtains before them. The temples in ancient, like the churches in modern times, were open from morning to night, with a small intermission at noon. The ancient sacrifice is succeeded by the sacrifice of the mass: the attending boys in white tunics are continued as in ancient times. The Mozzetta and Sottana of the priests, from the latter of which our cassock is taken, are both dresses of the priests of antiquity. The subject of the ancient sacrifice was called Hostia; the modern mass, Ostia.

The custom of using the aspersorio to sprinkle the people with holy water before the mass begins, the *chaunting* of the service, the ringing of little bells during the ceremony, are all Pagan

---

[1] The real Scotch bagpipe. [2] See Pausanias passim.

usages. The ceremony of putting ashes on the head, on Ash-Wednesday, is a continuation of the festival of the Fordicidia, which was celebrated at Rome on the 15th and 21st of April. The Catholic modern processions are exact imitations of those of the ancients, which were attended with music, tapers, successions of images, companies of attendants, streets hung with tapestry, &c., &c. The mendicant monks are merely a continuation of the priests of Isis, who, like them, lived by begging, and were great dealers in relics of the Gods, and who often pretended to possess the bodies of the Gods. The priests of Isis had their dresses made precisely of the same fashion as those of the Franciscan Monks: the sandals are the same. The tonsure of the priests of Isis and Serapis, or the practice of shaving the crown of the head, so as to leave only a ring of hair, is exactly continued by the modern monks. In short, the Franciscan Monks are evidently the priests of Isis.

The ceremony at Rome on Good-Friday, called the "Agonie," is nothing more than the Pagan ceremony alluded to in Scripture,[1] called the women weeping for Tammuz. The charms or amulets of the ancients are still strictly continued in Italy by all classes of people. The funerals are also in many respects the same as those of the ancients. The Protestant practice in England of throwing three handfuls of earth on the coffin, and saying, *earth to earth, ashes to ashes, dust to dust*, is a copy from the ancient Egyptians,[2] and the continuation of a Pagan ceremony, to satisfy the Gods below, in which the priest threw earth *three* times upon the body—" injecto ter pulvere curras."[3] The ancient offerings made at the sepulchres of friends are now succeeded by the sacrifice of the mass, for which payment is made to the priest. It is a sacrifice of prayer and incense, and is more or less expensive in proportion to the wealth or poverty of the deceased. In short, the ceremonies of torches, holy water, prayers for the dead, and the other forms used at funerals in many Christian countries, are nothing but imitations of similar customs observed by the Pagans; so that, in fact, there is not a single ordinance of the Christians which they can properly call their own; all is a servile imitation of the much-abused and calumniated, though, like Christians, in many respects blameable, Pagans.

The Jews fasted, and flogged themselves in the temple; the votaries of Isis did the same. In Trans. Acad. Ins. An. 1746, Tome IV., it is shewn, that almost all ancient nations had the practice of fasting.

The Persians used incense after the manner of the Jews, copied by the Christians.[4]

For nearly the whole of this section the Author is indebted to a small treatise on the ancient Customs of Italy and Sicily, by Mr. Blunt, of St. John's, Cambridge. Much more of the same kind might be discovered; but why multiply examples, when the case is proved usque ad nauseam?

In the front of most of the churches in Rome are placed very large obelisks or single pillars. Man is no doubt an imitative animal, and these may have been raised, by the modern Romans, merely out of imitation of their ancestors; but I am inclined to believe, that they were raised for the same reason that all the Pagan ceremonies which I have described were adopted—their Pontifex Maximus, &c. They were a part of the esoteric ancient religion, and, as such, were adopted. Two of these obelisks, covered with hieroglyphics, are ascertained not to have come from Egypt; but the hieroglyphics are said to be forgeries. Then why were they raised; and why were the hieroglyphics placed upon them? Did the modern Romans understand the hieroglyphics? I do not believe that they would be at the expense of engraving them, merely to pass off the obelisks as Egyptian, as, at the time that they were done, every one must have known of the forgery.

---

[1] Ezek. viii. 14. [2] Spineto, p. 148. [3] Horace, Lib. i. *Ode* xxviii. *l.* 36. [4] Hyde, de Rel. Vet. Pers. Cap. iii. p. 99.

Then what are we to make of them? I can scarcely believe that the hieroglyphics are known in the conclave; but it is next to imposible to ascertain what is known there. It is very certain, that if the knowledge of these hieroglyphics be a religious secret, a masonic secret, no attempt to discover it would be successful. For, if a Pope or Cardinal were to violate his oath, (without any object of self-gratification as it would be,) he would be rendered infamous; and the strong-nerved arms of millions of monks would be ready with their daggers instantly to give him his reward. If any man were to violate such a secret, I have no doubt that hundreds of priests in Rome would be ready to teach their fanatical devotees, that it would be the highest of all meritorious acts to assassinate or poison such a man. These obelisks were Lingas, adopted for the same reason that all the other rites and ceremonies of Heathenism were adopted.

In reply to what I have said a certain class of persons will exclaim, Oh, but these are nothing but the abuses of the Papists! But I think my reader will soon be convinced, if he be not convinced already, that between the Protestants and Papists there is very little difference. The priests of the latter have been obliged to give up certain absurdities which they found their flocks would no longer tolerate, keeping some as great as any they surrendered, and indeed keeping all as long as they possibly could. The Athanasian Creed and part of the service for the ordination of priests is as bad as any thing which the Papists profess. The truth is, that the Romish religion is nothing but a renovation of the old Pagan or Gentile religion, and the Protestant is only a part of the latter. But neither of them can properly be called the religion of *Jesus of Nazareth*, as I shall shew in a future book.

The fact of the identity of the Christian and Gentile rites and ceremonies has been so evident that the Romish writers have not been able to deny it, but have been obliged to have recourse to explanations. Baronius[1] says, "It is permitted to the Church to use, for the purposes of piety, "the ceremonies which the Pagans used for the purposes of impiety in a superstitious religion, "after having first expiated them by consecration—to the end, that the devil might receive a "greater affront from employing, in honour of Jesus Christ, that which his enemy had destined for "his own service." I suppose it is for this reason that the Romish Church has not any dogma, rite, or ceremony, which is not Pagan!!!

Polydore Virgil, who was much praised by Baronius and other learned men of the Roman Church, who call him a celebrated historian, and say that he was well instructed, and drew his information both from the ancients and moderns, says,[2] that the church has taken many customs from the religion of the Romans and other Pagans, but that it has rendered them better, and employed them to a better purpose.

Fauchet, in his antiquities of Gaul,[3] avows, "That the bishops of that kingdom employed every "means to gain men to Christ, availing themselves of their ceremonies, as well as of the stones of "their temples to build their churches."

Eusebius, in the Life of Constantine, admits that he, for the sake of making the Christian religion more plausible to the Gentiles, transferred to it the exterior ornaments which they employed in their religion. Pope Gregory I., surnamed the Great, who, Platinus says,[4] was the inventor of all the ecclesiastical service, followed this method, as every one can see, by the instruction which he gave to a priest called Augustin, whom he sent into Britain to convert the English. "It is not necessary," said he, "to destroy the temples[5] of the idols, but only the "idols, and to substitute the holy water, to build altars, and to deposit relics. If their temples

---

[1] An. 36 of the Annals. [2] Baron. Vol. IX. an. 740, Sect. 15; Pol. Virg. Lib. v. Cap. i.
[3] Liv. ii. Ch. xix. [4] In Vitâ Greg. I. [5] Greg. in Regist. Lib. ix. Epist. 71.

"have been well built, it is proper to divert them from the service of dæmons to the service of the true God, in order that the Pagans may be more easily induced to come to worship at the places where they have been accustomed.". He added, " That in the place of sacrificing beasts, they should have festivals to the saints or to the founders of the churches, and thus celebrate religious banquets; that thus having the use of some exterior observances they should be more easily drawn to the interior doctrines."

But how completely is this in opposition to the doctrine of Paul, that evil should not be done that good might ensue; (Rom. iii. 8;) to his advice to the Corinthian converts to flee from idolatry; (1 Cor. x. 14;) and to that of John, " Little children keep yourselves from idols"! (1 Ep. v. 21.) And how much at variance is it to the praise given by St. Ambrose to Theodosius, when calling him another Josias for destroying the temples of the infidels![1] How completely different is all this from the known practice of the first Christians, who would rather submit to be torn to pieces by wild beasts, than place even a sprig of laurel over their doors on a Pagan festival! Besides, how absurd is it to suppose that the single corrupt order of a Gregory should be able to engraft into the Christian religion not only the festivals but the doctrines and the sacraments, and the most obscure and abstruse metaphysical doctrines of the Pagan religion! The cause is not commensurate with the effect, and some other cause must be sought.

It is said that those superstitious practices were not adopted in the earlier times of the church, but were introduced afterward in the middle and dark ages. In order to form a correct judgment upon this point, it may be useful to ascertain at what time the Pagan superstitions actually ceased. It is well known that they had been laid aside in all the great cities as early as the time of Theodosius, and that they were banished to villages in remote situations, whence their followers were designated by the opprobrious name of Pagani. Now as it is improbable, and actually contrary to common sense to suppose, that a considerable interval should have intervened after the cessation of those superstitions of the Pagans, and their renewed adoption by the Christians, in compliance with the vulgar prejudices of the former, it follows that they could not be the produce of the dark ages of monkish superstition and ignorance. To take an example: Romulus was thought by the Heathens to be peculiarly favourable to young children, and it was the custom at Rome to present them at his shrine, to be cured of their complaints; afterward when the temple was converted into a church, it was dedicated to Saint Theodorus, who had been, like Romulus, exposed in his infancy, and therefore was supposed to be particularly fond of young children, who yet continue to be brought to his shrine to be cured of their diseases. When they recover, a miracle is alleged to have been performed; when they do not, the reason assigned may probably be, that the saint is not propitious to the parents. This exhibition is not in a remote place, but in the centre of the Papal city.

Now, as Theodosius destroyed or converted into churches such of the Heathen temples as Constantine had spared, this Christian superstition can hardly be dated later than the time of the former, and therefore it cannot well be attributed to the middle ages. Besides, if the almost solitary act of Gregory may be pleaded for a few of the local customs of Britain, it is perfectly incompetent to account for all the numerous Pagan doctrines and rites which have been pointed out in this work. It is evident that the story of Gregory, though perhaps very true, is a mere subterfuge, and is by no means adequate to account for the well-known facts, of the continuation of the Pagan rites and superstitions.

---

[1] Theodoret, Hist. Eccles. Lib. v Cap. xx.

CHAPTER III.

BETHLEHEM, BIRTH OF JESUS CHRIST.—BIRTH, DEATH, AND RESURRECTION OF ALL THE GODS.—PASSOVER.—LAMB OF GOD.—GENTILE CRUCIFIXION.—JESUS CHRIST WAS NOT CRUCIFIED.—JEWISH INCARNATION.—PYTHAGORAS.—OBSERVATIONS.

1. I SHALL finish this branch of my subject by shewing, that the birth, death, and resurrection of the body of the incarnate God, was common in almost every temple of Paganism, and that he was not only put to death, but also that he suffered on the cross, and rose again from the dead.

It is impossible to move a step in the examination of the rites and ceremonies of this religion without meeting with circumstances of greater or less importance connected in some way or other with the religion of Mithra or the Sun. Ænon, where John baptized, was sacred to the sun,[1] and had a temple dedicated to it.[2] Again, when Christ was born, he was sought for and worshiped by the Magi, who had seen *his* star in the East. Here is an evident allusion to astrology, properly so called, as distinguished from astronomy,—the calculation of nativities by the stars, which in all ages has been closely connected with magic and necromancy. The magi having arrived at Bethlehem, directed not by A star but by HIS star,[3] made their offerings, and celebrated with pious orgies, along with the angels who appeared at the same time, the nativity of the God, the Saviour, in the stable where he was born: but the stable was a cave, and it is still more remarkable, though it has never been pointed out by priests to their gaping congregations, that at THAT very time, the 24th December, at midnight, throughout all the Mithraitic caves of Persia, and in the temples throughout all the world, the same orgies were really in the act of being celebrated to the honour of the God Iαω—the Saviour. And it appears that these orgies did not cease for very many years after the death of Jesus, according to St. Jerom, in this very cave, and if we may believe Dr. Lightfoot, they may not have ceased to this time. The latter says, "Eusebius reports that "Bethlehem, from the times of Adrian to the times of Constantine, was profaned by the temple "of Adonis: for the asserting of which he cites these words of Paulinus: *Hadrianus, supposing* "*that he should destroy the Christian faith by offering injury to the place, in the place of the passion,* "*dedicated the image of Jupiter, and profaned Bethlehem with the temple of Adonis :* as also like "words of Hieromè: yet he confesses the contrary seems to be in Origen against Celsus: and "that more true. For Adrian had no quarrel with the Christians and Christianity, but with the "Jews, that cursedly rebelled against him."[4]

Of Bethlehem Jerom says, "Bethleem nunc, nostram, et augustissimum orbis locum de quo "Psalmista canit.[5] *Veritas de terra orta est,* lucus inumbrabat Thamus, id est, Adonidis : et in "specu ubi quondam Christus parvulus vagiit, Veneris Amasius plangebatur."[6] And Clarke[7] tells us, that the Christian ceremonies in the church of the nativity at Bethlehem are celebrated

---

[1] See Vol. I. p. 110.   [2] Bryant, Heath. Myth. Vol. I. p. 51, 4to.

[3] Every Amid or *Desire of all Nations* had a star to announce his birth to mankind. Thus Abraham, Cæsar, &c., had each his star.

[4] Lightfoot, Vol. II. Chap. li. p. 48, folio ed.   [5] Psa. lxxxiv. 12.

[6] Hieronymus, Epist. ad Paulin, p. 564.   [7] Vol. IV.

to this day in a Cave, and are undoubtedly nearly the same as they were celebrated in honour of Adonis in the time of Tertullian and Jerom; and as they are yet celebrated at Rome every Christmas-day very early in the morning.

From the fact, seemingly here established, that the temple of Adonis existed at Bethlehem before the time of Adrian, as it is admitted by the learned and Rev. Dr. Lightfoot, it is very probable that it must have existed before the time of Jesus; and the possession of droves of swine by the Gergesenes, and many other circumstances, induce me to suspect, that the religion of the Canaanites and the Phœnicians never was entirely abolished, but tolerated in different parts of the country among the descendants of the original inhabitants. If this should be found to be the case, I can readily believe that Magi, Magicians, Necromancers, came from a distance on a pilgrimage to worship, and to celebrate the rites of, the new-born God and Saviour; and that shepherds from the mountains should also have assembled there, precisely at the same day and hour, as they yet do at Rome for the same purpose, every 24th of December. Indeed, it is probable that something of the kind happened every year, at this season, at the shrine of Adonis.

The reader will recollect what was said before by the well-known oriental Christian, Abulfaragius or Bar Hebræus,[1] that there was a prophecy in the oracles of Zoroaster, "That a sacred "personage should issue from the womb of an immaculate Virgin, and that his coming would be "preceded by a brilliant star, whose light would guide them to the place of his nativity."[2] It is pretty clear that this is a copy from the Gospel histories, or that the Gospel histories are copies from it, or both from a common mythos. And it must be observed here, that the story of the Magi is contained in a part of the Gospel history which the Nazareens, Ebionites, Marcionites, Socinians, and most of the modern Unitarians, maintain to be spurious. If one be a copy from the other, which is copied must be left to the reader. After all that he has seen he will probably find little difficulty. This prophecy is evidently alluded to in the Gospel of the Infancy, which says, speaking of the Magi guided by a star, Quemadmodum prædixerat Zorodustht— as Zoroaster had predicted. This Gospel was received by the Nestorians, of whom Buchanan says, there are now about 50,000 in Malabar.[3] It is a striking circumstance, that the gifts brought by the Magi, gold, frankincense, and myrrh, were what were always offered by the Arabian Magi to the sun.

This prophecy is again noticed by Chalcidius in the third century. Commenting on the Timæus of Plato he says, "Stella quam a Chaldæis observatam fuisse testantur; qui Deum nuper natum muneribus venerati sunt—a star which is attested by Chaldean astronomers, who immediately hastened to adore and present with gifts the new-born Deity."[4] Christians have wished to make a Christian of Chalcidius, but the way in which he speaks of this Chaldean tradition, or whatever it was, shews clearly enough what he was. The observations of Chalcidius were probably made upon the story of the three Magi, who, according to Plato, came from the East to offer gifts to Socrates at his birth, bringing gold, frankincense, and myrrh.[5] One or both, or the union of the two stories, may have formed a foundation for the story of the three kings coming to Herod; and they have probably both derived their origin from the Hindoo religion. This story of the Magi having been applied to Socrates, by Plato, evidently proves that it was part of the ancient

---

[1] Hystoria Dynastarum, p. 54, ed. Oxon. 1663. Although I have given the substance of what will be found here from Abulfaragius, I think it expedient to repeat it. See Vol. I. p 561.

[2] Maur Ind. Sceptic-confuted, p 50.   [3] P. 136.   [4] Maur. Ind. Scep. confuted, p. 62.

[5] This story of Plato's I cannot point out in his works, but I was told it by a most respectable clergyman at Cambridge.

mythos of the renewed incarnation now lost. We have seen that it is found in Babylon, in Athens, and in Syria, and very nearly the same in India.

M. D'Hancarville[1] says, "Les Hymnes attribués à Orphée, mais rédigés par Onomacrite plus "de 500 ans avant notre ère, sont des espèces d'oraisons, que Scaliger croit avoir été récitées "dans les mystères............Ce livre singulier est reconnu par un docteur en Sorbonne, pour "être le plus ancien de tous ceux où il est parlé de l'Immaculée Conception de la Vierge *(Sura,* "iii. 88) appelée *Bibi-Mariam,* ou *la Dame Marie,* par les Turcs, comme elle est appelée "*Notre-Dame,* par les Chrétiens. Ces derniers, employant à sa louange les prières qu'ils répètent "sur le chapelet, en ont sanctifié l'usage apporté de l'orient au tems des Croisades, avec le dogme "de la Conception Immaculée. Mohamet le prit des Scythes ou des Tartares; Scythes, le "chef de cette nation, étoit fils d'une Vierge, suivant Diodore.[2] On prétend aussi que le Dieu "LA des LAMAS est né d'une Vierge : plusieurs princes de l'Asie, entr' autres l'Empereur *Kien-* "*lung,* aujourd'hui regnant à la Chine, et qui est de la race de ces Tartares Mandhuis, qui "conquirent cet empire en 1644, croit, et assure lui-même, être descendu d'une Vierge." I have no doubt that the whole mythos exists in China, and that it formerly existed in the books of the Jews, from which it was taken after the Christian æra, because the Christians applied the passages to their Messiah—a fact which has been very satisfactorily proved by Mr. Whiston.

Benjamin Constant says, "Ce système se rapproche sous quelques rapports de la doctrine "Indienne sur les incarnations successives qui ont lieu toutes les fois que Dieu veut faire con- "noître aux hommes la vérité. Il est assez remarquable qu'on retrouve une idée analogue dans "une hypothèse Juive. Les Juifs attribuent la même ame à Adam, à Abraham, et à David, et "croyaient que cette ame sera celle du Messie. Ils prétendaient encore qu'il ne fallait point "distinguer Élie de Phinès, fils du grand prêtre Eléazar, et que le prophète qui a vécu parmi "les hommes, tantôt sous le nom de Phinès, tantôt sous celui d'Élie, n'était point un homme, "mais un ange toujours le même qui s'incarnait pour donner ses conseils au peuple de Dieu."[3]

Mr. Faber,[4] speaking of the prophecy of Zoroaster, which I have formerly noticed, says, "The "Magi of Persia had a prophecy handed down to them from Zeradusht, (Zoroaster,) that a Virgin "should conceive and bear a child; that a star should appear at noon-day and lead them to it. "*You, my sons,* exclaimed the seer, *will perceive its rising before any other nation. As soon there-* "*fore as you shall behold the star, follow it whithersoever it shall lead you; and adore that* "*mysterious child, offering him your gifts with profound humility. He is the almighty* WORD, "*which created the heavens.*"

Now, Mr. Faber truly contends that this prophecy cannot be a Christian forgery, among other reasons, because it is found with the ancient Irish; whose history states, that it was made by a Persian called Zeradusht, and that it was brought to them by a Daru or Druid of Bokhara. The actual identity of the rites and tenets of the Irish with those of the ancients of the East, as well as their existence in Ireland previous to the Christian æra, has been so clearly proved by Borlase, Davies, Vallancey, &c.,[5] that no more need be said about it. "Therefore," says Mr. Faber, "this cannot be a Christian forgery." The first consequence which seems to follow from this well-founded argument is, that Zeradusht was a prophet, and that his work, the Zendavesta, must be admitted into the canon of the church. This not suiting, Mr. Faber supposes that the Persian must have seen the prophecy of Balaam or *some* other of the ancient prophecies, and have adapted it to his system; but he very wisely omits specifying which prophecy, as neither that of Balaam

---

[1] Rés. sur l'Origine, &c., p. 186. [2] Bibl. Lib. ii. [3] Benj. Constant, Vol. I. p. 171.
[4] In Hist. Orig. of Pagan Idol. Bk. iii. Ch. iii. [5] And by myself in my Celtic Druids, pp. 278, &c.

nor any other says a word about it: for though Balaam speaks of a star to arise out of Jacob, he says nothing like the story of a star coming from the East and guiding any persons.

Mr. Faber's mode of accounting for the history may be very satisfactory to the person who is blessed with a lively faith; but the story is plainly nothing but a part of the ancient mythology of the Magi and Brahmins respecting Cristna; who was believed to be an incarnation of the Supreme Being, of one of the persons of their holy and mysterious trinity—to use their language, *the Lord and Saviour—three Persons and one God.*

Mr. Faber's argument to prove the antiquity of this prophecy, as given at length in his book, seems quite satisfactory.

The reason why the three Magi who came to adore Jesus at his birth were called kings was, because the heads of the Magi were always called kings. It was a title of honour, like what we have in our Heralds' Office, *Kings at Arms*. " De non assumendo sacerdotio, testimonium dat
" Cicero, in libro De Divinatione referens : ' Nemo potuit esse Rex, antequam coluerat disci-
" 'plinam Magorum : nec magis ut quisque esset Magus quàm ut esset Rex.' Istorum itaque
" erat non tantùm reges in rectâ religione instituere, sed et eos inaugurare, ut in Christianismo
" fieri solet." [1]

" Ex hujusmodi Persarum Magis, celebriores aliqui fuerunt illi qui nostrum Salvatorem
" Christum in infantiâ visitatum venerunt ex Perside in Bethlehem." [2]

" Ab isto itaque Rege missi sunt (vel saltem, eo haud inscio, venerunt) Magi. Nam quòd
" Persis revelata fuerit Christi nativitas, certi sumus ex Evangelio: et præterea plerique autores,
" iique doctiores, idem statuunt." [3]

The real skulls of the three kings of the Magi are to be seen at Cologne: they were called Caspar, Melchior, and Balshazzar. It may here be observed, that the Magi were an order of men, not a nation, as is vulgarly imagined.

It has been before observed [4] that the Trinity of Plato was correctly the Trinity of Jesus, as described in the Gospel of John, and that the two accounts travelled *pari passu*, until they arrived at the famous *verbum caro factum est*. This is just as much a part of the Trinitarian system as the remainder, as is proved by the Brahmin history of the incarnation of Cristna, from which it was evidently originally taken. The idea of an incarnate God being among us now in modern times few persons (the followers of Johanna Southcote excepted) can entertain; but it was common to all ancient nations. Osiris, Bacchus, Adonis, were all incarnate Gods: taught by the priests; despised by the philosophers; believed by the rabble. They were probably all derived from the story of Cristna born in the eighth month, which answers to our December, on a Wednesday at midnight, in the house of Vasudeva, his father, and Devaci, [5] his mother. [6]

Thus the *verbum caro factum est* is not peculiar to the Christians, but was in fact acknowledged in almost every nation in the world. This was the Logos of the Persians and the Greeks, whose birth was originally fixed to the moment of the winter solstice. This Logos, we have seen, [7] was the second person of the Trinity—the Iao of the Gentiles.

Tertullian, Jerom, and other fathers of the church, inform us, that the Gentiles celebrated, on the 25th of December or on the 8th day before the calends of January, the birth of the God Sol, under the name of Adonis, in a cave, like that of Mithra, (in Persia *Mithra*; in Egypt, Phœnicia, and Biblis, *Adonis*,) and that the cave wherein they celebrated his mysteries was that in which

---

[1] Hyde de Rel. Vet. Pers. Cap. xxx. p. 373.   [2] Ib. Cap. xxxi. p. 381.   [3] Ib. p. 385.
[4] Vol. I. pp. 121, 160, 627.   [5] Ib. p. 139.   [6] Maur. Bram. Fraud. exposed.
[7] Vol. I. pp. 119—122.

Christ was born in the city of Bethlehem, or, according to the strict meaning of the word Bethlehem, *in the city of the house of the sun.*¹ This God Adonis is really and literally the Hebrew word אדן *Adn*, yet retained in the Welsh Celtic *Adon*,² which is translated into Latin *Dominus*, into Greek Κυριος, and into English *Lord*, the peculiar name of honour given to Jesus Christ.

On this day, at the moment of its commencement, the followers of Mithra began to celebrate the birth of their God. He was born in a grotto or cave precisely as Jesus Christ was. For though, in our Gospels, he is said to be born in a stable, yet in the holy land, at Bethlehem, the place exhibited is *a cave*. The stable no doubt was in a cave. The early fathers of the church acknowledge that the most probable of all the suppositions of the Pagans respecting the origin of the religion, was that of those who derived it from the Persians.

The same God was believed, by the inhabitants of Persia, Asia Minor, and Armenia, under the name of Mithra, to have been born in a cave on the 25th of December, to have been put to death, and to have risen again on the 25th of March. In their mysteries the body of a young man, apparently dead, was exhibited, which was feigned to be restored to life. By his sufferings he was believed to have worked their salvation, and on this account he was called *their Saviour*. His priests watched his tomb to the midnight of the vigil of the 25th of March, with loud cries, and in darkness; when all at once the light burst forth from all parts, and the priest cried, Rejoice, oh sacred *initiated*, your God is risen. *His death, his pains, and sufferings have worked your salvation.*³

In every case the God is supposed to become incarnate: in every case the place in which he was actually born was exhibited to the people. The night of the 24th December the Persians call the *Night of Light*. Stukeley observes, that the worship of Mithra was spread over all Gaul and Britain. The Druids kept this night as a great festival, and called the day following it Nollagh or Noel,⁴ or the *day of regeneration*,⁵ and celebrated it with great fires on the tops of their mountains, which they repeated on the day of the Epiphany or twelfth night. The Mithraic monuments, which are common in Britain, have been attributed to the Romans, but this festival (in consequence of its being kept by the Druids) proves that the Mithraic worship was there prior to their arrival. The Romans took nothing from the Druids, but on the contrary persecuted them, and put all whom they could make prisoners to the sword.

At the first moment after midnight of the 24th of December, all the nations of the earth, by common consent, celebrated the accouchement of the Queen of Heaven, of the Celestial Virgin of the sphere, and the birth of the God Sol, the infant Orus or Aur, the God of Day, called by the Gentiles *the hope and promise of all nations, the Saviour of mankind* from the empire of Ahriman and darkness.

The Egyptians celebrated the birth of the son of Isis on the 25th of December, or the 8th day before the calends of January. This Eratosthenes says was the God of Day, and that Isis or Ceres was symbolical of the year. The son of *the Holy Virgin*, as they called Ceres, was Osiris he was born on the 25th of December. At his birth, Plutarch says, that a voice was heard, saying, "On this day is born the *supreme Lord of the universe*, the beneficent king Osiris." On this day, at the same moment, the Romans began to celebrate the feast of the Brumalia in honour of the

---

¹ Dupuis, Tome III. p. 51, ed. 4to.

² And, from this word, all the rivers called *Don* have derived their names.

³ Dupuis, Vol. II. p. 194; Vol. III. pp. 41, 51, 62, 84.

⁴ Noel is the French name for Christmas-day.   ⁵ Vall. Coll. Hib. Vol. III. p. 464.

birth of the God of Day—of the Sol invincible—Natalis Solis invicti—described in vast numbers of very old pictures in Italy, with the legend Deo Soli, perhaps mistaken by the monks, and thus retained; or perhaps having a secret meaning.

It is remarkable that we have very few examples of infant Gods among the Greeks and Romans, though we have them in innumerable instances in Egypt; but I suppose them all to have been converted into Madonnas. I have no doubt whatever that great numbers of the examplars of the BLACK Mother and Child were infant Jupiters, or at least infant Gods; indeed, I should think every one of them: for, wherever there was a black child painted on an old wall, if it were renewed, it was painted like its predecessor *black*. This I myself have seen done in Italy. Cicero says,[1] "Is est hodiè locus septus religiosè propter Jovis *Pueri*, qui lactens cum Junone Fortuna "in gremio sedens mammam appetens, castissimè colitur à matribus." Bryant notices an inscription in Gruter:[2] Fortunæ Primigeniæ Jovis Pueri, D. D.

Again, Bono Deo Puero Posphoro.[3]

All the boy Gods which were not destroyed, were adopted as Bambinos.[4]

Nothing is more common in the North of England for the sign of an inn, than *the black boy*. I very much suspect, that the little Negro, as he is always described, is an infant Cristna.

Perhaps it may be thought by some, that the observations which I shall have to make on the celebrated lamb of God ought to have come here, but on consideration I have judged it better first to make a few observations on the resurrection.

2. Throughout all the ancient world we have seen that the birth of the God Sol, under different names, was celebrated on the 25th of December,[5] the day of the birth of Jesus. Thus, in similar accordance with the history of Jesus, the God Sol, on the 23d of March, was, by one means or another, put to death: and exactly three months succeeding the 25th of December, viz. on the 25th of March, he was believed to be raised to life again; and his resurrection was celebrated with great rejoicings.

The most important of all the different parts of the complicated system of Christianity, are the Crucifixion of Jesus Christ and his Resurrection from the dead. It will now be my duty to shew whence the collectors of traditions drew these particulars respecting him; where the *great men*, the *venerable fathers*, who believed that there were *four* Gospels because there were *four* winds— that men were raised from the dead sæpissimè—that boys were defiled and girls became pregnant by demons—found these traditions, and applied them to a person said to be put to death in Judea.

The reader has already seen that Jesus was mistaken for Iao or the Sun, and that all the Gods —Bacchus, Osiris, Hercules, Adonis, &c., were personifications of that great luminary. As Jesus and Iao were both born on the 25th December, it follows that as Jesus rose again on the 25th of March, the Vernal Equinox, after being cruelly put to death; so the different incarnations of Iao, from whom his birth was copied, should be found to have been put to death in a similar manner: and this we shall presently find was exactly the fact.

The resurrection of the human body to life and immortality, which was one of the leading doctrines of the Persian Magi, is of such an artificial nature, and includes in it so many circumstances apparently contrary to the evidence of our senses, that it is the acme of absurdity to suppose, that two nations should arrive at the same result by any common chain of reasoning.

---

[1] De Divin. Lib. ii. 41. [2] lxxvi. n. 6 and n. 7. [3] Gruter, lxxxviii. n. 13.
[4] See Bryant's Anal. Vol. I. p. 125. [5] Dupuis, Vol. III. pp. 117, 118. ed. 4to.

Hence it is evident, where such coincidence is found one must have copied from the other, or they must have drawn from a common source.

It must be recollected that it is not the mere resuscitation of a person newly deceased to life: it is the re-collection of the parts of a body long since reduced to a mass of filth and corruption, or scattered in dust by the winds or waves, eaten by animals of various kinds, and thus by becoming component parts of them, and converted by man to the support of his life, they form fresh subjects for resurrection to immortality—each part by some miraculous process unknown to us still supporting its identity: each man, though by this process forming parts of thousands of other men, and they again parts of thousands or millions of others, still retaining his absolute original identity, and the thousands or millions whose bodies had been partly composed of his body or of the bodies of each other in succession, all, like the original first man, rising to life and immortality. The subject is appalling: the divines say, when pressed upon it, that at the resurrection the body will be changed in the twinkling of an eye, into a spiritual body. As the word spirit is in meaning exactly the opposite of the word body, substance, or thing, they may as well say, that a *some*-thing will be raised to life and immortality in the form of a *no*-thing. But we must leave this to the divines; those of them are the wisest who pronounce it a mystery, and therefore beyond our comprehension—a thing to be believed, not to be discussed or reasoned about.

We are told by Diogenes Laertius, that the ancient Persians or the Magi believed in the resurrection of the body. To go no further, his evidence is unquestionable. But the following extract from Beausobre[1] will place the matter out of the reach of doubt:

"The Sadduceeism of Manes did not consist certainly in denying the existence of spirits, (des "esprits,) their immortality, and the punishments and rewards after death. So far from this, "that Sharastani puts among his dogmas not only that thought, *but that the sensible faculties of* "*seeing and hearing are never lost.* It follows, then, that he could not have denied the resurrec- "tion of the body. In fact, *the Magi believed in the resurrection*, as Diogenes Laertius testifies.[2] "It was one of the articles of the religion of Zoroaster.[3] Mr. Hyde had no doubt that the Magi "had taught the resurrection of the dead; and, besides the testimony of *the ancients*, whom he "produces to confirm it, he cites a relation which had been sent to him from the Indies, in which "the ancient faith of the Persians is explained and the resurrection positively taught.[4] If I am "asked, what idea the Persians had of the resurrection, I answer, that, apparently, they had the "same idea as the Jews: with bodies, the same as at present; with the same organs; the "same animal functions; (I know not any that were excepted;) to drink, to eat, to have women: "to live a tranquil and delicious life upon the earth, purified by fire, was the hope of the Persians, "as was that of the Jews, who never spoke so clearly of the resurrection as since they were "captive with the Assyrians. It is only since that time that the sects of Pharisees and Sadducees "existed."

Here we see the resurrection of the dead proved to have been the doctrine of Zoroaster or of the Persians, upon evidence of the most unquestionable kind. It seems impossible to doubt the fact. This is not a mere future state of life; it is the actual resurrection of St. Paul, with a real

---

[1] Tome II. Liv. ii. Ch. iv. p. 204.   [2] Diog. Laer. in Proem.

[3] Idem. p 383 "Credunt etiam resurrectionem mortuorum, et ultimum judicium, in quo boni à malis distinguentur," &c, Hyde, de Rel. Vet. Pers. Cap. xxviii. p. 355.

[4] Idem. p. 293, and Appendix, p. 537.

body, but yet with a spiritual body, i. e. a body purified by fire, as it is here described. It is an exact picture of the enjoyments of the Christians during the expected Millenium, and the reign of Jesus upon earth for a thousand years—the Hindoo renewal of the cycle of the age of gold.

But a belief in the resurrection was not confined to Persia; it extended, like the doctrine of the immaculate conception and solstitial birth, to every nation in the world.

Osiris was cruelly murdered by his brother Typhon, on his return from a progress in which he had performed many great actions for the benefit of mankind. The place of his burial was claimed by different provinces of Egypt. Relics of him were shewn in the temple of Philæ. To swear by those relics was the most sacred oath of the Egyptians.[1] In their caves or the adyta of their temples they annually, during the mysteries of Isis, celebrated the misfortunes and tragical death of Osiris, in a species of drama, in which all the particulars were exhibited; accompanied with loud lamentations and every mark of sorrow. At this time his images were carried in procession covered, as were those in the temples, with black veils.[2] On the 25th of March, exactly three months from his birth, his resurrection from the dead was celebrated, as already mentioned in reference to other Gods, with great festivity and rejoicings.

The birth of Horus, the son of Isis, was also celebrated, in another part of Egypt, like that of Osiris, and at the same time. His death and resurrection were, in a similar manner, celebrated on the 25th of March. They were the same Gods, in fact, only under different names.[3] This was the reason why these religions seldom occasioned any intolerance, persecution, or religious wars.

The birth-place of Bacchus, called Sabazius or Sabaoth, was claimed by several places in Greece; but on mount Zelmissus, in Thrace, his worship seems to have been chiefly celebrated. He was born of a virgin on the 25th of December; he performed great miracles for the good of mankind; particularly one in which he changed water into wine; he rode in a triumphal procession on an ass; he was put to death by the Titans, and rose again from the dead on the 25th of March: he was always called *the Saviour*.[4] In his mysteries, he was shewn to the people, as an infant is by the Christians at this day, on Christmas-day morning in Rome. On the 23d of March, the dead body of a young man was exhibited, with great lamentations, and on the 25th it was supposed to be revived,[5] when grand rejoicings took place, as in the other instances already specified.

In Crete, Jupiter Ammon, or the Sun in Aries, was painted with the attributes of the equinoxial sign of the lamb. This Ammon, who, as Martianus Capella informs us, was the same with Osiris, Adonis, Atys, &c., had his tomb and religious mysteries; and, though I have not found so much respecting his birth, death, &c., as of some of the others, they were probably all alike.

Apollo had his tomb at Delphi, where his body was deposited after he had been killed by Python. Three women bewailed his death, analogous to the three women, Mary Magdalene, Mary the mother of James, and Salome, who bewailed the death of Jesus. He was called the Logos, the light which had come into the world to enlighten it. Python was the great serpent of the pole, which annually brings back the autumn, the cold, the snow, and darkness—over which Apollo

---

[1] Maur. Ind. Ant. Vol. III. p. 214, 8vo. ed.

[2] At this time of the year the images in Italy are all covered, in like manner, with black veils, even to this day: as any one may see who will go thither a little before Easter.

[3] Dupuis, Vol. II. Liv. ii. Pt. ii. p. 194.   [4] Ib. pp. 195, 197, and notes.   [5] Ibid.

triumphs when he returns to the sign of the lamb at the vernal equinox, thus restoring the empire of light, with all its blessings. Pythagoras engraved on this tomb some mysterious verses,[1] which proves that he was a devotee or follower of this God, who was Apollo of Claros, of whom I have formerly treated.[2] The three Marys, of whom we read so much, were known in Gaul long before the time of Christ; and in England, for there is an altar at Doncaster, *Tribus Matribus, tribus Mariebus*.[3]

Three Goddesses, called *Mairæ*, were worshiped at Metz.[4]

In front of a temple at Metz was the following inscription:

" In honore Domûs Divi
Naëdis Mairabus
Vicani vici Pacis"[5]

In the following extract, from an anonymous author, the same story is shewn to exist in India:
" The Eleusinian mysteries are applicable to the mythological account of Buddha, the son of
" Maya, who, as the God of Love, is named Cam-deo, Cam, and Cama: signifying 'desire:'
" evidently the Grecian Eros: in this character, the Hindoos profess that he aimed an arrow
" from his flowery bow, at the heart of the supreme God, Maha-Deo: for which offence he was
" punished by a flame of fire descending and consuming his corporeal nature. Then follows a
" procession of priests, who accompany his widowed consort: the beloved Keti, who bears an
" urn, containing the ashes of the God, amidst the tears and lamentations of the people. Heaven
" and earth are said equally to lament the loss of '*divine love :*' insomuch that Maha-deo was
" moved to pity, and exclaimed, ' Rise, holy love !' on which Cama is restored, and the lamenta-
" tions changed into the most enthusiastic joy. The heavens are said to have echoed back the
" exulting sound, that the deity, supposed to be lost, was restored, '*hell's great dread, and
" heaven's eternal admiration.*' "

" Thus *Meru* is the worldly temple of the Supreme Being, in an embodied state, and of the
" Trimurti or sacred Triad, which resides on its summit, either in a single, or threefold temple, or
" rather in both, for it is all one, as they are *one* and *three*. They are three, only with regard to
" men involved in the gloom of worldly illusion: but to men who have emerged out of it, they are
" but one: and their threefold temple, and mountain with its three peaks, become one equally.
" Mythologists in the West called the world, or *Meru*, with its appendages, the temple of God,
" according to Macrobius. This worldly temple is also considered, by the followers of Buddha,
" as the tomb of the son of the spirit of heaven, whom I conceive to be the first man, re-emerging
" in every calpa, or the first lawgiver, often confounded with the first man. *His bones or limbs
" were scattered all over the face of the earth, like those of Osiris and Jupiter Zagræus. To collect
" them was the first duty of his descendants and followers, and then to entomb them.* Out of filial
" piety, the remembrance of this mournful search was yearly kept up by a fictitious one, with all
" possible marks of grief and sorrow, till a priest announced, that the sacred relics were at last
" found. This is practised to this day by several Tartarian tribes of the religion of Buddha: and
" the expression of the bones of the *son of the spirit of heaven* is peculiar to the Chinese, and some
" tribes in Tartary."[6] The latter part of this passage identifies the worship of Buddha with that of Osiris, Adonis, Bacchus, and the other Western Gods, whose followers observed this ceremony.

---

[1] Dupuis, Vol. II. Pt. ii. pp. 2, 195.   [2] Vol. I. pp. 324, 325.   [3] Ibid. pp. 310, 593.
[4] Montf. Ant Explained, Pt. ii. Liv. v. Ch. v.
[5] Trans. Acad. Ins. Anno 1733, p. 35. [See a nearly similar inscription in the Author's *first* volume, p. 310. *Ed.*]
[6] Asiat. Res. Vol. X. p. 129.

It is peculiar to the worshipers of the Bull. The Lamb, Hercules, or Cristna, was slain, but his bones were never in this manner collected.

The same account is given of Atys. His worship prevailed more particularly in Phrygia. Various histories were given of him in different places, but all terminated in the usual way with his being put to death, and being raised to life again on the 25th of March. As Jesus was said to be *suspensus in ligno*, so was Atys. It is useless to enter into particulars; they may be found WITH ALL THE AUTHORITIES cited by Dupuis under the head Atys;[1] as may those of Osiris, Mithra, Bacchus, &c., under their respective heads. It has, I think, been sufficiently proved, that Bacchus and Hercules answered to the Buddha and Cristna of India, and that the Western nations were only copyists of those of the East. If the reader will turn back to Volume I. pp. 144, he will see there, that Cristna was made " périr sur un bois fatal (un arbre), où il fut cloué d'un coup de flèche, et du haut duquel il prédit les maux qui allaient fondre sur la terre."

Certain priests of the Church of England account for the location of the birth of Jesus Christ on the same day as that of Adonis, Mithra, &c., by saying, that it is known not to have been his actual birth-day, but that it was adopted by the church the more readily to draw the Pagans to the true faith. The only answer necessary to be given to these persons is, that those of them who have any information at all upon the subject *know*, that the question of the day was a subject of great dispute among the early Christians, and THEY KNOW also very well, that the reason they assign has not a word of truth in it.

In ancient authors we constantly read of the burials and funeral obsequies of the Heathen Gods, and we are told that their bodies were interred at different places. Now I think this is a mistake, and that these obsequies were only the originals, and, in fact, were precisely of the same nature as the obsequies of the Romish Church for deceased kings and popes. At the time I am writing this, those rites have been celebrated for the deceased Pope Leo the Tenth at various places in Christendom. Except the great Pyramid, where the bones of the Beeve were found, be one of them, I have never met with the ruins of any monument which could be considered those of one of the Gods.

3. The resurrection of Christ was fixed precisely to the time of the Passover of the Jews, of which passover I shall now treat.

Cedrenus fixes the primitive creation to the 25th of March. The first day of the first month, he says, is the first of the month Nisan, which answers to the 25th of March of the Romans. In this day Gabriel gave the salutation to Mary to conceive the Saviour. On the same day the God, the Saviour, rose again from the dead—that day which the ancient fathers called the passover or the *passage of the Lord*. The ancient fathers fixed the second coming of the Lord to take place on the 25th of March. Cedrenus represents Christ as having died in the nineteenth year of Tiberius, on the 23d of March, and to have risen again on the 25th. From this comes the custom, he says, of celebrating the Passover on the 25th of March. On this day the true light rose from the tomb. Though the festival of the resurrection is now on the Sunday after the full moon of the equinox, it was formerly on the 25th of March, as Cedrenus asserts. This is confirmed by Theodore of Gaza.[2] This festival is known *in the writings of the fathers* by the name *pervigilium paschæ*. St. Augustin has a sermon entitled, De Esu Agni in pervigilio Paschæ. " It is on this " day," says this father, " that the Lamb who takes away the sins of the world is slain for the " salvation of man. On this day our gates ought to be marked with blood. Let us prepare for " the immolation of the Lamb." Isidore, of Seville, speaks in the same manner of the *Pervigi-*

---

[1] Asiat. Res. Vol. X.   [2] Dupuis, Vol. III. p. 56.

lium Paschæ. Lactantius says the same thing, and fixes the middle of the night for the rising of Christ from the tomb. Constantine was accustomed to cause the town where he was at this time to be illuminated, so that it was as light as noon-day.

The following passage from Georgius will shew, that the crucifixion and resurrection of Buddha took place *precisely at the same time* as all the others : In plenilunio mensis *tertii*, quo mors Xacæ accidit.[1]

Sir William Drummond has endeavoured to shew that the Mosaic account of the creation, in Genesis, and also various other parts of the Pentateuch, had allegorical meanings, and were descriptive of the correction of the ancient calendar, which, in consequence of the precession of the equinoxes, had fallen into great confusion, and had caused great confusion also in the mysteries and festivals of the Jews. It seems from almost every part of his work, that previous to the time of Moses the Bull must have been the equinoctial sign, though it may, perhaps, have ceased to be so for some time. The signs of the Zodiac, taken as the standards of the tribes, and Taurus, Leo, Aquarius, (or the man carrying water,) and Scorpio, being evidently the signs of the equinoxes and solstices, are a proof of it. The four equinoctial signs in the chariot, as it is called, of Ezekiel, is another proof of it.

The signs of the Zodiac, with the exception of the Scorpion, which was exchanged by Dan for the Eagle, were carried by the different tribes of the Israelites on their standards ; and Taurus, Leo, Aquarius, and Scorpio or the Eagle, the four signs of Reuben, Judah, Ephraim, and Dan, were placed at the four corners—the four cardinal points—of their encampment, evidently in allusion to the cardinal points of the sphere, the equinoxes and solstices, when the equinox was in Taurus. Aben Ezra says, that the cherubim in the temple had also the faces of those four signs. See Parkhurst's Lexicon. These are evidently the cherubim described by Ezekiel, and also the beasts described by John, full of eyes before and behind, and having the likenesses of a a *Calf*, a *Lion*, a *Man*, and an *Eagle*. All these coincidences prove that this religious system had its origin before the Bull ceased to be an equinoctial sign, and prove also, that the religion of Moses was originally the same in its secret mysteries with that of the Heathens—or, if my reader like it better, that the Heathen secret mysteries were the same as those of Moses.

It is also clear that the equinoctial sign must have changed from Taurus to Aries, before Moses ordained that the beginning of the year should open with the month Nisan. I can scarcely conceive how any proof can be more convincing of the change which Moses was carrying into effect.[2]

If any unprejudiced person would read the accounts of the plagues of Egypt, the passage of the angel over the houses of the Israelites, when the first-born of the Egyptians were slain, the hardness of Pharaoh's heart, &c., &c., and give an honest opinion, he certainly must admit that they are absolutely incredible. Then what are we to make of them ? The fact is, they are parts of an astronomical allegory—if not invented, at least compiled or written about the time allotted to the reigns of the first three kings, Saul, David, and Solomon. The whole history of the plagues, &c., keeps pace very well with the Labours of Hercules, the Conquests of Bacchus, the Argonautic Expedition, &c. ; each literally believed by the people, and each in its literal sense despised by the CHIEF priests, whose object in that age, as in this, was and is to keep mankind in ignorance and darkness.

Sir Wm. Drummond has shewn very satisfactorily that the feast of the Passover, veiled under the story of the Exod from Egypt, is nothing more than the Egyptian festival which was cele-

---

[1] Georg. Alph. Tib. p. 510.   [2] See Dupuis, Vol. III. p. 240.

brated at the vernal equinox;[1] in which, under one emblem or allegorical personage or another, two natural events were celebrated—the triumph of Ormasdes over Ahriman, of light over darkness, the ascension of the God Sol from the lower to the higher hemisphere; and the passage of the vernal equinox from Taurus to Aries. The same allegory applies with great truth and precision to both; and I am quite certain it was meant for both.

The same festival we also found in the Yajna sacrifice of the Hindoos.[2]

In the accommodation of the history of the Exod from Egypt to the passage of the Sun, we have a striking example of the mythic spirit. When we consider that this passage festival of the Sun is celebrated at the same moment with the Jewish festival, with nearly the same rites and ceremonies by almost all the nations of the world, and we consider also the way in which the triumph of the sun is celebrated in them all by a history of human actions, how is it possible to be blind to the identity of that of the Jews with all the others? In all of them the secret object of the festival was to celebrate the praises of the sun, or of that higher principle of which the sun is the emblem and shekinah.

The universal dissemination of this worship is worthy of the most attentive consideration. We have already seen that in Hindostan and Britain the procreative power of nature was celebrated on the day of the vernal equinox by Phallic rites, Huli festivals, May-poles, and April fools, and is even yet continued in these extreme points of East and West—of India and Britain—where the young girls with their swains little suspect the meaning of their innocent gambols—gambols which, if our devotees understood, they would view with horror. On the same day, in Persia, as I have just observed, the triumph of the Good over the Evil principle took place, the triumph of the victory of Light over Darkness, of Oromasdes over Ahriman. At the same time in Egypt, Phrygia, Syria, were celebrated the deaths and resurrections of Osiris, Atys, Adonis. In Palestine, again, we find on the same day the Jews celebrating their Passover, the passage of the equinox from the sign of the Bull to that of the Ram, or of the Sun from the inferior to the superior hemisphere; and, to conclude all, on this day we Christians of Europe still continue to celebrate the victory of the God Sol, known to all the nations above enumerated by his different names—by us, "the Lamb of God which taketh away the sins of the world"—on Easter Sunday having risen to life and immortality, triumphing over the powers of hell and of darkness.

4. Although the identity (not the similarity merely) of the modern systems of Christianity and the systems of the ancient Persians, and other worshipers of the God Sol, must be admitted, and indeed cannot be denied; yet many persons may have a difficulty in forming an idea how or by what steps the two systems became amalgamated or consolidated; so as either to form an imaginary human personage in one case, or in another case to attach themselves to the character of a real human being, or a divine person who appeared on earth in the shape of a human being. It is very certain that the same circumstances which took place with respect to the Christian religion, took place in the religions of Bacchus, Hercules, &c., in former times. Histories of these persons with miracles, relics, circumstances of locality, suitable to them, were as common, as well authenticated, and as much believed by the devotees, as were those relating to Jesus Christ. And where can be the difficulty of conceiving, that that should happen again, which we know from experience has happened before? To this it may be replied, that though it may be believed to have taken place, yet the means by which it has been effected are not so apparent. No person can be very much surprised that the *modus operandi* should not be very apparent, who gives due attention to the indisputable fact, that the priests, with all the powers on earth at their disposal, have been

---

[1] Œd Jud. Dissertation on the Paschal Lamb.   [2] See Vol. I. pp. 260, 389, 446, 584, 718.

employed for fifteen hundred years, in garbling, forging, and suppressing evidence, to prevent this *modus operandi* from being discoverable: but, notwithstanding all their efforts, a reference to some of the facts which have been detailed in this work will in a great measure remove the difficulty. Until the time of Luther and the Protestants, tradition was the grand support, and indeed the most powerful of all the engines used for the raising of the Romish Christian edifice. This engine was discarded by the Reformers, because their object was to take down part of the building, not to increase it; and the only difficulty was, to know where to stop—to know how much or how little was to be removed without endangering the whole edifice. It was evident that if they allowed the powerful engine *tradition* to remain, that edifice was impregnable. The Romish priests were well aware of the importance of their engine, and therefore exerted all their ingenuity to protect it: and for this purpose they found it expedient to give up some part of its power to secure the remainder. It is evident that nothing can be more liable to abuse than tradition. The tradition which the Jesuit of the present day will describe as the tradition of the church, is very different indeed from the tradition which was *in reality* used in the early ages of darkness. Every idle rumour circulated by ignorance and credulity became tradition, if it happened to suit the views of the priests. The frightened rabble, genteel and ungenteel, always timid in proportion to its ignorance, had not the most distant idea of any thing like biblical criticism. In order to secure its salvation, this rabble was only anxious to believe enough. It might believe too little, it could not believe too much. This cause operated in the ancient religions, as much as in the modern. Dr. Hyde[1] justly observes, that the ancients, always fearful of believing too little, kept constantly increasing their rites and ceremonies from surrounding nations. " Existimando melius esse " religione suâ abundare, potius quàm in aliquâ ejus parte deficere sic enim erat eorum mos, nova " quævis amplecti, eaque veteribus accumulare." This was exactly the case with the Christians. This cause is extremely powerful, and is the more dangerous because its power is not easily perceiveable. This cause continues to operate as *really* as it ever did in former times, and exactly in proportion to the ignorance of the people. And it is evident that it will continue to operate so long as belief or faith is held to be a merit: for, if belief be meritorious, unquestionably the more a man believes, the more he merits; therefore to make salvation secure, it is wise to believe as much as possible—to believe every thing. If a person believe every thing, he must believe the the truth—which can only be a part of every thing—of the whole.

Notwithstanding the strenuous exertions of the priests, for the last two thousand years, to eradicate every trace of the means by which their various doctrines, rites, and ceremonies, have been established; yet they have not entirely succeeded. Circumstances, apparently trifling in themselves, may sometimes be met with which have escaped their vigilance, and which will enable the impartial and unprejudiced inquirer to form a pretty correct idea how such of them, as he cannot discover or exactly point out the origin of, may have been produced. Remains of the ancient superstitions may occasionally be observed, on which most of the rites, ceremonies, and doctrines, have been founded; and the priests seem to have overlooked the circumstance, that the ordinances themselves for the destruction of others of them, if remaining, would serve to prove the fact of their previous existence, in a way fully as satisfactory as if we had them now before us.

The adoration by the ancients of the celestial bodies, and in its turn of the constellation or sign of the Zodiac, Aries, or the Ram, is so well known that it is needless to enlarge upon it. M. Dupuis, in his treatise, *Sur tous les Cultes*, has settled this matter. The manner in which this constellation came to be personified, or applied to the person of Jesus, may, at first, be

---

[1] De Rel. Vet. Pers. Cap. vii. p. 139.

difficult to conceive. Like almost every thing connected with religion, this effect was not produced by design, but by accident: that is, by the favourable combination of unforeseen circumstances.

This constellation was called the *Lamb of God*. He was also called the *Saviour*, and was said to save mankind from their sins. He was always honoured with the appellation of *Dominus* or *Lord*. He was called the *Lamb of God which taketh away the sins of the world*. The devotees addressing him in their litany, constantly repeated the words, *O Lamb of God, that taketh away the sins of the world, have mercy upon us. Grant us thy peace.*[1]

The following passage of Frickius *de Druidis* will prove that "the Lamb that taketh away the sins of the world" might very well be prophesied of by the Sibyls before the time of Christ. It will also complete the proof that the Jesus of the Roman Church was no philosopher of Samaria in the time of Tiberius. It proves also that our Litany is part of the ancient Pagan ritual, and as such gives it a new degree of interest.

"Rem dico admirabilem, omni tamen fide dignam, quam faciunt antiquissima Carnutensis
"ecclesiæ monumenta fastique, ac qui ex illis erutum tanti prodigii memoriam typis vulgarunt
"probatissimi scriptores; et in recentioribus quidem P. Franc. Poyraeus, acri judicio vir,
"integritate singulari, ac tenerâ in Deiparam pietate insignis, qui *triplicem coronam*, quæ hodie
"est omnium in manibus, pio sane et religioso artificio excellentissimæ, potentissimæ, optimæ
"matri contexuit.

"Itaque sic à majoribus acceptum referunt: signum Carnutensis virginis, quod hodieque visitur,
"quondam excisum esse in sacrâ Carnutum sylvâ, et Prisci regis, procerumque illius gentis
"unanimi consensu per Druidum manus, sanctiore quodam in antro collocatum, ac consecratum
"*virgini pariturae:* sive id mysterium ex oraculis Sibyllinis aut propheticis intellexerunt, sive
"acceperunt divinitus, extraordinariâ revelatione.. Moriens Priscus coronæ ac ditionis suæ
"Carnutensis heredem scripsit *virginem parituram*. Quæ autem occasio novæ illi religione fecerit
"initium, ita narratur·

"Quùm inter Gallos magna quædam exorta esset dissensio, nullâque interpositâ magistratuum
"auctoritate graves iræ sedarentur, ac jam eo ventum esset, ut omnia publicis contentionibus labe-
"factata pessum ruerent, cuipiam viro gravi, ad restinguendum tantum incendium, si quis alius,
"idoneo, imago coelitus est oblata, cujus in basi hæc inscripta verba: Agnus Dei, qui tollis
"peccata mundi, miserere nobis. Hanc ille imaginem quùm Gallis, qui in unum convenerant,
"palam ostendisset, paucis, quæ sibi monstrante Deo, revelata fuerant, præfatus, sic derepentè om-
"nium animos affecit pernovitque, nemo ut abeundum sibi domum putaret, priusquam reconci-
"liata pax esset. Ergo alii alios arctè complexi, sibi invicem, quicquid peccatum erat, condona-
"runt. Porro ad perennem tam fortunatæ reconciliationis memoriam, PARITURÆ VIRGINIS
"IMAGINEM EXPRESSERUNT, quam summo deinceps honore sunt prosequuti. Hæc ferè RIGOR-
"DIUS."[2]

Of this remarkable passage, I submit the following translation:

"I will relate an extraordinary circumstance, which, however, is worthy of all credit, on the authority of the most ancient monuments and annals of the church of the Carnutes, and of the most approved writers, who have thence derived and printed the records of so great a prodigy. Among the more modern of these authors is P. Francis Poyræus, a man of acute judgment, of singular integrity, and remarkable for his affectionate piety towards the Mother of God; who, by

---

[1] On an ancient medal of the Phœnicians brought by Dr. Clarke from Citium, noticed in Vol. I. p. 224, he is described with the *cross* and the *rosary*, which shew that they were both used in his worship.

[2] Frickius de Druidis, Cap. x. pp. 99, 100.

a pious and ingenious artifice wove the triple crown which is in every body's hands, for the most excellent, most powerful, and best of mothers.

"It is thus related, as handed down from antiquity—that an image of the Carnutensian Virgin, which is seen to this day, was formerly carved in the sacred grave of the Carnutes, and, with the unanimous consent of king Priscus and the nobles of that nation, was placed, by the hands of the Druids, in a certain holy cavern, and dedicated to the Virgin of the Conception. This mystery they either learned from the Sibylline or prophetic oracles, or they received it by an extraordinary revelation from heaven. When Priscus was dying, he named the Virgin of the Conception the heiress of the crown and dominion of the Carnutes. But the event which gave rise to the new worship is thus narrated:

"When a great dissension had arisen among the Gauls, and the authority of the magistrates had not interposed to quell the excitement, and it had arrived at such a height that every thing was falling into confusion through the public contentions, an image was sent down from heaven, to a certain grave personage, who was more likely than any other person to extinguish such a flame— on the base of which were inscribed these words: "O LAMB OF GOD, THAT TAKEST AWAY THE "SINS OF THE WORLD! HAVE MERCY UPON US." When he had publicly shewn this image to the assembled Gauls, and had repeated a few words which had been revealed to him by God himself, he so instantly affected and moved the minds of all, that no one thought of returning home till peace was restored. Each, therefore, embracing the rest, they interchanged forgiveness of all injuries. Moreover, in order to perpetuate the memory of so happy a reconciliation, they made an Image of the Virgin of the Conception, to which they thenceforth paid the highest honour.—Such nearly is the account of Rigordius."

Rigord, quoted above, by Frickius, and whom L'Escalopier also quotes, mentions, that among the Gauls, and especially in Chartres, there existed, a hundred years (N. B.) BEFORE the birth of our Saviour, the prophetic tradition of a Virgin that was to bear a son—VIRGO PARITURA.[1] He also observes, that the Egyptians held the same persuasion, "and not only worshiped such a "future virgin mother, prior to the birth of our Saviour, but exhibited the effigy of her son lying "in the manger, in the manner the infant Jesus was afterwards laid in the cave at Bethlehem.[2] *"Deinceps Egyptii* PARITURAM VIRGINEM magno in honore habuerunt; quin soliti sunt puerum "effingere jacentem in præsepe, quali POSTEA in Bethlehemeticâ speluncâ natus est. For this "passage L'Escalopier quotes a saint of the church, *Ephiphanius;* I say quotes, because his own "authority is very slender."[3] The sacrifice of the Agni or the Yagni sacrifice of India already described, was allusive to the Lamb of Isaiah and of Gaul.

I think I may now assume that I cannot be accused of very gross credulity in believing, that the son of the Virgin of Isaiah, and the Lamb of God that taketh away the sins of the world, were the same—both existing long before the time of Jesus of Nazareth.

When I reflect on the many circumstances, new and extremely curious as they appear to me, which I have observed, I am tempted to ask, Can it really be that I have a clearer sight than others, which causes me to see what others overlook? If this be true, to an absence of prejudice only can it be attributed. Such is the sensation I experience when I observe such circumstances as the following; I cannot shut my eyes to them: in every part of Italy I observe pictures of the holy family, of extreme antiquity, the grounds of them often of gold. Of course they are said to be of a date subsequent to the time of Christ; but when I see them inscribed with the words Deo

---

[1] L'Escaloperius, de Theologiâ veterum Gallorum, Cap. x.   [2] As in Luke ii. 7.
[3] Cleland's attempt to retrieve Celtic Literature, pp. 102, 103, 1766, 8vo. See Vol. I. pp. 169—171.

Soli, I cannot help doubting. These pictures represent the mother seated with a child on her knee, and a little boy standing close by her side. The lamb is generally seen in the picture. This is the very description of what Mr. Payne Knight calls Isis and her offspring, who were worshiped in Russia by the ancient Muscovites. And who was her offspring but Horus? He adds, they have in other pictures the symbol of a *golden heifer*, which is a symbol of the same person.[1] After reading the account of the Isis in every part of the North of France and England, of the Virgo Paritura, of the Lamb that taketh away the sins of the world, I cannot doubt that this is the same mythos in honour of the Beeve, which followed two thousand years after, in honour of the Lamb—a renewal of the same mythos for every new sign of the zodiac. Sometimes it was a Bull, then a Ram, and lastly, two Fishes, tied together by the tails on Popish monuments.

The first symptom of the worship of the lamb among the Israelites is to be found in the substitution of the Ram in the place of Isaac, by Abraham, for a sacrifice. When Joseph had become prime minister of Egypt, he married Asenath, a daughter of the priest of On or Heliopolis, the capital of Goshen, which word Goshen, Mr. Bryant states, means *the house of the sun*. Lucian[2] states, that the persons initiated into the mysteries of that temple sacrificed a sacred sheep, a symbol of the animal of the first sign, or of the equinoctial sign, which they ate as the Israelites ate their Passover,[3] On the ancient monuments of Mithra, in the different collections, we see the Bull, whose blood is shed to take away the sins of the world. The Bull is now succeeded by the Ram, *the lamb without blemish*, by whose blood the soul is purified from sin. On an ancient Christian monument the lamb is seen slain at the foot of the cross, the blood of which is caught in a cup.[4] This is a copy of the rite described in the celebrated Mithraitic monument of slaying the bull.[5]

Some of the coins of Gallienus are stamped with the figure of a Lamb and the legend *Jovi Servatori*. And in another ancient medal is seen the legend *Ammoni Servatori*.[6]

The Egyptian God Jupiter, with the horns of a ram, the Ammon, is but the sun at the equinox, which is confirmed by Martianus Capella, who maintains, in his hymn to the sun, that the God lamb or ram is but the sun. Then if Christ be the sun, Christ, in the moment of his triumph and reparation, ought to be as the sun, figured by the symbolical lamb. This symbolical sign is essential to his triumph over the prince of darkness and the works of the serpent. But, in effect, he has this form. He is designated in the Scriptures by the mystical name of the Lamb, the Saviour. His mysteries are those of the lamb without fault; nature is restored by the blood of the lamb. Every where the blood of the lamb, which takes away the sins of the world, is presented to us. When the priest presents to the initiated the mystic bread which contains the Christ, he says, "Behold the Lamb of God, which taketh away the sins of the world." He calls it "the Lamb" which has been "slain from the foundation of the world."[7] Every part of the Apocalypse turns upon the triumph of the Lamb over the powers of hell and darkness. The symbolical type of the sun, the redeemer, or of the first sign in which the sun had his exaltation and completed his victory over the powers of darkness, has been carefully preserved in the religion of the Christians, so that to name Christ or the Lamb is the same thing as to name the Redeemer.

---

[1] Class. Journ. Vol. XXVI. p. 269. [2] De Deâ Syriâ, p. 913. [3] Dupuis, Tome II. pp. 250, 4to.

[4] Casalius de Veterib. Christ. Ritib. Cap. ii. p. 4, or Cap. v. p. 48.

[5] St. Paulin, Bishop of Nola, Epist. 12 ad Sulpit. Severum, says, Sub cruce sanguineâ niveo stat Christus in agno.

[6] Dupuis, Tome III. p. 325, 4to.

[7] Rev. xiii 8. The Apocalypse is proved to be of very great antiquity by its having fixed the year to only 360 days.

Instead of the Crucifix, Christ is often represented over the altars on the continent as a Lamb. There is one at Cologne.

It follows, then, that the mysteries of Christ are the mysteries of the Lamb, and that the mysteries of the Lamb are mysteries of the same nature as those of the Mithraitic Bull, to which they succeeded by the effect of the precession of the equinoxes, which substituted the slain *lamb* for the slain *bull*. The Christian mysteries of the lamb are proved to be taken from the mysteries of Mithra, of the Persians, by the circumstance that the Persians alone have the lamb for the symbol of the equinoctial sign: the other nations have the full grown Ram.

M. Dupuis observes, that the lamb was a symbol or mark of initiation into the Christian mysteries, a sort of proof of admission into the societies of the initiated of the lamb, like the private sign of the free-masons. From this came the custom, in the primitive church, of giving to the newly-initiated or newly-baptized, the seal of the Lamb, or an impression in wax, representing the Lamb.

Christians even now make their children carry about their necks a symbolical image of the Lamb, called an Agnus Dei.

There are not many circumstances more striking than that of Jesus Christ being originally worshiped under the form of a Lamb—the actual lamb of God which taketh away the sins of the world. "Though many churches in this age were adorned with the images of saints and martyrs, "there do not appear to be many of Christ. These are said to have been introduced by the Cap- "padocians; and the first of these were only symbolical ones, being made in the form of a Lamb. "One of this kind Epiphanius found in the year 389, and he was so provoked at it that he tore it. "It was not till the council of Constantinople, called *In Trullo*, held so late as the year 707, that "pictures of Christ were ordered to be drawn in the form of men." [1]

Priestley is perfectly right: the custom of exposing the symbolical Lamb to the veneration of the people continued to the year 608, when Agathon was pope, and Constantine Pogonat was emperor. It was ordained, in the sixth Synod of Constantinople, [2] that, in the place of the figure of a lamb, the symbol used to that time, the figure of a man nailed to a cross should in future be used, which was confirmed by Adrian the First. But the Pope Adrian the First, in the seventh council, in his epistle to Tarasius, Bishop of Constantinople, had approved the representation of Christ under the form of the Lamb and adopted it. [3]

In the decree of the council of Constantinople quoted above, the knowledge of a most important fact is preserved to us by the decree passed for the express purpose of concealing it. If instead of this formal decree, forbidding the votaries in future to represent Christ as a Lamb, the practice had been merely discouraged by verbal communications, through the medium of the corresponding societies of monks, it would have been as certainly abolished, and this curious link connecting the ancient and modern superstitions would never have been discovered. It would have been irretrievably lost.

The following are the words of the decree, which I obtained in the Vatican Library, that mighty treasury of secret learning. [4]

In the Roma Sotterranea of Antonio Bosio, [5] Dell' Imagine di Christo in Figura di Agnello—"In

---

[1] Priestley's Hist. Corr. Vol. I. p. 339; Seuer, A. D. 707.   [2] Can. 82.

[3] Dupuis, sur tous les Cultes, Tome III. p. 61, 4to.

[4] The French supposed that they examined it. Silly fellows! The church took care that they should find as little of *secret learning* in the Vatican as they found of real *jewels* at Loretto.

[5] Lib. iv. Cap. xxix.

" quibusdam sanctorum imaginum picturis agnus exprimitur, &c.[1] Nos igitur veteres figuras
" atque umbras, ut veritatis notas, et signa ecclesiæ tradita, complectentes, gratiam, et veritatem
" anteponimus, quam ut plenitudinem legis accepimus. Itaque id quod perfectum est, in picturis
" etiam omnium oculis subjiciamus, agnum illum qui mundi peccatum tollit, Christum Deum
" nostrum, loco veteris Agni, humanâ formâ posthac exprimendum decrevimus," &c. See
Canon 83.[2] From this decree the identity of the worship of the celestial lamb and the Romish
Jesus is certified beyond the possibility of doubt, and the mode by which the ancient superstitions were applied to an imaginary personage or to a real human being, Jesus of Nazareth, is
satisfactorily shewn. Nothing can more clearly prove the general practice than the order of a
general council to regulate it.

It requires no very great exertion of the imagination to form an idea in what manner the
ignorant and fanatical devotees, when they applied the worship of the Lamb that taketh away the
sins of the world to the man Jesus, should seize hold of and apply to him every doctrine, rite,
or ceremony, which the idle traditions of the vulgar attributed to the Lamb in different countries
where they happened to prevail. The God Sol, Mithra, and Iao, being the same as the Lamb of
God, it seems natural enough that the ceremonies, &c., of the being passing under those names
should be adopted by his followers. Hence it is that we find them all mixed together in the
worship of Jesus. And, as the worship under the name of Mithra prevailed most in the different
Western countries of the world, it is not surprising that his peculiar doctrines and ceremonies
should most prevail in the new religion.

We have seen that Mr. Bryant, Dupuis, and others, have shewn that the worship of the
constellation of Aries was the worship of the Sun in his passage through that sign, and this
connects with the worship of the Lamb the different rites which were used by different nations in
the worship of the God Sol—the Dominus Sol—under the different names of Hercules, Bacchus,
Mithra, Adonis, &c., &c., their baptisms, oblations of bread and water, their births, deaths, resurrections after three days, and triumphs over the powers of hell and of darkness. In all this can a
person be so blind as not to see the history of the God $Ia\omega$, IHS, $I\eta\sigma\eta\varsigma$, the α and ω—the
incarnate God—the Lamb of God sacrificed to take away the sins of the world? As might be
expected, we find this Saviour originally described and adored under the form of a Lamb. In
many places of Italy, particularly at Florence, he is described as a Lamb, with the cross held by
his fore-leg. But, in most places, these representations have been destroyed in compliance with
the bulls or decrees above-named, which unwittingly let us into the secret, which, without them,
we might have guessed at, but could not have certainly known.

Over the high altar of the cathedral at Mayence, on the Rhine, is a golden lamb, as large as
life, *couchant*, upon a book sealed with seven seals, and surrounded with a glory. Over the high
altar of the cathedral of Bon, also, there is a Lamb in silver, as large as life, couchant on a book,
sealed with seven seals, and surrounded with a golden glory. In the gateway of the Middle
Temple in London may be seen one of these Lambs: he holds a cross with his fore-leg, and has
the sun for his head, with a lamb's face. This is a relic of the ancient Knights Templars. In
the late repairs of their building the lawyers have shewn much good taste in not destroying it.
I rejoice that such of my countrymen as cannot go abroad, may see this remnant of the ancient
superstition at home. I advise the Masonic Templars to add this to their eight-point *red* cross.

5. I will now shew my reader that the crucifixion of Christ is, like all the remainder of the
Romish mythos, a close copy from Paganism.

---

[1] S. Io Damasc. Orat. 3, de Imag.   [2] Baron. Annal. Tom. VIII. ann. 680, 692.

"Plato died about 348 before our æra. The beginning of John's Gospel is evidently Platonic. This philosopher was himself believed to have been born of a pure virgin; and in his writings had drawn up the imaginary character of a DIVINE MAN, whose ideal picture he completed by the supposition that such a man would be crucified"[1] —a supposition under which the *secret* mythos was evidently concealed, but which would be clearly understood by the initiated. Having penetrated into the mysteries, *we* understand it.

Prometheus is said to have been nailed up with arms extended, near the Caspian Straits, on Caucasus. The history of Prometheus on the cathedral of Bourdeaux here receives its explanation. Here the history of the Garuda, of the crucified Prometheus, in the Christian church, is accounted for: proved by the name of the river Garumna, in the department of the same ancient name, not to have been so called from any superstition of the middle ages. In our versions of the tragedy of Æschylus, Prometheus is always fraudulently said to be Bound. It is called *Prometheus vinctus*, He was nailed up in the form of a cross, with hammer and nails. The object of this impudent fraud need not be pointed out. In this case Protestants and Papists are all alike.

"The Prometheus Bound of Æschylus was acted as a tragedy in Athens, 500 years before the Christian æra. The plot or fable of the drama, being then confessedly derived from the universally recognized type of an infinitely remote antiquity; yet presenting not one or two, but innumerable coincidences with the Christian tragedy; not only the more prominent situations, but the very sentiments, and often the words of the two heroes are precisely the same." "Prometheus made the first man and woman out of clay"—"was a God." He "exposed himself to the wrath of God, incurred by him in his zeal to save mankind."[2] He was crucified on a rock, instead of a beam of timber.

Æsculapius was the son of Coronis. This *Coronis* was the first of the Jewish Sephiroth, *Corona*, and answered to the Brahm-Maia of the Brahmins. Æsculapius was Asclo-ops, οψ, οπος, Logos, *voice*—as *fire* and solar emanation, described by the numeral letters, *klo*=600. Thus: ׀=500, ל=30, y=70=600. He was the voice of the solar cycle, or the voice of the mundane fire; for *cycle* and *mundane*, I think, are convertible terms. Or, judging from the serpent with which this Saviour God is always accompanied, I should say, the *serpent of the solar cycle*—As-clo-οφις.

Æsculapius is always conjoined with the serpent; and generally with a serpent coiling round something—*en-cir* or *en-cycling*, something.

The serpent not only tempted Eve, but the name Heva meant *serpent*. Αργας means serpent; Argha, the emblem of the female generative power, and Αρχα, the ship in which the germ of animated nature was saved.

The Serpent, the Eva, the Argha, the Ship or Nau, the Cycle, the X=600, and the God, are all brought very near together if they be not identified:

> Once, as the sacred infant she survey'd,
> The God was kindled in the raving maid;
> And thus she utter'd her prophetic tale,
> Hail, great physician of the world! all hail.
> Hail, mighty infant, who, in years to come,
> Shalt heal the nations, and defraud the tomb!
> Swift be thy growth, thy triumphs unconfined,
> Make kingdoms thicker, and increase mankind.

---

[1] Taylor's *Syntagma*, in answer to J. P. S. [Dr. John Pye Smith?] p. 95, note. [2] Ibid. pp. 97, 98, and note.

> Thy daring art shall animate the dead,
> And draw the thunder on thy guilty head;
> Then shalt thou die, but from the dark abode
> Shalt rise victorious, and be twice a God.[1]

Mr. R. Taylor has stated, that he thinks the healing God[2] was related to the Therapeutæ, or Physicians of the Soul, as they have been called—as the name meant. And most certainly there are expressions in the verses of Ovid which shew a reference to the superstition of Virgil, and to the Christian, Promethean, and Hindoo incarnations and regenerations.

The following is an account given of the rites of Tammuz or of Adonis, or of the Syrian or Jewish אדן *adn* or אדון *adun*,[3] by Julius Firmicius: "On a certain night (while the ceremony of "the Adonia, or religious rites in honour of Adonis lasted) an image was laid upon a bed, and be- "wailed in doleful ditties. After they had satiated themselves with fictitious lamentations, light "was brought in: then the mouths of all the mourners were anointed by the priest, upon which "he, with a gentle murmur, whispered,

> " Trust, ye saints, your God restored,
> " Trust ye, in your *risen* Lord;
> " For the pains which he endured
> " Our salvation have procured.

> " Θαρρειτι, μυσται, τε θιε σισωσμινε,
> " Εσται γαρ ημιν ικ πονων σωτηρια.

"Literally, 'Trust, ye *communicants:* the God having been saved, there shall be to us out of "pains, salvation.'" Godwyn renders it, "*Trust ye in God, for out of pains, salvation is come* "*unto us.*"[4] Parkhurst[5] gives the translation from Godwyn, and says, "I find myself obliged to "rank Tammuz, as well as the Greek and Roman Hercules, to that class of idols which were "originally designed to represent the *promised Saviour, the Desire of all nations.* His other name "*Adonis,* is almost the very Hebrew אדוני *Adunı* or *Lord,* a well-known title of Christ."

On these rites of Adonis the Editor of Calmet says,[6] " Now these rites seem to be precisely "the same with those described in the Orphic *Argonautica,* where we learn that these awful "meetings began, first of all, *by an oath of secrecy, administered to all who were to be initiated.* "Then the ceremonies commenced by a description of the chaos or abyss, and the confusion atten- "dant upon it: then the poet describes a person, as a *man of justice,* and mentions the orgies, or "funeral lamentations, on account of this *just person;* and those of Arkite *Athene* (i. e. Divine "Providence); these were celebrated by night. In these mysteries, after the attendants had for a "long time bewailed the death of this *just person,* he was at length understood to be restored to "life, to have experienced a resurrection; signified by the readmission of light. On this the "priest addressed the company, saying, 'Comfort yourselves, all ye who have been partakers of "'the mysteries of the Deity, thus preserved: for we shall now enjoy some respite from our "'labours:' to which were added these words, 'I have escaped a sad calamity, and my lot is "'greatly mended.' The people answered by the invocation Ιω Μακαιρα! Λαμπαδηφορος! "'Hail to the Dove! the Restorer of Light!'"

---

[1] Ovid by *Addison,* ap. R. Taylor's *Diegesis,* p. 148.
[2] That is, the Suli Minerva of Bath.
[3] " *Hence the idol Adonis had his name*"—Parkhurst, in voce דן *dn,* p. 141.
[4] R. Taylor's *Diegesis,* p. 163.
[5] In voce תמז *tms,* p. 789.
[6] Fragment, CCCXVII. pp. 21, 22.

Here, I think, from this little scrap, which has escaped from the Argonautic mysteries, we see enough to raise a probability that in them were acted over, or celebrated, the whole of the Mosaic and Christian mythoses—the whole of what we have found mixed together in the rites of the Brahmins of South India, as given by the Jesuits, the mythos of Moses, and of the person treated on by the Erythræan Sibyl. It appears that these rites were celebrated in the autumn, to which they must, of course, have been removed by the precession of the equinoxes. We have seen before, Vol. I. pp. 822—824, that it was admitted by Clemens Alexandrinus, who had been himself initiated, that the mysteries of Eleusis were taken from the books of Moses. An interesting account of the tomb of Jesus, as it now is at Jerusalem, may be seen in the travels of Dr. Clarke. But in the writings of some traveller, but by whom I have now forgotten, an account is given that a miraculous fire descends from heaven at the festival of the resurrection, and nearly all the same ceremonies are gone through by the Christians at this day, as I have just now shewn were practised in honour of Adonis; which word Adonia, it may be observed, is nothing but the Jewish Adonai, which is always translated Lord in our Bible, in order to disguise the truth from its readers. This Adonis or Tamas was the same which we found at the tomb of St. Thomas, and the town of Adoni, in South India.

Adonis was the son of Myrra, which word, in the old language without points, would be nearly the same as Maria. He was said to have been killed by a boar in hunting. This will not, on any account, agree with the verses of Julius Firmicius; therefore there must have been some other history to which he alludes. We know that there were very few of the heathen gods which had not several different histories of their births, deaths, &c., and there must have been another of Adonis which has not come down to us.

It is said, that the Christians of Malabar are called Christians of Nazaranee Mapila, or Surians of Surianee Mapila. From this, when I consider that almost every other town named in the Christian mythos has been found, both in India and the West of Asia, I cannot help thinking it probable that a town called *Nazareth* will be found; as it is evident from the above, that there *is* or *was* a country called Nazarenee. As I have formerly observed, in the mountains at the back of the country where these Christians are found, upon the river Kistnah, is a town called ADONI, and another called Salem.[1] Let it not be forgotten that Adonis was Tammuz, and that Kistnah is Cristna.

The Christians of St. Thomas, as they are called, yet retain many of the old Brahmin customs, and are very different and quite distinct from the modern converts.[2] Part of them are said also to be rather lighter-coloured: this bespeaks them a tribe from the colder country of Cashmere or Afghanistan.

When I reflect upon what I have written respecting the Erythræan Sibyl, and that Justin Martyr says she told all the history of Christ, almost every thing which had happened to him, and that I have found the Tammuz or Adonis in the part of India where the Christians of St. Thomas were found, and compare it with what Parkhurst has said above respecting Tammuz, Adonis, &c., I can come to but one conclusion.

I must request my reader to look back to the description of *divine love* crucified, (Vol. I. p. 497,) and reconsider what has been said respecting Baliji, Wittoba, or Salivahana, the cross-borne, (ib. 667, 750, 764,) respecting the deaths and resurrections of Adonis, Æsculapius, &c., &c., &c.; and I think he will not be surprised to find a crucified Saviour among the Romans. This he will now see has been handed down to us on evidence in its nature absolutely unimpeachable. Minu-

---

[1] Vol. I. p. 666.   [2] Ibid. pp. 665, 666; and Asiat. Res. Vol. VII. p. 367.

tius Felix, a very celebrated Christian father, who lived about the end of the second century, in a defence of the Christian religion, called Octavius, has the following passage:

"You certainly who worship wooden Gods, are the most likely people to adore wooden crosses, "as being parts of the same substance with your Deities. For what else are your ensigns, "flags, and standards, but crosses gilt and purified? Your victorious trophies, not only represent "a simple cross, BUT A CROSS WITH A MAN ON IT. The sign of a cross naturally appears in a "ship, either when she is under sail or rowed with expanded oars, like the palm of our hands: "not a jugum erected but exhibits the sign of a cross: and when a pure worshiper adores the "true God with hands extended, he makes the same figure. Thus you see that the sign of the "cross has either some foundation in nature, or IN YOUR OWN RELIGION: and therefore not to be "objected against Christians."[1]

To whom could Cicero believe the acrostic of the Sibyl, mentioned in Volume I. pp. 574—576, applied? I now answer, to the crucified person commemorated on the standard, and who that might be, I ask the priests—for it is their order which has destroyed all the evidence respecting him. But I think few persons will now doubt that it was the BLACK crucified person whose effigy we see in thousands of places all over Italy—the Saviour crucified for the salvation of mankind, long before the Christian æra.

I think no unprejudiced person will doubt that the practice of the Romans, here alluded to by Minutius, of carrying a crucified man on their standard, has been concealed from us by the careful destruction of such of their works as alluded to it; and that its existence in the writing of Minutius is a mere oversight of the destroyers.

I cannot entertain any doubt that this celebrated Christian father alludes to some Gentile mystery, of which the prudence of his successors has deprived us. Perhaps the crucifixion of *divine love* in the person of Ixion, or Prometheus, or Semiramis. As I have shewn above, in the beginning of Christianity, Christ was not represented on a cross, but in the figure of a Lamb. This is proved by the decree of the Pope, which we have just seen, that he should no longer be represented as a Lamb, but as a Man on a Cross.

How great must have been the caution of the priests in leaving not a single Gentile, or, at least, Roman remnant of this crucified person, or any thing which could lead us to him, so that to this solitary, though very complete, Christian evidence, we are obliged for our knowledge of him! This consideration is quite enough to account for *lacunæ* in our copies of Tacitus, of Livy, of the Greek plays of Æschylus, Euripides, &c., &c.: for, to copies made by the hands of priests, we are indebted for every work of these authors which we possess.

How very extraordinary that not a single icon should be left! For their deficiency, there must be some other cause besides the astute care of the priests; and that cause is readily explained—the icons have become Christian crucifixes. Of these great numbers are to be seen in all Romish countries, which have every mark of extreme antiquity. It is the same with the very old pictures carrying the inscription, Deo Soli, and Soli Deo Mitræ, and Nama Sebadiah, which we have found in Kaliwakam, in the Tamul language in India, noticed in Volume I. p. 776, *note*, p. 779, and in the Appendix, p. 835. However, it is certainly proved as completely as it is possible in the nature of things for a fact of this nature to be proved, that the Romans had a crucified object of adoration, and this could be no other than an incarnation of the God Sol, represented in some way to have been crucified. It cannot be doubted that to mere accident we are indebted for the passage of Minutius Felix.

---

[1] Min. Fel. Sect. xxix.

How can any one doubt that this was the Lamb slain from the beginning of the world—the Solar Lamb incarnate? The Lamb of God slain as an atonement for the sins of the world may be Romish Christianity, and it may be true, but it is not the Gospel of Jesus, the Nazarite of Samaria.

I have no doubt whatever that there has been some mythos of the Χρηςος in the Greek and Roman Pantheons, which has been destroyed; and that, in innumerable places, the Χρηςος, in being copied by the priests, has been converted into Christos; and very greatly indeed are we indebted to Dr. Clarke for having honestly given us the inscription at or near Delphi.

I now beg my reader to look back to Vol. I. pp. 549—553, and there he will see the account of the prophecy of Apollo of Miletus. This Apollo was called Didymæus; Didymus means Twins. In this country there was a place called Thamas. There was also a town called Cresto-polis. There was a river Indus, a place called Sinda, a town called Calinda, also the city of Erythræa, an island of Calymna or C. lamina,[1] Mount Chalcis, Larissa, and the island of Crete,[2] called Candia[3] and *Icriti*.[4] I think in the Apollo Didymæus and the oracle of the incarnate person crucified by the Chaldæans, we cannot be blind to the mythos of Cristna and Salivahana, and the Calli-dei of South India at Çalamina, or St. Thomas, or the *twins*. Close to Rhodes is Portus Cresso, the Crestian Port.

In this country also is a Patara. Wherever we have an Apollo we have a mythos of Pataræ, or Patricius, or Patrick. Gen. Vallancey has traced the Miletii from Spain to Ireland. The people of Miletus are called Miletii. On this coast is an island of Calydonia, and a cape Kelidoni: I cannot doubt, though the colony might stop at some place in Spain, that it first came from this country, at which time came Calydonia to Scotland, and Patrick to Ireland, who brought the mythos of the God incarnate crucified by the Chaldæans—the God Icriti or Critika, which was both *bull* and *ram*—the God alluded to by Apollo of Miletus.

Col. Tod says, "When Alexander attacked the 'free cities' of Panchalica, the Poorus and "Hericŭlas, who opposed him, evinced the recollections of their ancestor, in carrying the figure "of Hercules as their standard."[5] Here, I have no doubt whatever, was the crucifix of Prometheus, of Ixion, of Cristna—the crucifix of Balii or the Lord (if Bal meant *Lord)* Ii—the crucifix which Father Georgius found set up at every cross road in Tibet—*(not observed by our English travellers,* though the Jesuit could see it)—the crucifix of Minutius Felix, and the crucifix *black* or *copper colour* at every point WHERE ROADS CROSS IN ITALY, (which will be accounted for by and by, when I treat of the Etruscan Agrimensores,) and in hundreds of the churches. In short, it was the peculiar emblem of the Pandean or Catholic religion; for *I have no doubt whatever,* that both these words have the meaning of *universal;* and *I suspect* that the perfect mythic history is yet secreted in the recesses of the conclaves of Tibet and Rome: and that, in ancient time, it was the doctrine of the Panionian temple at Ephesus, in Asia Minor, of the Pandion of Athens, and of the Ceres or Χρης of Eleusis and Delphi. In short, it was the universal *esoteric* religion of the world. Every common Catholic priest will swear to-day that he knows this to be false, and to-morrow he will get absolution for his oath, *for he knows nothing about it.* It is confided to very few persons—whether to TWELVE of the Cardinals may be matter of doubt. Here we see the reason why the Catholic Popes have every rite and ceremony of the ancient Heathens, as they are called, in their religion—the CATHOLIC religion. If I am mistaken, then the

---

[1] See Vol. I. p. 810.   [2] The French Chrétien.   [3] Candy or Ceylon.
[4] Evidently the Indian Kritika.   [5] Hist. Raj. Vol. I. p. 51, *note.*

Brahmins of Italy are precisely in the situation of the *Brahmins of India*, and have lost their secret system.

Where my friend Col. Tod learned the fact he has stated, respecting the standard, I do not know; but I suppose he borrowed it from Arrian, who says, that the troops of Porus, in their war with Alexander, carried on their standards the figure of a man. This must have been a Staurobates or Salivahana, and looks very like the figure of a man carried on their standard by the Romans. This was similar to the Dove carried on the standards of the Assyrians. This must have been the crucifix of Nepaul.

Georgius says,[1] " Ad hoc planè tam impiæ ac fœdæ superstitionis caput referri debent, quæ " de *secunda Trinitatis* Tibetanæ Persona narrat ex P. Andrada La Crozius in H. Chr. Ind. p. "514: ' Ils conviennent qu'il a répandu [Cho Conjoc] son sang pour le salut du genre humain, " 'ayant été percé de clous par tout son corps. Quoiqu'ils ne disent pas qu'il a souffert le " 'supplice de la croix, on en trouve pourtant la figure dans leurs livres : Leur grand Lama " 'célèbre une espèce de sacrifice avec du pain et du vin dont il prend une petite quantité, et " ' distribue le reste aux Lamas presens à cette cérémonie.' "

The Cambridge Key says, " Buddha, the author of happiness and a portion of Narayen, *the* " *Lord Haree-sa, the preserver of all,* appeared in this ocean of natural beings at the close of the " Dwapar, and beginning of the Calijug : He who is omnipotent, and everlastingly to be contem- " plated ; the Supreme God, the eternal ONE, the divinity worthy to be adored by the most pious " of mankind, appeared with a portion of his divine nature."[2] Jayadeva describes him as " bathing in blood, or sacrificing his life to wash away the offences of mankind, and thereby to " make them partakers of the kingdom of heaven. Can a Christian doubt that this Buddha was " the type of the Saviour of the world?"[3] Very well, I say to this learned Cantab, I will not dispute that the Cristna crucified, Baliji crucified, Semiramis crucified, Prometheus crucified, Ixion crucified, were all types of the Saviour, if it so please him; but let me not be abused for pointing out the facts. Type or not type must be left to every person's own judgment. On this subject I shall quarrel with no one. But then the Gentile religion must have been a whole immense type. This will prove Ammonius right that there was only one religion.

In the Apocalypse or Revelation, ch. xi. ver. 8, is a very extraordinary passage. It has two readings. In one it says that *your Lord* was crucified in Egypt, in the other, the received text, it says *our Lord* was crucified, &c. Griesbach says of the former *indubiè genuina*. This evidently alludes to the man crucified of Minutius Felix, who was thus crucified at Rome, in Egypt, Greece, India, at Miletus, &c. This is obviously a piece of Heathen mythology, of which, in the West, the priests have nearly deprived us ; but there is no room to doubt that it is one of the Salivahanas, Staurobateses, Baliis, Wittobas, Prometheuses, Semiramises, and Ixions, of the East. If we take the passage to mean *our Lord*, we have the Heathen or Gnostic cross-borne of Egypt, (for Christians do not pretend that Jesus was crucified in Egypt,) grafted on the Romish Christianity, like all their other rites and ceremonies. I have little doubt that the crucifixion of every Avatar, as it passed, was simultaneously celebrated at each of the five temples of Solomon in Egypt, wherein the Jewish prophet declares that the name of the true God shall be praised.

I have *some suspicion* also that the cross of Constantine was a crucifix. When he and Eusebius

---

[1] Alph. Tib. p. 211.

[2] In the Haree-sa, *the preserver of all*, we have the Hebrew הרה *ere* geneatrix, and ישׁע *ieo* the Saviour ; and in the Haree or Heri we have also the Greek Ερως, Divine Love, the Saviour of all.

[3] Camb. Key, Vol. I. p. 118.

were lying, (as Lardner has proved they were,) it was only taking the matter by halves not to take the *body* with the *cross*. However, this suspicion imports but little, as it is very clear that a *crucifix* was the object of adoration from the Indus to the Tibur; and I suspect even to the *fire tower* at Brechin, in Scotland.[1] Col. Tod says,[2] "The Heraclidæ claimed from Atreus: the "Hericûlas claim from Atri. Euristhenes was the first king of the Heraclidæ: Yoodishtra has "sufficient affinity in name to the first Spartan king, not to startle the etymologist, the *d* and *r*, "being always permutable in Sanscrit." Surely the identity of the Greek and Indian Hercules cannot be doubted, nor the identity of their ancestor Atreus?

It seems to me quite impossible for any person to have read the preceding part of this work with attention, and not to have felt convinced that there has originally been one universal mythos, repeated in a vast number of different and very distant places. It cannot be expected that the *whole* original mythos should be found any where; the eternal law of change forbids this: nor can it be expected that it should be found in every respect the same in any two places. This again the law of change forbids. For the mythos must change in *all* the places, and it is a million to one that in any two it should be found after several thousand years to have made in each the same change, so that at this time they should be exactly similar. But a sufficient degree of similarity is found to mark the fact, in great numbers of them, and in some really much greater than could have been expected. What can be more striking than that which we have found in Rome and Tibet?

In almost every mythos we see the same immaculate conception, the same ten months' pregnancy, the same attempts of an enemy to destroy the infant, the same triumph of the infant, his glorious and benevolent character and life, his final violent death, and his resurrection to life and immortality; and all this constantly connected with a town on seven hills, &c., &c., &c.

When I reflect deeply upon certain facts which cannot be disputed, and upon the identity of the worship of Tammuz, in Western Syria, of Tammuz in Egypt, and Tamus both in Northern and Southern India, that is, the two Eastern Syrias; upon the high probability, (shall I not say certainty?) that the Esseneans of Egypt and Western Syria were Pythagoreans and followers of the Χρης, that is, *Christians*, before the time of Jesus of Nazareth; upon the account of Christian doctrines in Southern India, given by the Jesuits—and upon the extraordinary fact that, when the work of Eusebius is properly translated, as given by the Rev. R. Taylor, the whole doctrine and church establishment of the Christians is found among the Esseneans in Egypt; I cannot help suspecting that the church of the Pagan Christian Constantine was nothing but the transplantation of the Essenes to the West, and that the secret, allegorical doctrines of these monks were those of the God Adonis, or Thamas, the Saviour re-incarnated or renewed every new cycle.

6. I presume it is well known to my reader, that in the first two centuries the professors of Christianity were divided into many sects; but these might be all resolved into two divisions— one consisting of Nazarenes, Ebionites, and Orthodox; the other of Gnostics, under which all the remaining sects arranged themselves. The former believed in Jesus Christ crucified, in the common, literal acceptation of the term; the latter, though they admitted the crucifixion, considered it to have been in some mystic way—perhaps what might be called *spiritualiter*, as it is called in the Revelation: but notwithstanding the different opinions they held, they all denied that Christ did really die, in the literal acceptation of the term, on the cross. These Gnostic or Oriental Christians took their doctrine from the Indian crucifixion of which we have just treated,

---

[1] See Celtic Druids, Introd. pp. xlvi. xlvii.　　　[2] Hist. Raj. Vol. I. p. 51, *note*.

as well as many other tenets with which we have found the Romish Church deeply tainted. This my reader must see will enable him to account for many extraordinary things.

I have already remarked, that the Pagan Roman crucifix was purposely concealed; for no one can doubt that there must have been some history connected with it. And persons may believe or not believe as the impressions on their minds or their prejudices may dictate; yet the evidence of the fact—the authority of Minutius—is complete and cannot be disputed, on any principle of sound criticism. And the fact must have been purposely concealed, or we should have had notice of it in some of the Roman historians or writers. I know that for honestly bringing forward this and many other facts, it will be said that I am not a Christian; at least by great numbers of those who will not allow any person to be a Christian who is not of their sect. I shall be accused of not believing the crucifixion, except as an allegory. But I may doubt this fact (though I expressly say, I do not here state my opinion upon it), and yet be a Christian, as much, at least, as the celebrated Christian Saint, Apologist, and Martyr, the orthodox writer against heresies, the Bishop of Lyons, Saint Irenæus, from whose works I have extracted the following passage. I think I surely have a right to call myself a Christian, if I am of the religion of this orthodox Saint and Martyr: but I repeat, at present, I do not state my opinion.

Lib. ii. Cap. xxxix. of Dr. Grabe's Irenæus has the following title: " Ostensio quod uno anno "non præconiaverit Dominus post baptismum; sed omnem habuisse ætatem." And it contains the following passage: " Omnes enim venit per semetipsum salvare: omnes inquam, qui per "eum renascuntur in Deum, infantes, et parvulos, et pueros, et juvenes, et seniores. Ideo per "omnem venit ætatem, et infantibus infans factus, sanctificans infantes: in parvulis parvulus, "sanctificans hanc ipsam habentes ætatem, simul et exemplum illis pietatis effectus, et justiciæ, "et subjectionis: in juvenibus juvenis, exemplum juvenibus fiens, et sanctificans Domino. Sic et "senior in senioribus, ut sit perfectus magister in omnibus, non solum secundum expositionem "veritatis, sed et secundum ætatem, sanctificans simul et seniores, exemplum ipsis quoque fiens: "deinde et usque ad mortem pervenit, ut sit[1] *primogenitus ex mortuis, ipse primatum tenens in* "*omnibus* princeps vitæ, prior omnium, et præcedens omnes. Illi autem, ut figmentum suum de eo "quod est scriptum, *vocare annum Domini acceptum*, affirment, dicunt uno anno eum prædicasse, "et duodecimo mense passum, contra semetipsos obliti sunt, solventes ejus omne negocium, et "magis necessariam, et magis honorabilem ætatem ejus auferentes, illam, inquam, provectiorem, "in qua edocens præerat universis. Quomodo enim habuit discipulos, si non docebat? Quo- "modo autem docebat, magistri ætatem non habens? Ad baptismum enim venit nondum qui "triginta annos suppleverat, sed qui inciperet esse tanquam triginta annorum: (ita enim, qui "ejus annos significavit Lucas, posuit: Jesus *autem erat quasi incipiens triginta annorum*, cum "veniret ad baptismum): et à baptismate uno tantùm anno prædicavit; complens trigesimum "annum, passus est, adhuc juvenis existens, et qui necdum provectiorem haberet ætatem. Quia "autem triginta annorum ætas prima indolis est juvenis, et extenditur usque ad quadragesimum "annum, omnis quilibet confitebitur: à quadragesimo autem et quinquagesimo anno declinat jam "in ætatem seniorem: quam habens Dominus noster docebat, sicut Evangelium ' et omnes "' seniores testantur, qui in Asiâ apud Joannem discipulum Domini convenerunt, id ipsum tradi- "' disse eis Joannem. Permansit autem cum eis usque ad Trajani tempora.' "

Και παντες οι πρεσβυτεροι μαρτυρουσιν, οι κατα την Ασιαν Ιωαννη τω τυ Κυριυ μαθητη

Coloss. i. 18.

συμβεβληκοτες,[1] παραδεδωκεναι ταυτα την Ιωαννην· παρεμεινε γαρ αυτοις μεχρι των Τραιανε χρονων. Quidam autem eorum non solum Joannem, sed et alios Apostolos viderunt, et hæc eadem ab ipsis audierunt, et testantur de hujusmodi relatione."

"A demonstration that the Lord preached after his baptism not (merely) for one year; but that he employed (in preaching) the whole term of his life. For he came to save all through himself: all I say who through him are born again to God—infants, little children, boys, youths, and old people. Therefore he came (preached) in every stage of life: and made an infant with infants, sanctifying infants: a child among children, sanctifying those of the same age as himself: and at the same time supplying an example to them of piety, of justice, and of submission: a youth among youths, becoming an example to youths, and sanctifying them to the Lord. So also an elder among elders, that the teacher might be perfect in all things, not only according to the exposition (law or rule) of truth, but also according to the period of life—and sanctifying at the same time the elders, becoming an example even to them: after that he came to *death* that he might be the first-born from the dead, he himself having pre-eminence in all things, the prince of life, above all, and excelling all. But to establish their own forgery that it is written of him, *to call* (it?) *the acceptable year of the Lord,* they say against themselves that he preached (during) one year (only?) and suffered on the twelfth month (of it?) They have forgotten—giving up every (important?) affair of his, and taking away the more necessary, the more honourable, and, I say, that more advanced period of his, in which, teaching diligently, he presided over all. For how did he obtain disciples if he did not teach? And how did he teach—not having attained the age of a master (or doctor?) For *he* came to baptism who had not yet completed thirty years of age: (for thus Luke who indicates his years lays it down: and *Jesus* was as it were entering on thirty years when he came to baptism:) and after (his?) baptism he preached only one year:—(on) completing his thirtieth year he suffered (death) being as yet only a young man, who had not attained maturity. But as the chief part of thirty years belongs to youth, (or, and a person of thirty may be considered a young man?) and every one will confess him to be such till the fortieth year: but from the fortieth to the fiftieth year he declines into old age, *which our Lord having attained he taught* as the Gospel, and all the elders who, in Asia assembled with John the disciple of the Lord, *testify,* and (as) John himself had taught them. *And he* (John?) remained with them till the time of Trajan. And some of them saw not only John but other apostles, and heard the same things from them, and bear the same testimony to this revelation."

Although this passage is very difficult to translate, arising probably from a wish of the translator out of the Greek into the Latin, to disguise the true meaning; yet it is evident that Irenæus accuses the other party of FORGERY, in representing Jesus to have been put to death only one year after he began his ministry. But I shall discuss this more at length in a future book.

I do not doubt that what I have said respecting the evidence of Irenæus will excite great surprise, and probably smiles of contempt in many persons; but I call upon all such individuals, not to give way to their vulgar prejudices, but to try this evidence by the rules by which evidence is examined in a court of justice. This is the only way of bringing the matter to a fair decision; but I believe there are very few, of even educated persons, who ever think upon the nature or value of evidence, or know that the consideration of the subject is of any consequence. This is the

---

[1] "(Συμβεβληκοτες) Ita Eusebius loco citato et Nicephorus, Lib. iii. Cap. ii. Sed in Georgii Sincelli Chronographia p. 345, edit. Paris, 1652, excuderunt συμβεβηκοτες, et ne quid varietatis dicit, in margini posuerunt συμβεβιωκοτες."

reason why so much nonsense is found to be believed, even by persons who, on other topics, evince a sound and discriminating judgment.

From this passage of St. Irenæus's, which has so fortunately escaped the hands of the destroyers, we learn the fact which cannot be disputed, that the doctrine of Christ crucified, preached in so pointed a manner by St. Paul, was, to say the least of it, a *vexata questio* among Christians even in the second century: this shews that we are merely a sect of Paulites.[1]

If Col. Wilford may be believed, the orthodox were not the only persons who disputed the age of Christ. Speaking of the sectaries, he says, " Some insisted that he lived *thirty, thirty-three, forty,* and others nearly but not quite *fifty*-years. Stephanus Gobarus has collected many of these idle notions, in the extracts made of his works by Photius."[2] They may be idle notions in the opinion of Col. Wilford, but they support the evidence of Irenæus, and what I have said, that it was a *vexata questio*.

Every oriental scholar knows, that Sir William Jones, Wilford, &c., have proved that the God Indra, of India, is the Jupiter Pluvialis of Greece; and I have proved that Jupiter is the God Iao of the Hebrews, and the Jesus of the Romish church. Then we have Iao crucified on a tree,[3] in Nepaul. See my figures, Number 14. I beg my reader to turn to the map; he will there find, in the Golden peninsula or Chersonesus, the Crysen or country of $X\rho\eta\varsigma$,[4] the kingdom of Judea and Mount Sion at the top of it. In Nepaul and Tibet there are the Eastern Pope and his monks, &c., and a *crucified* God. Again, in the promontory of India, in the South, at Tanjore, and in the North, at Oude or Ayoudia, there are the crucified God Bal-li, St. Thomas, Montes Solumi, sons of David, icons of Noah, Job, Seth, &c., &c.: and again, in the West, there are Bacchus, Osiris, Atys, &c., &c., all put to death and raised the third day; and this done, let him declare what he thinks of it. If he be satisfied, with Parkhurst, that all these things are *types or symbols of what the real Saviour was to do and suffer,* then I ask him to say what he thinks of the evidence of Irenæus, that the real Jesus of Nazareth was not crucified by Pontius Pilate. Perhaps he will not believe Irenæus: then do I tell him, that Irenæus, in a court of justice, is evidence conclusive, that he heard, as stated, from the old men of Asia, &c., &c., and, if the reader do not believe him, he entertains an opinion contrary to evidence. I maintain, that the evidence of Irenæus is the best evidence which we possess of the death of Jesus Christ; because it is the evidence of an unwilling witness. This brings to recollection the doctrine formerly noticed, of certain heretics maintaining, that Christ was crucified in the heavens; that is, I suppose, in the רקיע rqio of the second verse of Genesis. It also reminds me that Justin Martyr, after Plato, maintained him to have been described on the world or universe in the form of a cross.[5] All these facts, which tend to one point, cannot, I think, mean *nothing;* and this leads me to a suspicion, that there lies hidden under them a most important and profound part of the esoteric religion. The Chrēstos, $X\rho\eta\varsigma$-ος, was the Logos; the Sun was the Shekinah or Manifestation of the Logos or Wisdom to men; or, as it was held by some, it was his peculiar habitation. The sun was crucified when he seemed to cross the plane of the Equator at the vernal equinox. He was slain at every passover; but he was also slain in his passage, at the vernal equinox, from Taurus to Aries; and this is described by the young man slaying the Bull in the Mithraic ceremonies, and the slain lamb at the

---

[1] Paul was, however, preceded by *Peter* in preaching *Christ crucified.* (See Acts ii. 23, 24, 32, iii. 13—18.) Might not believers in the doctrine of " Christ crucified," therefore, be as justly denominated " merely a sect of *Peterites*" as " of *Paulites*"? *Editor.*

[2] Asiat. Res. Vol X. p. 93. [3] Georgius, p. 202. [4] Ibid. p. 348. [5] Vol. I. pp. 788, 789.

foot of the cross in the Christian ceremonies. The man Jesus was the Logos, or Divine Wisdom, or a portion of Divine Wisdom incarnate: in this sense he was really the sun or the solar power incarnate, and to him every thing applicable to the sun will apply. He was the Logos crucified in the heavens; he was the being described, according to Justin, in the heavens, in the form of a cross, and when the man Jesus taught the Chrèst Χρηστ *crucified*, this, or something like it, I suspect, was the doctrine which he taught. When we find from Irenæus that he was not murdered or killed, all we can make out of our four gospel-histories is, that they were allegories, parables, apologues, to conceal the secret doctrine. The evidence of Irenæus cannot be touched. On every principle of sound criticism, and of the doctrine of probabilities, it is unimpeachable. The doctrine I here suggest unites all the discordances of every kind. I know that a great outcry will be made at me for saying that Jesus Christ was the sun. In the *vulgar acceptation* of the words, I can only say that this is not true. But that Jesus or the Logos was believed to be a portion of ethereal fire by every one of the early fathers, is a fact; whether their belief was true or not, is another question. He was the Χρης of India; He was the χρης-αν of the Tamul, which had *en* for its termination; the Cres-us of the Sanscrit, and the Chres-us of the Latin, which had *us* for their terminations.

The ancient philosophers being much too refined and correct in their ideas to take up with the vulgar opinion, formed in a comparatively barbarous period, that the world was created by *spirit*, that is, *air in motion*, (the correct and *only proper meaning* of the word spirit, if it have any definable meaning) were driven to have recourse either to a refined igneous principle, in fact, to fire, or to use the word *illusion*. And they came to the last, because they found, on deep reflection, that they could form no idea of the First Cause; but of the emanations from it, they could; and, therefore, they conceived that the Creator was a refined fire, emanating from the Το Ον, or from the *illusory* unknown being. All the mistakes of moderns arise from inattention to Locke's unquestionable doctrine, that man can possess no ideas which he does not receive through the medium of his senses; consequently, man erroneously fancies he has *an idea* of an unknown existence, called spirit or a spiritual being—an unknown existence, which he chooses to call by a word that means *air in motion*. This unknown Πατηρ αγνωστος the philosophers called the Το Ον—surely a much better word than that which only meant *air in motion*. But, in fact, by this nonsensical word, the moderns contrive to deceive themselves, and gratify their malice by separating themselves from the ancient philosophers, who, if alive, would be very much ashamed to be of their company.

The view which I here take of this subject perfectly reconciles the passage of Irenæus in question, with the passages where he quotes our four gospel histories. I cannot conceive any other mode of reconciling them. Let those who disapprove it produce a better. All this is in perfect keeping with the whole of the esoteric doctrines of Jews, Gentiles, and Christians; and all this will be confirmed still more by the examination of our four gospel histories into which I shall enter in a future book, and which I shall shew were intended for the purpose of concealing a secret system. No one can deny that these books are full of parables: *without a parable spake he not unto them*. The whole is a parable, which covers the esoteric religion—a parable which it was impossible for the popes to explain to persons afflicted with insanity, like Luther and Calvin.

7. In the Old Monthly Magazine, in the numbers for October 1803, p. 221, Nov. 1803, p. 305, May 1815, p. 308, will be found a curious inquiry into the question, Who wrote Wisdom? In the same Magazine for December 1815, p. 407, August 1817, p. 35, Nov. 1817, p. 313, Who was the author of Ecclesiasticus? And in January 1818, p. 505, and in August 1818, p. 36, Who was the author of Sirach? A careful perusal of those essays will clearly shew, why these books have been

determined by the church, or rather, I should say, by modern priests, to have been written after the time of Jesus of Nazareth. They are *refused* by Protestants because they never knew any thing of *esoteric* Christianity. They were *received* by the members of the Romish church, because they understood the *esoteric* Christianity. I must beg my reader to recollect what I have said, in Volume I. p. 198, of the renewed avatars or incarnations of the Jews, then I think he will see from the following essay, January 1818, p. 505, an example of a crucifixion before the time of Jesus Christ among the Jews to match the crucifixions of Buddha and Cristna, and the Christ of the Romans.

"The claim of the son-of-godship at Jerusalem, however legally vested in the house of Hillel,
" was practically usurped by the house of Herod. If the representative of David was king *de jure*,
" the tetrarch was king *de facto*. In the eye of the reigning dynasty, whoever claimed to be Son
" of God advanced a treasonable claim; and under a constitution so strictly theocratic as to iden-
" tify the sovereign and the Lord, (see, for instance, Exod. xxxv. 30,) would technically be in-
" dicted for blasphemy. Some such accusation (xi.) our Jesus incurred, was in consequence
" crucified, interred, and rose again from the sepulchre. Here is his own account of this extraor-
" dinary and momentous incident of his life.

" ' By an accusation to the king from an unrighteous tongue, my soul drew near even unto death,
" and my life near unto the hell beneath. They compassed me on every side, and there was no
" man to help me; I looked for the succour of men, but there was none.'"—Ecclesiasticus li. 6 and 7.

"They said, 'He professeth to have the knowledge of God, and he called himself the child of the
" Lord. He was made to reprove our thoughts: he is grievous unto us even to behold; for his
" life is not like other men's,—his ways are of another fashion. We are esteemed of him as
" counterfeits: he abstaineth from our ways as from filthiness: he pronounceth the end of the just
" to be blessed, and maketh his boast that God is his father. Let us see if his words be true;
" and let us prove what shall happen in the end of him: for if the just man be the Son of God, he
" will help him, and deliver him from the hand of his enemies. Let us examine him with despite-
" fulness and torture, that we may know his meekness and prove his patience: let us condemn
" him with a shameful death; for by his own saying he shall be respected.'—Wisdom ii. 13—20.
" ' Thou art my defender and helper; thou hast preserved my body from destruction, and from the
" snare of the slanderous tongue, and from the lips that forge lies, and hast been my helper against
" my adversaries; and hast delivered me from the teeth of them that were ready to devour me,
" and out of the hands of such as sought after my life, and from the manifold afflictions which I
" had,—from the depth of the belly of hell, from an unclean tongue, and from lying words.'—Ecclesiasticus li. 2, 3, 5.

"But one inference is possible: there cannot have been two Menechmi[1] at Jerusalem, both
" named Jesus; both born of a virgin, to whom a miraculous conception was imputed; both edu-
" cated in the temple; both sent into Egypt; both undertaking a mission to reform the Jewish
" church, and lecturing to that effect in Solomon's porch; both claiming to be the Son of God at
" Jerusalem; both arraigned for blasphemy; both crucified; both interred; and both reserved for
" resurrection from the sepulchre. Yet all these things are true of the son of Sirach by his own
" shewing." But there *were* two Menechmi at Jerusalem. I do not doubt that there were nine or ten of them. They were all Jesuses or Saviours.

---

[1] Construed *comforters*: but I suspect we have here the Celtic word mannus and חכמ *hkm, man of wisdom*. I think it probable that the word has had both meanings.

I think no person will be surprised at the above, or will have any difficulty, who recollects the proofs which I have given of the identity of the Jewish and Gentile systems; and the numerous immaculate conceptions, crucifixions, and resurrections, of the Gods of the Gentiles, of the East and West.[1]

The book of Ecclesiasticus, or the wisdom of Jesus, the Son of Sirach, is much corrupted, and its parts dislocated. It was written by a different author from the book of Wisdom. As we might expect, it is called *the book of parables*.[2] The translation of this book of the Romish church was not made by Jerom, but is found in what is called their older Vulgate, but by whom that book was made they do not know. Jerom says he saw it in Hebrew.[3] But the learned Calmet makes a most important observation, the effect of which he does not see, which at once proves that the translation is much older than the Christian æra. He observes, that the translator uses *obsolete words*: thus he puts *honestas* for riches, *honestus* for a rich man, *respectus* or *visitatio* for the punishment of God on wicked men; *supervacuitas* for vanity or vain glory; *animalia supervacua* for dangerous or noxious animals. When I consider that we have the Mosaic mythos intermixed with that of the Gentiles in the Sibyl, which contained all things related of Jesus Christ,—that Clemens let out, that the same mythos[4] was to be found in the mysteries of Eleusis, and many other circumstances described in the preceding parts of this work—I cannot help suspecting that the counterpart of the crucified person described by Minutius, is to be found in these two works. It is a very important fact, that the whole of the mythos which I have given from the Monthly Magazine is taken in part from the book of Ecclesiasticus, and in part from that of the Wisdom of Solomon, hereby affording a high probability, that the whole mythos was originally in each of them; but that it has been destroyed, or at least so much mutilated in each book as to render it in each case unobservable on slight inspection. In fact, after the time of Christ, it would be disliked equally by Jews and Christians. Of course the Jews have not these books in their Canon, because they have no books in their Canon after Haggai, who lived long before the entrance of the sun into Pisces, or the time when this eighth or ninth avatar was supposed to have lived; but the two books most clearly prove that, in the secret history of the Jews, they had the history of the crucified Avatars like the Gentiles, and that it was *their secret doctrine*.

I now beg my reader to look back to the Appendix to Volume I. p. 832, and to observe what I have said respecting the Gospel of John, found in the vault under the ancient Jewish temple. I have there noticed a pillar under the Temple of Jerusalem, on which we are told, by Nicephorus Callistus, that the Gospel of John was found, to which I beg my reader to refer. I have there said, that I thought nothing was more likely than that this gospel should have been concealed there from a time long anterior to the Christian æra. Here were concealed, in the temple, the leading Gnostic doctrines as displayed by me in the last chapter of the first volume, and the history of Jesus the son of Sirach, which we have just read, and which would as evidently apply to the history of the Jesus of the *eighth* age, as to the Jesus of the *ninth* age. The Christians have evidently got possession of this book, and have accommodated it to the history of Jesus, the Nazarite of Samaria. It is of no use to meet this by shewing parts in John's gospel which would not apply to Jesus of Sirach. Mr. Evanson has proved, (in his Dissonance of the Gospels,) that this Gospel was never written by persons connected with Judæa, and that it is full of interpolations, almost from

---

[1] See Calmet's Dict. on the word WISDOM, for some information on this subject. This reminds me of the account in Enoch of the *Elect one slain*, noticed in Volume I. p. 549.

[2] Rees's Ency.   [3] Ibid.   [4] Vide Appendix to Vol. I. p. 838.

one end to the other. It was accommodated to what was wanted, though in some respects awkwardly enough; for the first chapter betrays the Gnosis and Cabala in every line.[1]

Perhaps I shall be told, that the story of the book of John having been found in the crypt of the ancient temple is a forgery of the Papists'. Protestant devotees easily dispose of unpleasant facts, and blind themselves by such kind of assertions; and undoubtedly their brother Paulites of Rome have given them plausible grounds enow for them. But it must be asked, in this case, Why the Christians, after the time of Constantine, should wish to teach that *the Jews* concealed the Gospel of John, in so solemn a manner, in this the most sacred place of their temple? Here I am quite certain, if persons would put aside their vulgar prejudices they would see, that there is a high probability that the story of Nicephorus, as far as the finding of the book goes, is true, and that all the remainder of his story is made up to accommodate the fact to his gospel history or Christian faith. I believe it is maintained both by the Papist and Protestant churches, that the gospel history of John was not written till after the burning of the temple. But whether written before or after that event, who should put it into the Jewish crypt? It was directly against the *interest* of the Christians to have put it there, as well as against that of the Jews, unless it formed a part, as I have suggested, of the Jewish secret Cabala. Supposing the Gospel of John to have been put into the crypt by the Jews, what could have been their object? If they believed the book, they were instantly Christians. If they did not, they must have detested and not venerated it. All Christians hold that from long before the time of the writing of John, the gospel histories of the other three evangelists had been written, and universally dispersed in the world, and that the book of John had been in like manner dispersed from the time it was composed.

The books of Ecclesiasticus and Wisdom most clearly prove, that the Jews had the mythos, and that it was a secret also. All this tends wonderfully to support the whole of the theory of the secret doctrines and mythos which I have been unfolding.

Suppose it a pure, unadulterated lie of Callistus': for what object did he lie? People seldom lie without some object. It could add no credibility to the genuineness of this book, written, as every one must know, in that day, if it were the fact, long after the destruction of the detested temple. It is very improbable, given as that age was to lying, that Callistus should risk so absurd and so unnecessary a lie. The probability is, *on the evidence*, that the story is true, and that all the appendages told about the temple by Callistus, are awkward lies to endeavour to account for this disagreeable, and, to him probably, unaccountable fact.

We are not to suppose that the book found and called the Gospel of John would be, word for word, the same as that which we have; a loose and general resemblance would be quite sufficient to cause and to justify the assertion of Callistus. The whole, in a very striking manner, supports and justifies what I have said in Volume I. p. 188, respecting the Jewish incarnations; and it also supports, in a striking manner, the doctrine which I have held, that the $\chi\rho\eta\varsigma$-tian mythos was the secret mystery of Eleusis, Delphi, and, indeed, of all nations.

The observations of the learned Calmet that the Latin language, into which the books of Ecclesiasticus and Wisdom are translated, was obsolete, is very important, as tending to shew, that the doctrine of a crucified God existed in Italy from a time long anterior to the Christian æra.

---

[1] I refer those persons, who cannot reconcile their minds to the dearth of information in the Jewish books respecting the different avatars, to Mr. Whiston's *Essay on the True Text of the Old Testament*, for a decisive proof that these books have been very greatly corrupted since the Christian æra, and corrupted, too, *for the express purpose of concealing every thing respecting our Messiah or any Messiah or Avatar*. I have on another occasion praised the Jews for not corrupting their books; more inquiry has proved to me, that my praise was very unmerited.

I must now beg my reader to review all the different accounts of the mythos which he has seen in all quarters of the world—lastly, taking that of Tibet, the part of the world whence the Ioudi came, and let him consider all the proofs of the identity between it and Rome—the same monks and monasteries, nuns and nunneries, by the same names of Beguines, (Romish monks and Beguine nuns, as it will be said, founded by Nestorians,) the same *tria vota constantialia*, the same tonsures and dresses, the three sacraments of orders, eucharist, and baptism, and many other things,—and I think he will at once be obliged to allow, that there are in both the remains of the same mythos which I have been describing. In Rome, in its rites and ceremonies, it remains almost perfect, and in Tibet nearly the same.

8. I now request my reader to turn to the history of Pythagoras, given in Volume I. pp. 150, 151, and to consider carefully all the particulars enumerated respecting him, as they so remarkably coincide with the gospel history of Jesus Christ; then to p. 168; then to p. 210, and observe the close connexions of the Indian avatars and the date of Pythagoras; and, lastly, to pp. 95, 96, of this book, and I am quite certain he must admit the identity of the two mythoses, histories, parables, or whatever he may choose to call them, of Jesus and Pythagoras. Mr. Kuster, Dr. John Jones, and other devotees, have endeavoured to disguise to themselves the fact, by assuming that Porphyry, Jamblicus, and others, who have written respecting Pythagoras, have copied the life of Jesus Christ in order to run down the Christians: but unfortunately for these writers their fine-spun web is at once broken to pieces by the observation of *honest* old Maurice, that the most important facts are taken from the works of authors who lived before the Christian æra.

Now I contend that, when all the peculiar circumstances are taken into consideration, there is a high probability that in the *man crucified* of Minutius, we have Pythagoras; and that the Christians, from whom we receive all our books, have suppressed the history of the crucifixion, and inserted in the place of it the story, that Pythagoras was burnt in his house by the populace. We must not forget that he established his school at Cortona, which I have shewn, in Volume I. p. 787, was the same as Cristona, and that we learn from Jerom, that one of the earliest of the names borne by the Christians, was the same as that of South India, Crestons,—of India, whence we have seen the Camasene, the Loretto, the Pallatini, the Saturnia, &c., &c., came to Italy.

There can be no doubt that wisdom is a quality of man which can never be desired too much, or appreciated too highly. An idle attempt has been made to divide what is called the wisdom of man from the wisdom of God, and the wisdom of man has been called foolishness. It is only necessary to say to this, that if it be foolishness, it is not wisdom. Nothing can be wisdom, that is, *really wisdom*, which does not include within it every thing necessary to man's WELFARE in the most extensive sense of the word,—*welfare* here and hereafter. Hence it is very apparent that man can only *approximate* to a state of wisdom. From this beautiful and refined view of the subject has arisen the idea that this godlike quality, in fact, well deserving to be classed among the Divine attributes, was incarnated in some degree in every human being. This gives us the explanation of the Hindoo assertion, that there have been hundreds of thousands of incarnations. Whenever we get to the bottom of the doctrines of these people, we are sure to find that they, the *sages* of old, possessed no small or common share of the quality we here treat of.[1]

But though, on a superficial consideration of this subject, we may be led to assign this attribute

---

[1] Probably the *seven wise men* of Greece were the Genii or divine incarnations of Wisdom or the Logos of the seven cycles, misunderstood by the Greeks, which had preceded the times of the authors who lived in the cycle preceding the Christian æra, which made the eighth before Christ. Of the person who was the Hero of that age, of course they could not speak with certainty. Perhaps they sought him in Alexander the Great.

to the Supreme Being, yet the profound sages of India, the Pythagorases of the East, did not dare to assign it to the Supreme as an attribute or quality; but they assigned it, in the only way they could do so, viz. by way of an emanation, from the Supreme to the Trimurti or Trinity. If it be said by objectors, that the Supreme, the Πατηρ αγνωςος, could not cause it to emanate from him, if he had it not; the reply is, that substance and all matter are, according to the doctrine of these objectors, in the same predicament; and here we arrive again at the true meaning of the *illusion*. How can WE know what are the attributes of the To Ον—of the Πατηρ αγνωςος; how vain and monstrous to attribute to Him any thing of which we have only received a knowledge through the fallible medium of OUR senses! All above the Trimurti is *illusion*, as is indeed the Trimurti itself. It is impossible to conceive a word more appropriate. It is the Maia; it is the Brahme-Maia.

I now beg my *learned* reader to bear this in mind, and then to turn to his Cruden's Concordance and read the texts which he will find there under the head of Wisdom. My *unlearned* reader, not used to consult Cruden, if any such should ever dip into this passage of my work, may consult the Apocryphal books of Wisdom and Ecclesiasticus; and, lastly, he may consult the book of Ayub or Job,[1] brought from Upper India to Arabia; from which beautiful and sublime allegory, if he understand it, he may really learn Wisdom,—a wisdom more precious, indeed, than the compass to the mariner,[2]—wisdom, indeed, above all price—the wisdom of patience and submission to the Divine decree—an humble resignation and contentment with our lot, and a firm reliance on the goodness of the Supreme Creator, as designing ultimately, although perhaps through temporary misery, to bring us to eternal happiness.[3]

Whenever the Holy Ghost was described as given to man, it was in the form of fire, if visible to the eye. Its effects always were, wisdom accompanied by power; but the power was never supposed to exist independently of the wisdom. This wisdom was the Holy Ghost, as we have seen, and whenever we closely analyse this, we always find the igneous principle at the bottom. Is it, then, a wonder, that we find the ancient Indian, Chaldean, or Collidean Ioudi, and the Persians, in the earliest and most uncorrupted state of their religion, offering their adoration to the solar fire, either as the emblem of the creative wisdom and power, or as the Wisdom and Power itself? Is it not surprising that the popes, in their anxiety to support this doctrine, should have yielded to the popular wish in adopting the rites and ceremonies with which the ancient system, in fact the system of the real γνωσις, was always accompanied?

To understand perfectly all the beauties of the doctrine of Wisdom, much and profound meditation on the word is necessary. It must be considered in all its bearings, which are almost innumerable.

---

[1] The least attention to the names of the actors in Genesis and Job will shew that they are parts of the same mythos.

[2] Job xxviii. 18: "*For the price of wisdom is above rubies.*" This ought to be rendered, *For the price of wisdom is above the loadstone* or *magnets*, (see CELTIC DRUIDS, p. 113,) and, consequently, above the mariner's compass, well known to the ancients. But how beautiful is the simile of the magnet or loadstone to the Supreme and to wisdom—causing to emanate and its invisible power or influence to draw to it the iron—and, again, pointing at its pleasure to its favourite north—where it "sits in the sides of the north," guiding amidst the dangerous shoals and quicksands the benighted mariner! All this, and much more, is lost in the nonsensical *rubies*.

[3] If we consider the Chaldee language of South and North India to be the same, and that language to be the origin of the Tamul, we shall have no difficulty in thinking it probable that the principal actor in the book of Job, Eliphaz the *Teman*-ite or Tm-an-ite, was a Tamulite; the syllable *an* in To-man being only the terminating *en*, which we know was a peculiarity of this language. We must not forget the Tamul Kaliowakim, which can, in fact, be called nothing but a book of wisdom, if the book in our canon deserves the name. The Persians had their book of Sophi or Wisdom; so had the Jews; and so had the Tams—no doubt written in their alphabet of sixteen letters. See Jeremiah xlix. 7. The Goddess Cali was from the Greek Καλος *beautiful*, and the Latin Calleo and Callidus, *a cunning* or *wise person*.

9. If we turn our minds back to what we have seen, we shall find with the Romish church every rite of Paganism; every thing which has been disguised by being charged to the Gnostics is found there, without a single exception. Irenæus was evidently a Gnostic. If he were not, how came he to place the Zodiac on the floor of his church? a part of which, not worn away by the feet of devotees, is yet remaining. He was of the sect of the Christ *not* crucified. How is all this to be accounted for, except that what the first Christian fathers all taught was true, namely, that there was an *esoteric* and an *exoteric* religion? A great part of what I have unfolded, indeed almost the whole of it, applies to the Gnostics; that is, to the Jesus described by the disputed chapters of Matthew and Luke—to Jesus of Bethlehem. St. Paul preaches, in a very pointed manner, *Christ crucified;* this was in opposition to the Christ *not* crucified of the Gnostics; and, in later times, of the Manichæans and Mohamedans. Gnosticism was the secret religion of the conclave. They had Jesus of Bethlehem for the people, Jesus of Nazareth for the conclave and the cardinals. For the people, they had and have *Jesus crucified;* for the conclave, Jesus *not* crucified. This will appear to many persons at first absolutely incredible. Most fortunately the church has been guilty of the oversight of letting the passage of Irenæus escape. One of the earliest, most celebrated, most respected, and most quoted authority of its ancient bishops, saints, and martyrs, tells us in distinct words, that Jesus was *not* crucified under Herod and Pontius Pilate, but that he lived to be turned fifty years of age. This negatives the whole story of Herod and Pontius Pilate. This he tells us on the authority of his master St. Polycarp, also a martyr, who had it from St. John himself, and from *all the old people of Asia.* It will, perhaps, be said, that Irenæus was a weak old man. He was not always old, and he must have heard this when young, under his master Polycarp, and have retained the knowledge of it during his whole life, and thus must have had plenty of time to inquire into the truth of what he had heard; and, weak or not, he was a competent witness to the dry matter of fact, viz. that he was told it by St Polycarp and the elders of Asia.

The escape of this passage from the destroyers can be accounted for only in the same way as the passage of Minutius Felix. Two passages escaped, among, probably, thousands destroyed, of which we know nothing, under the decrees of the Emperors, yet remaining, by which they were ordered to be destroyed.

We have seen great numbers of remains of the mythos of the different incarnations of the Buddhas, Cristnas, Salivahanas, &c., in India, recurring again and again in each cycle, as foretold by the Cumæan and Erythræan Sibyl, before the time of Christ. We have seen all the things which happened to the Χρεισος foretold before his birth. We have seen that the mythos of the crucifix was common to all nations, before the time of Jesus of Nazareth, from Thule to China. Whenever our travellers in India found any nations holding the doctrines of this universal mythos, the history of Adonis or Tammuz, which, of course, though substantially the same, vary in the detail, they instantly determined them to be corrupted Christians. A similar effect took place in Italy. The ancient proofs of this mythos were either destroyed as *corruptions,* or *adopted:* the latter was the case in vast numbers of very ancient crucifixes and paintings of the Bambino, on which may be seen the words *Deo Soli.* Now these two words can never apply to Jesus Christ. He was not Deus *Solus* in any sense, according to the idiom of the Latin language and the Romish faith. Whether we construe the words to *the only God,* or to *God alone,* they are equally heretical. No priest in any age of the church would have thought of putting them there. But finding them there, they tolerated them. Without examination they took for granted that they could apply to no one but their God, and endeavoured to explain away their *Unitarian* meaning as well as they were able. These considerations most satisfactorily account for the disappearance of the *heathen*

VOL. II.   s *crucifix* in Italy, India, and Britain. Where it was not destroyed it was adopted. The passage of Minutius Felix places its existence out of reasonable doubt.

Upon the fire tower at Brechin, described in my CELTIC DRUIDS, pp. xlvi., xlvii., plate 24, we have the man crucified and the Lamb and Elephant. As I have said there, I thought these completely proved the modern date of the tower, but I now doubt this; for we have, over and over again, seen the *crucified man* before Christ. We have also found " the Lamb which taketh away the sins of the world" among the Carnutes of Gaul, before the time of Christ. And when I couple these and the Elephant, or Ganesa, and the ring, and its cobra, Linga, Iona, and Nandies, found not far from the tower on the estate of Lord Castles, with the Colidei, the Island of Iona and Ii, and the Hebrew names, &c., found in Wales, I am induced to doubt my former conclusion. The Elephant, the Ganesa of India, is a very stubborn fellow to be found here. The ring, too, when joined with the other matters, I cannot get over. All these superstitions must have come from India whilst the Hebrew, that is, Celtic language, was in use.

That the ideas of the Trinitarian character of the Deity should be taken from the doctrines of the ancient philosophers, will surprise no one who considers how much they are praised by the most respectable of the Christian fathers—I speak of Clemens Alexandrinus, Justin, Ammonius Saccas, Origen, &c. Clemens expressly says, that the rudiments of celestial wisdom, taught by Christ, may be found in the philosophy of the Greeks; this is Esoteric Christianity. And Justin says, that Socrates was a Christian, and that, before the advent of Jesus Christ, philosophy was the way to eternal life. He calls it $M\varepsilon\gamma\iota\varsigma o\nu$ $\kappa\tau\eta\mu\alpha$, " a thing most acceptable in the sight of God, and the only sure guide to a state of perfect felicity." The opinion of the early fathers on this subject may be seen at length in Vol. II. of Vidal's translation of the Commentaries of Mosheim, note, p. 114.

The division of the secret Christian religion into *three* degrees, the same as the division at Eleusis, namely, *Purification, Initiation,* and *Perfection,* described in my *first* Volume, p. 822, is of itself sufficient under the circumstances to prove the secret religions of the Christians and Gentiles to be the same.

In Mosheim's Commentaries, Cent. II., may be found almost innumerable proofs, that a double meaning was universally, or very nearly universally, acknowledged to be contained in the gospel histories, until after the middle of the second century. But it is Mosheim's object to represent this as an innovation, introduced about that time; he therefore very skilfully assumes that no Christian writers before the time of Justin held this doctrine, though he is obliged to admit that it was held by Philo and the Jews. Mosheim must have well known, that the double meaning was held by all authors whom we possess before the year 150, as well as, I believe, by all after it, for many years. I challenge any polemic to produce to me the undisputed work of any author before that year, in which it is not expressly supported. But I object to pretended quotations from the works of the ancients by Paulites. If the reader will peruse Mosheim's Commentaries, keeping in mind that his object is to represent the *Arcani disciplina,* or, as he calls it, *that more secret and sublime theology styled by Clement of Alexandria* $\gamma\nu\omega\sigma\iota\varsigma$, as a new doctrine, he must, I am certain, be obliged to see that Mosheim most abundantly, but unwillingly proves, that it was the received doctrine from the beginning, and *no new thing.* In fact, the literal exposition was not adopted by the higher classes of society, till all classes were equally degraded in intellect; then the literal meaning of both the Old and New Testaments was, for the first time, received by the higher ranks; and the existence of a secret doctrine began to be denied.

The favourite objects with Ammonius, as appear from the disputations and writings of his disciples, which I stated in Volume I. pp. 824, 825, were those of not only bringing about a reconciliation between all the different philosophic sects, Greeks as well as barbarians, but also of producing a harmony of all religions, even of Christianity and Heathenism, and of prevailing *on all the wise and good men of every nation* to lay aside their contentions and quarrels, and to unite together as one large family, the children of one common mother. With a view to the accomplishment of these ends, therefore, he maintained, that divine wisdom had been first brought to light and nurtured among the people of the East by Hermes, Zoroaster, and other great and sacred characters; that it was warmly espoused and cherished by Pythagoras and Plato, among the Greeks; from whom, although the other Grecian sages might appear to have dissented, yet that with nothing more than the exercise of an ordinary degree of judgment and attention, it was very possible to make this discordance entirely vanish, and shew that the only points on which these eminent characters differed were but of trifling moment, and that it was chiefly in their manner of expressing their sentiments that they varied.[1] Surely nothing could be more desirable than the objects aimed at by Ammonius, or more deserving of the exertions of a good man.

Amidst all the confusion of sects, two leading doctrines may be perceived—that of those who held the literal meaning, at the head of which was Paul; and that of those who held the allegorical or learned, of which were Pantænus, Clemens, Origen, Justin, Philo, and Plato.

In reply to these observations I shall have some foolish explanations pointed out to me, given by or attributed to Clemens, Origen, &c., of the allegories. This mode of treating the subject may serve to blind readers of little thought, but can never change the facts, either that allegory, i. e. parabolic reasoning, was meant, or that it was attributed to these writings by the first Christians. The foolishness of the explanations (probably only given as a matter of *state policy*) may be fairly urged against admitting allegory, but against the fact that the writings were intended to be allegorical, it can never be urged.

The more I reflect upon Gnosticism, the more I am convinced that in it we have, in fact, the real science of antiquity—for a long time almost lost—but, I trust, by means of our oriental discoveries, yet to be recovered. Perhaps, from being placed in a situation to take a bird's eye view of its various departments, we may be better qualified to form a just estimate of it than any of our predecessors for some thousands of years past. In order to do this, we must, I think, divest our minds of the respect with which we have been accustomed to look upon the early Christian authorities, and to consider them as in reality no better guides than we consider the leaders of our sects of Ranters, Jumpers, and genuine Calvinists; and, I apprehend, though a Wilberforce and a Halhed may sometimes be found in modern, as an Origen and Clemens Alexandrinus were in ancient times, yet no philosopher will think of placing even those persons in the same grade of intellect with the learned and profound Locke, or the unlearned glove-maker of Salisbury,[2] or the printer of America.

Ammonius Saccas, the greatest of the early fathers, held Jesus Christ in veneration, as a person of a divine character and a teacher of celestial wisdom.[3] It was not till after the time of Justin Martyr that the Paulites of Rome began to prevail against the philosophers of Alexandria, where, in its catechetical school, the original *Christianity* was taught; and from the hands of such men as Plato, Philo, Pantænus, and Ammonius, it fell into the hands of such men as Calvin, Brothers, Wilberforce, and Halhed; and the consequence was, that instead of a religion of refined philosophy and wisdom, it became a religion of monks and devil-drivers, whose object, by the destruction of books and their authors, was to get the upper hand of those they could not refute, and to reduce all mankind to their own level. With these people, the popes, who were equally desirous of power, formed an alliance, and, to conceal this, fabricated the Acts of the of the Apostles, the

---

[1] Mosheim's Comm. Cent. ii. p. 132.   [2] Thomas Chubb.   [3] Mosheim's Comm. ut sup. p. 127.

Latin character of which is visible in every page: for a proof of this, Mr. Evanson's Dissonance of the Gospels may be consulted.

The sect of early Christians, the lowest in intellect of all, having, with the assistance of an unprincipled conqueror, obtained possession of the supreme authority, did precisely what the followers of Cranmer, the Ranters, and the Calvinists, would do at this day if they had the power,— they destroyed all their superiors in science, and burnt their books; and we, following after them, being in fact their children, inherit their confined and mistaken views. Our minds, by the viciousness of our education, are unable to form a correct estimate of our own feebleness; and until we are convinced of this truth, we shall in vain endeavour to search after the lost science of antiquity. I have found the difficulty of unlearning the false learning of my youth, much greater than that of acquiring the real learning which I possess. Very truly has Thomas Burnet said, SAPIENTIA PRIMA EST, STULTITIA CARUISSE.[1]

M. Matter has observed, that, in real knowledge, we are very little in advance of the ancients on that kind of subjects on which we treat; that, though we are very verbose upon many which are of a trifling and unmeaning import, upon great ones we are silent.[2] For an instance of what I mean, I ask, Whence comes the soul, and whither goes it? How is it combined with matter, and how is their separation effected? The observation of M. Matter is very just. Fortunately, perhaps, for me, the discussion of these points is not in my plan; I have only to notice the history of the attempts to remove the difficulties with which, in all ages, they have been surrounded: and, I think, whether true or false, the candid reader will allow, that the system of the oriental GNOSIS was, as I have called it, *beautiful* and *sublime*.

Throughout the whole of my work, it has been my sedulous wish to conduct my abstruse investigations with the strictest impartiality, and never to flinch from a consideration of imaginary injury to religion; for, if religion be false, the sooner it is destroyed the better; but if it be true, there can be no doubt that *veritas prævalebit*, and that it is very well able to take care of itself. But I will not deny, that when I meet with any theory which takes religion out of my way, and leaves to me the free investigation of the records of antiquity, I receive great pleasure; for my object is not to attack religion: my object has been to inquire into the causes of innumerable facts or effects which have hitherto baffled the efforts of the most industrious and learned inquirers. Such is the observation made by the learned Parkhurst on the subject of Hercules and Adonis,[3] that they are symbols or types of what a future Saviour was to do and suffer. It must be obvious, on a moment's consideration, that all the histories of the births, deaths, resurrections, &c., of the different Gods, may be easily accounted for in the same manner; and if this be granted, it is equally obvious, that the nearer they are to the history of Jesus Christ, the more complete symbols they become; and thus the development of the ancient histories, to those who admit the doctrine of symbols, becomes a handmaid instead of an opponent to the religion.

I am well aware that the doctrine of Mr. Parkhurst comes with but an ill grace from priests, who have never ceased to suppress information, and that the time of the discovery by Mr. Parkhurst is very suspicious. But notwithstanding this very awkward circumstance, I beg my philosophic reader to recollect, that the want of principle or the want of sense in priests cannot in fact change the nature of truth, and that it is very unphilosophical to permit such want of principle or want of sense to influence the mind in his philosophical inquiries.

---

[1] See the passage quoted, in Vol. I. p. 29. *Ed.*

[2] That may be very justly said of us which Sallust said of the Roman Senate, *Satis eloquentiæ, sapientiæ parum*.

[3] In voce יד or V. pp. 520, &c.

On the reasonableness of Mr. Parkhurst's doctrine I shall give no opinion: to some persons it will be satisfactory, to others it will not be so. But, as the opinion of our church, I have a right to take it. If any ill-judging member of the church should deny this doctrine of Parkhurst's, then I desire him to account to me in some better way for what we have found in the histories of Buddha, Cristna, Salivahana, Pythagoras, &c. If he fail in his attempt, let not the honest inquirer for truth blame me. I have fairly stated Mr. Parkhurst's opinion and mode of accounting for the facts which I have developed, because I consider them the best which I have seen, and because I should not have acted with fairness and impartiality had I not stated them. They have a tendency to promote the interests of science, not to injure them.

In his first chapter and seventeenth verse Matthew says, "So all the generations from " Abraham to David are fourteen generations; and from David until the carrying away into " Babylon are fourteen generations; and from the carrying away into Babylon unto Christ are " fourteen generations." Surely nothing can have a more mythological appearance than this. We must not forget that the Bible says, the age of man is seventy years; by which we have already seen that the sum of seventy-two years is almost uniformly meant. These three series of generations make 42, which multiplied by $71\frac{1}{2}=3003$. If we add 14 more generations before Abraham to the $42=56$, we shall have $71\frac{1}{2} \times 56=4004$, the correct orthodox chronological period. If we then add, in the same manner, 28 for two series more, making $84 \times 71\frac{1}{2}$, we shall have six series for the 6000 years, which completes the mythos. Nimrod says, "As " to their Manichæan romance legends we may observe, that the succession of Great Abad, " (Bauddha, or Abaddon from the bottomless pit,) and the thirteen Abads, implies the thirteen " generations of Solimans or theanthropic rulers from Adam to Nimrod."[1] Now the Great Abad or Buddha and the *thirteen* make fourteen, and this makes up the correct number to complete the mythos, as it is evident, from Nimrod, that the Manichæans made it out. Besides, it appears that the reckoning, by periods of *fourteens*, is exactly in character with the gospel history. The author of the Cambridge Key has made an observation which shews, in a very striking manner, the universal nature of the mythos: "I may observe, that of the first fourteen dynasties of " Manethon, seven are without names; and that in the first fourteen dynasties of every other " nation the same omission is observable. The Hebrews only give the names of Adam, and the " six princes in the race of Seth, who *reigned* in succession. The Hindus and Chinese give the " first created, and six princes in the same line: the Chaldæans those in the race of Cain: each " nation omits the names in the other race, that is, the names by which they were known as " sovereigns. The Old Chronicle, which treats of Upper Egypt, gives the dynasties, or more " properly reigns, complete, *making Noah the fourteenth.*"[2] This accounts for the series of fourteen before Abraham not named by Matthew. It is probable that the difference between the Samaritan and Hebrew chronology has arisen from a corruption of the Hebrew, to make it suit to certain mistaken times of the equinoxes or solstices of the Greeks and Romans, of eight or nine days alluded to by Columella, who is doubtful whether it was eight or nine days— all which will be noticed at large presently. To prove this, if we take 56 generations and multiply them by 72, and add for the 8 days and part of 8 days, in all 9 days—9 generations—$9 \times 72 = 648$, we shall have 4680.[3] But if we take the nearly correct time for the precession in one sign, $+2153+2153, +357\frac{1}{2}+16\frac{1}{2}=374=5$ degrees, and a fraction of one degree, we have 4680; and if we take another fraction of one degree, we have $2153+2153+357\frac{1}{2}+36\frac{1}{2}$, we have 4700. If we multiply the more correct Manwantara, $71\frac{1}{2}$ by 56, the number of generations, we have 4004. Here we see the real cause of the difference between the Samaritans and Jews. The former took the

---

[1] Vol. II. p. 509. [2] Vol. II. p. 135. [3] See Vol. I. p. 191.

correct time by the precession, which did not cause the error of the Greeks and Romans of 9 days; the latter took the common erroneous Greek and Roman, and thus got their 4004 years. It seems to me impossible to devise any thing more satisfactory than this. We must not forget what I have said formerly, that these calculations will all be right if made in round numbers, if the error do not exceed 71 or 72 years, which mode of calculation, for the festivals, is justified by the state of the case, as well as by the observation of Columella. This we shall see presently.

An Antara, often called Outar[1] by our travellers, of India, means a generation or age, and a Manw-antara is an age, that is evidently *an age of man*, and consists of seventy-two years, or of seventy-one and a fraction—rather better than a *half*—the age of man spoken of in the Bible. Here we have the fifty-six Manwantaras exactly agreeing with Usher. It will not have been forgotten that, in our calculation of the cycles, we always deducted for the precession of one sign, 2160 years. An age or generation was also thirty years. The Persians said, that there were seventy-two Solomons, that is, seventy-two *wise men* before the flood: these were 30 × 72 = 2160, the years of the precession in one sign. In these cases the Solumi were probably incarnations of wisdom or the sun, reigning in the towns where the temples of Solomon were built. Mr. Niebuhr has contended that, from the peculiar division of the first kings of Rome into astrological periods, making up the number 360, combined with other circumstances, it is apparent that not a real history but a mythos must have been intended, and this reasoning has been received by learned men with almost universal approbation. Now, in consequence of meeting with the history of Solomon and Saul, (or Talut[2], as he is called both in India and Western Arabia,) and many other particulars of the Jewish history both in India and Western Syria, the use of astrological numbers in the history of the Jews, and the extraordinary and unaccountable fact, that Herodotus never names the magnificent empire of Solomon, it is apparent that the whole Jewish history is an allegory, is, in fact, the same kind of history as that of the first three hundred years of Rome.[3] It is one of the parables of the Christian religion, in the gospel histories of which Jesus Christ is made, in so peculiar a manner, to teach his doctrines. The peculiarity of the fourteen numbered periods at once proves that this was not meant for real history. It is totally incredible that such round numbers should come out in real life and complete the sum of the 6000 years. The Mathematicians or Chaldeans, as I shall presently shew, were the only persons who really understood the principle of the mythos in the time of Cæsar, which induces me to believe that the whole Χρησ-tian mythos was a Masonic or Rosicrucian mystery; first, in part, let out by the publication, under *Ptolemy*, of the Jewish Scriptures, (or of what were perhaps only a part[4] of the Jewish Scriptures,) and never, in fact, all openly known in any thing approaching to a whole—never put together or explained openly, until now so done by me. It would originally be known at every great temple, like Delphi, Eleusis, Dodona, &c. As time advanced, parts of it got out by the treachery, indiscretion, or insanity of the initiated, and all became every day more doubtful, in consequence of the neglect of intercalary days, which was throwing the system into confusion.

---

[1] The word Outara means *an age*, and a Man-outara is *an age of man*. [2] See Vol. I. pp. 546, 740, 741.

[3] The Abbé Bézin says, "No Grecian author cited Moses before Longinus, who lived in the reign of Aurelian." Phil. of Hist. p. 159. This seems a very curious and important observation indeed.

[4] The book of Genesis shews evident marks of its being a compilation, and of mutilation. The way in which the tree of life is named, ch. ii. ver. 9, shews that some account of it, now wanting, must have preceded. The amalgamation of the Χρηϛ-tian with the Jewish mythos in North and South India, in which they differ from the present canonical mythos of the Jews, which does not include the crucifixion, resurrection, and ascension, &c., shews that we have not the whole; but we have it clearly in the Apocrypha, which proves that the mythos was a secret doctrine. This is confirmed by the extraordinary circumstance of the whole mythos being found, as we have seen, in Mexico—Book I. Chapter IV.

Whenever we get back to the earliest point to which we can go, we always find the Chaldei or Mathematici—those persons who are said by Josephus to have handed down the cycle from the Antediluvians, the persons, I think, (as shewn by Mr. Hammer,) who, under the name of Mathematici, were certainly Freemasons. The historical evidence that the Chaldeans were Chasdim, or that the Chasdim were Chaldeans, is clear; but I think Mr. Bryant's objection to the etymological derivation of Chaldean from Chasdim is well founded. The fact, probably, was, that the Chasdim or Chasidim, were persons of the college of Casi, which was in Ur of the Chaldees, or Callidiia, or, in the country of the di-cali or ia of the the holy Cali. We have a Casi to which students in medicine went to study the Chaldean language in two places in North India: Benares, anciently called Casi, and the temple of Solomon in Casi-mere.[1] This order of Cyclopes or Calidei or Mathematici were the builders of Stonehenge and Abury in the West, and of Dipaldenha, the temples of Solomon, the Pyramids, &c., &c., in the East, beginning with the simplest of all temples, a Gilgal, that is, *stone circle*, and ending with the highly finished York Minster, The Chasdim or Kasdim or Casi-di-im were Ka¦ideans, and both the same as the Callidei or Chaldei or Chasidim. The Chalidi were followers of Cali, the female deity of love; the Casideans were from חרס *hrs*, as we say *Chrs*, Ερως, the male deity. In my opinion that the Chasideans or Kasideans were Chaldei and Mathematici and Freemasons, I am supported by Scaliger, who makes them *knights of the Temple*, to whom the duty was specially devolved of maintaining that structure. Scaliger says, that they were *not a sect, but an order or fraternity*, and consisted of men of great wealth and power.[2] The circumstance that the Kasideans or Casi-deans were an order, and not a sect, is very important; for this accounts for their being found in several sects or religions, like Freemasons, and for the Templars being Kasideans. The description applies to the Freemasons in every particular; and this accounts for their being found among the Essenes, in consequence of which they have been thought to have been Essenes. I have some suspicion that the Caraites were a branch of them, and were named after the district called Cozar or Cæsar, whence the Caspian sea was called Kisr. I think we may be pretty certain that the Kasideans were masons and successors of the Cyclopes, the fabricators of the stone circles, cromlehs, &c.[3] It is very curious to observe, that not one in a thousand of the inquirers into the antiquities of nations ever condescends to bestow a thought on the authors of these very numerous edifices, and the most stupendous monuments on the face of the earth—to be found in all countries, even of the *new* as well as of the *old* world. I find from Mr. Sharon Turner,[4] that the year of the Anglo-Saxons began on the 25th of December. The night before that day, they called Moedrenech, *Mother Night*. It was spent in religious ceremonies. Our month of December was called Giuli, or Œrra Geola, and the month of January was called Œftera Geola. Bede says, the Saxons called the months above-named Geola from the turning of the sun on that day.[5] Now there does not seem any reason to believe that they had learned this from either the Romans or the Christians; and, if this be admitted, we have here, in the correct fixation of the solstice, a decisive and triumphant proof that the *Barbarian* Saxons were better skilled in astronomy than either the Greeks or Romans, in the time of Cæsar. This affords strong presumptive evidence that the priests or Druids, or Callidei, were descendants or had derived their learning

---

[1] See Vol. I. p. 702.   [2] Basnage, Hist. Jews, B. ii. Ch. xi. p. 126.

[3] The numerous circles which are found in India are said by the inhabitants to have been erected by a race of people called Chæones or Chaons, who are said to have been pigmies. Why they are supposed to be pigmies I cannot imagine; but the word Chæon is only the aspirated Æon or the Greek Αιων, and has the meaning of *cycle* as well as *emanation from the sun*, and is thus a cyclop, one of the Pi-clo or of the Cyclops.

[4] History of the Pagan or Anglo-Saxons, Vol. II. Ch. iv.   [5] The Geola is evidently our *goal*, used in racing.

from the Chaldæans of Tartary, or Eastern Scythia, or North India. There are only two ways of getting over this. The first is, to attribute it to accident. The second is, to suppose that these ignorant barbarians took their Festival from the corrected calendar of the Romans—with whom they were at perpetual war. Man was considered a *microcosm* by the Mystics; and as he was made after the image of God, and as God was the Kosmos, Mundus, he was made after the image of the world, the Το Παν, the Το Ον. We have before observed, in numerous instances, his close connexion with the renewing cycles, and on this account the first race of one-eyed beings, called Cyclopes or Κυκλωπες, made after the image of God, *the sun*, had only *one* eye. After some time, and for the same reason, the Hero Gods—Jupiter in the West, and Vishnu in the East, came to have *three* eyes in imitation of the supposed image of the Trimurti. In strict accordance with this was the renewed incarnation of the Solar Deity, the Λογος, in every cycle, in every neros, in which every thing was supposed to be renewed—new Argonauts, new Troys, &c. Thus the Genius of each cycle, every year as it revolved, was celebrated microcosmically. In allusion to this, he was born with the new-born Sun on the moment when the sun began to increase on the 25th of December, and he was feigned to die, and be put to death, and to rise from the grave after three days, at the vernal equinox. The God was continued by renewed incarnation till he came again, till the cycle ended and was renewed, till the end of the 6000 years. This is still exemplified in the Lamas of Tibet, and in the Popes, in all things yet more similar than, from the lapse of time and their great distance, could be expected. Here we find the reason why some of the Popes, intoxicated with silly vanity, let out the secret and called themselves Gods upon earth; and this is the reason why, as incarnations of the Creator of Heaven, Earth, and Hell, they wear the *triple* crown. The ceremonies of the Romish church consist almost entirely of scenic representations of the acts of Jesus Christ. All his history is acted over every year; a measure well calculated to keep the mythos in the minds of the people, for which our reading of the gospel histories has been substituted. Of the same nature were our sacred dramas, or mysteries as they were called, of the middle ages. Of the same nature were the plays of Æschylus, in which, as I have before remarked, we have the Prometheus *bound*, so called to disguise it, but which ought to be the Prometheus *crucified*. After his resurrection Jesus is said to have gone before his disciples into Galilee;[1] that is, Γαλ-αλ-ia or גל-אל-יא *gl-al-ia*, the country of the circle or revolution. We must not forget that Sir William Drummond proved that all the Hebrew names of places in the holy land were astronomical. I have no doubt that these names were given by Joshua when he conquered, settled, and divided it among his twelve tribes, and that all those names had a reference to the solar mythos. The same mythos prevailed in almost every country, and this is the reason why we find the same names in every country. They were the sacred or religious names, the places, probably, having other common names, and were necessary for their religious rites; their search for the members of Bacchus, of Osiris, &c., or for the journey of the Mary's to look for the body of Christ. We must not forget that we have the three Mary's in Britain and in Gaul, one of them the *Virgo Paritura*, and at Delphi, as well as in Palestine. All the great outlines of the mythoses were evidently the same, though, of course, in a long series of years, they varied in small matters. But the similarity, as we find, would continue the longest in the names of places and countries,—though, as I have just said, I do not suppose those sacred names were those in common use. I have no doubt that every country and place had *two* names at least. Each independent territory had its sacred mount or Olympus, &c. In time, as one state or tribe

---

[1] Mark xvi. 7.

conquered another, or as a country of twelve tribes divided, the two mythoses would be thrown together or divided, and perhaps a new mount adopted by part of the tribes, as a new mount was adopted at Jerusalem. It was not in the nature of things that either the twelve tribes or their mythos should always continue. We have hundreds of Jupiters or Gods I E, יה or Jah; all the Gods were Jah and Rajah, or Roi-Jah. We have numbers of Mithras, Bacchuses, Herculeses, &c., &c. Sometimes they were multiplied by the genii of the nine cycles, all going by the same name. Sometimes, as in the case of Bacchus or Hercules, by the God or Genius of one cycle taking the same name in many different countries. All this has led to the confusion which, in these matters, has hitherto prevailed, and necessarily prevailed. In my opinion the singularity of the regular periods observed by Niebuhr sufficiently proves the mythos; but there are traces of another period, of which Mr. Niebuhr had no knowledge, to be found in Cato,[1] who gives a different account, and says, that Troy was taken 432 years before the foundation of Rome. Here we have evidently the two numbers on which the cycles of 2160—21,600—432,000, are founded. In the multitude of our researches we have very often met with the word sam סם sm or סמ sm; as a name of the sun. I feel greatly surprised at myself that my mind should have never been turned to this curious and important word, evidently the Roman Sumnaut.[2] Its numeral power is $\Sigma=200$, M$=40=240$. For reasons which we shall soon see, this has probably been its meaning in the Latin or Etruscan. But as I have, in a future book, established the fact on as good evidence (viz. a high probability) as these matters will admit, that the last three letters of the alphabets were interchangeable as far as regards their powers of notation, we may consider the Hebrew meaning to be the same, namely, 240. In the Hebrew, as a verb, it means *to place in order*. In its plural, it is applied, in the first verse of Genesis, to the *planetary bodies*, and, generally speaking, I believe it may be rendered a planetary body, ranking the sun as one—for it is constantly used for the sun. Mr. Parkhurst observes, that probably the idol Chemin of the new world was the same word, as it had the same meaning. As a name of the sun, it came to denote *the trinity* (as Mr. Parkhurst shews that it did). In strict keeping with all my previous doctrines, it means *to place in order with great care*, and *to make waste* and *utterly desolate* and *in disorder*; herein exhibiting the Generator and Destroyer. It meant an *onion*, from the regular disposition of the involucra or integuments.[3] An onion was considered to be αιων των αιωνων.

I must now request my reader to turn to Volume I. pp. 647, 648, 658, and he will see it proved, by various authorities, that the fish Oannes was in name the same as John. John was the cousin of Jesus. Now, I think, there can be no doubt, that Arjoon, of the Indians, is the same as the John of the Christians. His name with the prefix Ar, which I do not understand, is the same. Arjoon was the cousin of Cristna, and nearly every thing which was said of Rama is said of Ar-joon. It is remarkable that Cristna and Rama are said to be the same. Then, if Rama is the same as Arjoon, Arjoon and Cristna must be the same. John is the cousin of Christ, Arjoon of Cristna. Christ is represented both by the Lamb and by a Fish or the Fishes. The Lamb is Ram, the Fish is John or Oannes. In the state of the Planisphere at the ninth cycle, John or Oannes or Pisces, had been running 360 years, or was declining before Jesus, in the ninth cycle of the Neros, had begun. Though different cycles, they were, as forming a part of the whole large one of the Zodiac, or 2160 years, the same. Thus John had passed 360 years, more than half of a cycle of 600, when Jesus began his cycle. All the cycles of the Neros would be cycles of the Ram or Lamb, whilst the equinox was passing

---

[1] Antiquit. Rom. Lib. 1. Sect. lxxiv. p. 59; Hom. et ses Ecrits, par D'Urban, p. 41.

[2] Refer to Appendix of first Volume, p. 833, for corruption of Tam, Sam, Cam; it shews Sam to be the original.

[3] Numb. xi. 5; Parkhurst in voce; Hutchinson's Works, Vol. IV. p. 262.

T

through Aries; and of the Fish, whilst it was passing through Pisces. Thus Rama and Cristna were the same. Joannes=240, and RM=240, the name of the sacred number of Rome, or the city of Rāma, as pointed out by Niebuhr. The period of 360 years, which John or Pisces preceded Jesus, will form a cycle with the 21,600, as well also as Rome's sacred number of 240. Thus we find Ramas in the history of all the cycles connected with Cristna, and subsequently we find Johns. I think the Eastern nations, in a particular manner, attached themselves to the number 6, the *vau*; and the Western to the number 5. (We must never forget Pythagoras's doctrine of numbers.) The first, to the 6×12=72, and 72×6=432. The latter, to the 5×10=50, and 60×10 =360. The 6, the vau, the even number, was for the *female*; the 5, the odd, for the *male*; and the two united formed the cycle or sacred number, 4320. The five is the ה or He, the male in Saxon and Hebrew. The two together make the *Evau*; and also the אוה, *iiuaa*,=28. Although I cannot exactly explain how or by what steps it arose, yet it is clear to me that the sacred number, 240, of the Romans, arose from שם *sm*=240; and, in the plural, their God Saman. Mr. Niebuhr has shewn how both the number of 360, and the number of 240, were used by the Romans, in each case making up their number of 1440, from the destruction of Troy to the founding of Nova Roma, by Constantine, on the seven hills, in the Thracian Romelia or the Romelia of Thrace, where the widows were burnt on the funeral piles of their husbands—in a country called Sindi, having the religion of the Χρης. Although I cannot explain how it was made out, I think I can see a high probability, that this mythos of the Romans and of Constantine was closely connected with, or was an integral part of, the mythos of the East, of Virgil, as we might expect from the doctrine of Ammonius Saccas, that, in the main, all the religions were the same. I must now make a few observations on the want of *absolute accuracy* in round numbers, which shews itself in almost all the calculations; but, if we look closely into the matter, we shall observe, that this is an effect which, in most cases, must necessarily arise from the primary numbers of nature, on which they are founded, not being accurate. Thus, for instance, the Millenium is founded on the Neros; but the correct Neros depends, by nature, on the fraction of a second of time: and the question often presents itself, whether we are to take 2153 or 2160. It is obvious that, by taking a fraction, I could easily bring out my whole round number of 6000; but *cui bono?* It is sufficiently near for the vulgar runners after the Millenium. It is evident, or in a few minutes will be so, that all these little errors were perfectly well known to the Chaldeans. In addition to these considerations I shall shew, in a future book, that the Chaldeans foresaw that a Comet would affect the earth in more than one of its progresses; and, by its disturbing force, necessarily cause an irregularity, from its nature unknown, but, on the whole, even of several years. This is perfectly justified by the retardation which astronomers observed to take place in Jupiter when the Comet [of 1680?] approached that planet.[1] I think these considerations are quite sufficient to answer the above *small* objections for the present; and I shall now proceed to the complete development of the *secret* Romish system.

If my reader will revert to Volume I. pp. 175, 182, 191, he will observe that the Indian scholars agree in stating it to be the unanimous doctrine of the Brahmins, that their Cali Yug began 3101 years before Christ, that, at that time, the flood took place, and that the sun entered the zodiacal sign Aries at the vernal equinox. Here, in the date of the sun's entrance into Aries, there appears

---

[1] The Author's apparently premature decease prevented his filling up the blank he had here left in his MS. If he referred to the Comet of 1680, (as submitted in the brackets,) his statement is directly opposed to the conclusions of Dr. Halley, who, "having observed that" it "came very near Jupiter in the summer of 1681, above a year before its last appearance, and remained several months in the neighbourhood of that planet, judged that circumstance alone sufficient to have considerably retarded its motion and prolonged the duration of its revolution."—Essay towards a History of the principal Comets, &c., pp. 64, 65, *Glasgow*, 1770.—*Editor*.

to me to be an error of nearly 600 years, which has never been observed by any of our oriental astronomers. The Brahmins, when questioned upon this point, say, Those events happened when the Sun and Moon were in a certain position, which was observed at the time it took place, and *that* time is only to be known by back-reckoning. This error is of great moment, and, if I be right, it is a most extraordinary circumstance that it has been overlooked by all the orientalists: for the Sun certainly did not enter the sign Aries until about 2520 years before Christ. If our orientalists did not observe it, the fact proves with how very little attention they read, and how very superficially they consider these subjects. At all events I believe they have never made any observations upon it.

I will now try to explain the error, and to shew how it arose. " Columella says,[1] the 17th of " December the sun passes into Capricorn; it is the WINTER SOLSTICE, as Hipparchus will have it. " The 24th of December is the winter solstice, AS THE CHALDÆANS OBSERVE."[2]

Now it is well known that Cæsar, with the assistance of a celebrated Chaldean astronomer from Egypt, called Sosigenes, ascertained the winter solstice to take place on the 25th of December, at thirty minutes past one o'clock in the morning. And it is a striking circumstance that he appears from the expression of Columella to have availed himself of the reckoning *of the Chaldeans*, whom my reader will recollect I have shewn to have come, with Abraham, or the Brahmin, from India, and whom our historians affect to treat with contempt, as having, in the time of Cæsar, become mere charlatans or conjurors; but who were, as appears from the facts above-named, in reality the only persons who had a sufficient knowledge of astronomy to correct the calendar, which had fallen into the utmost confusion. This any one may see by looking at our common globes, where he will find the Vernal equinox fixed to the 30th of Aquarius, which makes the equinox to fall on the 25th of Pisces, or March, 1800 years ago, by calculating back the precession 25 degrees, at 72 years to a degree. Now, from the 17th of December (the solstice, according to Hipparchus) to the 25th, according to the Chaldeans, there is a space of 8 days, which answers to 8 degrees, and as the solstice precedes a degree in 72 years, it makes in time, calculated on these data, an error of 576 years: $8 \times 72 = 576$. The Brahmins at this day, as we have formerly shewn, fix the entrance of the equinoctial sun into the sign Aries and their Cali Yug, 3101 years before the time Usher fixed for the birth of Christ; in which he made a mistake of four years. Now, if we allow for this error of Usher's of four years, the time to the date of the Cali Yug is 3096 years B. C., and the error of the Brahmins is exactly 576 years. For, from the 25th of Pisces, reckoning back to the first of Aries, there are not 43 degrees, as the Brahmin calculation would require, but 35 degrees only; which number, multiplied by 72, gives 2520; and this sum added to 576 makes $3096+4=3100$. This proves that the present Brahmins, when they fix their Cali Yug by back calculation, are exactly in the same error as Hipparchus, the Greeks and the Romans were, as to the time of the solstice.

The next question which arises is, How the Brahmins fell into this error of *eight* days in the date of the solstice, and into its consequent error of 576 years? And now, I think, we shall find another striking and curious coincidence, which will go far towards proving that the Hindoo system must have been founded on observation, near 5000 years before Christ. We have seen that there were *eight* Avatars believed to have passed in Siam, and eight Sæcula believed to have passed at Rome, at the birth of Christ. These eight Avatars and Sæcula I have shewn to be Neroses.[3]

Lalande, in his astronomy,[4] says, "Si l'on emploie la durée de l'année que nous connoissons, et

---

[1] Book xi. Ch. ii.
[2] See Vol. I. 175—177, 215.
[3] Bentley, Hist. Ast. p. 281.
[4] Tome II. Ast. 1570, ed. 3.

" le mois synodique tel que nous l'avons indiqué ci-devant, c'est-à-dire, des mois de 29ᴊ, 12ʰ, 44',
" 3", chacun, l'on aura 28ʰ, 1', 42" de trop, dans les sept mille, quatre cent, vingt-une lunaisons:
" ainsi la lune retarderoit de plus d'un jour au bout de six cents ans." If my reader will look back to Volume I. p. 169, he will find the above passage quoted, and a promise there made that I would return to it. From this observation it appears that there was, in fact, an inaccuracy in each Neros or Sæculum of more than one day in calculating it exactly at 600 years; which, if the solstice were settled, as of course it would be by the cycle invented for the purpose of settling it, but without taking the error into the account, would, in *eight* Sæcula, cause it to be fixed to the 17th day of December, instead of the 25th, and produce the mistake of the eight days, and the consequent error of 576 years. To keep the reckoning right, a day and part of a day ought to have been intercalated every 600 years.

The truth of what I have just now stated may be shewn in another way. In reality the space the sun passed through, that is, preceded, from his entrance into Aries to the time of Christ, was thirty-five degrees, which make or answer to two thousand, five hundred, and twenty years: $35 \times 72 = 2520$. The time the Brahmins fixed for their Cali Yug and the entrance of the Sun into Aries being 3100 years B. C., 3100—2520=580, which was their mistake. But 580÷72=8, with a remainder of 4, which, Usher's mistake corrected, is 576, the exact number. it ought to be. The eight degrees answer to the eight days which the solstice, in the time of Cæsar, was wrong.

In or about the year 3100 was a remarkable conjunction of the planets, as Sir W. Jones, Bailly, and others, profess to have ascertained. This is the pivot on which all the Brahmins' calculations hinge; and as the MODERN Brahmins reckoned by the Neros to the time of Christ, *without understanding the principle of the calculation*, they thus got wrong in their solstices eight days.

The difficulty which Figulus,[1] and others found in making out the true time arose from inattention to, or ignorance of, the necessity of making the requisite intercalation; and the error had reached, in the time of Figulus, to within a very few years of an entire sæculum. This would increase the difficulty, and, in fact, would render the number of cycles doubtful,—that is, whether the new cycle—that of Christ—was the *ninth* or the *tenth*. This accounts for Virgil's policy in writing in such an equivocal manner, that his prophecy might answer either to the latter part of the current cycle, or to the last cycle.

Now, I apprehend, after the philosophers found that the cycle of the Neros made a cycle with the number of years of the precession in ten signs of the zodiac, namely, in 21,000 years, they adopted the plan, in calculating their time, of starting from the flood or the Cali Yug, both backwards and forwards, as a kind of fulcrum, and of deducting the sum of 2160 years, the precession for one sign, because at that period a new system of calculation necessarily began upon a new principle. The former calculation was made upon the cycle of 360, the days in a year, and the lunar time of 30 days in a month. These two formed a perfect cycle: no intercalations would be wanted: and all the knowledge of astronomy, as far as was of any consequence to the first inhabitants, would be known and reduced to the smallest space imaginable. They found, that if they calculated backwards by the periods of years of precession in a sign, (as they must in future calculate forwards by them, if they meant to keep their time correctly,) these periods would exactly agree backwards with the calculation forwards; so that they could calculate backward before the Cali Yug, as correctly as forwards, from it,—the 360 days in a year making a perfect cycle, and these years, in periods of 360 or 720 or 2160 years, making a perfect cycle backward, in a circle to the 21,600 the years in ten signs, as they were obliged to calculate forwards to the same period. In short, by this contrivance, notwithstanding the great change in the lengths of the

---

[1] See Vol. I. pp. 185—187, 233.

year and month, which I shall explain hereafter, the calculations backwards would be perfectly assimilated to those forwards, and would, supposing the equinox to precede only about 50" in a year, or on the average or in mean time to precede after this rate, and that the Soli-lunar period of 600 years was correct, be also perfectly true. Thus they would be able to calculate by signs round the circle of the zodiac backwards, as they did in like manner by signs forwards, and, correctly too, for any length of time. It is also very worthy of observation, that the cycle of 360 makes a perfect cycle with the great precessional one of 25,920 years.

Now, if the reader will examine carefully the different astronomical calculations which I have made in the fifth book of the first volume, he will find no satisfactory reason given for the fact of the different arithmetical sums coming out correct from the calculations, the sum of 2160 years being first deducted; though the coincidence of the numbers shewed that it could not be the effect of accident, but that they must be true, whatever might be the cause. Here we find the whole satisfactorily explained, and an adequate reason assigned for the conduct of the astronomers. Very certain I am that I shall prove, all the ancients believed that the year was originally only 360 days long. Whether this be true or false, I contend, that I have raised the very highest probability, that, in their calculations of time, they proceeded upon this belief, and that its admitted duration had changed in a later day.

The lustrums *five* and *six* were the roots of all the calculations. The *five* was the lustrum when the year was 360 days long: the *six* when it came to be 365. In the first case the precession of the equinoxes was supposed to have taken place after the rate of 36" in a degree, and of 36,000 years in the circle. Thus we find the sum of 36,000 to be called *the great year*. (The Neros 600, and the Millenium 6000, make cycles with this.) In the second case, when the precession was supposed to take place in 50", and 25,920 in the circle; 25,920 was *the great year*. But with this the former number will not make a cycle; therefore, as said formerly, *ten signs* were taken, which, at 50" to a degree, and 72 to a sign, make 21,600; and with this, both the *five* and *six*, and the old numbers, all make cycles. Now, it is worthy of observation, that the *five* and its multiples make a cycle with the great precessional year 36,000; and the *six* and its multiples make a cycle with the great artificial year of 21,600, the united cycle of the two, with the great year of 36,000, and with the still greater artificial cycle of 432,000, as well as with the real cycle of 25,920.

The Romans must have had two computations of time, both of which were wrong. For, besides the misplacing of the solstice, which we have learnt from Columella, their "*year differed by an* "*excess of 67 days from the true time.*"[1] Now, although some of their festivals, which they did not understand, might be wrong 67 days, we cannot believe that the solstice could get so far wrong. We may almost as soon suppose they would mistake the equinox for the solstice.

It is worthy of observation that the persons employed by Cæsar were the Chaldeans, and that these mere *fortune-tellers* and *conjurers*, as our priests call them, were so well informed, that they could fix the time of the solstice to half an hour—to half past one in the morning. It is evident these Calidei, or Chaldeans, or Casi-deans, or Chasidim, or Mathematici, or Templars, or Rosicrucians, or Nousareans, or Mandaites, or Iobnites, or Essenæans, or Carmelites, or Freemasons, were then the best calculators and astronomers in the world.

Columella[2] says, "Nor am I ignorant of Hipparchus's computation, which teaches, that the "solstices and equinoxes do not happen in the eighth, but in the first degree of the signs. But "in this rural discipline, I now follow the calculations of Eudoxus and Meton, and those of ancient "astronomers; which are adapted to the public sacrifices; because husbandmen are both better

---

[1] Niebuhr, Vol. I. p. 208, ed. Walter. [2] Book ix. Ch. xiv.

"acquainted with that old opinion which has been commonly entertained: nor yet is the niceness and exactness of Hipparchus necessary to the grosser apprehensions and scanty learning of husbandmen." From this it is evident, that the festivals were not fixed with *niceness*, to use the words of Columella; but, we may fairly suppose, in whole numbers, which will justify me in doing the same. Thus, like Columella, I have calculated roughly and by round numbers; but this was not the way the Chaldean magicians or conjurors reckoned. They formed their calculation to a minute—to thirty minutes past *one* in the morning; consequently they must have known that it would be necessary to intercalate one day and part of a day every 600 years: and this I have no doubt that they did, wherever they had the regulation of the festivals in their Judæan, secret, masonic, Χρησ-tian festivals.

If my reader have attended closely to what he has read, he will have observed that there is an error of a day and a part of a day, about one-eighth of a day, every 600 years, and that I have only accounted for the day.

This remaining error I shall now account for. I think it will not be denied that I have unveiled a pretty large number of curious mythoses; but the most curious of all I have now to unfold. We have seen that all the Buddhas, Cristnas, Salivahanas, Adonises, Atyses, Mithras, Bacchuses, Herculeses, were put to death and rose again from the grave, part certainly, and all probably, after *three* days,[1] to life and immortality. We have seen from the unquestionable testimony of the Roman Saint, Bishop, and Martyr, Irenæus, that the real Jesus of Nazareth was not put to death. But yet, according to the Romish gospel histories, he was actually put to death by crucifixion. In the gospel of the Romish Jesus, we merely have the account that he was a part of three days in the grave. But tradition informs us that he was buried on the evening of Friday; he continued in the tomb till midnight of Saturday was past, and rose the moment the morning of Sunday commenced. Thus he occupied the tomb in three successive days, though for only one day of 24 hours, and a part of a day of 24 hours' duration. This professed entombment is meant figuratively to represent a certain time that was considered necessary to be intercalated, in the neros, as I shall now describe.[2]

There is an error in the Soli-lunar cycle of the Neros of one day and a part of a day in every

---

[1] In the case of Osiris in Egypt, and of St. Denys or Bacchus in Gaul, whose limbs were scattered in forty places, and sought forty days, I apprehend the last three were the days of the processions only—the days on which the parts of generation were sought.

[2] Whether or not the Author be right in his conclusion, the following anecdote, in Farrar's *Life of Howard*, the Philanthropist, may serve to illustrate the oriental custom of reckoning days: "Mr. Howard found, on arriving at Constantinople, in 1786, that the chief topic of the day was a summary and sanguinary punishment which had recently been inflicted on the grand chamberlain. The particulars were these:—the grand vizier sent one day for the grand chamberlain, who had the charge of supplying the city with bread. Yielding immediate obedience to the summons, this officer arrived at the palace of the minister in great state; and being introduced into his presence, was asked why the bread was so bad. He answered that the harvest had been but a very indifferent one. 'Why,' continued the vizier, apparently satisfied with this excuse, 'is the weight so short?' 'That,' replied the chamberlain, 'might have happened by accident to two or three, amongst such an immense number of loaves as are required for the supply of so large a city;' but he assured his highness that greater care should be taken for the future. Without further observation the vizier ordered him to quit his presence; but no sooner was he obeyed, than he commanded an executioner to follow the unhappy man and strike off his head in the street, where his body was publicly exposed for a day and a half, with three light loaves beside it to denote his crime.

"When the circumstance was related to Mr. Howard, he was told that the chamberlain's body had lain *three* days in the street, on which he expressed his surprise that it had not bred a contagion, and then he learnt that in point of fact it had not been left so long, as they were not entire days. It was evening when the head was struck off, and this was reckoned one day; it remained the whole of the second, and was removed early on the succeeding morning, which was accounted the third day. The eastern mode of computation is the same now that it was in the time of the crucifixion and burial of Jesus Christ, when three days were similarly reckoned." Pp. 195—197. *Editor.*

cycle, as we have seen; and this space of time it is necessary to intercalate every 600 years, in order to correct the error. This required intercalation is figuratively described by the burial of all these Gods, and of Jesus Christ. Every 600 years they were put to death, remained buried a day and part of a day, after which they rose again to new life—a new six hundred years commenced—a new Phœnix arose from its ashes.

We have before seen that the year of the sun was 600 years; that the Phœnix[1] lived 600 years; that the Phen or, in Irish, Phenniche, meant 600 years. As much as the cycle got wrong, it was necessary to intercalate. For this period the God was buried. In the six thousand years he would be mystically or feignedly buried ten times. And I have very little doubt, that when the old Phœnix burnt itself, a certain time elapsed before the young one arose from its ashes. But it was not to be expected that the priests would tell us this, if, indeed, they knew it. I have somewhere read, I believe in the work of Mr. Faber, a work which has no indexes, though paid for by subscription, that, in the ceremonies of the initiation into the mysteries of Buddha, a man was *supposed to be killed; and, aft.* r *lying on the ground some time, was simulated to be raised from the dead.* This is very like the practice in the Romish church of imitating, in their ceremonies, all the recorded acts of the life of Jesus Christ. This is in accordance with the resurrection described in Georgius and in my plates, figure 14.

The same ceremony is stated by the Abbé Bazin[2] to have taken place in the mysteries of Eleusis. He says, "These mysteries were, *according to Tertullian*, somewhat tarnished by the "ceremony of regeneration. It was necessary for the initiated to appear to revive; it was the "symbol of the new kind of life he intended to lead. A crown was presented to him, which he "trod under foot; the Hierophantes then drew forth the sacred knife, and the initiated, whom he "pretended to strike, also pretended to fall dead at his feet: after which he appeared to rise "again, as it were, from the dead. A remnant of this ancient ceremony still exists among the "Freemasons." In the Gospels we have the following statements respecting the burial of Jesus: *Matthew* (xxvii. 57, 62) says, "When the even was come:—now the next day that followed the the day of preparation," &c. *Mark* (xv. 42), "Now when the even was come, because it was the preparation, that is, the day before the Sabbath." *Luke* (xxiii. 53, 54), "And he [Joseph of Arimathea] took it down, and wrapped it in linen, and laid it in a sepulchre that was hewn in stone, wherein never man was laid before. And that day was the preparation, and the sabbath drew on." *John* (xix. 42), "There laid they Jesus, therefore, because of the Jews' preparation day."

The Gospels all agree that Jesus rose on the Sunday morning, and pointedly and unnecessarily, unless there was a particular meaning intended to be conveyed, say, "very early before day-light." But the tradition is, that he rose the moment after midnight of the second day. At Rome, in some of the churches, the ceremonies begin at this time, and in Syria, in commemoration of the resurrection of Adonis; and now, in the same place and at the same time, the ceremonies of the resurrection of Jesus Christ begin to be celebrated.

If the calculation of the mythos be commenced on the moment of the conjunction of the sun and moon, and the neros last 600 years, $28^h\ 1'\ 42''$, there must be, to make it come right, an intercalation in every neros or 600 years, of $28^h\ 1^m\ 42^s$. Then this will make the life of the sun end precisely in such a manner, in such a part of a day, as will be $28^{h.}\ 1^{m.}\ 41^{s.}$ before a third day begins, making it go one second into the third day to complete the $28^{h.}\ 1^{m.}\ 42^{s.}$. Thus the reason

---

[1] The Greek word φαινω or φαινω *to shine* came from the name of the sun φπ=600, or φηπ=608
[2] Translation by Wood Gandell, p. 220.

why he is in the grave, as it is called, three days, is apparent. The Millenium cycle was supposed to have begun at such an hour and minute of the day on which the sun first entered Taurus at the vernal equinox, as would make the eighth cycle or neros end at an hour which may be found by close examination of the history. It is said that Jesus was buried before the *sabbath began*; that would be before *six* on Friday evening. Then if he were the shortest time possible in the grave, to be consistent with the history, he would be there from six to twelve, or the last *six* hours of Friday, *twenty-four* hours of Saturday, and say *one second* of Sunday, and he would rise *very early*, as the text says, on Sunday morning. This makes one day, six hours, in the grave. Now what is the time necessary to be intercalated to correct the error to a second of time? It is one day, four hours, one minute, forty-two seconds. Then the authors of the mythos were in error the difference between $1^d \cdot 4^h \cdot 1^m \cdot 42^s$ and $1^d \cdot 6^h \cdot 0^m \cdot 0^s$. This is $1^h \cdot 58^m \cdot 18^s$, which, on 7421 lunations, the number there are in the cycle, makes an error in the moon's period of somewhat less than one secomd. This, I think, is bringing the matter pretty nearly to a point.

If the reader look back to Volume I. p. 175, he will find the Brahma period stated to begin 3164 years before Christ. We will try to find how this arose. By calculating backwards and allowing a day and part of a day for the error every six hundred years, the calculators made, in the eight neroses, *nine*, but not *ten* days: thus $9 \times 72 = 648 + 2160 = 2808 + 360 = 3168 - 4 = 3164$. This seems to me to be a real arithmetical proof of the truth of my explanation of the three days, or, more correctly, the day and part of a day in the grave.

From Taurus to Aries,	2160	3164
Aries to Pisces	2160	2160
Pisces to Jesus Christ,	360[1]	
9×72	648	5324
	5328	
	4	
	5324	

The history of the sun, I repeat, is the history of Jesus Christ. The sun is born on the 25th of December, the birth-day of Jesus Christ. The first and the greatest of the labours of Jesus Christ is his victory over the serpent, the evil principle, or the devil. In his first labour Hercules strangled the serpent, as did Cristna, Bacchus, &c. This is the sun triumphing over the powers of hell and darkness; and, as he increases, he prevails, till he is crucified in the heavens, or is decussated in the form of a cross, (according to Justin Martyr,[2]) when he passes the equator at the vernal equinox. But before he rises he is dead for one day and about four hours. This is nearly the time necessary to be intercalated every six hundred years, to make the calculation come right; at the beginning of the third day he rises again to life and immortality. The twelve labours of Hercules are his labours in passing through the signs of the zodiac, which are so similar to the

---

[1] Mr. Bentley states, p. 52, that the sun entered Pisces at the vernal equinox, 746 years B. C. He is here in a great error, or Cæsar and Sosigenes were in a great error in fixing the solstice to the 25th of December; and our globes are equally in error now in fixing the equinox to the first or thirtieth of Aquarius. This seems a mistake of Mr. Bentley's which I cannot comprehend. The sun certainly only entered the sign Pisces five degrees, or $5 \times 72 = 360$ years B. C. I will not assert the fact, but I have very little doubt that the intentional fraud Mr. Bentley speaks of in the Brahmin astronomers, all arose from the mistake of the 576 years, and the neglect of the intercalary days, of the necessity for which the modern Brahmins were ignorant.

[2] See Vol. I. p. 789.

history of Jesus Christ, as to induce the reverend, pious, and orthodox Parkhurst to declare them *types of what the real Saviour was to do and suffer.* These celestial images are what induced the learned Alphonso the Great to declare, that the whole history of Jesus Christ might be read in the stars.

No doubt this explanation of the three days' descent into hell will be separated from the other explanations of the mythos, and thus, taking it alone, it will be represented as extremely ridiculous. But, I ask, What were the entombment and resurrection of Bacchus, Atys, Apollo of Miletus, of Adonis, of Cristna, of Buddha, &c., &c.? Were these real deaths and resurrections, or astronomical mythoses?

In this book I think I have proved, that every rite, ceremony, and doctrine, which is found in the Christian religion, was a close copy of that of the Gentiles. Mr. Mosheim[1] is obliged to admit this, nearly to the extent here stated, and he endeavours to disguise and palliate it by pretending that they were taken into the Christian religion. But as I have proved that every rite, ceremony, and doctrine, of the Romish church is taken from the Heathens, and existed before the time of Jesus Christ, I beg leave to ask, Where is the remainder which is not Pagan, and which is to constitute the Christianity of the present day? The Christianity of Jesus Christ, from his own mouth, I shall exhibit in a future book, in its native and beautiful simplicity, unalloyed with Pagan, Paulite, Romish, Lutheran, or Calvinistic nonsense.

That which I have written is intended for the use of philosophers, as I have said in my Preface. How should the generality of mankind, occupied in the affairs of life, be expected to understand such a book? No, no; let them attend to their secular concerns, count their beads, and say their prayers, resting content with the religion of their ancestors, and be assured that God is equally present with the pious Hindoo in the temple, the Jew in the synagogue, the Mohammedan in the mosque, and the Christian in the church. Peter said, very wisely, *Of a truth I perceive that God is no respecter of persons; but in every nation he that feareth him, and worketh righteousness, is accepted with him.*[2]

I must fairly admit, that I cannot read what I have written without an indescribable melancholy. In what a state of delusion have four-fifths of mankind been kept, and still are kept, by the dishonesty of the remainder; and, in the teeth of my humble and feeble efforts, I fear always will be kept! But, at all events, I have done my duty; I have endeavoured, with no little labour, to draw aside the veil. I know what I deserve; I fear, I know what I shall receive, from my self-sufficient and ignorant countrymen. But yet, a new æra is rising. There still is hope in the bottom of the box. But one word more I must say of the Eternal City, before I close this article; it may serve for a warning.

It is a striking circumstance that the Pagans themselves boasted of the greatness of Rome, not only as the capital of the empire, but as the head of their religion, of which it was the centre; on account of which it was called by Atheneus Ουρανοπολιν, or the Holy City, Ruma Mamma, the residence of the Gods.[3] It was called the Goddess of the earth and of the nations, at the very moment that the axe was laid to its root, and that, by the treason of Constantine, its altars were about to be overthrown, its religion destroyed, and it was to be degraded to the rank of a provin-

---

[1] Comm. Cent. ii. Sect. xxxvi. n.

[2] Acts x. 34, 35.—For most of the articles in the above parallel between the rites of the ancient and modern Romans, I am indebted to a small treatise lent me by my friend Ed. Upham, Esq., entitled, "Les Conformités des Cérémonies Modernes avec les Anciennes. Imprimé l'An 1667.

[3] Lucan, lib. i., Deûm Sedes, Mart. lib. xii. Epigrorum. 8; Claud. de Laud. Stilic.

cial town. Thus, at this time, when loaded with corruption, its religion rotten to the core, and evidently at its last gasp, still, as in former times, it calls itself *eternal;* its pompous, empty, tawdry cardinals, bending beneath ermine, fat, and ignorance, waddle about their grass-grown streets and crumbling ruins, which would long since have yielded to the pest which surrounds them, had not the remnant of the fine arts of Greece procured to it a temporary respite. But, proud Rome, thy race is nearly run—thy day is nearly over. One century more, and, like haughty Babylon, the curious stranger, probably with fear and trembling, will ramble round thy ruins, and say, This *was* the eternal city! Here *was* Rome!

> Sure as the shaft that slayeth in the night,
> The pestilence glides slowly, robed in light.
> All-glorious Italy, o'er thy fair champaign
> The smiling fiend extends her silent reign.
> And desolation follows. Lo! she stands
> On the proud capitol, with noiseless hands
> Showering the secret ruin on the dome
> Of thy great temple, everlasting Rome!
>
> HERBERT's *Pia della Pietra*, p. 12.

(147)

BOOK III.

CHAPTER I.

ORIGIN OF LETTERS. — MOON'S PERIOD. — NAMES OF LETTERS. — SOUCHER. — DR. WAIT ON SANSCRIT. — CYCLE OF FOURTEEN. — THOTH. — OM. HOMER. — TARGUMS. — DR. YOUNG. SOL. — JOSEPH, PROTEUS. STALLS. — SOLOMON. SINDI. PETER. — CRYPTOGRAPHY, INDIAN. — VOWEL POINTS. — ACROSTIC. ANAGRAM. METATHESIS. THE NUMBER NINE. — ARABIC LETTERS. — THE GOD XANGTI. —'Εις, μια, ἑν. — SIGNETS. — SIGMA TAU. — ADAM. GENESIS.

1. THE following book will chiefly consist of a development of the mode in which the most important of all the various branches of human science, the art of writing, was discovered and brought to perfection. But before my reader begins to examine it, I must beg him to reperuse and reconsider the Preliminary Observations in Volume I., which have relation to the origin of letters and figures. Those Observations, chiefly taken from my work on the CELTIC DRUIDS, I inserted there, for the purpose of assisting in this investigation.

When I go back to the most remote periods of antiquity into which it is possible to penetrate, I find clear and positive evidence of several important facts. *First*, no animal food was eaten—no animals were sacrificed.[1] *Secondly*, it is recorded, and it seems probable, that the Gods had no names, and that no icons were used;[2] and almost all ancient nations had a tradition, that they once possessed sacred writings in a long-lost language. The possessors of these writings and this old language, I think, must have been the people who erected the Pyramids, the gigantic stone circles, and the other Cyclopæan buildings, which are found of such peculiar character and size all over the world. The language of these nations, or, in fact, the lost language which they used, we will now try to discover—assuming, that it was the first written language of man.

In the Preliminary Observations, Section 31–47, I have shewn how I suppose the Latin, Etruscan, or Phœnician, system of describing numbers by right lines arose—each number described by a collection of these lines, having had the name of a tree given to it. I find my opinion on this subject strongly supported by a passage of Vallancey's, which, when I wrote the Preliminary Observations, I had overlooked or not observed.[3] He says, "The Romans used literary characters "as numerals, and in alphabetic order as the Chaldæans did, so late as Julius Cæsar's time. In "the sixth century a Julian kalendar was dug up at Rome, on which the days of the month were "numbered by letters in alphabetic order, beginning with A at the first day of January, B to the "second, and so on to H, or the eighth day, which was their *Nundinæ*, from which day they "began again with A B C D E F G H, instead of I. II. III. IV. V. VI. VII. VIII., which were the "Phœnician and Palmyræan vulgar numerals."[4] If we could be certain that Palmyra was built by Solomon or the Jews, we should have a very good reason, indeed I may say a certainty, for

---

[1] Sacrifice—Sacrum Festum—sacrificium.
[2] This was because the God of Wisdom, or the *wise* God, was worshiped.
[3] Coll. Hib. Vol. V. p. 186.
[4] Vide Scaliger de Emend. Temp. p. 160.

u 2

believing that the right-lined numbers of the Phœnicians were also those of the Jews. As it is, we have a very high probability that they were so.

Before we begin the following speculation we will suppose that man had advanced so far as to have given names to trees, and to have called a certain tree Elm, another tree Birch, and others by appropriate appellations, and had called his first number, described by the mark I, *Ailm*, and his second number, described by the mark II, *Beth* or *Birch*, &c. In this case I would denote an idea of number, viz. *one*, and a sound, viz. *Ailm*; and II would denote an idea of number, viz. *two*, and a sound, viz. *Beth*; and each would denote a tree generally, and the two would also denote two peculiar trees, as distinguished from others, viz. the Elm and Birch: so each arithmetical figure or little collection of lines would have five significations. It would denote a number, a tree generally, a Birch tree, and a sound; and, after the discovery of alphabetic writing, a letter. Thus there would be a language like what the Chinese language and the Runes of Scandinavia are at this day. That is, there would be a symbol for every sound or name of a thing, for the thing itself, and for a number, and the number would, by association of ideas, be closely connected with leaves and trees. Thus this language of symbols would have five meanings, exactly as the language of the sacred books of the Tamuls is said to have had; and a question naturally arises, whether this language of numeral symbols may not have been the very language referred to by the Tamulese, as that in which their sacred books were written. This induces me to make a few observations on the Tamul language before I proceed further. At first, the distance of the place in which we find the Italian and the Phœnician right-lined letters or figures, from the country of the Tamuls, South India, certainly seems very great, but it becomes less, when it is recollected that we have exhibited individuals miscalled Christians, but who, in fact, were the followers of Tammuz, in South India, using the Pushto language of Syria, and the absolute identity of the worship of the *fishes* in both countries.

Dr. Babington says, "I cannot touch on the Tamil characters without remarking, that their extreme simplicity seems one among many circumstances which indicate that the language is of high antiquity. The Sanscrit of the South of India is written in characters (the Grant'ha) derived from the Tamil." The learned Doctor then proceeds to give reasons for the Tamil having an independent origin, at least equal in antiquity to the Sanscrit itself.[1] The name of the Tamul language is Pushto, and the root of this word Push, which I shall examine hereafter, means *a flower*, and this system of letters was sixteen in number, like that of the ancient Jews. The language of the Chinese, which we have just observed is a language of symbols, was called *the language of flowers*.[2]

I consider my system to receive no small support from the following passage of the Universal Ancient History:[3] "That the ancient language of the Chinese was pretty nearly related to the Hebrew, and the other tongues which the learned consider as dialects of it, notwithstanding what has been advanced to the contrary, we own ourselves inclined to believe. Ludovicus Thomassinus, Philippus Massonius, Olaus Rudbeckius, and Augustus Pfeifferus, seem to have proved this almost to a demonstration." M. Balbi, in a late learned work, has turned the arguments of the above-named persons and our Edinburgh historians into ridicule; but my experience teaches me, that ridicule is never had recourse to, till argument fails. Near Gaya, which is the place where Saca or Sacya finished his doctrine and became Buddha, is a tree called by the Chinese *Poo te choo* or the *Tree of Knowledge*.[4] The Chinese in a particular manner call their written

---

[1] Trans. Asiat. Soc. Vol. II. Part I. p. 264.
[2] Vol. XX. p. 131.
[3] See Vol. I. pp. 482, 738, 750, 753, 775, 779.
[4] Neuman, Catechism Shaman, p. xix.

language the flowery language, which I suppose is the language of *flowers* or *leaves*.¹ I apprehend this comes from their numeral symbols having had the names of plants.² This tree of knowledge seems to have been the Pushto, or Push, or Pote-sato. Every thing tends to raise a probability, that the Chinese and the Western languages of symbols were the same. I will now proceed with my theory, but I shall return to the Pushto and Chinese presently.

After man had used the right lines for some time, he would discover the art of making a figure to use instead of the collection of lines, and we will suppose him to have made or invented twenty-eight figures for the twenty-eight numbers which I have supposed him to have discovered; how this was done I will presently explain. We have an example of this in the tree alphabet, Table I. Nos. 8 to 10, and in the Runic alphabet, in THE CELTIC DRUIDS, pp. 4, 5.

We have thus, I think, very easily found how it is probable that the first *symbolical* system of writing was invented; but we have not yet found out the grand secret—the art of syllabic or alphabetic writing—though we have symbols for ideas and sounds.³

On this art Mr. Astle⁴ says, "Those authors whose learning and ingenuity entitle them to the " highest respect, and whose writings have furnished many useful hints towards the discovery of " alphabetic characters, *have not filled up the* GREAT CHASM between picture writing and letters, " which, though the most difficult was the most necessary thing for them to have done, before " they could attempt to account for the formation of an alphabet!" Mr. Astle does not pretend to have filled up the chasm. I think I shall be able to do it.

2. For the reasons given in the Preliminary Observations, (pp. 2, 3,) I cannot have any doubt that one of the first recorded ideas would be the moon's period, for which the twenty-eight numbers would be used, and perhaps one of the first *things* recorded would be the moon herself, by means of these numbers. In this case the record would be described by XXVIII, and by its component parts called Iod (i. e. Yew) pronounced twice, and Eadha (i. e. Aspin) once, and Ailm (i. e. Elm) three times. The use of these symbols for the twenty-eight numbers would soon lead to the formation of arbitrary signs for other things; and, in short, to the present Chinese writing—a mark or symbol for every word: and on this plan the Chinese have proceeded, exerting all their ingenuity, as we know, for thousands of years, having never left their first habit, or changed their first style of writing; the reason for which, I think, we shall discover hereafter.

The Western nations took a different course, and fell into the habit of making their letters for sounds instead of ideas of things, and thus in some way, which we will try to find out, the syllabic system arose. We have supposed that they first described the moon by marks which would represent twenty-eight units, that they would write it thus XXVIII; and, I suppose, that they would perform the operation in the following manner: if a man had to desire his neighbour to assist him to record the moon, he would say, make on the stone tablet or in the sand the mark Iod (yew), and he would make X. The speaker would then say, make or mark another Iod, and again

---

¹ Neuman, Catechism Shamas, p. 63.

² It seems to me that a language of symbols is totally unfit to communicate *proper names*, for which reason in translating from the Chinese, if the written account is to be followed, that is, the idea of the thing to be given, our names ought to be rendered as we render them. If the sounds used by the Chinese in speaking, for our names, are to be described, then a writer may copy the sounds as well as he is able. I suspect it is from a wish to do both, that Mr. Neuman has rendered proper names in so odd a manner. England is called *Ying keih le*; the Russians are called *Go lo sse*.

³ In the symbols for sounds began the first idea of music, an art considered by the ancients, and particularly by Pythagoras, as of much greater importance than it is with us; the reason for which I shall try to explain by and by.

⁴ Origin and Progress of Writing, p. 11.

he would mark X; now make an Eadha, and he would make V; now make an Ailm; and this order would be repeated twice, and he would make three lines III, and it would form our XXVIII. But neither the speaker nor the writer would pronounce this word, however much he might wish it, except by repeating the names of the trees—any more than we can pronounce 10, 10, 5, 3, as a word. Here, however, we have clearly a written, but an unspoken language of symbols.

We may now ask, How man, in the experiment which we have supposed him to try on the moon, would write the XXVIII? We know from history that it would not be horizontally, but perpendicularly, and must have been in one of the following ways:

$$\text{XXVIII} \quad or \quad \text{XXVIII} \quad or \quad \text{IIIAXX} \quad or \quad \text{XXVIII}$$

Suppose we write the word in our letters, but in the name of Celtic Irish trees, and in the above Etruscan or Italian numbers and manner, to see how it will look. We shall have them thus, beginning to read on the left side of the page:

Iod		‏od	X	X		Ailm		— X		—
Iod		‏od	X	X	Iod, Iod, Uearn, Ailm, Ailm,	Ailm		— X		—
Eadha	or	ᴇ adha	V	V	or	Uearn	or	ᴄ V	or	ᴄ
Ailm		ᴀ ilm	I	I	Another example	Iod		ᴀ I	ⁿ	ᴀ
Ailm		ᴀ ilm	I	I		Iod		ᴀ I	ⁿ	ᴀ
Ailm		ᴀ ilm	I	I						

Here, writing from the top downwards, and turning the paper to read—accordingly as we turn it, to right or left, we read in the Sanscrit and Greek manner, or the Hebrew and Arabic manner. Here we have the exact mode of writing, and of turning the paper, which is yet used in the Syrian, that is, the Pushto or Estrangelo language, as I learn from Dr. Hagar—writing it from the top to the bottom, but turning the paper and reading from right to left. This is confirmed by Vallancey, who shews, that it was the habit of the Tartarian nations, and quotes Forster, who says, "The " characters and mode of writing of the Calmucks, Moguls, and Mandschurians, are taken from " the Uigurian, and these again from the Syrian. These Syrians also still continue, to this day, to " write exactly as the Calmucks do, viz. they begin at the top, and draw a line down to the bottom, " with which line the letters are in contact from the top down to the bottom of it; and so they " continue to write one line after the other, at each line going farther on to the right, and carrying " their writing from the *top to the bottom*. But in reading, the Moguls and Calmucks, in like man-" ner as the Syrians, turn the leaf sideways and read *from the right to the left*."[1] These Calmucks and Moguls, who have characters taken from the Syrian, that is, I suppose, the Pushto, are generally called Tartars. It may be remembered, that we formerly found the Fossiones *Tartarum* in Italy, the country in which we found the first right-lined letter figures of Syria or Phœnicia.

Mr. Forster says, "This perpendicular way of writing was not unknown to the Greeks, who " called it, as *Bayer* observes, χαιμαι φορον, and was usual among the Syrians too, who, accord-" ing to Abraham Echelensis, wrote in this way."[2] The Greeks, as I have formerly observed, also called this Tapocon.

---

[1] Forster's Hist. of Voyages and Discoveries, &c., note, p. 106; Vall. Coll. Hib. Vol. VI. pp. 173, 174.
[2] Dr. Hagar on the Alphabet of Corea, Or. Col. Vol. III.; Vallancey, Coll. Hib. Vol. VI. p. 173.

"Tapocon Græci soliti sunt appellare genus scribendi deorsum versus, ut nunc detrorsum scri-
"bimus."[1]

And it appears from a letter of Gen. Vallancey's to General Pownall, that the ancient Irish also wrote in the perpendicular line.[2] And to these nations I have to add the Ethiopians. "Ethiopi-
"bus olim hunc modum (meaning the writing from top to bottom) familiarem quoque fuisse,
"docet Alexander ab Alexandro."[3]

I suppose that the experiment above mentioned, as made by man on the Moon's cycle, would, after some time, lead him to attend to the sounds of the trees' names, and that he would necessarily fall on the sounds of the first letters of the words, and be induced to try if he could call this word XXVIII by them: this he would do with ease, on the very first attempt, by pronouncing (a

$\overset{XXVIII}{}$ $\overset{XXVIII}{}$

very remarkable word) IIEA, I I EAAA, or in the other way, I I V AA, which was the word chaunted by the Bacchantes of the Greeks, in their nocturnal orgies—Evohe, Evohe; and, in short, Eva, addressed to the Moon; and also the word Yeve or Yeye, chaunted by the Hindoos in their ceremonies.[4] I have seldom been more surprised than I was when I discovered this process to bring out the Moon's name; but yet, when I consider the matter, it appears only natural if my theory be well founded. This word is also nothing more than the name of Ieue, described in Genesis by the word in the feminine gender אלהים aleim. In this extraordinary word we have united, first the monograms of God *I* and *II*, by which he is called in the Chaldee targum, and secondly בוא or וא היה *hue*, the two names of the male and female principles of nature. We may now see another reason why the letter or symbol I and the tenth letter, the jod, came to be considered the symbol of the Self-existent Being, and how the irregular verb היה *eie* or היה *hie* of the Hebrew arose, and came to mean self-existence.

In the first two letters of this word " *ii* we have the name given in the Annals of Ulster, and in sepulcral monuments now existing, to the island of Iona or Columba, in Scotland, the name of which island, I shall hereafter shew, meant the *generative power*. It is also remarkable that this word " *ii* is always used in the Targum for the name of the Creator instead of IEUE. But I can find the grammatical explanation of it in no Lexicon or Grammar, and I believe it cannot be shewn that it belongs to any verb or noun.

I believe that this word, from its connexion with letters, which I have just pointed out, and with the soli-lunar cycle of 28, came to be the name of the Creator of the male generative power, and the *vau* to be the name of the female. I believe that the jod י *i* has the same meaning in Hebrew and English; and that the word *is* which we use for the third person singular of the present tense of the verb personal *he is*, must be the first person singular of the present tense of the Hebrew helping verb יש *is*, and means *I am*, or I *is*, being the same as *I exist*. It probably must be the same in the first, second, and third persons singular. It also means, Parkhurst says, *substance*, and, as we might expect, from the word which describes the Self-existent Being, PROFOUND WISDOM; and this I consider very deserving of consideration.

I could not have wished for any thing more proper for my purpose, than that this word should, in this very extraordinary manner, from the names of trees and the powers of their numbers combined, thus unexpectedly give out the name of the moon as used by the Bacchantes—the name

---

[1] Festus *de Verbor. Signific.*, Hager, Babyl. Bricks, p. 51.   [2] Pownall on Ant. p. 219.

[3] Genial. Dier. Lib. ii. Cap. xxx. Synopsis Universæ Philologiæ, Godofredo Henselio, p. 104. Drummond says, that the Ethiopian language was Chaldaic. Punic Inscriptions, III. 24, 40, 75; and Vallancey has undertaken to prove the ancient Irish to be a colony from Phœnicia.

[4] See Vol. I. pp. 325, 452.

described by numerals having the number of the cycle peculiarly appropriate to it, which I shall presently shew that all the other heathen Gods also had; and also the name of Jehovah IEUE the Chaldæan God, and PROFOUND WISDOM. It amounts to a proof of the truth of the system much more complete than could have been reasonably expected. It forms a very strong presumption that I have actually fallen upon the very process which must have taken place. But this will be much strenghtened presently.

3. To return to the symbols. After man discovered the art of recording numbers by right lines, in the way already described, to the amount of twenty-eight, he would endeavour to find out some means of recording additional numbers, at the same time that he would try to simplify the process; and I suppose that after making one line thus, I, for *one*, he would, instead of making two lines for the *two*, make one straight lined symbol thus ⅃, and again call it by the name of *Beth*, the name of a tree (Birch); that for *three* III, he would make a symbol thus ᒣ, and call it *Gort* (the Ivy); that for *four* IIII, he would make a symbol thus Δ, and call it *Duir* (the Oak): and that thus he would proceed with the remainder of the twenty-eight numbers, making twenty-eight single right-lined and angular forms for his twenty-eight numbers. And I suppose that during the performance of this operation, which might take many years, (for in nations which actually made some progress in this process it never was completed,) he found out the means of recording additional numbers by discovering the decimal notation or arithmetic—the contrivance of beginning anew, when he got to *ten*, till he reached *twenty*; then beginning anew with tens as he had done with ones or units; thus I was ten, K was twenty, Λ was *thirty*, and so on. Thus he contrived a symbol for each figure. But if we consider this process carefully, we shall find, that each symbol was not only the representative of a thing or idea, namely, in the case of the second number, or chequers, of two stones, or of two lines on the bark of a tree or in the sand, but it was in each case also the representative of a sound, and of that sound which was the name of a tree, Beth, the Birch; and the representative of a number, *two*; and, in several instances, of a high and powerful number; as for example, Σ for 200.

This is all strengthened by the *facts*, that the first Celtic Irish and Hebrew letters were called after the names of trees, and that the first Greek letters were in lines, γραμμα, to use their word for them, and actually still continued to be called πεταλα, or leaves, after the knowledge of the reason for it was lost; and they will justify the inference that the theory which I have suggested above is well founded, because the theory shews a probable reason for the name of πεταλα having been adopted. If the letters of the Greeks were not originally *leaves* like the Hebrew[1] and the Irish or Celtic, why should they have given them the name of *leaves?* What connexion on any other scheme is there between πεταλα, leaves, and letters?

We have found that the Chaldees had their letters in *lines* or *gramma* also; and, as the Hebrew letters had the names of trees, and as the Greeks had their letters from Syria, nothing is more likely than that they should have originally called them after trees as the Hebrews did. But Pezron has shewn that the Greek came from the Celtic, that is, from the Hebrew. But if the Hebrew names of the letters had not, in later times, in the Greek language, the meaning of trees, this makes nothing against the system, because we may readily suppose in the long time that the Greeks may have existed before the arrival of the Cadmæan colony, they may have lost them. Vallancey has said, that the Chaldaic was only used as numerals, not as letters; that the Chaldee

---

[1] It must not be forgotten, that I assume I have proved that the Celtic and the Hebrew were the same. See Vol. I. pp. 461, 518, 709.

language is the same as the Estrangelo, which is the Pushto. This is also stated by several other learned men.

The word for letter in Latin is *litera*, which has been said to be derived from the Arabic لطىف *letif*, which signifies *an occult or mysterious meaning*. This Arabic letif is evidently our *leaf*, and shews that it is highly probable, as I have supposed, that the Arabic letters had the same names as the Hebrew. In fact Hebrew and Arabic are the same. Here in the old Latin or Etruscan *litera*, as in the Greek, the Hebrew, and the Celtic, we have the *leaves*.

Dr. Lingard, in his history, says, "I would attribute to these ancient priests the Rhŷn or mys-"terious language, so often mentioned by the bards (of Wales). To every tree and shrub, to their "leaves, flowers, and branches, they seem to have affixed a fanciful and symbolical meaning; and "these allegorical substitutes for the real names of beings and their properties must have formed, "in their numerous combinations, a species of jargon perfectly unintelligible TO ANY BUT THE "ADEPTS."[1] But why did not Dr. Lingard try to find the meaning of this jargon?[2] The Rbŷn here alluded to, is the Rhythm or the Arithmos of the Greeks; it was the Arithmetical system of letters formed by straight lines, having the powers of numbers and the names of leaves, and carried, I doubt not, to a much greater length than the first twenty-eight of the Arabians. It was the language of trees, of leaves, of flowers. It was in truth, probably, the first original Pushto, or language of flowers, corrupted, which I shall discuss by and by.

A learned writer, in the Universal History,[3] maintains, that the Syrian or Assyrian characters, (or Pushto,) which he calls the Estrangelo or Mendæan, in the time of Darius Hystaspes, were used by the old Persians, Assyrians, Syrians, Arabians, and Mendæans or Chaldæans, and that from this letter all the others in the East were derived; and Mr. Bayer has maintained, that, from the Estrangelo, the Brahmin characters were derived. Now we know that the Estrangelo, called also Pushto, was the letter of the Tamulese, and was in all probability older than the Sanscrit. Mr. Bayer also comes to the conclusion,[4] that the square Chaldaic character was the primigenial letter of the East. As he comes to this conclusion without knowing any thing of the fact—that it was the vernacular letter and tongue of a tribe, namely, the Christians or Crestans of Malabar, his opinion seems to deserve the greater respect. I apprehend that the square Chaldee letter was the primeval letter of the East, because it was, as Vallancey says, a letter of numeral symbols, of the first written but unspoken languages. Bayer maintains that the Pehlevi, which he calls Parthic, is derived from the Assyrian alphabet, called Estrangelo.[5]

I beg my reader to observe, that if the unspoken language of numeral symbols were written from the top to the bottom, the consequence would be, that when those symbols were used for syllabic letters, they would necessarily come, in different countries, to be used in different directions— sometimes from right to left, and sometimes from left to right; so that the same word would come to be pronounced in ways totally different: for instance, *cor* might be *ros*, and *ros* might be *cor*.

4. After I had finished what the reader has seen on the origin of language, I met with a passage in Boucher's Glossary, appended to Webster's Dictionary,[6] which supports every thing which I have said respecting the ancient Hebrew language in these islands, in a remarkable manner. Indeed, whenever any learned man undertakes to shew the similarity of any two old languages, he

---

[1] Vol. I. p. 18.

[2] Ogum craobh, "the branch writing," is surely decisive as to the correctness of the opinion of those who advocate the *Three* system. One of the three Seronyddion (Saronides?) of Britain was Gwyddion, *the Diviner by trees*. Cambrian Mag.

[3] Vol. I. p. 81, n. [4] Ib. p. 82.

[5] See Act. Erudit. Jul. 1731; Hagar, Babyl. Bricks, p. 14. [6] P. xxxv.

is always right. The principle applies as well to language as to geometry—things similar to the same are similar to one another. "If any language can be pointed out to which the Welsh is "materially indebted, it is the Hebrew;[1] for, there are several radical words that are the same in "both languages; there is also a similarity of sound in certain letters of both alphabets; and "they are likewise alike in some peculiarities of construction, especially in the change incident to "several letters in the beginning of words. The analogy between the Welsh and the Hebrew "proves, that since (as far as any negative can be proved) the former was not the original lan-"guage, it must be indebted, in a very considerable degree, for its origin, to the latter; for ac-"cording to Rowland,[2] *there are more sounds in the Welsh that agree with the Hebrew, than there* "*are in all other languages put together.* And it is extremely remarkable and peculiar, that the "Welsh has no resemblance to, nor coherence in, sound and signification (its own immediate "cognate dialects excepted) with any other language in the world, now known, except the "Hebrew." I must now beg my reader to refer to my CELTIC DRUIDS, Chapter II. p. 63, where he will find full and *complete proof* that the Welsh is really Hebrew. He will there find not a few words sufficient to support the assertion, according to the doctrine of Dr. Young, but actually a whole sentence from the Psalms of David, where the Welsh and the Hebrew words, when written in the same letters, are identical. I must now beg my reader to turn to the Plates in Volume I., Figure 26, the coin on which has a Hebrew inscription. To which I have to add, that some time ago, in one of the books of antiquities, but which I have forgotten, I met with a description of a Hebrew inscription on a large stone in some part of Wales. And now I wish to ask any one how a coin with the head of Jesus Christ and a legend, *in a language obsolete in the time of Jesus Christ*, should arrive in Wales and get buried in an old Druidical monument? I contend, that the probability is, that it is a memorial older than Jesus Christ, of the son of that individual of the three Marys, to whom, in his infancy, the line referred, which Mr. Davies suppressed, as stated by me in Volume I. p. 593, the Son of the Virgo Paritura of Gaul. Whether this medal represents the son of the Virgo Paritura, found in the Western countries long before the Christian æra, or Jesus Christ, cannot be reduced to a demonstration. Many things of this kind, I believe, have been found in different times and places, but always immediately discarded, as merely superstitious works of devotees of the middle ages. Thus truth is disguised, without any ill intention, by well meaning persons. In like manner Sir I. Floyer *throws out* the acrostic from the Sibyls, because he says it is a Christian forgery. In like manner Mr. Davies,[2] in a translation of a Welsh bard, leaves out the last two lines, because he says the bard had introduced a Christian idea representing *the son of Mary as the pledge of his happiness.* This Mary was probably one of the three Marys of Gaul, and her son, the Lamb of the Carnutes, the Saviour,[4] or one of the three Marys found upon an altar of Hercules at Doncaster. In this feeling of authors, influencing them for thousands of years, I doubt not may be found one of the chief causes of the disappearance of the Judæan mythos.

In addition to the above, and as a strong support of what I have elsewhere said respecting the Saxon language, I cite the following passage, which is in p. xxxviii. of Boucher: "For, by the

---

[1] "See Lhuyd's comparative etymology in the *Archæologia Britannica*, where he shews that the Celtic, itself from "the East, was the common parent of all the languages of Europe. See Pezron, Dr. Davies's preface; Holloway's "Originals, and lastly, Rowland's Comparative Table of Languages, in which he hath paralleled three hundred Hebrew "words, with an equal number taken from the ancient languages of Europe, corresponding therewith, both in sound "and signification, more than one half of which three hundred words, are shewn to have a surprising affinity and "resemblance with the Welsh."

[2] "See his *Mona Antiqua*, &c., p. 271."   [3] Celt. Myth. p. 253.   [4] See *supra*, p. 108.

" operation of one of the simplest figures in rhetoric, metathesis or transposition, i. e. merely a
" different arrangement of the same, or nearly the same letters, many Celtic words, even now,
" might easily be made Saxon: thus *draen* readily becomes *dern* and *thorn*, and *daear* no less
" naturally *erd* or *earth*." This arises merely from the different ways in which the line has been
turned when the writing was changed to the horizontal from the perpendicular. The Celtic reading
from left to right, instead of from right to left, of course places these words in contrary ways,
as found here. But if I have shewn (in my Celtic Druids), as most assuredly I have, that the
Celtic is Hebrew, this proves the Saxon to be Hebrew. For the Saxon being Celtic, and the Celtic
Hebrew, the Saxon must be Hebrew.[1] Things like to the same must be like to one another.
Besides I beg the doctrine of Dr. Young on probabilities may be applied to this. It is extremely
curious to observe how learned men labour to exclude themselves from the benefit of the real
learning of their predecessors. This arises from various causes; one of which is, the great antipathy which almost all philosophers have to the oldest books in the world—the books of Genesis;
and this dislike arises from the manner in which these books are made subservient to their selfish
purposes by both Jewish and Christian priests. For fear, therefore, of aiding them, the philosopher can never be brought to examine those books like any others; but the moment they are
named, off he goes; he will neither examine them, nor listen to any one who does. Therefore if
any person attempts an impartial examination, he is instantly poh-pohed down; the philosopher
is instantly aided both by Jews and Christians, for they have as much objection to a fair examination as the philosopher. This extends to the language in which the books are written, to the
Hebrew, because the priests endeavour to bolster up their interests and their fooleries by maintaining that the Hebrew language is the *oldest*, and therefore the *sacred* language. No man has
been more successful in his antiquarian researches than Vallancey; but, I really believe, merely
because he has traced the old Gods, &c., of the Irish to the Phœnician or Hebrew language, the
philosophers have been foolish enough to join the priests in running him down. The latter soon
discovered that Vallancey was likely to discover too much for them; and almost all the English
joined in decrying the literature of the Irish, because they envied them the honour of it, and because they hated the nation they oppressed and plundered. Of all this Mr. Adrian Balbi, in his
Ethnography, furnishes a fair example. For, in treating of the Mexican language, notwithstanding the close affinity between the Hebrew and the Mexican, which, in defiance of monks and
priests, has been so clearly proved, he never notices it. He acts in nearly the same manner with
regard to the Irish alphabets, and says, " De grands historiens et des philologues profonds ont déjà
" apprécié convenablement ces rêveries historiques, et ont démontré que ces alphabets, qu'on
" prétendait être antérieurs à l'alphabet Grec, ont été fabriqués par de pieux moines dans le
" moyen âge." If M. Balbi had looked into Vallancey's works, at the Irish alphabets, the Bobeloth
and the Bethluisnion, of which I have given copies in Vol. I. p. 9, and had used his understanding,
he would in one moment have seen, that they both possess the digamma or vau, which the Greeks
never used after the time of Aristotle, and, therefore, that they could not have been copied from
their alphabet by the monks of the middle ages; and secondly, that they both possess correctly
and simply the Cadmæan letters; and therefore it is totally incredible, that the monks should

---

[1] The Celtic is PROVED to be Hebrew in the Celtic Druids, (p. 63,) and in the Monthly Magazine, Vol. II. p. 609, and Vol. III. p. 10. The Celtic and the Hebrew are proved to be the same, in the Universal History, Vol. XVIII. p. 363, Vol. V. p 411. See also Diss. on Hist. of Ireland, Dublin, p. 48, 1763. I also beg my reader to turn to Vol. I. p. 109, and *supra*, Chap. I. p. 4, and to consider well what the well-known excellent Hebrew and Saxon scholar, Dr. Geddes, has said, in his Critical Remarks, respecting the identity of the Hebrew and Saxon.

have copied them only, leaving out the additional or new letters. The two facts taken together prove, that the old Irish or Celtic letters were not taken from the Greek, but were the same as the sixteen-letter alphabets of the Hebrew, the Tamul, and the Pushto or Peshito. Speaking of Gebelin, Balbi says, " Parmi les fautes grossières dont il fourmille, et que ses partisans ont répandues " dans un grand nombre d'ouvrages, on y lit, entr' autres, que le Persan, l'Arménien, le *Malais* et l'Égyptien sont des dialects de l'Hébreu." But very certain I am, that, notwithstanding the dogmatical assertion of the learned Balbi, this must not be classed among the mistakes of the learned Gebelin. The Count Gebelin is right; because all the languages of the world contained in syllabic writing, unless the Sanscrit be excepted, may be traced to one, and the Synagogue or Samaritan Hebrew is nearer to that one, merely from the accidental circumstance of its concealment in the Syrian temple. Wherever it and the Chaldæan priests went, there the remains of it will be found. It was the language of Ayoudia. It was the language of Pandea, in India, of Ceylon, Scotland, Ireland, and of Syria. Whenever a learned man attempts to shew the affinity of any two of *these languages*, he always succeeds; in the same manner he always succeeds in shewing their affinity to the Hebrew. No doubt it may be shewn more clearly in the languages of some nations than in those of others,—for instance, in Arabic and Celtic, than in Indian. This I attribute in a great measure to the fine Sanscrit having by degrees superseded it. Only in the broken dialects of India can it be expected to be found, and upon all these the Sanscrit has exercised an overwhelming influence. The observation of the Count Gebelin, respecting the MALAYS' speaking Hebrew, noticed just now, forcibly recalls to my recollection what was said by my learned friend Salome, respecting the Hebrew-speaking Malays, found by him in the dépôt of the English India house.[1]

All that I have said respecting the Hebrew I think may be said to be *unwillingly* admitted by the learned Balbi in the following words: " Dans ces dernières, l'Hébreu *surtout* offre, pendant " une longue suite de siècles, une étonnante fixité, soit dans les formes, soit dans les mots : fixité " qui est d'autant plus remarquable que, durant ce long intervalle, les Juifs subirent les plus grands " changements politiques."[2] This astonishing *fixité* of language, I have shewn, had its reason or cause in the accidental preservation in the temple, combined with the dogma which forbade all change. Had we any other sacred book of any one of the mysterious temples, we should probably have found it the same. Though the manuscripts might be torn and dispersed in the time of Jerome, yet still they were parts of the old book. Various opinions have been held respecting the primitive race and language, which have been often confounded, though by no means necessarily so; but unquestionably the great majority of learned writers have come to the opinion, that the Hebrew, as a written language, is the oldest, and this without any regard to religious considerations.

I mentioned in the note of p. 1, that Dr. Wait had observed " there were an IMMENSE NUMBER " of Chaldee roots to be found in the Sanscrit" language. I surely need not point out to the reader of this work what an amazing support the disinterested evidence of this learned man gives to my theory. It almost amounts to a proof that the ancient Tamul, the Estrangelo, the Pushto, must have been the Hebrew-Chaldee-Ethiopian-Syriac on which the Sanscrit was built. That is, it actually proves the truth of the hypothesis advocated by me in the above-mentioned note, that the Sanscrit was, in a great measure, founded on the Hebrew—a proof which I was not able to give in consequence of my ignorance of the Sanscrit, but which Dr. Wait has supplied. In the Sanscrit language there is scarcely a single word connected with mythology, which will admit of a

---

[1] See Vol. I. pp. 432, 442, 596, 665, 751.   [2] P. 58.

rational etymological explanation. All this class of words was formed long before the Sanscrit language, and they were only the old words written in the Sanscrit letter: from this it naturally follows, that they are inexplicable by the artificial rules of Sanscrit grammar—by the general application of which rules to every case, Sanscrit scholars run into the greatest absurdities. With the Brahmins it has become a point of faith to hold up their fine Sanscrit as absolutely *perfect*, and, in this, they are followed by some of its modern professors. This is with the Brahmins exactly the same as it is with the Jews and their *points*; but wherever faith begins, the use of reason ends. It is always their object to refer any word to a verbal root; but to accomplish this, they are obliged to neglect the signification, and often, also, to run into the most absurd and arbitrary assumptions with regard to the form of the words. A few examples will best illustrate this. The word swan, the Greek *xvwv a dog*, they derive from the root Si, (pronounced like the English word See,) *to sleep*—third person present *sete, he sleeps*—and they assign as a reason for the derivation, that a dog sleeps, or is a lazy animal. I think it will be allowed that nothing can be more forced than this. As a second example, Aswa (Latin equus, a horse) they derive from the root As, *to eat*, because a horse eats.

The Rajah Rammohun Roy informs me, that the word Age in Sanscrit means *to go*, and *quickness* or *velocity*; and thence, as fire is *quick*, it came to take the name of Agni or Yajni. Every thing in nature, the Rajah says, was supposed to have an angel presiding over it, according to the system of the Jews, which was also the system of the Hindoos—the angel being called a *deus*. Thus the Angel or Deus of Fire or of Agni came to be the God or Deus Agni. This is exactly the Jewish regimen. Now here, I think, we have an example of the Sanscrit scholars' losing a word by attention to their artificial grammatical rules, by which they conceive themselves strictly bound in accounting for the origin of any word, and by which they become involved in inextricable difficulties. It is almost evident to me, that the assumption of claims to absolute originality in the Sanscrit is a modern assumption. I apprehend the word age, *quick*, is the Latin Ago, which means *to move*, and the Greek αγs which has a similar meaning. It is certainly not impossible that the word *αγνος hostia pura*, or agnus *lamb*, being a burnt-offering, may have taken the name from the *fire*, and thus the Agni may have come to mean Lamb. Innumerable are the absurdities into which the Brahmins are obliged to run, in order to compel the language to bend to their artificial grammatical rules, and by these processes they can and do coin words which are found in their modern Lexicons, (and their Lexicons are all comparatively modern,) but in no other books; but to account for this, the roots are said to be obsolete.

As there are many words thus formed which probably never had in reality any existence, so there are many left out of the Lexicons which are in the books, but which are left out perhaps, because they cannot make them bend to their rules.

The following are obsolete Sanscrit words, occurring in the learned Dr. Rosen's Rig-Vedæ Specimen, and not to be found in any Sanscrit Dictionary:

प्रथान	*prat'hána*	glorious, celebrated.
वोहु	*vohla*	host, army.
अजिरं	*gíram*	quickly, speedily.
चित्	*chit*	and.
दम	*dama*	house, dwelling.

दमे	damé	at home (domi).
गृभ्	gribh	to seize, to take hold of.
पृत्सु	pritsu	in war, in battle.
भर्गिस्	bhargas	light, lustre.
चर्षणि	charshani	man, human being.
दोषा	doohá	by night, during the time of night.
वस्तर्	vastar	by day-time.
बिश्पति	vispati	a lord of agriculturers, i. e. a prince, a king.
मीहू	míhlu	wealth, riches.
ईला	ilá	food, nourishment.
सध	sadha	with, together with.

The Irish word Ogham and the Acham of the Sanscrit I have shewn to be the same. When we consider this we shall not be much surprised to find the language of Scotland called Sanscrit, or Gael-doct, that is, *learned Gael*—but this we shall find by and by. I suspect the Acham of the Sanscrit is nothing but חכם *hkm*, the Jewish word for *wisdom*. Door is in Sanscrit Dwara or Dura,[1] in Saxon *dora*. It is found nearly in all languages, and is no doubt an original word. In Greek it is δυρα. In Chaldee it is תרע *tro*.[2] The Sanscrit word to walk is *valg*: this is evidently English, that is, Saxon or Hebrew.

It has been observed by my friend, Professor Haughton, that all barbarous languages form their words of great length, and the observation is very correct, as we are in the habit of representing them by letters. But I think this only applies to unlettered languages. I much suspect that the fact of the languages having come to be described by syllables and letters, has had the effect of making all of them assume the difference of character which we see between them and the Polynesian and Mexican languages. The arts of writing and reading are so difficult to be learned, that efforts would naturally be made at first to render them as simple as possible; and it is on this account that we find all the first alphabets consist of right lines. It is perfectly clear that after most of the words of a language had been put into writing either by letters or symbols, whether confined to a high class or not, that language would naturally become more fixed than it was previously. Ben. Wasigh, of whom I shall speak presently, has let us into the secret of the monstrous complication in their forms, by having shewn us that all these forms were adopted for the sake of secrecy. The fact which he gives us is supported by tradition, by analogy, and by the general character of secrecy which was adopted all over the world. But though this made the forms of the letters complicated, it had no tendency to make the spoken languages so. The same cause which would make the spoken language of a barbarous people rich or complicated, would make the written language of its first inventors poor; for in writing, I think, as little labour as possible would be expended upon it, as it must have been

---

[1] Tod, Vol. I.   [2] See Webster on word Door.

an extremely difficult thing to accomplish. Every kind of contrivance would, therefore, be adopted for the sake of brevity, which would also tend to secure its secrecy.[1] It is perfectly clear that all the principal written alphabets of the world are the same in principle—have all been originally derived from one, and, it is probable, that that *one* was the numeral alphabet of the Arabians. In obedience to the eternal law, it would, of course, have a tendency to change—for nothing stands still. It would be pronounced by various nations in various ways, and we, by following their pronunciation, endeavour, as far as in us lies, to augment the mischief arising from the law of change; we labour to increase the change instead of endeavouring to decrease it as far as we can. For instance, suppose we take the letter *y o*, which, by its power of notation, *seventy*, is clearly fixed to the omicron of the Greeks, by their o, and by no other letter ought it to be described, and certainly not, as some persons would do, by the *ng*. This is clearly what we ought to do if we mean to denote the same idea as the Greeks and Hebrews by the same symbol. The sound has little to do with it; the idea is what we ought chiefly to attend to in these investigations.

We constantly find that travellers meet with persons of all classes speaking what they call the Arabic language. Now, if I be right in my idea respecting the identity of the Arabic and Hebrew languages, how is it likely, if not written, that they should be *distinguished* in India. This accounts for the Christians speaking Syrian in Malabar. The case with the Hebrew and Arabic languages is exactly the same as that of the six dialects of the British Celtic—the French, Manx, Irish, Welsh, Cornish, and Scotch, notoriously all the same, but now become nearly unintelligible to one another, although the common meaning can be perceived by any person who understands them all. But no person in the more civilized parts is able to understand a person of any of the other countries without great difficulty. This is, in the case of the Hebrew and Arabic, much aggravated by the artificial modern letters, in which they are written. It is perfectly clear that the Sanscrit is like all other languages in this, that it had its infancy, and was brought to perfection by degrees. The progressive state which the several Vedas shew, puts this out of all doubt. The most learned Brahmins now can scarcely read and understand the first Veda. The circumstances attending the Yajna sacrifice, and that the meaning of it is lost, are decisive proofs, either that a part of the language is lost, or that this sacrifice, which, when it is offered, is now *public*, was formerly secret.[2]

I must here beg my reader not to forget that the old Syriac or Estrangelo or Chaldee is called, though not the letter of the leaf or tree, yet very near it, the *letter of the flower*—Pushto—and which must be considered really the same: in this it is similar to the Welsh Celtic, lately noticed from Dr. Lingard. But I shall discuss this farther by and by.

The first Greek letters being in lines or γραμμα and called leaves or πεταλα, and their notation being yet in right lines, and the Etruscan or Italian being also in right lines; and the Irish and

---

[1] In my observations on Hieroglyphics I have overlooked an important notice of them by Ammianus Marcellinus, lib. xvii. 4, who says, that a certain Hermapion had written a book containing translations of hieroglyphics into Greek. From this the learned Heeren comes to the conclusion, that he must have understood the hieroglyphic writing and language. Now it so happens, that from this I come to a conclusion quite the reverse, namely, that like M. Champollion, he only pretended to understand them, but really knew nothing about them. If he had understood them, they would all have been instantly translated. Had they been used as the Edinburgh Review says, for the purposes of common life, Hermapion would have had no occasion to make a book of translations. He was evidently a pretender, to whom no attention at the time was paid, and he would not be worth a moment's notice if he did not add to the proofs already given by me, that they were lost at the time of the conquest of Egypt by the Greeks, and that therefore the discovery of the names of Ptolemies and Cæsars proves M. Champollion's discoveries to be all delusions. I think it is evident that Hermapion attempted to explain or translate them as M. Champollion has done.

[2] See Vol. I. pp. 260, 389, 640, 667, 707, 718.—For Sanscrit see Drummond's Orig., Vol. IV.

the Hebrew having been in right lines, and having both the names of trees, are not theories but facts, and will justify the conclusion that my theory is in substance correct. All this is strengthened by the numerous allegories in the old Arabic, Syriac, Welsh, and other languages relating to the tree of knowledge and of letters—Arbor in medio Paradisi, &c., and we shall find presently, that the first system of letters of the Chinese consisted of right lines. I think it must have been this numerical system which they had. Each of the numbers would constitute, correctly, one of their symbolic letters. We may be pretty certain it was the same as that which the people of Sumatra used, and we know from Jambulus that it consisted of 28 figures.[1]

I believe that no person who has studied the subject ever doubted that there has been one original, universal language. Mr. Bryant says, "There are in every climate some shattered fragments of original history, some traces of a primitive and universal language; and these may be observed in the names of Deities, terms of worship, titles of honour, which prevail among nations widely separated, and who for ages had no connexion."[2] On this subject a very learned and ingenious treatise, by Mr. Sharon Turner, may be consulted, in the first volume of the Transactions of the Royal Society of Literature. I have no doubt that in very early times a sacred or secret written language of numeral symbols existed, which was in use over the whole world, and that that language, as was a natural consequence, consisted of a definite number of words and ideas, each word and idea represented by a number. As long as a certain pontifical government lasted, which I shall shew was the first government, and was the inventor of this symbolic letter, this would remain. By degrees the priests of this order, but of distant nations, would add words to it, till the number became cumbersome, and then the discovery of syllabic writing being made, the numeral system would by degrees be deserted. This would be the first language both written and spoken, used in all nations. By degrees in each nation new words would be formed in addition to the old, and often exchanged for the old; so that we might expect what we find, namely, some of the old first words in every language. From the observation of Cluverius, that he found a thousand words of other languages in the Hebrew, and from the circumstance that it is in a less changed state than any other written language with which we are acquainted, an effect which has arisen from the accidental concealment of it, in the recesses of the temple of Syria, I am induced to fix upon it as being the nearest to the original language.

In the twenty-eight angle-shaped forms or arithmetic figures, there was evidently an unspoken symbolic language, or language of symbols. It is highly probable that after man had got thus far, he would very soon multiply these symbols by making new ones, as the Chinese have done—a symbol for each idea—or by making drawings of the objects of nature as the Mexicans have done with their hieroglyphics.[3]

6. We have seen how, in the name of the Sun and Moon, we obtained the first word of literal syllables. We will try another example or two. The Jews and Egyptians had a cycle of *fourteen* days.

Suppose man wanted to record the cycle of *fourteen*, he would write the sign which stood for *ten* and the sign which stood for *four*, calling one *Iod*, *Jod*, or *Yew*, and the other *Duir* or *Oak*, and

---

[1] Vide Prel. Obs. in Vol. I. p. 5, Sect. 22.   [2] Vall. Coll. Hib. Vol. VI. p. 4.

[3] The Mexicans must have gone from the old world after the decennary system of notation was invented, but before it proceeded to symbolic writing. If symbolic or Chinese writing had been invented and known to them, they would not have fallen back to hieroglyphics. Their hieroglyphics are not a secret system, but known to all; in this, differing from that of the Egyptians. I have no doubt that the periods of the planets were among the things first recorded—the recording signs at first being used as figures of notation, and not being representatives of sound, and therefore the signs

BOOK III. SECTION 6.   161

he would get I△ or *Iodur, Iodi* or △I *di*, the Hebrew די *di*,[1] which came to mean *holy* or God. Thus would be surmounted the immense difficulty of finding out the art of making signs for letters or syllables instead of things. And now every sign would stand for a number, a sound, a thing, a letter, and a syllable. The signs for things would be soon lost, the signs for letters and syllables remaining; and I fix upon this word △I *di* as likely to be the first written word in the first syllabic language, as we find it in the oldest languages.[2]

In the St. Kilda dialect; and also in that of Mexico, Di means Great and Lord. It is also written Ti. This justifies the explanation of Ti-bet by Georgius. It is the word of numerals Di=14. From this, as Malcolme says, probably came the name Dey, the King of Algiers.[3]

When a man had got the collection of *three* stones or lines, or the sign standing for them, to be called Gort, and in like manner the parcel of *four* to be called Duir, I can easily conceive how he would come to describe the word Dog by the signs for the 3 and the 4, called Duir and Gort. I think if he endeavoured to describe the animal by signs as he had done the cycles, he could do it no other way than by using the signs of the numbers, whose names had their beginnings with the sounds which he wanted to describe. The number of units in a cycle led a man naturally to describe it by the symbols, but nothing of this kind could lead an inquirer to fix upon any figures to describe the word dog; but in the place of this the sounds of the first letters would instantly present themselves; and thus he would describe it by the symbols for 4 and 3, because these numbers had names which began with D and G. He would find from this that, by taking the symbols of each number[4] and putting them together, he would produce a certain useful method of recording any thing he wished. Thus he discovered the art of giving sounds as letters, or of converting into letters the symbols of the numbers. This, I think, is the mode by which the most useful discovery in the world may have been made. All this is confirmed by ancient medals.

In the way which I have described, a symbolic language would be formed, each symbol standing for a number, and also for an idea. Men would understand one another perfectly, though the language could not be spoken. Every symbol for an idea would be a monogram. This is nothing but Chinese writing—the powers of notation of the respective signs having been lost when the Arabic system of notation was discovered; for the monograms would continue useful as writing, but be useless as numbers. The memory would be greatly assisted, at first, by the powers of notation, in the learning of such a language: and it is evident that, however varied the forms of the symbols might become, as long only as the ideas of the powers of notation remained unchanged, and however varied and unintelligible to each other the languages of men might become, yet the system of writing would be understood by all.

Supposing the written language of symbolic figures to have been in use for several generations, the spoken language must have been gradually changing; and then, if we suppose the syllabic language to have been brought into use by priests writing into it the words before preserved by them

---

which afterward became vowels would sometimes be used. Thus the Sun would be called Sul or Suli, as the case might be—as 336 or 366 was meant to be represented.

[1] I must apprize my reader that he will not find the Hebrew word די *di* in Parkhurst construed to mean God, but I feel no hesitation in giving it this meaning, since he allows that the Celtic De, Di, Dia, the Latin Deus, and the Greek Δια, and the Goddess Δηω, Ceres, were derived from it. See Greek and Hebrew Lex. in voce.

[2] Lord Kingsborough shews that God is called *Dios* by the South Americans. Antiq. of Mexico, Vol. VI. p. 68.

[3] From the די *id* came all the mounts called by us *Ids*, by the Hebrews ידו *ido* : i=10, d=4, o=70=84.

[4] If this be thought complicated, we shall presently find man to have recourse even yet to a practice much more complicated, described by Sir S. Raffles.

in unspoken symbols, we may easily conceive how differently the words would be spelt in different countries. The only surprise to me is, that any similar words should be found. Sure I am, that many more instances of identity of words in different languages have been found than could be expected.

We have not yet found why BD, as observed in Vol. I. p. 155, came in almost all nations to mean Creator. Buddha is, I have no doubt, the first God, whose written name we possess. Among other names we find him called *Bad*. This I think may perhaps have been his first name, and it may be AB or BA, meaning *father*, joined to the cyclic word *di*, making *Holy* Father. The *Ba* is the numeral emblem of Buddha, because the two letters represent the number *three*, the Trimurti, which was incarnate in father Buddha, or in the holy father. But here in *Bad*, we have the word for Wisdom, Logos, Divine Love, to mean evil. This was for the same reason that *hostis*, a host, and a peace-offering, meant enemy; and as the city of *On* or the Sun, or the generative principle, was called *the City of Destruction*, all these mistakes arose from confounding the creating and destroying powers. But the word BD may be derived from another source, which I will now explain. We have formerly found PD, as well as BD, to mean *giver of forms*. The Jews had a cycle of 14,[1] which they multiplied by 6, and thus made a cycle of 84, which must have been in this case, not BD, but PD; P=80, D=4=84; Pad or PD, the name of Adonis, and of the river Don, the Po, and the Ganges, evidently one of the names of Buddha—Pod-en[2] who was supposed to live 84 years. Though formerly puzzled to know why BD, or PD, should mean *creator* or *former*, we may here, perhaps, find the reason.[3]

Rapin[4] states, that the ancient Britons used a cycle of 84 years. This, in a very remarkable manner, connects the Eastern and Western world, and is on this account of the greatest importance. I shall return to this cycle in a future page.

We have seen that the first division of time or first cycle would be into a period of 28, the days of the moon's age, called cycle or circle from its constant renewal. The second would be into fourteen ID 10+4=14 or XIV, and the 28 might be two fourteens—ID ID—which became afterward the Syrian AD AD, and the יהד *ihd* treated of in Vol. I. p. 392. Man's first conception of God, after he acquired the idea of his existence, would be, of a being *one* and *holy*, and this *one* or *monad* he would describe by the figure which he used to describe the tree after which he called his first number or unit or digit[5] or *one*. Having, I suppose, found or made the D or Di stand for the name of the first cycle of *fourteen*, or in fact of the sun, of God, it almost necessarily followed, that the initial of the name of the monad, when man got to the use of letters, should be joined (to form the name of the God) to the general term for the idea: thus A was joined to the DI or D, and he got *Ad*. This was the *Ad* of North India, Eastern Syria, and also of Western Syria—*Ad ad* corrupted to *Hadad*. The *ID* was *Di*, the Hebrew די *di*; and from this we have the DI and D prefixed or post-fixed to words as Di-va, Maha Deva, the great Goddess Vau, or the mother Goddess Vau or Va. But *ad* might be a=1, d=4=5, the root of the cycle of 60. The Vau we have before found called Venus or the Mother:[6] thus we have *di-va* or *Di-eva*, *Deva*. This sacred cycle of

---

[1] Basnage, p. 436.   [2] See Vol. I. p. 153.

[3] But the BD may also come from B=2, D=4=6, which is the Vau, or, as we say, Eva, the mother of all living. Eva is only Vau, and the emphatic article *the*—making *the Vau*. Thus the Vau was the female generative principle. It was the root from which sprung all the various cycles depending on the number 432. It cannot be objected to the meaning given to the *Eva*, that the first letter is the Heth and not the He; because the Heth is not one of the old sixteen, but a new letter, and we have formerly seen that these two letters were commonly substituted for one another.

[4] Vol. II. Ed. Eng. B. III. p. 67.

[5] The very word digit for the numbers under 10, shews the origin of the figures.   [6] Vol. I. 221.

fourteen is no theory. Plutarch tells us it was the Egyptian sacred cycle of Isis and Osiris—*derived*, he says, *from the moon*—14 solar revolutions of the moon; therefore, properly a Luni-solar cycle. It was, I suppose, as above described by *id* 10+4, and thus it became the name of God and holy, being the first natural cycle. The reduction into its still lower cycle of seven, by dividing it, does not make a natural cycle like the fourteen light and fourteen dark days of the Moon. Thus came *Da* or *Di* to mean *holy* or God.

From די *di, holy,* came *do* to give, and *donum* and *divus,* in fact *the giver*—in Hebrew תן *tn*.— In the word A joined to the D=5, I think we have the first syllable of the word Ad-am, and in M, or Om the second. Or the second might be *ma,* great. It was the 5, the odd number and the male, in opposition to the אוה *eua,* the vau, the 6, the even number, the female. Our word *od* is ad=5, our word *even* is the vau=6, Eve with the Tamul termination. It is a remarkable fact, and of the first importance in this inquiry, that the names of the trees in the old Irish alphabet should all begin with the letters which give the sounds required to make the words that constitute the names of the letters. For instance, the Ivy, called Gort, to stand for the sound of G; the Oak, called *Duir,* to stand for the sound of D. This was because the number 4 was called Duir, meaning Oak. Thus the number was first called Duir after the Oak, then the letter was called Duir after the tree and the number. This is not the case in any language except in the ancient Celtic Irish, and just enough in the Hebrew, which was Celtic, to shew that the same rule obtained in the formation of its alphabet. A necessary consequence followed from this, that the letters, whose designations arose in the manner I have suggested, should have the sounds of the first letters which we now find in those names of trees, and no other: for instance, that the Duir should give the sound of D, and not of O or of any other. This chiefly contributed, perhaps entirely caused, the discovery of alphabetic writing; and it seems to me to be a very striking proof of the truth of my theory. But if what I have said in the Preliminary Observations (Volume I. pp. 13—15) be carefully considered jointly with what I have said here, I think no doubt will remain that the Hebrew, and consequently also the ancient Arabic, (which are, in fact, the same language,) had originally the same names of trees as the Irish. It is impossible to believe so many trees to have had the names of letters and this quality to have arisen from accident.[1]

The two Greek terms for letters, viz. πεταλα from πεταλον *a leaf,* and γραμματα from γραμμη *a line,* confirm what I have said, that letters were originally *leaves* and *right lines.* A book is called in Irish *barac* or *barc,* which also means a leaf, which Vallancey says[2] came from the bark of a tree.[3]

---

[1] The Morning Herald for April 16th or 17th, 1827, states, that the Bible Society in Ireland was giving Hebrew Bibles to the native Irish, because they found that they understood them in the Hebrew quicker than in the English. What I have said respecting the Hebrew and Irish names of trees seems to furnish a satisfactory reason for this, if the Herald be correct. And my theory is very much strengthened by what I have shewn from the preface to Boucher's Glossary, and from other authorities, that the Welsh, which was originally the same as the Irish, had a very close relation to the Hebrew, but to no other language; in fact, it was really Hebrew. It may be observed, that they were the humble peasantry of Ireland to whom the Hebrew was intelligible,—people removed from towns and improvement, and consequently change. I lately learned in Scotland, that the people of some of the most remote parts understand the people of the Western coast of Ireland, but the more civilized and cultivated parts of each population do not now understand one another. I was also told that some Miners came out of Cornwall to Mr. Pennant's slate quarries, and they understood, though with some difficulty, the Welsh who were working there.

[2] Coll. Hib. Vol. V. p. 134.

[3] We have found Bacchus called Liber, and Boc or Book; we have found him called Kiakiak in Siam; (Vol. I. pp. 639, 643;) and we have found him called by most of the Cycles, as Nss=650. The Hebrews called writing די די *di-di.* We have found him, in Ceylon or Siam, called Dak-po. This is Dg-Padus or Po. I believe the Kiakiak is

7. When we reflect upon the general tradition that Teut, Thoth, or Hermes, was the inventor of letters,[1] and that in the very old histories they are always connected with the idea of something magical, the following observation of the Abbé Guerin de Rocher will be thought striking: "Il " est surprenant que quantité de savants, qui ont fait des recherches sur Thoth ou Athoth, n'aient " pas observé que c'est le même mot qui en Hébreu (אתות *atut* sigma, אתיות *antiut* litteræ) sig- " nifie signes et lettres, parce que les lettres sont des signes des mots. *Athiuth*, qu'on prononce " *othioth*, et qui vient *d'athut* ou *othoth*, signes, est le mot constamment employé dans toutes les " grammaires Hébraïques, pour signifier les lettres. Ce mot nous indique donc que bien des " choses attribuées à Thoth ou Athoth, chez les Egyptiens, peuvent avoir rapport aux signes des " Hébreux: et le mot de signe, chez les Hébreux, signifie quelquefois des signes naturels, quel- " quefois des signes miraculeux, et enfin des signes artificiels, tels que les lettres. Je montrerai " en effet par-là l'origine d'un Thoth aussitôt après le déluge; d'un autre dans Moïse, qui a bien " droit à ce nom, et par les signes miraculeux qu'il opera, et par les signes ou lettres sacrées qu'il " écrivit. C'est que je développerai et prouverai dans la suite des règnes."[2]

I have formerly observed that I thought that letters were secret and considered magical. This opinion is confirmed by this observation of Guerin de Rocher, that the word used for letters or symbols of notation is also used for the idea of miracle, and is used in Genesis i. 14, as signs to divide the times. When a person considers the astonishing effect or power of letters and figures of notation, he will not be surprised that they should have given name to any miraculous effect. Nor is it surprising that the signs TT, which described, in the first symbolic letters, the soli-lunar cycle, should come to mean signs or letters generally, letters being considered the conveyors of the knowledge of Wisdom or TT, or OM.

We have found (*supra* pp. 8, 163) Bacchus called Liber, a book, and also the bark of the tree whereon letters were written. Now the אתות *atut* spoken of above by the Abbé, is evidently Tat or the name of Buddha. But TT is here a letter, and Tiut, or the plural, letters: this is Thoth, which is clearly nothing but the Hebrew plural of Tut. Vallancey[3] says, "Literarum verò characteres " in animalium, ARBORUMQUE figuris invenit THOTH."[4] Again he says, "תתא *tta*, in Chaldee, " means Vates and Haruspex; this is Tuatha in Irish;" and he gives an Irish verse thus trans- lated:

        Vates (Tuatha) Hiberniæ vaticinabantur
        Adventurum (tempus) pacis novum.[5]

Here, as usual, we have the prophecy of a new age. I beg my reader to refer to p. 23, *supra*, and to consider what is there said of the Thoth, Tat, and Bacchus, among the Mexicans.

Our word Book is evidently a diminutive of the word Boc, Bac, Bacchus. Bacchus is liber, *a letter, a book;* the bark of the tree on which the book was written is liber. אתות *atut* is תות *tut* and the emphatic article: it means Buddha and a letter. By the *tree* comes salvation, life; the inner bark or the liber on which the law was written, is the life of the tree, as anatomists say. Thus the tree is *the book of life*.

Cicero[6] says, that Hermes or the fifth Mercury, whom the Egyptians call Thoth, was the in- ventor of letters. This is nothing but the renewed incarnation of Hermes or the fifth Buddha in Egypt.

דקדק *dkdk*, and that it meant a cycle, for which we have not yet found a God—unless it be Dag-on. p=20, ד=4=24. Here I suppose a corruption of the p for the ב *c* or *k*. As this is contrary to my system, I name it as a suspicion, but nothing more.

[1] See Vol. I. p. 269.   [2] Hist. des Tems Fab. Vol. I. p. 54.
[3] Coll. Hib. Vol. VI. p. 174.   [4] El. Sched.   [5] Coll. Hib. Vol. VI. p. 312.   [6] Natura Deor. lib. iii.

The Oak and Beech gave out oracles at Dodona or Bodona. They were called *arbores loquaces* by Julius Valerius, Vol. III., and Firdausi mentions *speaking trees*, which revealed the decrees of fate to Alexander. These were books; liber, a book, was a tree—its leaves the leaves of the tree. A book is a prophet. What do we mean when we say, Consult the prophets, but the books of the prophets, to see what is foretold?[1]

Can any thing be more nonsensical than the story of the trees giving out oracles? This affords a fine example of the absurdity of the moderns in taking the mythological stories of the ancients to the letter, instead of giving them credit for what they assuredly possessed—common sense—and instead of endeavouring to discover the hidden meaning of their ænigmas! The Runes of Scandinavia, and the ancient Greek letters, were inscribed on triangular pieces or staves of Beech wood, and the word Buch signifies both a book and a beech tree.[2] Thus we see why the Beeches of Dodona spoke and gave out oracles. The word Rune, in the Anglo-Saxon, means, whispering, secrecy, magic. The word Runeh is Phœnician, or, more properly, Arabic. In Hebrew רנה *rne* means *a song* or *to sing*.[3] We must recollect that Olen was the first who celebrated the praises of the God at Delphi, with song or poetry.[4] I have read somewhere, but where I have forgotten, that on the pedestal of the God at Delphi was a frog. In Latin *Rana* means *a frog*. Here we see the same mystic play upon the word. There is a peculiar kind of small green frog which, in the spring, keeps a up continual singing, very different from the croaking of our frogs; and what is remarkable, it lives at that time not in the ditches, but on the tops of the Beech-trees. I have heard it often in the Netherlands on the banks of the Lower Rhine. Ladies in Paris keep it in a bottle for a weather glass. In fine weather it comes out to the top, in bad, it is at the bottom.

The staves of wood on which the Greeks wrote are called by Mr. P. Knight[5] Tablets; but he gives the Greek Δελτοι. I suppose they had this name from the similarity of the top of the stave to the Greek Δ delta. However the tripods might become changed in form in later times, when the Greeks lost all knowledge of the meaning or origin of their mythology, I have little doubt that, originally, they were nothing but these three-sided pieces of wood, the writing on which enabled the prophetess to give out her oracles—and thus the Beech-tree spoke.

From the word אלף *alp* joined to the second word Beta, the Alphabet evidently has its name. It means *chief, principal, leader*. It means *a guide*, and in this it is easy to see, that it means *knowledge* or *wisdom*. It also means a principal number; this I believe is mystical, and, in fact, means, as the first, the fountain of number or numeration. It means both a Lamb and a Beeve. The Elephant or Ganesa being the God of Wisdom, that beast had his name of Ελεφας from this word. He was the *first* and *wisest* of Beasts: from all this, when read in the Greek style from left to right, פלא *pla* came to mean the word Pallas or Minerva. In the Egyptian language, the island of Elephanta was called Philoe or Elephant.

The first word of the Alphabet is often *one*; which one is often described by the monogram I. Here the idea of *unity*, the To Ον, and *self-existence* are united. The number ten is also the same monogram, and means *excellence* or *perfection*, and has the same reference to the hundreds that the 1 has to 10, and constantly describes the To Ον. In Arabic numerals, *one* and *ten* were the same—1. They are the same in Roger Bacon's calendar.[6] In French we have the Ie in the pronoun je, I. All this exactly agrees with what we learn from history—that the first Etruscan

---

[1] Sir W. Ouseley. See Trans. Soc. of Lit. Vol. II. p. 11.
[2] Foreign Quarterly Review, No. XVIII. p. 439, May 1832.   [3] Fry's Lexicon.
[4] See Celtic Druids, Chap. IV. Sect. III. p. 121.   [5] Prol. to Homer.
[6] Astle on Letters, p. 189.

and Scandinavian or Runic letters or numbers were right lines; that with the Irish[1] they were called after trees; that with the Greeks they were carved on staves—Axibus ligneis—and that they were formed of right lines and called Γραμματα or Πεταλα or leaves, or petalōn or leaf (I believe tree); and that they are found with the mythos of Virgil and the leaves of the Sibyl, and in the Rythms or Runes of Wales. Now all this leads to the important result, that this system was not at first intended as a record of language but of ideas. We see in the Arabian and Hebrew alphabets perfect order as concerns numbers, but perfect disorder as concerns letters for names of letters or of sounds; and we shall find presently all the planetary bodies and astronomical periods described by numbers, as, upon my system, they ought to be found; for I suppose the use of numbers, for sounds and the formation of words, was not discovered till long after arithmetic and astronomy; and that the letters, selected at first without any regard to system in reading, though afterward altered by the Greeks, in their system, to accommodate it to a certain mythological superstition, very evident in the 6, 60, 600, ss, samach, xi; again, in the 9, 90, 900, Teth, of which I shall treat at large presently. In addition to this, I am quite convinced that an attentive consideration of the plates of letters given by Mr. Astle, will satisfy any person, that not only have the ancient systems once been all the same, but the forms of the letters have been nearly so. It will also shew the remains of the practice of making the letters from top to bottom, and of their being read sideways; as, for instance, the S M, the 8, ∞, and many others.

There are several parts of my system which are *facts* not *theories*. They are facts, that in that system of letters which we have, and that probably the oldest, viz. the Irish, the letters are called after the names of trees; that there are enow of the old Hebrew yet so called, as to raise a very high probability that they were all so originally; and that each tree's name begins with a letter answering in sound to the sound of the letter. It is a fact, that the moon's name in numbers, as above, is the name by which it was invoked in the orgies of Bacchus. It is a fact, that the Greeks called their letters gramma and petala; that the letters of all the oldest languages were in right lines, at angles, (though some of the nations certainly corrupted their alphabet to humour the mythos,) and that, at first, they mostly wrote from the top to the bottom.

If a person will impartially consider the great number of duplicates in the Arabic, he will at once see how unnecessary they must have been for a new-formed language: 4 symbols for d, 4 for Z or S, and 3 for T. All these were necessary for numbers; but, in an unformed language, must have been incumbrances; and thus, when numbers grew into letters, *as letters* they were dropped. With the Greeks the vowel v became f, and, in consequence, they were obliged to use for their figures two ς s, and place the vau at the end. We have seen the Chaldee or Hebrew written language traced to North India, the land of the Sacæ, and we have here the same alphabet of *sixteen* letters, brought by a tribe, as their history says, from the same place. If this was a forgery, how came its authors not to copy the Latin, the Greek, the Hebrew, of *twenty-two* letters, or the Arabic of twenty-eight? It is out of all credibility that the monks or bards of the middle ages should have known of the *sixteen* letters.[2]

---

[1] See the Callan Inscription, Celtic Druids, Figure 13, p. 5.

[2] No one can doubt, I think, that the following are all one language:

Sanscrit,	Ec,	Dwau,	Traya,	Chatur,	Pancha,	Shat,	Sapta,	Ashta,	Nova,	Dasa.
Hindoo,	Ek,	Dwau,	Teen,	Char,	Panch,	Ch hu,	Sat,	Ath,	No,	Dos.
Latin,	Unus,	Duo,	Tres,	Quatuor,	Quinque,	Sex,	Septem,	Octo,	Novem,	Decem.
Greek,	Εἱς,	Δυο,	Τρεις,	Τεσσαρες,	Πεντε,	Ἑξ,	Ἑπτα,	Οκτω,	Εννεα,	Δεκα.

8. It is now expedient to suspend our search into the origin of Letters, and to resume our inquiry (from Volume I. pp. 685, 686) into the origin of the most remarkable of all the mysteries of the world—the meaning of the Om of Egypt, of Syria, of India, of Delphi, of St. Peter's, of the Kremlin, of Lambeth—or, the Om of Isaiah, of Buddha, of Cristna—of the sacred, never-to-be-spoken *Om*. Inquiries among the most learned of the Jews of the present day incline me to suspect that they really have lost the Cabalistic meaning of the letter M. They all know that it had a secret meaning, and, in order to conceal their ignorance, they say it is the thirteenth letter, and assert that it is used in the middle of a word to denote thirteen attributes of God, which they pretend to find in Leviticus. This is manifest nonsense. But I am quite satisfied that there is no part of the Cabala, properly so called, which had not a rational and useful object, and the object in this use of the letter was the same as that of using a fringe of a peculiar number of knots, to keep in remembrance the beautiful cycle of 600 years. I have little doubt that the fringe was invented before the art of syllabic writing. They say that the M, the middle letter, means 40, that A, the first, means 1, and T, the last, means 400; then, by taking off the ciphers, they make 9, the emblem of eternity, and form the word אמת *amt*. This is exactly like the Greek Apocalyptic Alpha and Omega, and the Chrismon Sancti Ambrogii. It brings us again to Om-Amet, Om the desire of all nations. It has already been stated, (supra, p. 162,) that the first word of infant man was probably Ab or Ba. On examining the numeral powers of this word we find they mean A=1, B=2=3. Every where we find this word figuratively applied to the divine nature. God, or the

In Greek ψηφος is *a pebble*, and ψηφιζω *to calculate*. We learn from Herodotus, that the Egyptians made use of small pebbles or little stones to calculate.

	Gaelic.	Latin.	Greek.	Welsh.
1	Aon	Unum	'Εν	Un.
2	Do or Da	Duo	Δυο	Dau.
3	Tri	Tria	Τρια	Tri.
4	Cether	Quatuor	Τεσσαρα	Pedwar.
			Attic Τετταρα	
5	Cua-co-cooe	Quinque	Πεμπε or Πεντε	Pimp.
6	Sia	Sex	'Εξ	Chuech.
7	Seche	Septem	Επτα	Sailh.
8	Oche	Octo	'Οκτω	Uilh.
9	Naogh	Novem	Εννεα	Nau.
10	Dec	Decem	Δεκα	Deg.
11	Aondec	Undecim	'Ενδεκα	Un ar deg.
12	Dodec	Duodecim	Δωδεκα	Dau deg.
13	Tridec	Tredecim	Τρισκαιδεκα	Tri ar deg.
14	Cetherdec	Quatuordecim	Δικατεσσαρες	Pedwar ar deg.
15	Cusecdec	Quindecim	Δικαπεντε	Pun deg.
16	Siadec	Sedecim	Εκκαιδεκα	Un ar pim deg.
17	Sechedec	Septemdecim	Επτακαιδεκα	Dau ar pim deg.
18	Ochedec	Octodecim	Οκτωκαιδεκα	Dau nau.
19	Naoghdec	Novemdecim	Εννεακαιδεκα	Pedwar ar pim deg.
20	Fighed	Viginti	Εικοσι	Ygen.

James Grant, Origin of Gael. p. 47.

The 28 Arabian letters consist now of only 17 figures; the other letters are made out by points. The old Arabic of Mohamed is not now commonly understood. Enc. Lond. Vol. XII. 164. It is studied at Mecca, like Latin at Rome. We continually hear of letters being invented by different people. I do not doubt that there were almost as many letters as writers; but there was, in fact, one system at the bottom of all, which is yet clearly visible in every civilised nation. There have been many forms of letters, but there have never been but two alphabets or systems, the symbolic numeral Chinese, and the Cadmean or sixteen-letter system. If there has been a third, it must have been the Sanscrit.

Male generative principle, is always called Our Father. The numeral meaning of the word in a very striking manner applies to the Trimurti or Trinity. The coincidence visible here I attribute purely to accident; and a question may arise, whether the coincidence does not vitiate the theory of the origin of the numeral language; or the origin of the first infantine language which I have laid down. Applying to this the doctrine of probability laid down by Dr. Young as applicable to language, as stated in Volume I. p. 449, and which will be equally applicable to this case, I reply, I think it does not vitiate it, but on the contrary, as I will now shew, confirms it. I have stated the fact that, in almost all written languages, the word Ma or Am is found to mean Mother—to mean also Goddess, the female generative power—the Alma Venus—the עלמה olme—the mother of the Gods.[1] If this M, Am, or Ma, should be found accidentally to dovetail into the Mythos, in the way the word Ab accidentally fits into it, then, upon Dr. Young's principle, two such accidents will certainly vitiate my theory of the origin of the first language. But if, on the contrary, the numeral system do not dovetail into it in any way, but on examination is found to have been forced from its original simplicity as taught by me, to make it fit to the first language; then, on Dr. Young's principle, it amounts to almost a mathematical proof of the truth of both the systems. Two accidents could not be received, and the chances or probabilities would have been as a thousand to one that the names of Ba and Ma had been given to suit the mythos, but were not among the first written words of man: but the fact, that the alphabets are forced to make them suit the mythos, places the chances the other way. If we examine the alphabet we find that the M is not the centre letter of the twenty-eight, but a letter is thrown out in the Hebrew to make it so, and the letters are reduced from their natural or original number 28 to 27. By this means the M becomes the central letter, and this was done to make the Ma or Am the navel, the Delphus, the Omphè, the central letter,—the Mia, the female of Plato's Tὸ Ὀν. The original numeral alphabet of the Indian Arabians had 28 letters or forms. The Jews changed the number to 27, to make the M the centre. The Greeks changed their number to humour a superstition, the same in principle, and to make the two letters which described their cycle, the cycle of 650, the centre letters. If we examine this closely, it is exactly the same as the plan of the Jews. The benignant dæmon of the cycle was the Son of Man, MN=650; and thus arose the generic name *of the species*—Man, Mannus, the Male, afterward joined to the female, making Am-mon or Om-an; and, when aspirated, Homo, hominis, hominem. In accommodation to the same mythos, the Greek vau or digamma or number six, was written ϛ having the *sound* of the number ξ=60, three lines or three ϛ s or ξes, and the number χ=600. In like manner the M final and 600 of the Hebrews was constituted of the Samech, the 60 and 600, and the vau was, as the Vulgate calls the mother of the race, *Eva*. The E and U, the 5 and the 6, were the generators of all the cycles. They were both Lustrums. Thus came Eva or Eve, the mother of the race of *MN*, the root of Homo, of Man, the root of Mun-di, *holy cycle.*[2]

The manuscripts of the Poems of Homer are now all written without the digamma; but it is a fact admitted by all Grecian scholars, that when they were *composed* (not necessarily written) they must have had it. No satisfactory reason has been given to account for this extraordinary anomaly. I suppose when these poems were composed and sung, the use of letters was not known; but that when they were committed to writing by Pisistratus, the letters had been so long invented as to have given time for the *vāu* to have been excluded (probably for the mystical reason above-mentioned) from its place in the alphabet, and therefore they were written without it. In the whole story of their collection and committal to writing by Pisistratus, the knowledge of let-

---

[1] See Vol. I. pp. 110, 111.   [2] The sacrifice of *a woman* is called aumoman, woman, euaman.

ters is assumed, as no new invention; therefore, it is probable that they had been in use a sufficient length of time to have given an opportunity to make the alteration of the expulsion of the vau. It is almost certain that if this sacred poem had been written before the *vau* was rejected, it would not have been improperly written by leaving that letter out. It is impossible to account for the omission of the vau except from some mystic reason. The strong probability is, that if the vau had been in use when the poems were first written, they would have been written with it, and would never have been written without it. They alone would have kept the letter from being lost. It seems to me a strange thing that we should call this letter digamma, when it was evidently nothing but the Hebrew vau. I know scarcely any thing more absurd than calling the Hebrew *vau*, which is now only used in the powers of notation, in the Greek language, by the name of digamma. It is evidently our letter F, come from where it would; but it would not have looked learned to have merely called it F. It proves that Bentley and those who gave it that name, with all their boasted knowledge of the Greek language, actually did not in the least understand the principle of it. What they call digamma is nothing but the Hebrew *vau* growing into the sound of V, hard f. The sounds UV and VU are both the same.

When I reflect upon all the circumstances attending the knowledge of letters, I feel no doubt that they were not only considered to be magical, but that they constituted a great part of magic itself. Let us consider, only for a moment, what miracles, as figures of notation in solving problems in arithmetic, they would enable their possessors to perform. Let us consider alone the foretelling of eclipses, and let us add to this the knowledge of the periods of some of the comets, which I think I shall shew in a future book that the early literati did possess. In the passage quoted in Volume I. p. 675, from the Revelation xiii. 17, 18, the whole of my theory both of wisdom and of the system of using numbers for symbols and letters is, in one sentence, clearly expressed. The knowledge of the number is called *wisdom*, and the letters are called *marks*, that is, monograms or symbols, names, and numbers. Daniel (ix. 2) says, he knew a thing בספרים מספר *bsprim mspr*, *from* or *by* the letters in the book.

From ספר *spr* a letter, or symbol of notation, comes סף *sp* or Sup, or Soph, *wisdom*. The idea of wisdom and of letters is never separated.

Vallancey says,[1] that storia is an Egyptian word, meaning what we should call *news*. It seems to have been the Hebrew שטר *str*, which I think meant a scribe.[2] I believe the scribes were a learned order, a kind of priests, and that they were the only people who understood the art of writing.

In the very learned and ingenious work of the Marquis De Fostia D'Urban,[3] my attention was drawn to a passage of Josephus,[4] wherein he states, "That they pretend that they have received "them from the Phenicians and from Cadmus: yet is nobody enabled to shew that they have any "writing preserved from that time, neither in their temples nor in any of their public monuments. "This appears, because the time when those lived who went to the Trojan War, so many years "afterward, is in great doubt, and great inquiry is made whether the Greeks used their letters at "that time: and the most prevailing opinion, and nearest the truth is, that their *present way of* "*using those letters was unknown at that time*. However, there is not any writing which the "Greeks agree to be genuine among them older than Homer's poems," &c., &c. Now I conceive that

---

[1] Coll. Hib. Vol. V. p. 209.

[2] ספר a scribe has several significations in scripture—a secretary, a commissary or muster-master of an army, an able or skilful man, a doctor of the law, a man of learning, &c. Calmet in voce.

[3] Homère et ses Écrits, p. 111.   [4] Whiston's Joseph. ag. Ap. Book i. Sect. 2.

this opens the door most decidedly to my theory. The expression, *the most prevailing opinion was*, that the use of writing was not such, in the time of Homer, as that which obtained at that day, instantly produces the question, Then, what was the kind of writing alluded to? P. Knight says,[1] "The age of Homer is, however, so much anterior to all monuments of art, or authentic "records of history, that we cannot even tell whether or not he had the knowledge of any letters, "there being but one passage in his works where writing is mentioned, and that is so equivocal, "that it may mean either symbolical or alphabetical writing." The following is the passage to which Mr. Knight alludes. Parkhurst, under the word ספר *spr* may be consulted for the authors who have discussed it.

Πεμπε δε μιν Λυκιηνδη, πορεν δ' ὁγε ΣΗΜΑΤΑ ΛΥΓΡΑ,
ΓΑΡΨΑΣ εν πινακι πτυκνῳ, θυμοφθορα πολλα·
Δειξαι δ' ηνωγει ᾡ πενθερῳ, οφρ' απολοιτο.

"To Lycia the devoted youth he sent,
"With *Marks*, expressive of his dire intent,
"Grav'd on a tablet, that the prince should die."

It appears to have been a common opinion that some unknown kind of writing had existed, though it seems to be implied in the words of the text, that it was then unknown. If we suppose that the works of Homer were first written into the language of numeral symbols, a written but not a spoken language, many difficulties respecting them will be removed.

When we recollect the Indians admit, that the meaning of their celebrated and most sacred word Om is actually lost by them, I think we are allowed great latitude in our investigations; and if I be right, that the ancient Hebrew or Chaldee, the old sixteen-letter Tamul, Pushto, and Afghan language was the original dialect of India, it is not absurd to seek this celebrated word here. Then its ancient sacred representative would be simply the letter מ=600, so mystically found in Egypt, in M-om-ptha, and in Isaiah, in Om-nu-al, Om, *our God.* We have lately seen that the number *fourteen* described the first name of God. By the insertion of the final Caph, the letter M forms the fourteenth letter. I am by no means certain that a mystical connexion has not existed between the M and the cycle and the Ερως *divine love* and Ma, *mother*, and Amo, *I love*, and Eri, *the Saviour*. I believe both Venus and Cupid were called Ερως, like the Canya of India, and the Cama. Surely my mysticism is not more mystical than this! All the sixteen-letter languages ought to be considered but as dialects of each other, unless the artificial Sanscrit be excepted; and this assertion I feel confident that I should clearly prove, had I lexicons from English into Hebrew, Greek, and Sanscrit, as I have from these languages into English.

The monogram for the Virgin Mary—the Regina Cœli, is the M. Some of the early fathers called her a fourth God, an adjunct to the Trinity. But the most beautiful emblem is the Mother suckling the infant. See my Fig. No. 8. Here, in this beautiful icon of Buddha, I have no doubt, the male and female principles are described.

On reflecting deeply on what I have written in my Celtic Druids, (pp. 197, 198, 201,) respecting the word IEUE, and in several places in this work,[2] I am convinced that I have been hastily led into a mistake by the modern Jews. They hold that the sacred word IEUE is the word which ought never to be spoken. On reflection I think this was only formerly told to the vulgar Jews to satisfy them, and to evade their inquiries; but that the word of the Indians, Om, was the sacred word. It is probably, with most of the rest of the Cabala, lost.

---

[1] Ess. Gr. Lang. p. 19.   [2] Vol. I. pp. 67, 107, 158, 319, 320, 323, 430; and *supra*, pp. 5, 17, 137, 151.

The Jews could not be taught the Decalogue, nor could they read the Bible in the synagogues without violating the very law they were learning, or which Moses was repeating to them, if the secret word were IEUE. I believe that the real *secret* meaning of the text has reference to the word OM; and that it means *Thou shalt not speak the name of thy God* IEUE irreverently, meaning the secret name. Or the text may be correctly translated, *thou shalt not speak the name of the self-existent God* (IEUE meaning *self-existent*), and that the word referred to was the Om of Isaiah, described every where by the monogram M, as M-Om-ptha. When Moses asks God by what name he is to describe him to the Jews, he is told, that he is to describe him by this supposed forbidden name. How could this be? Here is a direct contradiction! It is said, the Jews write the word יהוה *ieue*, but pronounce it, in English, Adonai. But though it may be very pious to call him after the Gentile God Adonis, it is directly contrary to the command of God, who tells them what they are to call him, not what they are to write him. My explanation removes this difficulty.

Surely nothing can be too absurd in religion! God tells Moses he will be called *Ieue* by the Jews; in strict obedience Moses goes to them and tells them, they are to call him Adonis! The Jews say it is written *one way* and spoken *another*. When God is said to speak to Moses, there is no question about *writing*. The account in writing of the scene between Moses and God is altogether a different matter.

9. But this raises in my mind some questions respecting the Jewish Targums. If it be true, as Gen. Vallancey maintains, that the Chaldee letter never was in common use as a letter, but only as figures of notation, how came we to have the *Targums*, as they are called, in that letter? The story that they were written for the use of the Jews, when the old Hebrew was no longer understood by them, does not seem very probable, because, not the *Chaldee*, but the *Syriac*, was their vernacular dialect in the time of Christ. Gen. Vallancey says, this never was the letter of the Assyrians of Babylon, and this is confirmed by the fact I have noticed in another place, that no inscription was ever found in this letter at that place.[1] But this letter and dialect are found even to this day in use in the country of the Callidei in North and South India, with all the mythos of the Jews, joined with the mythos of a crucified Saviour or Messiah, (as is the case in Mexico,) foretold by name in these Targums, over and over, in the clearest terms. It is said that they were read in the Jewish synagogue alternately with the old Hebrew, first a verse of one, then a verse of the other, for the accommodation of the Jews after they had lost the old Hebrew. I do not know what is meant by the old Hebrew letter, for we have only the Samaritan, the Syriac, and the Chaldee letters; and the Syriac was the spoken language of the Jews. I begin very much to suspect that the Targums have been brought from the East, and that they are the sacred books of the Callidei of the East, suitably accommodated or corrupted—retouché.

A person who fancies himself very learned has triumphed greatly over my ignorance in not knowing that the Targums were written about the time of Christ; for, in my *Celtic Druids*, I have placed them after the time of Origen. Before I delivered my opinion I examined these books with very great labour and very little profit; and carefully inquired into their history. They were, in my opinion, more favourable to the Christian cause against the Jews than any books which I had ever read;[2] but that, notwithstanding they must have been informed of them by the Jewish converts if they had existed, yet neither Jerom nor any one of the ancient fathers before him ever quoted them: therefore I said, and I say again, that there is every reason to believe that they did not exist before the time of these authors. I do not wish to praise my own learning, but I feel

---

[1] Vol. I. p. 778. [2] Onkelos foretells the Messiah *twice*.

bound to say, that this is not the only time I have been accused of *ignorance* for knowing rather too much.[1]

A great mystery hangs over the Targums. It is acknowledged that there is no certainty when or where or by whom they were written. It is very extraordinary that neither Origen, Jerom, Epiphanius, nor any other of the early Christian fathers, knew any thing about them, particularly Jerom and Origen. Prideaux and Michaelis[2] will bear me out in this, that they are written in the Syro-Chaldaic dialect, that which was used about the time of Jesus Christ, and was in short the last language spoken by the Jews whilst a nation, and it is the language now used in South India. Their *professed object*, we are told, was to enable the unlearned Jews to have the consolation of reading and understanding the divine word. If these Targums had been written for this purpose, as it seems not to be doubted that they were, I think there can be no question but that some or other of the Jewish proselytes would have informed the Christians, Origen, Jerom, &c., of them. All the reasons which Dean Prideaux gives for their concealment by the Jews, are in favour of their publication or exposure by the converts from Judaism to Christianity, even supposing them to have been concealed. If a single convert had been made of any respectability, the secret must have come out, that the Jews had some books which they were charged to conceal from the Christians. But how could they be concealed, if they were in common use by the unlearned Jews?

Origen and Jerom both lived in Palestine for some time, the latter a very long time, expressly for the sake of gaining information respecting matters of this kind, and he wrote commentaries[3] in which the Targums, if known to him, must have been of the very first importance to his argument. Then how does it happen that neither of them has ever, in all his voluminous works, noticed them in the slightest degree? Epiphanius also understood Hebrew, or Syro-Chaldee, yet he never notices them. Several fathers of eminence in the Christian church were converted Jews; then how is it possible to believe that they would have failed to notice the Targums after their conversion, which would both have aided them in their arguments against their countrymen, and have justified themselves for their conversion.

Respecting Jerom and his search for the Bible in Judæa, whither he went to collect information, the author of the Revue Encyclopèdique gives the following account : " À la solicitation du Pope " Domase, ce père de l'église parcourut plusieurs païs. Il fut obligé d'apprendre le Chaldéen " pour recueillir les copies les plus authentiques que les Chaldéens avoient eu des Juifs. Il dit " qu'après bien de veilliés, de fatigues et de recherches même les plus exactes, il rassemble beau- " coup de lambeaux dispersés," &c., &c.

The present Jews look upon the Targums of Onkelos and Jonathan with such high veneration, that they assert that they were delivered to Moses by God himself from Mount Sinai, with the rest of their oral law. It cannot be doubted that these Targums are much more favourable to the Christians than the old Hebrew text or the Septuagint ; then, I think, when the Evangelists were quoting passages as prophecies of a Messiah, they would have quoted from them, or at least have noticed them ; and when Jesus was denouncing the oral law and traditions, he would have said something either for or against the Targums if they had been in existence. De Rossi, who is named in the Dissertation on the Poetry of Isaiah by Louth, professed to have *proved* that the present LXX is not the same as that translated for Ptolemy. Sabbathier collected all the passages which purported to be taken from

---

[1] It is not uncommon for a man, if he be more learned than his contemporaries, to be accused of ignorance. It would manifestly serve my purpose to uphold the great antiquity of the Targums ; but I reason for *truth*, not for *victory*. They shew the opinion of the Jewish church in the time I allot to them, which is enough for me.

[2] Ch. iv. Sect. vi.   [3] Prid. Con. Vol. IV. Pt II. B. viii. p. 633.

an Italian or Latin version of the Old Testament, made before the time of Jerom, or which he supposed were taken from it, as he did not find them in the Hebrew, the Vulgate, and the LXX; and he gave them to the world under the pompous title of an Italic-version; but I believe much which he collected was taken from the scraps of the sacred books of different Italian or other temples, which had escaped from their adyta. There is a copy of a Bible in Anglo-Saxon, in the British Museum, made by Aelfric in the tenth century, in which the variations prove that it can never have been made either from the Vulgate, the Italic, the LXX, the Hebrew, or the Samaritan.[1] The account of Ararat in Phrygia, proves that the Sibyls did not take their account from our Bible. The omission of Jacob, in Enoch, proves that he did not copy from our Bible, and the account of circumcision again proves that Aelfric did not make his translation from any of our books. The same argument may be applied to the accounts in China, in North and South India, and in Mexico. The same mythos is in all; but they have internal evidence that they are not taken from the Jewish books. All this tends to prove the truth of the remark, in the Revue Encyclopédique, that the books of the Jews were *lambeaux dispersés* at the destruction of Jerusalem. I cannot conceive how any one can look at the difference in the chronology, as given by Whiston, to say nothing of the other numerous variations, and not see that the histories are substantially different. How different must be the account in the Sibyls from that of the Jews, which places Ararat in Phrygia or old Room! All these speculations go to prove, that this Genesis, at least, was the secret book, or a book containing the substance of the first Pontifical government of all nations, and accommodated in some degree to their varied circumstances. Thus, when the Jewish Paulite sect arose, it could see nothing but the Jewish system or account of the mythos; all others, in its eyes, being copied from the Jews: and as this sect, through favourable circumstances, got possession of the power of the world, it succeeded in destroying almost every thing that operated against its system, or in corrupting, intentionally or unintentionally, all that it suffered to remain.

Mr. Sharon Turner, in the Transactions of the Society of Literature, to which I must refer my reader, has, at great length, endeavoured to shew that all languages must have been derived from one original. Every argument which he uses is strongly in favour of my theory of one original *written* but *unspoken* language; but this is nothing against his doctrine of one original spoken language also.

I think there can be no doubt that the use of letters was at first strictly confined to mythology;

---

[1] On this translation I have received the following information:

"The Anglo-Saxon translation alluded to was made by the celebrated Aelfric, Archbishop of Canterbury, elected to that see in the year 993; but this work was completed before that period, while he was yet a monk. It consists, 1st, of the *five* books attributed to Moses; and, 2dly, of the books of Josue and book of Judges. These seven books Aelfric styles the 'Heptateuchus.' They are preserved in a very ancient MS. in the Bodl. Lib., and thence published by Ed. Thwaites, dedicated to Hicks. To these he added Aelfric's translation of the book of Job, from a MS. in the Cotton Lib.; the Gospel of Nicodemus translated by an unknown author from Latin into Anglo-Saxon; and, lastly, a Fragment of the History of Judith, in the same language, completes the volume.

"The most important of these are the Pentateuch. Aelfric assures us, that he made the translation from Latin— from what Latin translation I know not. It does not agree with the Vulgate, nor yet with the ancient *Italic*, if Sabbathier's restoration can be relied on. It differs much from our common translation, and the differences are frequent and material. Yet where it does agree, the Anglo-Saxon is almost in every instance marked by superior brevity and clearness. In some instances it clears up passages quite unintelligible in our Version. Many passages are omitted in the Anglo-Saxon, and some most important laws—as that in the code of Sinai *for the circumcision of all males*. Aelfric's work does not, however, seem to me to be an abridgment, and I am inclined to suspect, that this law of circumcision was not an ordinance of Moses, because, if it was, why was it not obeyed during the time that the Israelites wandered in the Desert? but came first to be enforced upon their settlement in Canaan, as we are assured of in the the book of Josue. Be this as it may, this Anglo-Saxon translation may be of good service in some subsequent and better version."

and in consequence of this it is, that we find every really ancient mythologic name, when examined to the bottom, admit of explanation by numbers. Let the reader look at the definitions of the first book of Euclid, at the lines, and remember that all numbers, and all letters, were described by right lines. Let him think upon the Arabian Oriental Algebraic art, the date of which no one knows—the art of Geometry, the Pythagorean forty-seventh proposition of Euclid, and the letters, symbols of numbers, and lines, and doubt if he can, that this art was known to the great explicator of the universe, Pythagoras, who declared that all knowledge centred in numbers and lines, and who was burnt by his more wise and orthodox countrymen, for the wickedness of teaching this and similar doctrines.

The word Yoni is acknowledged to be the same as Iune. It is the same as the יונה iune of the Israelites, which means *dove*. It is the name of the islands of Java and Sumatra, which thus carry the same name as the island of Iona and of Columba, of the Hebrides of Scotland, both, no doubt, *sacred isles*. It is the same word as the Juno of the Latins.[1] It is a word composed of the Hebrew word יה *ie*, or the Syrian word *Io*, and the word *ni*, which I do not understand; but which, perhaps, may be only a nominal termination, like *en* in Cris-en, or *os* in Χρης-ος, or the Latin *us*, in Christ-us. It is the IE of the Apollo of Delphi. It is the Jan-nus and Ja-na of the Romans. It is the Diana or Di-ja-na or dwa-ja-na. It became, when the Greeks perfected their language, by the invention of a neuter gender, the To Ον, or the I Ον. It is the Hebrew יה *ie* or יהוה *ieue I am that I am*—or, grammatically,—*I shall be what I have been*; or a definition of the creative power. It is the root from which great numbers of the Sanscrit and Indian Gods have been formed. Yavana, is the *ie* and *vaha, to carry*, one of the meanings of the word *ana*, but which must have another meaning; because the word Ya-vana means a sect professing the superior influence of the female over the male nature;[2] and I believe it means *to bear* as well as *to carry*, and has precisely the same meaning as our word *to bear*, used to carry a burden—to produce a child. Hence we see why the Ya-vanas became Ionians. It is the root of Nar-ay-ana. Nar in Sanscrit is water, the Hebrew נהר *ner*, river or water, and the word means IE carried in the, or on the water.[3] It is Kanya; that is, Can or Cunia, &c., &c. It has the same meaning as the *Amba* of India,[4] and the Omphe of Greece, and the Om and Ammon of Egypt; these latter being of both genders, which, I am persuaded, answers to one sense of the Bya of India,[5] meaning Bis-Ja, Double-Ja—male and female. Finally it is the Argha.

The more I study my subject, the more facts I discover to prove that the Pythagorean doctrine was true, that all learning and science resolved itself at last into numbers. We find the Hebrew God called EI and I. We read much of Ion, of Ion-ia, of Jan-a, Jun-o, Iav-anas, and of Bet-on, בית-ון *bit-un*, and Beth-aven, בית-און *bit aun*. Now, how comes On to mean, as I have shewn, the generative principle? It is the neuter of the Greek pronoun ὅς,[6] meaning existence, which always carried along with it the idea of destruction, and necessarily reproduction, that is, the generative principle; and I-ον is the ON of I, and I, the jod, is ten, the X, the perfect number, the numeral meaning of the ten avatars, eternally renewed, of the creative God, the ΛΟΓΟΣ. It is also the To Ον, the Tau ON, that is, the cross of Ezekiel, with which the believers were marked in the forehead, after the manner of the Buddhists of India, and, indeed, of all the sects of India, who are marked with some sign or other. In the same manner the Christian priest, in baptism, marks the child on the forehead with the cross. If Plato had not made the ον the fountain of his mythos, I should have thought this too refined or mystical to be credited.

As the city of On or Heliopolis, or of the generative power, was called the *city of destruction*, so

---

[1] Asiat. Res. Vol. III. p. 364. [2] Ib. p. 358. [3] Ib. [4] Ib. p. 360. [5] Ib. p. 358. [6] Participle ων, qu.? *Ed.*

the Καλος or *beautiful* of Greece was the Cali or *Goddess of destruction* with the Indians. From this principle she became the Goddess of Time, because Time is the greatest of destroyers; and from her, the last age, when all was supposed to be destroyed or finished, was called the Cali-Yug or Cali-age. The same feeling in Europe which makes devotees deal in nothing but damnation, makes the Indian Goddess Cali a favourite, her devotees having first converted the *beauty* into *destruction*.

The meaning of the היה *ie* of the Hebrews, as I have repeatedly remarked, is *the self-existent*. It seems singular that, unless he were the Supreme, he should have this name. But the same thing happens in India, whence no doubt it came. The supreme Being in the second Veda says, "*From* " *me* Brahma *was born;* he is above all; he is *Pitama*, or the father of all men; he is *Aja*,[1] or " self-existing." From him, Col. Wilford says, they represent Adima (which word means both *first male* and *female*,) to have descended. She is the same as *Iva* or *I*, the female energy of nature, or descended from *I*—the same as Isa or Isi, male and female.[2] All these are nothing but Hebrew names written in Sanscrit.

If a person will think deeply he will have no difficulty in forming an idea how, when the art of writing was secret, a written word would be magical. A few lines scrawled in the presence of a person on a bit of leaf or bark might be given to him, and he might be told, whoever is a magician or initiated on seeing that scrawl, will know your name, or any other desired fact. A person must think deeply on this, or he will not see the force of the argument which arises from the dupe having no idea of the nature or power of conveying knowledge by symbols. As the Chaldæan priests were the only people who understood the secret of writing, it followed, that they were all magi or magicians; and when the secret did begin to creep out, all letters were magical or supernatural. This and some other secrets—the telescope, astronomy, the loadstone—made the Chaldæans masters of the world, and they became Moguls. Mogul is but Al-Mag, *The Mage*. On this account all the princes of India desire to be invested with the pallium by the old Mogul of Delhi, successor of Gengis Khan, of Tartary, the last incarnation of divine Wisdom. The mythos at last always reverts to its birth-place, Indian Tartary—the Mount Solima, the snow-capped Meru, where the Gods sit on the sides of the North. How the Mogul comes to be Lord Paramount of the world, I shall explain in a future book.

10. The observation of Dr. Young respecting probabilities is very important; for, as the *written* languages of all the nations of the old world contain a considerable number of words in common, the probability that they are all derived from one parent stock rises almost to a certainty. This leaves the question of the derivation of the genus *man* from one or more original pairs, nearly untouched. For the diffusion of the Pandæan, Catholic or Universal Buddhism, which seems evidently to have gone with the secret system of letters, will readily account for a certain number, and a considerable number, of the same words in all the different languages. It will also readily account for the variety which may be observed in their mixture. Wherever either the arithmetical or the first syllabic system extended, there a mixture of words might be expected; and it seems probable, from hundreds of circumstances, that the language of the Chaldæan Brahmin, which was that of which the Hebrew, Arabic, Ethiopian, Tamul, Pushto, and Syriac, were close dialects, was the language into which the arithmetical language was first translated, by means of the then newly-invented syllables. If we suppose the languages of the earth to have been at that time widely spread, and that dialects had begun to be formed, when the art of rendering the arithmetic into letters and syllables was discovered; the secret society of initiated who discovered it, in every

---

[1] Here is most clearly the Hebrew היה *eie*, or הי *ie*.

[2] Asiat. Res. Vol. V. p. 247.

country, would begin to translate it each into his own dialect. This theory, I think, will readily account for Hebrew and Indian words in Britain, and words of Britain in India. The possibility of a written, unspoken language is proved by its actual present existence in Java, which cannot be denied. The possibility of its existence by means of numeral ciphers must be admitted; and I am quite certain that the actual existence of the custom of using arithmetical signs to describe certain mythic words, and the possibility which I have shewn of many others having been formed from arithmetic, raises a very strong probability, that the arithmetical system has been general. Of a theory like this proofs can never be expected; probability alone must be looked for. To this theory *I* see no objection; but if there be certain difficulties which, when pointed out, I cannot explain, in such a case as this, they cannot be considered to invalidate it, as long as a possibility remains of an unknown explanation of them being discovered. If the theory be true, it is not within the scope of probability, that all difficulties should be removed, even if all the learning and talent in the world were employed upon it; much less when they are attempted to be removed by a solitary individual, who claims neither much learning nor much talent; and who, from the peculiarly recondite nature of his subject, can obtain no assistance.

I consider that it admits of no doubt, that all the written syllabic languages with which we are acquainted are the same, with merely dialectic variations; and that all the alphabets or systems of letters are one, only with the letters in different forms, as we have the English language and letter though one, yet WRITTEN IN DIFFERENT *forms*. The Arabic table of letters and numbers, compared with the Greek, proves this. We have here all the *numbers* in order, but the *letters* in disorder. We ought in considering these subjects never to forget, that all the various dialects of the world are like the spokes of a wheel, as we go back converging towards one another, till they meet in the centre; and, in a contrary direction, diverging, till at last they are no longer visible to one another. I believe that historical circumstances might be adduced, which would render it highly probable that, fifteen hundred years A.C., the people speaking all the then existing languages, could, though perhaps in some cases with difficulty, understand one another.

11. If we consider the effect of these numeral letters of this unspoken language, we shall immediately see that, when the numerals or ciphers became changed into letters, they would necessarily come to be read and pronounced, sometimes from right to left, and sometimes from left to right.

After man had made the discovery of the syllabic word liuaa, as described above, in Section 2, p. 150, perhaps the next attempt would be made on a word for the Sun, in the following manner. We will suppose a person wished to record the Sun, and to do it by means of numbers having the names of trees, these numbers, that is the numerical system, having so far advanced as to be simplified into a symbol or monogram for each number forwards—as we find it in Greece. He would then inscribe it thus, in right-lined angled symbols, having the meaning of one of the cycles which I suppose him to have invented.

Σ^1—$\sqsubset$ the sign of 300, called Suil.
U^1—V the sign of   6, called Uern.
L —L the sign of 30, called Luis.

336 the name of the Lunar Year.

I apprehend that the names of all things would be at the first monosyllables of the simplest

---

[1] It will be observed that the Author here, as in many other instances, conceived himself at liberty to use either Hebrew or Greek letters for his numerals. *Editor.*

BOOK III. CHAPTER I. SECTION 12.

kind; and that the first name of the tree called Suil, would be, not two syllables of four letters, but one of three—*Sul*, which, in numbers, gives the first lunar year of 336 days. Now, when a person wrote the three symbols ⌐V L, he could not very well help observing, that by pronouncing the three first sounds of the three names of the three trees, he would, by a fortunate and remarkable accident, have the sound of the name of the tree *Sul*. Here, then, we have correctly a sound, *Sul*, described by symbols or marks which were now, in this case, become letters, each mark or letter standing for a sound, and the three marks describing a sound, a number, a tree, the Sun, and the Lunar year—in all having five meanings. This would lead him to try if he could not describe other things as he described this tree (now unknown to us). We will suppose the Eg, as an example. He would look for a tree out of the twenty-eight, whose name should begin with the sound which we call E, and he would find Eadha, the sign of *five*, and having the mark or monogram E, and he would inscribe E. He would then try to find a tree which had a name that began with the sound which we call G, and he would find the Gort, having the mark or monogram ⌐ ; he would then inscribe that mark below the other, and he would have $\genfrac{}{}{0pt}{}{E}{\ulcorner}$ or $\genfrac{}{}{0pt}{}{\exists}{Eg.}$. Thus he would discover the art of using the monograms or symbols for numbers, or symbolic numerals, as letters to describe syllables, and letters, and sounds, and the symbols for the numbers would thus become letters.

Now the next word of letters discovered might be Suil or Suli, found in the same manner to denote the solar cycle of 366 thus,

ש s=300 Suil.
ו u= 6 Uern.
ל l= 50 Luis.
י i= 10 Iodha.
───
366

and thus the Sul changed into the Suli as science improved.

This is the Suli Minerva of Bath—the cycle that we find in the name by which Stonehenge was called in Welsh, *Emreis*—that is, ϵ=5, μ=40, ρ=100, ϵ=5, ι=10, σ=200=360; or, η=8, μ=40, ρ=100, η 8, ι=10, σ=200=366. In Su-li we have a word of two syllables; and thus we advance another step in literal and alphabetic writing. In the word שלש sls=630, salus, health, salvation, Salus-bury, we have another step; and our word Sun has probably been Sin=360, or Suni=366.

The word שלש means *three*. I cannot help suspecting this to refer directly to the Trinity. It has both the meaning of *three* and of *director* or *chief* or DISPOSER, as שמים *smim* in Gen. i. 8.[1]

12. Joseph was considered to be one of the divine incarnations or avatars for the salvation of the Egyptians. He was the Phoinix which appeared every 600 years. " Et vocavit Paroh nomen " Joseph *Saphenath Pahaneah*."[2] Και εκαλεσι Φαραω το ονομα Ιωσηφ, Ψονθομφανηχ, צפנת פענח *spnt-ponh*.[3] This passage is rendered by Jerom, "*Vertitque nomen ejus* (Pharao) *et* " *vocavit eum, Linguâ Egyptiacâ*, SALVATOREM MUNDI." And in Suidas Joseph is called by a name still more curious: " Cum autem FAUNUS insidiis appeteretur à propriis Fratribus in Egyptum fugit.[4] The Hebrew word has been rendered *Revealer* of the Secrets of the Stars. But I think no one can doubt what the Abbé de Rocher has pointed out—that the Faunus and פענח *ponh* is the

---

[1] Vid. Parkhurst in voce שלש *sls*, IX.
[2] Gen. xli. 45; see Vol. I. p. 502.
[3] Pagnin.
[4] Dict. de Suidas, verbo Φαυνος.

Roman Faunus and the Phœnix. But Joseph was also called by another name שלים *slit*. Gen. xlii. 6.[1] In the שלים *slit* and שלם *slt* we have a trifling *mispelling* (if any attention is to be paid to radical letters) of the feminine termination of the שלי=360, for the origin of Salus, Salutis, for the name of the Sun, the Phœnix, and the *Redemptor* or *Salvator Mundi*. And in old Irish our female *Sall*, *w s*=300, *l l*=30, *l l*=30=360, means a year.[2]

Several authors have thought that the Proteus of the Greeks, which word has the same meaning as שלי *slit*, was Joseph. This, I think, arose from his repeated incarnation in new cycles—different, but yet the same—in each cycle a Saviour or *Redemptor Mundi*; thus they made him a Proteus. His name Psonthom Phaneah, is our Proteus, or Phantom, and the Santon of the Orientals. The Phaneah is the Φηνν=608.[3]

The shrines in which the Gods were placed in India were called Stalls. These are the stalls of our Cathedrals, and of our Cow-houses. Hog, in his history of Cornwall,[4] says, that the sanctuary of the God *Hu*, or the Sun, or the Bacchus of the Druids, was an Ox-stall, where the God presided as a living animal,[5] or as the image of a bull. The name of the Bull, in the numeral symbolic letters, I have no doubt, was the same as we have found him so often.—Stll, or S=200, T=300, LL=100=600.[6] When the numerals became letters, the habitation of the *Stll*, by the regimen, came to be the place *Stll*. In this way, from this formation of the Hebrew, when in regimine, innumerable words took their origin. I believe the *Hu*, which is the common name of God in Wales, is only a corruption of the Hebrew pronoun הוא *eua*, meaning He. In India, the Gods are placed in the temples in stalla or stalls, that is, *recesses* or places of safety. In the West, the Gods were placed in Cellæ and CONCLAVIA. Hence come the cells and stalls in our cathedrals.[7] The Cell is the היכל *eikl*.

To be wise is to be enlightened. Lux is the Logos by whom all things were made; and the Logos is Rasit—Rst, ρ',σ',τ'=600. And Lux makes Lucis; then LX, χ'λ'=650. Again, L=50, ו *u*=6, ש *s*=300, י *i*=10, ש *s*=300=666.[8] The *Fleur-de-Lis* is the Lotus, the flower sacred to the Lux, or the Sul, or the Sun. The Auriflamme, the flame of fire or fire of gold,[9] was the standard. The three Lotuses or Lises were the coat of arms, emblems of the Trimurti, the three persons of the triple generative power, or of the Sun or Lux. שלה *sle*, Shilo, is probably של *sil*=360, or χ=600, λ=50=10, ו=6=666. This is Silenus. I have no doubt it was the invocation in the Psalms, called Selah, סלה *sle*.

The Greek word Ἡλιος is nothing but a variation of the Suli, Sul, and Sol. H, η, is the Hebrew emphatic article, and the word is soil, that is, suil, and *sli*=360 or 366, or *sul*=336; Sun in Sanscrit is *siona*, the first three letters coalescing into one. Hence evidently our Sun. Here we find the meaning of Mount Sion—Mount of the Sun; the same as Har-ol-ump, that is, Har-al-om,

---

[1] See Parkhurst in voce שלם *sls*. From שלשי the word Sultan is said to have been derived; but it is from the word *slt* or *xlt*.
[2] See Guerin de Rocher, Vol. I. pp. 113—120; Vol. II. p. 213; Vol. V. p. 22.
[3] See Vol. I. pp. 169, 181, 199, 500, 587, 507.   [4] Note on p. 158.
[5] This was the Welsh Bull with three Cranes on his back, called Budwas Trigeranon, answering to the Indian Buddha Trivicrama-ditya, or Buddha with triple energy, as explained by Col. Tod.
[6] Here, it will be observed, the Author again quits the Hebrew, and makes *stll* equal 600, partly by Greek and partly by Roman numerals. Yet see his note 5, *infra*, p. 187, and Chap. ii. Sect. 1. *Editor*.
[7] Jurieu, Vol. II. p. 248.   [8] On this mixture of numerals see note *supra*. *Editor*.
[9] We have formerly found (Vol. I. p. 600) the χρς and the χρυς connected. The χρυς was an incarnation of the *solar fire*. Here the *aurum* and *aur*, the *gold*, and the *fire*, are connected.

Mount of the God Om. Gebelin, in his Monde Primitif, has undertaken to prove, that the minuet was the *dance oblique* of the ancient priests of Apollo, performed in their temples. "The diagonal "line, and the two parallels described in this dance, were intended to be symbolical of the Zodiac, "and the twelve steps of which it is composed were meant for the twelve signs, and the "months of the year."[1] Little do our village girls, when dancing round the May-pole, and our fine ladies when dancing the Cotillon ✛ think, that they are exhibiting the most profound astronomical learning; but they are doing so nevertheless. Dancing was originally merely religious, intended to assist the memory in retaining the sacred learning which originated previous to the invention of letters. It began in sense, it is continued in nonsense. But why not? Does it not make them happy? Then merrily may the bonny lasses dance; they shall never be disturbed by me. Alas! disturbance will come soon enough, without me.

The Salii were Sulii or priests of Sul, who was worshiped with circular dances, whence the French or Franks, who were peculiarly attached to the dancing superstition, were called Salii. The president of the college of Salii in Rome was called Præsul—our officer is called Consul. Indeed I believe, that there were no parts of the rites and ceremonies of antiquity, which were not adopted with a view to keep in recollection the ancient learning, before letters were known. Thus, as I have just said, that which began in sense is continued in nonsense; for since the art of writing has become known, all forms and ceremonies are really nonsense. But it served the purpose of the priests to retain them, and that is the real reason of their continuance. It was the same in the ceremonies of the Jews. The whole system was held to be a microcosm of the Deity, the Templum, a part of it, and with reference to this every part of it had a meaning. But I shall discuss the microcosm at large in a future book. It may be enough to notice here, as one example, the fringe of the Jewish dress, which is formed of cords knotted in fives and sixes, and tens and twelves, of knots contrived, as the Jews say, so as to form, in their various combinations, the number 600, and the name of it is ציצת *zizit*, which is ת $t=400$, ' $i=10$, צ $z=90$, ' $i=10$, ת $z=90=$ 600. In these fringes, directed to be worn on the garments, and to be looked upon in a particular manner, (and called 600,) we have, if I mistake not, an example of Moses, under divine direction, practising that which Sir William Drummond called *buffoonery*.[2] But this word has several meanings, which are remarkable. As צי *zi* it describes exactly the carns of Tibet, of Scotland, of Ireland, and of Arabia also, a very striking and important identity.[3] It also means a flower, and a thin plate of metal.[4] The temple was a microcosm of the globe. The high priest in his pontificals in the Sanctum Sanctorum, surrounded with his Tzizit, was a microcosm of the tree of knowledge with its flowers, in the garden of delight. The flowers are said to be of the colour of the Hyacinth, as I understand, because it is blue; but I think this is not the meaning. The Lotus of the Nile is blue. I shall probably return to this. The parcels of knots in five and sixes, with their various combinations, are beautifully descriptive of the lustrums, and of combinations to form the double cycles of 360 and 432.[5] Here we see more proofs of what Pythagoras meant, when he said, that all science resolved itself into numbers.

13. We will now try to find the meaning of the word Solomon; often spelt Soleiman, Sulimon,

---

[1] Hog's Hist. Corn. p. 460.   [2] See Numb. xv. 38, 39; Deut. xxii. 12.

[3] Vide *Parkhurst* in voce.   [4] Vide *Fry*.

[5] The Catholic beads and a string of them called a Rosary are the same. The Rosary is from the word ras *wisdom*; the Bead, in like manner, is from the word Ved, or Wisdom. Beten, in German, is *to pray*.

Suleimon, and שלמה *slme*. Pezron has found the word Sol for Sun among the Celts, and I consider that, having it in Latin, we have it in the Etruscan. We have it also, I think, in the language of ancient Britain, in the Fons Solis at Bath. As we have just seen, the first word Sol, or Sul, or Suli, forms the cycles of 336 and of 366, and spelt with an X or ם final, probably of 666. The second word is the נם=90, and also ם‍נ=650. This MN or Menu was in a particular manner the symbol of mind. Minos or Menu or Numa was a wise lawgiver. The Mn formed the only animal in the creation possessing mind, called *man* for this reason. Thus the wisdom of the Sun became Solomon.[1] With reference to the same mythos we have the Lm 650, the Lam or Lam-da, holy LM, and L M B=72, and the Men-des or holy Goat, which is the same as the Sheep. And when science improved, we have the M=alone equal to 600. With reference to the same, we have the fig-tree called Lamed, the sacred tree of the Indians, which fructifies in its own peculiar manner something like the Lotus.[2] We have also Mount Meru, called by the Siamese Menu, or, at least, Maria called Mania, which, combined with the circumstances that we have seen relating to mounts and meres of the Aja or Lamb and Goat, justify a suspicion that Meru was Menu. With reference to this, the centre letter of the two Irish alphabets is in one called Moiria, and in the other Muin, substituting the N and R for one another, but each the centre letter. I cannot help suspecting, that all our Meres and Marias were corruptions of Menus or arose from them. I think it probable that Salman-asar was the Cæsar Solomon—Salmon-Æsar.

The second person of the Trinity being an incarnation of the solar power, the word של *sl* came to mean Saviour,[3] and from this comes the word שלום *slum*, and שלם *slm*, *peace*, and שלה *sle*, Shilo, Saviour, as is proved by his being called by Onkelos משיחא *msiha*, that is, THE Saviour or THE Messiah. From this we may now see where the Soli or Suli-Minerva of Bath comes from. She comes from the Saviour Minerva thus : Sol or Sul is Saviour, as the Sun is always called, therefore the Sul is both Sun and Saviour, and Miner is also Saviour.[4] פלץ *plz* is the same as the Pala noticed by me in another place, and is the origin of the Pallas.[5]

I imagine that the following is the true translation of 2 Samuel xii. 24 and 25 : "And he called his name Solomon (שלמה *slme*), and Ieue loved him. And Nathan the prophet put his hand upon him (וישלח-ביד *uislh-bid*) and called him after Ieue, (or *on account of* IE בעבור *bobur*) Jedidiah," (ידידיה *ididie*) that is, the most holy IE, or, in Hebrew idiom, Holy, Holy IE. Here we have the χειροτονια and Christening, or giving the Christian name, usually given with us at the baptism. I assume that the ד *d* in the word ביד *bid* ought to be ר *r*. With this the whole is *sense*, without it the whole is *nonsense*; and I think most Hebrew scholars who shall go through my work, and see all the proofs which I shall give of my theory, will agree with me that the emendation ought to be made.

The Milyans of Lycia were called Sólymi. They were also called Telmissi and Termillians.[6] They came from Crete. At Miletus was the crucified Apollo,—Apollo who overcame the serpent, פתן *ptn*, or the evil principle. Thus Callimachus celebrating this achievement, in his hymn to Apollo, has these remarkable words, lines 103, 104—

---

[1] I have little doubt that the monkey was called Hanuman from the same principle, and that the word Hanu was a a word of qualification, as perhaps, *half-*man or *inferior* man.

[2] Vall. Coll. Hib. Vol. V. p. 130.   [3] See Parkhurst under שלה *sle* and שלם *slm*.

[4] See Pausanias, and also Parkhurst in voce מנר *mnr* and פלץ *pls* II, where she is shewn to be the same as Venus, and to mean the generative power of the Heavens ; and the same as אשרה *asre* Venus or the Saviour. See Parkhurst in אשר *asr*, IV.

[5] Vol. I. pp. 629, 630.   [6] See Beloe's Herodotus, Vol. I. p. 236.

BOOK III. CHAPTER I. SECTION 14.   181

—— ειθυ σε ΜΗΤΗΡ
Γεινατ' ΑΟΣΣΗΤΗΡΑ ——

"Thee thy blest *mother* bore, and pleased assign'd
The willing *Saviour* of distress'd mankind." DODD.[1]

From this root also come the word פתר ptr, *to expound* or *interpret dreams*, and פתר ptur, *interpretation*, and *pateræ leaves*, i. e. the *divining leaves* of the Sibyl;[2] also the name of a town in Mesopotamia, (Numb. xxii. 5; Deut. xxiii. 4,) from an oracle at that place, and Patræ in Achaia, and Patara in Lycia, from an oracular temple of Apollo, whence Horace calls him Patareus. Hence also the priests among the Gauls were called Pateræ.[3] Whence also came the little images of the Phœnicians Παταικοι or Pataeci by Herodotus. In Python, the Serpent, may be found the destroyer, the Evil Spirit. Apollo was, I doubt not, the son of one of the females to whom we find the altars inscribed with the words *Tribus Mariebus*, who was the *Virgo Paritura* of Egypt and Gaul. Patra or Patta, in Sanscrit, means *a leaf*. The cups used in sacrifice in Sanscrit are called Pateras, and are made of a large leaf. The Greek word Petalon is the same as this.[4]

14. We may suppose another of the earliest words discovered, precisely in the same manner as the Sul, would be ⸁, ⸁, ⸁ , denoting 360. I suppose that the words which we found above, pp. 160, 161, to stand for the cycle of *fourteen*, namely, *di* or *id*, in order perhaps to imprint the day strongly on the memory, or from religious motives, had become sacred or holy.

Now we will suppose man called a certain river the river of the Solar orb: he would, in numeral letters, first call it the river of Sin, or 360, and next, the river of the *sacred* or *holy Sin*—and that would be *Sindi;* which was the name of a sacred river in Thrace, and of the river Indus in India—one the river of the Jews of Thrace, and the other the boundary of the great Mesopotamia of *Ioudia* or *Ayoudia* or *Judæa* of India.[5] But the important part of this observation to us, at the present, is, that we have got another name of two syllables.

Bud is B=2, D=4=6, the root of 432. Father is ab, abba. He is the first of all created and creating beings; thus he is B=2, A=1=3, the Trimurti, and the root of almost innumerable superstitious fancies about the generation of numbers. Thus, also, Ab-ba 3+3, the root again of the cycle of 432, a Roman Lustrum. I suspect Abba was both *parent* and *father;* as Beeve is both *cow* and *bull;* and as Khan was both *king* and *queen*.

We have found God called Ad, in India, and in Western Syria. A, is one, and d, is di—holy one or monad. And the word Monad is *Mn* 650, *di*, holy, A, one, *the holy one*, or To ON; that is, ON, the Generative power,[6] called Ἡλιος by the Greeks.

Every thing was microcosmic: Adam and Eve, made after the image of God, were a microcosm of Brahme and Maia,[7] their three sons a microcosm of the Trimurti. Noah, his wife, and three sons, were the same. It would have been singular if we had not found Adam and Eve in the arithmetical language. אדם adm, is I (or the Monad or root) of the di, *holy*, cycle of Om or M, —the God described on the fringe of the priest's garment.

---

[1] Parkhurst, p. 602.   [2] See Celtic Druids, p. 93.   [3] See Bochart, Vol. I. p. 666.
[4] Asiat. Res. Vol. VI. p. 499.

[5] The river Sind is also called Abba-Sin, or *father* Sin. (Tod's Essay on the Indian and Theban Hercules, Trans. Asiat. Soc.) I have little or no doubt from the word (Abyssinian) Abbassinian, that the Upper Nile was once called Sin-di, or Abba-Sin. The term father was constantly applied to the Nile in Egypt—as we say, *father* Thames.

[6] See Vol. I. p. 109.   [7] Ibid. p. 348.

In Volume I. p. 643, I say that the word עב *ob* has the meaning of Serpent, and that I shall explain this in a future page. The letter ב *b* denotes 2, and the letter ע *o* denotes 70, and the two denote the recurring cycle 72, the most common, and, perhaps, important of all the sacred cycles, but not more common or important than its emblem the Serpent.

Why did Jesus say he founded his church upon a *rock* or stone? I have shewn (in note 2 of Volume I. p. 346) the word stan or stone, both in India and Europe, to have the same meaning; therefore it follows, that it is a very old word, probably an arithmetical word. May it have been $\sigma=200$, $\tau=300$, $\nu=50$, $\nu=50$, *stnn* cycle of 600? It is very true, that the whole system was founded upon that cycle. What was the loadstone, which I have supposed carried in the Amphi-prumna as its mast, the mast of Cockayne,[1] of Minerva, of Wisdom, but L'-di-stone *the holy stone?* It was, most assuredly, of all inanimate things, the best emblem of Wisdom. What can be more precious than the magnet? This is highly figurative, no doubt; but who can deny that the language of Jesus was figurative, and as highly figurative too? This Lapis would be the Lapis of 600; then, by regimine, the lapis stnn.

I am quite certain that no one who considers that Jesus taught in parables, as he said, that he might not be understood, will think it unreasonable to go to an ænigma for the meaning of the ænigmatical expression to Simon Peter, Cephas, Pierre, *Thou art Peter, and upon this rock I will build my church:* Matt. xvi. 18. Now I think the stone on which Jesus meant to found his church, was Saxum, Sax, Saca, in short, *Buddha* or *divine wisdom*. This is in perfect keeping with other equivoques which Jesus is said to have used. The stone of Sax would become the stone Sax, with the Latin termination. Jesus Christ was a disciple of Buddha; that is, of Divine Wisdom. Who will deny this?- Thus we come at the first name of Buddha, *Saca.* Littleton says, Saxum a stone— σαξω πετρα, סלע *slo*. Κηφας, Chald. et Syr. כיפא *kipia*, Heb. כף *kp.* A play upon language, or an equivoque being *clearly meant*, no objection can be taken to an explanation arising from an equivoque. *Sax* is evidently divine wisdom, Buddha. It is also a stone, the anointed stone of Jacob, the emblem of the generative power or *wisdom*. Now, when I reflect upon the way in which our *c* has changed to *s*, and to *ς*, and upon the collateral circumstances, in defiance of rules of etymology I am induced to suspect that the כף *kp* is the ספר *spr* or letter, which we have found always connected with wisdom, and the Zephir or the Holy Ghost; and that it is also Sup and Soph.

15. The works of Fabricius shew that the Cryptographic writing by ciphers was common with the early fathers of the church; but this was practised in India to a much later date, as may be seen in Col. Tod's Rajahstan;[2] even to the year 1204 of the Hegira.

The work noticed by Col. Tod is said to have been written by a man who styles himself a *Shufeek* of Arungabad, or, as the Colonel says, "Rhymer of Arungabad." I doubt not that he was a poet, but he was also, probably, a *Shufeek* or *Sophee.* The work is called *Bisat-al-Gnaém,* or, in one sense, "*Display of the Foe;*" but it is meant also by these words, the Colonel says, to describe the year 1204, in which it was written. He gives "the numerical value of the letters which compose the title" thus:

"B. S. A. T. a. l. G. N. A. E. M.
2. 60. 1. 9. 1. 9.1000. 50. 1. 10. 40."=1183.

In Hebrew numerals it would stand thus:

---

[1] See Volume I. pp. 340, 344, 345.   [2] Vol. I. 235.

BOOK III. CHAPTER I. SECTION 15.   183

	ב	Beth	2	
	ס	Samech	60	
	א	Aleph	1	
	ט	Teth	9	
	א	Aleph	1	
	ל	Lamed	30	
No form[1]	ג	G.	1000	Bsat-al-Gnaim.
	נ	Nun	50	
	א	Aleph	1	
	י	Jod	10	
	מ	Mem	40	
			1204	

Here we have a writing containing two meanings. I suspect this was the case with the whole of Genesis; that it had a meaning for the learned and for the vulgar.

The Colonel observes, "as the total is only 1183, either the date is wrong, or a deficient value "is given to the numerals;" but the mistake is in giving the power of 9 to the Lamed instead of 30. This correction brings it right. Here we have the Cryptographic writing in a very late date, and it is in the Hebrew names of letters in India. I have not satisfied myself as to its real Hebrew meaning, but I suspect it means to compare the uncivilized or early princes of Mewar to a plantation or garden of wild grapes. But it furnishes a very strong support to my doctrine that the Hebrew was the root of all their Indian languages.

If figures were the origin of letters, that is, the first letters, all the original names of the Gods would naturally be numerical; and it seems natural that they should often remain as we find them; but not in like manner other names. It seems also natural, if notation were discovered by placing stones at the side of each other, as was probably the case, that addition, from perpendicular lines, should have been the first operation. The first of these operations would be to record time, moons, years, cycles,—and the collection would form the first name of the planet whose cycle it recorded. Thus the first name of the moon would be, as we have found it above, p. 151, Evohe, IIVAA=28.[2]

---

[1] May not ג have borne the same numerical value as ى in the cognate Arabic or Persian? As Col. Tod gives E=10, the Author seems fully justified in substituting י =10, in the word Gnaém. *Editor*.

[2] The Egyptians revered the Moon under the emblem of a Cat. Here, in our English, I doubt not that we have nearly the first name of the Moon. Káph=20, A=1, Teth=9=30—*Kat*. The Irish Phenniehe made 608; the φηττ=608; in Coptic, φm=600. The Chaldeans called the Phœnix פלן *Mo*—Caph final=500, Lamed=30, Oin=70=600. The Yug (or age as it ought to be called) of Cali or Clo=600. As we have found the famous State of Western Syria called Phœnic-ia, that is, the *Phenniche* of Ireland, (vide Celtic Druids,) and *is*, that is, country of *Phenniche* or of *Phenn*, it is very natural to expect its capital would have a name from the same kind of mythology: thus we have,

	s	ש =	300	
	i	י =	10	
	d	ד =	4	
	n	נ =	50	
Sidn			364	
Its daughter might be called	.	ת=	400	
		ר=	200	T. R. H. or Tyre.
		ה =	8	
			608	

[This, however ingenious, appears very doubtful, as Sidon or Zidon was not spelt with ש but with צ. See, in

16. I must now return for a moment to the subject of the ancient vowels. (The vowel points of the Hebrew I have long since proved in the Classical Journal, and in the Appendix to my first volume, to be *modern*.) It has constantly been said, that all ancient written languages were without vowels. This, I have no doubt, has passed down as a tradition from the earliest times, like many other old sayings without thought, by ignorant people. It is not true, and never was true of any of them, as a person may at once satisfy himself by looking into any of the old languages. But it was partly true. The least consideration of the manner in which I have shewn that the system of *figures* grew into a system of symbolic *letters* will prove, that it could not be otherwise than as it is, and this will tend strongly to prove the truth of my whole system. For it is evident that, after the trees acquired names, and the figures were called after the trees, and the first *unspoken* but written language was made by using the figures or ciphers, whether the words were composed out of the forms which were afterward vowels or consonants or both, as in the word *iivaa* for 28, it would be merely an effect depending, in each case, upon the contingency whether the names of the trees used began with a vowel or a consonant; this is the reason why, in the twenty-eight letters, we have several letters with the same sound, though of different powers of notation. In this case the names of several of the trees must have begun with the same letter; and this is the reason why, in the words of the first language, the vowels and consonants are mixed without any system whatever. In some words there are no vowels, others consist in part of vowels, and some of all vowels; and this takes place in the Celtic, the Hebrew, in fact, in every language which we have been able to trace up to a very remote antiquity, and among them was anciently included the Greek.

If I wished to form a word from the names of three symbols, and if those names began with three consonants, the word would have three consonants: if, of a consonant and a vowel, as Beth and Eadha, it would be written B E; if, of two consonants, as Duir and Luis, it would have no vowel, but merely two consonants, D L. In this manner most words would be written almost without vowels. But after some time the same cause which made man have recourse to the sound of the first parts of the names of trees, would occasionally induce him, in order to enable him to pronounce a word, to add a vowel answering to the sound in the words, where it could not otherwise be spoken. The first syllable of almost all words may be pronounced without a vowel, but not the second. Thus we have much oftener a vowel in the second part of a word than in the first; but there is nothing like a rule. It is evident that this process arose solely from the letters having been taken from the first sounds of the names of the trees of which the letters were formed; as, D from Duir. The order of the figures is natural, as it is natural that two should follow one, and three two; but the order of the letters arose solely from the names of the trees attached to the numbers having the respective sounds in their first letters. For instance; A is the first letter, because it is the beginning of the word Ailm, *which stands for the first number* or *number one*. If written language had been formed by the premeditation and reflection of Grammarians and Philosophers, we should have had the alphabet in a very different order; we should have had all the labial letters together, all the dentals together, all the vowels together, &c., and not, as it is now, in the order of notation. This orderly system in the Sanscrit tends strongly to prove it, comparatively speaking, a modern and artificial language. Indeed I think it does prove it to be so. I can readily suppose that, after man had found out how to make a syllable by taking the first letters of two words, as in the case of *Id* for 14, he would easily form other syllables by taking the sounds

---

Hebrew, Gen. x. 15, 19; Judges xviii. 28; 1 Chron. i. 13. Sidon or Zidon would, therefore, signify, in numbers, 154; and to justify חרה being considered as equal to 608, the ה must be taken for the Greek ή. *Editor.*]

of the first letters of words, or beginnings of words, to form other syllables; as I have shewn that he would take the first of Duir and the first of Gort, to make Dog or Dg.

17. The art of acrostic writing, which we find in the Tamul, the Psalms, the Runes of Scandinavia, &c., arose from the mode of making out a word from the first letters of numbers. The word IIVAA is really an acrostic; and it was this which led the ancients into the apparently foolish practice of acrostic writing, of which we find, in the languages and works above enumerated, so many examples. The words Bisat-al-Gnaim for 1204, lately quoted from Colonel Tod, are correctly an acrostic.

Mr. Mallet has observed, "that the ancient Scandinavian poetry abounded with acrostics of "various kinds, as much as the Hebrew;"[1] the Scandinavian, that is, the Saxon.

The practice to which our grammarians have given the scientific or technical name of Anagram, partly arose from the accidental transposition of the letters of a word, when changing the writing from the numeral system or system of ciphers, and from the top downwards, to the literal and horizontal, and partly from indifference as to the order in which the letters stood, when the language was in unspoken symbols. With respect to language, I believe our grammarians give too much credit to system, and by no means enough to what we call accident. A moment's reflection will shew any one that, in the unspoken language of numerical symbols, it was not of the least consequence in what order the symbols were placed. For instance, in the word Sul, whether it were Slu or Sul, precisely the same idea would be conveyed. This was the origin of Anagrams and Metathesis, to which we have given these fine names.

This explanation of the hitherto unexplained deficiency of the Hebrew and Celtic vowels, seems to me to be the most satisfactory of any part of my system, and to connect the whole together as perfectly as could be expected in cases of this kind. The number of characters in the old Arabic and other systems having the same names, for instance,[2] the three D's, shew, that they were originally never *intended* for *letters*, but merely for numbers.

I am of opinion that the Eastern or Cadmæan system, as the Greeks called it, was originally invented from the Arabic, and was kept a great mystery by the Masons, who were of the tribe or religion of the Chaldeans and of the Ioudi of Thrace. That the Ioudi were the persons who invented it, I shall endeavour to shew by and by. The irregular and unsystematic use of vowels shews that the change from the use of ciphers or figures or symbols to letters, was done without *any system or contrivance* which *had language or literature for its object.* The selection of the sixteen letters, both in Syria and in Greece, shews signs of the religious mystery, and in Greece, particularly, it shews that the leaf or petala system or practice was abandoned, in part, from compliance with the sacred mythos which prevailed. At first, after letters were discovered, the initial of the name of every number would form a letter, but several numbers being called after trees whose names began with letters having the same sounds, only one would be retained, and thus only sixteen or seventeen were kept in use. The characters of the trees also shew, that they did not arise from premeditation; for, if they had, such trees as the Spanish chestnut and the pine would have been selected. I can imagine no other cause for the selection but accident. But they are all inhabitants of high latitudes. They would thrive equally in Tartary and in Ireland.

Endless is the nonsense which has been written respecting the ten Jewish Sephiroths; but Moore has, perhaps, alone explained them. Their name, in fact, tells us what they are. They are well known to be ten symbols; and what is Sepher but Cipher?—the ciphers of notation up to ten, which, it is evident, contained in themselves, in the numeral language or language of

---

[1] Northern Ant. Vol. II. p. 144.   [2] See my Prel. Ob. Sect. 52.

ciphers, in its endless combinations, all knowledge or wisdom? This was really Cabalistic.[1] This was the meaning of the ænigma of Pythagoras, that every thing proceeded from numbers.

In this language of ciphers, every cipher or figure, to a certain extent, was, of course, the symbol of a word, viz. to 9 inclusive. At first this would be the case up to 28, and if we look to the tree alphabet, we shall see each of the grammata or lines, by means of the ligature, made into one. After the Arabic notation was invented, although all the figures from 9 to 99 would consist of two symbols, they were in fact representatives of but one idea. Basnage says, that the writing on Belshazzar's wall, interpreted by Daniel, consisted of but a letter or symbol for a word; this is correctly cipher writing. It is not surprising that the Chaldæan Daniel should have possessed this Cabalistic knowledge or the art of writing the symbols in some phosphoretic preparation, which should only be visible, perhaps, when shaded from the lights. M. Basnage remarks, that the same practice was observed on ancient inscriptions, where a letter or symbol stands for a word. For various mystical or superstitious purposes the Greek alphabet was varied from the Asiatic one, and if we look to other alphabets, we shall be able to perceive superstition at work, and the same superstition,—the same gratification of the passion or fashion of making riddles or ænigmas, which really seems to have been the leading occupation of the priests, or initiated, for many generations; in fact, in all time before Herodotus, who was called the *father of history*, from being its first inventor, i. e. of history as separated from the historic, mythologic ænigmas.

18. We will now consider the number 9.

The ט Teth of the Hebrew stands for *nine*. I have no doubt that we have this letter nearer the original in form in the Greek Θ Theta, a circle including a central point, though the Greek Theta is not unlike the Teth both in name and form. This has the same name as the Tha or Thas of the Egyptians, and the Φθας of the Copts. It is called the everlasting number, because, by whatever number it is multiplied, if the figures be added, they make 9. Thus $7 \times 9 = 63$, and $6+3 = 9$; or an equal number of nines, and for this reason it has the emblem of eternity for its figure, viz. a point and a circle. This Tha or Thas is the ninth or last number before the tens begin. The Tzaddi is the 90, the second nine before the hundreds begin; and the Tzaddi *final* is the third 9, standing for 900, before the thousands begin.

If the reader look to the Irish alphabets in my Preliminary Observations, Chapter I. Sect. xlvi. p. 9, he will find each of them to consist of seventeen letters, the ninth letter in each is the centre letter; it is the M. In the first it is called Moiria, that is, Maria; and in the second it is called the Muin=666, of which we have seen and said so much.[2] Can any one believe this to have been the effect of accident? And if it be not accident, can any one doubt that it is the effect of a secret system, and of the very system which I have been unfolding?

Georgius shews that the Pema or Lotus is the Padma softened to Pema. I suppose Padma is Sanscrit and means Pad, one of the names of Buddha, and Ma, mother; the same as Om, the male and female united in the Lotus flower. The word Ma or the M with a vowel, without which it cannot be sounded, was, as I have stated, the old word for mother or the female principle—the matrix; and, on this account, it might be that the central numeral letter of the alphabet came to have the name of M. It was the Ma or Om figure, and thus the tree figure or vine-tree came to be called MN, or Muin, or 666—M-vin the vin of M. It should be remembered that the Jews of the present day have numerous mysteries attached to the M as the central letter, (many more, probably, than I am acquainted with,) so that this is not merely a theory. A moment's inspection shews that the Arabic alphabet was constructed without any regard to the mythos. Mystery

---

[1] See Basnage, p. 199. [2] Vol. I. pp. 174, 273, 659, &c., also *supra*, p. 180.

itself is a mythos, as I have shewn—M-istory—perhaps, I-story—om—the Story of Om. This was correctly the case with all early history.¹ But it is quite clear to me that after the Hebrews had adopted the first sixteen letters, the others were added, without any regard to the wants of the language, as a moment's examination will shew. For what, then, could it be, but to humour this mythos?—partly, perhaps, out of regard to the Moon's cycle of twenty-seven days, partly to make the M the central letter; for, without the contrivance of the final letters, it would not answer. The final letters are not indispensably necessary, as most of the letters do without the finals. The Arabians kept all their numbers for letters, but it is evident that if they had been composed to serve the purpose of letters, they would not have had three letters T, or three letters S. I have before shewn that it seems probable that the Greeks at one time had the same number of numeral letters as the Hebrews, or letters having the same power of notation; but that they purposely contrived to leave out the Koph, in order that they might have the two centre letters for their monogram of Bacchus, Mn=650, eleven letters on each side. One effect of this would be to make the last three letters of their proper *old* alphabet have each, in succeeding times, two numeral powers.² I have taken great pains to prove, and I am certain I have proved, that the last three letters of the alphabet had each two numeral meanings. Here we have a satisfactory explanation of the mode by which that effect was produced in the Greek. After they had given names to gods or things, from the symbols having the original powers of notation, they would never be able entirely to destroy these first names and substitute new ones. If new ones were given, it is evident that both would continue.

Man in Sanscrit means *a human being*; in Chaldæo-Hebrew, *intelligence*.³

Mani is always called Mane: now this will give us nearly the numerical name.

$$\begin{array}{llll}
M=600 & M=600 & M=600 & H= 8 \\
A= 1 & N= 50 & I= 10 & M=600 \\
N= 50 & I= 10 & N= 50 & \text{———} \\
I= 10 \quad \text{or} & \{A= 1 & U= 6 & 608 \quad \text{Persian Hour.} \\
E= 5 & \{E= 5 & \text{———} & \\
\text{———} & \text{———} & 666 & \\
666 & 666 & &
\end{array}$$

Om—Mani—Pami or Pema—Om. One is nothing but the M=600. Mani is Numa or Minos or Menu. We have seen how the Nu is מ *Nh* or Noah,⁴ and I believe it is the NH—*Mn* 650.⁵

We constantly read of the *Son of Man*. I have often wondered why a human being should be so called. I have little doubt that by this was meant, *Son of the Solar Incarnation, Mn.*

Man was the image of God, of the being described by the number 650; in short, he was the microcosm of God. Mind was Sapientia; and this was only to be made perceptible by one man to another by means of the Logos or speech. Thus mind came to be described by the word Logos, the speech or anima in motion, the spirit of God, of which the Linga was the emblem. The organ of generation, for a similar reason, was called Linga, or Lingua, language, or speech, or Logos. Mind was the Το Ον. " Every thing tends to the Το Ον"—" to the centre." For this reason,

---

¹ Vol. I. p. 882, n. See Ἱστορια, Ἱστωρ, and Italian *Storia*.   ² ΑΒΓΔΕΖΗΘΙΚΛ-ΜΝ-ΞΟΠΡΣΤΥΦΧΨΩ.

² Volney, Res. Ant. Hist. Vol. II. p. 403.   ⁴ See Vol. I. pp. 234, 236, 420, 626, 649, 714.

³ Let it not be forgotten, that when I speak of these matters, I suppose the Greek and Hebrew letters to be the same or nearly so—not yet to have changed.

when the alphabet consisted of only twenty-four letters or figures, the two centre letters, the MN=650, formed its name. The name of that part of the Hom or Homo, which more immediately partook of the nature of the Τὸ Ὂν, mind and man-min-di, viz. *divus*, holy or sacred, that is, MN. After the sacred number, the Neros was found to be 600 and not 650, the number of the letters was reduced from 28 to 27, and the M=600 was the sacred number.[1] When this was the case, it is evident that those *who did not understand all the reasoning* might take either the LM or the MN for their sacred number 650. Thus came the *Lama* and the *menu*. Thus the Lamed came to be used indiscriminately with the Nun, as Ficinus tells us. And thus, as we might expect, Lama, Menu, and Mani, were all the same. The Lamed is, in fact, the LM-di, Holy or Sacred Lama.

At last, the Lama came to have the same name as the sheep, as the solar constellation, and as " the Lamb that taketh away the sins of the world," because, in the language of figures, it was was L=50, M=600=650. For a similar reason the Goat, which was the same as the Lamb, was called Mn-des, M=600, N=50=650.

The Indian Fig-tree was sacred to the Sun.[2] It was the tree of the Lam ; then, from the regimine, the tree Lam-di.

The reader may probably recollect the observations which I made in Volume I. pp. 606, 837, 838, that the Goat and the Sheep are the same genus of animal, and that they will breed forward, or continue the breed, like the Greyhound and the Pointer, not like the Horse and the Ass. This accounts for the Goat being often found where a Sheep might be expected. At last the two animals came to be equally adored, one as LM=650, the other as MN=650.

Parkhurst says, מדע *mndo*, knowledge, understanding.[3] From this root ידע *ido*, probably, comes the name of the Docetes. He says, דעת *dot*, knowledge.[4] I believe it was one name of the Gnostics, and from this probably came the Latin *Doctus*. We have found *munda* to mean a cycle or circle. I suspect this arose from the figurative similitude of the divine mind to the circle which we meet with every where, to the Θ, Τὸ Ὂν; and that man had this name from being an emanation from the divine mind. From the word ידע *ido* comes the word *idea*, which is so closely connected with understanding, knowledge, and mind. And thus the mounts Ida, of Crete and Troy, or Tr-ia, might, with little or perhaps no violence, be construed *mounts of knowledge* or *wisdom*.

The Iod has the meaning of hand and ten, and may be the root of the word Ioda or Juda. It is the ידע *ido* of the Hebrews, which means *to think*, and figuratively knowledge, Wisdom, in fact, our Idea. When a man has no ideas he has no wisdom. We have before seen the close connexion of letters and knowledge. Here, I think, we may find the meaning of Ayudia—*the place of wisdom*. The tribe of Judea may be nothing but the tribe of Judia or Idii. The Idei of Crete were Δακτυλοι, Dactyli, as the learned say, because they were *ten*, the number of a person's fingers. I apprehend they might also be so called from the Iodi or Idæi, that is, votaries, or the inventors or possessors of the system of letters, and also from the word Iod *a hand*. We have here several meanings similar to what we found in the Tamul. From the Hebrew word ידע *ido*, Idea, the ideas of letters, knowledge, wisdom, head, cannot be separated. The French *Tête* is Tat, Ras, head.

---

[1] Thus, when it was desired to retain the allegory of the tree of knowledge and letters in the alphabetic numeral system, and the mansions of the moon and the days of the moon's period were found to be more correctly described by 27, the letters were reduced to 27.

[2] Vall. Coll. Hib. Vol. V. p. 130.   [3] In voce ידע *ido*, VII. p. 274.

[4] Ibid. p. 273. In a future page we shall find the language of Scotland called *Gael-doct*. The latter word came to Scotland with the Jewish abstinence from Pork, and was derived from this word, meaning learned Gael, or Sanctum Scriptum.

The Cretans of Mount Ida were said, by the Greeks, to be Jews. They probably constituted the monastic body, the remains of which still continue as Christian monks on Mount Ida.[1]

Virgil seems to have known the true nature of this mythos from an expression in the Æneid, Lib. x.—

Alma parens Idæa Deûm.

This Idæa was the Maia of Greece. Proclus, upon Plato, uses the expression, Μαῖα Θεων ὑπάτη: Maia, the Sovereign or Supreme of the Gods.[2]

We know certainly that, after the use of the numeral symbols as letters commenced, the custom of using them as symbols did not cease; but, on the contrary, that they were continued in common use for superstitious purposes by the early fathers; and it is easy to imagine, that, after the numeral powers of the Coptic and Greek letters became changed, the Gods should, in some instances, be called, or rather be described, by the symbols in their new application. For instance, that what before was יה tr should become $\Sigma P = 600$. And, again, $T \Sigma P$ and $X \Sigma P$. I think each of the letters $P \Sigma T$ came to have two meanings. All this might readily arise in the infancy of letter writing, and during the gradual cessation of symbol writing. I think the very easy manner in which the unmeaning names of the Gods resolve themselves into numbers, and those the precise numbers which are required to describe the sacred cycle, as it advanced to perfection, and the way in which they are recorded in the numbers of pillars in the temples, and the way in which, as I have shewn, they were used to make up the periods of the Hebrew chronology, as taught by Usher, Marsham, and Eusebius; and the way in which the monograms descriptive of Jesus Christ are formed of the numbers of the three cycles, leave nothing wanting to the proof of the truth of my explanation of the system. The probabilities are as a million to one in favour of its truth.

It should also be recollected, that we are not to be tied down in our reasoning respecting the meanings of symbols and letters in the first years of their invention, in the same strict manner as we ought to be, when we reason about those of the fastidious Greeks, at the time when they had brought their beautiful alphabet to perfection, and fixed, with great precision, the power of every letter.

The attempts to tie down inquirers into the early periods of Greece, or any other country, to the strict grammatical rules adopted or formed in later times, when these countries had become highly civilized and their language fixed by these grammatical rules, can only serve, if permitted, to conceal truth. There is no reason to believe the ancient languages different from the modern with respect to their uncertainty; and how uncertain are they! The following passage of Sir John Maundeville, a learned Englishman in the fourteenth century, will shew in how short a time even a written language changes: "Aftre that thei ben zolden (yielded) thei sleen hem alle, and "kutten of hire eres, and soween hem in vynegre, and there of thei maken gret servyse for "Lordes." Similar examples may be found in every language.

I must also beg my reader not to be surprised if he should find several etymologies for a word. He must recollect that I pretend *to prove* nothing, only to raise different degrees of probability in each case; and when I give two explanations, the reader may take which he chooses; I believe he will find either of them consistent with the remainder of the theory. But I think it probable that, in many cases, words were designedly so formed as to have several meanings. It must also be recollected, that the meanings of words would change with time.

---

[1] For Iod *hand*, see Ouseley's Coll. Vol. III. pp. 62, 105, 418.   [2] Jurieu, Vol. II. p. 91.

19. After man began to theorize on the First Cause, he naturally designated it by the Monad or Unit, which was at length described by a point: on this arose many most refined speculations. It was on the Monad, on which was erected all the other numbers, till we get to ten; the whole of the fingers which formed one circle or whole, as it contained in itself all numbers. Then, by the invention of adding the other numbers over again, all numbers are formed. Thus the point came to be the foundation of both series, and the • or pruktos, or prick, or point, ׳ or jod, to be descriptive of self-existence, and of both one and ten, and from this in time might arise the Hebrew verb היה eie, to be or exist; with its irregular forms, and its ׳ i existence and יה ie, or, Syriacè, י׳ io, joined to ד׳ di, יד iud, and the people of Io-di, the holy Io; and, Chaldaicè, ידא iuda, and God self-existent, thus formed from the root • the Ailm, on which all letters and numbers were carried or formed, and consequently all knowledge. Thus it was the creator, and the foundation or mother of figures, letters, and knowledge: from this, the Iedi of Judi were the followers of the holy I, or Ie, or Io. From this being the origin of letters as well as of creation, the golden fleece (holy wisdom) and the apple of the Hesperides, apples of the tree of knowledge, holy wisdom came.

The first figure would, of course, be what we find it, I: when it got to *ten* it was X or ׳ in Hebrew, that is, Iod—Io-di—the *sacred Io* in the Syriac, or יה *ih* in the Hebrew, translated into the Greek IH of Delphi, or the XH=608. Jesus Christ, Basnage says, was described by IH. This shews that the ΗΙ of Delphi was written both HI and ΗΙ. In several of the old languages the *first* number is described thus, I, and the *tenth* in the same manner; and sometimes both by a point. This is the Hebrew Iod, and the Latin Iota. This is, I apprehend, the Το Ον of Plato. Iod is *hand*, and also, in Hebrew, the Ivy, which is called the five-finger-leaved tree, and the Plantavita.[1]

In the Dalmatian or Illyrian alphabet, the form of the I is X; and this, I cannot doubt, was originally the Roman, and the I or j was the *ninth*, and the X the *tenth*. The small variations in the alphabets shew, I think, that they have in most countries got into use by degrees; escaped, in fact, from the crypts, before any thing like grammar was thought of.

Duret says, "*Que Dieu est le chef de toutes les choses, tant de celles qui sont, que des autres qui doivent estre et ne sont encore.* Aussi ceste note de nullité 0, qui est circulaire et résoluble en soy mesme. Sans fin, et commencement, ne fait rien de soy, mais avec l'unité constitué le nombre de 10. Et de-là se va multipliant en la compagnie des autres, jusques à l'infini."[2] Or, it may be the Jewish and British and Indian cycle of 84—I=10, O=70, D=4=84. But I rather prefer the former. From this numerical theory, the Io of Syria, arose the Jewish irregular verb היה *to be*. As the *i. d.* or 10 and 4, made the half of the moon, when the year was supposed to be 336 days long; so the יה *i. e.* or 10 and 5, made the half when the year was supposed to be 360 days long.

The ׳ *Iod* is the tenth letter of the old alphabet of figures, the מ *mem* is the tenth of the new one of letters.

The sacred tetragrammaton might be either יהוה *ieue*, or Ὁ ων, και ὁ ην, και ὁ ερχομενος; or it might be, איהה *aeie*, which comprehends them all.

I apprehend the origin of notation, or of figures or arithmetic, is very fairly represented in the Preliminary Observations, and the beginning of this book. We will now try to find how the Arabic system was discovered, or I had, perhaps, better say, how the systems of calculation, by calculi or cowries, or right lines, was perfected. —For, though I have spoken of calculi or little stones

---

[1] Vall. Coll. Hib. Vol. V. p. 131. [2] Origin des Langues, p. 159.

only, yet I apprehend the African and Indian and Chinese custom of using little shells or cowries, and which are yet used in all the oriental countries, soon came into use instead of the calculi. I suppose that man, after a certain experience of the use of lines or cowries for numbers, proceeded to invent arbitrary figures for each parcel of lines or cowries, and thus he made a 2 for two cowries or lines, a 3 for three, and a 9 for nine of them; each of these parcels answering to a part of his fingers, and the 9 to nine of them. I have no doubt that in the forming of all these symbols, fanciful or mystical reasons would influence the formation of them, and when he came to the last finger or digit, and he cast about to determine what sort of a figure he should make for it,— for it, which was the total of the fingers,—he formed the sign of the circle as, in his opinion, the most proper; and this it really was, for many reasons, so evident, that I suppose I need not repeat them. Thus he got the 1, 2, 3, 4, to 9 and 0. When he examined this, he would find that he had one total. He laid his cowries or inscribed his lines one below another, and he found if he took three of them thus,

$$\begin{array}{r} 1 \\ 1 \\ 1 \\ \hline \text{they made 3...... } 3 \end{array}$$

and four would in like manner make 4. If he took ten of them, in like manner they made 10 or 0. That is, they made one 0, or one total, that is, 1. 0. This brought him instantly to simple addition, as far as to nine figures, and perhaps to ten. He would observe that the one total, or 10, was descriptive of all the cowries he had in his hand, and that the figures on the right described *ones* answering to his fingers or digits, and the next figure on the left ten digits. He then took two parcels of cowries of ten each, and he said,

If one of these parcels is described by one total.................... 1 0,
two of these parcels ought to be described by two totals................. 2 0,
that three might be described by three totals........................ 3 0,
and so on till he got to nine totals 9 0,
and, at last, that a hundred cowries would be described by ten totals, thus,.. 10 0.

This would immediately shew, that the first number on the right described digits, the next on the left tens, and the next on the left, parcels of ten tens each. In the above we have the sums—ten, twenty, thirty, &c.

About the same time that man got so far as to form the 10, and to describe the sums 20, 30, 40, &c., he would observe, if *one* and a *circle*, made one total,[1] and that the one in the second line to the left always answered to ten, that, if instead of the 1 and 0, he put 1 and 1, he would describe the eleven cowries, which he had in his hand; and if he put 1 and 2, he would describe the twelve cowries which he had in his hand; and hence he discovered how to describe 11, 12, 13, &c., to 20, or two totals. In this manner, again, he was led to discover, that the first line on the right was digits, the second to the left tens, the third to the left, parcels of ten tens, or what we call hundreds. After this, I think the mode in which man would proceed with the combined assistance of his cowries and figures, to underwrite the number of the odd digits on the right, carry-

---

[1] The word *Total*, which I have made use of, is al-tat; the tat or tot meaning ττ=600, and has come from the cycle of the neros, the perfect and complete cycle, including the whole time which the sun and moon took to come from any point to that same point again. It formed the Latin *totus*.

ing over the overplus parcels of tens to the next line, or to the tens, and the overplus parcel o. tens to the next line or the hundreds, is so easy to be imagined, that I need not pursue the analysis any farther. In the same manner, by taking one collection of cowries from another, he discovered subtraction, and in a similar manner division, and multiplication—using cowries, as they are yet used, even in the most complicated astronomical calculations, in India and China, a very interesting account of which may be seen, in the Kala Sankalita of Col. Warren. If a person will only take a parcel of pebbles or shells, he will soon find how very easily the art of arithmetic must have sprung from the combined use of calculi or cowries, and the infant art of writing, by numeral symbols, and of letters, when the latter were in the act of being discovered, and were coming into use along with the former.

20. The Chinese are said to have a God called Xangti, whose name is kept a profound secret, never mentioned on any occasion, but entrusted alone to those in the higher mysteries, who meditate on it with the most profound reverence. Here we have the exact history of the OM of the Indians, and of the IEUK of the Jews of the twentieth chapter of Exodus, which, when properly and mysteriously translated, means, as I have already stated, "Thou shalt not mention the name of ה א יה IEU, that is, of THE *Self-existent* Being." I mentioned above, p. 190, that, in the ancient language of ciphers, the *first* and the *tenth* figure were the same, I, and Θ; but the tenth was also represented by the mystic X. From this the X, the monogram of God, came to be confounded with the I, or ⓘ, also the monogram of God, and therefore may be here put for the I: and the *a* is the Hebrew ה *e* and the ע *o* corrupted into the ng. This produces the *Iao*. The ti is די *di*, Holy *Iao*. In Tibet they have the same God; he is called Xiang-siouph. This is more correctly reported and is the monogram X and Iao—the *soph* or *wise*, or the wisdom of Iao, and they have him also called Jang ti.—Divus Iao.[1] Here I suppose I shall be accused of taking etymological liberties. But it may be observed, that I do not entirely depend on the explanation or analysis of the word, but much more *on the history and the circumstances attending it.* These, in the analysis, or etymology, as it is called, of words, ought never to be lost sight of, and, I flatter myself, are never lost sight of by me. I think it must be allowed to me to take much greater liberties of this kind, with words which, by those liberties, dovetail into my system, when that system is shewn to be nearly established and supported by hundreds of other circumstances, than I could be allowed to take without them. It may be recollected that I have formerly shewn from Georgius, that the *Ti* meant *di* or *holy*, in the word Tibet. This being premised, I must add that, after I had written the above, I found the following passage of D'Herbelot: "*Ng* est une lettre Chinoise, qui répond "à l'*ain* des Hebreux; Monument de Christianisme en Chine." I think I could not well wish for any thing more to my purpose than this; and here we see a striking proof of the utility of adhering to the simple forms of the Hebrew alphabet, as given by me, and regulated by the powers of notation. Ie or Io was Logos, a tree was wisdom. Wisdom was letters, letters were a tree. Thus a tree was wisdom, because its leaves were letters; יע *ios* was the word used for letters. *I* was one, 1; one and a circle were 10, X; one and a circle were Io, which were IH or XH, the circle 608; one and a circle were a dot and circle, the emblem of the eternal monad—Θ. It was Θ, 9 9, the emblem of the eternal number, as they called it. A circle is a cipher; it is the emblem of eternal wisdom; it is שיפ—סופ *sup* or חיו *sup*, Σοφ, wisdom. Theta was nine, because 9 was the emblem of eternity; conformably to this, the first letter of the hieroglyphic alphabet was an *owl*, the emblem of wisdom. I must be permitted to repeat, that Ida is ידע Id-o, idea, mando, (vide Parkhurst,) מנדע *mado*, knowledge, wisdom, a circle, a cycle, a cipher. Stars were letters,

---

[1] Yao, volo, *I will do*; τυχσυ. Web. on Greek and Chinese Language, p. 35.

but each star was dedicated to a certain tree, or each tree to a certain star. A constellation was a wood, שׁתל *stl*, *satal*, whence *stella*, a star, or σ'=200, τ'=300, ρ'=100=600; and the Hebrew, English, and Sanscrit, *stl*, stalla, place of rest or settlement, σ'=200, τ'=300, LL=100=600; and the Mexican Ttl=650, Teotl. Mndo is מנדו=650—ד *di*, holy Mandaites, followers of Wisdom. They were Nazoureans or Nazarenes, therefore Nazorenes were followers of wisdom—therefore Jesus's followers were followers of wisdom. Jesus was a Natzir or flower of Nazareth, but the place where it grew was in *Carmel*, in the garden of God. Of this more presently. Buddha was crucified for robbing the garden of a flower: this, perhaps, we may understand by and by. The union of the mythos and the numeral symbolic alphabet, I think, can alone explain why the wood or grove in which the Gods were worshiped, the niches or stalls in which they were placed, and the groups of stars into which they were changed, should all have the same name—Stall.

In our Bibles we every where find the writers reprobating the adoration of groves or trees, which are ordered to be cut down and burnt. Mr. Landseer, in his Sabæan Researches, has most superabundantly pro ed, that those things which we call *groves*, and which in the Hebrew are called אשרה *asre* and אשירה *asire*,[1] were some kind of instrument of the nature of our celestial globes or armillary spheres. From these words, in fact, come the Latin *aster* and our *star*, and the Asteroth of the Sidonians, and the Goddess of the Saxons called Eoster. The word Asre came to mean a tree, because those instruments were covered with groups of stars, each star marked with a letter, which letter had the name of a tree. They were formed upon a microcosmic system, which I shall explain in a future book; by this, the earth or globe was divided into tenths, from which the tithe that I shall shew was paid by all nations came to be called Ashera. We constantly read of the fortunes of men told by the stars, of the life and actions of Jesus Christ being recorded in the stars, &c., &c. Every star having the name of a tree, it would also be a letter and a numerical symbol, and a group of them was called a constellation, of which there were two kinds. Of one kind, which had the names chiefly of animals, there were forty-eight: the other kind consisted of divisions formed by lines, each line distant from another five degrees, which would divide the sphere into seventy-two parts, as described by Plutarch. These lines, if taken from North to South, or from East to West, would divide the surface of the sphere into parallelograms seventy-two in number. By means of the forty-eight hieroglyphics and the numeral symbols, it would be no difficult matter to record a history, the parts of which would present themselves consecutively every night, so as to finish the story in a year, or in a period of years or cycle, at pleasure. Thus we have the labours of Hercules described in the zodiacal signs, as they are so satisfactorily explained by M. Dupuis. If the history of Hercules and his labours could be portrayed and described by the constellations, so might the history of Jesus Christ: and these labours are so similar to the sufferings of Jesus, that the reader must remember that the pious and Rev. Mr. Parkhurst has been obliged, much against his inclination, to acknowledge, that "they "were types of what the real Saviour was to do and suffer."

The word stella has the same meaning as aster, and is the same as the word שׁתל *stl*, which means both a group of stars, i. e. a constellation, and a wood. All these varieties arise from a similar cause, namely, from the stars being marked by letters or symbols, which letters had the meaning and names of trees. I have very little doubt that the Zodiacs of Esne and Dendera were instruments of this kind of perpetual almanack. Of course, if those instruments were set up in the temple, they must have been set up by the priests, by the initiati, and they must have appeared to the ignorant as something very extraordinary, as they would seem to enable the priests

---

[1] See Parkhurst, p. 47.

to foretell eclipses and other matters. Thus it is very natural that they should become objects of terror to the ignorant, who, in consequence, destroyed them when they obtained power.

Maimonides (in More Nevoc. ch. xx., Townley's translation, p. 263) says, "But the Zabii " being ignorant of the nature of the true God, and regarding the heavens and the heavenly bodies " as that eternal being who was free from all privation, and supposing that from thence all kinds " of power flowed down into images and certain trees, called in the law asheroth אשרות *asrut*, con- " cluded that those images and trees inspired the prophets with the prophetic language which " they uttered in their visions, predicting good or evil." These Asheroth are the instruments of which I have just treated.

We every where find the later Jewish writers, and particularly the prophets, reprobating the Ashres, but yet we find them in their Temple under the best of their rulers: they are repeatedly said to be set up *under trees*. And Abraham set up an *Ashera* in *Beer-sheba*. This shews that the Jews had their sects like the moderns. When an ignorant race of devotees, like our evangelicals, obtained power, they destroyed the images, burnt the books and Ashres or astronomical instruments, as John Knox and other Reformers did. Our books are come to us from this race of people, and for this every philosophical inquirer ought to make allowance. No doubt, like the Protestant reformers, many of them were honest, and destroyed some gross abuses, such for instance as the human sacrifices of prisoners of war, ordered by the law, of which proof enough may be found in "the devoted thing, both of *man* and beast," Lev. xxvii. 28, 29; also Lev. x. 14; Exod. xxix. 28; Numb. xxxi. 41; the *heave offering* of the men prisoners.[?] But if they reformed abuses, they indulged in their antipathy to learning, without judgment or discrimination, and this is proved by their destruction of the Asherim or astronomical instruments. Our modern devotees are surely not less inimical to learning, than were Jewish and Protestant Reformers.

I beg my reader to pause here, and to reflect upon the state in which he would be placed at the end of a period of 600 years, if he had had no historical account of what had precede that time; and, again, if he had a tradition or a writing giving an account of the immaculate conception, of the adventures of a divine person, and a dogma that this was to be renewed every 600 years; that, in short, all the affairs of the world were to be renewed periodically. He will at once see, that his very limited experience would not enable him to correct any chronological error.

The stars, the lights in the firmament of heaven, were, by the omnipotent voice of the Elohim himself, appointed to be "for signs and for seasons, and for days and years." The proper use of the asherim was, no doubt, in part for ascertaining and manifesting the movements of those signs, seasons, &c., and I imagine that they were used to foretell the political events which would happen, (as the mythos dictated,) as well as eclipses, conjunctions of planets, &c.; and men must have been very different from what we have ever known them, if priests and rulers did not make them subservient to their selfish purposes. This would, of course, expose them to the attacks of reforming fanatics.

In the case of the Hebrews we have an example of a temple whose sacred writings have escaped to us—in all others, of temples whose writings have not escaped; and in this, at last, consists the great difference between them. It is evident that struggles were constantly taking place between the patrons of images and iconoclasts—between reformers and anti-reformers—and our writings are those of the iconoclastic party, which at last prevailed. From this circumstance, and from being educated as partisans of this system, every thing takes in our eyes a suitable colour.

I have very little doubt that the stars were allotted to the numeral symbols, so as to make them into a kind of calendar or perpetual almanack, and this is what was meant by the declaration of the great astronomer, that the life and actions of Jesus Christ might be read in the heavens. It was contrived either for a year or six hundred years. Either the Roman Catholic system of portraying the actions of Jesus every year, or the system of Virgil in his new Troys and new Argonauts every six hundred years, was adopted. Vallancey and several others have had a glimpse of the truth, but they have had no success in making it out.

No person can look at the Mem final without seeing that it is the Samech, and the example in the word לִמְרְבֵה Imrbe of the use of it for the Mem, sufficiently justifies and proves, at least in mystic inquiries, its indiscriminate use. So far I consider that we are certain, independent of the innumerable other proofs of it which I have given.¹ It is the same as the Greek hissing ξ' which stands for sixty, and the חכם hkm, wisdom. The Sa is the ξω or ψω iso or Saviour or the 600: the same mystic system goes through the whole. With reference to this, the Six was described by what we call the Episemonbau or Vau, the hissing ς'. The first cycle was 6; the second 60; the third 600; the next 6000. The following passage will shew a similar kind of superstition of the Mohamedans in a late day, when in fact the knowledge of letters had rendered all such theories absolute folly and nonsense, but which, *before their discovery*, deserved rather to be called *wisdom* than *folly*.

The following is a metrical account of the verses, &c., of the Koran, taken from a very beautiful copy, once the property of the unfortunate Tippoo Sultan, but preserved in the public library at Cambridge. It was copied by me from a manuscript of Professor Lee's, lent me, at his request, by the secretary of the Royal Society of Literature.

> " The verses of the Koran, which is good and heart-delighting,
> " Are six thousand, six hundred, and sixty-six.
> " One thousand of it command, one thousand strongly prohibit.
> " One thousand of it promise, one thousand of it threaten.
> " One thousand of it read in choice stories,
> " And know, one thousand of it to consist in instructive parables:
> " Five hundred of it in discussions on lawful and unlawful;
> " One hundred of it are prayers for morning and evening.
> " Know sixty-six abrogating and abrogated.
> " Of such an one, I have now told you the whole."

In the 6666 and the 6600, exclusive of the abrogated part, I think may be seen the remains of the cyclic system.

21. We will now inquire into the famous Ἑις, μια, ἑν, commonly called the three genders of the Greek numeral adjective, which word describes our idea of unity.²

---

¹ See Vol. I. pp. 168, 172.

² Grammarians call it an irregular noun. In all the written languages except the Sanscrit, there are many words which grammarians can bring into no rule of grammar, and this gives them much trouble, because they proceed upon the idea, that language, both written and verbal, is to be accounted for on principles of what are called philosophy, when, in reality, they are much more the effect of what is called accident. Grammarians and Philosophers never had any thing to do with them, till they were come to a very advanced state. The more I inquire and think upon the subject, the more I am induced to have recourse to what we call accident, in the case of language.

Plato, who lived in the fourth century before the Christian æra, was the first that considered Grammar; Aristotle the first who wrote on it, and reduced it to an art; and Epicurus the first that publicly taught it among the Grecians. If an inquirer will only think one moment upon these facts, he will be obliged to admit that what I have said of Homer's poems must be in great part correct. They must be indebted almost entirely to Aristotle and his companions for the perfection of their language. According to Suetonius, the art of Grammar was first brought to Rome, about 170 years B. C., by Crates Malotes, the ambassador from king Attalus, to the Roman Senate. (Pref. to Bosworth's Saxon Grammar, p. xxiv.) If these facts be considered, we shall instantly see the absurdity of being tied down to observe the niceties of the language of the later Greeks and Romans. For, most assuredly, before the invention of Grammar, there could be nothing like precision in language. It seems quite certain from this, that the poems of Homer must have undergone a great dressing up by Aristotle, to bring them to their present perfection. But an ob-

I have shewn that the first recorded ideas of man were probably numbers. I think I may assume, that all written language came from Asia to Greece, and that the Greek language was formed from the oriental. Now I think we may observe something very striking in the Greek word for the idea of unity. A Greek grammarian would tell you, that the word for one is ἑις, and that it is irregular, making μια in the feminine, and ἑν in the neuter. But it is evident these words are not formed from one another, but are three separate and distinct words, for three separate and distinct ideas. If I be right in the primary formation of numbers, they may be sought for among the most ancient languages, and I think we shall find the Greek words above alluded to to have come from the East.

Priscian says, that in the Greek word Mia for *one*, *I* is considered the principal letter, and the M as mute. We constantly read in grammarians of words being paragogic and heemantive and formative. In nine cases out of ten these learned words are only used and contrived as a screen for ignorance. Almost all the words connected with mythology are of so old a date that their origin is totally unknown in all countries, and this is because they were formed before the art of syllabic-writing was known; and before this book is concluded, I feel confident I shall satisfy every reader, that they took their names from the first numeral art of writing which I have been unfolding. The mere assertion of Priscian, that the letter *m* is mute, is by no means satisfactory, as my reader can hardly fail to admit, when he has considered the circumstances which I shall disclose. I suppose that the word consists of the monogram M and the Hebrew IE, or, I, *self-existent*.[1] This opens a door to the explanation of many other words. I do not doubt that in the Mute, M, we have the monogram of the Om of India—three words coalescing, to use Sir W. Jones's expression, and forming the word O-M, or M, the Mem final of Isaiah. In a similar manner we have the Monos, which is the Latin *unus* with the Monogram prefixed.

This seems to restore this important word to something like rationality. 'Εις, in the Hebrew, may be שיא ʙɪs, ᴛʜᴇ *is* or *ens, existence* in the masculine; היא ʙɪe ᴛʜᴇ *ie, existence* in the feminine; and ἑν *the* ον, Το Ον, of Plato, in the neuter, or the *ens*. I have not a doubt that, when these words were formed, grammar rules had never been either heard or thought of. There is not in the world any thing like a written or spoken language formed by rule, except the Sanscrit, and in this very formed rule, its modern character is evident. Every language written and spoken is the child of circumstance, improved by grammarians, as our language and all languages of civilized nations are improving every day.

Some time ago, p. 190, I observed, that the M was the tenth letter of the new or Cadmæan alphabet of letters, and answered to the jod, the tenth letter of the old alphabet of numbers, which was often described by the hissing X. Our learned men say the numeral letter *six* was described by two digammas thus, F ⊎ or ⊐. Now I think it has been originally the same as the French hissing C with the sedilla under it thus, F Ç. This is the hissing *sixth* letter. The *tenth* hissing letter was the X, and the *sixteenth* letter was the Samach, or the terminating form of the tenth alphabetic letter M, and was formed by three lines or forms Ξ ξ, or three Çs, and denoted 60 and 600, and called by the hissing word Xi and Chi. We have no alphabetic name for the pre-

---

servation made by Mons. Dugas-Montbel, in the Journal des Savans, September 1831, that "Plato, Aristotle, Pʟᴜᴛᴀʀ-ǫᴜᴇ, citent des vers de l'Iliade; de l'Odissée, que nous ne retrouvons plus dans les manuscripts et les éditions d'Homère," proves, indeed, that they have been *recensés* in later ages.—Homère et ses écrits par Marq. Fostia D'Urban, p. 252.

[1] He says L was often used along with the N for 50. This we know to be true. Supp. Ency. Brit. Vol. I p. 522.

sent numeral letter 6. I suspect it was originally called *Sam,* the name of the Sun in various dialects, and that the name for the number 60, Samach, was Sam and אכם *akm,* and the same for the 600; and the form of it in the Greek was made to describe the triple power, of which the Sun was the emblem—the triple wisdom. That much mystery is hid under these words, cannot be doubted; whether I have suggested a probability as to its *true explanation* I leave to my reader.

At the head of all beings and their works the Oriental or Gnostic sects placed the Monad, Μια αρχη, also called Πατηρ αγνωςος, which M. Matter truly observes, was found in all the doctrines of India and Persia, and of the ancient world.[1] And who was this *feminine* Μια αρχη, who was also the masculine Πατηρ; I answer, the androgynous Brahme-Maia of India. This Monad, μια, is the feminine of the Greek word εις, μια, (or Ionicè ia,) εν *unus.* The word εις may be a formation of the Hebrew אש *ais,* substance, or the verb אש *is, he is.* It is joined with both genders and numbers. Εν, as used here, as the oriental language had no neuter, must have been purely Greek. But as it is the neuter of εις, *one,* it may be substance or matter, which was with the Persians and many of the Gnostics the origin of evil, or the destroying or evil principle, and may have been only a dialectic variation of the word *ον.* The neuter of the word for the idea of Unity can evidently be nothing but matter; that is, in idea it cannot be separated from matter. We derive our idea of number solely from matter. If I be right that all languages are derived from one, it seems not unreasonable to search for the roots of the originals of words in different languages. When the surprising manner in which ancient languages have become changed is considered, it cannot be expected that any thing like an entire original language should be found any where. But I think with skill and diligence, and the absence of prejudice, it is not out of probability, that the original language might be nearly recovered; but yet I think we are at present a long way from it. As an example, the Greek word εις would be the Hebrew אש *is,* the word μια the Indian *Maia,* and the word εν or ον the Hebrew אן *an.*

The example of the words εις, μια, εν, being oriental, is exactly similar to that noticed in my Essay on the Celtic Druids, in the Eleusinian mysteries, of the three sacred words ΟΜ ΠΑΞ ΚΟΓΞ,[2] commonly used both in India and Europe. No one will doubt, I think, that all these things have an intimate connexion. The three words used at Eleusis were purely Sanscrit; yet the Athenians would have been much offended to have been told that they were *barbarous,* though they admitted that they did not themselves understand them. They were brought to this temple when the name of the Sinde was brought to the river in Thrace, and the custom of burning the widows, and the name of Χρης given to the God. They were a form, like our Amen, which the priest at last used like the talk of a parrot, without thought; till, like our *amen,* its meaning was forgotten. The language kept changing, the form remained fixed. It is like the case of the words *Ite, missio est,* at the end of the Roman mass, the meaning of which is now unknown.[3]

But I have one more observation to make on this subject. The Εις, Μια, Εν, are descriptive of the Creator, Preserver, and Destroyer. The first is the male, the אש *is,* self-existence, PROFOUND WISDOM; the female is the Μια, the Λογος, both male and female, and Μια αρχη—πατηρ αγνωςος, the Εν or Ον is the neuter symbol of matter, the Destroyer. In Exod. iii. 14, God says, Εγω ειμι ὁ Ων· Ὁ Ων απεςαλκε με προς ὑμας.

When I consider the great number of Druidical, that is, of Cyclopæan, buildings in every part of the world, all having nearly the same generic character, I feel surprised at the fact, that there is not on one of them any thing to be found like an inscription. The facts of many of them, the

---

[1] Hist. Crit. du Gnost. Vol. II. Ch. iv. Sect. ii. p. 266. He also observes, that this was the Θεος αγνωςος which St. Paul found at Athens; and if he be right in this, he here curiously unites the Christian and the Heathen religions.

[2] Beausobre, Vol. II. p. 350, n. 198; Asiat. Res.; and in Vol. I. p. 253.   [3] See *supra,* p. 61.

Pyramids for instance, displaying great astronomical knowledge, and the stones of the circular and elliptic buildings, like Stonehenge, Abury, &c., having the numbers of the ancient Cycles, the Neros, that of Meton, &c., being considered, I am sometimes, notwithstanding what I have lately said on the subject of secrecy, inclined to suspect, that the knowledge of astronomy preceded the knowledge of syllabic letters much longer than we have been led to believe. I confess it is difficult to believe that astronomy should have so preceded; but yet it is difficult to account for the fact, that there is no such thing as an inscription on any really very ancient building. And the Orientals still continue, notwithstanding their knowledge of the Arabic figures, to work very difficult problems, and to make long arithmetical calculations, by means of their cowries.

22. We will now inquire a little farther into the ancient history of Signs or Seals or Crests or Monograms. We have found that the M, and the I, and the X +, were all commonly prefixed to words, for the sake of mystery, as it is said, but, as it ought to be said, for some cause which is unknown. It is a very common practice with all authors in writing, to assert or to say, a thing is so or so, without any qualifying word or clause to express doubt or opinion, when they merely mean to express their opinion. This is constantly done without any ill intention; but it is afterward quoted as authority, it being assumed that it is not opinion, but the assertion of a known fact, which thus obtains credit from the respectability of the assertor; and thus falsities are established and truth is concealed. It is one of the thousand ways which nature has devised to prevent our knowing too much of the realities of by-gone ages. It is often very difficult to discover whether an author is asserting a fact or delivering an opinion. When the saint, and bishop, and martyr—Irenæus, asserts a fact from his own knowledge, in which he has no interest, or in which his assertion is against his interest, we may believe him; but who would give a farthing for his *opinion* on any subject, where sense or judgment was required? Thus to apply this reasoning to the case before us, when an author says, "the *I* is prefixed for the sake of mystery," he evidently knows nothing about it. When it is said, "it is put into a word for the sake of the metre," this looks more like a certainty, because the truth of the assertion may be examined and the fact known. But if it were inserted for the sake of the metre, it was selected because it had a secret meaning. It is like the *M* and the *X*, a monogram, a sigillum, a seal. I believe the *I* was the sign of the *male* generative principle, called in the Targums *I* or *II*, and came from the word II in the word *ieva*,—that the *M* was the sign of the *female*, and that the *X* was the sign of the *united two*. Each might be a mark of sect. The Romish bishops all continue to use the X before they sign their names. It was the origin of seals. Those who could not write used their seal; sometimes with *ink*, sometimes with *wax*, to express their assent to a deed. In the same manner it was used as a crest; it was a Crestian distinction. I believe the use of a sacred name, called a Crestian name, descended to us from the most remote antiquity, although it may only have been used in modern times as a signature in signing the name. Lords and bishops, even now, do not use it. The monograms were all of the nature of crests, or seals, or ciphers, as we call them. And I believe there are vast numbers of words beginning with the *I*, the *M*, and the *X*, the meaning of which we do not discover, because we do not separate the monograms from them. What should we make of Bishop Doyle's X Doyle, if it were written in one of the ancient languages, in which there is no distinction of *capital* from *small* letters, and no separation of words, and his name had happened to have been Adoyle? We should then have had him Xadoyle. Thus it is with the *Momptha* of Egypt, and the *Iixthus* of the Sibyl, and probably the *I-χιον*—the *crucified* Ixion.[1] These monograms arose, as we have seen, from the first numerical letters, and constituted a small part of the endless ænigmatical science of the ancients. Almost to our own time, every useful art,

---

[1] See Vol. I. pp. 500, 503.

every science, every new discovery, was concealed, as far as possible, to a chosen few. The possession of a useful secret, I do not doubt, would be a passport into some of the secret crafts. All this, however, is now nearly gone, and in another century it will not be believed to have existed. From a careful consideration of the word SACRED, I am quite satisfied that it is a plant of modern growth. It was originally *secretum, secret*. By degrees secret matters came to be looked on with awe or fear; from this arose our *sacred*. I have some suspicion that the word sacred has no definite idea annexed to it. I consider the subject of monograms to be extremely curious, and to deserve much more examination than I have bestowed upon it.

23. After what I had written on the word Χρης in the first volume, (pp. 580—589,) was printed, I met with a passage of Mr. Payne Knight's,[1] which completely bears me out in what I have said respecting the Sigma-Tau, and the substitution of the T and Σ for one another. After representing that the Σ is classed separately by itself, as being neither mute, aspirate, nor liquid, and that it was commonly used by the Lacedæmonians and Aristophanes for the Θ, he says, "In " other instances both the Dorians and Æolians employed the T for the Σ, as in the pronoun ΣΥ, " which they wrote ΤΥ. The possessive, however, derived from it, was written with either letter, " indifferently, by the poets, as suited best with their Rhythm and Metre." Again, "Both the " English and French now sound the T as an Σ before the I in many instances, particularly in the " abstract substantives derived from the Latin." Again, "The case is, that Σ *being only a T* " *aspirated in a particular manner, would naturally be confounded with it* in the different modes of " pronunciation which habit or caprice gives rise to *in languages not fixed by any established rules* " *of orthography, which the Greek was not till the Macedonian conquest*, when the later Attic be- " came the common dialect."

Mr. Payne Knight has also observed, that the Lacedæmonians commonly used the R for the S,[2] which I have elsewhere shewn, was the constant practice with the Hebrews. This has a strong tendency to support my hypothesis, that the R, the S, and the T, all had two numerical meanings. If Mr. Knight be correct as to the unsettled state of the Greek language till the Macedonian conquest, as I have no doubt that he is, how absurd is it to tie up inquirers into its earlier history by the rules adopted to fix the meaning of the language in later times![3]

When in other cases I find the letter *s* changed for the *t*, and the *t* for the *s*, as Sur for Tur, and Tur for Sur,—and I consider the practice of writing every thing in numbers, I am induced to suspect that *Tam* is a corruption of the solar name, in Sanscrit *Sama*, and in Hebrew שם *sm*, on which I treated above, p. 197, and means ס Samech=60, ש Shin=300=360; and that, from an application to this mythos, in some way or other, the Hebrew שש ss=360, became שש ss=600; that the Greek 'Εξ and our *six* came from the same source; and that the name of the Greek Ξ the *trilinear* and triformed letter, was called Xi or perhaps IX. But *I* was the ancient emphatic article of the Saxons.[4] This at once accounts for its use in many cases which we have discussed, and it must have been once the same with the Hebrews, if what Dr. Geddes said was true—that

---

[1] Hist. Gr. Alph. p. 14.   [2] Ibid. p. 125.

[3] The Dorians and Æolians changed the σ into τ, as τυ for συ, as stated by Mr. Knight; but the Æolians also changed the Σ into Ρ, as μαρτυρ, for μαρτυς, ισπερ for ισπες, αφιρ for αφις. Dores, pro συς, σα, συν, dicunt τυς, τια, τιων—τ et ρ pro σ, in atticâ dialecto σ pro ξ. (App. Scapulæ, pp. 64, 65.) Attica dialectus mutat σ modo in τ, modo in ξ—θαλασσαν, θαλατταν—συντλαν, τευτλαν.—Σ pro ρ utitur; nam pro θαρσος, θαρσος, &c. Scapula. Hhapats in Hebrew (*to desire*) in Arabic (*to incline*) is, in Syriac, Hhapet. Thus the Greek μαζα, a kind of cake, the same as the Hebrew Matza, was pronounced by the Bœotians μαδδα. South M. As. R. Again, τεσσαρα in the Attic is τετττερα. Thus the Latins have the *tu* from συ.

[4] See Etym. Dict.

Saxon was Hebrew. It is very remarkable that the emphatic article should so often be the name of God: Arab. *Al*, Coptic *Pi*, Hebrew ח *e*, and *I*, and *II*.

In his late work, the learned Dr. Pritchard says, " In a variety of languages, either for the sake " of euphony, or from caprice or accident, sibilant letters have been interchanged with dentals. " The conversion of the Greek Sigma into Tau is familiar to all classical readers."[1] But I beg it to be observed that they *have* changed. Thus Χρησσος became Χρησος and *Chrétien*, and often ς, as Nesos from Nestos. They would change by degrees, and the -χϛηϛος on the monument of the Youth of Larissa is the middle of the change; from χρησσος to χρηϛος and to χρητος. He also observes, that the *r* and *s* are very often interchanged in the Indo-European languages.[2] It appears when those letters changed-as letters, they took their power of notation with them. So that the T came to represent 300, the S=200, &c.; but this must have been long after the mythic names had got into use, and this will account for and justify the explanation of them by the same powers as the Hebrew.[3]

In matters of this kind, after all our inquiries, nothing but a probability can ever be expected to be obtained, and I think a pretty strongly probable case is made out, that the last three letters of the old alphabet were, in the numeral powers, confounded with one another. It may also be observed, that if they changed in different periods, as we cannot now distinguish them, they will have all the appearance to us of being used in common, and the effects will be the same to us.

When I consider that the T and the S in the Chaldee and Hebrew, two such close dialects, were used indiscriminately for the same idea, the Sun in Sr and Tr, and Cushites and Cuthites, and that the S and T were in like manner used by the Greeks, in their Sigma-Tau, one for the other, and the singular and unaccountable variation between the last numbers of the Greek and more Eastern alphabets, and when I consider also the apparently universal practice of the ancients of describing names by numbers, and the great number of mythological words which might have then been explained by numbers, but which cannot, as they are now, be so explained, I cannot help believing that the Shin and Tau must have been used indiscriminately for numbers, as we find them for letters; that is, that the Shin must have been used both for 300 and 400, and the Tau for the same. I state this merely as a suspicion, and leave others to determine; but, for my own part, I cannot help believing that this was the fact; and before any person decides upon this point, I must request him to take his Lexicons and consider, in both Greek and Hebrew, how many words are spelt with similar letters—letters used for one another, Samech for Shin, Xi for Chi, and almost innumerable others. As I have before observed, it seems absurd to be tied down in our inquiries into the early ages, by the fixed rules of later times. There can be no rule on the subject. Thus, I think, that the Greek Σ came to represent both the Σ and T, and took the name of Sigma-Tau; and that *their* powers of notation, as well as that of the P or Rho, changed from what they were in the ancient Arabic. It is difficult, if not impossible, to say, with certainty, how the change arose. Perhaps, with respect to pronunciation, the change might arise from the same cause as that which caused the word πελασγος to soften into πελαγος, Christian into Chrétien, Casmillus into Camillus, Nestos into Nessos, &c., &c. There can be no doubt that the letters must have been at first in their numerical powers the same as the Hebrew and Arabic, and the reason why in the names of gods, cycles, &c., the Sigma may sometimes stand for 300, sometimes for 400, may have arisen from their having received their names before or after the change. Whatever might be the cause, I am persuaded the S and T, and S and R, came to have, in a considerable degree, as far as related to the powers of notation, a common meaning. No doubt in the

---

[1] Eastern Orig. Celt. Nat. p. 58.   [2] Ib. p. 59.   [3] See Lempriere in voce Salii.

early times of the first invention of the art of writing, where nations were separated by seas, variations would arise, as well as a great want of precision. It is very certain that the Greeks took their system of letters, either mediately or immediately, from Syria; then, finding the T and the S used indiscriminately for one another in the word for the Sun, might not this cause them to use those letters as numerals, indiscriminately, in the same manner? If this be admitted, the names of gods would, in several cases, turn out the mystic numbers. After I had come to this conclusion, I discovered that, in the epistle of Barnabas, there was authority for this, which I had overlooked.[1] If a Protestant should say the epistle of Barnabas is a forgery, I then reply, that the person forging it must have known whether or not the Hebrew Tau denoted 300. I believe that both in Hebrew and Greek the S and T were in common.

The reader has seen what I have said of the interchangeable character of the S and T, both as numbers and letters. If, then, we make ש $s=200$, ע $o=70$, פ $p=80$, י $i=10$, we shall have for the meaning of *Sopi*=360. Now, when the numerical meaning of so many other words is considered, I think this furnishes another presumptive argument, that the S and T were, as I have suggested, used promiscuously. No one will deny that Sophia is Greek. Will any one deny that it is Persian, in the case of the Sophees? We may expect to find the idea of Wisdom, the first emanation of the Solar power, described by every variety of numeral letters which will make up 360, 600, 608, 650, or 666, or any solar cycle. The name of Sumnaut, mentioned in Volume I. p. 792, is ס $s=60$, ו $u=6$, ם $m=600=666$, added to the word Neith, *wisdom*—Solar Wisdom.

The following will serve as examples of sacred numbers, if we consider the letters to have had two meanings.

$$\left.\begin{array}{l} \xi' = 60 \\ \rho' = 100 \\ \sigma' = 200 \\ \hline 360 \end{array}\right\} \begin{array}{l} \Xi\ P\ \Sigma \\ X\ R\ S \\ \text{Cross.} \end{array} \quad \left.\begin{array}{l} \text{Samaritan} + (\text{ת})\ 400 \\ \text{Resh} \ldots \ldots (\text{ר})\ 200 \\ \text{Vau} \ldots \ldots (\text{ו})\ 6 \\ \text{Xi, Samech} \ldots (\text{ס})\ 60 \\ \hline 666 \end{array}\right\} \text{Crux.} \quad \begin{array}{l} \xi' = 60 \\ \rho' = 100 \\ \iota = 5 \\ \sigma' = 200 \\ \hline 365 \end{array}$$

$$\left.\begin{array}{l} \text{ר}\ R = 200 \\ \text{ס}\ S = 60 \\ \text{ו}\ U = 6 \\ \text{ת}\ T = 400 \\ \hline 666 \end{array}\right\} \text{Wisdom.}$$

We have seen the Tau, or last letter of the alphabet, written $+XT$; in short, in every form of a cross. In the titlepage of my Latin Vulgate, given me by a Catholic priest, the name of Christ is thus written, $XP\Sigma$. It is placed on the breast of the Pope, surrounded with a glory. What can the secret meaning be, but the renewed incarnation in the person of the Pope? The mark above, of the sign ♎ Libra, at the autumnal equinox, shews that it is astronomical and equinoctial. I have never found a Catholic priest who could, or would, explain it to me. I have no doubt this monogram has several meanings. It is the sign of the sun, when in the equinox, in the sign of the Bull—this the ♎ shews most clearly.

---

[1] See Jones on the Canon; Vol. II. p. 424; and Basnage, Book iii. Chap. xxvi. Sect. iii.

The existence of the χρησολογια, both in Europe and India, long anterior to the Christian æra, I am quite sure that I have proved. By the Chrestologia, I mean the whole of the refined Gnostic doctrines which I have laid before my reader. It is also very certain, that this was not the public doctrine of the rabble in any country; then there remains nothing for it to have been, but the doctrine and object of the mysteries of Bacchus, of Apollo, of Ceres, &c. The χρησος on the tomb of the youth of Larissa really proves it. The χρησος on the tomb is an exact counterpart of the XPΣ on the Pope's breast, and of the Fishes tied together by the tails, of Italy. This beautiful and refined system, whether true or not, was at the bottom of every religion or mythos of the world, however diversified, and however, in later times, degraded. This was the religion of Pythagoras, of Plato, of Philo, and of Cicero. This was the religion of Jesus, of Moses, of Melchisedek, of Zeradust, of Cristna, and of Buddha. It was equally the religion of the Chinese and the Mexicans. There was no part of the world so celebrated for its mysteries as Delphi and Eleusis, and it was here the Χρης was discovered; and it is connected with India, by its Orphean Trimurti, its Buddha, its river Sinde, its burning of widows, &c., &c. I have clearly proved the system to have taken its rise in a very remote period. I have shewn how it is connected with the Cyclopæan buildings, with all the various mythoses, both Jewish and Gentile; and yet, as we find no account of it, in any of the books called histories, it seems to me impossible to avoid believing that it constituted a part of the far-famed mysteries. Although there be many things which I have not been able to explain entirely, and some which I may have mistaken, yet I am quite certain, that there is enough, not only to shew the reality of the system, but also the nature of it, and, in many respects, even the particulars.

23. I must now beg my reader to look back to what has been said in Volume I. pp. 505—509, respecting the Amazon, and of the male and female being formed originally in one body, and I think we shall perhaps find the origin of the word אדם adm, or, as we call it, *Adam*. This is Ad, the Eastern and Western Syrian name of God;[1] and the monogram M, the sign of the Om, the cycle of 600 years. The Ad is, A=1, D=4=5, the Lustrum.[2] Then *Adm* will be the holy M. Adm is Adma, or Ad-am, both *male* and *female*; and I suspect that Adam was supposed to be like the Siamese Boys; and when I consider the universal opinion, that the life of the first man was extended to many hundred years, I cannot help suspecting that he was supposed to have lived 600 years, or the length of one cycle. It is very clear that the book means to express, that he was not to eat of the fruit, and that if he had not eaten of it, he would neither have died, nor have propagated the species, and that it was only by eating of it, that he learnt to know his wife. Then I think this countenances my idea, that it was believed that he would live one cycle, and then be renewed, or absorbed into the Το Ον—similarly to what Virgil taught in the renewal of cycles. If it be said that the construction which I have put on the second book of Genesis is in contradiction to the first; I reply, that I cannot be responsible for this; but, if I be correct, the fact proves the want of wisdom in pretending to give a higher authority to those books than reason and sense will justify. Nothing can be more manifest than that the first chapter and first three verses of the second chapter of our Genesis, is a different work from the following parts; and the fact that the generality of Christians read them, and do not observe the circumstance, exhibits a striking proof, that the prejudice created by education is sufficiently powerful to blind mankind to the clearest daylight. The fairly-implied prohibition of animal food in the first, marks the humane and benevolent

---

[1] See Volume I. pp. 402, 519, 722; and *supra*, p. 181.
[2] Lustrum, L'Ustrum—ὑστερος *second*—ὑστερα *the womb*—עש *os*, factor—עשר *œr*, ten—שתי *ust*, two.

Buddhist; the permission, in the second,[1] to use it, though only in the sacrifice of the Lamb, as exhibited in the story of Cain and Abel, from which the pernicious doctrines of human sacrifices and the atonement have been justified or excused, exhibit the Brahmin school — followed, of course, as might be expected from such doctrines, by every species of atrocity. The persons found every where, but of whom we have no account, called *Aborigines*, an inoffensive, unwarlike race, I apprehend are Buddhists, the remains, probably, of the great Pontifical nation, whose history I shall exhibit in the next Book, reduced to barbarism by causes which will be there developed,—a barbarism which would have rendered them an easy prey to their Brahmin persecutors and conquerors,—to the successive tribes coming from the great central hive of Brahminism in North India or Tartary, called Celtæ, Scythians, Sacæ, Tatars, Huns, Goths, &c., if their bloodless and inoffensive habits had not otherwise done it. It is evident that a nation of Buddhists or Quakers, can only exist, as the Tibetians do, on the sufferance of their neighbours.

CHAPTER II.

DIS MARIEBUS.—SYSTEMS OF LETTERS.—LAST AVATARS. MOHAMED, &c.—NAMES OF THE GODS OF THE WEEK. — CHINESE WRITING: — ABACUS AND NABATHEAN ALPHABET. — JAVA. — NORTHMORE'S SYSTEM.— VON HAMMER'S BOOK. SAXONS.— BACCHUS. JANUS. OGHAM. — RHYME. BARDS. FATES. VEDS. — CHINESE. — IMMACULATE CONCEPTION OF SACA.—PALLIUM.—APOCRYPHA.—DEISUL.—HAMMER'S ARABIC BOOK.

1. We have seen, p. 180, that in Judia of Siam, Maria and Mania were the same. Maria was one of the persons whose altars are inscribed *Tribus Mariebus*, of which one was the Virgo Paritura. On the Heathen and Christian monuments the letters D. M. are constantly found. The Christians say, they mean Deo Maximo, and the Heathens say, they mean the Dis Mariebus, of whose history it is pretty clear they were ignorant. But in fact they were the same, and meant Dis Mariebus—the *holy three*, who had the care of the dead Christ, and embalmed him. They were the three Parcæ of the Europeans, who cut with their scissors the thread of life. On a Christian tombstone, in the Church of St. Clemens at Rome, they are *Dis Manibus*; however, the letters *is* and *anibus* have of late years been filled with cement to disguise them. But upon many Christian monuments the letters are, D. M. *Sacrum* XL.[2] This beats all our Christian antiquarians; they can make nothing of the XL. But it probably meant Deo M. 650. I think the three Marys or Parcæ were the Trimurti—Tri-mr-di, the holy triple Maria or Maia. One was Mary, *Sal* or *Sul*, Om; the second, Mary Mag (or Magna) di-Helen or Magdalen; and the third, Mary the mother of Jesus. The Mag is the same as Mogul—Mag-al—and the Almug-tree, of which the sacred part of the temple of Solomon was built, was the wood sacred to the *Mag-al* or *ul*, or great Gôd. From this, by the regimine, came the name of Mogul, as priests came to bear the names of their Gods.

When I consider the superstition connected with the M, the mystic nature of the M, the name of that letter *M-uin*, the other name of that letter Samach—Sam-*akm* or Akm-sa, the name of the next letter N-vin, and the Lamed, its name L-am-di, and that it has the same numeral power as the N, viz. 50, I cannot help suspecting a great mystery in the LMN; that they are like the

---

[1] This ends with the last verse of the fourth chapter.   [2] Basnage, B. iii. Ch. xxiii. p. 237, Eng. Trans.

Alpha and Omega of Ambrose, called χρησμα, and the Staff of Osiris ⚱, called χρηστηριον.[1] These three letters would be emblems of the Trinity; and I think these letters of the Greek alphabet have, at one period, been so contrived as to make them the three centre letters, (though they are not so now,) similar to the contrivance of the Jews to make the M the centre letter of their alphabet; and from this, the L and the N, came each to have the power of notation 50. The Lamb was the messenger of God; he was the first of the Αγγελλοι. The word Αγγελλ means 72, the same as LMB—L=30, M=40, B=2=72. If it were not on this account, why was the letter B put into the word *Lamb* for a young sheep? We constantly read of the Angels of God being 70 (read 72) in number. Here we find why they had the name of Αγγελλ. The LMN also describe the Etruscan cycle of 120. The central LMN=to 120, look very mythological.

"The letter H, in the old Greek alphabet, did not sound what we now call η, but was an aspirate like the English H. This was proved by Athenæus, and has been since further evinced by Spanheim, from several ancient coins; and there are no less than four instances of it in the Sigean inscription."[2] All this proves the early unsettled state of the language. The last learned observation made by the celebrated Porson, was on the letter H. He said, "If this be authentic, here is an additional proof that the η was anciently used and pronounced as we do our aspirated H." The reporter then adds, "I replied, It certainly was; and as to the authenticity of the Prænestine Pavement, I believed it could not reasonably be called in question."[3]

Herodotus says, he saw specimens of the Cadmæan letters on tripods, in the temple of the Ismenian Apollo at Thebes, in Bœotia. These tripods I believe to have been triangular blocks of wood, and the temple was that of שמשן e-smin—the Lord or Baal of the Planets, the leader of the heavenly host.

I consider that Carmel, on a part of which was the monastic institution of Nazareth, of the Rassees, or Essenes, or Carmelites, was called Carmel or the Vineyard of God, from the allegorical connexion of the vine with wisdom, as exhibited in the Greek Βοτρυς and Latin Racemus.[4] The settlement of the followers of the Rasit, in Syria, is beautifully described in the allegory of the Vine in the 80th Psalm, verses 8—16.

In great numbers of places in the Old Testament, the allegory of trees and letters is referred to. What was the Rod of Aaron which threw out branches or leaves or buds? What were the magical peeled rods of Jacob? What was the meaning of the branch from which the stem of Jesse was to arise? Was Jesse I-esa? The Gnostics frequently called Jesus *the Tree of Life*, and the *tree* itself *which grew in the middle of Paradise*, and, at other times, *a branch*. My idea that the fruit of the tree of knowledge was the acquisition of the knowledge of letters without initiation, is supported by the assertion of Enoch, that the wickedness of the world, which caused the flood, consisted in the attempts of men to obtain forbidden knowledge. It is also strengthened by a passage of Proverbs, Chap. iii. 13, 18, where Solomon says, "Happy is the man who findeth wisdom,"—"She is a tree of life to them that lay hold upon her." I suppose certain of the leaf-names of figures of notation were selected by a society, as a secret system of syllabic writing, after the symbolic system had been long in general practice, and that this society being spread about in different countries, slight differences in the mode of selecting the sixteen letters took place. Thus the religious mythos was not every where described in exactly the same manner; hence we see the small variation which shews itself between the Hebrew and the Greek:

2. We are in the habit of talking of the alphabet of Greece, and of the alphabet of Phœnicia, as if

---

[1] Basnage, 236.
[2] Classical Journ. Vol. I. p. 725. See my Vol. I. p. 236.
[3] Shuckford's Conn. Vol. I. Book iv. p. 225.
[4] See *supra*, p 9.

these countries had each one certain alphabet; while it is evident, that each country had great numbers of them; and yet they are all reducible into *two*, one of which is only a part of the other, that other being what we call Arabic, but anciently Cufic, and probably having its origin in the country of Arabia, between the Indus and Ganges, of the *thousand* cities of Strabo. In fact, every learned man had his alphabet—each differing from another in form, but each the same in substance. In the book of Ben Wassib, found by Mr. Hammer in Egypt, which contains the alphabet of Plato, we have upwards of seventy[1] of them. I have seen upwards of sixty more, in a manuscript of Sir W. Ouseley's; so that I have little doubt I could collect hundreds. Every man who was initiated into the mysteries, and who aspired to be a philosopher, is said to have had his own alphabet, in which he concealed his doctrines from all but his followers. At last, when writing became no longer a masonic or magical secret, each country acquired, by degrees, the habit of using some one of them. Their powers of notation, however, kept them all nearly the same, both in principle and order. (That they have all the same numerical power, has been proved by Gen. Vallancey in the plates to his fifth volume of the Coll. Hib.) And so, I have no doubt, they continued, to a very late day, with only the little variation in the last numbers of the Coptic and Greek. I think the probability is, that the order of men, (who were not, strictly speaking, priests, but nearly an order of priests, and some of whom might, perhaps, sustain the priestly office,) called Chaldæans, from central India, were the original inventors of the syllabic from the numeral system; and as for the numeral, I know of no people more likely than they to have been the inventors of it also. If the numeral were the system of the priesthood, it is not unlikely that the inventors of the syllabic system should have formed, at first, a new secret society, which I think would necessarily, by its superior talent, soon become possessed of sovereign power. There is no fact more certain than the general solicitude of the learned ancients to keep every part of science, as much as possible, a secret, each to himself, or his sect or followers. There was an unceasing struggle between the Bees, who tried to discover, and the Drones, who endeavoured to secrete; and, for thousands of years, the Drones succeeded in preserving their science and power, by admitting only the most talented or rich of the Bees into their order, which operated doubly in their favour; it took strength from their enemies and added it to themselves. It is impossible to deny that numbers of the alphabets are formed in unaccountably complex shapes; these were the alphabets of the drones, trying to envelop every thing in mystery. If the bees invented any, they would, for the sake of publicity, be of the simplest kind—like the first alphabets of the drones, made by them before the power and utility of the art were known, and before the necessity of using extraordinary care to keep it secret became manifest to themselves.

It thus appears that, in times which may be called almost modern, every learned man had an alphabet of his own, for the use of himself and the followers of his school. But I have no doubt that the art of writing was at first concealed, and was probably a part of the high mysteries, and most anxiously guarded from the public for many generations. In times such as these must have been, I need not point out what advantages such a magical possession would give to the initiated. After it became almost common, the learned had recourse to the inventing of new forms, to restore the art to secrecy, as far as it was in their power; but every form, unless the Chinese and the hieroglyphics are excepted, is founded on the first Cadmæan original. Though every philosopher or his school had an alphabet of a peculiar form, each alphabet was evidently founded on that of Arabia. The first alphabet was the Arabic alphabet of *numbers*, each number having the name of a tree, and amounting to twenty-eight. The second was the alphabet of *letters*, of Cadmus, which

---

[1] The first letter of the Hieroglyphic alphabet is, as I observed above, the Owl, the emblem of Wisdom.

consisted of the *sixteen* culled out of the twenty-eight. After some time, these sixteen were increased by adopting the whole twenty-two numeral Arabic letters, as they stand marked by the increasing numbers.[1] The more I meditate on thousands of trifling circumstances connected with these subjects, the more convinced I am, that, for many generations, the arts of reading, writing, and the higher branches of arithmetic, were in the hands of a ruling order, and this order was that of the priests of Ur of the Chaldees; that is, of the country Uria of Calida, that is, Calidi—country of the *holy Cali*. The high-priest and ruler has been the Mogh-ul from the most remote period. But the time when and the country in which the *first* letters were invented, is an ænigma which I fear must remain unsolved. However, I think we may be assured, that the place was East of the Indus, and West of China—probably in the tract of country between the Nerbudda and sixty degrees north latitude. I think we cannot come nearer than this to the place. Samarkand, Mundore, Oude, and Tibet, have nearly equal claims, and there does not seem to me to be much room for speculation on the subject.

If letters were kept as a masonic secret, as I suspect they were for many generations, the date of their discovery seems hopeless; we are then led into the inquiry as to the time when they first became publicly known. No where upon a Cyclopæan monument is any thing like an inscription, either in figures or in letters, to be seen. The first, perhaps, may be the Runes of Ireland and Scandinavia. These are evidently figure letters. The A is one line, the B is two, the C is three, and so on. I know not where or by whom the alphabet was discovered which is in Tab. II. Fig. 10, p. 5, of my Celtic Druids; but it seems to differ from the Callan inscription of which Dr. Aikin professes to have discovered the meaning, an alleged fact of which I entertain great doubt. Whether they were really cipher letters applicable to the sixteen-letter system or not, it is very clear that they would constitute such letters. The arrow-headed letters of Persepolis would evidently do the same. All circumstances tend to shew their great antiquity, and I cannot help thinking it probable, that they afford examples of the first figure alphabet. Almost all learned men endeavour to find the origin of languages by a comparison of the affinities of their forms and grammatical constructions. This seems to me to be a great mistake. For, as they advance down the stream of time, they generally keep improving, and, at all events, changing and becoming, in consequence, less like each other.

3. General Vallancey[2] has shewn, that the old Chaldee alphabet is strictly the same as the Estrangelo, (vide his Plates,) and *that* the same as the Phœnician, which is, in fact, Hebrew or Syriac. These are the languages which we have found (vide Vol. I. pp. 702, 765) in the College of Casi, near Oude or Youdia, or Benares, or at the Temple of Solomon, at the Mere or Mount of Casi, in Cashmere, the country of the crucified Indra. And again, a thousand miles to the south, in the country of the crucified Ball-ii or Wittoba, in South India, at Terpati or Tripoly or Trichinopoly, called Pushto and Syriac and Chaldee; in each place both the Christian and Jewish mythos are recorded—the two, in fact, are united in one. Again, we have found the same Hebrew language, and the same double mythos, amalgamated in Mexico, carried thither before the invention of letters or iron. The amalgamation of the Christian and Jewish mythoses, found in both India and Mexico, and the ignorance, in the latter, of the knowledge of iron and letters, are facts which can never be separated. It is impossible to have clearer proofs that the whole existed before the time of Christ. Can any thing be more striking than the fact so simply and, apparently, inadvertently permitted to escape, by the blind and prejudiced Buchanan, that he found a man, having the Jewish name of Joseph, celebrating what he thought to be some part of the Romish

---

[1] See Celtic Druids, p. 248. [2] Coll. Hib. Vol. V. p. 201.

religion in the TEMPLE OF JAGGERNAUT, in the Chaldee language, as he says, if my memory do not fail me. The above are indisputable facts; I submit them to my reader, and I beg he will reflect upon the way in which they all dovetail into the system of immaculate conceptions, deaths, and resurrections, and the renewals of cycles, of India and of Virgil. It is not improbable that in the temple of Jaggernaut, described by Buchanan, may be found the whole mythos. And if it should be found there, Europeans will be deluded as they have been in Tibet and Tartary, by being told, that its owners are Nestorian Christians.

The Bedoweens or nomade tribes of Arabia, are said to speak the purest dialect of Arabic.[1] The Bedoweens are nothing but Buddeens or Buddhists. These people are Tatars or Tartars, followers of Tat. In ancient times the tribe of Juda or Ayoudia was one of them. After a certain time it settled and established its capitol, first at Samaria or Gerizim, and afterward at Moriah. The tribe of Ishmael was another, an offset from the former; after some time it fixed its capitolium or acropolis at Mecca. They were like all other tribes, followers of the sacred Buddhist OM.[2] Titans are Tat-ans, i. e. Buddhists. The Tartars or Tat-ars, I doubt not, are both from North India, and the Sacæ, from the country of the thousand cities of Strabo. They are the Arabians of the Indus, and in Om-Ahmed, or the renewed incarnation, the last, the tenth incarnation or Avatar of Buddha, the M, the 600 in the arithmetical language, the desire of all nations, may be clearly seen the reason why these Eastern Tartars, Arabs, Afghans, were the first proselytes to Mohamed. Of what religion were the nomade tribes before the time of Mohamed? There is every reason to believe that they were for the most part Buddhists, though under some corrupted form probably—some, perhaps, of the same character as those called Christians of St. Thomas. And now we may begin to perceive why the wandering tribes, both of Asia and Africa, so readily came over to the Mohamedan faith. From European Christians the truth has been concealed by various causes, but not the least, the cunning of the priesthood, ending at last in its own as well as its devotees' ignorance. The system must have been well known, or we should not find the Asiatic princes all pretending to be Avatars, and perhaps each believing himself to be so. For, what opinion is too absurd for human vanity to entertain? Alaric, the Goth, was clearly so. Nadir[3] Shah's name shews him to have been one, and after him all the *Shahs* of the house of Ali: the Ommaides were the same. Genghis Khan was another.[4] But we must not forget that miscreant the GREAT Constantine the first, who, no doubt, affected the same thing, but did not succeed, at least with posterity. I believe that if the empire of any of these persons, except that of Constantine, had extended itself as Mohamed's did, we should have had in him an Om-Ahmed; and twenty years after his death there would have been no difficulty in making out a Koran from amongst his half rotten papers; and in telling the rabble, when it made its appearance, that it was an improved version of a former corrupted one; which it might perhaps be, in some degree. But I shall discuss this subject of imperial incarnations at large in a future book.

I have just said, that the Bedoweens, followers of Bedu,[5] whom we have found invoked in

---

[1] Van Kennedy, p. 58.   [2] See Vol. I. p. 652, for places, &c., with the Buddhist name of Om.

[3] Nerts $\begin{Bmatrix} N=50 \\ R=100 \\ T=300 \\ S=200 \\ \overline{650} \end{Bmatrix}$ $\begin{Bmatrix} N=50 \\ e=5 \\ e=5 \\ r=100 \\ u=400 \\ z=90 \\ \overline{650} \end{Bmatrix}$ Neruz   Netzir softened to Nadir $\begin{Bmatrix} N=50 \\ T=300 \\ S=200 \\ R=100 \\ \overline{650} \end{Bmatrix}$ Caph $\begin{Bmatrix} C=500 \\ R=100 \\ N=50 \\ \overline{650} \end{Bmatrix}$ NRS   [4] $\begin{Bmatrix} C(Caph final)=500 \\ N \ldots =50 \\ N \ldots =50 \\ \overline{600} \end{Bmatrix}$ Kan.

[5] See Vol. I. p. 584.

Thrace, were probably Buddhists under some corrupted form, perhaps Christians of St. Thomas. We have always heard of these Christians being Nestorians. Now the opinion of the Nestorians, or of the followers of that German, was, that Jesus Christ was a portion of God, incarnated in him; and, in short, his doctrine was very nearly the same as that of the followers of Cristna. On this account I do not doubt that, whenever the orientalists were met with, by Christians, holding these opinions, they were, without more inquiry, determined to be Nestorians. This seems to me to account satisfactorily for all the Nestorian nonsense in Asia, about which we read so much. I will now return to the subject of letters, from which I feel that I have too long digressed.

4. I believe the etymology of the names of the seven Gods of the Week has hitherto set all the learned at defiance. When I consider their very great antiquity, their priority to all other Gods, and the general practice of the ancients in calling their Gods after numbers, and that, if my theory be correct, they might consistently be called after the oldest cycle, I cannot help suspecting that originally they all meant the erroneous and oldest cycle of 666.

MONDAY may be—

$$\begin{array}{l} M=600 \\ I=10 \\ N=50 \\ U=6 \\ \hline 666 \end{array}$$ and in process of time $$\begin{array}{l} M=600 \\ N=50 \\ \hline 650 \end{array}$$

TUESDAY or *Mercury* may be—

$$\left.\begin{array}{l} T=400 \\ U=6 \\ Z=90 \\ Q=100 \\ O=70 \\ \hline 666 \end{array}\right\} \text{Tusco or Tuisco.} \qquad \left.\begin{array}{l} M=40 \\ A=1 \\ R=200 \\ K=20 \\ O=70 \\ L=30 \\ E=5 \\ S=300 \\ \hline 666 \end{array}\right\} \text{Markoles.}$$

Mercury in Chaldee is called כולס *kulis*, from כול *cul, to measure*. (Query, to *cull* or *count* or *select?*) May this have been כולום *kulos* or 666? It is not a very violent corruption.

The אתיות *atiut* is Thoth, the Egyptian inventor of Letters. Thoth is Mercury, called Tuisco. I think this may have been Tust, T=300, T=300, ו u=6, ס s=60=666. We have formerly seen that this word in Hebrew meant letters.[1] The Indathyrsus of Strabo is Bacchus,[2] T=300, R=100, S=200, ו u=6, ס s=60=666.

In WEDNESDAY or *Woden's-day* I fail, but I ought to fail if the system be right, because Woden, which has given name to this day, is not the original name of a God or cycle, but a corruption, as we have formerly seen, of Buddha.[3] But the word Mars, Martis, is the Αρης of the Greeks, with the monogram prefixed. Thus M. A=1, R=200, E=5, T=400, S=60=666.[4] He was also called Mavore, which I think was M. α'=1, υ'=400, ϟ=5, ר=200, ס=60=666.[5] He was also called Quirinus, Q=100, R=200, I=10, N=50, U=6, S (ש)=300=666.

---
[1] See *supra*, p. 164. [2] Cleland. [3] See *supra*, p. 4.
[4] T... is an old word for *father*. It is the Celtic Tat or Tad, the Greek Αρα. Pezron, p. 359.
[5] Here it must again be borne in mind, that the Author felt himself justified in referring to either the Hebrew or the Greek numerals in favour of his theories. *Editor.*

BOOK III. CHAPTER II. SECTION 4.

The THURSDAY is T=400, U=6, R=200, S (ס)=60=666—the day of the Bull.

We have found the German and Scandinavian Saxons called after their ancestors, the Sacæ, and they from their God Xaca, who was Woden, who was Buddha.[1] We have in the same country a tribe called the Frisii, whence came Friesland or Fries-ia; and these Northern tribes had a favourite Goddess called Freya, which I think was only the softened Freas-ia. Hence our FAIDAY. Then this will be in Greek and Hebrew—

$$\phi' = 500$$
$$\rho' = 100$$
$$\iota = 5$$
$$\alpha = 1$$
$$ס = 60$$
$$\overline{\quad 666\quad}$$

This Lady became, afterward, Αφρο-διτη, *the holy* φρη—that is, $\phi'=500$, $\rho'=100$, $\eta'=8=608$. She had a son, *divine love* or A-DON, *the* WISE, who was killed by a wild boar! Can any thing be more nonsensical? But this wild boar was an Apries, that is, A-φραις. This Phre was the solar title in Copt-ia or E-gupt-ia or Egypt. The mysticism of this is very profound. Divine wisdom, which has existed through all cycles, was killed by the hypostasis described by the number 666, A-φραις, the boar; but it rose again as the holy φρη=608, or the φην. This Adon was a resident of the country called Φην-icia or country of Phen. In this mythos, as in all others, the mother and son, the *male* and *female*, the Unity, Duality, and Trinity, the singular, dual, and plural, are all confounded or identified; for they are all three in one, and one in three.

In India, Saturn is called Sati. We all know how some of the Northern nations change the *an* into *iern*, as Christian, Christi*ern*. Then Saturn will be Satiern, and in Greek numerals—

$$\sigma' = 200$$
$$\alpha = 1$$
$$\tau' = 300$$
$$\iota = 10$$
$$\iota = 5$$
$$\rho' = 100$$
$$\nu = 50$$
$$\overline{\quad 666\quad}$$

Our sixth day is not called *Saturn*-day, but SATURday, that is, in Hebrew,

Samech = 60
Tau = 400
Vau = 6
Resh = 200
———
666

} which became in time with the Greeks {

$\sigma' = 200$
$\tau' = 300$
$\rho' = 100$
$\eta' = 8$
——
608

$\sigma' = 200$
$\tau' = 300$ } Satur-day.
$\rho' = 100$
——
600

$\sigma' = 200$
$\tau' = 300$
$\rho' = 100$
$\nu = 50$
——
650

} Whence Strn-ia.

---

[1] See *supra*, pp. 1—4.

NAMES OF THE GODS OF THE WEEK.

The Saturn of India is called Sani and Satyr, which latter is STR=600.[1]

We will now examine the names of some other of the Gods, keeping this principle in view. It would have been remarkable if we had not found the God *Osiris* in the arithmetical language. It is,

$y = 70$	$ı = 6$
$w = 300$	$σ' = 200$
$ı = 10$	$ρ' = 100$
$ר = 200$	$ס = 60$
$ı = 10$	——
$ס = 60$	366
——	
650[2]	

Mnevis is, M=600, N=50, U=6, I=10=666.[3]

In Ireland, the Chaldees were called Culi-dei. Here we have X'=600, L=50, U=6, I=10=666, or, in the epithet of *beautiful* or καλος, K=20, L=30, I=10=60. I doubt not that the Culidei came to Ireland before the beauty of the numbers 60 and 600 was discovered.

Pol, alluded to in Volume I. p. 652, is Pall, is Φλλυς,

$φ' = 500$		$φ' = 500$
$λλ' = 100$		$λ' = 50$
$ı = 6$	or	$λ' = 50$
$ס = 60$		——
——		600
666		

Pol means Head, Wisdom, Minerva Polias, and Palumba, *a stock-dove*.

The words Ras and Buddha are different from the other names of Gods, and might be only names of attributes. All the incarnations were Rasees, and I think the name of the first Buddha would be Xιυν=666—the Buddha or Ras of Siun or of the Sun. And, again, Xiun-sup, Wisdom of the Siun, or Sun, Solar Wisdom. Here I think I have the triumph of my system. The first name of the God was Xιυν=666.[4] He was the God of Sion, or of the Mount of Sion. When astronomical knowledge improved, his name was written with the Saxon emphatic article I-Xin—Xν-650. As it improved a little more, he became XH-608;[5] and at last X=600: and Basnage was not far from right when he said, " Would not any one have believed the Xn was Christ victorious ?"

We have Χαξs or Χξαs=666, or Ξχαs=666.

We have formerly seen that divine love was crucified under the name of Ixion.[6] · I have a great suspicion that this word was the monogram X and siun or X-sion or X-sun. Or might it be the monogram I, which has the same meaning as the X, and Xiun or Siun ? These are mere speculations; how far probable must be left to the reader.

The Tibetians have the word *Zin*, which is proved to be no other than *Xin*, called Zin viventem

---

[1] Camb. Key, Vol. II. p. 392.   [2] See Class. Journal, Vol. XX. p. 184.-

[3] The Egyptians are said to have had 666 kinds of sacrifices, which a learned writer in the Encyclop. Brit. voce *Sacrifice*, says, is incredible. This was, I suspect, merely a mistake. They had a grand sacrifice for every year, having some trifling variations relating to the year of the cycle of 666, which it shews that they had among them. Perhaps they killed as many animals as years of the cycle had passed, to mark the time, before the art of writing was known. Several of their Gods had the same name.

[4] See Etymol. Dict. voc. I.   [5] Vide my Vol. I. p. 224..   [6] See Ib. pp. 500, 503; and *supra*, p. 198.

et largitorem vitæ. A close attention to the pages 682 and 683 of Georgius (Alph. Tib.) will shew that the first of their names descriptive of God, Cjang-cihup vel cihub, is Kion or Kian, unde Hesych. χιονίαν, λευκαν η φωτωδη et Sinis Çan; in short, Sion and X*ιν*: and the second, *cihub* sive *cihuph*, is the Hebrew סוף or שוע or צוע *sup* or *zup*, *wisdom*, the root of the Greek Σοφια, and the meaning will be *the wisdom of Sion* or *Xin*,—the wisdom of the God described by the

$$X = 600$$
$$n = 50$$
$$\overline{650}$$

in the Coptic language, or the סן (סב) *sn* 650, in the Hebrew. When the peculiar manner in which the astronomical doctrine of the origin of the cycles 666, 650, 608, 600, and the sacred numbers of the Gentiles, together with the monograms of Christ, are considered, as dovetailing into one compact body, supported by many other circumstances, I think the truth of the system must be admitted to be demonstrated. Bring it fairly to the test of probability, and the arguments in its favour will be as a million to one.

When we consider the striking manner in which, as I have shewn, so many sacred names came from literal numbers, numerical letters, it is only reasonable to expect the same result from the roots of that most important word *Wisdom*. We have found the word Souphun among the Arabians. This is, $Z = 90$, $O = 70$, $U = 6$, $\phi' = 500$, or Σοφια. And our Wisdom is, W or $Y = 400$, $S = 200 = 600$, *di* holy—O*m*—Wisdom of the holy O*m*. Having found the word for the Sun *Sr*, also written Tr, the two indiscriminately used for one another, may it not be, that the Sr is only *RS*, read in the opposite direction? But SR is TR, and TR is 600. In this I am justified, by the unimpeachable evidence of Barnabas lately quoted.[1] Without this double power of the S be admitted, but I think it cannot be disallowed, I have not the ancient cycle in Ras. I have it, however, in ראשית or ראסות *rsut* the plural of Ras, thus: ר $r = 200$, ס $s = 60$, ו $u = 6$, ת $t = 400 = 666$, and we must observe whenever the word Rasit is paraphrased, either by the Jews or Samaritans, in the word החכמה *hkmut*, or by the Gnostics in the Acamoth, the word is always in the plural number. This shews us what the word Rasit ought to be, viz. the plural—and its plurality is allusive to the Trinity; and they are all feminine.

I believe we have the ancient Sacæ in the tribe of Rattores. They are, I think, Rats-ores,[2] the *ras* with an oriental sigma-tau. When their tribe settled in Germany, it founded Ratz-burg and Ratis-bon—ר $r = 200$, ת $t = 400$, ו $u = 6$, ס $s = 60 = 666$—Rtus-burg; or, perhaps, $\rho' = 100$, $\tau' = 300$, $\sigma' = 200 = 600$. The Persian Rustan is the same word Rstn—$\rho' = 100$, $\sigma' = 200$, $\tau' 300$, $\nu' = 50 = 650$.

In Ethiopia the prince is called *Ras*. It was so written, because when the Ethiopians turned their upright writing, they turned the word thus to read it; but the people a little lower down the Nile, whom we call Copts, turning the column the other way, as the Greeks did, have it *Sar*. Thus they have Sar-oub or Sar-Oph, or Prince *serpent* or *wise* Prince. Thus in Egypt, it is the Prince *Sar*, in Ethiopia, the Prince *Ras*.

I repeat that, if we reflect deeply upon the nature of the arithmetical language, which *was* not, and in its nature *could* not, be spoken, we shall instantly see, that it would make no difference whether a word was called Menu or Nume; and this fact will reasonably account for all the anagrams in proper names.

It seems to me, that the way in which almost all the names of the Deities are described by numbers or numerical letters, is a very decisive proof of the truth of the whole system. It is

---

[1] See *supra*, p. 189.   [2] As Hustimallo became Hatimalla, so Rastores became Rattores.

notorious that all proper names had meanings, but the names of most of the Gods are an exception to the rule, and this they ought to have been if their appellations were derived from the ancient cycles. A Deity might properly be described by every variety of numbers which would form any of his cycles, and, in respect to each cycle, by any combination of numbers which would form the sum of the cycle. Thus he might be called Sul—S=300, U=6, L=30=336; or Rqul—R=200, Q=100, U=6, L=30=336; or ww=600, or τ'τ'=600. And from this arose the multitude of Gods, all in fact being, as I have formerly proved, merely the names of the Solar Deity. And now, I trust, my reader will admit, I have fulfilled the promise I formerly made, that I should shew before I finished, that the custom of describing persons or Gods by numerals, was any thing but *buffoonery*, as Sir William Drummond called it. And here it must be obvious how easy it would have been to have reformed the religion of the Pagans, instead of burning its beautiful temples and murdering its votaries, by merely teaching them to raise their minds from the Sun to the sun's Creator. All the mischief arose from the pernicious, monopolizing spirit by which the priests endeavoured to keep all knowledge to themselves. But it gave them power and wealth, and this is the real secret.

I long endeavoured, but in vain, to discover why the planets were called by the same name, for example, Venus or Mercury, as that which designated God or the Sun; but I think I have, at last, discovered a probable reason for it. I think it is to be found in the poverty of ancient written language. I trust I have clearly made out, that the first cycle—that of 666—was the name, or perhaps I ought rather to say the designation, of every one of the planetary bodies. This was the name of the cycle and of the Divine creative power also, and this double effect arose from this fact, that if the Sun or the Deity was to be described in the arithmetical symbolic language, it was almost necessary that he should be described by some number connected with him, or in some way related to him; and *that* could be no other, because there was no other, than the length of the Lunar or Soli-Lunar year. Thus he became first Sli=360, next Suli=336 or 366. Upon the same principle he was afterward called by the name of the greater cycles as they arose. Now, by regimine, the planets would each be messenger of God, or messenger God, or messenger or Disposer Mars, or messenger Venus, &c.; the name of the God being, in arithmetical signs, 666. This is exactly similar to the priests' taking the names of their Gods by the regimine, as I have before described.

As it is evident, that God or the Creative Power might be called by whatever name arose out of any combination of numbers, which made up the sum of 666, as long as 666 was thought to be the number of his cycle, so it came to pass that God or Sol or the Creative Power had all these names, and that the old Gods, the Planets, each acquired one of these names. This is also supported by the fact, that the שמים smim or planets or disposers had at first no names, or icons either with the Druids or in Etruria or Greece or Syria or Persia or India. When the Hebrew language became lost in Greece, and the Greek arose, they acquired each a name described by 666, and it would necessarily be 666, if at that time 666 designated the First Power; and they changed as astronomical science improved. Thus we see how the words Saturn, Mercury, Mars, Ceres, Venus, &c., &c., arose. All this is much strengthened by the fact, that the names very seldom have any other rational etymology.

In a similar manner, kings and dynasties (Pharaohs for example) came to have the names of Gods. All kings were priests; in fact, they very often became kings or rulers, from their superior wisdom, knowledge, or cunning, and were thought to be emanations of the Deity, or persons endowed with a greater portion of the divine nature, mind, $\psi\nu\chi\eta$, anima; and they were emanations of $\varphi\rho\tau$, or emanations $\varphi\rho\eta$. Thus, by degrees, without being conscious of any thing wrong, they allowed themselves to be called by the names of their Gods, and also received the same honours. Thus, incarnation of God, or Apollo, or Mars—the incarnation God, Apollo, Mars. We every day do what is very similar without being conscious of any thing wrong. Henry the First would have been shocked to be called majesty, although it has become the name, the title of all our kings. To be called majesty is presumptuous enough, but I may be regarded as still more presumptuous, for I am *the God* Freya—Godfrey! If an age of darkness should arise, accompanied as it certainly will be, if it do arise, with a race of ignorant, evil-disposed fanatics, ready to misrepresent and distort every thing, William IV. and I may be abused for our presumption and wickedness.

As these effects arose by degrees without any formal record of their origin, it was soon lost. This is not *theory* but *fact*. It is similar to what we see every day. Many religious rites arose in the same way. For example, *fasting*. What could make *fasting* a merit? When foolish men quarreled, as we are told by all the Indian histories that they did quarrel, about the prevalence of the male over the female generative power in nature, the *female* was reprobated by the *male* devotee, and it became a merit to refrain from intercourse with the sinful creature. Thus arose monkish vows of chastity; and directly from this it came to pass, that fasting was recomended, as it was found, from experience, the most effectual device to assist men in the performance of their difficult task, keeping the vow of abstinence from the female. The cause or reason for the fast was forgotten, and the *fast itself* was esteemed a merit. Thus the thing which arose in sense is continued in nonsense; for it was founded in sense, that abstinence would keep down passion; it is *nonsense* to suppose that there is merit in refraining from a necessary or an agreeable quantity of food, and in taking only as much as will barely maintain life. From this abstinence all self-denial might have its origin, and come to be regarded as a merit.

When I look at the written representations of the numbers of all the ancient great nations, some barbarous oriental islands alone excepted, I instantly see that they formed one system, and were originally derived from one source; and the fact is precisely the same with respect to letters. But I find the forms of the figures of old Italy and Greece, to have been very different from the oldest forms of the figures of the oriental nations, which we possess. It is not improbable, but on the contrary it is very probable, that the colonies arrived from India in Greece and Italy before the art of notation had been committed to writing, but still not before the beautiful decimal system had been discovered, and not before the art of counting the moon's period of 28 days had been discovered. If this had not been the case, the Western nations would have had the Arabic figures 1, 2, 3, 4, 5, 6, &c. When I find these figures in use all over India, Tartary, and Persia, in their oldest books, I can feel little doubt that their antiquity is very great. Equally little doubt can I feel that the Cufic alphabet as figures (in some shape or other, for in the lapse of many years the shape of all written letters and figures must imperceptibly change) must originally, and for many generations, have served for the purposes of arithmetic as well as of letters, and for letters as ciphers. They must have been like monograms, symbols of words, very like the Chinese. Probably at first they would be confined to the 28 figures.[1] These would be the symbols of their cycles of the sun and the moon, and their number would be increased by degrees by the addition of other symbols. This would be an *unspoken* literature, as the literature of numbers and symbols in Algebra is still unspoken with us. I repeat, the letters would be symbols for *ideas*, not for *sounds*.

5. The language of the Tibetians, as found by Georgius, seems to exhibit a mixture of the system of the signs of the Chinese, and of the letters of the West. Sir W. Jones says, "It seems at

---

[1] The order of the ancient Cufic alphabet is the same as that of the Hebrew. (Univ. Hist. Vol. XVIII. p. 421.) This is an additional proof that Hebrew and Arabic were originally the same.

"present, from the influence of Chinese manners, to consist of monosyllables, to form which, with some regard to grammatical derivation, it has become necessary to suppress, in common discourse, many letters which we see in their books."[1] These were their figure letters, as was the case with the Arabic notation, which was reduced to 16, as letters. The Chinese, the Japanese, and the Siamese, are known to be all nearly the same; and Georgius has proved that the Tibetians and the Siamese are closely connected. This, I think, all goes to shew, that the Judæan mythos must (as found in China by Paravey) have gone thither before the letters were known or publicly used. I think a practice which still prevails in Japan is an admirable example of what the first universal language of figures would be. The Cambridge Key to the chronology of the Hindoos says, "The Japanese, by the use of symbols, continue to carry on, not only correspondence, but trade, with provinces, the inhabitants of which, were they to meet, would not be able to converse, from a total ignorance of the language of each other.[2] A convincing proof that a knowledge of letters does not necessarily militate against the use of symbols."

The people of Cochin China, Tonquin, and Japan, each speak a dialect of their own, very dissimilar from the Chinese; but all these nations, although they cannot understand each other by speaking, yet do so perfectly by writing. Du Halde says, their books are common to all of them. These characters, therefore, are a species of *arithmetical signs*, which each nation expresses by a different word, although among them all they *represent the very same number*, and excite the very same idea.[3] Here is evidently the first numeral symbolic language, which I have discovered without going to China for my information.

M. Abel Ramusat has imagined that he could point out the remains of Hieroglyphics in the Chinese letters. He has shewn very conspicuously both his own learning and ingenuity; but from such an infinite variety of figures as that of which the Chinese letters now consist, it necessarily follows, that an ingenious and industrious man may find almost any similitudes he wishes for.

There is the same system in Java. Sir S. Raffles informs us, that the natives of Java, that is, I think, the island of *Ieue* or *Jehovah*, call their ancient, now unused, language, Κάωι. This, I think, is merely the Iao aspirated. He says that, for many years, it was almost entirely confined to the family of the chief, and that the Javanese have a mystical language. He also says,[4] "For ordinary purposes, the Javans use a modification of some of the letters of the alphabet as numerals, but on occasions of importance it is usual to employ certain signs or symbols in lieu of these ordinary numerals, and this practice appears to be of great antiquity among them. These symbols consist in a certain number of objects, either represented in design or named, *each of which is significant of one of the ten numerals*. Of the former class are said to be those found in most of the ancient buildings and coins, which in that case usually bear no inscription." I think I see here, in the language of the island of Java, the original practice which I have been describing of a system of writing by ciphers. Though in this there is nothing absolutely to prove the truth of my system, there is what strongly tends to add to its probability, and probability is all that can ever be expected. Here, however changed in the space of four or five thousand years, are found the remains of the original first system of writing, and it is found among what must have been anciently the followers of Ieue or Iao, by whose Chaldæans I suppose the art of writing to have been first invented, and by whom I suppose it was kept a masonic secret for thousands of years. In consequence of this discovery of symbolic writing, the adoration of the *Al-ieu*, by his

---

[1] Asiat. Res. Vol. III. p. 11.
[3] Spineto, Lect. Hier. p. 273.
[2] Camb. Key, Vol. I. p. 396.
[4] Vol. I. p. 371.

original name, remains, although lost by all the rest of the world. The Javanese practice, or something very like it, is described in the following extract: "The characters of Cochin China, of "Tong-king, of Japan, are the same with those of the Chinese, and signify the same things; "though in speaking, those nations do not express themselves in the same manner; of conse- "quence the language of conversation is very different, and they are not able to understand each "other; while, at the same time, they understand each others' written language, and use all their "books in common."¹

The first Chinese written letters were formed of right lines, and were called, *Ukim* and *Yekim*, this is the emphatic article of the Sacæ I and the חכם *hkm* Wisdom—letters of *the Wisdom* or Wisdom of IE. Their invention is ascribed to Fo-hi,² whom we have formerly shewn to be Buddha. Bailly has observed, that from their division into fives,³ they appear to have been originally numerals, and the system founded on the number of the fingers on the hand repeated.⁴ The least attention to the Latin or Greek numerals will shew how applicable the observation is to them, I. V. X. XV. XX. The Ogham letters, or Ogum Craobh or branch-writing, of Ireland, have this peculiar character of division into fives, as well as the Runes of Scandinavia, that is, of the Saxæ or Xim or Sinenses, for the Chinese are nothing but the Sin, or Saxons, or Buddhists, having the whole mythos of the immaculate conception, the tree of knowledge, of life, the crucifixion, resurrection, &c., according to M. Paravey; all which had been previously related by Bergeron and De Guignes. "Bayer observes, that the Chinese letters consisted of nine simple characters, "five of which were plain lines, and the other four are two or three of them joined together." This is the exact description of the Roman numerals. The Irish Ogham is most unquestionably the Scandinavian or Saxon Rune, and they are all here identified with the Chinese and Eastern Xacæ, Saxæ, Sacæ, Xin, or Xin-di. Here we have the numerals and the letters identified in Runic letters.⁵

After I had finished what has been stated respecting the origin of letters, and cipher or numeri-

---

¹ Ency. Brit. Art. Philology, Sect. 117.

Dr. Morrison, in his "Chinese Miscellany," p. 1, thus confirms this striking fact: "The Chinese language is now *read* "by a population of different nations, amounting to a large proportion of the human race, and over a very extensive "geographical space,—from the borders of Russia on the north, throughout Chinese Tartary on the west, and, in the "east, as far as Kamschatka; and downwards through Corea, and Japan, in the Loo Choo Islands, Cochin China, and "the islands of that Archipelago, on most of which are Chinese settlers, till you come down to the equinoctial line at "Penang, Malacca, Singapore, and even beyond it on Java. Throughout all these regions, however dialects may "differ, and oral languages be confounded, the Chinese *written* language is understood by all. The voyager and the "merchant, the traveller and the Christian missionary, if he can *write* Chinese, may make himself understood through- "out the whole of eastern Asia."—Gutzlaff's Journal of Three Voyages along the Coast of China, in 1831, 1832, 1833, p. xxii.—*Editor*.

² As Fohi is said to have founded his kingdom 200 years after the deluge, perhaps we should be nearer the truth in supposing a more recent inventor.—"The written language of China, alike unique and ancient, is, from the singularity "of its structure, and the extent to which it is employed, one of the most remarkable that has been used amongst mankind. "The knotted cords, [see *infra*, p. 218,] originally employed as the record of events by them as well as many other nations, "in the first stages of their social existence, were superseded, at an early period in their history, by symbolic records. "The founder [*Vang-Vang*] of letters lived about 1100 years before the Christian æra, and the art of printing has been "in use among them for 800 years."—Gutzlaff's Journal, *ut sup.* p. xiv. See Vall. Coll. Hib. Vol. V. p. 102.—*Editor*.

³ We read constantly of *the Vau* or וו *Eos*, the Venus or mother, standing for 6, called Lustrum, L' str=600, or L included, 650; but from what Astle has said, p. 183, I have little doubt that the *five* also had this name. This community arose from their being the matrices of the cycles 360 and 432, and ultimately of the common great cycle, 432,000. As we should say, they are both mother numbers. Pliny divides the circle of the Heavens into 72 constellations or Lustrums. This makes them 5 each. I have already shewn that the L was emphatic, in Hebrew, as it is in French. I have lately met with a learned Jew who agrees with me on that subject.

⁴ Vallancey, Coll. Hib. Vol. V. p. 102. ⁵ Asiat. Res. Vol. II. p. 50.

cal writing, I met with an Essay by John Hoskyns, Vice P. R. S., July 17, 1686. He shews that the Abacus was really the same among the earliest Romans and Chinese, and exhibits drawings of each. He then goes on to explain the ancient numerals of the Chinese, and he describes one stroke or line to mean *one*; two lines to mean *two*; three to mean *three*; a cross to mean *ten*; two crosses *twenty*; three crosses *thirty*, and so on to a hundred. He then says, " Upon perusing " all the accounts I could meet with in books, I found very little satisfaction as to what I princi- " pally inquired after, which was, first concerning the method of the character, whether it con- " sisted of a certain number of marks methodically disposed like letters in a literal, or like num- " bers in a numeral, or like radicals in composite and decomposite derivations. 'Tis said to be " legible into a great many languages, considerably different one from another, but how this is " effected is not related, only 'tis said, that the marks *are of the nature of our arithmetical figures* " (which are become almost universal, at least to us here in Europe); and secondly, concerning " the number of these characters. To which I found as little satisfaction; for, by some relations, " I found that there were 120,000 of them."

I think no one can well doubt, that here we have a specimen of the first numeral system of writing by symbols, which I have been describing. Here is every thing required by the system which I had previously discovered—*first*, the right-lined characters; *secondly*, the decimal notation; and *thirdly*, the symbol denoting a number, an idea, and a word, but for a word which would be different wherever the words of two languages for one idea varied; by which means it comes to pass, that the different nations of the immense Chinese empire all perfectly well understand one another by writing. And here we see the reason why the Chinese have never adopted the literal style of writing; though, from what I shall presently shew, it is probable that the *sixteen letter* system, under some form, is known and used by them.[1] I think from what Mr. Hoskyns says, it is probable, that the numeral powers of the symbols being lost and only the ideas remaining, this will render the art of writing more difficult to learners. Of all the follies of Europeans, none has been more common than their abuse of the Chinese for not adopting the literal syllabic style of writing. We know very little of the Chinese; but the little we do know gives one reason to believe, that they are the wisest people in the world, and, perhaps, in nothing more wise than in keeping European pirates from their shores as much as possible. When they look to the conduct of all the European nations in India—the Dutch, the Portuguese, the French, and the English, and at their repeated attempts, by means of missionaries, to create disturbances in China, they can only consider them as pirates.[2] The wisdom of their government is sufficiently marked by the fact, that their immense empire has been at peace from foreign war for more than two thousand years, with little or no intermission, except when they were attacked and conquered by the Tartars. But in this, more than in all other matters, their wisdom was conspicuous; for their

---

[1] If I be correct in my theory, that the art of syllabic writing arose by degrees, they were necessary consequences that all the uncertainty and small variations which I have developed should be found in the different languages, both in the numeral and literal capacity of the letters, but still that the same system should, on the whole, be every where apparent.

[2] That Europeans are thus regarded by the Chinese is fully demonstrated by the following passage of Gutzlaff's " Journal (pp. 263, 264): " June 3, (1832,) Ma and his friend Le came again on board. He explained the reason " that we were treated with such suspicion. ' You are,' he said, ' very clever; understand making charts, are well " versed in the management of business, and always ready to act. We know all this, and are therefore on our guard. " Some Coreans were last year shipwrecked near us; we permitted them to travel through different provinces, allowed " them to see every thing, and to return by way of Leaou-tung to their native country; for this nation is stupid and " take no notice of the things which fall under their immediate observation. Nevertheless, if, by a proper statement " to the Emperor, you can prove that your sole object is trade, and not the acquisition of power, we will unite our " entreaties with yours, that trade to this place may be established.' "—*Editor.*

institutions and their conduct were such, that they, in fact, conquered their conquerors, and instead of becoming a province of Tartary, Tartary instantly became, and yet continues, a province of China; their enemies disappeared, and their celebrated wall became no longer of any use. Thus, by this despised system of writing, the Emperor's proclamation is intelligible in all the diversity of languages of his immense empire.[1]

It appears to me that in China, in India, and, in short, wherever the Jesuit missionaries went, they were at first encouraged by the governments of those countries—who must have seen that the religion of the Europeans was only their own religion, which, in some respects, was in a less corrupted state than it was in their own country; and the encouragement continued till the missionary fools, acting under the instruction of the rogues at home, shewed clearly that the object was to bring those countries under subjection to a foreign power. The object was probably first exposed by the claim of tithes—a claim which the church never surrenders on any account,[2] though it may permit it to be in abeyance. The cause of this will be clearly explained hereafter.

6. The Greek name of Numeration is Αριθμος—of Rhyme or Measure 'Ρυθμος. The Persians, according to Chardin, call it *Abged*, which word is evidently the a, b, g, d, of the Hebrew and Greek, and our a, b, c. And the symbolical letters of the Indian Algebra, are called Abekt, evidently at the bottom the same as the first letters of the Hebrew and Greek.[3] In the same manner the instrument used by the ancient Greeks and Romans to count with, and at present by the Chinese and Japanese, was and is called Abacus. Count Pararey observes, very justly, that the names *Abged, Abekt, Abacus, Apices*, prove the identity of figures and letters, and that the latter were derived from the former.[4] If persons would only gravely call to mind, how our own words are constantly going out of use, and how new ones are every day introduced, not only among the learned, by their coining them to answer to and supply the wants of new inventions and discoveries, but even among the vulgar, by their forming what we call *cant* or *slang* words, they would no longer be surprised at languages varying from one another in long periods. Thus we have often a word remaining in one nation which only remains as a name in another; such might be Draco, the Latin for Dragon, now only found in the name of the inexorable judge; and the matter must have been much worse in ancient times, before the arts of writing and printing were discovered.[5]

---

[1] " According to Pinkerton, it may now be considered as extending from those parts of the Pacific Ocean, called " the Chinese and Japanese Seas, to the river Sarason, or Sihon, in the west,—a space of eighty-one degrees, equal to " 4200 geographical, or 4900 British miles. From North to South, it stretches from the Uralian mountains, in North " latitude 50°, to the southern border, about 21°, being twenty-nine degrees of latitude, 1740 geographical, or nearly " 2300 British miles."—Gutzlaff's Journal, ut supra, p. xiv.—*Editor.*

[2] Had the Author lived to read the account of the rejection of the Irish Tithe Bill, in August 1834, by an overwhelming majority of Lords *Spiritual* and Temporal, his language would probably have been couched in terms of equal, if not greater, indignation. *Editor.*

[3] Vide Bija-Ganita of Bhascara.

[4] Essay on Figures and Letters, p. 59. In almost all nations we read of a learned lost language. No one will deny that Algebra must have been considered a profoundly learned science in all nations. The Greek letters were taken from the Hebrew or Arabic; then here we have the name of this Indian learning in the names of the Hebrew letters. This almost amounts to something more than a probability—to a proof—that the Hebrew was the first language of the Indians.

[5] In Java one of the alphabets reads from the bottom upwards. Crawfurd's Hist. Ind. Arch. Vol. II. p. 77.
In Malay, Kapala means *head*; this is the Greek Κεφαλος, and the Latin Caput. In Javanese, Sira means head: this, Hebraicè, is Rasi. Ib. 110.
Sakti, in Sanscrit, means *power* or *energy*; in the Polynesian languages it means *supernatural power*. Ib. 112.
The Chinese call the Sanscrit language the *Fan* language. This is, language of the Fanum, or the church, or the

I think, by means of the Greek or Latin numerals, a correspondence in an unspoken language would be readily carried on. But as soon as what are called the Arabic numerals 1, 2, 3, 4, &c.,[1] were invented, the process would be greatly facilitated. This might be the secret and forgotten language so generally spoken of. This would be an unspoken language at first. But I suspect that the tribe of the Yadu or Iod-di or Yo-di, or of the holy Io, or of the followers of the Cali-di or holy Kali or Cali, were the inventors of the Cadmæan system, and kept it to themselves, as a masonic secret. If we consider the extreme difficulty of learning the art of reading and writing, we shall instantly see the ease with which this secret might be kept by an order.

Although I cannot shew how, or into what language the system of ciphers was rendered, yet I think the Japan and Java practice is a decisive proof of its feasibility, and is probably a remnant of its first use. From the system of ciphers used as powers of notation arose written symbols, and the perfect, secret sixteen-letter system of the tribe of Ioudi or Chaldæans; and to them, I doubt not, it was confined for many generations—the Buddhists first, in like manner, keeping the system by figures unimproved.

Mr. Astle[2] informs us, that the first Chinese letters were knots on cords. Here we have the correct Quipos of the Peruvians, the country of Tanga-Tanga, treated of *supra*, p. 37.

After I had nearly finished what the reader has seen, I discovered in Hyde[3] what in a very remarkable manner confirms my hypotheses, but which will not surprise those who have read what I have written respecting the Judæan mythos of the Mexicans and Chinese. It is an alphabet of the Tartars who now govern China, and also an alphabet of the Mendeans, who, I suppose, are the Mandaites or Nazoureans or Christians of St. John or Nabathæans.[4] A moment's consideration will satisfy any Hebrew scholar, that they are both, notwithstanding the difference in the shape of the letters, correctly Hebrew. They do not differ even in a single letter. After this no one will be surprised to find the Judæan mythos in China. But this Tartar alphabet must be kept a secret as the use of letters is prohibited.[5]

7. Sir Stamford Rafflesis disposed to believe, that the island of Java, and not Ceylon, has been originally the Taprobane or ancient sacred island. It seems both the peninsula of Malacca and the other islands all carried the name of Java or Kawi. Sumatra was called *Jabadios*, that is, *holy-iava*. From what he says, I am inclined to think he may be right, but that, in fact, there were several islands, each, in a succession of years, claiming to be the *sacred* one. The temples have evidently been first Buddhist or Jain, succeeded by those of Cristna. The first, situate in the province of Kedú, which is a corruption of Iedu aspirated, in fact, of Judia or Juda, he calls Boro Bodo: this, I do not doubt, ought to be Bra Buddha, whose icon alone remains unmutilated.[6] The largest of the temples are generally in the form of a cross, and have been numerous and magnificent almost beyond credibility. It is curious to see them all tumbled into ruins by the hands of their owners, at the instigation, not by the command, of the followers of Mohamed; for hither

---

sacred building of the Latins. By Fan language is meant *holy*. It is the same as φην, often noticed before. The Latin word means holy or sacred building: in Greek Ναος or Σηκος. Neuman, Catechism of Shamans, p. 36.

A Nun in Chinese is called Pekewne; in Sanscrit she is called Bhagini. We have here the Beguins of the Romish church. (Neuman, Catechism of Shamans, p. 46.) Thus we have not only the same Papist Nuns in China, Italy, and Tibet, but we have them by the same names—of course carried thither and adopted by the *heretical* Nestorians, who account for every thing, but who, I believe, are not known to have ever had any Nuns.

[1] See Astle, p. 176.   [2] P. 164.
[3] De Rel. Vet. Pers. in a map at the bottom of the title of a Tartar book, in my copy, p. 358.
[4] Vide Ibid. App. p. 524.   [5] Ency. Brit. Vol. I. p. 727.   [6] Vide plates, fig. 34, in my Vol. I.

Mohamedan *conquerors* never came. Reason alone succeeded in converting the nation to the faith of the consummation of Christianity, in fact, of the Prophet, as I believe it did in most other places. The natives seem to pay little attention to the trumpery of the Koran, but they fix merely on the two great points of the religion, a belief in the Unity of God, and in the mission of the prophet; that is, that Mohamed was a Resoul or *Sent of God*—a belief which any philosopher may receive, if he will only ask himself candidly what, in the common exoteric religion, the word Resoul meant. Mohamed disclaimed all supernatural or miraculous power, and merely maintained that he was pre-ordained and sent to effect a reform in the debased religion of the world.

Jesus and Mohamed were philosophers, preachers of wisdom and morality to their countrymen, and, like Socrates and Pythagoras, neither of them left a single word of writing behind him. Some persons believe Jesus to have been murdered by the priests, others state that he escaped them; but at all events he seems to have offered no active opposition. Mohamed, on the contrary, when struck, returned the blow and beat his enemies. But in each case the moment the preacher was gone, books enow were manufactured by those whose interest it was to establish a dominion over their fellow-creatures. In each case, I have no doubt, the early actors in the dramas were well-meaning fanatical devotees. I doubt not that in India and in Europe millions went over from the religions of the two Cristnas (the God of India and the God of Rome), to that of the new Avatar, who, in the West, protected them by his arms against the sectaries of the old Avatar. For though the followers of the new Avatar never persecuted, the followers of the old one always did. It is not very surprising under these circumstances, that the new Avatar should have protected his followers by his arms. This would excuse, if it did not justify, the wars of Mohamed, and also account for his success.

Java is called by the natives *Tana* (the land) Jawa; or *Núsa* (the island) Jawa.[1] It is also called Zaba and Jaba, and Zabaja, that is, *ia-Zaba*, country of Zaba, and by Ptolemy, Jaba-diu. The term Jawa is also applied to the Malayan Peninsula and the Eastern islands.[2] The word Tana is the common term in the West for land or country, and the Nusa is evidently the same as the Greek $N\eta\sigma o\varsigma$. Sir S. Raffles shews, that Zaba comes from Java, Jaba; but Saba or Zaba in Coptic means Wisdom. We see from this, that the word Saba, whence come the Sabæans, has been originally nothing but a corruption of the Hebrew word Ieue; and here we see how it came to mean *wisdom*. Sir W. Jones acknowledges he does not know the meaning of the word Sabian or what was the Sabian faith.[3] I believe there never was an exclusive sect of Sabians; the word Sabian is merely a descriptive term. The Christians of St. John were Sabæans.[4]

In the fifth volume of the work of the Abbé de Rocher[5] it is said, "Selon *Horus* grammairien "d'Egypte, *Sbo* signifioit *érudition*. C'était ce que les Egyptiens appeloient *Sugesse*. Encore "aujourd'hui chez les Coptes ou Egyptiens modernes, le mot *Sabé* veut dire un *Sage*." I think from the above we may understand how the God *Ieue* became the God of Sabaoth,—how the planetary bodies, the intelligent disposers, were called Sabaoth, the plural of Saba, and whence the Sabæans had their name. From this also may come the French word *Savoir*.

In the middle ages the women of France had a nocturnal festival called the Réunion des Sabbats; this it is clear, from attendant circumstances, had nothing to do with the *day of rest*. I have little doubt that it related to the God of wisdom. It is said[6] to have related to the mysteries of the God Pan. I think it probable that the day set apart to the God of wisdom was called

---

[1] Raffles' Hist. Java, p. 1. [2] Ib. pp. 2, 3. [3] Asiat. Res. Vol. II. p. 8, 4to.
[4] Good's Job, Introd. p. lxxxvi. [5] P. 83.
[6] Hist. Phys. et Mor. de Paris, par Dulaure, Tome VIII. p. 90, ed 3d.

Sabbath or שבת *sbt*. From this it was a rest-day, and from this the word came to mean *to rest*. When I find the word Zäba or Saba in Coptic to mean *wisdom*, I can entertain little doubt that originally it must have had this meaning in Hebrew. But, indeed, Sir S. Raffles's explanation gives us a probable etymon in the corruption of the Hebrew name of God. This is similar to the corruption of the Hebrew *y o* into *ng*, as I have pointed out in the word Jaugti, *supra*, p. 192.

I must now beg my reader to turn to the Index of Volume I., and reconsider the several passages where the word Saba is treated of, and he will see that the discovery which I have made, with the assistance of the Abbé, that it means *wisdom*, will remove several difficulties, and furnish a link which was wanting in the chain of my theory. It will shortly be shewn why the Chaldæans were called Sabæans.

8. Until I had nearly finished what had been presented to the reader, I had not seen the plan of a gentleman of the name of Northmore, detailed in the Encyclopædia Londinensis.[1] It will there be found, that he has, in substance, actually and unconsciously hit upon the ancient universal language which I have been describing and proving to have once existed, without his having any idea that it had really ever been in use, viz. a language of ciphers. He thus describes it: "The character is real, not nominal; to express things and notions, not letters or sounds; yet to be mute like letters and arbitrary; not emblematical like hieroglyphics. Thus every nation will retain its own language, yet every one understand that of each other, without learning it; only by seeing a real universal character which will signify the same thing to all people, by what sounds soever each express it, in their particular idiom. For instance, by seeing the character destined to signify *to drink*, an Englishman would read *to drink*; a Frenchman *boire*; a Latin *bibere*; a Greek πινειν—a Jew שתה *ste*, and so on: in the same manner as seeing a horse, each nation expresses it after their own manner, but all mean the same animal." He then adds, "this real character is no chimera: the Chinese and Japanese have already something like it: they have a common character which each of these nations understand alike in their several languages; though they pronounce them with such different sounds, that they do not understand one another in speaking." It is then surely very remarkable that this Gentleman should choose the very same symbols, which I have detected in use by the first authors of any kind of written symbols, viz. what we have been accustomed to call the Arabic numerals. The following is a specimen of a sentence:

9, 8, .5,—7̂, 6̂. *I never saw a more unhappy woman.*

He undertakes to shew that 20 signs would be quite sufficient for 10,000 words; then, probably, my 28 Arabic numerals would give infinitely more than would be wanted. Although Mr. Northmore's plan is not exactly the same as that of the ancients, detected by me, yet an attentive reader will see that in principle they are strictly the same.

9. In my Celtic Druids, p. 311, I have noticed a book in the true Ogham character, and in the Arabic language, discovered by Mr. Von Hammer in Egypt, to which I also referred a little time ago.[2] I have a copy of the translation of that work, published by Nicol, Pall Mall, A.D. 1806. It contains upwards of seventy different alphabets. There are, among others, the alphabets of Plato, Pythagoras, Cleomenes, Socrates, Aristotle, and Hermes. On the alphabet of Hermes or of the hieroglyphics, the author says, "Every one of these kings invented, according to his own genius and understanding, a particular alphabet, in order that none should know them but the sons of *wisdom*." On examining these alphabets, they turn out to be every one of them founded on the Arabic, in fact to be Arabic, however varied the letters may be in shape. It is quite clear

---

[1] Vol. XII. p. 203. [2] Supra, p. 205.

that they all answer to the Arabic arithmetical figures, and will all suit to one key. It is, I think, also quite clear, that they will answer to a syllabic system, or to a symbolic one like Mr. Northmore's. Figure 1, in my plates (in Volume I.), is an example of one of them. The first figure of the hieroglyphical alphabet, as I have before remarked, was the *Owl*; the bird of Wisdom.

I must now notice a curious circumstance, overlooked by me before, which is this—We have seen how the doctrines of Plato are connected with the doctrines of the Trimurti, and of Emanations and the Jewish Cabala, and how all this is connected with the secret allegories of the tree alphabets and the Syriac, and the Tamul Pushto, and that the ancient sacred language of the Tamuls had *five* meanings. This premised, I have to observe, that the tree alphabet or Ogum Craobh or branch-writing, as it is called in Celtic Irish, given in my first plate, to which I have just referred, and found by Mr. Von Hammer in Egypt in the Arabic language, from which he translated it, is said by Ben Wassih to have been the Celtic used by Plato, and that each letter had several significations.

In Jeremiah xxv. 26, we read of a king called Sheshack. This person has puzzled the commentators very much. He has been thought by some, and correctly thought, to be king of the Sacæ.[1] This man was king of the Shepherds of Pallestini, who, I do not doubt, were Sacæ or Saxons, and Scythians, the conquerors of Egypt.

The Abbé Jacques-Jules Bonnaud[2] says, "Il faut encore observer que, suivant les auteurs "anciens, et Herodote lui-même,[3] les Perses donnoient à tous les Scythes en général le nom de "Saques." He shews,[4] that the Sesach, who pillaged the temple of Jerusalem, was one of these Saxons. In fact to call these tribes Saxons is the same as to call them *Buddhists*, or, as to call the natives of Europe *Christians*. But still, when our posterity read of great armies of Papists, of Greeks, of Protestants, of Lutherans, of Germans, and of Spaniards, they will read about those who were all Christians and all Europeans; and if they do not take more care, and exercise a better judgment than we have done, they will be in still greater confusion than we are.

To the early history of Java no attention whatever can be paid; nothing can be made out respecting it, except that a judgment may be formed and general consequences deduced from insulated facts. It is said, that among the earliest of the occupiers of Java was a race of *Rasaksa*;[5] but what these were, is, I think, no where explained. I suppose the word ought to be Ras-Saka. There is also mentioned an *Adi-Saka* or *Aji-Saka*, who is considered the same as a chieftain, called *Tritrestra*, who is said to have conquered the island. Here we have clearly the same mythos as that described by Georgius, in North India, which found its way to Europe, brought by people with the name of Saxons. Sir Stamford Raffles observes, that Saka means an *æra* in Sanscrit, and that Sir W. Jones says, very truly, that it is a name of Buddha.[6]

He further states,[7] that the word Saka was also applied to the founder of any æra—that Bala Raja of Guj'-rat was called Di-Saka, or Deva-Saka, which was a name of Salivahana—that the Caliyuga, or age of Cali, was divided into a number of Sakas. The fact was, that each God was Di-Saka, which, in regimine, meant God of the Saka; and Saka was 666—650—608, and at last 600. We read that the prince of *Rom* sent twenty thousand families to people Java.[8] I think it probable that this was an invasion of Brahmin religionists from Ceylon, which was called Ram or Rom, who, after several repulses, ultimately conquered the island, abolished Buddhism, and established the religion of Cristna, which seems to have united here, in some measure, with Buddhism,

---

[1] Vide Basnage, Hist. Jews, B. iii. Ch. xxv.   [2] Défense de l'Abbé Guerin de Rocher, p. 105.
[3] Herod. 7. 64.   [4] P. 101.   [5] Raffles, Vol. II. p. 67.
[6] Ib. p. 68.   [7] Ib. &c.   [8] Ib. p. 69.

the latter having preserved its temples. I think this may be inferred from the existence of the icons of both in the temples, as well as from their traditions. After Cristna comes the reign of the Pandus. The reign of the Pandus was probably nothing but a treaty of peace, or rather truce, under some Afghan conquerors, between the two sects, which ended the war of the Mahabarat and established the Holy Catholic or Pandæan faith—the adoration of the *double principle*, leaving each in the state in which it was at the moment of the truce, as we have seen was the case with the Amazons at Athens. This will account for all the anomalies which we have every where found. It is supported both by tradition and circumstances, and I think it is consistent with what we know of the character of man, from experience—after a storm there generally comes a calm.

The God to whom Thursday, or *the day of Jove*, or Iao or Ieue, is dedicated in India, our Orientalists call *Vrihaspati*. The true name of this God, I do not doubt, is to be found in the interesting history of Java, as described by S. Raffles. He gives it *Raspati*, that is, evidently, *Father of Wisdom*.[1] Arka, (this is the Greek Αρχη,) he says, means the sun.[2] The Javans have a celebrated poem on their mythology, called *Kanda*, that is, *Kan-diva*.[3] Sir S. Raffles declines giving it, on account of its indecency. One meaning of the word *kan* is pretty clear. This poem is also called *Pepakam*. This, probably, is *Pi-akm—The* Wisdom.

I can entertain little doubt that, if a fair and impartial examination were made, remains enow of the Judæan mythos would be found both about Jeddo in Japan, and in Java, to prove that it had formerly been established there. From the prejudice which every inquirer has hitherto had (without any unfair intention) against every thing of a Jewish appearance or tendency, the discovery of the mythos has had every disadvantage. In Siam it is so marked, that it cannot possibly be disputed; it is not probable that it should be established there, in China, and in North India, and not have extended to the sacred islands. Georgius says,

" Indorum *litteras, et linguam Balabandu* nuncupatum *ex Hebræo suam originum habere,* per-
" spicuè demonstratur, judice *La-Crozio* Epist. 32, ad Bayerum in Thes. Epistol. T. III., ex
" multis litteris Balabandecis, quæ si cum Hebraicis comparentur, ejusdem pene formæ videri
" possint. Simile quiddam in mentem mihi venit, quum de origine Tibetanarum à *Syriacis* for-
" tasse litteris deducenda cogitarem. Nam et hanc suspicionem La-Crozius ipse in animum mihi
" pridem injecerat. Quamobrem operæ pretium duxi earum complures, ne dicam omnes, cum iis
" conferre quas Syri Estranghelas appellant."[4]

Vallancey,[5] as I have before observed, says, the Estrangelo was the common alphabet of the Chaldæans, and that the present-used square Chaldaic letter was never used by the Chaldæans, except as numerals. I doubt the truth of what Vallancey says, if by Chaldæans, the society, not the Babylonian nation, be meant; but he probably does not mean this.

I have often before observed, that the most ancient historians, of all nations, speak of a primeval and sacred language, which in their time was lost. Pythagoras taught that all the ancient sacred

---

[1] Peti-ras-Urii. Hist. Jav. Vol. I. p. 475.   [2] P. 414.

[3] The first priests were called, in the old language, כהן ken, whence, I doubt not, came king. Kings who have received the χειροτονια are all priests. The Jews say their priests were called Cohens; under this is concealed the word ken. Among the Jews in London are certain honoured, but not very rich, persons called Cohens, who are believed to be lineal descendants of Aaron.° They still perform a peculiar service in the synagogue on the feast of the Passover. Khan is Cuning, Cunning, Kunig, King. Mr. Cleland has somewhere shewn that it was of both genders, meaning both king and queen, like our word sovereign, and that the Saxon word Cyning, a king, comes from ken, *knowledge*. In Yorkshire, *to ken* means *to know.* In Gothic, khaan meant king (αναξ in Greek); this was k=20, n=50, aa=2=72; or ך k=500, נ n=50, ג n=50=600. Again χγ=650. In almost every case these numeral names have two meanings—both appropriate to the circumstances.

[4] Alph. Tib. p. 583.   [5] Hib. Coll. Vol. V. p. 201.

learning was concealed in numbers. Almost as extended as the tradition of a lost language, was that of an universal empire—that of Pandæa. I apprehend that all these traditions referred to the universal language of numbers, in which the secret of the common mythos was concealed. Although this numerical language might not be equal to the present written language of any nation, yet I think it would be available for all the purposes of communicating and continuing a common mythos, which chiefly depended upon numbers. It would be correctly a cipher. The first language which it would represent would continue *fixed* for many generations, at the same time that the language spoken was dividing into dialects in great variety. This variety would still be increased, when this language of *numbers* began to be exchanged for a language of selected *letters* taken from the numbers. The latter would be so much more convenient that, in all the common concerns of life, it would soon supersede the other; from this it comes to pass that we have now no remains of the first language, except in the mythology. And here, in the names of Cycles, Gods, and Days of the Week, we have it. In truth, it may be in many other words, but we have not the means of detecting it. At first, it might be a representation of *ideas*, not of *words;* but it would not long continue so: the only word not strictly mythological, which I can fix on, is, I think, the ⊕ *ab*, for *father*.[1] But I think it yet exists, though greatly amplified, in the Chinese language. Except as a secret of the Tartars, the sixteen-letter system having never penetrated into China, a system nearly the primeval one yet remains. Of course the changes and variations which it must have undergone, to have suited it to the necessities of a great and civilised empire, preclude all hope of finding much of it among them.

I must now beg my reader to refer to Volume I. pp. 3, 4, 6, 30, 177, 653, 746, 763, and consider the theory which I have proposed for the origin of the cycles and the sacred numbers: then next to ibid. pp. 216, 221, 223, 224, 230, 499, 500, 590, and consider how this is strengthened by the monograms, and the use of the cross, and the records of all these sacred numbers, the number of the beast excepted, in the number of the pillars in the respective temples—and this done, when he has observed the manner in which all these things are connected together, and how they mutually account for and support one another, I defy him to doubt the truth of what I assert, that I have discovered and explained nearly the whole secret of the ancient mythology—that I have penetrated to the very inmost recesses, and laid open the most secluded of the mysteries of the temples.

10. It is, perhaps, unnecessary to remind my reader of the close, and hitherto unaccountable, connexion between the י״ן *iin* or wine or vine, and Janus and Noah, called Menu in the Bible, and the Indian Menu, and the fourteen various Menus, the Latin Mens, and the Greek Νοος, Mind, the Mannus or Man, the Mene or Moon, and the God Bacchus, to all which I have so often adverted already, but to which, together with several other matters, I must be permitted here again to advert. When I consider the close connexion of all these, and the failure of all attempts hitherto made to shew how it arose, and the avowed custom of the ancients, and particularly of Pythagoras, in describing all their mythoses by numbers, as, in so many ways, I have proved, I ask, may not this connexion have been described by numbers? Thus, $MN=650$, the number sacred to Bacchus, who was Menu, who was Noah, who was Janus.

In the Hebrew alphabet, I repeat, the centre letter M stood for 600. The modern Jews admit, that a great mystery lies under this. I have, in part at least, developed it. But in the Irish language, probably as old as any we possess, the Mem is called M-Vin or M-uin. This is the word Vin, or Oιν, or Ιιν, with the Monogram prefixed—in short, the name of Bacchus. But Bacchus was Buddha, Βοτρυς:[2] but Βοτρυς means *a grape*. Bacchus was also *wisdom*. In Latin, Race-

---

[1] This is correctly the first name for *God the Father* of the Jewish Cabalists—the Trimurti. See Vol. I. p. 70.
[2] See *supra*, p. 9.

mus means *a grape*, which is the Greek ῥαξ *a grape-stone* or *kernel*. Here the *ras* is evidently the *wisdom*; thus the word signified both Grape and Wisdom. It is very curious that in the Greek we should find the *Buddha*, and in the Latin the *Ras*; thus, from this double meaning, shewing how Bacchus became the God of wine. This might give rise to all the drunken revels and nonsense in honour of that God; and in a similar manner, probably, arose many of the absurd mythologies both in India and the West—amusing to the people, but contemptible to the philosophers and the initiated. Nimrod says,[1] "I conceive that the Feminine principle is adumbrated "by the vine and ivy which cling for support either to the ivy-mantled tower, or to the marital "elm, both of which alike designate the Arbos Antiqua Ithyphallus."

Now the M, as the centre letter, represented the M-phalos or Omphalos, the Ioni, (qu. Iωνι,) the Matrix, the Delphus, the Nabhi or centre of the earth; in fact, the female generative power. This M was the monogram[2] of M-ia, which was מ-יה *m-ie*, M the *self-existent*; and M-aia—the M-aia or Mother Ia, or Jah, and, as repeatedly remarked, with the Hebrews it was 600.

Now I have often wondered why the letter following the M-uin was called N-uin. If we examine the Greek alphabet we shall find that the Sanpi is not a letter, as it has no alphabetic sound attached to it, and all letters were once like this, and that the Greeks have only 26 forms for their letters, the two central ones being the M-UIN and N-UIN corrupted into Mu and Nu, from the Irish Celtic, which jointly make the number of Bacchus=650—the Me Nu, the Nu Ma, the Me Ne.

Noah is said to have had a fourth son born to him, called Inachus; this is Bacchus, Ιων— ינ-ה-כש *Iinekus* or ינ-א-כש *Iinakus*—Iin *the black* or *Ethiopian*; that is, the black or Ethiopian Jin or Jan, or Ian-us. Iacchus, I suspect, is Ia or Ie-chus or Ie-kus. As I have said before, I believe that the name of every God which was not a mere provincial or dialectic variation or corruption, was described by *a number*. Buddha was a Menu or Nu, or Menu was a Buddha, and Buddha lived, according to some of his followers, 56 years—N=50, U=6=56. One of the names of Buddha was the same as that of the famous Mani; and Mani was MN=650; and Mani was called Sin, or, in Chinese and Coptic, Xin, X=600, N=50.[3] But מנחם *nues* in Hebrew means comforter. From the same origin came the Mounts of Sin and Sion, and the river of Sin-de or *the holy Sin*; and the Sines or Chinese; for which see, at great length, Georgius as quoted above. He also shews the close connexion of the Hebrew words סוף *sup* and שׂוף *sup* with the words *sio* and *cyo*. Hence, he says, comes the Syriac *Sciuphoio*, (Scio-suph,) which means, with the Gnostics, &c., *purus spiritus*, which, he says, the religion of the Lama holds to migrate into human bodies for the salvation of man.[4] Here in Suph the *purus spiritus* we have WISDOM, and in Scio we have *I know, knowledge, sapientia*, and the island of Scio in the Mediterranean. This Zin, Sin, or Xin, Georgius shews is the same as the Σῆν *quod est* VIVERE, of the Greeks.[5] He shews that the Sio is the same as the *Siang* or *Sihang*, of the Tibetians, but without attempting to explain the reason why the *o* and the *ng* are substituted for one another. This is the Hebrew ע *o* corrupted into the *ng*, as in *Ganga, Jiam* Gang, &c., &c.; and the Çio and Sio are only the word Io aspirated. All this profound learning will be disputed on account of its depth; but I beg those who dispute it, on this account, to recollect, that it was not deep learning to those who invented it, and to whose inventive faculties it must have offered itself by degrees.

Vallancey[6] calls Ogham the God of Wisdom; this makes me suspect Ogham to be a corruption

---

[1] Part I. (1826) p. 271.
[2] Monogram as we call it, but called *Omen* by Martianus Capella. See Vol. I. p. 192.
[3] Georgius Alph. Tib. p. 681.   [4] Ibid. p. 683.   [5] Ibid. p. 682.
[6] Coll. Hib. Vol. IV. Part I. p. 416.

of חכם hkm. He adds,[1] that Ogham means עוגם ougm circles, and that Oga means an *explorer of wisdom*. I think the Ogham of Ireland and Acham of the Sanscrit, are nothing but modifications of the first חכה Akm. The Ogham of Ireland is certainly the knowledge of letters and of the tree of letters. Again, Vallancey says, "Had this Lexiconist known that Drui in Irish, and Daru in " Persian, signified *Sapiens*, and that it was the title of a Persian Magus of the second order, he " could not have been at a loss." He then goes on[2] to shew, that Seanoir, *a wise man*, from the root SHAN, is the epithet for a Druid, and that it has the same meaning as Ogham, consequently this makes the Ogham to mean *wisdom*, and the Ogham language or letter will be *the language* or *letter of wisdom* ; this justifies me in explaining the name of the Ogham of Ireland and Acham or secret letter or language of India to be the Hebrew חכם hkm.[3] Sean and De-Saine and Desanus were names of Hercules or the Sun. The above word Sean I believe to be a corruption of Sion, or rather, I should say, the same as Sion. Then the Mount of Sion was Mount of the Sun, of Hercules, or of Wisdom ; the sun being the shekinah of divine wisdom. Aga [*Ogga*] was a name of Minerva.[4] Is the Irish book of Lechem any thing but the book of the Ocham, L'Acham ? And from this Aga came Aga-memnon, and the Aga of the Janissaries. In an Irish MS., Vallancey says, Ogham is described to come from Guam, which means *wisdom*. In consequence of this I can scarcely doubt that Guam is a corruption of חכמה hkme. Thus, in endless variety, in all nations and ages, the doctrine of WISDOM is found to extend its secret ramifications.

11. The word Rhyme, I apprehend, comes from the Greek 'Ρυθμος, Rhythm, Rhyme, Rime, Rune. Much learned discussion has taken place to determine whether what we call Rhyme was invented by the Saraceni, i. e. Arabians, or by the Northern nations. After what the reader has seen advanced by me of the Oriental origin of the Scandinavian Sacæ, and of the Arabians from the North of India, he will not be surprised that I should entertain a suspicion, that it arose among the original inventors of letters, somewhere east of the Indus. All the sacred mythoses were in Rhyme, because at first they were unwritten. They were first written when syllables arose, and they were counted and subjected to rules for the sake of the memory—for the assistance of which music, chanting, and recitative, were invented. For the purpose of composing these verses and setting them to music, the Baids arose, and with them their Bedas or Vedas or Sagas—books or songs of wisdom. By regimine the singers of the Baids or Veds became themselves Baids or Vates; for the Bairds were formerly called Baids, i. e. Buds and Vates and Fates, *tellers of truth* or *wisdom*, and hence the Fetische of Africa. In this way, by the regimine, innumerable names had their origin. It rationally accounts for the effect, and no other cause will do it. Thus singer of Baid became *singer Baid* ; priest of Chryses became *priest Chryses*.

By the British the Druids were called Vates, by the Greeks Ouateis (Borlase). The origin of this name is preserved in the Irish Baidh, and Faith, but stronger in Faithoir or Phaithoir. The first was written Vaedh, a Prophet (evidently Veda), by the Arabs. Baid is the Chaldæan ברא *bda*, prædicavit, and בדים *bdim* Divini and mendaces.[5] This is evidently the Buddha of India.

The verses of the Vedas are the leaves of the holy tree.[6] The Ved, Bud, or Bed,[7] and Vaid and Baid and Vates, is, in Irish, *feadh, fiodh, fodh*, (i. e. *vodh*,) which means a *tree*, knowledge, art, science.[8] In Sanscrit, Veda means knowledge.[9] The Indian Vedas are never read, but only sung or chaunted. I believe that, like the Vedas or Bairda,[10] if the Pentateuch were not closely shut up in the temple, its perusal was confined to the order of priests.

---

[1] Coll. Hib. Vol. IV. Part I. p. 420.   [2] Ib. p. 416.   [3] Ib. pp. 420, 421, 432.   [4] Ib. p. 421.
[5] Ib. p. 427.   [6] Asiat. Res. Vol. I. art. xviii.   [7] As, indeed, it is sometimes called ; Georgius, p. 152.
[8] Vall. Coll. Hib. Vol. V. p. 147.   [9] Vide Asiat. Res. ut supra.   [10] Bairds, Forster's Travels, p. 41.

The collection of Persian books, called the *Dabistan*, the Cambridge Key tells us, are called Vedas;[1] and the first Veda of the Brahmins is called *Rich*. This is a corruption of Ras.[2] Reeshees, persons skilled in the Vedas.[3] The Jews call their first book of Genesis, from the first word, which means *wisdom*, Barasit; thus the first Veda is called Rich or Ras or Wisdom—Rich Veda.

I suspect that the seven Rishis of India, or the seven wise men, were the same as the seven wise men of Greece, and were the seven incarnate genii of the seven ages or Neroses, preceding that in which the authors lived, who wrote of them. It is remarkable that there should have been seven wise men in each nation. The Greeks having lost the meaning of their mythos, sought it among their men of learning, and, by some of the old authors, they were supposed to have all lived at one time; but it is evident that the Greeks were as ignorant of this as of all the remainder of the mythos. Many Hindoos believe the Vedas to have been written in a divine language, long since extinct.[4] I think this was the old Hebrew or Chaldee language, and the numeral symbolic letter—the language which furnishes an immense number of roots to the Sanscrit.

Van Kennedy says, *Veda* is derived from *vedati*, contracted *vetti*, he knows; whence comes *vidya* learning,[5] *vidivan* a learned man.[6] We have this in the Saxon *vidanti*, Greek ειδοντας, Latin *vident*, Anglo-Saxon *witton*, and the Indian God Wit-oba. But the *vetti*, he knows, is closely allied to knowledge, and knowledge is wisdom; and I think the Witton is a form of our wisdom, and hence comes our *Wittena-gemote*, or assembly of wise men.[7] From the same root comes video *I see* and vates *a prophet* or *seer*, κατ᾿ εξοχην, a *seer before*. From the same root comes ειδω and *idea*, which is *knowledge*, and the Hebrew ידע *ido*, and the mounts Ida, of Phrygia and of the island of Χρης or Crete, and of the French Chrétiens.

Sanscrit grammarians say, that the *b* and *v* in their language are permutable; this may, perhaps, account for the name of the God of wisdom being called Buddha, for it may be a formation, grammatically, from Veda. The same, without the digamma, is the Edda of the North, or of the Saxons or Scandinavians. The first name of Buddha was Saca, Saxa סש ss=360, afterwards followed Ttl=650, then תת Tt=600 or Tat.

Thus Buddha is Veda, and the Veda is the Vates or person wisely inspired: from the infallibility of the Vates came Fate; and from this mythos came the infallibility of the Pope, the inspired or incarnated divine Wisdom—the same as the Lama of Tibet.

The principle of the fates was this: The First Cause was believed to ordain a law, or foreordain, to each cycle what should happen. In every cycle the same things were repeated: the vates or fates only declared this law. Jupiter was bound by his own pre-ordained law, because, when he made that law, he, being omniscient, foresaw that he should not change it; he foresaw every thing, which, on the whole, was for the best, and, in agreement with that, he ordained every thing which would happen in the cycle, and for ever. However long the cycle may be, still if it be a cycle every thing will recur. This, although it may be false, is much more refined than our feeble conceptions, that God is changing every day, at the request or prayer of every fool who chooses to petition him; or, at least, as our book says, "when two or three are gathered together." What is for the best, the First Cause will enact, and if he enact it *in time*, he must enact it in a cycle, for time cannot exist out of a cycle; we can only form an idea of what we call *time* by means of our idea of circle or cycle. We know or believe from our senses that

---

[1] Vol. II. p. 129.   [2] Ib. p. 127.   [3] Ib. pp. 121, 122.   [4] Ib. Vol. I. p. 261.
[5] P. 210.   [6] This Vidya is our Widow—a knowing person—a person who has known man.
[7] In the Saxon, the sigma *sen*, is in fact found in the word for wise, which is Wit, *to know*, and Wist, *to know*; and, query, wiss? (Vide Lemon in voce Wi.) Is Witt-ox-mote *meeting of wise men of letters?*

events proceed in succession: how can we believe that events will proceed or succeed, for ever, without a stop? We may say we think they will, but of this we can form no idea, as we shall find, if we examine the course of our ideas closely. The Indians, meditating upon these matters, came at last, after the end of each cycle, to place the First Cause, as well as the Creator, in a state of absolute quietude; but what would this be, if continued, but Atheism? To avoid this, they made him rest a given time, then begin and enact anew the former order of things, to create happiness—begin a new cycle. I shall be told, that this will deprive man of free will, and perhaps God too. I cannot help this. It is not my fault that this theory of the ancients is attended with a dangerous result. My declaration of their opinion or faith does not change it, or make it. If my reader will try some other theory he will soon find himself in an equal difficulty; and this arises from the fact, that we here come to the extreme of our faculties. If we go farther, we go beyond the power of the human understanding, and then, if we talk at all, we necessarily talk nonsense, as all the profound metaphysicians, like Berkeley, and the professors of the Vedanta philosophy, do.

If the mind of man could be brought to the consideration of the subject of prophecy without prejudice, he would instantly see, that in its common and usual interpretation it involves the very acme of absurdity. For what is it that God the omnipotent chooses to reveal? Something to man for his good, which will happen in future; but, wonderful to tell, he always does this in such a manner, that man shall not know that it has been revealed, until the thing has happened. He gives it by the mouth of the priest, who is supposed sometimes to understand, sometimes not to understand it. But can any thing be more derogatory to the divine attributes? Why does not God make his priest speak out, intelligibly and clearly? Why did not the prophet tell the Jews, that their next Messiah should be a *spiritual* not a *temporal* Messiah, like all their former Messiahs? But every prophecy is an ænigma to be expounded by the priest. Here, again, we have the system of secrecy which prevails through every part of the ancient world. Every thing was allegory and ænigma, contrived for the purpose of supporting the power of the favoured initiated.

12. We have lately seen the Vedas, or books of wisdom or of the prophets, connected with the tree of letters. We will now return to the Chinese, with whom we shall find the same thing.

The Chinese have *si*, a tree, the root of *su*, a learned man. (The French have the word *savoir*.) *Sai* is learning, wisdom (whence comes Sci-en-tia); *su*, a book; also *siah*, derived from *soah*,[1] a tree. *Tsu*, doctus; *Xu*, arbor; *Sai*, doctrina; *Xi su*, literatus, doctus. The symbol at the top expresses a flower and books.[2] Here I think is Xaca.

Hio scientia, this is the *cio* of Georgius.

Xu, tsu, liber, epistola.

The word Shekia or Sakia שכיא *skia* in the Chaldee means prophet. This is because a prophet is a Vates, a Ved, a Bed, *wisdom*.[3]

Alvarez Semedo says, "The third sect (meaning sects of Chinese) is from India, "from the parts of Hindostan, which sect they call Xaca, from the author of it, concerning whom "they fable—that he was conceived by his mother Maia, from a white elephant, which she saw in "in her sleep;[4] and, for the more purity, she brought him forth FROM ONE OF HER SIDES, and

---

[1] Vall. Coll. Hib. Vol. V. p. 141.   [2] Ib. pp. 142—145.   [3] Hager, p. 8.

[4] Ganesa, the God of Wisdom, is always described with the head of an elephant, and certainly no emblem could be more appropriate. But we see here why the white elephant is adored by some of the Eastern kings. This superstition has been carried even to the extreme length of great states going to war for the possession of an elephant of this colour. This is not unlike the story that the siege of Troy was undertaken for the possession of a statue of the moon,

" then directly died, being but nineteen years of age: that he did penance in the snowy moun-
" tains under four masters *for twelve years*, so that by the time he *was thirty years* of age, he was
" accomplished in the science of *the first principle*. He took the name of Xekia or Xaca: he
" taught his doctrine *for forty-nine years*. He had many scholars who spread his doctrine through
" all Asia."[1]   After this Alvarez goes on to shew, that the *wisest* of the sect have a secret religion, " placing their whole intent on the understanding of the first principle, (which is properly
" the doctrine of Xaca,) whom they believe to be the same in all things; and all things to be the
" same with him; without any essential difference; operating according to the extrinsic qualities
" of the subject; as wax is formed into several figures, the which being dissolved by liquefaction,
" remain in substance the self-same wax." After this he shews that they use the tonsure, that
they have nunneries and monasteries, and several other customs similar to the Christians; and
that they believe in the metempsychosis. They are called Bonzes.

The Chinese hold letters in religious veneration, and, when they have done with any writing,
burn it with peculiar ceremony.[2]   Semedo says, that to form all their multitude of letters, they
use only nine strokes—compounding them for new significations.[3]   Their mark for *ten* is a cross.
It is difficult here to avoid seeing the Arabic system. It appears[4] that they understand and
practise the stereotype printing or printing from blocks.[5]

Saca being one of the names of Buddha, of course all the particulars of the life of Buddha are
told of him;[6] and Saca is proved, over and over again, to be the origin of the words Sacæ and
and Saxons. It follows, then, that when I say all Europe was Saxon, I use the same kind of expression as when I say, all Europe is Christian. Saxon is the name of the religion—Buddha is
merely an appellative, meaning *wisdom* or the *wise Saca*. I believe the word Cama is similar.
Cama is ama or am or Ma or Om aspirated; or, perhaps, X-ama, ama with the Monogram, meaning *maternal love*. Camaria and Cama, or Coma-rina is the same. Comisé is used for Pisces;
X-om-iso, the same—the appellative of divine love. It should be remembered that every God was
a *saviour*.

Thus we have Cama-marina, Cama-maria, Cama-deva, Cama-isé, and Cama alone. And, with
the monogram, it resolves itself at last into the mysterious *Maria* or Maia, and we may now ask
whether we have not this word in Mare, *the sea*, and in the sacred mere or lake, and the Mount
Meru ?—whether Maria was not the aria of *M*—that is, *place of M*,—residence of the female generative power ? I beg to refer to the passage which I have given from Mr. Payne Knight on the
word Ice, and to what I have said on the subject of sacred water, in Volume I. pp. 530, 531, and
supra, p. 19.

I much suspect that the Cama was a corruption of the ancient word שמש *sam*, the name of the
Sun, and that we here have the name of Sema of Hierapolis,[7] of Semiramis, of Camarina, Comorin,
and of Zamorin, of South India. We have found Semiramis and the Sema-Rama of India closely
connected with the dove. We have found the Samaritans also attached to the worship of the

---

Selene, (probably the Palladium,) or the war between Venice and Bologna, for a picture of the Saviour, painted by
St. Luke.
Man is said to have been made after the image of the God of wisdom. Surely the Fabricator must have failed
totally !

[1] History of China, pp. 89, 90.
[2] Jesus was born from the side of his mother. (?)   He was tempted for forty days, in the desert.   He disputed with
the doctors at twelve years of age.   He began to preach at thirty.   Irenæus says, he lived about fifty years.
[3] Vide Alvarez Semedo, Hist. China, p. 34.   [4] Ib. p. 33.   [5] P. 34.
[6] See note, *supra*, p. 215.   [7] See Georgius's index.   [8] Vide Vol. I. p. 497.

doye; and I have formerly (Vol. I. p. 596) noticed, that the Samaritans, in some versions, are said to place their Ararat in Serendive, though where I have read this account I cannot recollect, and find I have not noted the authority for it; but it seems to shew a connexion of the ancient Jews (i. e. the Samaritans) with South India, the country where we found the Mosaic mythos. Now I have a strong suspicion, that they took their name of Sama-ritans from this worship of the Cama or Sama of South India. When we recollect the Mosaic mythos at Trichinopoly, we need not be surprised to find the Ararat in the sacred island in the same neighbourhood. The Calida or Colchis, the Judaic mythos, and the neighbouring Serendive or Ararat, greatly add to the probability of the origin which I have given of the word Samaritan.

Ca is used for the pronoun I, in Siam; *Noca* in Peru; *Anok* in Egypt; *Ego* in Chinese, Greek and Latin; *Agam* in Sanscrit; *Aku* in Malay; *Ic* in Saxon.[1] All these are the X. In the Chinese language Y is one.[2]

Webb, in his essay to prove the language of China the primitive language, writes the name of the Supreme Being XEAN-TIA, on the authority of Texeira, a Spanish author; but according to Père du Halde, and the French way of writing Chinese words, it is written Chang-ti, and Tchan-ti.[3] This shews the extreme difficulty of finding the truth, among the misrepresentations, intended and unintended, of authors, for want of some system. The Xean-tia may be *di* or *divus* Sion, *God of Sion*, of the Siamese; or, it may be X-eao, the ng=o, or Georgius's *cio*.

For a proof that the Chinese had the doctrine of the Trinity and the Fall of Adam, see Bryant on the Logos.[4]

The Tartars are called Nestorians by Forster. But he confesses that they are professors of the religion of the Lama. They, that is the Nestorians, use the words Hom-Mani-Pema-Om. They also use the language of the country.[5] This shews that these pretended Nestorians are only followers of Cristna.

13. We have seen the mythological character of the Cæsari. The author of a memoir of a map of the country near the Caspian sea, says, that their chief was called, by the Byzantine historians, Χαγανός, which he translates Khan. But here we certainly have the Saga or Xaca. He says they built a town and called it Σαρκελ, Sar-kel. This is the ancient Scotch or Saxon Kel or Cil, for church, and *ras* wisdom. Here we have a colony of the Chaldæan or Cæsarean mythologists, called by their proper name, the people of Xaga, Xaca, Saca, Sagesse, building themselves a city for their capital, and their temple of course, the name of which was the *city of the* Kel (Cil) or *temple* of the (ras) *wisdom*. The name of Cæsar so universally spread in the world, the consultation by Cæsar of the Chaldæan astronomers, to reform the calendar, and many other circumstances, tend to shew that Cæsar was a Chaldæan or initiated person. The Arabian Khosru was Cyrus and Cæsar. From the ancient word in numerals, T. S. R. or Tzar or Cæsar, came the Hebrew word for King, שר *sr*, and for Queen, שרה *sre*. Tr. and Sr. were, as I have before remarked, convertible terms in the numeral language. From the *Tr* came the Greek word Tyrannus. The Queen of the Scythians was called Zarina.[6]

Vallancey says, "The Lamas persuade the people, that their God Xaca, or Tschaka, was incar-
"nated 2000 years before our æra, to be born of a Virgin whom they name Lam-Oigh-iupral, that
"is, the Lama or Luam of Oigh-a-breall, as the Irish would express the name; i. e. Virgo clitoris
"castæ. Xaca, says Mons. de Paw, should be written Ischaka, and signifies Lord."[7] Here we

---

[1] Sharon Turner.   [2] Ency. Brit. art. Philology, p. 530.   [3] Malcolme's Letters.
[4] P. 290, Appendix.   [5] Forster's Disc. on the North, p. 105, 4to.
[6] Diod. Sic. Lib. ii. Cap. xxxiv.   [7] Vall. Coll. Vol. IV. Part I. p. 451.

have again the immaculate conception of Buddha, i. e. of Xaca. The Ischaka is *isha* or יש׳ *iso*, *the saviour Saca*. It is the Arabic name of Christ, Ischa.[1] Ishaka, is Saca with the Saxon or Celtic emphatic article. But Ishaka means *a fish* in Irish, and חכמה *ise* means *wisdom*.

Arrian[2] names the country of the Assaceni and of Astaceni, whose capital, Massaca or Massaga, he calls a *great city*. By Strabo this city is called Magosa or rather Mosaga. I apprehend A-saceni means *the* Sacœ. The first syllable being the emphatic article, included, as usual, in the name, and Ma-saga is *the great Saca*. We have formerly seen, *supra*, p. 2, that Herodotus stated that the Scythians and the Saxons were the same people. The following extract from Mr. Oconnor's Chronicles of Eri, p. cl., note, will shew us how this arose: " In the sixth chapter of " Melpomene, Herodotus says, ' generally speaking, these people are called Scoloti, but the " Greeks called them Skuthai.' In Scoloti, the *i* is mere termination, and the letter 'o' is Gre-" cian, for euphonia, *ore rotundo*. Now, if you sound the comparatively modern mutation *Scott*, " *Sciot*, from the original *Sagiot*, you will readily recognise the identity of all the many literal " changes in so many different countries, through so vast a space of time." Mr. Oconnor's observation seems to me to be perfectly correct. The Scythians, the Saxons, and the Chaldæans, all had the same name. Cato, *de Originibus*, notices the Scythia Saga. The Sagæ and Caldai had the same name. In Ireland Saga signifies *a priest*.[3] Stephen, Byzant. and Pliny state the Sacæ and Scythians to be the same.[4]

Saca is probably found in Egypt in Saca-ra; and in the district of Saïs is found a town called *Siuph*, probably the town now called *Sauafe*—our word *safe*, from יש׳ *iso, to save*. In Siuph, I think we have Soph. Saïs has been thought to be connected with Saca. It is not improbable, when all is considered which we have seen of the close connexion between the Saviour, wisdom, Logos, that both the ancient words for Saviour יש׳ *iso*[5] and the word for wisdom Σοφια should have come from the Se, Sio, or Cio, Χιν, Xaca, &c.; Saïs, *Salvation*,[6] and חכמה *ise, wisdom*.

The canal of Joseph runs between the lake Mœris and the Nile; and between them also is a place called Beni Suef. I suspect that Suef is Σοφ. May not Joseph be Io-συφ, *wisdom of Io?* On the west of Egypt is the desert of Selimé, i. e. Solomon, שלמה *slme*.[7] This cannot have been named after the Jews of Jerusalem. Was not Selimé in the Montes Solumi or Mons Æsar of Ptolemy? This confirms the doctrines of the Abbé Guerin de Rocher.

Mr. Alwood[8] says, he thinks Typhon is the same as Suph-on, the word סוף *sup* of the Hebrews, meaning *destroyer*. This, as usual, comes from the Creator, Logos or Wisdom being the same as the Destroyer.

14. I have a suspicion, that the Amphibolus was the Pallium, and the same as the Sagum of the Saxons; and that their chief magistrate or *Cyning* was the Sophi, the Ras, or the Canning man, and at last the King. The Pallium is made of white lamb's wool, the lamb having been offered on the altar by the nuns of St. Agnes. The Amphibolus I have ridiculed in my CELTIC DRUIDS, p. 201, as the origin of the Saint whose adventures are told by the Romish church. This furnishes a good example of a mythos described under the guise of a history. But in fact under this guise

---

[1] See Vol. I. p. 583.   [2] See Hist. India, ch. i.
[3] Vall. Coll. Hib. Vol. V. pp. 11, 12, also p. 23.   [4] Ib.
[5] Of יש׳ *is* and יש׳ *isi* and יש׳ *ise* enough has been said—the same of *Lama*. I think Is-lam is the doctrine of the *Lama of Is*. (See the Appendix to Vol I.) The name of *Sinan*, the chief of the Assassins, was probably יש׳ *sin*—s=300, i=10, n=50=360—*Sin*. Saladin is probably Sul-ad-in, or Sul=336, and-Ad. I have little doubt that the ancient orientalists considered it religious to adopt the mystic names of God, as we do to adopt the names of our Saints, Matthew, John, &c.
[6] See Nimrod, Vol. III. p. 195.   [7] Rgyn. Herod. Vol. II. p. 165.   [8] P. 252.

much lies hid. When Elijah left his *prophetic* power to Elisha,¹ he conferred it on him or installed him in his office, by the *investiture* of the Cloak, or *Pallium*,—the power of the Vates, or Bed or Ved or Bud, or the Pall, the Pallas, the Palladium of Ter-ia, or Troy, was conferred on him; for all these words, applied to different purposes and several of them the same, only corrupted, mean *Wisdom*. In the Roman church, though a man may be elected by his suffragans, he is no Archbishop till he has the Pallium *from the God on Earth* or *the Vicar of God*, who has, *quoad hoc*, the power. It was the origin of the Palace or Pola or πυλις, or the King's-Bench, where he administered justice, and it is the Divan, Div-ania, *place of holiness* or חפש *spe* or Sopha, of Eastern despots—the *sacred* or *secret place*. In the middle ages, we read of great struggles between popes and kings—the latter wishing to have the power of investiture of the bishops with the Pallium, which the former never would grant. In fact, to part with this, was to part with an essential portion of their sacred character or power. If they had consented, they could not thereby have prevented the kings' having the power of communicating divine inspiration. I suspect the investiture with the Pallium was a higher species of χειροτονια.

As we might well expect, we find the Tam in the Greek word Θεμιςες, meaning *Laws*, ORACLES:² and Θεμις *the Goddess of Oracles*. חן *tm* has also the meaning of perfection, truth; this is closely connected with the Sacred Wisdom. It has also the same meaning as the אלפ *pla*—wonder, miracle. I have no doubt that it had the mystic meaning of wisdom; and, as it was the name of the Palm-tree, the tree, ever-*green*, supposed to be everlasting or to renew itself for ever from its roots, the favourite tree of the East, and the blessing of the Desert, it was carried before Jesus Christ, by his followers, in the procession to the Temple,³ as the emblem of *everlasting wisdom*. I have no doubt that the sacred or secret books of some sects, called the books of perfection, had also the meaning of *wisdom*. Of course all this is kept out of lexicons, by those who suppressed the meaning of the word Rasit.

Mr. Turner⁴ says, the leaves of the Palm-tree, in Tibet, are indestructible by vermin. If this be the case, here we see a beautiful reason for this tree being an emblem of eternity, and also of wisdom, engraved on its leaves, and of its connexion with letters.

We have seen that Cyrus was a solar epithet. Dr. Parsons says, "Between the Caspian and "Euxine seas there formerly dwelt two sorts of people, the one called *Rosci*,⁵ on the river Cyrus, "or rather on the *Ros*, *Ras*, or *Aras*, called by the Greeks Araxes.⁶ Here we have the solar title and the Ras or Wisdom identified; but, on the South-west of the Caspian, there is a town, called by Fraser⁷ Reach or Resht, the capital of Ghilan, in Mazanderan, which contains about 80,000 people. I beg my reader to recollect that the chief of the Assassins, the *tenth* Avatar,⁸ came from Ghilan. We see that the capital of the country which he left, to come to Western Syria, was called *the town of wisdom*. This countenances what I have said, that his object in coming to the West was to possess himself of the real city of Solomon.

The ancient Etruscans had a story of a certain Tages, who arose from the earth, and taught them all kinds of useful knowledge. The discovery that Etruria, the country of Itala or Vitula or the Bull, was originally called *Ras-ena* or the country of the Vine or of Wisdom, has nearly convinced me, that this Tages ought to be Sages, Sagesse, or Sagax.⁹ When the changes of the T for the

---

¹ "He took up also the mantle of Elijah that fell from him." 2 Kings ii. 13.
² See Parkhurst, in voce חן *tm*, p. 787.   ³ John xii. 13.   ⁴ P. 318.
⁵ The capital of Denmark was called Roschild. The son of Odin was called Sciold; the poets are called Scaldes.
⁶ Rem. of Japhet, p. 65.   ⁷ Travels in Persia, pp. 124, 151.
⁸ See Vol. I. pp. 700, 704, &c.   ⁹ Vide Creuzer, Vol. II. pp. 458—462.

S, and of the S for the St, &c., are considered, it will not be thought that I am very credulous, in suspecting that this famous Tages, who arose from the ground to teach the Etruscans learning and science, ought to be Sages or Sagax.

15. The doctrine which I have taught of an universal Catholic or Pandæan Judaic mythos having every where prevailed, I know from its singularity and its opposition to the priesthood of the present day, will, at first, be treated only with contempt: but there are certain facts which must be accounted for, or in the end the theory will prevail, or I ought rather to say the truth will be no longer doubted. It is a certain fact, that the temple of Solomon and the tomb of Moses existed in Cashmere when the Mohamedans arrived there, and were destroyed by them; therefore they were not named by them, or built by them. The city of Oude or Ioudia, the Montes Solumi, country of Daudpotri, &c., are in the same predicament if they are admitted to have had these names before the arrival of the Mohamedans; and this cannot be denied. It is not credible that these places should have been built, or had these names given to them, by the emigrant Samaritans, the bitter enemies of the system of David, Solomon, &c. The above are *proved* facts, not theories, and must be accounted for.

The same system is found near Cape Comarin; in Siam; in China; and in Mexico: all these things must be accounted for. It is true, the whole detail of the system is not found in the latter places to be exactly the same as it is in the former, because the system is accommodated to the country, and to existing circumstances in each case; but the fragments of it which are found, which, like the broken pillars and capitals when found, prove a temple anciently to have existed, render it highly probable that the very same system once existed. Indeed, they do more, they *prove* it: while the fact that, with these fragments the most important parts of the Christian system are found to have been amalgamated before the Christian æra, raises a grand obstacle to the truth of the Judæan and Christian system, *as at present laid down*. It may be fairly asked, How comes the Christian doctrine—the crucifixion for instance—if there was an ancient Judæan doctrine and the crucifixion was a part of it, not to be clearly found in the system of Moses and the Jews of Western Syria? I contend that the whole Crestian mythos was an esoteric system; the system concealed in the mysteries and in the Jewish unwritten Cabala; which, in this case, will have been, in reality, no way different from the ancient mysteries of the Gentiles. The opinion that there was a Cabala or unwritten doctrine among the Jews was never denied. If there were such a thing, it *must* have been taught somewhere, in some place, to its possessors, and this place *must* have been their temple, though we read nothing about it. Thus, in fact, there must have been Jewish initiations at Jerusalem as well as at Eleusis. We know that circumcision, baptism, confirmation, and I believe the eucharist, the doctrine of a murdered and resuscitated person, were all parts of the secret mysteries; the former three of these we know for certain were Jewish, and the Apocrypha tells us the last was.[1]

That there is not a more full account of the adventures of the incarnate God in the Jewish canon, proves a fact which is, indeed, proved by a thousand other circumstances—that the mythos was originally an unwritten secret, kept in all countries from the mass of mankind, or a secret kept in allegories or parables, but chiefly in the latter, the favourite resource of the religion. The knowledge of the regenerated and reincarnated God was probably never openly published, as long as it could be kept concealed. It was a great mystery. It constituted the high mystery in all the temples in which the high mysteries were celebrated. There is not a country where the

---

[1] The Author does not here quote any passage from the Apocrypha, but he probably had in view Ecclus. ii. 2, 3, 5, 6, 7, and Wisdom ii. 13—20. See *supra*, p. 124. *Editor.*

leading points of it are not to be discovered, and always, when discovered, found to have been carefully hidden—points sufficiently important and sufficiently numerous to warrant the conclusion, that the remainder of the system must have been known, though perhaps it is not now in our power to discover it. But I do not doubt when the very existence of the iconoclastic temple became endangered by the violence of the idolaters, the books of the Apocrypha, or secret doctrine, were written to preserve it, if possible, from being lost. But though we do not find the *eight* Saviours clearly made out in the books of the Jewish canon, yet we have found one of them in the Apocrypha;[1] and they are most clearly and repeatedly foretold in the Targums by the term Messiah. The Jews were always expecting this Messiah. They believed Julius Cæsar, and, afterward Herod, to be the Messiah. But, as neither of them restored the kingdom of Solomon, he was no longer regarded as a Messiah; he passed away and was forgotten. But their books clearly state, that Cyrus *was* a Messiah: that was, because he restored their Temple.[2]

16. I some time ago made an observation on the attachment of Pythagoras and the ancients to music. I have no doubt that music was closely connected with religion. All the ancient unwritten mysteries, (and all mysteries were once unwritten,) were originally preserved in rhythm or metre, and *set* to music, or *contained* in or *preserved* by music. Rhythm, metre, and music, were all invented for the purpose of aiding the memory—of assisting it more correctly to retain the sacred numbers, &c. For many generations after the use of letters became public, there were no writings in prose: all were in poetry or rhythm. All the stone pillars in the temples, erected or placed according to the numbers of the cycles, were partly for this same purpose. The sacred dances and scenic representations were for the double purpose of doing honour to the God and aiding the memory;[3] precisely as the scenic representations of the acts of Jesus Christ by the Romish church originally were, or perhaps are at this day; and of which the plays called mysteries in Elizabeth's time were a remnant. The Bards were an order to preserve and regulate the choirs, the Salii to preserve and regulate the dances. The origin of the Salii was, in fact, unknown to the Romans, and they were equally ignorant of many other of their institutions. The Salii were originally twelve in number. Their chief was called Præ-Sul,[4] which serves to shew that they were properly Sul-ii—*priests of Sol.* They had an officer called Vates, *a musician:* they were probably all Bards. But the most important of these rites were the processions, or voyages of salvation, or what were called the Deisuls.[5] In these, I have no doubt, that the whole life and adventures of the incarnate God were represented—from his birth to his resurrection and ascension.

The exact process which took place in the formation of the Bardic order cannot, perhaps, be clearly made out; but there can be little doubt that it became almost exclusively devoted to the composing and singing of the sacred songs. Originally all sacrifices were feasts, and feasts were sacrifices in honour of the Deity; at these the Bards sung their sacred songs. And it was not till these matters became common, that the Bards descended to celebrate the praises of love and war. At first, these feasts were strictly confined to the temple, and to the elect; but, as the labouring

---

[1] The Author again omits quoting any passages in proof of his assertion; but he probably had in view those referred to above, and as given at length in p. 124. *Editor.*

[2] See 2 Chron. xxxvi. 22, 23; Ezra. iv. 3, v. 13—17; Isaiah xliv. 28, xlv. 1—4. *Editor.*

[3] It is observed by Niebuhr, that the ancients never grounded their tragedies on real, but on *mythic* history only. Rom. Hist. Vol. I. p. 341, Ed. Walter.

[4] These were priests of the Sun; and I suspect they were πρεσ-συλ, and from hence our word priest might be derived. See *supra*, p. 179.

[5] See *supra*, pp. 20, 21.

classes became more enlightened, they insisted upon joining their superiors; and, by degrees, they discovered all the secrets: till, at last, *horribile dictu*, there is now scarcely a secret left! I have formerly stated that Clemens confessed that the Judæan mythos was in the ceremonies of Eleusis.¹ These were the continuation of the celebration of the mythos from the time when it was really secret. What else could cause them to be in the secret mysteries?

17. I believe, as I have repeatedly remarked, that for many generations the arts of reading, writing, and the higher branches of arithmetic, were secret, sacred, and astrological; that they were solely confined to the priesthood, which, chiefly by their means, ruled all nations; that one system of *sixteen* letters pervaded the whole world, and the priesthood was probably that of which we read so much in the Indian books, described by the name of the empire of Pandæa. If at first the written language were the same as the spoken, yet a moment's reflection will shew, that the latter would diverge in a variety of ways, in different countries, as time advanced. This is the allegory of the *confusion of tongues* mentioned in Genesis. We every where read of a sacred, *lost* language. We find this tradition with the Tamuls, with the Brahmins, with the Greeks, with the Druids, indeed, with all nations. And I am quite certain, that if the language of numeral symbols was not the lost language, the Synagogue Hebrew, in consequence of the state of seclusion in which it has been kept in the temple, is now nearer to it than any other.

The doctrine of probabilities, taught by Dr. Young,² respecting languages, is very important, and applies in a very marked manner to almost all my speculations. He has remarked, "that nothing could be inferred with respect to the relation of two languages from the coincidence of the sense of any single word in both of them, that is, supposing the same simple and limited combination of sounds to occur in both, but to be applied accidentally to the same number of objects, without any common links of connexion; and that the odds would only be three to one against the agreement of two words; but if three words appeared to be identical, it would be more than ten to one that they must be derived, in both cases, from some parent language, or introduced in some other manner from a common source. Six words would give near 1700 chances to one, and eight would give near 100,000; so that, in these last cases, the evidence would be little short of absolute certainty." Now, admitting that there are 339 words in Greek and Sanscrit identical;³ what are the odds? But admitting this fact, that there are 339 Greek, and 263 Persian words, the same as in the Sanscrit, what is the doctrine of chances? And again, admitting that there are in the Sanscrit and the German 163 words identical, how stands the doctrine of chances? Is it probable that the Sanscrit is derived from the *three*, or the three from *it*, or all the *four* from a common source?

We may always calculate upon the same causes, in similar circumstances, producing the same effects. We every where see, that spoken language becomes so completely changed, in a very few years, as to have merely a resemblance to what it was a few years preceding. This we see in all illiterate tribes, and to a considerable degree even in nations which have their languages fixed by dictionaries and grammatical rules. Now in all the written languages, even those which are the most distant from each other, we find a surprising identity of words having the same meaning; for instance, we will take the Sanscrit and English, as in the Sanscrit word *sam*, and English word *same*, both meaning, *like, similar*. This I suppose to have arisen from the secret, unspoken language of ciphers or figures having extended over the whole world, and continuing fixed for many generations, after all similarity in the spoken languages had disappeared. I think the words which we find reduplicated, in the different and distant languages, are the words of the secret, numeri-

---

¹ See Vol. I. pp. 822—825.   ² See *supra*, pp. 175, 176.   ³ See Vol. I. p. 449.

cal, or sacred language, accidentally fallen into common use. I think the example of the seventy-three languages or systems of letters, all having the Arabic for their foundation, treated of in the work found by Mr. Von Hammer in Egypt, raises a strong presumption that Arabic (which I consider to be, in fact, Hebrew) was the parent of the whole, when in its early Cufic state, though now, no doubt, in every way changed. The fact that almost all the roots of the Hebrew are found in the Arabic, proves them to be only close dialects of one another. This idea also is supported by the place to which I have traced the Arabic—North India—where we found an Arabia and a Suracena. I need not remind my reader, that the Syriac is a close dialect of the Arabic and Hebrew; and it is scarcely possible to believe that its names of Pushto and Estrangelo should be given to the ancient *sixteen* letter language, (now called Tamul,) without its being, or having originally been, the same language.[1] Let it be remembered that the Judæan mythos is found in both North and South India. It is also expedient to retain in recollection, that the Thamas is, in a very peculiar manner, found both in Western Syria and in the Tamul-speaking part of India.

After I had come to the conclusion, that the first language must have been a language of ciphers or symbols, I was informed by a very learned orientalist, who had never heard of my theory, that, after long and careful examination of many of the unknown characters in which vast numbers of inscriptions in India are written, he had made up his mind that they were written in cipher. Here we have an admission which might reasonably be expected, if my theory be true. These inscriptions are remains of the first system now forgotten. They are examples also of the commencement of the practice of putting inscriptions on buildings. This cryptographic system is not yet entirely disused in India.

When we consider the great number of letters having the same sound, and therefore totally unnecessary, the truth, that the system was formed for *numbers* and not for letters, becomes more apparent. In the seventy examples in Mr. Hammer's work, we find, in fact, seventy examples of the original, *first* numerical alphabet reduced to practice as letters, but all evidently founded on the Arabic system of notation, ending, at last, with hieroglyphics. The fact of the Mexicans having the knowledge of the powers of *notation* and not of *letters*, confirms what I have said. In reality, the hieroglyphics of Mexico must have been like these seventy alphabets, and as easily read. No person originally inventing an alphabet would ever think of inventing so many letters for the same sound as are found in these alphabets. The difference between the Mexican and Egyptian hieroglyphics is this: the former are meant to be public, the latter are meant to be secret to all but the initiated. These seventy alphabets are seventy examples of learned men, converting the Arabic numeral system to the purpose of literature, each, as the book says, to contain and conceal his peculiar doctrines; but which any person would be able to read into a certain given *written*, though, perhaps, *not spoken* language, who understood the notatory key which I have given in the numbers in figure 1, of my Plates.

I consider the chequers still used in our exchequer (as I am told)[2] a remarkable example of the first custom of counting by stones. The calculi of Italy we call chequers, as well as the squares on a table. Mr. Von Hammer says the numerical signs (called by us Arabic, and, by the *Arabs*, more properly *Indian numbers*), *used, vice versâ, for letters*, form an alphabet, which is generally known, and particularly used in the daftardam, or treasury office, for accounts.[3]

Isaiah (xxxiv. 4), when properly translated, says, "The heavens shall be rolled up because they are *a book*." Postellus says, "whatever is in nature, is to be read in the heavens." Sir W.

---

[1] Vide Georgius, Alph. Tib. p. 583.
[2] Hammer on Anc. Alph. p. vi. Lond. 1806.
[r] Their use was abolished in 1834.

Drummond, on the prophecy of Jacob, has almost proved this. I suspect that the whole was of the nature of a perpetual almanac for the cycle of the neros, and that the Zodiacs of Esne and Dendera were also for this purpose, only in an earlier day. On this principle it is that the Janampatri of Cristna will be found to give his birth, as Mr. Bentley admits, for the 600 years before, or the 600 years after Christ, or at the birth of Christ. But still I think the workmanship of the long zodiac will prove to have been executed, when the midsummer solstice was in neither Leo nor Virgo, but just changing from one to the other,—was a Sphinx, half Leo, half Virgo. If there be any thing like strong probability respecting this monument, it is, that it has its date, as now fixed by me, from the work of Sir William Drummond on this subject.

For thousands of years man would want to record nothing but cycles, and of these he would have daily and most pressing need; the knowledge of them from their very difficult and abstruse nature would necessarily be a secret. They are, in fact, a secret in this enlightened country. How few persons in Britain could of themselves make out the length of the solar year! This is a natural effect of a natural cause. The knowledge of this abstruse science would fall, of itself, into very few hands, and it would give its possessors the dominion over the remainder. The regulation of their seed-time and harvest, and all their religious festivals, would be with the Cyclopes.

Cicero calls the country where the Chaldæans lived Syria; and Lucian, who was born in Syria, calls himself sometimes a Syrian, and sometimes an Assyrian.[1] Of this country, Heliopolis was the capital. It was anciently called the city of Zobah. This was Saba, *Wisdom*. The province was Cyrrhestica (Crest-ica).[2] The temple at Heliopolis had its sacred *fishes* and *tank*, exactly like those of India at this day; and its temple was surrounded with forty pillars.[3] Its kings were called Ad, and Adad. In front of the temple was an immense Linga. Syria and Assyria seem to have been confounded together. Its language has been thought the oldest in the world, because places and persons named by Moses are better derived from the Syriac language than from any other.[4] It has twenty-two letters, which, with only a difference in shape, are evidently the same as the Hebrew. The Universal history says, "The Syriac was not only the language of "Syria, but also of Mesopotamia, Chaldæa, (for there is no more difference between the Chaldee "and the Syriac than between the English and Scotch,) Assyria, and, after the Babylonish capti- "vity, of Palestine."[5] Dr. Hagar says, "The Estrangelo or ancient Syriac, which is also called "Chaldaic."[6] This Syriac character consisted of lines at angles; the following is a specimen of it:

ܐܟܒܓܕܗܘܙ[7]

Sir William Jones says, "The gross *Pahlavi* was improved by Zeradusht, or his disciples, into "an elegant and perspicuous character, in which the Zendavesta was copied; and both were "written from the right hand to the left, like other Chaldaic alphabets, for they are manifestly "both of Chaldean origin."[8] Again, he says, "The oldest discoverable languages of Persia were "*Chaldaic* and *Sanscrit*."[9] Again, "The square Chaldaic letters found on Persian ruins, appear "to have been the same with the Devanagari before the latter were enclosed in angular frames."[10] When we consider that the Chaldee and the Hebrew are really the same, and we find the Sanscrit here using the Chaldee forms of their letters, only with the addition of a frame as it is called, how

---

[1] Hagar on Bab. Bricks, p. 12.
[2] Univ. Anc. Hist. Vol. I. p. 347.
[3] Asiat. Res. Vol. II. p. 57.
[4] Anc. Hist. Vol. II. pp. 285, &c.
[5] Ib. Vol. II. p. 292.
[6] Ib. p. 54.
[7] See Maundrell.
[8] Bab. Bricks, p. 37.
[9] Ibid. p. 44.
[10] Ib. p. 58.

can we well doubt that the Chaldee or Hebrew must have been the original root of the Sanscrit? Again, "His Pahlavi (i. e. Anquetil's) strongly confirms my opinion concerning the Chaldaic origin " of that language."¹ Again, "Examination gave me perfect conviction that the Pahlavi was a " dialect of the Chaldaic."² Again, he says, "The ancient letters of Cufah, had unquestionably " a common origin with the Hebrew or Chaldaic."³ Nothing can be more certain than that the Syriac letter is a varied form of the Hebrew; and it is nothing but the inclination every one feels to multiply and divide ancient matters of every kind which prevents this being seen.⁴ Sir W. Jones says, that the Armenian language was originally the same as the Zend and the Pahlavi.⁵. When we consider that all the Judæan or Chaldæan mythos is here, this is what we might expect.

I believe the most common of all the causes of confusion in languages has arisen from the almost universal mistake of learned men, in supposing that, because they see different forms of letters, they see different original alphabets. If they could be brought really to consider them all the same (the different forms of letters making no difference) with only some trifling corruptions, as is really the truth, they would instantly see what a mass of confusion would disappear. I may as well be told that our three forms of capitals, small capitals, and small letters, (to say nothing of our *written* characters,) are three alphabets, or that the Greek two forms $ΑΒΓΔ$, $αβγδ$, are two alphabets. Mr. Von Hammer's book has completely established the fact, that all the nations had one alphabet anciently, as the French, German, and English, have only one alphabet now.

On the Syriac language, Mr. Astle says, "It was also the language of Mesopotamia and Chal-" dea.—As to the arts and learning of the Syrians, they were by some anciently joined with the " Phenicians, as the first inventors of letters; but without entering into this matter, certain it is " that they yielded to no nation in human knowledge and skill in the fine arts. From their happy " situation they may almost be said to have been in the centre of the old world; and in the zenith " of their empire, they enriched themselves with the spoils, tribute, and commerce, of the nations " far and near, and arose to a great pitch of splendour and magnificence. Their language is pre-" tended to have been the vernacular of all the oriental tongues."⁶ Again, he says, "The Syrians " therefore are supposed to have been the first people who brought the Persian and Indian com-" modities into the west of Asia."⁷ Their letters are of two sorts—the Estrangelo and the Fshito.⁸ I think neither of these words is understood; but the word Fshito, into which the word Pushto is written, is an excellent example of the mode in which modern writers caricature ancient words.

---

¹ Asiat. Res. Vol. II. pp. 52, 53. ² Ib. p. 52. See also p. 64. ³ Ib. p. 7.
⁴ Ancient Arabic letters are the same as Cufic, twenty-eight in number. The present Arabic characters were invented by Ebn Moklah, 300 years after Mohamed. Ency. Brit. Vol. I. p. 727.
⁵ Asiat. Res. Vol. III. p. 12. ⁶ P. 38. ⁷ Ib. ⁸ See Univ. Anc. Hist. Vol. II. pp. 293, 294.

(238)

CHAPTER III.

ROMA. FLORA. PUSHTO.—ALLEGORY OF THE FLOWER CONTINUED.—GENERAL OBSERVATIONS.—ALLEGORIES.—ALLEGORIES CONTINUED.—RETROSPECT.

1. WE have seen the way, or something very like it, in which man first discovered the written language of numerical symbols, and by what steps he probably proceeded to discover the art of alphabetic, syllabic writing. After he had discovered the advantage and followed the practice of calling the sun by the different combinations of figures which made up his first cycle of 666, and which, as I have shewn, proceeded from unthought-of and unforeseen circumstances, he would begin to try to form the next words or the remainder of his written language, whether it were symbolic or syllabic, upon some system; and I think we have an example of this in the connexion of the various words having a relation to the first superstition, that is, to the adoration of the female generative principle, in the words Flora, flower, flour, pollen, Pallas, &c., &c. We shall discover examples of this in the history of the name of the *eternal city*, Roma, which we shall find to have a near relationship to the letters of the Tamuls of India.

Though the Tamuls now chiefly reside in the southern part of the Peninsula, yet it will not be denied, I think, that the Tangut and Tangitani of the North of India are the same in name as the people of Tangiers, and Trichinopoly, and the Telingana country, or Trilinga[1] of the South.[2] We have found in North India the country of Daud or David or Daoudpotra,[3] or the country of the children of David. On the coast of Coromandel, or the Taujeer or Tanjore coast, we have, in the country of the Telingana language, a district called Dravida, from which, no doubt, our fortress there has very properly taken the name of Fort St. David. In the same way the Portuguese, settling near the tomb of the holy Tamas, called it, and properly so, the settlement of St. Thomas. One name of Tibet is Pue-achim or Puek-achim. The meaning of the word Achim is clear; the Pue or Puek is probably the same as Push, meaning *flower*. It is said to mean North,[4] but it evidently is, either the country of the wisdom of the flower, or of the flower of wisdom. But here we see obvious signs of the universal mythos. The learned Georgius shews, that the language of the Tangutani was probably that called *Estrangelo Syriæ*: here, by another road, we arrive at the Pushto again, for Pushto was the name both of the Syriac language, and of that of the Tamul in South India. And it may be well not to forget the Tanga-Tanga of South America, and the traces of the Hebrew language which we found there, and that the Pushto has a manifest resemblance to the Chaldaic. Sir William Jones says, the language of the Afghans in North India is called Pukhto or Pushto,[5] and it is EVIDENTLY Chaldaic. The chief town of their country is called

---

[1] We may be permitted to ask the meaning of the words Telingana and Trilinga. The second at once offers us the meaning of triple language; but I think this is not its import, and that it will mean the *triple Linga*, the emblem of the Trimurti; and that Telinga means only the country or *ana* of the Linga, by the Hebrew name of תלפן *told* or תולד *tuld*, which has the meaning of Linga. In English, we have the word in tali or tally. Telinga is the same word as Kalinga, but it is written and pronounced by the islander *Kaling*. Crawfurd; Ind. Arch. Hist. Jav. Vol. II. p. 226.

[2] Vide Hamilton.

[3] Daud is Dis or Di-oud—the *holy* man of Oud or of Ayoudia. From reference to this, he is called the "man after God's own heart." This is similar to the Talut of Saul, noticed in Volume I. pp. 546, 740, 741.

[4] Ency. Lond. in voce Tibet.   [5] Asiat. Res. Vol. II. pp. 68, 76.

BOOK III. CHAPTER III. SECTION 1.

Paish-wer, or Paish-or, that is Paish-town.¹ It is situated 34°. 6′. N. L., 71°. 13′. E. Lon., on the Cabul, and was built or more properly rebuilt by Akbar. The Afghans are said to be partly Sunnis and partly Shiahs:² whence I conclude, though they may be Mohamedans, they are of neither sect, but of the Sofees, who existed before Mohamed, one of whom I have shewn him to have been. They are called Rohillas and Solaimani, and also Patans,³ and I believe Battanians. They dwell on the Mount of Solomon.

A writer in the Oriental Repertory⁴ says, the Afghans or Avghans have a language called Peshtu. *It has a peculiar character,* and seems *to be* FULL OF OLD PERSIAN. They are settled near Aud, where they are called Rohillas, and in the Deccan they are called Patans.⁵ The *proper* name, that is the *old* name of the Afghans, is Pooshtoon, and in the plural Pooshtauneh. It is also called Pookhtauneh, whence the name Pitan, by which they are known in India.⁶

I sought long, and inquired among my oriental friends, for the root of Pushto or Pushpo; but nothing like a root could I find, till I had recourse to the system of figures, and there I found it; and it is very remarkable that not one of the names of the first Gods, which I have found in figures, is to be traced to any rational or intelligible etymon. Nothing could well be more in favour of the system than this: Pusto is P=80, S=200, T=300, O=70=650. Pustp is P=60, U=6, S=200, T=300, P=80=666. Petalon is P=80, T=400, L=50, O=70, N=50=650. I will thank any friend to give me an intelligible etymon, either of Pusto or Petalon.

Thus the language of the Syrians and the Tamuls, of the Afghans and the Arabians, the Estrangelo, or of the Chaldæans and the Jews, was the language of the Flower—650: and what flower was this, but the flower which grew in Carmel, the garden of God, which grew in Nazareth, or in the place of the Natzir? What flower was this but the flower of which we so often read; which gave a name to the capital of Persia—Susiana or Susa—the Lily or Lotus? What flower but the water rose, the rose of Ise, Iseur, Isuren, of Sharon? "Susan, Lilium vel Rosa, Uxor Joachim."⁷

This was the flower κατ' εξοχην, described in Parkhurst by the פץ אז with a mutable but omissible ה *e*, meaning *to open* or *burst open*, and by the word פצה *psx, to open,* and by the word פץ *zx, to break open as a flower,* and as a noun פץ *ziz, a flower.* Here in the word פצה *psx* we have the Push-to. The word פץ *zx* is translated in the LXX. by the word πεταλον, a leaf, which Parkhurst says ought rather to have been a flower; and that flower, I doubt not, was the Lotus.⁸

An old picture found in Palestine by Dr. Clarke induced him to make some remarks on the Lotus or Lily, which, he observes, almost always accompanies the figure of the Virgin. He says, that Nazareth, at this time, signifies *a flower,* and, from St. Jerom, that Nazareth in Hebrew signifies *a flower.* This is the Lotus, equally sacred in India, Egypt, Greece and Syria. The bean which it produced in the Nile and Ganges, was that which, when the mythos was lost, was believed by the votaries of Pythagoras to be forbidden, in his mystics, to be eaten,⁹ but which he really never forbade.

The reader has seen the explanation of the Lotus or Lily, given by Mr. Knight, in Volume I. pp. 339, 340, and the reason why it was an emblem of the prolific powers of nature. We see that

---

¹ From this probably comes the title of Pesihwa.   ² Asiat. Res. Vol. II. p. 74.   ³ Ib. 73.
⁴ Vol. II. p. 249.
⁵ The circumstance, that the Hebrew, Samaritan, and Syriac or Pushto, have each twenty-two letters, and these the same letters, shews their original identity.
⁶ Elph. Cabul, Vol. I. p. 242.   ⁷ Vall. Coll. Hib. Vol. IV. Part I: p. 264.
⁸ I beg my reader to refer to the Virgin and the Rose, in Mexico, *supra*, p. 32.
⁹ Clarke, Vol. II. p. 411, Ed. 4to.

Dr. Clarke says the Lily is an emblem of Christ, because the word Nazareth means *a flower*. But if I admit this means *lily*, does it not mean *a flower?* Clarke states, that " Marinus Sanutus " says, ' Hæc est illa amabilis civitas Nazareth, quæ *florida* interpretatur: in quâ flos campi ori- " tur, dum in Virgine Verbum caro efficitur........Ornatus tamen illo nobili flore, super quem " constat spiritum Domini quievisse. Ascendet, inquit Isayas, flos de radice Jesse, et requiescet " super eum Spiritus Domini." It is surprising that Dr. Clarke should have forgot, that the Lily was sacred in Greece, in Egypt, in Syria, in the Jewish temple, and in India; and the bean of the water lily every where among the Pythagoreans. Christ was called a Nazarene because, according to Jerom, Nazir means *a flower*.[1] Fuller, in his Palestine, calls Christ both *rose* and *lily*.[2]

Nazareth, the town of Nazir or Ναζωραιος, *the flower*, was situated in Carmel, the vineyard or garden of God. Jesus was a flower; whence came the adoration, by the Rossicrucians, of the Rose and Cross, which Rose was Ras, and this Ras, or knowledge or wisdom, was stolen from the garden, which was also crucified, as he literally is, on the red cornelian, the emblem of the Rossicrucians—a Rose on a Cross. This crucified flower-plant was also liber, a book, a letter or tree, or Bacchus or IHΣ. This IHΣ was Logos, Linga, letters, L'FR=650. The God was also called Rose or Ras, because he was R=200, O=70, Z=90=360; or *Rose*=365; RS=RST=600; the Rose *of the Water*, or *Water-rose*, as it is called to this day. But this Rose of Sharon, this Logos, this word, was called in Arabic and Chaldæan *werta* and *werd* the same as our *word*.[3] Thus it was both the Linga, the generative principle, and Lingua, a word, or words, language. How curiously the system is interwoven, like rods of willows into a basket! It was Flora, Φλρ =650, which was the Flora of the Romans, and the פרח *pre* of the Hebrews, both meaning *a flower*. The famous Hesperides was the Hebrew עץ *oz* פרי *pri*. The פרי *pri* means *flower*, but the עץ *oz* means *letters* as well as *à tree;* and, I have no doubt, is closely connected, in some secret way, with the allegory of the Arbor magna, cujus rami sunt literæ, &c. Push-to and Push-pa are the same. Push, which means flower, is the root of both. The corruption is not greater between Pushto and Pushpa, than between Pema and Padma,—names of the Lotus. We have found Buddha called Pema, Padma, the Lotus, a flower. We have found him called Potisato; therefore Poti-sato meant *flower*. This strengthens my conviction that the Pushpa and Pushto were the same, and that, in consequence, the languages of Western and Eastern Syria, and Tamul, were the same, or at least had the same name. I have observed, (in p.   ,) from the Universal History, that the Mendæan alphabet was the Pushto or Estrangelo. Now the alphabet given by Hyde, and said by him to have been carried into China by the Tartars, is called the Mendæan. It is clearly the Hebrew in system.

The root פר *pr*, פרה *pre*, or פרח *prh*, in Hebrew means fecundus, fruit, blossoms; and from this as Parkhurst teaches, by a corruption, probably comes the Goddess Flora, or it is the same as the Goddess Flora. See Parkhurst, in voce, פרח *prh* II. and פרה *pre*. Sir William Ouseley[4] says, Flora Φορα—Flora fertility—פרה *pre* fertility, a young heifer, a flower; he says, they call the Euphrates φορα, which means *flower*. The Hebrew פרה *prh* meaning *flower*, I have little doubt, was the origin of the name of the Euphrates. I cannot help suspecting that Flora was an anagrammatic corruption of L'phora, that is, ל-פרה *L-pre*. I should not venture to derive Flower or Flora from Phora, had I not Parkhurst's authority, but I think his reasons quite justify him.[5]

---

[1] Tom. I. Epis. 17, ad Marcellam. [2] Book ii. Ch. vi. p. 143.
[3] Asiat. Res. Vol. II. p. 53.   [4] Trans. Soc. Lit. Vol. I. p. 112: he cites Josephus, Antiq. Jud.
[5] When I observe that the Apocalypse is almost filled with praises of the slain lamb, with which, in a remarkable manner, it connects the cycle of 144; that the ceremony of the slain lamb is connected with the flower and the pollen.

BOOK III. CHAPTER III. SECTION 1.

In addition to what I have said in several places respecting the similarity of Cristna and Jesus Christ, I now request my reader to observe (what I formerly overlooked), that the celebrated Arjoon, the brother of Cristna, is nothing but John with the epithet *Ar* prefixed. And I learn from Rammohun Roy[1] that he was not the elder brother of Cristna, as I have formerly stated, but, as John was to Jesus, he was his cousin. He assisted him in his labours for the good of mankind, and when he was killed, the Sun stood still to hear the lamentations of Cristna for his loss.

All the names of Rome are female—Roma, Flora, Valentia: nearly its first and greatest Goddess was Vesta. Heyne suggests Roma to be Ruma.[2] No person has puzzled all inquirers more than the Indian Rama,[3] the cousin of Cristna. He has frequently been observed to have been to Cristna what John was to Jesus;[4] and the similarity is so striking, that it puts the identity of the two mythoses out of all question. Rāmā is always written with the *a* long like the *o*. Then it is Raamaa: R=100, aa=2, m=40, aa=2=144, a number so celebrated in the Apocalypse, or the prophecy of the coming of the Ram-Lamb to take away the sins of the world. Lamb, we have before seen, is L=30, M=40, B=2=72, another number peculiarly sacred to the Lamb. On the word Ram, Georgius says,[5] "רם *Ram* vero, et *Rém* excelsum designat. Et quoniam שרא *Rum* Samaritanis caput, et vertex capitis dicitur, petunt fortasse ut in eorum summitate capitis arcana illa ac mystica precatione oriatur splendidus et corruscans Mani." When I trace Ram to the vertex capitis, and recollect the Caput and Ras of the Arabians, I cannot help suspecting the arcana doctrina to have the same meaning in each country.

Mr. Niebuhr has shewn, from the numbers of the Roman periods, that their early history is a mythos. He observes that they have a peculiar and sacred number in 240. This makes, in the numerals, RM or Ram, R=200, M=40=240.

The country of Rome and the ancient city built upon the capitol, according to Virgil, was called Struia, country of the cycle of 650, or Satiern-ia, country of the cycle of 666, or of King Lateinos 666, according to Irenæus. Now the country of Roma would be Romaia, not Romelia, nor yet Romania.

Although it be difficult, perhaps impossible, to prove the fact, I suspect that, some way or other, as the Protestants say, (but my reason is not theirs,) Rome had the name of *the beast*.[6] The Orientals called the country of Phrygia, which had the same name with it, the country of Room. Might it be a Tamul name, and be Rome, with a Tamul termination, thus—Rouma-en? The Satur-en is exactly in the Tamul style.

I cannot help suspecting that the Pushto is the same as the name Pesach, of the festival of the slain lamb; that Pesach, that is פסח *peh*, ought to be פסד *ped*=144; and that this *Ped* afterwards became *Poet* or *Peto*. It is the union of the peculiar circumstances which renders this admissible as a probability; especially as we know of many other changes much greater than this. I am quite satisfied that, according to all the rules of rational probability, we can never calculate too much on the stories and names containing the most abstruse enigmas.

[1] This great man died, near Bristol, on Sept. 27, 1833. *Ed.*   [2] See Vol. I. p. 376.

[3] We have not yet found the origin of the word Ram the brother of Cristna, and of the animal of the zodiac. Now, in the first language of numbers, we find in the Hebrew the Samach and the Mem final to stand for the same number—the famous number 600. From this mutual convertibility I think the Ram and the Ras have been the same.

[4] See Vol. I. pp. 648, 649.   [5] Appendix III. p. 716.

[6] When it is recollected that almost every heathen God had the name of 666, we need not be surprised that the first Christians should call it *the number of the beast*.

ROMA. FLORA. PUSHTO.

R = 100
O = 70
U = 400
M = 40
A = 1
E = 5
N = 50
―――
666

If this could be proved, I should have no doubt that the Ram and Rama of India, which meant both Beeve and Sheep, had originally the same name. All these things I leave to my reader, who must determine whether a number of *little* probabilities will amount to a *great* one. But all these effects ought to be found if figures were the first letters. Much curious matter respecting the secret names of Rome and Athens, may be seen in the third volume of Nimrod, from pp. 194—206.

Αρωμα, *the sweet smell*,[1] means also a flower, that is Pushpa or Pushto. This was the language of the followers of the Phasah or the Lamb—it was the language of the Flower, of the Natzir, of the Flos-*floris*, of Flora, of the Arouma, and of the flour of Ceres, or the Eucharistia. It was the language of the pollen, the pollen of plants, the principle of generation, of the Pole or Phallus, of the Pole which opened the Gate of Salvation, and it was the Gate itself, the Arca-polis, place of deposit of the sacred things of the state, which were the emblems of the Αρχη or *divine wisdom*,—it was the Pala, the Pallas, (the divine wisdom,) and the Palladium or pallium of Elijah, or of the Lamb of God.[2]

Ερως is amor, and this is ama, which ama aspirated is C-ama. Amor is Roma. Ερως is Sora or Sura,[3] the Sun. (Sora-Cora-mandel.) Ερως being Cama is also Ama or Venus; in India, Cama-rina, Cama-marina, Sea-Goddess. Thus Venus and Cupid or Dipuc, that is, the Virgin mother and Child are the same; these are the *black* Madonnas and Bambinos of Italy. If Rama be Roma it is Amor or *divine love*, and is the same to Cristna as Arjoon or Jnana, *wisdom*, cousin or assistant of Jesus, is to Jesus.

There is a plant called Amomum or the Jerusalem Rose. Littleton says, " Cum sit Assyrius " frutex, nomen etiam ipsum ab oriente sumpsisse vero simile est. Quippe Arab. voce אמאמא " (*hamama*) Amama dicitur, ab המאם (*hmam*) i. Columba, cujus pedem refert. M. The herb " called Jerusalem or our Ladie's Rose." With the leaves of this plant *the Phœnix built her nest*. The Egyptians used it in embalming their dead; whence Mummy, Momia, Mumia, Amomia. *Voss*.—Here we have mystery enough. I do not doubt that this was *Ama* or *Amor* or *Om*, and that this is closely connected with the famous *Om* and *M*. All inquirers have agreed that the first sound of love was *ma*. The cycle of 600 was an emanation of divine love, whence it was identified with the central letter, M, and thus prefixed as a monogram to the vin. Of all the parasitical plants, there is no one more lovely than the vine creeping up and embracing the marital Elm or Alma.[4]

―――

[1] Jones's Lex.   [2] ροϲε Sax., Rose Fr., Rosa Lat., Ros or Rhos Celtic, ῥεύσιος [ῥόδον?] Greek, Rose English.
[3] The Persians call the Sun Συρη. See Vol. I. p. 136. From the Am or Ma comes, by a beautiful genealogy, I love. *Lascivus* is from Laschmi the wife of Cristna. I suspect that Core and Cyrus and Συρη and Ras and Ros-e and Sir, and O-sir-is and שרק *srq*, a choice vine, were all mystically connected. Joachim was Abbot of a place called Flora or Sora, in Calabria.
[4] See Pezron, pp. 245, 257—259.

BOOK III. CHAPTER III. SECTION 1.

Piromis, in Coptic, signifies *a man*, and is Pi-romi.[1] Here Romi evidently means *Man*. Brahma or Brama is often called Birouma, which is nearly the Pi-romi of Egypt, and Pi-romis of Greece, which, Herodotus says, means καλος. " Indeque nata videtur Singalæorum vox Pirimiia " La-Crozio, Pirimijaa Relando, mendosè fortassis Pirimha."[2] It is probable that the Piroma, the Pi Brama, is the Bacchus, Bromos, Bromios, Bruma; that Pi-rouma is the Pi-Roma, and th is Roma, that is Brama, means *former* or *creator;* and, that the words Bra and Pra, *to form* or *reform* or *reformer*, was the first emanation which flowed or emanated from the Supreme, and is the same as the Greek ῥεω *to flow*—Pi-roma the efflux, κατ' ἑξοχην, of the Supreme. The fact that Piromis means καλος connects it with the Indian Cali and the Calidei or Chaldæans, The original word for Brahmin may have been ברא *bram*, in the plural בראמין *bramin*. The word may come from בר *br*, which means *to create*, or *a creator* or *giver of forms*. *Bra* means *factor* and *fecit;* and as the priests, in consequence of the regimen style, i. e. the rude, unfinished, inartificial style of writing, took the names of their Gods, so came the name Brahm. A Bram, or one of the Bramin, was a priest of *Bra* or of the *factor* M or OM, or the *factor* M or OM. Let it be recollected that I have shewn, it was from the invention of the cycles, that all these religions or superstitions had their origin. The cycles with the *high* priests produced astronomy, with the *low* priests and the vulgar, superstition. Br *Son*, by the reg. Son of Br, has been converted into Son Br.

Georgius says, that Amida or Omyto, maximus Deus Japonensium, is un emblême de la révolution des siècles.[3]

To the celebrated society of the Rossicrucians or Rosé-cruxians I have before alluded.[4] I am not a member of this society, therefore I cannot betray any secrets. This society is closely allied to the Templars; their emblem or monogram or jewel, or as malicious and bigoted adversaries would say, their object of adoration is a Red Rose on a cross, thus—

When it can be done, it is surrounded with a glory, and placed on a Calvary. When it is worn appended and made of cornelian, garnet, ruby, or red glass, the Calvary and glory are generally omitted. This is the Naurutz, Natzir, or Rose of Isuren, of Tamul, or Sharon, or the Water Rose, the Lily, Padma, Pema, Lotus, crucified for the salvation of man—crucified in the heavens at the vernal equinox: it is celebrated at that time by the Persians, in what they call their Nou Rosé,[5] i. e. Neros or Naurutz. The word Nou is the Latin *novus*, and our *new*, which, added to the word *Rose*, makes the *new* Rose of the vernal equinox, and also makes on the Rose of the PΣΞ Rss=360; and the ΞPΣ Xrs, or cross, or crs, or, with the letter *e* added, the *Rose*=365; in short, the God of Day, the Rss or *divine wisdom*, X, PΣ,[6] Cross-Wisdom (Ethiopicè). When

---

[1] Univ. Hist. Vol. I. p. 426.   [2] In Tom. VI. de Ritib. Relig. Ind. p. 295, Georg. Tibet. Alph. p. 99.
[3] Alph. Tib. p. 131.   [4] Vol. I. pp. 723, 809.   [5] Malcolm's Hist. Pers. II. p. 406.
[6] The monogram with which the title-page of the Latin Vulgate is ornamented, which, as I have stated, was given me

the word רשית is used in the first verse of Genesis, instead of שׁ rs, it may either be in the plural or the s and t may be used, like the Greek Sigma-tau,[1] joined to the very common practice of inserting the sacred name of God I or jod, as our learned men say for the sake of metre, (in which, I doubt not, *sacred writing* was originally written,) but the learned Jews say it was thus used for the sake of a mystery. The word is, then, really *Rst*.[2] . Templars, Rossicrucians, Royal Arch Masons, you all know that there is nothing incredibly recondite in this.

2. Buddha is said to have been crucified for robbing a garden of a flower. He is also, like the emblem of the Rossicrucians, called a Flower, a Rose, a Padma, a Lotus, a Lily, and Jesus Christ is called *a flower*. The Virgin in the pictures of the annunciation, is always presented with a flower by the ministering angel, and that flower is the Lotus or Lily. In Mexico the same thing is done, only the flower is *a rose*.[3] I account for the fact that Buddha was both the *flower* and the *robber* of the *flower*, from the *regimine* of the language; (the Indians admit their ignorance;) from which the robber of the flower became the robber-flower. If this were the case, it would be naturally aided by the beauty of the simile. The admitted ignorance of the Indians opens the door to this explanation, as a probability, till something more satisfactory is discovered. He was a flower, because as flour or pollen he was the principle of fructification or generation. He was flour, because flour was the fine or valuable part of the plant of Ceres or wheat, the pollen which I am told, in this plant, and in this plant alone, renews itself when destroyed. When the flour, pollen, is killed, it grows again several times. This is a very beautiful type or symbol of the resurrection. On this account the flour of wheat was the sacrifice offered to the Χρης or Ceres in the Ευχαριςια. In this pollen we have the name of pall or pallium, and of Pallas, in the first language meaning *wisdom*. From this, language, logos, linga, wisdom, all came to be identified with letters, the tree, liber, Bacchus. Thus when the devotee ate the bread he ate the pollen, and thus ate the body of the God of generation: hence might come *transubstantiation*.[4] From this it came to pass, that the double allegory of the knowledge of good and evil, and of the knowledge of the generative power in the female, then in the male, and the knowledge of letters and of wisdom arose, and were blended into one.

I cannot help suspecting, that from the association of ideas the words flour and flower, and *to flow* as the secretion of the female flows, the root of the word flour came to be connected with those different mythic subjects, and to have meanings, though evidently by association, connected, yet in almost every respect different. What do we mean by deflowering a woman? and whence arose the phrase? Surely the least reflection will tell us.

The Raj is an emanation of the Solar power, a Ray or Ras, wisdom. As the principle of generation he was the Push or Pollen, thus he was called a flower. The Raj may have been the Rose or Flower.

Professor Haughton says, in his Laws of Menu, "The translator, in rendering the word *Rajas* "by 'blood' has made the legislator adopt a vulgar prejudice to which he was superior. That "word does not mean blood, but, according to the Hindus, the fructifying medium; they apply it "equally to the pollen of a flower, or the monthly secretion of a female; both being indispensable

---

by a Catholic priest. It is placed on the breast of an allegorical figure which wears *three crowns* — three crowns, not solely, if it be at all, emblematical of Heaven, Earth, and Hell, but also emblematical of an incarnation of the Creator, the Preserver, and the Destroyer—an incarnation of the Trinity or the Trimurti.

[1] See Vol. I. p. 54—the word *cut* for *cus*.
[2] The Rst is the Persian mythological name Rust-an. If there was such a man he took the sacred name.
[3] See *supra*, p. 32.
[4] See *supra*, p. 64.

"to precede production, the one in all vegetable, and the other in the human, and in some animal
"bodies. One of the terms by which this appearance is known in Sanscrit viz. *pushpa* a flower,
"will strikingly support the idea of an ancient connexion between the popular opinions of the
"Gothic and Hindu nations."[1] I beg my reader to look back to Volume I. n. 261, where he
will find something which I did not then choose to explain.

Podov means a Rose. I cannot help suspecting that the word *pod* had its origin in the idea of Ray, Rad-ius. The Rose of Sharon being the Sun or Rhadius, Scythian reix, Punic resch, Spanish rey, French roy, all according to Postel from the Hebrew ראש *ras*, rosch, chief, head.

Radha[2] was the wife of Cristna: if the wife were Radha, the husband would be Radhus, i. e. Radhus, or the Sun, was Radius. The crucified *rose* and the crucified *solar emanation*, convince me of the close connexion, indeed of the identity, of the mythoses, though I cannot exactly connect them together.

The Buddhists, the natives of Tibet hold the Grand Lama to be always the same person—same Buddha only reincarnated, or renovated, in a new mundane case or body. And I believe that Jesus Christ was considered by some Christians to be a renewed incarnation from Adam and Noah, and that this was *one* of the reasons for the careful setting-forth of his pedigree, in the New Testament. Thus he was, in fact, Adam. But Adam sinned, and for his sin he was, in the person of Jesus Christ, crucified. He ate the forbidden fruit, the consequence of which was that he immediately learnt that he was *naked*, yielded to temptation and stole the flower of the garden. But the flower which he stole was of a very different description from the common flower; he stole the flour, the pollen, of an animated plant. After his theft, in that plant there was no more pollen. In the natural circumstances of the first pair there would never be any more flower to be seen. The female plant would produce no more pollen. In the natural healthy state she would produce children so quick as to prevent the exhibition of more till it finally ceased. For this robbery he suffered death. The theft of this flower brought sin and death into the world. There was no sin before this theft.

My allegorical explanations will not be thought too recondite by persons who have studied the character of the oriental nations in these matters; many examples might be produced, but I shall cite only one. A Vizir having divorced his wife Chemsennissa, on suspicion of criminal conversation with the Sultan, her brothers applied for redress to their judge. "My Lord," said they, "we had rented to Féirouz a most delightful *garden, a terrestrial paradise;* he took possession of "it *encompassed with high walls, and planted with the most beautiful trees that bloomed with flowers* "*and fruit.* (Compare Cant. iv. 12—14.) He has broken down the walls, plucked the tender "flowers, devoured the finest fruit, (comp. Cant. v. 1,) and would now restore to us this *garden,* "robbed of every thing that contributed to render it delicious, when we gave him admission to it." Féirouz, in his defence, and the Sultan in his attestation to Chemsennissa's innocence, carry on the same allegory of the *garden.*[3]

3. I must now request my reader to look back to Volume I. pp. 428, 429, and he will there see a description of Callida or Ur of the Chaldees, and he cannot fail to be struck with the flattering account which is there given by Col. Tod without his having the slightest idea of what he was giving a description, namely, of the country and ancestors of Abraham. It well supports my opinion, that the Chaldæans were the first possessors of the knowledge of letters, and indeed of magic

---

[1] Haughton's Menu, Note 66. [2] See Vol. I. p. 586.
[3] Parkhurst's Lex. in voce גן *gn*, which means *garden*. This word seems to be the origin of our word *garden*, which was probably more like the ancient word; for words seldom grow longer by age. From this root came the Sanscrit protector of gardens—Gan-isa-ן ג גן יש *iso*: the Sanscrit from the Hebrew, as might be expected.

and astrology, which, in fact, were but the knowledge of that, a part of which I shewed, in Volume I. p. 677, to have been possessed by Roger Bacon. As the knowledge of these things gradually became public, they gradually ceased to be mysteries, until at last there were scarcely any left. And as this effect took place by very slow degrees, during thousands of years, it would not any where be recorded. In fact, it would not be perceived by the mystics themselves. The secrets of Roger Bacon were the last of them.

The learned Bailly, after years of patient inquiry and close investigation, came to the conclusion, that all the learning of the Greeks and of the Eastern nations was but the débris of learning of a nation of scientific persons who had lived in a former time; and I have no doubt that had he not been prematurely cut off by the miscreants of Paris, he would have proved the truth of his doctrine. This, however, appeared so paradoxical to his countrymen, that I believe no one has attempted seriously to follow up his discoveries. The more I examine the more I become convinced that there was a race of antediluvians, and that they were a very learned race.

I believe the ancient mysteries, like almost all religious rites and ceremonies, arose by degrees from circumstances, and from the natural failings and feelings of mankind. It cannot be denied, that man has a natural propensity to monopolize and appropriate to himself what tends to distinguish him from his fellow-creatures, and to elevate him above them. From the gratification of these feelings, when the art of writing was, by degrees, discovered, it was closely concealed, and became what we call, or a part of what we call, the magic art. I believe the ancient mysteries consisted in the knowledge of letters and the higher branches of arithmetic, astronomy, and the theory of cycles which I have described; and in other branches of natural science, such as the use of the loadstone, compass, the telescope, &c.[1] In short, every part of science which could be concealed, and as long as it was concealed, was a mystery.

If I be right in my idea, and I know no other way of accounting for many anomalous facts, that writing was made originally from the top-downwards, was by symbols, was secret, and escaped from the mysteries by degrees, the extraordinary way in which proper names in all languages are mixed or written, which our grammarians have honoured with technical terms, such as *anagram* and *metathesis*, may be easily accounted for. Of this the name of God in Chinese, Tien or Neit[2] is an example. This will account, in a satisfactory manner, for the different directions in the styles of writing, as well as for the confusion in the powers of notation of the latter numbers of the Hebrew and Greek alphabets, and it will also explain the reason why we have so many places called by the same names. They were all, originally, secret and religious names, which by degrees came into common use. Every country had names of places to suit (in its religious ceremonies, processions, &c.) the universal mythos; but each must also have had other names, some only of which have come down to us. We now hear much more of the *sacred* names, than of the *common* ones, because all the ancient books, before Herodotus, were sacred books. Originally, writing was used for nothing but the affairs of religion. This theory, and I think I may say this verified theory, will account for every difficulty. The doctrine of secrecy which I here suggest, is in perfect keeping with what we know of all the habits of the ancients, and, indeed, of all mankind. Have we not in every trade a craft or mystery? The examples which I have already given of scientific discoveries secreted, which had no concern with religion, made by such men as Newton, strongly support me. There is no reason to believe that Pythagoras ever made public his knowledge of letters, even if he possessed it. He left not a written sentence behind him, though he dealt so largely in numbers—arithmetic and geometry. This is borne out by the positive testi-

---

[1] See Vol. I. p. 341. [2] See Ib. p. 429, and *supra*, p. 36.

mony of the treatise found by Mr. Von Hammer in Egypt—that every learned man had a letter of his own, in which he endeavoured to conceal his doctrines. This book of Ben Wassih's is as good evidence of the fact as can be expected; and, all circumstances considered, it is really good evidence. The attempt to monopolise knowledge seems to have been one of the most predominant passions in all ages; and it is easily to be accounted for, as knowledge is power. The vanity of man is flattered also, in being wiser than his neighbour.

I once more repeat, that the sacred mystic dances, music, poetry, or the art of composing in rhythm or lines in certain numbers of short and long syllables, and acrostics, were all inventions for aiding the memory, before the art of writing in syllables was discovered. I find great difficulty in believing that the persons who possessed the astronomical science, evinced by their knowledge of the neros, by their placing of the pyramids, and by the cycles displayed in many of the Druidical monuments, such as Stonehenge, Abury, &c., can have been ignorant of the art of writing—and these facts, among other circumstances, induce me to think it was known long before it was made public. Although the Chinese language is called the flowery language, or language of flowers, it appears in this to include trees, so that it would have been better called *language of plants*.[1] They considered a tree to be a symbol of knowledge.

4. There can be no doubt that one of the meanings of Genesis was, that by eating of the fruit of the forbidden tree, the tree of wisdom or knowledge, a knowledge of the sexes was acquired, and the consequent propagation of the species. And when I consider again the numerous allegories drawn from trees, that the Hebrew word עץ oz means a fruit-tree, and עצה oze and יעץ ioz counsel, i. e. wisdom, all evidently the same, I cannot help seeing that the allegories allusive to trees and letters, are drawn from the second book of Genesis, or the allegory of the second book of Genesis, the tree of knowledge, &c., is drawn from trees and letters, and which of these is the case is a curious subject of inquiry.[2] There is great probability that the allegory of the tree and letters arose from natural circumstances. The bark, the leaves, and the stem of the tree, became vehicles for conveying wisdom by means of letters, from the fortuitous circumstance of being the most convenient substances on which to inscribe them. I suppose about the time the ciphers or numeral letters were invented, the plan or custom of using the bark of a tree on which to inscribe them would be also adopted. Perhaps the circumstance of the leaf of each tree being used to express a number, might give occasion to the first numeral letters to have the names of trees, and from a union of these causes might arise all the beautiful and almost innumerable allegories of Genesis, and of the Eastern nations. The origin of the idea of the tree being the emblem of wisdom is very clear.

Under the magical symbols which we call ciphers or letifs, leaves, letters, all science or learning or wisdom was concealed; and it is perfectly clear that the words letif, leaf, and letter, were really the same. But I do not see how the knowledge of *wisdom* should make man know that he was *naked*; this, I think, might be merely the gross and literal meaning of the text; and, from a consideration of all the concomitant circumstances, I am induced to suspect that this gross meaning was only used to conceal the beautiful and refined doctrines contained in the mysteries relating to trees and knowledge, but which would be converted, as far as possible, according to the prevailing fashion, into allegories also. All these allegories respecting trees must have been totally incomprehensible to persons who did not understand the nature of letters and writing. They

---

[1] See Vall. Coll. Hib. Vol. V. pp. 144, 145.

[2] It may be observed that it is not necessary that the allegory in the first book of Genesis should be the same as the allegory in the second. As there are certainly two histories, there are probably two allegories.

must indeed have been *an impenetrable mystery;* but I am quite certain that there are two clear and distinct allegories.

As I have just said the mysteries themselves arose from natural circumstances. I suppose the knowledge of the Trimurti and the other doctrines of the Gnosis or Wisdom, the branch of the Cabala called Berasit, explained by me, was the secret of secrets, the grand arcanum; that, along with this, one of the first secrets was the knowledge of the art of writing and reading. From the extreme difficulty of acquiring the art of writing and reading, it would almost necessarily be a secret science even without any intention at first of making it so. The knowledge of Wisdom became the knowledge of letters. All wisdom was conveyed by letters, by the liber, the leaves, the bole, the stem of the tree; thus the tree became the tree of knowledge to make man wise, forbidden to all but the initiated. I believe that all the deep sciences were mysteries—astronomy, astrology, the higher branches of arithmetic, and mathematics, were, at first, all mysteries—mysteries which decreased in number as these sciences or secrets were discovered by the mass of mankind; and all these sciences were concealed in letters, and letters themselves were concealed in the names of the leaves of trees. I believe that one class or caste, called by a variety of names, but by us Chaldæans, were, as I have repeatedly remarked, the possessors of the secret. Hesychius says, Χαλδαιοι· γενος μαγων παντα γινωσκοντων.[1] The observation is very important. It shews the character which those persons had in his time. They were like the Freemasons of the present day; they became divided into different bodies, as we have Masons, Rossicrucians, Templars, &c.; and even each body, in different places, having some difference in their ceremonies as our Masonic societies have; but still the same general characteristic features are at the bottom. Such, for instance, as we see in the names of places in all countries, and all countries having the general mythos of the *ten* avatars to finish at the end of the six thousand years, and to begin again, and be renewed in sæcula sæculorum. It is the natural course of events, that, in different nations and in different periods considerable variations should arise, and not more have arisen than might be reasonably expected, allowance only being made for these natural causes. The Casideans, the Chaldæans, the Essenes, the Therapeutæ, the Mathematici, the Freemasons, the Carmelites, the Assassins, Magi, Druids, were all the same, and all held the Chreestian doctrine, and received, at their rite of baptism, which was universal, a Chreestian name, and, by this rite, were admitted to the first step of initiation into the mysteries. Here was the reason of the universal toleration after the union of the two great sects of the Linga and Ioni took place.

On admission into the highest mysteries, the rite of circumcision was administered, or, perhaps, originally, it was the general rule, that every one who was intended for the order, should be circumcised in his youth. The word circumcised, as I have before observed, has the meaning also of initiation. It is known that into the high mysteries of Egypt and Eleusis no person was admitted who was not circumcised,[2] though neophytes were constantly admitted. Besides, every person once admitted would choose to have his children admitted, and thus the order was kept alive; and thus it was that the order, as we have found, was both hereditary and not hereditary. The Monks constituted a class or order, at first perhaps the elect or perfect, or only the persons admitted into the very highest mysteries. Perhaps only the persons who performed the functions. In the Culdees of Iona and in Wales, there were both married and unmarried members of the convents; but probably this was an abuse. Pythagoras became a neophyte, and was admitted by the ceremony of circumcision.

We will now return to the flower. In India, Buddha, as already stated, robbed the garden of a

---

[1] Hesych. Lex. voce Χαλδαιοι. Hager, Bab. Bricks, p. 21.   [2] See Vol. I. pp. 304, 724, 759.

flower, for which he died. In Western Syria the female presents the fruit of the tree of the garden of love or wisdom to the male, by which means the death and regeneration of man ensue, and without which the species would not have passed on to futurity. Now what were the flowers of which the male deprived the garden of delight alluded to above? If my reader will carefully consider every meaning which the word flower or flour or pollen possesses in plants and animals, in short in all nature, he will then readily answer the question. And if he wish to know what was the kind of fruit presented by the female to the male to produce the prolongation of the species, he may ask any naturalist, or even village surgeon, and he will tell him that the apples of love, the ova, are not the produce of the male, but of the female. They were the apples of knowledge, because, by being presented to the male and tasted by him, he acquired a delicious knowledge which he never knew before, and he caused the renewal of the animal, from generation to generation, to be ultimately absorbed in the To Ov. Here we have the apples of knowledge in the *garden of delight*. The flower spoken of above was that without which there would be no generations or regenerations, it was the grand ornament of the garden, and, in this sense, the flower or plant of wisdom or knowledge. Without its stimulating and nourishing power there would be no fructification. The plant was worthless without it. It was the flower of wisdom—אלפ *Pla*, Pallas, Palladium, Pallium, and the Pollen of every plant; and, with men who did not possess the recondite knowledge of anatomy, it became, by mistake, the Phallus. I suppose I need not point out to my reader what, in this allegory, constituted the garden, the Can-ia, the Γυνη.¹ The female presented to the male the apples of love, the ova.² He tasted and fell. With the increase of the species, cares and sorrows arose, the ground became overrun with thorns and briars, and the garden of delight faded away. From this first act came all the good and all the evil in the world; without it there had been neither good nor evil. The being man, mannus, homo, was [allegorically] not an animal; it was a plant. It is the only being in whom red blood circulates, who at the same time masticates food and produces flowers—which flowers bear fruits—of which flowers the male despoiled the female, and thus propagated the species. There is yet one other animal which, circulating red blood, bears flowers: but what is its Indian name?—Hanu-man, the Monkey or Ape.

The Greek was first written without vowels, and from top to bottom, and called Petalon. But Petalon means *a leaf*, or, as I suspect, *a tree*, and πεταλα would be *trees*. From this came the petals of flowers. Æneas descending to the Shades, passed an elm-tree loaded with *dreams*. The alpha, in Irish ailm or elm-tree, was the trunk of the tree of letters, and has evidently a close connexion with the elm-tree of Virgil, and with the Greek style of writing, called *petalon* or *leaf writing*. Nothing can be more striking than that the Greek upright writing should be called *a tree*. But the letters were written upright, *asibus lignis*, or on stems of trees. If we look at and consider these figure systems, evidently all identical, we must observe, that the first and tenth and hundredth forms are all the same. The *a* is the first letter of the tree elm, ailm, and answers to the figure *one*. I suspect that the first name of the elm was ilm; that there was originally no vowel *a*, but the *oin*; that it was afterward added to the *ilm* when found to be wanted; and that this tree was called, at various times, ailm, ilm, elm, or oeilm, or ulm. Being the name of the monad To Ov, it naturally came to have the meaning of the first solar cycle, M=600, U=6,

---

¹ We read that the garden was robbed of its flower. Was this garden Eva? I think the Hebrew גן *gn* was not only *garden*, but it was also γυνη. Here we have the same story, only somewhat differently told.

² As the woman possesses the seed, the ova, not the man, that text is peculiarly proper which says, "the seed of the woman," not the seed of the man, "shall bruise," &c.

VOL. II. 2 K

I=10, L=50=666; and I suppose that the Sacæ or Saxons called their famous city *Ulm* after it, as they called their city in the Siamese Judia, and in Western Syria, the city of Sion or Siun or Xiun=666, or Sioun=336, or Siun=366, or Sin=360, or Xn=650. When we consider that the leaves of a book were really the leaves of a tree, the allegory of the tree of knowledge almost rises as a natural consequence. In the Syriac tongue Oden is Adonis; but the O, in Syriac or Pushto, (which we have found, is the same as Tamul,) was the emphatic article THE. Then Oden would be *the* Dn,[1] *Dun* or *Don*; but Don, we have found, meant wisdom or knowledge. Thus we come again to the tree of knowledge or of the garden of knowledge, or garden of Adonis. When Adam was in his first state he knew all that was necessary; he was an emanation from the Supreme; he was the divine incarnation: his descendants were obliged to cultivate letters, described by the sterility of the earth, to obtain knowledge—a difficult task as we all know. Here we see the reason why a tree was selected as the ground of the allegory, for trees were literally books. The tree was very appropriately in the garden of delight or knowledge or wisdom—the tree, the alphabet, by means of which all divine science was known—the tree by the study of which the favoured youth, selected for instruction in the secret mystic art, became one of the royal SACRED caste, enjoying the contemplation of all the higher branches of knowledge, particularly astronomy. The gardens of Adonis, of Syria, I really believe were all Edens, (Eden is Adon,) delightful groves, seminaries of education in the secret sciences, delightful retreats for study, imitated by the Domus Templi of the Templars at Cambridge, and the college of Hassan Subah at Cairo. The stories which we are told of the hanging gardens convey the idea of the greatest absurdities. I suspect they were of the nature of amphitheatres, for the purpose of giving and receiving lectures in the sciences; that the seats were planted with trees to shade the auditors from the sun. Nimrod has shewn that their form was probably amphitheatric, and, except for the object which I have named, they seem to have been very absurd.

We read that the tree of knowledge *(i. e.* wisdom) produced twelve fruits—one for each month. This was, I suppose, when the twelve ages or neroses were believed to make a cycle with the time of precession in the twelve signs. I think, at least in Greece, the style of writing from the top downward, in right lines, must have been the oldest, and this style called *petalon*, or that of the *leaf* or *leaves*, gives strong support to the antiquity of the Irish custom of calling their letters by the names of trees; for the practice of *upright* writing, as well as the use of the word *leaf*, were common to both.

Knowledge and wisdom, though not, perhaps, strictly identical, are constantly confounded. This arises from the consideration that wisdom is really the perfection of knowledge. In fact, perfect knowledge *is* wisdom. Jesus Christ is constantly called the branch, and the vine—the way of salvation, the way or door of life, the shepherd, the tree of life, the tree in the middle of the Garden of E-don or of wisdom. In the title-page of the Alcoran des Cordeliers, St. Francis is likened to Jesus Christ, by drawing him as a tree. Christ was Wisdom, and Wisdom was the " arbor magna in medio Paradisi, cujus rami dictiones, ulterius in ramos parvos et folia, quæ sunt " literæ extenduntur;" the great tree in the garden of Eden, whose leaves were letters, and whose branches were words. How could the practice of calling letters by the names of trees be better described? Buddha was Wisdom; Jesus Christ was Wisdom; consequently he was Buddha. Christ was the tree of life and of wisdom or knowledge; Buddha was Veda; Veda was wisdom—the book of life. Christ was the true vates or prophet; and the contents of the Veda were but

---

[1] The Mohamedans call Religion *Deen*; this is *Dn* or Wisdom. Malcolme's Hist. Pers. Vol. II. p. 219. The ה׳ *ie* of the Hebrew changed, in the Syriac, into Io. In the same manner the e changed into the o with the Ethiopians, and Christus or Chrestus or Χρητος became Chrostos. Geor. Alp. Tib. p. 748.

the vates or true prophetism. Vates is evidently a corruption of veda, or veda of vates. Hence, in fact, the Greek root χρης means both χρησος benignus, mitis, καλος and vates or ουατες—and in the word καλος we have the root or origin of the deity Cali of India, and of the Cali-dei or Cali-divi or Caldæans. As χρης, vates, *perfect wisdom*, he KNEW or KNOW-ed every thing past, present, and future. In the Veda was recorded all knowledge—past, present, and future—the knowledge of the generations or re-generations of the man, the knowledge of the renewal of cycles in sæcula sæculorum, that is, of cycles of cycles—the esoteric meaning of sœcula sæculorum, or αιων των αιωνων, æones, emanations of divine wisdom. Our book which we miscal Genesis, or *the book of generations*, ought to be Barasit—that is, Wisdom—that is, Veda or Buddha. Thus it is called by the Jews.

But there were two trees in Paradise—the tree of knowledge and the tree of life. What was the tree of life? We are told, that if Adam had eaten of the fruit of the tree of life he would have *lived for ever!* What does this mean? (Of course I assume that no person reading this book is so weak as to admit the literal meaning.[1]) A part of the text seems to be wanting. May it mean that, by the knowledge of the system of regenerations without having obtained such knowledge by previous *initiation* into the secret use of letters, of the Vedas, the Sophias, the רשות rsut, or of the knowledge obtained by means of letters, man would have become assured of his eternal existence; or, that, by knowing the sacred truth, he would have been induced so to modify his conduct as to ensure himself a speedy absorption into the Το Ον, to shorten the period or number of his transmigrations? Was the fruit of the tree of life the consequence of the admission into the sacred, i. e. secret, mysteries which, by producing fruits meet for salvation, produced or hastened the salvation of the initiated? We know initiation was said exoterically to produce the most perfect happiness. The effect of initiation was, reformation of manners, the future practice of the most sublime virtues, the rendering of a man perfect—(" If thou wilt be perfect, sell all that " thou hast, and give to the poor"—) inducing him to desert all the little, narrow, selfish gratifications of this life, for the purpose of securing those of a life to come. These, at least, were its tendency and its object. I say not that this was certainly the meaning of the allegory of the tree of life; but it seems to me, that it must have been this, or something very like it. At all events, I think the explanation of the second part of the allegory is in good keeping with, and is not unworthy of, the first; and they are both *beautiful,* perhaps *true.* All this is strictly masonic. I trust I am not improperly betraying the secrets of the craft, of the *Megalistor Mundorum,* when I state, that the designed effect of all masonic initiation is to render a man more virtuous—consequently more happy. A perfect Mason, if such a thing could be, must be a perfect Buddhist, a perfect Jew, a perfect Christian, a perfect Mohamedan. They are all Χρης or Χρης-oi or Christs.[2] And, from the most remote antiquity, a man in every new cycle has been looked for, who should be in a peculiar manner Χρης, to teach glad-tidings, divine wisdom, to mankind. Moses; the conqueror of Babylon, called for this reason Cyrus; Pythagoras, Herod, Cæsar Augustus, Jesus; *Mo* or *Om* AHMED the cyclar *desire of all nations;* St. Francis; were all thought, each in his day, to be Χρης-oi by their followers; and the vital principle which constituted a man, in each

---

[1] After nearly the whole of the first volume had been printed, I met with an observation of Mr. Christie's, (Essay on Worship of Elements, p. 25,) that Dr. Kennicott had shewn that only one tree standing in Eden was forbidden: this induced me to examine the question more carefully than I had done, and I saw at once that Dr. Kennicott was right. The whole context, of all the tracts of which Genesis is composed, relates only to one tree, except one short passage at the end of the third chapter.

[2] Christians were first called Christs. *Bingham.*

age, a member of this religion, and not a heretic, was a belief that this Χρης was come at that time, or had previously come.

I just now asked the question, whether the attempt to acquire illegal knowledge, or knowledge acquired by the possession of letters, was not the tree of life. Enoch says, the great sin of the old world, and that for which it was destroyed, was the attempt to obtain forbidden and illegal knowledge. This I consider of great importance.

In Genesis it is said, that man acquired knowledge—tasted of the fruit of the tree of knowledge of good and evil—illegally, illicitly, contrary to the command of God; in consequence, the ground was cursed, and in future he had to earn his bread by the sweat of his brow. Allegory or gross inconsistency is on the face of the story, respecting the curse of sterility fixed on the ground, in consequence of man's disobedience; for, it is said just before, that he was placed in the garden *to dress and till* it; and every one knows that the ground was not cursed: the sweet chestnut and the filbert, the plants of wheat and barley, bring forth their fruit, and are succeeded by the orange, the fig, &c., before they are decayed, as freely now as they always did. Then what does this mean? May it allude to the discovery by the people, by the uninitiated, of the art of writing, of letters, of the tree of knowledge, of the secrets of the priesthood? May it mean, that the people, as in Tibet, were taught the effect of good conduct by the initiated, but were not initiated into its arcana; and that, in future, the arcana would be known to those only who had gone through the labours of initiation? The expression of Enoch seems to favour this conjecture.

I think it probable that in the allegory of the trees of knowledge and of life, the latter was only to be obtained from first having tasted the former, or otherwise the devil must have been a very great fool indeed, in not first persuading Eve to taste of the tree of life, by which means he would have completely beaten his Creator. No one would have contrived to make the cunning devil so great a fool. This being admitted, and there is nothing in the text against it, the eating of the forbidden fruit of the tree of knowledge must have been the acquisition of the knowledge of letters by the uninitiated, and the fruit of the tree of life must have been the knowledge which was acquired by reading, by having tasted the knowledge of letters, of the eternal state of happiness intended for man by absorption into the Το Ον—happiness to be hastened by religious rites, mental abstraction—in fact, by the possession of a portion of wisdom or knowledge only to be obtained by initiation in the mysteries, and incarnated in the initiated by the Samach, χειροτονια, or imposition of hands, or investiture with the pallium. By this knowledge the initiated learned, that, by good conduct and the practice of virtue, they could hasten the period or shorten the sum of transmigrations.[1] This was only known to, and was a most invaluable privilege of, the favoured initiated few. This opens to us a most beautiful view of the ancient mysteries, a view in every respect justified by masonic mysteries of the present day, and anciently obscured by the unfortunate corporate and monopolising spirit, which excluded the mass of mankind from the invaluable secret, and thus kept them in a state of debasement—a weakness which seems inherent in the human character, at least a weakness attaching to the character of the great men of antiquity

---

[1] The ancient fathers generally believed in the metempsychosis, which was thus a part of the religion. Let me not be understood to mean that the professors of these doctrines really believed that, by the Samach or χειροτονια, a real inspiration was communicated. No: this was never imparted till after examination had shewn, that the neophyte had imbibed from his instructor—or that he had really acquired the divine knowledge of the divine wisdom—that he was imbued with divine wisdom—that, in short, divine wisdom suitable to the degree to which he aspired was incarnate in him, for it could not, of course, be in him, without being infused into him. It is exactly the same with our ordination of priests and bishops. The superior gives the χειροτονια—but it is not till after, by examination, he has ascertained that the divine knowledge or the knowledge of divine matters, is actually, or professedly, possessed by the neophyte.

with very few exceptions. In these exceptions we may place Socrates, Pythagoras, Jesus, who are said to have all lost their lives, not for divulging the secrets of the initiation; but, without being guilty of that offence, for endeavouring to teach the mass of mankind what the few learned from initiation, namely, that a virtuous life would secure eternal happiness; and probably for endeavouring to abolish the system of secrecy or exclusion. It has been always held to have been the object of Jesus, to open the Jewish religion to the whole world—that must have been the secret religion, the Cabala. The above was the simple and unadulterated doctrine of the philosophers of Athens, Crotona, and Nazareth. This was the Chreestism, as Justin Martyr said, taught equally by Socrates and Jesus of Nazareth. And one of the great objects of this work is to restore the doctrines of Socrates and of Jesus,—to draw aside their veils, as well as that of Isis.

5. Persons may dispute about the allegory of the tree, the arbor magna in medio Paradisi, and say this or that is not the meaning of the text; but I am certain that no philosopher will deny there is a high probability that the exposition which I have given of it, was the exposition of the ancients, and that upon which their secret system was founded. The sacred book of the Tamuls, as I have before stated, (in p. 15,) is said to have had *five* meanings. In India the mythos says, that the eldest son of God, the Adonis, the male, at the instigation of the female, robbed the *garden* of a flower, for which he was crucified; but that he rose again to life and immortality, and by this he wrought the salvation of man. May this be, that he secured the continuance of the generations of man? In the allegory of the fall of man, Adam and Eve having tasted of the fruit of the tree of knowledge, knew that they were naked and covered themselves with the leaves of the fig-tree, Ficus Indicus. I have no doubt it is on this account that the Indians give the name of Rawasit, that is, ראשית *rasit*, knowledge or wisdom, to that tree:[1] a tree peculiarly sacred to Xaca or Buddha.[2] And from a peculiar property which the *fig* has of producing its fruit from its flowers, contained within its own bosom, and concealed from profane eyes, its leaves were selected by Adam and Eve to conceal the organs of generation. Most of what has been said by Messrs. Maurice and Knight respecting the Lotus,[3] may be said of the fig-tree. The emblematic fruit of the tree of knowledge has been generally considered to be the apple; but it was very often described by the *grape* growing on, or hanging to, the elm. On ancient cameos the tree of knowledge is constantly described by a vine, producing its fruit among the branches of the marital elm. There is nothing in the *apple* or its mythic history to favour its pretensions: but what was the *grape*, the fruit of Bacchus, but the Greek βοτρυς, or wisdom; and, again, *the* Wisdom, in the Latin Rac-emus?[4] The Greeks made out the *apples* of the Hesperides and the *golden fleece* from this mythos. In the oriental language the fruit was Souph or Wisdom; and as Souph meant also wool, of course they took the gross idea, and instead of sacred wisdom, Χρης, Souph, made *golden fleece*. And their word for fleece, μαλλος or μαλον, meaning also apple, thus they got their golden apples. In a similar manner arose almost all the vulgar mythologies of the elegant Greeks—a very elegant but generally very unscientific nation. And this leads me to return to the *esoteric* meaning of the most beautiful, and, I am persuaded, the most general, of all the religious rites of antiquity—the Eucharistia—the sacrifice of *bread and wine*. We all know that Ceres was bread, Bacchus, wine. Love grows cold without bread and wine; "Amor friget sine Cerere et Baccho." What is bread? It is the flour of wheat, the most useful plant in the world—of that plant, which, by a peculiar blessing of Divine Love, has alone the property of renewing its pollen or flour, when destroyed by any accident. Thus the flour of wheat or bread is the most appropriate emblem of

---

[1] Georg. Alph. Tib. p. 509.   [2] Ib. p. 17.   [3] See Vol. I. pp. 339, 340.
[4] Was the Vine hanging on the Elm, *Racemus* or *Bothrys*, M-Om crucified?

divine love; bread is the produce of the pollen, as the renewed or regenerated man is the produce of another flower, the infant man, the cupid, the pledge of love—the produce of the fruit which the female solicited the male to taste, and which he, by tasting, fecundated, at the same time that he became wise to joys hitherto unknown to him, and by which he caused the continuance of the species, regenerated for periods, αιων των αιωνων. The wine was the grape, the βοτρυς, the *racemus*, the emblem of *wisdom* or *knowledge*—the fruit of the tree of knowledge, of the elm, the first letter of the alphabet, which bore on its trunk all the tree of letters, of the vedas, in which were concealed all sacred knowledge. The two united formed the Eu Ca Ri STia or Eu X a P ι Σ-[1] dia, the good deity Χρης, or Ceres: and from this the body and blood of the initiated or Gnostici arose. And, in allusion to this, Jesus is made to say, "I will drink no more of the fruit of the "vine until that day that I drink it new in the kingdom of God."[2] That is, I shall no more give you lessons, or join you in the search, of wisdom; no more initiate you into the divine mysteries of the Βορϱυς or the Racemus, till we meet in a future life, in my Father's kingdom; till we are all reunited to our eternal Father, absorbed into the To Ov. I call this most beautiful allegory, not more mystical than Jesus's calling Peter *a stone*, nor more equivocal in language; but no doubt it will be gall and wormwood to those who, in spite of the lessons of wisdom, continue to teach their countrymen, that God really failed to kill Moses at an inn. Fabius Pictor says, "Jani ætate nulla "erat monarchia, quia mortalibus pectoribus nondum hæserat ulla regnandi cupiditas, &c. Vinum "et far primus populos docuit Janus ad sacrificia: primus enim aras et pomœria et sacra docuit." "In the time of Janus there *was no monarchy*,[3] for the desire of rule had not then folded itself "about the hearts of men. Janus first taught the people to sacrifice wine and bread: he first set "up altars, and instituted gardens and solitary groves, wherein they used to pray; with other holy "rites and ceremonies."[4]

In every thing I observe that, the more deeply I search, the more I discover marks of the profound learning of the ancients, till I gradually mount up to the To Ov.

I am told, (by persons who *believe* and who require me to believe on the most doubtful of records and evidence, that the water rose fifteen cubits above Chimborazo, and that God wrestled with Jacob, and walked in the garden,) that I have no proof of the learning of the first nation. But the proof which they require cannot, in the nature of things, be obtained. Every thing in ancient history resolves itself into probability. In scarcely any instance can a proof, or any thing of the nature of proof, be produced; probability is all that can be expected. Innumerable are the facts that we meet with which are totally unaccountable on any of the anciently received systems, but which are all rationally accounted for by the theory that I have produced, if it be true; and I beg to observe, that it is not *merely a theory*, but that it is supported by innumerable facts and circumstances dovetailing into one another. Whether its truth be probable must be left to my readers; and nearly as various as the readers will be their opinions. One thing I would ask, which is, that no one would form an opinion who has not read the whole book. But a compliance with this request is not to be expected from the generality of mankind, who will find, if they will examine themselves closely, that nine times out of ten they decide questions not from their knowledge, but from their ignorance. Nothing is more common than to hear persons saying, upon questions they have never had the means of investigating, "I do not believe such a thing, because

---

[1] From this the word χαρις might have its origin. [2] Will any one say that this is not figurative?

[3] Except a sacerdotal government, to be treated of hereafter—the empire of Pandæa.

[4] Raleigh's Hist. Par. I. p. 91.

"I have never heard or read that it is so;" and in this manner they set up their opinion against those who have investigated a subject, or who have heard or seen it discussed.

6. The consideration of the great length of time through which I have passed with my reader, the vast space of country over which we have travelled, and the great variety of subjects which we have discussed, or occasionally adverted to, in the course of our progress, suggest to me one or two observations, which seem to be interesting, and which I will take the liberty of offering to his consideration before I conclude this book.—In extent and complication of matter, perhaps no work has exceeded mine. To have amply discussed every subject would have required a thousand volumes; and large as the work is, it can be considered as only a collection of the results of the lucubrations of philosophers on each subject. But this state of the case is not without its advantages. The philosophers of the world have been the industrious ants bringing in the grains of corn to be stored by me, as far as it was in my power, and placed in order in galleries for the use of the commonwealth. We have got a good store, gentle reader; and now we will take a walk together through the galleries, and review a small part of what we have accumulated. A deep consideration of what we have seen, must, I think, satisfy any one, that an uniform system may be perceived to have pervaded the whole world, and to have come down to us from the earliest time. We must always recollect that a certain degree of uncertainty and doubt is inherent in the nature of these inquiries. If this uncertainty did not exist, with most of their interest, they would lose all their utility. We seem to be fighting against a law of Providence, which says, "Man, "thy power of vision is limited; thou shalt not look too far either behind or before thee." Our circle of vision, too, is narrowed not alone by Providence; the cunning and all the evil passions of priests, and the prejudice of man, caused by his being educated by them, are leagued with his weakness to impede our progress, to embarrass our subject, and to render more doubtful, researches which, in their own nature, are sufficiently doubtful. When the priest cannot darken or throw into confusion, he burns, he forges, and he lies; speculating, according to a theory or plan charged on the philosophers by Mr. Faber,[1] but which that gentleman appears to me to have practised himself in the case of M. Volney, and on the old proverb, that *a lie* uncontradicted for a fortnight, is as good as *a truth*. Therefore we must be content with probabilities, and not expect mathematical demonstrations.

In the foregoing disquisition, there is, upon the whole, no part so curious or so important in its results, as the *origin of languages and letters*. All the systems of the world seem to be intimately interwoven with them, or at least so connected as not to be separated. This naturally arises from the circumstance, that the systems of antiquity are only preserved in the letters of the different nations, and are only to be found in detached parts, a little in one, and a little in another.

In all the vast variety of systems or religions it appears to me, that no where is an original one to be found. All seem to be founded upon something which has preceded, and to have arisen out of it. If we consider the state of the human understanding, this seems natural; for the mind of man is always jealous of being deceived, to a certain extent, and so far as generally to detect forgeries attempted *de novo*. We have several examples of the detection of attempts of this kind; and I think there is reason to believe that none have succeeded. I am quite certain, that an un-

---

[1] "It is said to have been a regular part of the atheistical system, on the continent, to misquote and misrepresent "ancient authors; and the honest principle of it is this: where one reader is capable of following the citer, ten will be "incapable; of those who are capable, where one takes the trouble to do it, ten will not take the trouble; and of those "who detect the falsehood, where one steps forward to expose it, ten will be silent. It may, therefore, never be de- "tected; and if it be detected, the voice of a single individual, when the efforts of a whole conspiracy are employed to "drown it, will be heard to a very little distance." Pag. Idol. Vol. III. p. 650.

prejudiced examination of every religion or sect will result in the conviction, that it was founded on somewhat which preceded it, and, generally, that it was got up more by fools than rogues; though I must not be understood to deny, that the fools were, in many cases, abundantly roguish. But there was, what they believed to be, truth at the bottom, which it was thought good or right to support, and in the support of which a little fraud was considered to be excusable, and, indeed, often meritorious. And under this pretext they ran into the greatest extremes of fraud. If we consider this, and admit it to be a fair representation of the case, we shall find it leads us naturally to the conclusion, that there can be no system existing which may not be traced to some other system which has preceded it; and this satisfactorily accounts for their all running back to the most remote antiquity. It follows as a necessary consequence, that they must do so; for, according to this theory, they would have been detected if they had been modern. The systems are like languages—both like the radii of a circle, diverging from a centre, as they advanced down the stream of time, but merging into a centre as we recede upwards. The origin of letters is a theory, and nothing but a theory, and so it must always remain. We have not any thing like a record of their invention; but from the discovery of the right-lined alphabets, I think a probability arises, that they have not been of an extreme antiquity. It may be doubted whether we possess sufficient data to justify a belief in their greater antiquity than two thousand years before Christ. Yet it is possible that they may have been much older. But if we admit this, I think we must suppose them to have been a magical or masonic secret.

On reconsidering the theory of the origin of letters and arithmetic, and their close connexion with the sacred numbers, and the division of the year and circle into three hundred and sixty parts, I can find nothing improbable; indeed, I can find nothing in ancient or modern times more probable than that which I have suggested; and I am quite satisfied I have proved, that all written languages had originally only one system of sixteen letters; (I speak not of the Chinese;) and the renewed reflection of each recurring day more and more serves to convince me, that it was of the nature of a masonic system, and kept a profound secret for many generations. I conceive that it was the first discovery of this secret art which gave rise to the castes of antiquity, thus making the initiated a race really superior to the remainder of mankind. We have a perfect example in Tibet of what they would be—the priests, the initiated idlers, ruling the uninitiated labourers.

The early monuments of man, in their scientific and gigantic character, every where display power and science too great to exist without letters and arithmetic, and in the unity of their character they prove that one system must have extended over the whole world. What can be more striking than the cromlehs, carns, and the circles round them, constantly used to describe the cycles and vernal festivals, equally found in India and Britain, and found also in all the intermediate countries? Had the science of letters not been a masonic secret, when the builders of Stonehenge and Abury were recording their astronomical cycles upon them in the numbers of the stones, they would have inscribed some letters upon them, as they are said to have done upon the pillars of the Siriad in later times.

What can be more striking than the universal adoration paid to the sun, in his character of Creator, Preserver, and Destroyer, or as the emblem of the Triple Deity, the Trimurti or Trinity —of Buddha, of Moses or Genesis, of Orpheus, and of Jesus of Nazareth? Is there a corner of the old world which has not been stained with the blood shed on account of this beautiful, but often-misunderstood, doctrine? The proofs are complete of its existence in the Aleim of the first verse of Genesis or Wisdom.

The doctrine of the androgynous nature of the Deity is as universal as the Trinitarian doctrine. There is no part of the old world where it is not found; and in the observations on the word

Aleim, the plural feminine of the word AL, it is shewn to have existed as really with the Jews as with any other nation. All these, and many more, were the doctrines of the Cullidei or Chaldæans or Mathematici, evidently the most learned race in the world, as I have repeatedly intimated, and as I shall more satisfactorily prove.

In the Buddhist history of Wisdom, or, as we call it in Greek, Genesis, we have an account, and the first account, of the people called Chaldei. In India there are clearly found two Urs of the Chaldees, or Urianas of Collida, from either of which the Chaldei may have come. This Buddhist book expressly says, that the Brahmin who founded the Judæan state in Western Syria came from the East; therefore, if we are to believe it, they must have come from one of the two Urs which were in the East; and this is an admission of this book to which we cannot refuse our assent,—every circumstance, all history and all probability support it. And I think it must be concluded, that the Chaldei, both of the West and of Cape Comorin, were equally colonies of the Chaldei of central Asia or Upper India. And a little reflection may induce the belief, that settlements of Chaldei were also made even as far as Ireland, and the island of Columba or Iona.

In the Chaldei we have, most fortunately, preserved to us the name of these people from the most remote antiquity; so that this is not a matter entirely arising from inference. It is of the nature of a circumstantial proof of an historical fact, and its consequences are most valuable and important. It serves as a chain to connect together all the scattered scraps of ancient history, and the various detached parts of the one universal Pandean or Catholic system of religion, through all its varieties in different parts of the world: and, through all its varieties, carrying with it one generic character, that of the affectation of secrecy—a perfect Proteus, but still, at the bottom, Chaldaic and secret—mysterious to the end, even in its last dying speech in the Lodge of Antiquity, at Freemasons' Tavern, in London. I do not pretend to say I have *proved* that the art of writing was a masonic or magical secret for many generations. In the nature of the case it is not capable of *proof*, but I think this may, with great probability, be inferred. However, I shall assume that it has been proved, and in my next book I shall endeavour to shew the nature of the universal system above alluded to, and of the Pontifical dominion which the philosophers, in consequence of their possessing the knowledge of letters, acquired over the whole world; and, in the book following, a doctrine which they held will be developed—a doctrine which is now lost, or known only by effects totally unaccountable to us in consequence of our ignorance of their cause.

(258)

BOOK IV.

FEODAL OR FEUDAL TENURE.

UNIVERSAL PONTIFICAL GOVERNMENT.—RELIGION OF TIBET.—CHARTRES' STONE—THE LINGA.—ISLAND OF IONA.—FEODAL OR FEUDAL TENURE.—GAVEL-KIND.—FRANK-AL-MOIGN.—LANDS IN DEMESNE.—BURGAGE TENURE.—TENURE BY KNIGHTS' SERVICE.—ORIGIN OF MONKS AND NUNS.—LAND TAX OF INDIA.—THE SCYTHIANS.—THE ARABIANS.—MYTHIC DIVISIONS OF COUNTRIES, WITH THEIR OFFICERS.—TRADE, CRAFT, RAS OR CASTE.—CATHEDRALS, &c., WERE DRUIDICAL, THEN ROMAN, TEMPLES.—INGS LANDS.—ALLODIAL LANDS.—HISTORY OF THE ISLAND OF ii, OR IONA OR ICOLMKILL.—CEYLON.—CAL.—VITRIFIED FORTS OF SCOTLAND.—MYSTERY, WITTENAGEMOTE.—THE SCANDINAVIANS.—GERMAN ROSSICRUCIANS.—DI-OM, D'OM, DOMUS, OM.—CERES, BETHLEHEM.—CHIVALRY.—SEA KINGS, RUNES.—GOLDEN AGE.

1. THE object of the two following books of my work will be to shew, that in very ancient times, of which we have scarcely any notice, a very powerful *pontifical government* extended its sway over the whole world; that it was learned as well as powerful; and that it must have been the author of the ancient Druidical works every where to be met with, and was probably the empire designated in the Indian books by the name of Pandea. I suppose this was an empire of Saca or Buddha; that it was first established to the north of India; and that it extended itself by sending out tribes or colonies under the command of its own order, which, availing itself of its superior intelligence, easily conquered the Aborigines, (who were a people, as I shall shew, that had escaped from a flood,) and established every where its dominion. I shall shew that the Supreme Pontiff was, in some respects, similar to the Lama of Tibet and the Pope—supposed to be a Vicramaditya or Vicar of God, and probably thought to be a divine incarnation of the Trimurti of India, or Trinity. I shall shew, that there were several floods, and point out, probably, the times when three of them happened, and that they were caused by a comet in its several returns.

2. No person has turned his mind to the consideration of the religion of Tibet, which is the only country in which we have the Buddhist religion in any thing like its original purity, who has not expressed his surprise at the wonderful similarity between its religion and that of Rome. But if we divest our minds of prejudice we shall see that they are, in fact, precisely the same, only disguised by our sectarian nonsense. Jesus Christ was supposed to be the *ninth* Avatar, (as they had the ninth Avatar in the East,) with the expectation of the *tenth*, till the failure of the millenium destroyed it; but a remnant of it remains among some persons, such as the followers of Brothers and Southcott, and Faber, Irving, &c., who expect a re-incarnation of Jesus Christ.

The Dalecarlians of Sweden have a dialect of their own, which is considered to be a relict of the Gothic, the Anglo-Saxon, and the Irish languages, with which it has a great similarity. Holsenius says the same analogy exists, with many other languages, such as English, Greek, Spanish, and Italian; and Dr. Thomson, who travelled in Sweden, tells us, that a Dalecarlian who spoke this dialect, being landed near Aberdeen, was understood by the inhabitants. The Swede was understood because his language was the Celtic Hebrew—the parent of all the languages in a state almost primeval. Every where, when we go back to the most remote times, one language seems to have prevailed, and that, the Celtic-Scythic-Saxon-Hebrew; for, in those very early times, they were one. I also beg leave to draw my reader's attention to the fact, that the name of the crucified Is, by which the Scotch island is called, which is precisely the name of Jehovah in the Targums, who was believed to be incarnate and to appear in the person of the crucified Jesus Christ, is also the name of the incarnate Bal or Lord Is, who was the crucified God of the temple of Tripetty, on the promontory not far from Ceylon. It was in the country where we find this God, that we found some persons calling the language Chaldean, and all calling it Pushto or Pushpa, the name of the Syrian tongue; and here it was that we found the story of St. Thomas and the Crestans, and all the mythos of Moses, &c., as described by the Jesuits, and also the story of Robertus de Nobilibus turning Brahmin.

3. It cannot well be doubted that the stone at Chartres is precisely the same as the Linga in the cave at Bhobanéser, in the Carnatic, forty feet long, as described by Stirling in the Asiatic Researches.[1] In the dialogue between Justin and Trypho is the following passage: "For Christ is "said to be a King and Priest, and God, and Lord, and Angel, and Man, and Captain of the Host, "and STONE."[2] Now, if the stone here do not refer to the stone in the crypts of the temples and Christian churches, I should be happy to be informed to what it does allude. The equivoque of the *stone* and *Peter* evidently refers to the same thing. Trypho is made to say, "Suppose it be "true that Christ was to be called a stone." This alludes to the Stone, Linga or Logos.

I understand Duchesne was one of the most celebrated antiquarians of France, and now ranks with our Selden. The following particulars were given me by my friend Robert Hannay, Esq.—CHARTRES, *its Antiquity*.[3] " Cette ville est l'une des plus antiques, non de l'Europe, mais de toute " la Terre. Les Gomerites envoyés pour peupler la Gaule Celtique, en jettèrent les premiers " fondemens du temps de Noé, ce second père et ancêtre de la race des hommes, sous la con- " duite du grand Samothes.—Aujourd'hui la ville de Chartres se glorifie de son Eglise Cathédrale " comme du plus ancien temple de la Chrétienté.—Avant que Cæsar l'eût assujettie à la gran- " deur de l'Empire, par tant de diverses guerres, les Seigneurs et Roitelets qui eurent la reserve " de son gouvernement avoient puisé quelque créance dans la doctrine des Druides que d'une " Vierge devoit naître au monde le Rédempteur des humains. Créance qui occasionna le gou- " verneur Priscus de la faire tirer et figurer embrassant un petit enfant, lui donner rang parmi les " statues des ses Dieux et lui offrir des sacrifices." Here Duchesne recounts a miracle which occasioned the building of a temple to the Virgin: "Miracle qui l'emporta aisément avec Priscus " au bâtiment d'un temple à l'honneur de cette Vierge laquelle n'avoit encore vu la lumière du " Soleil, et qui ne la vit de plusieurs centaines d'ans après.—St. Pierre, chef des Apôtres, délégua les " bien-heureux saints Savinian et Potentian en la Gaule, les quels s'étant arrêtés à Chartres, trou- " vèrent que ce peuple honoroit déja la mémoire de la Vierge, qui devoit nous produire le Fils de " Dieu, et que pour relever davantage son honneur et sa gloire ils lui avoient superbement bâti " ce temple. C'est pour quoi ils imprimèrent aisément le caractère de la croyance Chrétienne " sur ces tendres âmes et consecrant leur temple au nom de la sacrée Mère." He then, among other matters, observes, that the church had seventy-two Chanoines.

After the above, Mr. Hannay gives me the following curious history, and I think few persons will doubt that we have here, in the capital of the ancient CARNUTES of Gaul, a repetition of the

---

[1] Vol. XV. p. 311.   [2] Sect. xxxvi. Ed. Brown, p. 146.
[3] Extracted from Les Antiquites et Recherches des Villes, &c., par André Duchesne, 1609, pp. 292, 294—296.

Linga worship of Buddha, and of Delphi, and of Jerusalem, named in the Appendix to my first volume. I request attention particularly to what I have said respecting the Carnutes and the Carn in Vol. I. p. 835, and to the Virgo Paritura, in the extract of Duchesne.

"Of the various histories of the Cathedral of Chartres not one have I been able to find in the British Museum, otherwise my notes on its Druidical remains might have been much extended. In the absence of authority allow me to offer my own evidence in proof of a very ancient and singular relict of the Druidical religion still extant there. In 1825, I spent some days at Chartres, when there happened a festival of that church. On Sunday the cathedral was crowded with the people of that city and its neighbourhood. At the close of the service I observed that no one left the church without kneeling and making a short prayer before a small pillar or stone, for it was without polish, base or capital, placed in a niche, and much worn on one side by the kisses of the devout; after prayer each embracing the stone and imprinting with reverence a kiss upon its left side. Curious to know something of this strange ceremony, I inquired of an official of the cathedral, who informed me, that this stone was of high antiquity, even earlier than the establishment of Christianity—that for many centuries it had remained in a crypt of the cathedral, where lamps were kept constantly burning; but the stairs leading to this vault having been worn away by the great resort of pilgrims to this sacred spot, to spare the expense of repairs and avoid the accidents frequent in descending, the stone had been removed some time ago from its original site to where it now stands in the cathedral above. Upon further inquiry into the motives for this singular adoration, I was assured that this was no common stone, but a miraculous stone, and that its miracles were performed by its intercession with the Virgin Mary.

"ROBERT HANNAY."

I need not repeat that Delphi means *the navel*, and that it was called the centre and navel of the earth. In that temple there was a stone pillar to which the priests paid the most profound respect.[1] How can we doubt that here there were the same pillar and navel of the earth as we found at Jerusalem, Chartres, &c.? As we find the Lingas both in the temples at Jerusalem and Chartres were in vaults, so we find the Linga of the Rajahs of *Kesari* at the temple of Bhaskaresar, or Bhobanéser, Maha-deo, is placed in a "subterranean vault" as far as possible; but, from its immense size, it projects out to a great height.[2] In the adoration of the Linga we have a very remarkable example of the diffusion of this religion—in the Kara-corums or stone circles and lingas or pillars. We have it first in Tartary, probably its birthplace; then we have it described at Bhobanéser in Orissa,[3] in the Carnatic, in the Lingas and the name of the country; we next have it in the Gordyæan mountains; next in Carnac, in Egypt; next in Troy, with its Mount Gargarus, its stone circle and palladium, or sacred stone; next in the Temple of Jerusalem, as described by Nicephorus Calistus, with its stone pillar concealed in the cellar;[4] next in Rome, with its Etruscan Agrimensorism; next in Chartres, the capital of the Carnutes, the exact picture of that described by Nicephorus Calistus; next in Choir Gaure or Stonehenge; and lastly, in the Linga and Yoni and Kara-corum of Scotland, with its sacred stone from Scone. To these must be added the fire towers of Ireland, Scotland, and, indeed, many other of the fire towers, as they are

---

[1] Paus. Bœotic. 25; Const. Vol. II. p. 343.   [2] Asiat. Res. Vol. XV. p. 311.

[3] Ibid. Vol. XV. p. 306. Bhobanéser is also called Bhuvanéswara, and also Ekam-rakanuma, or Ekamra, or Ekamber. I have no doubt this was, as the city of the Linga, the city of the generative principle, the city of מאן Aām, the God of Wisdom.

[4] See Vol. I. p. 832.

ostensibly called, in many parts of Europe, and also the towers of India, of the Callidei, or Culdees, or Cala-Desa, which are almost exact pictures of those in Ireland. In some instances, where they are very large, iron bearers, of a size almost beyond credibility, have been used; as for example, at the ancient desecrated temple of Jaggernaut. "But, in general, the architects "have resorted, in the construction of their roofs, to the method of laying horizontal layers of "stone, projecting one beyond the other like inverted steps, until the sides approach sufficiently "near at the summit to admit of other blocks being laid across."[1] This, which is the most ancient mode of covering now remaining in the world, is precisely the same in the towers of Ireland and India. Not far from the famous Jaggernaut is the village of Kanarak: this is evidently the same name as the Carnac of the Carnutes in the West. It is called the Arka. Here was a famous temple of the sun. It was in the same style of building as those described above, and it tends to confirm what I have formerly said of the mystic use of the loadstone, that its roof, formed of overhanging stones, is capped with a large LOADSTONE; and in order to support such an enormous mass, bearers of beaten iron, which are yet remaining twenty-one feet in length and eight inches square, have been used. The stones of the roof have been fifteen or sixteen feet long, six feet deep, and two or three feet thick.[2] These stones must have been raised nearly two-hundred feet high. The building is formed into a cross by its two magnificent porches. Each side, we are told,[3] is sixty feet long. This would be, in feet of Cairo or of antiquity, at 8.7552 inches to the foot, about seventy-five feet. But when I consider the careless mode in which our travellers often make their measurements, I cannot help suspecting it has been seventy-two feet. It must have been a difficult matter correctly to ascertain the length of such a mass of ruins, amidst the jungle, the tigers, and the snakes. My friend, Professor Haughton, very nearly lost his life in attempting to penetrate to them through the jungle. In the front of the building stands a most beautiful pillar of one stone,[4] which cannot fail to remind a spectator of the pillars in front of the churches in Rome, particularly that in front of Maria Maggiore, for the location of which no satisfactory reason can be, or at least ever is, given. The Indians call these stones Jaya Stambhas or Pillars of Victory. But I believe their name has descended from a very remote antiquity, when they were called, in the language of the Chaldeans or Callidei or Culdees, Pillars of יהוה ieue or יהוה ieis, the Self-existent God, commonly called in the Bible, the God of Sabaoth, of Armies, of Hosts, and of VICTORY. Jagannath is saluted with cries of—Jye Jagannath, which they say means Victory to Jagannath; but it is evident that this is the Hebrew יה iis or is, always called the God of victory; and in both cases it really means, God the Creator, or the God of Wisdom, or Wisdom of the great Iu or Creator. But it had probably both meanings, one private, the other public. The ancient Hindoo bridges, built of *overhanging* instead of *radiated* stones, are very common in South India.[5] A history is to be found in Persia, evidently similar, though we have only a part of it. Benj. Constant[6] says, "Lors de la destruction de Persépolis par les Mohamédans, on découvrit " dans les *fondements* d'un des principaux temples de cette ville, une pierre précieuse appelée " Tutya, qui n'existe qu'aux Indes, sans que rien indiquât comment elle avait pu y être apportée." I think, after reading the accounts of the stone in the crypt or vault in the Carnatic, at Jerusalem, and in the capital of the Carnutes, no one will deny that there is a high probability that all these were for the same purpose, viz. to conceal the Cabalistic doctrines of the first chapter of John,— the adoration of the Logos, the Linga, or the Honover, as the Logos was called in Persia.[7]

---

[1] Asiat. Res. Vol. XV. p. 307.   [2] See Vol. I. p. 765.   [3] Asiat. Res. Vol. XV. p. 329.
[4] Ib. p. 320.   [5] Ib. pp. 336, 337.   [6] Vol. II. p. 24.
[7] See Ouvrages de Zoroastre, Vol. I. Part. II. pp. 86, 87, where the Word is invoked. See also pp. 138, 139, (which is very like John i. 1,) and Vol. II. p. 239, where may be seen the I AM, *i. e.* of the Hebrews. Trans. Bombay, Vol. II. p. 318.

4. We will now pause a little, and reconsider a few of the circumstances connected with the island of Iona. Artimodorus says, that there was an island, near to Britain, where sacrifices were offered to Ceres and Proserpine, the same as in Samothrace. We have seen how Ceres or Cres is identified with both Bacchus and Apollo, and it may be recollected how a sacred hyperborean island is said to have adored Apollo. It may also be recollected how we found in the East, close to Ceylon, on the promontory, the adoration of the crucified God, the Χρης, and the Callidei or Cullidi or Culdees, with their three Sacraments—of orders, baptism, and the eucharist—and also the Christians of St. Thomas. Let it also be recollected, that Diodorus tells us, Apollo was adored with dances, and that in this island the God danced all night. Now, from the Phœnician Ireland, of Mr. Henry O'Brien, (p. 227,) I learn, that the Christians of St. Thomas, till a very late day, celebrated their Christian worship with dances and songs. It may be recollected, that we have all these matters repeated at Delphi, where Dr. Clarke found the tablet with the Χρης. The reader must recollect the Linga and Nabhi in the cave at Bhobanéser—the Linga in the ancient temple of Jerusalem—in the cave at New Grange, in Ireland,[1] and at Delphi, and with the Carnutes of Gaul, whose monstrous temple was Carnac, and that this eastern country is called Carnate and Carnatic, that the languages of these countries were called Gael and Sin-gall and Sanscrit. He must recollect also the Camasene in India, Cape Coma-rin and Italy, and, what *we* have almost lost sight of, the April-fool and May-day festivals equally celebrated in Britain and India. The heathen custom of celebrating the rites of Thomas with singing and DANCING is, in fact, of itself, almost enough to prove the Thomas to be Tamuz, without the proofs which I have given in the first volume. But, as Mr. Baber[2] and our travellers give us no account of this dancing, it appears to have been suppressed since the arrival of the Protestants: hence we see how much more effective our Protestant missions are than those of the Papists, to suppress all the truths which may be of any real service to discover the nature of ancient history.

5. Perhaps among the circumstances which tend to shew the ancient connexion between the Eastern and Western nations, and to support my theory, that an universal sacerdotal empire extended its sway over the old world, there is not one more curious and striking than the existence, in the most widely separated parts, of the same artificial mode of occupying land, called in this country the Feodal or Feudal Tenure or system. This system is found equally in Britain and India. I apprehend it was first brought to the West from the latter, in very remote times, by a tribe of the followers of Xaca,—that is, by the Sacæ or Saxons. As the system is found both in Gaul and Scandinavia, it may have come hither by way of the former, or of the latter country. Every one knows that after the time of the Romans, in, comparatively speaking, a recent period, tribes of Saxons came to this country from the latter, but originally they came to both from Asia. Richardson truly says, " the feudal system in Europe is an exotic plant, but in the East it is indigenous, " universal, and immemorial. In India, Persia, Tartary, and other Eastern countries, the whole " detail of government, from the most ancient accounts down to the present hour, can hardly be " defined by any other description than feudal." D'Ancarville says, "Asia was then a fief depend- " ing on Scythia: it was the first governed by this kind of constitution, and here may be dis- " covered the origin of the FEUDAL SYSTEM, brought into Europe by these very Sacæ."[3] The system of feudal tenure supposes the natural state to be a state of rest—of peace—rest and peace to be the rule, and war the exception; and the granting of Jagheers or military fiefs—creating tenants by knights' service, is perfectly consistent with this.[4] It is curious to observe the principles of

---

[1] Vide O'Brien, p. 320.   [2] See Vol. I. p. 668.   [3] Vall. Coll. Hib. Vol. V. pp. 33, 228, 317.
[4] The Jagheer is said to have been a Mohamedan institution; Patton on Principles of Asiat. Mon. p. 203; but this

the feudal system admitted to be lost equally in India and Europe, and the lawyers in each of these countries to be in perpetual strife about them, yet making out nothing satisfactory at last. Before letters, livery of seizin was the practice. When we look to the great countries of Asia we find every where immense military fiefs, or fiefs partly military and partly hierarchical; we generally, I think, see the priests grow into kings: in some we see the seat of the priest occupied by the general, who, having forced the priest to give him the unction or χειροτονια, thus becomes sacred majesty. In Europe we see the system falling to pieces in different ways—the municipia growing into free states—some more, some less assimilated to the despotisms of Asia. In France and Germany, principalities arose,—in Italy and Greece, republics. Mr. Patton, who is the most sensible writer I have ever met with on these subjects, observes, "The circumstance of land being "common or the property of the society, and never possessed by individuals among the *pastoral* "*tribes*, which has been so frequently pressed upon the attention of the reader, seems to offer a "natural explanation of the rise and progress of the Asiatic constitution of monarchical govern- "ment, which is uniformly and unalterably despotic. These peculiarities have been shewn to "depend upon the absolute property of the land being vested in the sovereign, which precludes "the rivalship of power through the means of great land-proprietors, who cannot possibly exist "under such circumstances. But how this absolute property, of all the land of the state, came "originally to be vested in the monarch or sovereign, *is the question which it is so difficult to* "*answer*. If we suppose the pastoral state of society to have universally preceded the agricultural "state in Asia, a supposition not void of historical support, a very obvious explanation seems to "result from it. Among all pastoral tribes, the monarchical form of government is prevalent: the "chief is the representative of the public, and, in time of war, is absolute. The first and earliest "transition from the pastoral to the *agricultural* state of society, must always remain a subject "for conjecture."[1] Notwithstanding the multitude of writers of great eminence, both Jurists, like Spelman, and antiquarian philosophers, like Montesquieu, Dr. Stuart, &c., who have written respecting the origin of feodal tenures or fiefs,[2] it cannot be denied, that they have all failed to give a satisfactory explanation of it. It cannot be denied that something is still wanting.[3] I flatter myself my theory will supply it. Mr. Patton observes, that Bernier, Manuchi, Thevenot, Chardin, Tavernier, all with one consent assert, that there was no private landed property in India—that the emperor was sole proprietor of all the lands within his empire.[4] In China, the same appears to have been the case, and only a tenth of the produce was taken;[5] and in Persia or Iran the same.[6] And, again, the same in Siam or the Burman empire,[7] which, in the laws of Menu, is called Dhassa-meda. The Dhasa, is the Latin *decima*, and the Meda the Latin *modius* or *measure*, and the whole the *tenth measure* of the grain or other produce. Of the word feoud or feod or feud, I have not seen and cannot give any satisfactory explanation. But if the tribes of Ioudi and the Sacæ were the same, I suggest for consideration whether *feudal tenure* may not be lands in the tenure of Pi-Ioudi, תהּ Ioudi. And in favour of this is the circumstance, that, the part of the country whence the Ioudi came, namely, the Mesopotamia formed by the Indus and Ganges, is precisely the country were the Feodal system retains its greatest vigour at this day. Vallancey says, in old Irish Faoi-ud means, one under

---

I can scarcely believe. The word Jagheer seems old: גר יא *ia,* literally, country within a circular inclosure, a district, as districts in Ceylon and Germany were called *Circles.*

[1] Patton on the Principles of Asiatic Monarchies, pp. 268—270. [2] Ibid. p. 297.

[3] Many interesting observations on the ancient feodal tenures may be found in Vallancey's Coll. Hib. Vol. V. pp. 23—33, 228, 229, 318, 321, 322.

[4] Patton, p. 200.   [5] Ib. p. 229.   [6] Ib. p. 231.   [7] Ib. p. 264.

covenant,[1] and Feudal tenure, in Irish, is *Achusac,* in Arabic, Akhezet. This must be the Hebrew אחז *ahz,* possedit, obtinuit,[2] and the Acherah of the Mohamedans, that is, the payment of the tithe. In Irish *Achusac* also means *possessio,* and *Sean-achas* was a judge of a feodal code. I do not much doubt, that the Sean-ach became Senate. The first redditio was of the tenth of the produce, as the word asera implies, and this was paid to the patriarch at the head of the pontifical government, or his assigns, by nearly the whole world. The word Feud or Feudal is a generic term as applied to the occupation of land, of which there are several species. The first I shall notice is called *Soccage* and Free Soccage, which Blackstone says has been thought to be derived from the Saxon Soc, *a plough;*[3] but he thinks better, from Soc, liberty, privilege. However, I think it was from Xaca or Saca. It was the land of Saca, for which only the service of the plough or an agricultural return was required by the priests,[4] in opposition to the knights' service, for which, services of war or services which infringed upon personal liberty, were required by the military governors. The former were the lands of Xaca, Saca, Saga, Sagax, of Wisdom.[5] Socage or Soccage has been defined to be a determinate service, the render for which was precarious, unlimited, and uncertain. This was certainly its nature; but it was not from this that it had its name. I believe that *originally* soccage estates descended to all the children: but certainly, in Henry the Third's time, primogeniture in soccage lands came to prevail very generally. There were *Soc-manni* and *Boc-manni.* The first were Seculars—the second the Regulars, the Moines or Monks or Book-men. The mannus was descriptive of the order of Menu, or sacred or secret order—from the secret writing. The Soc and the Boc describe the division of the caste into *first* functionaries, and *second* those whence the functionaries were taken, into first, Regulars, i. e. Boc-manni, initiati or ordered; and second, Seculars, not regulated, not ordered. The word initiated marks the distinction. In order to separate and know themselves, they initiated or circumcised themselves: this was the secret, i. e. sacred rite. Is not sacred, Soc or Sac-rid, *to be-rid,* quit of —free from the rule of monks, as well as free from the rule of military service?

When Joseph was the prime minister of Egypt, it is clear that, whether his history be taken figuratively or literally,[6] a state of feodal tenure was established by him; the state of society described is exactly that which existed in India and Europe, after the sword divided from the crosier, and was beginning to prevail over it. (In the first ages of the tribe of the Jews the crosier alone prevailed.) This was the independent, or partly independent, state of the king at Thebes or Memphis, about the time when the priest at Philoe had power at his pleasure to order him to commit suicide.[7] The king was not of the description of our officers bearing that title. He was only the general in chief of the sacerdotal forces. We must recollect that the Rev. Robert Taylor has proved, in his Diegesis, that all the different degrees and orders of priesthood, or of the Christian hierarchy, formerly existed in Egypt.[8] This premised, I suggest that Free

---

[1] Vall. Coll. Hib. Vol. V. p. 229.   [2] Ibid. 229, 265.   [3] Blackstone's Com. B. ii. Ch. vi.

[4] After the sword had divided from the crosier, or the two castes of soldiers and priests, the origin of which I shall explain by and by, had arisen.

[5] The Sacæ are called Sagæ, Vall. Coll. Hib. Vol. V. p. 34; hence come sacrum, sacrificium, sacerdos. The Romans had a priest called Sagart, from the word Sag. There could be no sacrifice without this officer. From this word Cleland says came the Sac-erdos. Cleland's Spec. p. 22.

[6] *Literally* as I would fain flatter myself, at least in great part, for I cannot part with the beautiful story without much regret. If it be not meant to be literal, it must be of the same nature as the Cyropædia. It contains, in the latter case, a parable, to inculcate some very fine moral doctrine, which, whether true or false, it teaches.

[7] This is the exact case of the Grand Seignior and his Pashas at this day.   [8] See *supra,* p. 71.

Soccage is the Soccage in Egypt of Φρη, פרה pre or Phre¹ or of Pharaoh, or of the Solar deity; and, in the North, of the Scandinavian Freisia, and the Swedish Frij. The occupiers of the lands of the priests, when the crosier divided from the sword, held of the God Phre, and thus were freemen or men of the God Free, and exempt from military service. Thus, probably, arose the words *free* and *free-men*. They were men or tenants of the God Liber—of Liber-tas, or Liber-ty, (Liber-di, or God or *holy* Liber,) because the God Free or Φρη was Bacchus, and because Bacchus was called Liber. From his close connexion with the tree of knowledge and letters, he came to be called by the name of liber, *a book;* from a similar cause the bark of a tree, on which the letters were written, was called liber, all which I have before shewn at great length, *supra*, pp. 163, 164. In the *state* of the world which I now contemplate, the present *state,* in fact, of Tibet, the Priests were the Lords of the creation. Their tenants, paying only *a tenth* of the produce as rent, must have been in a very easy and comfortable state. Here is one of the reasons of the state of freemen, so much envied. Those are the *Liberi-Sokemanni*.² (We must not forget, and I shall presently resume the discussion of the mythological meaning which I have shewn that the north country word *mannus* or *man* always had, and its connexion with the Om or Hom of India and Persia.) They were the men or manni of Liber or Soke or Saca. They were said to be in FREE soccage for the reasons just now assigned, and they were in a later day said to be in COMMON soccage, because the priests of whom they held, having become monks, possessed every thing, and yet possess it in Tibet in COMMON, in community. They held of the community. From Blackstone's expression it is evident, that he considered the word *soc* to have the same meaning as *liber*, and he calls it *free*. This all arises from the application of Liber not being known.

6. I believe what Glanville says is true, that all lands held in free soccage were held in Gavelkind:³ "Si vero fuerit liber Socmannus, tam quidem dividetur hæreditas inter omnes filios quot-"que sunt per partes æquales; si fuerit Soccagium ut id antiquitus divisum." The *natural* process is for a man to divide his property among his children; the artificial is, by knights' service, to give it all to the eldest. I think the term Gavel-kind is formed from the British Gafaelu tenere or Gafael tenura, and the word kind-red. The land was held by right of kindred, and not by grant from the Lord or King or Soldier; in return for which, service of war was rendered. It was held of the Priest, who did not care how it went, so that he got his vectigal. From this it would come to pass, in many cases, perhaps in all, that the occupiers of lands would do suit and service to one lord and pay tithe to another. Gavel-kind land did not escheat in case of the felony of its occupier. It was Folkland and Allodial, which terms I shall explain presently. It did not escheat, because it was not the property in any sense of the occupier. But it would escheat for the felony of the person of whom the occupier held it; in such a case, however, the occupier would not necessarily be disturbed, as our farmers are not disturbed for the treason of their landlord. They pay their rents to the new landlord. If they have leases the landlord's treason does not affect the rights granted by their leases. The nature of the general tenure of land in ancient times is perhaps no where better exhibited than in the grant of land made by Xenophon to Diana. He gave up to her the land, reserving to himself the cultivation and enjoyment of it, but this, subject to the payment of a tenth of the produce to her. Here she was Lady of the soil, for the use of

---

[1] I have formerly shewn that the word *Phre* denoted the God of Wisdom, in numerals, that is, in ciphers; *supra*, p. 209.

[2] Blackstone, B. ii. Ch. vi. Liberi and Soc-manni both have the same meaning: Liberi-Socmanni is a pleonasm, very common in language, arising from the terms not being understood.

[3] The Gavel-kind tenure of Kent (Cantia, Qy. of Kanya, or *ia* of *Cuni—Bel?*) Ran. Glanville de Leg. Ang. Lib. vii. Cap. iii. p. 49.

which she retained the tenth. The land in like manner was THE LORD's in Palestine; but for him the Levites received the tenths. Niebuhr says, "So a tenth is the portion the state seems in general to have levied on corn, as the Roman republic did whenever it exercised its right of ownership."[1] Gilbert Burnet, in his history of the rights of princes, p. 115, has shewn that in the time of Clotaire the kings of France received the tithes or tenths, and that after they had given them up to the church, they took the tenth of the remainder, (if I understand him,) which was called the ninths. This, combined with the power of excommunication possessed by Charlemagne, seems to shew that the kings of France had some claims independent of the Popes, not now understood; and this is strengthened by the history of the disputes respecting the freedom of the Gallican church, which has always been involved in great difficulties. Sir Thomas Munro says, "among the *only* Hindoo chiefs unsubdued by the Mohamedans, the Rajas of Ceylon, Travancore, Cochin, and Coorg, the land-tax is still but ten per cent."[2] Mr. Cleland, without having the least suspicion of my theory, or that there ever was an universal system, has maintained there are proofs that, in very ancient times, almost all the lands in Europe belonged to the order of the Druids or Priests. I need not point out how this supports my theory. How the state of the world which I shall now describe arose, I shall endeavour hereafter to shew, but I believe that, in very early times the priest and king were the same, and that all the land belonged to the former. He was *jure divino* proprietor of the soil, and received from the cultivators, to whom he granted it, one tenth or the tithe of the produce for the use of it. The cultivators or Grantees answered to what in India are now called Ryots, and, in process of time, collectors were appointed who answered to the present Zemindars, who, at first, collected for the priests, and at last ended in renting the tithes of districts. The King-priest possessed the soil of the land, was Lord of the soil, as vicegerent of God. This was before the sword divided from the crosier; perhaps at the time now spoken of the sword was scarcely known. This might be the Golden Age of the Poets. The theory was, that the whole world belonged by divine right to the person who escaped from a great flood, who is called in the books of the Jews *Noah*, that he divided it or enfeoffed it to his three sons, and they to their children. And in subservience to this system, whether founded in truth or not, the monarchs of the East deduce their pedigrees from one of his three sons. This system I shall unfold in my next book.

7. The next tenure I shall notice is that of Frank-al-Moign. When two classes of priests arose, namely, the Seculars and Regulars, the lands in Frank-al-Moign were the lands held of the latter—held of the monks—les moines, or al-manni, both still being lands of Frank or Liber. The Seculars had that name from the Soc or Sac, both of which had the meaning of $αιωνος$. All priests were originally Seculars: the word Frank-al-Moign arose in time to distinguish the tenure of the Monks, the Regulars, from the tenure of the Seculars. The whole land was originally the property of the priests, as vicegerents of the Divine Power, Vicars of God, as the Pope claims to be the possessor of all lands, and claims the tithes of them as his tribute. They were Vicar-manni, which probably became corrupted, when its meaning was lost, into Vicrama, and Vicrama-ditya, perhaps Vicar-om-Manni. From the Priests the Soc-manni just named held their lands; and to them only were they amenable or liable in any way to account for their conduct; and they had their own tribunals. When in later times the right of the Pontiff was lost sight of and great conquerors gave away extensive districts to their followers or feodal Barons, in the interior of which lands occupied by the priests were of course included, the Barons claimed from the priest a service tribute or acknowledgment of superiority; but whenever this was granted, it was done

---

[1] Niebuhr, Vol. II. p. 136. [2] Briggs, p. 400.

through fear, and a mental or verbal reservation of the rights of the church was always annexed to it; and as the extent of these rights was unknown, the claim, which in no case was ever given up, was a source of the most violent animosity. In consequence of this, in later times, an unceasing strife for power always existed between the Barons and the Priests; the priests by the terrors of purgatory generally at last prevailing. The Franks were first heard of on the Rhine as Ale-manni. The word Frank means *free*, and is probably a corruption of the word Φϱη or Free—Liberi Sacæ. It was the religious name of the tribe, and in fact Saxons, as all the tribes probably were. Φρη and Freyas were arithmetical names of the same cycle, in its different stages of improvement, 666 and 608. From the word פרן *pro* Parkhurst derives the words Frank and Franchise, and the Franks, (who had a king or dynasty called *Pharamond*,) which tends to confirm what I have said. From this root may come our word Freehold, that is, land held of the God ΦPH. Our Freeholds are all held of a superior; in theory they all have suit and service to perform to the liege Lord, Priest or King, whichever it may be; that is, Khan or Pri-est, or Φρη-est, meaning *the real priest*. The word *est* is here a mere intensitive—the very Φρη. La Loubère[1] says, in the Siam language, Sion, that is, *Sun*, means *free*. On this account *the natives maintain that they have the same name as the Franks*. Their Pra means Creator; this is the Φρη of the Coptic and Greek. But Pra and Bra in the Siamese language are the same, and mean God; and here we come to the origin of the word in the numeral language—Φρ, and Φρη=600 and 608.

When, as I have lately said, the kings (as our William the Conqueror for instance) granted out large tracts to their generals, the latter claimed supremacy over the whole district; but they could not succeed against the priestly monks, who always denied the power of the kings to dispose, even by conquest, of the property of the church. But a struggle took place, whence arose the lay appropriations, in which the soldiers or laymen succeeded. When scruples of conscience and a refusal of absolution compelled the laymen to leave the patronage of the churches to the monks, the monks did not, until restrained by statutes, appoint rectors, but only curates or vicars keeping the tithes, which they claimed as the right of the order, to themselves. It is probable that the mode by which the orders of monks and seculars, after the Roman times, after having been divided, became united into one, was soon unknown to themselves. All we know is, that for a great number of years there was every where a marked separation of the two orders, and that there were perpetual divisions and disputes. Rapin says, the Franci and Saxons were the same, and he quotes Sir William Temple as authority;[2] and, the languages of the northern tribes were so near, that *they could all understand one another*, and that, as might be expected, their laws were all the same.[3] I need not point out how this tends to confirm the whole of my system. The five dialects of the British Celts are become so changed, that the different tribes are now, in general, no longer intelligible to one another; that is, with the exception of some of the inhabitants of the most remote and secluded places. D'Ancarville undertakes to prove, "that the mythology of the Egyptians, Brahmins, Chinese, Japanese, and all other oriental nations, had that of the Sacæ as their basis".[4] In his fifth volume of the Collectanea, Vallancey has given many striking proofs of the identity of the eastern and ancient Hibernian customs, which confirm D'Ancarville. " Franci et Saxones apud antiquos Socii et Amici, donec in diversas partes traheret imperii libido." Again, "Saxonum et Francorum nomen commune videtur aliquandiu fuisse gentibus, quemad- " modum adhuc nostra ætate in orientis partibus universæ Europæ gentes dicuntur Franci."[5] I feel no doubt that the Franks and Saxons were the same race of people. Perhaps the Franks

---

[1] Pp. 6, 7.   [2] Vol. I. p. 207.   [3] Vol. II. p. 138.
[4] Vall. Coll. Hib. Vol. V. p. 35.   [5] Themis Ambrica Petri Frid. Arpi, pp. 244, 246.

might be a tribe of the Sacæ, as the Macdonalds are a tribe of the Scotch. But still the one were Sacæ and the other are Scotch. Thus the Franks were Saxons. In a very early age I think they may be found in Italy. Italy had its name from Vitulus a Bull, and every one knows the story of its Saturnalia; it was the country of Saturn; but the Saturnalia were festivals of Saca. Selden says,[1] "Sesach Numen est apud Jeremiam .... ab eo (sic volunt viri doctissimi) "Sacea, festum Babyloniorum, dicta, seu ἡμερας Σακεας, uti apud Romanos Saturnalia à Saturno. "Atque ut Saturnalibus, servis epulantibus famulabantur domini, ita et in diebus Saceis; qui "quinque erant continui." When we recollect the striking manner in which the Saturn-ja is found in North India, (see Tod's map of Rajast'han, the country of the Sacæ or Buddas,) and the similarity of his Sacæa to the Saturnalia of Babylon and Italy, and we consider what Jeremiah has said respecting the king Sheshach, we cannot doubt, as I formerly remarked, that Shesach was the Scythian king, and that the followers of Saturn and the Pallestini were Saxons.[2] But from Herodotus we know that the Saxons and Scythians were the same; and in my Celtic Druids I have shewn that the Celtæ were both Scythians and Galli or Gauls: but I shall discuss this, which is very important, by and by, when I again treat of the Scotch island of Iona. The persons who held lands in Frank-al-moign would have no grants, charters, or other title-deeds, to shew for them, as their owners were by descent successors of the first appropriators or possessors; and, in consequence of this defect of title, they were often exposed to the demands of the Barons; who, when their consciences would not let them dispute the right of the church to the seignorage or lord-paramountship, called upon the monks to prove their right to the usufruct of particular parcels as individuals or separate bodies by the exhibition of some title; and as the modern principle, that no title-deed, or immemorial possession, is the *best* title, was not established, they were obliged to have recourse to a measure which neither is nor can be denied, viz. a general forging of grants and charters. This was a trick easy enough to the liberi, Boc-manni—Book men, impossible to be detected by the Barons, probably not one in a thousand of whom could read. I have spoken of the Moines or Manni as the same. We have seen the derivation of Homo for man or vir. I apprehend this was originally the name only of the Monks; they were the Manni Om, the first word in regimine. Whenever the word Mannus is found, it seems always to have a relation to something mystical, to the secret or mysterious doctrines. The Om-manni does not seem very unlike the Moines.

8. It is an important circumstance, that the Saxon kings claimed to have all the lands of their kingdom in demesne.[3] This is precisely the Indian system; and in the claim of the fee or the soil, and the edict giving the tithes to the church, a compromise seems to have taken place between the sword and the crosier. The statute of Ethelred, which gave the tithes to the priests, was, in fact, nothing but a declaratory statute. I perfectly agree with Cleland, who says, "The result of "my researches has been, that the feudal system is at this moment very little understood. Most "of the writers whom I have seen upon that subject, have mistaken the monstrous depravation of "that system, for the system itself."[4]

9. Burgage tenure is nearly the same as the Soccage tenure, but applicable to towns. In this, the *house* of which the family property consisted, went to the youngest son, the rest having gone off or colonised or enlisted in the military class. It is a practice strongly marking the identity of the Sacæ of Tartary and Britain, it being common to both.[5]

10. The next tenure to be noticed is that of tenure by Knights' service. Probably the Saxons

---

[1] De Diis Syriis, ch. xiii. p. 342.   [2] Vide Morning Watch, No. IX.   [3] Hallam, Hist. Vol. II. p. 179
[4] Spec. Add. art. p. xii.   [5] Vide Du Halde, Hist. of China, and Blackstone, B. ii. Ch. vi.

had tenures by Knights' service as well as the Romans; but a moment's consideration will shew why we hear not of Knights' service after the Norman came, except as service to him. There are, therefore, no more old remains of it now to be found. Those which were not strictly Norman, and at that time new, merged into the service due to the Normans or Northmen. If Saxon knights did not do their service to the new king, they threw off their allegiance, they forfeited their lands, and a Norman took them. To do military service to another would have been rebellion, treason. The only lands in free Soccage or Burgage tenure left by William, as indeed they probably were before, were lands held of the Priests. See the exchange of lands named in Blackstone,[1] by the Archbishop of Canterbury, from tenure by Soccage to tenure by Knighthood. At first, when Priest and King were identical, all lands were held in Soccage, held, I repeat, as they are now in Tibet, of the Monks. I think when the Archbishop changed the tenure of his lands, the object in holding them of the king was, to secure them from the claim of the Barons, to whom he could not exhibit any title to them. They had descended to him from his Druidical predecessors. Judge Blackstone[2] very properly and very distinctly admits the Saxon origin of the feudal or feodal system, though he overlooks the almost inevitable consequence that, after the arrival of the Normans, the old Saxon tenures by Knights' service must necessarily have disappeared—a fact which he seems at a loss to account for. The ancient Folkland, or estates held in villeinage, Blackstone says, was strictly neither feodal, Saxon nor Norman. The reason of this was, because their owners were the first possessors before the arrival of the later Saxons and Normans, and if any lands were left to them they could only hold of the new Lords. The old Lords were either gone or sunk into the class of villeins by the arrival of the new comers. They became the Helots; they were the folks—οἱ πολλοί. Several other kinds of tenure arose in later times, but they are not worth notice.

11. Perhaps the Monks did not exist till the quarrels respecting the two principles began to arise. Then, *as usual in all such cases*, the two parties ran into the most absurd extremes, till they covered the Eastern world with blood. It seems probable that the war lasted for many generations; in short, I believe it never entirely ceased till both parties were conquered by the Mohamedans. From extreme devotion to the *male* principle, it is likely that both the Monks and the Eunuchs might arise. The last person of the second class perhaps may be found in the celebrated and learned Origen. On the other side, in opposition, might arise the Nuns. I believe there are no Monks among the Brahmins; they are, I think, solely among the Buddhists. The followers of Buddha affected the *male;* the followers of Cristna the *female.* But it is very possible that in India, as in Europe, after the two sects united and the cause of their existence was forgotten; still, as the religious principle of abstinence from sexual intercourse, which had become established as a meritorious act, remained, monastic institutions of both religions may have been founded. Nothing is more difficult to eradicate than a religious principle of this kind, when once established. Monachism is of such a nature, that *if not molested,* silently and peaceably, by stealth as it were, it will, in no very long time, by possessing all real or landed property, possess itself of the government of every country. Tibet is a striking example of the truth of this remark. The Papal see is now essentially monastic. I have no doubt that the first governors of nations were priests—Melchizedeks, Royal or King-Priests. After a certain time, when the difference to which I have just alluded between the followers of the two principles took place, the Monks arose, and, by degrees, got possession of the governments. No doubt, the ancient priesthood would not like this, and probably petty wars and contentions would arise between the parties, similar to what we

---

[1] Com. B. ii. Ch. vi.   [2] Ibid.

know took place in the early ages of the European Papacy. But when the *male* and *female* sects coalesced, the Seculars and Regulars, though perhaps hating one another, would have a common interest against the remainder of mankind. In the dark ages of Europe we read of great contentions between the Popes and the Monks; but I think, at last, the Monks prevailed, having first received modern Christian ordination from the Popes. If we read the histories we shall find that the Popes, the Seculars, prevailed; but in the imprudent admission of the Monks to orders, according to their own, i. e. the secular form, they opened to them the doors of the Vatican.[1] Once admitted, they soon proceeded to the election of Bishops, subject, it is true, to the approbation of the Pope, and to investiture by him; but in a very short time they themselves became Bishops, Cardinals, and Popes; and although there is yet a good deal of jealousy between them, yet a common interest always induces them to join against the remainder of mankind. Thus they both united heartily against the Kings, when the latter wanted to acquire the appointment of Bishops. Here we see the reason why the monastic establishments of Deans and Chapters have the appointment of Bishops and Archbishops. All the orders of our Cathedrals and Minsters are monastic institutions—successions, in most cases, of the ancient Roman priesthood, and they of the Druids. As might be expected, the Monks, successors of the Essenes, Carmelites, &c., were in a particular manner addicted to the allegorical nature of Christianity. This may be seen in their defence of Origen,[2] who was evidently one of them, holding the doctrines of emanation, and that of an esoteric meaning in the Scriptures. He said "the Scriptures were of little use to those who under- "stood them literally, as they are written."[3] This is one of numerous instances to prove that the monks were the oldest Christians; the Seculars of modern times, put into power by Constantine, were the followers of Paul. The way in which their hierarchy arose is pretty clearly made out.

We are told that the first Monks arose, in the second century, in Egypt. The persons who say this, mean *Christian* monks; and that they were the first *Christian* because they were the first *Paulite* Monks. They were, in fact, Essenes or Carmelites, but became followers of the Paulites and Popes. It was held, that no person could be a priest except through the medium of the popes; and once a priest, he could never be unpriested, though he might be deprived of his functions—that is, of the power of performing the offices of the religion. But he always remained of the sacerdotal order or caste. In the brawls respecting Origen the true character of the religion may be seen. By our historians we are taught to believe, that the Popes and the Church were established in early times. The fact is, that until Constantine gave a preponderance to the Popes and Paulites, no party had any real superiority. Paul was the teacher of the literal meaning; Origen and the Monks of the Platonic Gnosis or mystery. As I have before said, the parties united; and this is the reason why we see in the churches of the middle ages the odd mixture of Gnosticism and Paulism, why we see the Deans and Chapters electing Secular Bishops. We are told that the monks were not priests. The truth is, they ordained one another or initiated their brethren on admission, after serving their noviciate. Ordination is nothing but initiation into the mysteries. We have an example in the Culdees of Iona. When the Popes ordained the monks anew, they said, they admitted them to orders, because they did not allow the legality of the previous ordination. With the admission of the Carmelites, Essenes, Therapeutæ, &c., into the Roman church, there entered all the rites and ceremonies of Gentilism, of which these were sects.

---

[1] The example of the overthrow of the power of the Seculars in the Papacy by the Regulars, has not been without effect. The Pope permitted the talented fanatic Loyala to establish his order; but the monastic spirit shews itself beautifully in the rule which excludes all Jesuits from the Papacy.

[2] Mosheim, Hist. Cent. iii. Ch. ii., Cent. vi. Ch. iii.   [3] Ib. Ch. v.

Their ancestors were puritanical seceders from the corruptions of Gentilism. As usual, time cooled the ardour of the sects, and they became fond of corruptions or show, &c. Are not our devotees doing the same thing? The Scotch are admitting organs into their churches, and every new church, in London, has a wicked cross, the mark of the scarlet whore, as the sect in power politely calls the chief Bishop of their countrymen, at the top of it. Whether the monastic order, that is, the regulation of binding themselves by the three vows took place before the sword divided from the crosier or afterwards, I do not know, and perhaps it may not now be possible to ascertain, but certainly the Royal priests were never supposed to be bound by those vows; they probably never took them. The custom of calling the chief sacrificer a king, in Rome, Athens, &c., was a remnant of this state of things. No man but a king[1] could offer a sacrifice. The real origin of the monastic order is unknown; in some instances it probably swallowed up the Seculars, as in Tibet; in others it failed. I am quite of Mr. Cleland's opinion, that priests were the first governors, kings their generals, who, at last, usurped the supreme power of their employers. A little consideration of the circumstances will suggest a very simple explanation of the way in which the four ancient castes may have arisen. The *first* must have been the priests; the *second* the military, their soldiers, who, by degrees, in many countries, got the command of the priests. The caste of trades must have been the dwellers in towns; the farmers would be the shepherds or pastors, having, at first, no fixed habitations, (like the Bedoweens,) and at last settling down as agriculturalists. Thus we have the *four* castes, all jealous of one another; and thus coming, at last, to be completely divided, as they were in Egypt, and are in India. The natural tendency of mankind to run into castes may be observed in Britain. Our nobles are the soldier caste; our clergy the priests; the squires and their tenants the agricultural caste; the tradesmen in towns the trading caste; and the paupers and lowest order, as in India, the *out*-caste. How early the tribes of Saxons came to the West we cannot discover; but they were first heard of by the name of Saxons about the year 604 of Rome, 150 years B. C., when the Consul Caius Papirius met them in Noricam, defeated them, and drove them into Gaul.[2] In process of time, when wars arose, the Liberi-Sockmanni, and tenants in Frank-al-moign, protected by the priests, remained at home, free from war and military service. They were the Sacæ or Saxon men of the book, of Liber and Bacchus.

The words Liber *free*, the solar Φρη of Egypt, and Liber *a book*, being, as I have shewn, closely connected—the bookish men, the men of Bac, Boc, Bacchus, were comparatively free from the rule of the warrior class, both in a civil and military point of view, and thence comes our *benefit of clergy*. If a man could read, it was at once a proof that he was initiated into the sacred order. If the benefit of clergy depends on a statute, it has probably been obtained by the priests to put their privilege out of doubt. It has been a declaratory statute. Although perhaps every man who was initiated could not read and write, yet I believe that every man who could read and write was initiated—these arts being taught to the initiated only in very early times. It has been said, that the privilege of clergy was granted to encourage learning. I believe it was used as a test, as a proof, that a man was of or immediately belonging to the sacred tribe, and therefore exempt from the jurisdiction of the court in which he had been tried. If he were acquitted, he said nothing; if found guilty, he pleaded his order and his reading. I have little doubt that the knowledge of reading and letters was a masonic secret for many generations, and that it once formed a part of the mysterious knowledge of Eleusis and of other temples. The triangular staves

---

[1] He must have been the Sag-art. [2] Southern North Am. Rev. No. X. p. 339.

on which the runes were commonly written were called Bogstav, or Buchstab, Book-staves.[1] Here is clearly our book.[2] A great seminary of learning in North India is called the place or city of the Book—Boch-ara. Rapin[3] calls Freelands, Bocklands, thus confirming much of what I have said above. In very ancient times all taxes were paid by a portion of the produce of the land—stamps, excise, and customs, were unknown. From the account given by Col. Briggs, it appears that this was always the case in India till very recent times, and the prosperity of the country seems to have depended in a great measure on the proportion of the produce which was taken by the government. It seems latterly to have varied. Du Halde describes this practice as still continuing in China. In the early times of the priests and rulers, a tenth was taken from the cultivators of the soil and no more—hence the origin of tithes; and there can be no doubt that, under this arrangement, a country would enjoy great prosperity. Mr. Cleland, as I stated above, is of my opinion, that priests were the first rulers of nations. He says, "It may, perhaps, at first sound " rash and unwarrantable, that the words Ecclesiastical, Diocese, Dean, Cardinal, Bishop, Priest, " and even Religion itself, do not originally mean any thing purely spiritual; being, in fact, in " their origin, all terms of judiciary import, in those times when the law was absolutely blended " with divinity, from which the law was proud of receiving its support. The law of the country " was also its religion."[4] This was the Druidical system and that of the Jews; it is that of Mohamedism, and was that of ancient India. At first, before the invention of writing, every country had a *lex non scripta*, of which some remains may every where be found. After the discovery of writing, the religious code was the law of the land. When Sir Henry Spelman calls the *feodal system* the law of nations of the Western world, he might have gone a little farther; for it was most certainly the law of the extreme East as well as of the West.

12. In the address of my friend Lieut. Col. Briggs to the India Company on the subject of the Land Tax of India, innumerable facts which he has adduced have satisfactorily proved that a system, in every respect the same as our feodal system, must, at one time, have prevailed throughout that country; that the soil of the country was always admitted to belong to the sovereign, and to be held by tenants by the render of service in some way or other. The fact noticed by Col. Briggs, p. 84, from Arrian, of Alexander the Great, on his conquest of the Sacæ or Saxons, restoring their country to their chiefs, to be held by them by delivery of standards, (as the Dukes of Marlborough and Wellington hold their land of our king,) and by their consenting to do suit and service, and to supply a body of troops when required, is very striking. It sufficiently accounts for the existence of the feodal tenures in the West, wherever tribes from the eastern countries, like the Saxons, settled. Feudal lands had seven incidents—heriot, relief, escheat, wardship, scutage, marriage licence, and homage. These were precisely the same in India and Europe.[5] Fee-udal might be land held of *the Iud in fee*. The Heriot was the payment of a sum of money, or some other thing, for the investiture in the fief. By this payment, the man saved his land. It was from the old words Eri and Heri, which in Greek and Arabic, consequently Hebrew and Sanscrit, meant *saviour*. It cannot for a moment be denied that the whole of our ancient common or unwritten law[6] is most closely interwoven into the Feodal system. It appears, from a speech made by Lord Brougham in the House of Peers,[7] that it has been a question among our old

---

[1] The island of Staffa is the island of Staves. This can be understood only by those who have seen it.
[2] Mallett, Int. Hist. Den. p. 227.
[3] Vol. II. pp. 152, 172—174.
[4] Specimen, Pref. pp. vii., viii.
[5] Briggs, p. 90, and Tod's Rajast'han.
[6] It was unwritten because it was established before the art of writing was generally known.
[7] "He alluded to what had taken place in the ancient kingdom of Scotland, of which the laws in former times,

lawyers, as the ancient law of Scotland was identical with the law of England, which of them copied from the other. The real fact was, that neither could be said to copy from the other. No doubt these laws were even older than our later Saxon ancestors. Let us look but for one moment at the states of Scotland and England after the last Saxon arrival, and consider whether at any time after that event there be the least reason to believe that either of these countries, in a state of perpetual enmity, would copy the laws of the other. In my mind this Indian polity must have come along with an oriental tribe much before the Saxons arrived from the Baltic. And I consider the " Regiam Majestatem" of Sotland as a decisive proof of the great antiquity of the system. When the lawyers of England and Scotland disputed respecting the superior antiquity of their laws, it never entered into the minds of either of them that they might both descend from a common source. They came when the Indian Gods came to Ireland. I suppose that this common source was a previous tribe of Sacæ, of the nation of Pandæa, or of the Buddhist religion, and who were the builders of Stonehenge, Abury, &c. The Saxon Heptarchy did not extend to Scotland, but the Lowlanders are called Saxons by the Highlanders. They were Yavanas or Ioudi, that is Sacæ, and Scythæ. I very much doubt the fact that the Romans governed here by their own laws, as asserted by Selden.[1] They probably governed their own people by their own laws, but the natives by theirs. The laws of Edward the Confessor were only declaratory laws. I believe our common law and feodal law both came from India at the same time. I believe what Fortescue says is true, that the customs or common laws of England, were the same under the ancient Britons that they are now; for though the Romans, Saxons, Danes, and Normans, successively reigned here, yet he tells us, that notwithstanding all these several mutations, the general customs or common law of England remained fixed and immutable, at least not actually changed, for so are his words,—In omnibus nationum harum et regum eorum temporibus regnum illud eisdem quibus jam regitur consuetudinibus continue regulatum est.[2]

13. We have yet said nothing of the Scythians; and it may very properly be asked, How, in regard to time, my Saxons or Sacæ would be related to them ? All difficulties with respect to them, as in any way opposing my system, are at once done away by a passage of Herodotus, who declares that they were two names of the same people.[3] From this I think there can scarcely be any doubt that the Celtæ, the Scythians, and the Saxons, were all tribes of the same people, succeeding one another, with some trifling variations which would naturally arise, in the lapse of time, from the natural tendency which every thing has to change. It may now be fairly asked, what has become, in modern times, of the mighty nation which was so numerous in ancient times as to send off successive swarms or colonies almost without end or number ? I apprehend we had them formerly under Alaric, in the Goths, who were driven forwards to the West by the semi-human Huns. (Semi-human, if fairly represented by their enemies, but this I do not believe.) Afterward the same race are found in the

---

" widely as they differed now from the laws of England, were so identically the same with those of this kingdom, that
" the oldest treatise on law in each of the two countries is said to be a translation from the other, there being a dispute
" between the lawyers of England and those of Scotland as to which was the original. He was bound, as holding alle-
" giance on a higher tie to the bar of England than to that of Scotland, to say—and he was happy to add, that he could
" really say it conscientiously—that he believed the treatise on English law to be the original. The treatise of Glan-
" ville, who was Lord Chief Justice in the reign of Henry II., was that from which the 'Regiam Majestatem' of Scot-
" land was taken—a clear proof that at that early period of our history, the principles of the Scotch law were the same
" as those of our own."—*The Times*, Dec. 3, 1830.

[1] Vide Ioan. Seldeni notas ad cap. xvii., Fortescue de Leg. Ang. Num. 6, p. 9.
[2] Fortescue de Legibus Angliæ, cap. xvii., p. 58, edit. Seldeni, 1616.
[3] Guerin de Rocher, Vol. I. p. 152; see *supra*, p. 2.

Tartars, who conquered China, and they dwelt in the country, a part of which contained the thousand cities of Strabo, of which mighty ruins, though scarcely any thing but ruins when compared to their former magnificence, yet remain—the country to the east of the Caspian, and extending ten or twelve degrees north and south of Samarkand. Σακαι-τες Σκυθας ετω φασι.[1]—Scytharum populi—Persæ illos Sacas in universum adpellavere.[2] D'Ancarville says, the Sacæ were also called Sagæ. After having reflected upon the Sofees of Mohamedism, who, in fact, make it nothing but a continuance of the doctrine of Wisdom, which existed thousands of years before the time of Mohamed, we shall not be surprised to find our Saxon ancestors bearing the same name as Mohamed. The kings, as a proper name, were called Clytones, and their sons Clytonculi. It is worthy of observation, that the ancient system seems to have been forgotten about the same time in India and Europe, and about the same time to have run into all manner of complicated machinery. I think reflection on the natural course of events—of effects and causes—will lead to a conviction that these were the effects which naturally arose from a system such as we have seen attempted to be shrouded in secrecy, before the art of writing was generally known; and I think we need go no further for the origin of the wish to keep it secret than to the natural desire of all men for power and pre-eminence. It was always as true as it is now, that knowledge is power. The men who began to possess knowledge, soon perceived that it gave them power, wealth, and ease. The endeavour to keep knowledge to themselves was a natural consequence of the love of power. I shall by and by shew there is a high probability, that there were several floods, and that many people escaped the last, who constituted what are constantly called *aborigines*, and along with them also escaped a few of a learned and superior caste, who soon became the tyrants or governors of the others.

14. The Arabians assert, that there are two races of men in Arabia.[3] This seems probable. I believe in every country there will be found at least two races of men. I believe, when Plato says there was an original race of men drowned by the flood, who had a language long since lost, he alluded, in fact, to such people as those Helots in Lacedæmon, who were the remains of a race drowned by the flood, but who were originally little better than barbarian, or became so in consequence of that catastrophe. It cannot be denied that the languages of the Chaldeans, of the Jews, and of Job, that is Arabians, were most closely connected dialects of one language. The Arabic of Job passes in the Jewish Canon for Hebrew. Parkhurst's Lexicon serves at once for the Hebrew, the Chaldee, and the Arabic of Job. Now, all the nomade tribes of Africa and Asia have a language called Arabic; and these tribes, from the peculiarity of their habits of life, have probably never had a foreign language imposed upon them, a fact which can be stated of scarcely any other nation. In South India, the lowest class, not the Parias or Outcasts of the Brahmins, but what Col. Briggs[4] calls the Aborigines, are the most ancient; they have no distinction of castes, and have nothing to do with the present Brahmin religion. After them come the Brahmins from North India. The same people whom Col. Briggs calls Aborigines may be discovered in ancient Syria; in Greece, in the Helots just mentioned; in Italy, Germany, &c. It is from this purity of blood, as I may call it, that the Arabs of the deserts have retained the old language. In this they would be much assisted, wherever Mohamedism prevailed, by having the standard Koran to keep the language fixed. I believe no Englishman who is a good Arabic scholar, and who is quite master of the Chaldee alphabet, would have much difficulty in translating Hebrew or Chaldee into English. These Arabians I have traced from an Arabia on the Indus.[5] Every where the yet nomade tribes

---

[1] Stephen. Byzant.
[2] Good's translation of Job, Introd. Diss. p. iii.
[3] Plin. Lib. vi. Cap. xviii.; Vallancey, Coll. Hib. Vol. V. p. 23.
[4] Essay on the Land Tax of India.
[5] See Vol. I. p. 416.

have the name of Bedoweens or Bedouins. Have they derived their name from being originally Buddists of North India, like the Saxons from having been Sacæ from the same countries? I suspect it is so. Buddha, it has been shewn, was called Saca, his followers Sacæ. The most learned Mussulmans allow that there was an esoteric Mohamedism. This was Sopheism, which was Buddhism from North India—from the Afghans. The reason why there are no castes among the Bedoweens is because they are the shepherd caste, whose habit necessarily is to wander about. After a tribe of shepherds took possession of a country and settled in it, the distinction of castes would begin to arise. Caste is a natural effect, not an artificial institution. It is the produce of circumstances, and not of design. When I contemplate the surprising similarity between the feudal system of North India and Europe, I am compelled to look to some cause, for I cannot retreat to accident. Therefore I am compelled to believe either that Europe copied from India or that India copied from Europe, or that the same effect took place in both, arising from some peculiar and unobserved quality in the human character. As I cannot discover the latter, and as I know the copying cannot have taken place in modern times, I am obliged to believe that these tenures are of much older date than is generally imagined; that the same mistake has happened with respect to them as to many other things, and that they are said to take their rise when they are first noticed, and then only, because then we have the first notice of them. I believe that they were the effects of, or parts of the Pontifical government, known in India by the name of Pandæa, which extended over the whole world, and of which all the lands were held by feudal tenure. I have mentioned before, (p. 4,) what Dr. Geddes said of all the words of the Saxon language being to be found in the Hebrew or its cognate dialects. The feudal system came with the Sacæ or Saxons. Alfred and Edward the Confessor were Saxons: and might not the Norman convert Saxon institutions to his own purpose? It was strictly according to the custom of the country which he had left. Normandy was conquered by a tribe of Scandinavians or Northmen.

15. I believe that wherever a nomade tribe made a settlement, the mythos of their ancient country was established, and this is the reason why we have so many Merus or Moriahs, Parnassuses, Olympuses, Acropolises, &c. They were all Mounts of Meru in miniature; they might be all said to be microcosms of the great one of North India. They are very perceptible in Greece; but I think we have the best examples of the system in Egypt and Syria. In the latter, in the astronomical names given by Joshua. Gerizim was clearly the sacred mount, the national cathedral; the twelve tribes were the religious districts or divisions. The same divisions into *twelve* prevailed in Attica, in Asiatic Ionia, in Etruria, and on the Po, and in several other places. From this we may see, that the division of the country into twelve parts, was one of the parts of the mythos. Whether Palestine was subjected to any minor divisions does not appear, but certainly there were places of worship called Proseuchas and Synagogues—the latter, probably, erected for districts like our parishes. In Egypt we have the mythic division complete; and the Rev. Robert Taylor has shewn, that the whole of our hierarchy existed there, among the Essenes, absolutely in perfection.[1] And as we know that these Essenes existed in Syria as well as in Egypt, the same system probably obtained in both. I take the Essenes in each case to have been the professors of the highest order of the Cabala, the *perfecti*—the prophets of the Old Testament, and of Elias, their superior. The Essenes were Carmelite monks. What has become of them? When did the order die? But it did not die: it yet exists in the Carmelites. When Jerusalem or Mount Moriah was set up against Gerizim, the prophets of the two mounts got to quarrelling.[2] The five temples of

---

[1] Supra, p. 71.   [2] See Vol. I. p. 428.

Jehovah in Egypt,[1] I have sometimes suspected, were cathedrals of the Essenes. All these were what we call collegiate churches. They all had temples, and each had its *domus templi*. These assertions are all proved by what I have shewn—that every rite, order, and ceremony of the Romish religion was an exact imitation of a similar institution among the ancient Gentiles.[2] Wherever the Pandæan or Catholic religion prevailed, every state had its divisions, and, if large, its subdivisions; each subdivision had its temple; and each temple its domus templi, for the education of youth. In this way, I believe, arose the corporate towns of Europe, and they were closely connected with the astrological superstition of the Pandæistic mythos. We are told that our corporate towns associated to protect themselves against the tyranny of the barons and military chiefs. This I believe is quite true; but they first existed under the priests, who joined the people in procuring charters to grant them privileges and confirm what they had possessed from time immemorial, so as, in fact, to have no deeds to shew for their lands. In such cases, the charter granted their lands by name. All these became Liberi, Sockmanni. It is in consequence of this that we find the mystic Chaldæan numbers to prevail in all our corporations—the *twelve* aldermen and and *twenty-four* councilmen. All this is closely allied to the feodal tenures established by the first settlers from the East. Wherever these people settled, they established their temples, their tenures, &c., &c. I suppose at first there were no other parishes than what are now comprised in the limits of our corporate towns. We know how, in later times, feudal chiefs established smaller parishes around their castles: hence arose our common parishes, our peculiars, &c., &c. At first, I have no doubt, every cathedral or Druidical circle had its sacred mount for its processions, called Deisul or procession of God the Saviour, Dei Salus, Salutis, an imitation of the progress of the God Sol from East to West. In fact, each had its Olympus, small or great, according to its means, which often afterward became a fortress, as Clifford's Tower at York. We find a mote, hill or Olympus in most old towns. At Cambridge and Oxford they yet remain. Sacred processions were made from the cathedral[3] round these mounts, and they are yet continued in all Romish countries. On these mounts was a cross, and round this the fairs and markets were held every Dies Solis; and when the barons established little parishes in opposition to the others, they fixed their markets in the churchyards. The clergy or liberi of the barons, the Seculars, were always in opposition to the Regulars, or liberi bookmen, or the monks, who possessed the other parishes. It is very certain that whenever a feodal chieftain wished to establish a church and parish, it would be an encroachment on the monks; and as it would be in opposition to them, and as he could make no priest, he would be glad to avail himself of the aid of the Pope. The same reason would operate with the kings to procure bishops from Rome, and thus, by degrees, the Seculars got established. But certainly there are the most striking proofs of all the collegiate churches having once belonged to the monks. "The ecclesiastical polity of the Romish church is, to this " moment, almost wholly Druidical. And as that ancient religion of Britain and the Gauls had " its Pope, its Cardinals, its Bishops, its Deacons, &c., who were succeeded in their spiritual or " temporal power and possession by the Christian Clergy, these last assumed identically those " titles of which the others had been deprived," &c.[4] Cleland says, the word Shire is from the Celtic *Hir, Cir, Chur,* Sir, &c. Each Shire was a distinct state, subdivided into Baronies, Parishes, Pareichs, or Bareiches. *Par* and *Bar* meant *a judge; reich, a region.*[5] From Cir, or Shur, comes our She-riff. The Cir is the Hebrew גר *gr.* We have found the circles or counties in the

---

[1] See supra, pp. 15, 16.   [2] Supra, pp. 58—75.
[3] Rapin maintains, that each diocese had only one church, and was, in fact, only one parish. Vol. II. p. 131.
[4] Cleland's Spec. p. 102.   [5] Ib. p. 8.

island of Ceylon;[1] we have the circles again in the five northern Circars, a country on the West side of the Bay of Bengal, called the coast of Coromandel, from the fifteenth to the twentieth degree of north latitude. I have before shewn that Cora-mandel means the circle of Core.[2] This pleonasm has arisen from the intermixture of the countries, and from one word having come to have two ideas; for the Sur meant the solar circle, the cycle, as well as the sun. In these Circars may be found almost an exact representation of the circles of Germany, and the patriarchal system which I shall develop in my next book is well marked. Every district which Hamilton[3] calls a village, is a perfect and complete municipium or urbs, orbis, a little world within itself, with all its officers from the highest to the lowest degree, in which state it has continued from the most remote antiquity. The account given by Mr. Hamilton is very interesting. I shall return to it in my next book, and merely add here, that India Proper was divided into these districts, and that the expression Northern clearly shews there has been a Southern, and probably a middle Circar or district. I think the term Deccan, which is called Daschnia in the Sanscrit, and which answers to the Decapolis of Western Syria, has been another division under the same system, and similar to the tithings of King Alfred in England. Cleland[4] says, Ridings, Radtings—governments; Radt, a provincial ruler. A Council was called the Raadst, whence he who had most influence ruled the roast. The state into which the world was brought, when the Pontifical system, from the usurpation of its kings or other causes, began to fall in preces, is well marked in North India. Col. Briggs says, " The subdivision of the territory into townships, as described in the time of Alex-
" ander, still obtains everywhere. Each of these petty states maintains its municipal legislation,
" independently of the monarchy; and every state presents the picture of so many hundreds or
" thousands of these minute republics."[5] In Greece we see the remains of this system. In the Amphictyons we have the Wittenagemote. But we must not expect that any two countries would decline and a new order of things arise exactly in the same way. Mr. Cleland says, "The
" whole order of the law, temporal and spiritual, sprung from our colleges. The greatest part of
" the Gauls, of Germany, but especially of Britain, was College-land, Glebe-land, Parish-land, all
" which are better expressed by the word DOMAIN, at bottom a Celtic word, equivalent to *Barony*
" or *Government-land*, which maintained the Bishops, the Judges, the subordinate militia and its
" officers."[6] He shews that the *Maire Dom* or Mayor of the Palace was the Judge, the word Dom meaning Judge. From this, in the law-glossaries, the Domesday book is called *Liber Judicatorius*.[7] From this the day of Judgment became Domesday. Mr. Hallam[8] says, " The pro-
" vincial cities under the Roman empire enjoyed, as is well known, a municipal magistracy, and
" the right of internal regulation. It would not have been repugnant, perhaps, to the spirit of the
" Frank and Gothic conquerors, to have left them in the possession of these privileges. But
" there seems no satisfactory proof that they were preserved in France, or in Italy; or, if they
" existed at all, they were swept away, in the former country, during the confusion of the ninth
" century, which ended in the establishment of the feodal system." (Here I think he ought to have said the RE-establishment.) " Every town, except within the royal domains, was subject to
" some Lord. In episcopal cities, the Bishop possessed a considerable authority, and in many
" there was a class of resident nobility." The old Lords were all of the nature of the Prince Bishops, or Palatines of Germany. The Thane was the same as the Optimas or Baro, and answered to the Antrustiones or Fideles or Drudes or Drudi. They were, I doubt not, originally of the Druid order, bearing arms, perhaps not having any religious functions,—perhaps not having re-

---

[1] Vol. I. p. 753. [2] Ib. pp. 760, 762. [3] Gazetteer, in voce Circar. [4] Spec. p. 7.
[5] P. 99. [6] Add. to Spec. p. xiv. [7] Second Add. p. 13. [8] Hallam, Middle Ages, p. 210.

ceived the Samach, as there are Brahmins at this day who are not priests. The Thanes, I believe, originally were the only tenants *in capite*. When a Druid was employed to command an army, and he usurped the throne, many of his barons would be Druidi. The observation of Mr. Hallam that the Edict of Milan, by Constantine, in the year 313, recognises the existence at that time of ecclesiastical corporations,[1] almost justifies what I have said of our towns being the Roman Municipia, and of the existence of Monasteries; for what else could these ecclesiastical corporations in Italy have been? and, if in Italy, probably in Britain. The fact is, I think, that the municipal towns may be discovered as far back as we can go; although, perhaps, subject to suit and service to some superior: but this, so far from proving that they had no previous existence, raises a presumption to the contrary. Their possession of charters of incorporation, of certain dates, by no means proves, for several reasons, their previous non-existence, and the previous existence under the forms expressed in those charters. I have no doubt that our corporate towns in general are the municipia of the Romans, and also of a system previous even to them. We have seen that the Sacæ occupied almost all Europe, and that they were the Palli; from these came the Palatinates and the Bishops Palatine, our three prince Palatine Bishops of Chester, Durham, and Ely, (Lancaster was not old,) and the prince Bishops of Germany. I believe these were originally all mitred Abbots, with archiepiscopal authority given to them by the Popes, exclusive of their Abbeys; that they were Abbots exclusive of the Popes; that their chapters made them Abbots; that then the Popes made them Bishops, the object of which was, to get them, the Monks, in fact, into the pale of the Vatican. But the Popes probably did not foresee that this would open the door of the conclave to the Monks, which would enable them, at last, to get possession of it, and convert the Papacy into a monastic institution, sinking the Seculars into a second class. Function was not necessary to a Bishop. Episcopacy was an order. Mr. Hallam[2] expresses himself in terms of surprise that the Monks should have been so rapacious for wealth which they could not enjoy, and that they should hesitate at no fraud or forgery to obtain it. The reason of this rapacity is to be found in the doctrine, that the Supreme Pontiff, or head of the Priesthood, was entitled to the land of the whole world, as Lord of the soil; and these cunning and long-headed persons could not fail to see that, if let alone, the whole land would, in a few centuries, quietly and without struggle, come into their hands, and that then they would again become the rulers of the world, as, in the most ancient times, they had been. Mr. Hallam says, the tithes were not paid originally as at present, but all were received by the Bishop and distributed by him to the clergy. These were, I suppose, the chapter-elected Abbots, made Bishops by the Pope, who received the tithes as heads of the monasteries, and sent priests to perform service where they thought it necessary. We know that monasteries in later times endowed Vicarages, when they themselves took the great tithes. The circular buildings of large stones, of which the Sacæ, Saxons, brought the pattern from North India, where vast numbers of them yet remain, were the first Druidical temples. When the Romans drove out the Druids and took possession of the vacant lands, the stones, in many cases, were broken up to build their more finished temples; and after them, when the Christians prevailed, their temples were in great measure used for Christian churches and monasteries. Thus only such Druidical temples are left as were not subsequently converted into Roman or Christian temples. Perhaps there is not a more striking point of similarity between the feudal laws and customs of the East and West, than that of the trial by a jury of twelve persons. Richardson shews this to have come from the East; that it was common to the Chinese, and to the Mexicans, which made Grotius say, the Mexicans must have been from Scandia. Hornius[3] says, " Quod vero Grotius infert, ex

---

[1] Hist. Mid. Ages, Vol. II. p. 2; Gibbon, Ch. xv. and xx.   [2] Hist. Mid. Age, Vol. II p. 6.
[3] De Orig. Gent. p. 270.

"Scandiâ ortos Mexicanos, quia Gotti et Saxones olim duodecemvirale tribunal habuerunt, id
"leviculum est: nam apud *Mexicanos* et *Sinenses* solum regium consilium eo numero constabat."[1]
Cleland says, "that most of the ecclesiastical terms of the Romish church, *as Parish*, &c., are
"Celtic, in which light it may be said, that the primitive Christians, for rearing the fabric of their
"church, took what suited them, of the ruins of demolished Druidism, for a scaffolding ; which they
"struck, and put out of the way, as soon as they had finished a nobler building."[2] When I recollect that the adoration of the Virgin and Child—Virgo Paritura—were common to Gaul and Egypt,
I am not surprised at the observation of Cleland. The parishes, &c., were equally common in
Egypt and Europe, and Mr. Taylor's exposé of them, in the former, is no surprise to me. The
description of Eusebius is incontestible, viz. that the Essenes were Christians, and the whole
together shews the original system most beautifully. Very justly has Bishop Lloyd observed that
Christianity flourished here before the time of Constantine; but he might have added, also before
the time of Christ.[3]

16. In India, every trade was a secret, and called by the word Ras, secret wisdom or knowledge.
Trades in general constituted one great *ras* or *caste;* each trade again a little subcaste; it had its
own Ras; each Ras had a Pontifex. Each trade or craft or caste admitted persons to its *ras* only
on payment of a fine and serving an apprenticeship. Every trade, as well as that of Mason, was
a craft: thus we have our crafts. This word is found in the κρυπτος of the Greeks. When a
person was taught the craft, he was admitted to be a *liber* or *free* or *soc* man, of that craft. Every
man who dwelt in the town was not a freeman; but those only who understood the liber or craft.
All the crafts were originally bound together by religious ties or initiations; in which the doctrines
of the Trinity, Baptism, and the Eucharist, are generally very prominent. Initiation itself was, in
fact, ordination. Here we have the three sacraments of the Christians of St. Thomas, and of the
Culdees of Iona, of Ripon, and of York. These religious rites among the crafts, in their initiations, have long entirely disappeared in Britain; but they remained till very lately in France and
Germany,[4] possessing almost all the outward appearances of Freemasonry, and being constantly
objects of jealousy and persecution by their governments. The circumstance of the Culdees being
found at York and Ripon can in no other way be accounted for, than by giving to those institutions
an antiquity much greater than modern antiquarians are willing to allow. The fact, indeed, carries them farther back than the Christian æra. I believe the Minsters were all Monastic establishments of Carmelites or Essenes or Therapeutæ or Cullidei. *Myn* meant stone. Stonehenge
Meyn ambre. Hence came minster and and monasteria.[5] They were all Gnostici. I think that
almost every very old church, of any magnitude and grandeur, was the work of monastic masons,
built by and for Monks—for the Regulars, not for the Seculars; that, originally, the country was
divided into districts, over each of which presided one of these institutions; that these were the
first Parochiæ, called, in the Celtic language, Bareich; and that the monks possessed the tithes of
the whole country. Ethelwolf was the first who passed a declaratory law in England, in 855, to
make the whole kingdom liable to tithes; but traces may be found of their payment, under the
Heptarchy, long before. In a similar manner a declaratory law was passed in the year 586, at the
Council of Mascon, by King Guntham. I think the castes, in early times, must have been nearly
the same in Europe as in India, and that they arose from the same natural cause. I have already
shewn how the four great castes arose, in India, and that every trade is also a caste. These, as I
have already intimated, are very nearly our crafts or companies of tradesmen taking apprentices;

---

[1] Vall. Col. Hib. Vol. V. pp. 321, 322.   [2] Attempt to revive Celtic Lit., p. 102.   [3] Ib. p. 105.
[4] Vide Dulaure, Hist. de Paris, Tome VIII. Livraison XV.   [5] Cleland, p. 144.

but the children generally succeeding their parents in the same trade, they were both hereditary and not hereditary. Guilds, Chantries, and Free-chapels, were suppressed by 1st Edward 6th. The Guilds are said to have been established to offer prayers for the souls of the deceased. They were poor persons who associated to procure this advantage. The Franchise or Liberty and right of Sanctuary arose from the double and confused use of the word Liber. A friend has observed, It is surprising that this has never been discovered before, if it be true. To which I reply, It would have been surprising if it had. For *first*, in early times, no one ever attempted to give a history except those whose object it was to conceal the truth, if they knew it, which, in most cases, is very doubtful. *Secondly*, they were men of the meanest understandings, incapable, from extreme bigotry, of taking an extended view of any subject. *Thirdly*, they had not the means of taking a bird's-eye survey of the world, as we have at this day. *Fourthly*, if what I have stated be the truth, they would have been instantly persecuted, like Roger Bacon, if they had published it. And, *lastly*, for want of the knowledge which we have obtained from India, only within the last thirty years, it was quite impossible that they could ever have arrived at the truth. The popish writers, enemies of the monks, tell us, and as usual we believe the evidence of enemies, that, in the early times, the monks were not priests; that is, because they assume that there can be no priest except by descent of cheirotonia from the Pope: this the monks could not shew; therefore their ordination was denied. The only instance we have of any thing like monks in their pristine state are the Collidei of Iona or Columba in Scotland; and it appears that they ordained one another before the Romish priests came among them; and, what is very remarkable, were permitted by the Romish priests, after they seized their monastery, to continue it. It is also very remarkable, that these Collidei or Chaldæans had the three sacraments which the Collidei or Christians of St. Thomas or of Tamul had, and no more, viz. Orders, Baptism, and the Eucharist; but taking with them also, or some of them at least, the three vows of chastity, poverty, and obedience. I take it, that I shall presently satisfy every one that the town of Columbo, in the island of Ceylon, and the town of Columba, in the island near Scotland, had each its name given by the same sect or people. I believe the Roman Senate was an hereditary sacred order or priesthood, like that of the Jews, and that of the Chaldæans or Cullidei, which married; but it was necessary, in all cases, to go through the ceremony of the χειροτονια, previous to performing the functions of a priest. The word Gosen or Goshen of Egypt, and Gosaen of India, read from right to left, instead of from left to right, described the land of the Soc above-noticed by Blackstone, and the Sag of Scandinavia; and I have a suspicion too, that all the Celtic tribes were Xacæ or Saxæ, so denominated from the name of their religion.

17. I can entertain little doubt that our cathedrals and churches, as I have already remarked, descended from the Druidical temples, and that by a very natural process. When the Romans overran Britain, they would find these places, with the lands belonging to them, *appropriated* to religion, or as seminaries of education, numbers of which we are told that the Druids possessed, but the remains of which are no where else to be found. The Romans would naturally use them for the same purposes: the building materials would be on the place; and, after the Christian religion overthrew the altars of the Romans, the same reasons which had operated with them, when they succeeded the Druids, to continue the appropriation of their institutions to religious purposes, I have no doubt, operated with the Christians in their succession to the Romans. We are told that our Collegiate Churches, and Deans and Chapters, were established in the eighth century. These, I have no doubt, were the remains of the colleges above alluded to, which underwent some change or regulation at that time. I do not doubt that they were monastic: the remains of the cloisters, dormitories, &c., about our cathedrals, prove this. I think it very likely that the junction between the Monks and the Pope, in this country, may have been effected by

giving them the appointment of Bishops. When the Romans left Britain, in the latter end of the fourth century, I suppose that Christianity pretty generally prevailed, though it might perhaps be of the mongrel kind which we find in Constantine, and probably the collegiate establishment which had existed in the time of the Druids had been succeeded by or converted into similar Christian establishments. I believe that, properly speaking, we have the remains of only one temple of the Romans in Britain, which is at Bath; and I think it very probable that, after they had completed their conquest of England, they treated the native religion indulgently, as they did the Egyptian. Their enmity to the Druids was occasioned by the Druids being enemies to them. What we read about human sacrifices, as the reason of the enmity of the Romans, is nonsense; for they practised this themselves, till the time of Claudius. I believe the Romans occupied Britain, as the Turks have occupied Greece, and that, after the conquest, they left the natives in possession of their religion, which would, in principle, be the same as their own, though differing in some small matters. It was what had been brought by the first tribes of Celtæ or Sacæ, in fact, by the Chaldees or Cullidei, who were, in reality, nothing but a sect of Druids, and similar to the Christians of Malabar. The Romans had altars in their castra, (caster, chester, &c.,) but they built no temples, unless in the former part of the four hundred years they were here. The corrupted Roman pillars, which we call Saxon, might be parts of temples which served both them and the natives. At the time of Constantine, the Roman religion was undergoing a radical reform, by changing to what we call Christianity: and, I believe, when the latter tribes of Sacæ or Saxons came, the religion of Britain was pretty much that of the Cullidei of Iona, York, and Ripon, possessing its colleges, formerly Druidical. The latter Saxons probably brought a new corruption or variety from Scandinavia; but we have no evidence that they interfered with the religion of the natives, (except with such of the Druids as were in rebellion,) and the two probably not very dissimilar. When the Romish priests or monks, under Augustine, came, then began the struggle between the Seculars and Regulars, the Cullidei and the Papists—the Cullidei, with their three sacraments, denied to be, or at least scarcely allowed to be, Christians, by the Papists."[1] The Cullidei were monks; but yet some of them married. Here we have the remains of the first patriarchal religion. By degrees the Papists prevailed, and from the struggles for mastery between the two parties arose the very great variety which a close observer must see in our ecclesiastical polity: our collegiate churches sometimes without bishops, sometimes with them; the tithes sometimes possessed by Seculars, sometimes by Regulars; Bishops sometimes appointed by Kings, sometimes by the Chapters; the variety of the livings, donatives, peculiars, &c., &c. We have no history of these times except by Romish writers, whose object was to support their own party and to conceal the truth, when it happened to be against them. Before the sixth century, all Monks were Carmelites; but I do not think there was at that time any one head of the order over them all; this, however, is a point involved in darkness. In the dispute, (noticed in Volume I. p. 768,) which took place between the Bishops of York and Canterbury for precedence, it appears,[2] that the Archbishop of York grounded his pretensions on an assertion, that his see was founded by Scotch Monks, with which Canterbury, founded by Augustine, had no concern. Here, 'I believe, we have the Cullidei; and that in the northern parts of the island, the old religion, as we might suppose, was less changed, corrupted, by Romans, Danes, later Saxons, than in the southern: that, in fact, it was Cullidæan Christian, when Augustine came to Kent and converted the Saxons, whose religion perhaps had

---

[1] We are told that the Saxons were not Christians. Thus it is often said, that the Unitarians of this day are not Christians; and it is always said, that the Mohamedans are not. But what signifies such nonsense?
[2] Rap. Vol. II. B VI.

become much more Pagan or corrupt, to the Romish Christianity, or to the faith of the *seven* instead of the *three* sacraments; the simple and first religion of Abraham, of Iona, in short of Buddha.

18. I apprehend in the most early times land was not appropriated, as it is now, except to religious uses, or at least to the use of the priests; but, that it was held more in the manner of our Ings lands, which changed hands every year. The remains of this ancient custom are yet to be found in many parts of Britain. The policy of nomade tribes, which arose from circumstances peculiar to their mode of life, must have been greatly against the appropriation of lands in perpetuity, and it was this policy which produced the custom of changing the land to which I allude. I believe oats and barley were the grains chiefly cultivated, as they required only a few summer months to bring them to perfection. At first, such tribes as were entirely nomadic would have no arable land. After a certain time they would invent a plough, and, in spring, would turn up a few strips of the waste and sow them with barley or oats. These strips (or *lands* as they are yet called in the north of England; in the common town fields one strip is a land) being appropriated only during the summer that they were growing the crop, and then being thrown open to the general pasturage. It would naturally happen, that (if the tribe remained in the same neighbourhood) the same lands would be repeatedly ploughed. This would arise in consequence of the greater ease with which the work would be done; a fact of consequence to those who had only such indifferent tools as the Hieralpha,[1] which we find in the hand of the Indian Hercules, at Muttra, and every where described on the Egyptian buildings. After some time it would be found that the lands had become exhausted, and fresh parcels would be resorted to—the old ones being left to become grass. This is the present practice in the Campagna di Roma. The same process took place with pasture land when dried grass became used. Each individual had a strip allotted to him, which varied every year. This is no theory.[2] Before a late inclosure of the parish in which I live, I had land in both these conditions. In this country, in my recollection, they were very common; and in this way, I have no doubt, that lands in many countries were anciently cultivated. As nomade tribes settled themselves in villages, small parcels of land would become inclosed around them, and I conclude that a parcel would always be appropriated to the temple and the priests, for their occupancy and residence. I think it is probable that these first villages would be formed of the aged and infirm who were unable to travel: these villages would by degrees grow into towns. At last the old, the rich, the priests, would stay at home, and the young would be sent off to the distant pastures, as the sons of Jacob were sent off to a distance, when Joseph was despatched by old Jacob to visit them. Thus, in many countries, Syria for instance, we find the wandering tribes yet mixed with the cities. When these wandering tribes quarrelled about the pastures, by degrees weapons would be invented, wars would arise, and with them generals and kings, disputing power with the priest in the city. The state of half appropriation of land described above, to be found with numbers of trifling customary variations in many parts of Britain, is a direct descendant of similar customs, upon a large scale, in North India and Germany. With many of the tribes of the Afghans, the lands change possessors after certain short periods. Mr. Elphinston particularly describes as an example the tribes of Eusof and Munder. The whole land of the clan or tribe seems to be in the possession of the chief, who, by necessity, can be no other than their trustee. At particular times a great meeting takes place, the whole is divided

---

[1] See Vol. I. p. 239.

[2] Tacitus (Germania, cap. i.) says, that the Germans cultivate sometimes one district, sometimes another, and often make new distributions of their lands.

among the subordinate clans by lot, who again divide it, at, under or in petty meetings, among the persons having a right to portions of the land. In some cases the lands are held for several years, in others only for one. All the people of a tribe are not entitled, but certain known persons, having the right; the others are in the situation of villains.[1] Mr. Elphinston observes,[2] that there are traces of this custom to be found in Khorasaun. Volney noticed the same in Corsica. Tacitus thus describes it with the ancient Germans: " Agri pro numero cultorum ab universis per " 'vices' occupantur, quos mox inter se, secundum dignationem, partiuntur : facilitatem partiendi " camporum spatiæ præstant. Arva per annos mutant." (Germania, xxvi.). Cæsar also has the following passage : " Neque quisquam agri modum certum aut fines proprios habet; sed magistra- " tus ac principes, in annos singulos, gentibus cognationibusque hominum qui unà coierunt, quan- " tum eis, et quo loco visum est, attribuunt agri, atque anno post, aliò transire cogunt." The description given by Mr. Elphinston is exactly the description of the process in my village of Skellow, called Sconhalla in Dom Bec. The persons having rights met at the Mote-hill, now remaining around the Cross on the top of the Calvary, once a year, on St. John's day, the day of wisdom, when, at the mote or meeting, the lands of the *ings* were distributed, by lot, among those having rights. From mote comes the word meeting; and from this being the *lotting* day, the meeting was called the Leet. From this comes the letting or allotting of lands, and the moting or mooting of subjects of discussion at meetings; for, at these meetings, all parish matters were moted or moved. In level countries, to make a mote-hill it was necessary to make a ditch, out of which came the materials for the mote ; hence circles of water called *Moats*; and as this ditch, in most places, would be a nuisance, when the hill became disused, the hill would be thrown down again into the ditch and thus it would disappear. The meeting was a miniature Wittagemote. After finding the ancient Gods, &c., of India, correctly described by their names in Ireland, long before they had arrived here from our East-India possessions, and therefore not possible to be modern copies, we shall not be surprised to find the tenures of lands similar to those which we have found in India, also in Ireland. From the Brehon laws it may be observed, that anciently the lands, at certain times, entirely changed their possessors. They were given up to a common stock, and a new division took place. The feudal customs of reliefs, wardships, trial by Jury, &c., may be perceived—all of them strong signs of the same ancient system which we have traced from India, and by no means proofs, as has been alleged, of corruptions of the Brehon laws.[3] I think it probable that the only land which would not be subject to change would be that of the priests. It would evidently be their policy to have their tenants fixed, and it would as evidently be the policy of the lay-lords or soldiers, when they arose, to have their tenants hold *their* lands by an *uncertain* tenure, which would not prevent them, on a sudden, marching to war or moving to fresh grounds with their Lord. Thus, by degrees, from the first, the class or caste of the priests arose; from the second, the caste of the soldiers or shepherds; and the stationary or resident occupiers of the lands of the priests would very naturally form the third class or caste of farmers : the residents of the towns, around the temple, would form the trades or fourth caste. A fifth caste or out-caste, or a certain unfortunate class of slaves or villains of no caste, the slaves of all the other castes, is every where to be met with. These slaves or villains were the performers of a variety of base or degrading works for the higher classes. In many cases they were what were called *aborigines*. By degrees they had small portions of land given to them, particularly by the priests, for which they rendered no suit or service like the other castes, being, in fact,

---

[1] Elphinston, Cabul, Vol. II. p. 17.   [2] Ib. p. 21.
[3] Hallam, Const. Hist. of England, Vol. IV. pp. 189—191.

a kind of slaves before they received them. When the higher castes rendered their suit and service, they rendered for these villains also—the villains were included. Thus, by degrees, they acquired lands without suit or service, and in this way arose the Folk lands, of which we read; but, I believe, no where find, at least I never found any. These lands were evidently part of the lands of the sacerdotal class.

19. It is very clear to me that the nature of *allodial* property is not understood by any one. In India it is called Bhoomia.[1] This word is spelt by some Bhumia. This is, *ia-h-om, land of Om*. Col. Tod thinks the Bhoomias were the predecessors of the Zemindars, and the scions of the native princes. The word Allodium is not a Latin word. Littleton gives the meaning of the word to be a Freehold—to be land for which a man owes no suit or service.[2] It is *al-di-om, land of the-holy-Om*. It is also called Boc-land, that is, *book-land*,[3] because it was originally a part of the land of the priests. I believe the Folk land was originally a part of it; but, in many places, it probably became a favourite mode of tenure. I believe that it was land originally held in occupancy by the priests, consequently it neither did suit and service, nor paid tithe. Ecclesia non solvat ecclesiæ. On this account it was the land of God—of אל *al*—די *di*. In India it was land held Bhoomia—that is, land held by the right of *Om*. And when other lands changed every year, it was stationary—as *Om* signifies. From the Pandæan system the name of God, אל *al*, came to mean *all;* and from the *Om* having relation to the same doctrine, came the *Om*-nis, having the same idea. In India the holders of this property have no title-deeds to shew for it, but hold it without title, from immemorial antiquity. As it has no suit or service to render, it goes not to the eldest, but in equal divisions among all the children, like our Kentish Gavel-kind lands or freeholds. Allodial property passed by inheritance, both in India and Europe, without requiring any relief or investiture, or the performance of homage. Salian Franks were the Franks of Sul. In England, if the learned Burton[4] may be believed, "no subject can hold land in direct or allo-"dial dominion."[5] This, I have no doubt, was once the case of every country in the old world. All was granted to tenants by the Supreme Pontiff, and the vectigal or tithe was the return, except from the priests, for land in their actual occupation. This holding was in Soccage. Upon this, all the other kinds of tenure were engrafted. Whatever encroachments were made on the system were probably done away with by William the Conqueror. Scheffer and Pontoppidan[5] say, that Odhal or Udal signifies *land free from tax*, and is the origin of Allodial, and is in opposition to pasture land called *Scattald*, which paid tax. From this comes the scotted or taxed lands, in many parts, and particularly in Hatfield Chace, near Doncaster, in Yorkshire. Scheffer says, that allodial is *odh proprietas*, and *all* totum. If it be correct that only the pasture paid the tax, we see a reason for the use of the Etruscan Agrimensores and the crosses to divide the open, uninclosed wastes, in order to collect the vectigal—of which I shall treat at large in the next book.[6] The crosses of Italy are found in the Scandinavian *Mark* stones of the Scottish isles.[7] I beg this may be recollected. The view which I take of the subject seems to be confirmed by an observation of Mr. Hallam's, that "the ecclesiastical hierarchy never received any territorial endowment by law, "either under the Roman empire, or the kingdoms erected upon its ruins."[8] The fact is, I have no doubt, that every cathedral was a species of college or monastic establishment, of extreme antiquity, which formed, at last, when the Monks became Christian, or rather, I should say, Romish, priests, a bishopric or archbishopric. It is not difficult to imagine how the Abbot would, when

---

[1] Tod's Rajast'han, Vol. I. p. 168.
[2] Vide Dict.
[3] Rapin, Vol. II. p. 196.
[4] On Real Property, Sect. i. Chap. vi. Col. 65, a
[5] Norway, Vol. II. p. 290.
[6] See Hibbert's Shetland Isles, p. 180.
[7] Ib. p. 182.
[8] Vol. II. p. 4.

once ordained, consent to rise to a mitred Abbot [1] or Bishop, or an Archbishop. I take a mitred Abbot to be an abbot with the order of bishop, but often *without functions*, out of his convent. They have been succeeded by Bishops in Partibus. By this means the Popes brought all the Carmelites or Essenes, and their property, into the church, and in return, the Monks ultimately, as I formerly remarked, brought the Papacy into subjection to them. As soon as the Monks got possession of the Papacy, either absolutely or by influence, they shew it, by repeated exemptions of monasteria from the power of the Bishops of their districts.[2] But this was after the kings had acquired the power of appointing them. In the opinion which I have stated here, I quite agree with Rapin,[3] who thinks the allodial lands were those of the priests, and that they were not subject to any feudal services: they were the domain of the priests. He derives Allodial from A, *non*, leud, *lands*. This is not satisfactory. The Allodial lands were those which the priests did not grant or subinfeudate to tenants, but which they themselves in part occupied, and in part let their servants occupy or cultivate. In Mr. Hallam's various attempts to explain the origin of the *feodal tenures*, the admitted earliest tenures of mankind in many parts of Europe, it is very extraordinary that it never should have occurred to him to ask the simple question, whether they might not have descended, in the whole or in part, from that people who must have been great and powerful, who built Stonehenge, Abury, and Carnac. Like all our historians, he has never thought it worth his while to ask himself the question, by whom these monstrous structures were erected. He has fallen into an error, very common with almost all antiquarians, that of determining that a thing certainly *did not previously* exist, because he finds no proof of its previous existence. But a thousand circumstances may render it probable that it did exist. If I find one arm-bone of a man, though I have no proof, it is, I think, probable that there has once been another. This, I think, has led him to place the establishment of several feodal abuses in late times, when the existence of the same abuses in India raises a strong probability, that the European abuse was only a continuance or renovation of earlier practices. The abuses to which I allude are not such, I think, as were likely to arise in different places merely from the similar state of the human mind under similar circumstances. But I do not deny that several abuses may be pointed out, owing their rise, probably, to the latter cause. Mr. Hallam,[4] when acknowledging the universal extension of the feodal tenure, attributes it to importation into the different places by immigrant tribes in modern times, while I think what he observes are only the wrecks of the universal feodal state, which were continued by those tribes who found and preserved laws and customs such as they had left at home.

20. And this brings me to an inquiry into the history of the island of Ii, or Iona,[5] or Columba, or Icolmkill, or Sodor, in Scotland.

The establishment on the island of Iona arose from an ancient Druidical settlement, and probably became one of the most celebrated seats of learning in the western world. Very extensive ruins are yet to be seen upon it. It is singular that this island should be called Iona and Columba, the former meaning *Dove* in Hebrew, the latter *Dove* in Latin. The Dove has always been the emblem of the Holy Spirit, of the Anima Mundi. A *black* dove came from the Hyperboreans to Delos and Delphi,[6] where the priestesses were in a particular manner endowed with the Holy Spirit. When the Holy Ghost or Spirit descended upon Jesus Christ, at his baptism, it was in the form of *a dove*, and always a female dove. I have shewn that Venus was identical with Ceres, Hecate, and she was *black*—in fact, the Mother of the Gods as such. She had two doves. She

---

[1] The mitred Abbots had seats in parliament as of right; but in right of *what* I think does not appear.
[2] Hallam, Vol. II. p. 30.   [3] Hist. Vol. II. p. 197.   [4] Ch. ii. Part. II.
[5] See Vol. I. p. 385, and *supra*, p. 262.   [6] See Vol. I. pp. 137, 434, 502.

was the Νες of Plato, one of the persons of his Trinity, in reality the Holy Ghost. The island of Iona, the island of the Dove, or, in Latin, of the Columba, is directly identified with Jehovah or Ieuε, by being called in the annals of Ulster Ii, the identical name by which Jehovah is always called in the Jerusalem Targum. On the most remarkable part of the word Ii-va, or Ii-vaa, see supra, p. 151.[1] The word Iona also means the female generative principle or the female organ of generation. In the cemetery of the convent or monastery of Iona, which was dedicated to the Saint or Holy Mary, the ruins of which remain, lie *forty-eight* kings of Scotland, *four* of Ireland, *eight* of Norway, and *one* of France, besides a vast number of other persons of great consequence, both known and unknown. Near the landing-place there were formerly a great number of CARNS. These were probably the most ancient burying-places, when this island was inhabited by Buddhists, who yet, in Upper India or Tibet, pursue the practice of making carns or large heaps of stones over their friends.[2] Of this island Dr. Garnet says, in his Tour to the Islands,[3] " We had " now examined the principal ruins of this island, and though they may be inferior in magnitude " and grandeur to many that are to be met with, yet when we consider the situation of the island, " the time when the buildings were erected, as well as the disadvantages under which they have " been undertaken, they may be looked upon as the greatest curiosities of the kind in the British " empire, especially when we connect with them the circumstances which have been already men- " tioned, viz. the flourishing state of learning at the time when the rest of Europe and of the world " was wrapt in the dark cloud of ignorance and barbarism." The learning is proved by their library destroyed at the Reformation, and the scarcity of Druidical remains is easily accounted for by the the stones used for erecting more modern edifices, at the time when it had grown into a Christian monastery and college. The island is called, in an inscription on a grave-stone, Ii. It says, " Johannis, Abbatis de Ii facta," &c. In another, " Hic jacet Johannes Macfingon, Abbas de Ij," &c. In another, a Nun is called " Prioressa de Iona." These inscriptions yet remaining on tombstones prove the truth of what I have said in my Celtic Druids respecting its name of Ii, which I quoted from the Annals of Ulster.[4] Respecting the great curiosity of this island and its remains, Dr. Garnet has not said a word too much in the extract which I have given above. There is also a St. Columb or Columba or Columbes in Cornwall, which took its name from a St. Columba, a female saint and martyr. It is reckoned a sacred place. There are nine sacred stones set up in a line near it, called *the nine maids*.[5] In Pegu and Ceylon Buddha is generally, when sleeping, overshadowed by *nine* Cobras. In other parts of India he commonly has *seven*, but in others only *five*. The number was probably regulated by the number of cycles of which he was the emblem at the time. This, I have no doubt, was the case with the number of the *Curetes* or Saviours, and the *Muses* or Saviours of Greece. Had the Cobras been meant to designate the planets, I think they would not have varied in number. The discovery of new icons, with different numbers, is no argument against this, as the devotees constantly make them after old patterns; they do not pretend to understand any of them.

The Roman Catholic historians account for the names Iona and Columba by the histories of Saints who were formerly bishops of the island, and for a very long time I was totally unable to reconcile the apparent strong testimony in favour of a St. Columba and a Saint Iona having really lived, with the evident mythological meaning of these names. At last it occurred to me, that it must have arisen from the absurd custom yet retained by our bishops of calling themselves after

---

[1] A particular account of this island may be seen in my Celtic Druids, Ch. v. Sect. xxxvii. p. 196.
[2] See Vol. I. pp. 409, 685. [3] P. 264.   [4] See the reference, ut supra.
[5] Hog's Fabulous History of Cornwall.

their bishoprics; thus we have Reginald Calcutta, instead of Reginald *of* Calcutta, and William Jamaica, instead of William *of* Jamaica. Of this sort of fooleries there is no end. This will account for the entries in the Saxon Chronicle and all the other difficulties; so that there may have been men who performed many of the acts recorded, and who signed themselves *Iona* and *Columba*. When this absurd custom began I believe no one can tell, and I apprehend it must have arisen from the regimine of the old language, by which Bishop *of* Iona, became Bishop Iona. This mistake of Bede and others is not more extraordinary than many other of their mistakes. A proper attention to the regimine—a natural effect of the poverty of the ancient language—I have no doubt will account for many mythological difficulties which have hitherto been totally insurmountable. It very satisfactorily accounts for the priests having the names of their Gods; and as in almost every case the king was the high-priest, it accounts for his being described by the name of the God, in the pontifical writings, which, in fact, are the only writings of these times that we possess. In every case in which a priest of any country using the old language is treated of, in the language of a country that had acquired the habit of forming its genitive case by inflection or by article, the consequence almost necessarily followed that the priest would have the name of the God given to him. In the neighbourhood of Iona there are many places with mythic and oriental names; and almost all the Indian Gods are found in Ireland.[1] The islands of *Bute, Arran, Ila*, and *Skye*, are thus called from *Buddha, Arhan, Ila* the consort of *Buddha*, and *Saca* or *Sakya*: the island of *Man* from *Man-anan* or *Mahi-Man*, or *Menu*.[2] All these were sacred islands, the same as Iona or *Columba*.[3] The names of *Buddha, Arhan, Man, Mahi-man*, were well known to the ancient Celts. The first month of the Egyptians, August, was called *Thoth* in honour of the God. The first of August, in old Irish, is called the day of *La Tat;* that is, the Buddha. The *Saman*, or *Somono* or Sumnaut of the East, is found in Ireland in *Saman, Samhan*, and *Shamhna*.[4] Vallancey says, in the old Irish language Budh, Buth, Both, means the Sun, Fire, the Universe. The Budh of Ireland was of the family of *Saca-sa*, or the bonus *Saca*. This is the Sacya, from whom the Buddha Muni of the Hindoos was descended. But though Sa may mean *good*, yet I do not doubt that it also meant *Saviour*. Many remains of the Buddhist religion are to be found in Ireland. He had a temple at *Budda-fan*, or *Butafan*, now Buttevant. פוט *Put* was the Apollo of the Chaldeans according to Bochart. *Abbuto*, or *Pater But*, is the Apollo of the Japanese. *Phutios* was an old Grecian epithet of the sun and Jupiter, according to Hesychius. It is said in the Asiatic Researches,[5] "there is a luminary, which rose, like fresh butter, from the "ocean of milk, churned by the Gods: the offspring of that luminary was Buddha, or the wise." Tradition gives Iona the character of having been a place very celebrated for education. It is probable that most of our Cathedrals, as I have before said, arose from Druidical or Buddhist institutions for education, founded about the time of Stonehenge; that they were Culdee establishments; for, in these, the Culdees were last found, as at York and Ripon. I am also of opinion that Cambridge, with its river Cam or Ham, its Castle Hill, its round church or Templum, its legend Alma Mater Cantabrigia—and Oxford, with its river Isis, its coat of arms, the BULL OR OX, its great tumulus at the end of the town, its Mithraic monument noticed by Stukeley, were both of them Druidical or Buddhist foundations. The reason why there are no pillars or columns, at those two places, like Stonehenge, is because they have been worked up into buildings since the time of Christ. If it had so happened that a college had been continued at Stonehenge, there would not now be any great circles of stones there. The tumuli only would have been found,

---

[1] See Celtic Druids, p. 183. [2] Fab. Pag. Idol. B. iv. Ch. v. [3] Celtic Druids, pp. 199—201.
[4] Faber, Pag. Idol. Ch. v. p. 365. [5] Vol. III.

wherever the establishments continued, though Culdees might remain as at Ripon and York, or legends or tumuli as at Oxford or Cambridge;[1] yet all the rough stone monuments would necessarily disappear. The same cause produced the destruction of the old temple and the production of the new one. The stones were ready and the lands unappropriated to private use, or rather, perhaps, I should say appropriated to sacred use. Thus monasteries and saints arose in Italy and Iona, on heathen temples. The great and rich foundations became cathedrals, the little ones churches or convents.

21. There are some circumstances relating to the island of Ceylon which we will now notice. The most rational part of its history states, that a conqueror, from the north of India, overran the Peninsula, advanced to Ceylon, and established there the religion of Guatama or Buddha the Second, as he is called by persons who do not understand the mythos. In this island is found a mount called Adam's Peak; in Cingalese called Himmaleh. In it there is also the mark of a foot, which Christians call the foot of Adam; but the Buddhists say it is the mark of the foot of Buddha. This is, because Buddha, who robbed the garden of a flower,[2] was a renewed Adam. There is a river of Calany and a temple of Calany, and, about six miles from it, a town called Columbo.[3] Its old name is called Serendive or Serendib. (Ararat, as I shewed in Vol. I. p. 428, is called Serendib in the Samaritan version.) There is also a mystical mount called Zian, which means place of repose.[4] At Rangoon is a God called Dagun.[5] The God Kandi-kumara, that is, the holy Khan of Cuma, is called a Rabbie.[6] This is correctly Hebrew, and means *prophet* or *seer*; that is, a seer forwards, a person who could see into futurity. It is remarkable that in the language of the ancient Gael the word Ii, the name of Ieue, should mean an island, and should be also the name of the sacred isle of the West—of Iona or Columba—and that Devi, in Sanscrit, should mean an island and be the name of God, and of the island of Ceylon. But I believe it means Dev or Div, that is, holy or saint I, shortened from Ii, the name of the crucified God at Tripetty, on the continent, not far from Ceylon, called Ball-Ii, or Bal-Jii. This will not be thought improbable when all the other coincidences between the sacred islands of the East and of the West, which I shall now disclose, are considered. That in the languages of the East, the word for island should be the same as that for God, and that a similar peculiarity should prevail in the sacred isle of Iona and all isles in the West, viz. *Ii*, I cannot attribute to *accident*, especially when I find the Popes claiming all islands as the peculiar patrimony of God.[7] The great islands of Java, Ceylon, Japan, Sumatra, or Javadios, were all sacred islands. The language of the sacred isle of the West, Iona, was called Gaeldoct; the name of the sacred isle of the East, where we find the Point de Galle, was Sin-gala. Here we have the same Gael, but with the appellative *sin* instead of the *doct*. The same cause operated in causing the Chinese to be called Sinæs, and in giving a similar name to the Sin-gala, also to the river Sinde in North India, and to the river Sinde in Thrace, to Mount Sinai, and to the desert of Sin in Arabia, to Jehovah Nis-si, and to Bacchus, Deo-nissi, which I noticed in Vol. I. pp. 423, 606. I shall resume the inquiry into the Sin presently. The monastery of Iona was occupied by Culdees or Cullidei, or Callidei. I am persuaded that it was once the religious capital of Caledonia; and if we do not now find Ceylon called Callida, it most likely was so formerly, as we find a Callida now grown into Cochin upon the neighbouring promontory, to which it was doubtless formerly joined. But the Cal in the word Cali and the Gal

---

[1] For the origin of Cambridge, see Cleland's Specimen, p. 71. He considers Cambridge to have been a College before the time of the Romans.
[2] See supra, p. 244. [3] See Vol. I. pp. 596, 671.
[4] See Upham's Hist. of Buddhism of Ceylon, Int. pp. 66, 74. [5] Ib. p. 17. [6] Ib. 53.
[7] Hallam's Hist. Mid. Age. Vol. II. p. 57.

were the same word corrupted, as is decisively proved by the name of the Prince of *Orugallu*, given in the Madras Transactions,¹ for he is called the prince of the Gallu or Gael, which is the same as the Cal of Ur or Urii. Having shewn the Celtic to be Hebrew, that is Chaldee, and these languages to be vernacular in South India, we have all the difficulties to the doctrine of identity of race and language in Scotland and India removed. An interesting account is given in the abovementioned Transactions² of the opening of some Tumuli and Carns, which shews them to be the very same as those found in many places in Britain; but, perhaps, no where more satisfactorily than in the neighbourhood of Inverness. The observation of Dr. D. Clarke, quoted in the Transactions, that they are the works of a people of whom we have no history, is quite correct. My reader may refer to the Carn in Fig. 18, and to Vol. I. p. 241, *note*, for the account of the Cromleh given by Sir Anthony Carlisle. If my reader will look back to Volume I. p. 527, he will there see that the word Selene means the female generative principle, the same as the Yoni, or Iune, the name of the Scotch island. He will remember that the Island of Iona is called also Columba. This observed, we must recollect that the ancients often treated of the sacred islands, but where these were situated was always a matter of much doubt; some persons placed them in the West, some in the East. I consider the Iona or Columba of the Hebrides to be the Western sacred isle, and the island of Ceylon, or one of the Eastern isles, to be the Eastern one. Lempriere says, "The name of Salice, which we learn from Ptolemy to have been the native denomination of the "island, is preserved in that of *Selen-dive* compounded of the proper name Selen, and the appel- "lative for an island in the Indian language." But the word *dive* means God and *holy* as well as *island*. Here, then, we have one word in each island meaning the generative power, viz. Selen and Iona, and one word in each I or Ii, and Dive, meaning God or holy; and what is still more remarkable, the name of the capital of Iona is Columba, and of Ceylon it is Columbo. And if the reader will consider the word Ceilan or Coilan or Ceylon, another name of this island,³ he will see that it is nothing but the accusative case of the Greek word Κοιλος, (the meaning of which I need not explain,) who was the father of Helen, the mystical mother of the Roman Constantine the First, and also the Latin name of heaven. If my reader be credulous enough to believe, that all these etymological coincidences are the effect of accident, he had better shut the book; it is not fit for him. It has been observed by Dr. Townley, that בעל *bol*, Bal, Baal, Bel, who was, in so particular a manner, the object of worship with the Irish, (who probably derived it from the Carthaginians,) was peculiarly the object of worship in Ceylon. He says, "Traces of this worship "are still found in the island of Ceylon, where it is termed Baliism, a word of uncertain etymo- "logy, but which will remind an antiquary of the names of Baal, Bel, and Bal, given to the sun⁴ "by the Chaldæans and other ancient nations, and the Baltan, or Bealteine fires of Ireland and the "Highlands of Scotland. These Singhalese worshipers of the Stars are few in number, and gene- "rally conceal their opinions. The worship consists entirely of adoration to the heavenly bodies; "invoking them in consequence of the supposed influence they have on the affairs of men. The "Singhalese priests are great astronomers, and they are believed to be thoroughly skilled in the "power and influence of the planets."⁵ Townley knew nothing, when he wrote the above, about the crucifixion and worship of Bal-iji⁶ in the promontory of India, not far from Comorin.

---

¹ Vol. I. p. 19.   ² Pp. 30—32.

³ Mr. Adrian Balbi has observed, that the small number of places from Ceylon to the Himmalaya, having names connected with the Brahmin religion, and the great number connected with the Buddhist religion, depose contrary to the Brahmin doctrines, that the religion of Buddha is the oldest (p. liiij). The observation is striking and conclusive.

⁴ See Selden de Diis Syriis.   ⁵ Townley's Diss. on Maimonides, p. 44.   ⁶ See Vol. I. p. 667.

But the circumstances of coincidence are wonderfully striking. The Rev. Mr. Whiter[1] says, "The race of the *Cymri* was supposed to have been brought by *Hu Gadarn*, into the island of Britain, from the land of *Hav*, called *Defrobani*, as Mr. Davies has observed in his Celtic Re- searches, pp. 154, 165. This information is derived from the Welsh Triads.........Defrobani is the Taprobane of the ancients or the island of Ceylon. This island is likewise called Serendib. In Sanscrit, *Div* is an island, and *Seren* is quasi Selan, the island of Ceylon." The circum- stances and coincidences which I have pointed out above I think give a great degree of credit to the Welsh Triads, quoted by Mr. Davies. Bochart says,[2] "De Taprobana Diodorus: *venerantur ut Deos cœlum quod omnia cœlestia*. Item: *In festis et precationibus recitant et canunt hymnos et encomia in Deos: imprimis vero, in Solem quem insularum et sui ipsorum dominum profitenter.* Ptolemæus notat ad ortum Portum Solis, et ad Aquilonem insulam Κωρυ, quæ Plinio est insula Solis. An à decurtato כורש (*curs*) *Cores*, id est, Cyri nomine, quod Solem interpretantur Plutar- chus et alii, Κωρυ dicta sit ea insula videant doctiores." We must recollect that near this island is the coast of Coromandel, which I formerly explained. For the meaning of the Κωρυ and כורש *kurs* and Coromandel, and St. Thomas, and the Χρης-ians having the three sacraments, the same as the Cullidei of Iona, the reader must look back to Vol. I. pp. 759, 760.

The Linga and Yoni are the peculiar objects of adoration in Ceylon. The language of the sacred island of Iona, of Scotland, is the Gaelic, but it is also called Shan Scrieu or Sanscrit.[3] Here we have, most clearly, the worship of the Yoni of India and its language. I have shewn in Volume I. p. 448, from Cleland, that the word Sanscrit was called *Sanscort* or *Sanskroutan* in the Celtic, or *Sanctum Scriptum*. In which of the six Celtic dialects he had found it in this form, he does not tell us; but it was probably in Irish. In my CELTIC DRUIDS, p. 60, I have given it San-Scriobhte, in which Mr. J. Logan, a good Celtic scholar, tells me I am right; but, that the *bh* in the last word, in speaking, are not pronounced. Professor Haughton says, that the word Sanscrit is de- rived from the preposition *San* (like con, *with*) and Crita, *done, made*, and has an *s* interposed for euphony; that the Latin concretus is from the same root, but has a different sense,—for the word in Sanscrit means perfected, adorned, embellished, CONSECRATED. Here in the last word we come to the true idea, which is *sanctum scriptum*. *Sanscrit* are like *Greek* scholars who, not attending to what Plato told them, that most proper names came from the *barbarians*, never travel out of Greece for their explanations; for which reason they are seldom right. Thus the Sanscrit scho- lars go no further than the Sanscrit. I tell them to go to an earlier language for the datoos or roots from which their fine language is derived. In the Scotch Celtic we have seen it is Shan Scrieu or Shan Scrief. In the Irish *Sean* and *Sun* mean old, venerable, holy; and Vallancey con- firms this, and says, in many places, that *sean* means the Sun. Here, at last, we have the origin of the word. Seanach, in Irish, means a high priest, a Druid; this is, Sean and Akme, chief priest. In Hebrew שן *sn* means the revolving sun and the tropical year. The Scrief is evidently the Latin Scribo, Scripsi, Scriptum. Then Sean or San-Script will be *writing of the Sun* or *holy writing*. In Hebrew סופר *supr* is a scribe, and כתב *ktbi* scribo, scripsi, scriptum. It is not diffi-

---

[1] Etym. Univer. Vol. I. p. 118.
[2] Phaleg, Lib. Prim. cap. xlvi. p. 697.
[3] While travelling lately by coach, in the Highlands of Scotland, an old gentleman told me the Gaelic language was called *Sanscrit*. On the coach-door being opened by the waiter, when we arrived at the next inn, the old gentleman asked him, in English, if he understood the Gaelic, and what was the name in Gaelic of the language: his answer was, *without a moment's hesitation*, Sanscrit! There could be no imposition here, the old gentleman was an entire stranger in that part, and had not had an opportunity to speak to the waiter. He told me he spoke the language very well, as it was his native tongue, but he never had been taught to write it, therefore would not undertake to write it correctly; but he wrote it in my pocket book, *Shan Scrieu.*

cult to see, though rather difficult to explain, how, from the two, the word *scriobhte* or *scrit* in the Sanscrit, was derived. This is a very good example for shewing how all these languages revolve back into one, when examined to the bottom, where, at last, we always find the Hebrew, the language into which the first numeral symbols were written.

At a little distance from the Scotch island of Iona is a small island, called by the sailors the Dutchman's Cap, which looks exactly like the Calvaries on which the Crosses are usually placed. It has three steps, having every appearance of being formed by art, cut out of the rock by manual labour. In old maps it is called Linga. I have no doubt that in ancient times a linga was at the top of it: whether any remains of it are now there I know not. Here we have the worship of the Linga and Ioni, and the female generative power, called Columba or the Dove, more clearly marked than we have found it heretofore. Thus the worship of the Linga and Ioni was equally prevalent with the Callidi of the East, of Comorin and Ceylon, as with the Callidei of Calidi-onia or Scotland. I suppose that the origin of the name Linga arose from the equivocal nature of the Logos. The idea of word and language cannot be separated. It is very certain that the Deity could not proceed to action *in any way of which we could form any idea*, except by creating or forming or producing, nor could he do this in any other way than by willing, nor could he exhibit this will except by speaking. He spake the word or he gave the word, and the world existed,— by the Word he formed or created it. Thus the Word or Linga came to be the generative power, or emblem of the generative power. I am persuaded that the *dove was a female;* and it is remarkable, that the Hebrew name of Dove is always female—יונה *iune*.[1] The word Aleim has a feminine termination,[2] and Haggai foretells the *promised desire of all nations* by a feminine word, the Amid or Om, or Mo-hamed,[3] and the Mohamedan crest is a Crescent, always the emblem of the *female generative principle*. From this I am induced to suspect, that I have considered the Mohamedans to have been more exclusively devoted to the *male* generative principle than, in reality, they were. Perhaps it is the Turks and not the Saracens, or perhaps the followers of Othman or Omar only, and not those of Ali, who have the Crescent. The island of Iona I find is called Sudor, and there is a priest called the *Bishop of Sodor and Man*. The Western islands were divided into two classes, and called Sodoreys or Sudoreys, and Nordoreys or Nudoreys, which, translated, are Southerns and Northerns. I feel no doubt that Sudor or Iona was once the capital of the Southern state. In which of the islands the capital of the northern one might be I do not know. These islanders became great pirates; and, under the name of *Sea-kings*, constantly made war upon the Highlands. The Norde-roy is North-king; the Sudor-roy is South-king. They probably came from Norway—Nor-ia. As a protection against these people, the vitrified forts were built; and this consideration will induce me presently to make a few observations respecting them. The name of the Scotch language, Gaeldochd, is very similar, when examined, to the word Shanscrieu, as we have found it is still called. We must recollect that we found a place in Ceylon called the Point or Promontory of Galle; this proves that the island was called Galle. Pray whence had Ben-gal, that is Beni, sons of Gall, its name?[4] In a note on Scott's *Chronicles of the Canongate*, Chapter X., is this passage: "The Deasil must be performed sunways, that is, "moving from right to left. If misfortune is imprecated, the party moves withershins, (German, "Widdersins,) that is, *against the sun*, from left to right." Here we have the *sin*, as it ought to

---

[1] See Vol. I. p. 112.   [2] Ib. p. 64.   [3] Ib. p. 679.

[4] In ancient Italy Mount Alba preceded the Capitol as *the sacred Mount*. Scotland was called Alba. Much is said about a *white sow* of Alba, which was called by Cassandra *blach*. See *supra*, p. 34.

be, for the sun—Sin=360.¹ I apprehend the word Sin came to mean Lion, when the Lion was the emblem of the Sun at his summer solstice, when he was in his glory, and the Bull and the Man were the signs of the Sun at the equinoxes, and the Eagle at the winter solstice. Gael is the Hebrew גל gl, and means *circle*, and the sacred island of Serindive or Ceylon, where, as stated before, there is the Point de Galle, and the sacred island of Scotland, where there is the language of the Gael or Gaeldoct or Sanscrit, is the island of Singal or of the Solar Cycle, or Circle of the Sun. The people of Ceylon are called *Singalese*, not *Ceylonese*. I am satisfied that all the ancient names of places, which had any connexion with the mythos, had meanings: therefore, I am induced to try to find the meaning of the word Singala—the name of Ceylon; and, forced and absurd as my explanation will at first appear, I cannot help suspecting that I am right. We have found the word Gael or Gal in Ben-gal, and the Gaelic language in Scotland. Suppose we read the word Sin-gal, Hebraicè; then we have Log-nis. The explanation of the Nis or Sin, the name of Bacchus or the Sun, we have seen before, meaning 360. Bacchus we have also seen was called Liber and Bac, Boc, Book. He is also the Linga or generative power and the Logos, that is, the Log, the root of Logos: then I think Singal is the language of the Sin, or of Nis, or of Bacchus, or the Logos, or Lingua or Linga. The Gael shews itself in Ceylon in every way. We have not only Point de Galle, but Tengalle, Battigaloe, Galkisse, Bengaly.

As we might expect, we have the *feudal tenures* in Ceylon. Cordiner informs us, that the possession of the soil was in the chief of the government.² Each *corle* or district was governed by a *coral*. Here we may have our earls. It means al-corl,³ *chief of the corle* or *circle*. The officers were remunerated by a portion of the produce of the land,⁴ called *accommodesan*, that is, in other words, by a composition, in lieu of the vectigal. From this comes our word accommodate. I have read somewhere, I think, in Marsden's History of Sumatra, that Ceylon was once conquered by the Chinese, or the Sin. Then it became, probably, the Gal of the Sin: the word Sin meaning also Sun, as I have just shewn, and coming at length to mean the Lion, the emblem of the Sun at the summer solstice. The coat of arms of the Son of the Sun—the Emperor of China—and of the Egyptians, the natives of Alba-Sin, was a Lion. The capital of Scotland was Pere or Bere-gonium. It is now nearly gone; the cottages in its neighbourhood having the name of streets, prove that it was once *large*. Near it is the highest mountain of Scotland, called Ben-Nevis; that is, Ben-Navis. Here we have the same name as the Mount Ararat, Mount Baris, or Naubunda,⁵ or Mount of the Ship. The top of this mount is seldom free from snow, and is nearly covered with stones, though not very large. I think it probable that it formerly had a ship-temple. The persons who destroyed the temple would not fail to roll the longest ones down the sides of the mountain, as was probably done with the Linga in the island of the Linga. Was Ben-Lomond, Son of Le-mond? Was Alfred, who divided the kingdom into tithings, *Al-phre-di?* The tithings shew that this was an ecclesiastical division. The tithings of the Saxon Alfred are exactly like the tithings of the Chinese, each responsible for its own policy. Was the word Bareich—the name of Parish—Bar-roi—rey-rex? Were the Condés or Counties or Earldoms 72, and the Parishes 360? England, including Wales, has 52 counties. Did Scotland make up the other 20?—Of the peculiarities of the Jews perhaps there is not one more marked than their hatred of *pork*. It is very remarkable that, in the Highlands of Scotland, to the North of the Caledonian Canal, until within a

---

¹ See Vol. I. p. 606. ² Hist. of Ceylon, pp. 18, &c. ³ Whence come our Curls and Churls?
⁴ Hist. of Ceylon, p. 19. ⁵ See Vol. I. pp. 203, 235, 293, 335, 347, 759.

very few years, there was no such thing as a head of swine. It was detested, and this all Scotchmen will allow. But whence this dislike no one can tell. The Christians never had any dislike to swines' flesh. It came, I apprehend, with the Sanscrit and the Gael-docht from Sin-galla, and the Indian promontory, where we have found all the Mosaic mythos in the temple of Jaggernaut. But in this we have a strong circumstance to support my theory of the existence of a Judaism totally independent of the Judaism of Western Syria, and, in addition, of its existence all over the world, long, very long, before the time of Christ. It beautifully supports my theory, that the original Judæan mythos had its birth in India, and that the Western Syrian Jews were only a colony from the first great hive. This mythos came to Scotland when the Gael, Celtic, and Hebrew, were all one. I cannot help suspecting that the famous Scotch warrior Fingal ought to be Singal, and this is strengthened by the fact, that his bard, Ossian, was the son of OM. I have long suspected that if Macpherson had understood the nature of Ossian's poems, he might have made them into an epic poem, something in its nature similar to that of Homer. I think they are a series of epics, like the tragedies of Æschylus, or the historical plays of Shakspeare. The history of the poems of Homer is very simple, when the mist in which the learning of men, who are too learned to see any thing in a simple and natural way, has enveloped them, is cleared away. According to the written accounts which we have, they were songs to celebrate a continuous history, as I have just remarked respecting the tragedies and plays of Æschylus and Shakspeare,[1] and were first collected by Lycurgus, then by Pisistratus, and at last by Aristotle and a company of men who, by inserting parts where needful, formed them into the poem which we have. They are sacred poems. They are the praises of the unknown God, or songs about the God Om—becoming the songs of Om—the mythos concealed, as we have so often found, under a history.[2] They were the same, I suspect, in Mœsia, the land of the Mystery, in Asia Minor, and in Caledonia in Scotland. The SANSCRIT word Eri or Heri, added to the Om, makes it Om the Saviour. We must not forget that we have found the subject of the poem described in this Sanscrit word (for Om-eri is Sanscrit) in India; for example, Achilles, Ulysses,[3] the Argonauts; and, in the Bible, Solomon, Iphigenia,[4] &c., and the history of the Bible in India, and both again in Egypt.[5] I have little doubt that the prejudice to which I have alluded in the latter end of my preface, has kept from us the truth respecting the father of Ossian, or has made Ossian the Omer, into the Son of Om. I beg my reader to recollect the manner in which the Vau changed into the F, and the F into the Ç, on which some very curious observations may be seen in Bishop Marsh's Horæ Pelasgicæ, before he determines whether it be not possible that the Fingal of Scotland may have been Singal. But what is Gaael? Is it 60? We know that this word is always pronounced unusually long, correctly as it is written here: G=3, AA=2, E=5, L=50=60. Thus Cali may have been Caall: K=20, AA=2, L=50=72, or Caph final=500, LL=100=600. But it is often in India written Kalee; this will be, K=20, L=30, EE=10=60, or Kli, K=20, L=30, I=10=60. I must now refer my reader to the CELTIC DRUIDS, p. 63, and there he will find several whole sentences taken out of a Welsh Bible, with the Hebrew words above them, letter for letter. He will also find, in pp. 59—61, a great number of Celtic, Sanscrit and Latin words which are evidently identical, which, according to Young's doctrine, PROVE most superabundantly, that the Hebrew is Welsh, and that the Welsh is both Sanscrit and Latin; therefore, that the Hebrew is

---

[1] Vide what I have said in Vol. I. pp. 360—366; and pp. 542—544.
[2] From the deceitful and false character it always assumed we have our Hum for *deceit*, and Humbug for *Big hum*.
[3] See Vol. I. p. 519.   [4] Ib. pp. 364, 615.   [5] See *supra*, pp. 17, 18.

Sanscrit. Thus we have the vernacular language of Cape Comorin and of the Celtic Hebrew all proved to be the same, in the same country. Here in Carnate we have the Mosaic mythos, and the two Mosaic dialects, the Chaldee, the Hebrew and the Gael, in Ceylon, called Singala and Sanscrit, and in Scotland Sanscrieu and Gaeldoct.[1] The Singala is Gala or Gael Nis. And I must repeat that, in India we have Mount of Nau-banda, *ship-cabled mount ;* in Scotland we have Mount Nevis, or, I should say, Mount Navis, and Loch Ness, and Inver-ness ; that Sin, when read Hebraically, is Nis, the name of Bacchus, of the river Sinde, of the president of the Jewish Sanhedrim ;[2] and, in short, of the Sun, as shewn in Volume I. p. 606, having the numerical power of 360. Dr. Babington says, that the Sanscrit of South India is written in characters derived from the Tamul ; and he and Mr. Ellis both agree in opinion, that the Tamul is a language not derived from the Sanscrit. Wilson says, it is not derived from any language now in existence.[3] I believe there were many Sanscrit languages ; it was an appellative term, and applied equally to the Gael or Celtic in India, and in Scotland. The Scotch Gael or Celtic, was the Gael of Singala, of Beni-Gael, of Point-de-Galle, of Oru Gallu, of the Syriac or Hebrew or Pushto. This very ancient and *first-written syllabic language* was, I cannot doubt, the Sanscrit or *holy writ*, and thus it is found in Scotland. This language, I confidently believe, was Hebrew or Chaldee, Syriac, Arabic, Ethiopic—in each country diverging a little, every year, from its first original, till it is now scarcely perceptible in any of them. After the Brahmin or Cristnu sect arose, it formed the Sanscrit, to distinguish itself from the others—which, originally secret, had become common, the effect of natural causes. And now the Sanscrit is, as I may call it, the victim of similar causes, and is public. After its sect acquired the sovereignty of India, it was a natural consequence that its Sanscrit, or Sanctum Scriptum, should become THE *sacred script*, particularly as the old sacred script every day became more nearly obsolete. We have precisely the same process in the Western Syria. The ancient sacred script, the Hebrew, became dead and a learned language, and no longer understood by the natives. The Arabic of the Koran is precisely the same : it is now a sacred script, or dead language, not understood by the mass of the people ; but is studied as we study Latin. Thus all languages, written and unwritten, change. It is only the natural effect of a cause, and that cause is the first law of nature—that every thing should be in perpetual motion, that nothing should stand still, *except* the one First Cause, the Tὸ Ὄν, the ☉, the circle being, whose centre is every where, and whose circumference is no where—Illusion.[4] Every thing is in perpetual motion, in the act of emanation from the First Cause, or in return to it. By this all the apparent aberrations and irregularities of the system are accounted for. At the beginning of each system all would be in order ; but still, it would possess within itself the principle of change, which we call disorder ; although it is only *disorder* to our narrow views. If a person without prejudice would only give himself time to think upon the way in which spoken language is always changing, and upon what must necessarily happen when the names of places, gods, and persons, come to be put into writing, in widely-separated nations, he would soon see that the same person or place must come to be very variously written ; and, in consequence, that, for the discovery of truth, we do not generally allow too much latitude, but too little. We will take as an example the words Callidei, Calidei, Chaldæi, Collidei, all which and many more words are meant to designate the same people. It is possible that sometimes, in taking the latitude I contend for, I may confound two persons or places ; but all these cases must depend upon collateral circumstances,

---

[1] See Vol. I. p. 736.   [2] See ib. p. 722.   [3] See ib. p. 736.
[4] See ib. pp. 162, 530, 643, 803, 814, 818, 826—828.

on which the degree of probability attached to each case must depend. Demonstration is not to be expected;[1] it is contrary to the nature of things. But, by not taking this latitude, I am certain, if we do not make an occasional mistake, we shall do what is much worse—we shall make a darkness—we shall learn nothing as we have hitherto done.

22. I beg my reader to refer to Vol. I. p. 709, for the word Bathkol בתקול *betql*, and he will find it explained, after the Jews, to mean the *daughter of voice*. This completely puzzled all commentators. It is evident that this word may also mean *daughter of* WISDOM, the word Cal meaning both *wisdom* and *voice*; from the words *to call*, as voice, and *calling*, as wisdom. Now we come at something like sense.[2] Now we come to the reason why the votaries of this mythos are every where found under the word Chaldeans and its variations. These people were the followers of *wisdom*, and thus the Goddess Cali, whom we have found near Cape Comorin, was Wisdom; and the Calidei of Iona or Columkill were followers of *wisdom*; and the language of these people was Hebrew, which was Celtic, which was the Gael, of Scotland and of Singala, and Bengal, and of the kingdom of Orugallu. It was the Gael-doct and the Sanscrit, Sanctum Scriptum—the Cel[3] of Celtic and of Cal changed into the Gel and Gal (as Camel and Gamel). Thus the language of the Gael-doct would be the language of *the learned wisdom*, that is, the learned Celt or Hebrew, the language of Abraham, of South India, and of the Chaldæans; and this, at last, brings us almost to a conclusion, to which we have come by a variety of other ways, that the Hebrew was the sacred language, and was probably the first language into which the mythos was written. I am almost certain that the Synagogue Hebrew was the universal language of the world when the syllabic writing was first used, and this, being used only for the mythos in the temples, remained as it was—but that it was soon deviated from in speech, and thus it came to be the secret language of all nations; that the Jews never spoke it, but that the Syriac was their vernacular tongue. They learn it, as we learn Latin, but they speak it no where. It became the dead and secret language from circumstances; but it never would have been more different from the Chaldee and Pushto, than the Celtic of Scotland is from the Celtic of Ireland, if it had not been written in letters of different forms. Sanscrit scholars constantly endeavour to tie me down to the strict orthography of that language, as at present settled in their lexicons and grammars. This is not the way to discover the truth. They cannot deny that that language, like all others, was once very different from what it is now, and, as I have shewn, has partly become lost; and that it was, in fact, when the first Veda was written, in a state of comparative rudeness. On this account the strict modern orthography must not be permitted to stop inquiry, or to determine the identity of words, against circumstances and probability. In the beginning of all nations their orthography must have been as wild as the winds. It is a very curious and striking circumstance, that the Cambridge river, the *Cam*, should also bear another Indian name, that is to say, *Granta*. We have had enough of the Cama of Cape Comorin; but the letters of this country are called the letters of the Grantha, which are said to have been derived from the Tamul, the meaning of which is, that they are the same as the Tamul. Is it possible to believe that the river Cam being also called *Granta*, can be the effect of accident? I think not. I believe that the Bede's houses, or houses of Buddha or wisdom,[4] had this name given to them when the river was called both Cam and

---

[1] People who do this, set up a system radically absurd, and contrary to all probability; and, in order to overturn this system, they require the most rigorous proofs.

[2] I believe that Mimra has been M-om-rah.

[3] The churches were called Kil or Cel: this was *house* or *temple of Kel* or *Cel*: and as the temple at first consisted solely of a circle of stones, the word came to mean *stones*.

[4] See Vol. I. p. 833.

Granta. In the Madras Transactions,[1] the words Cusuma-pura, Pushpa-pura, *the city of flowers*, and Pātāli-pura, are said to be synonymous. I believe that the word *Cusuma* answers to our Camasa and Camasene,[2] and that the Patali is the Greek Petalon. It is now expedient to recollect, that France, where we found the Bhoees, the Garuda, the temple of Carnac, and the Pattarini, is called *Gaul*, and the Welsh or English, *Celts, Galles*.[3]

23. I will now trouble my reader with a digression respecting the ancient *vitrified forts* of Scotland. That the vitrified forts were made for the purpose of places of refuge or defence cannot be doubted. The plate which I have given, No. 38, in my CELTIC DRUIDS, gives a very good idea of most of them. Several circumstances, which have been overlooked by those who maintain that they are mere beacon stations, prove this. They are much too large in general for mere beacons. The fort near Inverness is above eighty yards long and above twenty wide, and that above-named, in my Celtic Druids, is considerably larger. The quantity of wood which would be consumed before the wall would be vitrified, by filling it with wood as a beacon, is immense. Not only the whole wood of the mount on which it stands would be consumed by one fire, but the wood of several such mounts would be required. These forts run all round the coast, in several places across the island, and are in sight of each other, so that, to alarm the whole country, certainly not more than the size of a common *tar barrel* would be requisite on each. But it is not to be supposed that when one fort was attacked, it would raise a fire to alarm its neighbours. Supposing them beacons, for what use was the wall? Would not the wood lie on the top of the hill without the very expensive vitrified wall to inclose it? The Inverness fort is situate on a ridge, rising to a point on the West, around which the rock has been scarped away, and of the material which has been produced by this labour, the wall has probably been formed. This operation must have made the *west* end and the two sides inaccessible. The *east* end, by which the fort was entered, rises by degrees, and is defended by a double wall, in a somewhat similar way to the fort described in my Celtic Druids. It has been said, that the walls are more perfectly vitrified within than without. This was a natural consequence, and could not be prevented. I cannot conceive how it was possible to vitrify them, placed as they are, on the edge of a precipice, without producing this effect. I have no doubt they were made before the art of building with stone and mortar was discovered—when the natives lived, as they do yet in many parts of Switzerland, in houses built of timber, and pisé, as in Devonshire and many parts of France. Of these materials very good and even large houses may be built; but it is very clear that they would not be used for fortresses, as they would be burnt in a moment. When the art of building with stone and mortar was discovered, the vitrified forts went out of use, and the castles were built—the ruins of which yet remain—placed, like the old forts, in such situations on the banks of the Friths and Lakes as to communicate with one another. I have no doubt that the whole of the Highlands and Islands, north of the Caledonian Canal, might have been alarmed either from the old or the new castles, in a few hours, except in very foggy or misty weather. In those times, the temples were formed of large stones placed upright in circles, and the prodigious number of them which their remains shew to have once existed, prove, or render it highly probable, that a much greater population than what it has at present once inhabited this country. At that time, the ridge and fur form of the land, which I am told is yet to be seen in many places, now covered with heath, was made. From this country very large quantities of fish, corn, and cattle, are every year exported, in exchange for bills or gold, which are sent away to pay the rents of absentee landlords, but which, if paid to resident landlords, in kind or service, as it was formerly paid, would again raise a numerous

---

[1] Vol. I. p. 55.   [2] See Vol. I. pp. 760, 777, 788, 808.   [3] See ib. pp. 384, 745, 757.

BOOK IV. SECTION 23.

population, and again soon restore the heath-land to the plough. By the present order of things, in lieu of the population of the country, we have the population of Manchester and Birmingham. I do not mean to say that the present order is not *the better* of the two; I only mean to say, that *thus it is*. The gentlemen who have maintained that the vitrified forts were beacon stations, have been enabled to support their theory very plausibly, because they would necessarily be used as beacon stations, as no doubt all the castles, by which they were succeeded, occasionally were. They must have been very uncomfortable as places of residence, and on this account they were succeeded by the castles, which were equally strong, and perhaps stronger, as soon as iron and the arts of cutting stones and using mortar were discovered. I suppose that, at first, the stone pillar was the object of veneration, and was adorned with flowers and anointed with oil. The Ganesa [1] of India is now constantly anointed with oil. When the father, the Abba, the head of the tribe, made his residence stationary, it became the Bital [2] or Fanum. He was the Abbé, the wise man, the king and priest. When science and letters became known, and of course known more particularly to him than to most others, he associated with him such as he pleased,[3] to whom were confided the secrets of initiation, and as one reason for the better securing of these secrets, celibacy may have been established; and to the same end poverty, that is *community of property*, and obedience, may have been enforced. In our Colleges, evidently remains or revivals of Druidical institutions, we have the Abbé, or Rabbi, that is, a contraction of Roi, or Ray-Abbé, R'Abbé, or the Maître or Maistre, the Dean, &c. The Abbé, with the prepositive particle, was S'Abs, which thus came to have the meaning of *wisedom*.[4] The fellows, &c., were all celibats or monks; but when one of these monks went off to found another college or Bareich or Parish or Borough, he was allowed to marry, as he was then the Abba or Prior. St. John's-day was Midsummer-day. This John was Juana or Wisdom, and Wisdom was the Sun; hence the longest day was selected for his festival.[5] The day of the Sun (Sunday) was particularly the day of instruction by the Druid *Sabs*;[6] whence it obtained the name of *Sab-aith*, the preachment of the *Sages* or of *the wise*; consequently that day, when the Sun was most predominant, was held in the greatest veneration. It was called the Great Sunday. From this day the sun decreased. Mr. Cleland observes, that it was in allusion to this, that John the Baptist is made to say, " He must increase, (who was born on the winter solstice,) but I must decrease," John iii. 30. "On the Sab-aith the Saronide preached to the people, in the Kirk Meyn or T'impul or Ey-cil-Lys, barbarised into Église and Ecclesia."[7] The assembly was called Sabat; and in the name Sabbatines given to lectures on science or wisdom, in the colleges (on any day, not Saturday only) of France, the original name is yet retained. In the above names the Sar-onide is nothing but Ras, with a termination which I do not understand; the Kirk is the circle; the T'impul is *the temple* of the Templars, the origin of which we find here as well as of the circular churches of the Templars. But the words Église and Ecclesia are only the Hebrew word קהל kel. In allusion to this, and to their being

---

[1] See Vol. I. pp. 351, 420, 518, 651.   [2] Ib. p. 759.

[3] The number of circumcised or initiated by Abraham, 318, explained in a way which cannot be disputed by Sir W. Drummond, (Æd. Jud. p. 103, quoted by me in Vol. I. pp. 214, 215,) furnishes an admirable example of numeral and astrological allegory.

[4] Cleland's Specimen, p. 56.   [5] Ib. p. 94.

[6] "When Mr. Humboldt was in Cumana, in 1800, says Lavaysse, he constructed a fine sun-dial there. The Cumanese say, on passing it, 'We owe this sun-dial to the learned Humboldt.' The word Sabio, which they employ on this occasion, signifies, in the mouth of a Creole of the Spanish Colonies, both wise and learned. They always apply the word Sabio to this illustrious traveller." Globe Newspaper, Aug. 2, 1832.

[7] Cleland's Specimen, pp. 96, 97.

the builders or repairers of the temple, the Templars are *megalistors* of the temple—humble imitators of the architect of the temple of the universe—of the system which has the cross, with many points at the top of it, the pole-star of Juda. This is the reason why the cross of the Templars has not a line for the four cardinal points only, but many lines or points, now generally eight, probably allusive to the original eight planets. No doubt the cupola was the most glorious part of the temple; it was the top—the archè. It was also arched; this was the first arch. Was it from this *arch* or *pons* that the high-priest took the name of Pon-tifex? Did he not only place the *first* stone at the bottom, but did he also place the *last* on the top? I believe that he did, and that from this he became Pontifex Maximus. He was a microcosm of the Megalistor, M-wisdom, finishing the arch of the universe. It is curious enough to find the Mohamedans rebuilding the Jewish Temple, and the Christians adopting into its sanctuary the society of Templars, as the conservators of that building, which ignorant, uninitiated Christians hold that God repeatedly destroyed by a miracle (Titus and Julian) to avenge their cause. I beg my masonic reader to enter the new room at Freemason's Tavern, when lighted up, and there he will see what must have been the nature of the Cupolas at Komulmer[1] and Eleusis, when, as Chrysostom says, the ceremonies were celebrated under them, with light *music, dancing, and poetry*. The high-priest was the builder of the cupola or temple, which was only an imitation of the vault or arch of heaven. An arch is a pons. From this, as I have just now said, I suspect that the high-priest was called Pontifex. If my reader should think this far-fetched, I then request him to give me the reason why the high-priest is called bridge-maker or pontifex. The cupola is a diminutive of *cup*, which, though I can produce no authority for it, I believe meant the vault of heaven, and that *pons* had the same meaning. Cup, in Welsh, means *top*, the same as *ras* and $αρχη$. But all these explanations are very doubtful. The Abba was king and priest; in some cases his monks were his assistants; Abraham, *the stranger*, had 318 of them, and when he returned from the war he submitted himself to the Abba of the country for permission to remain there. These monks were the liberi, the men of letters, the initiated, the circumcised, the possessors of the secret, that is, of the sacred lore; they were the persons who anointed the linga with oil, and crowned it with flowers. They soon became *sacred*; and, when they thought proper to save a criminal, they admitted him among them, and thus arose the sanctuary. These king or patriarchal priests were the owners of all the land, and received the *tenths* as rent, for the purposes of government and religion. In Britain, we find their successors, the monks, appointing vicars, when the increase of population required them. In Yorkshire there are two small towns on the Roman road, called Aldborough and Boroughbridge. The meaning of their names admits not of doubt. The first was the ancient capital of the Brigantes, called by the natives *Iseur*, by the Romans *Isurium*—that is, *Saviour town*, and in later times called *the old borough*. For proofs of this see CELTIC DRUIDS.[2] The name of the other is the bridge of the borough or burgh. They are distant about half a mile from each other. They each returned two members to parliament. The first is now an insignificant village, the second can raise a market, but with difficulty. When *Iseur* was the capital of a great state they must have been in one city. This city was destroyed by the Romans, and there can be no probable reason found for its ruins returning members to parliament, except that, before the arrival of the Romans, it returned them to the old Wittagemote of its own state or to that of the nation; but probably from the unusual number of *four*, it returned them as being the capital of the nation, as London now returns four; and when the Romans withdrew, and the old Britons resumed their power, and the Wittagemote was restored, it resumed the exercise of its rights or duties. I think, from the ac-

---

[1] Tod, Vol. I. pp. 670, 671.   [2] Pp. 152, 195.

counts which we read, that the Romans left the country by a kind of convention, it seems probable that the two nations never amalgamated, and that when the Romans went away, the old system, in great part, revived. It seems to have ceased to send members at one time, but to have resumed its right in the time of Philip and Mary.

24. The Greek word μυϛηριον comes from the Celtic word *wist*, or *wise*, though this is rather contrary to the definition of secrecy.[1] It signifies *knowledge*. It is the radical both of history and mistery. A play was called a *History* or Mystery, from its being an historical representation.[2] In the middle ages sacred plays, called Mysteries, were performed. This was isteries, with the sacred M prefixed, and originally this was the case with all history. It was a mystery, a representation, in the form of parable or mythos, of the history of the sacred, never-to-be-spoken M or OM. The general assembly of the ancient Britons was called Witt-age-mot or Witten-age-mote or Witte-mote. This is, I believe, Witt, *wise—os*, letters, and mote, *meeting*.[3] This *Witte* is the same as the first part in the name of the crucified God of India, *Witto-ba*;[4] and *ba* is *ab*—both together meaning *father of wisdom*. The word wisdom is *Witte* or *Wis-di-om*. Wittage-mot is *wise*-mot. Wittage may be one of the very common pleonasms met with in language. Oga is a name of wisdom or Minerva. Wittage, witt-age or witt-oga, is the same as Cortage—Cor-Cir-age, *circle of wisdom*. Mr. Cleland, in his Specimen and in the Appendix, in various places, has shewn that the Holy Ghost was well known to the ancient Celts; that their public councils were always opened by an invocation of it, and that their decrees were held to be inspired by it. There was a class or sect of people among the Gentiles called *Pneumatomachi*.[5] The Salic laws were seventy-one or seventy-two in number: they were enacted in a place or field called Salicam, in Latin Salius, or Sali campus. They were proposed by the Saloghast, Wiseghast, Bosoghast, and Undoghast, which meant Holyghost; Wisdom of the Spirit; Voice of the Spirit; Will of the Spirit.[6] I think the Sali-ghast is the Ghost of Sali or Suli of Bath, which I have explained in Volume I. p. 609. But here we have the Trinity and the seventy-two, the microcosm, of which I shall treat in the next book. By the imposition of the hand on the head of the candidate, the *Ghast* or spirit of authority was conveyed.[7] This is literally the Hebrew Gas, spiritual fire, whence comes Ghost—Galvanic, Electric fire, the Magnetic fluid. I am convinced that the emanation from the To Ον was believed to be this fire. I am of opinion that all the ancient fathers of the church believed God to be a Spiritual Fire.[8] Although the town of Salusbury is probably modern, being removed by Edmund the bishop from Sarum, in the beginning of the 12th century, it doubtless took the ancient names along with it; as it was not considered to be the building of a *new* town, but the removal of the *old* one.[9] Salusbury was called also Saresbury; this is, town of Sar or Sur, in fact, Sura or Syr-ia, *place of Sur*.[10] The God of Wisdom was, in a peculiar manner, the God of Abraham the Chaldæan, or of the Callidei, or of Callida of India; it is in connexion with this that we have callidus, meaning *wisdom* or *cunning*. *Call* in Celtic, Cleland says, means *learning*;[11] whence comes a man's *calling*. Cleland says the L is the Celtic præpo-

---

[1] See note *infra*, on the last page of this book. *Ed.*
[2] Cleland's Specimen, p. 124. See also Vol. I. p. 822, *note*.
[3] I much suspect that the letters called Ogam or Agham of Ireland and India are the עץ *os*, meaning *trees* or *letters*, and Om, that is, the letters of Om, having the names of trees. When I consider that the same word meant both trees and letters, and that the leaves were letters, and the substance whereon letters were written were leaves of trees, and the bark of trees, I am not surprised at the allegories from trees. See supra, pp. 148—153.
[4] See Vol. I. pp. 145—147, 750. [5] App. p. 32. [6] Cleland's Sup. to Specimen, p. 30.
[7] Cleland's Spec. pp. 10, 11. [8] See Vol. I. p. 113. [9] Vide Rapin, Vol. III. B. viii.
[10] See Vol. I. p. 669. [11] Specimen, p. 124, *note*.

sitive article.¹ This tends to strengthen my assertion that it is the same in Hebrew. The Osci were T'Usci or THE Uscans or Tuscans.² Cleland, as I stated in Volume I. p. 822, *note*, explains the word parable to be *par-habul* by way of Fable. Habul gives the word Cabala used in Italy for a fable. He says from this comes the Pythagorean precept—*abstineto à fabis*. The beans of Pythagoras have puzzled all commentators: when he ordered his disciples to abstain *à fabis*, he meant from *fables*, not from *beans*.³ In fact, that they were not to take the parables in religion literally. I consider the veil of Isis to be a parable. Under that veil lay hid the book of wisdom. She was called Neith, which meant *wisdom*.

25. The traces of the oriental system of the Sacæ are evident in the Scandinavian kingdoms, in their traditions, customs, and names; for instance, in the name of the king, Hakim, the Crymogæa of Arngrimus;⁴ Thule, that is, *The* Iule; Finland or *Vin*land;⁵ and in the confraternities, which are the sodalitates of Italy, and are but a variety of the monastic establishments of North India, of Tibet, or of the Sacæ. The custom of sending round the cup, of saying the grace, and of pledging or drinking to the health of each other as the cup goes round, is nothing but a variation of the Eucharistia.⁶ It is the exact picture of Melchizedek and Abraham. Melchizedek first blesses God or invokes, or addresses a prayer to, God, that is, says grace; then he blesses or wishes blessings to his guest; drinks to his guest, who pledges him. The confrères of Scandinavia were all sworn friends, in sickness and health, in peace and war. They were the Culdees. The Saxons of Denmark had three cups, one to Odin, one to Niord (query Neith or wisdom, the Logos), one to Freya, and a fourth sometimes to Braga, the deity of eloquence and poetry, when the brave boasted or bragged of his exploits, in the presence of the fair—whence comes our word to brag or boast. The Scandinavians had their machinery of Demigods, who arose after the manner of those of the Romans and Greeks, by degrees, as the knowledge of the Trimurti faded away; and they, in like manner, became Christian saints. In fact, there was very little change; they were first χρης-iani Divi; they afterward became Christ-iani Divi. The division into districts is also most clearly to be perceived in their Seigneurs and Seigniories, which came into Britain from them. Mr. Mallet has observed, that the Seigniors or Seigneurs were always members of the confraternities, and that this continued till 200 years and more after the rise of Christianity, as may be seen in a MS. of the 13th century, cited by Bartolin.⁷ This means no more, in fact, than till the Papist missionaries penetrated into these northern regions. I have no doubt (as Mr. Mallet suspects), that they were the originals of the confraternities of the present Rossicrucians, freemasons, &c., in Germany and many other countries. The Papist convocations and councils, from the earliest time, have always had a most bitter enmity to these societies; but they have never succeeded in putting them down.⁸ the true reason of this enmity probably was, because they were Christians before the rise of Romish Christianity. In Volume I. p. 106, I explained the origin of our Sir, Sieur, Mon-sieur, Mon-seigneur, from the Egyptian O-sir-is and the Indian Iswara. The Seigniors and Seigniories are all the same, both in name and substance. Seignior is Lord, and Seigniory is Seignior-ia, *place of the Lord*. In Hebrew it would be written שיגנור siegNur as corrupted, but as in the Synagogue *sieour*. The ancient Britons divided the country into tithings, or into districts containing *ten* Fraternities, with a Lord of a Manor at the head of each; in the towns, ten fraternities of craftsmen or ten guilds. The tithing court, the lowest division, consisted of ten heads of families, who were mutual sureties for one another, as each, in particular, for all that were under him.⁹ The presidents of ten tithings formed a superior court,

---

¹ Cleland's Specimen, p. 140.   ⁴ Ib. p. 196.   ² Ib. pp. 1, 212.
³ Mallet, Int. Hist. de Dannemarc, pp. 169, 170.   ³ Ib. 173.   ⁶ Ib. p. 195.
⁷ Ib. p. 196.   ⁸ Ib.   ⁹ Rapin, Vol. II. p. 155.

and were called *sapientes* and Witan or Wites, i. e. *wise men*. Rapin observes, that this system is exactly that of China, that is, of Chinese Tartary, or of the Pallestini or Tartars, some of whom we formerly found at the mouth of the Po; in fact, the Sacæ. He adds, " the conformity is so " great between the practice of the Chinese and the Anglo-Saxons with regard to these tithings or " reciprocal pledges, that one can't but wonder, how two nations so remote from one another, " should agree so exactly on this point."[1] The Lords of Manors inherited their power, and I think they were originally ecclesiastical. The very name Lord or Seignior shews it. They were heads of a sacred caste, from which, the persons invested with the functions of religion were selected. They were the original of such establishments as the Prince bishop of Liege, Osnaburg, &c.

26. The Rosicrucians[2] of Germany are quite ignorant of their origin; but, by tradition, they suppose themselves descendants of the ancient Egyptians, Chaldæans, Magi, and Gymnosophists; and this is probably true. They had the name of *illuminati*, from their claiming to possess certain secret knowledge, and, from their secrecy, they were also called *invisible brothers*. They use as a mark of distinction or monogram the three letters F. R. C., which probably mean *Fratres Rosi Crucis*.[3] Luther took for his coat of arms, a cross rising from a rose. They are said to hold that an universal spirit pervades all nature, which they call Argheus.[4] Here is evidently the Indian Argha. Under an old Carthusian convert at Baden, is a very curious series of secret prisons; they are said, in the town, to have belonged to the Inquisition; but I have not been able to discover that it was ever established there. On this account, and for some other reasons, I am induced to suspect that they belonged to these *invisible brethren*. The circumstances of the gradation of ranks, the initiation, and the head of the order in Persia being called the Grandmaster,[5] raises a presumption that the Sophees were, in reality, the order of Masons. The most eminent of them are called Sheik, which is said to mean *reverend*, and this has the same meaning as *worshipful*. They are said to maintain, that the dissolution of bodies by the power of fire is the only way in which men can arrive at the first principles of things. Here I think we may perceive the resolution or reabsorption of all emanations into the First Principle, the Spiritual Fire, the Τὸ Ὄν. The word Ros is, in English, dew; by means of the similarity of this word to the word Ras, or wisdom, they seem to have deceived their enemies, and sent them upon a false search. But I think there is no doubt that along with other matters they were also Alchemists. I am quite of opinion that Roger Bacon was one of them. The name of the Deity was probably at first Lar, which was the origin of the Latin Lares; and Lar-di was holy or divus Lar, or Lord. After this, in the usual course, Priest of Lar-di (from the regimen) became Lardi and Lord. This was probably like our Majesty, the name of the Sovereign and of God, and of the priest or sacred Lord of the Manor; and from this, in time, came the lay Lords of Manors. The Lord was the Earl, that is, anagrammatically, *the Lar*, E-Lar-di. The writing anagrammatically is only a remnant of the Hebrew mode of writing from right to left. The Lar or Lord or Seignior resided at or presided over the Manor or Manor-ia, place of *Mnr*, of Minerva or Wisdom; or over the Lordship or Seignior-ia or Seigniory. The Earl or Lar or Lord was also the Spanish Conde, and Count and Compte, and County, that is, Count-ia, district of the Conde—the same as we found in Ceylon, in Volume I. pp. 753, 754; and the Conde is the Can, Khan, or Kan of Tartary, with the title divus or sacred, holy, can-di. Kan or Kin, in Celtic, means *head*.[6] The words Censeo, Census, include the idea

---

[1] Vol. II. p. 157.   [2] See Vol. I. pp. 723, 809; and *supra*, p. 243.
[3] Rather *Fratres Rosæ Crucis*, if from *rosa* and *crux*?   *Ed*.   [4] See Ency. Brit. voce Ros.
[5] Ib. voce Sop.   [6] Cleland, Spec. p. 114.

of telling by the head.¹ Censeo, I opine, derives from Kan, the head, as penser from *pen* the head.²
Khan is originally Ken, knowledge or wisdom. I ken a thing, or I know it; whence came γινωσκω.
Y is the Celtic prepositive article, and stands for THE.³ If my memory do not deceive me, Cleland has shewn that the word Khan—the Khan of Tartary—was the origin of our word King, and that it was a sacred or pontifical title, and was both male and female.

27. Every temple was a *tecte* or *house* of God. Jacob's stone was a house of God or of Om—D'om—thence came Domus for *house*. In the northern language Dom meant *a judge*.⁴ Dominus was inus-Dom, that is, inus=366—Om. The Cathedrals were called Duomo, or translated Casa Santa. The Dome is the Domo; it is the Arch formed of large stones, overhanging one another, with a flat stone at the top. It is the house, the Domus. It is the place D'Om, D'Am, D'Ama, or Di-Om, Di-Am, Di-Ama, of the *holy* OM; thus it grew into D'om; and thus, as usual, the name of God, *di*, came to be the emphatic article, and thus the house of Di-am or Di-om became Domus; Δις *holy*, [Jupiter] δῶ for δῶμα, *a house*—δι-ωμ-ia, *place of holy Om*. The stone on which the Vaid or Druid stood to preach was called Βωμος: this was like B-ras-it—*By Wisdom*. Βωμος was B-om, stone or altar of Om. Thus Bacchus was ΩM-adios, *the holy Om*. The country or district of the Lar, Lord, Count, was his Domain. This was Domania; that is, ama or ia-d'-om. His kingdom was Kin-d'-om, kyningdom, and Earl-d'-om, whence Bishopdom; and the record in which the particulars of his estate were entered was called Dombec—that is, Liber or Book or Bec-d'-om. This, in a later day, was imitated by our William the Conqueror, from whom only we have the word Dom-bec. At that time it is probable that the surveys of the priests were called Bec-Dom as a proper name. Thus William had a Boc-Dom. Dom-day-book was originally the D'om-d-nia, a record of the land of the Sacred Om, of the land which paid its tenths. This shews that there must have been at the time some which did not pay; and I apprehend these were glebes belonging to priests or convents. I beg my reader to look to the Celtic Druids, pp. 128, 129, to Vol. I. pp. 173, 232, 665, 729, and *supra*, pp. 68—71, where he will find it explained, that when the Jew received the χειροτονια, as Aaron received it from Moses, he was said to be *samached*, to receive the Samach, that is, the brand for 600, which the Samach of the Hebrew denotes. The Christian, in his Baptism, receives the Cross, X; this, again, is the mark for 600. But the Samach, as I have frequently remarked, is the M final—in fact, the OM. For a proof that Om, or Iom, meant also 360 days, or a year, see Vallancey.⁵ There is scarcely one of our very ancient customs, when examined to the bottom, which has not marks of the rule of the priests. Look at a coronation, in any of the ancient kingdoms. Every thing bespeaks the appointment by the priest of his Lieutenant or Vicra, or Vicar, after he has undergone the χειροτονια, or is samached, or anointed with oil, from the vessel called Ampulla. (Am is OM, and pulla is אלפ pala, or *wisdom*—the vessel of the wisdom of Om.) By the priest, he becomes his Vicra-ditya or *holy vicar*, or Vicra-ma-ditya—*holy* or *sacred grand Vicar*. With us rebellious wretches the Priest does homage to the King; not so in Rome and Tibet, where things move in their proper sphere—there the King does homage to the Priest. "OMM. Ce mot Arabe, qui signifie Mère, a plusieurs "significations, selon qu'il est joint à d'autres mots. OMM Alketab : la Mère du Livre, ou des "Livres. Le Protocolle, ou Original. Les Musulmans appellent ainsi, la Table, ou le Livre des

---

¹ To Calculate, to count. Xal. XI, x=600, 1=50, and clo. Count, ken, censeo, I think. Cen Xn=650—a census.
² Cleland, Spec. 114. See also Lemon, *voce count*.
³ Cleland, Spec. p. 197.
⁴ Cleland, Add. to Spec. p. 13.
⁵ Coll. Hib. Vol. VI. p. 393.

"décrets divins;[1] où ils prétendent que le destin de tous les hommes, est écrit en caractères
"ineffaçables, au quel ils donnent encore le nom de Louh al-Mahfoudh, qui signifie, la Table
"gardée, ou secrète.

"Le même titre d'OMM alketab, est encore attribué par les mêmes Musulmans au premier
"chapitre de l'Alcoran, que l'on nomme ordinairement, Soutat al-Fatehah." It seems in a particular manner to mean Mother. Thus, "OMM alcora: la Mère des Villes. C'est le titre que les
"Mohamétans donnent à la Mecque, parcequ'ils regardent cette ville comme la Métropole du
"Musulmanisme. L'on trouve cependant que la ville de Balkh a porté aussi le nom de Cobbat
"aleslam, qui signifie, le DÔME, ou la Voûte du Musulmanisme.—Quelques-uns ont donné aussi
"ce titre à la ville de Bokara."[2] The circumstance of the Koran being called Om, and the observation respecting the Vault of Mohamedism connecting it with our Dom-bec, with the Duomos
of Italian churches, and with the Dome or Cupola at Eleusis, under which the mysteries or ceremonies (which Clemens says were copied from Jerusalem) were celebrated; and the title of Dominus
given to the Archpriest or A chierist, make me suspect that the word Pontifex is only a translation of the word Dom. This suspicion is also strengthened by the circumstance that the first and
last stones of these buildings were always laid by the hand of the chief-priest, with great religious
ceremony.

28. Perhaps there is no word more deserving of consideration than the word Bethlehem בית *Bit*,
לחם *lhm*. When I consider the very remarkable manner in which this house of Ceres is connected with the person whom I think I have pretty well proved to be the Male Ceres—the χρης
—the R S T or ΤΡΣ—the 600, and the Om=600, I am induced to suspect this word to be the
emphatic article ל *l*, and חם *hm*, a formation or corruption of the *Om*. The sacrifice offered in
ancient and modern Italy to this God, described by ΧΡΣ or ΤΡΣ consisting of bread, is called
Mola; this would be Hebraicè al-om. It is remarkable that this God is called יי *ie* or the God of
victory in Hebrew and Sanscrit; and this Hebrew name of לחם *lhm* means also pugna, or victory, a warrior, a captain.[3] From this the Lucumones are thought to have come. I think from
all this the house of L-hm was house of the Om or Χρης or Ceres. I have frequently stated that,
in the Greek and Hebrew, the word for country is *aia* or *ia*; and that, in the West, it was *ana* or
ania. Mr. Cleland[4] has observed, that originally in Gaul, Germany, and Britain, the greatest
part of the land was College land, Glebe land, Parish land, which maintained the bishops, judges,
subordinate militia, and its officers; that it paid *tenths*, not as to priests, but to government, and
was called by the word *Domain*: but he attempts no etymon of the word. I conclude from his
silence that his system did not here assist him; but I think my explanation will give the etymon.
I think the word Domain came with the Umbri, and with them the names of the river *H*-umber,
North-umberland, C-umberland,[5] &c., and that it is *aia* or *ania* d'om—land of Om. And this, I
think, brings me back very near to the Indian-Saxon time, when the king and priest were identical—before the sword divided from the crosier—when all the land was the property of the king
and priest. Is it possible that when these Umbri or Ombri arrived here, and that, perhaps after
a long time, they had stocked the country with inhabitants, the sword was not invented?

29. And now I come to the origin of our Chivalry, which I think is to be found in the adoration
of Freya, the third person of the Scandinavian Trinity, the female generative power, the Creator

---

[1] This comes from the cycle of the 600 being the Om, and from its being the period in which every thing was believed, by the vulgar, to be renewed—the new Troys, new Argonauts. It was, in fact, a perpetual almanack.

[2] D'Herbelot, Bibliothèque Orientale.   [3] Parkhurst, in voce, IV.   [4] Sup. to the Specimen, p. xiv.

[5] See Vol. I. pp. 111, 408, 535.

and Destroyer, the Cali of India. From Freya, in the character of Cali, the day dedicated to her, our and the Romish Friday, become a day of misery, of fasting and humiliation—as the Sunday, or day of the Sun, was a day of rejoicing. But from this lady in her good character came our Chivalry—exhibited in devotion to the female sex—devotion, as Mr. Mallet has shewn, existing from a very remote time with the Northern Scandinavians.[1] Among that people, this and many other customs were retained, whilst in Britain, during the stay of the Romans they were in a kind of abeyance, ready to be restored, as, in fact they were, on the departure of the Romans and the coming of the Saxons, with whom, in their Scandinavian country, they had continued without any cessation. In the same manner all the Saxon customs and names I have exhibited above were easily renewed. Chivalry did not first *arise*, it *rose again*, in those times. It flourished, perhaps, the most, when the gallant but unfortunate Boadicea led her knights, 80,000 in number, to the combat; then it was, before the brave had fallen, before the city of Iseur was reduced, that chivalry took its rise. But with that Queen it fell; and with the return of the Saxons it revived. The Saxon architecture of the pillars under the chancel of the present minster, shew that the temple at Evora was of a more recent date than that of the remaining pillars at Iseur, when it was destroyed by the Romans. The Britons, by soi-disant antiquarians, are said to have gone naked, and to have painted their bodies. Very true; but if these short-sighted persons had looked a little farther, they would have seen, that the Britons went naked only in the day of battle, when they were painted to distinguish clan from clan, and different ranks from one another. Tacitus, in the first book of his Annals, has spoken concerning the nakedness of the Germans. Gebauer, in his work called Mantissa,[2] has shewn, that the Latin expression *nudum corpus* only meant uncovered; without armour; and this may probably have been the meaning of the nakedness of the Britons. But, as I have just said, it is likely that, as they fought naked, their bodies were painted or tattoed to distinguish them from their own officers or from their enemies. The Northern Picts were men *painted*. "To investigate this point fairly and authoritatively, it is even in " those remote ages, antecedent to Julius Cæsar's invasion, when, by the falsest of all conse- " quences from the plainest of all premises, the Britons are imagined to have been little better " than savages, though, in fact, they were, even at that time, under the most admirable of all human " governments; but, like all other human things, not exempt from faults."[3] Cleland then shews, that the island was conquered from being divided into federative governments, without a sufficient bond of union; and, in the same manner, western Europe will, perhaps, be conquered. It took the Romans many years to conquer Britain.[4] The Russians, since the time of Peter, have made much greater strides. In fine, in the beautiful account given by Mr. Mallet,[5] of the Cromlehs, the Carns, the circular temples of enormous stones, and the *custom of burning the most beloved of the widows* of the prince on his funeral pile, sufficiently establish the identity of the Indian and Scandinavian Sacæ. I have just now expressed an opinion that the word Pict was meant to describe a painted man, like those referred to by Cæsar in speaking of the Britons. This is confirmed by a fact which I did not know before, that a class of persons in Scotland were called *black* Gauls, that *Aulaif* was killed by *Black Gauls*. But it also appears that he was killed *per Albanos*. I think, from the designations Black—*pict* or *painted*, and *white* or *albus*, the tribes were

---

[1] P. 200.   [2] De Nud. Vet. Germ. Sect vi, p. 369.   [3] Cleland, Spec. p. 32.
[4] The Romans depended on armour, discipline, and Russian tactic—gold; the Britons on valour; and had they been united under one head, instead of being divided into clans and weakened by petty jealousies, the Romans would never have conquered them. The Britons were to the Romans, as the Europeans in general are to Russia.
[5] P 213.

thus described from their colours in battle. If a person wish, with little trouble, to form an opinion of the *inextricable* confusion of the early history of the North, he may peruse article IX. in No. XXXI. of the Westminster Review. It is very curious to observe how generally the custom of conveying knowledge by apologue, ænigma, allegory, fable or parable, prevailed in the world. We have it in India, in the fables of Æsop, and in the Queen's riddle to Solomon, in Syria; and in the history of Samson; and it was the common practice of the Scandinavians.[1] Anagrams and acrostics were parts of the same system. The facts themselves have nothing in them remarkable; but the universality of the practice, for so great a number of years, is very remarkable. In the absence of every other kind of amusement or occupation, not filled by war or hunting, the art of making parables or riddles filled up the time of the rich in all nations. It was in itself very good; it injured no one; it kept people out of mischief, and it sharpened the intellect. It was better than smoking.

30. Every inquirer into our ancient histories has read of the Sea Kings, who invaded the northern parts of the island from Scandinavia. These were the people who had the Sagas for their sacred books. How came they to be Sea Kings? Were they like the Royal Shepherds of Egypt—all kings? The Sea Kings were the Sagara or Sea Kings of Rama, in the island of Ceylon. The island of Iona had its name of Columba, from ancestors of those sea kings, who so often invaded Scotland in a later day.[2] Mr. Mallet, by shewing that the ancient Runes[3] were known to and used by the inhabitants of Tartary, (where inscriptions in them are yet to be found, and where no Christians, in the common acceptation of the word, ever lived,) long before the Christian æra, and by a variety of other strong arguments, proves that Ulphilas was not the inventor of them; but that, in fact, they are of an antiquity totally unknown; that they were brought with the Sacæ, and that for many ages they were considered secret, sacred, and magical, as I believe they were in all other nations which possessed the knowledge of them. A spell is a magical contrivance: this was the art of discovering the meaning of a word. Mr. Mallet also shews, that the oldest of the Runes were written in the manner of the Chinese—from top to bottom—afterward in the Boustrophedon style; and, at last, from left to right. In the antiquity of their poetry, he shews, that they vie with Hesiod and Homer, and I have a strong suspicion that in their fable of the Dragon and Thorab, we have the Tora of the Hebrews, and in their Scalds a corruption of the Chasdim or Chaldæans or Culdees of Iona, or Columkill, where their kings were buried, and where their tombs yet remain. But it was in the times when the immense circular temples[4] were built, probably before the invention of the Runes, that the instruments were made with which they worked their mines, which have had iron edges, but the handles of which are gold;[5] thus proving what I have suggested in my CELTIC DRUIDS, p. lxvi., that *gold* was once "the common metal for useful domestic purposes," and " Iron, from its great superiority of *real* value, the precious metal."[6]

31. Is it not possible that a golden age may really have existed; that is, an age when there were no wars;—that a scientific or learned race of priests, like those of Tibet, holding the system of the renewal of cycles—re-incarnations—which I have shewn existed in every part of the world, may have governed the whole?—If it be true, that a great flood destroyed the world, except a few fortunate individuals, and these grew into great nations—is it not evident that, by the time they had increased to any considerable number, the earth must every where have been in a situa-

---

[1] Mallet, p. 244.
[2] See Celtic Druids, p. 33.
[3] See various exemplars of them in cabinets in Sweden and Denmark, and Jacob on the precious metals.
[4] Vide Col. Tod's Hist. Raj. Vol. II. p. 218, note †.
[5] Ibid. pp. 230, 233, 237—239.
[6] Vol. I. p 452.

tion so favourable for occupancy as almost to have absolutely forbidden strife or wars of any magnitude for the sake of property? If a dispute arose between two tribes emigrating from the parent hive, it would terminate like that between Lot and Abraham—one, under the mediation of the common father, the head priest or patriarch, would go to the East, the other to the West. The abundance of excellent land would be so great, that it would not be worth contending for. Thus the world, without war, would become peopled. I can readily conceive too, how a privileged and learned order, keeping to itself its mysteries, in such a state of things, might enjoy supreme power for many generations, claiming to be proprietor of the soil, and receiving its tenths, which, in such a state, would be no oppression—but, on the contrary, it would constitute a government to mankind the most beneficial, perhaps, that can be imagined. And I can readily conceive, that this state of things would continue until the land of the world, by being fully stocked, would become scarce; then, and not before, the sword would be invented—then would end the golden age, of which, alas! we have nothing now left but the tradition—but it is an *universal* tradition. During this age it was that the circular temples were erected, in cyclar numbers, to do honour to the Deity, and, at the same time, to record in imperishable monuments, as far as human means could avail, the cycles on which all the system depended—the cycles which equally regulated their festivals and the time of the agricultural labours, to which they looked for their subsistence. These labours became of daily increasing importance, as land became scarce, and as the golden age of peace and plenty began to decline—till it ultimately faded away and left no traces of it, but a dream. If we suppose the cyclic system to have been established before the flood which drowned Atlantis happened, and a few persons only to have been left, why may not all that I have suggested have taken place, and the learned class who must have known the fact by tradition, for many centuries, have adopted the invention of the cyclic temples, to record their knowledge as far as lay in their power? Look to the remotest period, and every thing tends to support this theory. Insulated facts innumerable meet us at every step, none of which can be accounted for in any other manner, but for all of which this theory readily accounts. All tradition, all history, sacred and profane, support it—natural philosophy, facts and circumstances, all combine to support it. This was really the golden age; it was the age of $X\varrho\eta\varsigma$ and $X\varrho\upsilon\varsigma$—for there were no wars, and there was no iron. Gold was the common metal—iron was not known—and here we may observe how curiously the truth of the tradition appears. The ages were of Gold, Silver, Copper, Iron![1] and it is very evident to me, that this is correctly the order in which the metals were discovered: thus it is actually the fact, that *the age of gold* would be the age of piety and happiness. If we consider carefully the nature of the animal *man*, and at the same time the nature of the circumstances in which I have supposed him to have been placed after the flood, it seems to me that, in the state of the world which I have suggested, the golden age would almost necessarily arise. The difficulty we have now, is to believe in the absence of wars, for so great a length of time as my theory requires; but when fertile land was so plentiful as to be worth nothing, the whole world being agrestic, what should men fight for? Was it not better to remove than to fight?[2] Trifling border squab-

---

[1] See Celtic Druids, p. lxvi., as quoted above.

[2] In the book of Numbers (xx. 17, 19) we have an account of Moses, with his tribe, asking leave to pass through the lands of the King of Edom, and offering to pay for what he wanted. Here we have an exact example of what must have taken place in nearly the earliest times of which I have been treating. The first people would extend their borders by degrees, till they increased to a great size, covering a vast extent of country. Then those in the central part would want to ease themselves of their superabundant population, and would send off swarms in succession—each succeeding swarm settling as near the borders of the settled country as it could, and asking leave to pass through the lands of its predecessors, till at last the swarms would arrive at the ends of the earth. I think this was what happened to the Canaanites when driven out by Joshua. They passed through Lower Egypt, along the settled coast of Africa, till they

bles, no doubt, would arise; but an Abraham or a Lot would easily settle them. In such a state of the world many of our passions and follies would not exist. Would there be such a thing as the honour of nations? Would there be any jealousies arising from competition of trades? Would there be any wars or feuds of religion? The system of Buddha, of renewed incarnations to end at the remote period of 6000 years, would, for a long time, prevent them. When the first religious war, probably that of the Maha-barat, arose, then ended the golden age—the age of the universal religion. The universal prevalence of Buddhism is a fact, not a theory. I think I may almost say the same of the wars of the Maha-barat and the origin of sects. Every where as we advance in time, the remains of a decayed system, in endless variety, display themselves, and support the truth of the tradition of the story of *the golden age*—the universal tradition of all ancient and profane history. Every where we find the original system, and every where signs of its decay. I think attention to the nature of man will again let us into some secrets—will account for some effects which have hitherto been unaccounted for. We every where find works called the histories—History of Romulus, of Cyrus, of Theseus, of Bacchus, of Hercules, of Cristna, &c., &c.—at the bottom they are all identical, though, at the same time, each pretends to be a real history of a hero of the country where we find it, which, from the general identity, is evidently impossible. How is this? If one secret universal system, that of Buddha, prevailed, we may be very sure that as man, the *uninitiated* man, began to advance, by degrees, to his present state, he would begin to inquire into the origin of things—of the temples—of the religion—of the privileges of the favoured caste; and then it was that these mythic histories were produced to satisfy his curiosity, and to silence his inquiries. From various circumstances I think this process began in India, and by degrees became co-extensive with the system. The same policy is every where evident, along with the same system—but the system and its history varied in little matters to suit local circumstances, and to suit every new cyclic Avatar. This theory satisfactorily accounts for their similarity, and, at the same time, for their variety. It is not necessary to suppose a general agreement to account for this. Every where, as the 6000 years advanced, man would have the same curiosity, and, from state to state, the contrivance to repress it (having been once invented) would extend itself. Man, priests, and corruption, in all states, have been the same. As food became scarce, man became more unprincipled and priests more cunning. The earth every day produced more thorns and thistles, Gen. iii. 18, and the very remembrance of the golden age at last faded away with the absolute failure of the Millenium. If we figure to ourselves the first invention of a mythos of an immaculate conception, of an infant exposed, of his escape, of his victory, of his death, and of his resurrection after three days; or, under a parable of this kind, the passage of the Sun, from the winter to the summer, to be described, I think we may very readily suppose how, with the system of renewed cycles, this story would be every where propagated. From the peculiar circumstance, probably in its effect unforeseen, of the renewed cycles, it would require no superintending head to keep it alive. It is in its nature peculiarly calculated for duration; nothing could prove its falsity but time, and almost always a long future time, at least during almost all the time whose antiquities we have examined. Its system of mystery, masonry, and monachism, also tended strongly to its preservation. It also became, after a certain time, the universal test, the profession, the possession and bond of union of a peculiar order, that order in all states, after the union

---

got to the Straits of Gibraltar, where they erected the pillars described by Procopius, (vide Appendix to *Celtic Druids*, p. 314,) which forms the best proof now existing of any fact of so ancient a date as the Exod of Moses—a proof so strangely overlooked by all our priests, an oversight which can only be accounted for from their absolute ignorance of the nature of historical evidence. The history stated by Procopius is beautifully strengthened by the fact, that in the country on the opposite side of the Strait we find the City of Medina Sidonia.

of the Linga and Ioni, having an interest in opposition to the rest of mankind,—every where struggling with the sword for superiority—an order varying in different times and different states in small matters, but in great ones the same. Thus, for several thousand years after the wars of the Maha-barat ceased by the union of the Linga and Ioni, until the Christian æra, when the system began to be lost, we hear of scarcely any religious wars. About this time the mind of man had outgrown the mythos, the fable, the parable, which, as man improved, deteriorated till it became too bad any longer to be endured: the mystery then assumed a new shape—in the *vulgar* Christianity, and, after a time, in the *vulgar* Mohamedism; and in both religions, after the mythos and the mystery have both expired with time, we still cling to the ruins of the system, and look out for the millenium. As long as Buddhism lasted in its full extension, one ecclesiastical head, like the Lama of Tibet, resident somewhere, I think, superintended the whole, and kept it uniform, as I shall shew in the next book; but when the zodiacal cyclic incarnation of the Lamb succeeded to the Bull, and Cristna arose, then arose sects, varieties, and miseries, of every kind. Truly, indeed, do the votaries of Cristna maintain, that *he* came with the Cali Yug—with the *age of iron!* It comes out at last, that we have a $\mu\nu\theta$ος and a $\mu\nu$ς$\eta\rho\iota\text{ον}$. What is the *mythos?* What is the *mystery?* What is the parable, the fable? What is the secret doctrine? The mythos, the parable, is the fable under which the mystery is concealed; the mystery is the *secret* doctrine taught by Pythagoras, by Jesus,[1] by Mohamed—the renewal of cycles, the inspiration with the *holy ghost* of persons, in every cycle, to teach mankind the doctrine of a future existence of happiness or misery, according to their conduct in this life. Inspiration by the *holy ghost* is evidently a mere figure of speech, describing a person more enlightened than his neighbours. Whether this future life was taught by Jesus to be by a hell or by a metempsychosis, and an ultimate absorption into the To Oν, I know not. With hope and humble resignation I await the event; and thus, gentle reader, I conclude this book.

---

[1] *Secret* as his words in the Gospels prove over and over again.—[Matt. xiii. 11; Mark iv. 11; Luke viii. 10.—It is remarkable that these are the only passages in the Gospels in which the words *mystery* and *mysteries* occur, and that in each case they are accompanied by an explanation which proves that the doctrines taught were *secret* or *mysterious* only because the hearers were gross in their understandings and disinclined to investigate the evidences of their truth. Paul, who, in many of his Epistles, uses the terms *mystery* and *mysteries*, obviously does so in the sense of a *secret*, a thing or things which had been unknown till then, but were now made *known*; not that the doctrines of the Gospels or of his or the other Apostles' letters, were *mysteries*. "Secret (things belong) unto the LORD; but those *revealed* unto us and our children," (Deut. xxix. 29,) as much under the Gospel as under the Mosaic dispensation. *Editor*.]

BOOK V.

CHAPTER I.

OBJECT OF THE MYTHOS.—BOOK OF ENOCH ON THE EARTH'S AXIS.—NOAH AND SHIPS OF THE ANCIENTS. —CAUSE AND EXTENT OF THE FLOOD.—CHANGE OF THE EARTH'S AXIS. — FLOODS OF OGYGES AND INACHUS.—COMETS HELD TO BE PLANETS. — SEVEN-DAY CYCLE AND LENGTH OF YEAR.—WHISTON ON YEAR OF 360 DAYS.—WHISTON ON LENGTH OF ANTEDILUVIAN YEAR.—WHISTON ON COMET OF 1680. —COMET OF 575¼ YEARS' PERIOD THE CAUSE OF THE FLOOD.—PERIODS OF COMETS. — ENCKE'S COMET.—DRS. GREGORY AND HALLEY ON WHISTON'S THEORY.—DR. KEILL ON WHISTON'S THEORY.— COMET OF 575¼ YEARS CONTINUED.— M. ARAGO ON COMETS.— LEXALL'S COMET.— GENESIS, IN SUBSTANCE, FOUND IN MANY COUNTRIES.— AGENCY OF COMETS.— DIGRESSION ON GAS, SPIRIT, INSPIRATION, THE SOUL.—COMET AND FLOOD RESUMED.—THE WORLD'S HISTORY RENEWED.—EARLY HISTORY A MYTHOS.—SARASIT AND MERCAVAH.

1. HAVING exhibited proofs innumerable of the reality of a general mythos, it now seems to be necessary, in order to complete the whole, that I should exhibit the object for which the mythos was formed. We shall find that this was invented, as might be expected, for the support of the dominant priesthood; and that for this purpose circumstances were made subservient. When favourable circumstances were not to be found in *true history*, they were invented. Thus the Jews tell of Noah and Tibe, the Egyptians of Menu (which is but Noë) and Tibe, and both describe their three sons, followed by a train of lineal successors. I think I shall not be accused of giving way to idle superstition; but, despite of incurring this accusation, I must say, that there appear to me, when all the circumstances which I have laid before my reader are considered, much truth and very great plausibility in a passage of Dr. Woodward's discourse on the Ancient Egyptians: " The colonies all carried these customs along with them to their several abodes: and there were " from the very beginning *priests*, sacrifices, temples, festivals, and lustrations, as well among the " ancient Germans and Gauls, in Peru and Mexico, in Siam, China, and Japan, as in Egypt." What can be more striking than the custom of circumcision among the Tamuls, in Mexico, in Colchis of Armenia, in Egypt, and in Guinea and the kingdom of Congo, on the coast of Africa?[1] It is also very remarkable that this rite is found in all these places to prevail only among the Priests. This tends strongly to support the opinion which I entertain, that the order of Chaldei, a learned order, *did* escape from a flood, and, by means of their superior intelligence, *did* establish an universal pontifical empire, getting the command of the Aborigines all over the world, who were unarmed Buddhist barbarians, who also had escaped the flood; and, that the rite of circumcision, or initiation, as it was called, was invented before the art of writing was known, in order to distinguish that order from the rest of mankind. I think the knowledge of the art of writing

---

[1] O. Lopez, Hist. de Congo, ch. v.; Woodward on Wisd. of Egypt, p. 82.

and reading succeeded to it as a *test* in later ages. The fact that circumcision and initiation had the same meaning is very striking.[1] The universality of the practice also tends greatly to support my idea. When we look into the Jewish books we find that the Jews occupied Western Syria, precisely as the noble class of Romans did Italy, and as the Turks have done Greece—that is, as a separated and superior class or caste—the great mass of the ancient natives being left, as a species of Helots. The whole of the Jews were circumcised, because they are said to have been a *priestly nation*; and, if the history of Abraham can be believed, the Jews, properly so called, were all descendants of that Chaldæan Brahmin, and of the 318 persons said to be bred in his own house, who probably constituted the whole of the tribe, or of the high caste of the tribe, who had come with him from India. Though, for particular historical knowledge, memory, without writing, would reach but a very small space, yet for a simple story, or for a small collection of simple stories, closely connected with religion, or for any single, grand event, I think it would reach a long way back.[2] Such for instance as a great flood—like that of Noah—concerning which I must now make some observations.

2. We are told in the book of Enoch, that "the earth laboured and was shaken violently;" and in Chapter lxiv. Sect. xi., that "Noah saw that the earth became inclined, and that in consequence destruction approached." I think few persons who have read the book of Enoch will deny, that this is a most curious and striking tradition.—It is a tradition of common sense, supported by all the outward natural appearances of the earth. Enoch afterward says, verse 11, that the earth was destroyed because hidden secrets had been discovered; and in chap. lxvii. he makes Noah say, that he, Enoch, gave Noah the *characteristical marks or signs* of the secret things inscribed in his book, and *concealed in the parables*. I think it will not be denied, that I could scarcely have wished for any thing more to my purpose than all this, which is evidently no copy from the Bible. It directly admits the existence of symbolic (or numeral) writing, and that it had been kept secret. I ask, is it not possible that, from some cause, the axis of the earth may have been suddenly changed, as Enoch says in Book ix. Chap. x.? Every natural appearance strongly supports the doctrine, that the change has been sudden; and a sudden large change no more operates against the fact of the earth being governed by general laws, than a breaking out of a volcano so operates. And I am of opinion that the *diminution* of the angle of the planes of the two axes is not the effect of a periodical oscillation, but is the effect of the conservative power which we every where see around us, operating to restore the globe to the first state from which it has been moved. I believe one of the most powerful obstacles, with many persons, to the reception of the opinion, that the change in the axis of the earth was the effect of what we vulgarly call accident, is to be found in their conception of the greatness of the event or effect. They acquire this idea from a comparison of that event with themselves, and with every-day facts, like volcanic eruptions. But the idea is a delusive one. They ought to compare it with the motions going on among the innumerable suns and worlds moving in the starry firmament, which our astronomers know, by means of their telescopes, are changing every day—some suns appearing to rise into existence, and some to be destroyed, or to disappear. If persons would think upon this, they would see at once, that the change in the axis of the earth is only a trifling matter. It will be said, that if the two planes coincided, the equatorial regions would not be habitable from *heat*, and the polar regions from *cold*. Well, and what then? Are the poles habitable now? The heat of the one is

---

[1] See Vol. I. pp. 304, 305, note 4.
[2] It was to remedy this defect that such great numbers of the Druidical temples were built, with their pillars in cyclic numbers, and that the arts of epic and dramatic poetry, music, and dancing, were invented.

no more an objection than the cold of the other. But, after all, is this so certain? All these considerations are mean and contemptible to the person who duly estimates the immensity of the universe, the diminutive character of our globe, and the little nests of quarrelsome pismires which infest it, and fancy themselves somebody.

3. All the traditions maintain, that a person whom we call Noah, by some means, no matter what they were, foresaw that destruction approached. Tradition says, that he erected pillars with inscriptions in the land of Syriad or the holy Sura. This might be the Syria of India or of Palestine or of Egypt, which was meant. It also says, that he buried the sacred books in the city of the book Sephora. We have a Biblos in Palestine, and the city of Boc-hara in North India, both meaning *city of the Book*. Every philosopher, and every fool, knows, that floods have taken place; and if we consider them independently of mythology, and if we use our endeavours, their nature and effects may, perhaps, in some degree, be collected out of the scraps of traditions left to us; for I see nothing improbable in truths having come down to us concealed in fictions or parables, since we know that the use of parables is one of the most striking characteristics of the religion which is contained in these histories. Now, if we suppose that the ruin did not happen in a moment, but that a year, or even more time, was required to effect the whole by successive earthquakes, is it not possible, if such a scientific and sacerdotal government existed as I have contemplated, that the supreme Pontiff and his court may have saved themselves and their secret literature in a ship or floating house? (If such a case were to happen, in Europe, half the people being destroyed, and tremblings of the earth still going on, before the end of the year, where, and in which of our great men of war would KING WILLIAM and the Archbishop of Canterbury be found?) And if by this, or any similar contrivance, they saved themselves, and they never moved far from the ruins of the city they previously occupied, why should it not be the city of Boc-hara —the city of *letters* or of *the book*? No person who has read the essay of Governor Pownal on the ships of the ancients, will doubt that they had ships nearly as large and nearly as sea-worthy against a rushing flood, as ours. Suppose there were several or many of these ships, and that only one or two were saved; the probability is, that the Pontiff or Patriarch would be in one of them, because *he* would secure the best. Why should not this ship have been built upon the Caspian Sea? It was the best situated of any place to preserve the ship in a flood.—But why should not the axis of the earth have become changed to its utmost extreme by various shocks? Why should not some of the earliest and most violent shocks have taken place hundreds or thousands of years before? and why should not the last shock have been only a very moderate one, just enough to sink Atlantis, or to break the banks of the Euxine, though lasting, at intervals, for a year or more? If religious prejudice did not stand in the way, I am quite certain that some theory, not very dissimilar to this, would be universally thought probable. The probability in the last case is, if it be probable at all, that it happened after the discovery of writing by symbols, but before its discovery by syllabic letters. The Druidical circles mark the numerals, but nothing like letters, and it is worthy of observation, that the word Sephor, which is the Hebrew name of the town where the books were said to be preserved, means much more properly a *cipher* or *figure of notation*, than *a letter*. By a little forcing *letter* may be made out of it; but its meaning is, *symbol of notation*. It is also worthy of observation, that the word used by Enoch for the signs of the secret things in the book, is not translated by Bishop Laurence *letter*, but *characteristical marks*, Chap. lxvii. And by a note on the latter word, it is explained by the word SIGNS; this shews that, in the Bishop's opinion, letter is not meant. His explanation can apply to nothing but symbols similar to those of the Chinese.

4. Such persons as may feel disposed to take offence at my doctrine, that the flood may not have been universal, or think that the theory which I have proposed in Volume I. pp. 293, 294

of this work unsatisfactory, I refer to Diss. VI. of Vol. III. of the Morsels of Criticism, by Mr. Edward King, who will not be accused of want of piety and orthodox religion. Mr. King shews very satisfactorily, that, in the flood of Noah, according to *the fair construction of the Mosaic text*, the whole surface of the world was not covered with water, nor the whole of mankind drowned. What I have said respecting the violent change is perfectly in accordance with Cuvier's observation, that the revolutions of the world have not been gradual, but sudden and violent;[1] and what I have said above respecting the flood not having covered the whole world, is perfectly in accordance with what he has observed, that the marine remains are *not to be found* on the tops of the highest mountains.[2] Thus I have both the first geologists and first divines on my side in this matter. We might speculate to eternity, but it is impossible for us to know how a sudden change in the earth's axis would operate, or what would be its effects. The Pyramids of Egypt are of such a nature, that I think it not impossible that they may have escaped entire when every other building in the world was tumbled down. But my reader is not to suppose that I mean this to be the flood which threw up Mount Blanc or Chimborazo, but a much later one, which I have supposed laid bare the Delta of Egypt and broke down the banks of the Euxine, &c. If we suppose this to be the case, we readily account for the Druidical and Cyclopæan buildings found every where, and for the apparently long interregnum of darkness which seems to have taken place between their being built and that of the oldest of the modern ancient edifices and empires. It may be that most anciently the planes of the equator and the ecliptic coincided, that they were placed at an *angle* by a convulsion, that this angle was considerably larger than it is at this moment, and that it is gradually decreasing. In that case the polar regions must have formerly been much warmer than they are now, and, in consequence, may have been fit for the residence of plants which we now find only in warmer climates. For any thing we know, the reduction of this angle may have proceeded more rapidly at first than it has done in later ages, and this would account for the remains of plants which are not found growing there now. No doubt the change in the earth's axis would cause very great mischief; but the assertion, that the least check to the motion of the earth would cause *infinite* mischief, is but a gratuitous, dogmatical assertion, necessarily made in ignorance. I have a right to suppose only just so much retardation to take place as would produce the effects which we see and experience. Besides, the change might be along with, rather than against, the earth's motion, and this would make a great difference. That our country is gradually growing *colder* is proved decisively by the records of the suits in the exchequer between the parsons and the farmers for the tithe on wine. Every body knows that the northern and central parts of Britain, indeed, not any part of it, can now produce good wine.

An ingenious writer in an American journal has made some striking observations on the Deluge. He says, "There are many indications that a powerful current has passed over the continent of America from north to south, and the author of this article accounts for these appearances, by supposing that a change has at some period taken place in the velocity of the earth's motion on her axis. The surface of the earth at the equator revolves at the rate of more than 1,000 miles per hour, or 1500 feet per second, which is about the velocity of a cannon ball. We have no idea of circular motion like this. A wheel of wrought iron, of three feet in diameter, will fly in pieces before it reaches a velocity of 400 feet per second. Supposing the earth should be slightly checked in her daily motion—the Pacific Ocean would in a moment rush over the Andes and Alleganies into the Atlantic—the Atlantic would sweep over Europe, Asia, and Africa—and in a few hours the entire surface of the earth would be covered with rushing torrents, excepting the

---

[1] Jameson's Cuvier, pp. 15, 16, 4th Ed. 1822.   [2] Ib. p 18.

" vicinity of the Poles. The appearances presented on the surface of the earth are precisely such " as we would [might] expect after such a catastrophe."—*Silliman's Journal*. The probability is I think, that a great flood did take place more than two thousand, but not more than about three thousand, years before Christ, which destroyed the greatest part of mankind, leaving only a few persons in different places. I am very much inclined to believe that, at the bottom of perhaps every mythic history, there exist some truths. Now, nothing could be more easy to transmit by memory than such a bare fact as that of the sinking of an island, or that of a great flood. And I know nothing more likely than that it should have been made into a mythos—that it should have been made subservient to the purposes of the priesthood. Beyond the æra of Nabonassar, or about the first Olympiad or the founding of Rome, which is as far back as the memory of man may be supposed to extend, and before Herodotus, the first historian, wrote, history is mere mythos, as Diodorus Siculus properly represents it. In some instances, as in the case of Rome, instead of *history*, the *mythos* was continued to a much later date. It is possible that the inhabitants of the world, at the time of the last flood, may have had traditions of former floods having taken place a few, perhaps four or five, hundred years previously, which may have served to warn them, together with some symptoms of which we know nothing, that another concussion was likely to happen. The words of the book of Enoch imply that Noah and others learned *from secret science* that it would happen. If the change were caused by a comet, is it not possible that the persons who were so profoundly skilled in astronomy, as to be the inventors of the Neros, may have been able to calculate the period of one, and to foresee that it would come near enough to the earth to cause the mischief? Enoch says, " Respecting the MOONS have they inquired, and they have known " that the earth will perish with those who dwell upon it." Again, " They have discovered " secrets, but thou art free from the reproach of discovering secrets." Chap lxiv. Sect. xi. If the word translated *moons* had been planetary bodies, it would have been instantly applicable to the knowledge of comets; and I think there is a strong probability that such ought to be the translation. In numbers of places the book of Enoch shews a knowledge of judicial astrology, and speaks of reading the course of events in the stars, similar to the expression of Jacob and his children. All these expressions might really, though perhaps secretly, be meant to apply only to the future planetary motions. Under all the circumstances I cannot think it improbable that the change in the axis of the earth should have been caused by a comet, nor that its approach to the earth and the mischief which it was likely to cause, should have been known to the antediluvians —persons learned enough in astronomy to be the inventors of the cycle of the Neros. Reason, natural philosophy, and sacred and profane tradition, all support the justness of this conclusion. In aid of history and astronomy we can also cite the opinion of some of the first geologists: MM. Cuvier, Deluc, and Dolomieu, affirm "that, if there is any circumstance thoroughly esta- " blished in geology, it is, that the crust of our globe has been subjected to a great and sudden " revolution—not farther back than five or six thousand years ago ;"—that the countries now in- habited had been before inhabited, if not by mankind, at least by land animals ; consequently, one preceding revolution, at least, had overwhelmed them with water ; and that if we may judge by the different orders of animals, whose remains are found therein, they had perhaps undergone two or three irruptions of the sea.[1]

5. The assertion of the book of Enoch, that the axis of the earth was changed, was supported by Plato,[2] and the inclination of the earth's axis was well known to the Greeks, and was called

---

[1] Jameson's Cuvier, pp. 173—175, 4th Ed. 1822.
[2] See Volume I. p. 203. N. B. The suspicion which I have stated in the page here referred to, that the word Λοξιας related to the elliptic orbits of the planets, must be considered as erroneous—to be unfounded.

Λοξιας. This inclination was also well known to the Indians. There is a very remarkable passage in Plutarch: " It was the doctrine both of Diogenes and Anaxagoras, that after the creation
" or primary constitution of the world, and the production of animals out of the earth, the world,
" as it were of its own accord, was bent or inclined towards the South. And truly it is probable
" this inclination was the effect of Providence, on purpose that some parts of the world might be-
" come habitable, and others uninhabitable, by reason of the difference of the frigid, torrid, and
" temperate climates thereof."[1]

6. " Varro places the deluge of Ogyges, which he calls the *first deluge*, 400 years before Inachus,
" (à priore cataclysmo quem Ogygium dicunt, ad Inachi regnum,) and consequently before the first
" Olympiad. This would refer it to a period of 2376 years before Christ, and the deluge of Noah,
" according to the Hebrew text, is 2349—only twenty-seven years of difference. This testi-
" mony of Varro is substantiated by Censorinus *de Die Natali*, cap. xxi."[2] Here we have a most
important Gentile confirmation of the Mosaic record, affording a very strong *probability*, indeed,
when united to the singular circumstance of a comet which I shall presently notice, a *proof* of its
truth. The dates are as nearly identical as can be expected by any one who pays due attention to
the difficulty of keeping a record of time in those remote ages, and this without making any allowance for disturbing forces, which may be expected to have operated. This western evidence is
again confirmed by evidence in the East. But those who have read what I have stated of the
Mosaic mythos in China,[3] will not be surprised to learn, that the time of its first king or emperor,
Yao, who drained and rendered the country habitable, is placed about the year 2333 B. C. Here
we have, evidently, the flood and the God Iao of the Jews.[4]

7. Aristotle says,[5] " that the Pythagoreans held a comet to be one of the planets which appears
" after a long interval of time, and which, at the apex of its very elliptical orbit, is at as small a
" distance from the sun as the planet Mercury. Now the Chaldæans held comets to be planets;[6]
" *and the Egyptians predicted their returns.*"[7] We must not forget this observation of Sir William
Drummond's, that the Egyptians predicted the returns of comets, and for a reason which my
reader will find hereafter, I think it right to remind him, that it was a Chaldæan astronomer, called
Sosigenes, from Egypt, who corrected the calendar for Julius Cæsar. Professor Anthom, in his
Lempriere, says; " Plato informs us, that in the time of Atreus the motion of the firmament had
" changed in such a manner, that the sun and all the stars had begun to rise where formerly they
" had set, and to set where they had been accustomed to rise; in a word, the machine of the world
" was moved in a way contrary to that in which it had been before. It is evident, from the seve-
" ral parts of his relation, that he speaks of a confused and perplexed, and consequently a very
" ancient tradition. In his Timæus, however, he makes the Athenians to have first learned it from
" Solon; which would seem to favour the idea that the latter had, like Herodotus, received it from
" the priests of Egypt. Pomponius Mela speaks of the same tradition, as also Plutarch, Achilles
" Tatius, Solinus, and many other writers. Astronomers, however, insist, that the idea of such
" an interruption of the regular motion of the earth, as this phenomenon would have required, is
" not for a moment to be entertained, and that if it had taken place, it would have left physical
" traces behind; besides, the figure of the earth shews, they maintain, that its revolutions have
" been uniform since the flood. We leave the present subject with them and the ancients."[8] —

---

[1] De Placitis Philos. Lib. ii. Cap. viii. apud Whiston's Theory, B. II. p. 107; where, in pp. 102, 103, may be seen the confirmatory opinions of Leucippus, Laertius, Democritus, and Empedocles.
[2] Jameson's Cuvier, p. 205, 4th Ed.   [3] See supra, pp. 19, 36, 97.   [4] Jameson's Cuvier, p. 239, 4th Ed.
[5] Meteorolog. Lib. i.   [6] Senec. Quæst. Nat.
[7] Diodor. Lib. i., Drummond, Class. Journ. Vol. XVI. p. 157.   [8] Lempriere, in voce Phaeton.

With whom *I* will not leave it. Very true it is that the motion has probably been uniform since the catastrophe of the flood was *finished;* but this, THE FLOOD, is the very thing which we are talking about. It by no means follows, that there has been no flood since the throwing up of Chimborazo. Again I repeat, it is clear that there have been different floods, and we can never *know*, at least we do not *know*, whether the last flood did or did not throw up Chimborazo, although there may exist circumstances enough to decide our opinion. The author says, that if the motion of the earth had been interrupted, it would have left physical traces behind. Good God! what can this gentleman mean? Are there not physical traces every where? Are not Chimborazo and Mount Blanc physical traces? Can we take a single step without treading on them? The difficulty is not in finding *no* traces, but in finding too large ones, and too many of them. I speak not now of the processes by which the strata of the earth were deposited; but every thing tends to shew that the last change has been sudden and violent.

8. I now beg my reader to look back to what I have said in my CELTIC DRUIDS, p. 8, and in the Preliminary Observations, (Vol. I. p. 2,) respecting the origin of the seven-day cycle; then in pp. 27, 28, 291, 293, and 273, *note*, for what has been said respecting the flood or floods; to consider the universal tradition that it was caused by the sudden change in the direction of the earth's axis, as I stated in the note, in Vol. I. pp. 29, 30; and that, in consequence, the length of the year was changed from 360 to 365 days, and the length of the month shortened from 30 to 28 and 27 days. Now it is remarkable that, in Mexico, they have two weeks, one of 3 and one of 5 days, but not one of 7 days. This seems to shew that they separated from the old world before the change of the axis took place. This will make no material difference in my theory of the invention of figures and letters; because, instead of dividing the moon's period into fourteen and seven, they would act precisely on the same principle, and divide it into fifteen, and three fives, and ten threes.[1] The Javanese have the week of five days: on every first, they have their market, as was anciently the case with our Sunday; and they say, that the origin and names of the days of their week are unknown; but they have a tradition, that they were taken from *colours* and the division of the horizon. This is evidently the zodiac, when the two planes coincided. The evidence concerning this question of the change in the earth's axis is one thing, the belief of most persons respecting it is another. With the latter I do not concern myself; to the former, the evidence is clearly in favour of a sudden and violent change having taken place, which caused a very great flood; but this must have been before the building of the Pyramids, and must also have been before the flood which destroyed Maha-balipore; and yet, of course, it must have been since the creation of man. I can readily imagine an overflowing so great as, in a very small space of time, to have rushed over nearly the whole earth, in successive waves, so as not to have destroyed *every* individual, but to have left alive a very few persons, and that few to have perpetuated the race. One flood might be occasioned by successive convulsions of the earth, bursting the crust of the globe as we see it. There requires no miraculous interposition, if we suppose that in the intervals between the shocks of earthquakes, when the face of the globe might indicate renewed convulsions, a few of the more easily frightened inhabitants might be able to save themselves in boats or on rafts. Perhaps a few of them, cast on elevated lands by the wave and left there on its recession, might be able to save themselves in several parts of the world; and, in the same manner, a certain number of the animals might be preserved, and others lost, of which we now have only the remains. And the same effects may have been produced if we suppose the crust of the earth to have been burst by

---

[1] Crawfurd, Hist. Ind. Archipel. Vol. I. p. 289.)

the irruption of the central water from below, which may have been occasioned by the conjunction of a body with the moon, thus causing an immense tide. Had the change in the axis of the earth been asserted in Genesis, we should never have heard the last of the wisdom of that book. All the world, philosophers and devotees, would equally have received the assertion; but, because it is not there stated, though a consequence of it is, viz. the year having only 360 days, it is believed by none, notwithstanding all ancient tradition, natural history, and circumstantial evidence, are in its favour. Forster[1] says, the Hindoo year is 360 days. M. Adrian Balbi, in his Ethnography of the Globe, says, "Il est bon aussi de rappeler à nos lecteurs que les Mexicains avaient des semaines ou petits périodes de 5 jours, comme les peuples du royaume de Benin et les anciens Javanais, de mois de 20 jours, des années civiles de 18 mois, des indictions de 13 ans, des demi-siècles de 52 ans, et des siècles ou vieillesses de 104 ans." Here we have the year of 360 days.

We will now inquire what the ancients thought upon this subject.

9. I had collected a variety of authorities to prove that the ancients held, that both the civil and tropical year consisted of 360 days, and the month of 30 days, when I obtained WHISTON's *Theory of the Earth*,[2] in which I discovered that this had been proved by NEWTON,[3] and that he had already demonstrated the truth of my doctrine. As I consider this of great importance, and my reader may not be able easily to obtain Whiston's work, and if he could, he would find the proofs encumbered with much unnecessary matter, I shall copy them on this point, though they are rather long, and give those proofs instead of my own.

"The most ancient *civil* year in most parts of the world *after* the deluge; and also the *tropical solar* and *lunar year before* the deluge, contained just twelve months of thirty days a-piece, or 360 days in the whole.

"First.—I shall endeavour to prove, that the most ancient year in *civil* use, almost throughout the world, for several ages *after* the deluge, contained exactly 360 days, or 12 months of 30 days a-piece. Secondly.—That *before* the deluge, not only the *civil* year, but also the *tropical solar* year, wherein the sun passes through the ecliptic to the same point from whence it began; and likewise the *lunar* year, consisting of 12 Synodical months, each from new moon to new moon, or from full moon to full moon, were severally just 360 days long, and consequently that the *lunar* month was exactly 30 days.

"And, first, I am to prove that the most ancient *civil* year and month were of this length in most places *after* the deluge.

"(1.) This appears by that testimony mentioned in Georgius Syncellus, which informs us, that the additional five days, even amongst the Egyptians, one of the most ancient and learned nations in the world, were not originally added to the 360 days, or 12 months of 30 days a-piece, of which their year consisted, but were introduced about a thousand years after the deluge; so that till that time, their ancient year appears to have been no more than 360 days.

"(2.) This argument from the latter introduction of the five additional days, receives some confirmation from the *place* they always possess in the year, even after they were introduced in the *Egyptian* and thence in the *Nabonassarean* form, which was at the *end* of the whole year, as additional or superabundant days; which manner of adding them at the year's end seems naturally to imply, that the several months had been so long stated at 30 days a-piece, and so the whole year at just 360 days, that they could not think fit to alter them, but only ventured to add

---

[1] Sketches of Hindoos, p. 40. [2] Hypotheses, Book II. pp. 144—181.
[3] Vide Rev. Dr. Barret's Enquiry into the Constellations, pp. 8, &c.

" five days at the end of the year, which indeed were scarce accounted a part of it: still implying
" and supposing that the ancient and stated year was made up of 12 months of 30 days a-piece,
" or of 360 days in the whole, and no more.

" (3.) And what is but conjectured at in the last argument, is particularly asserted in a famous
" tradition in Plutarch, from whence it appears that the ancient *Egyptian* year was no more than
" 360 days, and that the five *Epagomenæ* were not looked upon as proper parts either of the year
" or of any of its months; but as days belonging to the nativities of five several Egyptian deities,
" who, as this present piece of mythology supposes, *were to be born neither in any year, nor in*
" *any month,* and that thereupon, these five days were added to the ancient year; which, there-
" fore, before this addition was made, contained no more than 360 days.

" (4.) That the most ancient *Chaldean* or *Babylonian* year was just 360 days, appears by that
" number of furlongs for the compass of the walls of Babylon, which, as Q. Curtius and Tzetzes
" affirm, were built in a year. a furlong each day. For though some who wrote about the time of
" Alexander the Great, and seem to have known, either that the solar year was 365 days long, or
" the astronomical year at Babylon itself was of that length, do say that the compass of the walls
" was 365 furlongs; yet Ctesias, who wrote before that time in the reign of Artaxerxes Memor,
" says with greater probability, that the number of furlongs was but 360. And since even those
" later writers add, that Babylon was as many furlongs in compass as there were days in the year;
" 'tis more than probable that they erroneously concluded from thence, that because the tropical
" year (or the astronomical year of Nabonassar) had 365 days in it, therefore Babylon was 365
" furlongs in compass. Thus then we see the testimonies of several authors that the walls of Ba-
" bylon were as many furlongs in compass as there were days in the year; and that the oldest
" and best testimony asserts that they were 360 furlongs in compass; wherefore it must be
" concluded highly probable at least, that the most ancient Babylonian year was exactly 360 days
" long.

" (5.) All this is more fully confirmed by a contemporary author, the Prophet Daniel, who lived
" and wrote in Babylon, in the reign of Nebuchadnezzar, who built those walls. For Daniel by
" his *time, times and a half,* or three years and a half, as we are sure from St. John's exposition of
" them, means 1260 days; and consequently by a single *time* or one year, means no more than
" 360 days; according to the usual computation of the age and nation in which he lived.

" (6.) We find also several footsteps and remains of this old year in the Medo-Persian monar-
" chy which subdued the Babylonian. As in the 360 channels which Cyrus cut to make the river
" Gyndes fordable for his army, when he went on his expedition against Babylon; and (if Jose-
" phus be not mistaken) in the 360 Satrapæ which Darius set over so many provinces of his em-
" pire. Thus also the sacred historian assures us, that *King Ahasuerus made a feast unto all his*
" *princes and his servants many days, even* 180 days, i. e. a just half-year's feast, that number being
" exactly half 360. Thus also the Periodus Magorum, mentioned by Scaliger, was 360,000 years,
" i. e. days, or a just millennium. In all which instances a plain reference is had to the year of
" 360 days then in use.

" (7.) That the *Persian* year contained but 360 days is still more evident from the testimonies
" of Plutarch and Q. Curtius, who affirm that the number of royal concubines to more than one
" of the Persian kings, was just 360. And we know both from Scripture and Herodotus, that
" they went in constant courses to their kings. And since their number answers so exactly to
" the days in the ancient year, according to the other testimonies; since also a year is so natural
" and obvious a length for one of those courses; nay, since Diodorus Siculus directly affirms that

"the Royal concubines were just as many as the days of the year, it is plain, the Persian year
"had just 360 days. Nay, even in much later times we find in the Arabic historians, that *Ardshir*
"*Ebn Babec*, who was king of Persia, in the third century of Christianity, was the author of the
"play which we call Tables; in which he appointed twelve houses or Areolæ to correspond to the
"12 months of the year, and 30 calculi or Tablemen, to answer to so many days in every month:
"a plain instance (if not of the then present length of the Persian year and months, yet at least)
"of the tradition they still retained, that originally the Persian year was just 360 days, containing
"twelve months of 30 days a-piece.

"(8.) There is also no small probability, that the most ancient year of the Mexicans in North
"America (who seem to have had their original from some of the *eastern* nations) was also exactly
"360 days. This people (as Joseph Acosta, amongst others, informs us) 'divided their year into
"'months, to [each of] which they gave 20 days, *wherein the 360 days are accomplished, not com-*
"'*prehending in any of these months, the 5 days that remain and make the year perfect.* But they
"'did reckon them apart at the end of the year, and called them *days of nothing*; during which
"'the people *did not any thing*, neither went they to their temples, but occupied themselves only
"'in visiting one another, and so spent the time. The sacrificers of the temple did likewise cease
"'their sacrifices.' Since then the Mexicans, even till these later times, esteemed as nothing
"those five days that were added to the 360 at the end of the year, and accordingly spent them
"in mere idleness; it is very probable they did this to signify that those additional days were not
"to be looked upon as any real part of the year, as they certainly were not of any of its months;
"or at least, to signify that they did *not originally* belong to the year, but were added to it in
"later times, to make it more agreeable to the solar year. And if so, it must be allowed that the
"primitive year of the Mexicans contained just 360 days, and no more.

"(9.) The only year among the ancient Greeks, and the nations descended from them, that can
"come in competition with this year of 360 days, is the tropical year or a year made very nearly
"equal to the tropical by cycles of years, or proper intercalations of months or days in certain
"revolving periods. And that this year was not originally in civil use amongst them, appears
"very probable from the most ancient manner of determining the seasons of the year, which was
"not done by the names of the months and days of the civil year, but by the heliacal rising and
"setting of the fixed stars, as is well known to all that are conversant in the old poetry and astro-
"nomy. Now, if the tropical year, or a year made equivalent to it by proper intercalations, had
"been the civil year, it can hardly be imagined that the easy and obvious method of reckoning the
"seasons by the months and days of the civil year should be entirely neglected; and so odd and
"troublesome a method as that of fixing them by the heliacal rising and setting of the fixed stars,
"should be entertained in its stead. And in confirmation of this reasoning, Diogenes Laertius
"says, that Thales the Milesian was the first of all the Greeks who discovered the length of the
"four seasons of the year, and that the tropical year was 365 days in length. And though Solon
"is said to have made the month conformable to the motion of the moon at Athens, yet even he
"himself was utterly ignorant of the tropical year, if he really had that discourse with Crœsus,
"king of Lydia, which Herodotus relates he had. For he there supposes, that if the year of 360
"days had an *embolimary* month of 30 days added to it every other year, it would thereby become
"equal to the tropical year. Whereby it is plain, he took the tropical year to be 375 days long,
"which is above 9 days and 18 hours more than the truth. Wherefore I think it may be con-
"cluded, that till after the time of Solon (or if this discourse with Crœsus be feigned by Herodo-
"tus under Solon's name, then even till Herodotus's time, which is above 100 years later) the

"ancient Greeks were generally ignorant of the true length of the tropical year; and, conse-
"quently, the most ancient Grecian year was not equal to the tropical. And if so, the following
"ancient testimonies will be undoubted evidence that it was of no other length than 360 days.

"(10.) That the ancient year of Greece, Lydia, and the Grecian colonies in Asia, was just 360
"days, appears from several testimonies. There is a clear intimation of this in the 360 gods,
"which (as Justin Martyr assures us) that most ancient poet and philosopher Orpheus intro-
"duced; one, it seems, for every day in the year. The same thing may be concluded from the
"before-cited testimony of Herodotus, (of Halicarnassus, a Grecian city in Asia,) who introduces
"Solon discoursing with Crœsus, king of Lydia, where, he says, that 70 years, (viz. either Asia-
"tic years, even till Herodotus's time, or at least Lydian years in the time of Crœsus,) contained
"25,200 days; from whence it follows, that a single year, at the same time, contained just 360
"days. This also is proved from the riddle of Cleobulus, tyrant of Lindus, a city of Rhodes.
"*There is*, says he, *one father who has 12 children, and each of these has 60 daughters, 30 of them
"white, and 30 of them black, all of them being immortal; and yet mortal continually.* By which
"all agree, that the year is meant with its 12 months, and each of their 30 days and 30 nights.
"Thus also Hippocrates (of the island of Cos, in the Egean sea) affirms, that 7 years contain 360
"weeks, and so one year 360 days. And also that 7 months are 210 days; and 9 months and 10
"days are just 280 days; and elsewhere, that 9 months contained 270 days, according to the
"computation of the Grecians. From all which it is evident, that 30 days were then allowed to a
"month, and 360 days to a year.

"(11.) That the most ancient year at Athens in particular, was 360 days, and the month 30 days,
"appears from the very original constitution of the city of Athens itself, which, as we learn from
"Harpocration, Julius Pollux, and Suidas, was divided (to use the words of the last) into four
"tribes, in imitation of the 4 seasons of the year; which tribes contained 12 $\phi\rho\alpha\tau\rho\acute{\iota}\alpha\varsigma$ correspond-
"ing to the 12 months; and each $\phi\rho\alpha\tau\rho\acute{\iota}\alpha$ had 30 $\gamma\acute{\epsilon}\nu\eta$ answering to the 30 days of each month;
"so that all the $\gamma\acute{\epsilon}\nu\eta$ collected together were 360, as many as the days of the year. Which words,
"in the opinion of a learned man, do not only demonstrate the true length of the primitive Athe-
"nian year, but also give the reason of it, from the original constitution of the city itself. That
"they demonstrate the true length of the primitive Athenian year, I acknowledge is very plain;
"but (with submission) they are so far from deriving this year, with its 4 seasons, 12 months, and
"30 days in each month, from the constitution of the city, that they assert on the contrary, the
"city was so divided and constituted in imitation of the year, and of its 4 seasons, 12 months, &c.
"And if Athens was a colony of the Egyptians, as seems exceeding probable, there can be no
"doubt but that the ancient year of 360 days and 12 equal months, (the only year and months the
"Egyptians then made use of) gave birth to the aforesaid constitution of that city, and so were
"evidently the primitive year and months in civil use at Athens.

"(12.) That the Athenians retained the year of 360 days, and the month of 30 days, till after
"the time of Alexander the Great, (either solely, as some learned men hold; or at least, together
"with the Lunæ-solar year, as Theodorus Gaza was of opinion,) may be proved from the books of
"ancient Athenians yet extant, as well as by other authorities. Thus Xenophon, in his excellent
"discourse of the revenue of the state of Athens, always takes it for granted that a year did then
"contain 360 days, and no more, as his late translator in his notes, particularly, observes and de-
"monstrates. And Plato, in his 6th book de Legibus, would have the Senate of the new Com-
"monwealth he is there describing, *to consist of 360 men, to be divided into 4 parts of 90 each;* in
"this alluding plainly to the year of 360 days, and its 4 quarters. And Aristotle expressly assures
"us, that the 5th part of a year was 72 days, and the 6th part was 60 days; and so by plain con-
"sequence, the whole year must have been 360 days. Lastly, Pliny, Laertius, and Varro, inform

"us, that at Athens, Demetreus Phalereus (after the time of Alexander the Great) had just 360 statues erected to his memory, the year at that time (as Pliny says expressly, and the other two as expressly as he, if their testimonies be taken jointly) not having any greater number of days in it than 360.

"(13.) This ancient year of only 360 days, appears also to have been the first Roman year before Numa Pompilius's correction. For Plutarch, in the life of Numa, says, that 'during the reign of Romulus, some months were not 20 days long, and others contained 35 days or more, the Romans not then sufficiently understanding the true length of the solar or lunar periods; but only providing for this one thing, that the whole year should contain just 360 days.'

"(14.) That this was the primitive Roman year, will appear very probable also from the Julian Calendar itself, which intercalates the Bissextile day immediately after the Terminalia, the last day of the ancient year; that is, immediately before the 5 last days of February, the last month in the ancient year; so that the 5 last days of February every common year, and the 6 last every Bissextile year, are to be reckoned intercalary, or additional days to the other 360. And, indeed, St. Austin, speaking of those who reckoned the Antediluvian years to be no more than 36 days, the 10th part of the lunar year, which he supposed to be 360 days, to which the 5¼ days were afterwards added to fill up the solar year; directly says, that the Romans called all those five (or six days in a Bissextile year) intercalary days. And though an intercalary month in the times immediately before the Julian correction, was inserted in the same place where the Bissextile day is inserted now; yet it is probable from what St. Austin says, and indeed from the agreeableness of the thing itself, that the first correction of the ancient year of 360 days, was made by adding the five days aforesaid to the end of it.

"(15.) That the original Roman year was exactly 360 days, is farther proved, because a tacit year of that length was retained in the Roman Empire for the anniversary celebration of some particular solemnities, long after the establishment of the Julian year, as appears from some inscriptions in Gruter; concerning which hear the words of the famous Cardinal Norris.—'In harum Inscriptionum unâ dicitur Nonius Victor cum Aurelio Victore, *Datiano Cereale Coss.* tradidisse LEONTICA XVI. KAL. APRIL. Et in alterâ memorandum iidem, *Eusebio & Hypatio Coss.* iterum tradidisse LEONTICA IV. IDUS MARTIAS. Erant sacra anniversaria, quæ anno evoluto, ab iisdem instaurata fuerunt. Priora peracta sunt Anno Christi 358, die 17 Martii: altera anno 359, die ejusdem mensis 12, jam evolutis diebus a prioribus Leonticis, 360.' This reasoning, from such undoubted authorities, is so plain and convincing, that nothing farther need to be added to it.

"(16.) This computation of 30 days to every month, and so of 360 days to a year in ancient time, is also confirmed by that length of a month all along in the old histories, as has, in great measure, been proved already, and is confirmed by these farther testimonies. When Queen Esther would express her absence from King Ahasuerus for an entire month, she expresses it thus: 'I have not been called to come in unto the King these 30 days.' And when Darius's courtiers in Daniel solicited him to prohibit prayers for an entire month likewise, they expressed it thus: that 'none should ask a petition of any god or man for 30 days.' And this month of 30 days did certainly continue in civil use at Athens till Solon's time at least. Diogenes Laertius and Plutarch agree, that he was the first who accommodated the month to the motion of the moon, and called the last day of it (which before was named τριακὰς, the 30th day) ἐνηκαινία, *the Old and New day*, as belonging partly to the old moon, and partly to the new. And Proclus also adds, that Solon was the first that made the month less than 30 days. Nay, even in later times, about 200 years after Solon, the ancient astronomers Euctemon, Philip, and Calippus, in those very cycles which they made for adjusting the years and months to the motions of the sun

" and moon, did constantly allow 30 days to each month, and then threw out every 63rd or 64th
" day, as is particularly explained in Geminus; who himself also expressly asserts, that the ancients
" constantly allowed 30 days to a month. Lastly, Julius Pollux, Galen, Cleomedes, Orus Apollo,
" Achilles Tatius, and St. Austin, do each of them assure us, that by a month, in the vulgar way
" of speaking, is meant 30 days. Nay, the four last express themselves so as if the lunar month
" itself were exactly of that length. And St. Austin carries the matter farther, and takes the lunar
" year, or 12 lunar months, to contain just 360 days. And even Dionysius Exiguus, above 500
" years after Christ, reproves many of this error, of taking the lunar month to be just 30, and the
" lunar year just 360 days. And it cannot be easily imagined how so great an error should so
" universally obtain, unless the most ancient year and month had been just 360 and 30 days in
" length respectively.

10. " And thus I think I have clearly proved the first particular which I undertook, namely,
" that the ancientest year in use in most nations of the Postdiluvian world was exactly 360 days,
" and the month exactly 30 days. I come now to shew, that even in the Antediluvian world, not
" only the year in civil use, but also the solar year, and the lunar year too, were each of them 360
" days in length, and exactly commensurate to one another. And here, if the reader will make
" allowances for the distance and obscurity of the times I am now about to treat of, and for the
" scarcity of any records belonging to them besides the Holy Scriptures, I believe he will find as
" much evidence, even for this second particular, as can reasonably be expected, and what is
" abundantly sufficient to satisfy him of the truth and reality of it.

" And (1) since we have found, that the most ancient Postdiluvian year in civil use in most
" countries was exactly 360 days, consisting of 12 equal months of 30 days a-piece; it is a strong
" presumption, that the Antediluvian civil year was of the same length. For it cannot easily be
" imagined how this year should so universally obtain after the deluge, except it had been in use
" before it; especially, since it is neither equal to the present solar year, nor to the lunar. If the
" first nations after the deluge had made any change in their year, they would certainly have en-
" deavoured to make it conformable to the motions either of the sun, or of the moon, or both;
" which appears to be the practice of every nation, when they undertake to correct or alter the
" year in civil use. And, therefore, since neither the year of 360 days, nor the month of 30 days,
" is agreeable to any of the celestial motions, it must be granted that the Postdiluvians were not
" the first framers of this year; and, therefore, that it was used before the deluge also.

" (2.) This farther appears by that most ancient and most valuable testimony of Moses, whereby
" we understand, that from the 17th day of the second month, when the flood began, till the 17th
" day of the 7th month, when the ark rested, were just 150 days, or just 30 days for every inter-
" vening month. The words are these: ' In the 600th year of Noah's life, the second month, the
" ' 17th day of the month, the same day were all the fountains of the great deep broken up, and the
" ' windows of heaven were opened. And the waters prevailed upon the earth 150 days. And
" ' after the end of 150 days the waters were abated; and the ark rested in the 7th month, on the
" ' 17th day of the month, upon the mountains of Ararat.' So that hence it is evident that five
" months, viz. the 2d, 3d, 4th, 5th, and 6th, had just 30 days a-piece; and by consequence it is
" most probable that all the rest had so likewise, and that therefore the whole year had no more
" than 360 days.

" *Lemma* to the third argument. The ancient succession of kings in Berosus and Abydenus,
" whose reigns are counted by Sari, governed some part of the Antediluvian world, and ended at
" the deluge. All this is asserted by the historians themselves. Nay, farther, Xisuthrus, the last
" king, appears evidently to be the same with Noah, since almost the whole history of the flood,
" and of Noah's being saved in the ark, may be found in the remaining fragments of Berosus and

" Abydenus, if you only change the name of Xisuthrus for Noah. As particularly, that 'God re-
" ' vealed to Xisuthrus, that a great deluge should destroy men from the earth, and begin on the
" ' 15th day of the month Dæsius, and therefore Xisuthrus was commanded to save himself and
" ' his family by entering into an ark or ship, and to take with him into the ark all sorts of birds
" ' and beasts, with necessary food for himself and them. Which being done, the deluge came, as
" ' predicted. And after the rain had ceased, Xisuthrus sent out a bird, to see if the waters were
" ' abated, which returned to him again, having found nothing to rest upon. And after some time,
" ' he sent out another, which returned likewise, but with dirty feet, whereby he knew the waters
" ' were abated. Lastly, he sent one out the third time, which returned not to him again. That
" ' afterwards, Xisuthrus opened the ark, and saw the ground was dry; so he and his wife came
" ' out and raised an altar and sacrificed to the gods. His children also came out and sacrificed,
" ' and found that the ark rested on the Gordyean mountains in Armenia, and part of it still con-
" ' tinued in being when this account was written. Afterwards Xisuthrus's children journeyed
" ' towards Babylon, built many cities, and founded temples, and particularly built Babylon.'
" These circumstances are so agreeable to the Scripture history of the deluge, that many have
" been tempted to think that Berosus transcribed this account from thence. But that cannot
" easily be, because amongst these truths there are some mistakes and falsities intermixed, which
" I thought it not worth the while to relate. But from those falsities, and from the idolatry in
" this history, it appears that it was collected and put into writing some few years after the
" deluge, namely, after the rise of idolatry amongst the Postdiluvians. And yet it is very proba-
" ble this was done long before the lives of men were fixed to the present standard, while some
" that had conversed with the sons or grandsons of Noah were still alive; because the particulars
" of the deluge are more accurately related therein, as we have seen, than could be supposed pos-
" sible, had the tradition passed through very many hands before it was committed to writing.

" (3.) That the Antediluvian year was just 360 days long, appears from the reigns of these Ante-
" diluvian kings, which, as I said, are not reckoned by years, but by Sari. And our authors tell
" us, a Sarus is 3600 years; that is, as some ancient Christian writers understood them, (and as
" appears by the great length of the particular reigns, some of them amounting even to 18 Sari
" a-piece,) 3600 days, or ten years of 360 days each. And the Hebrew or Chaldee expression of a
" Sarus confirms this assertion. Hhazâr is ten; and the first letter being such a guttural as could
" not well be pronounced by the Greeks, they would naturally express the word by $\Sigma\alpha\rho\sigma\varsigma$, which
" is therefore literally *a decad*. For the lives of the Antediluvians being generally at the least ten
" times as long as ours, they found it more convenient to reckon their own lives and the reigns of
" their kings, rather by decads of years than by single years. Now, if a Sarus or *decad* of years
" contained 3600 days before the deluge, it is plain that each year contained just 360 days.

" (4.) If it be proved by the preceding arguments, that the civil year before the deluge was just
" 360 days, and the civil month just 30 days; it will be thence very probably concluded, that both
" the tropical year and the lunar month were each of the same length respectively. The great
" probability of this will appear, whether we suppose the civil year and month to have been of
" human or of divine institution. For, 1st, if they were of human institution, what could induce
" the Antediluvians to make use of this form of year, if it varied as much from the motions both
" of the sun and moon as it does at present? The Antediluvian earth was extremely fruitful, the
" lives of its inhabitants extremely long, and the air at that time extremely clear; so that the
" inhabitants of the old world wanted neither leisure nor time, nor opportunity to make multi-
" tudes of observations, in order to discover the true length of the year and month; which, if they
" had discovered, the great conveniences visibly consequent upon the use of them must needs
" have induced the civil powers to have enjoined and established them accordingly. Now, since

"it appears by the former arguments, that in fact the civil year before the deluge was just 360 days, and the civil month just 30 days; it will be highly probable, from what is here alleged, that (if the same civil year and month were of human discovery and institution) the tropical year and lunar month were of the same length also. But, 2dly, if, on the other hand, God himself revealed to mankind the true length of the year, it will be still more evident that the Antediluvian tropical year was exactly 360 days long, and the lunar month exactly 30 days; for God cannot deceive his creatures; nor would he institute a form of year which was less convenient and proper for attaining the end for which it was instituted, when nothing hindered but that the *most* convenient and *most* proper; that is, the true tropical year and lunar month might have been as easily ascertained by divine revelation, as any others. Since, therefore, it is before proved, that the civil year was just 360 days before the deluge, and the civil month just 30 days; if God taught mankind this length of the year and month; then it plainly appears, that the tropical year and lunar month were just 360 and 30 days long respectively. And upon the whole, whether the Antediluvian civil year and month were of divine or of human original, (and of one of the two they certainly were,) it appears either way highly probable, that both the tropical and lunar year were just 360 days each, and the lunar month exactly 30 days.

"(5.) And that the primitive solar year was really no more than 360 days, and contained just 12 lunar months of 30 days a-piece, appears farther, by the most ancient division of the solar course into just 360 degrees, and those distributed into 12 signs of 30 degrees a-piece. For the only natural reason that can be given why the zodiac or solar circle was at first divided either into just 360 degrees or 12 signs, and why just 30 degrees were allotted to each sign, must be, that when this division was made, the sun ran through the zodiac in just 360 days, which were also 12 lunar months, 30 days being then the exact length of every month. And this division of the zodiac or solar circle into 360 degrees was so very famous and remarkable in old time, that astronomers and all other mathematicians have transferred that number of degrees to every other circle which they considered, and still have supposed them divided, every one, great and small, into 360 degrees. And this division of a circle has continued ever since, to this day, as a standing memorial of that most ancient tropical year which obtained when this division was made. I called this division of the zodiac a most ancient one, because it appears to have been made long before the earliest accounts of astronomy that we have; they all still supposing it, and not at all mentioning any thing of its first introduction. And since this division was first made when the true solar year was no more than 360 days in length, and contained just 12 lunar months of 30 days a-piece; it was therefore older than the deluge; since we are pretty certain that, generally speaking, since the deluge the solar year has been some hours longer than 365 days, and and the lunar year some hours shorter than 355. If, then, the zodiac was thus divided before the deluge, in correspondence with the true solar and lunar year; it is evident that before the deluge they were each of them just 360 days, and subdivided into 12 lunar months of 30 days a-piece.

"*Lemma* 1, to the sixth and seventh arguments. — Manetho's *most ancient succession of the Gods, as he calls them, reigned before the deluge, and ended at it.* Manetho divides his dynasties into those of the *gods, demi-gods, heroes, and men.* In this place I only speak of the first of these, because none of the rest do contribute any thing to the present argument. Now by gods here, Manetho (as he elsewhere explains himself) means only mortal men, who, for their wisdom and goodness, were severally promoted to the regal dignity, and afterwards made immortal. And Diodorus Siculus also speaks to the same purpose. But I shall not take upon me to defend every thing that Manetho, or any other writer, has advanced concerning these very ancient times. It is sufficient for my purpose, if I prove that these kings, whom Manetho calls

"Gods, reigned over some part of the Antediluvian world, and ended at the deluge; their memory being preserved by the old Egyptian records, and their history committed to writing not many years after the dispersion from Babel. I shall therefore endeavour to prove this Lemma; first, by the authority of several ancient Christian chronographers at least, if not by the direct assertion of Manetho himself; secondly, from a consideration of the *first* king; and, thirdly, from a consideration of the *last* king in the same succession.

"And, first, I am to shew what authority may be produced to prove that these kings reigned before the deluge. I observe, then, that both Africanus in the third, and Eusebius in the fourth century of Christianity, having spoken of the former sorts of Manetho's dynasties, and of the Gods among the rest, do each of them prefix this title to the following dynasties of men, [of the Egyptian dynasties after the deluge,] which clearly intimates that the preceding ones (and therefore also the gods) were before the deluge. And Panodorus, in the beginning of the fifth century, supposes both the gods and demi-gods to have reigned before the deluge. And Georgius Syncellus, though he rejects Manetho's authority in this particular, yet he every where allows and takes it for granted, that they were to be taken for Antediluvian kings, and supposed to be so even by Manetho himself. And indeed the length of some of their reigns is entirely disproportionate to any Postdiluvian times, and when allowance is made for Manetho's way of reckoning (which I shall presently explain) will be found very agreeable to the longevity of the Antediluvian patriarchs.

"Secondly, the succession of the gods appears to have been before the deluge, because Vulcan, the first king, was so. Tzetzes says, he was contemporary with Noah, whom he supposes to be the same with Osiris; but by the same argument he ought to have concluded, that the Egyptian Vulcan was long before Noah, since he was long before Osiris, as all will allow, and as it particularly appears from this very succession of the gods. And, indeed, Vulcan seems to be no other than Tubal-Cain in Scripture. Their names are near akin to each other, and the same character belongs to both. The Scripture says, that 'Tubal-Cain was the instructor of every 'artificer in brass and iron;' and Vulcan is famous in profane authors, not only for his artificial working in all sorts of metals, but also for his instructing mankind therein. And it is remarkable, that this is the more peculiar character of this Vulcan here, in the Egyptian succession of the gods, than of any other.

"Thirdly, the same thing may be proved from some considerations upon Typhon, the last king of this succession, namely, that he reigned immediately before the deluge, and perished therein. This will clearly follow from what is before proved, if compared with the following Lemma. For if Vulcan be Tubal-Cain, this succession must necessarily end at the deluge, the number of years it contains not permitting us to suppose it could possibly end any considerable time before it. But this will farther appear, 1st, because many circumstances of the deluge are mentioned in the history of Osiris and Typhon, in Plutarch and others; as particularly the very day when the deluge began, or when Osiris (who is taken for Noah) was shut up in the ark, viz. the 17th day of the 2d month after the autumnal equinox, as has been observed before. And other circumstances of the deluge there are in Typhon's history, some of which I shall have occasion to mention presently, and others will be produced under the following hypothesis; 2dly, the very name of Typhon also, according to some learned men, signifies a *deluge* or *inundation*; whence the Egyptian priests (as Plutarch says) called the sea Typhon. 3dly, Typhon (whom the Latin poets more frequently call Typhœus) is represented as a monstrous giant who fought against heaven, and was at last overcome by Jupiter; and as one says, lies now submersed in water. "From all which it appears very probable, that he was one of those giants who, as the Scripture says, were in the earth before the flood; one of those mighty men which were of old, men of

" renown, whose wickedness was so exceeding great, as might easily give occasion to the ancient
" tradition of their fighting against God. And, lastly, Typhon's being said to be overcome and
" submersed in water, seems evidently to proceed from his perishing in the deluge, which was
" brought upon the earth by the great wickedness wherein he and, indeed, all the Antediluvian
" world had involved themselves. So that upon the whole, it cannot easily be denied that this
" succession of the Gods ended at the deluge, and that Typhon, the last king of it, perished therein.
" [See another notion of Typhon in the III Appendix to the Essay for restoring the True Text of
" the Old Testament.]

" Lemma 2, to the 6th and 7th arguments. *The reigns of the gods* in Manetho *are not expressed
" by years, but partly by lunar months, and partly by ὧραι or seasons.* The probability of this
" *Lemma* Diodorus assures us of, that when it is said that some of the first kings of the succession
" of the Gods reigned about 1200 years, so many lunar months are understood thereby; and when
" it is said that the latter kings of the same succession reigned 300 years or more, there the sea-
" sons of the year are understood, reckoning 4 months in every season, and 3 seasons in every
" year, namely, Spring, Summer, and Winter. And these two sorts of Egyptian computations for
" years are also observed by Plutarch. And particularly as to the former, Varro, Pliny, Macro-
" bius, and Suidas, do all agree that the Egyptians of old computed a lunar month for a year.
" And Julius Africanus speaks also of several that computed the reigns of the most ancient kings
" of Egypt upon this hypothesis. And Eusebius also asserts, that this method of reckoning a
" month for a year, was practised by the most ancient Egyptians. Add, that Eudoxus also asserts,
" that the Egyptians formerly used a month for a year. And some ancient Christian chronogra-
" phers were so fully persuaded of this, that they have extended it too far, and supposed that all
" the reigns of the Gods in Manetho were reckoned by months only, and on that supposition, have
" reduced them to tropical or Julian years; whereas it appears from Diodorus, that only the long
" reigns of the first kings are to be computed by lunar months, and those of the rest by seasons
" of 4 months a-piece, or the third part of a year. And this computation of 4 months for a year, is
" not only attested by Diodorus and Plutarch as before, but also by Censorinus, Solinus, and St.
" Austin, who each of them affirm that the Egyptians of old used this way of reckoning.

" (6.) That before the deluge the lunar year, at least of 12 lunar months, and very probably the
" solar year too, was just 360 days, and each month just 30 days, will appear from some reigns
" in this Antediluvian dynasty of the gods. This I shall prove by shewing, first, that the lunar
" year was then exactly 12 lunar months, or 12 synodical revolutions of the moon, without any
" embolimary month; secondly, that the tropical solar year contained 12 months also; and, thirdly,
" that each lunar month contained exactly 30 days. And, first, the lunar year was exactly 12
" lunar months long; for Vulcan, in Manetho, is said to have reigned 9000 years; that is, as I
" have proved, 9000 revolutions of the moon, which make up 750 years of 12 months each, or, if
" you please, 75 Sari. From whence it appears, that each year had in it 12 lunar months exactly;
" no embolimary month being taken in for 750 years together. 2dly, the tropical year contained
" 12 months also, as appears from the years of the latter kings of this same succession of the gods,
" which are said to be each of the three seasons of the year, viz. Spring, Summer, and Winter,
" each containing 4 months. From whence it follows, that the tropical year (for it is a year
" determined by the seasons) was exactly 12 months also; which months must in all reason be
" supposed to be of the same sort with those which were before spoken of, namely, lunar months.
" So that it is highly probable, the tropical year at that time was just 12 lunar months in
" length. 3dly, each month at the same time contained exactly 30 days. This is attested by
" many ancient authors. Thus Varro, speaking of these large numbers in the records of ancient
" time, says, the Egyptians therein do reckon lunar months for years, and allow 30 days to the

" time in which the moon finishes its menstrual course. And Diodorus Siculus speaking of those
" who reckoned the reigns of the gods in Egypt by lunar months, expressly asserts, that they
" computed 30 days to a month. And in like manner, when Eusebius (speaking also of the long
" reigns in the Egyptian succession of the Gods) says, that the most ancient Egyptians reckoned
" by lunar months, instead of years; he adds, in the same place, that those lunar months consisted
" of 30 days a-piece. And Panodorus seems to intimate, that before the deluge, not only the civil
" but also the lunar month was exactly 30 days, and that the reigns of the gods in Manetho were
" computed by lunar months of 30 days a-piece. To these testimonies I need not add St. Austin
" here, as having already produced what he has spoken on this subject. Since then it appears by
" the first part of this argument, that, during this Antediluvian succession, there were exactly 12
" lunar revolutions in the year; and since it appears by the 2d part, that there were exactly 12
" (and those very probably lunar) months in the tropical year also; and since it appears by the
" 3d part, that there were just 30 days in each lunar revolution at the same time; it is evident
" from all three taken together, that before the deluge, the lunar year at least, and very probably
" the solar also, consisted exactly of 12 lunar months of 30 days a-piece, or of 360 days in the
" whole.

" (7.) That not only the civil, but also the tropical year of the sun, and the lunar year of 12
" synodical lunar months too, were each of them 360 days, and exactly equal to each other before
" the deluge, is farther attested by a famous piece of ancient mythology preserved in Plutarch, which
" I have had occasion to mention before; that about the times of Osiris and Typhon, that is, about
" the deluge, there happened such an alteration both in the month and the year, that the moon
" lost a 70th part of each day, and the sun gained it; whereby the lunar year became above 5
" days shorter, and the solar above 5 days longer, than each of them were before. Wherefore,
" since the solar year is now somewhat more than 365 days, and the lunar year somewhat less
" than 355 days, it is most evident, that before this change, both the solar and the lunar year were
" just 360 days, and exactly equal to each other. Nay, more, it is evident also, the change made
" in the solar and lunar revolutions, from their original to their present state and periods, hap-
" pened at the deluge."

Almost innumerable references to, and many passages from, the original authors are given by Mr. Whiston, but I have not thought it necessary to reprint them. I now apprehend that the opinion of the ancients cannot be a matter of doubt. After shewing this, Whiston undertakes to prove that their opinion arose from a knowledge of the fact handed down to them by tradition, and which was really a fact, that the change in the length of the year and month was caused by the near approach of *the* comet which last appeared in the year 1680, and whose period is about 575¼ years. Treating of this comet he says,

11. " The period of this comet most exactly agrees to the same time, I mean to 7 revolutions in
" 4028 years, the interval from the deluge till its last appearance, 1680. For, as Sir Isaac Newton
" first observed, from its elliptic curvature before it disappeared, that its period must be in gene-
" ral above 500 years; so as he and Dr. Halley since observed, that the same comet has been seen
" four times, viz. the 44th year before Christ, A. D. 531 or 532, A. D. 1106, and A. D. 1680, and
" that by consequence it makes a revolution in about 575 years. Now if we make but a very
" small allowance for the old periods before Christ, and suppose that, one with another, it has
" revolved in 575¼ years, we shall find that 7 such periods amount to 4028 years, exactly, accord-
" ing to that number since the deluge. . This is so remarkable an observation, and so surprising,
" that it will deserve a particular demonstration from the original authors themselves."[1] He

---

[1] Whiston's Theory, 3d ed. p. 191.

then proceeds to give authorities which prove that the comet was first noticed on the death of Cæsar, 44 years B. C., *and has been correctly noted three times since.* But for his proofs I must refer my reader to his work, as this does not seem so very material, because the mere facts cannot be disputed.

12. The flood of Noah is stated, by Usher and the Hebrew version, to have taken place in the year B. C. 2348; this added to A. D. 1680, gives 4028, the number required for the last appearance of the comet. Now, I apprehend, this coincidence is of such a nature as to raise the highest probability of the influence of that comet in causing the flood. But there are several other circumstances relating to this matter of the greatest importance. It is surely another very striking circumstance, that if we take eight revolutions of the comet, of 575¼ years each, they bring us to the commencement of the system—to the entrance of the Sun into Taurus, at the Vernal Equinox; the 44 years before Christ (the time when the comet appeared) being added, as of course they ought to be—

$$575\tfrac{1}{4} \cdot 8 = 4604 + 44 = 4648. \qquad 65 \times 71\tfrac{1}{4} = 4647\tfrac{1}{4}.$$

Now, I contend, that this renders it probable that, at the time when the Sun entered Taurus, one of the violent revolutions or catastrophes took place which have manifestly happened to the globe at different times. It also raises a probability that this very comet is the agent which has produced these effects. Again, every one knows the fact, that a great discrepancy exists between the Samaritan and the Hebrew chronology. Mr. Whiston contends,[1] *that the more exact Hebrew chronology,*[2] by which he means the more exact chronology of the children of Israel, placed the flood in the 2926th year B. C., which was the very year in which the comet must, in its proper period, have arrived in our system; and that by its appulse to the earth, at that time, it must have caused the deluge. He goes at great length into the subject, and endeavours to prove this fact astronomically from the tables of the Sun and Moon, and by various arguments, (not necessary for me to copy,) to within a day or two of the day of the month of the year named by Moses, Berosus, and Abydenus, and to a single day with the express testimony of Plutarch—all which, as he observes, is an "exactness of coincidence not a little remarkable." He supposes that the original circular orbit of the earth was made elliptical by the appulse of the comet, and the year lengthened from 360 to 365 days. It is not only, as Whiston says, *not* "a little remarkable," but it justifies me in concluding either that the ancients knew of the flood from experience, or they knew of the periods of the comet, and invented or fixed the time of the flood to suit them. The apparent contradiction between the chronology of Mr. Whiston's two accounts is reconciled, in a great measure, by a very surprising fact, that the 2926, (the year which he says the astronomical tables prove the comet to have come,) is the exact time of the eighth revolution of the comet, instead of the year 2348, which was the seventh; and, as he justly observes, when all the disturbing forces and other circumstances are considered, the trifling discrepancy which may be perceived is of such little consequence that, if there be any thing surprising in it, the surprise ought to be, that the discrepancy is not much greater instead of its being so little. It *is* a very remarkable circumstance, that one period seems to answer nearly to the Samaritan computation, and the other to the Hebrew. Mr. Whiston, on the Old Testament, says,[3] "It will not be amiss to set down here a "canon of what I now take to be the true chronology, from the beginning of the world till the "Christian æra; I mean this, upon the joint consideration of the Samaritan, the Septuagint, the "present Hebrew, and the old Hebrew used by Josephus." This is, in fact, the Samaritan calculation, as he *proves* the others to have been most excessively corrupted.

---

[1] New Theory, &c., Book II. pp. 217, 218.   [2] True Text of the Old Testament, p. 214.   [3] Pp. 213, 214.

	Years
(1.) From the autumnal equinox next after the creation of Adam to that at the end of the deluge.	1556
(2.) Thence to the departure of Abraham out of Haran	966¼
(3.) Thence to the Exodus out of Egypt	430
(4.) Thence to the foundation of Solomon's temple.	479 1/11
(5.) Thence to its conflagration.	464¼
(6.) Thence to the beginning of the Christian era	587⅓
	4483⅛
	1556
Deduct 1556 and we shall have the space from the flood to the Christian æra	2927
Then multiply the period of the comet 575¼ by 5, and add 44, the year B. C., in which it appeared, and it gives 2921¼	2921¼
	...5¼

and we shall have a coincidence of periods within 6 years; which, when all the disturbing forces are brought into calculation or allowed for, is a difference so small as to raise the probability of *the truth of the theory* much higher than if the numbers had actually coincided. For, we may readily suppose, indeed we must suppose, that such a disturbance as that caused by the comet, would take several years to subside.—The following will exhibit another curious coincidence. The Hebrew states the flood to have taken place 1656 years after the creation, and as it makes the birth of Christ 4000 years from the creation, it makes the flood 2344 B. C. Now, if we take 1656 and add to it four periods of the comet at 575 or 2300, and also the years it came B. C., 44, we shall have exactly 4000. This justifies the inference that the Jews or Chaldæans knew the the period of the comet, but made a mistake in calculating backwards, taking it to have touched the earth in one period later than that in which the Samaritans supposed it affected the earth, and they accommodated the reigns of their kings, &c., to suit that hypothesis. I think no unprejudiced person can doubt that the comet of 1680 is really the same comet as that which appeared 44 years before Christ. Now, if we refer to the Samaritan chronology, we shall find that the flood is stated to have taken place 1656 years after the creation; this is confirmed by the Hebrew, which, in this, exactly agrees with the Samaritan. If we add four revolutions of the comet to 44, and their sum to 1656, we have exactly the sum of 4000 years—the time from the creation to the birth of Christ. It is remarkable that 2348 is the date which our chronologers give (Usher's 4 years corrected) for the flood before Christ, according to Hebrew calculation: this is exactly 44 added to 2300, or to four revolutions of the comet, so that the Jews make the flood to have happened in the *fourth* revolution of the comet, and the Samaritans in the *fifth*. It is not possible to believe this to be the effect of accident. If we suppose the inventor of the mythos to have understood the period of the comet and the precession of the equinox, he contrived the entrance or the beginning of the sign Taurus to suit it, and made it to begin exactly with the eighth revolution, counting *backwards* and counting *forwards* it would end 44 years B. C., thus, 575½ × 8 = 4604 + 44 = 4648. Then, 65 degrees at 71½ = 4647. It seems probable that this was the principle, and that it was from the conjoined knowledge of the *precession*, and of the *periods of the comet*, that the mythos was formed. The Bible says, the flood happened in the year B. C. 2348. The year of the comet in its 4th revolution is 2344 [2346?] years B. C., counting its periods at 575½, and 2348 counting it at 576; in its 5th revolution it is 2919 years, and in its 8th revolution it is 4648 years. Now, I suppose the comet caused floods in its 4th, 5th, and 8th revolutions. Whiston undertakes to prove that the corrected Samaritan chronology makes the flood to have occurred 2926 years B. C.: this is only 6 or 7 years from the year of its return as above, 2919;[1] and it is as near as could be expected. I think it is evident that the Samaritan chronology has been meant to answer to the 5th revolution. When the great confusion or violent interference with the regular course of the globe is considered, and this immense disturbing power is compared with the disturbing powers which the planetary bodies are believed to exert upon each other, surely the allowance of so small a space as six or seven years upon the three approaches of the comet is very little! The ancients never calculated by fractions, but always in whole numbers. They must have seen, if, as I suppose, they knew and calculated the comet's periods, that it was perfectly nonsensical to expect absolute correctness in the return of the periods, and that, therefore, to encumber themselves with fractional calculations was a proceeding worse than useless. It was a million to one that the disturbing power exerted *three* times, should, in six thousand years, come to less than six years. If we take the comet's period at 576 years, it will make a cycle with the 4320, the double of the 2160, in 75 revolutions. Here we see another reason for the long periods or cycles of the ancients. If we give Noah and his Chaldæans credit for as much knowledge as Mr. Whiston, and gained like his, by observation, or rather, I should say, by reasonings on recorded observations, we may very readily give him credit for knowing, as Enoch says he did know, by a calculation of moons or by a calculation by lunar periods, *that the flood would come.* I shall shew in a subsequent part, that the ancients knew the moon's period to within *half a second of time.* If the man we call Noah, were a great and powerful prince, living near the Caspian sea, and possessing this knowledge, there is nothing improbable in his having built a great ship or floating house, and in his having saved in it his family and a few domestic animals. We know from experience that this would be quite sufficient upon which to ground the fable, and that it was perfectly in keeping with the character of the ancients to have founded a fable upon it. The division of the zodiac being artificial, it is evident that the formers of it could make it begin where they pleased; and it is evident also, that they made it begin with the Bull—fixing it as near as they could to the time of the comet. It is probable that they arbitrarily fixed it to a certain point in the circle, which they called Taurus, and it followed of course, that the precession would make the post time correspond (as it does) to it. Why the signs of the zodiac came to bear their respective names we do not know; but they were probably the produce of a high latitude, where the *camel* and *elephant* were not much in use. I think it is evident that the first of Taurus was the beginning, to proceed *forwards*, of our system; but probably the ancients had some mythic history which went *backwards* from that period, to which the respective signs bore a relation, as the three signs of Taurus, Aries, and Pisces, bear a relation to our mythos. Mr. Whiston says, " We know, by the exactest calculation from the" present " Hebrew copies, if, with all the ancients, we suppose Abraham born in the 70th year of his father Terah, that the entire 4000 years till the days of the Messias will end about A. D. 60."[2] Now this gives us to the year 1260 for the millenium, and shews that the 1260 of Daniel was calculated to begin from the commencement of our present æra, as two Neroses added to the 1260 complete the sum required. I shall be told, that though the comet comes in the periods I have pointed out, yet calculation shews that the earth and moon would not be in a situation of their orbits to be affected by it. To which I reply, it is very true that so it may appear by our calculations; but it is more probable that our calculations do not apply, or are wrong, or that there is something in the motions of the comet unknown to us, which makes our calculations wrong, than

---

[1] Here the reader will perceive that the Author omitted the *five* half years. These being added, there would remain a difference of only 4½ years between the Author's statement and the Samaritan chronology. *Editor.*

[2] On Old Testament, p. 227, ed. 1722.

that the above three simple arithmetical calculations should accidentally agree with the precession of the equinoxes, with the book of Genesis, with the return of the comet, and thus with the whole of my theory or system. As comets move in different planes, this comet may, by moving in a different plane, have been made to come in contact with the earth. Its plane may have been altered, without any material alteration of its period, by some body coming in collision with it in the further part of its orbit, as it came into collision with our earth. These suppositions are much more probable than that Mr. Whiston and I should be wrong. We calculate upon data, of which we have almost a perfect knowledge: they who oppose us, upon very uncertain and almost unknown data. Almost any supposition is more probable than that we should be mistaken.

13. Our astronomers will assert, without hesitation, that they can calculate the periods of several of the comets. They would have fixed, without the least hesitation, a year ago, the time when Encke's would appear;[1] but it has disappointed them,[2] and shewn that their knowledge in this branch of their science is far from complete. I contend that the coincidence of the times of the periodical arrival of the comet, of 575¼, with the dates 4648, 2926, and 2348, the *first* the entrance of the Sun into Taurus, the beginning of the system of chronology, the *second* the date fixed by Whiston, and the *third* the date named in the Hebrew Bible for the flood, raises a high probability that the ancient Chaldæans, who were said to have invented the Neros, and whose knowledge was displayed by Sosigenes to Julius Cæsar, really understood the theory of the comets; and all the circumstances combined render it much more probable that our astronomers are mistaken, and in ignorance, than that such a coincidence of the facts displayed above should have taken place, without a knowledge of the system by the persons writing the accounts, and also without the system being true. If our astronomers talk to me of planes and periods, I tell them, their error in the case of the Encke comet, and the extraordinary coincidences pointed out by me, render it much more probable that the ancients were right in their *practice*, than that they are right in their *theory*. What periodical changes take place in the motions of the comets we do not know. They may keep their periods, yet change their planes in some way unknown to us. The comets are of various kinds; some have atmospheres, some have not: some have tails, some have not; some are all transparent, some are only partly so. They are of different colours, and they move in different planes, and in reality our astronomers know very little about them. The ancients may have discovered the laws which rule that of 575¼ years' period, and not the others. The knowledge of this and of the recurring Neros, would be quite enough to have given to a fraternity like the Chaldæans the empire of the world, which, under one name or other, Brahmins, Magi, &c., they obtained. I am sometimes induced to ask, may not the ancients, availing themselves of this knowledge, have made up a system? But they cannot have made the equinox to precede neither more nor less than about 71¼ in a degree. They cannot have made the arrival of the comet, in its proper period, to have arrived exactly when the Sun entered Taurus at the equinox. According to our astronomers, they know all these matters perfectly—all the laws of gravitation are perfectly understood by them; but when I go back to the Ptolemaic system, I find its professors exactly like our present astronomers, foretelling the eclipses, &c., &c., and teaching that their system was demonstrated by the clearest proofs. Prudence tells me to recollect that there are some of these clearly demonstrated doctrines which are disputed by persons as clear-headed as any of themselves, though poh-pohed down with noise and clamour—Sir R. Phillips, Frend, &c.

The following are opinions in favour of Mr. Whiston's system, given by several astronomers of great eminence :

---

[1] See Morning Chronicle, Sep. 1st, 1832.
[2] Mrs. Somerville says, "Its re-appearance in the years 1825, 1828, and 1832, accorded with the orbit assigned by M. Encke." *Connexion of the Physical Sciences*, p. 380, 2nd edit. It seems, therefore, that the Astronomers were not disappointed. *Ed.*

14. On Mr. Whiston's theory that a comet may have caused the flood, Dr. Gregory says,[1] "Alius etiam erit quandoque cometæ sive effectus sive usus : si nempe cometa prope planetam transeat, (ita ferentibus eorum orbitis et motibus,) hunc ita attrahet ut ejus orbita immutetur, (mutata etiam ex mutua actione cometæ orbita,) unde planetæ periodus etiam mutabitur. Sed et satellitem ita per attractionem deturbare poterit cometa, ut, relicto suo primario, ipse evadat primarius, circa solem deinceps rotatus. Præterea, mutationes multo maximas in ipso planetæ globo producere poterit, non solum prolectando fluidum, si quod sit, sed per alias etiam qualitates ; si v. g. corpus tam vastum, et, si ex solis vicinia prodeat, ignitum, tellurem nostram è propinquo prætervehatur." On Mr. Whiston's theory Dr. Halley says,[2] "Inter omnes nullus priore appulsu terris minatus est quam ille anni 1680. Hic inito calculo non amplius ad Boream distabat ab orbe nostro annuo quam semidiametro solari, (sive radio lunaris orbitæ, uti existimo,) idque Novemb. 11° 1ʰ 6′ P. M. Quo tempore, si terræ quoad longitudinem conjunctus fuisset, parallaxis sane lunari æqualis in cometæ motu observari potuisset. Hæc astronomis dicta sunto ; quæ vero ab hujusmodi allapsu vel contactu, vel denique collisione corporum cœlestium (quæ quidem omnino non impossibilis est) consequi debeant; rerum physicarum studiosis discutienda relinquo."

15. Dr. Keill, who was an adversary of Mr. Whiston's work and doctrines, gives the following testimony: "I cannot but acknowledge that the author of the New Theory of the Earth has made greater discoveries, and proceeded on more philosophical principles, than all the theorists before him have done. In his Theory there are some very strange coincidents, which make it indeed probable, that a comet at the time of the deluge passed by the earth. It is surprising to observe the exact correspondence between the lunar and solar year, upon the supposition of a circular orbit, in which the earth moved before the deluge. It cannot but raise admiration in us, when we consider, that the earth at the time of the deluge was in its perihelion, which would be the necessary effect of a comet that passed by at that time, in drawing it from a circular to an elliptical orbit. This, together with the consideration that the moon was exactly in such a place of its orbit at that time, as equally attracted with the earth, when the comet passed by, seems to be a convincing argument that a comet really came very near, and passed by the earth, on the day the deluge began."[3]

16. But I must dwell a little longer on this subject. Whiston undertakes to prove, except the comet of 575½ years, "(1.) That no other of the *known* comets could pass by the earth at the beginning of the deluge.[4] (2.) That this comet was of the same bigness with that which passed by at that time. (3.) That its orbit was then in a due position to pass by at that time. (4.) That its descending node was then also in a due position for the same passage by. (5.) That its period exactly agrees to the same time; or, in short, that all the known circumstances of this comet do correspond, and that it actually passed by on or about that very year, and on or about that very day of the year, when the deluge began."[5]

I do not pretend to answer for the validity of the proof of *all* the other matters which Mr. Whiston professes to have proved; but I believe it will not be denied he has proved, that the comet of 1680 has a period of about 575 years, and was seen 44 years B. C.; and it is of great importance to observe, that the learned Dr. Keill appears to have examined, and to have admitted the truth of, the part of Mr. Whiston's theory the most essential to my system. Then, if the

---

[1] Gregory's Astron. p. 481, apud Whiston's Theory, p. 443.
[2] Act. Philosoph. pp. 1898, 1899, No. 297, apud Whiston's Theory, p. 444.   [3] Whiston's Theory, p. 445.
[4] He means in 2926.   [5] New Theory, p. 188.

reader admit this, and calculate backwards, he will find that the comet must have come, as I have already remarked, in its 4th revolution B. C., in the year 2349, and its 5th revolution, which Whiston says was the year of the flood according to *the more correct chronology*, in the year 2926. Now, it is very remarkable that the year 2348, the year allotted to the flood by Usher, Blair, &c., is not very far, viz. 172 years, from 2520 B. C., the period of the real entrance of the Sun into Aries at the Vernal Equinox, and the date of the flood as held by the modern Brahmins, when an error into which they have fallen of 576 years is corrected, and which I shall account for and explain. Every one must confess the confused state of the history of the Hebrews. This being admitted, I have no hesitation in saying, that if Mr. Whiston be correct in his calculations, which I cannot controvert, but of which I do not profess myself to be a judge, the flood must have taken place really in the year B. C. 2926. Had it not been for the high character which Mr. Whiston bears as an astronomer and mathematician, and the admission of his learned opponent Dr. Keill, I should, of course, have fixed its arrival to that year in which our chronologers fix the flood, viz. 2348 B. C. Mr. Whiston appears to me, but I do not profess to be a judge of his difficult astronomical reasoning, to have proved that the comet of 1680 must have come so near the earth in the year 2926 as to have necessarily caused some mighty effect, and this could be nothing but a flood. It is a striking circumstance that the 4th and 5th periods of the comet should fall, one on the corrected chronology of Whiston, the other on the chronology of the Jews, according to Usher. It looks very much as if chronology had been accommodated to one of them, by persons believing that the flood was caused by the comet, but by persons not knowing correctly in which period it had happened. It is also very remarkable that the period of what Whiston calls the corrected chronology of the flood, 2926, should be so very near the 3100, which the Brahmins now commonly fix for it. The result of the whole appears to be, that the Brahmins have had a mistaken tradition that the flood took place when the Sun entered Aries, at the Vernal Equinox, and that this has misled them. But I beg leave to suggest to astronomers, whether the comet may not have caused a *first* flood at the entrance of the Sun into Taurus about 4650 years B. C., and again the flood of Noah in 2926, and have come sufficiently near in 2348 to have caused another and a still less flood. We know so little of comets, that I think astronomers cannot safely assert that this may not have happened. We really know nothing except the *periods* of this comet and of some few others, and that their orbits are elliptical. If astronomers say that the effects alluded to could not have been produced by the comet of 575½ years' period, because the earth would not be at those times in a proper situation to receive the influence of it, they presume that it must have always moved in the same plane as that in which it now moves, and that, in other respects, it must have been subject to similar laws. I think it is much more probable that the comet may be subject to some law unknown to us, which keeping its period, brought it in collision with the earth at the times required by my hypothesis, than that the coincidences adduced should be the effect of accident. The doctrine of probabilities, I am persuaded, would shew monstrous odds against both accident and the infallible knowledge of our astronomers, and in favour of the hypotheses, that one or more floods have been caused by this comet, and also, that its period and influence were understood by the ancients. I think we have three well-marked floods; the last is the flood of Deucalion, or the Deus-Cali or holy Cali, and it took place 2348 years before Christ. The preceding one was really our flood of Noah, and it took place, as pointed out by Mr. Whiston, 2926 B. C.; and the first, or the flood of Ogyges, took place 4648 years B. C. This, perhaps, might be the flood which threw up Mont Blanc, Chimborazo, &c. The last mentioned year, 4648, was the time of the entrance of the Sun into Taurus: but I think the middle flood, in 2926, was that which altered the axis of the earth. The account in Genesis is a most valuable record of the tradition; but this is all that it is. The record of the tradition is for the philosophers, the detail for the rabble. It is for the man of science and for the philosopher to distinguish one from the other. This was formerly done in the mysteries. Mysteries are now out of fashion; the race of man has outgrown them; and all the secrets are already or must be soon laid open. Man must be treated like a rational being. Whether when so treated he will act like one, God alone knows. I fear for him; for I see his folly every where—I see his wisdom only now and then. I know what I have said on the subject of comets will be turned into ridicule by some of my brethren of the Astronomical Society; but I believe learned men are as liable to follies as other people. I have not forgotten that the truth of the Aristotelian philosophy was as little doubted for many generations, and its truth held to be as clearly proved by men of the first talent in the world, as the Newtonian is now. And this shews that learned men can dogmatise without any foundation in truth for their dogmas. If we want a proof of the folly of a learned man, we have only to go to the works of the great NEWTON, now in the custody of Lord Portsmouth. It would be no difficult matter to make a collection of the follies of the *wise*, which should exceed all other exhibitions of folly. I do not advance this with the intention of stigmatizing our present learned astronomers as foolish, but I most assuredly wish to repress that feeling of perfect certainty which leads to dogmatism, and to tell them, that they are liable to be mistaken like their predecessors and the remainder of mankind; and that they sometimes assume too much on the *certainty* of what they call demonstration, when that demonstration depends on theoretical or analogical reasoning, not confirmed by experience. In such cases I contend that they can assume nothing more than a high probability.

17. A gentleman of the name of Arago lately published a learned History of Comets; but although he ridicules Mr. Whiston, calling him *poor* Whiston,[1] yet he is not able to advance a single valid or plausible argument against Mr. Whiston's Theory, *as far as it is adopted by me.*[2] His argument to prove that the comet would not have the effect of producing a great tide, because it would pass by the earth (which he allows that it would do so near as twelve thousand miles) with great *rapidity*, is by no means conclusive against its causing one great instantaneous tide or rush of waters from the deep, and from all parts, to the side next to itself, and of course of a rush back again as soon as the moving cause was withdrawn, and probably of several oscillating waves. This is quite enough to cause the destruction of most of mankind, leaving the countries in a great measure as they were before; and this is much more consistent with the actual escape of many of the inhabitants, than from a long-continued flood, and it is quite enough to furnish the ground for the mythos of Noah, taking all the animals into the Ark, &c., &c. M. Arrago's treatise was written by direction of the French government to calm the fears of the people of Paris, and to satisfy them that there was no danger to be apprehended from the comet which was expected last year [1832].[3] Let us now speculate briefly upon the traditions which have come down to us. Suppose, instead of knowing that the comet would *not* come, our astronomers had known that it *would* come, and that they had been dwelling in Asia, as I suppose the ancients dwelling in Asia knew of the coming of the comet of 2920; is it absurd to suppose that the learned in the *secret science*, spoken of by Enoch, should have betaken themselves to the highest mountains of their country, should have built a ship, should have fastened it to the side of a mountain opposite to that in the direction in which the flood was expected to come, with a long cable, to let it rise as the water rose, and that this mountain should, from this circumstance, have acquired in later times the name of Naubanda or ship-cabled-mount? If I am not mistaken we are most of us in the

---

[1] Preface, p. ix.

[2] He confirms what I stated in the Appendix to my first volume, pp. 829, 830, respecting the Caspian sea, and shews that the depression is much greater and more extraordinary than I have represented it. It appears that the Caspian sea is nothing but an immense chasm into which the Volga discharges itself.

[3] Did not M. Arago's treatise on these *fears* apply especially to *Biela's* comet? This did appear in 1832. *Ed.*

habit of believing much more improbable things than this. Is it absurd to suppose that the people in possession of power at that time should take care of themselves, should do as the governors of Paris did last year, in their endeavours to calm the fears of the inhabitants, and secrete from them their danger? Is it absurd to suppose that they would be careful about their own security by fleeing to the highest mountain and providing their great floating house and fastening it to Naubanda? We are told, in substance, that, by calculation, they knew that a great catastrophe would happen to the earth; and we know, by astronomical calculation, that the comet which alone was capable of effecting any catastrophe did come. I should think, that persons who believe the Tο Ον walked in the garden, ought not to find a difficulty in believing this history. I ask my reader no belief in any miracle—in any thing contrary to the laws of nature, to reason or probability. I ask of my reader, only to treat the histories of Genesis and of Enoch as Niebuhr does the history of Rome, and as every reader does the history of Vespasian by Tacitus—that is, to believe the *credible* and to disbelieve the *incredible*. It is perfectly clear to me that before the time of Herodotus every history was a mythos or mystery or sacred history, the intention of which was to *perpetuate*, but to *conceal* the truth, to mean one thing, and to say another, that the mass of mankind *seeing might not perceive*, and *hearing might not understand*. We are told so in the Gospel. What more would we have? I beg my reader to reflect upon the admitted fact, that the comet of 1770 [1] [Lexel's] was retarded in its course by coming within the reach of the influence of Jupiter,[2] and upon the discovery of the asteroids in the vacant space where astronomers had long observed that a planet was wanting. In the latter case, as well as in the former, the probability cannot be denied, that an extrinsic force has been in operation, or that one body has operated on another. And surely no body is so likely as some kind of a comet, in a similar manner, to have caused a deluge on our earth at the time recorded. If there be waters on the planet Jupiter, I can have no doubt that they must have been greatly affected by the approach of the comet of 1770. Nothing is more likely than that, as changes took place in the motions of the comet of 1770, as described by M. Arago, the causes of which were not for a long time understood by our astronomers, so causes which may not be known to us may have operated on the comet of 575 years to cause it to affect the earth at the three times I have pointed out, and not either in the intermediate times of its return or since the year of the Hebrew flood, B. C. 2040.

18. At first sight it appears probable, that if a comet should be materially deflected from the plane of its orbit by any cause, its period also would be materially changed, and we know that it may be deflected since that of Lexel was twice deflected from the disturbance of Jupiter; but still we cannot be certain that its period *will* be much altered. As the orbit of Lexel's comet was first inflected towards the earth, by its approach to Jupiter, and again deflected from it by the same cause, so the comet of 1680 may have been so disturbed, in some way unknown to us, as to bring it three times to operate upon our earth, and this operation to be such as not materially to alter its period. I make this observation in reply to any objection which may be urged that, from calculation, it is known that the earth could not have been in such a part of its orbit as to have come into collision with the comet when it arrived. But I think the question will be one of probability, viz. is it more probable that our astronomers are in error or in ignorance, than *first*, that the coming of the comet should coincide with my theory of the entrance of the Sun into Taurus, at the Vernal Equinox, and *secondly*, with the beginning of my system, and *thirdly* and *fourthly*, with the two periods of the Samaritan computation and the Hebrew computation of the flood? I say, is it probable that all these events should coincide and fall out right, by accident? Is it

---

[1] See Arago, p. 22.
[2] See supra, p. 138, where the Author had left the date of the comet—of 1770—blank. *Ed.*

not more probable that the astronomers are ignorant, than that all the four events have occurred in a way suited to support my theory, by accident? It appears to me to be probable, that the fears of mankind, from the expected day of judgment and the termination of the millenium, may have been increased by the expectation, among such men as Roger Bacon, of the return of Cæsar's comet, or of the comet of 1680, in the twelfth century, but of the time of whose arrival they could not be certain, in consequence of their ignorance of what disturbing forces might operate upon it; but the existence of which disturbing forces such men as Roger Bacon might have readily had handed down to them, from Sosigenes and the Chaldæans who corrected the calendar for Cæsar.

19. No person, I think, looks at the question of the genuineness of Genesis correctly, or takes a correct view of the character of that book. It is very clear that it is in substance to be found, whether mythos or not, in almost every country, and that, as might be expected, the priests and people have accommodated it to their own purposes. It is impossible to deny that, stripping it of its nonsense, (which is a sort of thing found in every ancient history,) as we should strip the history of Vespasian of its miracles, the evidence is decidedly in favour of its authenticity. I contend that it is highly probable that a flood did take place, and that a man and his family were saved in a ship. If this were not the fact, then there must have been an universal mythos, or there must have been the fact, and it must have been accommodated to the universal mythos. That is, there must have been both true history and mythos. The peculiarity of the coincidences of the comet and the Mosaic chronology of the flood, almost put the fact of the *man saved* out of doubt. The strong proofs of the actual division of the world into three, and of its having been ruled by three potentates under one, as a supreme head, cannot be denied. It is quite impossible that so many traces of this system should remain without its having once existed. Ever since the Christian æra all accounts of countries and their inhabitants have been written by persons strongly prejudiced in favour of the modern date of the present system. The consequence has been, that they have generally left out or omitted to notice any thing which had a connexion with, or which would have shewn, the Christian or Judæan mythos. They believed all such matters to be merely modern, and only noticed such as appeared to them to have no connexion with the mythos. Hence, by degrees, almost every thing which could have shewn the universal system to have existed previous to the reputed time of Christ has disappeared. I am surprised that we have *so much* left, not that we have *so little*. In all our speculations and inquiries we have scarcely ever gone to *perfect accuracy*, so as to take in the consideration of fractions. Now a moment's reflection on the way in which the comets were connected with the system will shew the wisdom of this proceeding. For it is the very acme of absurd credulity to believe that a comet would throw the earth out of its proper plane and not cause some disturbance in the regularity of its period. That is, that its period should not be at least a little hastened or retarded at the time of the change. But by taking the calculations in whole numbers allowance is made for this, and no inconvenience can ever arise from it; as, for example, in calculating the precession by 72 years for a degree or day, there must be always room left to allow for the disturbance, necessarily unknown in quantity.

20. I apprehend that, in the primeval state of our system, the sun was in the centre, and the planetary bodies revolved around it in the same plane in concentric circles, in equal times, in the most perfect harmony and order, and that, including the earth, the primary planets were eight in number,—one probably being now split into the four new ones, called *Asteroids*. The system would then be very like a wheel; and exactly answer to the Mercavah or wheel of Ezekiel, which I shall notice presently. I see around me the ruins of a world. How is this? Can it be believed that the work of Wisdom is to go to decay? No, indeed! this I cannot believe. I must, therefore, form some theory to account for these ruins—to render them consistent with Omnipotent

Wisdom. I suppose that the comets may be the agents which have already effected great changes in all the planets, and that they may be destined to effect many others—till, in defined periods, the planets, by means of these agents, may be all reduced to a state of fusion or gas, and be at last reabsorbed into the To Ov, or be renewed again in some way unknown to us—in some way not to be understood by our limited faculties.

21. I know that in the following observations, (a digression from my subject,) which I will take the liberty to make, I shall venture upon very slippery ground; and, therefore, I beg they may be considered to be only conditional, and more for the sake of argument than for the delivery of an opinion. But before I proceed, I would observe to such philosophers as believe the universe or matter to be God, that if they be right, *he* must exist in his *more* refined, as well as in his *less* refined state; then my argument will apply. To such philosophers as think that the universe is *idea*, and does not exist in *reality*, I do not at present address myself. Gas is defined, *a substance reduced to the state of an aeriform fluid by its permanent combination with caloric*.[1] Then, pray what was it before it combined with caloric? Was it hydrogen? This Gas, I think, is what the ancient materialists (and all the fathers and Moses were materialists) considered to be the substance of the First Cause. I am forcibly impressed with the idea that the substance which we call *hydrogen*, by which is meant a substance which is the base of both *water* and *fire*, constituted that which the ancients called *spiritual fire*, and that from this arise the apparent contradictions in the designations of water, fire, and air, as the origin of things—for air the third (gas) is the first product, perhaps, of the union of the two former. Then in what will hydrogen differ from the To Ov? It is not *water*, though the base of water,—it is not *fire*, though the base of fire. It is not *air*, though air or gas arises from the union of its two products—shall I say, from the union of the *two emanations* from it? But here we may perceive the coporeal trinity of Plato. Whence came the baptism of water, fire, and air? From the FIRST (the To Ov, Illusion) emanated the base of hydrogen, which base was Maia; from Maia, or the base of hydrogen, emanated hydrogen, the base of *fire* and *water*. These first three constituted the first Trinity. From these, three in one, emanated the next Trinity, consisting of fire, water, air or gas, in their most refined forms—three in one, one in three—and from these emanated all beings in existence known to us,—all the beings of this our world, perhaps of the universe, perceptible by us. All this is ancient doctrine only put into *modern words*—Gas and Hydrogen: it is the doctrine of Macrobius. I greatly suspect that the electric, the galvanic, the magnetic, fluids and hydrogen, are all one substance; that the first *three* are *one*, is, I believe, a doctrine now scarcely doubted. Every thing in nature was supposed to be microcosmic: thus the second Trinity was a microcosm of the first. And now we come to the most refined of all refinements. As the hypostatic universe was a microcosm of the IMMENSE To Ov, so the minutest animalcule imaginable was a microcosm of the one above it: and thus, when we get to the least particle perceptible by sense, or even in imagination, how can we imagine any thing of this kind but by a circle, symbolised by a snake, with the tail in its mouth? What were the *second* and *third* of the first Trinity, but a picture, a reflection in a mirror, an idea, of the universe? All nature was a chain of trinities: the *third* person of the *first*, was the *first* person of the *second*; and so on, *ad infinitum*. Thus all nature was God; thus God was nature. Thus all matter at last was supposed to be resolved into the To Ov, and thus to be eternal. All nature was a ladder or a chain, the ladder of Jacob, with its 72 angels or æons, each a step, I doubt not—a ladder αιων των αιωνων, revolving like the period or number 432 for millions of millions of years. Saga, Xaca, and Saca, all most clearly mean Wisdom. The Isis of

---

[1] Webster's Dictionary.

BOOK V. CHAPTER I. SECTION 21.

Egypt was called Neith or Wisdom. סך sk in Hebrew means *a veil*, in Greek ΣΗΚΟΣ (very like Saca;. When the inscription says, *No one shall draw aside my veil*, does it mean, that no one shall explain my cabalistic doctrine of divine Wisdom ? This Wisdom was the second person of the Trinity—the Logos—the Saviour; and was constantly called *self-existent*. This is the Isa and Ma-hesa of India, the Hesus of Gaul, and שׁ *is, he is, profound wisdom*, and ישׁה *ise, existence*, ישׁע *iso, salvation*, and *Saviour*, of the Hebrews. From this came the Σωζω *to save* of Greece.

Faustus says, "Nos Patris quidem Dei Omnipotentis, et Christi Filii ejus et Spiritûs Sancti, "*unum idemque* sub triplici appellatione colimus Numen. Sed Patrem quidem ipsum LUCEM " incolere credimus SUMMAM AC PRINCIPALEM, ... Filium in hac secunda ac visibili luce con- " sistere; qui quoniam sit et ipse geminus, ... virtutem quidem ejus in SOLE habitare credi- " mus, sapientiam vero in LUNA: necnon et Spiritûs Sancti, qui est majestas tertia, AERIS hunc " omnem ambitum sedem fatemur ac diversorium ; cujus ex viribus ac spiritali profusione terram " quoque concipientem gignere patibilem Jesum."[1] When I recollect that Wisdom is the second person of the Trinity, that Isis and Neith are Wisdom, I think I can, from the above passage, discover how Isis became identified with the moon, and why the moon constantly bore the same name as the female, or rather androgynous, generative power. I think we may here also discover how the Holy Ghost or *third* person of the Trinity, came to be described as *breath* or *air in motion*, which we have never been able to ascertain before. I think it is probable that the Indians considered air in its most attenuated state, or hydrogen, or some similar fluid, to fill all space; and it seems not improbable, when we consider how their refined igneous matter was always combined with air, that they understood what we call *hydrogen*. However, whether or not they understood what we call hydrogen, they certainly understood that there was a principle of water, fire, and air, which answers to all our properties of hydrogen, and this they called Gas or Gast or Ghost.[2] But still I think they considered this gas to be the same as the electric and magnetic fluids. The Christians of the present day, almost all of whose minds are enfeebled by the prejudices of education, look upon the Brahmins and their learning and religion with contempt. These feelings they have inherited from the Greeks and Romans; but let me remind them of what the Brahmins say to this. They say, and say truly, that in their Vedas may be found all the logic of Aristotle and the philosophy of Plato, and that among their sectaries may be found the doctrines of Epicurus and of the Stoics; that it is no more just to run them down on account of the corruptions into which their religion has fallen, and the state of degradation into which their order has been reduced by foreigners' conquering their country, than it is to make the same charges against the religion and philosophy of the Western nations, on account of the corruptions of the Greek and Latin churches, and the present neglect of the philosophy of Plato, Epicurus, or Zeno ; that philosophers of these sects are to be found occasionally in India as in Europe; that, if we have our Spinoza, &c., they have their Vyasa; that with regard to religion, we have no right to say a word; that ours is radically the same as theirs, only that we have in some measure corrupted it, and have forgotten or lost its first principles which they, with all their misfortunes, have retained ; that our divine incarnation is the same as theirs; that, if the modern corruptions of the East and of the West be carefully taken from the two religions, they will be found to be identical—our Christ, their Cristna. These seem to me to be asseverations not easy to refute, as our missionaries know full well, and of their truth as far as concerns religion, the person who has carefully read the preceding part of this work must be very well qualified to form an opinion. The truth of the funda-

---

[1] Georg. Alph. Tib. pp. 278, 279.

[2] Which our Celtic ancestors invoked by the name of Iaye, Ghest, to preside over their Wittagemote.

mental principles of the religion, I think, every person who admits the existence of a God will allow, to be not improbable. Is not God the creator our preserver, and the regenerator of all nature? Does not every cycle and period return according to his divine law at its appointed time? What shall I say of inspiration? If a person feel a strong inclination to do a good act, is it very much out of the way to attribute it to the influence of divine goodness? If this be not divine inspiration, or if divine inspiration be not this, shall we have recourse to the learned Parkhurst and make it to be *air in motion?* (This may suit a narrow-minded priesthood, but the world has nearly outgrown it.) If this be not divine inspiration, shall we make a substance of it, and incarnate it? What is a divine incarnation, but a person endowed with more than a usual portion of the divine *spirit?* What, at last, is this, but a person having a more than common inclination to benefit his fellow-creatures? And if the *wind in motion* be given up, to this it must return—into this and into nothing but this, it will at last be resolved. Thus when religions are stripped of their grosser parts, they nearly resolve themselves into one. What, it may be asked, do you make of the renewal of worlds, and of the metempsychosis? I see nothing improbable or contrary to divine goodness in the renewal of worlds. The late discoveries of Laplace, and many other circumstances, give probability to the theory; and with respect to the metempsychosis, before it can be denied, many matters must be premised, which are of a nature attended with the greatest difficulty. Has man a soul? What is the soul? Is it substance or spirit? What is spirit? What is substance? Are not all these questions beyond the reach of the present human understanding? What is identity? Is man the same *to-day* that he was *twenty years ago?* He may as readily have existed in a former period and not be conscious of it, as he exists now and is unconscious of multitudes of things which happened to him twenty years ago. Thus we have a crowd of questions and difficulties which I shall not attempt here to resolve—questions to answer and difficulties to resolve, each of which have already, in vain, had hundreds of volumes lavished upon them.

22. We will now return to our subject. The circumstance that the year of the return of the comet, and the year of the flood according to Moses, should exactly coincide, raises a strong probability that a great deluge did take place at the time stated by Moses, and that it was effected by the agency of the comet. The testimony of all nations, that a flood did take place, strengthens the probability. Again, the appearance of the surface of the globe, as stated by Cuvier, tends to confirm it. Again, the testimony of Varro, respecting the flood of Ogyges, that it agreed in date with that of Moses, tends to confirm it. The union of these circumstances raises a probability that a deluge did take place at one of the two times stated—at one of the two approaches of the comet in its orbit, too strong to be shaken by any theories or mathematical calculations of philosophers at this day respecting the planetary motions, because it is impossible for them to know certainly how the cause would operate upon a system so different as our present one is from what it must have been formerly, before the catastrophe happened. The reasonings of philosophers can lead them to nothing more than a probability, and the final result of the two can only be probability against probability—and the question will rise, which is the stronger? But if the mathematical reasonings of philosophers should bring out a result favourable to the assertions or traditions of Moses and Varro and Whiston, then the probability will rise almost to certainty, indeed, as near certainty as can be expected in matters of this kind. A great catastrophe no one can deny. In fact, no one can deny several catastrophes. There is nothing, under all the circumstances, improbable in the doctrine, that there may have been two, or even more, of different degrees of magnitude, since the creation of man. It is not conclusive against the flood of Moses and Varro being at the time they name, or of its being effected by the comet of 1680, that its present motions, as now calculated by astronomers, if they should be so calculated, do not shew it would come into contact with the earth at that time; because it is very possible, that the concussion which

then happened may have caused its motions to be very different from what they now are: it may, after the great concussion of the bodies, have come into its present situation, and its habits of moving too, by degrees: if it be only moderately near, it is quite enough. If all the planets before this catastrophe moved in perfect order—all in their respective orbits, but all constantly in conjunction, and in one plane, it is possible that the same comet may have disarranged them all, and thrown the whole system into what appears to be disorder, at the same time. Every thing seems to shew periodical destruction and regeneration. What can be more probable than that comets should be the agents of these effects? Although the comet may not move in the same plane with the planets at this time, it may have done so before the concussion, or it may have come into the same plane by degrees, being previously ordained to do so, for the purpose of effecting great objects or changes. Although the present state of the system seems to shew disorder, it is probably only temporary or periodical, and all may return to order again. Ancient tradition and improved modern reason both support the probability of this doctrine. But in all this I contend, that I come as nea the truth, or certainty, as the astronomers do; only *I* do not come so near dogmatical assertion.

23. At first persons will wonder how any one could *believe* that, in every six hundred years, a space of time so short, the history of the world could be renewed; that new Argonautic expeditions, new Trojan wars, &c., could be re-enacted—a belief at first sight so absurd and so palpably repugnant to all historical experience. But I think this superannuated dogma passed down the stream of time, like other superannuated dogmas which, in our times, may be pointed out: the Millenium for instance. It was, like the Millenium, almost obsolete; partly believed, partly disbelieved—believed by some of the vulgar, despised by the enlightened. Like the Millenium, it was sought for every where, and its falsity, which was proved from facts, was attempted to be explained away. Before the invention of letters, there is no difficulty in accounting for the belief; the difficulty only arises afterward. This belief arose from natural causes. If we carefully examine the state of man before the invention of writing, we shall find that his memory would not reach even to half a neros, or to 300 years. Let us think of our grandfathers, great-grandfathers, and great-great-grandfathers, giving them forty years each. What do we know of them? What should we now know of them had we not possessed the art of writing and ciphering? No man who thinks deeply upon this will be surprised at a popular belief prevailing, that the same mischief would happen to *new* Troy, Rome, which had happened to *old* Troy, before the expected Great One would arrive at the end of the cycle, in thirty or forty years' time. And when Virgil wrote his 4th Eclogue, that was thought or feared by the vulgar to be the course of events. When the T. S. R. or Cæsar was really believed to have arrived, that part of the mythos, it would be said and thought, had been misunderstood before, as our devotees say the time of the Millenium was misunderstood formerly by those who expected it at the end of the first 600 years of our æra. This ought to have taught the fools wisdom. Are fools ever taught wisdom? When folly is once taught, it is very difficult to unteach it. I beg my reader to refer to what I have said, in pp. 262 —268, 330, respecting the origin of Deans and Chapters, and the whole of the Feudal system, and to observe the absolute darkness in which it is all involved, in an age thousands of years after the discovery of the art of writing. When he has done this, he will not be surprised at the ignorance of mankind before the art of writing was discovered, or if discovered, while it was kept a profound secret. Almost the moment the art of ciphering was found out, attempts would be made to make use of it to remedy the inconvenience which I have just mentioned. The first use would be to perpetuate the cycles or to register time, to perpetuate the knowledge on these subjects which, up to that time, had been acquired. In fact, to seize firmly and to secure that knowledge, that it should not, like other knowledge, escape them, of which they must have had daily experience, by

locating it in memorials as imperishable as possible; and this we find in the number of the stones in the stone circles, and probably in the stones of Carnac, to which a stone was added every year to record the time of the world, like the nails driven at Rome and in the Etruscan temple of Nurtia:[1] The next contrivance would be that of putting words into numbers. For though man could not write in syllables, it is very clear he must always, after he had obtained any skill in speaking, have spoken in syllabic words, and almost at the same time in which he learned to speak in them, he would learn the art of making rhymes, or composing lines ending in similar sounds. We have the first account of this in the poet Olen at Delphi,[2] and in the twenty thousand verses which the Druids of Britain caused their pupils to repeat. These were the first attempts to perpetuate facts. The very nature of them confined them to a caste or class, and made them secret and sacred. The next thing having the same object in view was to sing these lines or rhymes to a tune; and hence arose music. Hence arose the chaunting of Liturgies. Hence arose national songs. Hence arose among the priests an order or class of Bards, Muses, or Singers, singing or chaunting their Musas—singing or chaunting their doctrines or praises of the incarnate wisdom ;[3] books of Wisdom, or of Buddhas, in process of time, by the regimine, becoming books called Vedahs, or the books of the prophets. The vedahs are never *read* but *sung*. This is to prevent them from being corrupted.[4] After a mythos or history of a person was once established, the recollection of which was an object to be desired, it was, as I have just observed, made into a song, and sung or recited. After some time instrumental music was added: again, in time, action was added, and by degrees more persons than one were employed. Thus dialogue commenced, a chorus was adopted to make the matter more intelligible to the audience, and sacred theatres were built. It is difficult to imagine whether this preceded or followed the practice of making processions, or Deisuls, or voyages of salvation, through the districts of a country, where all the adventures of the person were acted—probably the infant exposed—the young man killed and resuscitated, &c., &c.,—a part of the adventures of the incarnate God performed each peculiar day, till the whole of his life and death was gone through every year. These were contrivances adopted to keep in remembrance the history or M-Istory before the art of writing by syllables, perhaps before the art of writing by numerals was discovered. For this purpose, after epic poems were invented, each poem was divided into twenty-four books, each book into a certain number of lines, each line into a certain number of words, and for this purpose also each syllable of each word was by practice fixed to be long or short, and each line was formed by a certain number of short and long syllables, placed in well-known order. Thus we have hexameters, pentameters, &c.

24. I have formerly said that there was originally one history, *that* history a mythos or a doctrine, and that the doctrine consisted of the arrival of a divine incarnation in each age, which the priests of each country persuaded the people must be renovated in their peculiar country, by exhibiting to them their former history, which, with a new cycle, would be renewed. The system of the renovation of cycles was an integral part of the mythos. The doctrine of the renewed incarnation is very distinctly visible in India, Persia, Syria, Greece, Italy, and even in China and Mexico. In consequence of the friendly intercourse which in the later times of antiquity existed among all nations with respect to their religious concerns, I am induced to believe that it was a part of the doctrine, that there might be more divine incarnations than one for each cycle—that more nations than one might be favoured with the interposition of the Deity in its behalf. I think if this had not been the case they would have quarrelled about them, which they no where did,

---

[1] See Vol. I. pp. 307, 476.   [2] See Celtic Druids, p. 121.
[3] The celebrators of the משה אש, by regimine, became themselves Musas.
[4] See Dr. Rosen's Translation of Parts of the First Veda.

until the secret meaning of the mythos was lost. However, whether one nation allowed another to have it or not, it is certain that each nation claimed to have it. Indeed, I have somewhere met with an account, that it is no unusual thing for the Brahmins to allow the truth of the divine incarnation of Jesus Christ. But they say, "You have had your divine incarnation, so have we. We do not deny yours, why should you deny ours?" "Ah! but" (we say) "our Christ was an incarnation of God himself, for the salvation of all who believe on him, proved by previous prophecies and by his miracles." "Very true;" (is the reply;) "we allow all you say. But our Christ-en or Christ-na was precisely the same for our salvation and the salvation of all mankind who believe on him, proved by previous prophecies and by his miracles." I imagine that this will be a very difficult argument to refute.[1] By representing to the people of Rome that its founder, Romulus, was descended from Troy—that he was deserted and saved from a tyrant, &c., &c., the priests could say to the people, "Is it not evident from this history, that you are a favoured nation, or one of the favoured nations?" On this account all histories were moulded to accommodate them to the mythos. This affords a satisfactory reason for all the histories being the same in some respects, and also for their having considerable differences. It also furnishes a satisfactory reason for each country having the same names of places. If it be said, that the tribes might have brought the names of places from the East, as our emigrants have carried our names of places to America, I reply, Not only are the names of places, but the mythos also, visible, where there are new names for the same thing. The indentity is much too extensive to be the unintentional produce of tribes merely settling. The system is uniform in all countries. The fact is, our emigrants take their sacreds, dedicate their churches to saints, &c., &c., and, if they yet had the Deisul, they would every where have had a sacred mount to perform it round, even in Australia. In every country which had any pretensions to have a *Saviour*, there was a Mount Meru or Olympus or Acropolis, with all its accompanying little superstitions. And all these places had secret and sacred names, probably not used in common life, until, by degrees, the secret came to be divulged to so many persons, that it was, in fact, no secret at all. What would the secrets of Masonry be, if every person in England was initiated? By degrees the mysteries became known, without its being perceived that they were divulged secrets; and it is clear that, if the initiated perceived they were their secrets divulged, they would, on no account, admit the fact; or at any rate they would conceal it if possible, and they would cease to be a part of their mysteries. We know that there were the greater and the less mysteries. In the less mysteries, the novice was admitted to only a certain portion of the mythos; to how much it is impossible to say. It is very clear that it was the establishment of the sect of the Christians—the sect of Paul—teaching the contradictory doctrine of a spiritual saviour, instead of a temporal one, but still of a human being actually crucified,[2] which caused nearly all the mysteries, remaining in Paul's day, to be lost *as mysteries*. A violent and furious sect of fanatics, like the modern Methodists, divided among themselves, but uniting upon certain great points, let out all the secrets of the temples, as far as in their power. Like Luther, they considered the breach of an oath or vow to be meritorious in a good cause. Under these circumstances the initiated who held to their vows could do nothing but abandon their mysteries altogether, and the celebration of them nearly ceased; but, as might be expected, we find them

---

[1] See, on the admissions of the Jesuits to the Brahmins, Vol. I. p. 560.

[2] The Author probably meant by "a *spiritual* instead of a temporal Saviour" one who was really to save from ignorance, sin, and death, instead of a metaphorical one, who saves only as wily priests teach, and as the ignorant many believe. In teaching the doctrine of such "a spiritual Saviour" there was, surely, nothing "contradictory"! for, who but a *human being* could be *actually crucified?* Let those who profess to believe that "the Eternal God *died*" as the real "spiritual Saviour" reconcile the apparent contradiction. *Editor*.

rising again under the fostering hand of Clemens Alexandrinus and of the reviving hierarchy, as soon as the sect began to improve in character. How much secret doctrine Clemens and his school may have taught, we do not know; but we do know enough to see that it was, at least, a part, and the best and most beautiful part, of the ancient system. The early Paulite Christians consisted of nothing better than what constitutes our Ranters, Jumpers, and Speakers with Tongues, in Mr. Irving's chapels at this day.[1] This Mr. Gibbon has satisfactorily proved. This Paul's first epistle to the Corinthians proves. They dreamt of nothing but an immediate kingdom of King Jesus—a sort of temporal or spiritual, visible king upon earth, at Jerusalem. As time advanced and proved the erroneousness of this dream, and as the sect improved in character, as all sects do in proportion to the rate at which their passion cools, their leaders, by degrees, went back to the old system,—the old mysteries began to revive, and they shew themselves almost as soon as we find any thing written respecting them in Clemens Alexandrinus. But the whole system could never be revived, because that which had been revealed to the whole world could not be unrevealed, viz. for an example, the multitudes of similar histories of the Avatars, &c., &c. But although the similarity of the histories is sufficiently striking, now that they are pointed out, they do not seem ever to have been publicly observed by the ancients. The fact could scarcely have been unknown in the mysteries; but it is never named by any writer, whose works remain to us; which seems to shew, that it must have been, if observed at all, a part of the secret system. Whatever knowledge the priests could keep to themselves, they most studiously kept. In the Western world, in modern times, no ancient institution or order has remained by whom it might be kept, unless it be in the conclave; but when the Europeans arrived in India, all the learning which remained to the priests, from their ancestors, they kept from the Europeans, and from all their countrymen except their own caste, with the greatest care possible; and, in a great many instances, they continue to keep it. Thus, to the escape of the secret knowledge, we are indebted for the destruction of the rule of the priests. I have no doubt that the sacred order which ruled the world possessed all science, and possessed it in a very high degree of perfection. When land became scarce and food difficult to acquire, men would become quarrelsome: to suppress disorders hired men would be employed, and their commanders, by degrees, would quarrel with their superiors. Then science would begin to creep out, and the veneration for the order to abate, till its rule would at last be overturned. Many causes would unite to produce this effect.

25. We have formerly seen in Vol. I. p. 264, that the Cabala consisted of two branches, the Barasit and the Mercavah. The latter is the knowledge of what are called sublunary beings, and might also consist of the knowledge of what we call natural philosophy, astronomy, the periods of the planets, the science of letters, high arithmetic, algebra, geometry, and some other secrets described by Bacon, as noticed in Vol. I. p. 341, *note*. The other, I think, probably consisted of the knowledge of all the profound doctrines of the Trimurti and the secret use of the system of cycles,—the meaning of the sacred *Om* and the Το Ον, and of Theogony. The word Mercavah is said to mean a *chariot*, and to refer to the chariot as it is called of the first chapter of Ezekiel (verses 15—21). The word which gives occasion to this, or which is translated chariot, is אופן *aupn*, the root of which is said to be אפן *apn*, but for the meaning of which Mr. Parkhurst refers to the word פנה *pne*. This, with a mutable or omissible ה *e*, he says, means *to turn*, particularly applied to the turn or the return of a day, or, of course, a period. He says also, that אפן *apn* means *a wheel*. This is justified by the

---

[1] It will be said, perhaps, that there were Josephs of Arimathea—men of a higher class—among the early Christians. This is very true—there were men of learning and wealth, like Mr. Whitfield, Mr. Wesley, Mr. Halhed, and Mr. Irving; but what, if admitted, does it prove against the argument? John Wesley was a talented and learned man; yet he believed he had miracles performed upon himself every day! But what were his and Whitfield's early followers?

context of Ezekiel, which treats much of a mysterious wheel, and upon the four cardinal points of the compass by the names of the Man, the Lion, the Ox, and the Eagle—the Equinoxes and Solstices. The generality of Jews give the first word of Genesis, *Barasit*, the common meaning given to it by the Christians, and though the greatest and the most learned of their philosophers, Maimonides, acknowledges the meaning of the two words is lost, yet, without any hesitation, they will tell you, that Barasit means *cosmogony*, and Mercavah the *moral doctrine*—thus transposing the two. Very certain I am, that this is a complete inversion. How they can make the wheels within wheels apply to *morality* I know not; but they aptly apply to *the planets*. In short, one, the Mercavah, was the doctrine of natural philosophy; the other, Barasit, the doctrine of moral philosophy. Mercavah taught astronomy, the use of the cycles, the history of the flood, and the cometary and planetary system, chronology, the secret principle or riddle of the millenium, and the microcosm, which I shall explain by and by, and with which the power of the initiated was most intimately connected, and which was, whether true or not, thought necessary for the government of mankind. The Barasit taught the doctrine of wisdom, the nature and attributes of the To Ov, the doctrines of the metempsychosis, of emanation, and of the reabsorption of every one into the First Being, hastened or retarded according to his good or bad conduct in this life; in short, every thing connected with morality, and the duties of man to his Creator.

CHAPTER II.

CÆSAR.—ALEXANDER.—GENGIS KHAN.—AKBAR.—NAPOLEON.—SUPREME PONTIFF.—RACES OF MAN. BLACK GODS.—TRINITARIAN DOCTRINE OF GENESIS. JEWISH POLITY. PRIESTHOOD.—SUPREME PRIESTHOOD.

1. I SHALL now proceed to shew more fully, that there have been many persons who have aspired to be divine incarnations.—Buddha, Cristna, Salivahana, Moses, Cyrus, Alexander, Julius Cæsar, Gengis Khan, Timur, Mohamed, Gregory, and Hakem Bemrillah, were all believed to be divine incarnations, as well as Jesus Christ, each opening a new age. Few persons who have read this work will doubt that the word Cæsar[1] must have some mystical meaning, and that meaning connected with the mysterious system which I have developed. I think the word in the first numeral letters has been, as the Pope of Rome calls himself, $XP\Sigma=600$. Having found from St. Barnabas, that X means 300 as well as 400, and from the other circumstances which I need not repeat, that the last three letters R, S, T, had each two meanings in common, and also that the last letter of almost all the alphabets, the Tau, was written indiscriminately with a cross, in fact, in any form of a cross; considering also, that we find the doctrine of Wisdom, or rather of the incarnation of Wisdom, to have been the secret doctrine of all nations; remembering also, that we are told, it was a common practice with the mystics of all nations to insert the letter I, the name

---

[1] See Vol. I. pp. 617—620; and *supra*, p. 95.

of God, into words, for the sake of a mystery,—I think it probable that the word Cæsar is the Hebrew word Rst or Rasit ; or rather that, originally, the word Rasit has been X or T. Σ. P., read from right to left, TΣP., and that from this, the Tzr of Muscovy has, by a little corruption, been derived. It is not half so mystical as the nonsensical mysticism which we find, from the letter of Barnabas, and many other circumstances, really did prevail among the ancients. My mystery is in better style, and is not nonsensical. Ras is called the root of the Hebrew Rasit; but whence comes the *it* at the end of the word? I shall be answered, perhaps, that it is formative, or a letter is heemantive or paragogic—all hard words invented to conceal the ignorance of persons too vain to confess their ignorance. I believe the word Rasit is a corruption of R. S. T., and that it is the original of the word Cæsar, and Tzar, and ΧΡΗΣ—the *mitis* or *benignus* incarnation of every age—Pater futuri sæculi—αιων των αιωνων. The letters for gold, for the word peaceful or happy, and for the benignant being ΧΡΣ, were the same in the first language of numeral symbols, and meant ΡΣΤ, the triune cyclar God or Genius—first, perhaps, ΧΡΙΣΤΝ=666, ΞΡΕΣΤ=60+100+1+5+200+300=666, corrupted into Crost; next to ΧΡΣΝ=650; next to ΧΡΗΣ=608; and next, as it yet remains, to ΧΡΣ=600 or ΧΡ=600.[1] Every thing which I have said respecting the ΧΡΣ or Crest is confirmed by an observation of Bingham's in his Christian Antiquities, that the Christians were not called by that name till the time of Ambrose; they were previously called Christs—*anointed*.[2]

It would be surprising if we did not find the Trinity among the Romans, and we have it in the Capitolium, (and it is not only Trinitarian but Christian too,) in its three altars or shrines "to the three Gods," called Συνναιοι, or, as this word is expounded by Nimrod, *the dwellers together*, the Dii Magni Samothraces, Θεοι μεγαλοι, Θεοι δυνατοι, ΘΕΟΙ ΧΡΗΣΤΟΙ. Tertullian says, that the three altars in the Circus were sacred triuis Diis, magnis, potentibus, valentibus; eosdem Samothracias existimant."[3] These altars were to Jove, Apollo, and Minerva. The Θεος Χρησος shews us what was meant when it was said in one of the gospel histories that the Christ descended and united itself to Jesus, at his baptism, and that he was Jesus the Christ, i. e. the Crest. We are all educated at this day with the impression that the AMID or *desire of all nations* was to be an actual God, or a person of the Godhead, and in consequence we can scarcely understand the situation or the feelings of a person who only looked for a man like himself, but endowed with a superior degree of the divine attribute of wisdom. I think this prevents us from entering properly into the feelings, and making a proper allowance for the natural and almost necessary weakness, of men placed in such situations as Cyrus, Alexander, Cæsar, Alaric, Mohamed, and Gengis Khan. I am convinced that every one of these believed himself to be the foretold person ; in several instances they were generally believed to be so by their followers; and in several instances, also, I have no doubt, that this was the chief cause of their victories.[4] We will now re-

---

[1] Lately, in the Curiosa Miscellanea, I met with another monogram, of which the author, Mr. J. Munro, says, he was not able to get any explanation from the priests, except that it meant something mystical; it was XP. It was found in the catacombs of Rome, on Christian monuments; but he says it was in use among the ancients long before the time of Christ. I apprehend it is the Hebrew and Samaritan Tau=400 and the Resh=200, jointly 600. But it may be the Greek Rho, in which case it will confirm what I have before proved from the epistle of Barnabas, that the last three letters of the old alphabet had each two meanings. We must not forget that the Tau in these old languages was written in every form of the cross.—See Vol. I. pp. 222, 223.

[2] Psalm cv. 15; Bingham, Book I. p 7.

[3] Nimrod, (Vol. I. pp. 243, 244,) who refers to Serv. in Æn. lib. ii. vers. 225, 297, and Tertull. de Spectaculis, Vol. iv. ch. viii p. 117. Semler.

[4] I think in the latter part of the life of Napoleon some slight symptom of this disorder—this hallucination—this monomania, may be perceived in that extraordinary man; but more on this point presently.

turn to one circumstance of the mythos of Julius Cæsar, to which I think, in Volume I. pp. 616—620, I have not done sufficient justice. It has always been understood that his mother underwent the operation, from her, denominated Cæsarean, and that her son Julius was extracted from her side. Now, when I consider that it was clearly a part of the mythos, both of the East and West, of that mythos, in fact, alluded to by Virgil, that the expected one, *the desire of all nations*, was to be born from the side of his mother, and not in the usual course of nature,—and when I consider the extraordinary circumstance of the connexion of his mother with the God in the form of a serpent in the temple of Apollo, and the aphanasia[1] or darkness at his death, &c., &c., I cannot believe in the operation, or attribute to accident the story of Cæsar's unnatural birth. I recur to the doctrine of probability—and I contend, that, under all the circumstances, the probabilities are as a hundred to one, that the story is a made-up one, to advance the claim of Cæsar to the sovereignty of the world—to support his claim of right by the *book* as well as by the *sword*. But I think the contrivance of the Cæsarean operation conveys with it a proof, that, though the doctrine of an unnatural or preternatural birth was meant to be taught, it was meant to be kept a secret. The more I meditate upon the numerous proofs scattered over the whole earth, which I have detailed in the preceding books of this work, the more am I convinced that the χρηστηριον[2] was the cabalistic or secret doctrine of all ages. In Volume I. p. 618, I have treated of a kingdom of Cæsar expected by the Jews in North India. Why should they expect a Cæsar? We must recollect that we found Cæsars in India; and all the princes of the Persian dynasty, who were overthrown by the Saracens, were Khosrus, which word was but a corruption of the word Cæsars. The popular belief that *a great one was to come*, must have been greatly aided by the uncertainty of the periods, from the difficulty of keeping a correct register of time. I think it very possible that Sosigenes persuaded Julius Cæsar to correct the calendar, by shewing him that he was born, if its errors were corrected, and it were put right, at exactly the proper time. Without the slightest attempt at a plausible reason for such an opinion, we find it general among the Romans, that their city was to be the seat of universal empire, the mistress of the world, and to be eternal. I have no doubt that this popular opinion greatly assisted towards its own fulfilment, and that it influences many of the persons who now inhabit that city, of a rank far above the vulgar. I have very little doubt when a spiritual kingdom came into fashion in the time of Constantine, this superstition influenced him in giving up the possession of the city, and, along with it, the right of ruling by the Book, to the successor of St. Peter. Pompey affected the same right or claim as Cæsar. His name shews it. All the world was ripe for it. It necessarily carried it with the destruction of the Republic and the establishment of a despotism. It was the secret doctrine of the Chaldæans and the mysteries, that a great one should come about that time;—the learned as well as the unlearned fools, against Cicero, Brutus, and the Philosophers. The mythos is very evident in the twelve successive Cæsars, like the Lucumones and Imams of Ali. I am by no means certain that the triumvirate was not an imitation of the division of the world among the three sons of Noah, and the three Samothracian Gods, the Dii consortes, or Θεοι χρησοι, of whom I treated not long since—the division of the great world into three parts, in imitation of the division of the little *Ager Romanus* into three parts in former times. Varro[3] says, " Ager Romanus primum divisus " in partes tres, à quo tribus appellatæ: Tatientium, Rammensium, Lucerum nominatæ, ut ait " Ennius, Tatienses à Tatio, Rammenses à Romulo, Luceres, ut ait Junius, à Lucumone." I believe that not only numbers of conquerors have thought themselves Messiahs, but that their followers have thought them so too. Is it less like'y that Cæsar should have followers of this kind

---

[1] See Vol. I. p. 612. [2] See Vol. I. pp. 319, 585—588; 758, 759; 786—788. [3] De Lingua Latina, Lib. iv.

than Brothers and Southcote? When time has brought with it not an age of happiness, but, as usual, one of misery, conquerors have died away and been forgotten. This is beautifully exemplified in the temples, &c., &c., erected to Cæsar; and, again, in the history of Mohamed. Nimrod[1] describes Antony as filling the East with his debaucheries; he shews that Antony called " himself the new Bacchus, the husband of Minerva and the lineal descendant of Hercules." He adds, " This personage, besides being generally addicted to the literature of the East, dabbled par" ticularly in the mysteries of the Jews, and consulted their doctor Rabenu Hacadosh concerning " the cabala of the Tetragrammaton and of the numbers 12 and 42." I cannot help suspecting that the profligate triumvirate divided the world into three in compliance with this superstition. Nothing is more common than the union of superstition and profligacy. I am quite satisfied that the opinion generally prevailed, that the world was to be divided into three parts, one of which was to have supremacy over the other two. The account of Antony shews the same mythos. These great men, dazzled, like Antony and Julian, drunk with prosperity, were easily taught the secret doctrines, and that each, in his own person, was the *promised one*: hence all the casting of nativities, the calculating of pedigrees, and making of Janam-patri.[2] These men were of the highest order of Patres Conscripti or Lucumones, and any one of them might have been the lineal descendant of the first Japetus. I go so far as to suspect that, after the world was divided into three by them, their quarrel was for the nominal superiority.

2. If the reader refer to Volume I. pp. 380, 381, he will see an account of the immaculate conceptions of various great men, and among them, of Alexander the Great, whose father was Jupiter Ammon, in the form of a Dragon. By the Persian historians he is called Iscander, thus shewing that the Al is merely the emphatic article: then we have a compound of Arabic and Greek—the Arabic *Al*, and *Ischa*, (the latter the Arabic name of Jesus, meaning *the Saviour*, and of Sarah, the wife of Abraham, of Eva,) and Ανηρ or Ανδρος the Greek for *man*. Mirkond[3] says, that, " in the " Ionian language, Iskander signifies Aksheed Roos, that is, Filusúf: which word is abbreviated " from Fila Súfa: as the Ionians call *love* Filá, and *wisdom* Súfa; according to which etymology, " Iskander means, *A lover of wisdom*." That is, we may see among other matters, that he was of of the sect of the Sofees or the Gnosis. The Filá Súfa is nothing but Φιλος Σοφιας. He was sometimes called a Roomite.[4] He by force made himself master of *Ros-heng*[5] and married her. His mother is said to have been delivered of him on a journey, and to have exposed him to perish in a desert, where sheep were fed. An *ewe* came and suckled him. The shepherd's wife, following the ewe, found him and brought him up. After a time, as usual in all these cases, his mother discovered him, brought him to the king, his father, &c., &c., &c. Here we have the usual mythos. In the account of the great battle with Dárá or Darius, Mirkond says, "*the blood ascended* " *from the back of the terrestrial Fish, to the face of the celestial Pisces;*" and, again, " *Streams* " *descended and ascended to Earth-supporting Piscis.*"[6] (I refer my reader to Vol. I. pp. 558, 559, and 635—637.) Alexander was said to be born in the year 360 before Christ, the year the Sun entered Pisces, at the Vernal Equinox.[7] According to Mr. Shea's translation, Mirkond makes Alexander

---

[1] Vol. III. p. 422.   [2] See Vol. I. pp. 183, 249.   [3] Translation by Shea, p. 366.

[4] Upon this word I must refer to the Index of Vol. I. for what is said in several places under the words *Roma* and *Rama*. Does this refer to the island of Roma, in Lat. 7. 35., Lon. 127. 20., and point to Romelia or Roma of Asia Minor, or of Italy, or of Rama of Western Syria?

[5] Translation by Shea, p. 369.   [6] Ib. p. 391.

[7] The mother of Alexander is called by the Greeks Olympias. We all know how Mount Olympus is said to be the residence of the Gods, and that it is figuratively used for the heavens. The Persians call Olympias *Rukia*; (Translation

declare, again and again, that *his* is a religious war for the glory of God, and to display the true faith.[1] I believe the translation has suffered much from Mr. Shea's having yielded to the prejudice to which I have alluded in the latter end of the preface to the first volume. I believe Alexander alluded to his claim to the legal sovereignty of the world, as the head of the descendants of Noah. We must not forget that Clemens Alexandrinus was initiated into the mysteries of Eleusis, and he let out that he found the Mosaic mythos there; from this, probably, Alexander learned that the kings of Macedon, that is, of Scythia, were the descendants of Japetus, so well known to Grecian story. Mirkond makes the word Khizar to mean *a prophet*.[2] The account of the squinting and the ugliness of Alexander's face is curious.[3] This reminds me of what I quoted, supra, p. 31, respecting the *marred face* of the promised one, in Mexico, from Lord Kingsborough's work. Mirkond describes Alexander, also, as a prophet. He was an Emperor or Embratur; that is, Om-bra-tur, which word originally meant *the reformer*, ברא *bra*, of the Tauric cycle of Om. The name of Alexander, when dissected, betrays the mythos. In the East he is never called Al-exander, but the emphatic articl. *Al* is left out, and he is called Iskander or Ischander. This, as I have just said, is nothing but the Arabic *Al-Ischa, the Saviour*, the name of Jesus Christ, in Arabic, and the Greek ανηρ, ανδρος, *a man*—a Saviour man, or a Saviour incarnate. When I combine this with his immaculate conception, &c., I cannot doubt the correctness of this etymon. I think no one who reads Pownal's treatise on the Study of Antiquities, pp. 91, 92, can well doubt that, had Alexander lived to old age, he would have established the finest commercial empire in the world. His views seem to have been guided by the most liberal policy; and I have no doubt that his conquests were as much the effect of a general belief that he was the *promised one* as of his arms. We must not forget that he was said to be born in the year the vernal equinox ceased to be in Aries, and a new sign commenced, viz. 360 B. C.; and that he was the produce of a connexion between his mother and the God Apollo, in the temple. Alexander, like Moses, was said to be horned, and indeed I believe he appears with horns on some of his coins. This proves either that he claimed to be *a divine incarnation*, or the belief of his followers that he *was one*. But I think the *Ram's* horns must have been given him by persons who did not understand the mythos, for he was *Pisces*, which had nothing to do with horns. His name *Ischa*, in Irish Celtic, meant *a fish*, the same word which in Arabic meant *Saviour*. From the Pisces being the emblem of the Saviour, the word ischa came to mean *fish*.[4] The anxiety of the princes of India to be the founders of cycles was great. When this is considered, along with the universal dissemination of the mythos and the belief that Alexander was a *divine incarnation*, it will not be thought surprising to find he had his æra. He was, as I have just stated, said to be born 360 years B. C.; but his æra began in the year 312. We know that the æra of neither Christ nor Mohamed began on the day of his supposed birth. Buddha's æra, in India, we have seen, in Vol. I. p. 192, was probably his supposed death. If Alexander was born 360 years B. C., and 312 was the time of his death, it would make him 48 years old. The title of the æra is *Yanane*; it is on a Persic MS. of the Gospels, at Cambridge. I cannot doubt that this *Yanane* is a formation from the Sanscrit Jnana—the Ioannes—Oannes—or the Fish of Assyria, and meant *wisdom*. This must be considered in concurrence with all the other mythic matters relating to this Ischander. The letter of The Old Man of the Mountain to Leopold, Duke of Austria, concludes thus:—" Sachez " aussi que les présentes ont été faites par nous à mi-septembre, dans notre château de Messiat

---

by Shea, p. 396;) this is the Hebrew רקיע *rqio*, which we translate *firmament*, and the "rack" or *flying clouds* of Shakspeare—*shall leave not a rack behind*. See Vol. I. p. 335, note [4].

[1] Ib. p. 405. [2] Ib. p. 424. [3] Ib. pp. 431, 432. [4] See references to Vol. I. ut sup. p. 346.

" (Massiat), la quinze cent-quinzième année depuis Alexandre."[1] If I knew the year of Jesus Christ, I could tell the date of the *birth* or *death* of Alexander, according to The Old Man's reckoning. Nimrod says, "Nor need I do more than shortly repeat, that the fable of Alexander's conception from an immense dragon is an exact copy from that of Nimrod the Dragon-begotten Bull, evidently made in order to conciliate the minds of the Orientals towards his design of setting up in Iran a new universal empire. 'He had a certain feeling of rivalry (saith Arrian) towards Perseus and Hercules, in as much as he traced his descent from them. And he did himself ascribe his own generation to Ammon, in like manner as the fables referred that of Hercules, and of Perseus, unto Jove. It was *for this purpose* that he took his journey to the temple of Ammon, namely, that he might more assuredly know, or rather *make pretence of knowing*, who he really was.' And I dare say that his real and authentic descent from Nimrod, (called Hercules in Greece, Perseus there and in Persia, and Sesostris in Egypt,) stood him in some stead with the Egyptians and Persians."[2] Again, Nimrod says,[3] "Dion relates *that immediately before the murder of Soæmis and Heliogabalus*, 'a certain dæmon, styling himself Alexander of Macedon, and having the very same features and dress, made his appearance on the banks of the Danube, and travelled over Thrace and Asia, like a Bacchanalian, with four hundred companions, who were adorned with the Thyrsus and fawn's skin. All those who were then in Thrace affirm with one voice, that lodgings and all necessaries *were furnished him at the public expense*, and no man, neither general, nor soldier, nor prefect, nor even the supreme governors of these nations, attempted to resist him. But he arrived in broad day-light, and, as it were, in a religious procession, at Byzantium, as he had prophesied he would. And he put over to Chalcedon, where he performed certain nocturnal rites, buried a *wooden horse* in the earth, and disappeared. I had been informed of all these things in Asia before Bassianus (i. e. Antoninus Heliogabalus) had been disposed of at Rome. Pp. 1365, 6.' I beseech the reader to weigh well these words, and by whom they were written, and he cannot fail to detect a deep and complicated scheme of imposture and mystic superstition." And *I* beg my reader to add to this, a consideration of what he has just read from Von Hammer, respecting the æra of Alexander, and I think he will not fail to infer with me, that we have but a very small part of the true history of these times. After this, Nimrod adds, that John Chrysostom complained that, in his time, people made their children wear medals of Alexander around their necks as talismans; that Julian maintained he had the soul of Alexander, by metempsychosis; and, that this was what urged him on in his war with the Persians.[4] Here we have a fine example of the monomania of which I have spoken in Julian, and of its leading on some persons to victory, and deluding others to their ruin; and, in his case, of its leading *him* to his ruin. Here it becomes apparent that it is for want of looking into, instead of despising, the secret histories of antiquity, that all our accounts of those times are so unsatisfactory, and that the conduct of many, indeed, of almost all, the chief actors in the dramas of those times is so unaccountable. In p. 283, Nimrod adds, "It was an old ambition of the Romans, or at least not a more recent one than the arrival of the Pessinuntian Great Mother and her Sodalities, that

" Avitæ
" Tecta vellnt reparare Trojæ.

" The place at which Mammæus's false Alexander prophesied he would arrive, and did arrive, was Byzantium. The son of Helena only accomplished what the son of Mammæa had first medi-

---

[1] Von Hammer on the Assassins, p. 346.
[2] Vol. IV. Part. II. p. 282.
[3] Nimrod, Vol. III. pp. 366, 367.
[4] Socrates, Lib. iii. Cap. xxi.

"tated."¹ Here, in the conduct of Constantine, we have a proof of the close connexion of ancient Paganism and modern Christianity. After this, Nimrod goes on to shew, that Origen and other leaders of the Christians were deeply implicated in the transactions of those times, connected with the mythic superstition: he adds, "The same system of mysterious doctrines animated the united Sophists and the imperial usurpers."¹ And, again, "It is remarkable that in the reign of Alexander Severus the Parthian empire was subverted by Artaxares, the son of Sassan, a man 'addicted to the ineffable mysteries. The workings of the same thing were towards the East as well as the West.'" This was repeated at the time of the Crusades. All this shews the going to pieces of the ancient system, and the struggles of the different persons, each to make out that he was this *great one* COMB. I have formerly noticed, en passant, the endless apparent nonsense of the Gorgon's head or head of Medusa, with hair of snakes, and the brazen head of Roger Bacon, &c. At great length Nimrod² has brought together, probably all, the stories of magical heads, which appear to have been as numerous as they were general over the world. All those stories are evidently closely connected with the most secret of the mysteries of the Γνωσις. I think a key to unlock all these cabinets will be found in the identity of meaning of the words שאר ras, a Head, and ras, Wisdom, and שפים spipn, Gen. xlix. 17, which means both *wisdom* and *a serpent—*sup-iphis or ophis, *wisdom of the serpent*. I shall not follow up this search—not attempt the disentanglement of this skein here, though, perhaps, I may return to it. But I may just observe, that Nimrod has pointed out that the Templars had a sacred head in the most remote crypt, and that they fabled much about the devil begetting the British *Merlin* on the body of a virgin, and the Dragon's head assuming, by prestige, the appearance of Gorloes, Duke of Cornwall, and engendering Arthur upon his wife Iogerne.³ When we consider the story of the connexion between the siege of Troy and the Gorgon's head of the Greeks, and all the mythos of immaculate conceptions in Alexander, Cæsar, and the Troya Nova of king Brute, &c., &c., we shall have no difficulty in seeing here the continuation of the mythos in Merlin, and in Arthur, with his round table and twelve knights—the secret mythos existing in Britain before the arrival of Cæsar, and passing down through the rule of the Romans to Arthur, to Alfred, and, at last, to Geoffry of Monmouth, who has fortunately preserved to us a remnant of it,—a remnant, which, instead of using, our short-sighted historians take all the pains in their power to destroy,—a remnant of a most important system, which yet continues to exert its secret influence upon all our institutions, both civil and religious. When my reader has well considered the above passages of Nimrod (Mr. Herbert), stripping them of the false colouring given by that gentleman, who can see nothing but devilish machinations in the simplest and most innocent matters; he, my reader, must be obliged to confess, that it is quite clear, that, in all our histories, we have in fact any thing but a real history of Alexander the Great. We have it just named, by Nimrod, to be ridiculed, that he said he was the son of Ammon. Just so far is said as will serve to justify the historian from a charge of fraudulent suppression; but, in reality, all the secret moving causes of Alexander's conduct and of that of his followers, is kept out of sight. The circumstance that an æra arose from him in Asia, shews how extensive the mythos must have been. I feel little doubt that, if I ever recover my health,⁴ I shall be able to unravel all these matters. I believe the claims of all the persons entitled *great*, and called *emperors*, were founded upon the system of Avatarism—of a believed descent from the eldest of the sons of Noah; or, if this plea could not be set up, upon the reception of the χειροτεσια from the lineal descendant, who was always believed to be known. In aid

---

¹ Nimrod, Vol. IV. Part II. p. 286. ² Ib. p. 219.
³ Gervas of Tilbury says, that King Richard used that sign on his standard. ⁴ July, 1833.

of this came the impregnation by the Python, or the Holy Ghost, in the form of a snake. Thus Alexander had, mystically, two fathers. The case was precisely the same in this respect with Jesus, of Bethlehem, and Alexander. They each had *two* fathers. Jesus was the son of the Holy Ghost, but still in the line of Abraham: Alexander also was the son of the Holy Ghost, or the Ghost of Ammon, but yet of the line of Japhet. It is extremely gratifying to me to find such learned men as Constant and Creutzer, although without having the most distant suspicion of the true nature of ancient history, coming to the same conclusion with me. The former says, " Plusieurs faits qui nous sont parvenus, bien qu'isolement, à travers l'obscurité des siècles et la " confusion des fables, semblent indiquer qu'à une époque encore antérieure à celle que nous nom- " mons fabuleuse, la Grèce fut subjuguée momentanément par un ordre de prêtres, soit indigènes " soit étrangers."[1] As this militates against his system, but cannot be denied, he endeavours to qualify it by the word *momentanément*. He then shews that Mr. Creutzer comes to the same conclusion, but by a different train of reasoning. The fact they could not deny, of the cause or the nature of this priestly government they were entirely ignorant. Mr. Schlegel says, speaking of the priests, " Dans les temps les plus anciens, la Grèce entière leur était soumise."[2] Again, " Plus tard, la caste des guerriers se souleva contre celle qui regnait au nom des dieux. " L'Iliade porte de fortes empreintes de cette lutte: la dispute d'Agamemnon avec *Chryses* et *Cal-* " *chas* en est un indice."[3] I suppose I need not point out the Χρης of Delphi and the Chaldæan in Calchas! Schlegel then goes on to say, that these priests were Pelasgi, and spoke a barbarous language. This was, I doubt not, the language which contained the Eleusinian mysteries, which we are told by Clemens Alexandrinus, were taken from the Jews—the language of the Synagogue, —the language on which the Greek was founded. Again, Mons. Constant says, " Nous ne ré- " poussons donc nullement la supposition qu'à une époque qu'entoure une nuit épaisse, il y ait eu " en Grèce une religion sacerdotale, et des corporations puissantes, crées par cette religion et " vouées à son maintien. Mais une révolution violente détruisit cette religion et ses pontifes, " avec toute la civilisation dont ils étaient les auteurs."[4] The facts of the pontifical government and the revolution he was obliged to see, the momentary violence is mere inference, mere dogmatism on a subject of which he was perfectly ignorant. The " corporations puissantes," were the municipal towns, wisely left to their own government by the pontifical order in every thing which did not concern its interests, contained in the productiveness of the vectigal—and on this account they were always prevented from going to war with one another. In the Areopagus of Athens we have the domestic legislature; in the Amphictyons we have the superintending one; this last, perhaps, assuming its form and power by degrees, as the superintending power of the distant autocrat fell away, or perhaps being the remains of the ancient pontifical government. M. Constant has treated at large on the Fétiches of the ancients. I think in these very low superstitions we have the religion of the Aborigines; but most certainly the higher ranks of society, and the professors of, or the instructed in, the cabala and the mysteries, cannot be suspected of believing such nonsense; though, occasionally, no doubt, a person or two might be found in the higher classes with understandings sufficiently mean to receive them. In my recollection the use of charms against witches, evil demons, and other similar nonsense as degrading as the fetiches of Africa, were common among the lower orders in Britain. No doubt as the doctrines of incarnations escaped from the conclaves they became mixed with the superstitions of the vulgar, till now it is difficult, perhaps quite impossible, to separate them. It is probable that when the high class increased, so as to be very numerous—too numerous to be initiated—they by degrees *descended* as

---

[1] Constant, Vol. II. p. 319.   [2] Ib. p. 331.   [3] Ib. p. 332.   [4] Ib. p. 336.

the Aborigines a little *ascended*, till the two nearly came together both in religion and intellect, and at last the distinction was entirely lost. Constant says, "Il ne faut pas confondre ces apo-théoses qui sont particulières à la religion Greque, avec les incarnations que nous rencontrerons fréquemment dans les religions sacerdotales : ce sont deux choses directment opposées."[1] In what particular cases the incarnate or solar mythos may have been attributed to real men, as we know it was to Alexander and Cæsar, it may be difficult to affirm or to deny, but I am persuaded that there never was a Bacchus, a Hercules, or a Jove.

3. When the time for the Millenium arrived, but no appearance of its actual arrival could be perceived, it was with the sect of Ali, as it was with the sect of the Christians—their whole system fell into pieces; and they were obliged to avail themselves of such resources as circumstances offered. It appears from a part of the Dabistan, translated by Professor Lee, and given by him to the Society of Literature, from whom I borrowed it, that the Mohamedans had a succession of twelve Imams, and that there was supposed to be yet one remaining in the world, though his residence was unknown. Of their *esoteric* system nothing can be made out, except merely, that there is *an esoteric religion;* but it seems to have some relation to the first doctrine of a divine Idea, according to which the world was formed. Along with the degradation of the human mind in most Eastern countries, the degradation of the doctrines has kept pace; till, really, in all those countries, unless China be excepted, their doctrines consist of nothing but the most inconceivable nonsense. If it were not for the hope of discovering the origin and nature of the learning of the early races of man, which keeps continually shewing itself in little detatched parts, all the Eastern learning in the world would not be worth the half-hour's trouble of a wise man. But, as a means to discover the learning of antiquity, it is worth every thing, and by its means I have no doubt that the secrets of antiquity will one day be all clearly made out. I flatter myself I shall have paved the way.[2] The Sheahs hold an inconceivable quantity of nonsense respecting their open and concealed Imams; but it is what one would expect to arise from the falling to pieces of the system in such a state of society. It may be even doubtful whether any thing approaching to the beautiful system of the ancient Gnosis or Sopheism now exists among them. As might be expected, they accuse the Sonnees of having corrupted the Koran. The Sheahs or the followers of Ali, are obliged to confess that the successor or lineal descendant of Mohamed is in existence; but because *they* have not possession of him, they say he is in secret: the Turks or Sonnites deny this, and not unreasonably; for, under the circumstances, it is not at all likely that he should have forgotten his pedigree. They say that he is now living at Mecca. The present Royal family of Persia are of the *Kajar* tribe of Turks.[3] This is the *Cæsar* tribe. Kai Khusrau or Cyrus is described by Mirkond[4] as a prophet, and is said to have disappeared suddenly from the earth—not to have died.

---

[1] Vol. II. p. 470.

[2] I think sufficient importance is not attached to the fact of the ignorance of the Indians. It is almost beyond credibility. They have nothing pretending to be a history, which goes back to two hundred years before the Christian æra. Their Vedas do not pretend to be this kind of work. Their 18 Puranas (Moore, pp. 441, 442) are 18 Cosmogonies; but, by whom or when written, they do not pretend to know. They acknowledge that they do not know what is the meaning of the word Vyasa. Their astronomical tables carry on their face marks of extreme antiquity, but their authors are all unknown. The first historical æra is that of Vicramaditya, fifty-six years B. C., preceded by a period of three thousand years, in which the Hindoos pretend to no "continuous accounts, either religious, traditional or historical." This three thousand years is a chasm which cannot be filled up. (Hist. Sketch of Sans. Lit., Oxford, 1832, p. 68.) This is perfectly true, and I suspect that all their pedigrees in the lines of the Sun and the Moon—Chandra and Soma—are really sheer nonsense, designed to flatter the petty princes of the present day; and, except for a very few generations back, are not worthy a moment's attention. The whole of their histories of Soms and Chandra are modern inventions. Gengis Khan and his successors knew better than to credit them.

[3] Translation by Shea, p. 192.   [4] Ib. pp. 260, 263.

Here is the mythos. This is the ascension. Mr. Briggs tells me, that "when Selim III. pos"sessed himself of the power of the Calif, he also got possession of his person, and took him
"with him to Constantinople, and ruled under his authority as long as he lived. But at his death
"the legal pontifical power descended to the heir of Mohamed, who is now at Mecca, and is in a
"private station there. That Mahmud Pasha now rules under his authority, and that he could
"cause the Grand Seignior to be excommunicated immediately by him if he chose it. That the
"act of excommunication by the Grand Seignior is a mere *brutum fulmen*, not having any influ"ence on the minds of the Mohamedans, who look solely to the lineal descendant of Mohamed for
"the right of excommunication." Now this is evidently only one side of the question. The
Turk must have another heir or he would not have pretended to excommunicate Mahmud Pasha.
The grounds of his claim to the power of excommunication I think we shall discover presently. I
suspect that the present is a struggle between the Turks and the Saracens; that, at the bottom,
the Turks claim to be descendants from Japhet, and the Egyptians from Shem.[1] Mr. Briggs
denies this, and says that Mahmud is an Osmanli. Mohamed, as we might expect, carried his
pedigree up to Noah.[2] Turk is the descendant of Japhet; Mohamed of Shem. The first Pacha-
lic of the empire is that of Jeddo, as Mr. Briggs says, because the holy city is placed there; but
why is it called Jeddo or Juda? What has Juda to do with the city of Ishmael? Why, but because it was the chief city of a tribe of Juda?—which Eusebius lets us know existed before Abraham, and which came from India before the tribe of Abraham, and some of whom he found at
Salem in Melchizedek. This was the tribe which gave the name of Judé to the Pole-star. When
the tribe got as far as it could, it built a city. After a time it passed over and peopled Abyssinia
and Upper Egypt. At this time the isthmus of Suez was a morass, or water, and the Delta had
not appeared in consequence of the subsidence of the Mediterranean. We must not forget, that
the Brahmins or Hindoos all maintain that they are a foreign race in India, and that they came
from Tartary. It is a fact, not hitherto explained, that the native Hindoo princes formerly solicited (and even yet, if the British did not prevent it, would solicit) investiture in their dominions
by the hand of the Mogul, at Delhi,[3] though he is a Mohamedan, and they are followers of Cristna
or of the Brahmins. The reason is found in his being supposed to be a descendant of Gengis
Khan, who was believed to be an Avatar, a Vicrama-ditya, and, as such, entitled to universal
dominion—a right to which dominion is believed still to exist in his lineal descendant.[4] The fact
of the Hindoo princes soliciting investiture by the hand of the Mohamedan Mogul may be accounted for by the theory which I advocate, that Mohamed also is considered by them to have been
an Avatar, as he was certainly considered by the Afghans. The preservation of the Lingas and of
the simple icons of Buddha, by the Mohamedans, when they destroyed all the idolatrous temples
of the Hindoos, strongly tends to support my suspicion, that the Moslems objected to the *corruption* of the religion, not to the religion itself. Their conduct is exactly similar to that of Cambyses
in Egypt, who left the Lingas when he destroyed the idolatrous temples. The ancient pilgrimages
of Hindoos to Mecca confirm this theory. The Sopheism of India and Mohamed were, no doubt,
originally the same. It is evident that the Mogul, the King of Siam, the Emperor of China, all
claim to be the descendant of the eldest son of the first Patriarch, and from him to have a right
to the empire of the world. From this we may see, that their titles of *king of kings*, &c., &c., are

---

[1] See Assiat. Journ. for Feb. 1833, p. 74.   [2] Sale's Koran.
[3] The city of seven gates, like the city of Thebes, governed by Al-Mage, *the Mage* or Mogul. Delhi, *city of The-
God-II*, D'-el-ii.
[4] Vide Hamilton's Gazetteer, 2d ed., 8vo. pp. 494, 499.

not examples of mere empty, fulsome adulation, but that they have a basis. On this rests their claim or title of *Son of the Sun* and *Moon*, which at first appears to us so monstrously ridiculous. The Empire of Gengis Khan was called the *wise government* or *the government of wisdom*, and his name was Zin.[1] Respecting this prince see, in the Ency. Brit. art. Mogul, pp. 299, &c., the pedigree from Japhet, the romantic account of his ancestors for 400 years, his inauguration by a prophet, the change of his name from Teninjin, and the belief of his subjects that he was entitled to possess the whole world. This inauguration of Gengis took place in the 13th century, when in Europe the Millenium was expected, when all men were looking out for some *one to come*. Gengis Khan marched into China in A. D. 1211.[2]

Ranking, in his history of Mexico, says, "Those who were most interested in the advancement " of Genghis Khan, have had the insolence to make him pass for the son of God: but his mother, " more modest, said only that he was the Son of the Sun. But not being bold enough to aver, " that she was personally beloved by that glorious luminary, she pretended to derive this honour " from Buzengir, his ninth predecessor: and his partisans reported, that Buzengir was the son of " the Sun." (This manifestly makes Gengis the tenth Avatar.)[3] " His mother having been " left a widow, lived a retired life: but some time after the death of her husband, Douyan-Byan, " she was suspected to be pregnant. The deceased husband's relations forced her to appear be- " fore the chief judge of the tribe, for this crime. She boldly defended herself, by declaring that " no man had known her: but that one day lying negligently on her bed, a light appeared in her " dark room, the brightness of which blinded her, and that it penetrated three times into her body, " and that if she brought not three sons into the world, she would submit to the most cruel tor- " ments. The three sons were born, and the princess was esteemed a saint." The Moguls believe Gengis Khan to be the produce of this miracle, that God might punish mankind for the injustice they committed.[4] The same mythos was applied to Tamerlane, whose mother was said to have had connexion with the God of day.[5] All this satisfactorily accounts for the wish of the native princes of India to receive investiture at the hand of the Great Mogul. Sumatra or Sabadios is a repetition of the same mythos, where there is a Delhi, in Lat. 3°. 46'. N., Long. 99°. 42'. E. The prince is called Sultan and "Allum Shah, which, being translated, signifies *the world's* " *king*."[6] Sultan is Sul-tania, *place of Sul*. Shah is Jah, and Allum is Al (Arab. THE) and Om, or All, i. e. GOD OM.[7] The Moguls trace their pedigree, with each particular ancestor specified, from Japhet.[8] I have little doubt that the Emperor who was descended or who claimed to be descended from each of the three sons of Noah—Shem, Ham, and Japhet—would claim for his an-. cestor to be the eldest son of Noah, and of course to be like Noah—Emperor of the whole world. This is confirmed by the doubtful state of the text of Genesis, which, though doubtful, evidently inclines to Shem. I have little doubt that the Tzar of Muscovy maintains, that neither the Emperor of China, nor the Emperor of India, is the legal successor of Noah, but that *he* is the man.

---

[1] Ranking's History of the Mongols, pp. 18, 65.

[2] The Christian æra is the best of all periods to make the fixed one, or the pivot of ancient and modern times, because being settled by the Chaldæan Sosigenes, it is a fixed epoch for all the ancient Eastern nations as well as for those of the West. Ptolemy fixed the precession of the Equinox at 36 seconds a year, the same as it was once fixed by the Indians.

[3] I suspect that Buzen-gir is gir-zaba—the cycle of wisdom. When I recollect that Sab or Zab is *wisdom* and that Zup or Suph is *wisdom*, and how Zab and the Zaboim or planets are connected with *wisdom*, I cannot help suspecting that Zup and Zab were originally the same word.

[4] Petis [Petit?] de la Croix, Book i. Ch. i.   [5] Hist. Res. into Mexico, by Ranking, pp. 177, 178.   [6] Ib. p. 501.

[7] See Vol. I. pp. 65—67, and 669.   [8] Abul Ghazi Bahadur, Part i. Ch. i.—iii., in Ranking, p. 385.

In the story of the mother of Gengis and her three sons, we have a confused account of the incarnation of the *triune* God—the expected and promised one—one who was to rule over the earth. I have come to a perfect conviction that this mythos has given rise to the pretensions of several of the great conquerors of the world, if not of every one of them; and I suspect that it secretly actuates the present Emperors of both Austria and Russia. This mythos is the foundation on which the divine right of kings, of which we have heard so much, is built. Richardson admits the feudal tenure to have prevailed in Arabia, and that Mahmud of Ghazni consented to solicit and receive investiture in his dominions from the Kalif Alkader. Richardson states the fact without understanding it.[1] Again, (in p. xv.,) Mr. Richardson gives a very striking description of the care of the great men of the East to make out their genealogies; at the same time, while he states the fact, he is obliged to attribute it in a great measure to fashion, or a natural impulse, not having the slightest idea of the real cause. Thus he states Tamerlane to have made out his pedigree to Gengis Khan, who pretended to be descended from Turk, the son of Japhet; and here we see in the descendants of Turk the sovereigns of Constantinople, ruling the world from the city of seven hills in Europe, as the Mogul, the descendant of Turk, affects to rule the world from the city of seven hills—Delhi—in Asia. And yet it is very curious to read the account given by Richardson of the suit and service done by Gengis himself, to a Tartar chieftain, called Thogrul or Prester John, the Khan of Cara-cum or Cara-corum, who must have been, in actual power, as nothing, compared with Gengis. But this can only be accounted for by supposing, that Thogrul claimed the right as an *elder branch* from Japhet. It is also very curious to observe all the great princes obeying the summons to assist Thogrul against his rebellious subjects; and all those inferior to Gengis, doing suit and service *to* Gengis.[2] In this example the whole *feudal system* of Germany, with its emperor and tributary princes, is complete. This example of Gengis doing suit and service to Thogrul, a person of whom we know nothing certain, except that he must have been very much the inferior in power to him, is exactly imitated by the Pacha of Egypt, in claiming to hold his dominion of an obscure individual, now resident at Mecca, and, under this authority, setting at defiance, as I have stated above, the excommunication pronounced against him by the Grand Seignior.

4. Every thing which I said respecting the tendency of the doctrine of expected or foretold Messiahs, or Avatars, or renewed Incarnations, in December 1832, after I had written what my reader has seen, I found confirmed in a very curious account, given in the Bombay Transactions,[3] by Col. Van Kennedy, of an attempt of Akbar, in the latter part of the sixteenth century, to establish what the Colonel calls *a new religion*. If we make allowance for the unquestionable fact, that, although the Colonel knew of the ten Avatars of India, yet that he was entirely ignorant of the real origin or nature of the mythos which I have been describing, and how they applied to modern times, and thus, for want of information, was deceived—we shall at once perceive, that Akbar probably believed himself to be the last Avatar—that Avatar which all the present Hindoos say is yet to come, and in which assertion they are still supported by the followers of Brothers, Southcote, &c., in the West. It appears that Akbar was called the *imperial wisdom*, the *accomplished apostle*, and the *perfect messenger* of God, *perfectly* skilled from the divine essence in all knowledge. Abul Fazl says, "When, through the good fortune of mankind, the season arrives for "the revelation of the truth, a person is endowed with knowledge,[4] upon whom God bestows the "robes of royalty, in order that he may lead men in the right way with absolute dominion: such "is the Emperor of our time." This shews that Abul Fazl either was, or pretended to be, a

---

[1] Pp. ii., iii.   [2] Richardson, p. xxxiv.   [3] Vol. II. pp. 242, &c.   [4] In other words Wisdom.

believer in him. After the above, Col. Van Kennedy goes on to observe, that Akbar was believed to have some peculiar and immediate communication with the Supreme Being;[1] but the mode in which this was effected was considered *a mystery, only confided to the higher orders of the initiated.* Here we have the gradations of the Sophees. He assumed the title of Khalifah Ullah, or Vicegerent of God, and his religion was called Iláhi,[2] or Godly. And in the place of the usual symbol of Islamism, the following was adopted: "*There is no God but God, and Akbar is the Khalif of* "*God.*" The Colonel gives a quotation from an Indian *Musselman author*, who, he says, *allows in bitterness of spirit*, that in five or six years not a trace of Islamism remained. The passage is very striking; and although the Colonel observes that the above author must limit his description of the propagation of the religion only to the court and the departments immediately connected with it, yet I think enough transpires to shew, that it extended over almost all his empire, and how or when it entirely ended, if it be ended, I think it will now be difficult to shew. It is a remarkable circumstance, that Akbar wished to abolish the slaying of animals,[3] and he made a pilgrimage to the tomb of Hadj. at Ajmir, *barefoot*. This does not look like *policy*, but *fanaticism*, —a return to the Buddhist system. But he was tolerant in the highest degree, permitting all sects to follow their own laws and customs, and on no account suffering them to be interfered with in religion, in any manner whatever. I should say he was very like Mohamed; but, like that great man, not entirely free from a mixture of fanaticism with his philosophy. We must, however, always bear in mind, that we really know nothing of what was taught to the *initiated in the mysteries;* but the Colonel says, that, after his death, when Jehangir re-established Mohamedism,[4] it is probable, that Akbar's followers concealed themselves *among the Sophees*, to whose tenets this religion *had a close resemblance.* I cannot help suspecting that the Sophee doctrines had more to do with this than Col. Van Kennedy had any idea of. We must not forget that it had its mysteries and its initiati. In the mode in which it extended itself, and, indeed, in every other respect, it was strikingly similar to the Evangelium Eternum and the St. Francis of the Romish Church. The thing lasted its little day, but various circumstances combined to prevent its continuance, as various circumstances, in a similar manner, had formerly aided the continuance of the Avatars of Cristna, Christ, and Mohamed. The first two of these were only required by the system of the mythos to be great men, bringing peace and happiness, each in his peculiar cycle,—and after the death, resurrection, and ascension of each, another was expected to come to complete the system. We may easily suppose in the case of Cristna, and we know in the case of Christ, that the mythos did not rise *to its highest prosperity* till an age of ignorance arrived. Though Christ may be said to have arisen in a time of high civilization, and in an improved state of the human mind, yet his doctrines did not make any great progress in the world till the human mind was in a rapid state of deterioration—till after the Council of Nice. No doubt the sect had some able followers, as the sects of Brothers and Southcote have had—such persons as Nathaniel Brassey, Halhed, Mrs. and the Honourable and Rev. Mr. Foley, and some highly respected personal friends of my own, whose names, out of regard to their relations now living, I do not choose to give. But there is this difference between the two: the circumstance of a rapid *decline* in the state of the human mind aided in converting Christ into a God; the present rapid *improvement* in the state of the human mind most powerfully operates against the mythos. The establishment of a priesthood by Constantine, so constituted as to be in a pecuniary manner greatly interested in its success, and who, as might be expected, left no stone unturned, and never stopped at any fraud to serve its purpose, favoured the mythos. The case might have been different had the Millenium been fixed at the end of

---

[1] Bomb. Trans. Vol. II. pp. 258, 259.   [2] I do not doubt *the* יהוה *ies*.   [3] Bomb. Trans. p. 257.   [4] Ib. p. 267.

ten thousand instead of the six thousand years. All these religions are the children of accident and circumstance. They all had their *origin* in the peculiar circumstance that the cycle of the Neros should form the cycle of the six thousand years, and the two again the cycle of 21,600, and 432,000 In the time of Christ, all persons were on the look-out for some one to come; such also was the state of the world in the time of Mohamed, and again, in the time of the Crusades. In the last case, however, the Millenium being expected to follow immediately on the appearance of the *promised one*, and this not arriving, the general expectation was disappointed, and the bubble burst. Brothers and Southcote had not these auxiliary circumstances in their favour, and so they died, and their pretensions were strangled almost in their birth: I cannot help thinking that Charlemagne claimed to be universal Monarch, as successor of Augustus.[1] It is admitted that he was controlled by his Barons, in temporal affairs, but that, in spiritual, his authority was paramount.[2] He exercised the power of excommunication, as appears from his chartularies.[3] Nimrod has observed the peculiarity of character which attached itself to Charlemagne, without understanding in the slightest degree the truth or the nature of it: he says, "Charlemagne's reign, like "that of Alexander and Arthur, was a favourite legend of secret anti-christianism, and a symbo- "lical vehicle for its mysterious meanings. His paladins were the round table, and Roncesvalles "the battle of Salusbury Plain over again."[4] My reader must have observed a difficulty in my explanation of the universal system, arising from the probability that the Gods Buddha and Cristna both describe the Sun; in fact, I think I may say not the *probability* only, but the *certainty* that they are meant to be either actually the Sun or that Higher Principle of which the Sun is the Shekinah, and the emblem. At the same time, we have almost as good proofs that these Gods were once actually men, exercising the functions of royalty and governing large nations. Still they were supposed to be men in whom a portion of the God was incarnated. I think, from a consideration of the history of Akbar, we may find how this arose. The mythos taught that some one was to come—then the devotees naturally looked out for some one by the adoption of whom they might gratify that gloomy passion which we see in all religious people—that state of fear of damnation which often makes life intolerable—that state which makes the Goddess Cali a favourite in India, and the predestined state of damnation of Calvin a favourite dogma in Europe. If, at the beginning of a cycle, some great conqueror or chieftain did not appear, whom weakness and the flattery of followers could not persuade, like Akbar, that he was an Avatar, the devotees in the cycle following were sure to apply it to some one, or to create some one, on whom it might be fathered: thus Avatarism was in any case sure to be supported, and where great men did not offer themselves, like Cæsar or Alexander, little men, like Brothers, or the living God, described in Vol. III. p. 64 of the Bombay Transactions, were continually arising in all ages. This is the reason why the Hindoos say, there have been thousands of Avatars. We hear much in the Indian histories of a *second* and a *third* Buddha. I have very little doubt that this is all to be accounted for from princes of the countries professing the Buddhist religion having pursued the same plan as Gengis Khan, Akbar, and several others, and called themselves Avatars. Thus we have in Siam a *tenth* Avatar. The original principle of the mythos being lost, this did very well with an ignorant and degraded race. We need not be surprised at this in Siam, when we find it answered so well with Akbar. But from this have arisen all the stories respecting the *second*, the *third*, the *eighth*, or the *tenth* Buddha. I feel little doubt that, as we have believers in the *tenth* Buddha, so there are yet believers in the *divinity* of Akbar, as the tenth incarnation. Among the Guebres of Persia

---

[1] Hallam, Hist. Middle Ages, Vol. I. p 11.
[2] Ib. Vol. II. p. 16.
[3] Ib. p. 32.
[4] Vol. IV. pp. 95, 96.

the same mythos is found.¹ This of course is accounted for by the Guebres having formerly been Christians, and having relapsed into Paganism. But those who have examined into their mysteries, say that, in fact, throughout the whole of their system marks of Christianity may be seen, though, as those Christian examiners say, *grievously defaced;* the annunciation, the magi, the massacre of the infants, the miracles of Christ, his persecutions, ascension, &c., &c., are all there. These Guebres are equally at enmity with Jews and Christians. After finding the mythos in China, Tartary, North and South India, and in Western Syria, it would have been surprising if it had not been in Persia. Of course, this will be attributed to the heresy of Nestorius, which the learned Nimrod has, I believe, very correctly declared to be Buddhism.² De Vallement³ says of Nestorius, "L'an 440, Nestorius parut sur les rangs et se mit à soûtenir que Jésus-Christ, né de la "sainte Vierge, n'étoit point Dieu, mais un pur homme, qui avoit mérité d'être joint à la Divinité, "non par une union hypostatique; mais par une singulière et excellente habitation de la Divinité "en lui." When I consider the late period at which this German made his appearance, I am compelled to believe, that wh.⁴ was called Nestorianism, was nothing but the same kind of Christianity which we have found on the coast of Malabar. It was, in fact, χρης-ism. In Horace¹ we find Augustus described to be the son of Maia. Here the mythos shews itself evidently. Thus in detached scraps, in loose expressions, it is discovered. It is difficult to believe that at the time when they were used, there was not much more before the public than we now find. Either this must have been the case, or the system must have continued a secret. In the former case, the evidence of it must have been destroyed by the Christian priests, when the old manuscripts were re-written by them; and this might easily be done—for we have not a single manuscript which has not passed through their hands. From the beginning of the modern system of Χρης-ism at Antioch, to the Council of Trent, the practice of destroying books has never ceased. The system may be said to have been established, on the burning of the books by the Council of Nice, testified by the picture of it in the church of St. Giovanni Laterano, placed there both to commemorate the glorious event, and to incite the faithful to similar meritorious acts. I am quite certain, that we do not give credit enough to the effects which may, nay must, have arisen from the unceasing and systematic exertions of an immensely powerful, corporate body, acting together for a thousand years to produce them,—a body, however discordant in other respects, yet, on the point of secreting evidence, united by both temporal interest and religious prejudice,—a prejudice even going so far as to induce the persons under its influence to believe that their eternal welfare would be compromised if they did not yield to it. I cannot help being apprehensive that, on this subject, I shall probably fail in exciting in the mind of my reader the same strong impression of its importance which I feel myself. In order to do justice to it, much more, and much more *deep* consideration of the history of the earlier part of the Christian æra is necessary than most persons will be prevailed on to give to it.

We have in the history of Akbar a perfect example of an Avatar, and I suspect that he announced himself as a *tenth* Avatar, putting back Mohamed as the *ninth.* On the doubt which I formerly mentioned to have arisen in the time of Virgil, respecting the *eighth* and *ninth* Avatar, we find room enough left for Akbar to have raised his pretensions. In Akbar we have the whole thing undisguised; it was not attempted to be secreted. I cannot help suspecting that, in one or both of the Cæsars, the system has formerly been equally displayed; but that the evidence of it has been destroyed. I contend that this suspicion, indeed, I may almost say belief, is justified on

---

¹ Art. Guebres and Gabres, Ency. Brit.
³ Du Secret des Mystères, p. 275.
² Vide Vol. I. of this work, pp. 808, 809.
⁴ Lib. I. Ode II. l. 43.

the truest principles of criticism and the laws of evidence, as applied to a calculation of the doctrine of probabilities.

A very beautiful picture of the Apotheosis of Akbar is in the possession of my friend, the learned [Sir] Greaves Haughton, Secretary of the Royal Asiatic Society. He asks a thousand guineas for it.[1]

5. To what I have said in Vol. I. p. 688, respecting Napoleon, I think it expedient to add a well-known anecdote of him. When his uncle, Cardinal Fesch, once expostulated with him, and expressed his belief that he must one day sink beneath that universal hatred with which his actions were surrounding his throne, he led his uncle to the window, and, pointing upwards, said, "Do you see yonder star?" "No, Sire," was the reply. "But I see it," answered Napoleon, and abruptly dismissed him.[2] What are we to make of this? Here we have the star of Jacob, of Abraham, of Cæsar. Here we have a star, probably from the East. The whole of Napoleon's actions in the latter part of his life bespeak mental alienation. I believe that he continued to retain expectations and hopes of restoration to the empire of the world, till the day of his death. Many circumstances unite to persuade me that he was latterly the victim of monomania. I cannot help suspecting that Napoleon was tainted with a belief that he was *the promised one*. It is not improbable that he should have indulged a secret monomania; nor is it more improbable that it should happen to him than to Brothers, Wesley, Swedenborg, Southcote, and many others. A great mind is as liable to the complaint as a little one. Sir Isaac Newton, most assuredly, laboured under the complaint in his latter days. Look at his Treatises on the Apocalypse. Except with the view of paving the way for some ulterior measures, it will be difficult to find a reason for the famous Sanhedrim which Napoleon caused to be held at Paris. With a view to this object, of which he never lost sight, in a former day he attempted the conquest of Syria. With a view to this he made the famous declaration to the Egyptians, for which he was so much abused by our priests, that he was a Mohamedan. I have no doubt he flattered himself that he would unite all the sects—bring all the stray sheep into his fold. He wished to play the same game as Akbar, probably without knowing that Akbar had played it before him. Victor Cousin says, " You will remark, that all great men have, in a greater or less degree, been fatalists : *the error is* " *in the form, not at the foundation of the thought.* They feel that, in fact, they do not exist on " their own account: they possess the consciousness of an immense power, and being unable to " ascribe the honour of it to themselves, they refer it to a higher power which uses them as its " instruments, in accordance with its own ends."[3] With the exception of the words in Italics, which I do not understand, I quite agree with M. Cousin. But how completely it bears me out in the assertion I have made, that the belief in each person that *he* was *the great one that was for to come* has led either to his success or to his destruction! It led Julian into the desert—Napoleon to Moscow. The more I consider the conduct of Napoleon, the more I am convinced that he laboured under monomania. Every action of his life bespeaks it. I learn from those who lived with him on the most intimate terms, at St. Helena, that he was what they call a decided fatalist. But this is by no means sufficient to account for the whole of his conduct, particularly in the latter part of his life, when he persisted in carrying on the *hitherto unaccountable* farce of being treated

---

[1] Akbar was poisoned, by mistake. His burial-place is at Scander, five miles from Agra. "Akbar the Second, " present heir and representative of the imperial house of Timûr, enjoys only the empty title of ' King (Padshah) of " Delhi,' without either royal prerogative or power." Extracted from Rammohun Roy's Work on the Judicial and Revenue Systems of India, Introduction, p. x., 8vo ; London, 1832.

[2] J. T. Barker, of Deptford, to Ed. of Morn. Chron., Oct. 12, 1832.

[3] For. Quar. Review, No. XXIII. July 1833, p. 202.

as an Emperor. It appears to me that, without some secret reason, his conduct was so absurd and childish that he must have laughed at himself. How he could carry the farce on without laughing I cannot comprehend, particularly after he had signed his abdication of the throne of France. Every action of his life is unaccountable, (although generally grand,) on the common known rules which actuate mankind; but allow the monomania for which I contend, and every action—his rise—his fall—are easily accounted for. I repeat, there is nothing to prevent a great mind from being subject to this malady any more than a little one. Only look back carefully into history and hundreds will be found to have laboured under this complaint. Endes, of Bretagne, for one. In Napoleon's case circumstances happened to be favourable, in other cases they were unfavourable. It is impossible to conceive any thing in our estimation more absurd than the conduct of the monarchs of Asia towards Europeans. In fact their conduct makes them, in our eyes, no better than idiots. All this arises from their principles of action, and from the motives of their conduct, not being understood by us. It arises from our ignorance, not from theirs. They are, or they suppose themselves to be, descended from the first three monarchs—the sons of Noah; and, on this account, as each entitled either to the sovereignty of his part, or, as eldest, to the Lord-paramountship of the whole world. On this account, every sovereign who does not claim as the descendant of one of the three, is, on his own shewing, a rebel, if, by his ambassador, as in case of our embassies to China, for instance, he refuses to do suit and service to his superior. The Emperor of China would say, either as descendant of Japhet, the eldest son, (or as having received the *cheirotonia* or *samaoh* or the *pallium* from the eldest son, and thus as his vicegerent or vicramaditya,) "I am entitled to suit and service from you." When our ambassador was required to go down on his knees, his answer ought to have been, "My master is not a rebel; he denies that "the person who granted investiture to Gengis, your ancestor, had any power,—was, in fact, the "direct descendant of Japhet. He denies, also, that Japhet was the eldest son." To this the answer would have been, "Even if Japhet was not the eldest, he was the one of the three who "had power over your country—Europe; and you cannot deny what all Asia knows, that the "K'an of Cara-corum is the lineal descendant of Japhet, as the Sheriffe of Mecca is of Shem."

All these claims, we may say, are now obsolete and contemptible; but this can scarcely be advanced by any impartial Christian person, who admits that the doctrine is believed and has a powerful moral influence over hundreds of millions of human beings—and, after all, is founded upon his own religion. For, if I shew a believer in the literal meaning of the Old Testament, that any specific persons now living are the lineal descendants of the three sons of Noah, it will be difficult for him to deny the divine right of those persons, each to the sovereignty of his share of the world. We may easily despise the claim, and turn the whole book and all or any of its separate parts into ridicule; but the Asiatics who admit the truth of the book, act much more consistently in admitting the claims of the Khan of Cara-corum and the Sheriffe of Mecca, and in receiving investiture in their dominions from them. Very certain I am, that the monarchs of Asia have a *rational*, not a *silly* or *foolish* claim to *divine right* (whether it be founded in truth or falsehood) to which our European monarchs have not the slightest shadow of pretence—for which reason it is silly or foolish in *them*. If any kind of divine right is pleaded by European monarchs, they ought to send ambassadors to China, or somewhere else, to do suit and service to their Superior Lord. I believe Japhet, if he could appear, would say, "You, the descendants of Shem and Ham, owe me "suit and service; but you are, in regard to each other, equals. You were each enfeoffed in your "domain by our common ancestor." I wish in a very particular manner to draw attention to the fact noticed by Mr. Von Hammer, that when the great meeting of Jurists took place in Bagdad, to discuss the claims of the different parties to the Califat, in the year 1011, its proceedings were secret. For what reason could this meeting, in the capital of one of the parties, be secret? Had

Mr. Von Hammer asked himself this question, it would probably have led him to much curious information. Why does the Tzar, the successor of the Tzarina who put Cyrus to death in ancient times, and who was the Queen of Cara-corum, call himself Tzar? Why is he treading on the Serpent?[1] Why does he affect the name of Constantine? Why does he maintain, that the Pope is a *schismatic*, and that he, or his patriarch, is the head of the Christian church? Why! but because both Constantinople and Rome are in the domain of Japhet. The circumstance that the persons claiming to be the personal representatives both of Japhet and Shem, are persons in humble life (comparatively speaking) who are known to be, or are acknowledged to be, such representatives by great monarchs, as well as by their neighbours and countrymen, strongly supports the probability of their claims being founded in truth.[2] I have little doubt that Mohamed believed himself to be, and was generally believed to be, the descendant of Abraham—that is, of Shem—after the failure in the line of Jesus, for want of heirs. It is from this mythos or true history, which ever it may be, that our veneration for the persons of our kings is derived. Superstition is hereditary: it has lasted in this case, as in many others, long after its cause has ceased to exist. This superstition is not natural to the human race, but entirely artificial. But it is at last dying away, and if once dead, it can never be restored. I suspect that few of my readers will be able to overcome their prejudices so far as to see the whole force and importance of this argument.

6. The Mohamedans of the East constantly call Constantinople *Room*,[3] and, as we might expect, its monarch, *emperor of the world*. To the pretensions of the different kings or emperors to this power, we are in the habit of paying no attention, treating them as mere ebullitions of empty vanity: but I believe this is the result of our *own* vanity. We are too apt to suppose that we know every thing, and this makes us too proud to look beneath the superficies of things to which we are not accustomed. I believe every monarch who assumes the title of Emperor, assumes to be the successor of one of the three patriarchal descendants of Noah; and then, I doubt not, base adulation steps in to persuade each individual that his line is the eldest, and that, of course, he is, by right, supreme over all. And I suspect that wherever a man has got the title of Great, it has been given him, by the advocates of this doctrine, as a distinctive badge. They are always *emperors*,—not merely *kings*. For this reason Napoleon was Emperor, not merely a King. It is a remarkable circumstance, that the horse on which Peter the Great is riding, on the famous monument at Petersburg, treads on the serpent. If the coincidence of this with my theory is the effect of accident, it is a very remarkable accident. It satisfies me that he was held, by the makers of the statue, to be an avatar, crushing the evil principle. The mythological nature of early history has been noticed by Cuvier. He says, "It would avail us nothing, if we now entered into an examination of the different traditions of Sardanapalus, in which a celebrated, learned man has imagined that he has discerned proof of three princes of that name, all victims of similar misfortunes:[4] and in the same way another learned man finds in the Indies at least three Vicramadityas, equally the heroes of precisely similar adventures."—Again, "In a word, the more I reflect on the subject, the more I am persuaded that there was no more an ancient history of Babylon or Ecbatana, than of Egypt or the Indies; and instead of explaining mythology historically, as Evhemere or Bannier, it is my opinion that a great portion of history should be considered as mythology."[5] This is precisely my doctrine. In Volume I. p. 42, I have stated that the third book of Genesis might be called, the book of the generations or regenerations of Adam. I might have added, or the book of the generations of Menu or Noah, or נח *nh* or mind, incarnated

---

[1] See infra, Sect. 6.   [2] See Vol. I. p. 832, and supra, 354.   [3] Vide Bombay Trans. Vol. II. p. 9.
[4] See Mem. of Freret, in Mem. Ac. Belles Lett. Vol. V.   [5] Cuvier ap. Jameson, pp. 130, 131.

in man. I apprehend Noah was held to be the first divine incarnation, at or after the flood, or in the new world. He was the first Archierarch, the owner of the whole world, and from him descended three others, who were, after him, Archierarchs, and for this reason it is that this book of Genesis gives a pedigree of his three sons, in a direct male line from him. But, because *our sacred* book is the sacred book of the tribe or line of the Archierarch Shem only, we have his pedigree continued forward, beyond only a very few generations. The account of the wickedness of Cain, by which he forfeited his birthright, and of the death of Abel without issue, is given to prevent any claim to the Pontifical power from any persons who might have escaped the flood, exclusive of those in the ark. The reader may recollect the assertion I formerly made, in Vol. I. p. 294, that "the text does not say, that the surface of the whole globe was covered," and the Rev. Edward King has *proved* in his treatise, that the Hebrew text does not justify our translation, that all the inhabitants were drowned. The observation of Cuvier, that diluvial remains are not to be found above a certain height on the mountains, shews that if the book do assert (which it does not) that all the mountains were covered, and, in consequence, all mankind drowned, it asserts what is not true. It is probable that a great number of persons, all over the world, escaped, who, I doubt not, are the people we have been accustomed to call *aborigines*.[1]

There is great difficulty in settling the proper places, according to their seniority, of the three sons of Noah, as all divines have allowed. I think it probable that Japhet was the youngest, and Ham the eldest, and that the story of his uncovering his father was only contrived to justify the claims of Shem to the high-priesthood and archierarchical sway over the others. The whole history looks as if there had really been such persons as those named,—that the account of them was substantially true, but that it had been accommodated to the system and circumstances of the Jewish priests and government, claiming supremacy from their ancestor, flattering themselves that, however obscure they might then be, a great saviour would come, to place them in the command of the restored Pandæan kingdom. This has, to a very considerable degree, succeeded in placing the Pope at the head of Christianity or modern Judaism, as it is in reality, though it is lost to the children of Shem. I think if there had not been something in it, we should have had a straight-forward declaration that Shem was the eldest, and that his descendants, the Jews, claimed to rule in that right. The pedigrees which we have of Jesus Christ are intended to shew his right, and his obscure situation is not unlike that of the present Calif, now resident in an humble situation, at Mecca, giving power to Mahmud of Egypt, and the case of the prince of Caracorum, which I described some time ago, in giving power to Gengis Khan. The reason why we call it or him Menu is, because each people having this mythos would maintain, that its ancestor was *the* incarnation of the divine mind, or the Man-nu, and that the other two were only men, or at least inferior incarnations under their Man-nu, and that *he* was entitled to universal empire. In like manner as we found the mythos of Noah, the ship, &c., in North India, so we find in the cases of the Grand Seignior, the Mogul, &c., the people tracing their pedigrees to a Noah. I doubt not, had we all their sacred books, we should find an accommodation of this mythos to their own peculiar circumstances, at every one of the temples of Solomon, by a little suitable change of the first part of Genesis, unless it be that *the Jews* have made the accommodation. And I think it very likely that this assumption (when the origin of the whole, as time advanced and nations were more and more separated, became doubtful) was the cause of the ruin of the Pontifical government. And here we have the reason why we not only find traces of what appear to us the doctrines of the little Jewish tribe of Western Syria, in all parts of the world, but what appear to us

---

[1] In the page above referred to, I suggested the probability that the Indians and Chinese escaped.

to be settlements of the same people, but without the books of Moses. They probably had their books, where their mythos was recorded, accommodated to their peculiar circumstances, but these have been long since destroyed by the Cambyseses, &c., and it is probably owing to the preservation of the books of Moses and his followers, that we have the Jewish tribe not dissipated like the others. In the fourteen Solumi we have probably an example of fourteen tribes, like that of Abraham or Moses coming from India, and each setting up for itself the Mosaic mythos in many places, and particularly in Egypt. All this is confirmed by the exposition which I have given. In the history of Abraham we have the history of the tribe leaving India, and arriving, after various removals, in Egypt, and of its settling there. In the history of Moses we have an account of its *exod* from Egypt, and of its endowment with the mythos detailed above, or of the leaders of the tribe settling up a claim, like many others, to the supreme priesthood. In Moses we have an example of one of the chief priests setting up for himself, when the supreme Pontiff and his Pontificate had, in fact, become obsolete. On contemplating the nature of such a pontifical government as I have described, it appears to me that, before the art of writing was publicly known, the priests, aided by the influence of education and by the general veneration for their characters, would have little difficulty for a very long time in preserving their power, and in preserving order: they would be the lawgivers, and the people would have nothing to do with the laws but to obey them. In reality, in one sense, the people would be slaves, the priests masters; but, as the services rendered by the slaves were fixed to a tenth of the produce of the soil, and nearly the whole population were cultivators, their rule must, upon the whole, have been very mild, and favourable to the increase of the people. But still there appears every where a class of Helots who were almost always treated with cruelty by the superior dominant classes. They were the aborigines, and slaves under slaves, and adscripti glebæ. It is evident that the feudatories or payers of the tenths, the ryots, would constantly improve in moral character, with improved agriculture; but the Helots would be very liable to retrograde in moral character. I have said, that the feudatories or cultivators were slaves; this must be considered only a figurative expression, as their service was fixed, and, if they rendered it, the priest would have no further demand upon them. They were correctly the ryots of India. The Zemindars were originally merely the collectors for the Pontiff, to whom the tithe was due, and who, at first, (before any of his caste got possession of lands as allodial property, or perhaps, in some cases, on the same tenure as the ryots,) divided it among them, as was done in Britain in the earliest time. When tradesmen arose in towns, the occupiers of houses must have held them of the lord of the soil. Thus burghs or municipia arose around what in most cases became a castle, with its great or little seigniory, according to circumstances. It is evident that the system, in different countries, would receive numbers of variations according to the circumstances of localities and other matters easily understood, all tending to cause variations,—but if the system *did* originally exist, the truth is likely to be discovered only by keeping the original in our view in our researches, always making proper allowances for the varieties alluded to above.

7. However various the races of man may have been, it is totally impossible to deny that marks the most unequivocal of an universal language, and of an universal polity, of some kind, are every where apparent. The Judæan mythos, in which the histories of Adam, Noah, Moses, &c., are mixed with that of Cristna, &c., or of which I had better say, the histories of Moses, &c., and of Cristna, &c., are parts, is to be found, in China, Mexico, Peru, Ireland, and Scotland—to be found every where. The multiplicity of the Divi or Gods of the Indians and Greeks, who arose in later times, are no more an objection to this, than the multitude of the Angels, Dæmons, and Saints, of the Christians of the West. If the doctrine of chances laid down by Dr. Young be strictly applied to all nations, there will not one be found where there will not exist a number of

Hebrew or oriental words much more than sufficient upon his theory to establish so high a probability of an universal language as to amount almost to mathematical certainty. Whether this was the symbolic or the first syllabic language, or both in succession, I will not pretend to say. Supposing aborigines of the white races of man to have been left scattered over the West and North-West, and in China, we can in no other way account for the Judæan mythos of black people being found in them, than by supposing it carried by persons whose colour has become changed by mixture with the white inhabitants. There is no reason to believe that the Judæan mythos was propagated as we now propagate the Gospel in distant countries. As far back as history extends, the Brahmins and Jews had an utter aversion to proselyting. In compliance with, or rather in submission to, the superior judgment of Mr. Laurence and other physiologists, on a subject on which I could not be expected to form an opinion upon anatomical grounds, namely, on the question whether there were originally only one or more than one species of man, in my observations respecting the black Gods, I treated them as one *genus* and one *species*; I now think it expedient to make a few additional observations to shew how my theory may be affected, supposing there was only *one* genus, (which is a fact which cannot possibly be disputed,) but *several* species.[1] If the latter should be the state of the case, as maintained by Mr. Ruish of Petersburg, who professes to exhibit the Rete-mucosum by which the blackness is produced in the negro, then I should suppose that there have been various races of *red* or *white* as well as the *black* one; but, that the originals of all the Gods have been of the black race, of the class of followers of Cristna, after the black race had become improved into the shape in which we find him—that, by the handsome black males constantly uniting with the most handsome black females, their progeny increased in beauty till it arrived at the degree of perfection which we find in Cristna; that the pontifical government did originally consist of this race; and that, in the East, the entire population consisting of this race, it continues black—still retains the rete-mucosum—though for the reasons before given by me, it is improved in shape: but that, in the West, to which it sent out numerous tribes, it mixed with the white races, the remains of inhabitants before the flood, called aborigines, the rich and powerful gradually marrying with the handsomest of the white races, till the whole race of the worshipers of the *black* God became white. We have daily experience of the black races, by this process, becoming white; but we have no example of the white race going back to the black. I pretend not to shew the cause of this latter circumstance, which is a fact—but the mere fact itself. This seems to shew that the aborigines were more numerous than the black colonies from the East; but this is, perhaps, no more than might be expected. For these reasons I think it must be allowed that, if the hypothesis that there was only one species be unfounded, yet the great argument and chain of reasoning which run through my work will not necessarily be in any respect overthrown. Nor do I perceive any difficulty in reconciling the apparent contradiction in it, if we only suppose what may have readily happened, that the high science attained[3] by the *black* Chaldæans was not discovered till the race had improved in form and faculty to the state in which we find the God Cristna. But even allowing the truth of the discovery of Mr. Ruish of the Rete-mucosum, and all that the Abbé Basin has said,[2] I see no reason whatever why the Negro of the corn-growing valleys of the Upper Ganges should not, from the causes assigned by Mr. Crawford, as detailed by me, in Vol. I. pp. 285, &c., have improved in faculty so as to have become highly civilised, and master of much, indeed of high, scientific information, before his form became moulded into that of Cristna. It is, in fact, strictly within the conditions of my argument, that

---

[1] See Vol. pp. pp. 51, 134, 138, 242, 253, 398, 418, 751.
[2] Philosophy of History, translated by Wood Gandell, pp. 6—10.

the syllabic writing should have been discovered, and indeed all the high discoveries made, before the last flood, by the followers of Cristna—for our calculation goes to establish the fact, that the last flood did not take place till long after the sun entered Aries, at the vernal equinox. And we must recollect that my argument requires, that, long before the sun entered Aries, the race should have advanced, by degrees, in improvement, to be very nearly as improved in knowledge as at the moment of the sun's entrance into it. If we suppose man to have arrived at a high point of mental culture five or six hundred years before the entrance of the sun into Aries, the calculation will shew, that this will give him time to have had a knowledge, from astronomy, of the approach of the comet in twenty-nine centuries. In consequence of the prejudice (for it is really prejudice) against the Negro, or I ought rather to say, against the *possibility* of a Negro, being learned and scientific, arising from an acquaintance with the present Negro character, I admit with *great difficulty* the theory of all the early astronomical knowledge of the Chaldees having been acquired or invented by his race, and that the Chaldees were originally Negroes. But this prejudice wears away when I go to the precursors of the Brahmins, the Buddhists, and when I reflect upon the skill in the fine arts which they must have possessed when they executed the beautiful and most ancient sculptures in the Museum of the India-house, and the knowledge of astronomy shewn in their cycles of stones, &c., &c. That the *Buddhists* were Negroes, the icons of the God clearly prove.

8. The reason for the difference between the Ioudi of the West and of the East, is to be found in the circumstance, that the Afghan Brahmin who came with his tribe from the East, to Syria of the West, was an iconoclast: he was opposed to the use of images, just beginning to prevail (and now so much prevailing) when he left India. He was of the religion or sect of Persia, and of Melchisedek; and it is very evident that almost all the *peculiarities* found in the laws and manners of the Jews, are what arose from the anxiety of their lawgiver, Moses, to preserve this hatred of images—an anxiety of a sect well depicted in the history and book of Esther, and also in the conduct of Cyrus, Darius, Cambyses, &c., in destroying the images in Egypt, but leaving the lingas— and in restoring the Jews and their temple. And I think *that* is very likely to be true which is told by the Jews, namely, that they were not permitted to read Genesis for fear that it should, (*i. e.* that the Trinitarian doctrine found there should, for there is no other the least likely to do it,) draw them into idolatry, as it is pretty clear that it had done their ancestors in the East. I think, to the Trinitarian doctrine of several Persons or Gods, as it must always have appeared to the generality of mankind, and to the renewed avatars or divine incarnations, the numerous Gods, both of Greece and India, may be easily traced; and the influence of the doctrine among the illiterate part of mankind justifies the fears of the Jews, and may furnish a plausible reason for the care with which they concealed their cabala. No one can deny that the, at first perhaps innocent, *adoration of images* and emblems, has ended in the degradation of all nations. In every part of the history of the Jewish polity the struggle between the priest and the king is apparent; and, that the books are those of the priesthood is equally apparent: but yet the controul of the king in their manufacture may be observed. For instance, though David was a man after God's own heart, yet the priests contrive to say that both Saul and he were given to the Jews as a punishment. The object of the Jewish history was merely to preserve the pedigree, to shew the exercised right of the ruling power to their little throne at the time it was written, and the dormant right of the priesthood with whom it was in abeyance, until it was finally lost in the time when they became merged as a province in the neighbouring states. Had it not been for the fortuitous circumstance of Jesus Christ being of the little party of the *two tribes*, we should now have known as little about them as we know about the former great party of the Samaritans—the *ten tribes*. The books which the Jews choose to call *canonical* bring the history no lower than about the year

400 B. C. Here ends what may be properly called their *mythical* history, and their *real* history begins in what is called the Apocrypha, the historical books of which I doubt not contain a real history, though perhaps full of exaggeration. The books of Ecclesiasticus and Wisdom are evidently intended for the purpose of containing and concealing their cabala, the secret doctrines of Wisdom.[1] They are, in fact, a sort of paraphrase or commentary on the secret history of Genesis, and on the renewed incarnations, as is evident from the renewed incarnation in Jesus, the Son of Sirach, discovered and pointed out by me, supra, p. 124. If the priesthood whom we have supposed to have ruled the world were content to take as their tribute, a tenth of the lands of the cultivators, and that there was no intermediate class, like our gentlemen, between the cultivator and the lord of the soil, (observe the word Lord, L'aur-di,) there would necessarily be a prodigious increase of population. It might thus become peopled in so short a space, that there would not be time for the language to become so much changed into dialects as to cause one part to be unintelligible to another. Under these circumstances the communication between the remote parts would be extremely easy. There would be scarcely any temptation to rob a traveller, for I do not believe that in that early time any thing in the nature of money would exist, or precious stones be known. The cultivators would be as little disposed to travel as our farmers; and suppose one of the high caste were desirous of passing from one distant place to another, he would want nothing for his journey. He would only want the arrow of Abaris, the Mariner's Compass. In this state of the world hospitality would be the result of feeling. The world would be peopled to a very considerable extent before man would require any thing in commerce. He would want nothing except the produce of his farm or flock; then of what was he to rob the traveller, particularly a priest; or for what was he to injure him? As men became numerous and were obliged to betake themselves to ungenial climates and unproductive soils, the arts of weaving wool, of building houses of wood and sun-dried clay, the art of ploughing and sowing, and the habit of dwelling in towns, arose by degrees. I can readily conceive these arts to have arisen to a great pitch of perfection before various languages existed, and before there would be any impediment to the most free intercourse between different parts of the world, to the persons who might be employed about an archierarchy, and the very few persons who would wish to perform long journeys. It is very clear that the first persons who acquired the knowledge of astronomy and other sciences, by whatever means they acquired them, would become an initiated, or separated class, as the necessary result of circumstances, by what is vulgarly called accident, without, at first, any intention on their part. By degrees they would constitute what we call a priesthood. In this state of things the art of foretelling an eclipse would give them the dominion of the world; but I think they would have arrived at this power before they possessed science enough to foretell an eclipse. I shall be told, that the history of barbarous nations does not justify this theory. I say in reply to this, I think that the discovery (call it *accidental* if you please) of the art of symbolic, and afterward of alphabetic, writing, is quite enough to account for the civilization of one part of mankind being higher than that of another, and gives an answer to this objection. This theory is completely borne out by a fact which cannot be disputed—the existence of the Druidical and Cyclopæan remains in EVERY part of the world, which this theory accounts for satisfactorily, and to account for which no theory has even pretended to account before. The Druidical, that is the stone circular, buildings would be the first. The Cyclopæan walls would arise, by degrees, as the world became crowded with inhabitants, food and land scarce, and man quarrelsome—in fact as the golden age wore away. Then arose soldiers hired by the scientific caste to keep order,—then arose disputes for superiority between the hirelings to keep order, and the scientific caste,—be-

---

[1] See Vol. I. pp. 755, 795.

tween the crosier and the sword; and, by degrees, from natural circumstances, the four castes of priests, soldiers, tradesmen in towns, and cultivators, arose. For some hundreds of years, perhaps, while the golden age was passing away, while these things were taking place, the languages would advance in their formation, and the world begin to be, as at present, no better than a tower of Babel. The passage of man through the different stages which I have developed has been beautifully and very appropriately described by the Golden, the Silver, the Brazen, and the Iron ages,—for, as I have before remarked, I do not doubt that this was the order in which the metals were discovered. Every thing betrays the going to pieces of an immense machine—a machine which went well enough as long as circumstances were favourable to it, but which necessarily went out of order as they changed, and they necessarily changed because the law of nature—of all existent beings—forbids them ever to stand still. As the change of the circumstances was varied by situation, climate, and many other incidents of every different country, so the effects were varied. In most Asiatic states we have *despotisms*; in the temperate European, we have *free states*; in many others, the settlement of clans, where the order of priesthood never shews itself except it be as priest and king, united at the head of the tribe or clan. In Abraham we have priest and king; in Melchizedek the same.

9. I formerly stated, p. 264, that in Egypt, the power of the high-priest was such that, if he ordered the king to commit suicide, he would be obeyed; and that this is what is done by the Grand Seignior to the Pashas every day. In the following account, by Mr. Heeren, the supreme priesthood shews itself very clearly:—" The priests of Egypt were the principal land-
" holders of the country, and besides them the right of holding lands was enjoyed only by the
" king and the military caste. Changes of course must have ensued, amid the various political
" revolutions to which the state has been subject, in this important branch of the sacerdotal power,
" yet none of such a nature as materially to affect the right itself, and hence we find that a large,
" if not the largest and fairest, portion of the lands of Egypt, remained always in the hands of the
" priests. To each temple, as has already been remarked, were attached extensive domains, the
" common possession of the whole fraternity, and their original place of settlement. These
" lands were let out for a moderate sum, and their revenue derived from them went to the
" common treasury of the temple, over which a superintendant or treasurer was placed, who was
" also a member of the sacerdotal body. From this treasury were supplied the wants of the
" various families which composed the sacred college. They had also a common table in their
" respective temples, which was daily provided with all the good things which their rules allowed:
" so that no part of their private property was required for their immediate support. For, that
" they possessed private property, is not only apparent from the circumstance of their marrying
" and having families, but it is expressly asserted by Herodotus. From all which has been said,
" then, it follows, that the sacerdotal families of Egypt were the richest and most distinguished in
" the land, and that the whole order formed, in fact, a *highly privileged nobility*."[1] The success of Robertus de Nobilibus and the Romish missionaries in making proselytes, both in South India and China, has been much reprobated by Mosheim[2] and others, because it is said to have been obtained by unworthy means; but the more I examine the question, the more I am led to believe, that these nuworthy means, as they were called, was in a great measure nothing but a real explanation of the ancient identity of the Indian and the Roman secret religions, as I have explained, supra, p. 127, which the Jesuits demonstrated to be the fact, when the corruptions which had been introduced into the religions of both Buddha and Cristna were removed from them. They are said (as if, in so doing, they had committed a heinous offence) to have persuaded the Chinese Emperor

---

[1] Heeren's Ideen, 2, 2, 125; Barker's Lempriere, in voce, Egypt.   [2] Eccl. Hist. Vol. I. pp. 20, &c.

and Nobility, that the primitive theology of their nation, and the doctrine of their great instructor, Confucius, differed in nothing important from the doctrine of the Gospel. They are further charged with inventing a variety of fictions, to shew that Jesus Christ had been known and worshiped in China many generations before. In all this, there seems to me to be a high probability that the Jesuits had discovered, or by some means had become informed of, the secret doctrine of the renewed avatars, which I have, so much at length, endeavoured to shew, existed in the conclave, and that they endeavoured, in South India, not to *destroy* the existing religion, but merely, its gross abuses corrected, to bring it into subjection to the Grand Lama in the West. And with respect to the Chinese who were Buddhists, they endeavoured to convert them to the faith of Cristna, substituting their own Grand Lama, the Pope, for the Grand Lama of the Chinese, at Lassa, in Tibet. I feel little doubt that had the Jansenists, the Dominicans, and the Franciscans, not interfered, the Jesuits would have effected the conversion of the Chinese, the Japanese, and the Indians; for it appears from Varenius,[1] that their religion was the same as that of the Chinese and the Tibetians, which I have already noticed—the same processions, statues, candles, perfumes, prayers for the dead, auricular confession, monasteries for both sexes, who lived in abstinence, celibacy, and solitude, &c., &c.[2] I have a great suspicion not only that the Jesuits taught the identity of the religions of Italy and India, but also believed them to be identical. And if they did believe this, they only believed what was true. Clear-sighted people like the Jesuits could not do otherwise. Modern Christianity, as exhibited at Rome and Petersburgh, is nothing but a continuance of the ancient religion of Rome, if it be stripped of many of the modern corruptions with which it has become loaded. But it is the ancient *Esoteric* religion of which I speak—at first attempted to be established in its *esoteric* character; but, from the failure of which attempt, the present system arose, a great part of the ancient secret system now forming the public one.[3]

---

[1] Descript. Japon, Lib. iii. Cap. vi. p. 10.

[2] Vide Mosheim, Hist. Vol. V. p. 34, *note*, and Charlevoix's Histoire de Japon, Tom. II. Liv. xi. p. 57.

[3] There are *two* clear and distinct Christianities—the *exoteric* and the *esoteric*. The exoteric consists of the atonement, imputed righteousness, &c., absurd degrading doctrines, and accounted for by an absurd story about a man eating fruit contrary to the order of God; but it is a story altogether intended for the vulgar. It consisted of the Gnosis or the doctrine of Emanations. It was Trinitarian, in the refined way which I have described in the latter end of the first volume. The reason why we do not find the Trinitarian doctrine clearly developed in the Gospels is, because it was found only by inference in the story of the tree and the fruit, because it necessarily requires the doctrine of a future existence which was not contained in the exoteric language of the Pentateuch. In *that* the people are attempted to be governed alone by threats of temporal punishments. It is strictly Unitarian; the doctrine of the Trinity and the Gnosis being no part of it, for they are couched in ænigmatical or equivocal language, for the evident purpose of concealment. It simply looked to the God ιευε, a local God, as the author of all. The *esoteric* doctrine was a secret. It might be meant to be described, but it was not meant to be explained. What little is found has escaped from the crypt, and coming into the hands of such men as Irenæus, Papias, Augustine, Athanasius, &c., it has ended in being what might be expected from such persons, incomprehensible nonsense. It is very curious to find the only class of persons who possess the smallest portion of philosophy, the Unitarians, struggling for the vulgar system against the system of the ancient philosophers, and getting over the difficulties in which this involves them, by throwing overboard some of the nonsensical doctrines—the atonement for instance. The Unitarians ask why the Trinity is not clearly expressed in the gospels. To this no reply can be given. But my hypothesis answers this at once—Because it was the secret doctrine. It was the cabala both of the orthodox Jews and the Chrestians. Upon reconsidering what I have said in the last section of the first volume (pp. 826, 827)—that the Μια αρχη was the chief part of the *esoteric* religion, I have come to a conclusion, that, in fact, the whole Trinitarian doctrine constituted the secret religion; and this is the reason why, in the writers of the first two or three centuries, we every where have it in such doubtful terms. The doctrines of Christianity were but the doctrines of the ancient mysteries becoming public, and applying to the circumstances of the cycles as they advanced with time. What can be more striking than the expectation of the Millenium, equally among Christians and Gentiles? This accounts for such persons as Papias, Irenæus, &c., travelling from place to place to discover the true gospel. Either the secret doctrine was lost in their day, or they were not trusted with it. It would probably have been as imprudent to trust it to Irenæus in early times, as it would have been to trust it to Luther or Calvin in later times.

We often read of Hilarion and others being the founders of monasteries or monastic orders. This is said either when a new order was founded, or when the members of an ancient Essenian monastery were admitted into the Romish church. Jortin[1] states that there were more than ninety-six thousand monks in Egypt, in the fourth century. The Buddhists and Brahmins are well marked by Porphyry.[2] He says, "There is one tribe of Indians divinely wise, whom the "Greeks are accustomed to call Gymnosophists; but of these there are two sects, over one of "which Brahmins preside, but over the other the Samanæans. The race of the Brahmins, how- "ever, receive divine wisdom of this kind by succession, in the same manner as the priesthood. "But the Samanæans are elected, and consist of those who wish to possess divine knowledge." Here, in the Samanæans we have the Essenes or Monks, and, I doubt not, also the Chaldæans. Originally the Sectaries of the Bull were followed by the Brahmins, the Sectaries of the Ram or Lamb; or I ought, perhaps, rather to say, they themselves, in many cases, changed and became Sectaries of the Ram or Lamb. The distinction between those who took by hereditary descent and those by election, well describes the two systems of the Buddhists and Brahmins. In the Archierarchy of the Buddhists we have the prototype of the Papacy. In the mixed system or democracy of the Brahmins, we have the prototype of the mixed system of the Protestants; and, in the innumerable sects of India, we have the prototype of the innumerable sects of Europe: in every case a similar cause producing a similar effect. It seems to me not improbable that, originally, Monachism might arise from a wish for retirement and the enjoyment of a contemplative life, which, by degrees, grew into all the present austerities and absurdities with which we are well acquainted. Abstinence from the *female*, without which families must have arisen to disturb the pursuits of science, would be among the first effects of the abuse of this praiseworthy propensity; and the appointment of a head or superior to keep order would at last finish the establishment. That it should become *religious* was a necessary consequence—for philosophy was religion. The knowledge of the το οντως ον [3] and his attributes was the religion, and the philosophy also. This knowledge was closely interwoven with the study of astronomy, as it has been frequently remarked in this work. After reading the account of the Essenes, of the Jews, and of the Samanæans, in Porphyry,[4] and also the account of the Christian Essenes, as given by Philo, Josephus, and Eusebius, I cannot for a moment doubt, that they were all *one*, with such trifling variations as time and change of language and country must necessarily produce. The Chreestian religion, or the religion of the Χρης, evidently existed from the earliest time; and Jesus Christ was nothing but the *ninth Avatar* coming in his proper order—Salivahana in the East, Jesus Χρης in the West. And, as the Brahmins make their Cristna, not the *ninth Avatar*, but *God himself*, so the Christians do the same with their teacher of Samaria. And though Mohamed and St. Francis were thought to be the *tenth* Avatar by their followers, yet the followers of Cristna and Jesus would not consent to abandon their favourite object of adoration. Thus, notwithstanding the Salivahana of India is well known, yet the Cristna continues to prevail. In the West, the only difference is, that St. Francis, as an Avatar, has been rejected for the former Avatar. But I have no doubt that Mohamed was accepted as the *tenth Avatar*, by many millions of persons, in the East. The view which I here take of the origin of Monachism is not, I think, in opposition to what I have said in a former part of this work, respecting the contest between the *male* and *female* generative powers. I think both causes aided each other. We have the Brahmin well marked in Abraham; and the difficulty of separating the two sects, in modern times, is easily accounted for

---

[1] Ecc. Hist. Vol. II. p. 22.
[2] Preface to Porphyry *de Abstinentia*.
[3] De Abstin. Book IV. Sect. xvii., Taylor's Trans.
[4] De Abstinentia, pp. 147, 148.

by several circumstances—the first of which is, their union, as far as the feud respecting the adoration of the *male* or *female* generative power separated them from each other. Another circumstance is to be found in the fact, that the partizans of the two religions of Buddha and Cristna were, in reality, the same, however much they might hate each other; exactly as the Mohamedans and Christians are, in reality, the same, though we know that nothing can exceed the hatred which they bear to each other. These causes are enough to account for the great difficulty of making out the history of the sects in the West. But this difficulty is increased by several adventitious causes. Supposing that a tribe came from the East to Palestine, bringing with it its Samanæans, or its proportion of religious, at that time established in its country; it is very certain that these persons, in the course of perhaps a thousand or fifteen hundred years, would change considerably, and would probably have but a slight tradition of their origin. Probably they would acquire a new name, with the change in the language of their country, and a name again changed, by being handed down to us in the language of a Western people, who, in fact, did not understand that of the people about whom they were writing. We have an example in our priests. In little more than a hundred years our word *parsons* is very nearly gone, and is become changed into that of *clergymen*. And for language, the five dialects of the Celtic furnishes a very good example—Irish, Scotch, Welsh, Manks, Cornish. No person who has inquired can doubt their original identity: but how surprisingly are they changed! The individuals using them are now almost unintelligible to each other, and thus, in fact, these dialects are become separate languages. I believe that, if no very great mundane revolution should take place, nothing more than the common course of events, in three thousand years a historian will have more difficulty in making out the history and origin of the present nations of the world than we have. I believe that, as the distinction between the Buddhists and Brahmins became lost in the East, so in the West, the distinction between Protestants and Papists will insensibly diminish, until it will nearly, if not entirely, disappear. This will be greatly aided by no one religion being the sole religion of any very large district. This is the state of the case in the East, where sects are mixed—Buddhists, Brahmins, Mohamedans, Christians—at the side of each other, and often within each other. These different leading sects being also split and divided, into under, smaller sects, as Greeks, Papists, and Protestants, are divided in the West. No man, perhaps, is so well qualified to write a general history of the world as I am: but, I believe, if such a man as Sir Walter Scott was would take my work and study it carefully, with a candid desire to correct its errors and supply its deficiencies, he would be much better qualified. It must not, however, be an attempt to pursue the line of kings in each country, as we pursue our line—shewing how *Mary* followed Henry, and *Elizabeth* Mary; but it must be more in the nature of a critical dissertation on the history of each period, perhaps of each century. He must begin with the origin of the Buddhist religion and the Pontifical, Pandæan kingdom, marking well the few *facts* which we possess, from the *probabilities*: and, perhaps, in this early period, the fact of the existence of this golden age, or universal government, the builder of Stonehenge and Dipaldenna,[1] as the only one which we have remaining. The fact of the discovery of the Druidical and Cyclopæan edifices in all parts of the world proves its actual existence in a manner which nothing can impugn. It is pretty clear that the Monks, the *Regulars*, are descendants of the Buddhists—the *Seculars* of the Brahmins. This is the reason why we find the Monks in many countries possessing the tithes. The feuds between the two are the last remnants of the expiring disputes of the sects, called wars of the Mahabarat in India.[2] The

---

[1] See Vol. I. pp. 160, 230, 733; and supra, p. 135. N.B. the Author's orthography variable. *Ed.*
[2] We constantly read of the Brahmins having come into India from the North, and of a Pandæan kingdom. I have

Buddhists were the Hierists and Archierists, and the Pope became so, as I have said before, in consequence of the surrender of *the book* by Constantine. *He* was the follower of Cristna; and we have no Pope in India, because there did not happen to be a Constantine. We know very little of the domestic economy of the Brahmin church; but they may have imitated their Buddhist predecessors in some places unknown to us. Probably the Archierarch has become a king; and this may be the reason why the Archierarchy has disappeared. I think it is to be found in the Grand Magus—the Great Mogul—from whom the princes of India hold their crowns. I believe the Papists were nothing but a sect of Paulites—followers of Cristna—and Paul such a man as Luther, Calvin, or Montanus, acquiring many followers, and his sect put into power by Constantine. The Monks of Europe were Buddhists, and came over to this sect, and united with it afterward. All the apparent anomalies and confused mixture of the orders arose from the going to pieces of the first Archierarchy, and the rising of the second. The Monks were the Samanæans or Gymnosophists. The same thing took place in Britain and Ireland in the West, as took place in India, or we should not have found the Buddha and the Cristna and the Callidei here. When Cæsar arrived in Britain, the first system had gone to pieces. The Buddhist government had been overthrown by that of Cristna, and the whole country had become divided among petty princes and tribes. Gaul was in the same state. All the oriental mythos is well marked in that country. I think it is very likely that Cæsar conquered both Britain and Gaul as Cortes and Pizarro conquered Mexico and Peru; that he was thought to be the Æsar *expected to come:* for, as we have found other parts of the mythos, it is not unreasonable to expect to find this. The reason why we have no account of this in the Greek and Latin writers, is the same as that which prevents our having any account of this mythos in the historians of the conquest of Mexico and Peru; and yet no one can doubt that the mythos existed there, and that it aided their conquest. When the first Pontifical government went to decay, (perhaps its decay was caused by the rise of the sect of Cristna,) different effects would take place in different countries; yet remnants of it may be expected to be found in all. What we do find is exactly that which, under the circumstances, might be expected to be found. But the numerous remnants of the first system, religion, or mythos, prove its original existence beyond a doubt. This admitted, all the rest is a natural consequence.

---

no doubt that this was the kingdom founded when the sun entered Aries. The wars of the Mahabarat were the struggles to establish this kingdom. I think it probable that the sect of Cristna arose in Tartary, and, after a struggle with, and the defeat of, its countrymen, it advanced to the South and conquered India. This is exactly what happened to Baber in a later day.

CHAPTER III.

NIEBUHR ON PONTIFICAL GOVERNMENT IN ITALY.—PATRIARCHAL GOVERNMENT IN CHINA.—MOHAMED.—PONTIFICAL GOVERNMENT.—THE ASSASSINS.—NIEBUHR ON LANDED TENURES RENEWED.—CONFEDERATED STATES UNDER PONTIFICAL GOVERNMENT.—LETTERS AND POPULATION.

1. WE will now return to Mr. Niebuhr, and to the remains of the Pontifical government in Italy, discovered by him, but not understood.[1] Mr. Niebuhr says, "It is the more probable that the "Roman kings, according to the general polity of states in the ancient world, levied a tenth off "the lands, the property of which vested in the state, as it did with the princes of Asia; because "even multiplied vassalage, without any considerable taxation, would have been inadequate to "execute their enormous buildings."[2] I have no doubt that over the whole world, wherever the Cyclopæan or Druidical buildings are found, and where are they not found? a patriarchal system extended, and that it was supported by the tenths of the landed produce. In the account of the almost obsolete, at least much neglected, Agrimensores of Italy, and of the *ancient Etruscans* we have probably the only written remains of the financial polity of the ancient Patriarchal priesthood. But we have plenty of substantial remains of it in the Druidical and Cyclopæan buildings, and in the innumerable stone crosses yet every where to be seen in almost all countries, at the crossings of the roads and in many other places. The reason given by Niebuhr for the use of the cross, the Cardo,[3] and the Decumanus,[4] decussated on the face of the world, correctly according to

---

[1] See Vol. I. pp. 375, 376, 620—623, and supra, 26, 27, 56, 134, 137.

[2] The Roman History, Vol. I. p. 470. Walter's Ed.

[3] The Patriarchs of tribes fixed their residence near the stone pillar, the object of adoration, the emblem of the generative principle. Most learned inquirers have seen that, of this, the *cross* was the emblem; but the reasons they have assigned why it became so have never been satisfactory to me. I believe it arose from the horizontal cross on the tops of the Cardos—the Gnomon.

[4] It is related that Josiah burnt the Ashre in the fields of the Brook Kidron. 2 Kings xxiii., &., &c. The root *Ash* means a *plant* or *tree*, and *one* or *the first*; it also forms the root of the word Ashera, which means *tenth* or *tithe*. We have seen the Alphabet to be a tree, and we have found, in the oldest languages, the figure 1, and the figure 10, to be denoted by the same form. I believe the *iod* for the letter *yew* and for 10, is only the holy I—*i-di*. In the translation of the forged Veda into French (Asiat. Res. Vol. XIV. p. 32) "*Une syllabe composé son nom*" is given as the translation of the Sanscrit word *Aoshara*, which Mr. Ellis says has not that meaning, but that it means *indestructible*, *infinite*, not considering that it may possibly have both meanings. He admits that it means letter. In the Arabic, I understand, it means *letter*. Robertus likens the world to *a tree*. In his imitation of the Veda the translator says, "Du système "qui donne au monde la figure d'une fleur et des grandeurs de la déesse Tārā, qui habite sur la première feuille à "l'Est." He then says, "La fleur qui compose le monde répondit la déesse est même composée de dix feuilles; je dois "me métamorphoser sur chacune de ces feuilles," &c. Then occurs an account of the first leaf of the flower, &c., which is followed by a refutation, and, in succession, each of the *ten leaves* of the universe, and the *ten avatars*. The Tenth or the Decumanus of the West is called Ashera, which was the ancient payment to which Mohamed restored that part of the world which came under his dominion. I have little doubt that the Ashre set up by Abraham were at the cross-roads or the capitols, precisely the same as the stone pillars of the West, called *decumans*, and were used for the same purposes, and might perhaps be in some respects of a more scientific character. I suppose they were, as Mr. Landseer imagines, of the nature of Orreries, and would make the line of the meridian correctly. From being covered with stars, marked with letters that had the names of trees, they came to be called *woods*, and from marking the divisions into parcels of ten degrees each, for the payment of the tithe, the word came to mean *ten*, and, from the payment of tithe taking the precedence of all payments, it came to mean *first-fruits*. I am of opi-

the four cardinal points, and evidently connected with the Etruscan religion, is very striking. Here, if I mistake not, is the origin of the Mercator's Chart. The whole world, I do not doubt, was divided into squares or parallelograms, and a cross was fixed at every intersection, as Italy is described, by Niebuhr, to have been.[1] These crosses pointing to the four cardinal points could never be removed or mistaken, for they corrected each other. The object of this mensuration was the collection of the tenths for the priesthood. The Patriarch, the Πα[τ]ηρ αρχη, Royal priest, as the Vicramaditya, the Vicar of God, was the owner of the soil of the whole world; the cultivators or consumers of the pasturage paid a tenth of the produce for the use of it. At first, with respect to the land, there were three persons concerned: first, the Arch-priest, who was the owner—Lord of the soil; secondly, the Cultivator or the Shepherd; and, thirdly, the Labouring Man, the Helot, the slave, *adscriptus glebæ* as he very soon became; and, after a certain time, arose the Soldier. This was the origin of Feudal Tenures.[2] After some time, of course, this state

---

nion that the Asbre were perpetual almanacks; and, from foretelling the times and marking the distances, they were called *stones of wisdom* or Lingas. For this reason, when they were lost in India, and a pillar with an Elephant's head formed their substitute, the Elephant came to be *the God of wisdom*, or the Elephant's head, the emblem of the God of wisdom, came to be their substitute on account of the wisdom of that animal.

[1] See supra, p. 117.

[2] "Les Saques, ou les Scythes, passoient pour un peuple très sage, et très modéré: ils n'imposèrent à l'Asie, conquise
"par eux, qu'un léger tribut, c'étoit plutôt une redevance, propre à marquer leur domaine, qu'une imposition, dont ils
"chargeoient des peuples soumis par la force de leurs armes.—'Asiam perdomitam vectigalem fecere, modico tributo,
"'magis in titulum imperii, quam in victoriæ præmium imposito.' (Justin.) L'Asie étoit alors un *Fief dépendant* de
"la Scythie. C'est le premier état gouverné pendant un longue suite de siècles, par cette espèce de constitution, dans
"laquelle on peut reconnoître l'origine du droit Feudal, apporté en Europe par les descendans de Saques, ou Scythes.
"Leur gouvernement étoit très doux, et leurs lois très justes, comme on peut le juger par ce qu'en disoient Justin et le
"poëte Chœrilus et bien mieux encore, par la manière dont l'Inde, la Chine, et le Japan étoient gouvernés par leurs pre-
"miers princes: car ces princes descendoient des *Saques*, et leur administration paroit avoir été reglée, sur le modèle
"du gouvernement d'une famille, dont le chef est regardé comme le père." (D'Ancarville, Rech. sur l'Orig. des Arts de
la Grèce.) It is really very extraordinary how every learned inquirer finds his way at last to Scythia or Tartary, or to the country about ten degrees to the North and South of 40°. N. L. In the above extract there appears to me to be a recognition in the way of a collection of facts of all my theories and doctrines. First we have the primary existence and the wisdom and moderation of the Sacæ: that is, of the followers of Japhet. All that appears to have been required was, an acknowledgment of superiority. This was because Japhet claimed to be the eldest son. This strongly confirms what Richardson said, that Asia was a Fief of Scythia. This was because Shem owed suit and service to his elder brother; and very justly (I do not doubt) it is observed to have lasted many generations, and to have been of the nature of a Patriarchal government, or the government of a family, of which the chief was the father. All this is precisely my theory of Genesis and its division among the three sons of Noah. M. Benjamin Constant says, "En parcourant
"l'Europe, l'Asie, et ce que nous connaissons de l'Afrique, en partant de la Gaule, ou même de l'Espagne, et en pas-
"sant par la Germanie, la Scandinavie, la Tartarie, l'Inde, la Perse, l'Arabie, l'Ethiopie, et l'Egypte, nous trouvons
"partout des usages pareils, des cosmogonies semblables, des corporations, des rites, des sacrifices, des cérémonies,
"des coutumes et des opinions ayant entre elles des conformités incontestables: et ces usages, ces cosmogonies, ces
"corporations, ces rites, ces sacrifices, ces cérémonies, ces opinions, nous les retrouvons en Amérique, dans le Mex-
"ique, et dans le Pérou.—C'est vainement que l'on voudrait assigner pour cause à ces conformités des dispositions géné-
"rales inhérentes à l'esprit humain. Il éclate dans plusieurs détails des resemblances si exactes, sur des points si minu-
"tieux, qu'il est impossible d'en trouver la raison dans la nature ou dans le hasard." (Pp. 197, 198.) If M. Constant be right, which I am certain no one can dispute, how can any one doubt that there must, at some former time, have been one universal system?—as he says, "D'un peuple primitif, source commune, tige universelle, mais anéantie, de
"l'espèce humaine." (P. 200.) "N'est-ce pas à ce peuple que nous devrions demander le point de départ de la reli-
"gion?" (P. 201.) Again he says, "Nous n'affirmons nullement qu'il soit impossible au travail, et au génie d'arriver
"un jour à la connaissance de la grande vérité, du grand fait, du fait unique qui doit servir à réunir les fragments
"épars de la chaîne brisée dont nous soulevons quelques anneaux." I am vain enough to flatter myself that I shall go far to fulfil the hopes of Mons. Constant. Of this ancient system he says, (p. 214,) "Il est vrai que la théologie phy-
"sico-mystérieuse prit naissance assez de bonne heure dans les pays où le sacerdoce exerça beaucoup d'influence: mais
"il est faux qu'elle ait d'abord été la religion populaire, et qu'elle soit ensuite devenue une doctrine secrète réservée

of affairs would vary in different countries; but, by slow degrees. In India, collectors were appointed by the government to receive the payments, and to dispose of them, in some way, for the use of the Landlord. Here we have the Zemindars and the Ryots. A similar state of things was detected by General Vallancey, in Ireland, and under the same names too. These Zemindars in time, in some places, became what our country gentlemen are—they received from the lands as much more than *a tenth* as they could extort—in most cases obliged to do this by the government, become *military*, for its benefit. In order to render these early payments available to the distant governors, the most valuable of the metals was at last brought into use as a medium of exchange or commerce. It is evident that, without something of this kind, the produce of the land could never be made useful to a distant government. The exact process by which this machine crumbled into pieces, in various countries, and new ones became formed out of its ruins, cannot now, probably, be discovered; but common sense teaches us, that different effects would be produced in different countries. In some, the priests would form a species of Aristocracy or Oligarchy: and I think Mr. Niebuhr has shewn, that this was probably the case with the Tuscan Lucumones in their first state, when symbolic writing[1] was used, and also when they became the Roman Senate. These hereditary Sacerdotes[2] got possession of the tenths; when allegiance to a distant superior ceased—appropriated them to their own use, and then taxed the remainder of the people for the support of the state: and this usurpation it was which caused all the disputes in Rome about what were called Agrarian laws. It was something similar to what is going on between the priests and people with respect to the tithes in Ireland at the present moment. This is very similar to the state of Egypt described by Mr. Heeren. (See sup., p. 264.) Judging from the traditions of a Pandæan kingdom—from the remains of the mythos in every country, visible in the sacred names of places—judging also from the peculiar style of the Druidical buildings found in all parts of the world—the Cromlehs, the Carns, and the circular temples, I am induced to believe that the system was an archierarchy—that somewhere there was a Papa or grand Lama, a divine incarnation, who superintended the whole. It seems to me very natural for such an Archierarchy originally to arise; and as the colonies went out, from a country which would flourish greatly under such a state of things as I have suggested, that it should extend its paternal influence over the whole world.[3] It is also very natural, after it had attained its utmost limits, that it should endure a certain number of years and then, operated on by the eternal law of change—containing within itself, as all systems do, the seeds of their own destruction—that it should go to decay and fall in pieces. But it was evidently a system very tenacious of life. After long depression we have seen it almost revive in Asia, under Akbar, and in Europe, under the Roman Papacy of the middle ages; and there is reason to believe, that it has never been entirely defunct at Lassa. After the 6000 years had passed away, it is very clear that some change in the system must take place; and now, neither in Rome nor

---

" aux philosophes et aux initiés. Elle a commencé par être secrète, et s'est répandue ensuite peu-à-peu, malgré les " prêtres." I need not point out to my reader how completely my doctrines are supported here. M. Constant afterwards observes, (p. 226,) that Lévêque, who has written a history of Russia, places the source of all religions in Tartary. In this I believe Lévêque is right. By every inquiry I make, I am drawn to Tartary, perhaps to Cara-corum, or China.

[1] This was before syllabic writing was invented. From an expression in Mr. Niebuhr's work it appears, that for some reasons which he does not give, he believes the Etruscans once used a symbolical writing, (Hist. of Rome, Vol. I. p. 92,) and afterward could transcribe their narratives in the more modern alphabetical characters. These symbols I do not doubt were the numeral letters. I regret exceedingly that Mr. Niebuhr has not given his reason or his authority.

[2] In the ancient language the priest was the possessor of the sacra-dos or sacred portion of the produce: from the regimine he became Sacerdos.

[3] I suspect the Oriental pontiff has resided at many places; for instance, at Oude, Agra, Benares, Delhi, Mundore, &c.

Tibet do we hear of the Divus, the Pater Futuri Sæculi, the αιων των αιωνων, but only of the vicramaditya or Vicar of God; in Rome receiving his authority from the last incarnation, passed by the hand of St. Peter. But yet the Pope holds in his poitrine the keys of the kingdom of heaven, and of supreme power over the whole globe."[1] He never yields either to Emperor or King. When he wished to subscribe to our oriental translation society, an insuperable obstacle arose. He could not consent that his name should be placed in the list of members *after* the king of England: we English could not consent to have his name *before* it. For a long time I was much at a loss to account for the Roman state, instead of the Pontifex Maximus and the priests, possessing the tithes; but this is to be accounted for by the circumstance that the first kings were in fact Pontiffs as well as Kings, and, I have no doubt, supported their throne by the proceeds of their *Domain* as it is called by Niebuhr, and by the tithes. After their expulsion, to have left the Pontiffs in possession of the Domain and the Tithe would have left them to be Kings; therefore, a Pontiff was appointed of the sacred caste or order, who was content to fill the office, (but, perhaps, still with a secret reservation of the *rights of the church*,) with an outward conformity to the new order of affairs—an officer, by some fiction, being appointed, called King and Sagart, for the sole purpose of officiating in the sacrifices. These Pontiffs were like our old act-of-parliament Bishops. I have little doubt that the family of the Julii always aspired to the office of Pontifex. A prophecy has a natural tendency to cause its own fulfilment. I think this might both stimulate the exertions of Julius Cæsar, and also operate upon the minds of his friends and devotees—upon the minds of those who looked for some *one to come* at that time. Speaking of the tenure of land in Italy and the tithe, Niebuhr says, "The footing on which the possession of land and the land "tax stand in India, supplied me with an existing image of the Roman possession, the Roman "*vectigal*, and the mode of leasing it. In India the sovereign is the sole proprietor of the soil: "he may at pleasure confiscate the land cultivated by the Ryot: nevertheless the latter may "transmit it to his heir, and may alienate it: he renders a larger or smaller definite portion of the "produce in kind: this the state leases or sells to the Zemindars: unless it has granted the re- "venue of a district or of a piece of ground to some temple or pious foundation for ever, or to "some of its vassals and officers for life.—This state of things is not peculiar to India: traces of it "occur throughout Asia: where, in ancient times, it prevailed far and wide in the most unequivo- "cal form: as it did in Egypt, where all the land was the property of the Pharaoh, and the mili- "tary class merely had the land tax remitted to them.[2] The Tetrarchs in Syria were Zemindars, "who usurped the rank of Sovereigns: as, through one of the most calamitous mistakes that ever "brought ruin on a country, notwithstanding the most benevolent intentions on the part of the "government, the Zemindars of Bengal succeeded under the government of Lord Cornwallis in "getting themselves recognized as dependent princes and absolute proprietors of the soil. In like "manner the agrarian institutions of Rome must not be deemed peculiar to it: they were un- "doubtedly common to all the Italian states: and many of the notions connected with them pre- "vailed even beyond the peninsula: so that there is the less reason for supposing that the coin- "cidence between them and those of India is accidental and therefore delusive."[3] In the above description Mr. Niebuhr makes a mistake respecting the land of the Ryot. I think the Sovereign had no right to resume possession of it, or confiscate it at pleasure, as long as the Ryot did his suit and service, and paid his vectigal. Mr. N. in many other places shews that the *vectigal* was originally a *tenth*; and that the Roman Patricians not only got possession of all the lands of the

---

[1] As possessing this power, he gave away Mexico.
[3] Vol. II. pp. 133, 134. Thirlwall's Ed.

[2] He here means tithe.

state, merely paying the *tithe*, but that at last they usurped the tithe also. It is pretty certain. that, with the present constitution of the human race, whenever a priesthood should get possession of sovereign power in a large and powerful state, the almost necessary consequence would be the separation from it of a new order of priesthood. The priests would become kings, and take with them the tithes, the right of the soil of the lands, granting to the officiating priests and temples, from time to time, portions for their support—they themselves every day more and more merging the character of priests in that of kings. Thus the Mogul, though not even professing the Hindoo religion, is looked up to as Lord paramount by the princes of India of the Brahmin religion. Thus, again, the Grand Seignior, who is descended from the Khans of Tartary, is looked up to by the little sovereigns of all the Mohamedan States who are not followers of Ali, as the Lord paramount and ecclesiastical head of the world. I consider the fact of the Hindoo princes of India soliciting investiture from the Great Mogul, as, in a very peculiar manner, supporting my theory—affording circumstantial evidence to its truth. Every thing tends to confirm the suspicion formerly expressed, (supra, p. 344,) that the mythos actually caused several conquerors to arise. For example, Cyrus, 600 years B. C.; Alexander at the entrance of the sun into Aries; Cæsar at the commencement of the ninth seculum; Gregory the Great; Mohamed; Gengis Khan; Attila; Akbar; and perhaps Napoleon—about the year 1800, the fourth sæculum from Christ. Amidst the inextricable confusion of Mr. Niebuhr's work, arising from his ignorance of the principle upon which the modern or republican disposition of the Roman lands was made, viz. the decay of an ancient system and the rise of something like a new system from its ruins, it does clearly appear, that a considerable part of the discontent of the people arose from the refusal of the Roman nobles to pay the tithe for the lands which, in fact, they had usurped.[1] It is very extraordinary that Niebuhr has filled many pages—several chapters—with a description of the unaccountable variety and complication of the constitutions of the Roman and Grecian states, in the course of which, he constantly exhibits his ignorance of the Roman and Grecian writers; but never, in any instance that I remember, does he attempt, on any rational ground, to account for this state of things. About the mythos, we have plenty of observations; and now and then a reflection on the amphictyons or the kingdom of Saturnia: but never does he attempt to examine what these may have been. Here he would have found, in the falling to pieces of the old polity, the reason of the difficulties which he meets with. South America is exhibiting something very like the state of Italy and Greece after the Pontifical kingdom went to ruin. The constitutions of France and Britain are something like the constitution of Rome: their origins are sought after by the antiquarians, but sought after with little success. They would succeed better if they went back to the Pontifical kingdom, and to the builders of Stonehenge and Carnac. It is surprising that Mr. Niebuhr was not led to the discovery of the Pontifical kingdom, when he was induced to observe, that the king had the sole power of convoking the senate and the people, and of proposing measures to them: that he had the absolute command of the army, and that he alone *could make a sacrifice for the nation*.[2] In an observation which he afterward makes, (p. 339,) that the Pontifical law and the Augurs were independent of the king, we have an example of a priest grown into a king beginning to lose his pontifical character, and the priests beginning to set up a power independent of him— to separate themselves from him. From the account given in p. 340, Vol. I. of Niebuhr's work, it appears that the Romans had a *lex non scripta* precisely as we have: the conditions or regulations of which were known only from adjudged cases, in old obsolete books of the priests, probably books not written for the sake of conveying legal information, but merely for the sake of the

---

[1] Hist. of Rome, Vol. II. pp. 164, 165. Thirlwall's Ed.   [2] Ib. Vol. I. p. 338.

mythos; similar, he observes, to the practice of the Eastern nations, and particularly the Jews, as exemplified in Numbers xxxvi.[?] I have little doubt that the Mohamedans have the same system; and when our travellers say they are ruled by the Koran alone, they are led to this by seeing no other written code. I do not doubt that the Koran always so far rules, that nothing is held to be law which is against its doctrines.[1] It is quite clear that the Jews had a *lex non scripta* before Moses partly composed, partly compiled, the Pentateuch; and because many of the sect in North and South India, Mexico, &c., who have not the Pentateuch, have part of the same laws as the Western Jews, I am satisfied the latter were only their old laws put into writing by Moses. Mr. Niebuhr's history is the only one which I know possessing the shadow of a probability of any thing like truth, and with him, in many of his conclusions, I cannot agree. His work is rather *a critical dissertation* than *a history*, a sort of thing which must either, really or mentally, have been produced by every historian before he put down in order the results of his speculations. But when we have, as is commonly the case with historians, nothing but the results, without the power of judging of the reasoning by which they are produced, we can expect only what we find, on examination, a tissue of falsities and contradictions. A great fault of all ancient historians is, that they never consider sufficiently the state of affairs which they find as an effect of some previous cause; yet the cause must be well understood before they can have any chance of understanding the true character of the people of whom they treat, and the nature of their institutions. Without a pretty correct knowledge of these particulars they must always remain in the dark. This imperfect knowledge, added to the almost universal practice (even Gibbon is no exception) of receiving unconditionally the evidence of partisans or of opponents, has made all history worse than a riddle.

2. Although we know very little of the internal economy of the Chinese empire, yet enough transpires from the persons who have written respecting it, to shew a high probability, that the universal feudal system and the payment of tithe prevailed there, as in other countries. As in all other countries the system has undergone great changes, so it has in China; but remains of the original may be perceived. The Rev. David Collie, principal of the College at Malacca, in a note on his translation of the Shang Mung, p. 75, has stated, that by the *Kung* plan in China, an average of several years' produce was taken, and the *tenth* part of that average was fixed as the permanent tax on the land. He then describes several alterations; that, at one time, a *ninth* was taken, that in some instances a portion of land was set out for the government, which was tilled by the farmers as a rent, for the eight or nine other parts, which they occupied. In some cases he states the land to be cultivated by companies who paid the *tenth* of the produce to government. Here, I think, the remains of the ancient Patriarchate are evident. I frequently suspect that the Chinese empire was the seat of the first patriarchal government—the Officina Gentium. It must have been either in China or in the country of the thousand cities of Strabo, in North India, nearly all of which have now disappeared. In the Chinese empire there is nothing of the nature of Knights' fees or of the Indian jagheers. This is what we might expect from the well-known unchanged state of that empire. It yet continues, with its Pontiff at its head, less changed than any state in the world. This is the state of the patriarchal government of China. And it was, probably, for the purpose of his receiving the payments in gross produce, that the wonderful canals were formed, which bring such immense tribute in fruits of the earth to the Emperor. I have no doubt that the Chinese exhibit the remains of the first patriarchal government, almost in every thing. We have

---

[1] I strongly suspect that the doctrine of predestination, held by the Mohamedans, had its origin in the doctrine of the *renewal* or *regeneration* of every thing *in cycles*. It is clearly subversive of *free will*.

in many nations examples of great works raised to gratify the foolish vanity or the idle superstition of man; but where, except in China, have we ever seen works executed by government for the encouragement of commerce, or for the promotion of human happiness? I fear, however, that even in China the canals were formed for the merely selfish purpose of receiving the tributes in kind, before money was in use.

3. I think there is every reason to believe that Mohamed considered himself to be the *tenth Avatar* or the *divine incarnation* of the *tenth age*. I now address myself to philosophers, and not to Paulite devotees. We must not forget that if he were merely a hypocrite, he deceived his wife, his slave, and the first four Califs—not weak men like the followers of Brothers, Whitfield, Wesley, and Southcote—but men of the greatest talent, who conquered and ruled a great part of the world with consummate skill. But how did these men live? Not in splendour, but in comparative poverty; walking on foot to the Mosque, without pomp or retinue, like the other citizens of Medina, and themselves performing, chaunting,[1] every day the simple service to the Deity required by the Mohamedan law. The simplicity of life, and the total neglect of every thing like personal gratification, exhibited by the first Califs, persuade me that they believed themselves the locum tenentes of a divinely inspired, or divinely commissioned, person. What should induce all these four men in succession, in the possession of immense wealth, and in the command of large armies and of the finest empire on which the sun ever shone, to affect, and really to practise, extreme moderation, if not poverty? But they went farther, and by the establishment of the Ashera —that is, the restoration of their empire to the simple payment of the tenth of the produce, rents and all other taxes and Roman exactions being abandoned—they proved themselves a blessing to the whole of their world, which, from a state of great misery, they restored to great prosperity, and, as far as was in their power, to the happiness it had enjoyed under the rule of the first Hierarchy, in the golden age. Every thing tends to prove that their conduct was an attempt to return to that primeval state. Each Calif thought himself the successor of Adam and Noah, and the brilliant victories of their generals confirmed the delusion. I have little doubt that the belief, that Mohamed was the Vicar of God, ensured his victories much more than the sword; and it was this moderation in regard to taxation which secured his conquests. The armies of the Prophet, like all other armies, pillaged their conquered enemies in the moment of victory; but submission made and the sword sheathed, there was an end of oppression: peace succeeded to ceaseless civil war, and the tenth of the produce of the soil was substituted for endless and ruinous taxes, which the conquered countries had been subjected to under their former governors. This was the state of the dominions of the first Califs, which lasted long enough to amalgamate their heterogeneous collection of materials into an uniform mass. The tenths, without any oppression of the people, enabled their later Califs, the patrons of arts, science, and literature, to support large armies and a regal state in the greatest splendour.[2] This favourable state of things continued for five or six hundred years, till the Turkish barbarians arrived from the North, from Tartary, and overthrew it —once more plunging their fine countries into barbarism and misery. Every thing tends to shew that the first four Califs believed that they were destined to restore the *golden age*. With Othman, the third, this opinion probably began to die away. A very sensible and important article is given in the Foreign Quarterly Review, No. XXIII. July 1833, on Mohamed and Mohamedism. The

---

[1] Ockley.

[2] It appears that, in Spain, when the Christians surrendered to the Moors, they were required to pay only a *tenth* of the produce; but when the cities were taken by storm, a *fifth* was demanded. It is evident, however, that even under this imposition, as it was all that was demanded from the cultivator of the ground, he could not be much oppressed. Thus the Christian monasteries increased under the Moorish sway. Cobbett, Vol. LXXV. No. XIV. p. 879.

author has come nearer to the truth than any person who has treated on this subject. But he has, in a very surprising manner, omitted the notice of several hitherto extraordinary and unaccountable facts, which, in estimating the character of Mohamed, cannot reasonably be passed over. He never notices the fact, that the Koran, as it is admitted, was made up after his death, in a moment of confusion and civil strife, partly from papers in a state of rottenness, and partly from the *memories* of his followers; and that, twenty-two years afterwards, it was again made up or redacted by Othman. Thus it can be called no better than a forgery. But the learned Reviewer admits, that it contains evident marks of two religions, which he divides between the time previous to the flight to Medina, and the time posterior to that flight, while I think he ought to have allotted the first to the true Koran of Mohamed and the first four Califs—commanding, as I have stated above, immense armies, but walking on foot to the mosque, to chaunt the praises of God, in such simple ceremonies as might be expected from an "eclectic reformer: a reformer in the truest sense of "that abused term."[1] The Reviewer says, "the Koran contains two very distinct religions: the "first, a system of pure theism, as perfect as the age could produce, inculcating severe morals and "stoical submission..... The second teaches a sanguinary propagandism." Here we have the Koran of Mohamed and the first four sincere and zealous patriarchs, and the Koran of the conquering and magnificent Saracens—puffed up with pride and vanity. The Koran of the eclectic philosopher was not likely to suit the conquerors of Asia. A new one must be grafted on the old, to find a justification for their enormities. I must make another observation upon the Reviewer's rather unfair description of the vision of the passage on the Borak, or flash of lightning, through the seven heavens, to the throne of God. As Mohamed passes along the several heavens, the different patriarchs request him to intercede with God for them; but when he comes to that nearest the throne, where Jesus Christ was placed, the scene changes, and Mohamed begs Jesus to intercede for him—hereby, in a very marked manner, placing Jesus Christ above himself, and declaring himself a Christian. This is in perfect accordance with the Mohamedan doctrine—that through the excessive depravity of man, the mission of Jesus—of love—of peace—of benevolence—having failed, a strong one—that of the sword—must follow.

Most assuredly, in the sixth century, nothing could be further from success as a mission of peace, than the mission of Jesus. It is quite inconceivable into what a state the whole eastern world had then fallen. One of the great causes of the rapid success of Mohamedism was the bringing into one body of peace all the jarring elements of that period. I shall be reminded of the accounts, in the Koran, of Mohamed's violation of his own laws of morality with respect to women. But when was there ever great and unexpected success without its being attended with a species of intoxication? Mohamed was just as liable to this failing as other men. But this does not make him an impostor. To have obviated the ill effects of these errors of conduct in the minds of the first four califs, &c., there must have been something very interesting in the character of Mohamed, if, indeed, the stories were not foisted into the *second* Koran to palliate some later Saracen outrage by the prophet's example. But the stories might probably be true. They are in character with what we know of the human animal from experience. Whether we attribute the second Koran to a change in Mohamed, or to the knavery of the later Saracens, to justify the conquest of the world, they are both in character, and may be, in part, both true. The Reviewer, (p. 204,) says, "We "have already said that the Koran contains two distinct religions, the one containing the germs of "*purity* and *illumination*, the other fraught with maxims of bigotry and intolerance." I doubt it not. One was the religion of Mohamed the Sophee, the follower of divine wisdom, (treated on at

---

[1] Foreign Quarterly Review, p. 196.

large by me, in Vol. I. pp. 678—685,) the other was, or might be, the doctrine of the conquering Califs. It is very certain that there is no effect without a cause; and it is no way surprising that with such a mind as Napoleon's must have been, he was curious to know what could have been the cause of the wonderful success of Mohamed. It is easily to be pointed out; we will stop a moment to reconsider it. In the first place, Mohamed was believed to be the person promised by Jesus Christ, and also *the promised one* of the Jews. Besides, a great person was believed to have been promised, and was expected about his time by all the higher class of Gentiles, that is, the initiated part of mankind, particularly in the eastern world, who should be the *tenth incarnation*;[1] so that the minds of men were by this means prepared for the reception of him and his doctrines. This conduced to his success. Again his first success was the cause of a second; for success was very reasonably considered to be a proof of the truth of his mission. The next cause was the state of peace and security which was enjoyed by the nations under the Mohamedan sway. It appears that the occupiers of lands paid the Ashera or Zacal,[2] as it is called by Ockley,[3] to the Calif, who was the sole propr.^tor of the soil, exactly like Julius Cæsar by right of the Sword and of the Book—by the union of the Royal and Sacerdotal power, exactly like the Egyptian Pontiff. Thus, as there were no persons to form a class like that of our gentlemen, the whole country was circumstanced as our country would be if, by an edict, all taxes were abolished and the occupier of every farm was declared the owner of the land he occupied—paying to the government the value of a *tenth* of the produce. In addition to this, every person who did not occupy land paid a poll tax; this was what I think, in the Romish church, was called Peter's pence. It appears that this, in Egypt,[4] was two ducats a year. What proportion this might bear to a man's labour I know not; but it evidently must have been very small. When these circumstances are taken into account, and the peaceful and happy state of the countries under the Califs is considered, in comparison with the wretched state of the countries governed by the Greek emperors, it does not appear very wonderful that the temptation should have operated to the making of converts. *That* must never be forgotten, in considering these matters, which our priests always contrive to put out of sight, namely, that neither Jew nor Christian was required to give up a single iota of his faith when he turned Mussulman. The Mussulman religion was held to be the *completion of both*—the abolition, or, in fact, the changing, of neither. These were the causes which, at the death of Omar, in the twenty-third year of the Hegira, had given to the Saracens the empire of Arabia, Syria, Assyria, Persia, Egypt, and a considerable part of eastern Africa. These great conquests must have been made in less than fifteen years. After the death of Othman, the Califate became so split into parties that it is extremely difficult, perhaps impossible, to make out any thing that can be received as certainly true. The bigotry and malice of the Christians render every assertion they make *doubtful*: and when they quote a Mohamedan writer they almost always do so, as a contrivance to convict the Mussulmans of some enormity on their own evidence. As the sects of Mohamedans, of one or other of which every writer was a member, had as much hatred for each other as the Christians had for the whole of them, there can be no difficulty in Christians' finding a Mohamedan proof of what they want. And if we apply to any of the most respectable of the early historians, and consider them exempt from the failing of prejudice, it is impossible to avoid seeing that they have composed their

---

[1] See Vol. I. pp. 187—190, and 678—680.

[2] I suspect that the word Zacal is only il-saca, THE *Saca*, which is formed by the regimen—the payment or the right of Saca, become *the Saca*.

[3] Vol. I. p. 12.   [4] Ockley.

histories without taking the circumstances above detailed into consideration, and without the exercise of any thing like critical acumen. Suppose an Arabian author was to write the history of Europe; would he want materials to blacken the Popes, if he went for his facts to Luther or Calvin? But he could say, See what is admitted by Christian historians themselves! Thus Christians and Mohamedans were equally liable to misrepresentation. In both cases, when there was a lack of true enormities, which I fear seldom happened, there was no lack of falsities. Before the precious metals were known, and afterward, while gold, as it was in Mexico and Peru, was the only metal and coin not invented, the Supreme Pontiff could receive very little or no profit from distant possessions: the offerings must have been like those we read of, as being sent by the Druids of Britain to the temple of Apollo, at Delos, wrapped in wheat-straw. By degrees, this sort of homage would die away, or nearly so. This is the case with respect to Mohamedism. The Deys of Egypt, Tunis, Algiers, &c., all admit the Grand Seignior's or the Sultan's supremacy; and he, as the superior Lord, claims, though he does not receive, the *tenth* of the produce. But he does receive an acknowledgment. The country in the vicinity of the residence of the Pontiff, I doubt not, paid its tithes to him, and he consumed them. But as the tithes must have been in the form of perishable produce, they could be consumed in distant places by the initiated only who resided there, and who thus became the priests of every country—all appointed, originally, by the Supreme Lord. We constantly read accounts of most powerful Pashas submitting, without the slightest murmur or resistance, to an unarmed messenger, with the bow-string, when carrying the Grand Seignior's firman. This is the exact counterpart of the Egyptian High-priest's authority, spoken of in p. 366. It is precisely the same mythos—brought from Tartary. I believe the Grand Seignior claims the whole world, not as *king*, but as *Pontiff Seignior*, as a Divine incarnation; and all who do not acknowledge his authority, are rebels. On this account, I believe, he never makes a *peace*—only a *long truce*. A peace is a contract between equals: conceiving he has no *equal*, the Grand Seignior cannot submit to make a peace. It is perfectly clear that the Emperor of Germany always claimed the supreme power, and considered all the other kings of Europe, and I do not doubt of the world, as his vassals, in the same manner as Cæsar and Augustus did. He claimed superiority over the Pope, and the Pope claimed it over him. The Emperor of Russia maintains the same claim. These do not profess to be claims of *force* so much as of *right*. They claim as uniting in their persons both the right of priest and king—the book and the sword—as successors of the Cæsars.

4. I think, obscure as is our view of early Mohamedism, we may see, besides the adoption of the Ashera, other signs which cannot be mistaken, of an attempt to return to the primeval patriarchal government. In the Imams of Persia we have the 12 Lucumones; in the 72 Ansär or Helpers, who assisted the prophet on his arrival at Medina, I think we have the 72 of the Jewish Sanhedrim, the Amphictyons of Greece, and the Cardinales of Rome; and in the three Mohajee or Movers, who accompanied him when he fled from Mecca, we have the three sons of Adam and Noah, the three Flamens of Rome, and the three Patriarchs of Antioch, Alexandria, and Rome—imitators of the division of the kingdom of Saturn—and the three Archflamens or Archiepiscopates of Britain. It seems probable that an Hierarch should have been appointed for each district or nation, as conveniently marked out by natural boundaries, with priests in various departments under him, who would receive the tithes and convert them to their own use, and change them into money, as soon as money was invented. This Hierarch would follow the footsteps of his Superior; and, by degrees, would claim and acquire the rights and privileges of Archierarch—the distant Lord, by degrees, as national intercourse became interrupted, might be lost sight of, and at last be forgotten altogether. When money was once invented, new questions would arise, and the Lucumones or Patricians, having been in the enjoyment of the produce before the invention of money, would

very naturally wish, and claim, to keep it; but still they would not desire to throw off all allegiance to their Spiritual Father, who, at last, by desiring more than he had been used to receive, would cause the ruin of the system. Thus, by degrees, as even the knowledge of a very distant Lord faded away, the Hierarchs of kingdoms would grow into Archierarchs; and, in many cases, the character of Pontiff would be lost in that of King—priest and king—like Melchizedek. I think, from the Jewish Sanhedrim and their tribes; from the twelve Lucumones of the Etruscans; and from several other institutions and circumstances before treated of, which my reader must remember, it seems probable, that a powerful body and a well-organised system originally prevailed over the whole world. The uniform character of the gigantic circular temples shews this; they cannot be accounted for without something of the kind; and this powerful body must have had *immense funds* in money, or other means at its command, or it could never have erected those stupendous edifices. Mr. Niebuhr justly observes, "the drains from the Lake Copias, cut through "thirty stadia of solid rock, and the cleaning out of which surpassed the strength of the Bœotians, "in the time of Alexander, were assuredly the work of a people antecedent to the Greeks."[1] Here Mr. Niebuhr stops: not the slightest attempt does he make to ascertain who those people were. Similar works may be found in the temples of Pæstum[2] and the Gallery of Pausilippi. I think that there was in all countries a Pontifex, a cabinet of 12, and a counsel of 72 Cardones or Cardinales, divided among the districts, each superintending one of them. We have this division already marked in Genesis. In the appointment of an Hierarch, the Cabinet would, at first, *recommend* to the Archierarch; at last they would *elect;* and of course the choice would generally be one from their own number. It is easy to imagine how all this would arise. By degrees, the 72 would begin to wish to have a voice in the election; and, after a time, the people occupying the lands and rendering the different feudal returns, whether they were in money or in services, would put in a claim. Of all this we see evident traces in Italy, Greece, and India. The process which I have here described, took place, I have no doubt, all over the Pandæan kingdom: but as the change arose from circumstances, it is also quite clear that it would occur in no two places in *exactly* the same manner. I have no doubt that the Cardinales and the Decumanni were attached in some way to the collection of the tithes, the Decumanni, particularly, as their name seems to imply—perhaps men of *the tenths* or *tithes,* the operatives under the Cardinales. All the receivers of the tenths were at first priests or initiated. By degrees, those only, who exercised the functions which arose and became the rites and ceremonies of the religion, would be, strictly speaking, *priests.* But the others would form a privileged or sacred caste—a caste more or less marked in different places, and more or less divided from the general mass of tithe takers, according to circumstances. It is not unlikely that these functionaries were monks, and that monks became, after a time, the sole and proper priests. In the sect of the Paulites we have a pretty clear account how its establishment arose—evidently in imitation of the Essenes of Egypt. It imitated the other old system, as closely as it could; but it did not unite with its advocates till several centuries had elapsed. Its early separation, its ultimate union with the monks, are well marked.

5. In Volume I. p. 700, I observed, that Mr. Von Hammer was attempting a history of the Assassins, and that he had every qualification for the task, with the exception of *an enlarged and unprejudiced mind.* He has, since that time, completed the work, and has shewn that I formed a just estimate of his character. His work is, in fact, one great untruth, founded on one great mis-

---

[1] Roman History, Vol. I. pp. 119, 120. Walter's Ed.
[2] See Vol. I. pp. 432, 433, 563, 586, 777, and especially p. 625 on Niebuhr's silence on the builders of the *Cyclopæan wall* found under the ruins of the Colosseum. *Ed.*

take. He commences his inquiry with a thorough conviction that the objects of it, namely, the Assassins, were the most detestable of monsters; and, actuated by this opinion, he is blind to every thing in their favour, tortures the most insignificant and indifferent things to their prejudice, and not seldom sees proofs of guilt in parts of their character or history where any impartial person would see proofs of merit. Though I do not charge him with having wilfully stated a fact which is without foundation, yet the whole is really a misrepresentation. His history came into my possession at the moment the printer was finishing the Appendix to my first volume. It is a very able performance: and, as is usual with histories of this kind, under his skilful management there appear to be few or no difficulties in it; all is simple, plain, and detestable—a mass of straightforward, pure, unadulterated wickedness. These people are said to have first appeared about the year 1086, and existed till finally destroyed by Houlakou, the third successor of Gengis, the Khan of Tartary, in A. H. 654, i. e. A. D. 1256, a period of about 170 years.[1] It appears from Mr. Hammer's account, that the same general expectation of the end of the world prevailed in Asia, in the twelfth and thirteenth centuries, that prevailed in Europe, and caused the Crusades, as I have formerly described; thus, in a very satisfactory manner, supporting the truth of my ideas on that subject. If my theory were true, the same sentiment would prevail in both, about the same time. It appears, I think, first to have been expected in A. H. 489, i. e. A. D. 1095, on the conjunction of the planets, that year, in Pisces; and again in A. H. 582, i. e. A. D. 1186, on their conjunction in Libra.[2] This expected catastrophe was evidently attributed to an anticipated unfortunate collision of the planetary bodies. And I think we may readily suppose that the ancient belief in the collision of a Comet and the Earth may have given way to a belief that the mischief was to be caused, in some way, by a collision of the planets. Learned as the great Astronomer Naszireddin de Thous was, he might not know that the Comet of 1680 was to appear in 1106. But after it had appeared without any accompanying catastrophe, the general belief, the origin of which might be unknown, would settle itself upon the planets. It is certainly a very extraordinary circumstance that we should find this great astronomer, when basking in royal favour at the court of the Calif, and abounding in wealth, played the traitor both to the Ishmaelites and to the Calif; and, in fact, succeeded in delivering them both into the hand of the Khan of Tartary. I think this can be attributed to nothing but a religious motive. He exhibits a perfect picture of a renewed Daniel, for he appears, after the fall of his first master, to have been soon after a great favourite at the court of the Khan, the successor of the Calif, employed in making catalogues of the stars, and in doing other things for the good of mankind. I think it is not impossible, that the founder of the sect of the Ishmaelites, as Hassan Sabah became, may have been the last descendant in the right line or elder branch of Fatima, the favourite daughter of Mohamed.[3] Such he was, or such he claimed to be. The particulars of the journey of Hassan Sabah from the court of Seldjoukide, Sultan Melekshâb, to Reï,[4] and at last to Ispahan, and his dialogue with his host, Aboulfasl, where he is represented to offer his opinion to him, that, if he had only two friends,[5] he could overthrow the Califate, may be all substantially true; but yet it is so represented as to be substantially untrue. I believe the story wants the addition, that the reason why he thought, if he had

---

[1] Hammer, pp. 255, 263.   [2] Ib. p. 256.
[3] In the various claims to power, founded on hereditary and feudal rights, we may see the reason for the attachment of all the ancients of the East to the preservation of their pedigrees.
[4] Hammer, pp. 70, 72.
[5] "Que s'il avait seulement deux amis fidèles et dévoués, il aurait bientôt renversé la puissance de ce Turc et de ce payean." (Ib. p. 72.)

two friends, he could overthrow the Califate, was to be found in the moral influence which he would possess over the minds of the people of Asia, by making known the truth that he was the *lineal descendant of the prophet,* and the last real Imam. If this were the fact, or the true statement of the case, it is perfectly clear, that in either case it is a truth which would be most studiously concealed by every one of those who have written respecting him and his followers. I believe the Templars were Assassins, because they were Sophees. In the spread or dissemination of the Sopheistic doctrines is the reason why the Assassins are every where to be found. Here is the reason why what appear to be emissaries from the Assassin chief are found every where, in every country. Whether really connected with them or not, every Sophee would have the appearance of being one of them—and every Sophee would be their well-wisher, and would, at any time, be very easily brought into their pale. Every Assassin might be a Sophee, though every Sophee might not be an Assassin. Here we have the reason of the great moral influence which they acquired, and of the constant assemblage in the Eagle's Nest of all the great and celebrated philosophers, astronomers, and literati of the world. How is it possible to believe, for a moment, the representation of Mr. Hammer, that they were a band of miscreants, so bad as to be totally void of all good; and, at the same time, to believe, that they should be sought after even in their den by the great and good of all countries? It does not appear to me that they claimed to be the eldest of the lines or representatives of the eldest of the descendants of Noah, but to have ceded that rank to the rulers at Caracorum; and this is the reason why they were not destroyed by Gengis Khan, who evidently claimed to hold his power as vicegerent or vicar of the Khan of Caracorum, from him from whom he received investiture into his dominions after he had first won them by the sword. He knew the value of the moral power, though our people (in relation to the great Mogul) cannot be made to see it. By the investiture with the Pallium, as Elijah invested Elisha, or else by the χειροτονια, as Moses invested Aaron, he received power from the rightful possessor of all power at Caracorum, and in return he did suit and service to him for his dominions.[1] To Gengis I think there can be no doubt that the Calif at Bagdad paid tribute and did homage. The feudal system shews itself, unconsciously to Mr. Hammer, in several places. I think there can be no doubt that both the Calif and the Chief of the Assassins agreed in the first instance to pay tribute to Gengis Khan. Mr. Hammer says, " Le renversement du Khalifat n'entrait point, à pro-
" prement parler, dans les projets du Khan. Les ordres qu'il avait transmis à son frère Houlakou
" en sont une preuve : il lui avait prescrit de ne demander au Khalife que sa soumission, et des
" troupes auxiliares."[2] Here the Feudal principle shews itself in correct practice; and though we do not read any account of it in Mr. Hammer's pages, we may be very certain that the numerous castles of *the man of the mountain* would not have been left in peace by Gengis had he not done his suit and service; and it was the refusal of this reddition, under the traitorous advice of Nassireddin de Thous, which probably brought on the ruin both of Bagdad and Almaut or Almont.

I think the great point of the heresy of the Templars may be found in their secretly holding the Pope to be only the representative of Shem, while they admitted that Japhet or the Caracorum gentleman was the Lord Paramount. The Manichæans certainly denied the Supremacy of the Pope, and the Templars were most assuredly Manichæans. This accounts for their Christianity,

---

[1] I learn from Mr. Briggs, our Consul at Alexandria, that the present Pasha of Egypt (April 1833) claims to hold his dominions not from the Sultan, but from the Sheriff of Mecca, who is in no higher a station than that of a private gentleman. But he derives his descent from the Prophet. It is quite out of all question, I think, to suppose that the person at Caracorum can pretend to have any power from Mohamed, and if I be right in this, of course we have no where else to go for it than to Japhet.

[2] Hammer, p. 284; see also pp. 294, 301, 302.

and for a certain degree of submission to the Pope; for he was their immediate Lord—but the Lord of Caracorum was their Lord Paramount. When I find the house of Fatima ruling in Egypt, and always consisting of Ishmaelites, I am sometimes induced to suspect that there was a claim set up by them on the part of Ham. Of this we hear nothing, for the same reason that we hear almost nothing of the system any where—that is, because none of the despots can now establish a claim to it, which makes them all put it out of sight; for, to bring it forwards, would only shew that though *they* had no right divine, yet some one else might have it. The letter of the Old Man of the Mountain, or Le Vieux, to Leopold, Duke of Austria, extracted from Rymer,[1] though determined by Mr. Hammer to be spurious, contains, I think, evident marks of genuineness. I think had the Ishmaelites not really had the æra from Alexander, which we find in that letter, it would not have been there.[2] I think no Mohamedan, no Christian, forging that letter in the eleventh century, would have thought of such a thing. Certainly such an æra may have been common in Asia, though unknown to us, for we are really suprisingly ignorant, and so we shall always remain, unless we can lay aside some of our narrow-minded prejudices. We may see from this admitted æra why Philip, the king or emperor of Macedonia or Scythia, sought to be acknowledged by the Amphictyons, and why, before his son marched to attack the descendants of Shem, he received his appointment, or at least was acknowledged as Lord, or Sovereign, (as we know he certainly was,) over Greece, and probably over the remainder of the dominions of Japhet; and also, probably, as Lord Paramount over the dominions of Shem and Ham, which he soon after conquered. We are greatly too much given to attribute the attempts at universal dominion of the ancient conquerors to avarice or ambition. No doubt these vices acted most powerfully; but there was always, at the bottom, a *claim* and generally a *belief* too in a right. They generally had the moral as well as the physical power with them, or they endeavoured to have it.

Every thing relating to these matters is put out of sight as much as possible by both Christians and Mohamedans, because now, in Europe at least, it all operates against the right divine of reigning despots and the priests. Mr. Hammer admits, (p. 3,) that the organisation of the society of Ishmaelites can be compared to no other of the secret associations of *brigands* or *pirates* which have preceded or followed it. " L'histoire de ces dernières ne nous présente que de " malheureux essais ou d'infructueuses imitations." The reason why the society of the Ishmaelites can be compared to no other society of brigands or pirates is, because it was not in *any respect* like a company of brigands or pirates. No doubt, like all other societies, it had faults, and great faults, and, like them all, committed great crimes; but this admission will not go the length to justify Mr. Hammer's description. His zeal against modern secret societies has made him mistake the character of those of the ancients altogether. I have little doubt that the society was not called Assassin from being a *murderous* one, but that a murderer was called from it an Assassin. The proper meaning of the word I have given in Volume I. p. 723. The accounts of them were, as we might expect, before they were taken in hand by Mr. Hammer, incomplete—"Ces détails si incom- " plets par eux-mêmes, nous ont-ils été transmis *sans suite, sans ordre, sans aucune* vue claire et " précise." In my first volume (*ut supra*) I have described them as Chasdim or Chaldeans descending from a very early period. In one sense I am quite correct; but they probably did not assume that character which entitled them to the name of Ishmaelites till the time of the Imam Ismaël, the son of Dschafer.[3] It was certainly a very remarkable accident, if it were an accident, that the Califate should become divided into three empires. The family of Ommia reigned

---

[1] Given in Hammer, pp. 345, 346.   [2] See supra, pp 347, 348.   [3] Hammer, p. 9.

at Granada, in Spain; the family of Abbas, at Bagdad, on the banks of the Tigris; and that of Fatima, at Cairo, on the Nile.¹ . Here we have the three divisions of Shem, Ham, and Japhet—Europe, Asia, and Africa. "Aujourd'hui encore, les princes des familles de Katschar et d'Osman occupent
" avec le même titre les trônes de Téheran et de Stamboul; les droits de ces derniers-à un pareil
" titre sont légitimes, car, après la conquête de l'Egypte par Selim, les insignes du Kalifat, l'éten-
" dart, le glaive et le manteau du prophète, qui jusqu'alors se gardaient au Caire, furent confiés à
" la garde de saintes villes de la Mecque, où il naquit, et de Médine, où était son tombeau. C'est
" pour cela qu'ils s'appellent gardiens des deux saintes villes. Padischah et Schah, empereur et roi,
" Sultan-al-berrein et Khakan-albahrein, sont des mots qui signifient dominateurs et seigneurs de
" deux parties du monde et de deux mers: ils pourraient aussi facilement se dire les *protecteurs de*
" *trois saintes villes*, les maîtres de trois parties du monde, et les dominateurs de trois mers, car
" Jérusalem, le Mecque et Médine sont en leur possession. Ils commandent en Europe, en Asie,
" et en Afrique: enfin, la mer Noire, la mer Rouge, et la mer Blanche, baignent des contrées
" soumises à leur pouvoir."² 'Where the account above does not exactly dovetail into my system, I cannot help attributing the discrepancy to Mr. Hammer's ignorance of the system, and I suspect that when the Pope caused the Mohamedan confession of faith to be placed on the chair of St. Peter, he was preparing Rome to become again one of the three holy cities. Hannibal had shewn that a march from Granada to Rome was not impossible. There is no doubt that Jerusalem, Mecca, and Medina, were considered holy; but when I recollect the circumstances which I have adduced in my first volume to shew that Mohamed wished to restore the world to its primeval patriarchal state, I cannot help suspecting that the capitals of the three quarters of the world were originally called THE sacred cities. When the attempt to restore the system failed, and the system became nearly forgotten, the Mohamedans having failed in conquering the *whole* world, the three cities of Asia might come to be substituted for the others. I cannot help considering the division into three, and into seventy-two sects, with the seventy-two helpers, and twelve advisers of Mohamed, and twelve Imams, to be similar to the Triumvirate of Rome, the twelve Cæsars, and the seventy-two free towns. These are odd *accidental* coincidences.³ I believe that the Ishmaelites were correctly the followers of Ham, and that is the reason we find them among the Fatémites of Egypt, who were all Ishmaelites. The Persians are the followers of Shem, and the Turks of Japhet. How the three connected themselves, whether in some way by descent or by the imposition of hands, with the three ancient patriarchs, I do not know; but the coincidence of circumstances is much too complicated to have been the effect of accident. The Ishmaelites were at war with the Califs and the Christians, because they both usurped a part of their dominions. Both Syria and Egypt were the domain of Ham; and the story of the uncovering of the patriarch by Ham, as indeed the book almost says, was invented to palliate or justify the usurpation or superiority of the other brothers. How the different Califs of Cairo, Bagdad, and Granada, made out their claims is very uncertain; but it appears that, in A. H. 402, and A. D. 1011, a great meeting was held at Bagdad, when the claims of the Fatémites to the Califate were declared to be null and void. "Sous le règne du Khalife Kadir-Billah, tous les légistes tinrent à Bagdad une assemblée
" SECRÈTE, dans laquelle les plus célèbres d'entre eux déclarèrent que les prétentions des Fatémites
" au Khalifat étaient nulles et sans fondement, et qu'il n'y avait rien de vrai dans ce qu'ils allé-

---

¹ Hammer on Assassins, pp. 21, 22. ² Ibid. p. 22.
³ No doubt it will be said, that these numbers might be adopted from the same kind of unmeaning custom which makes us talk of *scores* and *dozens;* or, if we have a large number to name, to say *a hundred,* instead of ninety-six or ninety-seven or one hundred and one. The probability of this will depend on collateral circumstances, and must be left to the reader's decision. I believe that our habit of talking of, and in preference adopting, such numbers, has descended to us from the microcosmic superstition, the nature of which is now forgotten.

" guaient sur leur descendance."[1] Here I think we may see why, in the mouths of the other two divisions, from whom alone we have the history, the Ishmaelites were Assassins. If we had the Ishmaelian account, although the others would not be called Assassins, Chasdim, or Chaldæans, they would be called robbers. Here, in the secrecy of the meeting, the true character of the whole shews itself—escapes out of the crypt—to our view. What could be the reason for keeping secret this meeting held in Bagdad, the capital city of the enemies of the Ishmaelians or Fatémites? The circumstance of secrecy here is in perfect keeping with what I have maintained throughout the whole of my work, that there were originally an esoteric and an exoteric system.

I very much suspect that Mohamed, before he died, pretended to divide the world into three parts, or that his followers pretended that he had divided it anew, and that this was done in consequence of the lines of Ham and Japhet having failed, and that therefore he had made a new division, as survivor of the eldest line, through the son of Abraham, by the *princess* Hagar. We must not forget that the Mohamedans maintain, that Hagar was not a *slave*, but a *princess*. We make her a slave to obviate Mohamed's claim. In Mr. Hammer's attempt to clear up the claims of the descendants of Mohamed to the Califate I see nothing but disputes and confusion. In the *secret* meetings, or the meetings charged with *secrecy* or *secret objects*, of great bodies of delegates from all parts of Asia, I confess I can see nothing but men meeting to bolster up the divine claim of the person calling them together. But still, it is observable that the object *was* secret. Why was it secret, if the whole system was not a secret one ? It looks very like an acknowledgment of the different despots, that a real right existed somewhere, but each of them fearing that he should not be able to make out his own claim. The whole object of Mr. Hammer's work is to shew, from the example of the Assassins, the danger or the mischiefs which must arise to society from *secret* societies; in short, that secret societies must necessarily be leagued against the welfare of mankind. And, in the original distribution of mankind into the professors of an *esoteric* and *exoteric* religion, he is perfectly right ; but it by no means follows that those societies which were formed upon, or arose from the ruins of, the ancient system, can be so considered. It was the possession of secret doctrines which makes Mr. Hammer angry, and he is angry because he cannot help seeing, that in this very society was the origin of the Free-Masons, Templars, &c., of Germany, of which he and his master are both afraid. He says, " Hassan " qui jusque-là avait cherché en vain un centre où il pût établir le siège de cette puissance " qu'il rêvait, s'empara enfin de la forteresse d'Alamout, dans la nuit, un mercredi, 6 du " mois de Redscheb, 483 ans après la fuite de Mohammed, 1090 ans après Jésus-Christ, et " sept siècles avant la révolution Française, dont les premiers auteurs furent des membres de " sociétés secrètes, qui, *comme les Ismaëlites, ne voulaient que le renversement des trônes et des* " *autels.*"[2]   In page 95 he says, " C'est ainsi que, pour atteindre un but presque semblable, les " Pythagoriciens et les Jésuites durent employer les mêmes moyens que les Assassins." Mr. Hammer represents the kings of Egypt to have been the servile tools, the mere generals, of the Priests, " dont le Lituus, la crosse de nos jours, était le véritable sceptre ;" that these priests taught idolatry to the populace, whilst they concealed the true dogmas under hieroglyphics and symbols ; that their great secret was the knowledge of a future state ; that the popular belief was confined to a terrestrial life, the pretence for which was to prevent the mass of mankind from having their minds diverted from the necessary pursuits of social life by refined and abstruse speculations respecting the future.[3]   He adds, " Moïse, initié à la politique des prêtres de l'Egypte " et à tous leurs secrets, conserva quelques-unes de leurs sages institutions, et cacha à son peuple " la doctrine de l'immortalité de l'âme ; aussi la connaissance en fut-elle en Egypte, réservée d'une

---

[1] Hammer, p. 34. 　　　[2] P. 82. 　　　[3] Pp. 61, 62.

" manière presque exclusive à la caste des prêtres, du moins nous n'en trouvons aucune trace dans
" les livres des Hébreux, excepté dans le poëme Arabe de Job, qui encore n'en fait pas partie." [1]
He then goes on to shew, that the great object of the Priesthood was to direct the energies of the
people to the good of the state. " Les mystères, véritables bienfaits pour les initiés, n'avaient rien
" de nuisible pour les profanes. La doctrine occulte du moyen âge de l'Egypte était d'une nature
" tout opposée : la première ne songeait qu'à affermir le trône et l'autel, la seconde qu'à les ren-
" verser.[2] La grande différence qui existe entre la construction de l'ancienne Memphis et celle
" de la nouvelle Kahira peut nous servir de point de comparaison entre la doctrine secrète de l'an-
" cienne *Académie d'Héliopolis* et celle de la *nouvelle Maison des Sciences*." [3] I have no doubt
that Mr. Hammer is nearer the truth than he himself is aware of. The same doctrines of the
Cabala or the Gnosis I firmly believe were taught in the old and the new academy of Egypt. The
ancient philosophers knowing very well that the belief of the truth of a dogma (such, for instance,
as that of the Trinitarian nature of the Godhead) can never be meritorious, nor the disbelief of it
criminal, were not able to see in what manner speculations on such subjects were to benefit those
whose whole time was required to procure the comforts of life. The reasons here assigned seem
probable; they are consistent with what we know of the weak and selfish character of man. The
Lacuna, in the system of the Hebrews, is beautifully supplied by what I have taught respecting
their Cabala. The example of the great Temple of this little mountain-tribe, whose secret books
have fortunately reached us, may be considered only as one example of the other great temples of
the world. It is very interesting to observe Mr. Hammer lauding the ancients for keeping their
fellow-creatures in debasement and ignorance, for the support of the throne and the altar, but
reprobating the same system in modern Egypt, because it was not the system of his own sect.
Hakem Beinrillah, whom Mr. Hammer calls (p. 54) the most stupid of tyrants of whom the history of Islamism speaks, who was the sixth of the Fatêmite Califs, about A. D. 1004, established
or greatly enlarged the college or lodge at Cairo, called Darol-Hikmet or *the house of wisdom*,
which he abundantly provided with books and mathematical instruments, and celebrated professors, and a revenue of 257,000 ducats. In this institution all the sciences were publicly taught,
AS WELL AS THOSE OF THE SECRET DOCTRINE, which the Koran was believed to contain. The
secret doctrines or mysteries were only taught by degrees, or initiations or gradations from lower
to higher ranks. "Dans le sixième, on enseignait que toute législation positivement religieuse
" devait être subordonnée à la législation générale philosophique. Les doctrines de Platon,
" d'Aristote, et de Pythagore, étaient citées comme des preuves logiques et fondamentales." [4]
Mr. Hammer, after this admission, goes on to shew, that the secret doctrines were of the most
pernicious kind; but, as they were secret, it is very certain he can know nothing about them, and
what he says must be looked on as mere calumnies. The college built at Cairo was (like that at
Cambridge, and the Temple church in London) only rebuilt in or about the twelfth century, A. D.
1123. As the society of Assassins and Templars were (I have no doubt) of the same philosophy
or religion, the previous existence of the College at Cairo raises a strong ground for belief that
they existed, in fact, long before the building of it. It appears that, in the beginning of the
twelfth century, *the house of wisdom* at Cairo was destroyed, but soon after restored, though in a
new place. This was about the time when the London Temple-church was rebuilt, in a new

---

[1] Hammer, p. 63.

[2] In simple English, according to Mr. Hammer, one was to enslave the people, the other to liberate them. But whether the latter deserved this unconscious eulogium may be doubted.

[3] Hammer, p. 64. [4] P. 58.

place, and I think also when the churches at Cambridge and Northampton must have been rebuilt on their ancient Saxon foundations. This causes me to suspect that about that time there must have been some general persecution of the order and destruction of their buildings; and, perhaps, on its nominal renewal, it may have taken the name of Teutonic or St. John or Templar. These were in fact all the same societies, as much as modern Templars, Rossicrucians, and Masons are; for they are really very little more than different lodges of one order. They have as little variation as could be expected in two long and distantly-separated lodges. Mr. Hammer shews that the Assassins were not a dynasty, but a *confrérie*, an order. "C'était simplement un ordre comme " celui des chevaliers de Saint-Jean, des chevaliers Teutoniques ou des Templiers." (P. 90.) Again, " Les Chrétiens et les Infidèles, les ordres chevaleresques et celui des Assassins se conju- " rèrent en même temps pour renverser l'Islamisme et les princes de cette religion." (P. 103.) After censuring D'Herbelot and Deguignes for considering the Assassins as a dynasty, Mr. Hammer says, "Tout ne prouve-t-il pas au contraire l'existence d'un ordre? Les Assassins n'ont-ils " pas des Prieurs, un Grand-maître, des règlemens, une religion spéciale tout comme l'ordre des " chevaliers Hospitaliers, celui des chevaliers Teutoniques et des Templiers?" (Pp. 197, 198.) Again, "Nous avons plusieurs fois indiqué les analogies qui existent entre l'ordre des Assassins " et d'autres ordres contemporains ou postérieurs : c'est vraisemblablement par l'influence des " croisades que l'esprit de l'Orient s'est réflechi dans celui de l'Occident. L'ordre où ces analo- " gies sont plus frappantes est incontestablement celui des Templiers: *leurs statuts occultes*, " spécialement ceux qui concernent le mépris de la religion positive et l'accroissement de leur " domination par la conquête des citadelles et des châteaux forts, paraissent avoir été les mêmes " que ceux des Ismaïlites. Les Assassins portaient des habits blancs et des bandelettes rouges, " les Templiers un manteau blanc et une croix rouge ; c'est encore un point de ressemblance très- " remarquable." (P. 339.) I have no doubt of the identity of the two orders, and that the Sophee or Gnostic doctrines were the bond of union. While Mr. Hammer (pp. 89, 90) represents the chief of the Assassins to have been neither priest nor king, and only to have taken the title of Scheik or Sage or Old Man of the Mountain, he yet asserts that *he claimed all power*. This is very like what we may perceive of the person at Caracorum, when the puissant Gengis Khan applied to him for inauguration, and is at the present moment claimed by the Sheriff of Mecca, in the dispute between the rulers of Egypt and Constantinople. (April, 1833.) In several places [1] Mr. Hammer distinctly admits, that the secret doctrines of the Ishmaelites existed at Cairo before the existence of the society of the Assassins founded by Hassan Sabah. All that this amounts to is, that he was the first person who got possession of the castle of Alamout or Almont, and of many others in the mountains near the Caspian Sea. Hammer also says, "Le Grand-maître, ses " Prieurs et ses missionnaires allaient partout répétant qu'ils voulaient la domination non pour " eux ou pour l'avantage de l'ordre, mais au nom de l'Imam invisible, dont ils se disaient les en- " voyés, et qui paraîtrait à la fin lui-même pour proclamer ses droits à l'empire du monde entier." (P. 143.) Here creeps out the claim of the followers of Ham, the Fatémites, to the first rank, to the archierarchy: and here the doctrine of the Millenium shews itself. It is admitted, (p. 176,) that Hassan, the second, assumed to be the real Imam. But this was, I think, after the failure of the Fatémites of Egypt. But in the order of their historical accounts there is much difficulty. It appears that some of the Assassins were men of high intellect, and that Hassan "assez instruit " dans les théories philosophiques, il se croyait *l'unique savant* de son temps, dans cette branche " de connaissances comme dans toutes les autres." Here *the unique savant* alludes to Hassan's

---

[1] See Hammer, p. 136.

being, in the opinion of his followers, a renewed incarnation of divine wisdom, like the Pope, or the Lama of Tibet. In every part of the history of the Assassins the most devoted fanaticism shews itself —a fanaticism which, if a tenth part of what Mr. Hammer has said be true, never has, perhaps, been exceeded. "Nous possédons *de lui un grand nombre de traités de philosophie et de jurisprudence, mais* "*ce n'est pas le lieu de les citer.*" (It is unfortunate that no place has been found to cite these curious works; but it is a valuable admission that they exist or have existed.) "Ces études étaient "un homage rendu non-seulement aux institutions du fondateur de l'ordre, *qui profondément versé* "*dans les sciences mathématiques et métaphysiques,* avait amassé au château d'Alamout" or Almont "une précieuse collection de livres et d'instrumens, mais encore à l'esprit de son siècle, pendant le "cours duquel la civilisation de la nouvelle Perse atteignit son plus haut degré et la philosophie "et la poésie prirent le plus brillant essor. Son règne de 46 ans vit naître et mourir une pléiade "de poètes Persans plus illustre que celle des Alexandrins sous les Ptolémées et que celle des "poètes Français sous François 1er." (Pp. 176, 177.) And yet we are taught to believe that these Assassins, the authors of these fine works, around whom all the worth and talent of the world appear to have been collected in the castle of Alamout or Almont, were a mass of infamy, unmixed with any thing of good. What fools Mr. Hammer takes all his readers to be! The true character of the whole history shews itself in the account of the great meeting of savants which was called in Persia by the Abbassides, against these people, their doctrines, and their claims. But every nerve is strained by Mr. Hammer to persuade his readers, that the whole was a temporal struggle for power, not one of religion or principle. Speaking of the death of a great philosopher, (p. 179,) he says, "Comme sa doctrine était considérée *par le collège des légistes comme* "*philosophique,* C'EST-A-DIRE COMME ATHÉE, chacun pouvait le tuer avec impunité." Here we see a probable reason for the assassinations by the Assassins—for I think there can be no doubt that they did commit them in great numbers as reprisals—but that they, with the *aid of fanaticism,* which was wanting to their opponents, who were as guilty as themselves, beat them at the game. It was not mere villany which made seventy thousand Fédawis (pp. 210—212) await the orders of the old man or Imam[1] to throw themselves from the battlements of his castle to shew their devotion to him.[2] It was fanaticism or religious principle alone which could do this. We are taught to believe that the writers of the fine works above alluded to were the enemies of mankind, though these works were calculated to be generally useful. The whole concludes with a general denunciation of their works, not a refutation of them; and, at last, when they are conquered by the sword of the successors of Japhet from Caracorum, by a general ignition of these works. (P. 239.) Yet it seems some of them have yet escaped; but we must not expect to obtain them through the medium of Mr. Hammer. He says (p. 198), "Ce qui donne encore à notre opinion plus de force "et de probabilité, c'est l'existence des écrits de Raschideddin, qui, jusqu'à ce jour, ont été conservés in Syrie par un reste des Ismaïlites."[3] "On y voit clairement que l'auteur avait une con-"naissance étendue des livres sacrés du Christianisme." (P. 199.) It appears that the Mogul gave directions to the historian Atamelik Dschowaïni to search the libraries of the Ishmaïlites at Alamout, and to destroy, in fact, every thing which could make known the truth. "Il mit à part "les Korans et d'autres livres précieux, et livra ensuite aux flammes, non-seulement tous les

---

[1] It is a singular thing that the origin and meaning of the word Imam should be totally unknown.

[2] Whatever was the age of the chief of the Assassins he was always called *old man.* This arises from the mistake in later and ignorant writers in not perceiving that what we call a Sage, did not necessarily mean an *old man;* but only a sage one—a possessor of wisdom. This is the reason why the Buddha of Wales, Ireland, Scotland, and India, is always called Old Man.

[3] Extraits d'un livre des Ismaélis par M. Rousseau, tiré du LII cahier des Annales des Voyages.

" ouvrages philosophiques et impies de l'ordre des Assassins, mais même tous les instrumens qui
" servaient à l'étude des mathématiques et de l'astronomie." (P. 278.) After the history of this destruction Mr. Hammer informs us, (p. 279,) that the historian preserved documents from which he formed a short biography of the founder, Hassan-Sabah: "Cette esquisse a servi à tous les
" auteurs Persans, entre autres à Mirkliond et à Wassaf, qui ont l'un et l'autre traité ce sujet avec
" assez de talent, et l'ont *souvent mis à profit*. *Nous-mêmes, nous avons suivi pas à pas ces deux*
" *historiens*." I think, after this development of the source whence the history of the Assassins is drawn by Mr. Hammer, my reader will not be much surprised at the account which he has seen is given of them. The war between the Calif of Bagdad, the Imam of Alamout and the Emperor of the Mogols, or Schâh of Khowaresm (probably Korasan) is said to have arisen in consequence of a preference given to the standard of the Calif before that of the Emperor of the Moguls or Mongols.¹ "Ce dernier s'approcha de LA VILLE DU SALUT, à la tête d'une armée de
" trois cent mille hommes," to attack the Calif, who sent the famous Schehabeddin-Seherwerdi, who, to his harangue, received the following answer: "C'est bien: l'homme qui revêtu du man-
" teau de prophète, règne comme son successeur sur les fidèles, devrait posséder toutes ses quali-
" tés: mais je n'en trouve aucune dans les descendans de la famille d'Abbas." - (P. 224.) For some reason, the real nature of which we may easily guess, Hassan Sabah, the second, prétended to burn his books; but it appears that he only pretended to do it, or if he did it, he kept copies. This Mr. Hammer stigmatises as a shocking act of hypocrisy. There was probably something good in them which the despots in league against the Assassins could not refute, and durst not expose to the view of their subjects. It is perfectly clear to me that there must have been something good, and very good, or professing to be very good, in the system, or it would not have caused seventy thousand persons to be ready at all times to sacrifice their lives in its support, at the nod of their leader. We ought never to forget that a person who is not a hypocrite, but a sincere fanatic, always imagines that his cause is good.—A fanatic in intentional evil never existed. I think, if we divest our minds of prejudice, we shall see that all the great emperors or conquerors were devotees—fanatics. They were generally also fatalists. If we do not take these considerations into the account we shall form but a very imperfect idea of the real state of the ancient, and particularly the eastern, world. I think it is very likely that superstition as well as policy moved Gengis Khan to go for investiture to Caracorum. We ought never to lose sight of this fact, that, whether mere mythos or matter of fact, the doctrine of Genesis has been the moving cause of the conduct of almost all the world from the very earliest time. It was not a book confined to the Jews, but a book of the secret mysteries of the whole world, which appears to us to be confined to the Jews, because their secret books are those only which have been preserved.

We have direct and unquestionable proof that the mythoses of Jerusalem and Eleusis were the same; then what must the history of this mythos have been? "La puissance des Ismaïlites
" était détruite, les châteaux forts du Grand-maître avaient été conquis, leur troupes massacrées
" et dispersées, et leur doctrine publiquement condamnée. Toutefois, elle fut encore enseignée
" en secret: l'ordre des Assassins, comme celui des Jésuites, subsista long-temps encore après
" avoir été supprimé, surtout dans le Kouhistân, province hérissée de montagnes et peu favorable
" aux recherches de persécuteurs." (P. 320.) But now arises the question, What was taught in secret? Was it merely to murder? I know not what it can have been but the secret doctrines of Sopheism—so universally disseminated, and so universally persecuted. Mr. Hammer says, (p. 330,) that "Les débris de l'ordre des Ismaïlites se sont maintenus jusqu'à ce jour en Perse et

---

¹ Pp. 223, 224.

" en Syrie. Mais uniquement comme une des nombreuses sectes d'hérétiques, qui se sont élevées
" du sein de l'Islamisme, sans prétention au pouvoir, sans moyen de recouvrer leur influence
" passé, dont du reste ils paraissent avoir perdu le souvenir. La politique révolutionnaire, et la
" doctrine mystérieuse de la première loge des Ismaïlites, ainsi que la meurtrière tactique des
" Assassins leur sont également étrangères : *leurs écrits sont un mélange informe de traditions em-*
" *pruntées à l'Islamisme et au Christianisme, et de toutes les folies de* LA THÉOLOGIE MYSTIQUE."
Here, in the last sentence, we have good grounds for *suspicion*, or, perhaps I ought to say *belief*,
that we have a proof of what I have before said respecting the Sopheistic character of the Ishmaelites ; and that, however corrupted it may still be, they retain a remnant of the ancient Gnosis.
They still remain in existence as a sect, and are scattered over extensive countries as far as India ;
they still have an Imam at their head, " qui réside sous la protection du Schâh à Khekh, village
" sur le territoire de Roum. Comme d'après la doctrine des Ismaïlites, l'Imam est un rayon
" incarné de la divinité, l'Imam de Khekh a encore aujourd'hui la renommée de faire des
" miracles, et les Ismaïlites — vont en pélerinage, des bords du Gange et de l'Indus, pour
" recevoir à Khekh la bénédiction de leur Imam." (Pp. 330, 331.) Mr. Hammer says, they
are called Souweidani, which I call Soufidani or Sophees, and Khisréwi, which I call Cæsareans or Kaisar-ians. He adds, " Ils sont ainsi appelés, ceux-là du nom d'un de leurs anciens
" Scheikhs, ceux-ci à cause de leur vénération particulière pour le prophète Khiser (Elias), le gar-
" dien de la source de vie." (P. 331.) Here we have the Carmelites, the Essenes, and, probably,
the real origin of the name of Cæsar. The doctrine of the Ras, the Gnosis, connects them all.
They dwell about Mount Masziat, which is thus called as the mount of the Saviour.[1] Their Imam
is only a little Lama, like him of Tibet. Nothing can be more mean or contemptible, perhaps
detestable, than the state to which they are now reduced. Mr. Hammer, near the end of his
work, thus concludes : " La constitution de la loge du Caire, la série graduée des initiations, les
" dénominations de *maîtres*, de *compagnons*, *d'apprentis*, la doctrine publique et la doctrine secrète,
" le serment d'obéissance passive, nous retrouvons tout cela dans ce que nous avons vu, lu ou
" entendu de nos jours, sur les sociétés secrètes qui ont été les instrumens de tant de révolutions ;
" et si nous cherchons des comparaisons dans l'histoire moderne, nous verrons que la procédure
" des tribunaux secrets de plusieurs ordres d'Allemagne offrait aussi quelque ressemblance avec
" celle de l'ordre des Assassins."[2] (P. 340.) And here we may see the secret reason which influenced Mr. Hammer to adopt every calumny against, and to misrepresent, the Assassins.

6. Mr. Niebuhr, speaking of the landed tenure of Italy, says, the "*general characteristic* was the
" principle that all landed property is derived from the State, and that the Conqueror acquires a
" title to it ; so that the exercise of his acquired ownership depends entirely upon his own will
" and pleasure, whether he shall tolerate the original occupants or not, on condition of a rent."[3]
Here, I apprehend, is the identical system of India and Europe, in its most simple form—the
farmers or ryots or feudatories holding their lands by payment, a *redditio*, of part of the produce,
and many facts unite to prove that *part, a tenth*. I have no doubt that the first GREAT *wars* (Mahabarats) were between the sovereigns or High-priests or Pontiffs about the presidency over the
whole world—as to which was the representative of the elder branch. With these the cultivators
or feudatories would have little or no concern. In those early times there was no such thing as
our land-holder or country gentleman. We see here the origin of the thirst after universal empire.

---

[1] This word is spelt Maszīat, Mésiade, Masiaf, Masiath, and Mosiab. (P. 363.) In the time of the Crusades it was
the chief place of the Assassins. When I recollect their doctrines of the metempsychosis and a divine incarnation, I
cannot doubt that I have, above, given its true meaning, in the word *Saviour*.

[2] " De Kopp, Constitution des Tribunaux secrets en Westphalie."   [3] Roman Hist. Vol. I. p. 122. Walter's Ed.

This gave rise, after some time, to what Mr. Niebuhr has noticed—that " it was a peculiar notion of this people, that every war conferred this right, though waged without any appearance of extermination, but on the ordinary grounds; and this right existed also between nations of one stock."[1] It has been judiciously observed by a writer in the Philological Musæum,[2] that Niebuhr has shewn, that " the primary and essential distinction between the patricians and ple- "beians, who were not an aristocracy and a rabble, as the writers of the Augustan age, and, as " following in their wake, all the historians of modern times imagined, but two several nations— " the one domineering, the other dependent, like the Normans and Saxons, to take an instance, " during the first centuries after the conquest, or like the English settlers and the native Irish." Here we have the exact picture of the Chaldæan or Druidical or Brahmin caste, with greatly and out-of-all proportion superior knowledge, and therefore superior power, coming from the East and taking possession of the countries occupied by the Aborigines—ignorant, naked, and defenceless; split, probably, into numbers of little, unconnected tribes, and, perhaps, after the first alarm, grateful to their conquerors for peace and security.—This may remind us of Abraham and his 318, trained or initiated in his own house, who, in his war with the five kings, probably employed under their command thousands of mercenaries! But it is very difficult to discover in the Roman state the difference between the Plebes and the Clientelæ or Tenants. Mr. Niebuhr acknowledges that they became amalgamated into one. I apprehend the Plebes were the occupiers of the lands, whose ancestors were what we call tenants *in capite* of the first Pontifical government. The Clien- teies were occupiers to whom the sacerdotal order, who were the successors of the Pontiff, let their domain lands, or the lands of which they had acquired the possession, at first, probably, under the pretence of supplying their families with necessaries, (as our Parsons possess their Glebes,) but which were by degrees increased, till they possessed large tracts. The remains of the caste are well marked in the prohibition of the marriage of Patricians with the class of Equites or Plebes. The Roman state was essentially agricultural. It had originally neither trade nor navy; and when it admitted other towns to the freedom of Rome, I believe this was confined to the plebes or occu- piers of lands only, except in some particular instances where the nobles of those towns were admitted to Roman citizenship; but in this case, I think, they were admitted into the class of Patricians, if not into the Senate, or among the Patres Conscripti. Mr. Niebuhr correctly observes, that the Clients were to the Gentes, what the tenantry were to the Lairds in the Highlands of Scotland. I apprehend the family of the Julii or of Cæsar is an example of a foreign noble admit- ted to the right of citizenship. The Ælii, the Fabii, the Lamii, perhaps furnish other examples; and I suspect that when great numbers of these foreign nobles became Roman citizens, the old Pa- tricians adopted the devise of enrolling themselves as sole members of the senate, to keep out the others, who, though admitted into the state, were nevertheless excluded from the exercise of the powers of Government—whence the Senators were called *Patres Conscripti*. They were our En- glish House of Peers—the foreigners were our Scotch and Irish Peers. The latter would vote only as Knights. The knights in all states, I believe, were the same. They answer to the military caste of India. They were the richest of the Plebes, who could afford to arm themselves and serve on horseback. By degrees they grew into a separate caste; and, I think it not unlikely, that they might, in some cases, have the vectigal remitted to them for their services. Thus we have, as in India, the priests, the warriors, the farmers, and the οἱ πολλοί constituted the fourth class. The same natural cause produced nearly the same natural effect in India and in Europe. We have nearly lost the fourth caste; but it may just be seen, with its subcastes, in the crafts or corpora-

---

[1] History, Vol. I. p. 122. Walter's Ed.

[2] No. I. p. 199.

tions of our towns. We must never forget that the Roman writers, such as Festus, &c., [1] acknowledge that those matters were only pretended to be understood by *erudite lawyers*. Although there was, I think, no legal distinction between a Plebs and a Client, each being entitled to vote in the assemblies, yet I do not doubt that there was a very great and marked distinction between them, arising from the absolute independence of the former, and the dependence of the latter on the noble under whom he held his land. I have little doubt that the Plebes or farmers, or occupiers of the lands, to whom they were let or granted by the sacred order, could sell or part with the lands as they pleased, the new owner always continuing subject to the vectigal. In this manner individuals of the Plebes became very wealthy. The struggles between the Patricians and the Kings, the *traditions* of which, and nothing more, remain to us, were only the natural contests between the high-priests, as to *who* should be *king* and *priest* when the great pontifical government fell to pieces. The whole mythos—the immaculate conception, death, &c., is found in the History of Servius Tullius.[2] Servius Tullius was the first who had the glory. Mr. Niebuhr has observed, that every city in the West, from Tyre to Gades, had a senate and general assembly, and that all the confederacies of early nations were based on religion. This is, no doubt, true, and for many generations this principle secured to the noble priesthood, the initiated or sacred caste of nobles, the empire over their fellow-creatures. As the first system went to pieces, of course systems differing in some respects would arise in different countries. I must again remind my reader, if he should ask why we have not accounts of the system which I endeavour to disclose, that the Roman writers all acknowledge, that every thing connected with these subjects was involved in darkness and doubt. Niebuhr[3] says, the accounts of the historians "differ materially from each other, because neither" of them "was explaining the institutions of his own times, or those nearly approximating, but " matters entirely obsolete, and rendered the more obscure because things wholly different in " nature had assumed the ancient names." The very terms of law, respecting the nature of the possession of lands, were, like every other matter relating to them, subjects of dispute with the lawyers. Thus Festus gives one definition of *possessio*, Javolenus another.[4] All these doubts arose from the fact, that the original principle of the sacerdotal, feudal system was lost, like the original of our own common law, and was endeavoured to be made out, like our law, from unwritten tradition and decisions of former judges, and from reasoning upon the two. I think there can be little doubt that the Sacerdotal order was at first strictly hereditary, and for some time this would answer very well; but I believe we may take it for a settled matter, that an exclusive order, of the nature of an aristocracy, will not last a long time, but will dwindle away—first into an oligarchy, and at last die. This tendency, I imagine, was the cause of the admission of persons into the order by initiation, which was adopted as a mode of keeping up the numbers. In Vol. VI. p. 111, of Lord Kingsborough's Antiquities of Mexico, an account is given of a correspondence between Cortes and the Emperor, recommending him to get a grant of the tithes from the Pope, Alexander the Sixth, which was refused; but the Emperor hereby acknowledged the right of the Pope to the tithes. This shews the truth of the theory I advocate. The Pope is said to have given all the new-found countries to the Spaniards; but, in fact, he enfeoffed the king of Spain in them—reserving to himself the Vectigal or Ashera. Protestants never cease abusing the Pope for his arrogance in *giving away* those countries: the truth is, they have not the slightest idea of *the nature of his claim*. It is very certain that the vectigal was not a payment of rent: it was the rendering of a portion of the crop—and *that* Niebuhr has, over and over again, shewn to be *the tenth*. And although this mode of exacting a rent is, as when with us it comes to be a tenth

---

[1] Niebuhr, Vol. I. p. 249. Walter's Ed.   [2] Ib. pp. 261, 262.   [3] Ib. p. 279.   [4] Ib. Vol. II. p. 363.

added to a third, the most pernicious imaginable; yet, when it consisted, as in all ancient states, of only a *tenth*, I can scarcely imagine that it would be found to operate at all against the great prosperity of agriculture. Mr. Niebuhr says, " The Patrician occupants of the domains still con-"tinued to pay no taxes. Livy, IV. Cap. xxxvi."[1] Here we have an example of the priests being themselves the occupiers, and, no doubt, cultivating the lands by means of their servants or slaves. And when the state conquered a country, they claimed to be owner of the land, as head of the state, and to receive the vectigal. One great object of the struggles of the tribunes was, to compel the nobles to restore the payment of the tax or tithe for these domain lands, which, when held in domain, were supposed not to be liable. As representatives of the Supreme Pontiff, the Patricians claimed *all* the soil, and, as his representatives also, the redditio or vectigal, though this only as trustees, for the use of the state. They came to stand in his place; and in return for the vectigal, maintained the government of the nation. Besides this, they had the lands in domain; these being in their own occupancy, paid no vectigal. Ecclesia non solvit ecclesiæ. When the Romans conquered a country, they said, the land is the property of the Roman Sovereign, who then stood in the place of the sovereign whom they had conquered. " Yes," said the nobles, " it " is the property of us, the representatives of the Archierarch, and we shall receive the vectigal, " as trustees for the state, leaving the lands in the hands of their old occupiers." But both the Patricians and Plebeians said, "Our state being now the sovereign of this new country, we will " take a part of it—as much as we please—from the old occupiers, and give the occupation of it " to our own citizens." " Good," said the Patricians, " we will take it among us, and cultivate it " by our slaves, and pay the vectigal to the state." " No," said the poor people, and the soldiers who had won it, " you shall give it to us; we will cultivate it ourselves, and pay the vectigal to " the state;" for, no doubt, it had long been found, that the tithe or *one tenth* only being paid, a great profit was to be made out of the other *nine tenths*, after all the expenses. Thus I apprehend there were two subjects of complaint—the people complained that the nobles did not pay the vectigal for the land held in domain, while they had got possession of large vectigal-paying tracts, cultivated by their slaves, which the people said ought to be theirs to cultivate and occupy, they paying the vectigal. Most, if not all, of the land of Italy is held by the Nobles, and cultivated by their serfs or labourers on their account. It is the same in Russia. Niebuhr says, " When " the consulate was divided between the two orders, the Patricians demanded the exclusive pos-" session of the jurisdiction, because the civil, no less than the religious law, was the science of " their caste, and more especially of the pontifices, who could only be nominated from their " body."[2] But how this came to pass it is clear no one knew. This civil law was obviously, at first, a *lex non scripta*; and the knowledge of this being confined to the Patricians, would evidently give them the opportunity (particularly when combined with the power of interpreting the religious law according to their pleasure) of deciding every great case in which the landed property of the state was concerned, according to their own interest. Every endeavour to account for this state of things has hitherto failed. Mr. Niebuhr does not seem to have attempted it: he has contented himself with merely setting out the state of the case. I apprehend my theory of the falling to pieces of the Pontifical Government will afford the requisite explanation.

7. The confederated towns or states of Ionia, of Attica, and of Etruria, being in the precise number *twelve*, sufficiently shew method and design, and therefore, probably, that their confederation was formed under the superintendence of the Pontifical government, and not the effect of a few states confederating for mutual defence. System, not accident, is evident. Then arises the

---

[1] Rom. Hist. Vol. II. p. 197. Walter's Ed.   [2] Ib. pp. 415, 416.

question, Where and what was the system? and I think I have a right to reply, that it was part of the policy of the Pontifical government thus to form the nations under its sway, leaving them in the exercise of their municipal rights, but exercising a controul, so as to prevent wars; or, if wars arose, to make them speedily be at peace again. I think a careful examination will satisfy the reader, that none of the sovereigns aspiring to be the supreme Pontiff ever made peace. If the rebels to their authority did not submit, they only made a truce. This, as I have already remarked, is the practice of the Grand Seignior. Mr. Niebuhr has pointed out the same system of confederated states among the Celts of Gaul, as we have just noticed in Greece and Italy. Indeed, I think the system is plainly perceivable in the Druidical polity.[1] I cannot help suspecting that one great reason why Rome was saved after the Gallic capture was this, that it was maintained to be the original emporium, the Capitolium or religious head of the Italian, if not of the European, Pontificate; and, as such, was looked up to by all the other states, with no little veneration. Though it had banished its kings, yet in the person of its Pontifex Maximus, it possessed within itself the right to the sovereignty of the world. The tradition of its right to the sovereignty, which we always find it most strenuously claiming, might readily continue, after the real particulars of the history of its origin were forgotten. However, the claim, the superstition, is always well marked by every historian; but no one, I think, has ever given the shadow of a plausible reason for its prevalence. Mr. Niebuhr thinks Cære was the parent city of Rome.[2] He adduces the long state of peace between the two states, and the opinion of the Romans themselves, that their religious rites came from Cære; of which they adduced the word Cærimonia as one proof. When the Romans were in distress they always sent their sacred things, and their riches, to Cære. It appears not unlikely that Cæres is a formation from the $X\rho\eta s$ of Delphi. I think there can scarcely be a doubt, that the city, which originally stood on the seven hills, was extinct for a time: if it was deserted, as some persons have thought, in consequence of a volcanic eruption, the inhabitants or government may have removed to Cære, and afterwards returned. I can hardly account for the peculiar sanctity of Rome, if Cære had ever been the peculiarly sacred place, or the first Cardo. I think we are quite in the dark on this part of the subject. I think we may see that, in early times, when soldiers first arose, they received no pay. In the great empires, in which the general of the Priest or Pontiff usurped the power and made himself Khan (כן cn Cohen), the lands were granted to his followers, on condition of finding a man and horse, i. e. himself equipped for war.[3] I have no doubt that the kings received the vectigal as both King and Pontiff; and hence came their funds for erecting buildings and making war. When the kings were expelled, Mr. Niebuhr[4] shews, that these funds were embezzled by the nobles to the great impoverishment of the state. I think there can be no doubt that the nobles were the caste which had come from the East, and whether the people whom Niebuhr[5] names as living after the time of the capture of Veii were their followers merely, or an earlier race of aborigines, or a body composed of both, it may be very difficult to determine.

8. If we carefully consider the first state of man, we shall find that he must have been in a situation peculiarly favourable for increase in numbers. Suppose, with Whiston,[6] that the eight persons in the Ark increased to about 2000 in one hundred years; and if we double them every twenty-five or thirty years, which I am convinced is not unreasonable, in 600 years there would be 100,000,000, in 650 years, 500,000,000 of people on the earth.[7] In whatever state we choose to place the world

---

[1] See Rom. Hist. Vol. II. pp. 258, 259. Walter's Ed.   [2] Ib. Vol. I. p. 194, *note*, and Vol. II. p. 467.
[3] Ib. Vol. II. p. 220.   [4] Ib. p. 221.   [5] Ib. pp. 222, 223.   [6] Univers. Hist. Vol. I. p. 262.
[7] Professor Leslie, of Edinburgh, states the *square feet* on the globe to be 5,482,584,878,284,800.

when the numeral symbolic language, which I have proved to have existed, was invented, it is very certain that when once a close society had formed its system and assigned numeral symbols to a given number of words, as long as that society existed and used those symbols, that language would continue in a great degree fixed. 'I think there is every reason to believe that this system would be co-extensive and contemporary with those peculiar cyclic or Druidical buildings which we find all over the world. I suppose we may safely believe one language to have continued intelligible to the whole world for five or six hundred years, or until the population rose to two or three hundred millions. The probability, I think, is, that the Druidical temples were erected when the numeral alphabet was in use, but when the syllabic alphabet was a secret, if it was discovered at the time. The numbers of the cycles described by the pillars, clearly prove the astronomical knowledge. The squared Trilithons at Stonehenge shew a much more recent work than the rude pillars at Abury—and the finely-executed temples at Pæstum, a date still more recent. The more I reflect on the subject, the more I am disposed to believe in a kingdom of Pandæa. This kingdom may have arisen in various ways. I can readily imagine an order rising to power—the effect of its superior intelligence—and, from a secret society of equals, growing by degrees into an Archierarchy; I can imagine this order continuing to govern by its influence for a long time,—its *secrets* gradually growing into *sacreds*, (the similarity and peculiar relation of these two words make me suspect them of very great, almost primæval, antiquity,)—its president acquiring power, and at last sovereign sway over his equals. Or if we suppose a college of priests or possessors of wisdom, with a president, at last obliged to employ a general—a soldier, to keep order, and that he should seize the crosier of his employer, in many cases, the only effect would be like that which happened at Rome with Cæsar—the Pontifex would become a warrior. With the change of the man, the archierarchy would only acquire more power—as the Chinese acquired more territory by being conquered by the Tartars. The Tartars annexed their own state as a province to the Chinese Empire, which it yet remains.

I conclude this chapter with repeating, that I cannot help suspecting, if we could come at the truth, that we should find in China strong marks of the *patriarchal government*, and, perhaps, of the first government of man. I have little doubt that originally, the monarch of the celestial empire was thought to be an incarnation of the solar Ray; whence he is brother of the Sun and Moon. The integrity or identity of its institutions has been preserved from the earliest time by the use of its symbolic alphabet. If we suppose that it was the original patriarchal state, we may easily conceive the natives of Uria or Callida to have discovered the syllabic system, and to have been unable to prevail against the strong patriarchal government which had become established in the East—by degrees, to have formed and established a new Archierarchy, extending itself to the West, and ultimately prevailing over all the western world. It may be said, that this must have been after the establishment of the Judæan mythos, because we find it established in China; but the present Mosaic or Judæan mythos is nothing but a branch of the first Buddhist or Tauric system of cycles; or, perhaps, I should say, a collection of the remnants of the first system, established when the symbolic numeral alphabet was in use, and destroyed by the wars of the Mahabarat. After this, probably, the syllabic letters and the Chaldæi, as an order, may have arisen, in Callida. I think in the Callidei of North and South India, we have a decisive proof that they actually possessed the dominion of all India, or ruled or prevailed over it, in some way—either by the *sword* or the *crosier*.

CHAPTER IV.

MICROCOSM. — ATOMS. — CHINESE MICROCOSM.—THE WORLD, &c., DIVIDED INTO THREE.—SACRED NUMBERS.—MERCAVAH AND CAABA.—MEASURES OF THE ANCIENTS.—ETRUSCAN AGRIMENSORES. TEMPLUM. MOUNT GARGARUS. COR. CARDO. AGRIMENSORES. TERMINI.—THE BRITONS.—THE SAXONS.—TITHES RESUMED.—THE ATHENIANS.— DIVISION INTO CASTES, INTO THREE, &c. — ARCHIERARCH, SANHEDRIM, AMPHICTYONS.—RELIGIOUS DANCES. POETRY. MUSIC.

1. AMONG the ancient philosophers there was no superstition or doctrine more universal than that of the MICROCOSM, though it is now nearly lost. The fragments of it lie scattered around us in the greatest abundance. We occasionally express our wonder at them, but we never think of inquiring into their cause or object. I must try whether I cannot, for a little time, arrest their progress towards oblivion.

The Microcosm is most intimately connected with the Cabalistic doctrines of the Trinity and of Emanations. It is seen every where, when once attention is drawn to it. The most ancient author, I believe, who has treated of it, is Plato, and he has named it only once to my knowledge, and that is in his Timæus.[1] It is very remarkable that it has acquired so great an influence, that all nations, without being conscious of it, constantly act from the impulse given by it in former times. We every where find it in what the ancients called *sacred numbers*; but no one has ever been able to give a satisfactory reason for these numbers having the sacred character affixed to them. Magic has been assigned; but nobody can tell what Magic was or is; nor are the sacred numbers in any way connected with it, except some few of them with that branch of it called *judicial astrology*. The origin of the Microcosm may, perhaps, be found in Genesis, i. 27, *God created man in his own image.* Every thing was supposed to be in the image of God; and thus man was created double—the male and female in one person, or androgynous like God. By some uninitiated Jews, of about the time of Christ, this double being was supposed to have been created back to back; but I believe, from looking at the twins in all ancient zodiacs, it was side to side; precisely as we have seen the Siamese boys,—but still *male* and *female*.[2] Besides, the book of Genesis implies that they were side to side, by the woman being taken from the *side* of man. Among the Indians the same doctrine is found, as we might expect.

Brahma was *scientia excellentissima*, because he was *humani generis propagator:* idemque etiam est rerum universarum architectus et opifex, summe potens, summeque intelligens. *Hujus vero symbolum, et ænigma erat apud veteres homo.*[3] Thus Man or Mannus was in the image of God; and thus, after God—Om—he was called Hom-o. Every thing was microcosmic. In the Tauric cycle we have Adam and his wife, and Cain, Abel, and Seth. In the Arietic cycle we have Noah and his wife, and Shem, Ham, and Japhet—a new trinity every 1800 years at first, then every 2160. When the mystics could not make the number come right, they made Noah live in *both* worlds.[4] The To Ov was supposed to be *duplicate*—then from the *two* to *triplicate* himself. From him proceeded the male Logos, and the female Aura or Anima or Holy Ghost—in ancient times always

---

[1] See Stanley's Philosophy, p. 208.
[2] Georg. Alph. Tib. p. 116.
[3] See Vol. I. p. 505, *note*.
[4] See Index to Vol. I. for references to Noah.

female. In microcosmical imitation of this, man, animals, and plants, and, in short, all animated nature, were believed to be formed of both sexes. Thus the To Ov was supposed, in himself, to possess the two principles of generation. Thus we have Adam and Eve; from them, Cain and his wife; Abel and his wife; and, afterward, Seth and his wife. Again, Noah and his wife; and Shem, Ham, and Japhet, and their wives. Cain, the eldest, was supposed to have forfeited his right to supremacy, by his misconduct. And on the believed fact, that Nöah really escaped from the flood, the mythos is contrived to shew, that, in consequence of the misconduct of Cain, he had a right to the supremacy; and, again, in consequence of the misconduct of the eldest son of Noah, that the second, Shem, inherited the right; that, in that line, the Pontificate should proceed; that, in that line, the Avatar saviours, kings, and priests, should always be found; and that, in that line, should all mankind be blessed.

2. In all the speculations in which I have indulged, my reader must have observed, that I have confined myself strictly to describing the doctrines or opinions of others, carefully retaining my own; but I cannot here resist the opportunity of observing, in what an extraordinary manner the probability of the truth of the ancient doctrine of the Microcosm is supported by the discovery of modern physiologists—that, when the seed of any animated being is examined in its minutest development, it seems to have the full or complete form of its parent, and that generation is, at last, but accretion. I suspect it was held, that the minutest atom was but a microcosm or miniature existence of some future being; and that, probably, every atom in its turn would be both the germ and the increment of other beings, till every atom had taken its turn.[1] The *atomic* doctrine of Pythagoras was learnt by him (as we are told) from the Phœnician or Judæan or Chaldæan, called Moses or Moschus, the name in both cases equally corrupted. The doctrines of Pythagoras and Moses, with very little exception, appear to have been identical. This was the philosophy revived, in a later day, by Des Cartes, with some additions, on the truth or falsity of which, I, as an expositor merely of the doctrines of the ancients, am not called upon to give an opinion. But this much I will say, the Cabalistical doctrines of Moses, of Pythagoras, and of Jesus, were the same: and the Sopheism of Mohamed, and the name of his temple Caaba or Caavah, the same as the Mercavah[2] of the Jews, raise a strong probability that *he* held similar doctrines.

3. An expression is dropped in a learned paper in the Asiatic Journal,[3] from which it appears, that the Chinese have among them the doctrine of the Microcosm: the author says, "By the Chinese, Man is considered a Microcosm: the universe is man, on a large scale: this is all we find positively stated on this subject. Human reason is the reason of the universe. The holy man, or the sage by eminence, is like the great pinnacle, and spirit as *he* is. He is the first of all beings. His spirit is one with the heavens, the master-work of the Supreme Reason, a being perfectly

---

[1] Colonel Wilford says, "It is to be observed, that, in general, the Hindus believe that all living beings originate from an atom-like germ, endued, virtually, with life; but inert till placed in a proper medium; when it becomes actually a *punctum saliens* or an embryo. It is indivisible, and cannot be destroyed by any means whatever; but will remain till the end of the world. *When a man dies, his body restores to the earth, and to the other elements, all that augmentation of substance, which it had received from them:* but the atom-like germ remains the same...... This atom-like germ is called in Sanscrit *atibahica*, and is mentioned in the Garudapurana. It is called also *omyaviyam*, because it goes faster than the wind. They say, that it is exactly the sixth part of these atoms, which we see moving in the rays of the sun, when admitted into a dark room, through a small aperture." (Asiat. Res. Vol. XIV. p. 431.) The part which I have marked with italics, shews that Col. Wilford has misunderstood his subject. It is a pity he had not gone deeper into it. I suppose the original of the word *ozyaviyam* has been the Latin vivo—vixi—disguised by the formation according to the artificial Sanscrit rule. I cannot help suspecting that the abuse of those artificial rules not only leads the modern Sanscrit scholars into great absurdities, but entirely shuts the avenues to ancient learning, and by this means has been one of the causes of their present lamentable state of ignorance.

[2] See *supra*, p. 342, and *infra*, p. 401.   [3] No. XXXVI. New Series, Dec. 1832, p. 306.

"unique." The Chinese system begins like all others; and, in this, it instantly displays its identity with all others. The doctrine of Taou Tsze says, "*Taou* or 'Reason' produced *one*; one "produced *two*; two produced *three*; three produced *all things*."[1] Here we have the doctrine correctly, as I have, in part, described it in Vol, I. pp. 594, 703, 757, &c. This last passage is taken from the work called *Taou tĭh king*, a Latin version of which is in the Library of the Royal Society, and which was executed by a missionary who had devoted his whole life to the study of it.

4. To return to our subject.—The world was divided among the descendants of Noah into *three*, and again into *seventy-two*. These were as follow: Japhet, the youngest, had *twelve*; Ham, the second, had *twenty-four*; and Shem, the eldest, had *thirty-six*.[2] This induces me to return to an observation in Volume I. p. 474, where I ridiculed Sir W. Jones's division of the languages of the world into *three*, those of Shem, Ham, and Japhet. I now think it right to observe, that it does not seem unlikely, when the world came to be divided into three sovereignties, that the universal language should, in its grammatical forms, have run into three dialects, which would shew themselves in a marked manner. On this point, therefore, I may have been under a mistake. In similar microcosmic manner the period which I have formerly described of 21,600 years was divided into *three*. The libration of the planes of the Ecliptic and Equator was supposed to take place in 7200 years. It was thought to librate three times in the 21,600 years; seventy-two small cycles of 600 years, or 72 large cycles of 6000 years, in 432,000 years. In this manner all the cycles were microcosmic. Thus, microcosmically, also, the surface of the globe was arranged. From Adam proceeded Cain, Abel, and Seth; and from them proceeded all mankind: yet we know not how the *first* world was divided; but we shall, by and by, find circumstances which will lead us to believe that it must have been divided as the second was divided. After the Flood, came Noah, and Shem, Ham, and Japhet. Their *posterity* was divided into *three*, and these were subdivided into *seventy-two* races. In like manner the *world* was divided into three parts—the portions of Shem, Ham, and Japhet; and these again, as appears from Genesis, into seventy-two districts, occupied by the seventy-two races spoken of above. In this way Noah was the patriarchal Archierarchal Pontiff while he lived, and, under him, his three sons, as Hierarchs, one for each division. After his death, they became three Archierarchs—one, perhaps, at Oude or Babylon, for Asia; one in Egypt, for Africa; and one, probably, at Rome, or at Thebes, in Bœotia, for Europe. In later times the heathen kingdom of Saturn was divided, in like manner, into three parts—one at Antioch, for Asia; one at Alexandria, for Africa; and one at Rome, for Europe. Now insulated facts and circumstances like the Amphictyon, scraps of records like Genesis, and analogy, raise a probability that this was the foundation of the universal microcosmic mythos. Perhaps a religionist will say, It was a literal truth. We will now point out what will add to the probability of its existence, whether *mythos* or *truth*. I believe the above is chiefly mythos; but I believe that an Archierarch did arise, who was what was thought to be the first incarnation, and will represent Buddha and the Pandæan kingdom; and that, under him and his successors, the world was ruled in peace, till the equinoctial sun passed into Aries—till the festivals required correcting,—till, perhaps, a great flood happened—and that, during this time, the Druidical circles were erected—the microcosmic mythos was invented or RENEWED and acted on, as we shall presently find. I see no impossibility in the first Archierarchy having arisen before the sun

---

[1] Asiatic Journal, No. XXXVI. New Series, Dec. 1832, p. 303.

[2] Genesis x. 21, ought to be rendered thus: "Unto Shem also, the father of all the children of Eber, and the brother of Japhet, *the elder to him*, were children born." Here, as we might expect, the sacred book not only makes the ancestor of the Jews the *eldest*, which would give him the tithes of the whole world, but it gives him as many kingdoms in domain as the other two put together.

entered Aries, in what we call the æra of Buddha; and if this were the case, I see no improbability in an archierarchy having succeeded by descent from the first King-priest who lived after the deluge, and in such Archierarchy having continued during many generations. I have just intimated that Buddha would represent Noah. There are a hundred circumstances, and, if my memory do not deceive me, some authorities, in favour of Buddha being Menu; but Menu was Noah, therefore Buddha would be Noah. Here I think we have the amalgam of the systems of Genesis in the East and West—Buddha, Divine Wisdom incarnate in Noah. Menu and Buddha are but qualities, appellatives personified.

5. In all our inquiries we constantly find men actuated by an opinion that some numbers are more *lucky* than others, but we no where meet with an explanation why they should be so considered. I believe the general conclusion is, that this opinion arose from magic; but how this could be I believe no one can shew, and I think it only arose from no one knowing what magic was, and thus it served to conceal ignorance. It appears that man and every thing else was believed to be made in the image of God, or of that first pattern which proceeded from the To Ον, after which the universe was formed. The more nearly a person imitated this pattern, the more pious, or perfect, or excellent he was esteemed; and, on this account, the more an individual was withdrawn from the flesh and abstracted from the world, the more he assimilated himself to God; and, in like manner, all the numbers connected with the microcosm of the world, were holy and fortunate. For this reason, as far as possible, every human work was assimilated to the great work of God, by the adoption of the sacred numbers. As Noah divided the world to his sons—Shem, Ham, and Japhet; so Saturn divided the earth to his three son—Jupiter (Ham), Pluto (Shem), and Neptune (Japhet).[1] As the kingdom of Saturn was divided into *three*—Asia, Africa, and Europe; so the world, as then known, was divided, after the death of Christ, into three Patriarchates—the chiefs of which resided at Antioch, Alexandria, and Rome. I suspect that the division of the world among his three sons, by Constantine, was a compliance with the mythos of Noah and Shem, Ham, and Japhet. I believe the Pope will allow that Cæsar held both by the *book* and the *sword*. When Christ came, the Emperors only held by right of the sword. The successor of Christ, the Pope, held by right of the book. When Constantine had given Italy to the Pope, he held it by right of both the book and the sword. He was king and priest of Italy. But he held all the remainder of the world by right of the book. He was not king of it, but he had a right to the tithes of it, which his ancestor, Noah, retained, when he granted the land to his three sons. As heir of the eldest son, the Pope was Lord Paramount of the soil. The kings were his vicegerents, his feudatories, bound to do him suit and service, and to pay him the *tenths*. The Emperor of Germany was successor of Constantine, and claimed all his rights. And, in like manner, I have no doubt that *each* country was divided. Mr. Hallam[2] states this of England. The old British historians tell us, that, in the time of Lucius, about A. D. 180, there were three Archflamens, viz. of York, London, and Carleon (Chester), who, when Lucius was converted to Christianity, became Archbishops.[3] Here we have the country divided into *three*, in imitation of the three divisions of the world. The Romans divided Britain into five dioceses. Brutus, grandson of Eneas, having killed his father Sylvius, fled from Italy, and after joining himself to some emigrants from Troy, in Greece, and *undergoing many adventures*, he landed at Tot-ness, in Devonshire. The island was inhabited by Giants; he conquered them and seized the island. He had, as I stated in Vol. I. p. 367, three sons—*Locrin* or *Loegrin*, to whom he gave Loegria, that is, England; *Camber*, to whom he gave Wales, hence called *Cambria*; and *Albanact*, to whom he gave Scot-

---

[1] Vide Calmet, in voce Japhet.   [2] Hist. Mid. Ages, Vol. II. pp. 20—23.   [3] Somner's Ant. Cant. p. 228.

land, which from him was called Albania. Here we have the old mythos—the going out, the adventurous journeys, and the Father—Brutus—and three sons; like Adam, and Cain, Abel, and Seth; or Noah, and Shem, Ham, and Japhet. This history is found in Geoffrey of Monmouth, and is now always regarded as a fiction of the monks of the middle ages; but the single fact of the Game Troy in Wales, being noticed by Pliny, joined to the names of the countries, raises a strong probability that Geoffrey did but repeat the tradition which he found. The Game Troy seems to me decisive upon this point.[1] Tot-ness is Tat-nesos, or nase or town of the promontory of Tat, Taranis, or Buddha. It stands very near a remarkable peninsula or promontory. The Scots have a similar story of Gathelus, a king of Athens, but it is not worth repeating, and is noticed only to shew the existence of the mythos. It may be seen in Rapin. In the respective histories of Brutus and his Sons we have the exact repetition of the mythos. If we look back to Vol. I. pp. 615, 616, we shall find the history of the life of Virgil to be an exact copy of the history of Homer. Thus, not only was the history of nations always a renewal, a repetition, of a former one, but the history of their musas or bards was a repetition. There is nothing *new* under the sun, said Solomon. In the reign of William I., England is said, by Selden, to have been divided into thirty-seven shires.[2] These included, I doubt not, the disputed town and county of Berwick upon Tweed. By statute 35 Henry III.,[3] Wales was empowered to send twenty-four members to the English parliament. If it were *one* for each county, it would leave *twelve* for Scotland, to complete the seventy-two, and give her only twelve counties. If it were *two* for each county, then it would leave Scotland twenty-four. But it is of no consequence to me, in either case; the probability is, that the whole for the island was seventy-two. The microcosm creeps out, which is all that interests me. Mr. Hannay observes,[4] that the municipal governments of our towns dated their beginning centuries before the Norman or even the Saxon conquest, or, I believe, the Roman invasion. I have no doubt that they may date with Troya Nova, or Trinobantum.

6. I mentioned, near the close of the first chapter of this book, that I should explain the microcosm of the word *Mercavah*. Maimonides and other learned Jews say, that the Mercavah refers to the chariot of Ezekiel, chap. i. vers. 15—21, and ch. x. 9—16; now, what is this Hebrew word which is substituted for the word used by Ezekiel אפן *apn*, and alleged to mean chariot? It is מרכב *nrkb*, and is said to be derived from the root רכב *rkb*, or Recab, meaning *to ride*, and *a carriage*. But here is the *M* unaccounted for. When I recollect that all this writing is invented to record and continue, but yet to conceal, that which ought not to be written, and which was originally preserved in verses unwritten, and that the intention is to make the meaning as difficult as possible to be discovered,—when I also recollect the context of the four animals of the cardinal points, and their connexion in the text with the wheel, and what we have seen of the *Om* of Isaiah, of the cabalistic meaning of the monogram *M* and the custom of using it as a monogram, I suspect that one part of the Mercavah refers to the cycle of the Om; that by the translated term Mercavah is meant, a vehicle or conveyor of the secret of the Om, of the doctrine of the renewal of cycles, with all its various concomitant mythoses. The word Caaba was derived from the last part of the word Mercavah or Mercaba—from the noun Recab. It was the temple[5] of the cabalistic cycle or circle

---

[1] See Vol. I. pp. 377, 385.   [2] Hannay's Hist. Rep. p. 46.   [3] Ib. p. 184.   [4] Ib. p. 166.

[5] A Temple was the circle or wheel of the heavens. The Caaba, with its 360 pillars around it, was the temple of Mohamed (like the temple of Solomon) or circle or wheel of Mohamed, or of Om, *the desire of all nations*. Mercavah or מרכב was the רכב *rkb* of Om. To have called it temple of Mercaaba would have been a tautology. All the oldest temples of Zoroaster and the Indians were caves, acknowledged to be in imitation of the vault or circle or wheel of heaven. From all these considerations I am induced to believe that the word Mercavah is formed of מ M, חר or

of the sun or the heavens, the temple of Recab. For this reason it had a circle of 360 stones around it, and the black stone in the inside of the circle is still adored as the emblem of the sun, the generative principle. Originally it had a dove or lune, as an object of adoration: this is said to have been destroyed by Mohamed himself. (The temple in the sacred island of Iune or Iona of the West, was surrounded with 360 stone crosses; but, within the larger circle, it had a smaller one of 60 crosses; and close to it is the island of Linga. Here is the same mythos in the East and West. After this, if there were no other reason, we should scarcely be surprised to find Mohamedism connected with the ancient mythology and modern Christianity.) Notwithstanding the story of the destruction of the Dove, the use of the crescent induces me to believe, that Mohamed adopted the double principle. The Caaba is said to have been planned originally in heaven. This is, in fact, after the pattern of heaven,—the circle of the sphere. Mr. Low has observed, that a considerable analogy appears to exist between the shape, construction, and ornaments of the tabernacle and altar described in Exodus, and those of the Caaba.[1] This is what we might expect. Every temple was a microcosm of the universe. In imitation of this, the temples were surrounded with pillars.[2] The temple of Mecca had 360. The temple of Iona had 360 in the outer circle; and 60 in the inner one, wheel within wheel; and three revolving globes. The temple at Ana-mor, in the county of Fermanagh, in Ireland, has 48, the number of the ancient constellations, in its outer row, placed in an ellipse, and 9 in a circle within, to shew that 9 cycles were passed, or the ninth cycle was arrived when it was built.[3] The ellipse and the small circle of 9, placed in one of its foci, seem to shew, that the elliptic orbits of the planets were known to its builder. But the most common number of the pillars was 40. I suppose this has been 38, and 2 at the entrance, marked in some way to distinguish them from the others, as at Stonehenge. Probably the *two* have been the Jachim and Boaz—emblems of the *male* and *female* generative powers, standing in front of the temple. I do not think it improbable, that the persons who knew from the calculation of the moons and secret science, that the earth would become inclined and the flood ensue, should have known the exact number of the Planets. Sir William Drummond believed, that the ancients counted them to 16 in number. I believe that there was originally only one pillar before the temples, and that this, the Cardo or Cross or mete-stone, increased to two, when the union of the sects of the Linga and Ioni took place. But there is a single obelisk in Egypt, before the temples, as also in Rome, before all the churches. In most cases, in Rome, the obelisks are the sacred ones brought from Egypt. But in one case, before the church of Maria Maggiore, a Corinthian column is placed, that is, a column ornamented with Rams' horns and Palm-leaves, which was, I believe, the pillar chiefly used at Jerusalem.[4] The Temple at Hierapolis, now Balbec, that is Bal-bit—*house of Bal*, has 40 pillars,[5] and in the magnificent plan of the temple of Ezekiel, published by Solomen Bennet, the four oblong buildings in the middle of the courts have each 40 pillars, and the four oblong buildings at the four corners, which have no grand entrances, have each 19, the number of the metonic cycle so common in the circles in Britain and Ireland. All this is in perfect keeping with the minor, and, I may venture to say, nonsensical, parts of the Cabala. But the religion of the Cabala proceeded, as all other religions have pro-

---

(meaning chief or אפך) בכ *eb, cav* or *cavah*—the chief or head circular vault of M. The idea of wheel applied to the revolving planetary bodies is peculiarly appropriate. The Cavah is the origin of our word *cave*.

[1] Trans. Asiat. Soc. Vol. III. p. 123.   [2] See Vol. I. p. 703.   [3] Vide Vall. Coll. Hib. Vol. VI. p. 400.
[4] There is a Corinthian pillar at Benares, in the temple of Vis Visha. (Hodges, p. 62.)
[5] See the plan in Maundrel's Travels.

ceeded, and always will proceed, while the mind of man has its present constitution, from simplicity to complication, till it arrived at the fooleries which we meet with in such endless variety, described in Montfaucon, &c., called Gnostic emblems: for Gnosticism was nothing but the doctrines of the Cabala corrupted and becoming publicly known. I have no doubt that the metestone, mentioned above, was the father or generator of 600 other smaller measures. This metestone was the sacred stone called Mudron. For a great variety of information respecting sacred stones, the sixth chapter of the Celtic Druids may be consulted. From association, the boundary, or mete-stone, being the emblem of the generative power, the word *dud* and *dd* came to mean the paps of a woman and love; and from the same came our word Madam. By association might also come the name which we give to the substance out of which the globe was supposed to be formed, called Mud; and, again, the Muth or Mother, the name which the Egyptians gave to Isis; and, as Mr. Webster says, truly,[1] in this is a proof of the identity or common origin of the Phœnician, the Celtic, and the Teutonic languages. In this manner, by the association of ideas, almost all language may be traced to its source, and the origin of every word be shewn.

7. The learned and Rev. Mr. Gabb, whom I have quoted in Vol. I. pp. 296—298, in his Finis Pyramidis, has gone at great length into the examination of the measures of the ancients, and though I doubt the truth of his idea, that the great Pyramid at Giza, was built solely for the purpose of forming a standard measure of length and capacity, yet I have no doubt whatever that, from a comparison of it with some of the ancient Temples and the Nilometer at Cairo, the oldest, the most perfect and universal of the measures of the ancients may be ascertained. All nations have originally had certain names of measures—the digit, the finger, the palm of the hand, the foot, the pace—which are still in use in most countries; and it is evident that they were originally so called from a reference to the human body. Five digits or inches made the palm; two palms the foot; three feet the pace. The ancients had also the cubit and the stadium. I shall begin my observations with the foot. My reader, however, will recollect that my object is not to treat of the ancient *weights* and *measures*, but merely to shew that they were founded on the microcosmic principle, or that it may be discovered in them. It appears that the sarcophagus or *parallelopiped* in the great pyramid of Giza consists of two cubes, which together are equal in length to the one hundredth part of the side of its base. This chest is divisible into ten parts, each of which constitutes a foot, and into four parts, each of which constitutes a cubit; thus each cubit is two feet and a half, and the whole chest or sarcophagus is ten feet, or four cubits, or the little stadium,[2] and the side of the base of the Pyramid is four hundred Nilometer cubits, or one thousand feet, which make the great Egyptian stadium. The ten feet, the length of the chest, the little Egyptian stadium or the Hebrew fathom, is the measure by which the Parthenon at Athens, the temple at Ephesus, and the temple at Jerusalem, were built, and which was a measure anciently used by the Romans in their temples.[3] This foot of the ancients is (I believe with Mr. Gabb) correctly represented in our inches, by 8.7552 *in.*, and in our feet by 0.7296, and two such feet by 1 *ft.* 5.5104 *in.*[4] The foot used by Archimedes and the Syracusans was probably the same, as

---

[1] Dict. in voce Mud. See Vol. I. p. 336, note ³.

[2] I consider the Pyramids to be of late erection compared with most of the Druidical circles. This I think is proved by the workmanship. The art of using the chisel was probably scarcely known when most of the circles were erected; but still, when I recollect that Moses orders the pillars set up not to be touched with the chisel, it occurs to me that a religious principle may have operated against its use.

[3] The front of the Parthenon Hecatempedon at Athens, destroyed by Xerxes, was one hundred feet. Gabb, pp. 38, 44.

[4] Gabb, p. 102.

it differed from the Egyptian foot only $\frac{1}{1000}$ of an inch.[1] Mr. Gabb says, (p. 48,) "And 400 cubits, which equal 1000 Pyramidic feet, are equal to the side of the Pyramid's base, and is the stadium of the Egyptians. 200,000 cubits are equal to 500,000 Pyramidic feet, which are equal to a meridional degree, if taken very near the equator: of course 72,000,000 of cubits are equal to 180,000,000 of Pyramidic feet, which are equal to the circumference of the earth." To which I add, (in order to make the microcosm clear,) or 360,000,000 palms,[2] (two of which equal a pyramidic foot,) are equal to the circumference of the earth. I think the Microcosmic system no one can doubt here. And from the whole which has been written upon this subject by Mr. Gabb, Sir Isaac Newton, Mr. Whiston, and Sir W. Drummond,[3] there can be no doubt that the ancients had a standard of measure, taken from the mensuration of a meridional degree at the equator, more correct than the French have at this day, after all their attempts, with their modern scientific improvements, and that both they and the English would have shewn their wisdom if they had adopted Mr. Gabb's advice, and taken the chest at Cairo, the old standard, as their standard of measure.[4] I feel little doubt that the palm was the universal measure of all the very ancient temples, and was the invention of the first Pontifical race, and probably descended with them and with the Neros, as Josephus says, from before the last of the three floods, perhaps before the second of them. If the reader return to the Preliminary Observations, Vol. I. p. 6, he will find that I have there divided the circle of 360 degrees into 180, then the 180 into 90, then the 90 into three times 30, then each thirty into three tens, and each ten into two fives, or each 30 into 6 fives; and he will remember that in the *five* we have the Lustrum of the old Italians. Pliny divided the circle into 72 constellations; these were the lustrums; then, as there were 360,000,000 palms in the circle, there would be 72,000,000 of lustrums. Picus, of Mirandola, thus describes the Microcosm of Plato: "Plato asserts, (In Timæo,) that the Author of the world made the mundane and all other rational souls, in one cup, and of the same elements, the universal soul being the most perfect, ours least; whose parts we may observe by this division. Man, the chain that ties the world together, is placed in the midst; and as all mediums participate of their extremes, his parts correspond with the whole world: thence called Microcosms."[5] Man is the stadium,[6] the fathom, the standard. The first man was an incarnation of Wisdom, and down, step below step, to animals; animals, step below step, to plants; plants, step below step, to metals, stones, the minuted particle of matter, the invisible gas, the ethereal or spiritual fire. Above him, souls of men, dæmons, angelical minds of various degrees, angels, arch-angels, principalities, God.

I am not certain that the stadium, in strict analogy to the above, was not considered, in mensuration, as the standard or chain placed in the midst, which tied the world together. The ancients divided the globe in the following manner:

$$360{,}000{,}000 \text{ palms} \div \begin{cases} 2 &= 180{,}000{,}000 \\ 3 &= 120{,}000{,}000 \\ 4 &= 90{,}000{,}000 \\ 12 &= 30{,}000{,}000 \\ 36 &= 10{,}000{,}000 \\ 72 &= 5{,}000{,}000 \\ 360 &= 1{,}000{,}000 \end{cases}$$

---

[1] Gabb, p. 44. [2] See *infra*, p. 405. [3] Classical Journal, Vol. XVI. [4] See *Gabb*, p. 55.
[5] Stanley's Hist. Phil. Pt. V. p. 208.
[6] The stadium comes from *ito* to *stand*, whence also come stans and standard. From the crosses of the Agri-

Again,

$$360{,}000{,}000 \text{ palms} \div \begin{cases} 5 &= 72{,}000{,}000 \\ 10 &= 36{,}000{,}000 \\ 15 &= 24{,}000{,}000 \\ 30 &= 12{,}000{,}000 \\ 40 &= 9{,}000{,}000 \\ 60 &= 6{,}000{,}000 \\ 120 &= 3{,}000{,}000 \\ 360 &= 1{,}000{,}000 \end{cases}$$

The first measure was 1, Digit, Finger, or Inch.

5	Fingers or Inches made	1 Palm or Hand.
2	Palms or Hands, or 10 Fingers............	1 Foot.
2¼	Feet or 5 Palms	1 Cubit.—Πηχυς.
2	Cubits, 5 Feet, or 10 Palms	1 Cube, Yard, Pace, or Stride.
2	Cubes, or 4 Cubits, or 20 Palms, or 10 Feet	1 Chest, Stadium, Fathom, or height of a tall man.[1]
100	Chests, Stadia, or Fathoms, or 1000 Feet, or 2000 Palms.........................	1 Pyramid, or Great Fathom, or Stadium.
50	Pyramids, or 50,000 Chests, or 500,000 Feet, or 1,000,000 Palms	1 Degree.
360[2]	Degrees, or 360,000,000 Palms	1 Circle.

Thus the man is the *fathom* or *stadium* or *standard* by which all measurements were made; and all temples, and parts of temples were built in equal numbers of this measure, or some equimultiples of this measure. In the same manner, the circle of the heavens, and the circle of the earth, were divided into equimultiples of this measure. I think, as I have before intimated, that all temples were anciently believed to be microcosms of the world. Whiston, on the Old Testament, p. 85, says, " It may not be amiss to set down here the exact length of the old Egyptian and " Jewish cubit, as our great Sir I. Newton has determined it from the measures of the Pyramids " of Egypt, taken by the learned Greaves; and as I have found it also most agreeable to the mea- " sures of the sepulchres of the house of David, still remaining at Jerusalem, in Maundrel's " Travels; and to the measure of the table of Shew-bread upon Titus's Arch at Rome, in Reland's " discourse thereon. I mean, that in inch-measure it was=20. 7936 inches, and in foot-measure= " 1. 7325 feet, or 1 ft. 8 in. 7·9·/1·0·." The reason why Mr. Whiston and Sir Isaac Newton did not come to the same conclusion as Mr. Gabb, with respect to the length of the Jewish and Egyptian measure, the fathom, the stadium, and the foot, was because they took the account from Mr. Greaves's measurement of the Pyramid, which was taken, where only he could take it, from the

---

mensores being put up of the size of one stadium, they were called stans or stones; and from the collections of dwellings round these stones, towns came to be called stan—as Penistan, in England; Bagistan, in Persia. Stadium may be also Standiom—Stan-di-Om—Stone of the sacred Om, or Hom, the height of a man. Fathom may be Father-Om. A fathom is equal to ten pyramidic feet, which are equal to about 80 of our inches, or 6⅔ feet, the height of a tall man.

[1] An Irish Giant or a Goliath.

[2] The 360, I apprehend, were also divided into three parts of 120 each; these into two of 60 each; these into two of 30 each; these into two of 15 each; and three of 5 each; and the 30, into five of 6 each. Thus we come at the two lowest lustrums.

side, and not from where the French took it, at the foundation or widest part of the triangle. But the identity of measurement shewn by Mr. Gabb in the length of the base of the Pyramid, with the construction of the Nilometer of Cairo, with the temples at Jerusalem, Ephesus, Athens, and Rome, furnish a proof very superior to the theories of Greaves and Newton—indeed, they leave no room for any doubt on the subject. The discovery had been made by the French Savans before it was observed by Mr. Gabb, and it is astonishing that they failed to make it useful. One of them says, "The monuments of Egypt have something mysterious, which betrays ideas worthy of our " admiration. Each side of the base of the great Pyramid 500 times multiplied gives 57,075 " toises, which complete a geographical degree. The cube of the Nilometer 200,000 times multi- " plied gives exactly the same result."[1] I believe the ancients took their measurement of the degree in the island of Jaba-dios, or the island of the holy ISUB, or Sumatra, in, perhaps, the province of Rome-lia, and near the city of Rome, which was probably there. This circumstance may justify the inference, that they knew, that the degree was less at the Equator than near the Poles. Indeed, this is in perfect keeping with their knowledge of the periods of the comets, and of other important facts, which every where shews the superiority of their learning to ours. In accordance with the system of microcosmic numbers, the oriental philosophers have determined, that a man in health makes 360 respirations in a Ghari of time; six such respirations, therefore, must equal a Pal, or the sixtieth part of a Ghari, and, in the course of 24 hours, a man, in health, will make 21,600 respirations. The Ghari is the sixtieth part of a day and night, which sixtieth part is further divided into sixty other parts—called Pal, and the latter, again, subdivided into sixty other parts—called Bebal. The Greeks had two standards of square measure, called the Aroura and the Plethron, the latter known to be the double of the former. I think as there were two stadiums or measures of length of one name, Stadium or Fathom, there were two Plethrons and two Arouras. The small Aroura was 720 square feet, and the large one 1440, and the other was 5000 square feet for the small Aroura, and 10,000 for the large one.[2] If we allow for the mistake, probably of the printer, of 722 for 720, we must see here the microcosm and the whole system. The 720 square feet are evidently only the double of 360 palms. The 5000 and 10,000 are from the base of the Pyramid. Again, the Egyptian Aroura was the square of 100 cubits, or 10,000 square cubits; and the Plethron 20,000 square cubits.[3] Pliny calls them *jugera*, and says the largest Pyramid occupied 8 of them, which produce an area of 160,000 square cubits. The discovered dimensions prove this perfectly correct: for the side of the base of the Pyramid being 400 cubits, these multiplied by 400, give 160,000 square cubits. The granite chest 25 times repeated, gives a length, of which the square is the Aroura, or 10,000 square cubits. Although none of our writers have given us the inside capacity of the chest, or the exact thickness of its sides, we may be very certain that it formed the measure of capacity. Indeed, after a standard of length is once fixed, there is no difficulty with a standard of rain-water. Mr. Gabb has observed, that the ancient jugera were the lowest standard or unit of land measure, and meant not only any inclosed position, but what we call lands, that, is balks or strips of land, in the open town-fields.[4] We have here the use of the Agrimensores measuring and granting out the land of the Lords to their feudatories, and the origin of our town-fields. The same system may be perceived in the measurement of the lands by the Etruscan Agrimensores. Niebuhr says, "The jugerum was, as its name indi- " cates, a double measure;" and the proper unit of the Roman land measure is the actus of 14,400 " square feet, a square of each side of which measured one hundred and twenty feet. A quadrangle

---

[1] Paucton, Métrologie. Paris, 1780. Muller's Univers. Hist. Sect. iii.
[2] See Gabb's Fin. Pyram. p. 75. [3] Ib. [4] Ib. p. 73.

"containing a superficies of fifty jugera comprised the square of ten actus within its area, and is certainly a century, not indeed of a hundred jugera, but of a hundred actus."[1] In the 120 and 14,400 the mythos is evident. Again, Niebuhr says, "The Etruscan and Umbrian versus, of *ten* ten-foot rods, bore the same proportion to the square root of the Roman actus or fundus, *twelve* ten-foot rods, as the cyclical to the civil year of the Romans. ...... A century, therefore, of a hundred actus, contained one hundred and forty-four versus, i. e. the square of twelve."[2] The Pythagoreans, as well as the Platonists, (in fact, they were the same, only successors of each other,) held the doctrine of the microcosm; but I think it was a part of their secret system. Indeed, the whole of the system which I have developed contains innumerable facts which can be accounted for only from a desire of secrecy. The theory that Man was the centre of the animal or animated mundane system, is pregnant with many curious circumstances. It seems that the race of men was like the race of animals, which was thought to descend from the Ganesa, the Elephant, the wisest of animals, to the lowest,· to the point where it connected with the race of animated plants, which in like manner descended. As the highest of the race of animals descended to the lowest, and thence to the highest of the race of plants, so the highest of the race of man was thought to have descended to the lowest—from the Newtons and Lockes to the idiot—or rather, I should say, from the incarnation of divine wisdom in the Supreme Pontiff, in Noah and his successors; in fact, in the Chaldæans, who inherited the supremacy of the whole world. And from this, after the theory was lost, from the effect of custom or tradition not understood, all the claims of kings by *divine right* have descended. From this, too, the desire of all kings to trace their pedigree up to Noah has arisen. The corresponding committee of the Asiatic Society, of which Sir Alexander Johnstone is the chairman, have been so obliging as to make inquiries for me into the dimensions of some of the old temples of India. The subject of ancient weights and measures is a very comprehensive one. At a future day I shall probably return to it, when I may be able to ascertain whether what I suspect is really true, viz. that the old temples in China, Mexico, India, Syria, Greece, Italy, and of Stonehenge and Abury, were all built by one measure, and were intended, each in its own peculiar way, to be a microcosm of the universe.

8. We will now return to the Etruscan Agrimensores, from which, indeed, we have made a very long digression. All the operations of the Tuscan Augurs or Agrimensores, for they were both one, were of a religious nature. Their first unit of measure or ager, our acre, was a microcosm of a greater. It was called a temple, and every temple was a microcosm of a greater, of a wheel within a wheel, till it became a microcosm of the globe, and the temple of the globe was a microcosm of the planetary system, and *that* of the universe.[3] The Cardo, the Decumannus, and every part of the duty of an Agrimensor, was religious, and intended to regulate the collection of the tithe: this arose from circumstances and was continued by policy. The word-Templum or Temple is a very important word, and may serve to throw some additional light on the origin and secret meaning of the Templars and their doctrines: indeed, I think a proper understanding of it will, in a great measure, open the door of their sanctuary. When an Etruscan Augur began his divinations, he "used to rise in the stillness of midnight to determine in his mind *the limits of the celestial temple.*"[4] This temple was evidently a something in the heavens,

---

[1] Hist. Rome, Vol. II. p. 389. Walter's Ed.   [2] Ibid. pp. 389, 390.

[3] I doubt not that the refusal to pay the tithe was denounced as a great sin. By what process, or by what cunning manœuvre, the Roman priests got the custom established of taking *auguries* before any assembly could proceed to business, I do not know; but the object evidently was, to have the power at all times of controlling them. This power gave the Pontifex Maximus a negative upon all the proceedings of the state. It was, in effect, *a veto.*

[4] Niebuhr, Hist. Rome, Vol. I. p. 221. Thirlwall's Ed.

perhaps the hemisphere, and again shews that the word *templum* had some meaning much more sublime than a humanly-erected building. But the celestial vault was the Templum erected by the CHIEF MASON, the Megalistor Mundorum. Here I stop. Templars are nothing but masons, and there are some of their secrets I would not divulge if I could; but perhaps I do not know them. I may be in error, but this I will say, they are so closely connected with masonry, that it is very difficult to separate them. Very certain I am, that they are under some very great mistakes, and I can set them right, if I choose. The temple of Ieue at Jerusalem was called היכלבית *eiklbit*, but often היכל *eikl* only—the second word בית *bit*, which means *house*, being omitted; it is, in fact, a pleonasm, very common in the Hebrew; a habit or defect, perhaps, of writing, which probably arose when the written language was known as a secret science to very few, in the recesses of the temple, and but ill understood even there. The word כל *kl* has the meaning of ALL, and probably in its origin is כ *k*, *as*, and אל *al*, meaning *as all, as God.* The word כל *kl* answers to the Latin *omnis*, and OM has the same idea, from the sacred word for God, whence I think it had its derivation. But כל *kl* has also the meaning of the *heavens*, and here we have the Latin coel-um. I must now request the very close attention of my reader, and his excuse for a long quotation from Mr. Parkhurst,[1] without which he will not understand this most recondite subject. "היכל *eikl*, the middle and *largest* part of the *temple* of the Lord, the *sanctuary.*—It is "applied to that *high* and *holy* place where Jehovah peculiarly dwelleth; otherwise called the *holy* "*heavens*, or *heavens of holiness*—מהיכלו *meiklu*[2]—*From his Temple,* Ps. xviii. 7. Mr. Merrick, in "his annotations on this text, observes, that this expression is applied to *heaven* by heathen authors, "from whose writings the following passages are cited by *De la Cerda*, in his commentary on "Virgil, Georgic iii. p. 389:

"'—— *Cæli tonitralia* Templa.'—LUCRET. lib. i.

"'*Qui templa Cæli summa sonitu concutit*.'—TERENT. Eun."

"So also *Ennius*, quoted by *Delrio*, on *Seneca's* Herc. Fur. p. 217:

"'*Contremuit* templum *magnum Jovis altitonantis*.' And,

"'*Quanquam multa manus ad cæli cærula* Templa

"'*Tendebam lacrymans———*.'"

These texts clearly prove, that with the ancients the word templum had a meaning much more grand and refined than merely the building on the earth, or the *bit* or *tectum* built by human hands, which was always considered to be a microcosm of the temple of the firmament. Thus, in the oldest monuments of the Druids, we have the circle of stones, in the number 12, the signs in the circle—signs of the zodiacal circle, with the arch of heaven for the cupola; and, in fact, the divisions of the heavens marked in a great variety of ways. I know some persons will say this is fanciful; but they cannot deny the facts of the numbers in the monuments; and there must be some cause for their peculiarity. With respect to the fancifulness, I quite agree with the objectors that nothing can be more fanciful than almost all the recondite doctrines of the ancients appear, when taken without the remainder of the system of which they form a part being considered, and without the *necessity* for them being also considered.[3] This *necessity* arose from the

---

[1] On the word הכל *ekl* I. and III.

[2] From this comes our Saxon word mickle for *much*; and, in some cases, used for *all*, as, Micklegate, York—the *sole* or *only* road into the city, and over the bridge from the south.

[3] In the Pantheon at Rome, with its open top, we have a beautiful example. Here we have the plan of the oldest temples, as they would be built, before the art of building a key-stoned arch was discovered—this would be an approximation to it.

ignorance of the ancients of the art of writing, which left them no other resource to register these most important parts—groundworks of all their theories, systems, and festivals. Under the law of Moses, when the religion was confined and intended to be confined to one little country, a place was fixed on and a temple built for the worship of God; but when the Saviour of the whole world invited all people to a participation in his favours, this attachment to one place was done away, and every place was considered equally good for his service. Jesus Christ had no predilection for the temple at Jerusalem or at Gerizim. In whatever place his people shall assemble, in his name, he will be in the midst of them. Accordingly, the first Christians assembled indifferently in houses or other places where they happened to be; and it cannot be doubted that, if Jesus Christ had thought temples necessary, he would have said so: but the poor man's religion wanted no such superstitious adjuncts. The beautiful globe was his τεμενος, and an humble and contrite heart his temple. This was the doctrine of the Buddhist, of the Pythagorean, of the Essenian philosopher of Samaria. This was the doctrine which the Samaritan Nazarite taught, as I have pointed out in my preface to the first volume.[1] Here we have no gorgeous temples, no trumpery shows, no sects, nor the possibility of forming them. Here we have no firebrand creeds or symbols of faith to incite men to cut each other's throats. Here all is peace and brotherly love. Here we unite all religions.

To return from this digression. Every thing was divided into *two*. The heaven was divided into two hemispheres, and the globe we inhabit into the North and the South—the Dark and the Light—the Good and the Evil. Man, in like manner, was originally believed to have been formed in *two* parts in *one* body—male and female[2]—the higher and the lower—the good and the evil. In the same way time was divided—the day and night, the winter and summer. Thus we read much in the works of the Brahmins of *the day of Brahma* and of *the night of Brahma*. All the cycles were made up of the multiplication of the *five* and *six* together—the *He* and the *Vau*—the male and the female—from whose union and conjunction all the race of man descended. We have found the cycles of 360 and 432 originally founded on the two numbers *five* and *six*—the *two lustrums*; and the two cycles 360 and 432[3] to have been united at last in one larger cycle. Now, I think, all this had reference to, in fact was closely interwoven with, the theological system, as the cycles may be said to have been interwoven into one another. There was the one, the Τὸ Ὂν, generally marked in a very peculiar manner.[4] Then there were the *three*;[5] then the other cyclar numbers as described in my Celtic Druids, Sect. XXIII., and I feel little doubt that the microcosm, after the one and three, was made to depend on, or was regulated by, the foundation number *five* or *six*; and these two arose from the change in the length of the year (and consequently in the length of the cycles) from 360 to 365 days—the number 432, the cycle formed by the six being to unite with the cycle of 360, and together to form one whole, and thus to retain both. The temple of Stonehenge is a production of the $5 \times 12 = 60$, &c.; the temple at Abury in its number of 650 included both in its system. Both these are in good keeping with the remainder of the system, but we cannot come to any determination respecting them, nor do I know that it is of any consequence. The division of the nations named in the tenth chapter of Genesis,[6] which was into 72, is alluded to most clearly in 32nd ch. and 8th verse of Deuteronomy, where the Most High is said, in the LXX., to have

---

[1] Pp. xvii. xviii.   [2] See *supra*, p. 397.   [3] Vol. I. pp. 6, 7.

[4] This in Stonehenge may have been the altar-stone as it is called, but which must have been merely for the Eucharistia, as I believe there is no appearance that a large fire has ever been lighted upon it: or it may have been the single stone at a *little distance*, like the crosses in our churchyards—the Lingas or Phalluses.

[5] The altar-stone and the two stones at the entrance, or the three stones standing outside the circle.

[6] See Vol. I. p. 265, and *supra*, p. 399.

divided the nations according to the number of the Angels of God, and not, as in our text, according to the number of the children of Israel. Now, I think this division of the world is a microcosm of the division of the heavens. We know the stars are commonly called *angels*, and that Pliny said there were 72 constellations, or groups of stars, called by the names of animals or other things. I suspect the stars here alluded to were constellations, and that the surface of the earth was divided microcosmically after the heavens. I have not been able to make out, from examples, in any one country, a perfect or nearly perfect system; but this is not to be expected; nor, indeed, have I been able, as the Irish did with their *elk*, to put all the parts collected from different quarters into a whole; for this reason, at present we can consider it as only a proposed theory, to remain for examination, with such a degree of weight annexed to it as each reader may think it deserves. But yet I think the existence of the microcosm is rendered probable, by facts still existing. Mr. Niebuhr has observed, that every cardo or stone cross set up, where the lines of the agrimensores crossed each other, was called a Templum. But in every country there was one grand Templum or Cardo or Cross or Capitolium or Acropolis or Stonehenge, whence all the others proceeded, or by which they were regulated; and it is evident that this must be a microcosm of the temple of the globe, of the temple of the planetary system, with its its beautiful pole-star, or the star of Juda or cross with many points, the Templars' cross at the top of it. We every where read of nations adoring large rude stones, in such a manner as is almost incredible of rational beings. I believe this was a species of $\delta v \lambda \epsilon \iota a$ paid to the Cardos, the nature of which had become forgotten; and perhaps it might, in some instances, be transferred to other large stones by credulous devotees, who, in all ages and all nations, are perpetually at work to increase the objects of their devotion—always at work to find something new—something to make them more worthy than their neighbours of the favour of God. These cardos or termini or mere-stones were all poles—polises, and the first from which all the East and West branched off, was the arco or acropolis. From these came our Maypoles. The villages grew up around these poles, as they are found at this day, and hence arose the name of $\pi o \lambda \iota s$ for *town*. I suppose the Umbrians of Italy had 360 of them, as we know Persia had, and as I believe all other nations had; and that it was 300 of these which the Etruscans conquered.[1]

9. In Volume I. p. 527, I have alluded to the stone circle on Mount Gargarus by the Indian name or epithet Cor-Ghari, treated of by Mr. Faber.[2] Here is evidently the Welsh name of Choir Ghaur, of Stonehenge, applied to Gargarus of Troia. I think no human being will doubt this. The passage noticed in my Celtic Druids, Ch. VI. Sect. XXI. p. 237, where Homer describes the chiefs meeting in the circle, must allude to Gargarus, and to the stone circle seen by Dr. D. Clarke, upon that mount.[3] The Monks called Stonehenge Chorea Gigantum. הגגור *hg-gur* is *place of the circle*: the two form the terminations of Indian towns ending with *urg* and *uggar*, and our *burgs*. The word *Cor* is evidently the *Choir* and the same as the Cor, the centre of the measurements in Italy. Cor also means the heart; and, probably, from being the *heart* or *centre*, in Persia, it described the Sun. I think from this it is probable that the Cardinales or centres of measurements of Britain began at Stonehenge, or if, as is probable, Britain was microcosmically divided into *three*, that it was one of the three. One of the names of Stonehenge is Main Ambres or Ambrose. Cleland has shewn that Meyn means *stone*, and was the origin of our Minsters, and Monasteries. Main of Am, or Om-bra, *stone of Om the Creator*. The famous Rocking stone in Cornwall was called Main Ambre. This is the same. I suspect the *bra* was the same as *divus*, and at last

---

[1] Vide Niebuhr, Hist. of Rome, Vol. I. pp. 112, 113. Thirlwall's Ed.
[2] Anal. Vol. III. pp. 31, 229.   [3] See Vol. I. pp. 229, 360, 362, 423.

meant *holy*. Ambrosia was the liquor of the holy or creative power Om. The oil was that of the holy or creative power, whence comes the French Ampulla. Professor [Sir Greaves] Haughton says, Cor Gharri may be analysed into Cor-Ghirry, the mountain Cor: for Ghirry means a mountain, as you may have heard of Nilgherries or blue mountains. If the G is pronounced hard, as in gift, no *h* is wanted, and it would then be Giri, and sounded Ghirry. Stonehenge seems to mean no more than *the hanging* or *suspended stone*. Cor Gawr is the old British name, which means the circle of the powerful ones, from Cor, a circle, and Cawr or Gawr (Gaor), the Mighty One, the Great One. But I think we have another Gargarus or Choir Ghaur in the celebrated Carum Gorum, of Tartary, whither Gengis Khan went to receive investiture in his dominions. This was the residence of *the Prestre John*, or the Priest of the God of Wisdom. The kingdom of Gengis called itself in a particular manner the kingdom of wisdom. Hence I believe that Carum Gorum is etymologically the same as Choir Ghaur and as Gargarus, and that it had the same meaning. But I think we have, as we might expect, another Choir Ghaur, in Scotland, in the mount of Carum Gorum, [cairn gorm?] whence the precious stones of that name are procured, in the county of Perth. They are all mounts of the Cor or circle or heart or wisdom. They were all acropolises, capitoliums, of the divine incarnation.—I must now return to what I have said, that Carnate probably had its name from the two Carns of St. Thomas,[1] and observe, that, in consequence of finding the word Carn in such very general use all over the world, I am obliged to seek for some other meaning; and I think I have it in the word Cor, which, when read Hebraicè, meant *wisdom*; and I think, from allusion to this name of God, the piles of stones called Carns, which are generally surrounded with circles of upright stones in the numbers of sacred cycles, (vide several in the neighbourhood of Inverness,) had their names.[2] From Mr. Claproth's excellent map of Asia, I learn that the country between 40 and 50 degrees of N. Lat., and 100 and 120 E. Long. by French reckoning, the country of Caracorum, in the year 232, was called the country of *Sian pi Libres*. (Sion the Free. In Siam, it may be remembered, that the natives say the French have the same name as themselves—*free*.) In 302 it was called kingdom *des So theou* (or of the holy Saviour) or *Tho po* (the God). In 425 it was the empire of Joan Joan. (This, I do not doubt, was Prestre John, or the Priest of Jnana, *wisdom*.) In 565 it was the empire of the Turks. In 632 it was the kingdom of Thop Khiu (God Khiu). In 679 it was the country of Hoei He, or Ouigours or country of Thou khiue (Circle of Iao or the Ieo). In 745 it was the empire of the Ouigour, or the Hoei He, or the encampment of the Kakan. In 865 it was the country of Kirghiz or the Tartars. In 1125 it was the empire of the Kin or Altoun Khans. Next it was the Mongols. In 1290 it was the empire of Khorin, or Caracorum, or Ho-lin. It really appears probable that from this remote country in the earliest time all our mythology has come. We have found an Ararat in the Il-avratta of India. According to the theory of Agrimensorism, both the Ararats ought to be Cardos. In India we have this in Mount Meru. In Western Asia it is very clearly made out by Cellarius, in his Geographia Antiqua. He shews that the part of Taurus, which separates *Sophene* from Mesopotamia, was called the Godyean mountains. On these the Ark of Noah was supposed to have rested. Berosus says, the Ark rested on the mountains των κορδυαιων. The Targum of Onkelos on Gen. viii. 4, uses the word Kardu, which the Targum of Jonathan, by metathesis, calls Kadrun. Elmacinus calls it the Mountain Cordi. It has also the name of Baris, which means *ship*.[3]

---

[1] See Vol. I. pp. 757, 765.

[2] The word Gard, which means *place*, as Stutgard, Chunigard, &c., or *district*, was the Hebrew גיר *gir* and די *di*, *holy circle*. Hence comes our small inclosure called *a yard*. Hence come the circles of Germany, which were all religious divisions, formed in the time of the pontifical government.

[3] I have little doubt that the Mount Nevis, which is close to Beregonium, the ancient capital of Scotland, and within

Here, in the name of this very remarkable mountain, I think we have a Cardo in chief to complete the mythos. It was the Cardo of Noah. Baris or Ararat, or the Mount of Kardi, was believed to be the highest in the world; and from this mountain, as a centre, Noah was supposed to divide the world among his three sons. The Gar of Gargarus, the Giri of India, the Gaur of Choir Gaur or Stonehenge, the Cor of the Mounts of Cordi or Kardu, or Ararat, and the Cardo of Italy, are all the same word and have the same meaning. They are all central points round which circles of some kind were built or supposed to be built, (and here we have the *cir* of circle,) and they were also acropolises or capitoliums, and had the meaning of Cor, *heart*, as the centre of measurement round which the 72 and 360 districts were laid out; as our system is placed round the sun. The change in letters, such as in the G, the C, the K, &c., will not be objected to by any person who makes a due allowance for the absolute uncertainty of all old languages, before the invention of grammar, and the constant use of what we learnedly call the anagram and metathesis, which were originally mere corruptions, habits, or styles of speaking or writing. As we have seen the Roman Cardinals called *hinges*, so the Choir Gaur was called for the same reason the Stone-hinge. It was the pontifical capital, the pivot on which all the districts of Britain depended or turned, when England was under the jurisdiction of its three Arch-flamens. And I have not a doubt that there was a similar Cor-giri somewhere for both Scotland—Albania or Caledonia—and for Cambria. When I find the Om the object of adoration of all nations—the emblem of the creative power, the temple of Stonehenge, by means of the cycles, the emblem of the same mythos, and the Hebrew language of Britain, it is not unreasonable to go to the Hebrew language for the explanation. The whole is evidently in keeping. The parts are in character with one another.[1] I beg leave to draw my reader's attention to the names of Gargarus and Stonehenge being the same (Choir Ghaur and Cor-Ghari) in the Sanscrit and the old English language, and also to the Cor of the Etruscans. This, of itself, almost confirms my theory of the ancient system, the crosses, &c. These two names for Stonehenge are similar to the word Sanscrit of India and Scotland, and Sanscort of the Celts. Every inquirer into the antiquities of nations knows, or ought to know, how much labour the learned Vallancey took to prove that the Irish were a tribe from Spain, but which previously came thither from the East. We have seen that the Sibyls say that Mount Ararat was in Phrygia, in Asia Minor, which Phrygia was adjoining to Mysia or the country of the *Mystæ*, or Troy. But I think it probable that the whole of Asia Minor was Mysia, or mystic land, the land of Room. In Asia Minor we have Calinda, Calamina, and Calida, places of India, connected with the mythos of Ararat. We have also a nation of Brigantes, and Briges, whence Drummond[2] supposes the name of Phrygians came, and the word Free, and the Scandinavian Phriga or Freya. From this root we have formerly observed that the Siamese say the Franks or French have the same name as themselves. There is also a place called Caledonia and an Albania, and Milea or Miletia, and a Mount of Solyma.[3] In Britain we have Brutus, descended from Æneas, and his three sons, and Trinobantum or Troya Nova, and Albany, and Caledonia, and the Brigantes, and the Calidei, and the Miletii, and Patrick in Ireland. Can any one doubt that the same mythos or the same people have been in both places? But Asia Minor was both *Mysia* and *Room*, the mystic name of the city in which the Pontifex Maximus, or chief Bridge-builder in Italy dwells. Sir W. Drummond has observed, that the name of Brigantes comes from Briges, and that Phryges and Briges,

---

sight of the island of Iona, meant Baris and Navis. Like the Baris and the Cordi, the centre of the Agrimensorium of Asia, it was the centre of Scotland. Vide Bochart Geo. Sac. B. I, and Whiston's Theory of the Earth, B. II. p. 135. 3rd ed.

[1] See CELTIC DRUIDS, Ch. VI. Sect. XVIII. p. 231. [2] Origines, Vol. IV. pp. 356, 357.
[3] See Vol. I. pp. 594, 810.

according to the Greek authors, are the same, and that these people came from Thrace, where we have formerly found the Sindi and the other Indian names. He then (p. 355) observes, that the Thracian name for a *pons* was *Brig* or *Briga*, the very name the same useful contrivance bears in North Britain, where some of the common people, even at this day, believe that the arch is held together by sorcery or magic. Cor was the Latin name for both heart and wisdom. Here we see why the Bulla, treated of *supra*, p. 87, was in the form of a heart: originally, I have not a doubt, from the name בעל *bol* באל *bal* Bull-a, in form of a Calf, as it has been and is yet in modern times in form of a Lamb—the Agnus Dei. From this came the word Cardo, αχμη. We have the meaning of it in the cor januæ quo movetur, as hinge, regulator of the door;[1] and, as regulator, it gave name to the line drawn from North to South,—the pole or axis of the earth, used by the Etruscan Agrimensores to make their squares for the collection of the sacred tenths or tithes. This line regulated all others. The word is cor-dis-di—*divus*, and from this it came, that where the Decumanus, the line, crossed it from East to West, the point of intersection at which a cross was set up, was called *cor*, or ardo, car-di. It was in each district the centre, the heart, of all their operations: it was, from circumstances, the Arca-polis, the Caput-olium. From this point of intersection two roads always branched off, which is the reason why we have a cross or merestone in the centre of every village, which arose by houses collecting round the sacred X: for this was, for many evident reasons, declared most sacred and holy, and in suitable places the temples arose around or over these crosses. The whole circle was divided into 360 parts; and, beginning at the Equator, the Decumanus was drawn at every ten of these parts to North and South, whence it had the name Deca. In a similar manner, I believe, the mensuration by the Agrimensores took place in every country. The Decumanus would always be the same, but the Cardo would in one sense vary. A Cardo would run through every capitol or principal town, which of course would divide the land into parallelograms of different lengths. The lengths would vary according to localities. Our system is the same: the parallels of Latitude never vary, the Longitude each nation reckons from its own cardo. It was from being the superintendants or curators of the Seventy-two Bareichs, parishes or cardinal divisions, into which the city of Rome was divided, that the Roman cardinals had their names. I have no doubt originally, perhaps even yet, Cardinales of the whole of the 72 divisions into which the patrimony of St. Peter may have been divided: for the patrimony of the Resoul, the Vicra-ma-ditya, the Vicar of God, extended over the whole world. That it *was* divided into 72, is clearly proved by the division of the 72 nations of the earth, mentioned in the tenth and eleventh chapters of Genesis. The author of that book perfectly understood the doctrine of Agrimensorism. That book was never written by Moses, though it might be adopted by him. The adoption of the number of seventy-two arose out of the divisions of the circle. The Gaelic word *coir*, genitive *choir*, signifies a space of ground inclosed on all sides. It is the Greek χωρα, *locus*.[2] We have the *cor* in *cortex*, the bark of a tree, and χαρτης, charta, and the Gaelic *cart* and *chart*. It is curious to observe the cart, by its wheels only distinguished from the sledge, and the chart, connected both with letters and the agrimensorial measurement of land. In the Celtic language *reich* meant *ruler of a country:* from this came the Rex, and both are the same as Ray. Gor is *a circle;* Gor-reich *the ruler of a circle,* like the German circles.[3] The Ager of the Romans is our acre (that is, measure of land or τεμενος). It is the Hebrew נור *gur* הג *hg*, originally *place of the circle.* I have no doubt that this was a cross in a circle; that is, a circle divided into four. The Roman territory was called Ager Romanus; and at first, as we might expect, it was divided like the globe—like

---

[1] Litt. Dict.   [2] Grant's Thoughts on the Gael, p. 169.   [3] Cleland's Spec. Ap. p. 33.

India—like Britain—like Scotland—and probably all other countries—into *three parts*. It may be asked why the word Cor just spoken of came to have the meaning of *Wisdom*. What has the heart more than any other part of the body to do with Wisdom? In the ancient Etruscan language, read from right to left, it was Cor or Roç, that is, Ros or Ras, and the country where we find this, we are told, was called Razena; that is, country of Ras or wisdom. It was ras, not " à curâ, quia in eo omnis solicitudo et scientiæ causa manet."[1] From this came the cardo, car-di; the c in these words answering to the g, and the g answering to the c and k, and the acra or ακρα or αρκα of the acropolis, the origin of the Ager. It was the heart as the centre of the operations of the Agrimensores, the point of intersection of their Decuman and Cardo; and as *wisdom* or scientia it was the regulator or pivot or hinge on which the two right lines to the cardinal points extended. As the point which directed and regulated all the operations, it was closely allied to mind, or intelligence, or wisdom. The *cor* is also the root of concors, concordia; from this comes also the word *to care*, that is, to interest one's-self about, and the Gaelic word *car*, affection, *cardias*, friendship, and the Greek καρδια, in place of caredia, and the Latin *carus* dear. And, finally, it is the Persian name for the *Sun*; thus, again, uniting the centre, the To Ον, and wisdom.

We constantly say a thing hinges upon this or that, hereby evidently considering a hinge as a regulator, as it regulates a door. Ainsworth says, a Cardo means a way crossing through the fields from North to South. This is also often called a *balk* by Niebuhr, and is a word at this time in common use for the strips of land in open town-fields in Yorkshire, and in other parts. Now this shews us that these cultivated lands or strips were regulated by these balks, which were not subinfeudated by the Lord, but always were, and yet are, his property. On the inclosure of my Manor of Skellow many years ago, I, of course, as Lord, claimed land for the balks, and had it allowed to me, as it is usual in similar cases. Hence we see that one of the great employments of these agrimensores must have been to protect the Lords' balks from being destroyed or stolen, to which they were very liable. The ridge of mountains which *divides* North India or Oude from Tartary, is called Balkan: this may mean Bal-ania, *land of Bal*. A similar ridge called Balkan divides the Sindi of Thrace from Scythia or Tartary. They were both Sindi—followers of the holy Xin. From Cardo we have, as I have before remarked, the cardinal points of the compass; and, as the line from North to South was first drawn, it evidently regulated the others. We know that the magnetic needle has varied for a great number of years back. The needle, I think, anciently pointed North and South, without any variation; that this variation is like the variation of the angle made by the planes of the Equator and Ecliptic; that, at the time *they* were displaced, it also was displaced; and, like them, it is gradually coming right again—though, like a pendulum put in motion, they may both oscillate some time before they get right. The Indians thought the oscillation was *great*, M. La Place thought it *small*. It may at first have been *large*, now *small*, and thus both the Indians and La Place may be right. At the boundaries of districts and where roads meet in Britain are the remains of the ancient termini, which were *crosses*, and, in the time of the Romans, priapuses, in different forms; all these were emblems of the generative power. The boundary, from being an emblem of the Ter-Menu, was called *terminus*; it denoted the creative power, of which also Apis or the Bull was the emblem: it was called Pra or Bra Apis—Priapus. Apis was but Ab or Ba *the father*. The Father, the Creator, was the triune principle—A=1, B=2=3. The Terminus was Ter-omen-us. An Omen was a kind of projector or foreteller or giver of warnings, and might be good or evil. Ter-omen was the *triple* omen, or omen of the Triune God. Martianus Capella tells us, that the cycle of Om—M—608, was called OMEN.[2] The

---

[1] Isid. ap. Litt. Dict.   [2] See Vol. I. p. 192.

Pillar with a cross at the top, placed on a Calvary of three steps, was an emblem of the Trimurti with the To Ov above it. I have just said that the crosses were the emblems of the generative power. These central stations, and particularly the first, was the generative point whence all the measurements proceeded; on this account, in a particular manner, it became the emblem of the generative power, as well as of the *heart* and of *wisdom*; it produced, generated, all the others. Every one is aware into what a variety of grotesque, and often indecent, forms, the termini of the Romans degenerated; but they all had a reference to the generative principle in some way or other, and in all cases their origin was in the sacred cross of the Agrimensores. In India, the same cause produced the same effect. A writer in Tait's Edinburgh Magazine says, "Gun-putty, "with an Elephant's head, that shews itself on various milestone-like appurtenances at the side "of an Indian road."[1] From this passage it is evident that the same termini remain in India and in Europe, as might be expected. The termini were considered the special protectors of gardens. Gun-putty is a figure with the head of an Elephant, the emblem of wisdom, or magical knowledge or science. Judging from the drawings and icons of him, I suspect his proboscis often formed a *gnomon*. The name is a compound of גן *gn* for garden, and *petti* father, *the father of the garden*. This is of importance, as it shews the same compound doctrine of agrimensorism, of wisdom, and of the generative principle, in India and in Europe. Let it be recollected, that in India Buddha is said to have been crucified for *robbing a garden!*[2] From being the emblem of the Om, the obeliscal pillar came to be called עמד *omd*, that is, om-di—emblem of the *holy Om*. This renovating cycle was itself the emblem of the Self-existent; whence עמדי *omdi* came to mean *self-existent*.[3]

I will now draw my reader's attention to another natural effect necessary to be attended to in order to obviate some objections. If we consider that great principles were originally laid down, general rules to be at first attended to, it followed that, after the system went to pieces, and all communication between the distant parts ceased, those principles would be carried into operation in a variety of ways,—still all endeavouring to keep to the system. Thus it is we have the great cycles described and supported in different ways. In some countries of the East we have the 600, in others the 60. In Italy we have the 240, and 360, and 120; but all coming to the same conclusion. In a similar way, in the building of temples, the pillars had different microcosmic numbers—8, 12, 38, 19, 360, &c., &c. In a similar manner some people built the choirs of their cathedrals crooked; some, perhaps, having lost all knowledge of the astronomical import, would, on rebuilding their temple, make it, as they thought right, by building it straight. Thus it is that we have an endless variety; and, in fact, there is scarcely an ancient monastery or cathedral in foreign countries, which does not retain some fragment of the old system, lost by most, and often not understood by any of the inhabitants. As various as the numbers of pillars in the stone circles are, I have little doubt that they have all once had their respective allusion to the principle, in some way unknown to us. Besides, it is possible, that some of the circles may have been erected after the system went to pieces, and the principle was no longer understood.

10. After Cassivellaunus was defeated by Cæsar, he disbanded all his army, except the warriors of 4000 chariots, with which *he retreated to the woods*. What a barbarian the man must have been to have had 4000 chariots; and how little skill he must have had to manage them in woods inaccessible to the Romans, and in a country *without roads!* Nothing but prejudice can have caused the belief in the Roman accounts of the barbarism of the Britons.[4] I have no doubt they bore to the Romans pretty much the same relation that the Mexicans did to the Spaniards: but who will say

---

[1] No. I. p. 32.   [2] See *supra*, pp. 248, 249.   [3] Parkhurst in *voce*.
[4] It is a beautiful example of the absurdity of historians in taking as true the evidence of enemies.

the Mexicans were *barbarians?* The human sacrifices were the same in both Rome and Britain; and if they prove the Britons to be *barbarians*, they prove Augustus Cæsar to have been one, for he offered up 300 human victims in one night at Perugio; and human sacrifices were not laid aside till the time of Claudius. The 20 towns, said to have been conquered by Vespasian, I suppose to have been part of the Municipia alluded to above, in fact, to have been so many of our old Borough towns, which sent their deputies to the Wittagemote. We are told that the military roads which we find in England and other countries were made by the Romans. I believe these were the roads originally set out by the sacerdotal agrimensores, but continued and increased by those of the Romans, who seldom destroyed the works of art in the countries which they conquered. I cannot believe that a people like the ancient Britons were barbarians, as they were sufficiently civilized to bring into the field of battle large bodies of charioteers and cavalry, and to manœuvre them, as Pownall has shewn, exactly in the manner practised by the Greeks and Asiatics.[1] The fact of these chariots is alone sufficient to prove that the natives were not in the state of barbarism which has been described. This and the science displayed in the temples negative all the story of the barbarism of the Britons. I believe that many of the right-lined roads were what were travelled on by these chariots, and were originally formed when the builders of Abury and Stonehenge held sway. But it must not be understood that I mean to say that the Romans did not make new roads, or that ignorant devotees in later ages might not set up crosses from pious motives, and in ignorance of the original intention of those they imitated. I do not doubt that they did. On the tops of modern crosses I think will be found an upright cross, or the hole in the centre where it has been fixed. On the tops of ancient ones will be found horizontal crosses; in fact, the dials and gnomons of Ahaz, always inscribed with right-lined Etruscan figures, or, as Vallancey has shewn them to be, Phœnician figures, which we still continue to use. The gnomon was to indicate the cardinal points. In all the accounts of Britain we read of a Supreme Pontiff or Archdruid. I have no doubt there were three Archflamens under him, who became the three Archbishops spoken of, *supra,* p. 412.

11. It cannot be denied that the attempts of Mr. Hume and all our other historians to account for many circumstances in the history of the early constitutions of our Saxon ancestors have been attended with very little success; and the difficulty, as he justly observes, has been greatly increased by some of the most important provisions having become objects of party dispute. But I think this has, in a great measure, arisen from the confined view which the historians have all thought proper to take of their subject. It seems never to have entered into their minds to inquire what became of the population left by the Romans; and whether some customs or laws of the mighty people, for mighty *they* must have been who raised Stonehenge and Abury, might have remained. Indeed, the fabricators of these buildings seem never to have once entered into their minds. Mr. Hume says, "the language was pure Saxon; even the names of places, which often " remain while the tongue entirely changes, were almost affixed by the conquerors."[2] In order to get rid of the old inhabitants, he represents them to have been nearly exterminated; and, then, to account for the Saxon names, he represents them to have been given by the *new* Saxons, when, in all probability, they only resumed their old Saxon names in the few instances where others had been given by the Romans. We have reason to believe, from the numerous Roman names of towns yet remaining, that the later Saxons did not change the names. I think when the Saxons came, they found the remains of their ancestors, who had, five or six hundred years before, built Stonehenge, &c.; and if our historians could have ascended a little higher in their researches, they

---

[1] Stud. of Ant. p. 274.   [2] Vol. I. Ap. I. p. 262.

would have found sufficient, probably, to have removed all the difficulties of the Saxon constitutions and laws.

I think circumstances tend to shew, that the great Barons were limited in number by the necessary offices which they held; for they were not like our present peers, mere animals of ornament,—each had some place or duty assigned to him. We are told that they consisted of from *fifty* to *eighty* persons;[1] but when I consider the mysterious numbers in the towns, I cannot help suspecting that, originally, they were, like the cardinales of Rome, 72 in number; and that, consequently, the nation was divided originally into 72 Earldoms, which would be, perhaps, the Domain of as many Municipia, with each its 12 Aldermen and 24 Common Councilmen. Each Earldom had its Urbs—a microcosm of the world. I think the Aldermen or Eldermen have been confounded with the Earls. The Earl was חלאר *elar*, THE *lar*, and was the same as the Heretogh or Duke, who was the ארץ *eartz*, עיי *oje*, Aga of the land.[2]

12. Pownal[3] says, "From the nature of that branch of revenue, the tithes, which arose from "the *Agri Decumani*, and by an inquiry how this branch was transferred to the Christian church "on its political establishment, may be discovered, I should guess, the true origin of tithes, as "they, in fact, came to the church." The person who has read this work thus far, will not, I think, require teaching the means by which the tithes descended to the Christian church. Allodial property was, in the first instance, only that *occupied* by the priests, and thus subject to no return of any kind. As these priests or initiated increased, with the decay of the system they would, by degrees, keep getting possession of more of the Agri Decumani, till they came to form a very large part of the productive lands of the country. By degrees, as the priests lost the character of functionary priests, only keeping the character of sacred caste, they began to acquire more land than they could occupy, and they subletted it in soccage, &c. The initiated or priests by degrees formed an aristocracy: they were, in fact, the non-officiating priests—gradually losing their sacerdotal character, like the Prince Palatines or Bishops of Germany. On the division, or, perhaps I should rather say, on the rise, of the military aristocracy, when they began to settle and to form a second aristocratic branch or class or caste, I think they enfeoffed their followers in the lands not previously occupied, in their own countries, and in conquered countries by force of arms in such districts as they chose to take from the conquered; but in every case the church or priesthood claimed, though they might not always obtain, the possession of the tithes. The priesthood claimed the soil as representatives of the vicar of God, and the tithe was the return to the Lord. In due season, in order that he might unite the right of *the book* to the right of *the sword*, the man of the sword compelled the priest to give him the χειροτονια; but this the priest always did accompanied with the open or mental reservation of the rights of the church. And it is exceedingly curious to observe the tenacity with which the obnoxious words *rights of the church* were always inserted in treaties or in rendering homage or in swearing fealty, when the priests were obliged to succumb to the violence of the kings or barons, and the anger of the latter at these words, because, as they very properly observed, they could not understand them. The fact was, the right of the church was the Lord Paramountship over the soil of the whole world; and, for the permission to the laity to the use of it, the moderate return of the tithe was required. For this reason it is that the tithe precedes all—kings' taxes—landlords' rent—military services—tithe comes before all. The right is maintained to be inalienable, indefeasible — nullum tempus occurrit ecclesiæ. And when we find the tithes in the hand of the prince, it is where the Bishop has become Prince, and has lost his sacerdotal character. But in this case we always find the officiating priests claiming,

---

[1] Hallam, Const. Hist. Eng. Vol. I. p. 6. [2] Hume, App. p. 266, n. [3] Stud. of Ant. p. 115.

and at last receiving, the tithes.¹ I suspect that after the agrestic life in a great measure ceased, all lands which were not held by one of the other tenures came into the hands of the priests, who granted off or disposed of their *usufruct* as circumstances called for them, in return for the payment to them of tithe; and that this is the reason why very large tracts of waste lands are found by Mr. Hallam to have been in the hands of the Monks, who acquired great riches by bringing them into cultivation.

13. The same disputes took place among the Athenians as in the Roman state, respecting the oppression of the people and the division of lands, before the time of Solon.² The same stories are told as we hear in Italy about debtors, creditors, &c.; but at last the whole comes to this, that in neither country is the state of the case understood, unless Mr. Niebuhr has discovered it. Cecrops is said to have divided the Athenians into four tribes; these, I apprehend, were the four Indian castes, each tribe into three peoples, and each people into thirty parts.³

Before the time of Solon, the Athenians were divided into four castes—the sacerdotal nobles, the soldiers, the farmers, and the tradesmen, and, in fact, a *fifth*, the slaves or outcasts.⁴ Their state was divided into 12 districts; and the system is to be seen in the 360 persons who were called confrères. Respecting the question of debtors and creditors, of which so much is said both in Greece and Italy, I think there is yet something not understood. What connexion have debtors and creditors to lands, any more than houses or other matters? I suspect that the *debts* were demands made by the nobles upon the feudatories, for more than the tenths or tithes, to which the landholders would maintain that the nobles were not entitled. It is evidently a struggle between the nobles and the people for disputed debts, having, I think, some connexion with the lands. Tithes were paid to the priests of Delphi, and the similarity of the agrarian disputes at Rome and Athens seems to raise a probability that they both arose from the same cause. Dr. D. Clarke has observed, that it appears, from an inscription which he found in Bœotian Thebes, "That "anciently, in that city, as in London, there were different companies, or communities, established "for the different vocations."⁵ Here we have the same system as that which we have assigned as the foundation of our Municipia. At the time when we read of the Amphictyons, the sacerdotal system had evidently gone to decay; but yet in the 12 states sending their deputies to the council, and in the 360 confrères of the Athenians, we may see the fragments of it. Treating of the nobility of Athens, Mr. Niebuhr says, "There was indeed at Athens, in very remote times, a nobility "which traced their descent from the heroes and princes of the heroic age; *that* is the idea of an "aristocracy. Solon himself belonged to this class, and so did the later Plato, and Critias, and "the orator Andocides. The distinction of this nobility was ascertained by the ancient division of

---

¹ Aristotle states the tribute from the land in Greece to be a *tenth*. (Briggs, p. 11.) Persia paid *one tenth*. (Ib. p. 14.) Syrian Judea paid *one tenth*. (Ib. p. 9.) In China *one tenth* is paid. (Ib. p. 15.) In the Burman Empire *one tenth* is paid. (Ib. p. 16.)

The Laws of Menu expressly *admit the Sovereign to be lord paramount of the soil in India*. (Ib. p. 25.)

Bertolacci states, that the whole of the land in Ceylon is the property of the Crown, of which it is held by the payment of returns of various kinds. (Ib. p. 45.)

After a careful inquiry, Col. Briggs comes to the conclusion, that the Hindoo institutions at one time were similar and universal throughout India. (Ib. 81.)

In India the country was in a very particular manner divided into districts, each containing 84 sub-districts—similar to the hundreds in England. (Ib. p. 85; Tod, Vol. I. p. 141.)

The Aids in Orissa, Travancore, and Ceylon, are a *tenth* of the produce. Briggs says, it is this which probably gave rise to the prevalent opinion throughout India, that the demands of the king were once limited to the *tenth* of income or produce, in lieu of all other direct imposts. (Ib. p. 93.)

² Sabbatier, p. 32. Stockdale's Ed.   ³ Fêtes Court. de Grèce, Vol. III. p. 193.

⁴ Sabb. p. 48.   ⁵ Travels, Vol. IV. p. 56, 4to.

"clans, not altogether unlike castes; and the blending of these with the other citizens, was the "aim of Clisthenes' code of laws. In some of these families, as the Eumolpidæ and Butades, "there still existed a few hereditary but unimportant offices of the priesthood. The Aleuadæ, "like the Bacchiades,[1] were a numerous and widely-diffused royal Gens. There also existed in "Greece, oligarchies of the most odious description, frequently degenerated from the aristo- "cracy."[2] Here are evident traces of the first order of priests growing into an order of lay aristocrats; the different offices of the priesthood having become hereditary in families—the origin of which the families themselves had forgotten. This, before the art of writing was generally practised, would soon happen. Mr. Niebuhr observes,[3] that it was the general opinion of the philosophers as well as the people of Greece, that an older race had occupied that country, who had perished, and who were the fabricators of the walls of Tiryns, and other buildings called Cyclopean,—of the drains from the lake Copias, &c., &c.; but of whom they had no records whatever, except their works. How could this have been, if the art of writing had been known and in common use for the purposes of history? This early race were the people who came from India and conquered the aborigines, as we conquered the people of North America, and are conquering the people of Australia. The laws being unwritten, letters not being invented, an order of priesthood or a separate order would be required to keep them in remembrance; for this reason the courts, like the Areopagus of Athens, were constituted, which, I doubt not, answered to a lodge of Freemasons, and above them were the Amphictyons, who answered to the chapter. These were the men by whom the book of wisdom, or the Veda, Beda, or Saga, was compiled in each case, when letters came to be known, the object of which was to produce uniformity, as that began to fail after the system began to go to pieces. I think it not unlikely that the monks and monasteries might at first, after the sacred caste came to be numerous, arise from there being establishments for education, and for the preparation of novices for the priesthood. The books of religion and of law, I do not doubt, were what the Pentateuch and the Koran yet are, the codes both of law and of religion. The sodalitates or companies of brethren or phratries or crafts in Athens were 12 in number, in what were called 360 houses.[4] Here we have the remains of the Microcosm. In a very ancient history of the Umbrians, it was related that the Etruscans had conquered three hundred of their towns.[5] Here Mr. Niebuhr says, we ought to consider the three hundred to mean only a large indefinite number. The absurdity of three hundred towns, in the common acceptation of the word town, he could not get rid of. Pliny says, there were more than twenty towns in the Pontine Marsh, which is about twenty-five miles long. In each case (notwithstanding all the learned distinctions of the literati) between the different kinds of towns the towns were nothing but polises—the divisions of the Agrimensores, something like our townships, each divided from its neighbour by a Cardo. They were parts of the 360 subdivisions. The country villages of the Romans were called *pagi*; the real nature of these is explained by the Greek name which they bear in the history of Dionysius, where a *pagus* is called a περιπολιον—as we should say a *circumpole*.[6] These were, I doubt not, our Maypoles, where the priest treated the people (when they came to pay their tithes) with games and feasting, as the landlords in Britain have a feast on the rent day. I suspect the houses named above, called Φαραις, and by the Lombards *Fara*,[7] had their names from the same root as the Pharaohs of Egypt, and all had reference to the feudal

---

[1] In the Aleuadæ and Bacchiades I suspect we have allodial proprietors and bookmen—the scribes of the Jews.
[2] Niebuhr, Hist. Rome, Vol. I. p. 120. Walter's Ed.   [3] Ibid. pp. 118, 119.
[4] Niebuhr, Hist. Rome, Vol. I. p. 307. Thirlwall's Ed.   [5] See *supra*, p. 410
[6] Niebuhr, Vol. II. p. 248. Thirlwall's Ed.   [7] Ib. I. p. 305.

system. Mr. Niebuhr says, "The tribes in the states of antiquity were constituted on a twofold "principle: in some states the arrangement was regulated by the houses which composed the "tribes, in others, by the ground which they occupied."[1] On considering this observation, I am induced to suspect, that when tribes came from the East to settle a country, not only the land was set out according to the microcosmic principle, but the people had the lands allotted to them on the same principle; and that it was the remains of this which Mr. Niebuhr perceived. The existence of the castes he shews[2] to be clearly perceptible in Italy. From the whole of the early part of this chapter it is plain that Dionysius, Aristotle, and Polybius, were all equally ignorant of the origin of the tribes, fraternities, &c., of the Greeks and Italians, and that all their statements are mere attempts at theories to account for that state of which they had no historical records; and the reason of this was because they had their origin when the widow-burning first took place on the river Sinde in Thrace, and in the Saturnian kingdom in Italy—before, in fact, the use of letters was known. The whole are the scattered remnants of the microcosmic system—remnants probably retained only in the national poems or songs. In his chapter entitled, "The Patrician Houses and the Curies,"[3] Mr. Niebuhr has bestowed very great pain in his endeavour to explain the origin of the tribes and divisions of the Greeks and Italians: he has, however, quite failed. I think if he had possessed the knowledge of the Sacerdotal Government, and how the Feudal System was connected with it, he would have succeeded much better. He would have unravelled the mystery where I fail.

14. The division into castes may be observed in the very early history of almost all nations. It was an effect which naturally arose from the universal Pontifical Government. The same causes every where produced the same effect. Strabo says, the Iberians were divided into *four* ranks.[4] The old Irish were divided in a similar manner.[5] As the Lucumones of the Etruscans were *twelve* in number, so we find, in the oldest monastery of the world, of which we have any remains, that of Iona of the Culdees, that it had *twelve* and their Prior, by whom they were ordained.[6] In the 360 Satrapes, into which Persia was divided; in the 72 Solumi, and in the three counsellors of Darius, named in the third, fourth, and fifth chapters of the first book of Esdras, when he ordered the Temple of Jerusalem to be rebuilt, I think we may see traces of the Microcosm in Persia. Josephus[7] says, that Darius made the prophet Daniel ruler over 360 cities. The oldest division of South India was into three Tamul principalities,[8] herein exhibiting signs of the same mythos. But this was probably before the priests of either Cristna or Vishnu arose. The universal mythos shews itself in a very peculiar and striking manner in the islands of Java, Sumatra, and Japan. They are all called by the same name—Jabadios. This, as I have frequently remarked, is clearly the island of the Holy Ieue. In Sumatra, the king calls himself by the two names of Sultan and of Allum Shah, the latter of which explains the former. We are told that it means *the world's king*. I have been informed by a very intelligent and respectable traveller, that the Turkish cavalry are, in general, feudatories, and that they hold lands on condition of themselves serving or finding a man and horse when *called on*, or at specific times, according to the terms of the tenure. Mr. Klaproth, p. 156, states the Tatar nation to have consisted of 70,000 families. I have little doubt that we have here a sacred caste, limited to the sacred number of seventy-two. These were the tribes of Caracorum. The Turcomans of the Ottoman empire are divided, like the Roman Cardinales, into seventy-two tribes. In this, joined to several other circumstances which I have

---

[1] Niebuhr, Vol. I. p. 301. Thirlwall's Ed. [2] Ib. p. 302. [3] Ib. Vol. I. pp. 301—331. Walter's Ed.
[4] Lib. XI. Univ. Hist. Vol. IX. p. 609. [5] See Anonym. Diss. on Irish Hist. pp. 29—54.
[6] Jameson's Hist. Culd. Chap. III. [7] Book X. Chap. XII. [8] Trans. Mad. Soc. p. 18.

before noticed, we see a proof of the origin of the Turkish power.¹ (In the same work Mr. David observes, that the Nestorian Syriac literal character has a close affinity to the Ouigour.² This is because they are, in fact, both the Pushto.) The Grand Seignior has twelve Ulemas. Tacitus informs us that the Germans divided the year into *three*. In honour of Augustus Cæsar 70 cities in the Roman provinces were called Augusta.³ I can entertain little doubt that these were 72 ecclesiastical capitals of districts, into which the empire was divided, and they are continued in the Roman cardinals. It has before been observed, that the chiefs at the siege of Troy were 72 in number. The Universal History⁴ says, "So we find Chedorlaomer, King of Elam, to have presided over several Reguli or Phylarchs, who, notwithstanding this, exercised a sovereign authority in the district where they held their residence. In like manner, at the siege of Troy, all the petty Greek princes obeyed the orders of Aga-memnon,⁵ whom Homer represents as king of kings; and, that this form of government prevailed anciently in Arcadia, Numidia, Etruria, Tartary, &c., has already been evinced." Here we have marked traces of the Microcosm in Greece and the other states named. The name of Chedorlaomer reminds me that the 70 kings, whose thumbs and great toes were cut off,⁶ shew the mythos or microcosm in Syria. The Universal historian then goes on to shew that originally the same system prevailed in China, and that the feudatory princes formed a species of parliament, or, I should say, Wittenagemote, and *that they officiated solely in religious matters*. Ieou was the great prophet, lawgiver or saviour, of the Chinese; there he had seventy disciples.⁷ In like manner Iη-σες, that is IH, the ζω or Saviour, had 70 disciples. It is repeatedly observed by Mitford, in his history of Alexander, that all the Indian princes who were subjected to that conqueror, seem to have been feudatories to some grand potentate residing to the East; and there is an observation in the Universal Ancient History,⁸ that a Tartar Khan called Kiun Kan, before the time of Alexander the Great, divided his dominions among 48 princes. These, I apprehend, were subinfeudatories, or, in fact, tributary nobles, doing suit and service; and I think we may see, that these Khans were the ancestors of the Mogul, and claim to be the direct descendants of Noah and Japhet, to whom they trace their pedigree. I feel little doubt but that this Mogul claims to be one of the three, and the division into 48, the number of the ancient constellations, again shews the remains of the microcosmic system. Faria y Sousa says, the king of Bengal is the *heir* to all men.⁹ Among both the Greeks and Romans we read very distinct accounts of families possessing by inheritance certain offices or dignities, and among the priests particularly. But remains of this, I think, may be seen in most nations, when their ancient history is closely examined. In consequence of this system, the four great castes, as in India, became divided into a great number of little ones. All trades, all sciences, were hereditary. This seems to have answered very well; for, under the practice, all arts and sciences seem to have risen to a high state of perfection, and only to have declined with the destruction of it. Chevalier Ramsay, in his Cyrus, (p. 54,) has described the system to have been the practice of Ireland. I think it very probable that before the invention of letters it may have been the most eligible plan which could be adopted. It is difficult for us, brought up in the knowledge of letters, to judge of the state of the world before their invention. The Roman Pontifex Maximus, it is known, had a council, a kind of cabinet of *twelve* persons; but of what they consisted does not seem to be known. They were, I doubt not, the Tuscan Lucumones. The word *Lucuman* I suppose to be Lux-mannus or Lucis-mannus. They had also an order called the

---

¹ Vide Pref. to Lumley David's Turkish Grammar, p. xliii.   ² Ib. p. xv.   ³ Lemp. Augusta.
⁴ Vol. XX p. 124.   ⁵ The Aga of the Janissaries comes from the same title.
⁶ By order of Adoni-bezek, according to his own confession, Judges i. 7.
⁷ Collie's Trans. of Hea Mung, p. 117.   ⁸ Vol. I. p. 46.   ⁹ Hist. Ind. Vol. I. p. 416. Eng. Ed.

Flamens, originally only *three* in number, who were Flammæ-mannus. The Ager Romanus was divided into *three* districts. The microcosm is visible in the Pontiff, and in the Flamens or Augurs, confined to the number *three*; and, like the Supreme Pontiff, their persons were sacred, and they were accountable to the Pontiff only for their conduct. When I think upon the admitted obscurity in which the subject of the Roman early polity is enveloped, and I find that the knights were at first restricted[1] to *three hundred*, and afterwards increased to *six* and then to *eighteen* hundred, and that the Patres Conscripti were at first limited to *three hundred*, I am induced to suspect that the latter were originally three hundred and sixty, and that the remainder of the numerical mythos of seventy-two, &c., was originally in use, though now lost to us. The numbers in the formation of the Roman Legion, and other parts of their military establishment, clearly display the mythos. The case of the Microcosm or Macrocosm, whichever it may be called, to which I have so often alluded, is similar to the case of the Irish Elk, which I mentioned above. It is unreasonable to expect to find the whole system, or proofs of its former existence, in any one place; but I think it is not unreasonable by collecting fragments of it in different places to hope to make out the whole, as the Irish made out their whole Elk. However, of this I am quite certain, that if I cannot make out the whole, I can exhibit quite enough to prove both its actual existence and its general nature.

15. I think there is a great probability that there was an Archierarch and a council of *twelve*, and a senate of *seventy - two* in every country—the governors under a Pope at Oude, Agra, Mundore, Samarcand, or some other great capital. We see remnants of this system in different places. We have them in the twelve Lucumones of Italy; in the twelve heads of Tribes and in the seventy-two of the Jewish Sanhedrim, and in the seventy-two Solumi of Persia; in the twelve states of Ionia; and in the council of the Amphictyons, who were evidently a religious assembly, sent from twelve states of Greece. I suspect that the *three* presidents did not impart *all* their secrets to the Council or Chapter, or Conclave of *twelve*, or the chapter of twelve all their secrets to the *seventy-two*. These would be formed in every great natural division of the world, or in every one of the seventy-two divisions, as we have them laid down in Genesis—a grand council to superintend each division, and, under it, as many subdivisions as would be required by localities and circumstances—each having its Flamens, Lucumones, and Sanhedrim; and each having its sacred Mount or Cardo or Acropolis or Olympus or stone circle or τεμενος, around which the processions, the Deisuls, the voyages of salvation, were made, and the collection of the tithes would be paid, as at Delphi and Jerusalem. All this being strictly religious, all independent of any petty disputes which might take place between emigrating tribes, it would not be affected by them in the slightest degree. Thus we find the council of the Amphictyons unaffected even by the invasion of Xerxes.[2] This superior Sanhedrim, originally, I suspect, filled up by itself, as vacancies occurred, would leave to the respective subdivisions the management of their domestic affairs. It would seldom interfere with its civil concerns; but yet, I think, each government would be a kind of subinfeudation of the great one. Every district would have its archpriest. Of this we have remnants in abundance in our hierarchy, in our municipalities—succeeding to the Roman Municipia—in our Mayors and Corporations, which, by degrees, came to be formed; and, in the country, in our Lords of Manors, (Lords of Minerva,) originally, I have no doubt, all ecclesiastics, sacerdotes beginning to lose their sacerdotal character. In the council of Amphictyons,[3] at Delphi and Eleusis, we have the origin of our College of Heralds—a *sacred* (i. e. also *secret*) college, with its κηρυξ or messenger of peace;[4] and in the Druidical col-

---

[1] Niebuhr, Hist. Rom. pp. 255, 256. Walter's Ed.
[3] The word Amphictyon is, Am-phi-iction or Ixion.

[2] See Vol. I. p. 632.
[4] See Vol. I. p. 590.

leges—our universities—we have the places where youth were educated for the different situations of the priesthood. But I must still be understood to mean, that all these divisions went on as subordinate to the *three* Archierarchs—the descendants of Shem, Ham, and Japhet. I think it is probable that the first Archierarchical Government left the towns and the districts appertaining to them, generally, to the management of themselves ; from which the various free states of Greece and Italy arose. They were held in feudal tenure of the God Phree. Their business was to preserve the supreme power of their Pontiff, wherever he happened to reside, and to arbitrate disputes among the tribes. At this time and under these circumstances it is evident, that there could be none of the wars and national enmities, or causes of them, which at present exist. Whenever differences arose the Amphictyons would be the disinterested mediators. This we see most clearly in the Amphictyons of Greece. There would be no interest in these early Amphictyons to do injustice; their tithes would be known and certain; but it would be most evidently their interest to preserve peace, for the sake of encouraging the increase of the produce of the land, and the consequent increase of their tithes. As this system began to go to decay, they would begin to increase rites and ceremonies of religion to intimidate the people. Magic and juggling tricks of every kind would begin to arise. In the little republics of Greece, and in the same, or nearly the same, description of little states in Italy, we have the formation of societies for their own governance in secular affairs: in Greece, under the council of the Amphictyons—in Italy not so clearly marked, but probably under a Pontifex Maximus somewhere, and under the Lucumones and Cardinales. Remains of this system shew themselves every where, when ancient history is examined to the bottom; and the consentaneousness of the remains proves, that an universal system prevailed throughout the world. The traditions of the poets, are, in fact, in their foundations, true traditions—not as we have been accustomed to consider them, merely poetical effusions, for the sake of amusing idle people. The Golden Age was no figure of speech, but a reality.[1] In the history of the Phocian war, and the interdict pronounced against it by the council of the Amphictyons, we see the almost expiring power of one of the local conclaves. It is perfectly clear that the council possessed the supreme power, at least in every thing appertaining to religion; and that all the different states of Greece formed a whole subject to them. It is also pretty clear, from the different accounts given of the origin of this council, that it was, equally with the origin of the state of Greece itself, at that time unknown to their writers. This arose from its institution having taken place several generations before the use of letters, in an age said to be *barbarous*. So fine an institution bespeaks any thing but an age of barbarism! This is the reason that the states of Greece were all exactly in the same situation with respect to their early history, as the least impartial examination of it will satisfy any one. When Alexander the Great aspired to the sovereignty of the world, he applied to the Amphictyons, who acknowledged him as their Lord, or who took upon themselves to appoint him to the sovereignty of all Greece. This seems to be nearly among the last exertions of their supreme power. But I have little doubt it was with the understanding, that he was the *new incarnation ;* though this might be only secretly professed by the initiated. We must never forget, that the real system was kept *a secret* as much as possible. Amidst all the confusion in which the history is involved, it is very clear that Philip aspired to be chief of the Grecian states, only as general or officer of the Amphictyons. The Areopagus at Athens, I suppose, was the high ecclesiastical court of that state, and probably, originally founded on the same plan as its superior—the Amphictyonic council, to whom, no doubt, it was amenable. Although in periods of public calamity the Areopagus sometimes interfered in state affairs, this

---

[1] See *supra*, pp. 305—308.

seems to have been a stretch of authority. It took cognizance of all religious concerns, and, as such, of criminal actions, murder, &c. The origin of this court, like all other Grecian concerns, is lost in fable. I believe that the emblematical figures which are every where found in such great numbers in the East, had their origin before the knowledge of letters, and were invented for the purpose of assisting in keeping alive the mythos. As might well be expected, the meaning of them is now almost entirely gone. I have repeatedly observed in the course of this work, that the ignorance of the Latins and Greeks of their mythology and Gods is quite unaccountable; but on more mature consideration I think the invention and adoption of them, previous to the knowledge of letters, is quite sufficient to account satisfactorily for that ignorance. It appears to me, now that I consider it in connexion with their ignorance of letters, to be a necessary consequence. Their sacred poems would enable them to retain or preserve but a very small part of their mythology; and of history, for the *purpose of history*, they had none. Besides, sacred poems retained by memory, would answer very well as long as every thing proceeded peaceably; but the moment civil wars and revolutions of empires commenced, they would be no longer of any avail. I had nearly completed this work, in which I have so frequently expressed my surprise at the unaccountable union of ignorance and knowledge among the ancients, before it occurred to me, that many facts prove that science must have been, till a very little time before Christ, entirely confined to *secret* societies—each philosopher keeping his science as much as possible to his own followers. We must recollect that the total absence of every thing like reviews, magazines, and newspapers, must have rendered this comparatively easy. This will readily account for the Callidei or Chaldæans being the possessors of science, to the exclusion of others. This is supported by the book found in Egypt by Mr. Hammer, which says, as I have before-mentioned, that every learned man had a letter of his own.[1] I have frequently observed, that the religion of Buddha must have come to the West, using the epithet *Buddha*. I rather regret that I have so used it, as it may have a tendency to raise objections in the minds of some persons, who will revolt at the local superstition of India being brought to Britain and other western nations; but facts found in them sufficiently prove, that the same system really existed in both, and actually by the name of Buddha too. We find little of this system in *books*, because when syllabic literal writing began to escape from the adyta of the mysterious temples, the law of eternal change was operating to its destruction; but we cannot look a yard around us, without seeing remnants of it, from the village merestone, and the four-road cardinal-decuman cross to the mighty Stonehenges and Aburys yet existing, from Iona in Scotland, to Iona in Ceylon — from Tanga Tanga of Tartary and China, to Tanga Tanga of Peru.

16. Dancing is looked on with contempt by philosophers at this day; but I have no doubt that the dance was among the ancients really of much greater importance than has been suspected. It was generally accompanied with both music and poetry, and the original intention was to keep in recollection the sacred mythoses before the invention of writing;[2] and surely nothing could be better contrived for this purpose. All early sacred books are poetical. For the same purpose festivals, equally accompanied with dancing and poetry set to music, and sung to the dancing, were established to keep in recollection victories or other celebrated events. When this view is taken of those apparently frivolous arts, how surprisingly are they changed! Instead of sciences contemptible and demoralising, as they became after the art of writing was made public, we see that, when under the supervision of the first priesthood, they were originally most important, and must have been the firmest supports to patriotism, morality, and every generous virtue. We now

---

[1] See *supra*, p. 205. [2] See Vol. I. p. 404, and *supra*, p. 179.

see why they were patronised by the Socrateses and Pythagorases of antiquity. Although I give more credit than has been given by any one in modern times to the great change which must have been effected in the world by the knowledge of the art of writing having become general, yet I suspect I do not, by any means, give credit enough to it. To the knowledge of it I attribute, in a great measure, the conversion of those originally moral and delightful arts into causes of every kind of vice and impurity. With their utility they lost their innocence and simplicity. Being no longer necessary to preserve the recollection of historical events or mythoses, they were abandoned to those who practised them without understanding their meaning—merely for their sensual gratification. All the best feelings and refined sensations gave place to the gratification of the lowest passions, and the temples became no better than taverns and brothels, the places of resort for strumpets and bacchanals. That this was their state no one can deny. But though the later of the ancients admit the fact, yet it is quite clear that the abuse had crept on so imperceptibly, that they were utterly at a loss to account for it, and with the corruption of the mythology and religion, an absolute ignorance of their meaning very naturally ensued. As the knowledge of the art of writing crept out by slow degrees, and was used, without any previous system, to record only a few of the most important matters, its tendency would be to induce carelessness, and a relaxation of the efforts to explain the meaning of the dances, poems, &c., which would previously be bestowed, when there was nothing but the retention of them in the memory to depend upon.

" In a choral ode of Sophocles, he (Pan) is addressed by the title of Author and Director of the
" Dances of the Gods; as being the author and disposer of the regular motions of the universe, of
" which these divine dances were symbols. .... Among the Greeks, all dancing was of the
" mimetic kind: wherefore Aristotle classes it with poetry, music, and painting, as being equally
" an imitative art: and Lucian calls it a science of imitation and exhibition, which explained the
" conceptions of the mind, and certified to the organs of sense things naturally beyond their reach.
" To such a degree of refinement was it carried, that Athenæus speaks of a Pythagorean, who
" could display the whole system of his sect in such gesticulations, more clearly and strongly than
" a professed rhetorician could do in words; for the truth of which, however, we do not vouch, the
" attempt being sufficient. Dancing was also a part of the ceremonial in all mystic rites: whence
" it was held in such high esteem, that the philosopher Socrates, and the poet Sophocles, both
" persons of exemplary gravity, and the latter of high political rank and dignity, condescended to
" cultivate it as an useful and respectable accomplishment. The author of the Homeric hymn to
" Apollo, describes that God accompanying his lyre with the dance, joined by the other deities;
" and a Corinthian poet, cited by Athenæus, introduces the Father of Gods and Men, employed in
" the same exercise. The ancient Indians, too, paid their devotions to the Sun by a dance imi-
" tative of his motions, which they performed every morning and evening, and which was their
" only act of worship. Among the Greeks, the Cnosian dances (Q. Gnosian?) were peculiarly
" sacred to Jupiter, as the Nyssian were to Bacchus, both of which were under the direction of
" Pan; who, being the principle of universal order, partook of the nature of all the other Gods;
" they being personifications of particular modes of acting of the great all-ruling principle, and he
" of his general law of pre-established harmony; whence, upon an ancient earthen vase of Greek
" workmanship, he is represented playing upon a pipe, between two figures, the one male and the
" other female; over the latter of which is written ΝΟΟΣΣ, and over the former ΑΔΚΟΣ:
" whilst he himself is distinguished by the title ΜΟΛΚΟΣ: so that this composition explicitly
" shows him in the character of universal harmony, resulting from mind and strength; these
" titles being, in the ancient dialect of Magna Græcia, where the vase was found, the same as
" ΝΟΥΣ, ΑΛΚΗ, and ΜΟΛΠΗ, in ordinary Greek. The ancient dancing, however, which
" held so high a rank among liberal and sacred arts, was entirely imitative; and esteemed ho-

" nourable or otherwise, in proportion to the dignity of what it was meant to express."[1] David danced before the Ark,[2] and one of the Gospels[3] describes Jesus and the Twelve Apostles as having celebrated a dance after the *last supper*. It is difficult for us to enter fully into the feelings of the actors or spectators of the dance, or to comprehend the intensity of them, which would probably arise from the belief that they were the representations of scenes of real life. For want of experience we can form no idea of the effect which must have been produced. I have before observed that all the mythoses of antiquity were contained in poems.[4] I have no doubt that writing was originally used solely for the purposes of religion, and used only in the form of poetry, for the sake of aiding the memory,—prose being comparatively a late invention. This, I think, led to the universal degradation of the human character—of the human animal. In the first place, the memory deteriorated, and, in the next place, by the abuse of allegory, the minds of the uninitiated were brought, by degrees, to the reception of the most degrading puerilities. The common people finding such stories as those of Cristna believed by their superiors, the initiated, (but which, in fact, were not believed by them,) were also induced to believe them. Thus, in time, in all countries, arose the mythology, and in a similar manner the poems came to be considered to have divine authority, and to be, as inspired writings, infallible. I have no doubt that if the *Paradise Lost* had been written in the beginning of the Christian æra, it would have been regarded as of divine authority. Its mixture of puerile nonsense and beautiful passages is well calculated to attract a devil-driving age. The Marquis de Fortia d'Urban[5] says, " La prévention pour la coutume " a été, de tout tems, un obstacle au progrès des arts : La musique s'en est surtout ressentie. A " Lacédémone, où Lycúrgue avait joint la musique aux exercices militaires (Plutar. Apophthegmes " des Lacédémoniens, Chap. xxxi.); il n'était permis de faire aucun changement dans l'art de " célébrer les actions héroïques, quoique fort instruit des anciens usages, il ajouta une corde à la lire " pour varier les tons. Les Éphores condamnèrent cette nouveauté, et clouèrent sa lire à un " mur : tant on était attaché à la simplicité des accords !" says the Marquis. He then adds, " Le musicien Timothée ayant aussi ajouté deux cords à sa lire lorsqu'il disputa le prix aux jeux " CARNÉANS, un des Éphores vint, un couteau à la main, lui demander de quel côté il voulait que " fussent coupées les cordes qui excédaient le nombre de sept." He adds, " On voit par ces faits " l'importance que les anciens attachaient à la musique, au chant, et même aux instrumens." The Marquis may be perfectly assured that the Spartans might have sung to what tune they pleased, had not something very important depended upon it. All those exercises of the young Carneans were religious, as were all their games. How all the notes of music were made useful to record the mythos, it may be impossible now to discover; but when I recollect all the Pythagorean doctrines and praises of music, I cannot doubt that they were converted to such use, and were of the very first importance too. It seems probable that the class of persons called Rhapsodists, in Greece, were correctly the bards of Britain, Ireland, Scandinavia, and India; and the rhapsodies which they sung were the cyclic poems, or poems to celebrate the renewal of Cycles or Avatars—in songs carrying a double meaning—an *exoteric* and an *esoteric* meaning,— which was clearly the case with their tragedies.

It is a very important fact to be observed and recollected, in this disquisition, that, in reality, poetry was the only species of composition which could by possibility exist until the invention of the material of books, such as prepared skin or papyrus, was brought to a very considerable degree of perfection; and we have reason to believe that this invention in the West, at least, had no very

---

[1] PAYNE KNIGHT on Ancient Myth. p. 153
[2] See *supra*, p. 225.
2. Samuel vi. 12—16.
[4] Sur l'Orig. de l'Ecriture, p. 94.
[3] One of the *Uncanonical*. ED.

great antiquity. And here we see the reason why (as Mr. Niebuhr has observed) all the ancient pseudo-histories, but real mythoses, of Italy, appear to have been in verse or poetry. No doubt an exertion of memory surprisingly great must have been required for the composition of such poems as the Iliad and the Odyssey; but we can scarcely form an idea how different from ours may have been the retentive faculties of persons, the improvement of whose powers of memory formed the great and leading object of their education. I doubt not, as I have already intimated, that the art of *writing* has been the ruin of the retentive faculty of the human mind. I believe in every country the religious system, which included in it what might very properly be called also the philosophic system, was concealed or conveyed in ballads or feigned adventures of a person, from which, when historians arose, they formed their respective histories. As in each country, from the lapse of time and other circumstances, small variations in the ancient story must have arisen, so, in the respective histories, variations would take place, yet the universal mythos would still occasionally shew itself.

CHAPTER V.

MICROCOSM CONTINUED. VEDANTA AND NYAYA PHILOSOPHY OR DOCTRINES.—NATURE OF THE MICROCOSM.—PYTHAGORAS ON NUMBERS. CYCLES.—MYTHOLOGY. PATRON AND CLIENT. COLONIES. ISOPOLITY. NUMA POMPILIUS.—SYMBOLIC AND ALPHABETIC WRITING.—ADORATION OF ANIMALS. THE ONION. CREST.—THE ANCILE OF NUMA. CYCLIC MYTHOS. CLEMENS ALEXANDRINUS. ANCIENT MYSTERIES. BAPTISM, THE EUCHARIST, &c. DOCTRINE OF THE ANCIENT AND MODERN Χρης.—BAILLY, BUFFON, &c., ON BIRTHPLACE OF MANKIND. FORMER HEAT AT THE POLES. THE MYTHIC-CYCLIC-MICROCOSMIC SYSTEM. WHAT HAS HAPPENED MAY HAPPEN AGAIN. ILLUSION.

1. We have seen much respecting the contention between the advocates of the *male* and of the *female* principles of generation for superiority. Besides this, there was another source of dissension, which was the produce of it, and which was of the most refined and abstruse nature; indeed, it was of so refined a nature that, whoever has endeavoured to explain it has lost himself. The doctrine has agitated the schools as well in Europe as in India, from the most remote of times. It is the abyss in which deep thinkers and learned men have generally been shipwrecked. Their lucubrations have ended in *illusion*. This has arisen from their attempt to grasp what is evidently out of the reach of the mind of man. In Europe we have had it, in modern times, under the names of *Des Cartes* on one side, and of *Berkeley* on the other: in India it has been discussed chiefly by *Vyasa*; and it is called the doctrine of the *Vedanta* philosophy in opposition to the *Nyaya* philosophy. The word *Vedanta* is evidently a formation from the word Ved, which I have shewn to be the same as Bud, and to mean *wisdom*,[1] and it has acquired this name in India, because it was principally the doctrine of the ruling power, the Brahmins. This meant the doctrine of the eternal existence of matter or substance (the doctrine of *Des Cartes*); of which the First Cause, the יה *ie*, the *I shall be what I have been* was supposed to consist—the יהיה *ieie* chanted by the

---

[1] See *supra*, p. 4.

Brahmins in the word *Yeye*. The word *Nyaya* was the opposite of this, and is a formation, almost English, consisting of the negative *ny*, which is the English word *Nys*, (used, I believe, only by Spenser,) meaning, *none is*. It is the negative particle and the Hebrew *w is*, which jointly mean *not is* or *not wise*, and the Hebrew word יה *ie, existence*. The two doctrines in common terms may be defined those of Matter and Spirit—of Materialism and Immaterialism—called also Atheism and Deism.

The followers of the *Nyaya* were also the followers of the *female*, *Maia*—those of the *Vedanta* were followers of the *male*, Brahme. I think, in the Mahabarat war, the Buddhists were followers of the Nyaya, and the Brahmins of the Vedanta; but the two sects in later times, after the whole became merely a matter of the idle speculation of philosophers, in short a logomachy, and the meaning of the mythology was lost, were completely intermixed and so confounded one with the other, that they perpetually changed sides, and the followers of the Nyaya, the *spiritualists*, who were formerly considered the Atheists, are now considered the only Deists; and the *materialists* are considered the Atheists. The two doctrines are so nearly the same in principle, that it is very difficult to distinguish one principle from the other; and, if I understood Mr. [Sir] Greaves Haughton, the learned Secretary to the Asiatic Society, on the 2d of March, 1833, they are at the bottom the same. Under these circumstances I think I shall not be thought very paradoxical in thus stating my belief, that the modern Brahmins, in their endeavours to recover the lost learning of their ancestors, have done precisely what has been done by the Jews with the *Barasit* and *Mercavah*, in their Cabala, namely, they have substituted one for the other. The יה *ie* is clearly materialism, let the priests say what they will to the contrary; however, it is the dogma of the Brahmins; and Nyaya is nothing but the denial of the Yeye—the negative of it. But if I be mistaken as to the sects having changed, this will not alter the fact that one is a negative of the other. The יהיה *ieie* I am satisfied, was understood to be a spiritual fire, an *emanation* from the Supreme Being, and partaking of his nature—hereby making him into a material existence. I believe it will not be denied that the great feud between the Buddhists and Brahmins arose *in part* from the difference between the Vedanta and the Nyaya philosophies; which, as I have intimated, are called the doctrines of *materialism* and *immaterialism*, *matter* and *spirit*, and, as thence inferred, of Theism and Atheism, which, in Vol. I. p. 815, I have shown is an inference not possible to be supported.[1] From this the worshipers of God, under the names of Cristna or the *benevolent lamb*, or Vishnu the *fish*, gratifying their sectarian hatred, take occasion to call the Sacæ or Saxons or followers or worshipers of Saca, the God of wisdom under the name of Buddha, Atheists; and they find our learned men, such for instance as the learned Mr. Colebrook, blockheads enough to follow their example. I have little doubt that this feud arose as early as the division between the Buddhists and the Vishnuvites, whenever this might have happened, and that it was long before the perfecting of the Sanscrit language. Of course, as usual, (and after the manner of the Greeks formerly complained of by Plato,) Sanscrit scholars go to the Sanscrit for an etymology,[2] and they make of *Nyaya i*, to go, with the prefix *ni* into, *inference, argument, reasoning, logic*; and of *Vedanta*, from *Veda*, and *anta, the end*: the end, that is, the purpose or ultimate result and substance of the Veda. The above is the explanation of one learned Sanscrit professor: the following is the explanation of another :— "The word Vedanta is derived from Véda, *the Scripture*,

---

[1] I am well aware that what I have said in the passage quoted above, may be, and will be, disputed by the metaphysicians; but what are all their nice distinctions on these subjects, (which are in reality *above our comprehension*,) but a mere logomachy and nonsense?

[2] There are great numbers of words in the first Veda which are in no Lexicon; this is because their meaning was lost before a lexicon was made. Dr. Rosen tells me, the first lexicon was made about 600 years *after* Christ.

"and Anta, *end;* implying the end or object of the Veda. Nyáya, in its original sense, means "fitness, propriety; hence its applicability to express the same thing as we call *logic.*" These etymologies may be satisfactory to the profound searchers into these questions; they are not so to me. The following, I think a better explanation: the Vedanta is the patronised doctrine of the ruling powers in India; and I suppose they meant, that the doctrine has *wisdom* for its *end* or *object;* and that they affirmed, that this, that is, Ved, Bed, or Bud, is its doctrine, in opposition to the other, which is *not wisdom.* Now we have formerly seen that the Brahmins chaunt in their service the word Yeye,[1] which they do not understand; but say, they suppose it to mean *victory,* the word *ye* meaning victory. I have shewn that this is the name of the Hebrew God יהוה *ieie,* who is often called the God of victory, but the meaning of which is *self-existent God,* and is an epithet in a particular manner applied to the God of wisdom. I believe, therefore, as I have lately remarked, that the Nyaya is merely the Hebrew and Sanscrit word יהוה *ieie,* with the Celtic, Saxon, and Sanscrit negative, prefixed by the Brahmins to convert it into a term of reproach against their opponents, to make them deniers of the self-existent God, or to be *Atheists.* Then the first will be, the doctrine of *the wise;* the latter of *the unwise.* I repeat, that our Sanscrit scholars, in endeavouring to expound the meaning of *proper names* by the Sanscrit only, are exactly in the same situation as that in which Plato describes the Greeks to have been, in their endeavours to expound *their* proper names by their *own language,* instead of going to the Barbari. Sanscrit scholars also should go to the Barbari. I believe the names of all their Gods will be found in the Arabic, that is, in the Hebrew roots. Mr. Wilson says, "by Siva himself, the Pásupata writings were composed: Kanáda is the author of the Vaisheshika philosophy. The Nyáya originates with Gautama. Kapila is the founder of the Sánkhya school, and Vrihaspati of the Chárváka. Jaimini, by Siva's orders, composed the Mímánsa, which is heretical, in as far as it inculcates *works* in preference to *faith,* and Siva himself, in the disguise of a Brahman, or as Vyása, promulgated the Vedánta, which is heterodox in Vaishnava estimation, by denying the sensible attributes of the Deity."[2]

2. We will now inquire farther into the nature of the microcosm. From the To Ov proceeded the Creator, Preserver, and Destroyer—Brahma, Vishnu, and Seva; from them proceeded 72 Angels, and from them 360 others; these were the angels seen by Jacob, and these were the 360 Æons of the Valentinians, and the 360 tutelar saints of the Romish church, one for each day of the year, and the Divi of Macrobius. The seed of every living or animate being was believed to have been formed at the first creation, or to be a part of or an emanation from the To Ov, to have existed from eternity, to be a perfect animal in miniature, a microcosm of every animal above it, and at last, of course, of the first Great Cause. Every seed was a microcosm, i. e. a little world— was a world in miniature. Naturalists, by means of the microscope, perceive that the seed of every animate being, like the egg of the serpent waiting in the sand for the solar ray to develop its faculties, is a being complete, and only waits for the peculiar circumstances suitable to its nature to develop itself.[3] It is evident that without the solar heat no animate being would ever come into existence. Hence we see how the sun came to be regarded as the Creator, and why the ancients adored that luminary: and the prayer of Cyrus, though he was an Iconoclast, and of Martianus Capella, noticed in Vol. I. pp. 191, 192, shew that they could reconcile the adoration of the solar power under his various names with the adoration of one Supreme Being, at the head of

---

[1] See Vol. I. pp. 430, 468.   [2] Asiat. Res. Vol. XVI. p. 10.
[3] Here we have a microcosm of Brahme brooding over the deep, and of the Spirit of God moving on the face of the water, of *Genesis.* See *supra,* p. 67.

all. I consider it quite impossible for any one to have read this work with attention, and not to have seen that an universal mythos once prevailed; but I cannot help thinking that, if it had been a system regularly made out, and previously contrived in all its parts, we should have made it clearly out *step by step*. On this account I am induced to suspect that the mythos arose from circumstances, and was founded on, or consisted of, the microcosmic principle; and that from this, when applied to the cyclic system, which is most clearly microcosmic, the mythic histories took their rise, in all nations having a certain degree of resemblance, but in all nations, from the peculiar circumstance that the facts of real history were used to describe the *mythos*, it must of course vary, *i. e.* a certain quantum of variation must take place in the mythic history. Real facts could not be bent quite to fit; but they were bent to do so as nearly as possible. The bending of the real facts would be aided by the natural uncertainty of tradition, by which only they were handed down, writing being, I suppose, unknown. As story or a tale of facts was to be the vehicle, such leading facts as the native tradition preserved, must, of course, be used, and would be very easily made to bend. Thus we have, as observed by Nimrod, the Exodus or *going out* of all nations, probably the first migration of the tribe. We have this part of the mythos clearly in North India, South India, in Syria, Babylon, Troy, Rome, and in Mexico, perhaps the most remarkable of all.[1] In Genesis we have the microcosm of two worlds. We have the Patriarch, that is, the head father or Pontifex Maximus, and his three vicars, dividing the world into three parts; and the four in each case are microcosms of the To Ov, and of the Creator, Preserver, and Destroyer. In the first case, Cain was the *destroyer*. In the second case, Ham was the *wicked one*, or the *destroyer*, the *cursed one*—the father of the Canaanites or followers of the female principle—Γυνη, *Cune*.[2] Julius Firmicus Maternus says, "It is necessary to know, in the first place, that "the God, who is the fabricator of man, produced his form, his condition, and his whole essence, "in the image and similitude of the world. ...... And thus the Demiurgus exhibited man by "the artifice of a divine fabrication, in such a way, that, in a small body, he might bestow the "power and essence of all the elements, nature for this purpose bringing them together; and "also, so that from the divine spirit, which descended from a celestial intellect to the support of "the mortal body, he might prepare an abode for man, which, though fragile, *might be similar to* "*the world.*" Again, "So that the animal *which was made in imitation of the world* might be "governed by an essence similarly divine."[3] He was endowed with a portion of the first attribute of God or of the divine idea—wisdom. He had a portion of the generative power; he had a portion of immortality. Every animal, as I have already remarked, was a microcosm of man—beginning, probably, with the wise elephant, and descending to the meanest reptile. A portion of the same mind or wisdom, the same generative power, is visible in all. Every plant was a microcosm of the animal, and possessed a portion of mind. The sun-flower turns itself to the God of day; the pimpernel[4] opens to the sun, and shuts itself to the storm. The ash-tree planted on a bank, with one root hanging down, turns it inwards to the earth. The sensitive-plant, like the youthful maiden, at first shrinks from the touch of man. Every plant has the living principle and the organs of generation; and thus every thing descends, and the whole world, and each part,

---

[1] See *supra*, pp. 23, 24; Lord Kingsborough's Mex. Ant., Vol. VI. p. 237; and Nimrod, Vol. II. pp. 370—373.

[2] I stated in Volume I. p. 724, from Chrysostom, that when the Gentile mysteries began, a herald proclaimed "Procul! hinc procul este, profani," and that the Christians did the same thing, exclaiming "hence all *dogs*." Why make such a point of turning out the dogs, more than any other animal? I believe a mistake took place between the Γυνη and Κυων, Κυνος, and that it originally applied to followers of the *female generative principle*.

[3] Trans. by Taylor.

[4] In the case of the pimpernel, to evade the question or to disguise the fact, I shall be told some idle, inconclusive story, about the stimulating power of the solar ray or of light; but it is all true—it is matter acting upon matter.

is an image of God. How curiously is this connected with the first principles of the Το Ον, or Gnosticism or Wisdom, and how beautifully does all resolve itself into one system!

3. We may now see what Pythagoras meant when he said, that all things arose from *numbers*. In the first place, numbers, as we have seen, constituted the symbolic letters in which all the natural and religious learning of the ancients was contained. The learning of languages was not considered as any part of science or education with them; none being *dead*, all were *intelligible*. Grammar, with all its complicated rules, was unknown to them; but they must have had enough to do to be able to repeat the meanings attached to the numeral symbols. The second sense in which the expression of Pythagóras is explainable, is most clearly found in the microcosmic numbers, and in the doctrine of emanations and cycles; from *one* proceeded *two*, from the *two* proceeded *three*—in all *five;* and from these proceeded the seven planets, the constellations divided into 12, 24, 72, 360, 432, and all the immense cycles of which we have been treating, and which ultimately brought up all the aberrations of the planetary system, when every thing was reabsorbed into the Deity.

It is not to be supposed that the philosophers who taught this system expected the world to be renewed every 600 or 6000 years. These were but little cycles to enable them to keep their time and their festivals in order; they were used as religious contrivances to delude the vulgar. Very different renewals of all things were looked for by the philosophers—various floods, and, perhaps, after a year of Brahma, 4,320,000,000 of years, a restoration of a perfect globe, of the planetary system, and the universe of fixed stars to their first state. Our globe is evidently an effect, in part perfected; the effect, perhaps, of a third or fourth or fifth internal or mundane revolution. Nobody can suppose the globe will go to ruin or decay. It will most assuredly all come again to some perfect state unknown to us. It is like a butterfly; it will pass through all its stages—return to its egg—and run its course again. If the reader look back to Volume I. pp. 166, *et seq.*, he will find that the system of cycles which I have unfolded, is founded on two numbers, the number *five* and the number *six;* that from them arose the numbers 360 and 432, and that from these a cycle was formed which included them both, viz. 21,600. In many places I have observed that the first year of all nations was believed to have had only 360 days.[1] If this were the case, it is evident that the science of astronomy would, before the irregularity of the motions of the planets arose, and before the number of the years of the periods of the sun and moon became comprised in odd numbers, and in fractional parts of years, days, and hours, be comparatively easy. The 12 moons of 30 days each, and the 360 days, would make an exact Soli-lunar cycle, and the account of time would be kept regularly and without difficulty. And we may readily suppose this astronomical knowledge would be acquired without any very profound science or skill in observation. Now we may easily imagine that after the catastrophe of the flood, as soon as man found the system thrown into disorder, he would begin to devise means to correct the evil, and then astronomy would be improved by making cycles, as I have supposed in Volume I., and by experiments and observations, until he brought it to the perfection at which I have shewn that it finally arrived. Then it would be that the millennial system was formed by taking the period of time between the entrance of the equinoctial sun into Taurus and his entrance into Aries, and then carrying the cycles forward, as I have there explained. This seems to me to furnish a very satisfactory reason for the operation of first taking off the sum of 2160 for the precession in one sign. The existence of the fact I have there clearly proved. The reason of it we have here. If we suppose the flood to have happened and the Pontiff and his court to have escaped, it would be a very considerable time be-

---

[1] See, particularly, *supra*, pp. 316—326, and 409.

fore they would discover that the regular periods no longer returned; and, probably, by the time that they discovered the correct length of the new year and of the new month, they would have forgotten almost every thing, except that their year had been 360 days, and their moon's period 30 days. Under these circumstances it seems natural, as soon as they had found out that the precession of the equinox took place after the rate of 2160 years in a sign, that they should, when they formed their artificial system as we have seen it, go back for one sign and endeavour to make the two systems into one, as we have really found them to have done. This is the more probable, because the system would go on *pari passu* with the experiments which I have shewn probably took place to ascertain the real length of the new Soli-lunar period, the Neros. If the theory which I here propose, and it is the result of improved information and additional study, be thought probable, it will in a slight degree vary the theory advanced in Volume I. pp. 177, 178, for the discovery of the cycles; but though it will change the course of progression by which they were discovered, it will tend to confirm the system on the whole. We must recollect that, when I attributed shortness of memory to the early race, I suppose them to have had only the numeral symbolic, and not the syllabic, system of letters; perhaps not even *that*, but only the knowledge of figures of notation. I have much suspicion that all the periods consisting of the number *twelve* were formed when the year was actually 360 days long, and that the periods consisting of the number *ten* were formed when the new and compound cycle was formed of the ten Neroses and ten signs of the Zodiac. The Equinox, if it preceded at all, preceded after the rate of 54" in a year, a degree in 66 years, a sign in 2000 years, and the circle or 12 signs in 24,000 years. When the ancient astronomers discovered that, in consequence of the flood, the circular motions of the heavenly bodies were completed in broken periods, they probably invented the cycles out of the two systems to obviate the inconvenience which the change had brought about. And this is the reason why we have the sacred numbers sometimes from the *twelves*, the *old* system—and sometimes from the *tens*, the *new* one. And thus we have the system of the cycles of 21,600, of 43,200, of 432,000, and of 4,320,000, to unite the two systems. Sir W. Drummond says,[1] "If the "priests of Ammon were right, the antediluvians may have been so likewise, for Plutarch tells us, "that according to the former *the annual period has been continually decreasing*." This, in no small degree, tends to confirm my theory, that the year was lengthened by the change in the direction of the earth's axis, and that it is gradually returning to its former natural state.

When I read the critical dissertations of Mr. Niebuhr on the History of Rome, which every where betray the utter confusion in which the early part is involved, the total failure of the almost unceasing attempts of the later historians (such as Cicero and Tacitus) to produce any thing like order, or to account for the endless anomalies in the customs, laws, and constitutions of the respective states, which every where shew themselves, I am driven to seek some cause which they have not understood or to which they have paid no attention. I am thus almost compelled to have recourse to the ancient Pontifical government, about which I have already said so much, and to trace the difficulties of the Roman writers to their neglect to search into the few remaining circumstances of this ancient empire, of the importance of which they seem never to have formed a proper estimate. It is like ourselves: we are always looking for the causes of effects in times since the Roman conquest of Britain, which ought to be looked for in the times and in the state of things before their arrival—which state of things, in many respects, they left, unaltered, to their successors, when they quitted the island. Once, and I think only once, Mr. Niebuhr's[2] attention seems to have been drawn to what he calls the *influence of numerical forms* in the states of anti-

---

[1] Class. Journ. Vol. XVI. p. 156.   [2] Vol. II. p. 20. Thirlwall's Ed.

quity which, on that occasion, he says, *solves a puzzle;* but he almost instantly loses sight of it. He often observes the recurrence of the numbers 12 and 30; but it seems never to have once occurred to him to inquire further into the reason of this recurrence, which a moment's consideration would have taught him must have had a cause. He notices the tradition of the Alban and Latin states being formed of 600 families, and also that some of the very heavy and oldest coins, called *ases*, without inscriptions, have the head of a young man on one side, wearing *a Phrygian bonnet*, and on the reverse *a wheel*, with six spokes. The former figure he thinks represents Ascanius, the latter, the spokes of the wheel, the six centuries of the Lavinian Colony.[1] This may be true; but I can only conceive the regulation of the states by the number 600 to have the same reference as the spokes on the coin, viz. to the revolving cycle of 600, celebrated by Virgil. The bonnet or *mitre* marks the cycle as *sacred*. The formation of the legion by 6000 men, and its decuples 60 and 600, had reference to the same superstition. Niebuhr says, "At this time four " legions must have been 12,000 men: add to this 12,000 from the colonies and subject towns, " and 24,000 for the double contingent of each allied state, and the whole assembled force will be " 72,000 men. The legend peeps through in this wantoning with typical numbers, which it de- " lights to multiply enormously."[2] But Mr. Niebuhr, like our modern English historians, never once gives himself the trouble of asking what was the meaning of the legend which peeped through, and why they thus *wantoned* with certain peculiar typical numbers. After the knowledge of the system was lost, the legend was continued from habit, and we constantly talk of our *scores* and *half scores*, our *dozens* and *half dozens*, &c. Had this habit arisen from the nature of these numbers, we should have found a similar name for the number eight, which has the accidents that may be supposed to influence the numbers *twelve* and *ten* in a much more remarkable degree. Indeed, had arithmetic been the effect of learning, instead of what we call accident, there can be no doubt that eight would have been taken as the terminate number, instead of ten.

4. The microcosm is visible in the number of the Gods, as in every other part of the creation which is in any way subject to the genius of man. We have three at the head, in the capitol— Jupiter, Apollo, and Minerva. We have the 7 Dii Consentes, the Cabiri; the 12 greater Gods, and the 360, one for each day. It is true we do not now find the 72; but, as we found them distinctly marked in the 72 angels of the 72 nations of the world, and in the 72 angels ascending and descending the ladder of Jacob, we may be very certain they were once there. Mr. Niebuhr has taken great pains to exhibit the infinite variety in the minor internal forms, and in the outward relations of the several states and municipia of Italy and Greece with one another; but he scarcely ever attempts to account for such a state of things having arisen. All this, however, is a necessary consequence, or arises very naturally out of the state which I contemplate, of a supreme Sacerdotal or Patriarchal government overriding the whole, but leaving each to govern itself in its own way, to form its domestic regulations according to the circumstances of the localities, climate, &c., of each; yet, as we see in the Amphictyons, when necessary, exercising a paternal and mediatorial power of the most beneficial nature over them all. In consequence of the profits of this order of mediators being fixed to the unvarying *tenth* of the produce, its interest would, in a very peculiar manner, as I have before remarked, lead it to the preservation of universal peace. It would prosper with the prosperity of the sub-infeudate castes; it would suffer with their sufferings; it would sympathise with them in all their feelings. The system of patron and client would exist in the most amiable of forms.[3] And when at last the universal law of change began to

---

[1] Niebuhr, Hist. Rome, Vol. II. p. 19. Thirlwall's Ed. [2] Ibid. p. 40.
[3] Mr Niebuhr observes, (Hist. Rome, Vol. I. p. 119. Thirlwall's Ed.,) that "at Rome the relation between patron

operate upon the system, it would produce precisely what we read of in the rhapsodies or poetical works of the bards—first a Golden age, then an age of Silver, then one of Brass, and, at last, when the system went entirely to pieces, what has very well been called an age of Iron. The more I reflect, the more I become convinced that the theory, (a theory founded upon innumerable facts,) which I have laid before my reader, will rationally account for all the hitherto anomalous circumstances in which the world is placed: and, as my theory is upon the whole, or perhaps with some trifling errors, the truth, it is the only theory which will ever do it. There is no subject of which we hear more than that of the sending out of colonies, from both Italy and Greece; but they are all described to have taken place in very remote times. The actual going out, in every case, seems to have been forgotten. It is very natural that the patriarchal government should have promoted this system, to relieve the overflow of the population, which, by causing a scarcity of food, would cause vice and misery to prevail, and, with vice and misery, make the people more difficult to be governed, and thus to endanger its rule. And every new colony would add to the wealth and power of the Patriarchate. Among the Buddhists we have in a peculiar manner the monastic system, and under this system we may readily suppose the order of monks, which was kept up by taking children from the other classes, would be kept within such bounds as were thought desirable, and that it would be abundantly supplied with food, without ever being liable, except from an occasional scarcity—the effect of bad seasons—to the inconvenience of want. I think this celebrated system must have arisen by degrees, and have had its origin in various causes; but, perhaps, chiefly in the natural tendency of man to monopolise and secrete knowledge. And probably the institution of an order which should continue itself by descent, may have arisen from the going to pieces of the first system. We have the remains of the first of these in the monks of Tibet and Europe, and of the second in the Brahmins of India; we have the system also, in modern times, pretty nearly portrayed in the celibate Catholic, and the marrying Protestant, clergy. Mr. Niebuhr every where finds a system which he does not understand, or at least does not know how to account for, called Ισοπολιτεια or Isopolity. This was an interchange of rights among the different towns or free states. This again was a natural effect which would arise (as he finds it varied in many ways) from the general, superintending character of the Patriarchal government, leaving the respective towns to regulate their own domestic concerns, and it was the remains of that government falling to pieces by degrees. I think there is nothing of this kind left now any where. Perhaps the remains of it may be seen in the *Pale* of Germany and Ireland.[1] Livy, not understanding or adverting to the fact, that it was an effect of a previous cause, the remains of a former state of society, treats it as a *cause* instead of an *effect*. Livy calls it a hospitable relation entered into with a whole people.[2] But Niebuhr justly observes, that it "is a "feature of ancient tradition which no late writer could have invented." He represents the rights of the municipium to have been acquired in three ways—*by birth, by exercising isotely, and by manumission by a municeps*.[3] The first, is that of our sons of freemen succeeding their fathers; the second, our apprentice; and the third, our grant of the freedom of a town. In the Pale of Ireland, and the Pfahlbürger of Germany,[4] we have a remnant of the Pontifical or Patriarchal government which cannot be disputed. I have no doubt that the word was brought to both countries by the first tribe of Saxons. It comes from the Hebrew פלא *pla*, in its sense of *separavit*.

" and client was the feudal system in its best form." I mention this to shew that the system (or rather the remains of the system) made itself visible.

[1] Niebuhr, Vol. II. pp. 74, 75. Thirlwall's Ed.   [2] Ibid. p. 57.
[3] Ibid. p. 55.   [4] Ibid. Vol. I. p. 398; Vol. II. pp. 74, 75. Thirlwall's Ed.

To be in the *pale* was to be separated from something. I do not find the root in Hebrew for the Greek πυλη; but a moment's reflection shews that the *separavit* has essentially this idea. A door or gate cannot well be disconnected from the idea of *separating*. The word *iso*, I think, may have come from the root נצא *iza, egressus est*, and the compound word would mean *persons gone out from the pale*. We use the word *pale* in Yorkshire for a sheep-fold; and a vessel to hold milk, from the cow, a milk-pail. I think it probable, that when Numa Pompilius became governor of Rome, he found the state ruled by a portion of the customs or laws of the previous government, which had gone to decay, and left nothing but a chaos behind it: and he undertook to arrange and write down a certain part of what he found and thought necessary for the use of the infant state, then first beginning to assume the form of a settled government: but this would not exclude the deciding of such cases as his writing did not provide for, when they arose, according to the ancient customs; and these decisions would naturally form or *declare* (precisely as ours do) a *lex non scripta*. The great mistake of Niebuhr and many other writers consists in this, that they consider every thing to have taken its rise from the supposed date of the Roman city or state, while the city, state, and almost every thing connected with them, are effects of something preceding. From inattention to this circumstance, the whole of Niebuhr's explanation of the constitutions of the Romans and Grecians is a chaos, and particularly with respect to the occupation of the land. He clearly shews, that the same principle prevailed in both Italy and Greece. I have no doubt that whenever the conquering tribes of Chaldæan-Celtic Sacæ arrived in a country new to them, and in fact in all countries, from Tartary or Scythia, they established their own feudal tenure of land, either by subinfeudating the lands in part to the miserable, ignorant, savage, descendants of antediluvians, or aborigines as they were called, or to their own tribe entirely—reserving to the rulers, who were the priests, the *tenths*. Thus the whole world became subject to the same Patriarchate—a Patriarchate subdivided into three, and I doubt not each of the three having a book, like Genesis, which would shew that its was the eldest branch of the family of Noah, whether it was Ham or Japhet or Shem. The circumstances which Mr. Whiston has pointed out, that astronomical science shews the first race was preserved in that part of the globe called Tartary, and that Noah must have resided in China, tend to confirm this. But I must remind my reader, for my own credit, that I do not affirm the truth of any part of Mr. Whiston's system, except that which I expressly mention as adopting. I by no means wish to implicate myself in much nonsense which that amiable and learned person persuaded himself to believe. He exhibited a remarkable proof that *learning* does not, in every thing, carry with it *sense*.

5. I must now revert to a circumstance which would necessarily arise from the numeral symbolic writing in a downward direction, growing into horizontal alphabetic writing, in different nations, in which the spoken languages had so far changed as to be in part or almost entirely unintelligible to one another. I suppose the change from the symbolic to the alphabetic would take place by degrees, and the upright line would be turned sometimes one way, sometimes another; this would form entirely *new* words.[1] Thus Ras might become *sar*; and as we know the s became c, or was originally c, here we have the word car or cor,[2] for *heart* and *wisdom*—two ideas of things widely different. In this way many words would be formed, each of them sometimes having two meanings totally different from one another. Here it is evident that we have a class of words which

---

[1] See Vol. I. pp. 455, 484, 942; and *supra*, 153, on the word רש or *sur*. *Ed.*

[2] This is remarkably confirmed by what we find in Ethiopia and Egypt. In the former, in the Chaldee, it turned to the left; in the latter, in the Coptic, it turned to the *right*; but in both it had the same meaning—head, chief, prince, wisdom.

will bid defiance to all rational etymology. This is remarkably the case with *ras* and *cor*. *Sul*, the Sun, I think is another example. It would form Lus[1] or *Lux, lucis*. We must recollect, that in this reasoning I suppose what we know was the fact, that the first letters were right lines, perhaps some few at angles, in fact, the Runes, and the letters used by the Masonic Culdees, at York, as may be seen in their books now possessed by his Royal Highness the Duke of Sussex. If we consider maturely the situation of man in the first ages of the world, we shall immediately observe the paucity of words which, in a numeral symbolic language, would be requisite to carry on the common affairs of life, and how very much less would be required than is actually now in daily use in China. Sir William Jones has said, that, without any regard to grammar, if a person would learn to repeat or learn the meaning of three thousand words in any language, he would be able to speak it. I have no doubt that the knowledge of the meanings attached to a certain portion of numeral symbols constituted part of the learning contained in the twenty thousand verses which the Druids required the pupils to repeat in their colleges. Even after the world arrived at so advanced a state as to erect such works as Stonehenge and Abury, the number of necessary words would not be large. We may safely say that a *fifth* of what are requisite now, would not then be wanted—merely nouns, verbs, and pronouns. I am convinced that if a judicious selection of a thousand words, or rather ideas, was made and located to numbers, any two persons who learnt these might communicate without any difficulty, although speaking and knowing no languages but those which are the most dissimilar in the world. By being attached to numbers, the language would be remarkably stable and fixed, and by being formed of right lines at angles, it would require very little learning. What we call the Arabic figures, which are known all over the world, and which were probably known from almost the earliest period, might answer the purpose. In order to reap the benefit of such a system, at this day, it would not be necessary even that it should be generally learned to be *repeated*. A printed key might be circulated in each country. For example: if a vocabulary of the thousand Persian words were printed with the numbers annexed, the language would instantly become known to every one who could write the Persian language. They would be readily printed upon fifteen pages of a sheet of paper folded in octavo, leaving the sixteenth for the direction, to send it by post. It is very evident, that for the purposes of commerce, or science, by increasing the number of ideas attached to increased numbers, it might be carried to almost any extent. I here only describe the ancient system, a part, a remnant of which is yet found in China and Java. In the first language of numerals none of the little words which we use for the signs of cases of nouns would occur, and I think they were not used in writing till syllabic literal writing began to be practised. They came into use by degrees, which is the reason why, in the old Hebrew language, they all seem to have the same meaning. For the same reason it is that the word which has now become the exclusive emphatic article of one nation, may be found in the proper names of another: for instance, the Tusci were nothing but THE-osci—Thosci—Thusci—Tusci, inhabitants, I suppose, of Naples.[2] I much suspect that not only the high branches of Geometry and Mathematics were known to the ancients, but Algebra also. We are taught to believe that it was discovered by the Arabians in the middle ages.[3] When I find that it was known in Italy three hundred years ago, and that it was ascertained that it had been known *in a secret society* three hundred years before that time, I am immediately led to conclude, that it was a remnant of the science of the old Tuscan Augurs or Agrimensores—a part

---

[1] From this the Lotus, or flower of the Sun, the manifestation of. Wisdom, of Love, &c., came to be called *flower of Lus* or *Lys*—the Rose of the Water, of Ice, Isis, Isuren, Sharon.—See *supra*, pp. 6, 7, 32, 33, 44, 45.

[2] See Niebuhr's Map. [3] The science of algebra is nothing but a symbolic language.

of the ancient mysteries—of magic; for the answers to questions given by its means would, to ignorant people, be truly magical. Mr. Christie[1] has observed a passage of Diodorus, (Book I. Chap. I.,) which seems to refer to the first numerical symbols. He says, "At the time when "speech was indistinct and confused, ασημυ και συγκεχυμενης, they by degrees expressed "themselves in a more articulate manner, and appointed symbols to represent the objects under "consideration, by which means they were able to explain themselves intelligibly." This passage of the Greek Diodorus leads me to repeat, that we ought not to be tied down in our construction of Greek words in the early period when that language was naturally ασημος, in the same manner as when it became fixed, and when the Greeks, in respect to delicacy of speech, became the most fastidious people upon earth.[2] When I consider the vast variety of independent states in Greece, their continual feuds and jealousies, and the practice discovered by Mr. Hammer of every philosopher having a form of letter of his own,[3] I cannot much doubt that the Amphictyonic council of the *state* regulated the sacred letter in which all matters under its cognizance were recorded. This would naturally become in time the letter of the whole country, superseding the letter of the separate states. All this seems to account rationally for the great dissimilarity of forms with the uniformity of system, and for all the discordant or heterogeneous states of Greece having one letter—and the discordant or heterogeneous states of Italy another. Thus I think it probable that the Greek system of writing was for a long time confined to the caste of priests in Greece, the Latin to the caste of priests in Italy, as the Sanscrit was for a long time confined to the caste of priests in India. The above description by Diodorus is peculiarly applicable to the Synagogue Hebrew, and must have been equally applicable to all written languages in their early stages. I have frequently observed, that the dogma forbidding any change in the text has preserved the Hebrew, locked up in the Temple, in a state of purity.

6. But to return to the Pythagorean philosophy of the generation of numbers. This was the generation of cycles, ending or beginning with the Το Ον or One: for *one* is but *on*, and increasing or decreasing, as the case might be, like the coats of an Onion[4] *ad infinitum*, either way ending in illusion; for we are as incapable of forming an idea of the least atom as of the greatest substance; and the idea of number cannot be separated from or formed without matter. In no part is the system more beautiful than in the doctrine of the microcosm. We have an abundance of theories to account for the adoration of animals by the Egyptians and others, but none of them satisfactory. I believe it arose from the names of animals being unintentionally formed of the numeral symbols which also formed certain cycles, when the numerals grew into letters. Thus the numeral letters *clo*, which meant 600 in Chaldee, meant a *cat*—k final=500, l=30, o=70=600. Thus a Cat came to be sacred. In the same manner the Onion, on account of the similarity of its coats to the planetary spheres, was called—from being sacred to the Father of Ages—αιωνων—onion. It was also strikingly similar to the microcosmic principle. I much suspect that most of their sacred animals were adored for similar reasons. Thus every animal, the numeral letters of whose name described at once the animal and one of the planets or sacred cycles, came to be an object of adoration, and the animal was considered sacred to the God. Hence the explanation I have given above, p. 113, of *Æsculapius* from Asclo-οφις. The ops οψς, οπος, and ϙφις were in fact anciently

---

[1] Essay on worship of the Elements, p. 3.   [2] The same observation will apply to the Sanscrit.   [3] See *supra*, p. 247.

[4] The Onion was adored (as the *black stone* in Westminster Abbey is by us) by the Egyptians for this property, as a type of the eternal renewal of ages, and for this very reason, probably, called αιων των αιωνων, as our *settle* is so called from the Hebrew שתל *stl*, and our *order* from the Hebrew ערך *ord*. The Onion is adored in India, and is forbidden to be eaten. Forster's Sketches of Hindoos, p. 35. See Vol. I. pp. 193, 338, 449.

the same word, and meant Logos and Serpent. Thus the Logos is divine wisdom; and thus the serpent came to be regarded as the wisest of animals. Cyclops is the same—κυκλος and οφις—Serpent of the Cycle, or Logos of the Cycle. If it be objected that what I have said of the ουψ and οφις cannot be admitted, as they do not furnish proof—I reply, If there have been one original language, the different ancient words may be expected to be found scattered indiscriminately in all languages descended from that original, or formed upon it. I admit they do not furnish proof. Scarcely in any case can a proof ever be found; at the most a high probability is all that can be expected, and that I contend we have here. But this is a matter of opinion: every one must judge for himself. Hutchinson and Shaw say, that the *onion*, in Hebrew שם *sum* or שן *sun*, is a perfect emblem of the disposition of the heavens. Supposing the root and head to represent the poles, if it be cut transversely or diagonally, it will be found divided into the same number of spheres, including each other, counting from the sun or centre to the circumference, as the ancients knew the courses of the orbs divided this system into, and so the divisions represented the courses of those orbs. The Sanscrit word *Syâma* means darkness, black, black flowers; and *Syâmânga* means the planet Mercury or Buddha. This is formed from the Hebrew root שם *sm* which means *a planet*, plural שמים *smim* planets, rulers, and disposers. These planets were called messengers and αγγελλοι or angels. As we find so many Sanscrit words in the English and other languages,[1] I suspect that the *Syûm* and *ûnga* mean *the Angel Sam* or *Buddha*. From finding the word Sam[2] to mean the Sun, the Planet Mercury, darkness, and Buddha, and the Tam to mean a zodiacal incarnation, *i. e.* of the Sun in the sign of the Twins—and in several other cases from finding the T and the S to be interchanged, I am induced to suspect that the Tam is a corruption of the Sam—as I formerly suspected the Tages to be a corruption of the Sages. I have Parkhurst's authority for saying that the change of the ש into the ת was usual.[3] I am rather inclined to think the Onion was an emblem of the recurring cycles than of the planets; but as it would evidently suit for both, it probably was used for both. Notwithstanding the identity of the appellative (for it is merely an appellative) of Crēst or Χρης given to the two persons in India and Europe, at the head of the two divisions of the religion, it seems probable that the Western Crēstians descended directly from the Buddhists rather than from the Brahmins. It is true that we constantly meet with what appear to be traits of the Brahmins in the West, but we must not forget that the Buddhists and Brahmins were the same in all great points. Brahminism was but Protestant Buddhism, and the two assimilate to the Papists and Protestants, in the fact, that, in each case, the reformers, as they called themselves, abolished the Archierarchy which I have exhibited to my reader.[4] I have called them reformers, and so in both cases they were. For, in India, the effects of Brahmanism were, to reform the calendar, to make it assimilate to the changed state of the heavens, and thus, no longer to have Taurus as their emblem, but Aries. This was the case with Moses, who reformed the system of his tribe by abolishing the golden calf; and it was attempted to be restored by the *ten tribes*, who set up the Calves at Dan and Bethavon. In almost every point the Archierarchy of Rome and Tibet are the same. I think it seems probable that the Patriarchal government or the Archierarchy continued until after the time that the sun entered Aries at the vernal equinox, when the religious revolution took place; this was about the time when the flood happened—the axis of the earth became changed or inclined, and almost all the ancient learning of the world was lost. If this event happened about two thousand five hundred years B. C., and only very few persons escaped, in five or six hundred years, as I have

---

[1] See *supra*, pp. 166, 167, *note*.   [2] Ibid. pp. 199—201.
[3] Greek Lex. in voce ΘΤΡΑ.   [4] See Vol. I. pp. 161, 162; also *supra*, pp. 53, *et seq.*, and pp. 359, 360.

already shewn, they might readily have increased to five or six hundred millions of people;[1] and if the knowledge of symbolic writing and arithmetic remained with the heads only of the Pontifical government in the East, we may see a very probable reason why that body of men, by means of their colonies, became the rulers of the world, even long before the period of five or six hundred years had elapsed. If the Archierarchal system was established before the flood, it was very natural that it should have been revived after it. We have this well described in the histories of Adam and Noah. If the last great convulsion left a few people in every country, or in only most countries, they would stock the world, to a very considerable extent, in much less time than I have allotted to them; and if they were under a patriarchal government before the catastrophe, they would subsequently be prepared to submit more readily to its superiority, especially when it was introduced by the castes from the oriental hive, of whose arrival in the West, and their conquest of what have been called the aborigines, we have such abundant proofs. From the Eastern tribes being called Διοι Πελασγοι or *holy sailors*, it is probable that they brought peace and civilization to the aborigines. I think from the picture I have drawn of *the golden age*, this was probably the case. Their superior attainments would give them the superiority, and it would not be till they became corrupted, that they would reduce the aborigines into Helots. These Pelasgi or Sailors might be also Chalidei. The Pelasgi were, in a marked manner, said to be inhabitants of Crestona in Thrace. They are called Διοι Πελασγοι by Homer, because, says Eustathius in his Commentary, they were the only people who, after Deucalion's flood, preserved the use of letters.[2] This theory seems to me to agree very well with all the circumstances, such as the change in the earth's axis and the consequent flood by a comet, a fact established upon as strong a probability as in such a case could be expected. If we consider every person who was admitted to the high mysteries of the religion as, by that privilege, admitted to the sacred caste, we have no longer any occasion to seek for the reason of the great anxiety to conceal the doctrines. As these doctrines became known, the mysteries would fall off by degrees, till, in fact, there would be scarcely any left. High arithmetic, literal writing, astronomy, and other sciences, were what originally constituted the mysteries. We have almost the last examples of this exclusiveness and spirit of monopoly in the concealment of algebra in Italy. In all countries we have well-marked traditions of tribes coming from the East, and of their finding and conquering the aborigines, who were often supposed to have been indigenous, as they knew nothing of their own origin, except a few vague traditions, of which one always was, that they had escaped from or arisen after the flood. For want of the knowledge of letters this seems to be a consequence which would necessarily follow in five or six hundred years. I am convinced that this has every probability on its side. I consider the circumstances of coincidence between the comet of 1680 and the chronological date of the flood in the Indian, Jewish, and Grecian writings, (when their 3101 period is corrected and its mistake accounted for) to establish the reality of a flood at that time, on so high a degree of probability as to amount almost to certainty. However, it is a probability on which I have no hesitation in saying, that any philosopher may rationally found *a probable opinion*, and any devotee *a belief*. I have said above, that I think the Western Christians descended from the Buddhists, though we very often see traits of Brahminism in the West. I suspect that all the old Druidical monuments are antediluvian. I think this would not be thought improbable if persons could be brought to consider the fact of the flood divested of the mythic absurdities and mistranslations with which it is loaded in Genesis. These absurdities I have shewn were, in all ancient

---

[1] See *supra*, p. 395. [2] Grant on the Gael, p. 21.

books, contrived to conceal under them, and to preserve for the use of the initiated, certain great truths.

7. Before I venture upon another of what will be called, by persons of *little minds*, my *bold speculations*, I must beg my reader to recollect, that when the famous ancile came from heaven, sent by Pallas to Numa, five others were immediately made by that legislator, in order that the true one might not be known. This shield was to be the protector of the eternal city.[1] Thus there were to be five records of the mythos, at least of the cyclic mythos. In the Tamul, in which we found the Mosaic mythos, we have an account that their sacred writing had five distinct meanings.[2] Now what has happened to the ancient mythology of the Gentiles? Various persons have attempted its explanation, and it cannot be denied that several of them have succeeded with a considerable show of probability : for instance, one class of persons, the followers of Euhemerus, have made it into the history of *men*; another class, the Stoics, have explained it by allegory; by which process they have deduced from it *moral truths*. Now, I ask, is there not a probability that the first ancient sacred writing, before it became corrupted, might have been constructed, like the lost writing of the Tamul, to contain several meanings—so constructed for the purpose of gratifying the prevailing attachment to secrecy, so that no person might be able to say certainly what was its real meaning? May not Genesis have been this very Tamul book? Clemens himself has been supposed to have been initiated into the mysteries of Eleusis;[3] and this being admitted, he gives us a piece of information of the greatest importance to my whole system. He says,[4] *that the truths taught in the mysteries had been stolen by the philosophers from Moses and the prophets*.[5] That is, in other words, that they were the same, at least with some part of what is contained in the doctrines of those persons or in their writings. This is a piece of extraordinary confirmatory evidence of almost my whole system. In another place, speaking of the mysteries, he says, *here is an end of all instruction. We behold nature and things*.[6] Here is the Mercavah, which, together with the Barasit, I have little doubt contained all the mysteries—that is, the Grecian Cabala. Perhaps there is no point upon which the modern religious are more completely deceived by their priests than on that of the ancient mysteries. They are represented by all Protestants as matters of little moment, to which novices or only half Christians were admitted, when, in fact, they were for many generations held to be of the greatest possible importance, and must evidently have contained something very different from what is now celebrated or preached in our churches every day. They were taught by Clemens, Origen, and the higher order of Christians; but I believe they were not known to Paul or his followers, who, I think, had no concern with them. When the Paulites got possession of power, the mysteries were treated with contempt. I shall, perhaps, have passages produced to me to shew that Origen or Clemens acknowledged Paul. As well might passages be produced from my works to prove that I acknowledge Wesley, Wilberforce, Halhed, Southcote, or Brothers. Suppose I do acknowledge them all and their writings, and admit them to have been most excellent persons, and many of their doctrines to have been very good. What then? Does this make me adopt all their pernicious fooleries? It is quite impossible to maintain that the doctrines of the Trinity, of Baptism, and of the Eucharist, can be the secret doctrines which are so clearly declared, by Clemens Alexandrinus, to exist, because all these were openly explained to the world by Justin Martyr, in his Apology, addressed to Antoninus Pius, long before the time of Clemens, about the year 160. It therefore follows, that Clemens must allude to some

---

[1] See *supra*, pp. 145, 146.
[2] Ib. pp. 15, 148.
[3] Euseb. Præp. Evan. L. ii. Cap. ii. p. 61, παντων μεν δια πυρας ελθων ανηρ.
[4] Strom. V. p. 650.
[5] Ouvaroff on Myst. of Eleusis, transl. p. 44.
[6] Strom. V. p. 2; Ouvaroff, ib. p. 42.

other secrets or mysteries; at the same time, I think there can be no doubt that many of the Romish fathers did affect to make a secret of their explanation of Baptism, the Eucharist, &c. But the public explanation of Justin shews that this was not the principle of the church. The fact was, I have no doubt, that after the Paulite fathers got power, they began to wish for mysteries, which, when their sect was in adversity or a state of weakness, they affected to despise; thus they attempted to make mysteries of the doctrines which I have shewn were not so considered by Justin. What constituted the *whole* of the Christian mysteries will probably never be discovered; but their existence cannot be denied. I consider the *eucharistia*[1] as a solemn pledge of secresy—to preserve faithfully the secrets which the Master had been communicating to the elect; and as we have found it in almost all nations, it was probably in this manner originally used in all. It cannot be denied that the Eucharist was celebrated by Jesus in his last supper *in secret*—it was confined to the twelve; and in the Roman church of the Paulites it was kept a secret from the rabble for several hundred years. I do not, as I have just said, consider it so much a secret, though still it was a secret, as a pledge of the faithful keeping of the secrets or mysteries at that time just celebrated. In the mode in which we have found this Melchizedeckian and Pythagorean ceremony celebrated by the ancient Latins and the modern Jews, we have an example of a mystery having become, as it is now with us, public. This is the case with all the Judæan mythos which we have found in Mexico, China, India, Syria, &c., &c.[2] Augustin, Theodoret, Basil, Pope Innocent I., and others, have treated of the mysteries of the Christians, of which they clearly say, that Baptism, the Eucharist, and the meaning of the other Sacraments, constitute a part; but their words generally imply that they were only a part. Innocent says, "Reliqua vero, *quæ scribi fas non est*, cum adfueris, interrogati poterimus edicere."[3] Now we know very well that the *scribi fas non est* must apply to something besides the sacraments, about which it was common to all these fathers to write. It may be observed, that there is scarcely a single dogma or rite of the Romish church which I have not already shewn to have been equally in use among the Gentiles;[4] therefore, on this account, it seems to follow, that there must have been something else: and what can this have been but the secret doctrines of Wisdom and the Gnosis, which I have shewn were the secret doctrines of all nations? In our endeavours to ascertain the cause why the Judæan Χρης-ian mythos, which I have discovered in so many nations, was not treated of in ancient authors, we never give sufficient credit to the exertions of the ancients to keep secret their mysteries, of which this χρηςηριον was the chief part. It was not only forbidden to reveal the mysteries, but it was forbidden either to write OR EVEN TO SPEAK ABOUT THEM. And whenever they were so spoken of or written about, it was always held to be *contra bonos mores*—contrary to good taste, and was, in fact, enough to exclude the writer or speaker from good society, and to consign his writings to oblivion. They were regarded by almost all persons in the same way as a great majority of persons in England consider the writings of Payne or Carlile. The word mystery took a new meaning, as it has done with us. We call Baptism, the Eucharist, &c., mysteries; but by this name we do not mean to describe them as *secrets*. This is proved by the circumstance of Justin having published them all. In fact there are *public* and *private* mysteries. We must not forget that we have found that part of the mythos which consists of the crucifixion among the Jews, where we might expect to find it, if it were a secret system, namely, in their books of *the secret doctrine,* called Apocrypha—in Wisdom and Ecclesiasticus.[5] Every thing tends to shew,

---

[1] I have no doubt whatever that the banquet, which always follows a Masonic Lodge or Chapter, is the remn.. of the Eucharistia.
[2] See *supra*, pp. 28, 214, 218, 232, 235.
[3] De Vallemont, Du Secret des Mystères, p. 55.
[4] See *supra*, pp. 129, 145, 276.
[5] See *supra*, pp. 124—126, 232.

that the part consisting of the deaths and resurrections of the Gods were parts of a secret system, which, originally performed in the mysteries by the initiated alone, by degrees got out and became known to the vulgar. This satisfactorily accounts for the way in which we always find it wrapped up in an ænigmatical style of writing, as it is in Wisdom and Ecclesiasticus above named. If this history were a part of the ancient religion and mysteries, the state in which it is come to us in the different countries is what is a necessary consequence. That the apocryphal books are now only in a Greek translation, is no proof against their antiquity. If we suppose them forgeries, we must allow that the person forging them in Greek must have held them out as translations. We may as well say, that the works of Irenæus are not his, because we have them not in the Greek, but only in a Latin translation. I pay very little attention to the opinion of the Jews of the present day, who may as readily throw out ancient learning as they adopt modern; such, for instance, as the Masoretic pointing. But I have met with learned Jews who maintain that Wisdom and Ecclesiasticus shew from their idioms a translation from the Hebrew. St. Jerome went to Syria to study Hebrew, and I have seen it stated in the Revue Encyclopédique, that there is in his works an account of his, that he found the ancient writings of the Jews defaced and dispersed in fragments in different places, and that he collected them with great difficulty. The Jews are like other sects. As time advances they all arise from circumstances, and where they are not new, but old, they constantly change with circumstances, and each gives to its ancient books the construction most suitable to its modern ideas, which are the effect, in every case, of the new circumstances in which the sect is placed. Hoffman says, that the early Christians did wisely not to expose the mysteries to the profane view of the infidels. How futile these arguments appear, since I have shewn that there is no rite or ceremony now known among Christians which was not common to them and to the Gentiles! Even the famous transubstantiation we have seen was alluded to by Cicero.[1] It cannot be doubted that the mysteries alluded to by Clemens Alexandrinus, and delivered by Jesus Christ to the three, were very different from those heathen figments about which the Romish and Protestant priests have always made so great a noise. There can be little doubt that the construction given by the fathers to the words of Jesus, that the Apostles should not throw their pearls before the swine, meant, that they should not reveal the secrets of the religion. Dr. De Vallemont has proved, by authorities of the ancient fathers, the most numerous and unquestionable, that the later fathers endeavoured to make the doctrines of the Trinity, Regeneration, and the Eucharist, among others, into *secrets*, the most sacred, and they attempted to preserve them from the vulgar and the Gentiles with the greatest possible care. He has abundantly proved the same thing of the Gentile mysteries. The secreting of the Christian mysteries was but an attempt to restore the secrets of Paganism, which had been, by degrees, revealed by unprincipled persons, and which will always happen when society comes to that unhappy state in which an oath is no longer considered binding. The Pagan religion in the fourth century, and indeed long before, had become virtually dead; most of its mysteries had become known or were forgotten among the mass of the people; and where they yet continued and were noticed by the Christians, the latter were deluded by a story which suited their capacities well enough, that the Devil had been at work, and had copied from the Christian rites. This was, I doubt not, quite sufficient to satisfy the scruples of the few who were able to inquire or desirous of inquiring. The Christian, that is, the Popish, mysteries were in every respect similar to the ancient Gentile. I do not believe that they varied in any important particular. On the subject of the *real presence* in the Eucharist, De Vallemont has most undoubtedly the advantage in the argument with the Pro-

---

[1] See *supra*, p. 61.

testants. If the Protestants choose to argue the question of Transubstantiation on the ground of common sense, excluding the ancient practice and the authority of the ancient fathers, they beat the Papists; but they must then admit all other tenets of their religion to be argued on the same grounds; then down go Papism and Protestantism together, and we come to the Philaletheans and to Ammonius Saccas. De Vallemont says, "Y a-t-il de l'équité à chercher la créance des Pères " sur l'Eucharistie dans des discours, où il ne vouloient pas sur ce point être intelligibles à ceux qui " n'étoient pas du secret des Mystères ?"[1] No, indeed, it is not equitable; nor is it equitable to seek in the same way for the belief of Plato or of Philo or Jamblicus—to seek for their opinion in works written evidently unintelligibly to deceive the ignorant—works which have only been left to us by the Papists, because the secrets they were meant to conceal were as well those of the modern as of the ancient church. The whole of the work of Jamblicus *de mysteriis* is written to occupy the attention of inquirers and to mislead them. Nor shall we be surprised at works of this kind being fabricated, when we pay a due attention to the extreme anxiety displayed by the initiated both before and after the death of Christ, to conceal and preserve their secrets. And when we reflect upon the indisputable fact, that all the doctrines of modern Rome were the same as the open or secret doctrines of ancient Rome, we shall no longer be surprised at the Popes re-enacting all their rites and ceremonies. Nor shall we any longer be surprised at finding Χρης-ianity at Rome, at Delphi, and in Malabar. The doctrine of the Χρης was the secret doctrine of the ancients which we have known by the name of Gnosis. It had ceased to be a secret, and the doctrine of the modern Χρης was precisely the same which Clemens, Origen, &c., endeavoured, but endeavoured in vain, to restore. The secrets once divulged could never be entirely concealed again; and the increasing number of sects, and the growing use of letters, all conspired to defeat the project. From this arose the heterogeneous mass which became modern Christianity, a motley mixture—every sect wearing a dress peculiar to itself. When mysteries are communicated to too many persons, the profound respect in which they were previously held is lost in the eyes of educated persons, and they become incautious; this is the reason why we find Cicero letting out the secret of the Gentile transubstantiation. It cannot be denied, that the apology of Justin, addressed to the Emperor Antoninus, and to the Senate and people of Rome, wherein he explains the mystery of the Eucharist in pretty clear terms, must be allowed to be an exception to the course of the other fathers. What was the reason of this singular conduct in this celebrated martyr will probably never be certainly known. I have not seen any satisfactory excuse for it. The more I read, think, and inquire, the more I am convinced that Popery is nothing but reformed Paganism,[2] as Protestantism is nothing but reformed Popery, but with this marked distinction, that Protestantism cut off and abolished many important parts of Popery, while Popery retained every part of Paganism which could be considered of any consequence.

8. I beg my reader to recollect what has been said respecting the symbolic language of the Chinese, and the probability, indeed I may almost say the certainty, of its having originally been formed by numerals.[3] Numerals offer themselves so readily as the symbols, and must be so well adapted to aid the memory and to fix the meaning, that I really cannot imagine how they could be overlooked. But I have no doubt that they were, in fact, the origin or cause of the written language being discovered—the language was an effect of them. If this numeral Chinese language

---

[1] Du Secret des Mystères p. 116.
[2] This accounts fully for all the apparent half *Pagan*, half *Christian* eccentricities of Constantine the First. See *supra*, pp. 51, 119, 207, 281.
[3] See *supra*, pp. 160, 215, 216.

were the written language of the Pontiff, we see how easily he would communicate with the most distant nations, long after their spoken languages had deviated from the original, (which was not far from the sixteen-letter Hebrew,) so far as not to be intelligible to one another.[1] The knowledge of this would be confined, necessarily, to the sacred caste. Every thing tends to shew that the original of this language ought to be placed in Chinese Tartary, which Bailly, Buffon, Linné, and indeed all the most learned philosophers, agree in selecting as the birth-place of mankind. The symbolic language of which I have been treating is nothing but the language of China. About the beginning of the French Revolution, the celebrated philosopher Bailly published his history of ancient astronomy, in which he endeavoured to prove, that the first race of men, after the flood, had been situated on the East of the Caspian Sea, and thence had extended towards the South. In his treatise on the Origin of the Sciences in Asia, he has undertaken to prove, that a nation possessed of profound wisdom, of elevated genius, and of an antiquity far superior even to that of the Egyptians or Indians, soon after the flood, inhabited a country to the North of India *proper*, between the latitudes of forty and fifty, or about fifty degrees of north latitude, the birth-place of the book of Enoch,—a country of about the latitude of London. He proves that some of the most celebrated observations and inventions relating to astronomy, from their peculiar character, could have taken place only in those latitudes; and he maintains, that arts and improvement gradually travelled thence to the Equator. The people to whom his description is most applicable, are those near Mount Imaus and northern Tibet, a country in which very celebrated colleges of learned men were anciently established, particularly Nagracut, Cashmere, and Bocharia. Mr. Hastings informed Mr. Maurice, that an immemorial tradition prevailed at Benares, which was itself in modern times the grand emporium of Indian learning, and therefore the less likely to preserve such a tradition against itself, that all the learning of India came from a country situated in forty degrees of north latitude. On this Mr. Maurice says, " This is, in fact, the latitude of Samarkand, " the metropolis of Tartary, and by this circumstance the position of M. Bailly should seem to be " confirmed." Astronomical calculations, tradition, and the evidence of old writers, all confirm the doctrine advanced by Bailly. About or a little before the time when M. Bailly published his history, Buffon, Linné, and others, had published some very curious speculations respecting the origin and formation of man. They produced facts to prove that the earth had been originally much hotter at the poles than it is now; that it had gradually cooled; and that the cold was gradually and by imperceptible degrees increasing. This they endeavoured to account for by *a theory* which improved science, I think, has shewn to be unfounded; but the *facts* remain unshaken. From a very close attention to the nature of the ancient mythologies, all which are intimately connected with astronomy, they imagined that man had been created, and that the arts and sciences had take their rise, not far from the Arctic Circle, where the earth had first cooled— and that they had extended southwards as it became by degrees more and more cold. Many sepulchres and some very surprising remains of antiquity had been found in Upper Tartary, about the neighbourhood of Selinginskoi. These were supposed to be remains of an ancient people *previous to the flood*. M. Bailly concludes his argument in the following words: " These facts, then, " unite to produce the same conclusion: they appear to prove to us, that the ancient people who " brought the sciences to perfection, a people who succeeded in the great enterprise of discovering " the exact measurement of the earth, dwelt under the 49th degree of latitude. If the human " mind can ever flatter itself with having been successful in discovering the truth, it is when many " facts, and these facts of different kinds, unite in producing the same result."[2] The philosophers

---

[1] See *supra*, pp. 148, 149, 217.   [2] Celtic Druids, Ch. II. Sect. X. to XVI.

above-named accounted for the greater degree of heat which they thought they had detected at the poles, by supposing, that the earth had been in a state of fusion. I only concern myself with the fact, that they thought they had detected a greater degree of heat in the polar regions. The greater angle made by the two planes will rationally account for this,[1] as its decrease will rationally account for the increase of the cold in those regions, and the constant increase of cold in England. Sir William Jones and other short-sighted and narrow-minded persons have turned Bailly, Buffon, Linné, and other foreign philosophers, into ridicule, for teaching that man must have been created in Tartary, about the latitude of London, 51½. If my theory of the change in the earth's axis be true, that country must have had, soon after the flood, a much finer climate than it has now. Respecting that part of the theory relating to the cooling of the earth, I give no opinion, not professing to possess any skill in geology; but, independently of that part of the question, there are many circumstances to justify Bailly in his opinion. I suspect the great mythic-cyclic-microcosmic system, of which I have treated, was the foundation of the systems of all nations; but, as time advanced, and as heresies necessarily arose, the mythos would be made to bend in every new heresy to its dogmata. Every great sect or division had its book of wisdom; and, during the continuance of the division between the great sects of the Linga and Iohi, each sect would have had that book leaning to its paramount dogma. When the union took place, this would, in some measure, be corrected, but probably not entirely. Where the *female* was the favourite, as at Athens, we should find a leaning, even after the union, to the Minerva or Ceres; where the *male*, as in Jerusalem, the leaning would be to the Jupiter or Iao. The system of Cycles, an effect arising out of almost the first and most pressing wants of man, was in itself of a nature peculiarly proper to perpetuate this mythic system, and may be considered as the great cause which prevented, for a certain time, the divergence of the system, and of its present actual dispersion and disappearance. It lasted one period of ten ages, or 6000 years; it is now nearly dissipated and gone. It arose out of the wants of man; it was continued by those wants: it aided greatly in supplying or remedying those wants. Those wants being now supplied by the diffusion of great scientific knowledge, the system is gradually yielding to the law of change, of eternal regeneration—and to the law which forbids man to look too far either behind or before him. It is almost lost and forgotten. But a few ruins of the building—once beautiful—lie scattered around us. We have them distorted and corrupted in Papism, Grecism, in Sopheism, in Sonneism, in Lutheranism, and in Calvinism. What will come next no one can tell; but, perhaps, Solomon was right, that there was *nothing new under the sun*. Perhaps man is near his end. What has happened before may happen again. The *mastodon* is dead. Perhaps the comet of 1680 may come again: the tops of the mountains may be the bottom of the seas; and, in a thousand years more, philosophers, in some shape or other, may speculate respecting the properties of that extinct animal, the remains of which they will find, and which we call *man!* In the doctrine of Pantheism the Το Ον was every thing, and every thing the Το Ον. In its monad, in its least of all possible quantities as well as in its circle, whose centre is every where, whose circumference is no where, all was Το Ον: but what is this but *illusion?*

---

[1] It is said that, if the planes coincided, the equatorial regions would be uninhabitable. I believe that African Negroes would not find it too hot.

(446)

CONCLUSION.

In Volume I. pp. 824, 825, and supra, pp. 130, 131, I spoke of what was called the Eclectic philosophy. This I suspected was really the original Chrestianity. I shall now return to that subject. About the time of the Cæsars we find the mysterious secrets of Χρης-tianism beginning to creep out, to escape from the crypts, and to shew themselves to the world in various ways. We see this very particularly marked in the general expectation of the world, that some *great one was to come*. After a certain time, when the period of the new age was certainly passed, as it appears, from the passage in Juvenal,[1] to have been well known to be, a belief gradually arose that the great one, the Χρης, the Saviour, had appeared. The first effect of this was, to produce a feverish state of the public mind, rendered worse by the utter contempt into which the corrupt state of the heathen religion had fallen; and the next effect was, to produce a great number of sects, of what were called Christians, each inquiring if *the great one* had come. Some thought that *Herod*,[2] others believed that *Cæsar*, might be the person. Indeed, it is well known, that each of these was believed to be the person by vast numbers of devotees. Soon after this time, the destruction of Jerusalem, of its records, and of every thing which could give certainty to a report, having taken place, the popular voice fixed upon an individual who was said to have lived and taught there, and to whom was applied that part of the mythic mythos relating to the *crucifixion* and *resurrection*; and then it was found, for the first time, by the Paulites, that this Saviour was to be a *spiritual* not a *temporal* Messiah. It is impossible on reading the works of Plato, and perhaps of every one of the ancient philosophers, not to remark the nonsense with which their writings appear to abound: all this arises from their wish to keep their doctrines *secret*, and is well described by a passage in the Encyclopædia Britannica, in voce *Platonism*. Speaking of Plato, the author says, "After having "said that he meant to wrap up his meaning in such obscurity, as that an adept only should fully "comprehend it, he adds expressions to the following import: The Lord of nature is surrounded "on all sides by his works: whatever is, exists by his permission: he is the fountain and source "of excellence: around the second person are placed things of the second order; and around the "third, those of the third degree. Περι των παντων βασιλεα, παντ' εςι, και Εκεινου ενεκα "παντα. Εκεινος αιτια παντων των καλων. Δευτερον δε περι τα δευτερα, και τριτον περι "τα τριτα. (Opera, p. 1269.) Of this obscure passage a very satisfactory explanation is given "by Dr. Ogilvie." For want of attention to this principle, all translators have endeavoured to make these mystical works of the ancients to read into sense, and to find out from their *literal* meaning a system, which it is evident their authors never intended to teach. A system they had certainly; but it was not a system described or expressed by the common meaning of the words, but one which was hidden in jargon, purposely made unintelligible to common readers, when looking only to the common meaning of the words.[3] Few people, I am persuaded, are aware of the

---

[1] See Volume I. pp. 187, 579.   [2] See *supra*, p. 233.
[3] Written originally in a language of numeral symbols or what we call ciphers.

extent to which this pernicious practice was carried. The moment the author of the above passage in the Encyclopædia has finished it he throws it aside; and, without any attention to the assertion of Plato, that he meant to couch his doctrine in obscure terms, he proceeds to reason upon their literal meaning, and to shew how they differ from the Christian Trinity. No unprejudiced person can doubt that the Trinity of Plato was substantially both the Trinity of the Christians, and the Trinity of the Hindoos, and no one but a devotee, who has sacrificed his understanding to fears for his future welfare, will doubt on the subject. The following is the account of the Eclectics,[1] and of the greatest of the sect or school, Ammonius Saccas, given by the Edinburgh Encyclopædia: "This learned man was born of Christian parents, and educated in their reli-
" gion: the outward profession of which, it is said, he never entirely deserted. As his genius was
" vast and comprehensive, so were his projects bold and singular; for he attempted a general coa-
" lition of all sects, whether philosophic or religious, by framing a system of doctrines which he
" imagined calculated to unite them all, the Christians not excepted, in the most perfect harmony.
" In pursuance of this design, he maintained, that the great principles of all philosophical and
" religious truth, were to be found equally in all sects; and that they differed from each other
" only in their method of expressing them, and in some opinions of little or no importance; and
" that by a proper interpretation of their respective sentiments, they might easily be united into
" one body. Accordingly, all the Gentile religions, and even the Christian, were illustrated and
" explained by the principles of this universal philosophy; and the fables of the priests were to be
" removed from Paganism, and the commentaries and interpretations of the disciples of Jesus from
" Christianity. In conformity to this plan, he insisted, that all the religious systems of all nations
" should be restored to their original purity, and reduced to their primitive standard, viz., the
" ancient philosophy of the East, preserved uncorrupted by Plato; and he affirmed, *that this*
" *project was agreeable to the intentions of Jesus Christ*, whose sole view in descending upon earth
" was, to set bounds to the reigning superstition, to remove the errors that had blended them-
" selves with the religions of all nations, but not to abolish the ancient theology from which they
" were derived. He, therefore, adopted the doctrines which were received in Egypt concerning
" the universe and the Deity, considered as constituting one great whole: concerning the eternity
" of the world, the nature of souls, the empire of providence, and the government of the world by
" dæmons. He also established a system of moral discipline, which allowed the people in gene-
" ral to live according to the laws of their country and the dictates of nature; but required the
" wise to exalt their minds by contemplation, and to mortify the body, so that they might be
" capable of enjoying the presence and assistance of the dæmons, and ascending after death to the
" presence of the Supreme Parent. In order to reconcile the popular religions, and particularly
" the Christian, with this *new system*, he made the whole history of the Heathen Gods an allegory,
" maintaining that they were only celestial ministers, entitled to an inferior kind of worship: and
" he acknowledged that Jesus Christ was an excellent man, and the friend of God; but alleged
" that it was not his design entirely to abolish the worship of dæmons, and that his only intention
" was to purify the ancient religion. This system so plausible in its first rise, but so comprehen-
" sive and complying in its progress, has been the source of innumerable errors and corruptions in
" the Christian church. At its first establishment it is said to have had the approbation of *Athe-
" nagoras, Pantænus, and Clemens the Alexandrian, and of all who had the care of the public
" school belonging to the Christians at Alexandria.* It was afterwards adopted by Longinus, the

---

[1] Eclectic, from εκλεγω, *I choose*. The Eclectics were called *Analogetici*, or, as Dr. Brewster says, never assumed any distinct name. Thus, under this designation, the ancient Christians have been hidden.

"celebrated author of the treatise on the Sublime, Plotinus, Herennius, Origen, Porphyry, Jambli-
"cus the disciple of Porphyry, Sopater, Edisius, Eustathius, Maximus of Ephesus, Priscus,
"Chrysanthius the master of Julian, Julian the Apostate, Hierocles, Proclus, and many others, both
"Pagans and Christians. The above opinions of Ammonius are collected from the writings and
"disputations of his disciples, the modern Platonics; *for he himself left nothing in writing behind
"him:* nay, he imposed a law upon his disciples not to divulge his doctrines among the multitude ;
"which injunction they made no scruple to neglect or violate."

In considering the above description, it should be recollected, that it is written by a person not only profoundly ignorant, if my idea of the philosophy be correct, but by a person whose prejudices lead him unconsciously to misrepresent it in every way. But yet enough transpires to shew us, that, according to this account, all the leading points which I have been advocating through the whole of my work are to be found in it; and, indeed, that the systems must have been the same with some trifling discrepancies, in which it is probable that both I and those who have represented to us the doctrines of Ammonius, may have fallen into mistakes. It were ridiculous to suppose that either I or they can have wholly avoided error; and I beg every candid reader to recollect, that the malicious exaggeration of trifling errors ought not to be permitted to influence his mind with respect to the remainder. In the list of the advocates of this system we have unquestionably the most illustrious names of antiquity, both Christians and Gentiles. It is worthy of observation, that we have in this list, persons said to be the greatest enemies of Christianity, which makes me suspect that these men were only enemies to the prevailing sect of the Paulites. Let it not be forgotten, that we have the works of Julian, Longinus, Porphyry, &c., only from the hands of the Paulites, who, we know, omitted nothing to misrepresent and blacken their enemies, having recourse to frauds and forgeries of every kind. For an instance, I have only to name the Philosophy of Oracles, forged in the name of Porphyry, as declared by Lardner. How can we know that the same may not have been done for Julian? In the account given by the Encyclopædia, there seems nothing in the system which may not easily be shewn to be rational and consistent with sound philosophy, except the part relating to dæmons, which was, in fact, the doctrine of the Romish church, under the name of angels. It may be collected from the latter part of the account that Ammonius fell into the usual error of all the philosophers, of endeavouring to keep the system secret, in consequence of which, it was not committed to writing; and, as might be expected, it was first grossly misrepresented, and then finally lost. In order the better to disguise the truth respecting its advocates, the Paulites called them *Eclectics;* but the name by which they called themselves was Philaletheans, or *lovers* or *friends of truth.* In not committing his doctrines to writing, we find Ammonius Saccas treading strictly in the footsteps of Socrates, Pythagoras, and his master—Jesus.[1] I think when the author of the above-cited article represents this system as new, it is obvious that he grossly misrepresents it, and that this was nothing but the oldest and original system taught by Jesus, and held by the enlightened part of his followers in the school of Alexandria; at least that it was held by them to be so. So far from being new, it is manifest that the Éclectic or Philalethean sect,[2] one of whom Jesus Christ was, existed before his time, and was previously taught by Potamon, who was succeeded first by Jesus, then by Ammonius. The doctrines taught by them both were the ancient, oriental, uncorrupted Gnosis or Wisdom, which I have shewn existed in all nations and all religions. We are misled in our estimate of it by seeing it through the prejudices instilled into us by our education in the doctrines of Paul, who founded one of the numerous and low or inferior sects. This sect, as I have frequently remarked, aided by

---

[1] See supra, p. 219.   [2] Of which sect I beg to be considered a member.

Constantine, got possession of all power, and thus was enabled to destroy or corrupt all evidence by which the truth might have been discovered.[1] We must not forget that, in these ancient systems, philosophy cannot be separated from religion—for philosophy was religion, and religion was philosophy. If we take this view of the subject, we may not find it difficult to discover the reason why, in all ages, the Paulite priesthood have been so addicted to fraud and dishonest practices; for it is evident that, without these infamous measures, they never could have succeeded in so completely deceiving mankind as they have done. This readily accounts for their systematic destruction of all books, Christian as well as Gentile, except the contemptible trash of their own sect. It seems pretty clear to me, that when we meet with the epithet *anti-Christian* applied to such men as Porphyry or Julian, we may almost always read instead of it the word *anti-Paulite*. It must not be supposed, I maintain, that there were not differences among the Philaletheans— for instance, between Clemens and Porphyry. No doubt there were differences; but though these differences are unquestionable yet it is evident they themselves maintained, that their doctrines were virtually the same.

I now conclude with a simple statement of what, (as it appears to me,) an unprejudiced, dispassionate inquirer after truth may reasonably believe respecting Jesus and his doctrines. If any learned and liberal-minded priest shall think that I have mistaken any fact, or erred in the conduct of any argument, or in any conclusion which I may have drawn, I shall be extremely happy to receive his correction. I shall notice it, with the respect it deserves, in an appendix, which I shall publish for this and other purposes.[2] In the time of Tiberius appeared a man of the name of John. He was a Nazarite, of the monastic order of the Pythagorean Essenes, and lived the life of a hermit. He was put to death by Herod, for rebuking him for his vices. About the same time lived a person, who was his cousin, whose original name has probably been changed, like that of Abraham, Jacob, Joshua, Pythagoras, &c., but who has since been known by the name of JESUS CHRIST. This person was also a Nazarite, of the same sect or monastic order—the Pythagorean Essenes. He, like his cousin John, was a philosopher, a teacher of morality and of reformation of manners to his Jewish countrymen. He was put to death[3] by the priests of the Pharisees, the prevailing or orthodox sect, at that time, in Judea, against whose vices he loudly declaimed, and whose hypocrisy he exposed. He was a person of a most virtuous life and amiable manners—the Socrates or Pythagoras of his day. We know that he taught a very strict and pure morality, the unity of God, the immortality of the soul, and that this life is only a state of probation for a state of future existence, in which every person will be rewarded or punished according to his merits or demerits. These are the facts which we know respecting Jesus and his doctrines,—and as I believe that the facts are real, and that the doctrines are true, I consider that I am his follower, his disciple, and *a Christian*.

---

[1] See *supra*, pp. 117, 173.

[2] "In the midst of *life* we are in *death*." Two years and a half before this sentence was printed, the Author was numbered with the dead! *Editor*.

[3] As this part of the Author's MS. was transmitted, by his direction, to the printer, *unaltered*, it may admit of doubt whether he was fully satisfied with the evidence adduced from Irenæus in proof that Jesus Christ was *not* crucified, but attained the age of *fifty*. See *supra*, pp. 120—123, 142, 228. *Editor*.

INDEX.

	Page
A, the first letter of Ailm, the *first or one*,	184, 249
Aaron, the rod of, what,	204
Ab or Ba, probably the first word of infant man,	162, 167
——, ☉—father—God the Father, the Trimurti,	223
—— or Ba, *the father*, Apis, from,	414
Abacus—the ancient Roman and Chinese, the same,	216, 217
Abad, the Great, or Buddha or Bauddha or Abaddon,	133
Abads, *thirteen*, the generations of Solimans,	133
Abaris, the arrow of, the mariner's compass, alone necessary to the early traveller,	365
Ab-ba, the root of the cycle of 432, a lustrum,	181
——, the, was king and priest,	297, 298
Abba-Sin—the Upper Nile once so called,	181
Abbas, the family of the Calif, ruled at Bagdad,	385
——————, declared by the emperor of the Mongols not to possess any of the virtues of the prophet,	390
Abbassides—a great meeting of learned men called by the, in Persia, against the Assassins, their doctrines, &c.,	389
Abbé or Rabbi, a contraction of Roy or Rey-abbé, R'abbé,	297
Abbé Bazin. See Bazin.	
Abbé Guerin de Rocher, the. See Rocher.	
Abbé Marolles, the. See Marolles.	
Abbot, a mitred, a bishop *without functions*, &c.,	285
Abbots, the mitred, made abbots by their chapters, and bishops by the Popes,	278
————————, their right to sit in Parliament,	285
Abbuto or Pater But, the Apollo of the Japanese,	287
Abekt—the symbolic letters of Indian Algebra,	217
Aben Ezra,	105
Aberdeen — a Delecarlian landed near, was understood at,	258
Abged, the Persian for numeration, our A, B, C,	217
——, abekt, abacus, &c., prove letters are derived from figures,	217
Abile or Calpe, the Straits of,	19
Aborigines, an inoffensive race, Buddhists,	203
——, the so called,	283
——, escaped from a flood—conquered by colonies, &c.,	258, 309, 361, 435, 439

	Page
Aborigines, the, of South India, have no distinction of castes,	274
——————, remains of, *white races*, more numerous than the *black* colonies sent out by the Pontifical government,	363
——————, the, ignorant, naked, and defenceless—their countries taken possession of, by the learned caste from the East,	392
——————, of Greece, conquered by a race from India, as we conquered the people of North America, and are conquering those of Australia,	419
Aboulfasl (the host of Hassan Sabah),	382
Abraham, 8, 10, 14, 16, 34, 45, 60, 61, 97, 110, 194, 245, 300, 329, 360, 386,	449
————, Zoradust or Zoroaster,	58
————, and Sarah, mythological character of,	81
————, his birth announced by a star,	95
————, supposed to have had the same soul as Adam, David, and the Messiah, i. e. an angel,	97
————, 14 generations before,	133
————, the Brahmin, 139, 257, 310,	364
————, an ashera set up by, in Beersheba,	194
————, the simple religion of—of the three sacraments,	282
————, the 318 circumcised or initiated of, an example of a numeral and astrological allegory, 297,	298
————, the God of wisdom, peculiarly the god of,	299
————, an, and a Lot, dispute between the servants of,	306
————, an, and a Lot, would soon settle a dispute in the Golden Age,	307
————, and his 318 men—the Jews descended from,	310
————, opposed to images—beginning to prevail when he left India,	364
————, priest and king,	366
————, the Brahmin well marked in,	368
————, the Ashra set up by, were probably at the cross roads or capitols—like the stone pillars of the West, called Decumans, &c.,	371
————, and his 318, brought up in his own house, in his war with the five kings, probably employed, under their command, thousands of mercenaries,	392

	Page
Abraham, St., and Mary his niece,	81
Abram,	58
Absolution—refused by monks, to compel laymen to leave church patronage to them,	267
Absorbed, absorption, into the To Ov, 249, 251, 254, 301,	336
Abstineto á fabis—abstain from *fables*, not, from *beans*, 239, 240,	300
Abulfaragius or Bar Hebræus,	96
Abul Fazl, on Akbar,	354
Abul Ghazi Behadur,	353
Abury, built by the Cyclops,	135
——, the rude pillars at, more ancient than the Trilithons of Stonehenge, &c.,	396
——, the temple at, in its number of 650, &c.,	409
—— and Stonehenge, the builders of, must have been a *mighty people*,	416
Abydenus, on antediluvian kings,	321, 322
————, on the time of the flood,	327
Abyssinia and Upper Egypt, peopled by a tribe of Juda, which came from India, before the tribe of Abraham,	352
Abyssinian Christians,	37
Accommodesan—a portion of the produce of land,	292
Accusamileuses, the,	30
Acham (Sanscrit) Ogham (Irish) הכמ (Heb) Wisdom,	158
Acherah—tithe among the Mohamedans,	264
Achilles,	293
———— Tatius,	314
————, on a month as 30 days,	321
Acosta,	30, 31
————, on the Mexican year,	318
Acropolis, an, in each country having any pretence to have *a Saviour*,	341, 422
Acrostic writing in the Tamul, the Psalms, and the Runes,	165
Acts of the Apostles, the, fabricated—the Latin character of, visible in every page,	131, 132
Actus or fundus, the Roman, twelve ten-feet rods, &c.,	407
Ad or Hadad, the, of Syria, is Buddha,	6
Ad ad corrupted into *Hadad*,	162
Ad, God so called in India and Western Syria; A is one, and d, is di—holy one or Monad,	181
Ad and Adad, the kings of Heliopolis so called,	236
Adam,	22, 133, 377
——, from A joined to D—5, and M or Om, or Ma, great,	163, 202
—— and Eve, a microcosm of

452 INDEX.

	Page
Brahme Ma'a, and their three sons a microcosm of the Trimurti,	181, 398, 399
Adam stole the pollen of the female plant, and, for the robbery, was crucified in the person of Jesus Christ,	245
———, an emanation of the Supreme,	250
———'s Peak—his foot—Buddha's foot-mark, in Ceylon,	288
———, from proceeded Cain, Abel, Seth, and from them all mankind—the first world how divided,	398
Addison,	114
Adima, the first *male* and *female*,	175
A-DON, THE WISE, of the country of Phrn,	109
Adonai (for Ieue) is the name of Adonis,	171
Adoni-bezek — his confession of cruelty,	421
Adonis,	102, 103, 132, 161, 171
———, his death and resurrection,	25, 106, 112, 115, 143, 145
———, his temple at Bethlehem,	95, 96
———, Bacchus, and Osiris, were all incarnate Gods,	98
———, ןדא *adn*, the Welsh Celtic Adon,	99
——— was a personification of the Sun,	100
———, his birth on same day as Jesus Christ's,	104
———, the rites of, or of Tammuz,	114
——— or ןודא *adun*, or ינדא *Adoni* or *Lord*,	114, 115
——— said to have been killed by a boar,	115
——— the son of Myrra or Maria, was Tammuz, or Tamas, or Thomas,	115, 119
——— or Tammuz, the history of, or universal mythos,	129
———, in Syriac, is Oden,	350
———, called the eldest son of God—robbed the garden of, a flower, was crucified, &c.,	253
Adonises, Atyses, Bacchuses, Buddhas, Cristnas, Herculeses, Mithras, Salivahanas, all the, put to death, and rose from the grave, &c.,	142
Adoration of saints, the,	81
Adrian, Hadrianus, to destroy the Christian faith dedicated the image of Jupiter, and profaned Bethlehem with the temple of Adonis,	95
———, before the time of, the temple of Adonis existed at Bethlehem,	96
Adrian I. (pope),	111
Adventurers, the, of the Incarnate God, acted in the Deisuls, and in the sacred theatres,	340
Aelfric's Anglo Saxon Bible differs from the Hebrew, Samaritan, Septuagint, Vulgate, &c.,	172
Æneas,	64, 74, 400, 412
——— descending to the shades, passed an elm-tree loaded with dreams,	249
Ænon,	66
———, sacred to the sun,	95
Æon, aspirated, is Chaon,	155
Æschylus's *Prometheus vinctus*, 113, 136
———'s Plays, cause of lacunæ in,	116
———, the Tragedies of,	293

	Page
Æsculapius — Asclo-opa, Logos, Serpent of the Solar Cycle, 113,	437
———, death and resurrection of,	115
Æsop's Fables,	305
Afghan Brahmin, the, (Abraham,) who came to Syria of the West, was an iconoclast,	364
Afghans, the,	238
———, partly Sunnis and partly Shiahs, are called Rohillas, Solimiani, and Patans; their language, called Peshtu, is full of old Persian,	239
———, the tribes of Eusof and Munder—the lands of, change possessors after short periods,	282
———, believed Mohamed to be an Avatar,	352
Africa,	2, 75, 312, 399, 400
Africanus, on Manetho's Dynasties, &c.,	324
Afflatus Numinis, the, or Holy Ghost, in ordination,	81
Aga—Ogga—a name of Minerva,	225
Aga, the, of the land,	417
Agamemnon,	18, 225, 421
———, his dispute with Chryses and Calchas,	35
Agatha, St., the festival of,	91
Agathon (pope),	111
Age of Gold or a Golden Age,	1, 266, 305—307, 365, 366, 369, 377, 323, 434, 439
———, an, of learning, peace, and civilization, once existed,	1, 305
———, the, would be an age of piety, &c.	306
Age of Silver,	306, 434
—— of Brass or Copper,	306, 434
—— of Iron,	306, 308, 434
———, the, of the Lotus, of Roses,	-32
Ager, our acre, the first unit of measure, was a microcosm of a greater,	407
———, i.e. measure of land or τεμενος,	413
——— Romanus, the Roman Territory so called, like the globe, like India, Britain, Scotland, &c., at first divided into *three parts*,	413, 414, 422
Αγιαλατρια, the, of Greek, Roman, and Protestant churches,	81
Agnes, St., the nuns of,	230
Ages of Gold, Silver, Copper, Iron,	306
Agni, אפי *iod*, the God of wisdom,	5
———, the sacrifice of the, or the Yagni sacrifice,	109, 157, 159
—— Dei, blessed by the Pope, &c.,	88
Agnus Dei, the, succeeded the Bulla,	87
———, Qui tollis, &c.,	108
———, worn by children,	87
Agonie, the, on Good-Friday, is the weeping for Tammuz,	92
Agra, Akbar's burial-place near,	358
———, a pope at, or at Oude, &c.,	422
Agrarian laws—cause of disputes about the, in Rome, and in Athens,	373, 418
Agri Decumani, the, got possession of, by the priests;	417
Agrimensores, the, Etruscan,	117, 284
———, in the account of, we probably have the only written remains of the financial polity of the Patriarchal priesthood,	371
———, the use of, in mea-	

	Page
suring out lands to feudatories—the origin of our *town* fields,	406
Agrimensorism—the author of Genesis perfectly understood the doctrine of,	313
———, wisdom, and the generative principle—the same compound doctrine of, in India and in Europe,	415
Ahasuerus—the 180 days' feast of, just half a year, &c,	317
———, queen Esther not called to, for 30 days,	320
Ala, Aja—Jah, Jave, Jove, &c,	5
Aikin, Dr., on the Callau inscription,	206
Ailm, ilm, elm, oeilm, or ulm,	249
———, the elm, the first letter of the Tree-alphabet,	148—150, 184, 249
———, all letters and numbers formed on the,	190
Ainsworth, on the word Cardo,	414
Air, fire, water, the Etruscans baptized with,	67
———, in motion, breath, spirit,	67, 123
Aurr, aspirated, is Chaeon,	135
Αιων των αιωνων,	51, 56, 251, 254, 336, 344
———, the, not heard of now, in Rome or Tibet, but only the Vieramadytia, &c.,	374
Aja — self-existing — a name of Brahma,	175
Ajax,	18
Aje-mere—its origin may be Aja,	5
Akbar believed himself, and was believed to be, the last Avatar; was called *perfect messenger of God*, &c., &c.,	354
——— assumed the title of Vicegerent of God,	355
——— his *divinity*, &c., yet believers in,	356
——— announced himself as the *tenth* Avatar, putting back Mohamed as the *ninth*,	357
——— poisoned by mistake—picture of the Apotheosis of,	358
———, the archhierarchy almost revived under,	373
——— the Second, enjoys only the empty title of King (Padshah) of Delhi,	358
Akme—perhaps the same as the American Sachem,	25
Al, God, *all*,	284, 408
Alaric, a supposed Avatar,	207
——— and his Goths—Scythians, Sacæ, &c.,	273
——— believed himself to be the person foretold,	344
Alb or *alba*, the, ordered by Numa, to be worn by a priest,	64
Alba, Mount, preceded the Capitol as *the sacred mount*,	291
———, white sow of, *black*,	34, 291
———, Sin, the natives of, the Egyptians,	292
—— Vestia,	79
Alban and Latin states, tradition of the, being formed of 600 families,	433
Albanact, to whom his father Brutus gave Scotland, hence called Albania,	400, 401, 412
Albanians—a name for Britons, or the English,	2
Alchemists,	301
Aldborough, the capital of the Brigantes,	298

INDEX.

Aldermen and Councilmen, whence their number, 276, 417
Aleim, the, of Genesis, or Wisdom, 256
———, the plural feminine of Al, 257
———, has a feminine termination, 291
Ale-manni, the Franks, 267
Aleuadae and Bacchiades, the, a numerous and royal Gens—probably allodial proprietors and bookmen, 419
Alexander, 17, 34, 36, 317, 319, 320, 356
——— conquered Egypt about 30 years before Christ, 17
——— de Symbolis Pythagoricis, 49
——— opposed by the Poorus and Hericulas, 117, 118
———, the Genius of his age, probably sought in, 127
———, decrees of Fate revealed to, by speaking trees, 162
——— conquered the Sacæ or Saxons, and restored their country to the chiefs, &c., 272
———, believed to be a divine incarnation, 343, 347
——— himself to be the person foretold, 344
———, his name from Al, Ischa (Arabic) and ἀνδρος, a man, 346, 347
———, said to have been born 360, B. C., the year the sun entered Pisces at the Vernal Equinox, 346, 347, 375
———, ascribed his generation to Jupiter Ammon, 346, 348, 349
———, declared his war a religious one, &c., 347
———, an æra of, in Asia, 348, 349, 384
———, had, mystically, two fathers, 350
———, why, before he marched, he was acknowledged as sovereign over Greece, over the other dominions of Japhet, and probably over those of Shem and Ham, 384
——— acknowledged by the Amphictyons as their lord, and as sovereign of all Greece, they probably regarding him as the new incarnation, 423
——— ab Alexandro, 51, 64, 76, 79
———, Pope, 88
——— VI., Pope, refused the Emperor a grant of the tithes of Mexico, &c., 393
———, Severus, 349
Alexandria, 22, 399, 400
———, colonies of Jews from, supposed to have gone to America, 22
———, the philosophers of, 131
Alfred, the tithings of king, in England, like the divisions in Western Syria, and in India—Decapolis and Deccan, 277
———, was this from Al-phre-di? His tithings were ecclesiastical, and like those of the Chinese, 292
Algebra—an unspoken language, 213
———, the letters of, from Hebrew or Arabic, 217
———, said to have been discovered, by the Arabians, in the middle ages—known in Italy 600 year—probably a remnant of the science of the old Tuscan Augurs or Agrimensores—in a symbolic language, 436
Algebra, a part of the ancient mysteries, of magic, 437
———, in the concealment of, an example of the spirit of monopoly, 439
Ali, the Shahs of the house of, 207
———, the followers of, 291
———, the Imams of, like the Lucumones and the 12 Cæsars, 345
———, the system of the sect of, fell into pieces, when the Millenium did not arrive, 351
Alkader, the Calif, gave investiture to Mahmud of Ghazni, 354
All Saints and All Souls, the Mexican festival of advocates answered to our, 31, 82
All Souls, the festival of, at Florence, 68
All Souls' Day—what the Irish call the feast of the fires of Baal, 82
Allegauies, the, 312
Allegorical meaning, the, held by Plato, Pantænus, Philo, Clemens, Justin, Origen, Philo, 131
Allegory, the double, of knowledge, and of the generative power, 244
——— on Chemsennissa, as a garden, 245
——— of trees and letters, 247
——— of the trees of knowledge and of life, meaning of the, 252
Allelujah, same as the Irish Ullaloo and the Mexican Hululaez, 27
Allodial Tenure, 265, 284, 285
——— Lands, the lands partly occupied by princes, and in part let—not subinfeudated, 285, 417
Allodium—al-di-om—land of the holy Om, 284
Allum Shah, i. e., Al the and Om, —Shah in Jah—the God Om, the world's king, 353
Almamon, 26
Almaat, Alamout, or Almont, the castle of the Assassins, 383, 386, 388—390
Almug-tree, the, the wood of Magal or Mag-ol—of the great God, 203
Alphabet, the first word of, often one, 165
———, each learned man had his own, 205, 220, 235, 424, 437
———, the first was the Arabic, of numbers, 205, 234
———, the second, of Cadmus, of letters, 205
———, anciently one for all nations, 237
———, the, a tree, &c., 371
———, the Tree, 148, 184, 186
Alphabetic writing, whether known to Homer, 170
Alphabets, the right-lined, probably not older than 2000 years B. C., 256
Alphabetum Tibetanum. See Georgius.
Alphonso the Great, on history of Jesus Christ read in the stars, 145
Alt, or atel, means water, 29
Alvarez, Semedo, 227, 228
Alwood, Mr., on Typhon, 230
Amama — Amomum — the Jerusalem Rose, 242
Amazon, (nature of the,) 202

Amazons, the, at Athens, 222
Amba, the, of India, 174
Ambrose (St.), 94, 344
———, the Alpha and Omega of, 204
Ambrosia—the liquor of the holy or creative power Om, 411
Amenti, the Egyptian, 7
America, 2, 22, 24, 33, 35, 38 —40
———, the printer of, 131
American and Basque languages, analogy of the, 27
——— Trinity, the father of, Om-equeturiqui, 23
Americans, the, adored the Sea, 30
——— South, ignorant of Letters and Iron, 33
———, the Ass and Horse unknown to, 35
———, their connexion with the old world, 37
———, Jewish rites, &c., known to, 39
———, supposed to be colonies from Tartary, &c., 40
Amict, an, 64, 79
Amid, the promised desire of all nations, 291, 344
———, every, had a star to announce his birth, 95, 96
Amida or Omyto, maximus Deus Japonensium, 243
Ammianus Marcellinus, 159
Ammon, Jupiter, the same as Adonis, Atys, and Osiris, 102
———, the sun at the Equinox, 110
Am-mon or Om-an, homo, man, 168
Ammoni Servatori, 110
Ammonius Saccas, 42, 118, 130, 138, 139, 443
———, his attempt to unite all sects, 131, 447, 448
Amomum, the Jerusalem Rose, 242
Amor or Roma, ib.
Amphibolus—the Pallium? 230
Amphictyon is, Am-phi-ct-on or Ixion, 422
Amphictyonic council, the, probably regulated the sacred letter, in which all matters under its cognisance were recorded, 437
Amphictyons, the, 277, 375, 380, 384, 419
———, the council of, unaffected even by the invasion of Xerxes, 422
———, would be disinterested mediators, when differences arose; it was their interest to preserve peace, for the increase of the produce of the land; interdicted the Phocian war; acknowledged Alexander as their lord; the Areopagus amenable to, 423
———, when necessary, exercised a paternal, &c., power, beneficial to all the states, 433
Ampulla, the vessel of the wisdom of Om, 302
———, the oil of the holy or creative power Om, 411
Amulets and charms retained in Italy, 92
Anacalypsis, the, 22
Anagrams and metathesis, origin of, 185, 246
——— and Acrostics, 305

INDEX.

	Page
Ana-mor (in Ireland), the temple of, has a circle of 48 pillars—the number of the ancient constellations—and, within, a circle of 9, to shew that 9 cycles were passed, or that the 9th was arrived, when the temple was built,	402
Anaxagoras—on the design of the earth's inclination,	314
Ancients, the, calculated by whole numbers,	329
———, the recondite doctrines of, appear fanciful when taken without the system of which they formed a part,	408
———, the, supposed to have known not only the high branches of Geometry, &c., but Algebra also,	436
Aucile, the famous, sent by Pallas to Numa—this shield was to be the protector of the eternal city,	440
Andalusian Pilot, the,	30
Andes, the,	39, 312
Andrada La Crozius, P.,	118, 243
Audrew's, St., Cross,	30
Androgynous, generative power, the,—the moon bore the same name as,	337
——— like God—man supposed to be created double, male and female in one person—side by side, like the Siamese boys,	397
Ange de S. Joseph, father,	77
Angels, fallen, the prototype of the,	88
——— of God—the nations divided according to the number of, i. e. probably, according to the stars or 72 constellations,	410
Anglo-Saxons, the, began the year on Dec. 25th, and were better skilled in astronomy than the Greeks and Romans of Cæsar's time,	135
Angoulême, Duchesse d',	70
Animal, every, a microcosm of man, &c.,	430
——— food, none eaten in early times,	147
Animalcule, the minutest imaginable, a microcosm of the one above it, &c.,	336
Animals, none sacrificed in early times,	147
———, plants, &c., believed to be formed of both sexes,	398
———, unsatisfactory theories to account for the adoration of, by the Egyptians and others.	437
Anna Pereuna, sister of Dido,	91
———, Sa. sister of the Virgin, or Petronilla,	91
Ausār or helpers—in the 72, who assisted the prophet at Medina, we have, probably, the Jewish Sanhedrim, the Amphyctions of Greece, and the Cardinales of Rome,	380, 383
Antara, an, or Oatar, an age,	134
Antediluvian year, the, was 360 days long, and the mouth 30 days long,	321—326
Anthou, professor,	314
Antioch, Alexandria, and Rome, the capitals of the three parts into which the kingdom of Saturn was divided among his three Sons—Jupiter, Pluto, and Neptune,	399, 400
Antioch, Alexandria, and Rome, the chiefs of the three Patriarchates of the Christian world, resided at,	400
Antiochus—the claim attempted to be set up by,	54
Antiquities of Mexico, &c., 21—41, 74, 161, 393,	430
Antonius—the pretended founder of monastic institutions,	46
Antony called himself the new Bacchus, &c.,	346
Antrustiones, the, or Fideles or Drudes or Druidi,	277
Anubis,	79
Aom-la-ania, the Mexican place or country of the Self-existent,	23
Aou, perhaps, אוּן agnu, with the t a prefix, Tangut,	7
Ape or monkey, and Brahmin, the same word in the Indian language,	9
Apex—the mitre is the,	53
Aphanasia, the, of Queealcoatle,	26
A'-φρας—the boar,	209
Ᾱφρο-δίτη—the holy φρη=608,	ib.
Apis or the Bull, the emblem of the creative power, from Ab or Ba, the father,	414
אפן apn,	401
Apocalypse—the crucified of the, in Egypt, 14, 15,	118
———, the, turns on the triumph of the Lamb, over the powers of hell and darkness; fixes the year to 360 days,	110
——— is filled with praises of the slain Lamb,	240, 241
———, the number 144 celebrated in,	241
Apocrypha, the, disliked equally by the Jews and by Christians,	125
———, has the mythos of the crucifixion, &c., which proves the mythos was a secret doctrine, 134, 232, 333, 441,	442
———, the books of the, probably written to preserve the secret doctrine, 233, 441,	442
Apocryphal Gospels, in one of the, Jesus said to be the son of a Dyer or Painter, &c.,	7
Apollo, 202,	213
——— killed by Python, and bewailed by three women,	102
——— of Claros, Pythagoras a follower of,	103
——— of Miletus, prophecy of,	177
——— ———entombment and resurrection of, 145,	180
———, the dance oblique of the priests of,	179
———, a hyperborean island said to have adored,	262
——— and Olympias—their connexion, 345,	347
——— described as accompanying his lyre with the dance, &c.,	425
Apologue, ænigma, allegory, &c., the custom of conveying knowledge by, once prevalent,	300
Apostles, the, 42, 43, 46, 71,	77
——— become Divi,	80
———' Creed, the, 42,	89
Apotheosis, the, of Pagans, canonization of Saints,	81
———, of Akbar,	358
Appius,	86
Apples of love, the, presented to the male, in the garden of delight,	249
Appollonius Tyaneus,	3
April-fool and May-day festivals, the, equally celebrated in Britain and in India, 106,	262
Apuleius, 61, 76, 78,	79
Aquarius, 139,	144
Arabia,	15
——— Felix,	19
———, Western,	134
———, the carus of,	179
———, other alphabets founded on that of, 205, 220,	221
———, an, in North India,	235
———, two races in,	274
Arabians, the, 77,	241
——— and Scandinavian Sacæ from North India,	225
———, traced from an Arabia on the Indus,	274
———, the, Algebra said to have been discovered by,	436
Arabic, the,	175
——— and Hebrew, the, the same, 153,	235
———, the old, allegories in, on tree of knowledge, &c.,	160
———, duplicate letters of, for numbers, 166, 185,	235
———, the old, of Mohamed, now not commonly understood,	167
———, the, anciently Cufic, 205, 213, 234,	237
———, notation, reduced to 16 letters,	214
——— numerals, the 28, would stand for more words than are wanted for a universal language,	220
———, the present characters, invented 300 years after Mohamed,	237
Arabs, Bedoween,	4
Arago, M., ridicules Whiston's Theory,	333
———'s History of Comets written to calm the fears of the Parisians, 333,	334
Ararat, Mount, 18,	321
———, the Il-avratta of India, 18,	411
———, placed by the Samaritans in Sereudive, 229,	288
———, Naubanda—Mount of the Ship, 292,	411
———, Ship-cabled Mount, 294, 333,	334
Araxes, the, Aras, Ros, Ras, or Cyrus river,	231
Arcadia, Numidia, Etruria, Tartary, &c., the same form of government anciently prevailed in,	421
Arca-polis, place of deposit of sacred things,	242
Argα, the ship in which the germ of animated nature was saved,	113
Archbishop, an, in the Romish church, though elected by suffrages, must have the pallium from the vicar of God,	231
Arch-Druid, the, in Gaul, held out his foot to be kissed,	55
Archdruid or Supreme Pontiff, the, of Britain, probably had under him three archflamens,	416
Αρχη—divine wisdom,	242
Archflamens, the three, of York, London, and Carleon (Chester), became Archbishops, when Lucius was converted,	400

INDEX.

Archierarch, Noah the first, and his three sons Archierarchs after him, ... 361
——— the rights and privileges of, gradually acquired by the Hierarch of each nation; and the distant Lord was at last forgotten, . . . 380, 381
———, there probably was an, with a council of 12, and a senate of 72, in every country, under a Pope, . . . 422
Archierarchical government, the first, probably left towns, &c., to their own management—hence the *free* states of Greece and Italy, . . . 366, 423
———, if the, was established before the flood, it would revive after it—the few persons remaining would readily submit to its superiority, . 435
Archierarchs, three, after the death of Noah, his three sons became; one, perhaps, at Oude or Babylon, for Asia; one in Egypt, for Africa; one at Rome or Thebes in Bœotia, for Europe, . 399
Archierarchy—very natural for an, to arise, and that it should extend its paternal influence over the whole world, . . 373
———, the first may have arisen before the sun entered Aries, in the æra of Buddha, and have continued during many generations, . . . 399, 400
———, the, abolished by Christ and Cristna—that of Rome and Tibet almost the same, . 438
Archierist, the, (of India,) may have been a king—hence the Archierarchy may have disappeared, ... 370
Archimedes and the Syracusans—the foot measure used by, 403, 404
Ardshir Ebn Babec, author of the play called Tables, . . 318
Areopagus, the, of Athens, courts like, answered to a lodge of Freemasons, &c., . . 419
———, was the high ecclesiastical court, &c., but amenable to the Amphictyons, 423, 424
Argha—serpent—emblem of the female generative power, 113, 174
Argheus—an universal spirit—evidently the Indian Argha, . 301
Argonautic Expedition, the, . 105
———, a, new, every 600 years, believed in by the vulgar, despised by the enlightened, ... 339
———, mysteries, 114, 115,
Argonauts, the, . . . 293
———, &c., new, 136, 195, 303
Arhiman—the evil principle, 83, 88, 106
Aries, . . . 138—140
———, the equinoctial sign changed from Taurus, to, before time of Moses, . . . 105, 106
——— personified, called the Lamb of God, applied to Jesus, and worshiped, 107, 108, 110
———, the worship of, the worship of the sun, . . . 112
———, till the equinoctial sun passed into, the world may have

been ruled in peace, by the Archierarch—till the festivals required correcting, &c., . . 399
Arietic cycle, in the, we have Noah and his wife, and Shem, Ham, and Japhet—a new Trinity every 1800 years, at first, &c., . 397
Aristites, Sacerdotum, the, &c., 3
Aristocracy, the sacred and military, ... 417
Aristophanes, . . . 199
Aristotle, ... 153, 314
———, the first who wrote on Greek grammar, . 195, 196
———, the alphabet of, . 220
———, on the length of the year, 319
———, on the tribute in Greece—a *tenth*, . . . 417
——— classes Dancing with poetry, music, and painting, as equally an imitative art, . 425
Aristotelian philosophy, the, once as little doubted as the Newtonian is now, . . . 333
Arithmetic (high), literal writing, astronomy, &c., originally constituted the mysteries, . 439
Arjoon, the cousin (or brother) of Cristna, . . 137, 241, 242
——— or Juana, the assistant to Cristna, ... 242
Ark, the, ... 361
——— of the Covenant, . . 10
———, the, Noah, and Thebes, have the same meaning, . 12, 13
——— of the Mexicans, . 27
———, increase of the 8 persons saved in, in 100 years, &c., 395, 439
Arka (Αρχα) in Javanese—the *sun*, 222
———, the ancient temple of Jaggernaut, at Kanarak, so called, 261
Arkite *Athene*, i. e., Divine Providence, ... 114
Armenia, . . . 4, 321
Armenian Christians, the, turned to the sun, in prayer, . . 89
——— language, the, originally the same as the Zend and the Pahlavi, ... 237
Arnobius, . . . 64, 80
Arouma, the, . . . 242
Aroura and Plethron, Egyptian and Greek standards of square measure, ... 406
Apoua, the sweet smell, a flower, pushpa, ... 242
Arran, the Isle of, so called from *Arkan*, consort of Buddha, - 287
Arrian, . . 118, 230, 272
Artaxerxes Memor, . . 317
——— was addicted to the ineffable mysteries, . . 348
Arteng, ... 8
Arthur's (prince) *round table*, &c., the mythos seen in, . 349, 356
Article, the emphatic, is often the name of God—*Al* (Arabic), *Pi* (Coptic), ה or ' or ה (Heb.), 200
Artimodorus, . . . 252
Arungabad, the Shufeek or Sophee or Rhymer of, . . 182
Ascanius and the Lavinian colony, 433
Asenath, the wife of Joseph, . 110
Aes, old Latin coins, without inscriptions, having the head of a young man, and a wheel with 6 spokes, &c., . . . 433
Ashera—*tenths*, tithe, . 193, 371
———, the, (restored by Moha-

med) established by the Califs; the (Mohamedan) world thus made as happy as under the first Hierarchy, . . 377, 379, 380
Ashera, an, set up, by Abraham, in Beersheba, . . 194, 371
Ashre, the, were burnt by Josiah; 371
———, were perpetual almanacks, ... 372
Ash-Wednesday, Shrovetide, &c., 59
———, the ceremony of putting ashes on the head on, a continuation of the festival of the *fordicidia* of the Romans, . 92
Asia, 4, 25, 39, 66, 69, 70, 75, 120—122, 312
——— and Africa, the wandering tribes of, readily came over to the Mohamedan faith, . 207
———, once a fief depending on Scythia, ... 262, 372
———, an æra of Alexander arose in, 348, 349, 385
———, the conduct of the monarchs of, towards Europeans, not understood—it arises from supposing themselves descended from the first three monarchs, the sons of Noah, . . 359
Asia Minor—the whole of, probably, was Mysia or mystic land, the land of Room: in it are Calinda, Calamina, and Calida, places of India, connected with the mythos of Ararat, . 412
Asiatic Journal, the, . . 352
———, on the Microcosm among the Chinese, 398
——— Researches, the, 7, 67, 103, 104, 122, 181, 214, 219, 225, 236—238, 240, 260, 261, 297, 371, 388, 429
——— Society, Transactions of, 148
Aspen, the, Eadha or E, in the Tree alphabet, . . . 149
Aspersorio, the, for sprinkling the people with holy water, a Pagan custom, ... 91
Asre, asire, ashres—groves—a kind of celestial globes, &c., 193, 194
Ass and Horse, the, unknown, in a state of nature, to the Americans, before the arrival of the Spaniards, 35
———, the golden, of Apuleius, 76
Assaceni or Astaceni, the, whose capital was Massaca or Massaca—A-saceni, *the Saca*?—Ma-saga, *the great Saca*? . . 230
Assassin, every, might be a Sophee, ... 383
———, the Society probably not called so, from being a *murderous* one, but a murderer from it, called an *assassin*, . . 384
Assassins, the, . 348, 381—392
———, Druids, Magi, &c., practised the rite of baptism, 248
———, their history, according to Von Hammer, is a mass of straight forward, pure, unadulterated wickedness, 382, 389
———, why every where found, ... 383
———, considered a dynasty by D'Herbelot and Deguines, as an order by Hammer, . 388
———, were profoundly versed in the *mathematical* and *metaphysical* sciences; their fana-

ticism, and the reason for their assassinations, the burning of their works, &c., 389
Assassins, their doctrine taught in secret; what was it?—the secret doctrines of Sopheism? 390
————, their doctrines of the metempsychosis and a divine incarnation, 391
Assours and Dewtahs — wars of Cristna with the rebellions, 88
Assyrians, the, 101, 171
————, the Dove their standard, 118
Asteroids—one planet probably split into the four new ones, 335
Asteroth, Astarte, Eostre, or Easter, 58, 59
—————————— from asre, 193
Astle, Mr., 149, 165, 166, 215, 218, 237
Astronomers, the ancient, more probably right in their practice, than the modern in their theory, 330
————; our, if dwelling in Asia, and knowing of the coming of the comet, &c., 333, 334
Astronomical Society, the, will ridicule the subject of Comets, as here treated, 333
Astronomy, the knowledge of, probably long preceded that of syllabic letters, 198
Aswa—horse—from As, to eat, 157
Atamelik Dschowaini, the historian, directed by the Mogul to search the libraries of the Ishmaelites, at Alamout, and to destroy every thing—their instruments, &c.—which could make known the truth, 389, 390
Athanasian Creed, the, 43, 93
Athanasius, 43, 367
Atheism and Deism, the Nyaya and Vedanta philosophies so considered—their advocates changed sides, 428
Athetistical system of quoting, on the continent, 255
Atheists — the Sacæ, Saxons or Buddhists, so called by the followers of Cristna, &c., 428
Atheneus, 145, 204
———— on a Pythagorean dancer, 425
Athenians, the, were divided into four castes—the sacerdotal nobles, soldiers, farmers, tradesmen—and a fifth, the slaves or outcasts, 418
Athens, 47, 97, 418, 419
————, the Pandion of, 117
————, secret names of, 242
————, the ancient year of, was 360 days, 319, 320
————, in the Areopagus of, we have the domestic, in the Amphictyons the superintending legislature, 350
Atibahica—an atom-like germ so called, in Sanscrit, 398
Atlantic, the, 312
Atlantis, the island of, 39, 40
————, the flood which drowned, 305
————, may have been sunk by the last of several shocks, 311
Atomic doctrine, the, of Pythagoras, said to have been learned by him from Moses, 399

Atonement, pernicious doctrine of the, 203, 367
Atreus, father of the Heraclidæ, 119
Atreus, in the time of, the motion of the firmament had changed, 314
Atri, father of the Hericlūs, 119
Attalus (king)—grammar brought by his ambassador—Crates Malotes—to the Roman Senate, 195
Attica, Ionia, and Etruria, the confederated towns or states of, 394
Attila, 375
Atys, 102, 104
————, suspensus in ligno, 104, 106
————, raised on third day, 106, 122, 145
Atyses, Adonises, &c., &c., put to death, &c., 142
Atzala Isurani, 7
Aube, an, 79
Augur—when an Etruscan began his divinations, he rose in the stillness of midnight, to determine the limits of the celestial temple, 407
Auguries—uncertain how the Roman priests got the custom established of taking them, before any assembly could proceed to business, &c., 407
Augurs, the, their power, 52, 53
————, the lituus of, because the crosier, 78
Augusta, 70 cities so called in honour of Augustus ; probably these were 72 ecclesiastical capitals of districts into which the empire was divided, 421
Augustine or Austin, 22, 37, 58, 65, 74, 76, 367
———— sent to Britain to convert the natives, 93
———— De Esu Agni, &c., 104
———— converted the Saxons of Kent, 281
————, on the Antediluvian years, and on the intercalary days, 320
———— on a month, as 30 days, 321, 326
————, Theodoret, Basil, and pope Innocent I., on the Christian mysteries, &c., 441
Augustinians, the, 76
Augustus, a title given to the Nile, 54
————, Octavius, 54, 56
————, the Auσν των αιωνων the Genius of the Ninth Sæculum, 56, 251
———— was called Divus, 80
———— ordered the Compitales to be honoured with garlands, 99
———— erected the temple of Jupiter Tonans, 91
————, described, by Horace, as the son of Maia, 357
———— Cæsar offered up 300 human victims, in one night, at Perugia, 416
Aulaif, killed by black Gauls, and by Albanos! 304
Aura placida, made into St. Aura and St. Placida, 85
————, Anima, or Holy Ghost—in ancient times always female—proceeded from the Tò Oν, 397
Aurelian, 134
Auricular Confession. — 34
———— enables rogues to tyrannize over fools, 74, 75

Australia, 2, 341, 419
Austria and Russia, the emperors of, probably actuated by the mythos of legal descent from Noah, 354
Author, the, right of, to the name of a Christian, 120, 449
————, object of, not to attack religion—his wish to be impartial, 132
————, a future life awaited by, with hope and humble resignation, 308
————, affirms the truth of no more of Mr. Whiston's system, than what he expressly mentions as adopting, 435
————, wishes to be considered a member of the Eclectic or Philalethean sect, 448
————, whether, he was fully satisfied with the evidence of Irenæus, that Jesus Christ was not crucified, 449
Autumnal Equinox, 83
Avatar (is probably Abba-Tur), 14, 38, 39, 51
————, Moses an, 14
————, Nero claimed to be the Tenth, 54
————, the crucifixion of every, 118
————, the new, the followers of, protected by arms, 219
————, the tenth, chief of the Assassins, came from Ghilan, 231
————, Gengis Khan, by his partisans, made out to be the Tenth, 353
————, the last believed to be yet to come, 354
Avatars, 40
————, or incarnations, 81
————, eight in Siam, 139
————, all Asiatic princes pretended to be, 207
————, the ten, 248, 354
————, of Cristna, Christ, and Mohamed, 355
Axibus lignois, or on stems of trees, 249
Axis, the, may have been suddenly changed, as the book of Enoch says, 310, 313, 332
————, may have been changed by various shocks, 311
————, sudden change of the earth's —the year changed in consequence, from 360 to 365 days, &c., 315
————, changed at the time of the flood, and almost all the ancient learning of the world lost, 439
Ayodia, the place of wisdom, 188
Ayodia, 16, 21, 36
————, or Oude, 122
————, language of, 156
————, Eastern, 16, 181
————, Western, 36
Ayub or Job, book of, from Upper India to Arabia, 128
Azores, the, 35
Aztekan, the, 26
Azteks, the, 31

B and v permutable in Sanscrit, 226
Baal or Bel, 74, 82
————, priests of, 74, 87
————, is Samhan, 82
Babel (tower of), 24, 25, 27—29, 324

INDEX.

	Page
Baber, Mr.,	262
Babington, Dr., on Tamil or Tamul characters,	148
Babylon, 12, 28, 46, 48, 97, 133, 146, 171,	350
———, mythos of, in Mexico,	28
———, Scarlet Whore of,	46
———, compass of the walls of, 360 furlongs, same as the year of 360 days,	317
———, built by Xisuthrus's children,	322
——— or Oude, the Archierarch-son of Noah—may have resided at,	399
Bacab, the Son, in the Mexican Trinity,	32
Bacchus, 6, 8, 9, 19, 23, 29, 40, 59, 103, 104, 106, 112, 137 164, 202, 224, 253, 271,	292
———, the Grecian—an Egyptian	19
———, cut in pieces on Mont Marte, 59,	8
———, tomb of, became church of St. Baccus,	74
———, worshiped as St. Denis, at Paris—as Liber or Liberius, at Ancona,	84
———, the temple of, now church of Holy Liberius,	91
———, Adonis, and Osiris, were all incarnate Gods,	98
———, was a personification of the Sun,	100
———, his birth-place disputed—was worshiped chiefly at Teimissus,	102
———, conquests of, like Plagues of Egypt,	105
———, raised on the third day,	122
———, the search for his members, 136,	142
———, strangled the serpent,	144
———, called Liber, Boc, Book—and, in Siam, Kiaklak,	163, 164
———, orgies of,	166
———, monogram of, Mn=650, 187,	223
———, was Buddha, Noah, Menu, Janus,	223
———, Bromos, Bruma, Piroma, Pi Brama,	243
———, liber, letters, language, logos, linga, wisdom,	244
———, was wine, Ceres bread,	253
———, Deo-nisi	288
———, was Om-adios—the holy Om,	302
———, Hercules, Jove, there never was a,	351
———, the Nysian dances sacred to,	425
Bacchuses, &c., put to death, &c.,	142
Bacon, Roger, 165, 280,	342
———, on the knowledge possessed by,	246
———, probably a Rosicrucian,	301
———, may have known of the disturbing forces of the comets, &c.,	335
———, the Brazen Head of, &c.,	349
Bactria, the Sacæ possessed themselves of,	4
Bad, a name of Buddha,	162
Baden—curious secret prisons under a convent at,	301
Bagdad, in the meeting of Jarissi, in 1011, the proceedings were secret; why?	359

	Page
Bagdad, the Calif at, probably, paid tribute and did homage to Gengis,	383
———, at a great meeting at, in A. H., 402, the claims of the Fatémites to the Califate declared null and void,	385, 386
Bagphps (Scotch),	91
——— of Calabrian shepherds,	90, 91
Baidh or Vaedh, a prophet,	225
Baids—vates, fates—tellers of truth or wisdom,	ib.
Bailly;	3, 140
——— on Chinese letters—division of, into fives,	215
——— on the learning of the ancients,	246, 444
——— on the first race of men, after the flood, having been situated east of the Caspian Sea—in a country between 40 and 50° of North latitude—possessed of profound wisdom, of elevated genius, and of an antiquity far superior to the Egyptians and Indians,	444
——— ridiculed by Sir W. Jones, &c., for teaching that man was created in Tartary,	445
Bala Raja of Gujerat,	221
Balaam, the prophecy of,	97, 98
Balbec (Bal-bit, house of Bal), the temple at, has 40 pillars,	402
Balbi, M., on Chinese related to Hebrew,	148, 155, 156
———, on the Buddhist religion,	289
———, on the works, &c., of the Mexicans, Javanese, &c.,	316
Bal-ii, the crucified God, 122, 296, 259,	288
Balisms, the, of Ceylon, and the Baltan fires of Ireland and the Highlands of Scotland,	289
Baliji, Balii, or Balji, 115, 118,	288
Balk and Bokhara both called Cabbat alaslam, the Dome or Vault of Mohamedism,	303
Balkan (may mean Bal-ania, land of Bal), a ridge of mountains which divides North India or Oude from Tartary, and another which divides Thrace from Scythia or Tartary,	414
Balks, strips of land, not subinfeudated, but the property of the Lord of a Manor,	ib.
Bal-Sab, Lord of Death, Samhan or Beelzebub,	82, 83
Bambinos,	100, 129
——— and Madonnas,	242
Baunier explained mythology historically,	360
Baptism, 64, 66, 67, 69, 70, 262, 279,	289
———, older than the time of Jesus—practised by the followers of Zoroaster, &c.,	64
———, practised by the Jews, Greeks, and nearly all nations, before the existence of Christianity,	65, 66, 232
———, Christening, and Confirmation, rites of the Magi,	66
——— with the Holy Ghost, with fire, water, and blood,	67
———, in doctrine and outward ceremony, Etruscan,	69
———, Christian, called the 'aver of regeneration,	ib.

	Page
Baptism of Bells—in China,	70
———, the rite universal, and a name given at, to the children of the Assassins, Carmelites, Druids, &c.,	248
———, the, of water, fire, and air—whence,	336
———, the Eucharist, &c., only part of the Christian mysteries, according to Augustin, Basil, &c.,	441
Βαπτισμα, baptism,	64, 68
Βαπτισμοι, washings,	64
Bar and Par meant a judge,	275
Baralt—wisdom—the first book of Genesis,	226, 251
———, probably the knowledge of the Trimurti, and the secret use of the system of cycles,	342
———, Jews and Christians say it means cosmogony; it taught the nature and attributes of the TrOr, the metempsychosis, emanation, &c.,	343
Bards, the, an order to regulate the choirs, &c.,	233
Bareich—Parish, 276,	279
———, was this Bar-roi or Barrex?	292
———, or Borough,	297
Baris (ship), Ararat,	411
——— and Cordi, the centre of Agrimensorius of Asia,	412
——— or Ararat, was believed to be the highest mountain in the world; from this as a centre, a cardo, Noah was supposed to have divided the world among his three sons,	412
Barker, J. T.,	358, 366
Barnabas, St.,	211, 343, 344
Barnes, Dr., Joshua,	19
Baronius (Cardinal), 52, 79, 94, 66, 87, 93,	112
Barons, the, claimed of the priests an acknowledgment of superiority—this granted with a mental reservation of the rights of the church.	266, 267
———, few of, could read,	268
———, the great, (not like our present Peers, mere animals of ornament,) said to have been from 50 to 80—but probably were 72 in number,	417
Barret, on the Zodiacs,	36
Barrett's, Dr., Enquiry into the Constellations,	316
Bartolin,	360
Basil, on Christian mysteries,	441
Βασιλευς also τον ανθρωπ,	51
Basnage, 37, 51, 83, 135, 186, 190, 201, 203, 204, 210,	221
Basque and American languages, analogy of the,	27
Bassianus—Antoninus Heliogabalus,	349
Bath, remains at, of only one temple of the Romans, in Britain,	281
Bathkol—daughter of voice—rather daughter of wisdom,	295
Bavani,	6
Bayer, on Greek way of writing,	190
——— on Brahmun characters from the Estrangelo, 153,	222
———, on the 9 simple characters of the Chinese,	215
Bazin, l'abbé, 17, 19, 134, 143,	363
BD, the Creator, the giver of forms,	162

VOL. II. 3 O

INDEX.

	Page
Bead (Catholic beads) from Ved or Wisdom,	179
Bealtine, feast of the fires of Baal,	82
Beans, the, of Pythagoras,	239, 240, 300
Bearded men and Negroes found in South America,	35
Beast, the number of the,	241
Beausobre, M.,	60, 65, 77, 101
Bed, ved, vates—a prophet, wisdom,	227
Beda or Veda means book,	8
Bedas or Vedas,	4, 43, 88, 225
Bede,	135
———'s houses—houses of Buddha or Wisdom,	295
Bedoween Arabs,	4
Bedoweens, the, speak pure Arabic, are Buddhists, Tatars, followers of Tat,	207, 208
——————, have no fixed habitations,	271
—————— or Bedouins, the nomade tribes of Africa and Asia,	275
Bédu (Buddha),	207
Beech and Oak, the, gave out oracles at Dodona,	165
Beelzebub,	82, 83
——— or Baal Zebub,	83
Beeve, the,	23, 110
———, both Cow and Bull,	181
——— and sheep; the Ram and Rama meant both,	212
Beguines, monks and nuns in Tibet,	127, 218
Belgic Suesones,	1
Belief or faith held to be meritorious,	107
Below,	180
Bellarmine,	69, 77, 88
Bellona,	74, 86
————, priests of,	74
Bells and pomegranates on highpriest of the Jews, and on the kings of Persia,	69
———, baptizing of, a bull issued for; practised in China,	70
———, four baptized at Versailles, in 1824, Louis XVIII. and Duchesse D'Angoulême being spousors,	70
———, ringing of a little, in worship, a Pagan usage,	91
Belshazzar, the writing on the wall of,	186
Belus, the tower of,	27, 28
Benares, anciently called Casi,	135
———, the college at,	206
———, in the temple of Vis Vishu, at, there is a Corinthian pillar,	402
———, a tradition at, that all the learning of India came from a country situated in 40 degrees of north latitude—that of Samarkand,	444
Benedictines, the,	76
Benefit of Clergy, used as a test, &c.,	271
Ben-gal, i. e. Beni — the sons of Gall,	291
———, the Zemindars of, recognized as princes,	374
———, the king of, *heir* to all men,	421
Beni-Gael—the Gael from the,	294
Beni-Suef,	230
Benjamin, the tribe of,	19
Ben-Lomond—was this, Son of Lomond?	292

	Page
Ben-Nevis, Ben-Navis, *Mount of the Ship*,	292, 294
Bennet's, Solomon, plan of Ezekiel's temple,	402
Bentley,	5, 139, 144, 236
———, on the digamma,	169
Bere-gonium, once the capital of Scotland,	292, 411
Bergeron,	215
Berkeley,	217
Bernier,	263
Berosus, on antediluvian kings,	321, 322
————, on the time of the flood,	327
————, on the Ark resting on the mountains των κορδυαιων,	411
Bertolacci, on the whole land in Ceylon, the property of the crown,	418
Beth, the birch, the second letter of the Tree alphabet,	148
Bethlehem,	95, 96, 98, 99, 109
————— profaned by Adrian,	95, 96
—————, the stable at, a *cave*,	95, 99
————— means City of the House of the Sun,	99
————, the house of the *male* Ceres, &c., from ♄ the emphatic article, and ⌂ח, a corruption of Om—house of Om,	303
Beverley (Mr.),	88
Bhobanéser, the Linga in the cave at,	259, 260, 262
Bhoees, the, Garuda, and temple of Carnac, in France,	296
Bhoomia—Bhumia—*ia-b-om*, land of Om,	284
Bhoomias, the, preceded the Zemindars,	ib.
Bhuvanéswara or Ekamra—city of ⌂ח hkm, the God of wisdom,	260
Bibi-Mariam ou *la Dame Marie*,	97
Bible, the,	27
———, on age of man,	133, 134
———, history of, found in India and Egypt,	293
———, on the time of the flood,	327, 328
Biblis, birth of the God Sol, as Adonis; celebrated at,	98
Biblos and Bochara, both mean *city of the book*,	311
Bingham says, Christians were first called *Christs*,	251, 344
Binothris, Bu-Thré or Ben-Terah,	14
Birmingham,	297
Birth, death, and resurrection, the, of the incarnate God, the doctrine of, common in Pagan temples,	95, 96, 98–100, 102
Bisnt-al-Guaém, "*Display of the Foe*," or the year 1204 of the Hegira,	182, 183
———, is an acrostic,	185
Bishop, Cardinal, Dean, Diocese, Ecclesiastical, Priest, Religion, in their origin, all terms of judiciary import,	272, 279
Bishops, Suffragan, baptized bells,	70
———, Secular, procured from Rome by barons and kings, in opposition to the Regulars,	276
———, Palatine, the, originally mitred Abbots,	277, 278
———, Arch, the, of York and Canterbury, dispute between, for precedence, why,	281
———, in Partibus	285
Bissextile day or days, intercalary, &c.,	320

	Page
Bital or Fanum, the, the first residence of the Abba,	297
Bithynia,	7?
————, the Christians of,	90
Black God, the, in the Casa Santa, at Loretto,	57
———— *Boy*, the, the sign of, probably an infant Cristna; Mother and Child,	100
———— *Gauls*, in Scotland,	204
———— races became white by intermarriages, &c.,	363
———— Gods, *genus* and *species*, &c.,	ib.
———— *Stone*, the, in Westminster Abbey, adored,	437
Blackstone,	264, 265, 268, 269
Blair, Dr., on the time of the flood,	332
Blond,	53
Blondus,	74, 76
Blunt, Mr., on ancient customs of Italy and Sicily,	92
Boadicea—Chivalry probably flourished most, when she led her 80,000 knights to combat,	204
Bobeloth and Bethluisnion Alphabets, the,	155
Boc, book, liber, name of Bacchus,	8, 163, 164, 265, 271, 292
———manni, Monks or Book-men,	264, 268
Boch-ara, the city of the book,	272, 311
Bocharia,	444
Bochart,	47, 59, 181, 287, 290, 412
——— on adoration of Saints,	31
Bochica, founder of the Peruvian nation,	34
————, the Mithra or Osiris of Bogota,	ib.
Bocklands—free-lands,	272, 284
Bogota, form of government given to, by Bochica,	34
Bogstav, Buckstab, Book-staves, (book,) the triangular staves on which the Runes were written,	272
Bokhara, mythos brought from, to Ireland,	97
Bombay Transactions, the,	355, 356, 360
Bœtus—the stone on which the Vaid or Druid stood to preach,	302
⌂ב״ן *bnim*, filii, confounded with ⌂ב״ן *abnim*, lapides; hence the story of Deucalion and Pyrrha having repeopled the earth with *stones*,	18
Bon, a Silver lamb, with a glory, in the cathedral of,	112
Bones of the Son of the Spirit of Heaven,	103
Bonnaud, M.,	18
————, the Abbé, Jaques-Jules,	221
Bono Deo Puero Posphoro,	100
Bonzes, the, use the tonsure, &c.,	228
Book, a, in Irish, called *burac* or *barc*,	163
Book, the Pope (by Constantine's gift) ruled Italy, &c., by right of the,	345
Book and *Sword*, Cæsar held by the right of the,	379, 400
————, right by the, claimed by the emperors of Germany and Russia,	380
Borak, the, or flash of lightning, on which Mohamed said he passed through the seven heavens, &c.,	378
Borlase,	97, 225
Boro Bodo—Bra Buddha,	218

INDEX.

	Page
Bosio, Antonio,	111
Bosworth's Saxon Grammar,	195
Βοτρυς, grape, 9, 204, 223, 253,	254
Bottarini,	25
Boucher, 153,	163
Boustrophedon style, the, the Runes once written in,	305
Boutta, Boto, Buddha,	9
Boy Gods adopted in Italy as Bambinos,	100
Boys, believed by the *fathers*, to be defiled by demons,	ib.
Bower,	58
Bowll, the, of India, probably the Piscina,	69
Bra or Pra, means *factor*, 243, Creator,	267
Braga—the deity of eloquence, &c., hence *to brag*,	300
Brahme or Bacchus or Liber,	8
———— Maia,	129
————, the *male*, the followers of,	42b
————, brooding over the deep, a microcosm of,	429
Brahma,	7, 8
———— means *leaf*—the same as Brahaspati,	8
————, the religion of,	58
———— as supreme God, surrounded with good and bad angels,	88
———— period, the, began 3164 years B. C.,	144
————, born from the Supreme Being,	175
———— or Brama, is often called Birouma,	243
————, the propagator of the human race, the architect of all things, &c.,	397
————, the *day* of, and the *night* of,	409
————, after a year of (4,320,000,000 of years), the philosophers looked for a restoration of a perfect globe; of the planetary system and fixed stars to their first state,	431
Brahmin, the, (Abraham,) who founded the Judæan state, came from the East—from Ur or Uriana of Collida,	257
———— church, little of its domestic economy known; may have imitated its Buddhist predecessors,	370
Brahminism was but Protestant Buddhism—the effects of, the reform of the calendar, to assimilate it to the state of the heavens —Taurus no longer its emblem, but Aries,	438
————, traits of, often seen in the West,	439
Brahmins, Brachmans, the, 48— 50, 98, 138—140, 409,	434
————, the, turn to the East at worship,	89
————, the rites of the,	115
————, of India and of Italy, secret system of the, lost,	138
————, the modern, ignorant of the necessity of intercalary days,	144
————, the, hold the Sanscrit to be absolutely perfect,	157
————, the most learned, can scarcely read, &c., the first Veda,	159
————, the call their first Veda, *Rich—ves* or *wisdom*,	226
————, the, on a lost language,	234
————, the, from North India,	274, 369

	Page
Brahmins, the, have a tradition that the flood happened when the sun entered Aries, &c.,	332
————, say, in the Vedas may be found the logic of Aristotle and the philosophy of Plato, &c.,	337
————, said to allow the divine incarnation of Jesus Christ; but contend, that Cristna, also, was incarnated for the salvation of all who believe on him,	341
————, or Hindoos, maintain that they came from Tartary,	352
————, averse to proselyting,	363
———— and Buddhists—the precursors of their skill in the fine arts,	364
————, in the democracy of, we have the mixed system of the Protestants; they receive divine wisdom by succession, &c.,	368
———— and Buddhists, the, changed sides, as Atheists and Deists. The Brahmins (like the Jews with *Baruch* and *Mercavah*) have substituted *Nyaya* and *Vedanta* the one for the other,	428
————, traits of the, in the West —Buddhists and Brahmins in all great points the same,	438
Bramin, a priest of Bra, the factor M, or Om,	243
Brassey, Nathaniel,	355
Bread and wine, sacrifice of, 58, 59	
————, converted into a horrible mystery, 63,	68
————, and water, sacrifice of,	59
———— and water, offered by the Magi, Essenes, Gnostics, Eastern Christians, and by Pythagoras and Numa,	60
Brechin, the *fire-tower* of,	119
————, the *man crucified*, and Lamb and Elephant, on the,	130
Brehon laws, the,	283
Brewster, Dr., on the Eclectics, or *Analogetici*,	447
Brigantes, the,	298
———— and Briges, of Asia Minor, whence the name of Phrygians, Free, and Phriga and Freya,	412
Briggs, Mr., (on Land Tax of India,)	266, 272
————, on the Aborigines of South India,	274
————, on the subdivision of territory in India,	277
————, on the heir of Mohamed, &c.,	352, 383
————, on the *tenth* paid in Persia, Judæa, China, &c.,	418
Britain, 4, 57, 70, 99, 106, 279,	281, 282
————, the worship of Mithra spread over,	99
————, Hebrew and Indian words in,	176
————, the castes in—the nobles, clergy, esquires, tradesmen, paupers—the *out-caste*, as in India,	271
————, conquered by the Romans —why,	304

	Page
Britain, gradually colder, proved by tithe suits, on wine,	312
————, the secret mythos existed in, before Cæsar's arrival,	349
————, the first system had gone to pieces when Cæsar arrived; the Buddhist government had been overthrown by that of Cristna,	370
————, its constitution like that of Rome,	375
————, divided into *three*, by the Romans divided into five dioceses,	400
————, the causes of effects, *since* the Roman conquest of, looked for; instead of those before the arrival of the Romans,	432
Britons, the ancient, divided the country into tithings, &c.,	300
————, went *naked*—in battle only—to distinguish clan from clan?	304
————, Roman accounts of the barbarism of,	415
————, if the, were barbarians for offering human sacrifices, Augustus Cæsar was a barbarian, &c.; sufficiently civilized to bring into the field large bodies of Charioteers, &c., and to manœuvre them in the manner practised by the Greeks, &c.,	416
Brothers, 131, 346,	358
————, &c., &c., the followers of, expect a re-incarnation of Jesus Christ—the *tenth* Avatar, 258,	354
————; Whitfield, Wesley, and Southcote—the followers of, weak men,	342, 377
———— and Southcote have had able, &c., followers,	355
————, had not the general belief of *the promised one*, in their favour,	356
Brute (king) and the Troya Nova, of,	349, 412
Brutus, grandson of Æneas, having killed his father Sylvius, fled from Italy, landed at Totness, conquered the island of Great Britain, and divided is among his three sons, &c.,	409, 412
———— and his three sons—here we, have the old mythos, like Adam, and Cain, Abel, and Seth; or Noah, and Shem, Ham, and Japhet,	401, 412
Bryant; 46, 58, 95, 100, 110, 112,	135, 160, 229
Bucer,	88
Buchanan (Dr.),	96
———— on the temple of Juggernaut,	206, 207
Buckingham,	65
Bud,	83
————, is B=2, D=4=6, the root of 432,	181
Budda, Old Man, the,	4
Budh, Buth or Both, in Old Irish, means the sun, fire, universe,	287
Buddha, 1—3; 7—9, 23, 31, 34, 36, 43, 56, 60, 103, 104, 148, 170, 202, 209, 210, 221, 225,	282
———— was Sacya, or Saca, 1, 3, 6, 27, 148,	226
————, statues of, spared by Mohamedans	2
————, Deus Bonsiorum,	5

INDEX.

Buddha, means book, 8—was Hermes, 31
——— son of Maya, 103
———, entombment and resurrection of, 103, 105,..142, 145
———, sacrificing his life, a type of *the* Saviour, 118
———, Bauddha, or Abad or Abaddon, 133
———, mysteries of, a man supposed to be killed in, 143
———, called Bad, from Ba *father* and Di *holy*, 162
———, divine wisdom, 182, 250
———, was a Menu or Nu, Mani, 224
———, means Veda, 225
———, said to have been crucified for robbing a garden of a flower, 244, 248, 249, 256, 415
———, the Linga worship of, 260
———, the followers of, affected the *male* principle, 269, 445
———, called Sacm, 275
———, in Pegu and Ceylon, *sleeping*, overshadowed by *nine* cobras, an emblem of the cycles, 286
———, who robbed the garden, a renewed Adam, 288
———, the system of, of renewed incarnations, &c., 307
———, believed to be a divine incarnation, as well as Jesus Christ, 343
———, his æra probably began with his supposed death, 347
———, the simple icons of, preserved by the Mohamedans, 352
——— and Cristna, the Gods, describe the Sun or the Higher Principle of which it is the Shekinah, but were probably men, governing large nations, in whom a portion of the God was incarnated, 356
———, stories respecting the second, third, &c., ib.
——— and Cristna, the ancient religions of, like the ancient Roman secret religion, 366
———————— the partizans of the religions of, the same, though hating each other, 369
———————— and the Callidel—we should not find the, in Britain and Ireland, had not the same thing taken place here, as in India, 370
———, the, of Wales, Ireland, Scotland, and India, always called Old Man, why, 389
——— and the Pandæan kingdom represented by the Archierarch—thought to be the first incarnation, 399
———————— would represent Noah-Menu. Buddha and Menu were qualities, appellatives personified, 400
———, the religion of, coming to the West—the idea may be revolting to some persons, yet facts prove it—from Iona in Scotland to Iona in Ceylon, from Tanga Tanga in Tartary and China, to Tanga Tanga in Peru, 424
Buddhas, books of wisdom, 4
———, incarnations of, 129
———, &c., put to death, &c., 142
Buddhism, 34
————, the Pandæan, Catholic or Universal, 175

Buddhism, the universal prevalence of, a fact, not a theory, 307
Buddhist religion, the, in Tibet, similar to that of Rome, 258
——————— many remains of, in Ireland, 287
———————, older than the Brahmin, 289
Buddhists, the, 4, 9, 10, 50, 221
———————, &c., marked with a sign, 174
——————— or Quakers, a nation of, can exist only on the sufferance of their neighbours, 203
———————, kept the system of figures unimproved, 218
———————, of Tibet, hold the Grand Lama to be Buddha reincarnated, 245
———————, when they inhabited this island, 286
———————, that *the*, were Negroes, the icons of the God clearly prove, 364
——————— and Brahmins, the, clearly marked by Porphyry, 368
———————, the distinction between, became lost, 369
———————, the, were hierists and archierists, 370
———————, during the Mahabarat, were followers of the *Nyaya*, the Brahmins of the *Vedanta*—but they afterwards changed sides, &c., 428
——————— and Vishnuvites, division between, ib.
———————, the, the monastic system among, how kept up, 434
——————— and Brahmins, in all great points, the same, 438
Budwas Trigeranos, 4
————————, Trivicrama-ditya or Buddha with the triple energy, 178
Buffon, Linné, &c., their speculations on the origin of man, on his being created, and the arts and sciences taking their rise not far from the Arctic circle, 444
———————, ridiculed by Sir W. Jones, &c., for teaching that man must have been created in Tartary, 445
Buffoonery, 179, 212
Bull, the, worshipers of, 104
———, equinoctial sign of, 105, 110
———, passage of, to Aries, 106
———, is succeeded by *the lamb without blemish*, 110
——— or Ox, the, of Oxford, 287
———, the sectaries of, became sectaries of the Ram, 368
Bulla, the, worn by Roman children, 87
———, in the form of a heart, originally of a calf, as now of a lamb,—the Agnus Dei, 413
Burckhardt, 65
Burgage, nearly the same as Soccage, tenure—applicable to towns—shews identity of the Sacra of Tartary and Britain, 268
Burman empire—one *truth* is paid in the, 418
Burnet, 42, 49, 50
———, T., said, SAPIENTIÆ PRIMA EST, STULTITIA CARUISSE, 132

Burnet, Gilbert, on Tithes, 266
Barton, on land in England in Allodial dominion, 284
Bute, the island of, so called from Buddha, 287
Butler, 81
Butts—Buddha, 3
Buttevant, Buddha-fan, Buddha had a temple at, 287
Buxtorf, 3, 89
Buzengir—gir-zaba, cycle of wisdom—was reported to be the son of the Sun, and the ninth predecessor of Gengis Khan, 353
Bya, Bis-ja, Double-ja, Male and Female, 174
Byzantium—the false Alexander arrived at, &c., as he had prophesied, 348

Ca, the pronoun I, in Siam, 229
Caaba or Caavah, the name of Mohamed's temple, 39?
————, derived from the end of Mercavah or Mercaba, the, with its 360 pillars, was the temple or circle or wheel of Mohamed, 401
————, the, besides the 360 stones around, had a *black* stone in the centre, still adored as the emblem of the sun or generative principle. Originally it had a dove or Iune, as an object of adoration. Is said to have been planned in heaven, i. e. after the pattern of, &c., 402
Cabala, the Jewish, 321, 350, 428
————, the, unwritten doctrine, 232
————, the object of Christ was, to open it to the world, 253, 409
————, the, consisted of two branches—*Bareset* and *Mercavah*, 342
————, on the Tetragrammaton, &c., 346
————, a reason for the care to conceal, 364
———— or Gnosis, the doctrines of, taught in the *old* and *new* academy of Egypt, 387
————, the religion of, its progress from *simplicity* to *complication*, 402, 403
Cabalistic Jews, the, 6
————, doctrines of Moses, Pythagoras, and Jesus, the same, 396
Cabiri, the, 433
Cadmean letters, the, in the Irish alphabets, 155
————, on tripods, 294
———— system, the, kept a masonic secret, 218
Cadmus, 169
————, sixteen-letter alphabet of, 206
Cæro, Niebuhr thinks, was the parent city of Rome. If it had been the first Cardo, the peculiar sanctity of Rome unaccountable, 395
Cæsar (Julius), 10, 27, 53, 54, 95, 141, 259, 266, 375
——— or Kaesar, grandson of Noah, 24
———, Kartuetia (Irish)—Ceartluetl (Indo-Scythian) joined to the Mexican Tiutli or Teotli, 25

INDEX.   461

Cæsar, name of the God Mars, 54
———, his birth announced by a star, 95
———, principle of the mythos known in the time of, 134
——— regulated the Calendar, 139, 140, 144, 314, 330, 335
———, on change of lands, among ancient Germans, 283
———, on the Britons' going *naked*, &c., 304
———, believed to be a divine incarnation, 343
——— himself to be the person foretold, 344, 446
———, a kingdom of, expected by the Jews of North India, 345
——— probably conquered Britain and Gaul, by being thought the *Æsar* expected to come, 370
———, the true origin of the name of, is probably Kaisar, 391
——— held by right of the *book* and the *sword*, 400
Cæsarean operation, account of the, a part of the mythos, &c., 345
Cæsari, the mythological character of, 229
Cæsars, the, 56, 446
———, as successors of the, claims made by the emperors of Germany, Russia, &c., 380
Cain, princes in the race of, 133
——— and Abel, the sacrifice in the story of, 203, 361
———, birthright of, forfeited by wickedness—and the death of Abel without issue, &c., 361, 398
———, in the first world, the Destroyer, 430
Cairo, in feet (measure) of, 261
———, the califs of, &c., 385
———, the college at, rebuilt about 1123, A.D, 387
Caius Papirius drove the Saxons into Gaul, 150 years B.C., 271
Cajetau's *Gods by participation*, the same as Plato's *made Gods*, 81
Cal, changed into Gel and Gal—as Camel and Gamel, 295
Calabrian Shepherds, 90, 91
Calany, a river and a temple, in Ceylon, 288
Caledonia—the religious capital of Iona? ib.
———, Albania, and a Milea or Miletia, and Mount Solyma, in Asia Minor—in Britain, Albany, Caledonia, and, in Ireland, the Miletii, 412
Caledonians—Saxons or Celts, 2
Cali, 28, 31, 83
———, the Goddess, from Καλος, *beautiful*, 128, 175, 243, 250
———, the female deity of Love, 135
———, the Goddess of Destruction, 175, 356
———, Cal and Gal in, the same word corrupted, 288, 289
———, may have been Caal=72 or 600, or Eli=60, 293
———, wisdom, 295
——— and *leo*—the God Cali, 28
Calidei, Chaldæi, Callidei or Collidei, the, 2, 135, 141, 171, 243, 261, 262, 294
Cali-dei, Cali-divi or Chaldæans, the 350
———, the, of Iona, were followers of wisdom, 295

Calif—each thought himself the successor of Adam and Noah, 377
———, the, sole-proprietor of the soil, like Cæsar, by right of the Sword and the Book, 379
———, probably paid tribute and did homage to Gengis, at Bagdad, 383
Califate, the, split into parties, after Othman's death, 379
———, why, Hassan Sabah said that, with two friends, he could overthrow the, 382, 383
———, the, was divided into three empires, 384
California, the Gulf of, 38
Califs, the first four, &c., deceived by Mohamed, if he were merely a hypocrite; but their simplicity of life, &c., prove they believed him a divinely commissioned person, 377, 378
———, of Cairo, Bagdad, and Granada, uncertain how the, made out their claims, 385
Caligula, 46
——— and Heliogabalus required the kissing of the foot, 55
Calijug or Caliyug, the, 118, 139 —140, 183, 221
——— the *Iron Age*—Cristna came with, 308
Calinda, 117, 412
Calippus, the ancient astronomer, 320
Callida or Ur of the Chaldees, the country of Abraham, 245, 289, 412
———, now Cochin-Ceylon probably once so called, 288
Calli-dei, the, of South India, 117
Callidei, the, thought to have possessed the dominion of all India, or to have prevailed over it, either by the *sword* or the *crosier*, 396
——— or Chaldæans, the exclusive possessors of science, 424
Callidia—country of the di-cali, or *is* of the holy Cali, 135, 206, 218
Callimachus—his hymn to Apollo, 180, 181
Callixtus.—See Nicephorus.
Calmet, 69, 114, 169
———, on the translation of Ecclesiasticus, and Wisdom, 125, 126
———, on the word Japhet, 400
Calmucs or Calmucks, the, 130
Calvin, John, 73, 131
——— and Luther, afflicted with insanity, 123
———'s dogma of predestined damnation approved in Europe, as the goddess Cali is a favourite in India, 356
——— could not be prudently trusted with the secret doctrine, 367
Calvinism, Grecism, Lutheranism, Papism, Sopheism, Socucism, remakes of the Cyclic system in, 445
Calvinists, genuine, 131
———, the, 132
Calx, calyx, 28
Calydonia of India, of Scotland, 117
Calymua and Calamina, 117, 412
Cam, the, and *Granta*, Indian names of the Cambridge river, 295
Cam-Deo, the God of Love—"Hell's great dread, and Heaven's eternal admiration," 103
Câma, is both Cupid and Venus, 6, 103
———, Cama-Deva, Cor X-sma, 6

Cama, and Cauya, 170
———, Camaria, Coma-rina, &c., 228, 295
———, Cama-rina, Cama-marina—Sea-Goddess, 242
Camasene, the, in India, Cape Coma-rin, and Italy, 127, 262, 296
Camber, to whom his father Brutus gave Wales, hence called Cambria, 400
Cambrians, the, Saxons or Celts, 2
Cambridge, the Domus Templi, at, 250, 287, 387
——— and Oxford—Druidical or Buddhist foundations, 287, 288
——— and Northampton, the churches at, rebuilt on Saxon foundations, 388
——— Key, the, 24, 118, 133, 210, 214, 226
Cambyses, 11, 13
——— left the Lingas, when he destroyed the idolatrous temples of Egypt, 352, 364
Cambyseses, &c., Destroyed books containing the mythos, 352
Camel and *elephant*, the, not in much use where the signs of the Zodiac were invented, 329
Campidolia, the, 74
Canaanites and Phœnicians, the, the religion of, never entirely abolished, but tolerated by the Jews, 96
———, the, when driven out by Joshua, passed along the coast of Africa, to the Straits of Gibraltar, &c., 306, 307
Canada, 28
Canals in China, the, probable object of their construction, 376, 377
Candles and lamps in churches copied from the Egyptians, 79
Candy or Ceylon, 117
Can-la, Γων, the, 249
Cannon ball, the earth's revolution, at the equator, about equal to the velocity of, 312
Canonization of Saints, the, the *apotheosis* of Pagans, 81
Canterbury, the Archbishop of, exchanged lands from tenure by Soccage to tenure by Knighthood, 269
Cantia (Kent)—of Kanya, or *is* of Cunī—Bel? 265
Canticles, the, 45
Capacreyme, festival of, 31
Cape Comarin, (Coma-Marina?) 6, 16
——— Comorin, 232, 257, 295
———, the vernacular language of, and the Celtic Hebrew, the same, in the same country, 294
Cappadocians, the, 111
Capricorn, 139
Car or Cor, for *heart* and *wisdom*, from *res* or *cor*—in Chaldee it read to the *left*, in Coptic to the *right*, but in both meant head, chief, prince, wisdom, 435
Caracorum—suit and service done to the Khan of, as the descendant of Japhet and Noah, 354, 361, 383
———, the Lord of, the Lord Paramount of the Templars, 384
———, the Khan of, invested Gengis Khan, 388
———, the country of, in the year 232, was called *Sten pi Libres*, Sten the Free; in 302

VOL. II.   3 P

INDEX.

des So theou, kingdom of the holy Saviour, &c., &c.; probably all our mythology has come from, 411
Caralites, the, named after Cozar or Cæsar, 135
Caras or Ociras, 14
Cardinales, the, of Rome, like Mohamed's 72 Ausâr or Helpers, 380
——— or centres of measurements, the, probably began at Stonehenge for Britain; or if it was divided into three, Stonehenge was one of the centres, 410
Cardinals, the, adore the Pope, 55, 56
———, so named from being curators of the 72 parishes, &c., into which Rome was divided; perhaps, as Cardinales of the 72 divisions of the Patrimony of St. Peter, i. e. of the whole world, 413, 420, 421
Cardo, a, ran through every capital or principal town, as every nation reckons longitude from its capital, &c., 413
Cardus or termini or mete-stones were all polises. The first, from which all the East or West branched off, was the arco or acro-polis, 410
Carli, 25
Carlisle, Sir Anthony, on à Cromleh, 289
Carmel (Mount), 44, 46, 58
———, the Vineyard or Garden of God, 44, 45, 193, 204, 239, 240
Carmelites, the, and Essenes the same, 44, 45, 141, 248
Carmes—les Druides, 44
Carn, probably the same as Cor—read Hebraicè it meant wisdom, 411
Carnac, in Egypt, 260
———, in Gaul, 261, 296
———, a stone added to, every year, to record the time of the world, 340
Carnate, in, we have the Mosaic mythos, and its two dialects—the Chaldee and Hebrew, 294
———, probably so named from two Carns of St. Thomas, 411
Caruatic, the, the Lingua of, 260—262
Carneaus, the games, &c., of the, were all religious, 425
Carne-vale, a farewell to animal food, 59
Carnival, the, and the Saturnalia, identity of, 86
Carns, they of Ireland, and of Tiber, 179
——— and Tumuli in India, the same as those in Britain, 289
Carnutenslau Virgin, the, 108, 199
Carnutes, the, of Gaul, 55, 87, 108, 109, 130, 259—262
———, the Lamb of, 154
Carthage, 17
Carthaginians, the, 269
Carthusians, the, 47
Carum Gorum (or Caracorum) in Tartary and Scotland — both, perhaps, etymologically the same as Choir Ghaur or Gargarus, 411
Casa Santa, the, at Loretto, 57
Casalius, 110
Casas, Las, 29, 30, 39
Casaubon, Isaac, 84
Cashmere, 4, 16, 24

Cashmere or Afghanistan, 115
Cashl-Mere, 4
Casi-mere, temple of Solomon in, 135, 206, 232
———, two places so called in North India, 135
Casideans, Chasidim, &c., the best calculators of time, 141
Casmillus changed to Camillus, 200
Caspar, Melchior, and Belshazzar, Magi kings, 98
Caspian Sea, the, 4, 24, (called Kisr,) 135
———, 229, (and Euxine,) 231
———, why not the ship (or ark) built on? 311
——— its depression —an immense chasm into which the Volga discharges itself, 333
——— castles in the mountains near, got possession of by Hassan Sabah and his Assassins, 388
Cassiodorus, 20
Cassivellaunus, after he was defeated by Cæsar, disbanded his army, except the warriors of 4000 chariots! 415
Cassock, the Sudra, Tunica, or Zone, 77, 78
———, the ancient Mozzetta and Sottana, 91
Caste—an effect, not an institution, 275, 279, 392, 420
———, the favoured, when their privileges began to be inquired into, 307
Castes, the four—priests, the military, dwellers in towns, and farmers, 271, 283, 392
Castello, 5
Castles, Lord, a ring found near his estate, 130
Cat—the numeral letters clo=600, meant a—thus a cat came to be sacred, 437
Cathedral or Monastery, scarcely an ancient which does not contain some fragment of the old system, 415
Cathedrals and Minsters, all the orders of, monastic—successions of the ancient Roman priesthood and of the Druids, 270, 276, 278, 280, 281, 287, 288
———, formed at last bishoprics or archbishoprics, 284
———, the choirs of, built crooked, &c., the knowledge of the astronomical import being lost, 415
Catholic processions are imitations of those of the Pagans, 92
——— Popes, the, have all the rites of the Heathens, 117
———, the holy, or Pandæan faith, &c., 222, 232
Catholics, the, 3, 72,
Cato, 137, 230
Caves—all the oldest temples of Zoroaster and the Indians, were—in imitation of the vault or wheel of heaven, 401
Caucasus, 413
Cavah, the origin of our word cave, 402
Cecrops said to have divided the Athenians into four tribes—these probably into three peoples, and each people into 30 parts, 418

Cedrenus, 104
Ceilan or Coilan—Ceylon—the accusative of Κοιλος, the father of Helen, the mystical mother of Constantine, and the Latin name of heaven, 289
Celestial empire—the monarch of, originally thought to be an incarnation of the Solar Ray—whence he is brother of the Sun and Moon. The integrity of its institutions, from the earliest times, preserved by its symbolic alphabet, 396
Celibacy, 47
———, the doctrine of Devils—in high esteem among the Pagans, ib.
Celibate Catholic, the, and the marrying Protestant clergy, are a copy of the monks of Tibet, and of the Brahmius, of India, 434
Cellarius, on Mount Taurus, 411
Cells or stalls, 178
Celsus, 80, 95
——— on use of images, 80
Celtæ, the, 203
———, were Scythians, and Galli or Gauls, 268, 273
Celtic, the, 20, 165, 166, 170, 171, 181, 197, 206, 230
———, five dialects of,—Scotch, Manks, Irish, Welsh, and Cornish, 20, 159, 267
———, or Hebrew, 130, 155
——— Hebrew, the, the parent of all the languages in a primeval state, 259
———, the, is Hebrew, i. e. Chaldee, and vernacular in South India, 289
———, the six dialects of, 290
———, of Scotland and Ireland, difference of, 295
———, the five dialects of, now different languages, 369
CELTIC DRUIDS, the, 82, 83, 119, 128, 130, 147, 149, 154, 155, 197, 206, 220, 286, 287, 290, 293, 296, 298, 302, 305, 306, 315, 444
———, see the, on Sacred Stones, 403
——— tribes, all the, were Xacæ or Saxæ, so called from their religion, 280
Celts, the, 62
———, ancient, opened their public councils by an invocation of the Holy Ghost, 299, 337
———, of Gaul—confederated states amongst whence arose the system, 395
Censeo, I think—Cen, Xn=650—a census, 302
Censorinus, 314, 325
Centeotl, is Cau or Canteotl, 32
Ceres, 77, 79, 86, 91, 99, 161, 202
———, Eleusinian mysteries of, celebrated twice a year, 91
——— or Χρης of Eleusis and Delphi, 117
——— identified with Bacchus and Apollo, 262
———, flour offered to, in the Eucharistia, 242, 244
——— or Proserpine, sacrifices offered to, in an island near Britain, 262
Ceylon, 9, (or Candy,) 117, 156, 165, 218, 221, 259, 262, 277, 280

INDEX. 463

	Page
Ceylon, its history, &c.,	288—294
———, the districts or circles of,	263, 303
C, G, and K, the change in, as, Cor, Gar, Kardu, &c.,	412, 414
Chaoties or Chaons, from *auv* aspirated,	135
Chair of St. Peter, signs of the Zodiac on the,	57
Chalcidius,	96
Chalcis, Mount,	117
Chaldæan loudi, the, adored *fire* as the emblem of creative wisdom and power, or as the Wisdom and Power itself,	128
——— priests, the, alone understanding the secret of writing, were all magi or magicians, and masters of the world,	175, 214
——— Celtic Sacæ, the conquering tribes of, when they arrived in a new country, supposed to have established their own feudal tenure, subinfeudating the land, in part, to the descendants of the antediluvians or aborigines, but reserving to the rulers — the priests—the *tenths*,	435
Chaldæans, the, 26, 28, 50, 139, 147, 362	
———, the incarnate God, crucified by,	117
———, on the race of Cain,	133
———, called the Phœnix בלב *klo*,	183
———, from central Asia, the inventors of the syllabic system,	205, 245, 248
———, why called Sabæans,	220
———, divided into different bodies, like Masons, &c.,	248
———, and other ancient nations, called the sun *Bal*,	289
———, held comets to be planets,	314
——— or Jews, the, knew the period of the comet, but made a mistake in calculating backwards,	328
———, inventors of the Neros, probably understood the theory of comets,	330
———, the *black*—high science of the,	363
Chaldean astronomers worshiped the new-born God,	96
——— magicians or conjurors,	142
———, Druidical, or Brahmin caste, from the East, took possession of the countries of the Aborigines,	392
Chaldeans, the,	2, 3, 138, 139, 141
———, were Chasdim, or the Chasdim were Chaldeans,	135
———, Jews, and Arabians, their languages connected dialects of one language,	274
Chaldee, the, the language of North and South India,	128, 135, 166
———, square letter, the primeval language of the East,	153
———, alphabet is Estrangelo, &c., &c.,	206, 239
——— or Hebrew, the original root of the Sanscrit,	236, 237
Chaldees, if originally Negroes, &c.,	364
Chaldei or Mathematici, the, Josephus says, handed down the cycle from the Antediluvians,	135
———, the first account of, in the Buddhist history of Genesis—both, of West and East, from Upper India,	257
Chaldei, an order of, escaped from a flood, and, by their learning, established a universal pontifical government,	309
Chalidi, the, followers of Cali,	135
Champollion, M.,	11
———, his discoveries all delusions,	159
Chandra,	83
——— and Soma, pedigrees in the line of, nonsense,	351
Chang-ti,	36
——— and Tchangti, the Supreme Being,	229
Chaons, the, 3, or Chæones,	135
Chardin,	217, 263, 268, 271, 272, 288
Charlots, the, of the Britons, probably travelled on many of the right-lined roads formed when Abury and Stonehenge were built,	416
Charisties, Caristies, Charistia, the festival of,	62, 64
Charlemagne, probably claimed to be universal monarch, as successor to Augustus; his paladins and Roncesvalles, &c.,	356
Charlevoix's Histoire de Japon,	367
Charms and amulets, ancient, retained in Italy,	92
——— against witches, evil dæmons, &c., once common among the lower orders, in Britain,	350
Chartres, the stone in the cathedral of, the same as the Linga,	259, 260
Chart (χαρτις) and Cart (Gaelic) connected with letters, the agrimensorial measurement of land, and with wheels,	413
Chasdim, the, or Kasdim or Casidi-im, were Kasideans,	135
Chasuble,	64
Chati, same as Sacti or Sakti,	6
Chemin,	137
Chemseunissa, wife of Feirouz, allegory on,	245
Chéphren or Chabyris,	13
Chequers, the calculi of Italy so called,	235
Cheres,	13, 14, 20, 21
——— or Chares was Moses,	14
Chérinus, or Menchérinus,	13
Cherubim, the,	10
Chia (Eve corrupted), the wife of Bochica,	34
Chibiriss, the mother of Bacab,	32
Children, of the same trade as their parents, in India,	280
Chimalman, the Mexican Virgin,	32
Chimborazo—the author required to believe that the water rose 15 cubits above,	254
———, the flood which threw up,	312
——— and Mount Blanc are they not physical traces? &c.,	315
———, might be thrown up by the flood of Ogyges,	332
China,	10, 28, 31, 35, 36, 39—41, 69, 173, 192, 214, 218, 223, 229, 232, 240
———, the Hebrew spoken in,	41
———, mythos of the crucifix common from, to Thule,	129
———, all taxes in, paid by a portion of the produce of the land,	272
China, the emperor of, called Son of the Sun,	292, 353
———, the renewed incarnation visible in,	340
———, the emperor of, as descendant of Japhet, would say, he is "entitled to salt or service from" European kings or their ambassadors,	359
———, canals in, for the encouragement of commerce, &c.; perhaps, rather for receiving the tributes in kind, before money was in use,	376, 377
———, gained territory by being conquered. Could we come at the truth, we should probably find strong marks of the patriarchal, and perhaps of the first, government of man in,	396
Chinese, the,	33, 36, 202, 205
——— use the expression *bones of the Son of the Spirit of Heaven*,	103
———, on the first created,	133
——— are Sin, Saxons, or Buddhists,	215, 220
———, have the whole mythos of the immaculate conception, &c., &c.,	215
———, the wisest people in the world, because they exclude European pirates,	216
———, or Sines,	227, 279
———, have *si* a tree, the root of *su*, a learned man,	227
———, hold letters in religious veneration,	228
———, hold the Trinity and the fall of Adam,	239
———, have trial by Jury,	278, 279
———, said to have once conquered Ceylon,	292
———, emperor and nobility, persuaded by the Jesuits, that the doctrine of Confucius did not differ much from that of the Gospel, &c.,	366, 367
———, who are Buddhists, attempted, by the Jesuits, to be converted to the faith of Cristna —why,	367
———, consider Man a Microcosm; the universe is man, on a large scale, &c.,	398
———, language, the ancient, nearly related to Hebrew,	148
——— is that of symbols, and called the language of flowers,	148, 149, 247
———, first system of letters, was of right lines,	160, 215
———, Japonese, and Siamese languages, the, nearly the same,	214
———, numerals, the, one stroke or line meant *one*, &c.,	216
——— language, the, is understood over a space of 4900 miles,	217
———, the symbolic language of the almost certainty of its having been formed by numerals,	443
——— empire, the, or the country of the 1000 cities of Strabo, probably the seat of the first patriarchal government,	376
———, Mexican, and North-Indian Mythoses, the,	35, 376
——— Records destroyed,	36

INDEX.

Chinese Tartary, 215
—, selected by Bailly, and by most of the learned philosophers, as the birth-place of mankind, 444
— Years, 26
Chiribians, the, 31
Chiribicheuses, 32
Chisel—the use of, scarcely known when the Druidical circles were erected; but religious principle may have operated against its use, 403
Chivalry—Its origin, &c., 303, 304
Chivim—Evites, Hivites or Ophites, 31
Cho Conjoc, the second person of the Tibetian Trinity, 118
Chod, God, is Od, Hod, 6
Choir Gaure } —Stonehenge, 260, 410
Choir Ghaur }
Choir Ghaur and Cor-Ghari, names of Stonehenge and of Gargarus, the same in Sanscrit and old British, 412
Chul, XL—650, 28
Cholula or Chululan, 26—28
— Tulan, 27
— temple at, like Tower of Babel, 27, 28
Chou-king, 36
Choul, Du, 64
Chreestian religion, the, existed from the earliest time, 368
Chrēst, the, crucified, 123
Chrestian mythos, } 16, 134
Χρηϛ-tian, }
Christianity, the original of, Plato, Philo, Pantænus, and Ammonius Saccas, 131
Chrétiens, les, 97
Chri, Χρι, 32
Christ, 17, 22, 25, 26, 33, 36, 43, 47, 50, 60, 61, 64, 71, 75, 84, 95, 109, 110, 137—140, 171, 211
— attained the age of nearly 52 years, 26—(or of 50) 120—123, 228
— conceived by a rose being smelt, 33
—, the Romish incarnation of Divine Wisdom, 44
—, the Passover of Christians, 60
—, hymns sung to, as a God—bowing at the name of, 90
—, worshiped by the Magi, 95
—, his nativity revealed to the Magi of Persia, 98
—, Lamb or Redeemer, represented as the Sun, at the vernal equinox, 110
—, the mysteries of, the mysteries of the Lamb, and of the Mithraitic Bull, 111
— worshiped under the form of a Lamb, ib.
—, pictures of, not to be a lamb, but a man on a cross, 112, 115
—, crucified, as preached by Paul, a varata questio, 122
— in the heavens, in the form of a cross, 122, 123, 145
— was the Χρηϛ of India, the Χρηϛ-αν of Tamul, the Cres-us of the Sanscrit, and the Chresus of the Latin, 123
—, on the generations from Abraham, to, 133
—, to be called a Stone—the Linga or Logos, 259

Christ, on the time of the flood before, 326—328
—, our, and Cristna, said to be identical, 337
—, the æra of, 347
—, when his doctrines made progress; how converted into a God, 355
—, when he came, the emperors held only by right of the sword: after his death, the world, as then known, was divided into three Patriarchates, 400
—, till a short time before, all science confined to secret societies, 424
Christening, Baptism, and Confirmation, rites of the Magi, of Mithra, or the Sun, 66
Christian, a, the Author entitled to the name of, as much as Irenæus, 120, 449
— a, not required to give up an iota of his faith, when he turned Mussulman, 379
— æra, the, a fixed epoch for all the ancient Eastern and Western nations, 353
Christian doctrines, the, 35, 37, 73
— to be found in the morality of Pythagoras, 49
— hierarchy, the, the same as that of the Essenes, 71
— fathers, the, taught an esoteric and an exoteric religion, 129
—, the early authorities, no better guides than Ranters, Jumpers, and genuine Calvinists, 131
— Monks, the, were Egyptian Essenes, 35
—, the, the polity of, a close copy from the Essenean, 43
— mysteries, the, taken from those of Mithra, 111
—, what constituted the whole of the, will probably never be known, 441
—, the secreting of the, an attempt to restore the secrets of Paganism, which had been, by degrees, revealed, &c., 442
— mythos, 10, 28, 34, 36, 37, 115
— religion, the, 35
—, same as the vulgar religion of the Gentiles, 42, 93, 145
—, parables of, 134
— and all the Gentile religions attempted to be explained and made one by Ammonius Saccas, 131, 447, 448
Christians, 3, 9, 25, 28, 39, 43, 45—48, 50, 58, 59, 62, 79, 71, 89, 90, 95, 96
—, of the Manichæan sect, 45
—, most of the rites and doctrines of the, existed before the time of Jesus of Nazareth, 50
—, Ευχαριϛια of the, 62
— of St. John, 66
—, modern, have adopted ancient monuments, &c., 68
— the hierarchy of, a close copy of the Persian, 71
—, the, of the Levant, all use the girdle, 77
— have adopted and adored the same persons or Gods as the Heathens, 80, 82, 90
Christians, the Early, prayed standing, 78, 104
—, would not call the days or months by their usual names, for fear of pollution, 84
—, pilgrimages of, imitated from those of the Pagans, 86
—, have a Saint as the Persians had an Angel for each day, ib.
—, the Early, were taken for worshipers of the Sun, by turning to the East, 89
— of the Church of England turn to the East, ib.
— of Bythinia, 90
—, have copied the names of Gods, 91
—, the Early, would not place laurel on their doors on a Pagan festival, 94
—, the Verbum Caro factum est, not peculiar to the, 98
— shew an infant on Christmas morning at Rome, 102
—, the, of Malabar, called Christians of Nazarence Mapila, or Surians of Surianee Mapila, 115
—, of the first two centuries consisted of Nazarenes, Ebionites, and Orthodox—and of Gnostics, &c., 119
—, at this time, a sect of Paulites, 122
— esoteric doctrines of the, 123
— have got possession of the Gospel of John, found in the ancient temple of Jerusalem, 125
—, one of the earliest names of, Crestons, 127
— and Gentiles, secret religions of, the same, 130
—, the sect of the early, the lowest of all in intellect, burnt books, &c., 132
— of St. Thomas, 208, 262, 279, 280
—, natives of Europe, are Papists, Protestants, &c., 221
—, the first called Christs, 251, 344
—, of the present day, their minds enfeebled by education, look with contempt on the learning, &c., of the Brahmins, 337
—, the Early, Josephs of Arimathea among, 342
—, the system of the sect of, fell into pieces when the Millenium did not arrive, 351
—, make the teacher of Samaria to be God himself, as the Brahmins do Cristna, 368
— and Mohamedans, in reality the same; their mutual hatred, 369
—, when the, of Spain, surrendered to the Moors, they paid only a tenth of the produce—when their cities were stormed, a fifth was demanded, 377
—, the bigotry and malice of, render their assertions (against Mohamedans) doubtful, 379
— and Mohamedans equally liable to misrepresentation, 380
— put out

INDEX.

	Page
of sight the true grounds of *divine right*, &c., why,	384
Christians, no rite now known among the, which was not common to the Gentiles,	442
Christianities, two,— the *exoteric* and *esoteric*—the first consists of the Atonement, &c., intended for the vulgar; the *esoteric* was a secret, not meant to be explained,	367
Christianity,	25, 28, 37, 61, 71, 95
———, the mythos of, in Egypt,	10
———, in Tartary, in North and South India,	28, 36
———, in China,	19, 36, 97
———, in Mexico,	28, 34, 36, 37
———, orthodox,	7
———, sacrifices for the Dead, coeval with,	74
———, modern systems of, identical with those of the ancient Persians,	106
———, flourished here before the time of Christ,	279
———, generally prevalent in Britain, at the end of the fourth century, when the Romans left it,	281
———, modern, if stripped of corruptions, a continuation of the ancient religion of Rome,	367
Christie, on Worship of Elements,	251
———, on a passage from Diodorus on speech and symbols to represent objects,	437
Christus or Chrestus became Chrestus,	250
Chronicles of the kings of Persia adopted into the canon of the Jews,	17
Chrysanthius, the master of Julian,	448
Chryses,	225
——— and Calchas—their dispute with Agamemnon,	350
Chrysostom, St.,	58, 61, 298
———, on the Gentile mysteries,	430
———, John, on children wearing medals of Alexander, as talismans,	248
Chubb,	131
Churula,	28
Cicero,	2, 52, 64, 76, 86, 98, 100, 164, 202, 236
——— on the power of the Augurs,	52
——— on Transubstantiation,	64, 442, 443
———'s property confiscated,	76
———, Brutus, &c., the learned and unlearned fools in Rome, against,	345
Cihnateocalli—i. e. semple of Cali, the God of Sina or Sian,	31
Cihnathe, temple of Sin, Sion, Sinai or Sina,	29
Cimmerians, the,	4
Cio or Cioch,	8, 31, 227, 229, 230
CIPATENAL, the WORD,	23
Ciphers, the language of,	185, 186
———, the written, unspoken language of, extended over the whole world, and was long fixed,	234
———, the language of, the first,	235

	Page
Cir—from גר gr—a circle,	263, 276
Circle, the, how divided, in Volume I.,	404
Circles, districts in Ceylon and Germany so called,	263, 303
——— and in the five Northern Circars,	276, 277
———, the, of Germany, were all religious divisions of the pontifical government,	411
Circular temples, in cyclar numbers, erected in honour of the Deity,	306
Circumcision, the law of, omitted in Aelfric's Anglo-Saxon translation of the Pentateuch,	173
——— means also Initiation,	248, 309, 310
———, the custom among the Tamuls, in Mexico, in Colchis of Armenia, in Egypt, in Guinea and Congo—prevails only among the priests,	309
Cjang-cihup—the wisdom of Sion or Xin,	211, 224
Claproth's, Mr., Map of Asia,	411
Clarke (Dr.),	95, 168, 117, 239, 240, 262
——— on Tumuli and Carns, in India,	289
———, on the companies established in Thebes,	418
Classical Journal,	110, 210, 432
Claude Duret,	3
Claudian,	145
Claudius,	76
———, human sacrifices offered by the Romans, till the time of,	281
Clearchus,	50
Cleland's Specimens, &c.,	55, 59, 62, 109, 222, 264, 266, 275, 277, 279, 290, 297, 299—302, 304, 413
Clemens Alexandrinus,	17, 20, 43,
Clement of Alexandria,	49, 50, 69, 79, 89, 115, 125, 234, 447, 449
——— on rudiments of wisdom taught by Christ, found in the philosophy of the Greeks,	130
——— held the *allegorical* meaning,	131
———, on the mysteries celebrated under the Cupola of Temples, &c.,	298, 303
———, and his school, revived and taught the best part of the ancient system of mysteries, &c.	342
———, on the Mosaic mythos at Eleusis,	347, 350
——— says, that *the truths taught in the mysteries had been stolen from Moses and the prophets*,	440
———, the mysteries alluded to by,	442
Clement VIII.	55
Cleobolus—tyrant of Lindus—his riddle on *the year*,	319
Cleomenes, the alphabet of,	220
Cleomodes—on a month, as 30 days,	321
Clients, the Roman, were to the Gentes, what the tenantry were to the Highland Lairds,	392
Clifford's Tower at York, formerly an Olympus,	276
Clisthenes' code of laws—the aim of, to blend the noble clans of Athens with the other citizens,	419
Clo=600, Cali or *klo* the Phœnix,	183

	Page
Clotaire,	266
Clytones and Clytoneuli,	274
Coatle, Mexican name of God,	32
Cobbett, on the Moorish sway in Spain,	377
Cobra, the,	130
———, the *nine* overshadowing Buddha, *sleeping*, emblem of the cycles,	286
Cochin China, Tonquin, Japan, and China, the characters of, the same, though the spoken languages differ,	215
———, Callida,	288
Cockayne, the mast of, *the loadstone?*	182
Codex Borgianus,	32
——— Vaticanus,	32, 35
Cœlum—how derived,	408
Cœnobites, the,	48
Cœnobium, Κοινοβιον,	47
Cohen (כן cn) the general of the Priest or Pontiff made himself Khan,	395
Coheels, a priest, a Cohen,	3
———, Sagan,	ib.
Coheus, the, Jewish priests, descendants of Aaron,	232
Coir, genitive *choir*, the Gaelic for a space inclosed on all sides, is the χωρα, place or land,	413
Colebrook,	88
——— and others blockheads enough to consider the Buddhists as Atheists,	428
Colldei, the,	130
College of Heralds, the origin of our, the council of the Amphictyons of Delphi and Eleusis,	422
Colleges, our, remains or revivals of Druidical institutions,	297
——— (celebrated) anciently established at Nagracut, Bocharia, and Cashmere,	444
Collie, the Rev. David, on the *Kung* plan in China, by which a *tenth* of the produce was fixed as the land tax,	376
———'s translation of Hea Mung,	421
Cologne, skulls of the three Magi kings at,	98
———, Christ as a Lamb, at,	111
Colonies from Italy and Greece, in very ancient times,	434
Colosse,	43
Colosseum—the *Cyclopæan* wall found under the ruins of the,	381
Colubra, Culebra,	31
Columb, St., or Columba or Columbes, in Cornwall—its sacred stones, called *the nine maids*,	286
Columba or Iona, settlements of the Chaldei made as far as the island of,	257
——— and Columbo of Ceylon, both so named by the same sect,	280, 288, 289
———, the learning of, when the rest of Europe was in ignorance and barbarism,	285
Columbo, in Ceylon,	263—290
Columbus,	33
Columella,	133, 134, 139, 141, 142
Comet, the, (of 1680?)	138, 382
———, of 575½ years' period,	327, 328, 330—332, 334
———, if a, caused the change of the earth's axis, at the flood,	313
———, the, of 1688, seen four	

VOL. II. 3 Q

INDEX.

times, viz. 44 B. C., 531 or 532, A. D., 1106 and 1680 A. D., 326
———, the probable cause of the flood, 327–332, 334, 338
———, periods of, to the Christian era, 328, 329
———, our astronomers will assert that they can calculate the periods of several of the, 330
———, the, may have effected great changes in all the planets, 336
———, the, of 1680, the coincidence between, and the chronological date of the flood, in Indian, Jewish, and Grecian writing, establish the reality of a flood at that time, on so high a probability, as to amount almost to certainty, 439
———, may come again—the tops of the mountains may be the bottom of the seas, 445
Comets—held to be planets, 314
Common Soccage—lands held in, 265
—— Law, the, of England and Scotland, established before writing was generally known, 272
—— and feodal law, the, of England, both came from India at same time?, 273
Comorin, Zamorin, or Camarina, 228
——, Cape, 232, 257, 295
Compitales, the, 90
Compitallcii, the games, ib.
Conception, *immaculate*, 21–23, 38, 42, 49, 96, 97, 102
———, crucifixion, and resurrection, the mythos of, in Egypt, 21
———, in India, Syria, Mexico, and South America, 22, 23, 38, 42
———, &c., in China, 215
Conclave, the, knowledge possessed by, uncertain, 93, 342
———, the secret doctrine of renewed Avatars (probably) existed in, 367
Conclaves, the, of Tibet and of Rome, 117
Concubines, the 360 Royal, of the Persian kings, 317
Conde is Can or Khan—Can-di, holy Can or Kan, 301
Confederated towns and states of Ioola, &c., being precisely *twelve*, shew method and design, 394
———— states, among the Celts of Gaul, 395
Confession, 73, 74
Confirmation, 66, 71, 232
———— by the girdle, 77
Confrères, the 360 of Athens, &c., 418
Confucius, 36
———, similarity of his doctrine to that of the Gospel, 367
Confusion of tongues, the, allegory of, 234
Connexion, the ancient, between the Eastern and Western nations, 262
Conquerors, numbers of, have thought themselves, and have been thought by their followers, to be Messiahs, 345
Constant, Benj., 44, 97, 261
———, on a priestly government in Greece, 350, 351
———, on similar customs, &c.,

&c., in Europe, Asia, Africa, and America, 372
Constantine, 26, 27, 33, 34, 51, 53, 54, 56, 90, 94, 105, 126, 138, 278, 279, 289
————, indictions of, 34
———— was both Christian and Pagan, 51, 119, 281
———— affected to be the Tenth Avatar, 51
————, alleged gift of Italy by, to the Church, 53, 54
———— ordered Sunday to be set apart in honour of the God Sol, 90
————, the cross of, probably a crucifix, 118
————, the treason of, 145
————, the miscreant, affected to be an Avatar, 207
————, gave a preponderance to the Popes and Paulites, 270, 449
————, how influenced to give the successor of St. Peter the right of ruling by *the book*, 345
————, the conduct of, a proof of the close connexion of Paganism and modern Christianity, 349
———— established a priesthood interested in the success of the mythos, &c., 355
———— was the follower of Cristna—no Pope in India because there was no Constantine there, 370
————, suspected to have divided the world among his three sons, in compliance with the mythos of Shem, Ham, and Japhet, 490
————, the half *Pagan* and half *Christian* eccentricities of, what accounts for, 443
————, Bp. of Constance, 80
———— Pogonat, 111
Constantinople, the council of, (*In Trullo*,) in 707, ordered pictures of Christ in the form of men, 111, 112
———— three days, how reckoned in, 142
————, the city of seven hills, 354
———— and Egypt, dispute between the rulers of, 352, 354, 361, 388
————, in the domain of Japhet; is called Room by the Mohamedans of the East, 360
Consulate, when the Roman was divided between the two orders, the Patricians demanded the exclusive jurisdiction of the civil and religious law, as it was the science of their caste, &c., 394
Cook, Captain, 38
Cooke, 48
Copias, the drains from the Lake, 381, 419
Coptes, the, 77
Cor (choir), centre of measurements in Italy, &c.; it also meant *heart*, and *wisdom*, hence probably, in Persia, it described the Sun, 410
——, *cor-die* or *di*, *dieus*—hence where the Decumanus or line crossed it, a cross was set up, &c., 413, 414
—— Gawr—the circle of the Mighty One, 411

Coral, a, (hence Earl) means al-corl, chief of the *corle* or *circle*, 292
Cora-mandel — Coromandel — the circle of Core, 277, 290
Cordiner, on the *corles* or *districts* in Ceylon, 292
Core, Cyrus, Χορε, Ras, Ros-e, Sir, and O-sir-is mystically connected? 242
Corea, the Chinese *written* language understood in, 215
Coreans, the, esteemed *stupid* by the Chinese, 216
Corinth, 43
Cornwallis, Lord, the government of, 374
Corporate towns, the, of Europe, existed under the priests—connected with the Pandæistic mythos, 276
Cortes and Pizarro probably aided in their conquests by the mythos, &c., 370
————, recommended the Emperor to get a grant of the tithes, from Pope Alexander VI.; this was refused,—why, 393
Cortona, 127
Cos, the island, Hippocrates on the years of, 319
Cosar, a kingdom of Jews, in the East, so called, 25
Cosmo, St., 84
——— and Damien, the church of, was the temple of Romulus and Remus, 91
Cotillon, the ⊕, dancing originally religious, 179
Council of Nice, the, 355
————, burning of books by the, 357
Counties or Earldoms, the, of Great Britain, were they 72, and the Parishes 360? 292
County, i. e. count-ia, *district of the Conde*, 301
Cousin, Victor, on all great men being *fatalists*, 358
Coxcox, saved on a raft,—perhaps Sasax or Saxas, 31
Craft, trade, or caste, each a secret, in India, 279
Crafts or trades, all originally bound by religious ties, ib.
Cranmer, 132
Crates Molates, brought grammar to Rome, 170 B. C., 196
Crawford, 9, 217, 238, 315
————, on the Negroes of the Upper Ganges, 363
Creator, Preserver, and Destroyer, the, 83, 244, 256, 429, 430
————, the, Logos or Wisdom, the same, 230
Crescent, the, always the emblem of the *female generative principle*, 291
————, from the use of, probable that Mohamed adopted the double principle, though said to have destroyed the dove or lune, 402
Crestian Port, the, Portus Cresso, 117
———— (Christian) name, a, derived from use of a crest or seal, 198
———— mythos, the whole an esoteric system, 232
Crestism, 9
Crestians or Christians, the, of the West, probably descended di-

INDEX.

467

rectly from the Buddhists, rather than from the Brahmins, 438, 439
Crestologia, 20
Crestons, one of the earliest names of Christians, 127
Cresto-polis, 117
Cretans, the, of Mount Ida, Jews, 189
Crete, 102, 180, 188, 226
——— called Candia and Icriti, 117
Creutzer, 7, 56, 62, 231
——— on a priestly government, in Greece, 350
Cristna, 5, 8, 9, 35, 43, 44, 48, 56, 57, 98, 100, 104, 133, 202, 218, 221, 242
——— the same as Samson, 8
——— and Jesus, identity of their history, 44, 241
——— birth of, different, according to Maurice, from that of Jesus, 49
——— the Saviour, 53
——— incarnation of, 98, 34.
——— the same as the Kistnah, 115
——— and Sallvahana, mythos of, 117
——— and Rama, the same, 137, 138
——— strangled the serpent, 144
——— entombment and resurrection of, 142, 145
——— after, came the reign of the Pandus, 222
——— the followers of, affected the *female* principle, 269
——— sects, varieties, and miseries of every kind, arose with— with *the age of iron*, 308
——— Christ-na or Christ-en, according to the Brahmins, incarnated for the salvation of all who believe on him, 341
——— the degree of perfection in the form of, arrived at by handsome *black* males constantly uniting with the most handsome *black* females, 363
——— by the Brahmins, made to be not the *ninth* Avatar, but *God himself*, as Christians make the teacher of Samaria, 363
——— and Buddha, the partizans of the religions of, the same, though hating each other, 369
——— the stories respecting, why believed by the common people, 426
——— (*the benevolent lamb*) and Vishnu (the fish), the followers of, call the Sacæ, Saxons or Buddhists, *atheists*, 428
Cristnas, incarnations of, 129
———, &c., put to death, &c., 142
——— the two, of India and Rome, 219
Cristona, 127
Crœsus, king of Lydia, 318, 319
Croix, Pet. de la, 353
Cromlechs and Carns, the, &c., 373
Crosier, the, carried by the Pontifex Maximus, 57
——— was the lituus of Roman Augurs, 78
——— and sword, the, 264
———, disputes between, 365, 366
Cross, the, 30, 34, 35, 37, 69, 88
———, venerated by the Cumans, 30
——— the God every where crucified and suspended from, 36
———, signing with, 69, 302
——— sign of, to drive away the Devil, 88

Cross, the sign of, a foundation in nature, 116
———, of the Templars, with eight points, why, 298,
———, the Cardo, and the Decumanus, 371
Crosses—pointing to the four cardinal points—their object, the collection of the truths for the priesthood, 372
———, Termini, or Priapuses, the, of the Romans (often indecent), emblems of the generative power, 414, 415
Crotona, 48
Croze, La, 118, 243
Crucified God, the, the doctrine of, in Italy, anterior to the Christian æra, 126
———, the adoration of, 262
Crucifix, the, of Balli, of Cristna, of Ixion, of Prometheus, 117, 118
———, at every cross-road in Tibet, 117
———, of Nepaul, 118
———, a, an object of adoration from the Indus to the Tibur, and even to Scotland, 119, 129
———, the Pagan Roman, purposely concealed, 120
———, mythos of, common to all nations, 129
———, *heathen*, disappearance of, in Britain, &c., 130
Crucifixion, Resurrection, Immaculate Conception, and Trinity, the, mythos of, found in Egypt, India, Syria, Mexico, and South America, 21, 22, 25, 33, 28, 42
———, the, the Author's opinion respecting, not stated, 120
——— of Adonis, 99, 100, 112
——— of Apollo, 102, 103, 180
——— of Atys, 102, 104, 106
——— of every Avatar, celebrated at the 5 temples in Egypt, 118
——— of Bacchus, 100, 102, 112
——— of the *black* Saviour, 32, 36, 37, 116
——— of Buddha, 103, 105, 118, 124, 244, 248, 249, 256, 415
——— of the Christ, 123
——— of Christ, 25, 122
———, the Christ of the Romans, 124
——— of Cristna, 104, 118, 124, 145
——— of the Dove, 114, 116
——— of Horus, 102
——— of Iao or Iao, 100, 112, 122
——— of Indra, 33, 296
——— of Ixion, 115, 118, 198
——— of Jesus, the Son of Sirach, 124, 232, 441, 442
——— of Jesus Christ, 104, 105, 112
———, and resurrection of, most important parts of Christianity—whence derived, 190
———, a close copy from Paganism, 112
———, believed in *literally* by the Ebionites, &c.,—but *spiritualiter* by the Gnostics, &c., 119
——— of Jupiter Ammon, 102
——— ——— Zagreus, 103
——— of the Logos, in the heavens, 123
——— of Mithra, 99, 100, 112
——— of Osiris, 100, 102, 136
——— of Prometheus, 113, 116, 118

Crucifixion, the, of Pythagoras, 127
——— of Queealcoatle, 32
——— of Salivahana, 115
——— of Semiramis as the Dove or Divine Love, 116, 118
——— of Sol, 99, 100, 112, 116
——— of Wittoba or Balliji, 115, 118
——— of Xaca, 105
Cruden, 128
Crusades, the,—the mythic superstition at the time of, 349
———, the Millenium expected at the time of, 356, 382
Crymogæa, the, of Aragrimus, 300
Cryptographic writing, by ciphers, 182, 183
——— system, the, not entirely disused in India, 235
Crysen (or Chrysen), the country of Χρῃς, 122
Ctesias—on the walls of Babylon, 317
Cufic alphabet, the, long served for *letters* and *ciphers*, 213
Culdees, the, of Iona and Wales, had married and unmarried members in their convents, 248, 280
———, at Ripon and York, 279, 287, 288
Culi-dei (Chaldees), Χλι=666, 210
Cullidei, Chaldæans, or Mathematici, the most learned race in the world, 257
———, Callidi, or Culdees, their three sacraments—Orders, Baptism, and the Eucharist, 262, 279—281, 290
——— ordained each other before the Romish priests came among them, 280
Cuma, on Cape Comorin, 6
Cumana, Humboldt's Sundial in, 297
Cumans, the, 30
Cumæan Sibyl, the, 129
Cunti, Centeotl, Can or Canteotl, Cup—the sending round of, &c., a variation of the Eucharistia, 300
Cupid, 5, 6, 103
——— and Venus, both called Ερως, *divine love*, 170
Cupola—from Cup, in Welsh *top*, same as *ras*, &c., 298
Curetes or Saviours, why *nine*, 286
Curioges—Curates, 53
Curls and Churls, our, from *alcorl?* 292
Curtius, Q., on the Walls of Babylon, 317
Cusco, 32
Cushites and Cuthites, so called from change of T and S, 209
Cusuma—answers to Camasa and Camasene, 296
———pura, Pushpa-pura, Pātāli-pura, *the city of flowers*, ib.
Cuvier, 39
——— on the revolutions of the world—sudden and violent, 312, 313
———, on the mythological nature of ancient history, 360
——— on diluvial remains, 361
Cybele, 47
Cycle of 360, 141
——— of *fourteen*, how written, 160
———, 162, 163, 181
———, the first was 6, then 60, then 600, &c., 195
———, of 666, was the name of every planet, 212
——— of *twenty-eight*, 149, 150, 162

468   INDEX.

	Page
Cycle of the Neros,	140, 198
———, the Metonic,	32, 198
——— of Om,	181
——— processional, the, of 25,920 years,	141
——— of 84, used by ancient Britons, is Jewish, British, and Indian,	162
	190
———, the same things renewed in every,	226, 227
———, of 600, an emanation of divine love,	242
———, does not every return, according to God's law?	338
———, of 600, marked as *sacred* by the bonnet or mitre on the head of the youth on the Roman *ass*,	433
Cycles, system of regeneration of,	36
——— and sacred numbers, origin of the,	223
———, the knowledge of, necessarily a secret,	236
———, with the *high* priests produced astronomy, with the *low* priests and vulgar, superstition,	243
———, described by Cromlehs and Carns, in India, Britain, &c.,	256
———, the, regulated festivals and agricultural labours,	306
———, renewed, the system of, calculated for duration,	307
———, all the, were microcosmic,	399
———, all the, made up by the multiplication of the *five* and *six*,	409, 431
———, the great, described in different ways—in the East, by 600 and by 50; in Italy, by 240, 360, 120, &c.,	415
———, of 21,600, of 43,200, &c.,	432
———, the system of, arose out of, and was continued by, the wants of man; it aided in supplying or remedying these wants; it is yielding to the law of change, and is almost forgotten,	445
Cyclopæan and Druidical monuments,	36, 147
——— no inscription found on any,	197, 198, 206
——— walls arose by degrees, as the world became crowded, food and land scarce, and man quarrelsome,	365
——— *wall* found under the ruins of the Colosseum — Niebuhr's silence on the,	331
Cyclops, the,	135
——— κυκλος and οφις—Serpent of the Cycle, or Logos of the Cycle,	438
Cyclopes, the, or Calidei or Mathematici, the builders of Stonehenge, Abury, Dipaldenha, the temples of Solomon, the Pyramids, &c., &c.,	135
———, one-eyed, after the image of God, *the sun*,	136
———, regulators of cyclic religious festivals, &c.,	236
Cymri, the, supposed to have been brought to Britain, by *Hu Gadarn*, from Defrobani — Taprobane, Ceylon,	290
Cyning, the Sophi, Ras, Cunning man—King,	220

	Page
Cyprian, St.,	58
Cyrrbestica—Crest-ica,	236
Cyrus,	51, 56, 57, 375
———, the Αμμυ τυυ αιωνων,	51, 56
———, a solar epithet,	231
———, a Messiah,	233
——— thought to be a Χρης,	251
———, the 360 channels cut by, to make the Gyndes fordable,	317
———, believed to be a divine Incarnation,	343
——— himself to be the person foretold,	344
———, was put to death by the Tsarina or Queen of Caracorum,	360
———, Darius, and Cambyses—their reason for destroying the images in Egypt, but leaving the Lingas, &c.,	364
——— (though an Iconoclast), why he could reconcile the adoration of the solar power with the adoration of the Supreme Being,	429
D and r permutable in Sanscrit,	119
Dan, the,	4
Dabistan—Persian books, called vedas,	226
Dad, dade, daddy, for father,	33
Dafterdam, the (treasury office), the numbers used in, form an alphabet,	235
Dag,	21
Dago and Taurico }	38
Dagon and Taurus }	
Dagun—a god so called, at Rangoon,	288
Δαιμονολατρεια or Δεισιδαιμονα, the, of the Gentiles, imitated in the αγιολατρεια of the Greek, Roman, and Protestant churches,	81
Dak-po (Dg-Padus, or Po), name of Bacchus in Ceylon,	163
Damascenus, John, S.,	112
Dan,	18
———, sign of, the Scorpion or Eagle,	105
D'Ancarville on mythology of Egyptians, Brahmins, &c.,	267
——— says the Sacæ were also called Sagæ,	274
——— on the FEUDAL SYSTEM,	262, 372
Dances, music, &c., to aid memory before syllabic writing was discovered,	247, 424
Dancing, originally merely religious,	179, 229, 262
——— approved of by Socrates, Sophocles, &c.,	425
———, the ancient, entirely imitative, and esteemed honourable or otherwise, in proportion to the dignity of what it was meant to express,	425, 426
Daniel, the writing interpreted by, a symbol for a word,	186
——— on *a time, times, and a half,* &c.,	317
———, not to pray for *a month,*	320
———, the 1260 of, calculated to begin with our present era,	329
———, a perfect picture of, exhibited by Nassireddin de Thous, at the court of the Khan of Tartary, &c.,	362

	Page
Daniel, made ruler over 360 cities, by Darius,	420
Darius—the 360 Satraps of,	317
———, solicited to prohibit prayers for 30 days,	320
——— and Alexander—in the battle between, *streams of blood* said to *have ascended from the terrestrial fish,* &c.,	346
——— made Daniel ruler over 360 cities,	420
Darol-Hikmet or *house of wisdom,* at Cairo, in which all the sciences, &c., were publicly taught,	387
Daru (Persian) Drui (Irish) a Persian Magus,	225
Data—the Sanscrit Dhatoos are,	1
Daudpotri,	232
David's (Lumley) Turkish Grammar,	421
David, (king,) supposed to have had the same soul as Adam, Abraham, and the Messiah,	97
———,	105, 232, 238
———, sons of, in India,	122
———, 28 generations from, to Christ,	133
———, Psalms of, a sentence from the, identical in Hebrew and Welsh,	154
———, Daud, Dis or Di-oud—the *holy* man of Oud or of Ayodia,	238
———, a man after God's own heart, yet given to the Jews as a punishment,	364
———, measures of the sepulchres of, still remaining at Jerusalem,	405
——— danced before the ark,	426
Davies, Mr.,	97
———, on *Son of Mary,* in a Welsh bard,	154
———, his Celtic Researches,	290
De, di, dia (Celtic), Deus, and *dea* and Αψω, the Goddess Ceres, from יד di—*holy,*	161
De Rossi, quoted by Lowth on the LXX.	16
Deans and Chapters, the origin of, involved in absolute darkness, thousands of years after the discovery of the art of writing, 280,	339
Deasil, the, must be performed *sunways,* &c.,	291
Debtors and creditors, the, of Greece and Italy—the debts were, probably, demands made by the nobles for more than the *tenths,* &c.,	418
Decalogue, the,	171
Decapolis, the, of Western Syria,	277
Deccan—Daschula in Sanscrit—answers to Decapolis, and to the Tithings of Alfred,	ib.
December 24th, at midnight, orgies celebrated in Mithraitic caves, and in temples generally, to the honour of the God Iao—the Saviour,	95
——— at Rome,	96
———, the Persians called it the Night of Light,	99
———, the accouchement of the Queen of Heaven, celebrated on, by nearly all nations,	ib.
——— 25th, the birth of the God Sol, celebrated on, by the Gestics, 98—100—of Osiris, 99, 102—of Adonis, Apollo, Atys, and Jupiter Ammon, of Crete,	102

	Page
December 25th, the birth of Horus celebrated by the Egyptians,	102
Decumanni, the, perhaps men of the *tenths* or *tithes*, the operatives under the Cardinales,	381
——, was drawn at every tenth part of the circle from N. to S., whence its name Deca; like the parallels of Latitude, these lines were always the same,	413
Deen, religion so called by the Mohamedans,	250
Deflowering, whence the phrase,	244
Del-para, and Panayia,	45
Deir, in Sanscrit, means an island; is the name of God and of the island of Ceylon,	288
Deisul, voyage of Salvation,	21, 276
Deisuls,	29, 64, 233, 422
——, whether sacred theatres preceded or followed the,	340
Deity, the doctrine of the androgynous nature of, as universal as the Trinitarian,	256
De la Cerda—his commentary on Virgil,	406
Della Salute, church of, at Venice,	91
Delecarlians, [Dalecarlians,] the, have a dialect of their own—a relic of Gothic, Anglo-Saxon, and Irish,	258
Delhi—city of the God Il—D'-el-ti,	332
——, there is a, in Sumatra,	353
——, the city of seven hills,	354
Delos and Delphi—a *black* dove came to, from the Hyperboreans —the priestesses of, particularly endowed with the Holy Spirit,	285
Delphi,	86, 102, 136, 202
——, Apollo's tomb at,	102
—— and Eleusis, the Χρης or Ceres tif,	117
——, mythos known at the temple of,	134
——, (means *navel*, the centre,) the Linga worship of,	260, 262
Delrio,	408
Delta, the, of Egypt, laid bare by a flood,	312
——, appeared at the subsidence of the Mediterranean,	352
Deluc—on the sudden revolution of the earth's crust,	313
Deluge, the, remarks on, by an American writer,	313
Demetrius, St.,	65
—— Phalereus, had 360 statues erected to his memory at Athens,	320
Demigods, the, of the ancients, are the Saints of the moderns,	81
Democritus,	47, 314
Demons, the, fire at the sound of the sacred bell,	70
—— or Manes,	74
D. M. S., Diis Manibus Sacrum,	74, 83
Dendera, the Zodiac of,	192, 256
Denis, St.,	84, 85
——, death and resurrection of,	85
——, church of, was the temple of Dionysus,	91
Denmark, the Saxons of,	360
——, instruments in the cabinet of, with edges of iron and handles of Gold,	365
Deo Soli,	100, 109, 110, 116

	Page
Deo Soli, Unitarian meaning of these words,	129
Des Cartes, with some additions, revived the philosophy or doctrines of the ancients,	393
—— and Berkeley in Europe, and Vyasa in India—the doctrines of,	427
De-Saine, Dessaus, names of Hercules or the Sun,	225
Desire of all Nations, the,	167, 251
——, to be born from the side of his mother,	345
Despotism in Asiatic states—the cause,	366
Deucalion,	18, 20, 439
—— (Deus Cali, or holy Cali,) the flood of, took place 2348, B. C.,	332
Annex, suavitas, dulcedo,—hence Deucalion,	18
Devaci, the mother of Cristna,	98
Devanagari, the,	236
Devi, in Sanscrit, means *an island*; is the name of God, and of Ceylon,	288
Devil, contrivances attributed to the, by Spanish Monks, in reference to Mexican and Peruvian doctrines and rites,	23, 24, 31, 33
——, the, and his fallen angels, the prototype of, &c.,	88
——, the cunning,	252
——, begetting *Merlin* on the body of a virgin, fable of,	349
——, said to have copied the Christian rites, when the Pagan mysteries were attempted to be restored,	442
—— drivers,	131
—— driving age, a,	426
Devils, the, busied themselves with the Eucharist,	60
——, set up baptisms,	66, 68
——, air cleared of, by baptized bells,	70
——, driven away by salt in holy water,	88
Dewtahs (bad angels), with whom Cristna, the Saviour, made war,	ib.
Deys, the, of Algiers, Tunis, &c., admit the supremacy of the Grand Seignior,	380
Dhasa-meda—decima and modius —the *tenth measure*,	263
Dhatoos, the Sanscrit, are data,	1
D'Herbelot,	77, 303
—— and Desguines censured by Hammer for considering the Assassins a dynasty,	383
Di, Da, *holy* or *God*,	161, 163
Di, in the St. Kilda and Mexican dialect, means Great Lord,	161
Diana,	47, 85
——, Di-ja-na, or Deva-ja-na, from Yoni,	174
Di, dives, the first name of God,	23
Dido, sister of Anna Perenna,	91
Dies Solis—markets and fairs held on, around the sacred mount with its cross,	276
Digamma, the, or Vau, not used by the Greeks after the time of Aristotle,	158
——, is the Vau growing into the sound of V, hence *f*,	169
——, two used for the numeral letter *six*,	196

	Page
Dii Consentes, the,	483
Dii Consortes, the,	344, 345
Diodore,	97
Diodorus (Siculus),	11—13, 29, 84, 229, 230, 312, 314, 317
——, on the most ancient succession of the Gods, &c.,	323, 325, 326
——, on speech, indistinct and confused, and symbols to represent objects,	437
Diogenes Laertius,	101
——, on the length of the year,	318—320
—— and Anaxagoras, on the design of the earth's inclination,	314
Διος Παλακναι, the, or *holy sailors*, eastern tribes, might be Chaldei —the only people who, after Deucalion's flood, preserved the use of letters,	429
Diomede,	18
Dion, on a certain demon, styling himself Alexander of Macedon, appearing on the Danube, &c., &c.,	348
Dionysius Exiguus, on the error of 30 days as a month,	321
—— Halicarnasseus,	51, 54
——, in the history of, a pagus is called a *ναρκπολιν*, as we should say a *circumpole*,	419
——, Aristotle, and Polybius, all equally ignorant of the origin of the tribes of the Greeks and Italians,	436
Διονυσος, Bacchus, worshiped, as St. Denis,	84, 85
Dionysus, the God, same as St. Dionysius,	85
Dipaldenba, built by the Cyclops,	135
Dipaldenna,	369
Dios, S. American name for God,	161
Dipus, or Cupid and Venus,	242
Di-Saka or Deva-Saka, Bela Raja so called,	221
Dis Manibus,	283
Dis Maribus,	ib.
Disorder, the, which the present system seems to shew, is probably only temporary or periodical,	239
Div, in Sanscrit, is an island; Seven, is quasi *Seiun*, the island of Ceylon—Serendib,	290
Divi or Gods, Divi or Saints,	91
—— inferiores, Roman and Christian,	80, 81, 83
Divine incarnations — Buddha, Cristna, Salivahana, Moses, Cyrus, Alexander, Julius Cæsar, Gengis Khan, Timur, Mohamed, Gregory, Hakem Bemrillah, were all believed to be, as well as Jesus Christ,	343
Divine Right, the claim of, by monarchs of Asia *rational*, if pleaded by European monarchs, they ought to send ambassadors to China, or somewhere else, to do suit and service to their Superior Lord,	359
——, of European despots and priests, what operates against,	384
——, all the claims of kings to, have descended from Noah, &c.,	407
Division into threes (the Mohamedan), similar to the Trimurtras, &c.,	386

VOL. II. 3 R

INDEX

Divus, 28, 80, 90
——— Augustus, Paulus, Petrus, 80
——— Petronius, 90
——— applied to Christian Saints, ib.
D. M., Deo Maximo or Dis Manibus or Dis Mariebus, 203
D. M. *Sacrum* XL, probably Deo M. =650, ib.
Dodona, 86
———, mythos known at the temple of, 134
———, the *beech* and *oak* gave out oracles at, 165
Dog, a, described by signs, 161, 185
"Dogs, hence all" and "Procul, hinc procul este, profani," 430
Dolomieu—on the sudden revolution of the earth's crust, 313
Dom, a judge, 277, 302
Domain—*aia* or *asia* d'om—land of Om, 303
Domase (Pope) solicited Jerom to search for the Bible in Judea, 172
Dom Bec, Sconhalla in, 283
——— bec—Book or Bec-d'om, 302
———-day-book—D'om-d'aia—a record of the land of the sacred Om, land which paid its tenths, ib.
——— tree, the, 65
Domesday Book—Liber Judicatorius, 277
Domingo, St., language of, corrupt Hebrew, 19
Dominos, 79
Dominus, Κυριε, Lord, name of honour of Jesus Christ, 99
——— ——— Mortis, or Bal-Sab, 82, 83
——— ——— Sol, the Saviour, 89, 112
Domitian wished the words *the Lord our God commands it to be used*, 55
Domus, from D'om, Di-om, the place of the *holy* Om, 302
Don, river, from יון *adu* Adon, 99
——— or Dun, *the Do*—wisdom or knowledge, 250
Doncaster, an altar of Hercules at, 154
Door, a, in Sanscrit *dwara*, Saxon *dora*, Greek, θυρα, 158
Double principle, the, adoration of, 222
Δελεια, a species of, paid to Cardos, their nature or design being forgotten. Devotees in all ages and nations strive to increase the objects of adoration, 410, 416
Douyan-Byan, husband of the mother of Gengis Khan, 353
Dove, the, Semiramis, 228
———, in Heb. *Iona*, in Lat. *Columba*, the name of Ii, Iona, Icolmkill, 285
———, in Hebrew, is always *female*, 174, 285, 291
Doyle, Bishop, X Doyle, 198
Dozens and *scores*, our, probably derived from the microcosmic superstition, the nature of which is forgotten, 385, 433
Draco, 217
Dragon, the, and Thorah, the fable of, 305
Dravida—hence Fort St. David? 238
Druid, a, brought the mythos from Bokhara to Ireland, 97
———, the Arch, in Gaul, field his foot out to be kissed, 55
———, probably had under him, three archflamens, 416
———, when a, commanded an army,

and he usurped the throne, many of his barons would be Druidi, 278
Druids, the, 31, 44, 50, 62, 54, 69, 71, 82, 83, 277, 278,
———, kept Dec. 24th and called the 25th Nollagh, 99
———, were persecuted by the Romans, who took (learned) nothing from them, ib.
———, of Gaul, worshipped the Virgo-Paritura, as the mother of God, 100 years before the birth of our Saviour, 108, 109, 259
———, taught by, or descended from, the Chaldæans of Tartary, or Eastern Syria, or North India, 135, 136
———, were called Vates, by the British — Ouateis by the Greeks, 225
——— or priests—almost all lands in Europe anciently belonged to the order of, 266
———, enmity of the Romans against them, why, 281
———, the 20,000 verses their pupils repeated, 340, 436
———, the, of Britain, sent offerings to the temple of Apollo, at Delos, wrapped in wheat straw, 380
———, in the oldest monuments of, we have the circle of 12 stones,—the number of the signs of the zodiac, &c., &c., 408
Druidical or Cyclopean buildings—no inscription found on any, 197, 198
——— circle, every, or cathedral, had its sacred mount, for the Detsul or procession of God the Saviour—of Sol, from East to West, 276
——— temples, the, became Roman and Christian temples or churches, &c., 278, 280
——— built, with pillars in cyclic numbers, to remedy defects of memory, for historic knowledge, 310
——— circles, the, mark *numerals*, but nothing like *letters*, 311
——— and Cyclopean buildings found everywhere, 312
——— remains of, in EVERY part of the world, 365, 373
——— edifices prove the existence of the Golden Age, under the universal pontifical government, 369
——— wherever found, there the patriarchal system extended, 371
——— temples, the, probably erected when the *numeral alphabet* was in use, but when the *syllabic* was a secret, if it was then discovered, 396
——— colleges (whence our universities) these, &c., subordinate to the *three* Archierarchs—the descendants of Shem, Ham, and Japhet, 432
——— monuments, all the old suspected to be antediluvian, 439
Drummond (Sir William), 48, 159, 236, 297, 314
———, on Hebrew names of places, &c., all astronomical, 105, 136

Drummond (Sir William), on *buffoonery*, 179, 212
———, on the knowledge of the ancients, respecting the number of the planets, 402
———, Sir I. Newton, Mr. Whiston, and Mr. Gabb, on the standard measure of the ancients, 404
———, on the Brigantes, &c., 412, 413
———, on the priests of Ammon, and the antediluvians, respecting the length of the year, 432
Duchesne, on the Cathedral, &c., of Chartres, 259, 260
Dugas-Monthel (Mons.), 196
Du Halde, on signs or symbols known to people of Cochin China, Tonquin, Japan, and China, 214
———, 229, 268, 272
Duir, the *Oak* and number *four*, 161, 163
——— and Gort, the first letters of, to make Dog or Dg, 161, 185
Dulaure, 219, 279
Dupaix, M., 28
Du Perron, 55
Dupuis, 6, 60, 66, 85, 99, 100, 102—105, 107, 110—112, 193
Duret, Claude, 3, 190
Dutch, the, conduct of, in India, 215
Dutchman's Cap, the isle of, called Linga in old maps, 291, 292
Du Verdier, 79
Dwapar, the, 118
Dwara (Sanscrit), *dora* (Saxon), θυρα, *a door*, 158

E, the, changed into O, with the Ethiopians, 250
Eagle's Nest, the—reason of the constant assemblage of philosophers, astronomers, &c., in, 383
Earl (Lord) E Lar-di, *the* Lar, 301, 417
Earldoms, the nation supposed to have been originally divided into 72, the domain of as many municipia, each with its 12 Aldermen and 24 Councilmen, 417
"Earth to earth," &c., is copied from the ancient Egyptians, 92
Earth, change in the Axis of the, 310, 311, 313, 315, 332, 438, 439
———, the revolution of, at the equator, about equal to the velocity of a cannon ball; and if she were slightly checked in her daily motion, the Pacific would rush over the Andes, &c., and the Atlantic over Europe, Asia, &c., 312
———, the, its figure shows its revolutions, &c., 314
———, that she would incline and the flood ensue—those that knew this, from the calculation of the moons, might know the exact number of the planets, 402
———, the surface of, *suspected to be* microcosmically divided, after the heavens, 410
———, the, supposed by Buffon, &c., to have once been in a state of fusion, 444

INDEX.

471

	Page
East, the, the emblem of the good Deity,	89
———, turning to, in worship,	89, 90
Easter, bloody wars respecting the time of celebrating,	58, 59, 90
——— Sunday, finding the *whole* God on,	59
———, victory of the God Sol, celebrated on, by Christians of Europe,	106
Easter Island and its images,	38
Eastern learning worthless, but as a means to discover the learning of antiquity,	351
Ebionites or Nazarenes,	60
Ebn Mokiah invented the present Arabic characters, 300 years after Mohamed,	237
Ecbatana,	360
Ecclesia non solvit ecclesiæ,	284, 394
——— or église, from Ey-cil-lys,	29.
Ecclesiasticus, Who was the author of?	123
———, why *refused* by Protestants—*received* by members of the Romish church,	124
———, much corrupted, but the translation of, older than the Christian era,	125
——— and Wisdom, probably had, originally, the whole mythos of the crucified Avatars, &c.,	125, 126, 128, 232, 441, 442
———, the books of, intended to contain and conceal the Cabala—the secret doctrines of Wisdom,	365
———, shew from their idioms a translation from the Hebrew,	442
Echelensis, Abraham,	150
Echvah, the Holy Ghost of the Mexicans,	32
Eclectic philosophy, the,	446
Eclectic or Philalethean sect, the Author wished to be considered a member of the,	448
Eclectics, the,	447
———, so called, by the Paulites,	448
Eclipse—the art of foretelling an, would give a priesthood the dominion of the world,	365
Edisius,	448
Editor, Notes by the, 32, 35, 43, 64, 65, 72, 73, 82, 90, 103, 122, 142, 174, 176, 178, 183, 184, 208, 215—217, 232, 233, 241, 301, 329, 330, 333, 334, 341, 369, 381, 449
Edmund, bishop of Sarum or Salisbury,	399
Edward VI.,	60
———, Liturgy of,	88
———, Guilds, Chantries, and Free-chapels, suppressed by the 1st of,	280
——— the Confessor, the laws of, only declaratory,	273
——— and Alfred, were Saxons,	275
Egypt, 4, 7, 10—13, 15—22, 34, 44, 45, 47, 48, 59, 66, 67, 98, 100, 105, 106, 118, 194, 205, 211, 219, 221, 230, 239, 275, 279, 281, 360
——— possessed by the Persians,	11, 12
———, a marsh, except the district of Thebes,	12, 13
———, history of, a Travesty of that of the Jews, or of Holy Scripture,	11, 15—18
Egypt, kings of, ending in *cheres*, were renewed incarnations,	13
———, the crucified of, *your* and *our* Lord,	14, 15, 116
———, five temples of, 15, 16, 118, 275, 276
———, a cashmouric district in,	16
———, ancient language of, the Coptic, which was Hebrew or Chaldee,	20, 243
———, the Essenes of, 43, 45, 46, 48, 49, 66, 135, 270, 381
———, infant Gods in,	100
———, the plagues of, incredible,— keep pace with the Labours of Hercules, and the Conquests of Bacchus,	105
———, conquest of, by the Greeks, meaning of hieroglyphics lost at the time of,	159
——— and Eleusis, the high mysteries of, none but the *circumcised* admitted to,	248
———, a *feodal tenure* established in, by Joseph,	264
———, history of the Bible found in,	293
———, the Mosaic mythos set up, particularly in, by a tribe from India,	362
———, the priests of, the principal landowners—they were *a highly privileged nobility*,	366
———, the poll tax in, was two ducats a year,	379
———, the kings of, were the generals of the priests, 264, 266, 380, 386
———, a single obelisk before the temples in—many of the obelisks brought to Rome,	402
———, Upper,	10, 12, 44, 45, 133
Egyptian proper names, all Hebrew,	18
——— Aroura, the, was the square of 100 cubits,	406
Egyptians, the, 11, 12, 15—18, 20, 25, 64, 77, 79, 177, 219
———, sacred letters of, Chaldaic,	20
———, supposed to have peopled America,	25
———, Gospel of,	45
———, appeared their Gods with prayers and incense,	79
———, their feast of candles,	86
———, celebrated the birth of the Son of Isis, the God of Day, &c., on Dec. 25th,	99
———, their most sacred oath to swear by the relics of Osiris,	102
———, celebrated the vernal Equinox,	106
———, worshiped the VIRGO PARITURA, prior to the birth of our Saviour,	109
———, had a cycle of fourteen,	160
———, used pebbles or small stones to calculate,	167
———, revered the Moon under the emblem of a Cat,	183
———, said to have had 666 kinds of sacrifice,	210
———, used the Amomum in embalming, &c.,	242
Egyptians, the, the first month of, called Thoth—August,	287
———, predicted the return of Comets,	314
———, the ancient year of, only 360 days,	316, 317, 319
———, the old, had two computations for the year, viz. by lunar months, and by three seasons, (Spring, Summer, and Winter,) each of four months,	325
——— (Saracens), claim to be descendants of Shem,	352
———, Napoleon declared to the, that he was a Mohamedan, why,	358
———, unsatisfactory theories to account for the adoration of animals by the,	437
Eichhorn,	43
Eight instead of *ten* would have been taken for the terminate number, had Arithmetic been the effect of learning,	433
היכל *eihl*—the *middle*, the largest part of the temple, the *sanctuary*, &c.,	408
'Εις may be חיש THE *is*, or *ens*,— existence,	196
——— שיא *ais*, *substance*, or שי *is, he is*,	197
'Εις, μια, ἑν,	195—197
———, three words with distinct ideas,	196
———, descriptive of the Creator, Preserver, and Destroyer,	197
Eléazar,	97
Elect one slain, the,	125
Electric, Galvanic, and magnetic fluids, the, and hydrogen, suspected to be all one substance,	336, 337
Elephant, the, or the Ganesa of India,	130, 165
Elephanta, called Philoe or Elephant,	165
Elephant's head, a pillar with an, used in India, instead of Lingas,	372
Eleusinian mysteries, the, of Ceres, celebrated twice a year,	91
Eleusis,	55, 130, 202
———, mysteries of, from books of Moses,	115, 125, 347, 440
———, a man pretended to be killed in the,	143
——— and Delphi, the Χρης or Ceres of,	117
———, mythos known at the temple of,	134
———, the three sacred words used at, purely Sanscrit,	197
———, initiations at,	232
——— and Egypt, the high mysteries of, none but the *circumcised* admitted to,	248
———, the ceremonies at, celebrated with music, &c.,	289
———, the mysteries of, copied from Jerusalem,	303, 350
Eleutherius, St.,	85
Elias, the prophet, the Superior of the Essenes or Carmelite Monks,	275
Elie, Eléazar,	97
Elijah invested Elisha with the cloak, pallium—the power of the Vates, Bud, &c.,	231, 383
———, the pallium of,	242

INDEX.

Eliphas the *Tmen-ite* or Tm-an-
  ite, a Tamulite, 128
Elisha, 231
Elk, all the parts of, collected from
  various quarters, by the Irish,
  said to have been put into a
  whole, &c., 410, 422
Ellis, Mr., on the word *Acahars*, 371
Elm (or alma), the marital, 242
Elmacious calls Ararat, the Mountain Cordi, 411
Elphinston, Mr., on change of
  lands, among the Afghans, 282, 283
Elphinstone, 239
'Ημερα τε 'Ηλιε, Day of the Sun, 90
Emigrants, our, take their sacreds,
  &c.,—had they the Deisul, they
  would have the sacred mount,
  even in Australia, 341
Empedocles, 62, 314
Emperor, embratur, Om-bra-tur,
  the reformer, of the Tauric cycle, 347
  ———, the, neither of China
  nor of India, but of Muscovy, the
  legal successor of Noah, 353
  ———, the title of, assumed, as
  successor of one of the sons of
  Noah, 369
Emperors, the Roman, as pontiffs,
  claimed as delegates of ΤΗΣ—
  drew imposts from all nations—
  wished to make Latin the common language—and permitted
  those devoted to the infernal
  Gods to be killed, 54
  ———, threw money
  to the people at their coronation
  —were adored by them, and had
  the title of Deus or Divus, 55
Emreis, Welsh for Stonehenge, 177
'Εν, *the On*—Το Ον of Plato, 196, 197
Eocratites, the, 60
Encyclopædia Britannica, the, on
  Platonism, 446
Endes, of Bretagne, his monomania, 359
Edinburgh Encyclopædia, the, on
  the Eclectics, 447
Eneas or Enéa, 18
Eneka, 29
Enfield, Dr., on baptism, by the
  Samaritans, 66
England, 10, 72, 149
  ———, called *Ying keih le*, by the
  Chinese, 149
  ———, the laws of, 272, 273
  ———, the constant increase of
  cold in, 445
English, the, 2
  ———, converted by Augustin, 93
  ———, conduct of, in India, 216
  ———, French, and German,
  the, on alphabet of, 237
Ennius, on the three tribes of
  Rome, 345
  ———, on the great temple of Jupiter, &c., 408
Enoch, the book of, 83, 173
  ———, on *Illuci One skin*, 125
  ———, on cause of the Flood, 204,
    252, 310
  ———, gave Noah the *characteristical marks or signs* of the secret
  things to his book, 310, 333
  ———, book of, discovers a knowledge of judicial astrology, 313
  ———, on Noah, &c., knowing *the
  flood would come*, 329
  ———, how his history should be
  treated, 334

Eoster, the Saxon goddess, 193
Eostre, Asteroth, Astarte, 58, 59, 193
Epagomenon, the five days belonging to five Egyptian deities, *to be
  born in no year, in no month*, 317
Ephesus, 43, 47, 66
  ———, the Panionian temple of, 117
Ephores, the, condemned any innovation in music in celebrating
  heroic deeds, and in the construction of the lyre, why, 425
Ephraim, the sign of, Aquarius, 105
Epic poems—divided into 24 books,
  each into a certain number of
  lines, &c., 340
Epicurus, the first who taught
  grammar among the Grecians, 195
  ———, and the Stoics—the doc-
  trines of, to be found among the
  sectaries of India, 337
Epiphanius, 50, 60, 78, 109, 111
  ———, does not notice the
  Targums, 172
Epiphany, the, 84, 99
Episemon-bau or Vau, 195
Equites or Plebes, the class, pro-
  hibited from marriage with the
  Patricians, 392
Eratosthenes, 12, 13, 99
Eri or Heri, the Saviour, 15, 170, 272
Ερε, 15, 103
Ερες, 5, 62, 135
  ———, Venus and Cupid both so
  called, 170
  —— is Sora or Sera and Cama-
  Ama or Venus, 242
Era, the origin of the Sanscrit Eri
  or Heri, 15
  —— or o-ers, city of the, or of ΤΗΕ
  Sun, *ib.*
Erythræan Sibyl, the, told all the
  history of Christ, 115, 129
Escolapier, L', 109
Esdras (the 1st book of), on the
  three councillors of Darius, &c.,
  traces of the microcosm, in Per-
  sia, seen in, 420
חשמל o-*smeh*, Lord or Baal of the
  Planets, 204
Esne, the Zodiac of, 193, 236
Esoteric doctrines, the, 22, 43
  ———, of Jews, Gentiles,
  and Christians, 123
  ——— religion, the, 92, 117, 122
  ———, as, taught by the
  Christian fathers, 129
  ——— Christianity understood by
  Catholics, unknown by *Protestants*, 124
  ——— Christianity, 130
  ——— religion, the, of the Mohamedans, 351
  ———, the ancient, now
  forms part of the public one, &c., 367
Esoteric and *exoteric* religion, the
  professors of the, &c., 336
  ——— an, and an *exoteric* meaning in the poems sung by the
  rhapsodists and bards, 426
Essenean Christians,—Χρηστιανοι, 45
  ——— monastery, an ancient—
  the members of, admitted into
  the Romish church, 368
Esseneans, the, 61
  ———, of Egypt and Western
  Syria, were Pythagoreans, followers of Χρης, *i. e.* Christians,
  before the time of Jesus of Nazareth, 119

Esseneans, Essenes, or Carmelites,
  43, 44, 75, 141, 204, 248, 275, 279
Essenes, Samaneans, and Christian
  Essenes, the, were all *one*, with
  trifling variations, &c., 368
  ———, were Egyptian monks,
  the same as the early Christians,
  43, 50, 66, 135, 331
  ——— or Therapeutæ, 45
  ———, were Christians before
  Christ was born, 46, 48, 49
  ———, relation between, and
  the Hindoos, 50
  ———, hierarchy of, same as
  the Christian, 71
  ———, turned to the East at
  worship, on Saturday, their day
  of meeting, 89
  ———, their doctrines those of the
  God Adonis or Thamas, the Saviour re-incarnated, 119
  ———, Carmelites and Therapeutæ, the, admitted into the Roman church, 270
Esther, 17
  ———, book of, part of the chronicles of the kings of Persia, *ib.*
  ———, the queen, not called to
  the king for thirty days, 320
  ———, the book of, well depicts
  the Jewish hatred of images, 364
Estoteland—di-sala-estotel, 29, 37
Estrangelo, the, or Pushto, 150,
    153, 159, 237
  ———, or Mendæan, or
  Pushto character, used by the
  Old Persians, Syrians, Assyrians,
  Arabians, Mendæans or Chaldæans, 153
  ———, same as Chaldee,
  Hebrew, &c., 226, 236
  ———, the common al-
  phabet of the Chaldæans, 222
  Eswara, Irish and Hindoo God, 83
  Eternal City, the, Rome, 145, 146,
    238, 440
  ——— life or happiness, the knowledge of, imparted to the initiated only, in the ancient mysteries, 252, 253
  Ethelred—the statute of, giving
  tithes to the priests, only declaratory, 368
  Ethelwolf, in 855, made the whole
  kingdom liable to tithes, 279
  Ethiopia, 211
  Ethiopian dialect, the, 175
  Etruria, 67, 212
  ——— Ras-ena—country of the
  Vine or Wisdom, 231
  ———, Attica, and Ionia, the confederated towns or states of, being precisely *twelve*, shew method
  and design: their confederation
  probably formed under the Pontifical government—not for mutual defence, 394
  Etruscan, the, 26
  ——— baptism, with the Holy
  Ghost, 54
  ———, with water, air,
  fire, and blood, 67
  ——— inscriptions, two, 68
  ———, the system of numbers,
  &c., by right lines, 147
  ——— right-line letters and notation, the, 150
  ——— Agrimensores, the, 112, 284
  ———, all the

INDEX.

	Page
operations of, were of a religious nature—intended to regulate the collection of the tithe,	407
Etruscans, the, 26, 53, 67—69,	231
———, the symbolical writing used by,	373
———, conquered 300 polises—probably the villages round the Cardos,	410
Eu Ca Ri STIa or Eu X a Pi Σ-dia, the good deity Ceres,	254
Eucharist, the, 37, 58—60, 62, 63, 232, 262, 279, 280, 441,	443
——— practised by Melchizedek, 58,	441
——— the Persians, 59,	60
———, as used by Jesus Christ, the most beautiful ceremony,	59
——— or bread-and-water sacrifice, was offered by the Magi of Persia, the Essenes, the Gnostics, by nearly all Eastern Christians, and by Pythagoras and Numa, 60,	253
———, was in use among the Celts and Druids,	62
———, the Trinity, and Regeneration, the later fathers endeavoured to make the doctrines of, secrets, and attempted to preserve them from the vulgar and the Gentiles,	442
Eucharistia, flour offered to Ceres in the sacrifice of, 242, 244,	300
———, the, considered a solemn pledge of secrecy—probably so used, originally in all nations—was celebrated by Jesus, in the last supper, in secret; in the Roman church it was long kept a secret from the rabble,	441
Euclid, 48,	174
Euctemon, the ancient astronomer,	320
Eudoxus,	141
———, on the Egyptians reckoning a month for a year,	325
Euhemerus, the followers of, on the Gentile mythology,	440
Eumolpidæ and Butades, the families of the,	419
Euphrates, the, from φαρα, a flower,	240
Eupolemus,	58
Euripides, cause of lænæ in,	116
Euristhenes (Eurysthenes),	119
Europe, 10, 31, 36, 37, 40, 54, 70, 106, 219,	312
———, Chrestologia existed in, before the Christian æra,	292
———, all Saxon, all Christian,	228
———, the feudal system of, copied from that of India,	275
———, western, like Britain, may be conquered from want of bond of union,	204
——— and India—the same natural cause produced nearly the same natural effect (classes or castes) in both, 275,	293
European pirates, wisely excluded from China,	216
——— monarchs,—their claim to divine right silly,	359
Europeans, the—all the learning of the priests kept from, on their arriving in India,	342

VOL. II.

	Page
Eusèbe de Salverte,	3
Eusebius, 8, 10, 25, 27, 29, 45, 46, 50, 80, 95, 118, 121, 189, 358,	440
———'s Eccles. History,	43
———'s Life of Constantine,	93
——— and Constantine fled according to Lardner, 118,	119
———, on Manetho's dynasties, &c., 324—326
———, on a tribe of Juda, from India, before the tribe of Abraham,	352
Eustace, 55,	75
Eustache, 64,	77
Eustathius,	3
Eutychius,	17
Euxine, the banks of the, broken down by a flood, 311,	312
Eva,	34
—— or Eve, mother of the race of MN, of man,	168
——, the Vau, Venus or Motherstanding for 6—Lustrum,	215
Evangelion of Zoroaster, of Mani, and of the Romish Jesus, the same in principle, and nearly in ceremonies,	65
Evangelium Eternum, the,	355
Evanson, on Dissonance of the Gospels, 125,	132
Evan or Hæa=28,	138
Eve, 31,	32
——, the Mexican, called Ysnextil and Suchiquecal,	32
——, Heva, meant serpent,	113
—— is Vau and the article the—THE Vau,	162
—— not persuaded by the Devil first to taste of the tree of life, why,	250
Even is Vau=6, Eve with a Tamul termination,	163
Evhemere explained mythology historically,	360
Evites, Hivites, or Ophites,	31
Evoho, ΗVAA=28, 183,	184
Exod, the, of Israelites, like the migration of the Mexicans,	24
———, the Egyptian festival at Vernal Equinox, 105,	106
———, a proof of, strangely overlooked by our priests,	307
———, or going out of all nations—probably the first migration of the tribe: the mythos clear in N. and S. India, in Syria, Babylon, Troy, Rome—and in Mexico, perhaps the most remarkable of all,	430
Exorcism,	88
Exoteric doctrines, 29,	283
——— religion, as, taught by the Christian fathers,	129
———, the,	219
——— and esoteric religion, the professors of the,	336
Extreme Unction, 72,	73
Ezekiel, the cherubim of,	105
———, the cross of,	174
———, the Mercavah or wheel of, 335, 342, 343,	401
———, on the four cardinal points of the compass, under the names of the Man, Lion, Ox, and Eagle—the Equinoxes and the Solstices,	343
———, in the temple of, the four oblong buildings have each 40 pillars, and at the four corners

3 s

	Page
have each 19—the number of the metonic cycle, &c.,	402
Ezra, Aben,	105
Faber, Mr., 29, 143,	258
———'s Orig. Pag. Idol., 39, 97, 98,	287
———, his treatment of M. Volney,	255
———, on Cor-Ghari,	410
Fabius Pictor on Janus,	254
Fable, by way of,—parable, from par-habul,	300
Fables — not becas — Pythagoras's disciples cautioned to abstain from, 239, 249,	300
Fairs and Markets held on every Dies Solis, around the sacred mount with its cross,	276
Faith without works, the doctrine of, pernicious,	73
Faithoir or Phaithoir, a vates or druid,	225
Fakirs, the,	74
Fall of man, meaning of the allegory of,	253
Fan, the Chinese name for Sanscrit,	217
———, holy, same as φρην,	218
Fanatic, a sincere, always imagines his cause is good. A fanatic in intention never existed. All the great emperors and conquerors devotees, fanatics,	390
Fara, the, of the Lombards, and the φαραις of the Greeks, probably from the same root as the Pharaohs of Egypt, and all in reference to the feudal system, 419,	420
Faria y Sousa, 25,	421
Farrar's Life of Howard,	142
Farre pio,—holy bread,	62
Fasting, the origin of—the reason forgotten,	213
Fasts, origin of the Romish,	77
Fate, principle of the,	225
Fatemirs, the claims of, to the Califate, in A. H., 402, at Bagdad, declared to be null and void, 385,	386
Fates, from mythos of the infallibility of the Vates,	226
Father, Son, and Holy Ghost, baptism in the name of, practised by the Manichæans,	65
Fathom, a, is equal to 10 pyramidic feet, or 6¼ feet English, the height of a tall man—an Irish Giant, a Goliath,	405
Fatima, the favourite daughter of Mohamed,	382
———, the house of, ruling in Egypt, were Ishmaelites, 384,	385
Fauchet (president), 86,	93
Faustus, on the Father, Son, and Holy Spirit,	337
Feasts of Purim,	17
———, the, of the Innocents,	83
———, made by Ahasuerus to his princes, &c.,	317
Februa, the Goddess, or Februata Juno, became the Purificata Virgo Maria,	82
February, the last month in the ancient year at Rome,	320
Fecundity, offerings by females, to procure,	85

474   INDEX.

Fédawis, seventy thousand (through fanaticism or religious principle) awaited the orders of the Old Man or Imam of Alamout, to throw themselves from the battlements of his castle, to shew their devotion to him, 389, 390
Fee-udal might be lands held of *the Iud in fee*, 272
Feirouz, the husband of Chemsennissa, 245
Female, the, presented to the male *the apples of love*, 249
Female, the followers of Cristna affected the, 269
―――, where the, was the favourite, as at Athens, a leaning, even after the union (of the sects of the Linga and Ioni) to Minerva, or Ceres, 445
Feodal or Feudal Tenure, in Britain and India, 262, 272, 275, 283, 285
――― system, the principles of, lost equally in India and Europe, 263, 268
―――, Saxon origin of, 269, 272, 275, 276, 278, 372
―――, the origin of, involved in absolute darkness, thousands of years after the discovery of the art of writing, 339
―――, the, prevailed in Arabia, 354
――― rights—claims to power, founded on, 382
――― system, the, shews itself, unconsciously, to Mr. Hammer, 383
Festival of St. Agatha, in Sicily, twice a year, 91
Festivals, the, of April-fool and May-day, equally celebrated in Britain and in India, 106, 262
Festum Dei Mortis (All Souls' Day) celebrated by the Buddhists of Tibet, by the Papists, and by the Protestant church of England, as by the Mexicans, 82
Festus—his definition of *possessio*, 393
Fête Dieu, the, 79
Fetiches, the, of the ancients and of Africa, 350
Feudal Tenure, lands in the tenure of Pi-Ioudi, *the Ioudi*? 263
―――, in Irish is Achusac, in Arabic Akbezet, the Acherah payment of tithe, 264
――― lands, the, had seven incidents—heriot, relief, &c., 272, 283
――― tenures in Ceylon, 292
Feudatories, the, or payers of *tenths*, under the Pontifical government, would constantly improve, &c., 362
Fewardentius, 5
Ficlnus, 188
Fig-tree, the Indian, sacred to the Sun, ib.
――― to Xaca or Buddha, 253
Figulus, 140
Figures, the system of, grew into symbolic *letters*, 184
Fila (*love*) súfi̇́ (*wisdom*) from Filusúf, is φιλος σοφιας, 346
Fingal, the Scotch warrior, should be Singal? 293
Finland or *Vin* land, 300

Firdausi mentions *speaking trees*, 165
Fire, adored by the Indian and Chaldæan Ioudi, and by the Persians, as the emblem of creative wisdom and power, or as the Wisdom and Power itself, 128
Firebrand creeds, to incite men to cut each others' throats, none in the religion of the Samaritan Nazarite, 409
Fire Towers, the, of Ireland, Scotland, and India (so called)—Lidgas, 260, 261
Firmament, the, motion of, said to have changed, so that the sun and stars rose where they had formerly set, &c., 314
Firmicius, Julius, 114, 115
First Being—reabsorption into the, hastened or retarded by good or bad conduct, 343
――― Cause, the, 226
―――, in absolute quietude, what but Atheism? 227
―――, every thing in emanation from, or in return to—nothing stands still except, 294
―――, Gas probably thought, by the ancient materialists, to be the substance of, 336
――― Great Cause, every seed a microcosm of the, 429
Fish, the, of Assyria — Ioannes, Wisdom, 347
Fishes, the two, worshiped after the Ram and the Bull, 110
Five temples of Jehovah, in Egypt, (probably cathedrals of the Essenes,) 15, 16, 118, 275, 276
Flagellants, the, 74
Flamen, the Romans made Romulus a, 53
Flamens, the three, the Diale to Jupiter; the Martiale to Mars; the Quirinale to Romulus, ib.
―――, the, clothed like priests, 79
―――, confined to *three*, their persons were sacred, and they were accountable only to the Supreme Pontiff, 422
Fleur de Lis, the Lotus, 178
Flood, the, caused by attempts to obtain forbidden knowledge, 204, 252, 310
―――, of Noah, not universal, &c., 312, 361
―――, a great, more than 2000 years B. C., leaving only a few persons in different places, 313
―――, the, which destroyed Mahabalipore, 315
―――, probably occasioned by *the* comet which last appeared in 1680, 326, 439
―――, happened in 2348, B. C., according to the Hebrew, and in 2925, B. C., according to the Samaritan Chronology, 327—329, 332
―――, highly probable that a, did take place, and that a man and his family were saved in a ship, 335, 438
―――, of Deucalion, 332
―――, of Ogyges, 314, 332, 338
Floods, several, probably occasioned by a comet, 258, 274, 315, 332, 338
Flora—flower, flour, pollen, Pallas, &c., 238, 242

Flora, a corruption of L'phora, פרה *pre*, fertility, &c., 240
―――, a name of Rome, 241
Florence, baptistery at, 67, 112
―――, festival of All Souls, at, 68
―――, churches in, covered with votive offerings, 87
Florida, 31
Flour offered to Ceres in the Eucharistia, 242, 244
Flower—Nazir, Natzir, Nazareth, and Puah, mean a, 239, 240, 242
Floyer, Sir J., threw out Acrostic of the Sibyls, 154
Fo-hi—Buddha—the invention of Chinese letters ascribed to, 215
Foley, Mrs., and Hon. and Rev. Mr., 355
Folkland, 265
―――, estates held in villeinage, were neither feudal, Saxon nor Norman, 269
――― lands—read of, but not found, 284
Fordicidia, the festival of, 92
Foreign Quarterly Review, on Mohamed, &c., 377, 378
Forster, 38, 150, 225, 229
Fortescue, on the common laws, &c., of England, &c., 273
Fortia d'Urban, Marquis de, 137, 169, 426
Fossiones *Tartarum* in Italy, 150
France, 70, 219, 277, 279, 286, 297
―――the kings of, received the *tenths*, afterwards the *ninths*, 266
―――the constitution of, 375
Franci, the, (Franks,) Liberi Sacæ, and Saxons, the same, 267, 268
Francis, St., thought to be a Χρης, 251, 355
――― the *tenth* Avatar, 368
――― I.,—the French poets, under the reign of, less illustrious than the Persian poets under the reign of Hassan Sabah, the founder of the Assassins, 389
Franciscan Monks, the, wore the tonsure like the priests of Isis and Serapis, 92
Frank means *free*, probably from Φρη, 267
Frank-al-Moign, a tenure, 266
―――, persons holding lands in, had no title-deeds, hence the Monks (against the Barons) often forged charters, &c., 268
―――, tenants in, 271
Franklin, the printer of America, 131
Franks, the Salian, were Franks of Sal, 284
Fraser, 231
Free — Freemen, probably from Φρη, Bacchus or Liber, libertas, Liber-di—*holy* Liber, 265
Freehold—land held of the God Φρη, 267
Free lands, i. e. Bock lands, 271
Freemasons, the confraternities of, 300
―――, the, or Mathematici, &c., the best calculators of time, 141
――― have a remnant in their ceremonies of a death and resurrection, 143
―――, Templars, &c., of Ger-

INDEX.

many—their origin traced to the Assassins, 386
Freemasons, Rosicrucians, and Templars, little more than different lodges of one order, 388
Freemasons' Tavern, when lighted up, 298
Free Soccage, 264, 265
Free States, in Europe—the cause of, 366
———, the, of Greece and Italy, held in feudal tenure, 423
——— Towns—the 72, like the 72 Helpers, &c., of Mohamed, 383
———will, 227
———, predestination subversive of, 376
Freisia, Frij (Sweedish), Freya, 265
French, the, overran Italy, 57
———, deceived at the Vatican, as at Loretto, 111
———, conduct of, in India, 21t
———, have a less correct standard of measure than the ancients had. The French and English would have shewn their wisdom by taking the Chest at Cairo for their standard of measure, 404
———, took the measurement of the Pyramid, at the foundation, 406
Frend (W., Esq.), 330
Freret, 360
Frey, 83
Freya—the northern Goddess, 209
———, *the God*, (Godfrey) the Author's name, 213
———, the third person in the Scandinavian Trinity—Chivalry arose from the adoration of? 303, 304
Frickius de Druidis, 108, 109
FRIDAY (Freya) and Φιταδ=666, 209
Fringe, the, of the highpriest's dress, the *zizit*, meant 600, 179
Frisii, the, whence Friseeland or Friesia, 209
F. R. C. (Fratres Rosi Crucis ?) the monogram of the Rosicrucians, *the illuminati* or *invisible brothers* of Germany, 301
Frog, a, on the pedestal of the God at Delphi, 165
Froissard, 55
Fry, 165, 179
Fuhito—the Pushto, 237
Fuller—calls Christ both *rose* and *lily*, 240
Future life, a, whether taught by Jesus to be by a hell, a metempsychosis, or by an absorption into the To Ὀν, uncertain, 308

Gabaa, la ville de, 19
Gabb, Mr., on the measures of the ancients, and on the Pyramid of Giza, as built for forming a standard of measure, &c., 403–406
Gabriel (the angel), 88, 104
Gaditan, the, temple of Hercules, 78
Gael, Sin-gall, and Sanscrit, the, 262
———, Celtic, and Hebrew, the, once all one language, 293
Gael-doct, the *learned Gael*, 158, 188, 292, 294

Gael-doct, the sacred language of Iona, 288
———, the language of *the learned wisdom*, &c., 295
Gaelic, the, is called Shan Scrieu or Sanscrit, in the Highlands of Scotland, 290
Galasius, 5
Gale, 46, 47, 53, 74, 81, 84
Galeb, or a month, as 30 days, 321
Galilee, Γαλ-αλ-ια, country of the circle or revolution, 136
Galien, on music in sacrifice, 64
Galli and Archigalli, the, 47
Gallican Church, the, its claims, independent of the Pope, 266
Gallienus, 110
Game Troy, the, in Wales, noticed by Pliny—Geoffrey of Monmouth, probably, did but repeat the tradition which he found, 401
Gandell, Wood, 19, 143
Ganes, 5
Ganesa, the, or Elephant, 130, 165, 327
———, is constantly anointed with oil, 297
———, animals thought to descend from, to the lowest in intellect, &c., 407
Ganessa, SAPIENTIÆ Deus, 5
Ganga, Jiam Gang, 224
Ganges, the, 239, 263
Gar, the, of Gargarus—the Giri of India—the Ghaur of Stonehenge—the Cor of mounts Cordi or Karda (Ararat)—and the Cardo of Italy, are all the same word; they were centres of measurement, round which the 72 and 360 districts were laid out, 412
Gard—means *place*, as Stutgard, &c., or *district*; the Heb. גיר gir די di—*holy circle*; hence the circles of Germany, 411
Garden, Buddha robbed a, of a flower, 244, 248, 249, 256, 258, 615
Garden of delight, the, 249, 250
———, Adonis robbed the, of a flower, 253
Gardeus, the, of Adonis, were all Eden, 250
Gargarus, Mount, 260
———, here probably are the Cor-Ghari, of India, and the Choir Ghaur, the British name of Stonehenge, 410
——— or Choir Ghaur—others in the Carum Gorum of Tartary and Scotland, 411
Garnet, Dr., his Tour to the Islands, 286
Garudapurana—the atom-like germ, mentioned in the, 398
Gas, (the Hebrew) spiritual firehence Ghost—Galvanic, electric fire, the magnetic fluid, 299, 337
——— and Hydrogen, a digression on, &c., 336
Gate of Salvation, &c., 242
Gathelus, a king of Athens—the Scots have a story about, 401
Gaul, 103, 252
———, the worship of Mithra spread over all, 99
———, all the oriental mythos well marked in, 370
Gauls, the, worshiped the *Virgo Paritura*, as the Mother of God,

100 years before the birth of our Saviour, 108, 109, 135
Gauls, *black*, in Scotland, 204
Gautama, the Nyaya philosophy originated with, 429
Gavel-kind, lands held in, were all in *free soccage*, 265
Gaya, 148
Gehauer, 304
Gebelin, the Count, on Malays speaking Hebrew, 156
———, on the *dance oblique*, 179
Geddes, Dr., 1, 4, 61
———, on identity of Hebrew and Saxon, 155, 199, 275
Geminus, on a month, as 30 days, 321
General of the Priest or Pontiff, when the, in great empires, made himself Khan, the lands were granted to his followers, on condition of each equipping himself for war, 395
———, if the, seized the crosier of his employer, as at Rome, with Cæsar, the Pontifex would become a warrior, 396
Generation but accretion, how rendered probable, 398
Genesis, 4, 11–13, 16, 19
——— and history of Egypt identical, 11, 12, 15
———, a Buddhist book, 83
———, allegorical meaning of, 105
———, names of the actors in, shew the mythos, 128
———, shews marks of compilation, and of mutilation, 134
———, the books of, the oldest in the world, 155
———, a, the secret book of the first pontifical government, 173
———, had two meanings, for the *learned* and the *vulgar*, 183
———, a Buddhist book, forbids animal food, 202
———, in ch. ii. to end of ch. iv. is Brahminical; it permits animal food in sacrifice of the Lamb, 203
———, the 1st and 2nd books of, have two histories and two allegories, 247, 248
———, should be called *Baratit*, i. e. wisdom, i. e. Veda or Buddha, 251
———, mentions not the change in the earth's axis, 316
———, the account in, a valuable record of the tradition of the flood, 332
———, how its history should be treated, 334, 335
———, the text of, inclines to Shem, &c., 353, 361
———, the 3rd book of, might be called the book of the generations or regenerations of Adam, 360
———, the text of, does not say the surface of the whole globe was covered—many persons, in different parts, may have escaped, &c., 361
———, the Jews not permitted to read, lest it should draw them into idolatry, by its Trinitarian doctrine, 364
———, the divisions of 72, &c., marked in, 381
———, the doctrine of, the moving cause of the conduct of almost all the world, from the earliest

INDEX.

time; it was not confined to the Jews, but was a book of the secret mysteries of the world, 390
Genesis implies that the first pair were created side by side like the Siamese boys—but still *male* and *female*—by the woman being taken from the *side* of man, 397
———, how ch. x. ver. 21 ought to be rendered, 399, 409
———, the amalgam of the systems, in the East and West, 400
———, the author of, perfectly understood the doctrine of Agrimensorism; not written by Moses, 413
———, a microcosm of two worlds in, 430
———, in, the fact of the flood is loaded with mythic absurdities and mistranslations, 439
———, may it not be Tamul, containing several meanings, constructed for secrecy? 440
Gengis Khan, 175, 375
———, an Avatar, 207, 352
———, believed to be a divine incarnation, 343
——————, himself to be the person foretold, 344
——————, his alleged miraculous birth—his name Zin, his empire called *the government of wisdom*—he marched into China in 1211, A.D., 353
——————— did suit, &c., to Thogrul, 354, 361, 383, 388
———, was probably moved by superstition as well as policy, to go to Caracorum, 390
———, went to Caracorum for investiture, 411
Genius, the, of each cycle—birth, death, &c., of, 136
Gentile monuments adopted by modern Christians, 68
——— τελεται, sacrifices for the dead, 73, 74
——— religion an immense type, 118
——— confirmation, a, of the Mosaic record of the deluge, 314
——— mysteries, when they began, a herald proclaimed, "Procul, hinc procul este, profani!" 430
Gentiles, the, 59, 60, 61, 79, 81, 84
——— celebrated the birth of the God Sol, on Dec. 25th, 98, 99
———, esoteric doctrines of, 123
——— and Christians, secret religions of, the same, 130
———, the higher class of, the initiated, expected the *tenth incarnation* about the time of Mohamed, 379
Geoffrey of Monmouth—the history found in, of the landing of Brutus, at Totness, 400, 401
Geola,—goal—turning of the sun, 135
Georgius, [his Alphabetum Tibetanum,] 1—3, 5—9, 31, 37, 105, 117, 118, 122, 186, 192, 211, 213, 214, 221, 222, 224, 225, 227—229, 235, 238, 241, 243, 250, 253, 337, 397
Gergeseues, 96
Gerizim, Mount, 207
———, the sacred mount, the national *cathedral*, 275
German and Scandinavian Saxons, the, from the Sacæ, 209

German, the, on words in, identical with Sanscrit, 234
Germans, the, 59, 221
——————, nakedness of, 204
——————, ancient, change of lands among, 282, 283
——————, divided the year into three, 421
Germany, 4, 70, 211, 277, 279, 282, 300, 411
———, the emperor of, always claimed supreme power, and considered all other kings of Europe, probably of the world, as his vassals, as Cæsar and Augustus did, 380, 400
———, the Freemasons, &c., of, feared by Hammer and his master, 386
———, in the pfahlbürger (pale) of, we have a remnant of the Pontifical Government, 434
Gervas of Tilbury, on the sign of Richard's standard, 349
Gessenius, 19
Ghari of time, a—a, man in health said to make 360 respirations in; a Ghari is the sixtieth part of a day and a night; how subdivided, 406
Ghilan, in Mazandaran, 231
Giam—hence Ganga or Janga, 7
———Jang, Deus Sapientiæ, ib.
Giants—Great Britain said to have been inhabited by, when Brutus seized the island, &c., 400
Gibbon, on the dreams of the Paulite Christians, &c., 342
——— no exception to the almost universal practice of receiving unconditionally the evidence of partisans or of opponents—hence history worse than a riddle, 376
Gilgal, a *stone circle*, the simplest of temples, 135
Girdle, and Sudra, 65, 66, 77, 78
Girls, (believed by *the fathers*,) to be pregnant by Demons, 100
Giuli, or Œrra Geola, month of December, 135
גל gl means *circle*, the Gael, 292
Glanville (on Gavel-kind), 265
Globe, the surface of, microcosmically arranged, 399
———, our, an effect, perhaps of a 3rd or 4th, or 5th interval or mundane revolution; will not go to ruin or decay, 431
Glover, 61, 69
גן gn, *a garden*, (hence Gan-isa, protector of gardens,) 245, 415
Gnios, Gnos, 5
Gnomon, the proboscis of the elephant on the Icon of Gun-putty, suspected to have often formed a, 415
———s and dials, the, of Ahaz, always inscribed with Etruscan or Phœnician figures, still used by us, 416
Gnosis, γνωσις, the, 5, 128, 130
———, the oriental, *beautiful* and *sublime*, 132, 351, 448
———, secret mysteries of, connected with magical heads, 349
———, the, or doctrine of Emanations, 367
Gnostic Christians, the, 10
Gnosticism—the real science of antiquity, 131

Gnosticism was nothing but the doctrines of the Cabala corrupted, and becoming publicly known, 403
Gnostics, the, 60, 75, 224
———, had Jesus of Bethlehem for the people—Jesus of Nazareth for the Conclave and Cardinals, 129
Goat and sheep, the, same genus, will breed forward, 188
Gobarus, Stephanus, 122
Go to see, Chinese name for the Russians, 149
God, Chod, is Od, Hod, 6
———, the Kosmos, Mundus, man made after the image of, 136, 228
——— equally present with the pious Hindoo, Jew, Mohamedan, and Christian, 145
———, is called *Dios* by the South Americans, 161
———, supposed to change every day, 226
———, almost every heathen, had the name of 666, 241
———, the author required to believe that He walked in the garden, and wrestled with Jacob, 254, 334
———, believed to be a spiritual fire, 299, 336
——— was nature, all nature God—how, 336
———, our creator, is he not our preserver, the regulator of all nature, &c.? 338
———, man, and every thing supposed to be made in the image of, 397
——— Sol, the, 98, 112
———, birth of the, celebrated on Dec. 25th, 99, 100
———, put to death on the 23rd and raised on the 25th of March, 100
———, said to be the father of Gengis Khan and of Tamerlane, 353
Godfrey (the Author's name) from the God Freya, 213
Godhead—a belief in the Trinitarian nature of the, not meritorious; the ancient philosophers saw no benefit in speculations on, to those who were labourers, 387
Gods, the, burial of all the, 143
———, had no names in early times, and no icons, 147
———, "sit on the sides of the North," on Meru, 175
——— of the week, names of the, 208
———, the names of, derived from cycles, 212
———, 360, one for every day in the year, 319
———, the originals of all the, have been of the *black race*, 363
———, the numerous, of Greece and India, easily traced to the Trinitarian doctrine, 364
———, the 12 greater, and the 360, one for each day, 433
———, the deaths and resurrections of the, parts of a secret system, by degrees made known to the vulgar, 442
Godwyn, 114
Gold, frankincense, and myrrh, offered by the Magi to the Sun, 96
———, while the, was the only metal, and coin not invented, 380

INDEX.

	Page
Golden Age, a, may have existed, when there were no wars,	1, 305
———, the,	266, 307
———, when and why it began to decline, &c.,	306, 365, 366
———, the fact of the existence of,	369
———, the first four Califs believed themselves destined to restore,	377
———, not a figure of speech, but a reality,	423
———, a, produced by the mild Sacerdotal government—then an age of Silver, of Brass, and, as the system went to pieces, an age of Iron,	434
———, probably introduced by the Διοι Πελασγοι, who brought peace and civilisation from the East,	439
——— Fleece, the—holy wisdom,	190, 233
Gomara,	30
Good (on Job),	219, 274
——— Friday, the "Agonie" at Rome, on,	92
Gor, *circle*—Gor-reich, *ruler of a circle*,	413
Gordyæan Mountains, the,	260, 411
Gorgon's head, the, nonsense of,	349
Gorlœs,	61, 67, 68
Gorlœs—the appearance of, assumed by the Gorgon's head, &c.,	349
Gort, the Ivy, *throu*,	161, 163
———, the monogram of, Γ,	177
Goshen, *the house of the sun*,	110
——— of Egypt, and Gossen of India,—the land of the Soc,	280
Gospel histories, the, from the scriptures of the Therapeutæ or Essenes,	45, 46, 96
——— of the Nazarenes,	63
——— Infancy,	96
———, the, on the mass of mankind *seeing*, they *might not perceive*,	334
——— of John, the beginning of the, Platonic,	113
——— contains Gnostic doctrines, the Gnosis and Cabala; found in a vault under the ancient temple at Jerusalem,	125, 126
Gospels, the,	64, 67, 73
———, four, because there are four winds,	100
———, intended to conceal a secret system,	123, 308
———, the Trinitarian doctrine not clearly developed in, why,	367
———, one of the, [apocryphal?] describes Jesus and the Twelve Apostles as having celebrated a dance after the *last supper*,	426
Gothic and Hindu nations, connexion of opinions between the,	245
Gotha, the,	293
———, (under Alaric,) were driven forwards to the West, by the Huns,	273
Grabe, Dr.,	5, 60
———, his Irenæus, Lib. II. Cap. xxxix.,	120

	Page
Γραμμα, the first Greek letters, in lines,	159
———τα,	163, 166
Grammar, first taught among the Greeks by Epicurus,	195
Grandfathers, great-grandfathers, &c., what do we know of them?	339
Grand Seignior, excommunication by, of the Pasha of Egypt, a *brutum fulmen*,	352
———, the, descended from the Khans of Tartary, regarded as Lord Paramount and ecclesiastical head,	375
——— or Sultan, the, as superior lord, claims, though he does not receive, the *tenth* of the produce; having no equal, he never makes a *peace*, but only a long truce, &c.,	380, 395
——— Vicar or Vicramaditya,	9
Grenta and Cam, the, Indian names of the Cambridge river,	295
Grantha, the letters of Cape Comorin so called,	ib.
Grant's Thoughts on the Gael, 413,	439
Grape, the, βοτρυς, 9, 204, 223,	253, 254
——— Stone, the, ραξ,	9, 224
Gravamena of Germany, the,	70
Great and emperor, the claims of all persons so called, founded on Avatarism, on a believed descent from Noah's eldest son, or on the χειροτονια received from the lineal descendant of,	349
Great One to come, the—struggles of different persons, each to make out that *he* was,	ib.
———, a belief that *he* was *the*, has led a conqueror to his *success* or his *destruction*: it led Julian to the desert, Napoleon to Moscow,	358
Greaves's measurement of the Pyramid,—where taken,	405, 406
Grecian history,	18, 19
Greece, 17, 19, 21, 35, 40, 47, 60, 87, 102, 118, 239, 275,	281
———, the Sages of, held the doctrine of purgatory,	73
———, the seven wise men of, 127,	226
———, the sixteen-letter system in,	185
———, colonies into, from India,	213, 419
———, Muses, the, or Saviours of, why nine,	286
———, Lydia, and the Grecian colonies, the ancient year of, only 360 days,	319
———, the doctrine of the renewed incarnation, visible in,	340
———, disputes in, between debtors and creditors, not understood,	418
———, writing in, probably confined, for a long time, and Latin to the caste of priests, in Italy, as the Sanscrit was to the caste of priests in India,	437
Greek, Hindoo, Latin, and Sanscrit names of numbers,	166, 167
——— alphabet, the, altered from the Asiatic for superstitious purposes,	185
———, the, on words in, identical with Sanscrit,	234

	Page
Greek, the, was first written without vowels,	249
——— scholars, like the Sanscrit, fail in their explanations, why,	290, 429
———, when that language was ασημος and συγκεχυμενη, &c.,	437
——— church, baptism in the, by immersion,	65
Greeks, the, 16—18, 20, 48, 49, 61, 65, 74, 86, 87, 130, 131, 133, 139, 150, 159, 189, 211, 221, 224,	337
——— and Romans, few infant Gods, among,	100
———, their error of nine days on the precession,	134
———, less skilled in astronomy than the Saxons,	135
———, admitted no writing older than Homer's poems,	169
———, had once the same numeral letters as the Hebrews,	187
———, ignorant of their mythos,	236
———, tropical year of,	318
———, had two standards of square measure—the Aroura and the Plethron; there were two of each of these measures,	406
———, among the, some families possessed hereditary offices—particularly the priests,	421
———, among the, all dancing mimetic — the Gnosian dances peculiarly sacred to Jupiter,	425
Gregory I., or the Great, on use of images,	69, 86, 93
———, his command could not ingraft all the Pagan doctrines, sacraments, &c., into the Christian religion,	94
———, believed to be a divine incarnation,	343, 375
Gregory Nyssenus,	84
——— Thaumaturgus,	ib.
——— XIII., as Pontifex Maximus, reformed the calendar,	52
Gregory's, Dr., opinion of Whiston's Theory, &c.,	331
Griesbach,	118
Grotius,	37, 276
Ground, the, *not cursed—it* still produces freely, &c.,	252
Groves, the adoration offered in, reprobated—what they were,	193
Gruter (Inscriptions of),	320
Guam—wisdom,	225
Guatama, or Buddha the Second, his religion established in Ceylon,	288
Guatimala,	33
Guebres, the, fire-worshipers,	83
———, the mythos found among—Christianity *grievously defaced*, &c.,	357
Guerin de Rocher, the abbé, 2, 10—17, 19, 163, 177, 178, 221,	273
Guinea, De,	36, 215
Γυνη, Can-ia, the,—*the garden of delight*, allegory of,	249, 250
——— and Kwn, probably a mistake between, as applied to the *profane* and to *dogs*,	430
Gun-puity — with an elephant's head, the emblem of wisdom, at the side of Indian roads—*the fe-*

VOL. II.   3 T

478 INDEX.

ther *of the garden*, from ‖ɔ gn, garden, and *petti* father; 415
Gautham, king, a declaratory law passed by, at the Council of Muscon, 279
Gushtasp, 77
Gutzlaff's Journal, 215, 216, 217
Gwyddion (one of the three Seronyddion), *the diviner by trees*, 153
Gymnosophists or Samaneans, the, 43—45, 368
———————, the monks of Europe were, 370
Gynæcocracy, 24
Gyndes, the river, made fordable for the army of Cyrus,—against Babylon, 317

H, ἡ, originally pronounced *h* as in English, 204
Habul, gives Cabala, the word used in Italy for *a fable*, 300
Hadad, is Idad or I-badad, 6
———, corrupted from *Ad od*, 162
Hadrian, 15
Hag, 31
Hagar—the Mohamedans maintain that she was not a *slave*, but a *princess*, 386
———, Dr., 150, 153, 227, 236, 248
Haggai lived before the entrance of the sun into Pisces, 125
——— foretells the *promised desire of all nations* by a feminine word, 291
" Hail to the Dove," &c., 114
Hakem Bemrillah, believed to be a divine incarnation, 343
——————, established or enlarged the college at Cairo, called Darol-Hikmet or *the house of wisdom*—provided it abundantly with books, mathematical instruments, celebrated professors, and a revenue of 257,000 ducats, 387
Hakim, 4, 7
———, the king, 300
Halde (Père du). See Du Halde.
Halfeld, 43
Halhed, Mr., 131, 342, 355
Halicarnassus, a city of Asia, 319
Hallam, 268, 288, 356
———, on feudal system, 277, 285
———, on ecclesiastical corporations, 278, 284
———'s Const. Hist. of England, 283, 417
———, on waste lands in the hands of the monks—riches acquired by bringing them into cultivation, 418
Halley, Dr., on the Comet of 1680; its revolution in 575 or 575½ years, &c., 326
———'s, Dr., opinion of Whiston's Theory, 331
Ham, probably Noah's eldest son, 361,
———, the story of his uncovering his father, why contrived, 385
———, a claim for (the *divine right* of) probably set up for the Ishmaelites in Egypt; the despots do not bring it forward, why, 384

Ham, both Syria and Egypt the domain of, 385
———, in the division of the world, had 24 parts, 399
———, the *wicked one*, &c., father of the Canaanites or followers of the *female* principle, 430
Hamilton, Sir W., 85
—————, 238, 352
—————, on the word Cirear, 277
Hammer, 205, 220, 221, 235, 237, 247, 424, 437
———, on the Assassins, 348, 381—391
———, on the meeting of Jurists at Bagdad, 359
———'s, Mr. Von, History of the Assassins, is one great untruth, founded on one great mistake, 381, 382
———, his zeal against modern secret societies, 384, 386, 391
———, his ignorance of the system respecting the three *holy* cities, &c., 385
———, lauds the ancients for keeping the people in ignorance; but reprobates the same system in modern Egypt, 387
——— followed Mirkhond and Wassaf in his History of the Assassins — hence his account is not surprising, 390
Hancarville, M., D', 97
Hannay, Robert, Esq., on Chartres, its Cathedral, and miraculous Stone, 259, 260
————, on the beginning of the municipal governments of our towns—their date, 401
Hannibal shewed a march from Granada to Rome was possible, 385
Hanuma, the monkey, *half*-man, 180, 249
Haquim, 4
Haree or Heri, the Greek Ερως, the Saviour of all, 118
Har-ol-ump, Har-al-om, Mount of the God Om, 178, 179
Harpocration, 319
Hassan Sabah, the college of, at Cairo, 250, 387
———, founder of the sect of Ishmaelites, may have been the last descendant in the right line of Fatima, the favourite daughter of Mohamed: his journey to Rei and Ispahan, and his dialogue with Aboulfasl, 328, 388, 390
———, the lineal descendant of the prophet, the last Imam, 383
———, made the fortress of Alamout the seat of his power, 386, 388
———, was, in the opinion of his followers, a renewed incarnation of divine wisdom, like the Pope, or the Lama of Tibet, 389
———, the second, assumed to be the real Imam, 388
———, pretended to burn his books; if he did, he kept copies. Something, probably, good in them, which the enemies of the Assassins could not refute, and dared not expose to view, 390

Hastings, Mr., on a tradition at Benares, 444
Hat, the chief ensign of the Flamens, 53
Hatfield Chase, the scotted or taxed lands of, 284
Haughton, Professor, [Sir Greaves], 158, 244, 245, 261, 358
—————, on derivation of the word Sanscrit, 290
—————, on Cor-Ghari or Cor-Ghirry, the mountain Cor, 411
—————, on the words *Nyaya* and *Vedanta*, 428, 429
Hayti, the God of, called Joeanna, 31
He, ה, the number 5, 138
——— and *Vau* (5 and 6), the *male* and *female*—all the race of man descended from the union and conjunction of, 409
Heathens, the inferior gods of the, 89
——— matched by saints, 90
———, names of the gods of, copied by the Christians, 91
Heavens, the, a book,—whatever is in nature, to be read in, 235
Hebrew, the, every letter of, had four or five meanings, 15
———, spoken in China, and the Hebrew and Christian system flourished there, 41
———, i. e. the Celtic, in Wales, 130, 154, 163, 176
——— and Samaritan chronology, the difference between, 133
———, the ancient Chinese nearly related to, 148
——— and Arabic the same, 153, 159, 213
———, is Celtic and Saxon, 155
———, and Mexican, close affinity between, ib.
——— Bibles given to the Irish, 163
———, the root of the East Indian languages, 183, 225
———, vowel Points of, modern, 184
——— and Celtic, deficiency of vowels in, 185
———, the first language of the Indians, 217
——— or Chaldee, the original root of Sanscrit, 236, 237
———, Samaritan, and Syriac or Pushto, have each 22 letters, 239
———, the first numeral symbols written into the, 291
———, the, according to Young, is Welsh, 293
———, the *sacred script* became a dead language to the Jews, 294
———, the, locked up in the Temple, preserved in purity, 437
Hebrews, the, 17
———, give only Adam and six princes in the race of Seth, 133
———, used R for S., 199
———, confused state of the history of, 332
Heeren, 10, 159
———, on the wealth, &c., of the Egyptian priests, 366, 373
Hegisippus, 46
Helen, the female generative principle, 51
———, the mystical mother of Constantine, 289

INDEX. 479

Helena—mother of Constantine, 348
——— St., Napoleon at, a decided fatalist, 358
Heliogabalus and Caligula required kissing of the foot, 55
——— Antoninus, 348
Heliopolis, or On, 110
——— the temple at, had its sacred *fishes* and *tank*, 236
——— its kings called Ad and Adad, ib.
——— the ancient academy of, 387
Hell, hot, cold, &c., 73
——— a, whether Jesus Christ taught a future life by, 308
Helots, the remains of a race drowned by the flood, 274, 310
——— the aborigines, a class of almost every where, were slaves under slaves, &c., 362
Henry of Navarre, 54
——— I., not called Majesty, 213
Heptarchy, the Saxon, did not extend to Scotland, 273
——— traces of tithes paid under the, 279
Heraclidæ, the, from Atreus, 119
Heraclitus, 47
Herbert, Lord, 30
Herbert, extract from, on "everlasting Rome," 146
Hercules, 8, 19, 21, 106, 112, 117, 132, 137, 154, 225
——— the Gaditan temple of, 78
——— a personification of the sun, 100
——— the Labours of, 105
——— the Greek and Indian, identity of, 119
——— strangled the serpent, 144
——— the Labours, &c., of, "types of what the real Saviour was to do and suffer," 193
——— the, at Mattra, and on Egyptian buildings, 282
——— Antony called himself the lineal descendant of, 346
——— Alexander traced his descent from, 348
——— was called Perseus in Africa and Persia, and Sesostris in Egypt, ib.
Herculeses, &c., put to death, &c., 142
Herennius, 448
Heresies, *twenty* before Christ, 50
Heri or Eri means Saviour, 15, 293
Hericülas, the, and Poorus, 117
——— from Atri, 119
Hermapion, 159
Hermes, 31, 131
——— Teut or Thoth, the inventor of letters, 163
——— or fifth Mercury or Buddha, 164
——— the alphabet of, 220
Herod, 96, 449
——— and the 3 Kings or Magi, 96
——— Jesus *not* crucified under, according to Irenæus, 122, 129
——— believed by the Jews to be the Messiah, 233
——— to be a Χρης, 251, 446
Herodotus, 2, 15, 19, 27, 28, 36, 54, 85, 167, 180, 181, 204, 221, 230, 268, 273, 314
——— really the *father* of history; did not discover the empire of Solomon, or the mountain tribe of Jews, 11

Herodotus's history and Genesis the same, 12, 13
——— was in Egypt about 400 years B.C., 17
——— never names the empire of Solomon, 134
——— all books before, were sacred, 246
——— history before, mere mythos, 313, 334
——— on Solon discoursing with Crœsus, 318, 319
Hesiod, 305
Hesperides, the apples of, the tree of knowledge, 190, 253
——— from פץ ox and מרי pri, *letters* and *tree*, and a *flower*, 240
Hhasār—*ten* in Heb. or Chaldee—Σαρς in Greek, literally *a decad*, 322
Hesychius, 248, 287
Hexameters, pentameters, &c., how they arose, 340
Hibbert's Shetland Islands, 284
Hieralpha, the, of the Hindoos, was the Lituus or Crosier, 79
——— in the hand of Hercules, 282
Hierarcha, the, of each nation, would grow into Archierarchs, as the knowledge of a very distant Lord faded away, 381
Hierarchy, the, of Christians, a close copy of that of the Persians, 71
Hierocles, 448
Hieroglyphic alphabet, the first letter or symbol of, an owl, 192, 205, 221
Hieroglyphics, 20
——— on two at Rome, not from Egypt, 92, 93
——— meaning of, lost in Egypt, 159, 160
——— the Mexican, known to all, 160, 235
——— remains of, in Chinese letters, 214
——— the Egyptian secret, except to the Initiated, 235
Hieronymus (Jerom), 16, 58, 77, 95, 96, 98
Hierophantes, the, of Athens, drank hemlock to render them impotent, 77
חכמה *hkm*, wisdom, 195, 215, 225
חכמה *Akme*, Guam, a corruption of, 225
Hilaali, 29
Hilarion, on the founders of monasteries, &c., 368
Hindoo doctrine, the, on the number of Incarnations, 127
——— Greek, Latin, and Sanscrit names of numbers, 166, 167
——— year, the, is 360 days, 316
——— princes, the, solicit investiture of the Mogul, though he is a Mohamedan, 352, 353
——— institutions at one time similar and universal throughout India, 418
Hindoos, the, 33, 69, 72, 73, 79, 81, 83, 103
——— their pristine religion that of the pure and ancient Catholic faith, 24
——— believe the Vedas were written in a divine, long-lost language, 226
——— and followers of Brothers, Southcote, &c., believe the last Avatar is yet to come, 354
Hindoos, the, say, there have been thousands of Avatars, 356
Hindus, the, give the first created, &c., 133
——— believe that all living beings originate from an atom-like germ, 398
Hio—Cio—scientia, 227
Hipparchus, 26, 139, 141, 142
Hippocrates, on the length of the year, 319
Hispaniola, 30
Histoire des Temps Fabuleux, 11, 12, 17
Histories, the, of Romulus, Cyrus, Theseus, Bacchus, Hercules, Cristna, &c., in reality identical, 307
History, the, of Rajast'han, 4, 39, 117, 119
——— before Herodotus—mere mythos, 313, 334
——— every, a mystery, *to conceal the truth, that the mass seeing, might not perceive*, 334
——— originally one, and *that* a mythos of the arrival of a divine Incarnation in each age, which the priests of each country persuaded the people must be renovated in their peculiar country, 340
——— a great part of ancient, should be considered as mythology, 360
——— of the world, few, perhaps, so well qualified to write a general, as the Author, 369
——— all, made worse than a riddle, how, 376
Hivites, Evites, or Ophites, the, 31
Hoffman, says, the early Christians did wisely not to expose the mysteries to the profane view of infidels, 442
Hog's History of Cornwall, 70, 88, 178, 179, 286
Hollowmas-day or La Samhna, 82
Holloway's Originals, 154
Holm or baum, the Phœnix, Phoinix or Palm-tree, 65
Holme, the, 69
Holsenius, on the analogy between English, Spanish, &c., 258
Holy Bread—the Pagans, says Tibullus, appease the Divinity with, 62
Holy Ghost, the, 20, 54, 65, 81
——— spiritus, Πνευμα, רוח, air, breath, 67
——— effects of, wisdom and power, 128
——— or Zephir, 182
——— or Spirit, descended on Jesus Christ, at his baptism, in the form of a dove—always a *female* dove, 285
——— of Plato's Trinity was Ne—Venus, 286
——— well known to the ancient Celts, and invoked in their public councils, 299, 337
——— breath or air in motion, 337
Holy One, the, in the West, incomprehensible, and one with the Tien, 36
Holy Trinity, the, 80

INDEX.

Hom—the Mexican Creator and Triune God, 23
Hom-eican—place of the Holy Trinity, ib.
——-ei-can—country of the Self-existent, ib.
——-eteuli—God of threefold dignity, ib.
——-eyoca—place of the Creator, the same as the Omorca of the Chaldæans, ib.
Homeyoca, the same as the Omorca of the Chaldæans, 28
Homer, 13, 17, 18, 64, 305
——, the MS. poems of, all without the digamma, 168
——, no writing older than, admitted by the Greeks, 169
——, his poems indebted to Aristotle, &c., for their perfection, 195, 196, 293
——, Om (the God) and Eri or Heri (Saviour)—Om the Saviour, 293
Honover, the Logos or Linga was so called in Persia, 261
Horace, 62, 77, 87, 92, 357
Horæ Sabbaticæ, 78
Hornius, on the Mexicans—from Scandia, 278, 279
Horse and Ass, unknown in a state of nature to the Americans, 35
——, the, viewed with horror when first seen by the Mexicans, but undeceived by the death of, 38
——, the, of the Revelation, 39
——, cow, and sheep, how conveyed to America, 40
——, and the Ass, will not breed forward, 188
Horus, son of Isis, his birth, death, and resurrection celebrated in Egypt, 102
——, worshiped by the Muscovites, 110 v
——, an Egyptian grammarian, 219
Hosanna, 31
Hoskyns, John, on Chinese numerals, &c., 216
Hostia, ancient sacrifice, 91
Houlakou, the third successor of Gengis, said to have finally destroyed the Assassins or Ishmaelites, in A. D. 1256, 382
Howard, the philanthropist, 142
Hu, God in Welsh—his sanctuary an Ox-stall, 178
Huehue, the Mexican first pair, 26
Hull festivals, at the vernal equinox, 106
Hum, *deselt*—Humbug, *Big Hum*, 293
Human sacrifices of prisoners of war, ordered by the (Mosaic) law, 194
—— sacrifices, offered alike in Rome and in Britain—they were not laid aside by the Romans till the time of Claudius, 416
—— race, the probable increase of, after the flood, in 500 or 600 years, 395, 439
—— reason, according to the Chinese, is the reason of the universe, 398
Humboldt, 25—28, 33, 34
——, the *learned* or *Sabio wles*, 297
Hume and other historians have failed to account for many circumstances relating to our Saxon ancestors, from taking too confined a view of the subject: the fabricators of Stonehenge and Abury seem not to have entered their mind, &c., 416
Hume, on the Aga of the land, 417
Huns, the, 203
——, drove the Goths towards the West, 273
Hutchinson, 137
—— and Shaw say, the Onion is a perfect emblem of the disposition of the heavens, 438
Hydaspes, the, 19
Hyde, Dr., 30, 61, 64—66, 70, 71, 77, 78, 83, 86, 89, 92, 98, 101, 218, 240
——, on the fear of the ancients of believing too little, 107
Hydranos, the, 65, 66
Hydrogen, probably constituted what the ancients called *spiritual fire*, the To Ov, &c., 7, 336
Hydropism, 7
Hymnes, les, d'Orphée, 97
Hyperborean island, a sacred, said to have adored Apollo, 262
Hyperboreans, the *black* dove from the, to Delos and Delphi, 285

I, a monogram, prefixed for mystery, 6
—, the form of is X, in the Dalmatian alphabet, 190
—, the Creator, the mother of figures, letters, knowledge, ib.
—, said to be prefixed for sake of mystery, (the sign of the *male* principle,) 198, 343, 344
—, the ancient Saxon emphatic article, 199
—, is Agam (Sanscrit), Aku (Malay), Anok (Egyptian), Ego (Chinese, Greek, and Latin), Ic in Saxon, &c., 229
Iacæa, festivals of Bacchus, 8
Iach Iach, the God of Siam, ib.
Iacch, lacché, ib.
Iacchus—Ia or Ie-chus or Ie-kus, 224
Iad or I-hadad, ib.
I am that I am, on front of the temple of Isis, at Sais, 17
Iao, 5, 192
— of Siam, 7
— the God Sol, Mithra, and the Lamb of God, the same, 112
—, } birth of, at winter solstice, 49, 95
Iaw }
— of the Gentiles, the second person of the Trinity, 98
—, Jesus mistaken for, or the Sun, 100
Ice—derivation of, 19
Icon of Buddha—the mother suckling the infant, 170
Iconoclasts, 194
——, the Jews a sect of, 16
Icons, Gentile, have become Christian crucifixes, 116
—— of Noah, Job, Seth, in India, 122
Icrid, Critika or Kritika—the God —both Bull and Ram, 117
Id=14, 184
Ida, mounts of, by the Hebrews called *Ido*, 161, 188, 226
Idæa—Mala—alma parens Deum, 189
Idei, the, of Crete, were Dactyli, because *ten*, 188
Identity of the Persian and Christian services, 78
——————— Christian and Gentile festivals, 84, 93
——————— Carnival and the Saturnalia, 86
——————— modern systems of Christianity and of those of the ancient Persians, 106
——————— of the celestial lamb, and of the Romish Jesus, 112
——————— worship of Tammuz in Western Syria and Egypt, and of Tamus in North and South India, 119
——————— of Jewish and Gentile systems, 125
——————— Tibet and Rome, in rites, &c., 127
——————— the ancient Indian and Roman secret religions, the cause of the success of the Jesuits, 366
——————— appellation of the Crēat or Χρης given to two persons in India and Europe, at the head of two divisions of the religion, 438
Ididi or Jedidiah, the most holy IE, 180
יהי *ido*, Idea, 188, 192, 325
Idols, the, of the Britons, ordered to be destroyed by Gregory I., 93
יהי *iv*, the *I shall be what I have been*, &c., 425
IE, 5, 6, 174, 175, 180, 190
— of the Hebrew changed into Io, in the Syriac, 250
יהיה *ieie*, the, chaunted by the Brahmins in the word *Yeye*, 427—429
Ieo, THE, L'Awu, 9
Ieu, the great prophet, lawgiver, or Saviour of the Chinese, had 70 disciples, like Ἰησους, the Zω or Saviour, 421
Ieoud, son of Saturn, 8
IEUE, 170, 171, 180, 219, 286
— or Iηo, the followers of, 214
IH of Delphi or the XH=608— Jesus Christ described by, 190, 192
IHS, Iησος, 112
——, Bacchus, Logos, Linga, letters; LTR=650, 240
Ignorance, the, of mankind, before the art of writing was discovered, and while it was kept a profound secret, not surprising, 339
I-ha-ho or I-ha-hou, the God eternal, 17
Ihid, 9
Ii, 7, 139, 200
—, the crucified God of Scotland and of Tripetty, 122, 206, 259, 288
— or Iona, inquiry into the history of, 285—288
— the island, and the name of Jehovah, in Hebrew and Gael, 286, 288
Ii-di, 7
Iinaa, 150, 176
IIVAA=28, Evohe, 151, 183, 184, 286
——, an acrostic, 185
ΙΧΘΥΣ is I-χθυς, 6, 198
Ila, the island, so called from *Ila* the consort of Buddha, 287
Ilâhi, *godly*,—the name of the religion of Akbar—probably from the יהיה *ieu*, 355
Ilas, 14

INDEX. 481

Ilas or Tulis, 14
Iliad, the, 18, 19
Ilium, 51
——— or New Rome, ib.
Illusion, 123, 128, 294, 336, 445
———, the lucubrations of learned men in Europe, as in India, have ended in, 427
Image of God — man, animals, plants, and every thing, believed to be made in the, 397, 400
Images, the use of defended by Arnobius and Celsus, 80
——— and emblems, *the adoration of*, has ended in the degradation of all nations, 364
Imam Ishmaël, (the son of Dschafer,) after whom the Assassins probably assumed the name of Ishmaelites, 384
——— the invisible, proclaimed by the Assassins, as about to demand the empire of the whole world: the origin and meaning of Imam unknown, 388
Imams—open and *concealed*, nonsense respecting, 351
———, in the, of Persia, we have the 12 Lucumones, 380
——— the 12, similar to the 12 Cæsars, &c., 385
Immaculate conception, an, or the, 21, 38, 42, 96, 194
———, the, of Suchiquecal, 32, 33
———, of Jesus, by his mother, different from that of Cristna, 49
———, story of, considered spurious by the Nazarenes, &c., 96
———, Zoroaster's prophecy of a—brought to Ireland by a Daru or Druid of Bokhara, 96, 97
——— of Bacchus, 102
———, the, of Buddha, Xaca or Saca, 227—230
———, of Cæsar, 345, 349
———, of Alexander, 347, 349
———, of Gengis Khan and his brothers, 353
Immaculate conceptions, crucifixions and resurrections of the Gods of the Gentiles, of the East and West, the, numerous, 125, 207
——— of Alexander and Cæsar, 349
Immaculée conception, l', de la Vierge, 97
Immortality of the soul—the knowledge of the doctrine of, confined almost exclusively to the priests, in Egypt, and hidden by Moses from his people, 386, 387
Inachus (son of Noah), the black or Ethopian Iis, 224
Inachus, 309, 414
Incarnate God, an, now believed in, 98
———, adventures of the, a great mystery, taught only in the temples, 232
———, the adventures of the whole life, &c. of the, represented in the Delsuls, 233
——— or solar mythos—in what cases attributed to real men, 351
VOL. II.

Incarnation of the Trimurti or Trinity, the Supreme Pontiff, supposed to be an, 244, 258
——— our divine, the Brahmins say, is the same as theirs, 337
——— a divine, what is but a person with more than a usual portion of the divine *spirit*? 338
———, the doctrine of the renewed, visible in India, Persia, Syria, Greece, Italy, China, and Mexico, 340
——— of Cristna, 98, 341
———, the, of the *triune* God, a confused account of, in the story of the mother of Gengis Khan and her three sons, 353, 354
Incarnations or Avatars, 81
Incas, the, had a cross, of Jasper,—held in great veneration, 32
——— of Peru, united in their person the temporal and spiritual powers, 34
Incense used by both Jews and Gentiles, 79, 92
Indathyrsus,—Bacchus, 208
India, 22, 36, 39, 79, 87, 97, 103, 106, 109, 118, 127, 134, 181, 192, 206, 207, 209, 210, 212, 219, 239, 278, 340
———, the sages of, held the doctrine of purgatory, 72, 73
———, words of Britain in, 176
———, Chrestologia existed in, before the Christian æra, 202
———, colonies from, into Greece and Italy, before the art of Notation was committed to writing, 213
———, the fire towers of, 260, 261
———, the feudal system of, 262, 272, 275
———, the principles of, lost in, 263, 268
———, proper, divided into three districts, 277
———, the holders of land in, have no title-deeds for it, 284
——— and Scotland, identity of race and language in, 289
———, the subjects of Homer's poems, and the history of the Bible, found in, 293
———, the priests of, kept all their learning from the Europeans, and from all their countrymen except their own caste, 342
———, the sects of, a prototype of those of Europe, 368
———, North and South, Mexico, &c., many of the sect in, who have not the Pentateuch, have part of the same laws as the Western Jews, 376
——— and Europe,—the same natural cause produced nearly the same natural effect (classes or castes) in both, 279, 392
———, the dominion of all, possessed by the Callidei, who ruled over it, either by the *sword* or the *crosier*, 396
——— divided into districts, each containing 84 sub-districts, like the hundreds in England, 418
———, the great castes of, became divided into many little ones, &c., 421
———, North or Tartary, 1, 2, 7, 19, 134, 171, 173, 376

India, South, 7, 19, 24, 134, 171, 173, 376
Indian Gods, the, in Ireland, 273, 287
——— princes, the, conquered by Alexander, seem to have been feudatories to some grand potentate of the East, 421
Indians, the, hold the waters of the Ganges sacred, 65
———, the earth's inclination known to, 314
———, probably understood what we call hydrogen, 337
———, ignorance of the, almost incredible, 351
———, probably escaped from the flood, 361
———, a tribe of, divinely wise, &c., 368
———, the ancient, paid their devotions (morning and evening) to the sun, by a dance imitative of his motion?, 425
Indies, the, 360
Indra, 27
———, crucified and raised from the dead, 83, 206
———, of India, the Iao of the Hebrews, the Jupiter Pluvialis of Greece, and the Jesus of the Romish Church, 122
Indus, the, 33, 117, 263
——— or Siudi—the holy river, 181
Infallibility, the, of the Pope, from the mythos of that of the Vates, 226
Infant Baptism, 67, 69, 70
——— practised by the Persians, 65
——— by the Assassins, Carmelites, Druids, Essenes, &c., &c., 248
——— in scripture, *in universali*, not *in particulari*, according to Bellarmine, 69
Ings Lands, the, changed hands every year, 282, 283
Innocent I., Pope, on Christian mysteries, says, "Reliqua vero, *quæ scribi fas non est*"—this must apply to something besides the sacramenta, 441
——— III., 52, 54
Innocents, the account of the murder of the, from India, 235
Inscriptions, many written in cipher, in India, 49
Inspiration by the Holy Ghost, a figure of speech, describing a person more enlightened than his neighbours, 308
Inspiration, what is it? Is it a substance, &c., 338
Io, 5, 6, 192
Iod is a point, the centre, 6, 190
———, hand, 189, 190
———, Ivy (Heb.) and *tenth* letter of the alphabet of figures, 190
———, is, perhaps, i-di, *the holy I*, 371
Iodia, is Ayoudia, 6
Iogerne, the wife of Gorloes, 349
Iohnites, the, &c., or Chaldæans, the best calculators of time; 141
I Ov, the Ov of 1. I, jod, is son, X, the perfect number, 174, 190
Iona, or Columba, 130, 257, 260
———, the Culdees of, 270
———, inquiry into the history of, 285—289

482 INDEX.

Iona, the island of, is called Sodor or Sudor, 285—291
———, the language of, is Gaelic and Shan Scrieu, 290
———, had its name of Columba from the ancestors of the Sea Kings, 305
——— or Iune (in the sacred island of) the temple was surrounded by 360 crosses or pillars, and 60 pillars in the inner circle—wheel within wheel, &c., 402
———, the monastery of, had *twelve* and their Prior, 420
——— in Scotland, from, to Iona in Ceylon, facts prove that the religion of Buddha came to the West, 424
——— and Linga, 130
Ionia, Attica, and Etruria—the confederated towns or states of, being precisely *twelve*, shew method and design; their confederation probably formed under the pontifical government, not for mutual defence, 394
Ioudi, the, 43
———, from Tibet, 127
———, Indian and Chaldæan, adored fire, 128
———, inventors of the Cadmæan system, 185
——— and Sacæ, the tribes of, the same, 263
———, Sacæ and Scythæ, were the Lowlanders of Scotland— Yavanas, Saxons, 273
———, the difference between the, of the West and East, found in the Brahmin coming to Syria being an iconoclast, 364
Ioudia, Ayoudia or Judæa of India, 181
Iphigenia, 21, 293
Ireland, 31, 82, 83, 97, 117, 156, 183, 210, 230, 286
———, the carns of, 179
———, settlements of the Chaldei in, 270
———, the fire towers of, 260, 261
———, Indian Gods came to, 273, 287
———, and Highlands, the Baltan fires of, 289
———, in the *pale* of, a remnant of the pontifical government, 434
Irenæus, 5, 57, 60, 142, 198, 241
——— on the age attained by Jesus Christ, 120—123, 228
——— on duration of our Lord's ministry, 120—122
———, a Gnostic, 129
———, Papias, Augustine, Athanasius, &c., letting out a part of the *esoteric* doctrine, &c., 367
Irish, the, pass their children through fire to Beal or Samhan, 82
———, light fires, like the Persians, on Nov. 2nd, 83
———, old Gods of, traced to the Phœnician or Hebrew language, 155
———, the old or Celtic letters of, the same as the sixteen-letter alphabet of the Hebrew, Tamul, and Pushto, 156
———, Hebrew Bibles given to, 163
———, letters in, called by names of trees, 166
———, the middle letter of the alphabets of, is M, 185

Irish, the, according to Vallancey, a tribe from Spain, but previously from the East, 412
Iron, not found till 188 years before the war of Troy, 22
——— and letters, the Americans ignorant of, 33, 40, 41, 206
———, bearers, of beaten, 21 feet long, and 8 inches square, in the temple of the sun at Kanurak, 261
———, once the *precious* metal—instruments with iron edges and gold handles, exemplars of, in Sweden and Denmark, 305
Irtish, the, 67
Irving, the followers of, expect a re-incarnation of Jesus Christ— the *tenth* Avatar, 258
———'s chapels—the speakers with tongues in, 342
Isa, Isi, male and female, 175
——— and Ma-hesa of India, the Hesus of Gaul, &c., 337
Isaac, 8, 110
Isaiah, Lowth on the poetry of, 16, 172
———, the virgin of, 109
Isan or Isuren of India, the Isis of Egypt, 7
Ischa, in Irish Celtic, meant a *fish*, the same as the Arabic for *Saviour*, 347
Ischaka, the Saviour Saca, 229, 230
Ischas, or Isca, or Ischa, the name of Sarah, and of Jesus, 60, 230, 346, 347
Iseur, 304
Ishmael, the tribe of, 207
———, what has Juda (Jeddo) to do with the city of? 352
Ishmaelites or Assassins, the sect of, 382—391
———, had an æra of Alexander, 348, 349, 384
———, the, were followers of Ham; at war with the Califs and Christians, because both usurped a part of their dominions, 385
———, the, why they were called Assassins, 386
———, the secret doctrines of, existed at Cairo, before the Assassins were founded by Hassan Sabah, 388
———, the sect of the subsisted, like the Jesuits, long after the open suppression of the order, particularly in Kouhistân, &c., 390
———, the, of the East, go on pilgrimage from the Ganges to the Indus, to receive, at Khekh, the benediction of their imam— regarded as an incarnate ray of the Divinity, 391
Ishuren or Sharon, the Rose of, 6, 33, 44, 239, 240, 243
Isidore of Seville, 104
Isis, 7, 19, 34, 61, 78, 84, 102, 110
———, rites of, by water, air, fire, and blood, 67
——— priests of, like Franciscan and Mendicant Monks, 92
——— and Serapis, priests of, wore the tonsure, ib.
———, with her son Horus, worshiped by the Muscovites, 110
———, sacred cycle of *fourteen*, 163
———, the veil of, a parable, 300

Isis, the, of Egypt; was called Neith, 336, 337
———, called Muth or Mother by the Egyptians, 403
Iskander or Ischander (Alexander) a lover of wisdom, exposed by his mother, suckled by a wolf, &c., 346
Islam—doctrine of the *Lama of Is*, 230
Islamism nearly destroyed by Akbar, in six years, 355
———, the princes of, attempted to be overthrown, by Christians, infidels, and the Assassins, 388
Ismenian Apollo, the, of Thebes in Bœotia, 204
$y\omega$' *iso*, the Saviour, 118; to save, 230, 337
Isopolity—an interchange of rights among towns or free states, 434
Ispahan, 382
Israel, the twelve tribes of, 19
Issachar, 1м
Isthmus of Suez, when a morass, 352
Ἰςορια, Ἰςωρ, Storia, 187
Isuren, 6, 7
Isurium, i. e. *Saviour Town*—Aldborough, why it sent two members to parliament, &c., 298, 299
Iswara and O-sir-is, our Sir, Sieur, &c., from, 300
Itala, Vitula or the Bull, country of —Etruria, 231, 268
Italy, invasion of, by the French, 57
———, votive offerings to Saints, in the churches of, 90
———, Bambinos in, adopted from *boy* Gods, 100
———, the Saviour adored in, under the form of a lamb, 112
———, the Camasene of, from India, 127, 262
———, colonies into, from India, 213
———, nuns in, the same as in China and Tibet, 218
———, its Saturnalia were festivals of Saca, 268
———, the crosses of, found in the Scandinavian *mark* stones of the Scottish isles, 284
———, the renewed incarnation visible in, 340
———, remains of a pontifical government in, found, but not understood, by Niebuhr, 371
———, the landed tenure in, identical with that of India, &c.; lands held by the payment of a part of the produce—a *tenth*, 391
———, in, as in India, there were priests, warriors, farmers, and οἱ πολλοι, who constituted the fourth class, 392
———, most, if not all, of the land in, held by the nobles, and cultivated by their serfs, 394
———, disputes in, between debtors and creditors, not understood, 418
——— and Greece—the relations of the states and municipia of, with one another, how they arose, 433
Ite, Missio est, 61
———, the, meaning of unknown, 197
Iva or I, the female energy of nature, 175, 28
Ixion, the crucifixion of, as *divine love*, 116, 210

INDEX. 483

Jaba, Java—Zaba from, 119
Jabadios (Sumatra), i. e. *holy Java*, 218
————, the ancients probably took their measurement of a degree, in the island of, 406
Jabe, Jave, Jove, 5
Jachim and Boaz—emblems of the *male* and *female* generative powers—probably represented by the two outer stones, as at Stonehenge, 402
Jacob, the testament of, 17, 18
————, the star of, 98
————, the omission of, in Enoch, 173
————, the anointed stone of, the emblem of *wisdom*, 182
————, the sons of, sent to distant pastures, 282
————'s stone, a house of God, 302
———— and his children, 313
————'s ladder, with its 72 angels or æons, &c., 336
————, the angels seen by, 429, 433
————, his name changed, 449
————, (Mr.,) on the precious metals, 305
Jagbeer, a military fief, 262
————, from בגר וא is, country within an inclosure, a circle, 263
Jagbeers, Indian, nothing of the nature of, or of knights' fees, in the Chinese empire, 376
Jagannath—the God of Wisdom, 261
Jaggernaut, 206, 261
————, the whole mythos probably to be found in the temple of, 207, 293
Jah, 5
Jaimini, by Siva's order, composed the Mîmânsâ, &c., 429
Jamblicus, 46, 48, 127, 160, 448
———— *de mysteriis*—his work written to occupy the attention of inquirers and to mislead them, 443
James, the Apostle, and St., 72, 73, 75
Jameson, 18
————'s Cuvier, 312—314, 360
————'s History of the Caldees, 420
Ja-na, Jan-aus, Juno, from Yoni, 174
Janam-patri, the, of Cristna, 236
————, the making of, 346
Janga or Ganga, from Giam, 7
Jang-ti, Divus Iao, 192, 220
Jansenists, Dominicans, and Franciscans, the—had they not interfered with the Jesuits, they might have converted the Chinese, Japanese, and Indians, 367
Janus, the keys of, transferred to Peter, 81
———— and Noah—Menu, 223
———— first taught the people to sacrifice *wine* and *bread*, 254
Jao, 5
Japan, 34, 39, 288
Japanese, the, correspond by symbols with other nations, 214
Japetus—either of the Triumvirate might have been the lineal descendant of the first, 346
Japhet—the Moguls trace their pedigree from, 353
————would say, the descendants of Shem and Ham owe him suit and service, &c., 359
———— and Shem—the representatives of both, are persons in humble life, 360, 361

Japhet, probable that he was the youngest son, 361
————, in the division of the world, had 12 parts, 399
Java, 49, 221
————, its written, unspoken language, 126—214, 218
————or island of Ieue or Jehovah, 214
————, Chinese written language, in, 215
————, one alphabet of, reads upwards, 217a
————, originally Taprobane? 218-
————, called by the natives, *Tana Jáwa*, 219
————, the early history of, 221
————, Ceylon, Japan, Sumatra or Javadios, were all sacred islands, 288
Javanese, the, have the week of *five* days, 316
Javolenus—his definition of *possessio*, 393
Jayadeva, 118
Jaya Stambhas, Pillars of Victory, 261
Jeddo or Juda—what has this to do with the city of Ishmael? 352
Jehangir, after the death of Akbar, re-established Mohamedism, 355
Jehid, 7, 9
Jehova, Jehovah, 5
Jehovah Nis-si, 288
Jephthah's daughter, 21, 293
Jeremiah, 221, 268
Jerom, St., 16, 58, 77, 98, 156, 171, 173, 177, 239, 240
———— or Hieronymus, 95, 96
————did not translate Ecclesiasticus, which he saw in Hebrew, 125
————, sought the Bible in Judæa, 172
————, found the writings of the Jews defaced, and dispersed in fragments, 442
Jerusalem, 28, 35, 45, 89, 137, 230, 446
————, claim of son-of-godship, at, 124
————, pillaged by Sheshach, a Scythian or Saxon, 231
————, initiations at, as at Eleusis, 232
————, the Linga worship of, 260, 261
————, Mecca and Medina—the three holy cities—and the Black, Red, and White Seas, are under the power of the families of the Califfs, &c., 385
————, the temple of, ordered, by Darius, to be rebuilt, 420
————, the Talmud of, 72
————, Rose, the, the Amomum, 242
———— or Mount Moria being set up against Gerizim, the prophets of the two mounts quarrelled, 275
————, Targum, the, calls Jehovah *H*, the name of the island Iona, 286
————, the temple of Ieue at, was called *eikhit*, but often *ekl* only—bit, *house*, being omitted, &c., 408
Jesuits, the, 76
————, at first encouraged, in China, India, &c., 217
————, all excluded from the Papacy, 270

Jesuits, the, their admissions to the Brahmins, 341
————, demonstrated the identity of the Indian and Roman secret religions, 366, 367
————, &c., employ the same means as the Assassins did, to attain their end, 386
————, like the Assassins, subsisted after their order was suppressed, 390
Jesus, 43—46, 49, 57, 59—61, 63, 68, 89, 120, 121, 136—138, 143
————, the Rose of Sharon, of Isurea, &c., 6, 33, 44, 239, 240, 243
————, in Apocryphal Gospels, called a Dyer, a Painter, or a Potter, 7
———— and Cristna, identity of their history, 44
————, immaculate conception of, 49, and birth at Bethlehem, 95—99
————, a priest of the religion of Melchizedek, 58
————, called Ischas or Ischa, 60, 230, 346, 347
———— and the sun, mixed worship of, 89
————, the Trinity of, the same as that of Plato, 98, 447
————, his reign on earth for 1000 years, 102
————of the Roman church, no philosopher of Samaria, in the time of Tiberius, 108
————, his tomb at Jerusalem, 115
————, time he occupied it, 142—144
———— the Iao of the Hebrews, 122
————, the man, probably taught the doctrine of the Chrêst *crucified*, 123
————, the, of the eighth and ninth age, 125
————, a disciple of Buddha, i. e. of Divine Wisdom, 182
————, called the *Tree of Life*, &c., by the Gnostics, 204, 250
———— and Mohamed left no writings behind them, 219, 448
————, like Xaca, born from the side of his mother, 228
————was wisdom—Buddha, &c., 250
————, said to have lost his life for teaching that virtue would secure eternal happiness, 253
————, would no more *drink of the fruit of the vine*—meaning of, 254
————, the Christ, i. e. the Crêst, 344
———— and Cristna, the followers of, consent not to abandon their favourite object of adoration, 368
————, his mission of love, peace, and benevolence having failed,— according to the Mohamedan doctrine—a strong one, that of the sword, must succeed, 378
————, what a dispassionate inquirer may believe respecting, and of his doctrines; the Socrates or Pythagoras of his day, 449
———— of Bethlehem, 56
————, passed down his power, through St. Peter, to the Popes, 57
————, mistaken for Iao or the Sun, 100
————, for the people, 129
———— and Alexander, each had, mystically, two fathers, 350

484   INDEX.

	Page		Page		Page
Jesus of Judæa,	60	temples necessary, he would have said so; the beautiful globe was his τεμενος, and an humble and contrite heart his temple,	409	Jews, the, their dislike of the Apocrypha—their secret history had that of the crucified Avatar, like those of the Gentiles,	125
—— of Nazareth, 50, 51, 58, 93, 109, 112, 124,	256
——, the Nazarite of Samaria, 117, 125,	409
——————, for the Conclave and Cardinals,	129	Jesus Christ, the charge of, to the Apostles, not to throw *pearls before the swine*, construed by the fathers to mean, that they should not reveal the secrets of the religion,	442	——, have no books in their canon after Haggai,	ib.
——————, a Nazir, or flower, 6, 193, 239, 240,	243	——, have, contrary to the author's former opinion, corrupted their books,	126
——, the Son of Sirach, crucified, &c.,	124, 125
——————, the renewed incarnation in,	365	—— was of the Eclectic or Philalethean sect,	448	——, and Samaritans, difference of chronology between, 133, 134, 327,	329
Jesuses or Saviours, nine or ten,	124
Jesus Christ, 16, 35, 43, 59, 65, 66, 87, 106, 142, 143, 189, 202, 285,	343	Jew, a, not required to give up an iota of his faith, when he turned Mussulman,	372	——, had a cycle of 14, 160,	162
——, have lost the Cabalistic meaning of the letter M, 167,	223
Jewish Cabala,	221
——————, a Nazarite, of the monastic order of the Pythagorean Essenes, 44, 46, 50,	449	————, unwritten doctrine,	232	——, reduced the 28 to 27 letters, to make M the centre letter,	168
———— Cabalists, the,	223
———— Canon, the, conceals the mythos of the adventures of the Incarnate God,	232	——, say that *Ieue* is written one way and spoken another,	171
——, the whole history or life of, may be read in the stars, 57, 145, 193,	194	——, say the Targums were delivered to Moses, by God, on Mount Sinai,	172
———— history,	11
———— travestied by the Egyptians, 11, 16, 17		——, of Thrace,	181
——————, beautiful simplicity of his character and life,	63	——, in the first ages of the tribe of, the crosier alone prevailed,	264
———— and Christian doctrines found in America,	35
——————, the first begotten,	72
——————, forbade long prayers,	87	————, *the secret*, had the history of the crucified Avatars, like the Gentiles,	125	——, spoke not Hebrew—Syriac was their vernacular tongue,	295
——————, his birth celebrated on Dec. 25th, like that of Mithra in Persia, and of Adonis, in Egypt, Phœnicia, and Biblis, 99,	104
———— Mythos, 10, 34, 36, 40, 97,	173, 232	——, occupied Western Syria, as the noble class of Romans did Italy, and as the Turks have Greece,	310
———— ——, in China, 19, 36,
——————, not crucified at *thirty*, but lived to be *fifty* years of age, according to Irenæus, 120, 121, 123, 142,	228	———— ——, in North and South India, and in Mexico, 34, 36, 134, 206,	229	——, make the flood to have happened in the *fourth* revolution of *the* comet (of 1680),	328
———— priests and government, the, claimed supremacy from them, flattering themselves that a great Saviour would place them in command of the restored Pandæan kingdom,	361	Jews, the, of North India, expected a kingdom of Cæsar,	345
——————, the life of, said to have been copied from the history of Pythagoras,	127
——, averse to proselyting,	363
——, their canonical books bring their history no lower than 400 B.C.,	364, 365
——————, held as a divine person by Ammonius Saccas, 131,	447
——————, symbols of the real history of, in the births, deaths, and resurrections of the Gods,	132	———— tribe, the, little—traces of the doctrines of, in all parts, but without the books of Moses, 361,	362	——, the peculiarities of, arose from Moses's anxiety to preserve a hatred of images,	364
——————, scenic representations of the acts of, in ceremonies of the Romish church,	136	Jews, the, 10, 11, 17, 20, 24, 28, 29, 34, 35, 38, 39, 43, 48, 49, 54, 59, 62, 64, 65, 69, 71, 72, 79, 95, 105, 106, 130, 133, 147, 148, 157, 189, 211, 223,	226	——, the *mythical* history of, ends with their canonical books —their *real* history begins with the Apocrypha,	365
——————, his history that of the sun,	144
——————, a coin with the head of, and Hebrew inscription, found in Wales,	154	——, had a *lex non scripta* before Moses partly composed, partly compiled, the Pentateuch,	376
————, Cabalistic,	6
————, a sect of iconoclasts,	16
————, colonies of, supposed to have gone from Alexandria to America,	22	——, Mohamed was believed to be *the promised one of*,	379
——————, palm-tree branches, as the emblem of *everlasting wisdom*, carried before,	231
——, in the Cabala, have substituted *Baraeit* and *Mercavah*, the one for the other,	429
——————, and Crisna, similarity of, 241,	242
——————, considered a renewed incarnation of Adam and Noah,	245	————, Christians, and Mexicans, similarity between,	23	——, the present, may as readily reject ancient learning (the secret doctrines of the Apocrypha) as they adopt modern—the Masoretic points,	442
————, said to have been cannibals,	31
——————, supposed to be the *ninth* Avatar; a re-incarnation of, expected by the followers of Brothers, Southcote, &c.,—the *tenth* Avatar,	258	————, inscriptions state that they came into China about the time of Confucius,	36
Jid,	7, 8
Joachim, abbot of Flora or Sora,	242
————, introduced their and the Christian rites into the Mexican religion,	37	Job, &c., icons of, in India,	122
——————, maintained by Nestorius not to be God, but a mere man, &c.,	357	—— or Ayud, book of, from Upper India,	128
————, the high priest of, with and pomegranates,	69
——————, his obscure situation, like that of the Khan of Caracorum and of the present Calif of Mecca,	361	————, had the rite of confession bells and held purgatory,	74	——, names of actors in, shew the mythos,	ib.
————, turned towards Jerusalem in prayer,	89	——, the Arabic poem of, alone (of all the books of the O. T.) contains the doctrine of the immortality of the soul,	386
————, fasted and flogged themselves, like the votaries of Isis,	92
——————, had he not been of the *two* tribes, we should know as little of them, as of the *ten*,	364
Jocanna,	31
————, attributed the same soul to Adam, Abraham, David, and the Messiah,	97	Jod, the, or point or pruktos, descriptive of self-existence,	190
——, the *ninth* Avatar— Salivahana in the East, Jesus Χρης in the West,	358
Johanna,	31
————, had the same idea of the resurrection as the Persians,	101	John the Baptist,	64—68, 95
——————, had no predilection for the temple at Jerusalem or at Gerizim had he thought		————, the esoteric doctrines of,	123	—— or Oannes, the Fish,	137, 138

INDEX.

485

	Page
John or Oannes, the cousin of Jesus,	241
———, meaning of his decreasing, &c.,	297
———, a Nazarite, of the monastic order of Pythagorean Essenes,	449
———, Evangelist and St., 67, 72, 120,	121
———, the beginning of his Gospel Platonic,	113
———, Cabalistic doctrines of the 1st ch. of,	261
———'s, St., exposition of the *time*, &c., of Daniel,	317
John, St., Christians of,	66
———————, Sabæans,	219
John's, St., Midsummer day,	297
———————, the Knights of, or the Teutonic, or Templars,	388
Johnstone, Sir A., his promise to make inquiries into the dimensions of Indian temples,	40
Jonas,	21
Johnathan, the Targum of,	172
Jones, Sir W., 122, 140, 213, 219, 221, 236—	238
———, on the division of the languages of the world into *three*, probably right,	399
———, on the number of words learned, which would enable a person to speak any language,	436
———, and others, ridicule Bailly, Buffon, Linné, &c., for teaching that man must have been created in Tartary,	445
Jones, Dr. J.,	127
———'s Lexicon,	242
Jones, on the Canon, 63,	201
———, on the language of the Tartars,	67
Jordan, the baptism by John, in,	65
Jortin, on the monks of Egypt, in the 4th century,	368
Joseph called *Seuft*, and a Saviour, 2,	16
——— שלו Shī,	178
———, the Proteus of the Egyptians and Greeks, called Redemptor Mundi—his name an appellative, 16, 177,	178
———, prime minister of Egypt,	110
———, canal of, in Egypt; Io-συφ, *wisdom of Io?*	230
——— established a feodal tenure in Egypt,	254
———, sent to his brethren, by Jacob,	282
——— and Mary, the flight of,	45
——— of Arimathea,	143
———, a man so called, in the temple of Jaggernaut,	206
Josephs,	21
Josephus, 45, 46, 49, 50, 135, 169, 317;	327
———, on the Essenes,	368
Joshua, his names for the tribes had a reference to the solar mythos, 136,	275
———, his name changed,	449
Josiah burnt the Ashre or groves, &c.,	371
Josias,	94
Jounas,	31
Jove—the fables of the descent of Hercules and Perseus referred to,	348
Javi Servatori,	110
VOL. II.	

	Page
Jovis Pueri, D. D.,	100
Juda or Ayoudia, the tribe of,	207
———, a tribe of, from India, passed from Arabia and peopled Abyssinia and Upper Egypt,	352
Judæa, 60, 100, 125, 172,	449
———, or Ayoudia, Eastern, 16, 21, 36, 122, 156,	181
———, or Ayoudia, Western, 36, 39,	40
Judæan, masonic, χρησ-tian festivals,	142
——— Mythos, 7, 10, 35, 40, 218,	222
———————, the, in China, before letters were known,	214
———————, the, probably to be found in Japan and Java,	222
———————, the, in the ceremonies of Eleusis,	234
———————, in both N. and S. India, 235,	293
———————, or Chaldæan, in Armenia,	237
———————, the, of which histories of Adam, Noah, Moses, Cristna, are parts, to be found in China, Mexico, Peru, Ireland and Scotland,	362
———————, the, of *black* people, how found among *white* races,	363
——— or Mosaic mythos, the, established in China, a branch of the first Buddhist or Tauric system of cycles, or a collection of remnants of it, when the symbolic numeral alphabet was in use,	396
——— mythos, the, found in Mexico, China, India, Syria, &c., &c.,	441
Judah, or Juda, 8, 9,	18
———, the sign of, Leo,	105
Judaic mythos, the, everywhere prevailed,	232
Jodaism, mythos of, in Mexico,	29
——— and in China,	218
Jadaizing Christians, the,	60
Jude, St.,	88
Judea, in the Chersonesus,	122
———, the tribe of, the tribe of Judia or Idii,	188
Judii, 7, 188, 218,	250
Jugera and Jugerum,—their contents, &c.,	406
Julian—the temple destroyed by,	298
——— (the Apostate), 346,	448
——— maintained he had the soul of Alexander, &c.,	348
———, when the epithet *anti-christian* is applied to, we may read *anti-Paulite*,	449
——— Calendar, the, intercalates the Bissextile after the Terminalia, before the last five or six days of February,	320
Julii—the family of the, always aspired to the office of Pontifex,	374
——— or Cæsar, the family of, probably an example of a foreign noble admitted to citizenship; the Ælii, Fabii, and Lamii, perhaps furnish other examples,	392
Julius Africanus—on the reigns of Egyptian kings, &c.,	325
——— Cæsar, 57, 147,	330

	Page
Julius Cæsar, as Pontifex Maximus, reformed the Calendar,	52
——— united the secular and ecclesiastical authority,	53
——— assumed the title of Cæsar,	54
——— held out his foot to Pompeius Pænus, to kiss,	55
———, believed by the Jews to be the Messiah,	233
———, the comet (of 1680) first noticed on the death of,	327
———, his unnatural birth, a made-up story, to advance his claim to the sovereignty of the world,	345
———, stimulated to exertions, and his followers operated on, by *some one to come* being then looked for,	374
——— Pollux,	319
———, on a month as 30 days,	321
——— Valerius,	165
Junius, on the three tribes of Rome,	345
Juno, from *Iune*, Yoni,	174
——— Jugalis,	82
——————— the miraculous conception of,	ib.
Junone [Junoni?] Fortunæ,	100
Jupiter, his love of Leda,	8
———, temple of, on Mount Carmel,	58
———, image of, carried in processions,	79
——— Stator,	86
——— Capitolinus, Sponsor, Tonans,	91
——— Ammon, the Sun in Aries, 102,	110
———, the father of Alexander, 346, 348,	349
——— Zagræus,	103
——— Pluvialis, the, of Greece, is the God Indra of India, the God Iao of the Hebrews, and the Jesus of the Romish Church,	122
——— with *three* eyes, the image of the Trimurti,	136
———, bound by his own pre-ordained law,	226
———, overcame the giant Typhæus or Typhon, 324,	325
——— (the planet)—Lexel's comet retarded by the influence of,	334
———, the father of gods and of men, represented as dancing,	425
Jupiters, infant,	100
——— or Gods,	137
Jurieu,	189
Jury, the Trial by, our, came from the East, and is common to the Chinese and Mexicans, 278, 279,	283
Justin Martyr, 4, 60, 61, 66, 67, 69, 89, 253,	319
——— calls Sunday not Sabbath, but *the day of the Sun*,	90
——— maintained that Christ was crucified in the heavens,	122
——— says Socrates was a Christian,	130
——— held the *allegorical* meaning,	131
——— and Trypho, the Dialogue between,	252
———, addressed his Apology to Antoninus Pius,	440
———, his explanation of	

3 x

INDEX.

the mystery of the Eucharist, in his Apology, forms an exception to the course of the other fathers—the reason of his conduct unknown, &c., 443
Juvenal, on the high priest of Anubis, 79
———, a passage in, 446
Jye Jagannath,—Victory to Jagannath, or God the Creator, or the God of Wisdom, or Wisdom of the Great Iz or Creator, 261

Kaca, 32
Kadir-Billah, the Calif—a secret assembly at Bagdad, held under, which rejected the claims of the Fatémites to the Califate, 385, 386
Kæmpfer, 39
Kaisar—probably the true origin of the name of Cæsar, 391
Kajar, i. e. Cæsar, tribe of Turks, the, 351
Kaling, Kalinga, the Telinga, 238
Kaliuwakim, the Tamul, a book of wisdom, 128
Kaliwakam—the Nama Sebadiah, in, 116
Kam, 5
Kam-deva, 5, 6
Kamschatka, 215
Kanarak, a village near the temple of Jaggernaut, 261
Kanda—Kan-diva—a Javan poem, 222
Kandi-kumara, the God—i. e. the holy Khan of Cuma—is called Rabbie, 288
Kanīche, 29
Kanyā, 5, 265
———, Can or Cunia, 174
Kdom, the ancient, unused language of Java, 214
Kapala (in Malay) κεφαλος, caput, head, 217
Kapila, the founder of the Sánkhya school, 429
Kara-corgns or stone circles, and lingas or pillars, 260
Kartuelta, the same as Cear-tlutli, i. e. Kæsar or Cæsar, the grandson of Noah, 24
Kasideans, the, an order, not a sect, 135
Κατ' ἐξοχην, 226, 239, 243
Katachar and Osman, the families of, occupy, with the same title, the thrones of Teheran and Stamboul, 385
Kawi or Java, also the name of the peninsula of Malacca, and of several islands, 218
Kedú, a corruption of Iedu, aspirated, &c., ib.
Keill's, Dr., opinion in favour of Whiston's Theory, 331, 332
Kel, église, and ecclesia, from the Hebrew, 297
Kelidoni, Cape, 117
Ken (נכה), the first priests so called—hence king, 222
———, knowledge, wisdom, 302
Kennedy, Van, 207, 226
———, on Akbar, 354, 355

Kennicott, on one tree only, in Eden, forbidden, 251
Kent—Gavel-kind Tenure of, 265, 284
Kesari, the Linga of the Rajahs of, 260
Keti, wife of Cama, 103
Kettle-drum, 70
Khakan or emperor, 67
Khan was both king and queen, 181, 222, 302
———, the, of Caracoram, the lineal descendant of Japhet, 359
Khekh, a village in the territory of Roum, in which the Imam of the Ishmaelites resides, 391
Khorasaun—traces of the change of land in, 283
Khosru—Cyrus—Cæsar, 229
———s, the, were Cæsars, 345
Khouhistān — the Assassins continued in, long after their order was overthrown, 390
Khowaresm, probably Khorasan, the Schāh of, ib.
Kiaklak, name of Bacchus in Siam, 163
Kidron, the brook, 371
Kien-loug, l'empereur de la Chine, descendu d'une Vierge, 97
Kil or Cel, the churches first so called, 295
King of the Age, the, 51
——— priest, the, was anciently lord of the soil, as vicegerent of God, 266, 269
———, none but a, could offer a sacrifice (for the nation) in Rome, Athens, &c., 271, 375
———, the, in Rome and Tibet, does homage to the priest, 302
——— and priest, the, identical, in Indian-Saxon time, 303
———, Jesus—the Paulite Christians dreamed of, as a visible King at Jerusalem, 342
——— of Kings, the title of, claimed by the Mogul, the king of Siam, and the emperor of China, 352
———, the Pontifical law and the Augurs independent of—an example of a king beginning to lose his pontifical character, 375
———, Mr. E., on the flood of Noah, 312, 361
Kings—several of Egypt, copies of Abraham, of Joseph, and of Moses, 16
———, at first, were generals of the priests, or of the sacerdotal forces, 264, 271, 272
———, fifty-one lie in the cemetery of the convent or monastery of the island of Iona, 286
———, or patriarchal priests, the owners of all land, 298
———, the divine right of, founded on the mythos, 354
———, the first were also pontiffs, 374
———, (the early,) received the vectigal as king and pontiff—hence their funds for building, and for making war, 395
Kingsborough's (Lord) History, &c., of Mexico, 21—26, 28—31, 34—37, 74, 161, 393, 430
———, on the marred face of the promised one, in Mexico, 347
Kirk Meyo—kirk is the circle, 297
Kissing, the, of the foot, 55
Kiun Kan, a Tartar Khan, said to

have divided his dominions among 48 princes—the 48, the number of the ancient constellations, shew the remains of the microcosmic system, 421
KL, Cal or Wisdom X, 2
——— is X = 600, L = 50 = 650, ib.
לב kl means ALL and heavens, &c., 408
Klaproth, Mr., on the Tartar nation, 420
Knight, Payne, Mr., 19, 70, 85, 165, 199, 228, 239, 253
———, on Isis and her offspring—Horus, 110
———, on whether Homer had the knowledge of letters, 170
———, on Dancing among the ancients, 425, 426
Knights' Service, 262, 265
———, the tenure of, 268, 269
———, the Roman, at first restricted to 300 (like the Patres Conscripti), were afterwards increased to 600, and then to 1800—the 300 should be 360, probably, 422
Knights Templars, the, 112, 388
———, the, in all states, thought to be the same; the richest of the Roman Plebs who could arm themselves, &c., 392
Knox, John, and other reformers, destroyed images, &c., 194
Knotted cords—superseded by symbolic records, 215
———, the first Chinese letters, 218
"Knowledge is Power" was always as true as it is now, 274
Komilmar, 28
Komulmer, the ceremonies at, celebrated with music, dancing, &c., 298
Kopp, Dr, on the Constitution of the secret Tribunals of Westphalia, 391
Koran (Tippoo Sultan's), metrical account of verses, &c., in, 195
———, the trumpery of the, 219
———, the standard of the Arabic, 274
———, the Arabic of the, a dead language to the mass, &c., 294
———, called Om, and the Dome, connect it with our Dombee and the Duomas of Italy, 303
———, so far rules, that nothing against its doctrines is held to be law, 376
———, made up after Mohamed's death, and, 22 years afterwards, redacted by Othman; said to contain two distinct religions—the first a system of pure theism; the second a sanguinary propagandism, &c., 378
Κωρυ,—Cores—Cyrus, 290
Kúmari or Komari on Cape Comarin, 6
Kuon, a dog, 159
Kuster, Mr., 127
Kyrie, Eleeson, 87

INDEX. 487

	Page
L, the, emphatic in Hebrew,	215
———, the præpositive article of the Celtic and Hebrew,	299, 300
L'Achm,	32
— often used with N, for 50,	196, 203
LA, le Dieu des Lamas, né d'une Vierge,	97
La Loubère,	267
La Place, M.,	26
———, the late discoveries of,	338
Lacedemonians, the, used the kettle-drum at the death of their king,	70
——————————, used R for S,	199
Lachim was L'hkm, *the wise*,	6
La Croze,	243
Lactantius,	80, 104
Lacuna, the, of the Hebrew system, supplied by what is here taught respecting the Cabala,	387
Ladder, the, of Jacob, of Mount Solyma, of metamorphoses—the Scala or Sacala, is Xaca-cio,	9
——————, or a chain, all nature was,	336
L'-di-stone, *the holy stone*,	182
Laertius,	314
Ααως, αφεσις, like Ite, Missio est,	61
Lakchmi,	32
Lake Copias—the drains from, not the work of the Bœotians, but of a people antecedent to the Greeks,	381
——————, no record of the fabricators of the drains of,—an early race from India,	419
Lalande,	139
Lam,	37
Lama, the, of Tibet,	1, 36, 57, 75
——— —————, and the Lamb of Rome, equally adored as God upon earth,	9, 75
———, when he dies, believed to remove to a new body,	58
———, Menu, and Mani, the same,	188
———, of Tibet, the inspired or incarnated wisdom,	226
———, the religion of,	229
——————, keeps the whole mythos uniform,	308
———, the Grand of the West, substituted, by the Jesuits, for the Grand Lama at Lassa,	367
——— a grand or Papa somewhere, who superintended the whole archhierarchy,	373
Lamas, the,	34, 97
———, of Tibet, exemplify the renewed incarnation, &c.,	136
Lamb or Llama,	35, 36
———, the—Hercules or Cristna, slain,	104
———, " of God, that taketh away the sin of the world," 55, 87, 104, 106, 108—110, 130,	242
———, Martin IV. addressed as,	55
———, worshiped 2000 years after the Beeve,	110
———, a golden, at Mayence—a silver at Boo—with the sun for his face, at the middle temple, London,	112
———, slain from the *beginning* of the world,	117
———, the, of the Carnutes,	154
———, the zodiacal cyclic incarnation of, why it succeeded the Bull,	308
Lamed, the, is L-M-di, holy or sacred Lama,	188, 203
Lam-Oigh-lupral, the virgin mother of Xaca,	229
Lamps and candles, the use of in churches, copied from the Egyptians,	79
Land, L'-anla-di, the holy country,	29
———, the emperor sole proprietor of, in China, India, Persia, and the Burman empire,	263
Land Tax, the, *ten per cent.* in Ceylon, Travancore, &c. &c.,	266
Lands—or strips of land—appropriated only in summer,	282
Landseer's Sabæan Researches,	193
Language, the first written, long lost,	147, 222, 234, 274
———, the, of numbers, exchanged for letters,	223
———, a *written, not spoken*, understood by one who had the notatory key,	235
——— and polity—marks of an universal, every where apparent,	362, 363
———, one, may be supposed to have continued intelligible to the world, for 500 or 600 years, till the population rose to two or three hundred millions,	396
———, an extensive, commercial, might be formed by 1000 selected words being attached to numbers, with a key,	436
———, in the first numeral, none of the little words for the cases of nouns occurred—probably not used till syllabic literal writing began to be practised,	436
Languages, all the, of the world, except Sanscrit, may be traced to the Samaritan Hebrew,	156
———, their liability to change, whether spoken or written, 234,	291
———, a book with 73, all founded on the Arabic,	235
———, all written, had originally only 16 letters,	256
———, the, of the world, divided into *three*—those of Shem, Ham, and Japhet,	399
Lardner (Dr.),	119, 448
Lares, the,	90
Larissa,	117
———, the Youth of,	51, 200, 202
Las Casas,	29, 30, 39
Lascivus, from Laschmi, wife of Cristna,	242
Lassa,	9, 367
———, the archhierarchy never wholly defunct at,	373
Latelmos, king,	241
Latin, Greek, Hindoo, and Sanscrit names of numbers,	166, 167
Laurence, Mr., on *one* or more than one species of man,	363
Lavaysse, on Humboldt's Sun-dial,	297
Law, the, of the country *was* the Religion, with the Druids, Jews, and ancient Indians, and *is* so with the Mohamedans,	272
———, the common, of England and Scotland, established before writing was generally known,	ib.
Laws (the common) of England and Scotland, which the older— derived from a common source— probably from a tribe of Saca, of the nation of Pandæa,	273
L'Awu or THE *Ico*,	9
Lawuh, a mountain in Java,	ib.
Lay Impropriations—whence they arose,	267
Learned man, every his own alphabet or language of figures or ciphers,	205, 220, 235, 246
Learning of the first nation, the author no proof of the,	254
Leda,	8
Lee, (Professor,)	195, 351
Leet, a, so called from *lotting* lands on St. John's day,	283
Legion, the Roman—the numbers in the formation of, display the mythos,	422, 433
Lempriere,	200, 314
———, on the name of Salice,	287
———, on the word Augusta,	421
Lemon, Mr.,	226, 302
Leo, Pope,	89
——— X., the obsequies of,	104
Leopold, Duke of Austria,	347, 384
Leslie, Professor, of Edinburgh, on the number of square feet on the globe,	395
Lessing,	43
Letif, leaf and letter, all learning concealed under,	246
Letter, litera (Lat.), letif (Arab.), a *leaf*,	153
Letters, the origin of,	147, 215
———, the knowledge of, a great part of magic,	169, 245
——— and numbers, all, described by right lines,	174
———, the secret system of,	175
———, the science of, a masonic secret, perhaps known to the builders of Stonehenge, &c., 256,	271
———, the knowledge of, acquired the philosophers a dominion over the whole world,	257, 258
———, without a knowledge of, the ignorance of the Latins and Greeks respecting their mythology and Gods, a necessary consequence,	424
——— and iron,	34, 35
———, unknown to the Americans,	33, 40, 41, 206
Leucippus,	314
Levant, the, all Christians of, go to church with the girdle,	77
Lévêque places the source of all religions in Tartary,	373
Lex non scripta, the Roman—the knowledge of, confined to the Patricians—was interpreted to their own interest,	394
Lexel's comet, retarded by the influence of Jupiter,	334
Lexicon, Sanscrit—many words in the first Veda, which are found in no—their meaning lost; the first lexicon made 500 years *after* Christ,	428
L-hm—from ל and חם—house of Om,	303
Lhyd,	82
Liber, Bacchus, 8, 163, (Boc, Book,) 265, 271, 292
——— or Liberius,	84, 91
Liberi Sokemanni—men of Liber, or Soke, or Saca,	265, 271, 276
Liberius, St., an Armenian,	84

INDEX.

Libration of the planes of the Ecliptic and Equator, supposed to take place in 7200 years—72 small cycles of 600 years, or 72 large, of 6000 years, in 432,000 years, 399
Lightfoot, 95, 96
Lilies and pomegranates, 45
Lily, the, or Lotus, 239, 240
——, of the Valley, Christ, 44
——, the emblem of the Trinitarian sun, 45
Linga, the, 33, 236
———, or Priapus, 7
——— and Ioni, wars on account of, 34
——— and Iona, 130
——— or lingua, language, speech, logos, mind, 187, 240
——— and Ioni, the two sects of, united, 248
——— and Yoni, and Kara-corum of Scotland, 260
———, objects of adoration in Ceylon, 290
——— or Logos, the generative power, &c., 259, 291, 292
———, the worship of, equally prevalent with the Caillidi of the East, and the Collidei of Scotland, 291
———, or stone pillar, adorned with flowers, and anointed, &c., 297
——— and Ioni, by the union of (the sects of), religious wars ceased for several thousand years, 308
———, when the union of the two sects took place, the Cardo, Cross, or Meto-stone probably increased to two, in front of the temples, 402
———, even after the union of the sects of, a leaning shewn to the *female*, as at Athens; or to the *male*, as at Jerusalem, 445
Linga, the old name of an island, near Iona, called the Dutchman's Cap, 291, 292, 402
Lingard, Mr., on the Rhyn or mysterious language of the Welsh bards, 153, 159
Lingas, the obelisks at Rome, were, 93
———, in the temple of Jerusalem, and in the cathedral of Chartres, were in vaults, 260, 261
———, of the Hindoos, preserved by the Mohamedans, 352
——— and Phalluses — like the crosses in churchyards, 409
Lion, a, the emblem of the Sun at the summer solstice, and the coat of arms of the emperor of China, and of the Egyptians, 292
Littleton, 242, 413
Liturgies—the chaunting of, whence it arose, 340
Lituus, the, 78
———, or the Crosier, was the Hieralpha of the Hindoos, 79
———, the cross, the true sceptre of the Egyptian priests, 386
Livery of seizin, 263
Livy or Livius, Titus, 76, 394
———, cause of *lacunæ* in, 116
———, not understanding Isopolity, treats it as a *cause*, instead of an *effect*, 434

Llama or Lamb, 35, 36
Lhyd's comparative etymology, 154
LM =650, 188
LMB =72, 204, 241
LMN, a great mystery in, 203
———, emblems of the Trinity, 204
לחרבה *herbe*, the ם used for ב, 195
Loadstone and telescope, the, known to the Chaldæans, 175
———, the, L'-di-stone, *the holy stone*, 182
———, compass, and telescope, the knowledge of, constituted part of the ancient mysteries, 246
———, a large one capped the roof of the temple of the sun, at Kanarak, 261
Locke, on ideas, 123, 131
Locrin or *Lorgrin*, to whom his father Brutus gave Loegria, i. e. England, 400
Logan, Mr. J., 290
Log-uis—Sin-gal (read Hebraicè), 292
Logos, the, 6, 46, 174, 178, 187, 197, 240
———, or Buddha, 8
———, the birth of fixed to the moment of the winter solstice, 98
———, Apollo was called, 102
———, crucified in the heavens, 123
———, re-incarnation of, in every cycle, every *neros*, 136
——— or Linga, a stone—Christ called a, 259
———, was called Honover in Persia, 261
———, the *male*, proceeded from the Τὸ Ὄν, 397
Lokman, 4
London, 36
———, every new church in, has a wicked cross, 271
Longinus, no Grecian author cited Moses before, 134
———, adopted the system of Ammonius Saccas, 447
Loo-Choo Islands, the, Chinese written language in, 215
Lord, the, (Jesus Christ,) duration of his ministry, 120—122
Lord—from Lar-di, holy or divus Lar? 301
Lord Paramount, 375
———, the Pope and the Khan of Caracorum both held to be the, 383
———, of the soil, the Pope the, as successor of the eldest son, 400
Lords of Manors, the, originally ecclesiastical? 301
——— (Lords of Minerva), all originally ecclesiastics, 422
Loretto, 30, 45, 80, 127
———, the Casa Santa at, 57
———, the Sa. Maria of, has forty names, 91
———, the jewels, sought by the French at, 111
Lot and Abraham—like the dispute between their servants, a dispute between emigrating tribes, &c., would terminate, 306
—, a, or an Abraham, would soon settle a dispute in the Golden Age, 307
Lotus, the, or Lily, 44, 45, 243
———, Age of, 32
——— or Water Rose, 32, 33, 436

Lotus, the, of the Nile, *blue*, 179
———, equally sacred in India, Egypt, Greece, and Syria, 239, 240
———, flower of the Sun, manifestation of Wisdom, of Love, &c., 436
Loub al-Mahfoudh — la table gardée ou secrète, the Mahomedan book of destiny, 303
Louis XVIII., a sponsor at the baptism of bells, 70
——, St., at the cathedral of, four bells destroyed, ib.
Λουτρον καλυγγενεσιας, 69
Love-feast or Eucharist of the Manichæans, 60
Low, Mr., on the analogy between the shape, ornaments, &c., of the Tabernacle, and those of the Caaba, 402
Λοξιας, the Author's former suspicion of its import, erroneous, 313
———, the inclination of the earth's axis, so called, 313, 314
Loyala, the talented fanatic, &c., 270
Lucan, 53, 145
Luceres, à Lucumone, 345
Lucian, 110
——— calls himself a Syrian, and an Assyrian, 236
——— calls Dancing a science of imitation, &c., 425
Lucius—when he was converted (about A. D. 180) the three Archflamens of Britain became Archbishops, 400
Lucretius, 408
Lucumon is probably Lux-maunus, &c., 421
Lucumones, the, 345
———, the Tuscan—became the Roman Senate; these hereditary Sacerdotes got possession of the tenths, 373, 380, 381
———, were *twelve*, 420
———, probably the cabinet of the Pontifex Maximus, 421
Ludovicus Vives, 53, 74
Luke, the Gospel according to, 46, 67
——, on the baptism and age of Jesus, 120
——, St., his picture of the Saviour, 228
Lunar year, the, consisted of 12 synodical months, of 30 days each, from new moon to new moon, before the flood, 316, 325
Lus or Lux (might be from *sul* the Sun)—hence the Lotus was called the flower of Lus or Lys, &c., 436
Lustrum, L'Ustrum—ἑστερος, *second*, 202
———, the, of the old Italians, viz. *five*, 404
Lustrums, the, of *five* and *six*, the roots of all calculations, 141, 168, 215, 409
———, 72,000,000, of, — or Pliny's division of the circle into 72 constellations, 404
Luther, afflicted with insanity, 123
———, his coat of arms—a *cross rising from a rose*, 301
———, could not prudently be trusted with the secret doctrine, 367
Lux, the Logos, Rasit, Rsi =600, 178
LXX., the, its great variations from the Hebrew—It was probably a

INDEX.   489

	Page
translation of the sacred books of the five temples of Egypt,	16
LXX., tho, its translation of Baal-Zebub,	83
———— of ΥΥ ss,	239
————, reading of, of Deut. xxxii. 8, on the division of the nations,	409, 410
Lycurgus, Pisistratus, and Aristotle, collected and reduced to their present form the Poems of Homer—at first *sacred poems*,	195, 196, 293
————, united music to military exercises,	426

M, a monogram, prefixed for mystery,	6, 198, 299
——, Cabalistic meaning of, lost by the Jews,	167
——, made the centre letter by the Jews,	168, 186, 187, 204, 242
——, monogram for the Virgin Mary,	170
——, the mystic nature of,	203
——, the M-phalos or Omphalos, Ioni, the centre,	224
— or Om, the sacred, never-to-be-spoken,	299
ɔ, the tenth letter of the new alphabet of letters,	190, 196
▭ = 600, 170, 180, 187, 188, 207, 223, 224, 242	
— final, is the Samach,	195, 241, 302
Ma or Am, *mother* in most written languages,	168, 170, 186, 242
Maccabees, the book of the,	4
Macdonald,	82
Macedon, i. e. Scythia, the kings of, descendants of Japetus,	347
Macpherson—did not understand the nature of Ossian's poems,	293
Macrobius,	103,
————, on a lunar month, computed for a year,	325
————, the 360 Divi of,	429
Madonna—Dolerosa—Vialis,	90
———— of the sun,	91
Madonnas,	100
———— and Bambinos,	242
Madras Transactions, the,	289, 296
Mæsades, the,	59
Magi, the,	48, 65, 66, 77, 95, 97, 301
————, religion of, corrupted,	58
————, offered gold, frankincense, and myrrh, to the Sun,	96
————, Magicians, Necromancers, and Shepherds, would come to Bethlehem to worship the new-born God, every 24th of December,	96
————, the heads of, always called kings,	98
————, the skulls of three kings of, to be seen at Cologne,	ib.
————, Persian, believed in the resurrection of the body,	101
Magic assigned as the origin of the Microcosm—nobody can tell what magic was or is,	397
Magnetic needle, the cause of the variation of the—may, like the planes of the Equator and Ecliptic, be gradually coming right	
VOL. II.	

	Page
again, and may again point directly N. and S.,	414
Maha-ballipore destroyed by a flood,	315
Mahabarat, the,	88, 369, 396, 428
————, ended in the establishment of the Holy Catholic or Paudean faith, &c.,	229, 370
————, probably the first religious war—when it arose, the Golden Age ended,	308
Mahabarats—the first GREAT wars —the, probably arose between the Sovereigns or High-priests or Pontiffs, about the presidency over the whole world,	391
Maha-Deo,	103
Mahdeus and Mahadeva,	7
Mahmud Pasha, of Egypt, said to have the heir of Mohamed under his authority, by whom he could excommunicate the Grand Seignior, &c.,	352, 354, 361, 388
———— of Ghazni received investiture from the Calif Alkader,	354
Mahomet, Life of, by Prideaux,	89
Maia or Maria, the mother of the Romish Christ,	44
—— or Brahme-Maia,	128
————, sovereign or supreme of the gods,	189
M-aia, mother Ia or Jah,	224
Maia, mother of Xaca, conceived from a white elephant,	227, 228
————, the base of hydrogen, &c.,	336
————, described by Horace as the mother of Augustus,	357
————, the *female*, the followers of, &c.,	428
Maimonides,	89, 194
———— acknowledges that the meaning of the words *Baratit* and *Mercavah* is lost,	343
———— and other learned Jews on the word Mercavah,	401
Main Ambres, name of Stonehenge (hence our Minsters and Monasteries) Main of Am or Om-bra —stone of Om the Creator,	416
Mairs (Marias?) three goddesses,	103
*Maire Doon—Mayor—*a judge,	277
Majesty—Henry I. would have been shocked to be called,	213
Malabar, 50,000 Nestorians in,	96
————, the Nestorianism of, was, in fact, Χρης-ism,	357
Malacca,	215
Malcom's History of Persia,	243, 251
Malcome's, David, Antiquities of Britain,	20, 30, 33, 229
Male, the followers of Buddha affected the,	269
———— and Female sects, the, coalesced,	269, 270, 445
———— powers —contest between the,	358, 369, 427
————, where the, was the favourite, as at Jerusalem, a leaning (even after the union of the sects of the Linga and Ioni) to Jupiter or Iao,	445
Mallet's Northern Antiquities, &c.,	165, 272, 304
————, on Seigneurs and Seigniories,	300
————, on the ancient Runes, as known in Tartary,	305
Μαλλος, μαλον, apple, fleece,	252
Mama-ja,	6
Mammacocha, the Sea adored as,	30

	Page
Mammæus's false Alexander, &c.,	348
Man, the Isle of, so called from Man-anan or Mahi-man or Menu,	287
Man, considered a microcosm,	136
————, in Sanscrit, *a human being*—in Chaldæo-Hebrew *intelligence*,	187
————, priests, and corruption, in all states, the same,	307
————, has he a soul? What is the soul? &c.,	338
————, his state before the invention of letters,	339
————, though he could not *write* in syllables, soon learned to *speak* in them, and to make rhymes,	340
————, various races of *red* and *white*, as well as *black*,	363
————, if he arrived at high mental culture 500 or 600 years before the Sun entered Aries, &c.,	364
————, the passage of, through different stages, appropriately described by the Golden, &c., Ages,	366
————, the first state of, peculiarly favourable for an increase of numbers,	395
————, supposed to be created double—*male* and *female* in one person, in the image of the androgynous God,	397
————, animals, plants, &c., believed to be formed of both sexes,	398
————, the chain that ties the world together; below him, animals, plants, metals, &c., &c.; above him, souls of men, dæmons, angels, archangels, God,	404, 407
————, the stadium, the fathom, the standard,	404, 405
————, believed to be formed two in one body—male and female—the higher and lower, the good and the evil,	409
————, perhaps, is near his end ; a thousand years hence, philosophers, in some shape, may speculate on the extinct animal *man!*	445
———— *of the Mountain*, tho—the castles of, were left in peace, by Gengis, why,	383
Mandaites, the,	141, 193, 218
Mandschurians, the,	150
Manes or Demons,	74
Manes held, that the faculties of *seeing* and *hearing* are never lost,	101
Manetho, }	
Manetho, }	11, 12, 14, 133
————'s a succession of Gods who reigned before, and ended at, the deluge,	323, 324
———— mentions their reigns by lunar months, &c.,	325, 326
Mangey,	46
Mani,	7, 8, 65
————, celebration of the eucharist, by the followers of,	59
Manichæans, the,	8, 45, 49, 60, 80, 129
————, baptized both infants and adults,	65
————, on the succession of Abads,	133
————, denied the supremacy of the Pope, and admitted the Caracorum gentleman was Lord Paramount,	383
Manichees, the,	48
Manle, Malac, Minu =666,	187

3 Y

490   INDEX.

Mannus—man—connexion of the word with the Om or Hom of India and Persia, 265, 268, 397
Manor—manor-ia—place of Mnr, Minerva, Wisdom, 301
Manuchi, 263
Manwantara, *an age of man*, 134
Manwantaras, (fifty-six,) 133, 134
March 25th, celebrated for the resurrection of Mithra, 99
———, celebrated for the resurrection of Jesus, of the god Sol, 100
———, celebrated for the resurrection of Bacchus, Horus, and Osiris, 102
Marcionites, the, 80, 96
Marco Paulo, 33
Maria, the lake of, 45
———, queen of heaven, 81, 82
———, aria, *place of M?* 228
———— Sa. degli Angeli—Anima-Consolazione, &c., 91
———, called Mania, in Siam, 180, 203
Mariebua, Tribus, 103, 181, 203
Mariner's Compass or the Loadstone, a wisdom more precious than, 128
Marinus Sanutus, 240
Mark stones, the Scandinavian, of the Scottish isles, 284
Markets and fairs held around the sacred mount, with its cross, on every Dies Solis, 276
———, anciently held on our Sunday, 315
Markoles = 666, Tuesday, 208
Marks, letters so called, and knowledge of the number called *wisdom*, 169
——— , whether Homer made, or knew alphabetic writing, 170
Marolles, the abbé, 53, 62, 79
Marriage, with ancient Persians, a religious service, like that of the Greek, Romish, and Protestant Christians, 71
——— *a civil contract* in Scotland, and in the United States, 72
Mars, 83, 212, 213
——— is Αρης, and the monogram M, 208
Marsden's History of Sumatra, 292
Marsh, Bishop, 43, 61, 67, 69
———'s Bishop, Horæ Pelasgicæ, 293
Marsham, 189
Martial, 145
Martiales, the priests of Mars, 76
Martianus Capella, 102, 110, 224
———, on the cycle of Om = 608, called OMEN, 414
———, adored the solar power, 429
Martin IV. was addressed thus, "O Lamb of God, who," &c., 55
Martinmas, the festival of, 86
Martyr, Justin, 4, 60, 61, 66, 67, 69, 89, 115, 144
———, Peter, 39
Mary, *Maria Stella, Mother of our Maker, glorious Virgin of Mount Carmel,* 45
——— Magdalene, the mother of Jesus, and Salome, 102
———, Mag or Magna di-Helen, 203
———, one of the *three* of Gaul, 154
——— followed *Henry,* &c., a general history must not be written with stating, that, 369

Marys, the three, 103, 136
———, or Parcæ, 203
Ma-Saga, *the great Saca*, 230
Mason, a perfect, must be a perfect Buddhist, Jew, Christian, or Mohamedan, 251
Masonic Templars, eight-point red cross of the, 112
——— or Rossicrucian mystery the whole Χρησ-tian mythos, 134
——— Lodge or Chapter—the banquet which always follows a, probably the remains of the Eucharistia, 441
Masonry—what would be its *secrets*, if all England were initiated? 341
Masons, the, kept the Cadmæan system in mystery, 185
Mass, the, 64
———, Latin for corn or bread, 61
———, is called the Host, 62, 91
Masses or services for the dead, 73
Massaca, Massaga, Nagosa, or Mosaga, a *great city*, 230
Massageta, the, 37, 67
Massonius, Philippus, 148
Mastodon, the, is dead, 445
Maszlat, Mount (of the Saviour?) called also Méslade, Maslaf, Maslath, and Moslah,—in the time of the Crusades the chief place of the Assassins, 391
Maternus, Julius Firmicus, on man produced in the image, &c., of the world, 430
Mathematici, the, were Freemasons, 135
———, Cyclopes or Calidei, the builders of Stonehenge, Abury, Dipaldenha, the Pyramids, &c., 135
———, calculators of time, 141
Mathematicians or Chaldeans, the, in the time of Cæsar, 134
Matribus, Tribus, 103
Matter, M., on the little advance in real knowledge, 132
———, on the Monad, 197
Matter—the doctrine of the eternal existence of, 427
——— and spirit, materialism and immaterialism, &c., 428
Matthew, the Gospel according to, 45, 60, 67
——— and Luke, disputed chapters of, 129
———, on generations from Abraham to Christ, 133
Maundeville, Sir John, 189
Maundrell, 236, 402, 405
Maurice, Mr., 49, 67, 69, 70, 83, 89, 96, 98, 102, 127, 253
———, on M. Bailly's position, respecting the first race of men after the flood, 444
Mavors and Quirinus—Mars, 208
Maximus of Ephesus, 448
May-pole festival (the vernal equinox in Taurus) still celebrated in Hindostan and Britain, 106
———, the, dancing round, 179
———day and April-fool festivals, the, in Britain and India, 262
———poles, our, whence, 410
———, where the priest treated the people with games, &c., when they came to pay their tithes, 419

Maya, (parent of Buddha, and God of Love), 103
Mayence, a golden lamb, with a glory, in the cathedral of, 112
Measures—how the oldest, most universal, &c., of the ancients, may be ascertained, 403
———, Digits, Palms, Feet, Cubits, &c., &c., 404, 405
———, Aroura, Plethron, &c., 406, 407
Mecca, 207
———, the mother of cities, 303
———, Medina, and Jerusalem, holy cities, 385
———, the temple or Caaba of, was surrounded with 360 pillars, like the temple of Iona, in the West, with 360 crosses, 402
Medina, 377
———, Mohamed's flight to, 378
——— arrival at, 380
——— tomb at, 385
———, Sidonia, the city of, 307
Mediterranean, the, the subsidence of, 352
Medo-Persian Monarchy, the, 317
Medusa's head, &c., the nonsense of, 349
Megabyzes or Megalobyzes, the, priests of Diana, 47
Megalistor, the, 27
——— Mundorum, the, 251, 408
———, the celestial vault, was the templum erected by the, 408
Μεγιστυ κτημα, the guide to felicity, 130
Melchizedeckian and Pythagorean ceremony—the Eucharist; in the mode celebrated by the ancient Latins and the modern Jews, we have an example of a mystery become public, 441
Melchizedek, 45, 202
———, Abram, Mithra, and Jesus, the religions of, all the same, 58
———, sacrifice of bread and wine, of, 59, 62, 63
———, says grace, drinks to his guests, &c., 300
———, at Salem, one of the tribe of Juda, which came from India, before the tribe of Abraham, 352
———, Abraham of the religion of, 364
———, priest and king, 366, 381
Melchizedeks, Royal or King-Priests, the first governors of nations, 269
Mem, the, in Irish called M-vin, M-ain, 223
Memory, without writing, cannot preserve historic knowledge, except of a simple story—as, of the flood, 310, 313, 339
———, the shortness of, in the early race, attributable to their having only numeral symbolic, and not the syllabic, system of letters—perhaps only the knowledge of the figures of notation, 432
Mencerinus or Menchérinus, 13
Mendæan alphabet, the, was Pushto, &c., 153, 240
Mendeans—Mandaites, &c., 218
Men-des, holy Goat or Sheep, 180

INDEX.

Men-des, holy Goat or Sheep— 650, 188
Mendicant monks, the, like priests of Isis, 92
Mendicants, the, 72, 76
——————, no other beggars in Rome, but, 72
Menochmal, two, at Jerusalem, both named Jesus, and both born of a Virgin, &c., 124
——————, the Celtic *mannus* and סנמ *Mn*, *man of Wisdom,* ib.
Ménès, 12, 13
Menu, Nume, 211
———, Janus or Noah, 223, 360
———, the laws of, 244, 263
———, Noē, and Tibo, 309
———, each people, having the mythos, would maintain that its ancestor was *the* incarnation or Man-ou, 361
——— Buddha; but Menu was Noah, therefore Buddha was Noah, 400
——— the laws of, admit the sovereign to be *lord paramount of the soil*, 418
Mercator's Chart—probable origin of, 372
Mercavah—the wheel of Ezekiel, 335, 401
——————, the knowledge of sublunary things, &c., 342
——————, by Jews and Christians, said to mean *moral* doctrine; it taught astronomy, the use of cycles, &c., 343
——————, and *Baruth,* meaning of lost, 343, 428
——————, and Mohamed's temple, called Caaba or Caavah, 398
——————, the microcosm of. Perhaps the vehicle or conveyor of the secret of the Om, of the doctrine of the renewal of cycles, 401
——————, from ם, מ or ני or (meaning *oppy* or chief) and בכ *cb, cav* or *cavah*—the chief or head circular vault of M, 491, 402
——————, the, with the Barasit, supposed to contain all the mysteries—the Grecian Cabala, 440
Mercury, 31, 312
Merlin, the British, begotten by the Devil on the body of a virgin, as fabled by the Templars, 349
Maroe, the island, 10, 44, 45
Merrick's annotations, 408
Meru (Mount), 21, 45, 73, 103, 175, 228, 411
———, perhaps Menu, 160
———, a mount, in every country having any pretensions to have a *Saviour*, 341
Merus or Meriahs, Parnassuses, Olympuses, Acropolises, &c., why we have so many, 275
Mesopotamia, the, formed by the Ganges and Indus, the feudal system vigorous in, 263
Mezala, 62
Messiah (Massiah) the château of the Old Man of the Mountain, 347, 348
Messiah, the, 14, 34
——————, of the Jews, 31, 97
——————, *a spiritual,* why not foretold? 227
——————, foretold in the Targums, 233

Metals, the order of the discovery of—Gold, Silver, Brass, Iron, 366
Metaphysicians, profound, talk nonsense, 227
Metempsychosis, the ancient fathers believed in the, 252
——————, whether Jesus Christ taught a future life by a, 308
——————, many matters must be premised, before it can be denied, 338
Meton, 141, 198
Metonic cycle, 32
——————, viz. 19, so common in the stone circles in Britain and Ireland, 402
Mets, 103
— Malrs, three goddesses worshiped at, 103
Mexican king, the, danced before the God, 31
——————, temples in the form of a cross, 32
——————, language full of Greek and Hebrew words, 35
——————, rites, &c., are almost the same as those of the Jews, 39
——————, language, close affinity of, to the Hebrew, 155
——————, and Polynesian languages, difference between, 158
Mexicans, the, their monuments, paintings, mythology; their triune God; their arrival from the West, 23
——————, their migration, led by the God of Armies, 24
——————, had fringes on their garments like the Jews; their chronology on the creation, deluge, confusion of tongues, nativity of Christ, &c., 25
——————, crucified a man at the end of 52 years, 26
——————, held that the world *was* inhabited by giants; chaunted the word *Hululaea*; their hieroglyphic annals extended backwards beyond Egyptian, Persian, Greek and Sanscrit history, 27
——————, their temple Xochicalco faced the four cardinal points, and they had no *iron,* 28
——————, their language similar to the Hebrew, 29
——————, baptized their children; had a fast of 40 days; honoured the cross; 31
——————, called God the Father, Yzona, 32
——————, had their mythology from Asia, and held the doctrine of regenerations in cycles, 33
——————, called their great God Yao, IHHVRABLE; expected a Messiah; their history of the flood, a close copy of Moses's; sacrificed their first-born; practised auricular confession, 34
——————, their courts had the same number of judges as those of the Jews, 37
——————, viewed the first horses of the Spaniards with horror, 38
——————, knew not the use of iron, 40, or of letters, 41, 32, 206

Mexicans, the, must have gone from the old world before symbolical writing was invented, 160
——————, their religion, 202
——————, knew notation, 235
——————, had trial by Jury, 278, 279
——————, must have gone from the old world before the change in the earth's axis, 315
——————, the most ancient year of, 360 days, 318
——————, and Spaniards, the relation between, like that of the Britons and Romans, 415
——————, who will say they were barbarians? 416
Mexico, 28, 29, 31, 34, 36, 39, 74, 171, 173, 232, 393, 430
——— and Peru, antiquities of, 21—41
——— or Mesi-co, the country of *Msih* or of *the Messiah,* 23
——— or Mesitli, 23, 24
——————, the same Hebrew language and double mythos in, 206
——————, the Virgin and Rose, in, 244
——————, two weeks in, viz., one of 3, and one of 5 days, but not one of 7 days, 315, 316
——————, the doctrine of the renewed incarnation, visible in, 340
——————, given away by the Pope, as supreme over the whole world, 374
——— and Peru, while Gold was the only metal in, and coin not invented, 380
Meyn Ambre, Stonehenge, 279, 410
——————, the Rocking-stone in Cornwall so called, 410
Mezeray, M., 54
Mi Dubh, month of sorrow or grief, 83
— Nolagh, month of the new-born, ib.
— Samhan, month of Samhan, ib.
Mia, the female of Plato's Τὸ Ὄν, 168
———, the monogram M and the Hebrew Ιω—self-existent, 196, 224
Μια αρχη and Παντη αγιωτις, the androgynous Brahme-Maia, 197
———, the, a chief part, &c., 367
Mickle for *much*—our Saxon word from the Heb. *Mikhla*. In some cases it is used for *all,* as Micklegate, York—the *sole* or *only* road into the city, from the south, 408
Michaelis, 43, 67, 172
Microcosm, man considered, a, 136
——————, the great, of North India, 275
Microcosm, the, 299
——————, no doctrine more universal than, among the ancient philosophers; fragments of it lie scattered around us; it is intimately connected with the Cabalistic doctrines of the Trinity and Emanations; its origin perhaps found in Gen. i. 27, 397
——————, the probable truth of the ancient doctrine of, supported by the discovery of modern physiologists, 398
——————, after the *one* or the *three* must to depend on the foundation number *five* or *six*, 409
——————, traces of, in the 70 or 72 cities called Augusta—

INDEX.

in the 72 chiefs at the siege of Troy—in the 70 kings whose thumbs and great toes Adonibezek ordered to be cut off, &c., 421
Microcosm, the, visible in the Pontiff and three Flamens, &c., 422
———, every seed was a, 429
———, visible in the number of the Gods—the *three* in the capitol—Jupiter, Apollo, Minerva, 433
Microcosmic numbers — *one* produced *two*, &c., 431
Migration, the first of the tribe—the Exodus, &c., 430
Miletli, the, from Spain to Ireland, 177, 412
Miletus, Apollo of, 117, 118
Military roads, the, of Britain, said to have been made by the Romans — but probably most of them were set out by the Sacerdotal Agrimensores, 416
——— aristocracy, when they arose, they probably enfeoffed their followers in lands not previously occupied, 417
Millenium, the, 102, 138, 141, 329, 388
———, with the failure of the remembrance of the *golden age* faded away, 307
———, is still looked for, 308
———, expected at the end of the first 600 years of our era —its falsity proved from facts, &c., 339
———, the non-appearance of, when its supposed time arrived, 351
———, expected in the 13th century, 353, 356
———, expected equally by Christians and Gentiles, 367
———, shews itself, with the claim of the followers of Ham, on behalf of the invisible Imam, 388
Milner, Dr., Apostolic Vicar, 58, 61
Mimra—has it been M-om-rah? 295
Mind was the Te Os, 187, 188
Minerva or Pallas, 5
———, Antony called himself the husband of, 346
Minos or Menu or Numa, 180, 187
Ministers—all monastic establishments of the Carmelites, Essenes, Therapeutæ or Cullidei, 279
Minutius Felix, on the man crucified, 115—119, 120, 125, (probably Pythagoras,) 127, 129
Miraculous conception, the, of Sachiquecal, 33
———, of Juno Jugalis, and of the Virgin Mary, 82
———, of two Jesuses, 124
Maia, the mother of Xaca, 227, 228
———, of the mother of Gengis Khan, and of Tamerlane, 233
Mirkond, on the birth, &c., of Iskander (Alexander), and his battle with Darius, 346
———, on Khizar, a prophet—describes Alexander as a, 347
——— describes Kai Khusrau (Cyrus) as a prophet, 351

Mirkond and Wassaf, Persian writers, relied on by Hammer in his History of the Assassins, 390
Misem, a name of Bacchus, 19
———, the Saviour, from ישע *iso* and ם m, *ib.*
Missio or Mass, the, 61
Missionaries, our, know of the similarity of the Brahminical to the Christian Religion, 337
M-istory—mystery, 187
——— or history of a mythos, kept in remembrance by songs, before the art of writing by syllables, perhaps of writing by numerals, was discovered, 340
Mitford's History of Alexander, 421
Mithra, 34, 58—61, 66—69, 104, 110, 137
———, the followers of, observed the sacrifice of bread and wine, 59, 60
———, rites of, by water, air, fire, and blood, 67
———, his followers turned to the East in worship, 89
———, his birth celebrated at the commencement of Dec. 25th, 99
———, believed to have risen from the dead, on March 25th, *ib.*
———, the mysteries of, 111
———, the God Sol, Iao, and the Lamb of God, the same, 112
Mithras, 137
———, &c., put to death, &c., 142
Mitre, the ancient, 77
MN, the centre letters of the Greek alphabet, 187, 188
MN = 650, 193, 223, 224
מנדא *mndo*, knowledge, understanding, 189, 192
Mndo מנדא = 650—רי di holy Mandaites, followers of Wisdom, 193
Mnevis, *Mnui* = 566, 210
Mo or Om AHMED, the cyclar *desire of all nations*, 251
Moedrenech, *Mother Night*, Dec. 24th, 135
Mœris, the Lake, 230
Mogul is Al-Mag, *the Mage*, 175
———, Mag-*el* or *ul*, Almug-tree, or great God, 203
———, the, supposed to be a lineal descendant of Gengis Khan, 352, and of Noah, 421
———, investiture by, sought by Hindoo princes, 352, 353, 375
———, the Great, in the, may be found the Archierarch, 370
———, the moral influence of investiture by, not perceived by our people, 383
Moguls, the, 150
——— trace their pedigree from Japhet, 353, 361
Mohajoo or Movers—in the, who fled with Mohamed, we probably have the three sons of Adam and of Noah, and imitators of the three flamens of Rome, and of the archflamens of Britain, 380, 385
Mohamed, 29, 33, 218, 219, 274, 375
———, a Saca or Sacaswara, 2
———, an incarnation of Wisdom, of Buddha, 3
———, thought to be "the Desire of all Nations," 167, 251, 291
———, the first proselytes of, were Eastern Tartars, Arabs, and Afghans, 297

Mohamed, the *secret doctrine taught* by, 388
———, believed to be a divine incarnation, 343
——— himself to be the person foretold, 344, 377
———, the era of, 347
———, the lineal descendant of, said to be living at Mecca, 351, 352, 354, 361
——— carried his pedigree to Noah, 352
———, the descendant of Shem, after failure of heirs in the line of Jesus, 360
———, thought to be the *tenth* Avatar, 368, 379
———, restored the ancient payment of the *tenth*, 371
———, his conquests secured by the belief that he was the Vicar of God, and by his moderate taxation, 377
———, in his passage through the heavens, begs Jesus to intercede for him, thus placing Jesus Christ above himself, &c., 378
———, causes of his success; thought to be the promised comforter, 379
———, wished to restore the world to its primeval, patriarchal state, 385
———, suspected of having pretended to divide the world into three parts, or that his followers said he had, in consequence of the lines of Ham and Japhet having failed. Nothing but confusion in Hammer's attempt to clear up the claims of the descendants of, to the Califate, 386
———, the Sopheism, &c., of, render it probable that he held the same Cabalistic doctrines as Moses, &c., 398
———, said to have destroyed the Dove or Iune, an object of adoration in the Caaba; yet, from the use of the Crescent, he probably adopted the double principle, 402
Mohamedan and Tartarian Conquerors, 35
Mohamedans, the, 35, 76, 83, 129
———, spared the statues of Buddha, 2
———, cut off the girdle of a proselyte, 77
———, superstition of, on the number 6, 195
———, conquered the devotees of the two principles, &c., 269
———, said not to be Christians, 281
———, less devoted to the *male* principle than at first supposed, 291
———, rebuilt the Jewish temple, 296
———, call Mecca the mother of cities, 303
———, had supposed one of their Imams remained—his residence unknown, 351
———, call Constantinople Roum—its monarch Emperor of the world, 369
——— and Christians, the, in

INDEX.

reality the same; their mutual hatred, 369
Mohamedans, the, probably have a *lex non scripta*, though travellers suppose they are ruled by the Koran alone; the doctrine of predestination, held by—its probable origin, 376
———, the writers of the sects of, hated each other, as much as the Christians hated the whole of them, 379
———, and Christians equally liable to misrepresentation, 380
———, maintain that Hagar was a *princess*, 386
Mohamedism, an *esoteric*, was Sopheism, Buddhism, from North India, 275
———, one great cause of its rapid success, 37
———, connected with ancient mythology, and with modern Christianity, 402
Mohamet, 97
Moines or Manni (Om-manni) the same, 268
Mola—bits of bread offered in sacrifice, 62
———, Hebraice is Al-om, 303
Molech—Baal, 82
M-om-ptha, 170, 171, 193
Monachism—its nature, &c., 269, 368
Monad is *Mn*=650—dl, *holy A, the holy one*, 181
———, the, or unit, point or jod, contained all numbers, &c., 190
———, the, placed by the Gnostics at the head of all things, 197
———, in its least quantities as in its circle, whose centre is everywhere, &c., all was To Ov, —what is this but illusion? 445
Monarchs, the, of Asia, have a rational claim, European monarchs not the shadow of a pretence, to *divine right*, 339
Monasteries, the Christian, increased in Spain, under the Moorish sway, 377
MONDAY may be *Mns*=656, or *Mn*=650, 208
Mongols,—the emperor of, advanced from *la ville de Sahn* to attack the Calif of Bagdad, declaring that he found in the family of Abbas none of the virtues of the Prophet, 390
Monkey, the, called Hanuma, *Aelymas*, 150
Monkeys, an army of, said to have assisted Cristna in his conquest of Ceylon, (but Brahmin and *ape* or *monkey* is the same word,) 9
Monks, the, use a girdle with 12 knots, 77
———, church patronage left to, by laymen, 257
———, and Eunuchs probably arose from devotion to the *male* principle—no monks among the Brahmins, but are among the Buddhists, 269
———, successors of the Essenes, &c., addicted to an allegorical Christianity, 270
———, were not priests in early times, not being ordained by the Popes, 280
Monks, the, were all Carmelites before the sixth century, 281
———, the Regulars, descendants of the Buddhists, 369, 370
———, it is likely, became the sole priests, 381
———, of Tibet and of Europe, 434
Mons Esar, the, of Ptolemy, 230
Mont Marte, 59
Montesquieu, 263
Montes Soldini, the, 122, 230, 232
Montezuma, 39
Montfaucon, 103
Month, the, shortened from 30 to 28 or 27 days, 315
———, the lunar, exactly 30 days long, before the flood, &c., 316—326
Monthly Magazine, the Old, 123, 125
Moon, the, and Isis, identified, &c., 337
Moon's period, the, the first recorded idea, 149, 150, 162, 183, 187, 188, 213
Moons, the word, in Enoch, should probably be translated planets, 313
Moore, on Ciphers, 185
———, on the Purabas, 351
Morea, the Morus or Mulberry—*sapientissima arbor*, 5
Morrison, Dr., on the extent of the Chinese *written* language, 215
Mosaic history, the, travestied in the Egyptian, 11, 15—18
———, found in Mexico, 34
———, China, 36
———— law, the, the model of European common law, 37
———— system, the, 63, 68
———— and Christian mythoses, the, in the Argonautic mysteries, 115
———— mythos, the, in the mysteries of Eleusis, 115, 195, 347
———, at Trichinopoly, 229
———, in the temple of Juggernaut, 293
———— record of the deluge, a Gentile confirmation of the, 314
———— or Judean mythos, the, established in China, a branch of the first Buddhist or Tauric system of cycles, 396
———— mythos, the, in the Tamul, 440
Moses, 19, 20, 24, 34, 40, 43, 44, 60, 67, 163, 171, 202, 256
———— was an Avatar, a Messiah, 14
———, a Saviour, 16
———, certain kings of Egypt repetitions of, 61
———— has the horns of Jupiter Ammon, 81
———, the mysteries of, the same as those of the Heathen, 105
———, by direction, practising *buffoonery*, 179
———, tomb of, in Cashmere, 232
———, thought to be a Xper, 251
———, God failed to kill, at an inn, 254
———, sacrificed Azron, 303, 383
———, with his tribe, asking leave to pass through the lands of the king of Edom, an example of other emigrations, 306, 307
———, on the flood, 321, 327, 353
———— and Alexander represented with horns, 347

Moses—an example in, of one of the chief priests setting up for himself, when the supreme Pontiff and his Pontificate had become obsolete, 362
———— initiated into the policy of the Egyptian priests, concealed from his people the doctrine of the immortality of the soul, 385
———, or Moschus (the Phœnician, Judæan or Chaldæan)—Pythagoras said to have learned the *atomic* doctrine from; their doctrines, with little exception, appear identical, 396
———, ordered the pillars set up, not to be touched with the chisel —the probable reason, 403
———, under the law of, religion was confined to one little nation, and a temple built, &c., 409
———— did not write, though he might adopt Genesis, 413
———, reformed his tribe by abolishing the *golden calf*—attempted to be restored by the *ten tribes* by the calves set up at Dan and Bethavon, 488
Mosheim, 49, 60, 66, 145, 270
———, on the double meaning of the Gospel histories, 130, 131
———, on Robertus de Nobillibus, 366, 367
Moslems, the, objected to the *corruption* only of the Hindoo religion, 352
Mosque—the first Calif walked barefooted to the, 377, 378
Moto-hill, the Calvary with its cross, &c., 283
Mother, the, of God, the Virgin, 76, 108
———, the great, of the Gods, 76
———— priests of, called Semiviri, 77, 79
Mother Night (Moedreneeth) on Dec. 24th, 135
Motion, the, of the earth, had it been interrupted, would have left physical traces, 314, 315
Mount Blanc — the flood which threw up, 312, 315, 322
———— Imaus, 444
———— Moriah, Maria (מריה), or Maia, probable origin of, 45
———, the capitol, &c., 297
———— Sion in the Chersonesus, 129
———, the Mount of the Sun, 178, 225
———— of Solyma, 9
———— of Solima, the, 175
Mountain Tribe of Jews, the, not discovered by Herodotus, 11
Muzzotta and Sottana, priests' dresses, 91
מרכב *murkb*, from רכב *rkb* or Rocab, *to ride* and *a carriage*, for *Merouah*,—the chariot of Ezekiel, &c., 491
מוסה *mseh*—the celebrators of the, by *regimine*, became Muses, 340
Motron—the sacred stone or meteor stone; hence, perhaps, mad, madam, Meth or Mother, the Egyptian name of Isis, 403
MUIL=666, 249, 250
Muin (Moiria i. e. Maria)=666, 186, 223, 224
———, Sam-skm or Akm-es, 224
M-uin, N-uin—Mu, Nu—Me Nu, Nu Ma, the Me Ne, 226

	Page
Muller's Universal History,	406
Mummy, Monia, Mumia, Amomia, from Amomum,	242
Mundaites, Nazoreens, Nazoureans, or Christians, the, of St. John,	66
Mundore,	205
———, a Pontiff or Pope, once at,	373, 422
Municipia, the rights of the, how acquired,	434
Munro, Mr. J., on the monogram XP, found in the catacombs, &c., of Rome, but in use long before the time of Christ,	341
Muscovites, the, worshiped Isis and Horus,	110
Muses, the, or Saviours, of Greece, why nine,	286
Music connected with religion,	233, 298
———, poetry, and painting, classed with *dancing*, by Aristotle,	425
———, Pythagorean praises of,	426
Mussulmans, the,	302, 303
Mussulman religion, the, held to be the completion of both the Jewish and Christian,	397
Μυςηριον, from the Celtic word *wist* or *wise*, signifies *knowledge*—is the radical of *history* or *mystery*, with the sacred M prefixed,	299
Μυθος and μυςηριον, the, what are the Mythos and the Mystery?	308
M-vin, the vin of M,	186, 242
Mylians, the, of Lycia, called Solymi, Telmissi, and Termillians,	180
Myn—a stone,	279
Mystery is a mythos—M-istory—perhaps I-story-Om, *the story of Om*,	187
———, the, the *secret* doctrine taught by Pythagoras, by Jesus, and by Mohamed,	308
Mysteries—plays of the time of Elizabeth,	233
———, the ancient, consisted, in part, of a knowledge of the Loadstone, Compass, Telescope, &c.,	246
———, plays, in the middle ages, so called,	299
———, out of fashion—the race of man has outrun them [?]	333
———, as such, lost by the establishment of the sect of Paul,	341
———, if every person who was admitted to the *high*, was admitted to the sacred caste, we need not seek for a reason for concealing the doctrines,	439
———, or secrets—the Eucharist used, perhaps in all nations, as a pledge of keeping the; it was forbidden to write, or even *to speak about them*,	441
———, Christian, the secreting of the, was an attempt to restore the secrets of Paganism,	442
———, when communicated to too many persons, the respect for them is lost,	443
Mystics, the,	136
Mythic-cyclic-microcosmic system, the great, suspected to be the foundation of the systems of all nations,	445
Mythology, the, of the Brahmins, Chinese, Japanese, &c., had that of the Sacæ as its basis,	267
———, of the Gentiles—	

	Page
one class have made it into a history of *men*, another have deduced from it *moral truths*,	440
Mythos, Christian (Chrestian,) the,	10, 14, 16, 34, 36
———, similarity of, in Tibet and in Rome,	119
———, almost every, has the same immaculate conception, &c., &c.,	119, 133, 307
———, the same, prevailed in almost every country,	136
———, of a crucified Saviour or Messiah,	171
———, the Chinese have the whole,	215, 314
———, when the mind of man outgrew the, it assumed a new shape—*vulgar* Christianity and *vulgar* Mohamedism,	308
———, a general—the object for which it was formed,	309
———, instead of history, continued, as in the case of Rome,	313
———, the, probably formed from a knowledge of the *precession* and of *the periods of the comet*,	328
———, the Christian or Judæan—all connexion with, omitted by advocates of the modern date of the present system,	335
———, or history of a person, made into a song, and sung or recited,	340
———, all histories accommodated to the,	341, 430
———, the, visible in the twelve Cæsars, like the Lucumones, and the Imams of Ali,	345
———, the Mosaic, set up by tribes from India, in various places, particularly in Egypt,	362
———, remains of the, visible in every country, in the sacred names of places,	373
———, the, probably caused several conquerors to arise,	375
———, an universal, once prevailed; arose from circumstances; founded on the microcosmic principle,	430
———, the cyclic—five records of the,	440
———, Jewish, the,	10, 34, 35, 49, 171, 173
———, in China, &c.,	19, 36, 97, 357
———, in Mexico,	26, 34, 36, 37, 134
———, Mexico and India,	206, 357
———, of Moses, all the, found at Tripetty,	259
Mythoses, all the sacred, were in rhyme—unwritten,	225, 426
———, the, of Jerusalem and Eleusis, the same,	390
Nabathæans, the, Mandaites, Nazoureans, &c.,	218
Nabouassar, the æra, &c., of,	313, 316, 317
Nadir Shah an Avatar,	207
———, Netzir, Nrtz, Neeruz—Nerutz—650,	ib.
Naga, or Hag,	31

	Page
Nagualism, an American doctrine,	ib.
Nails driven at Rome, and in the Etruscan temple of Nurtia, to record time,	340
Naked (Adam and Eve), meaning of,	245, 246, 253
Nama Sebadiah,	116
Nandies,	130
Nannacus,	18, 20
Napoleon—the monomania of,	344, 375
———, told Cardinal Fesch he saw "a star,"—declared to the Egyptians that he was a *Mohamedan*—in St. Helena a decided *fatalist*—his actions bespoke mental alienation,	358, 359
———, was Emperor, not merely a king, why,	360
———, was curious to know the cause of the wonderful success of Mohamed,	379
Nar-ay-ana, from *ner* (river or water) and IE—"IE carried in or on water,"	174
Narayen, the Lord Haree-sa,	118
Nassireddin de Thous, (the great astronomer)—why be delivered the Ishmaelites and the Calif into the hand of the Khan of Tartary; he exhibits a perfect picture of a renewed Daniel, &c.,	382, 383
Nathan (the Prophet),	160
Nations, the division of, into 72, named in Gen. x. 21, and alluded to in Deut. xxxii. 8, according to the number of the Angels of God,	409, 410, 413
Naturalists—their discoveries by means of the microscope,	398, 429
Nature, all, a chain of trinities: the *third* person of the *first*, was the *first* person of the *second*, and so on *ad infinitum*; thus all nature was God; thus God was nature,	336
Natzir, or flower of Nazareth, Jesus a,	193, 239, 240, 243
———, the language of the,	242
Naubanda, Mount of the Ship,	292, 411
———, *ship-cabled mount*,	294, 333, 334
Naurutz—Neros—the,	243
Navaretto, M., F. de,	30
Nazarene, Jesus called a,	44, 240
Nazarenes, the, the Gospel of,	63
———, or Ebionites,	60, 96
———, Marcionites, Socinians, and most of the Unitarians maintain that the story of the Magi, &c., is spurious,	96
Nazareth,	45
———, Jesus of,	50, 51, 58, 93, 109, 112, 119, 122
———, a town of, probably, in India,	115
———, the real Jesus of, not crucified,	142
———, the monastic institution of,	204
———, signifies *a flower*,	239, 240
Nazarite, Jesus a,	44, 240, 449
———, John the Baptist, a,	66, 449
Nazir or Natzir, a flower,	45
Nazoreens, Nazoureans, Mandaites, or Christians of St. John, the,	66
———, followers of wisdom,	193, 218
Ναζωραιοι, Ναζαρηνος,	44, 240
Neagorus, Thomas,	85

INDEX.

	Page
Nebuchadnezzar built the walls of Babylon,	317
Necia,	74
Negro, the, of the Upper Ganges, may have improved in faculty—become scientific before his form was moulded into that of Cristna,	363
———, prejudice against the *possibility* of a, being learned and scientific,	364
Negroes and bearded men found in America,	35
———, African, perhaps, would not find it too hot, if the planes coincided,	445
Neith—wisdom—Isis so called,	300
Neketali, in the Caribbee, means dead,	29
Nepaul,	7, 33
——— and Tibet, in, there are the Pope, his Monks, and a *crucified* God,	122
Nerbudda, the,	206
Nero, claimed to be the Tenth Avatar,	54
Neros, the, 29, 138—140, 141,	188
———, an intercalation in every, of 28th. lon. 42s.,	143
———, Naurotz,	243
———, the inventors of, profoundly skilled in astronomy, may have calculated the period of a comet,	313
———, said to have been invented by the Chaldæans,	330
———, several religions had their origin in the cycle of,	356
———, and the palm, as a measure, descended with the first pontifical race from before the last of the three floods,	404
Nessos from Nestos,	200
Nestorian Christians, the,	10
Nestorians, the, 60, 127,	218
———, received the Gospel of the Infancy,	96
———, believed Jesus Christ was a portion of God,	208
———, the Christians of St. Thomas, said to be,	ib.
———, the Tartars so called, are followers of Cristna, and use the words Hom-Mani-Pema-Om,	229
Nestorius,	32
———, his heresy was Buddhism,	357
Neuman, 148, 149,	218
Nevis, Mount—close to Beregonium—probably meant also Baris and Navis: it was the centre of Scotland,	411, 412
New Grange, the Linga in the cave at,	262
——— Trojan wars, a belief in, &c.,	339
New Troy, Rome—the same mischief to happen to, as to old Troy,	ib.
New Troys, &c., 136, 195,	303
Newton (Sir Isaac),	316
———, on the periods of the comet (of 1680),	326
———, proof of the folly of a learned man, in the works of, 333,	358
———, and Whiston—their conclusion with respect to the Jewish and Egyptian measure, &c.,	405

	Page
Newtons and Lockes, from the, dawn to the idiot,	407
Ng, a Chinese letter, answers to the Hebrew oin, 192,	224
Nice, council of,	80
Nicene Creed, the,	42
Nicephorus,	121
——— Callistus, 125, 126,	260
Nicol, Mr.,	220
Niebuhr, 26, 27, 56, 137, 138, 141, 233, 241, 334, 371—375,	432
———, on kings of Rome—astrological periods,	134
———, on the *tenth* levied by the Romans,	266
———, on the Roman kings levying a *tenth*, &c.,	371
———, on the Tuscan Lucumones,	373
———, on the Vectigal, and the mode of leasing it,	374
———, exhibits his ignorance of the Roman and Greek writers; observes on the mythos, &c.,	375
———, his *history* is rather *a critical dissertation*,	376
———, on the drains from Lake Copias,	381
———, on the landed tenure of Italy—that all landed property belongs to the State, and that the conqueror acquires a title to it,	391
———, says, every city, in the West, from Tyre to Gades, had a senate and general assembly; and, that all the confederacies of early nations were based on religion. Hence the initiated or sacred caste had rule over their fellow-creatures,	393
———, on the Roman Jugerum, &c., 406,	407
———, on every Cardo, &c., being a Templum,	410
———, on the nobility of Athens, tracing their descent from princes, &c., of the heroic age, 418,	419
———, on the twofold principle on which the tribes in ancient states were constituted; his ignorance of the Sacerdotal Government, &c.,	420
———, on the ancient pseudo-histories (but real mythoses) of Italy, all in poetry,	427
———, on the Alban and Latin families—on the legions, and on the whole assembled force being 72,000; "the legend," he says, "peeps through this wantoning in typical numbers;" but he asks not the meaning of the legend,	433
———, did not understand the system of Isopolity,	434
———, considered every thing to have taken its rise from the date of the Roman city or state—hence his explanation of the constitutions of the Romans and Grecians is a chaos,	435
Niemeyer,	43
Nile, the, 21, 211, 230, 239,	385
———, the sacred name of, was Augustus,	54
———, the Upper, once called Sindi or Abba-Sin,	181
Nilometer, the, at Cairo,	403
———, the cube of, 200,000	

	Page
multiplied, gives the length of a geographical degree,	406
Nimrod, 10, 24, 36, 42, 52,	344
———, on rulers from Adam to Nimrod,	133
———, on secret names of Rome and Athens,	242
———, on the character of Antony,	346
——— an Alexander,	348
———, on Magical heads, &c.,	349
———, on Charlemagne's reign, &c.,	356
———, on Nestorius's heresy,	357
———, on the Exodus or *going out* of all nations,	430
Niord—Neith or Wisdom—the Logos?	300
Nis or Sin—360, Bacchus or the Sun, 288,	292
Nisan, 104,	105
Noah, 12, 13, 15, 17, 18, 27, 133, 253, 354, 359, 360,	377
——— called, by Berosus, Sagan Ogygisan,	3
———, his grandson Kaesar or Cæsar,	24
———, icons of, in India,	122
——— and his Wife, a microcosm of Brahme and Maia,	181
———, their 3 sons a microcosm of the Trimurti, 181, 397,	398
——— enfeoffed the whole world to his three sons and their children, 266, 399,	400
——— saw the earth became inclined, &c.,	310
——— foresaw that destruction approached, and buried the sacred books in Sephora,	311
———, the flood of, 2349 [2348?] years B. C., 314, 327, 332,	334
———, probably the Xisuthrus of Berosus and Abydenus, 321,	322
———, supposed, by Tzetzes, to be Osiris,	324
———, the flood of, took place, according to the Samaritan chronology, in 2926 B. C., or, in the *fifth* revolution of the comet (of 1680) *backward*, 327,	332
———, if a great prince, living near the Caspian Sea, nothing improbable in his building a large ship and saving his family, &c., in it, 329,	335
———, divided the world among his three sons, 345,	372
———, the emperor of the whole world,	353
——— held to be the first divine incarnation—he was the first Archierarch over the whole world,	361
———, by the Mystics, made to live in *both* worlds; why,	397
———, according to the mythos, he had a right to the supremacy, in consequence of Cain's misconduct,	398
———, Buddha—Divine Wisdom—incarnate in,	400
———, the Supreme Pontiff—all the claims of kings to *divine right* have descended from,	407
Nobilibus, Robertus de, turned Brahmin,	259
——— and Romish missionaries—their success in South India and China,	366

495

	Page
Noca, the pronoun I, in Peru,	329
Noé,	18
Noel, Christmas-day,	83, 99
Nolagh, Christmas-day,	ib., ib.
Nomade tribes, the, of Africa and Asia, all have a language called Arabic,	274
———, the policy of, against appropriation of lands in perpetuity,	282
Nonius Victor cum Aurelio Victore, &c.,	390
ΝΟΟΣ, ΛΛΚΟΣ, and ΜΟΛΚΟΣ, mind and strength attending the god Pan,	425
Norde-roy, North-king, the,	291
Nordoreys and Sodoreys—the Northerns and Southerns, the Western Islands divided into the,	291
Normandy, conquered by a tribe of Scandinavians or Northmen,	275
Normans or Northmen,	269
——— and Saxons in Britain, like the Patricians and Plebeians in Rome—two nations,	392
Norris, Cardinal, on the length of the year, &c.,	329
North India, 19, 19, 31, 35, 36, 40, 135, 136, 152, 171, 173, 207, 225, 235, 238, 282,	300
———, mythos of, in Mexico, 28,	34
———, Chaldee language of, 128,	166
———, the empire of Pandea, first established in,	258
———, the great microcosm of,	275
———, the Jews of, expected a kingdom of Cæsar, why?	345
——— or Tartary, 1, 2, 7, 28, 136, 203, 221,	376
Northern Pacific Ocean, the,	30
Northmore, Mr., on a universal language of figures, 220,	221
Norway—Nor-la—the Sea-kings probably from,	291
Notation, the origin of—by calculi or cowries,	190—192
———, the art of,	213
Notes by the Editor. See Editor.	
"Nothing new under the sun," Solomon, perhaps, right in asserting there was,	445
Notre Dame, the Virgin Mary,	97
Nou Ross, i. e. Neros or Nazrutz, of the Persians,	243
Nousareans, the, calculators of time,	141
Nu, Nh or Noah, and Nh—Mn=650, 187, 223,	224
Nubia,	9
Nudum corpus, mount uncovered, without armour,	304
Nullum Tempus occurrit Ecclesiæ, 54, 75,	417
Numa, 60, 64, 74,	77
——— or Menu or Minos, 180,	187
———, when Pallas sent him the Ancile from heaven, immediately made five others, that the true one might not be known,	440
———Pompilius, 53, 62,	68
———'s correction of the Roman year,	320
———, when he became governor of Rome, probably found the state ruled by a portion of customs and laws of a previous government, and arranged, &c.,	435

	Page
Numbers and letters, all, described by right lines,	174
———, the sacred, and Cycles, the origin of,	223
———, sacred, connected with Magic—how uncertain,	397
———, lucky—some supposed to be more so than others,	400
Numeral symbols, in the unspoken language of, sor might be roa, and roe might be sor,	153
———, or the Synagogue Hebrew, the sacred lost language,	234
——— symbolic language, the, would contain long fixed; was probably co-extensive and contemporary with the Druidical buildings found all over the world,	396
Numerical forms, the influence of, in the states of antiquity,	432
———, Symbolic writing, in a downward direction, on growing into horizontal Alphabetic writing, would be almost unintelligible when spoken—as one might become sar, &c.,	435
——— language, the paucity of words in a, requisite to carry on the common affairs of life, less than is daily use in China,	436
Nun, a, in Chinese Pekeome, in Sanscrit, Bhagini,	218
Nundinæ, the, of the Romans,	147
Nuns (Papist) the same in China, Italy, and Tibet,	218
——— probably arose in opposition, &c.,	269
N-vin, 203, or N-uin,	224
Nyaya philosophy, the,	427
——— is the negative particle and the Hebrew אין is, meaning not is or not wise, and אין is, existence; it is the negative of Yeye: the the followers of, were those of the female,	428
——— is the Hebrew and Sanscrit איןie with the Celtic, Saxon, and Sanscrit negative to convert it into a term of reproach—Atheists—the doctrine of the unwise,	429

	Page
O, in Syriac, Pashto or Tamul, is the emphatic article,	250
———, total, al-tat, 600—cycle of the neros,	191
O'Brien, the Phœnician Ireland of,	262
O'Brien's Dictionary,	82
Oak and Beech, the, gave out oracles at Dodona,	165
Oannes the same as John,	137
Ob, serpent, the recurring cycle of 72,	182
Obeliscal pillar, the, called Omd, i. e. om-di, emblem of the holy Om,	415
Obelisks and single pillars in front of churches, at Rome, 92, 251, 402	
———, these were Lingas,	93
Ocaras or Caras,	14
Ockley, on the Califfs, &c.,	377

	Page
Ockley, on the Ashera or Zacal,	379
Oconnor, Mr.,	230
Octavius, Augustus,	54
———— Cæsar, united the offices of Pontifex Maximus and Emperor,	56
Octavius, the, of Minutius Felix,	116
Od is ad=5,	163
Oden is Adonis in Syriac,	250
Odhal or Udal (hence allodial?) land free from tax,	284
Odin, 4,	300
Œdipus Judaicus, on the Paschal Lamb,	106
Œftera Geola, month of January,	135
Offerings, Votive, 85—87,	91
Oge—an explorer,	225
———, a name of wisdom or Minerva,	299
Ogm or Agham, the, of Ireland and India—the letters of Om, having the names of trees,	299
Ogham (Irish) and Acham (Sanscrit) the same, 158,	225
——— is the Scandinavian or Saxon Rune,	215
——— character and Arabic language, the, a book found in,	220
———, the God of Wisdom,	224
———, the language or letter of wisdom,	225
Ogilvie, Dr., on Plato,	446
Ogum Craobh, "the branch writing," 153,	221
Ogyges, the flood of, 314,	338
———, took place 4648, B. C., and might throw up Mount Blanc, Chimborazo, &c.,	332
———, testimony of Varro respecting,	338
Ogygian Sagan, Noah so called,	3
Ouidiche Samhna, the night of Samhan,	82
Oil, anointing with—Extreme Unction,	72
Oin or ain, answers to the Chinese letter, ng, 192,	224
"O Lamb of God, who takest away the sins of the world," 55, 87, 104, 106, 108—110	
Old Man of the Mountain—his letter to Leopold, duke of Austria, 347, 348,	384
———, the, claimed all power, as the khan of Caracorum did, and as the Sheriffe of Mecca still does,	388
———, why so called, whatever his age,	389
Old and New Testament, literal meaning of the,	130
Oleo, first celebrated the died, at Delphi, with song,	165
———, on rhymes,	340
Oligarchies of an odious description, in Greece, degenerated from the aristocracy,	419
רתלעמ olme, Alma Venus, Mother of the Gods,	168
Ol-om-ris, three Gods, the same as Hom-etsull,	23
Olympiad, the first, 313,	314
Olympius—mother of Alexander—is called Rushia by the Persians, 346,	347
Olympus,	91
———, each independent territory had its,	136
———, an, in most old towns—	

INDEX.

	Page
remaining as at Cambridge and Oxford,	276
Olympus, an, in every country which had any pretensions to have a Saviour,	341
Om,	23, 34
——, the tree of the sacred,	65, 83
——, meaning of the, of Egypt, &c., the never-to-be-spoken,	167, 342
——, Om-Amet or Om-Amed, the desire of all nations, 167, 207, 251, 291,	401
——, meaning of, lost to the Indians,	170
—— of India, from Mia?	196
——, the sacred Buddhist,	207, 299
Om, not IEUE, the word never-to-be-spoken by the Jews,	170, 171
Om or Ammon of Egypt,	174
—— or Iom, meant 360 days,	302
Omadius,	19, 23
——, Bacchus,	302
Ombri, the,	53
Omen (monogram),	224
Ometeuchtli, the same as Bacchus,	23
Ommaides, the, were Avatars,	207
Omm alcora—la Mère des Villes—Meccque,	303
Omm Alketab—Mère du Livre, &c.,	302
——, 1' chap. de l'Alcoran,	303
Omnia, the family of, reigned at Granada, in Spain,	384, 385
Om-nu-al, (Immanuel of Isaiah,)	23, 170, 401
Omorca, the Hom-eyo-ca of Mexico,	28
ΟΜ ΠΑΝ ΚΟΤΗ, the three sacred words used in the mysteries in the Eleusinian mysteries,	197
Omphalos—M-phalos, Ioni, the centre, &c.,	224
Omphe, the, of Greece,	174
On or Heliopolis,	110
—— or the sun, the city of Destruction,	162, 174
On means the generative principle,	174, 191
One is On increasing or decreasing, like the coats of the Onion, ad infinitum, either way ending in illusion,	437
Onion, the, from the similarity of its coats to the planetary spheres—from being sacred to the Father of Ages, was called aurum—is adored in India, and forbidden to be eaten,	437
——, (in Hebrew בצל aum or בצל em,) a perfect emblem of the disposition of the heavens,	438
Onkelos (the Targum of) foretells the Messiah twice,	171
——, for Ararat, uses Kardu—that of Jonathan, by metathesis, calls it Kadrun,	411
"Only-begotten, the,"	72
Onomacrite [Onomacritus], the compiler of the Hymns of Orpheus,	97
Ophites, Evites, or Hivites,	31
ΟΦ and οφις anciently one word, and meant Logos and Serpent, and thus the serpent came to be regarded as the wisest of animals,	437, 438
Orarium, an Amict,	79
Order, our word, from ערד ord,	439

VOL. II.

	Page
Ordination, (χειροτονια, which see,)	68—71
——, nothing but initiation into the mysteries,	270
Oriental Pontiff, the, has probably resided at Oude, Agra, Benares, Delhi, Matadore, &c.,	373, 422
Origen, 4, 46, 80, 89, 130, 171, 172,	448
——, the founder of monastic life,	47, 269
—— against Celsus,	95
—— taught the Platonic Gnosis,	270
——, &c.,—implicated in mythic superstition,	349
——, Clemens, and the higher order of Christians, taught the mysteries—not known to Paul or his followers—yet Origen and Clemens acknowledged Paul,	440
Origin, the, of languages and letters, 254,	255
Oromasdes, the Good Principle,	83
——, light,	106
Orontes, the,	19
Orphée, les hymnes d',	97
Orpheus,	56, 97, 256
——, the 360 gods introduced by,	319
Ortelius, Abraham,	3
Orugalla, the prince of the Galla or Gael—same as the Cal of Ur or Uril,	289
Oru Gallu, the Gael or Celtic, from the,	294, 295
Orus,	14, 16
—— or Aur, God of Day,	99
—— Apollo, on the month, as 30 days,	321
Osci, the, were T'Usci—THE Uscans or Tuscans,	300, 436
Osiris,	7, 14, 16, 34, 103
——, death and resurrection of, 25, 59, 104, 106,	122
——, Adonis, Bacchus, all incarnate Gods,	98
——, son of Ceres or the Holy Virgin,	99
——, a personification of the Sun,	100
——, murdered by his brother Typhon,	102
——, scattered members of, search for the,	136, 142
——, sacred cycle of, of fourteen,	163
——, the staff of P, called χρησιμον,	204
——, in Hebrew numerals = 656,	210
O-sir-is and Iswara, Sir, Sieur, &c., from,	300
Osiris, supposed to be the same as Noah,	324
—— and Typhon, about the times of, or, about the deluge, an alteration in the length of the month and year,	326
Ossian (the bard), the son of Om,	293
——, his poems a series of epics, and like the tragedies of Æschylus or the historical plays of Shakspeare,	293
Ostia,	62
——, the modern Mass,	91
עשתרת Oshrt, Eostre,	59
Othman or Omar, the followers of,	291

4 A

	Page
Othman redacted the Koran—no better than a forgery,	378
——, after the death of, the Califate split into parties,	379
Oude or Youdia,	206
Ougn (ogham) circles,	225
Ουρανισαλιμ, the holy city Rome,	145
Ouseley, Sir W., 165, 189, 205,	240
Out-caste, the,	274, 283
Ouveroff on the Mysteries of Eleusis,	440
Ovid, 67, 74, 79, 90,	114
Owl, the, the first figure of the hieroglyphic alphabet, 192, 205,	221
עז oz, Parkhurst in voce,	132
Pachacama, Pi-akm-cama, i. e. Pi-Acham,	37
Pachacamack,	34
Pacific Ocean, the,	25
——, the Northern,	39
Pad or PD, name of Adonis, of the Po, Don, and Ganges, and giver of forms,	162
Pæstum—works in the temples of,	381
——, the finely-executed temples at, shew a more recent date than the Trilithons of Stonehenge,	396
Pagan religion, the, in the 4th century, virtually dead—most of its mysteries had become known—and where they were noticed or continued, the people were told, that the Devil had copied the Christian rites,	442
Pagani, the opprobrious name of village Pagans,	94
Paganism,	17
——, the Romish mythos, a close copy of,	112
Pagans, the, 64, 69, 74—76, 104, 145, 212,	448
——, called their chief-priest Sovereign Pontiff,	54
——, sacrificed covered with the Amict,	79
——, had processions for rain, &c.,	80
——, their festivals for local Gods,	81
——, used ceremonies like those of Christians on building temples,	85
——, at funerals, &c.,	92
Pagi, Roman villages,	419
Pahlavi, the, improved by Zerdusht,	236
——, a dialect of the Chaldaic,	237
Paish-wer, Paish-or, i. e. Paish-town,	239
Pal, the sixtieth part of a Ghari, &c.,	406
Pala, Pele, Peli,	5
——, Pállas, the,	242
Palace, pola, πυλις, the King's-Bench	231
Pale, the, of Ireland and Germany—the word brought to both countries by the first tribe of Saxons,	434
——, to be in the, was to be separated from something,	435

INDEX.

Palestine, 106, 136, 172, 226, 239, 240
———, the land in, was the Lord's — the Levites received, for him, the *tenths*, 266
———, if it had not sub-divisions, as parishes, it had Prosenchas and Synagogues, 275
———, supposing a tribe came to, from the East, with its Samanuans or Religious, &c., 369
Palladium, the, of Troy, 228, 231, 242
Pallas or Minerva, 5
———, from פלא *pla* or *alph*, 165, 189, 249
Pallatini, the, from India to Italy, 127
Pallestini, the, or Tartara, at the mouth of the Po—Sacæ, 301
Pallium, the, 230, 242, 244, 249, 383
Palm, the, probably the universal measure of all the ancient temples—the invention of the first Pontifical race, 404
Palms, 360,000,000 of, (agreeably to the microcosm,) equal to the circumference of the earth, or to 360 degrees or one circle, 404, 405
Palm-tree, the emblem of eternity—its leaves, in Tibet, indestructible by vermin, 231
Palmyra, 147
Pan, the God, 219
———, addressed as the Author and Director of the Dances of the Gods, &c., 425
Panayia and Dei-para, 45
Panchalica, free cities of, 117
Pandæa, 45, 278, 275
———, the empire of, that of Saca or Buddha, 258
———, a kingdom of—the more the Author reflects, the more is he inclined to believe in; it may have arisen in various ways, its *secrets* gradually growing into *sacreds*, 396
Pandæan empire, kingdom, &c., the, universal, 223, 234, 254
———, &c., system, affected secrecy, 257
———, each subdivision of, had its temple, and each temple its *domus templi* for the education of youth, 276
———, system, the, 284
———, kingdom, the Jews hoped to be placed, by a great Saviour, in the command of the restored, 361
———, the, probably founded when the sun entered Aries—the wars of the Mahabarat were struggles to establish it, 370
———, traditions of a, 373
———, process of the election of Hierarchs, all over the, 381
Pandorus, on the Gods and Demigods before the flood, 324
———, on the civil and lunar months, 30 days each, before the deluge, 326
Pantæneus, 131, 447
Pantheon, at Rome, with its open top, an example of the plan of temples, before the art of a keystoned arch was discovered, 408
Papacy, the, brought into subjection, by admitting the Monks, 285
———, prototype of, in the Archierarchy of the Buddhists, 368

Papias, 46
———, Irenæus, &c., letting out a part of the *esoteric* doctrine, it has ended in incomprehensible nonsense, 367
Papist Christianity, 40
——— Councils, &c., cause of their hatred to Freemasons, &c., 300
Papists and Protestants, the, little difference between, 93
———, the, scarcely allowed the Cullidei to be Christians, 281
———, a sect of Paulites—followers of Cristna, 370
Par and *bar*—a judge, 276
Para, is Bra, Creator, 6
Parable, from *par-habui*, by way of fable, 300
Paraclete, the, promised by Jesus, 51
Paradise or Tartarus, in Tartary, 73
———, the Zend brought from, 78
Paradise Lost, if the, had been written early in the Christian æra, it would have been regarded as of divine authority, 426
Para-sachti, Parasakti, Adisakti, Devaki, and Parakti, have all the same meaning, 6
Paravey, 36
——— on China, 214, 215, 217
Parasiti and Parasites, 53
Par-habui, by way of fable, is *parable*, 300
Parias, the, or Outcasts of the Brahmins — the Aborigines of South India are lower than, 274
Paris—the fears of the inhabitants of, calmed by M. Arago's *History of Comets*, 333, 334
Parishes (Bareiches, Pareichs), 275, 276, 279
Parkhurst, 2, 6, 6, 44, 48, 59, 83, 105, 114, 137, 145, 151, 170, 177—181, 189, 192, 193, 231, 239, 240, 245, 267, 303, 338, 342, 408, 438
———, on types and symbols of what the real Saviour was to do and suffer, 129, 132, 133
———, his Lexicon serves for the Hebrew, Chaldee, and Arabic, 274
Parsons, 37, 231
———, our word, nearly gone—changed to *clergyman*, 369
Parthenon Hecatompedon, at Athens, destroyed by Xerxes, 403
Parthian empire, the, subverted by Artaxerxes, 349
Passover, the, 31, 59, 69, 110
———, or *passage of the Lord*, 104—106
Pastoral tribes, a monarchical government prevails among all, 263
Patæci, little images of the Phœnicians, 181
Patans, (Pitan,) Rohillas, Schalmaul—the Afghans, 239
Patara, Pathare, Patrichm, or Patrick, the mythos of, 117
———, in Lycia, 181
Πατηρ αγιωτητε, the, 123, 128, 197
Pater Futuri Seculi, the, not now heard of in Rome or Tibet, but only the Vicramadytia or Vicar of God, 374
Patra or Patta (in Sanscrit), a *leaf*, 181
Patra, in Achaia, 5
Patriarch, the, Hairy ayxy, Royal Priest, as the Vicar of God, the owner of the soil of the whole world, 372
Patriarch, the, and his three vicars —the *four* a microcosm of the To Ov, of the Creator, &c., 430
Patriarchal religion, remains of the, in the Callidei, 281
———, government, the first seat of the, was probably the Chinese empire, or the country of the 1000 cities of Strabo, 376, 396
———, the, left towns, &c., to regulate their domestic concerns, according to circumstances, &c., 433, 434
———, probably continued, till after the sun entered Aries, 438
Patriarchate—every colony sent out by, would add to the wealth and power of the, 434
———, the whole world subject to the same — subdivided into *three*, each having a book like Genesis, to shew it was the eldest branch of Noah's family, whether it was Ham or Japhet or Shem, 435
Patriarchs, the, of tribes, fixed their residence near the stone pillar—the object of adoration, 371
Patricians, the Roman, got possession of all the lands, paying only the tithe, which, at last, they usurped, 374
——— and Plebeians, not an *aristocracy* and a *rabble*, but two nations, like our Normans and Saxons, 392
——— and Kings, the struggles between, were contests among the high-priests as to who should be *king* and *priest*, when the great Pontifical government fell to pieces, 393
——— and Plebeians, disputes between the, respecting the lands of conquered countries; the Patricians wished to claim them, as they did *all* the soil of Italy, as the representatives of the Archierarch, 394
Patron and Client, the relation between, when it existed in its best form, 433, 434
Pattarini, the, of Gaul, 296
Patton, on the principles of Asiatic Monarchy, 262, 263
Paul, St., 43, 66, 94, 197
———, his letters addressed to the Essenæans, 46
———, fanatical nonsense of, 73
———, called Divus, 80
———, the resurrection — as taught by, 101, a *vexata quæstio*, 122
———, taught *Christ crucified*, 129
———, the head of those who held the *literal* meaning of the Scriptures, 131, 270
———, the *mysteries* remaining in his day, lost by his teaching a *spiritual Saviour* actually crucified, 341
———, like Luther, Calvin or Montanus, acquiring many followers, his sect put into power by Constantine, 370
——— II. 52
Paulinus, 95, (bishop of Nola,) 110

INDEX.

	Page
Paulite Christians, the early, nothing better than our Ranters, Jumpers, &c.,	342
———, devotees not addressed (on Mohamed), but philosophers,	377
———, fathers, the, no doubt wished for mysteries, and made them out of doctrines not so considered by Justin Martyr,	441
Paulites, the,	122, 130
———, of Rome, against the philosophers of Alexandria,	131
———, or sect, got possession of power, and corrupted and destroyed, &c.,	173
———, the sect of, an imitation of the Essenes of Egypt,	381
———, when the, got possession of power, the mysteries were treated with contempt,	440
———, who, the first found that the Saviour was to be a *spiritual*, not a *temporal Messiah*,	446
Paulo, Marco,	33
Pausanias,	62, 91, 180, 260
Paw, Mons. de,	229
Payne Knight. See Knight, Payne.	
Payne (Paine) (Thomas), and Carlile, the writings of,	441
Peaceful and happy state of the countries under the first Califs in comparison with that of those governed by the Greek emperors,	379
Pedigrees, traced by monarchs of the East from one or other of the sons of Noah,	266
——— (the Hindoo) in the line of the sun and moon, nonsense,	351
———, reason for the attachment to, in the East,	382
Pegu,	45
Pehlavi or Parthic, the, derived from the Estrangelo,	153
Peirun,	39
Pema or Lotus, from Padma,	186, 243, 244
———, Buddha so called,	249
Penance,	72, 74
Penang,	215
Penn, William,	37
Pentameters, hexameters, &c., how the, arose,	349
Pentateuch, the,	31, 225
———, allegorical meaning of,	105
———, partly composed, partly compiled by Moses; many of the sect in North and South India, Mexico, &c., who have not the Pentateuch, have part of the same laws as the Western Jews,	376
——— and Koran, the, codes both of law and religion,	419
People on the earth—the probable number of, in 650 years after the flood,	395
Pepakam (a poem) probably is Pi-akm—*the wisdom*,	222
Periodus Magorum, the, or 360,000 years,	317
Perpetuam felicitatem made into St. Perpetua and St. Felicita,	86
Persepolis,	77
———, arrow-headed letters of,	225
———, the destruction of, by the Mohamedans,	261

	Page
Perseus—Alexander traced his descent from,	348
Persia,	73, 83, 102, 106
———, chronicles of the kings of, adopted into the canon of the Jews,	17
———, the Guebres of,	83
———, the oldest languages of, Chaldaic and Sanscrit,	236
———, the doctrine of the renewed incarnation, visible in,	240
———, the feudal system of,	262
———, the priests of, lords of the creation — their tenants paying only a *tenth*, were in a comfortable state,	265
———, the Royal family of, are Kajar Turks,	351
———, (and perhaps all other nations,) had 360 pollacs—probably villages, around the Cardos,	410
Persian Magi, the, celebrated the Eucharist with *bread* and *water*,	60
———, hierarchy, the,	71
———, sages, the, held the doctrine of purgatory,	73
———, on words in the, identical with Sanscrit,	234
———, year, the, contained 360 days,	317, 318
Persians, the,	34, 48, 58, 69—72, 83, 106, 197
———, possessed Egypt,	11, 12
———, Gospel of,	59
———, had the festival of Saka, Sakea or Sakia,	60
———, had their children baptized,	65
———, marriage with ancient, a religious service—and their sacristans, sacerdotes, præsules, and archipræsules, corresponded with presbyters, bishops and archbishops,	71
———, young, invested with the girdle,	77
———, had *four* days each month as Sabbaths or Sundays,	70
———, lighted fires, like the Irish, on Nov. 2nd,	83
———, had an angel, as the Christians have a saint, for each day,	86, 88
———, celebrated the resurrection of Mithra on March 25th,	99
———, had the same idea of the Resurrection as the Jews,	101
———, alone had the *lamb* for the equinoctial sign,	111
———, adored *fire* as the emblem of creative wisdom and power, or as the Wisdom and Power itself,	128
———, said, that there were 72 Solomons before the flood,	134
———, called the *San Συρυ*,	242
———, are followers of Shem,	385
Persons, a few easily frightened, may have saved themselves, in boats or on rafts, from a flood,	315
Peru,	30, 39
——— and Mexico, the Antiquities of,	21—41
———, while Gold was the only metal in, and coin not invented,	380

	Page
Peruvian nation, the founder of,	34
Peruvians, the, had the festival of *Capacrayme*,	31
———, believed in one Supreme,	34
Pervigilium Paschæ,	104, 105
Pesach (same as Pushto?) the festival of *the slain lamb*,	241
Pessinuntian Great Mother, the,	348
Petalon—Greek writing from top to bottom—a tree,	249, 250
Πεταλα or leaves — letters,	159, 163, 166, 249, 250
Peter, St.,	54, 56, 57, 122, 145
———, has the keys of Janus,	81
———, a rock, &c.,	182
———, his being called a *stone* mystical and equivocal,	254, 259
———'s, St., chair and church,	55—57
———'s Pence,	54
———, the, of the Romish church, probably the poll-tax paid in different countries by those who did not occupy land,	379
Peter Martyr,	39
——— the Great—probably regarded as an Avatar, crushing the Evil Principle, with his monumental horse—treading on a serpent,	360
Petersburgh and Rome—modern Christianity as exhibited at, a continuance of the ancient religion of Rome,	367
Petronilla, an epithet of Sa. Anna,	91
Petronius, Divus,	90
Petrus, Divus,	80
Pezron,	208, 242
Pfeifferus, Augustus,	148
Φαλυς from φυν=608, or φρυ=608,	143
Phallus, the,	242, 249
Phallic worship,	85
——— rites, at the vernal equinox,	106
Pharamond—a king or dynasty of the Franks,	267
Pharaoh, the hardness of his heart,	105
———, all the land of Egypt the property of,	374
Pharaohs, the, had the names of Gods,	212
Pharisees, the,	101
Φρυν and Phœnicushe (Irish)=608	
——— φυν=608 in Coptic,	143, 183
——— icia or country of Phen,	209
Phile, relics of Osiris shewn in the temple of,	102
Philalethean sect, the Author wishes to be considered a member of the,	448
Philaletheans, the,	442, 448, 449
Philaster,	50
Philip and Mary (of England),	299
———, the ancient astronomer,	320
——— of Macedon, why he sought to be acknowledged by the Amphyctions,	384, 423
Philippi,	43
Phillips, Sir R.,	330
Philo,	49, 50, 202
——— says nothing about Jesus Christ,	46
———, on double meaning, &c.,	130
———, on the Essenes,	368
Philos, the priest at, could order the king, i. e. the general of the sacerdotal forces, to commit suicide,	264, 266, 280
Philological Museum, the,	392

INDEX.

	Page
Philosophers, the, of Athens, Crotona, and Nazareth,	253
———————, renewals of all things look'd for, by,	431
Philosophy was religion, and religion was philosophy, in ancient systems,	449
Phiues, fils d'Eléazar,	97
Phocian war, in the interdict pronounced against the, by the Amphictyons, we see the almost expiring power of one of the local conclaves,	423
Phœnicia,	48, 98
———————, right-lined letter figures of,	148, 150
Phœnicians, the,	83, 96, 169
———————, ancient, paid tithes,	78
———————, had the Lamb of God described with the cross and the *rosary*,	108
———————, the right-lined letters or numbers of,	147, 148
Phœnix, the, lived 600 years, or a new cycle began,	143
———————, Phen or Phennicshe, meant 600 years,	143, 183
———————, built her nest with the leaves of the Amomum or Lady's Rose,	242
Phœnix, the, Joseph,	177, 178
———————, called *klo* = 600, by the Phœnicians,	183
Phota-Jah, Pho-tha, Phtha, or Thas,	5
Φωτισμος,	69
Photius,	122
φην αίθος, Αφρο-διτη the holy Phre,	209
—— and Freyas — names of the cycle as 666 or 608,	267
פרע *pre* or Phre or Pharaoh— the Solar Deity, God of Wisdom, Bacchus,	265, 271
Phrygia,	18, 47, 104, 106, 226
———————, called Room, by the orientals,	241, 412
———————, adjoining Mysia — the country of the Mystar or Troy,	412
Phrygians, the,	18
Phutios, old Grecian epithet of the Sun and Jupiter,	287
Picts, the, were men painted,	204
Picus, of Mirandola, on the microcosm of Plato,	404
Pilgrimages, imitated from the Pagans,	86
———————, the ancient, of Hindoos, to Mecca,	352
Pillars surrounding ancient temples — the most common number was 40, probably 38, and 2 at the entrance,	402
Pimpernel, the, opens to the sun, &c.,	430
Pinkerton,	217
Pipes or bagpipes, the, of Calabrian shepherds,	90, 91
Piromis (καλος) *a man,*—Pi-rouma is Pi-roma, Brama, *former* or *creator*,	243
Pisces, or John,	138
———————, the Vernal Equinox fell on the 25th of, 1800 years ago,	139
———————, the sun entered the sign of, 360 years B. C.,	144
Piscina,	69
Pisistratus,	168
Piregie, the feast of,	86

	Page
Pitima, the father of all men,	175
Pius II., called the cardinals Senators of Rome,	55
———— VI.,	80
Pla, Pallas, &c.,	165, 180, 249
———, *Pale*, the, of Ireland, &c., brought by the first tribe of Saxons,	434
Place, La, M., thought the oscillation of the planes, &c., *small*; the Indians thought it *great*,	414
Plagues, the, of Egypt, incredible; keep pace with the Labours of Hercules, and the Conquests of Bacchus,	105
Planes, the, if they coincided—what then?	310
———————, may have coincided anciently,	312
———————, when the, coincided,	315
Planets, the, may all be reduced to a state of fusion or gas, and be re-absorbed into To Or,	336
———————, the end of the world expected from a collision of,	382
Platina,	52
Platinus,	93
Plato, 43, 47, 48, 62, 93, 96, 113, 122, 168, 174, 189, 190, 196, 202, 205, 219, 221	
———, the Timæus of,	1, 397
———, the island of Atlantis, of,	39, 40
———, the Phædon and Republic, of,	73
———, the Θεοι γεννητοι, of,	81
———, the Trinity of, that of Jesus,	98
———, the original *Christianity* taught by,	131
———, the first that considered grammar,	195
———, the alphabet of,	220
———, on an original race drowned by the flood,	274
———, in the Trinity of, Νους or Venus was the Holy Ghost,	286
———, on proper names derived from the *barbarians*,	290, 429
———, on the inclination of the earth's axis,	313
———, on the change in the motion of the firmament,	314
———, on the division of the senate into 4 parts of 90 each, &c.,	319
———, the corporeal Trinity of,	336
———, Aristotle, and Pythagoras— the doctrines of, cited as logical and fundamental, &c.,	387
———, the most ancient philosopher who has treated of the microcosm,	397, 404
———, on all souls being made in one cup, of the same elements,	404
———, Philo, and Jamblicus—not equitable to seek for the belief of, in their works, written evidently unintelligibly to deceive the ignorant,	443
———, on the Lord of nature surrounded on all sides by his works,	446
———, the Trinity of, substantially that both of the Christians and of the Hindoos,	447
Platonics, the modern,	448
Platonism—the Encyclopædia Britannica on,	446
Platonists, the,	72
Plebes and Clientelæ or Tenants— the difference between; difficult	

	Page
to discover. Probably the Plebes were occupiers, as tenants *in capite*, of the first pontifical government; the Clientes as tenants of the sacerdotal order,	392, 393
Plinius,	3, 49
Pliny,	3, 50, 74, 274, 325
———'s account of Christians of Bithynia,	90
———, divides the circle into 72 constellations or lustrums, 215, 404, 410	
———, on the length of the year, &c.,	319, 320
———, on the Game Troy, in Wales,	401
Plotinus,	449
Plutarch, 8, 99, 193, 196, 314, 317, 325	
———'s Life of Numa Pompilius,	320
———, on circumstances of the deluge, in the history of Osiris and Typhon,	324, 327
———'s Apophthegms of the Lacedemonians,	426
Pluto,	7, 93
Πνευμα, רוח, *ruh*, spiritus, ghost, air, breath,	67
Poetry, in reality, the only species of composition, till the invention of the material of books, &c.,	426
Point de Galle, in Ceylon, 288, 291, 292, 294	
Polar regions, the, formerly warmer than now, and fit for plants found only in warmer climates,	312
Pole or Phallus, the,	242
Pole-star, the, named Judé by the first tribe of Juda, from India,	352
Poles—the earth supposed to have been much hotter at the, than it is now,	444, 445
Polycarp, St.,	80, 129
Pol—Pall—φαλλυς=666,	210
Pol—head, wisdom, Minerva Polias,	*ib.*
Pollen, the language of the,	242, 249
Poll-tax, a, once paid by every person who did not occupy land,	379
Polydore Virgil, 61, 64, 74, 79, 86, 93	
Polynesian Islands, the,	39
Pomegranates and bells on the garment of the Jewish high priest and the king of Persia,	69
Pompey claimed to rule by the same right as Cæsar,	345
Pomponius Mela,	314
Pons—the Thracian name for a, was *Brig* or *Briga*, the same as in the North of Britain, &c.,	413
Pontifex—is it a translation of Dom?	393
———, the family of the Julii always aspired to the office of,	374
———, a, with a cabinet of 12, and a council of 72 cardones or cardinales in each country,	381
———— Maximus, the, 52, 53, 56 —58, 76, 92	
———————, the king of the age,	51
———————, the title of, strictly Heathen,	55
———————, a microcosm of the Megalistor, M-wisdom,	298
———————, in the person of, Rome possessed the right to the sovereignty of the world,	395
———————, by auguries being taken, had a negative, a *veto* on all state affairs,	407

INDEX.

Pontifex Maximus, the, the chief bridge builder, 412
Pontiff, if he, and his court, escaped from the flood, 311, 431
——— or Pope, the oriental, has probably resided at Oude, Agra, Benares, Delhi, Mundore, &c., 373, 422
———, if the numeral Chinese were the written language of the, he would easily communicate with distant nations, long after their spoken languages were unintelligible to each other, 443
Pontiffs, the, 34, 52
Pontifical dominion, the, over the whole world, acquired by a knowledge of letters, 257, 258, 275
——— government — Constant, Creutzer, and Schlegel, on the, 350, 37?
———, under the, the priests, by their knowledge of writing, &c., would be masters—the people slaves, 362
———, the, originally *black*, sent out colonies to the West, which mixed with *white* races, till the worshipers of the *black* God became white, 363
———, the first, went to decay (perhaps by the rise of the sect of Cristna)—numerous remains prove its original existence, 370, 371
——— kingdom — antiquarians would succeed better if they went back to the, and to the builders of Stonehenge, &c., 375
——— government—the falling to pieces of, affords an explanation of the struggles of the Patricians and Plebeians of Italy; this, Niebuhr has not attempted, 394
———, a part of the policy of the, to form towns and states into a confederacy, 394, 395
Pontifices Maximi, the, had sovereign authority, 51—53
———, exercised authority as delegates of the THE, 54
Pontine Marsh, the, (25 miles long) —Pliny says there were more than 20 towns in; they were polices, divisions of the Agrimensores, &c., 419
Pontius Pilate, Jesus of Nazareth *not* crucified, under, according to Irenæus, 122, 129
Pontoppidan and Scheffer on the word allodial, 284
Poor man's religion, the, wanted not the adjunct of temples, 409
Pooahtoon, the old name of the Afghans, 239
Poo to Choo, the tree of Knowledge, 148
Pope, the, 52—54, 75, 81, 84
———, and court of Spain kept strangers from America, 22
———, throws money to the people when crowned, 55
———, is adored, 55, 56, 75
———, called himself head fisherman of Galilee, 56
——— (John XIV.), issued a bull for baptizing bells, 70
———, claims to be possessor of all lands, as Vicar of God, 266, 374, 400
Pope, the, secular bishops procured from, by barons and kings, 276
———, placed at the head of Christianity or modern Judaism, by the Jews claiming the high priesthood for Shem, 361
———, became the Archierist, by Constantine's surrender of *the book* to him, 370, 400
———, would not consent that his name should be put, in a list, after that of the king of England, 374
———, superiority over, claimed by the emperor of Germany, and by the Pope over him, 380
———, when the, caused the Mohamedan confession of faith to be placed on the chair of St. Peter, he was probably preparing Rome to become again, one of the *three* holy cities, 385
———, the, (Alexander VI.,) gave all new-found lands to the Spaniards, but refused a grant of the tithes to the Emperor : he reserved to himself the vectigal, 393
———, the, will probably allow that Cæsar held by both the *book* and the *sword*, 400
———, a, at Oude, Agra, Mundore, Samarcand, or some other great capital, 373, 422
Popery, is but reformed Paganism ; Protestantism is but reformed Popery, 443
Popes, the, and the Spaniards, 35
———, like the emperors, wished Latin to be common in all nations, 54
———, allowed those to be killed who were excommunicated, 55
———, claimed supernatural knowledge, 56
———, why some of, called themselves Gods, 136
———, and Monks, contentions between, in the dark ages,—the result, 270, 285
———, brought all the Carmelites or Essenes and their property into the church, 285
———, claimed all islands as the peculiar patrimony of God, 288
———, would an Arabian writer want materials, to blacken, if he went to the writings of Luther or Calvin? 381
Popish mysteries, the, in every respect similar to the ancient Gentile, 442
Population—a prodigious increase of, when the priest, as lord of the soil, took only a *tenth* of the produce ; little temptation then, to rob a traveller, there being no money, &c., 365
———, to relieve the overflow of, colonies sent out by the Patriarchal government, 434
Populifuga or populifagium, 24
Pork, hated by Scotch Highlanders, as by the Jews, 292, 293
Porphyry, 48, 50, 80, 127, 368, 446, 449
Porson, Mr., on q, as Λ in English, 204
Portsmouth, Lord, the works of Newton in the custody of, 333
Portuguese, the, 35, 238
———, conduct of, in India, 216
Portus Cresso, the Crestian Port, 117
Porus—his standard, 118
Posh or Push, the flower, 33, 148
Post-diluvian year, the, 360 days, and the month 30 days, 316—321
Postellus, on what "is to be read in the heavens," 235
Potamon, 448
Potisato, a flower, a name of Buddha, 240
Pot-Jid, Poto, Pot-Tit—Buddha, 9
Potter—on the Piscina, 69
Potyid, a name of Tibet, 9
Pownal [Pownall?] on Antiquities, 25
———, on the ships of the ancients, 311
———, on the charioteers and cavalry of the Britons as manœuvred in the manner practised by the Greeks, &c., 416
———, on tithes, &c., 417
Poyræus, P. Franc., 108
Pra or Bra means *factor*, creator, 243, 267
Prayers for the dead, 72—74, 76, 84
———, imitated from the Pagans, 92
———, long, forbidden by Jesus Christ, 87
Præmonstrants, the, 47
Prænestine Pavement, the, 204
Præsul, the president of the college of the Salii, 179, 233
Præsules et archpræsules, 71
Precession of the Equinox, the—the ancients could not have made it neither more nor less than about 71½ (years) in a degree, 330
———, calculating the, at 72 years for a degree, allows room for disturbance, &c., 335
———, the, fixed by Ptolemy and the Indians at 36 seconds a year, 353
———, the, at the rate of 2160 years for a sign, 431, 432
Prestre John or Joan Joan—Caracorum, in A. D. 425, was the empire of, 411
Priapus or the Linga, 7
———, from Pra or Bra Apis, 414
Priapuses of different forms, emblems of the generative power, at the boundaries of districts, in Britain, ib.
Prician on Mia, for *one*, 196
Prideaux's Life of Mahomet, 89
Prideaux, on the Targums, 172
Priest, the, when he cannot darken —burns, forges, lies, 255
———, the, and king, in early times, the same, 266, 269, 303
Pri-est or φρη-est, *the real priest*, 267
Priest and King — a struggle between, apparent in the Jewish history; Saul and David said to be given as a punishment, 364
Priests, the, of the Great Mother, called Semiviri, 77
———, of Eleusis, kept the commands of Triptolemus, ib.
———, for 1500 years, were employed in garbling, forging, and suppressing evidence, 106, 107

VOL. II. 4 B

	Page
Priests, tho, of the Sun—*ηγης-ονλ*, whence *priest?*	233
———, in Asia, &c., have grown into kings,	263
———, the first governors—kings their generals,	264, 271, 272
———, our ancient customs bear marks of the rule of,	302
———, sacrifices, &c., from the beginning, in Germany, Gaul, Peru, Mexico, Siam, China, Japan, and Egypt,	309
———, of Egypt—their great secret was a knowledge of a future state: why they concealed it from the people,	386, 387
———, by degrees, got possession of the Agri-Decumani, till they acquired more land than they could occupy, and sub-letted it, in sdccage; they formed at length an aristocracy,	417
Priestley, Dr.,	55, 78, 84, 111
Priestly nation, the Jews were a, —hence all were circumcised,	310
Primates, archbishops, and bishops,	53
Primeval and sacred language, a, lost,	147, 122, 223, 274
Primogenitus,	9
Prince Bishops or Palatines, the,	277, 301
——— Palatines of Germany—like the, the priests gradually lost their sacerdotal character,	417
Principles, the two, quarrels between the followers of,	269
Priscus, king, made the *Virgo Paritura* heiress to his crown and kingdom,	108, 109
———, built a temple to the,	259
Pritchard (Dr.), on sibilants letters interchanged with dentals,	200
Privileged and learned order, a, receiving its *tenths*, would constitute a beneficial government,	306
Processions, Catholic, imitations of the Pagan,	79
Proclus,	189
Procopius, on the pillars set up by the Canaanites, when fleeing from Joshua,	397
"Procul! hinc procul este, profani,"	430
Prometheus,	32
——— *vinctus*, crucified on a rock,	113, 136
———, crucified, as *divine love*, 116, and crucifix of,	117
Prophecy, the subject of,	227
———, a, tends to its fulfilment,	374
Proserpine and Ceres, sacrifices offered to, in an island near Britain,	262
Proseuchas and Synagogues, the, of Palestine,	275
Protestant Church, the,	54
——— ——— of England,	82
——— Religion, the, a part of the Pagan or Gentile,	93
——— missions more effective than Papist, in suppressing evidence of the truths of ancient history,	362
Protestants, the, 3, 43, 54, 72, 75,	84, 241
———, their dislike to monastic institutions,	46
———, their hatred of the Jews,	59
———, purgatory offensive to,	73

	Page
Protestants and Papists nearly alike,	93
———, the distinction between, will insensibly diminish in the West, as between Buddhists and Brahmins in the East,	369
———, the, abuse the Pope for his arrogance in *giving away* countries; but they have not an idea of *the nature of his claim*,	393
———, if the, choose to argue the question of Transubstantiation on the ground of common sense, they beat the Papists; but they must admit all other tenets of their religion to be argued on the same ground,	443
Proteus, the, of the Greeks, Joseph,	178
———, the Pandæan system, a perfect,	257
Proto-flamen, the,	53
Psalms, the, art of acrostic writing in,	185
Ptolemy—publication of the Jewish Scriptures, under,	134, 172
———, (the geographer,) the Mons Æsar of,	230
Sailoe—*Selen-dive*,	289
———, on Portus Solis,	290
Ptolemaic system—the professors of, like our astronomers, teaching that it was demonstrated, &c.,	330
פתר *ptr*, to *interpret* dreams,	181
פתר *ptur*, *interpretation*, *paters*, *the shining leaves* of the Sibyl,	*ib.*
Pukto or Pushto, the language of the Afghans,	238, 239
Puranas, the 18—are cosmogonies,	351
Purgatory,	72, 73
———, introduced into Italy by Æneas,	74
Purim, the feast of,	17
Push or pollen, a flower—monthly secretion,	244, 245
Pushto, the,	1, 5, 7, 221, 294, 421
———, the language of flowers,	148, 149, 238—240
———, or Estrangelo language, the,	150, 153, 159, 175
———, or Syriac and Chaldee,	205, 235, 236, 238, 259, 295
Pusto —656—Pustp—666—Petalon =650,	239
Put, the Apollo of the Chaldeans,	287
Pyramid—identity of the length of the base of, with the temples at Jerusalem, Ephesus, Athens, and Rome,	406
Pyramidic feet, 180,000,000 of, equal to the circumference of the earth,	404
Pyramids, the,	147, 198, 315
———, may have escaped, when every other building was tumbled down by the flood,	312
Pyrrha,	18
Pythagoras, 47, 63, 77, 133, 202,	246, 449
——— a Carmelite, 44, 45, 49,	58
———'s morality contained the doctrines of Christianity, 46,	253
———, a follower of Apollo,	103
———, the history of, said to have been copied from the life of Jesus Christ,	127

	Page
Pythagoras, probably the man crucified, of Minutius,	127
———'s doctrine of numbers, 138, 174, 179, 195, 222, 223,	431
———, on music,	149
——— left no writing behind him,	219
———, the alphabet of,	220
———, fond of music,	233
———, on beans forbidden by, to be eaten,	239, 240, 300
———, if he knew, he did not make letters known,	248
———, became a neophyte and was circumcised,	*ib.*
———, was thought to be a Χρης,	251
———, is said to have lost his life for teaching that a virtuous life would secure eternal happiness,	253
———, the *secret* doctrine taught by,	308
———, said to have learned the *atomic* doctrine from Moses; their doctrines appear nearly identical,	398
Pythagorean philosophy, the, of the generation of numbers, of cycles, ending or beginning with the Το Ον or One,	437
——— Essenes, John (the Baptist) and Jesus Christ, monks of the order of,	449
Pythagoreans, the, 47—49, 61, 62,	72
———, the bean of the *water lily* of,	239, 240
———, held a comet to be one of the planets,	314
———, and the Jesuits acted like the Assassins, to attain their end,	386
——— and Platonists, held the doctrine of the microcosm—probably a part of their secret system,	407
Pythagorists, the,	48
Python killed Apollo,	102
———, the, or Holy Ghost, impregnation by,	350

	Page
Quakers, the,	84
——— or Buddhists, a nation of, can exist only on the sufferance of their neighbours,	203
Queezalcoatle, the Mexican Saviour; his temptation, &c.,	24
——— disappeared at the end of 52 years,	26
———, his marred countenance,	31
———, nailed to a cross; crucified in the heavens,	32
Queen of heaven, the,	33, 61, 82
——— and king, *Khen* was both,	181, 222
Questions, often decided not from *knowledge*, but from *ignorance*,	254
Quetzalcoatle, the Mexican God of Air,	27
———, the inventor of *round temples*,	33
Quipos, the, of the Peruvians,	218
Quirinales, the, of Numa,	76
Quirini, the,	*ib.*
קרם *qrm*, feast, communion,	62

INDEX.

	Page
Raadst—a council,	277
Raamaa = 144,	241
Rabbits, Seven, the Mexican year of,	25
Rabbi Meir,	72
—— Simeon,	ib.
—— Solomon,	79
Rabenu Hacadoth,	346
Racemus,	253, 254
Radha, the wife of Cristna,	245
Radhas (Cristna) the Sun, was Radius,	ib.
Radt—a provincial ruler,	277
Raffles, Sir S.	161, 214, 218—222
Raj, the, an emanation of the Solar power, a ray, wisdom,	244
Rajahpoutana,	6
Rajahpoutans, the,	25
Rajas, not *blood*, but the fructifying medium,	244
Rajast'han, the country of the Sacæ or Buddhas,	258, 272
Raleigh,	254
Ram, the, worshiped before the time of Moses,	105
——, personified and called the Lamb of God,	106—108
——, his worship followed that of the *Bull*, and preceded that of *The Fishes*,	110
——, substituted for Isaac, by Abraham,	ib.
—— or lamb,	137, 138
—— Lamb, the coming of, to take away sin,	241
——, *rem excelsum*—ram, caput, vertex capitis,	ib.
——, the brother of Cristna—Ram and Ras the same?	ib.
—— and Rama meant both Beeve and Sheep,	242
Rama and Cristna the same,	137, 138
——, the cousin of Cristna,	241
Rammohun Roy, the Rajah, on *Age* (Sanscrit) *to go*, hence Agni or Ysgul,	157,
——, died (Sept. 27, 1833),	241
——, on title of Akbar II., king of Delhi,	358
Ramsay, the Chevalier, (in his Cyrus,) on trades, &c., being hereditary in Ireland,	421
Ramenses à Romulo, &c.,	345
Ramusat, M. Abel, on Hieroglyphics,	214
Ranking, on Gengis Khan's miraculous birth, &c.,	353
Rapin,	162, 257, 272, 284, 285, 299—301, 401
Ras, the,	3, 6, 224
——, (in Ethiopia) Sar, (in Egypt) prince,	211, 435
——, in the plural *Rasu*, allusive to the Trinity,	211
ראש *ras*, the origin of reix, resch, roy, roy,	345
Ras means *head* and *wisdom*, and שפטים ספים both *wisdom* and *a serpent*,	349, 435
—— or Sar, car or cor, cor or roe, would be pronounced, as read from *right* to *left*, or the reverse,	435, 436
Rasaksa, (Ras-Saka?) a race in Java,	221
Raschidoddin, the writings of, preserved in Syria, by a remnant of the Ishmaelites,	389
Ras-ena (Etruria), country of the Vine or Wisdom,	231
Rasit, meaning of, suppressed by lexicographers,	ib.
Rastores, Rattorei, Ratz-ores, the ancient Sacæ,	211
Ratis-bon—Ratz-burg,	ib.
'Raξ, the grape-stone,	9, 224
Rawasit (Rasis), wisdom—the Ficus Indicus so called,	253
Rayme,	31
Razacm or Razanui, children of Ras or Wisdom,	3
Reach or Resht, the capital of Ghilan,	231
Reader, the, requested not to decide till the whole book is read,	254, 255
Reading, writing, &c., the arts of, long in the hands of a ruling order—the priests of Uria,	206
——, long secret, sacred, astrological,	254, 246—248
——, formed part of the Mysteries of Eleusis and other temples,	271
Real Presence, the,	59, 61
Real Presence in the Eucharist—on this subject Vallemont has the advantage in argument with the Protestants,	442
Red Sea, the,	19
Rees's Cyclopædia,	125
Reeves, Mr.,	60, 66, 69, 89
Regifugia and Populifugia, a, a part of the mythos,	24
Regimine—a proper attention to, will account for many mythological difficulties — why priests had the names of their Gods, &c.,	225, 287
Reginal Calcutta, for Reginal *of* Calcutta,	287
Regulars (the Monks) and Seculars, the,	266
——, after having been divided, they became united,	267
—— and Seculars—the monks or bookmen, and the clergy of the barons, in opposition,	276
Rei,	382
Reich—a region,	276
Reland, on the measure of the Table of Shew-bread,	405
Religion, every, got up more by *fools* than *rogues*,	256
——, when its origin began to be inquired into,	307
——, originally an *esoteric* and an *exoteric*,	386
Religions—no original one found of the vast variety of,	255
——, when stripped of their grosser parts, nearly resolve themselves into one,	338
——, the source of all, placed in Tartary, by Lévêque,	373
——, two distinct, in the Koran—the one contains the germs of *purity* and *illumination*; the other is fraught with maxims of bigotry and intolerance,	378
Religious rites among crafts, in their initiations, lost in Britain, remained till lately in France and Germany,	279
——, the modern, on no point more deceived by the priests, than on the nature of the ancient mysteries,	440
Resoul or *Soul of God*, Mohamed a,	219
Resurrection, the,	21, 25, 33, 38, 42, 90
——, of the body, believed in by the Magi,	100, 101
——, those wisest, who pronounce it a mystery,	101
——, believed in by all nations,	102
——, at the festival of, a miraculous fire said to descend from heaven,	115
——, believed in *literally* by the Nazarenes, Ebionites, and the orthodox—but *spiritually* by the Gnostics, &c.,	119
——, pollen, in its renewal, a beautiful type of,	244
——, of Adonis,	25, 106, 112, 115, 142
——, of Apollo,	145, 148
——, of Atys, 104, 106,	122, 142, 145
——, of Æsculapius,	115
——, of every Avatar,	118
——, of Bacchus, 102, 104, 122, 142,	145
——, of Buddha, 103, 105, 142,	145
——, of Cama,	103
——, of Christ (Jesus), 104, 105,	136
——, of Cristna,	142, 145
——, of the Dove,	114
——, of Horus,	102
——, of Indra,	33
——, of Jesus, the son of Sirach,	124
——, of Mithra, 99, 104,	142
——, of Osiris, 25, 102, 104, 106,	122
——, of Salivahana,	142
——, of Sol,	100, 106
——, of Xaca,	105
Rete-mucosum, the, of the Negro,	363
Reuben, the sign of, Taurus,	105
Réunion des Sabbats, the festival of,	219
Revelation, the, or Apocalypse,	35
Revue Encyclopédique,	172, 173, 442
Rex Sacrificulus, the,	25
Rhapsodists, the, of Greece, like the Bards of Britain, Ireland, Scandinavia, and India — the rhapsodies were poems to celebrate the renewal of Cycles and Avatars,	426
Rhamsialites, history of the Architect of,	17
Rhine, the,	112
Rhyme (from ῥυθμος), Rune,	225
Rhymes—the repetition of, the first attempt to perpetuate facts,	340
Rhythm, metre, music, invented for keeping in memory the sacred numbers, &c.,	233
Rhyn, the, of Wales, the Rhythm or Arithmos of Greece,	153
——, the mysterious language of the Welsh bards,	153, 159, 166
Rice, a monk,	44
Rich or Ras or Wisdom,	236
Richard (King), the sign on his standard,	349
Richardson on the Feudal Tenure in Arabia, and genealogies,	354
Ridings, Radtings—governments,	277
Right, the, of the church, was the

INDEX.

	Page
Lord Paramountship over the soil of the whole world—Always openly or mentally reserved by the priest,	417
Rigordius,	108, 109
Ripon and York, the Culdees of,	279, 281, 287, 288
Rib, or Ram,—240,	241
Robertus likens the world to a tree,	371
Rocher de Guerin, Abbé, 2, 3, 10 —17, 19, 20, 177, 178, 212,	230
Rock, the, on which the church of Christ was to be built, Saca, Buddha or *divine wisdom*,	182
'Poδυ a rose, from job Ray, Radius?	245
Rogare et Donare made into St. Rogatien and St. Donatien,	86
Rom or Ram (Ceylon), the prince of, sent 20,000 families to, and established the Religion of Cristna, in Java,	221
Roma,	62
—— Nova,	138
——, the eternal city,	238, 345
——, the country of, would be Roma-ia,	241
——, the island of, in Lat. 7, 35, Long. 127, 20,	346
Roman Catholic Religion, the,	42, 93
——, nothing new in; is reformed or Protestant Gentilism,	42, 443
——, a renovation of the old Pagan religion,	93
—— Church, the Jesus of the, not a philosopher of Samaria, in the time of Tiberius,	108
—— Papacy—the Archierarchy almost revived under the, in the middle ages,	373
—— Pontiff, the, had the name of Papa,	54, 56
—— State, why the, instead of the Pontifex Maximus and the Priests, possessed the tithes,	374
——, the, essentially agricultural; originally it had neither trade nor navy; who were admitted to citizenship in,	392
—— Historians, the, differ about obsolete matters—the principle of the sacerdotal, feudal system being then lost,	393, 432
—— State, disputes in the, respecting the division of lands,	418
—— Year, the ancient, 360 days long,	320
Romans, the, and the ancient, 17, 27, 53, 64, 67, 74, 138, 139,	337
——, ancient and modern, their use of images,	80
——, ancient, had Jupiter Tonans, Sponsor, &c.; the moderu, have St. Pietro in Vaticano, —in Vinculo, &c.,	91
——, took nothing (in religion) from the Druids, but persecuted them,	99
——, began the feast of Brumalia on the 25th of Dec. in honour of the God of Day,	100
—— and the Greeks, had few infant Gods,	ib.
——, carried the sign of a crucified man on their standards,	116, 118

	Page
Romans, the, and the Greeks, the equinoxes of,	133
——, their error of 9 days, on the precession,	134
——, less skilled in astronomy than the Saxons,	135
——, had two wrong computations of time,	141
—— used literary characters as numerals, as late as Julius Cæsar's time,	147
——, did they govern Britain by their own laws?	273
——, used the Druidical temples,	278, 280
——, why their enmity to the Druids, as they themselves offered human sacrifices,	281, 416
——, destroyed Isurium or Aldborough,	298
——, left Britain,	296, 299
——, depended upon armour, discipline, and Russian tactic—gold; the Britons on valour,	304
——, believed their city was to be the seat of universal empire, and to be eternal,	345
——, an old ambition of,	348
——, had a *Lex non scripta* as we have,	375
——, when in distress, sent their sacred things, and their riches, to Cære,	395
——, and the Britons bore about the same relation as the Spaniards and Mexicans,	415
——, probably made some new roads in Britain,	416
——, among some families possessed hereditary offices — particularly the priests,	421
Rome, 22, 43, 44, 51, 57, 60, 74, 82, 90, 91, 118, 137—139, 143, 313, 399,	400
——, the early kings of, both kings and priests,	53
——, the sages of, held the doctrine of purgatory,	72, 73
——, no beggars allowed in, but the Mendicants,	76, 92
——, churches in, covered with votive offerings,	87
——, pillars in front of the churches in,	92, 251, 402
—— and Tibet, secret conclaves of,	117
——, similarity of mythos in,	119, 127
——, the Eternal City, 145, 146,	238, 440
——, a Julian Kalendar dug up at, in the sixth century,	147
——, all the names of, *female*—Roma, Flora, Valentia—nearly its first goddess was Vesta—had the name of *the beast*,	241
——, the king does homage to the priest, in,	302
——, in the domain of Japhet,	350
—— and Petersburgh, modern Christianity as exhibited at, if stripped of modern corruptions, nothing but a continuance of the ancient religion of Rome,	367
——, probably saved after the Gallic capture, by being considered the the Capitolium or religious head of the Italian, if not of the European Pontificate,	395

	Page
Rome, the obelisks before the churches in, mostly the sacred ones brought from Egypt; that before the church of Maria Maggiore, like that at Jerusalem,	402
——, all the doctrines of modern, the same as the open or secret doctrines of ancient Rome — hence not surprising that the Popes re-enact rites, &c.,	443
Romelia of Thrace,	138
Romish Christ, the, the son of Maia or Maria,	44
——, an incarnation of Divine Wisdom,	65
—— Christians, doctrines of the, similar to those of the Tibetians, 37,	75
—— Christianity (not the Gospel of Jesus),	117, 300
——, has the Heathen or Gnostic cross-borne of Egypt,	118
—— Church, the, 43, 44, 46, 72,	104
——, seven Sacraments of,	58—75, 282
——, its doctrine of the *real presence* more consistent than the Protestant doctrine of the Eucharist,	59, 61, 442
——, Marriage,	71
——, Extreme Unction, Penance, and Purgatory,	72
——, revenues of the priests of, the same as those of Pagan sacrificers,	76
——, origin of the feasts of,	77, 86
——, has processions for rain, &c., like the Pagans,	80
——, has every rite, &c., of Paganism, 139, 145, 276,	441
——, scenic representations of, of the acts of Jesus Christ,	136, 233
—— bishops, the, use X before their signature,	193
—— church, in the, an Archbishop must have the pallium from the *Vicar of God*,	231
—— Essenean monks admitted into the,	368
—— fathers, the, affected to make mysteries of Baptism, the Eucharist, &c.,	441—443
—— Jesus, the Evangelion of, the same as Zoroaster's and Mani's,	65
——, the worship of, and of the celestial lamb, identical,	112
——, the gospel of,	142
——, mythos, of the crucifixion of Christ, a close copy from Paganism,	112
—— religion, a part of, celebrated in the temple of Juggernaut,	206, 207
Romulus,	53, 76, 86
——, the tomb of, became the church of St. Theodorus,	74, 94
—— and Remus, temple of, now Church of Cosmo and Damien,	91
——, in the reign of, some months were 20, some 35 days long,	320
——, his history used by the priests, to shew that the Romans were a favoured nation,	341
Room, Phrygia so called by the Orientals,	241

INDEX.

	Page
Room and Mysia—Asia Minor was both,	412
Roomiz, a, Iskander or Alexander, so called,	346
Ros, in the unspoken language of numeral symbols, might be sor,	153
Rosary, the, from Ras, wisdom,	179
Roschild, the capital of Denmark so called,	231
Rosci, the, on the river Cyrus, Ros, Ras or Aras,	ib.
Rose, Ras, wisdom—the crucified,	240, 243, 245
—— on a cross, &c.,	240, 243
—— of Sharon, of lau-ren or Ishuren, Jesus the,	6, 33, 44, 239, 240, 245
Rosen, Dr., on obsolete Sanscrit words,	157, 158
——'s, Dr., Translation of Parts of the First Veda,	340
——, on the first Sanscrit lexicon,	428
Roses, the Age of,	32
Rossi, De, on the Septuagint,	16, 172
Rossi-crucians, or Templars, the,	6, 248
——, adoration of the Rose and Cross, by,	240, 244
——, their monogram surrounded with a glory, and placed on a Calvary,	243
——, the, Freemasons, &c., the confraternities of, Christians before the rise of Romish Christianity,	300
——, of Germany, suppose themselves descendants of the Egyptians, Chaldæans, &c.,	301
——, modern Templars, and Masons, are little more than different lodges of one order,	388
Roumaen—Rome, with a Tamul termination =666,	241, 242
Rousseau, M., an extract from, on the Ishmaelites,	389
Rowland, on Hebrew sounds in Welsh,	154
Royal Concubines, the 360, of the Persian kings,	317
—— Shepherds, Saxons,	25
——, the, of Egypt,	305
RST (רשית) the I or Jod inserted for mystery,	6
—— or TPZ the 600, and Om=600,	303
PZT, each of these letters had two meanings,	189, 199, 299, 343
—— Rasit, a corruption of ; hence Cæsar, Tzar, and Χρις,	344
RSUT=666—wisdom,	201
——plural of Ras, allusive to the Trinity,	211
PZH ros=360—HPS cross, or crs with the letter e Rose, =365,	243
Rudbeckius, Olaus,	163
Ruish, air., on genus and species of man,	363
Rukia (the Persians so call Olympias), is this the Hebrew regio—firmament?	346, 347
Ruma Mamma, Rome,	145
——, Roma,	241
Rune (Anglo-Saxon) is Runeh, Phœnician or Arabic,	163
Runes, the, of Scandinavia,	148, 163
——, acrostic writing in,	185

VOL. II.

	Page
Runes, of Scandinavia and Ireland, the, are figure letters,	206
——, their division into fives,	215
——, of Scandinavia, known to, and used by, the Tartars before the Christian æra,—brought with the Sacæ,—written from top to bottom, &c., &c.,	305
——, the letters were right lines,—used by the Masonic Culdees of York,	436
Runic alphabet, the,	149
—— letters or numbers were right lines,	166
Russia,	215, 304
——, History of, by Lévêque,	373
——, nearly all the land in, held by the Nobles, and cultivated by the serfs, on their account,	394
Russians, the, called Go lo see in Chinese,	149
——, their great strides since the time of Peter,	304
Rustan (Persian) rstn=650,	211
Rusticus, St.,	85
Rymer,	384
Ryots, the, cultivators or grantees of India,	266, 362, 373, 374
—— feudatories or farmers, holding their lands, in Italy, as in India, by payment of part of the produce, &c.,	391

	Page
Σ changed into P by the Æolians,	199
—— T by the Dorians and Æolians,	199, 438
—— perhaps both Σ and T, and hence called Sigma-Tau,	200, 201, 211
Sa is ζω or שיע or Saviour, or the 600,	195
Saba or Zaba (wisdom), whence Sabæans,	219, 220
Sab-aith—the preachment of the sages or of the wise,	297
Sabat, an assembly—Sabbatines—lectures,	ib.
Sabazius or Sabaoth, birth-place of Bacchus,	102
Sabbats, réunion des, festival of,	219
Sabbath, the day sacred to the God of Wisdom,	219, 220
Sabbathier,	172, 418
Saca, [the God of Wisdom] 1, 2, 9, 10, 31, 32, 275, 428
Sa-ca-akim,	2
——, Saca-ca, Sacya, Buddha, 1, 3, 6, 27, 148, 229, 428
Sacæ, the, or Saxons,	1, 4, 165, 203, 207, 228, 250, 275
——, the German and Scandinavian Saxons from,	209
——, the ancient, the Rattores,	211
——, Saxons, Scythians, conquerors of Egypt,	221
——, the Scandinavian, and the Arabians, from the N. of India,	225
—— or Saxons, the, brought the feudal system from Asia into Europe,	262, 372
—— and loudi, the tribes of, the same,	263
—— or Saxons, the, conquered by Alexander,	272

4 c

	Page
Sacæ, the, were the builders of Stonehenge,	273
——, were also called Sagæ,	274
——, occupied almost all Europe,	278
——, or Celtæ, Chaldees or Cullidei, the first tribes of, were Druids, like the Christians of Malabar,	281
——, traces of the oriental system of the, in Scandinavia,	300, 305
——, the, or Scythians—the wisdom and moderation of, i. e. of the followers of Japhet,	372
——, Saxons or Buddhists, called Atheists by the followers of Cristna, &c.,	428
——, the Chaldæan-Celtic, their conduct in new countries,	435
Sacala,	9
Sacas or Sagas—Sacas-ana, country of Sacas,	4
Sacerdotal caste, a, ruled the world,	1
—— empire, an ancient universal,	262
—— or Patriarchal government, a supreme, overrode the whole, but left each state to regulate its domestic concerns, &c.,	433, 434
——, a remnant of, in the pale of Ireland, and in the pfahlbürger of Germany,	434
Saceswara, Mohamed a,	2
Sachem,	25
Sachia, Sechia,	3
Sacraments, the three,—the religion of Abraham, of Iona, of Buddha,	283
Sacred—secret,	199
—— Soc or Sac-rid—to be rid, quit of rule, &c.?	264
Sacred majesty — the χειροτενια gives the title of,	263
—— order, the, which ruled the world, possessed all science,	342
—— Numbers—the microcosm found in what the ancients call the, &c.,	397
—— poems, retained by memory, would answer during peace; but, when wars arose, they would not avail for history,	424
Sacrifice—none but the king could make a, for the nation, at Rome,	375
Sacrifices for the dead, co-eval with Christianity,	74
——, all, were originally feasts,	233
Sacristan, Saxtan, Sexton,	71
Sacti, Sakti,	6
Sadducees, the,	101
Sadduceeism, the, of Manes,	ib.
Sagâ,	25, 34
—— and Saca, clearly mean Wisdom,	336
Sagan, Cohenia and Oggizan,	2, 3
—— Oggizan—Noah so called,	3
Sagart, no sacrifice without a,	2, 25, 264
Sagas or Sacas,	4, 34
Sagax, Sagexe,	3, 231, 232
Sages for Tages,	231, 232
Sagio,	2
Sagiot,	230
Sahagun,	23
Sai, learning,	227
Saints, the adoration of,	81

INDEX.

Saints, the canonization of, is the apotheosis of the Pagans, 81
St. Columba and St. Ions, said, by Catholic historians, to have been bishops of the Isle of, 286
Sais, Sausfo—*safe*, 230
Saka, Sakea, or Sakia, festival of, 60
———, an era, a name of Buddha, 221
Saladin, probably from Sul-ad-in, or Sul—360 and ad, 230
Sale's Koran, 352
Salem, 45, 58
Salic laws, the, their number and where enacted, 299
Salice—Ceyloo—the name preserved in *Salen-dive*, &c., 289
Sali-ghat, the ghost of Sall or Sull, of Bath, 299
Salii, the, were Salli or priests of Sul, 179
———, an order to regulate the sacred dances, 233
Salivahana, 9, 133, 221
———, cross-borne or Stauro-bates, 115, 116
———, the, of India, though well known, yet the Cristna of, prevails, 368
Salivahanas, 116
———, incarnations of, 129
———, &c., the, put to death, &c., 142
Salman-asar, Salmon-Æsar, Cæsar Solomon, 180
Salmon's Modern History, 22
Saloghast, Wiseghast, Bonoghast, and Undoghast, meant the Holy Ghost, 299
Salome, Mr., on the Malays speaking Hebrew, 156
Salvation, voyage and voyages of, or Deisul and Deisuls, 20, 21, 64, 233, 276, 422
——— wrought, by Mithra's resurrection, 99
Salverte, de, Eusèbe, 3
Sall (in old Irish) לַּל—360, means a year, 178
Sallust—Satis *eloquentiæ*, *sapientiæ parum*, 132
Salusbury—Sara or Syr-ia—*place of the Sun*, 299
Sam, a name of the sun, 137
———, of Mercury, darkness, and Buddha, 438
Samach, the final form of the *tenth* letter, M, 196
———, = 60, *Sam* (the Sun) and *aum*, 197
——— and mem final = 600, 241
———, imposition of hands, investiture, the, 252, 278, 359
———, Aaron received the, from Moses, 302
Saman, 31, 138
Samaneans, the, or Gymnosophists, 43–45, 50, 368
———, probably Essenes or Monks, and Chaldæans, 368, 370
Samaria, 36
———, capitol of the tribe of Juda or Ayoudla, 207
———, the Jesus of the Roman church, not a philosopher of, 108
———, the teacher of, made to be God *himself*, 368
Samaritan History or Pentateuch, the, 16
——— Nazarite, the, 43

Samaritan and Hebrew chronology, the difference of, 133, 134, 327, 329
——— Hebrew, purity of the, 156
——— Philosopher, Nazarite, Buddhist, Pythagorean, Essenean, the—the doctrine taught by, was all peace and brotherly love, 409
Samaritans, the, 5, 66, 133
———, correct times of the precession, taken by, 134
———, attached to the worship of the *dove*, 228, 229
———, Sama-ritane, worshipers of, Sama or Cama?—place Ararat in Serendive, 229
———, bitter enemies of the system of David and Solomon, 232
———, make the flood to have happened in the fifth revolution of the comet (of 1680), or 2926, B. C., 328
Samarkand, 206, 274, 444
Samhan, 82, 83, 287
Samhna, 82
Samnaut, 137
סמך = 666, and Neith *wisdom*—the Solar wisdom, 201
Samothrace, 55
———cian Gods, the three Great, 344, 345
Samson—Cristna, Isaac, 8
———, his likeness to Hercules, 21
———, the history of, 305
Samuel (the prophet), 45
Sanhedrim, the, called by Napoleon—reason for, 358
———, the Jewish, 380, 381
———, a, in each of the 72 divisions of the world, 422
Sangus, the statue of, 89
Sanpi, the Greek, not a letter, 224
San-script—*writing of the sun* or *holy writing*, 290
Sanscrit, the, 156–159
———, of South India, derived from the Tamil, 148, 156
———, held by the Brahmins to be absolutely perfect, 157
———, Hindoo, Latin, and Greek, names of numbers, 166, 167
———, comparatively modern and artificial, 184
———, called *Fen* by the Chinese, 217
———, on words in, identical with Persian, Greek, and Germain, 234
———, words, on, from the Hebrew, 245
———, called Sanscort or Sanskrontan, in Celtic, 290, 412
———, like *Greek* scholars, fail in their explanations, why, 290, 429
———, formed by the Brahmin or Cristna sect, for secrecy, but it also is become public, 294
———, the, was comparatively rude when the first Veda was written, 295
———, of India, end of Scotland, 412
Saphenath Pahaneah [Zaphnath-paaneah] Joseph, in the Egyptian, *Salvator Mundi*, 177, 178
Saques, les, ou les Scythes—their conquest of Asia, and mild treatment of, &c., 372
Saraceni, the, Arabians, 225
Saracens, the, have they, like the Turks, the Crescent? 291
——— and Turks, a strug-

gle between, as to the right of excommunication, 352
Saraceni, the, conquering and magnificent, puffed up with vanity and pride, 378
Sarah, 14, 16
——— called Ischas or Ischa, 60, 230, 346
———, the wife of the Brahmin, (Abraham), 81
Sarai, means *the* queen, 14
Sara-iswati, the, *Des Scientiarum*, 8
Sarcophagus, the, in the Pyramid of Giza—its length, &c., 403, 406
Sardanapalus—traditions of three princes of that name, 360
Sari—the reigns of ancient kings counted by, 321, 322
Sarkel—*kel* or *cil* church, and *ras* wisdom? 229
Saronide, the, is Ras, &c., 297
Saros, a, 3600 years, or rather days, &c., 322
Sasax, Saxax, 31
Saseuach, Sacon, Sessen, Saxenach, 2
Sassan, father of Artaxerxes, 349
Satiernia—country of the cycle of 666, 241
Satrapes, in the 360, and in the 72 Solumi of Persia, &c., we may see traces of the microcosm, 420
SATURDAY, Heb. *Str* = 666 — Gr. *Str* = 608 — *Str* = 690 — Sarn = 650, 209
Saturn, 8, 212
———ia or Saturnia, 62, 127
———, Satiern, in Greek numerals = 666, 209
———, called Sani, Sani, Satyr, in India, 299, 210
———, the kingdom of, divided into three parts—Asia, Africa, and Europe, 399
——— , to Jupiter (Ham), Pluto (Shem), and Neptune (Japhet), 400
Saturnalia, the feasts of Italy, were festivals of Saca, 268
Saturnia, the kingdom of, 375
Saul (king), 105
——— or Talut, so called in India, 134
———, as king, given as a punishment, 364
Savinian and Potentian, the Saints, in Gaul, 229
Saviour, the, 19, 24, 61
———, the acts of, sensically represented, 29, 136, 233
———, crucified, black, 32, 36, 37, 116
———, Aries was called, 103
———, a *spiritual*, instead of a temporal, actually crucified, taught by Paul, 341
———, in every country which had any pretensions to have a, there was a Mount Meru, Olympus, or Acropolis, &c., 8.
———, of the whole world, invited all people to a participation in his favours, &c., 409
——— (or Messiah), Cyrus, a, 233
Saviours, 21
Saxa, Saca, Xaca, Xim, Xis, Xin-di—Sinenses, the, 215
Saxon, the, is Celtic and Hebrew, 155, 260
——— kings, the, claimed to have all lands in demesne, 268
——— institutions, the history of

	Page		Page		Page
the, little understood by Hume, &c.,	416, 417	Scotland,	4, 156, 286	Selden,	65, 259, 268, 273, 289
Saxons, the,	1, 2, 4, 9, 32, 209, 231, 228, 250, 262, 272	———, (highland) the language of, called Sanscrit,	158, 294	Seldjouhide—Sultan Melekshâh,	382
———, Royal,	25	———, the carns of,	179	Selene, like Yoni or Iune and Iona, means the *female generative principle*,	289
———, the *barbarian*, better skilled in astronomy than Greeks or Romans, in the time of Cæsar,	135	———, the fire towers of,	260, 296	Selim III., said to have taken the Calif to Constantinople, and to have ruled under his authority,	352
		———, the laws of,	272, 273		
		———, the sacred islands of,	287		
———, ancient, the emphatic article of the, was I,	199	———, and India, identity of race and language in,	289	———, the conquest of Egypt by,	385
———, and Franci or Franks, the same,	267	———, was called Alba,	291	Selimé i. e. Solomon, the desert of,	230
		———, the *first written syllabic language* found in,	294	Selinginskoi—many sepulchres, &c., found near the neighbourhood of—supposed to be remains of a people *previous to the flood*,	444
———, and Scythians, the same,	268	Scott, Sir Walter—if such a man as he was, would study this work, with a view to correct its errors and supply its deficiencies, he would be qualified to write a general history of the world,	359		
———, first heard of in the West, about 150 B. C.,	271			Sema, of Hierapolis,	228
———, said to be not Christians,	281			Semedo, Alvarez,	227, 228
——— or Sacæ, the latter tribes of, in Britain — their religion nearly that of the Culldei of Iona, of York and Ripon,	ib.	Scribes, the, perhaps alone understood the art of writing,	169	Semiramis, and the Sema-Rama of India, closely connected with the dove,	228
		Scriptures, the,	10, 17, 18	Semler,	43
———, of Denmark, had *three* cups, to Odin, Niord, and Freya,	300	———, of the Therapeutæ or Essenes, the ground-work of the Gospel histories,	45, 46	Senators, the, of Rome, why called *Patres Conscripti*; they were like our English Peers; the foreigners like our Scotch and Irish Peers; these would vote as Knights,	392
———, with the return of the, to Britain, the Scandinavian customs, &c., revived,	304, 416	Scythès, âls d'une Vierge,	97		
		Scythes ou Tartares,	ib.		
		Scythia, Eastern,	136	Seneca's *Hercules Furens*,	408
———, the later, when they came to Britain, probably. found the remains of their ancestors, who had, 500 or 600 years before, built Stonehenge, &c.,	416	———, Asia once a fief depending on,	262	Sephiroth, the *ten* Jewish, were ten symbols or ciphers,	185
		Scythians, the,	2, 97, 203, 221	Sephora, (Sephor,) *city of the book*, more properly *a cipher*,	311
		———, Saxons, and Sacæ, the same,	230	Septuagint, the,	83, 327
Sbo—erudition, sagesse,	219	Sea-Kings, the, made war upon the Highlands,	291, 305	———, the, probably a translation of the sacred books of the *five* temples of Egypt,	16
Scala or Scale,	5, 9				
Scalds, the, a corruption of Chasdim, Chaldæans or Culdees?	305	Sean (Sion), name of Hercules, the Sun or wisdom,	225, 296	———, the present, not that translated for Ptolemy,	172
Scaliger,	64, 97, 135				
———, on the Periodus Magorum,	317	Sean-ach, hence Senate?	264	Seraph, the Saviour of Egypt,	14, 15, 87
Scault, a name of Joseph,	2	———, a high-priest, a Druid,	290		
Scander, the burial-place of Akbar,	358	Sean-achas, a judge of a feudal code,	260	———, thought to be the peculiar God of the Christians,	15
Scandia, Grotius thought the Mexicans from,	278	Sect or division, every great, had its book of wisdom, leaning to its paramount dogma,	445	———, the priests of, at Athens, had the head shaved,	78, 79
Scandinavia,	148, 252	Sects, all, improve as their passion cools,	342	——— and Isis, the priests of, wore the tonsure,	92
———, the Runes of,	165, 166				
———, — the confrères of, all sworn friends,	300	*Secret* doctrine, the, of Jesus—remarks on,	308	Serendive or Serendib, the old name of Ceylon,	288, 290, 292
Scandinavian poetry abounded in acrostics,	189	———, lost in the days of Papias, Irenæus, &c., or not trusted to them; it might have been as imprudent to trust it to them, as to Luther or Calvin,	367	———, Ararat placed in, by the Samaritans,	229, 288
——— Sacæ, the, and Arabians, from the North of India,	225			Serenus, Bishop of Marseilles,	80
Scandinavians, the,	3, 304, 305			Servius Tullius—the whole mythos in the history of the immaculate conception, &c., &c.,—he was the first who had the glory,	393
———, had their Demigods,	300	*Secrets* and *sacreds*—the two words suspected to be of almost primæval antiquity,	396		
Scapula,	199				
Scattald—land which paid *taw*,	234	Secular bishops,	270, 276	Sesostris,	12
Scheffer and Pontoppidan, on the word *allodial*,	ib.	Seculars, all priests were, originally,	266	Seth, &c., icons of, in India,	122
Schehabeddin-Seherwerdi, the famous, sent by the Calif, to the emperor of the Mongols, when about to attack Bagdad,	390	———, and meaks, the orders of,	267	———, princes in the race of,	133
		———, and Regulars, though hating one another, had a common interest against the rest of mankind,	270	Sethenæ,	14
				Settle, our word, from שתל etl,	437
Scheller, Dr.,	2			Seven Rabbits, the Mexican year of,	25
Schlegel, on an ancient priestly government in Greece,	356	———, the,—the clergy of the barons—were always in opposition to the Regulars, the Monks,	276	——— Sacraments, the, of the Romish Church,	58—75
Sciakam,	2, 25			*Seven wise men*, the, of Greece, probably the seven incarnations of Wisdom or the Logos of seven cycles,	127, 226
Sci-akham,	6, 7	——— and Regulars—struggles between, when the Monks, under Augustine, came to Britain,	281		
Sciold, the son of Odin,	231				
Scipio Africanus,	54				
Sciot, Scioi—from Sagiot,	230	———, the, the descendants of the Brahmins,	369	Seventy (or 73) languages, all founded on the Arabic,	235
Sciothi—Skuthai—Scythians, the,	ib.				
Scone, with its sacred stone,	260	*Seed of the woman, the,* "shall bruise," &c.,	249	Seventy thousand Fédawis were at all times ready—from fanaticism or religious principle—to throw themselves from the battlements of the castle of Alamout, to shew their devotion to the Imam, 389, 390	
Soonhalis in Dom Bee, at the village of Skeflow,	283	———, when the, of any animated being is examined, &c.,	398		
Scores and Dozens, our, probably derived from the microcosmic superstition,	385, 433	Seignior, the grand, and (power over) his pashas,	264		
Scotch, the,	220	Seigniory is *seignior-in*—place of the lord,	300	Seventy-two, the number, &c.,	299
———, are admitting organs into churches,	271			———, members of Parliament, for the whole island (of Great Britain)—the microcosm peeps out in that number,	401

INDEX.

Entry	Page
Seventy-two, the nations of the earth divided into,	409, 410, 413
Seventy-two, a senate of, probably in every country; the Jewish Sanhedrim, the Solumi of Persia, &c., &c.,	422
———, angels, the, of the 72 nations, &c.,	433
Severus, Sulpitius,	110
Sextus, V.,	54
Shakspeare, the historical plays of, like the poems of Ossian,	293
———, the "rack of," flying clouds,	347
Shan Mung, Rev. David Collie's translation of the,	376
Sharastani,	101
Sharon, Ishuren or Isuren, the Rose of,	6, 33, 44, 239
———, the Rose of, Jesus,	6, 42, 240, 243
Sharon Turner,	135
Shaving of the head and surplices borrowed from Egyptian priests,	78
Shaw,	82
Shea'e, Mr., Translation of Mirkond,	346, 347, 351
Sheahs, the, accuse the Sonnees of corrupting the Koran,	351
Sheik—said to mean reverend,	301
Shekia—Sakia—a prophet,	227
Shem—his claims to the high-priesthood, &c.,	361
——— owed suit and service to his elder brother, Japhet,	372
———, Ham, and Japhet, the three divisions of, in the families of Ommia, Abbas, and Fatima, ruling in Europe, Asia, and Africa,	384, 385
———, claim for, probably set up by Mohamed, the lines of Ham and Japhet having failed,	386
———, according to the mythos, in consequence of Ham's misconduct, inherited the right to the Pontificate; in his line the avatar saviours, kings, and priests were to be found, and all mankind to be blessed,	398
———, in the division of the world, had 36 parts,	399
Sheriffe, the, of Mecca, the lineal descendant of Shem,	359
———————, the Pasha of Egypt claims to hold his dominions from,	383, 388
Shesach, a Scythian, Tat-ar or Tar-tar,	2
Sheshach (who pillaged Jerusalem), the king of the Sacæ or Saxons, or Shepherds of the Pallestini,	221, 268
Shin and Tau both used for 300 and 400,	200
Ships of the ancients, the, nearly as large and as sea-worthy as ours,	311,
Shire—from the Celtic hir, cir, chur, &c.,	276
Shrovetide,	59
Shuckford,	201
Si, siab, learning, in Chinese,	227
Siakhim,	8
Siam,	31, 32, 45, 163
———, 8 Avatars in,	139
———, Judæan mythos in,	222, 232
Siamese Boys, the,	202, 397
———, the, and the Tibetians, closely connected,	214
Siamese, the, say the French have the same name as themselves, viz. free,	267, 411, 412
Sian or Siam,	31
Siang or Sihang, the, of the Tibetians, is Sio,	224
Sibyl, the, the leaves of,	166
Sibyls, the acrostic of the,	154
———, their account of Ararat not from the Bible,	173
Sicily, Siculia, or Xaca-elo-ia,	9
"Sides, the, of the north," where the Gods sit,	73, 175
Sidon, שידון =364,	183
Sigalion, Dieu de Silence,	18
Σιγη, Σιγηλος, Σιγαλεος,	ib.
Sigma-Tau, S and T substituted for each other,	199, 200, 211, 244
Signs, seals or crests, origin of,	198
Silius, on the rites in the Gaditan temple of Hercules,	78
Silliman, on the flood,	312, 313
Simeon, Jacob's son,	18
———, the Rabbi,	72
Simon Magus,	89
Sin, Sin-di, the holy Sin,	181
———, Saxons or Buddhists, the Chinese are nothing but,	215, 292
———, =360, or Xn =650,	250
———, Singala, sin instead of doct,	288, 292
———, =360 for the Sun—the Lion, as the emblem of, at the summer solstice,	292
Sina, Mount,	31, 288
Sinan—chief of the Assassins.	230
Sincellus, Georgius, the chronography of,	121
Sind, the river—Abba-Sin, father Sin—the Nile once so called, like father Thames,	181
Sinda,	107
Sinde, Sindi, a river of Thrace, and the Indus,	179, 181, 202, 224, 288, 294, 420
Sindi, the, of North India and of Thrace, both followers of the holy Xin,	414
Singal, the language of the Sin, or of Nis or Bacchus,	292
Singala, the, is Gala or Gael Nis, &c.,	294
Singapore,	215
Singhalese, a few of the, are worshipers of the stars,	289
Singing rhymes to perpetuate facts —singing or chaunting praises of the Incarnate wisdom,	340
Sion, i. e. the sun, in Siam, means free,	267
Sioun=336, or Siun=366, or Sin =360, or Xn=650,	250
Sirach, who was the author of the book of?	123
Siriad, letters said to have been on the pillars of the,	256
Sis, the numeral letter, how described,	196
Sixteen-letter system or alphabet,	148, 166, 167, 185, 205, 223
———————— languages, dialects of each other, Sanscrit excepted,	170
————————, the, probably known to the Chinese, 216, (as a secret to the Tartars,)	223
————————the, of the Ioudi or Chaldæans,	218
————————, the, pervaded whole world,	234
Sixteen-letter Hebrew, the, not far different from the original language, i. e. of China,	443
סך sk in Hebrew; means a veil—in Greek σηκος—very like Saca,	337
Skellow, a custom continued at the village of,	283
Skye, the Island of, so called from Saca or Sakya,	287
Slain Lamb, the, of the Apocalypse, connects with the cycle of 144, &c.,	240, 241
סלה sle, Selah,	178
שלה sle, Shilo, Silenus, 178, Saviour,	180
שלי sli=360,	178
Sli, Suli, the Sun,	212
שלים slit, a name of Joseph,	178
שלש sls, =630, salus, health, salvation, Salus-bury,	177
——— three, the Trinity,	ib.
Slu or Sul meant the same, in the unspoken language of numeral symbols,	185
שמים smim, the disposers, rulers, &c.,	177, 212, 432
Smith, Dr. J. P.,	64, 113
Smoking, what occupation or amusement is better than,	305
Soc-manni, the, were the Seculars,	264
————, holders of lands from the priests,	266
Soccage lands, primogeniture in, prevailed in the time of Henry III.,	264
———, Free, from Soc, a plough—or liberty, privilege—or, from Xaca or Saca?	264, 265
———, tenure by, lands changed to tenure by Knighthood,	269, 284
Sochi-quetzal, the mother of Quecalcoatle,	32
———, or Suchi-quecal, is both male and female,	ib.
Socinians, the,	96
Socrates (the scholastic),	77
Socrates,	96
———, his birth announced by a brilliant star, and gold, &c., offered to him by the Magi,	ib.
———, called a Christian by Justin,	130
———, like Pythagoras, &c., left no writing behind him,	219
———, the alphabet of,	220
———, said to have lost his life for teaching that virtue would secure eternal happiness,	253
Sodalitates or companies, &c., the, in Athens, were 12, in what were called 360 houses; here are remains of the microcosm,	419
Sodoreys and Nordoreys, Southerns and Northerns, the Western Islands divided into the,	291
Sofees, the, of Mohamedism,	274
——— or Gnosis, the sect of,	346
Soga-Nozo,	34
Sol, the Lord, execution of—the Saviour,	49
———, his rising to immortality at the Vernal Equinox,	100
———, the God, his mysteries celebrated on the Sunday,	89, 90
———, his birth at the Winter Solstice, 49, or on March 25,	98—100, 106
———, the, worship of,	112

INDEX. 509

Solaimani, the Afghans, dwell on the Mount of Solomon, 239
Solar and Lunar revolutions, the change made in the, happened at the deluge, 326
Soldier, when the, arose, 372
Soldiers hired by the scientific class, to keep order, 365
Soleiman, Sulimon or Suleimon, 179, 180
Soli Deo Mitræ, 116
Soli-lunar period of 600 years, 141
———— cycle of the Neros, 142, 163, 432
————, an exact, 12 moons of 30 days each, &c., 431
Solimans, 13 generations of, 133
Solinus, 3, 314, 325
Solomon, 105, 233, 293
————, his empire not discovered by Herodotus, 11, 124
————, the author of the Iliad, 12
————, uncertain whether he built Palmyra, 147
————, the sacred part of the temple of, built with the Almug-tree —the wood sacred to the Mag-al or ul, or the great God, 203
————, on wisdom—a tree of life, 204
————, the temple of, at Casi in Cashmere, 206, 232
————, the real city of, 231
————, the mythos accommodated, at every temple of, 361
———— said there was nothing new under the sun, 430
Solon, on the firmament, 314
————, on the length of the Tropical year, 318, 319
————, the first who accommodated the month to the moon's motion, 320
————, disputes among the Athenians, before the time of, 418
————, Plato, Critias, and Audocides, were of the noble class of Athenians, ib.
Solumi, temples of, 16, 134
————, probably incarnations of wisdom, 134
————, in the fourteen, we probably have an example of fourteen tribes, like that of Abraham, coming from India, &c., 362
Somaglia, cardinal, 81
Somerville, Mrs., on Enke's comet, 330
Sommona-cadam, or Sommona-kodam, of Siam, 3
Sommona-chutana, of Pegu, ib.
Somner's Antiq. of Canterbury, 400
Son of God, the, 33, 72
Son of Man—Son of the Solar Incarnation, Mn, 187
Son of the Sun, a title of the emperor of China, the Mogul, and the king of Siam, has a basis, 292, 353
————, Genghis Khan and Tamerlane were said each to be the, 353
Soæmis [Sommias?], the mother of Heliogabalus, 348
Sophee, every, would be a well-wisher to the Assassins, though he might not be an Assassin, 383
Sophees, the, 50
————, of Persia, probably Masons, 301
————, gradations among, of the Initiated, &c., 355

VOL. II.

Sopheism, the, of India and Mohamed, originally the same, 352
———— the secret doctrine of, probably what the Assassins taught in secret after the overthrow of their order, 390, 391
————, of Mohamed, and the name of his temple, Caaba or Caavah, like the Mercavah of the Jews, &c., 398
Sophocles, 62
Sopi = 360, Sophin, Sophees, 201
Sor, in the unspoken language of numeral symbols, might be ras, 153, 435
Sorbonne, the, 97
Sosigenes, the CHALDÆAN, corrected the Calendar for Julius Cæsar, 27, 139, 144, 314, 330, 335, 353
———— persuaded Julius Cæsar to correct the Calendar, to prove that he was the great one to come, 345
Soul—what is it? Has man a soul? 338
Souph, wisdom, wool, golden fleece, 253
Souphuu—σοφια, 211
South America, 22, 35, 238
———— exhibits something like the state of Italy and Greece, after the Pontifical kingdom went to pieces, 375
South Americans, the, ignorant of letters and iron, 33, 40, 41, 206
Southcote, Johanna, 98, 346, 358
————, the followers of, expect a re-incarnation of Jesus Christ, the tenth Avatar, 258, 354
———— has had respectable followers, 355
———— had not the aid of a general belief in the promised one, &c., 356
————, her followers weak men, 377
South India, 10, 19, 24, 36, 40, 171—173, 206, 228, 229, 238, 396
————, mythos of Mexico in, 29
————, Chaldee language of, 128, 289
————, the Sanscrit of, derived from Tamil, 148, 294
————, the lowest class in, called Aborigines, 274
————, the oldest division of, was into three Tamul principalities —exhibiting signs of the mythos, 420
Souweldani and Khisréwi, the, probably were Soufdani or Sophees, and Kaïsar-ians or Cæsareans, 391
Spain, 117
————, the court of, its jealousy kept strangers from South America, 22, 36, 37
Spanheim, 294
Spaniards, the, 30, 32, 38, 39, 221
Speech, when indistinct and confused, &c., 437
Spelman, 263
Spinoza, 337
Spineto, the Marquess of, 16, 25, 92, 214
Spirit, what is? What is substance? 338
———— of God, the, moving on the face of the water, 429
Spiritus, πνευμα, רוח, Ghost, air, breath, 67, 123
ΣP = 600, 169
Spring, Summer, and Winter, years reckoned by these three seasons,

4 D

of four months each, by the ancient Egyptians, 325
ספר spr, a letter, symbol of notation, a scribe, 169
Stadium (10 feet), the little Egyptian, or the Hebrew fathom—by this, the Parthenon, at Athens, and the temples at Ephesus and Jerusalem, were built, 403
————, from sto to stand,—hence stans and standard. It may be Standiom—Stan-di-Om, the Stone of the sacred Om or Hom—the height of a man, 404, 405
Staffa—the island of staves, 272
Stall, a, why so called, 193
Stalls, still = 600, 178
Stamboul and Teheran, the thrones of, &c., 385
Stan or stone (stan = 600?) 182
Stan—towns so called from the crosses of the Agrimensores set up, of the size of one stadium, and dwellings collected round them. Hence Penistan, in England; Bagistan, in Persia, 405
Standards, to be delivered, by the chiefs of the Sacæ, to Alexander, as the Dukes of Marlborough and Wellington do, 272
Stanley, 88, 397, 404
Star, every, had the name of a tree, 193
———— a, seen by Napoleon—the star of Abraham, 358
Stars, the life of Jesus read in the, 57, 145
————, were letters, 192
Staurobates, the cross-borne, Salivahana, Wittoba, the figure of a man on the Standard of Porus, 117, 118
Stephen, Byzant., 230, 247
Stirling—on the Linga at Bhobaneser, 259
שתל stl, satal, a constellation, stella, star, stalla, settlement, 193
————, our word settle from, 437
Stockdale's edition of Sabbatier, 418
Stoics, the, their use of the mythology of the Gentiles, 440
Stola, 78
Stone pillars, in temples, according to the numbers of the cycles, 233
Stonehenge, built by the Cyclops, 135
———————— Sacæ, 273, 416
———— and Abury, cycles displayed in temples of, 246, 256
————, by the Welsh, called Choir Ghaur, 260, 410
————, Abury, and Carnac-Hallam asked not the question by whom they were erected, 285
————, if a college at, there would now be no great circles of stones, 287, 288
———— and Dipaldenna, the builder of, the universal government, 369
————, the squared Trilithons of, shew a more recent work than the rude pillars at Abury, 396
————, the temple of, the production of 5 × 12, &c.; the altar-stone of, must have been for the Eucharistia, there being no appearance of fire, &c., 409
————, by the Monks called Chorea Gigantum, 410
———— seems to mean the hanging or suspended stone, 411

	Page
Stonehenge or Stone henge, was the pontifical capital, the pivot on which all the districts of Britain turned, when England was under the jurisdiction of three Arch-flamens—probably there was a similar one for Scotland, and one for Wales,	412
———— and Abury must have been built by a mighty people, yet Hume, &c., have not thought of them,	416
————————, even after the world had advanced so far as to erect such works, the number of words not necessarily many,	436
Stonehenges and Aburys, the, prove that the religion of Buddha came to the West, &c.,	424
Stones, 15 feet long, 6 feet deep, and 2 feet thick, in the roof of the temple of the sun, at Kanarak,	261
Strabo,	4, 26, 64
————, on the division of the Iberians into four ranks,	420
————, the 1000 cities of,	2, 205, 297, 274, 376
Struia, ancient name of Rome,—country of the cycle of 650,	241
Stuart, Dr.,	263
Stukeley,	48, 99
Su, a book, in Chinese,	227
Suarasuoti, Sara-iswati, Dea Scientiarum,	8
Suchiquecal, the Mexican Eve,	32
————, the queen of Heaven,	33
Sudra and Girdle, the,	65—67, 78
———— and Tunica—Cassock,	78
Suessones, the Belgic,	1
Suetonius,	55, 76, 195
Suidas,	11, 18, 177
————, on the four tribes into which Athens was divided,	319
————, on a Lunar month computed for a year,	325
Suil or Sul, the solar cycle of 366,	177
Sukey, from Ψυχη,	32
Sokub,	9
Sol—336 or name of the Lunar year, &c.,	176—178
Sul or Rqsl—336—שש—600—ד׳ע—600, numeral names of the Solar Deity,	212
——, the sun,	436
Sul-ii—priests of Sol,	233
Sull-Minerva, the, of Bath,	177, 180
Sultan—Sul-tania, place of the Sun—the world's king,	363, 420
Sultan-al-berrein ei Khakan-albabrein, &c.,	385
Sumatra, Jabadios, i. e. holy-lava,	218
———— or Sabadios,	353
————, the king of calls himself Sultan, &c.,	420
Sun, the, every thing, at last, centres in,	36
————, Lord and Saviour, the eucharist of,	60
———— and Jesus, the mixed worship of,	89
————, mysteries of, celebrated on Sunday,	89, 90
————, the birth of, at Winter Solstice,	98—100, 136
————, the, at his passage from Taurus to Aries, at the Vernal Equinox,	122

	Page
Sun, the history of, the history of Jesus Christ,	144
————, first recorded by rightlined, angled symbols,	176
————, probably once Sin=360 or Sini=366,	177, 181
————, Sol, Sul, Saviour,	180
————, stood still to hear the lamentations of Cristna, when Arjoon was killed,	241
————, universal adoration paid to, in his character of Creator, Preserver, and Destroyer—as the emblem of the Trimurti or Trinity,	256, 429
————, in the centre, in the primeval state of our system,	335
Sunday, prayers on, standing, by Persians as well as by Christians,	78
———— celebrated in opposition to the Jewish Sabbath, not as Dies Solis,	89
———— not called Sabbath by Justin,	90
————, the day of instruction by the Druid Sabs,	297
————day of the sun,	304
————, markets anciently held on our,	315
Sun-flower, Pimpernel, Sensitive Plant, &c., the,	430
Συνναοι (the dwellers together), the three Gods, or the Trinity of the Romans, &c.,	344
Sup, sup,	192, 224
Supernumeral, a,	79
Supreme Pontiff, the, (of the Pandæan empire,) similar to the Lama of Tibet, and the Pope of Rome—a Vicar of God,	258
————, the, entitled, as lord of the soil, to the land of the whole world,	278, 284
————, and his court may have saved themselves, &c., from the flood, in a ship,	311
————, could receive little profit from distant possessions, while gold was the only metal, and coin not invented,	380
————, the Patricians, as representatives of, claimed all the soil, and the vectigal, as trustees for the state,	394
————, none of the sovereigns aspiring to be, ever made a peace,	395
Sur used for Tur, and Tur for Sur,	199, 200, 211
Suracena, a, in North India,	235
Suslana or Susa, the lily or lotus,	239
Sweden—instruments with edges of iron and handles of gold, in the cabinet of,	305
Swedenborg, &c., the monomania of,	358
Swines' flesh, the dislike of, in the Highlands, probably came to Scotland from Sin-galia, with the Sanscrit,	293
Switzerland, houses in, of timber and pise,	296
Sword, before the, divided from the crosier,	266, 383
———— and crosier, a compromise between the,	268
————, the, and Book, the right by, of the Egyptian Pontiff, of Julius Cæsar, and of the Calif,	379

	Page
Sword, the man of, to unite the right of the book to that of the sword, made the priest give him the χειροτονια,	417
Syāma, in Sanscrit, means darkness, black flowers, &c.,	438
Syāmānga means the planet mercury or Budhha—probably the Syām and ānga mean the angel Sam or Buddha,	ib.
Sybil, the, Acrostic of,	116
————, all that related to Jesus Christ in,	125
Sybils, the,	45, 57, 74, 108
————, say Ararat was in Phrygia, in Asia Minor,	18, 173, 412
Sussex, His Royal Highness, the Duke of, books of the Masonic Culders of York, possessed by,	436
Sylla,	54
Syllabic or Alphabetic writing,	149
———— system, the, the inventors of, possessed of sovereign power,	205
———— writing arose by degrees,	216
————, &c., probably discovered before the last flood, by the followers of Cristna,	364
Sylvester (Pope),	78
Symbolic language, the, (of numerals,) that of China,	444
Symbolical language, how formed,	161
———— and alphabetical writing—the discovery of, accounts for the civilization and power of a higher class; &c.,	365
———— writing—before syllabic was invented,	373
Synagogue Hebrew, the, universal, when syllabic writing was first used—it was the secret language of all nations,	295
Synagogues and Proseuchas, the, of Palestine,	275
Syncellus, Georgius, on the year of the Egyptians,	316
————, on the antediluvian kings,	324
Syria, 6, 10, 15, 22, 39, 40, 44, 97, 156, 212, 236, 239, 282,	305
————, the resurrection of Adonis celebrated in,	143
————, Eastern,	162, 240
————, the followers of the Rasit, in,	204
————, the right-lined letter figures of,	150, 236
————, the sixteen-letter system in,	185, 235
————, Eastern and Western, and Tamul, the languages of, the same,	240
————, the doctrine of the renewed incarnation, visible in,	340
————, the conquest of, why attempted by Napoleon,	358
————, Western, 16, 24, 39, 40, 45, 119, 134, 162, 181, 183, 231, 232, 235, 240, 249, 250, 277,	310
————, the Jews of, a colony from India,	293
————, the mythos in,	357
Syriac, the old, allegories in, on the tree of knowledge, &c.,	160
————, the vernacular dialect of the Jews, in the time of Christ,	171, 172, 175
————, a close dialect of Arabic and Hebrew,	235
————, the language of Sy-	

INDEX.

	Page
ria, Mesopotamia, Chaldæa, Assyria, and Palestine,	236, 237
Syriac, the literal character, the Nestorian, has a close affinity to the Ouigour—In fact both are Pushto,	421
Syriad (Syria of India, Palestine, or Egypt); *Holy Sura*—Noah said to have erected pillars, with inscriptions, in,	311
Syrians, the,	77
———, write and read like the Calmucks,	150
Syrias, the two Eastern,	119
System, our—in its primeval state, the sun in the centre, and the planets revolved in the same plane, in concentric circles, &c.,	335

	Page
T changed for S, and for ST,	231
— or X =300,	20
Taboo or Bouta,	25
Tacitus,	86
———, cause of *lacunæ* in,	116
———, on change of lands among the Germans,	282, 283
———, on *nakedness* of the Germans,	304
———, says the Germans divided the year into *three*,	421
Tad, Taduys, Tas, Tat, Tetta, Tantah—father,	33, 208
Tages used for *Sages*—Sagesse, Sagax,	231, 232
——— probably a corruption of Sages,	438
Talmud, the Jerusalem,	72
Talut, Saul so called in India,	134, 238
Tam, perhaps a corruption of the Sanscrit *Sama*,	199
——— Sam,	438
Tamas, (St. Thomas,) tomb of the holy,	238
Tamerlane traced his pedigree to Gengis Khan—descended from Turk, the son of Japhet,	354
Tammuz, the women weeping for,	92
———, the weeping for, is the "Agonie" at Rome,	92, 96, 114
——— or Adonis, the rites of,	114
Tamul or Tamil, the,	148, 175
———, the ancient Hebrew-Chaldee-Ethiopian-Syriac,	156, 235, 294
———, acrostic writing in,	185
——— and the Grantha, of Cape Comorin, the same,	295
Tamuls, the, their sacred book had *five* meanings,	15, 148, 221, 253, 440
———, on a lost language,	234
———, their letter, &c.,	238
Tanga-tanga or Tangut, 32, 37, 39,	318, 238
——— Tanga of Tartary and China, from, to Tanga Tanga of Peru, proofs that the religion of Buddha came to the West,	424
Tangiers,	238
Tangitani, the language of the,	ib.
Tangut, the name of God, in Peru,	7
——— and Tangitani, the, of the north of India, the same in name as the people of Tangiers, &c.,	238

	Page
Tanguth, a ram offered in, as a ransom for the child,	33
Tangutia, Tibet so called,—*is tangut*, country of Tangut,	37
Tanjeer or Tanjore,	238
Taou Tsze, the doctrine of, says, "*Taou* or 'Reason' produced *one*; one produced *two*; two produced *three*; three produced all things,"	399
Tapooon, a way of writing, so called by the Greeks,	150
Tarasius, Bp. of Constantinople,	111
Targums, the, probably sacred books of the Callidei of the East,	171
———, not noticed by Jesus or the Evangelists,	172
———, not known to Origen, Jerom, &c.,	171, 172
———, on the term Messiah,	233
———, name of Jehovah in,	259, 286
Tartares ou les Scythes,	97
———, Mandhuis, the, who conquered China,	ib.
Tartars, Tatars, the,	24, 32, 36, 67, 150, 203, 207, 216, 223, 240
———, the, called Nestorians,	229
———, conquered China,	216, 217, 274
———, added their own state as a province to the Chinese empire,	396
Tartary,	40, 73, 103, 213
———, the Sacæ of,	1, 221
———, mythos of, in Mexico,	28
———, a province of China,	217
———, the probable birth-place of the Linga adoration,	260
———, the government of feudal,	362
———, the mythos in,	357
——— or Scythia—every learned inquirer finds his way to, for the origin of the Feudal system, &c.,	372
———, the source of, all Religions placed in, by Lévêque, and the Author drawn to, by every inquiry, or to Caracorum or China,	373
——— (or Chinese Tartary), man supposed to have been created in,	444, 445
———, or North India,	1, 2, 7, 19, 175
Tartarus or Paradise, in Tartary,	73
———, the *very bad* in,	ib.
Tat, a name of Buddha, 2, 23, 24,	164, 207
— is the name of the Tartars or Tatars,	24
— is Ras—head,	188
Tatar nation, the, said to have consisted of 70,000 families—probably a sacred caste, limited to the sacred number 72; these were the tribes of Caracorum,	420
Tatian, the followers of, used *water* in the eucharist,	60
Tatienses à Tatio, &c.,	345
Tau, the, written $+, X, T$,	201, 343, 344
Tauric or Vernal Equinox festival, the, commenced 4680 years before Christ,	84
——— cycle, in the, we have Adam and Eve, his wife, and Cain, Abel, and Seth—a new Trinity, &c.,	397, 399

	Page
Taurico and Dago—Taurus and Dagon,	38
Taurus, the vernal equinox in,	83
———, Leo, Aquarius, and Scorpio or the Eagle, the four signs of Reuben, Judah, Ephraim, and Dan,	105
———, the vernal equinox from, to Aries,	106
———, when the sun entered—a violent revolution probably happened to the globe, &c.,	327
———, Aries, and Pisces, the three signs of, bear a relation to our mythos,	329
———, the entrance of the sun into, at the vernal equinox, 4648 B. C.,—the time of the flood of Ogyges,	332
Taverniér,	263
Taylor, (Rev. Robert,) 44, 45, 64,	114, 119
———'s Diegesis,	43, 55, 57, 114
———'s Syntagma,	113
———'s translation of Jamblicus,	46
——— on the degrees of the Christian hierarchy, as having formerly existed in Egypt,	71, 264, 275, 279
Taylor's translation of J. F. Maternus,	430
Taxes, all, in ancient times, paid by a portion of the produce of the land, and now in China,	272
Tchiven,	
Teepaul, the, or stone,	24
Teheran and Stamboul, the thrones of, occupied by the families of Katschar and Osman,	385
Telescope, the, and loadstone, known to the Chaldæans,	175
Τελεται, sacrifices for the dead, 73,	74
Teleuteans, the, a Tartar nation,	31
Telingana or Trilinga, the country of the,	238
Telmessum or Telmissus,	16, 102
Templars, the, adopted by the Christians, as the conservators of the Jewish temple, rebuilt by the Mohamedans,	298
———, had a sacred head, &c.,	349
———, probably Assassins, because they were Sophees; they were also Manichæans; they acknowledged the Caracorum gentleman or lord, as their Lord Paramount,	382, 383
———, modern, Rossicrucians, and Masons, little more than different lodges of one order,	388
———, their origin, their secret doctrines, &c.,	407
———, are Masons. Some of their secrets the Author would not divulge; but could correct some of their mistakes,	408
Temple, Sir William,	267
———, the, of Jerusalem,	33, 298
———, every, a microcosm of the universe; hence temples were surrounded with pillars,	402, 407
Temples, the *five*, of Egypt, 15, 16,	118, 275, 276
———, all the oldest, of Zoroaster and the Indians, were *caves*,	401
———, all anciently believed to be microcosms of the world,	405
———, whether the old, in China,	

512 INDEX.

Mexico, India, Syria, Greece, Italy, and of Stonehenge and Abury, were all built of one measure, and intended to be a microcosm of the universe, 407
Temples, in the building of, the pillars had different microsmic numbers, viz., 8, 12, 38, 19, 360, &c., &c., 415
Templum or Temple—the word an important one—may throw light on the origin, &c., of the Templars, 407
————, the word, with the ancients, meant more than merely the building on earth—it was always considered a microcosm of the temple of the firmament, 408
Temps, les Fabuleux, des Egyptiens, 11, 12, 17
Tenth or Tithe, the, or Decumanus of the West, is called Ashera, the payment to which Mohamed restored that part of the world under his dominion, 371
————, the, of the produce, the fixed land tax of China, 376
————, a, added to a third, is with us oppressive; but in ancient states the tithe did not operate against agriculture, 393, 394
Tenth Avatar, the, 54, 258
————, Nero claimed to be, 54
————, Gregory the Great, thought to be, 343, 375
————, Alexander and Cæsar, each believed himself to be, 344
————, Mohamed thought, and believed himself, to be, &c., 3, 167, 251, 343, 344, 368, 377
————, Akbar, believed to be, 354
———— announced himself as—putting back Mohamed as the *ninth*, 357
Tenths, the, enabled the later Califs—patrons of arts, science, and literature—to support large armies, &c., 377
————, all the receivers of, at first, priests, 381
Teocalli, the Teo or God *Cali*, 28
Teotecpatl, the divine stone, 24
Teotl, the Mexican supreme and invisible God, 24, 193
———— signifies Sun and Age, 29
Teotle, the same as תלה *tit*=650, 24, 29, 35
Terence, 408
Termini—the same remain in India and Europe, 415
Terminus, the boundary, so called from being the emblem of the Ter-Menu — of the creative power, 414
Ter-omen, the *triple* omen or omen of the *Triune* God, *ib.*
Terpati, Tripoly or Trichinopoly, 206
Tertullian, 45, 61, 66, 68, 72, 74, 78, 87, 89, 96, 98, 143
————, on the Roman and Samothracian three *great* Gods—or the Trinity, 344
Testament, Old and New, double meaning of, 130
Tête is Tat, Ras—head, 188

Teth is 9—Tzaddi is 90—Tzaddi *final* is 900, 186
————, Theta, Tha or Thas (Egyptian) Θθας (Coptic) all stand for 9, *ib.*
Tetragrammaton, the sacred, 190
Tetrarchs, the, in Syria, were Zemindars, 374
Teut, Θεος, Teut-ates, 23
—— or Thoth or Hermes, the inventor of letters, 163, 208
Teutle, Mexican name for Θεος or God, 23
Θ, the emblem of eternity—a point and a circle, 186, 192
Thales, the Milesian, the first of the Greeks who discovered the length of the Tropical year, 318
Thamanim, 17
Thamas, a place, 117
Thames, *father*, 181
Thamus, 95
Thane, the same as Optimas and Baro, 277
Thanes—originally the only tenants *in capite*, 278
Thas, Phtha or Photha, 5
Thbe, Thebes or the Ark, 12, 13
Theatres, sacred, whether built before or after the Deisuls, difficult to imagine, 340
Thebais, the, 66
Thebes, 10, 13, 17, 20
————, the history of, a travesty of the Flood and of Noah's Ark, 12
————, with seven gates, governed by Al-Mage, *the Mage*, Mogul, 352
————, Grecian, 13
————, companies, anciently in, as in London, 418
Θεμις, the Goddess of Oracles, 231
Θεμιςις, Laws, Oracles—connected with Tam, *ib.*
Theocritus, 70
Theodore of Gaza, 104
————, on the year of the Athenians, 319
Theodoret, 5, 80, 94
————, on Christian mysteries, 441
Theodorus, St., 74, 94
Theodosius destroyed Heathen temples, or converted them into churches, 84, 94
Θεοι μεγαλοι, Θεοι δυνατοι, ΘΕΟΙ ΧΡΗΣΤΟΙ, 344, 345
Θεος αγνωςος, the, 197
Therapeutæ, the, or Essenes, their scriptures the groundwork of the Gospel histories, 45, 46
————, or physicians of the soul, 114
————, Mathematici, &c., the same, 248
————, the Essenes and Carmelites, admitted into the Roman church, 270
Therophantes, the, 47
Thessalonica, 43
Theuch, 37
Theut, an American God, *ib.*
Thevenot, 263
Thirlwall's edition of Niebuhr's History of Rome, 375, 407, 410, 419, 429, 432—434
Thogrul—Khan of Caracorum—service, &c., done to, by Gengis Khan, though much superior in power, why, 354

Thomas, St., 117, 122, 207, 259, 290
————, the Christians of, called Nestorians, 208
————, Tamuz, the Christians of, celebrated their worship with *dances*, &c., 262
————, the Christians of, have three sacraments—Orders, Baptism, and the Eucharist, 279, 280
Thomassinus, Ludovicus, 148
Thompson, Dr., 258
Thor, 4
Thoth, 3, 23
———— is Mercury, called Tuisco, 208
————, the first month of the Egyptians—August, 287
Thrace, 102, 346
————, the Ioudi of, 185
———— and North India, the Sindi of, both followers of the holy Xiu, 414
Three, the, marked in temples—the altar-stone and the two stones at the entrance, 409
Θρονυσις or Θρανισμος, 50
Thule, i. e. *the* Iule, 129, 300
Thursday is Tura=666—the day of the Bull, 209
————, the Indian God of, is *Vrihaspati*, 222
Ti or di, *holy*, 7, 192
Tibe—Noah or Menu, 309
Tiberius, 46, 104, 108, 449
Tibet, 1, 9, 31, 34, 36, 40, 54, 57, 75, 82, 206, 218, 231, 300, 305, 444
———— is Ti-bot, Ti-bout, Ti-boutta, or Di-Buddha, 7
———— called Potyid, *ib.*
———— called Tangutia, 37
————, society divided into *two* classes, in, 84
————, secret conclaves of, and of Rome, 117
————, similarity of mythos in, and in Rome, 119, 127
———— and Nepaul, in, there are the Pope, his Monks, and a *crucified* God, 122
————, the carus of, 179, 286
————, the people of, taught the effect of good conduct, but not initiated into the arcana, 252
————, the priests of, *idlers*— the uninitiated *labourers*, 256
————, lords of the creation, and their tenants paying only a tenth of the produce, as rent, are in a comfortable state, 265
————, all lands in, held by the priests in community, 269
————, the king does homage to the priest, in, 302
Tibetian Alphabet. See Georgius.
Tibetians, the, 9, 26, 203, 210, 224
————, doctrines, &c., of, similar to those of the Romish Christians, 37, 75, 367
————, their language a mixture of signs and letters, 213
————, closely connected with the Siamese, 214
Tibullus, 62, 87
Tien, the, the Holy One invisible, 36
—— or Niet, *God* in Chinese, 246
Tigris, the family of Abbas reigned at Bagdad, on the banks of the, 385

INDEX.

	Page
T'impul, the, temple of the Templars,	297
Timur, believed to be a divine incarnation,	343
———, the present representative of—Akbar II.,—bears only the empty title of King of Delhi,	358
Tippoo Sultan,	195
Titans, the, were Tatans,	24, 102
Tithe, the, precedes all — kings' taxes, landlords' rent, &c.,	417
Tithes, the payment of, to Melchizedek,	58
———, paid by the ancient Phœnicians,	78
———, the church never surrenders them,	217
———, how the, descended to the Christian church,—those of conquered lands always claimed,	417
———, paid to the priests at Delphi,	418
———, would be paid, in each country, as at Delphi and Jerusalem,	422
Tithings, ten, the presidents of, formed a superior court,	300
———, conformity between the Chinese and Anglo-Saxon,	301
Titlu—666,	29
Titus Livius,	76, 86
———, the temple destroyed by,	298
———'s Arch, at Rome,	405
Tle, Mexican names ending in,	35
———, these letters mean, in Hebrew, hanged or suspended,	36
Tod's (Col.) History of Rajast'han,	4, 39, 117–119, 158, 178, 182, 183, 185, 245, 268, 272, 284, 298, 305, 418
Toland's Nazarenus,	30, 72
To Or, the,	9, 123, 128, 135, 165, 168, 181, 188, 190, 196, 202, 249, 251, 252, 342, 414
———, " every thing tends to,"	187, 254
———, the T-rua Or,	174
———, whose centre is everywhere, &c.,	294
———, the First principle, Spiritual Fire—the re-absorption of all emanations into,	301, 308
———, persons who believe the, walked in the garden, &c.,	334
———, the planets may be re-absorbed into the,	336
———, supposed to be duplicate—to triplicate himself,	397
———, supposed to possess in himself the two principles of generation,	398
———, the one, is marked, in a peculiar manner, in the cyclar numbers,	409
———, from the, proceeded the Creator, Preserver and Destroyer—Brahma, Vishnu, and Seva; from them 72 Angels, and from them 360 others, &c.,	429, 430
———, in the doctrine of Pantheism, was every thing, and every thing the To Or,	445
To www Or, the knowledge of, and of his attributes, was the religion and the philosophy,	368
To Πav, the,	136
Torquemeda,	30, 33, 39
VOL. II.	

	Page
Total, O, one O, two O's, &c.,	191
Totness—Brutus, from Italy, said to have landed at,	400, 412
Tot-ness is Tat-ness, or ness or town of the promontory of Tat, Taranis or Buddha,	401
Tower of Babel, the,	24, 25
———, the Mexican temple, at Cholula, similar to,	27, 28
Townley,	194
———, Dr., on worship of Bal, Baal or Bel, in Ceylon,	269
TR and SR were convertible,	211, 229
Tr—600,	211
Trade, each, a secret, had its Ras, and each Ras its Pontifex,	279
Tradition, the grand support of the Romish Christian edifice,	107
———, discarded by Luther and the Protestants, in part,	ib.
Tragedies, by the ancients, grounded on mythic history only,	233
Trajan,	120, 121
Transmigration of souls,	82
Transubstantiation, ridiculed by Cicero,	64, 442, 443
———, might be derived from eating bread, the body of the God of generation—Buddha,	244
———, if argued on the ground of common sense, excluding the authority of the fathers, the Protestants beat the Papists, &c.,	443
Tree, the, of the sacred Om,	65
——— Alphabet, the,	148, 149
——— Alphabets, allegories of the,	221, 299
——— of knowledge and letters, close connexion of the, with liber, bark, a book,	163, 164, 265
———, the, i. e. wisdom, produced twelve fruits,	250
——— of Letters, the, with the Chinese,	227
——— of Life, the, what does it mean?	251
Trees and letters, allegory of, often referred to in the Old Testament,	294
———, the, of knowledge and of life, meaning of the allegory of,	252, 253
Tria vota substantialia, the,	48, 127, 280
Trial by Jury, our, from the East, is common to the Chinese and Mexicans,	278, 279
Tribe, the, of Abraham, from India, after various removals, settled in Egypt,	363
Tribes, the 12, were religious districts or divisions,	275
Tribus Mariebus,	103, 181,
———, Tri-ma-di, holy triple Maria or Maia,	203
Trichinopoly, the Mosaic, &c., mythos at,	239
Trichinopoly,	239
Trigranaos, Badwas,	4, 178
Trilings—triple language or triple flags?	238
Trimurti, the,	34, 168, 181, 221, 223, 238, 256
———, or sacred Triad,	103
———, all above, is illusion,	128
———, emblems of, were three Lotuses,	178, 244
———, Orphean,	222

	Page
Trimurti, the, as the knowledge of, faded away, Demigods or Saints arose,	300
———, an emblem of the, with the To Or above it,	415
Trina-cria or Trina-crios, the Triune Aries,	9
Trinitarian system, the, taken from the Brahmin history,	98
———, the, character of the Deity taken from the doctrines of ancient philosophers,	130
——— doctrine, the, of Genesis, likely to lead the Jews into idolatry,	364
———, why not clearly developed in the Gospels—because it was the secret doctrine,	367
Trinity, the,	36, 37, 42, 60, 177, 211, 229, 255, 279, 299
———, from all quarters of the Heathen world,	49
———, Holy,	80
———, of Plato, like that of Jesus,	98
———, incarnation of,	244
———, first and second,	336
———, found among the Romans, in the three altars to the three Gods, called Συνναοι—to Jove, Apollo, and Minerva,	344
———, and Emanations, the Cabalistic doctrines of, intimately connected with the Microcosm; a new Trinity every 1800 years, at first, then every 2160 years,	397
———, Baptism, and the Eucharist, cannot have been the secret doctrines alluded to by Clemens, these having been openly explained by Justin Martyr in his Apology,	440, 443
———, Regeneration, and the Eucharist, the doctrines of, the fathers endeavoured to make into secrets, and to preserve them from the vulgar and the Gentiles,	442
Tripety,	14
——— and Scotland, the crucified God II, of,	259, 288
Triptolemus, the three commandments of,	77
Tritrestra, — Adi-Saka or Aji-Saka,	221
Triumvirate—probably an imitation of the division of the world among the three sons of Noah,	345, 346
Tropical Solar Year, the, 360 days long, before the flood,	316
Troy, (Trole, or Tr-la,)	18, 137, 227, 231
———, new, (Rome), the same mischief to happen to, as to old Troy—the popular belief in, not surprising,	339
———, the Game, in Wales, noticed by Pliny,	401
———, the chiefs at the siege of, were 72—all obeyed Agamemnon—king of kings, &c.,	421
Troya Nova, the, of King Brute,	349
——— or Triuobantum—our municipal governments of towns, may bear date with,	401
Troys, new,	136

4 B

INDEX.

Troys, new, believed to be renewed every 600 years, 303
"Trust, ye saints, your God restored," &c., 114
Trypho and Justin, the Dialogue between, 259
T, S, R, Tzar or Cæsar, 229
Tsu, learned, in Chinese, 227
TT *letter*, Tiut *letters*, 164
Tt=600, or Tat, 226
Ttl=650, Teotl or Teotle, 193, 226
Tubal-Cain—probably the Egyptian Vulcan, 324
Tuesday may be Tuzqo=666, or Markelos=666, 208
Tulad, the male organ, &c., 24
Tulan Cholula, tower of, like the Tower of Belus, 27
Tulis, or Ilas, means *crucified*, 14
Tungusians, the, 39
Tunica, the, 78
Turcomans, the, of the Ottoman empire, divided into 72 tribes, 420
Turdetani, the, 26
Turk, the son of Japhet, 354
Turkish barbarians, the arrival of the, from Tartary, overthrew the favourable state of things introduced, &c., by the Califs, 377
————— cavalry, the, said to be feudatories, &c., 420
Turks, the, occupied Greece, as the Romans did Britain and Egypt, leaving the natives in possession of the religion, 281
—————, have they alone, the Crescent ? 291
—————, claim to be descendants from Japhet, 352
—————, are followers of Japhet, 385
Turner, Mr., 82, 84
—————, on the Palm-tree, 231
—————, Sharon, 135, 160, 229
T'Uscl, the Uscans or Tuscans, were the Osci, 300, 436
Tutelar Gods and Saints, 90
————— saints, the 360 of the Romish church, 429
Tutya, a precious stone so called, in the temple of Persepolis, 261
Twelve, divisions into, prevailed in Attica, in Asiatic Ionia, in Etruria, &c., 275
————— aldermen, and *twenty-four* councilmen of our corporations, were derived from Chaldæan mythic numbers, 276, 417
—————, a council of,—the Lucumones—the heads of tribes—the Amphictyons—the Conclave, &c., 422
—————, periods consisting of the number, supposed to be formed when the year was 360 days long —and those of *ten*, when the new and compound cycle was formed of the 10 neroses and 10 signs of the Zodiac, 432
————— and *ten*—why the names *score* and *dozen*, and no name for the number *eight*, &c., 433
Twins, the, in all the ancient Zodiacs, side to side, &c., 397
Two, every thing divided into— heaven into two hemispheres; the globe into North and South, 409
Types, &c., *of what the real Saviour was to do and suffer*, 122, 132, 193
Typhon, 8, (Suph-on, destroyer,) 230

Typhon, (signifies *a deluge* or *inundation*,) reigned immediately before the flood, &c., 324, 325
Typical numbers—why *continued* in by the Romans, 433
Tyre, חור =608, 183
Tyrians, the probable fabricators of the walls of, 419
Tzar and Tzarina, (Cæsar or Xesar,) 6
————— of Muscovy, the, probably maintains that Ac is the legal successor of Noah, entitled to rule the world, 353
————— why does he tread on the serpent ? why maintain the Pope to be *a schismatic ?* &c., &c., 360
Tzetzes, on the walls of Babylon, 317
—————, on Vulcan — Noah and Osiris, 324
Tzitzit, the *fringe* on the high-priest's dress, 179

Ukim and Yekim the first Chinese written letters, 215
Ulemas, the Grand Seignior has *twelve*, 421
Ullaloo (Mexican Hululaez), Allelujah ? 27
Ulm (the city of), 250
Ulphilas was not the inventor of the Runes, 305
Ulster, in the annals of, the island of Iona called H, 286
Ultima Thule, 14
Ulysses—the name of, found in India, 293
Umbrians, the, of Italy, had 360 polices—probably villages around the Cardos, 410, 419
Ungirt, unblessed, 77
Unigenitus, the Logos or Buddha, 7—9
Unitarians, the, 96
—————, often said not to be Christians, 281
—————, struggling for the vulgar system, ask why the Trinity is not clearly expressed in the Gospels. it was the Cabala of the orthodox Jews and Chrestians, 367
Universe—immensity of the, diminutive character of our globe, and the quarrelsome pismires who infest it, 311
—————, the hypostatic, a microcosm of the immense To On, 336
—————, the, according to the Chinese, is man, on a large scale —and human reason the reason of the universe, 398
Universal History, the, 395
—————, on feudatory princes, 421
————— mythos, the, shows itself strikingly in Java, Sumatra, and Japan, all called Jabadios, 420
Unspoken language of numeral symbols, in the, *sor* might be *ros*, and *ros* might be *sor*, 153, 436
—————, a written, possibility of, proved by its existence in Java, 176
—————, the, of ciphers, universal and fixed, 234

Upham, Ed., Esq., 145
—————'s Buddhism, of Ceylon, 289
Upper Egypt, 10, 12, 44, 45
Ur or Uril, of Cal or the Chaldees, the country of Abraham, 245, 289
Urago-Zoriso, (the Father,) Urusana, (the Son,) and Urupo, (the Spirit,) the American Trinity, 23
Urban V. (Pope), 87
Urban, D' (Marquis De Fortia), 137, 169, 196
Uria or Callida—the natives of, may have discovered the syllabic system; and, unable to prevail against the strong patriarchal government in the East, may have established a new Archierarchy, extending itself to all the western world, 396
Uriel (angel), 88
Urs of the Chaldees, two, in India, 257
Urus or Beeve, the, 23
Usher, 139, 140, 189
—————, his chronology agrees with the Indian Manwantaras, 134
—————, on the time of the flood, 327, 332
—————'s *four* years corrected, 228

Valencia, 62
Valentia, a name of Rome, 241
Valentinians, the 360 Æons of the, 429
Valg, in Sanscrit, *to walk*, 158
Vallancey, 2, 3, 8, 22, 24, 62, 82, 83, 97, 117, 147, 150, 153, 155, 160, 163, 164, 169, 171, 180, 188, 195, 205, 206, 215, 222, 224, 225, 227, 229, 230, 239, 247, 262—264, 267, 274, 279, 287, 302, 373,402, 412, 416
Vallemont, De, on Nestorius, 357
—————, de Mystères, 441—443
Varenius, on the religion of the Chinese and the Tibetians, 367
Varro places the flood of Ogyges, the first flood, 400 years before Inachus, 314, 338
—————, on the length of the year, 319, 320
—————, on a lunar month, computed for a year, 325, 326
—————, on the *Ager Romanus*, 345
Vasudeva, the father of Crisna, 98
Vater, Professor, 27
Vates—fates, bads, balds, *tellers of truth* or *wisdom*, 225
—————, a musician, an officer of the Sulli, 233
Vatican Library, the, 30, 111
—————, the procession from, to the Lateran church, 55
—————, could we get at the secret of, we should, probably find, &c., 57
—————, imprudently opened to the Monks, 270, 278, 285
Vau, the number 6, 138
————— or Va, Venus, the mother, or mother Goddess, 162, 215
—————, the, changed into F, and the F into C, 293
Vayavyam—its supposed Latin original *vivo*, 398
Vectigal or Ashera, the, of newfound lands, reserved to himself by the Pope, 393

INDEX.

	Page
Ved, bed, vates, a prophet,	227
Veda or Beda, means book,	8
———, knowledge,	225
———, Buddha,	226
———, the first, of the Brahmins, is called *Rich*,	ib.
———, was wisdom, the book of life,	250
———, the forged, on the *ten leaves* of the universe, &c.,	371
———, Beda, or Saga, the, compiled when letters became known, &c.,	419
Vedanta philosophy, the,	227, 427
———, the, from Veda, *scripture*, and anta, *the end*—the purpose, &c., of the Veda; the followers of, those of the *male*,	428
———, supposed to mean, the doctrine has *wisdom* for its end, &c., in opposition to Nyaya, *not wisdom*,	42
Vedas, the, or Bedas,	4, 43, 88
———, Indian, not read, but sung or chaunted,	225, 340
———, the Dabistan (Persian books) so called,	226
———, the, books of wisdom, connected with the *tree of letters*,	227
———, the, contain no history 200 years B. C.,	351
Vega, on the cross of the Incas,	32
Veil—*no one shall draw aside my*—does it mean, No one shall explain my cabalistic doctrine of divine wisdom?	387
Veils of Socrates, Jesus, and Isis,—the object of this work to draw aside, and to restore their doctrines,	253
Veneris Amasius,	95
Venice—remonstrance of Baronius to the city of,	52
——— and Bologna, a war between, for a picture of the Saviour,	228
Venus,	5, 6, 84, 212
———, Calva, Capitolina, Verticordia, &c.,	91
———, Van or Va, mother, or mother Goddess,	162, 215
——— and Cupid, both called *Epws, divine love*,	170
——— or the Saviour,	180
———, identical with Ceres, Hecate—she was *black*, the mother of the Gods,	285
——— was the *Nous* of Plato's trinity—the Holy Ghost,	286
Verbum Caro factum est not peculiar to Christians,	98
Verdier, Du,	79
Vernal Equinox, the,	83
Veron,	47
Verses, 20,000, committed to memory, and repeated by the pupils of the Druids,	340, 436
Versus, the Etruscan or Umbrian, of *ten* ten-feet rods, &c.,	407
Vespasian—the miracles of,	335
———, said to have conquered twenty towns—probably part of the *municipia* which sent deputies to the Wittagemote,	416
Vesta,	62, 91, 241
Viales, the,	90
Vicar-manni—probably corrupted into Vicrama, Vicramaditya—priests,	266
Vicarius Jesu Christi,	52

	Page
Vicars of God, on earth, united in Jesus of Rethlehem,	57
Vicramaditya,	9, 302
——— ———, Mohamed a, or a Saca or Saceswara,	2
———, the first Supreme Pontiff, supposed to be a, of the Trimurti,	258
———, the Vicar of God, was owner of the soil of the whole world,	372
———, or Vicar of God, the, alone heard of now, in Rome and Tibet,	374
Vidya, a Widow—a knowing person,	226
Vierge, l'immaculée conception, de la,	97
Vine, the, embracing the marital Elm or Alma,	242
———————————, was it M-Om crucified?	253
———, the *fruit of*, Jesus would not drink of,	254
Vineyard or garden of God, Carmel, the,	44, 45, 193, 204, 240
Virachocha, and Pachacamack, the Peruvian Creator,	34
Virgil, 9, 45, 47, 62, 64, 79, 83, 114, 138, 140, 166, 189, 195, 202, 207, 345, 408	
———, calls Octavius *God*,	55
———, the doubt in the time of, respecting the *eighth* and *ninth* Avatar,	357
———, the history of the life of, a copy of that of Homer,	401
———, the revolving cycle of 600, celebrated by,	433
Virgin, the, without spot,	33
———, Maria (or Maia),	45
———, and child, the worship of the,	49
———, Mother of God,	76
———, Mary, the blessed,	82
——— and child, the adoration of the, common to Gaul and Egypt,	109, 191, 279
———, Mary, the monogram for, is M,	170
———, intercession to, by the miraculous stone of Chartres,	260
———, figures of, accompanied by the Lotus,	239, 244
——— of the Conception, or Paritura, the,	163, 199
——— and Rose, the, in Mexico,	32, 239
Virginia,	28
Virgo, the zodiacal sign of,	5, 6
——— Paritura, the, 14, 108, 109, 136, 181, 203, 259, 260, 279	
———, the son of, in Wales,	154
——— Maria, Purificata,	82
Vis Visha, the temple of, at Benares,	402
Vishnu, with three eyes, the supposed image of the Trimurti,	136
Vitrified forts, the, of Scotland—remarks on their nature and design,	296, 297
Vives, Ludovicus,	53
Volney,	31, 187
———, how treated by Mr. Faber,	255
Vossius,	242
Votive offerings,	85—87, 91
——— tablets,	90
Vowel points, the, of Hebrew, modern,	184

	Page
Vowels, deficiency of, in Hebrew and Celtic,	185
Vows, the three—chastity, poverty, and obedience,	48, 127, 280
Vrihaspati—father of wisdom—the God of Thursday, in India,	222
———, the founder of the Chárváka school,	429
Vulcan—probably Tubal-Cain,	324
——— in Manetho, said to have reigned 9000 years, i. e. 9000 revolutions of the moon, or 75 years of 12 months each, or, 75 Sari,	325
Vyasa, (the Indian Spinoza,)	337
———, the meaning of, not known to the Hindoos,	351

	Page
Wait, Dr., on Chaldee roots in the Sanscrit,	1, 156
Wales,	4
———, Hebrew names in,	130
———, given by Brutus to his son Camber, hence called *Cambria*,	400
———, the Game Troy, found in, decisive of the mythos; by 35th of Henry III., empowered to send 24 members to Parliament,	401
Walsh, Dr.,	45
Walter (Editor of Niebuhr), 27, 371, 381, 391—395, 407, 419, 422	
War between the Calif of Bagdad, the Imaum of Alamout, and the Emperor of the Moguls or Mongols, because a preference was given to the standard of the Calif, &c.,	390
Warren (Col.), the Kala Sankalita of,	192
Wars, the first GREAT, (Mahabarats,) probably between the High-priests or Pontiffs, about the presidency over the whole world; in these wars the feudatories would have little or no concern,	391
Wasigh, Ben, on complications of forms of letters,	158
Wassih, Ben,	205, 221, 246
Water Rose, the, or Lotus,	32, 33, 420
Water, fire, and air—the origin of things—the baptism of—the first Trinity,	336
Webb, on Chinese the primitive language,	229
Webster,	153, 158, 192
———, on the common origin of the Phœnician, Celtic, and Teutonic languages,	403
Wednesday—*Woden's*-day,	208
Welsh, the,	2
———, or English, called Celts, Gales,	296
——— language, the, indebted to the Hebrew,	154, 163
———, the old, allegories in, on the tree of knowledge, &c.,	160
——— Triads, the,	290
———, the, according to Young's doctrine, is Hebrew, and both Sanscrit and Latin,	293
Wesley and Whitfield learned men; but what were their followers?	342, 377
———, the monogamia of,	358
———, Wilberforce, &c., &c., if

516 INDEX.

the Author acknowledge them most excellent persons, and many of their doctrines very good—he does not adopt all their fooleries, 440
West, the, the emblem of the Evil One, 89
Western Judea, 36, 39, 40
——— Syria. See Syria Western.
Wheat, alone, has the power of renewing its pollen, 253
Wheel, a, of wrought iron, will fly in pieces, before it reaches a velocity of 400 feet per second, 312
———, the, or Mercavah of Ezekiel, 335, 342, 343, 401
———, a, within a wheel, 407
Whiston, Mr., 97, 169, 173, 314
———, on the true text of the Old Testament, 126
———, on the year of 360 days, 316—326
———, on the comet of 1680; its seven revolutions, from its last appearance to the deluge, 325, 338
———, on the Samaritan chronology, as to the year of the flood, 327, 329, 332
———, and the Author, calculate on more certain data than those of their opponents, 330
———'s Theory—opinions of Drs. Gregory, Halley, and Keill, in favour of, 331
———, Mr., supposed the eight persons in the ark increased to 2000 in 100 years, 395
———, on the length of the old Egyptian and Jewish cubit, 405
———, on the first race in Tartary, and on Noah residing in China, 435
White race, no example of a, going back to the black, by intermarriage, 363
Whiter, the Rev. Mr., on the race of the Cymri, 290
Whitfield and Wesley, were learned men; but what were their followers? 342, 377
Widow, a, from Vidya, a knowing person, 226
Widows, the custom of burning, in Thrace, 197, 202
———, the origin of, 429
Wilberforce, 131, 440
Wilford, Col., 122, 175
———, on the belief of the Hindus, that all living beings originate from an atom-like germ, &c., 398
William IV. may be abused hereafter for accepting the title majesty, 213
——— the Conqueror—his grants of land to his generals, 267, 284, 392
——— Jamaica, for William of Jamaica, 287
WILLIAM, KING, and the Archbishop of Canterbury—in which of our men-of-war would they soon be found, if a flood were to happen to Europe? 311
William I., in the reign of, England said to have been divided into thirty-seven shires, 401
Williams', Miss, edition of Humboldt, 26—28, 32, 33

Wilson, Dr., on the flight of Joseph and Mary, 45
———, on the Pasupata writings, the Vaisheshika philosophy, &c., 429
Wisdom, an emanation, from the Supreme to the Trimurti or Trinity, 128
——— and letters, the idea of, never separated, 169
——— is W or Y=400, S=200, &c., holy Om—wisdom of the holy OM, 211, 299
———, the perfection of knowledge, 250
———, the doctrine of, existed thousands of years before Mohamed, 274
———, can the work of, go to decay? 335
———, the second person of the Trinity, the Logos, the Saviour, 337
———, the incarnation of, the secret doctrine of all nations, 343
——— and the Gnosis, the secret doctrines of, were those of all nations, 441
———, the book of, who was the author of? 123
———, why received by the Romish Church—refused by the Protestants, 124
———, probably contained, originally, the whole mythos of the crucified Avatars, &c., 125, 126, 128, 232, 441, 442
Wodehouse, the Rev. C. N., 67
Woden, 4
———, a corruption of Buddha, 208, 209
Wit, to know, the Saxon Sigma-tau in, 226
Witan or Wites, i. e. wise men, 301
Witherahins (in German widderstno) against the sun—sin for Sun, 291
Wittagemote, the, 283, 298, 299
———, our Celtic ancestors invoked the Ghost (or Holy Ghost) to preside over, 299, 337
Wittesa-gemote, the assembly of wise men, 225, 277
———, the feudatory princes of China formed a, but officiated solely in religious matters, 421
Wittoba or Bal-II, the crucified, 206, 299
———, ba or ab, father of wisdom, 299
Witt-os-mote, meeting of wise men of letters? 226, 299
Wolfang, St., with book of Saturn, 81
Woman, a, the sacrifice of, called cunoman, 168
Wood, Gandell, 17, 19, 363
Wooden horse, a, buried in the earth, &c., 348
Woodward's, Dr., discourse on the ancient Egyptians, 309
Word; our, is in Arabic werts, in Chaldean werd, 240
Words, if a judicious selection of 1000, were made, and attached to numbers, two persons might communicate without difficulty (with a key), though speaking different languages, 436
World—the empire of the, obtained by a knowledge of the recurring Neros, by Chaldæans, under the names of Brahmins, Magi, &c., 330

World, the division of, into three, ruled by three potentates under one, as supreme head, 335
———, divided among the three sons of Noah, and the division probably imitated by the Triumvirate, 345, 346
———, peopled to a great extent, before man would require commerce, 365
———, the author of a general history of the, must begin with the origin of the Buddhist religion, and the Pontifical Pandæan Kingdom—marking well the few facts from mere probabilities, 369
———, a general expectation of the end of the, prevailed in Asia, as in Europe, in the 12th and 13th centuries, 382
———, the, divided among the descendants of Noah, into three, and into seventy-two parts or races, 399, 400
———, the, as then known, after the death of Christ, divided into three Patriarchates, &c., ib.
———, the division of, into seventy-two, each division having its Flamens, Lucumones, and Sanhedrim, its Sacred Mount and its Delsuls, 422
Worlds, the renewal of, nothing improbable or contrary to the Divine Goodness in, 338
Writing, the art of, how discovered, &c., 148, 149
———, magical, 175, 205, 245, 256
———, the infant art of, 192
———, a masonic secret, 218
———, Reading, &c., the arts of, long secret, sacred, and astrological, 234, 246, 247, 274, 339
———, sacred, originally in metre, 244
———, originally from the top, downwards, 246
——— and Reading, a knowledge of the art of, probably succeeded circumcision as a test, 309, 310
———, the ignorance of mankind before the discovery of the art of, and while it was kept a profound secret, not surprising, 339, 424
———, if the art of, had been known, and in use, there would have been records respecting the fabricators of the walls of Tyrins, &c., 419, 420
———, before the invention of, Dancing was of great importance, to keep in recollection the sacred mythoses, &c., 424
———, great change which must have been effected by the art of—then Dancing, &c., with their utility, lost their innocence and simplicity, 425
———, the art of, the ruin of the retentive faculty, 427
Written syllabic languages, all, the same, with dialectic variations, 175, 176
Wytfleet, 30

INDEX.

X or Xaca, KL, cal or wisdom of X, 2
— in Etruscan, Oscan or Latin, stands for 10 or for 600, 6, 113
—, a monogram, prefixed for mystery, 6, 198
— or T=300, 20
— is I, in the Dalmatian or Illyrian alphabet, 190
—, a monogram of God, confounded with the I, 192
—, the tenth *hissing* letter, 196
—, the sign of the united *male* and *female* principle, 198
—, the sign in baptism—the mark for 600, Samach, 302
— means 300 as well as 400, 343
Xaca, 6, 8, 28
— called Cio, 31, 32
—, crucifixion and resurrection of, 16
—, Woden, Buddha, 208, 209
—, miraculous conception, &c., of, 227—230
—, or Xekia, taught his doctrine for 49 years, 228
— or Buddha, the fig-tree sacred to, 253
—, Saca, Saga, Sagax, Wisdom, the lands of, held in soccage of the priests, &c., 264
—, Wisdom, 336
Xaca-elo-la, Siculia or Sicily, 9
——Ischaka, signifies Lord, 229
——melech, Royal Shepherds or Royal Saxons, 25
Xacæ, Saxæ, Sacæ, Xin or Xin-di, the, 215
X-cesar or Cæsar, 6, 24
XACHA, 5
Xαγανος,—Saga or Xaca, khan, 229
Xaҕas, Xacas or priests of Wisdom, 34
X-al-hua, the Self-existent X, 27
X-ama, or Cama-deva, both Cupid and Venus, 6, 170
———, ama, maternal love, 228
Xamorin or Zamorin or Semiramis, 6
Xangti, a God of the Chinese—like IEUE and OM, never to be pronounced, 192
XEAN-TIA, may be di-Sion—God of Sion—of the Siamese, 229
Xaξι—Xξaι—Xχai=666, 210
Xειροτονια, 68—71, 180, 222, 231, 252, 263, 280, 302, 349, 359, 383, 417
Xelhua—the architect or giant, 27
Xenophon—grant of land by, to Diana—a *tenth* of the produce to be paid to her, 265
———on the revenue of Athens, 319
Xeques or Zaques, Peruvian priests, 34
XH =608, or the Greek IH of Delphi, 190, 210
Xι or Ιχ, the *trilinear* letter Η, probably so called, 199
Xiang-siouph, a god of Tibet—*the wisdom of Iao*, 192
Xin, Xim, Sinensea, Sacæ, Saxons, 215
—— (X=600, N=50) Sin or Mani, 224, 250
——, Xaca, Se, Cio, Sio, Sais—salvation, 230
——, the holy—the Sindi of North India and of Thrace, the followers of, 414
Xisuthrus, the history of, in Berosus and Abydenus, like that of Noah, &c., &c., 321, 322
Xiuh-tecutli, the Mexican God of *fire*, of years, the Everlasting One, 31
Xιυν=666, Buddha, or Ras of Sion or the Sun, 210, 250
XL or Chol=650, 28
Xn—Christ victorious? 210
Xochicalco, (*house of flowers*,) the temple of, faced the four Cardinal points, 28
Xochimileks or Xaca-melechs, *Royal Saxons*, 25
Xρης, 62, 119, 138, 197, 199, 202, 226, 314
———, Chri, 32
———, Egyptian kings, whose names ended in *cheres*, were renewed incarnations of the, 13, 14, 20
——— or Ceres (of Eleusis and Delphi), 117, 254, 262
———, country of, Crysen (or Chrysen), 122
——— of India, Christ was the, 123
———, the, and Xρυς, the *gold* and the *fire* connected, 178
———————, in the golden age of, no wars, 306
———, means χρησος, καλος, and ευατες, 251
———, a believer in, as come, not a heretic, 252
———, the, of Delphi and Chaldæa, seen in *Chryses* and *Calchas*, 350
———, the religion of, evidently existed from the earliest time, 368
———, the, of Delphi—Cæres (Cære?) probably a formation from, 395
Xρης—the doctrine of, was the secret one of the ancients, of the Gnosis—in vain attempted by Clemens, Origen, &c., to be restored, 443
Xρησιαν mythos, the, 16, 22
—————————, was the secret mystery of Eleusis, Delphi, and of all nations, 126
——— Judæan mythos, the, not treated of by ancient authors, because they were bound to keep secret their mysteries, of which the Xρηςηριον was the chief part, 441
Xρης-iani Divi, the, became Christiani Divi—saints, 300
Xρης-ianity—no longer surprised at finding, at Rome, at Delphi, and in Malabar, 443
Xρησιανοι, the, 46
Xρης-ians, the, having three sacraments, 290
Xρηςηριον (or X-ρστ=600), 20, 441
———, the staff of Osiris, 204
———, the Cabalistic or secret doctrine of all ages, 345
Xρης-ism, from the commencement of the modern system of, at Antioch, to the Council of Nice, old MSS. and books have been destroyed, to secrete evidence, &c., 357
Xρησολογια, the, existed before the Christian æra, 202
Xρηστος, converted by priests into Xριςος, 117, 174
Xρησ-τος was the Logos, 122
——— from χρησος, and changed to χρηστος, 200

Xρησ-τος, the, on the tomb of the Youth of Larissa, 200, 202
ΗΡΣ=360, Cross, 201
———, divine wisdom or Cross-wisdom, 243
☩
XPΣ, the name of Christ thus written, 201
——— on the Pope's breast, 202, 343
——— or TPΣ, the sacrifice offered, in ancient and modern Italy, to this God, consisting of bread, is called Mola—Hebraicè Al-om, 303
——— or XP=600, the benignant being—the triune cyclar God or Genius, 344
Xu, a tree, in Chinese, 227
X-umio, the mother of the Mexican Word, 23
XXVIII the first form of *recording* the first idea, viz. that of the Moon or her period, 149, 150, 227, 229

Y, in Chinese, is *one*, 229
—, the Celtic præpositive article, THE, 302
Yaca-tecutli, the Mexican God of Merchants, 31
Yadu, Iod-di or Yodi—holy Io, the tribe of, 218
Yagui sacrifice, the, or the sacrifice of the Agni, 109, 157, 159
Yajni, or Yagni, the sacrifice of the Lamb, 45, 157, 159
——— sacrifice, the, celebrated the passover or the passage of the vernal equinox, from Taurus to Aries, 106
Yao and Hom, the Mexican Triune God, or the Creator, 23
—, the Mexican great God, called INEFFABLE, 34
— volo, *I will do*, 192
—, the first king or emperor of China, drained and rendered it habitable, about 2333 B. C.— Here we have the flood and the God Iao of the Jews, 314
——teotle, the Mexican God of Armies, 24
Yavana—a sect in India, devoted to the *female* principle, 174
Yavanas or Ioudi, i. e. Sacæ and Scythæ, Saxons—the Lowlanders of Scotland, 273
'Τδρανος, *the waterer*, 66
'Τδωρ and Isis, 7
Year, the great or precessional, 3600 years, 141
———, the, originally only 360 days long, 141, 316—326
———, reckoned by the ancient Egyptians, sometimes by the lunar month, at others by the three seasons—Spring, Summer, and Winter, 325
———, divided into *three* by the Germans, 421
———, the first, of all nations, believed to have had only 360 days, 431
ΤΗΣ, the, =608, Bacchus, 23, 54

INDEX

	Page
Yew, the, Iod or I in the Tree alphabet,	149, 160, 371
Yoye, the יהוה irie, chaunted by the Brahmins,	427—429
Y-HA-HO, the most Sacred Name among the Egyptians,	17
Ying krih le, England so called by the Chinese,	149
Younne, the title of Alexander's æra—a formation of the Sauscrit Jnana, the Ioannes, &c., the fish of Assyria, *wisdom*,	347
Youi the same as *Iune*, the *door*, and as Juno—the Ja-na, the Diana, Di-ja-ua or Dwa-ja-na,	174
——, Iune, Iona, and Selene, alike mean the *female generative principle*,	289
Yoodishtra,	119
York Minster, ending in the highly finished, from a Gilgal or *stone circle*,	135
——, the Micklegate of,	408
—— and Ripon, the Culdees at,	279, 281, 287, 288
Young, Dr., his doctrine of probabilities,	154, 155, 168, 175, 293, 362, 363
——, on the derivation of languages,	234
Youdia or Oude,	206
Yxnextli (also Suchiquecal), the Mexican Eve,	32
Vzona, the Father—Bacab, the Son— Echvah, the Holy Ghost, so called by the Mexicans,	32

	Page
Zab, Zub, or Zuph, *wisdom*, probably the same originally,	353
Zaba and Jaba—the name of Java,	219
Zabii, the, believed images and trees inspired the prophets,	194
Zacal or Ashera—Zacal is, probably, only li-saca, THE *Saca*—the the payment of Saca became *the Saca*,	379
Zamorin or Xamorin or Semiramis,	6
——, Comorin, or Camarina,	224
Zaphnath-paaneah—Joseph,	177
Zaques or Xeques, Peruvian priests,	34
Zarina, the queen of the Scythians so called,	229
Zemindars, the, first collected tithes for the priests, &c.,	266, 362
——, were preceded by the Bhoomias,	284
——, in India and Ireland—became what our country gentlemen are, &c.,	373
——, under Lord Cornwallis's government, were recognized as dependent *princes*, and absolute proprietors of the soil,	371
Zendavesta, the,	78, 97, 236

	Page
Zeno,	47, 337
Zephir or the Holy Ghost,	182
Zeradusht, Zerdusht,	77, 97, 292, 236
Zian, in Pegu—the mount of Maria —Meru,	45
——, a mystical mount—means place of repose,	288
Zin ls Xin,	210, 211
——, the name of Gengis Khan— changed from Teningin,	353
Zoba—Saba—wisdom,	236
Zoradust, Abraham, the reformer of the religion of the Magi,	58
Zodiac, signs of the, on the chair of St. Peter,	57
——, Mosaic pavement of the, in a church at Lyons,	ib.
——, the signs of, probably the produce of a high latitude, where the *camel* and *elephant* were not in much use,	329
Zodiacs, the, of Esne and Dendera,	193, 236
Zone and Cassock, origin of the,	77
Zoroaster,	58, 64, 65, 77, 131, 261
——, prophecy of, respecting the son of an immaculate Virgin,	96, 97
——, taught the resurrection,	101
—— and the Indians, all the oldest temples of, were caves, in imitation of the vault, circle, or wheel of heaven,	401
Zorodusht or Zoroaster,	96

(519)

PASSAGES OF SCRIPTURE

REFERRED TO OR QUOTED.

BOOK	CHAP.	VER.	PAGE
GENESIS	xxii.	2,	8
	v.	29,	18
	xiv.	18, 19,	58
	ii.	9,	134
	i.	14,	164
	i.	8,	177
	xli.	45,	ib.
	xliii.	6,	178
	x.	15, 19,	184
	iii.	18,	307
	xlix.	17,	349
	i.	27,	397
	x.	21,	399, 409
Exodus	iv.	25,	38
	xxxv.	30,	124
	xxix.	28,	194
	iii.	14,	197
Leviticus	xxi.	5,	79
	xviii.	21,	82
	xx.	2—4,	ib.
	xxvii.	28, 29,	194
	x.	14,	ib.
Numbers	vi.	13—21,	44
	xi.	5,	137
	xv.	38, 39,	179
	xxii.	5,	181
	xxxi.	14,	194
	xx.	17, 19,	306
	xxxvi.	[?]	376
Deuteronomy	xxii.	12,	179
	xxiii.	4,	181
	xxix.	29,	308
	xxxii.	8,	409, 410
Joshua	v.	3,	38
Judges	xix.		19
	xx.		ib.
	xviii.	28,	184
	i.	7,	421
2 Samuel	xii.	24, 25,	180
	vi.	12—16,	426
1 Kings	xviii.	28,	74
	xviii.	26,	87
2 Kings	xxiii.	10,	82
	ii.	13,	231
	xxiii.	6, &c.,	371
1 Chronicles	i.	13,	184
2 Chronicles	xxxvi.	22, 23,	233
Ezra	iv.	3,	ib.
	v.	13—17,	ib.
Job	xxviii.	18,	128
Psalm	xxxiii.		58
	lxxxiv.	12,	95
	lxxx.	8—16,	204
	xviii.	7,	408
Proverbs	iii.	13, 18,	204
Song of Solomon	iv.	12—14,	245
	v.	1,	ib.
Isaiah	xix.	18,	15
	xliv.	28,	233
	xlv.	1—4,	ib.
	xxxiv.	4,	235

BOOK	CHAP.	VER.	PAGE
Jeremiah	xx.	1,	3
	xix.	5,	82
	xxxii.	35,	ib.
	xlix.	7,	128
	xxv.	26,	221
Ezekiel	xliv.	20,	79
	viii.	14,	92
	i.	15—21,	342, 401
	x.	9—16,	ib.
Daniel	vi.	10,	89
	ix.	2,	169
Ecclesiasticus	li.	2, 3, 5—7,	124, 232
Wisdom	ii.	13—20,	ib. ib.
MATTHEW	xiii.	55, 56,	49
	iii.	11,	67
	vi.	7,	87
	i.	17,	133
	xxvii.	57, 62,	143
	xvi.	18,	182
	xiii.	11,	308
Mark	vi.	3,	49
	i.	8,	67
	vi.	13,	72
	xvi.	18,	ib.
	xvi.	7,	136
	xv.	42,	143
	iv.	11,	308
Luke	iii.	16,	67
	xii.	35,	77
	ii.	7,	109
	xxiii.	53, 54,	143
	viii.	10,	308
John	i.	25,	64
	iii.	23,	66
	i.	14, 18,	72
	iii.	16, 18,	ib.
	xix.	42,	143
	xii.	13,	231
	i.	1,	251
Acts	xix.	1—7,	66
	ii.	23, 24, 32,	122
	iii.	13—18,	ib.
	x.	34, 35,	145
Romans	xvi.	16,	90
	iii.	8,	94
1 Corinthians	v.	7,	60
	x.	14,	94
Colossians	i.	18,	129
Philippians	ii.	10,	90
Hebrews	vii.	1, 10, 11, 15,	58
James	v.	14, 15,	72, 73, 75
1 John	iv.	9,	72
	v.	21,	94
Revelations	ii.	8,	15
	xi.	8,	ib.
	i.	5,	72
	xiii.	8,	110
	xi.	8,	118
	xiii.	17, 18,	169

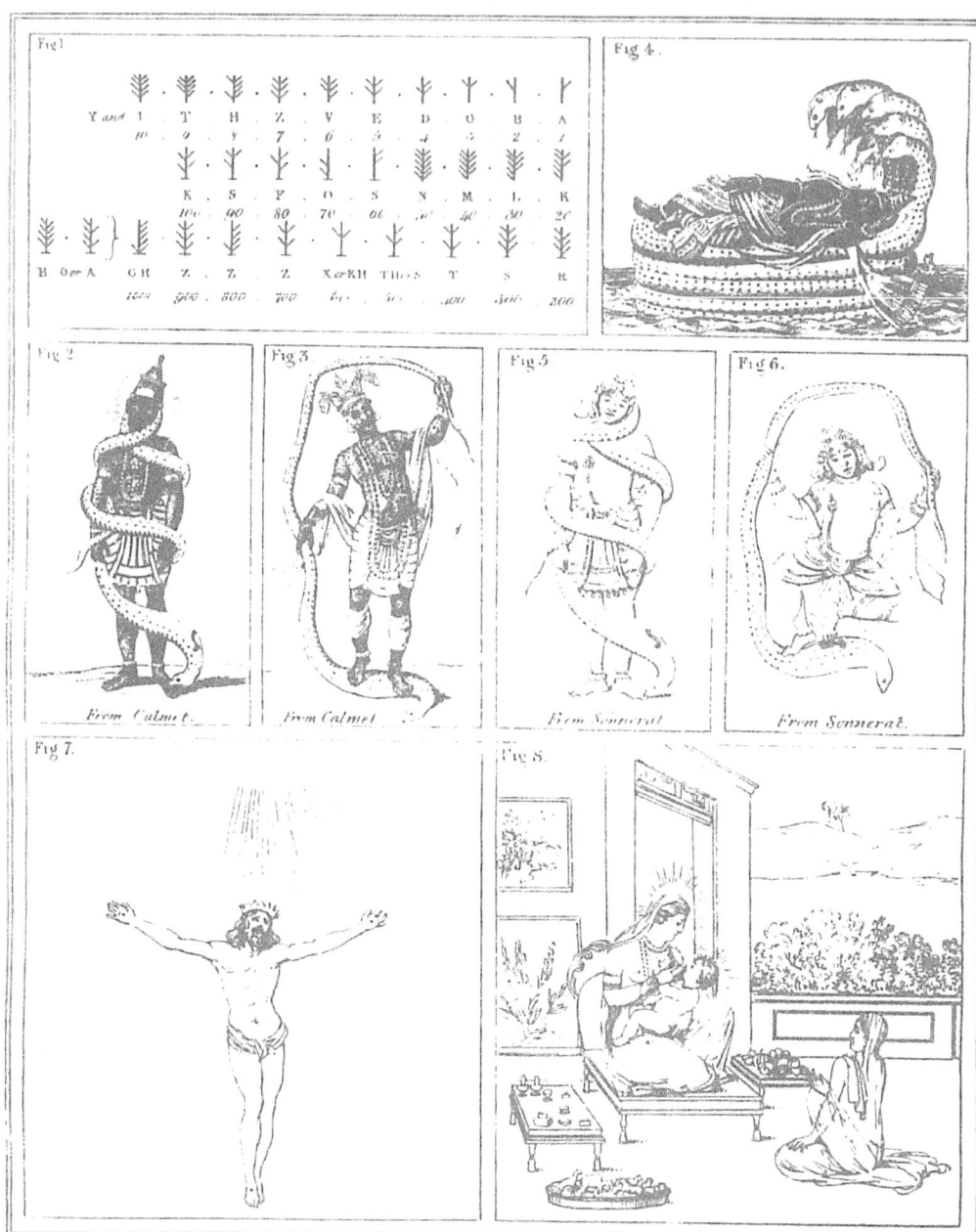

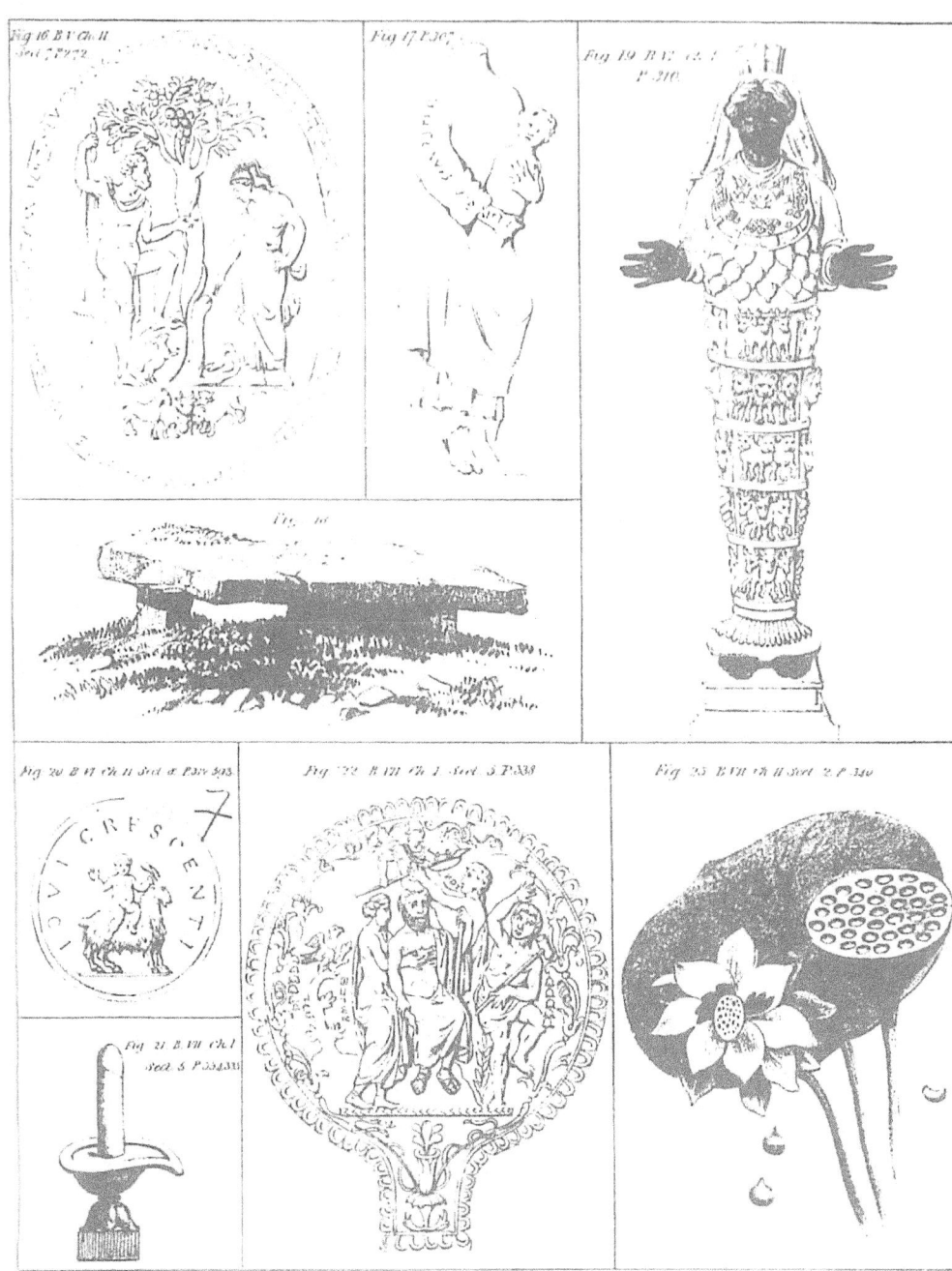

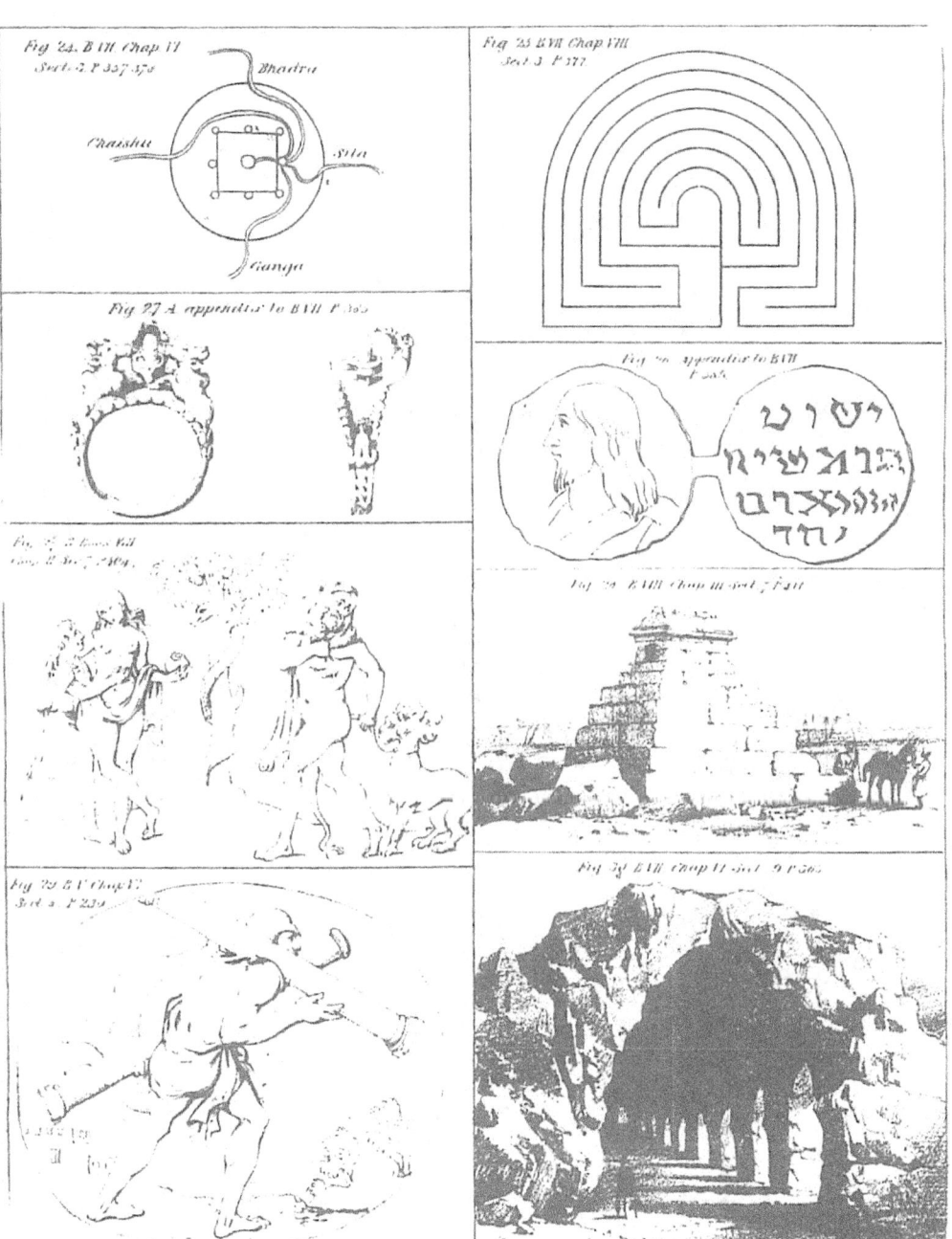

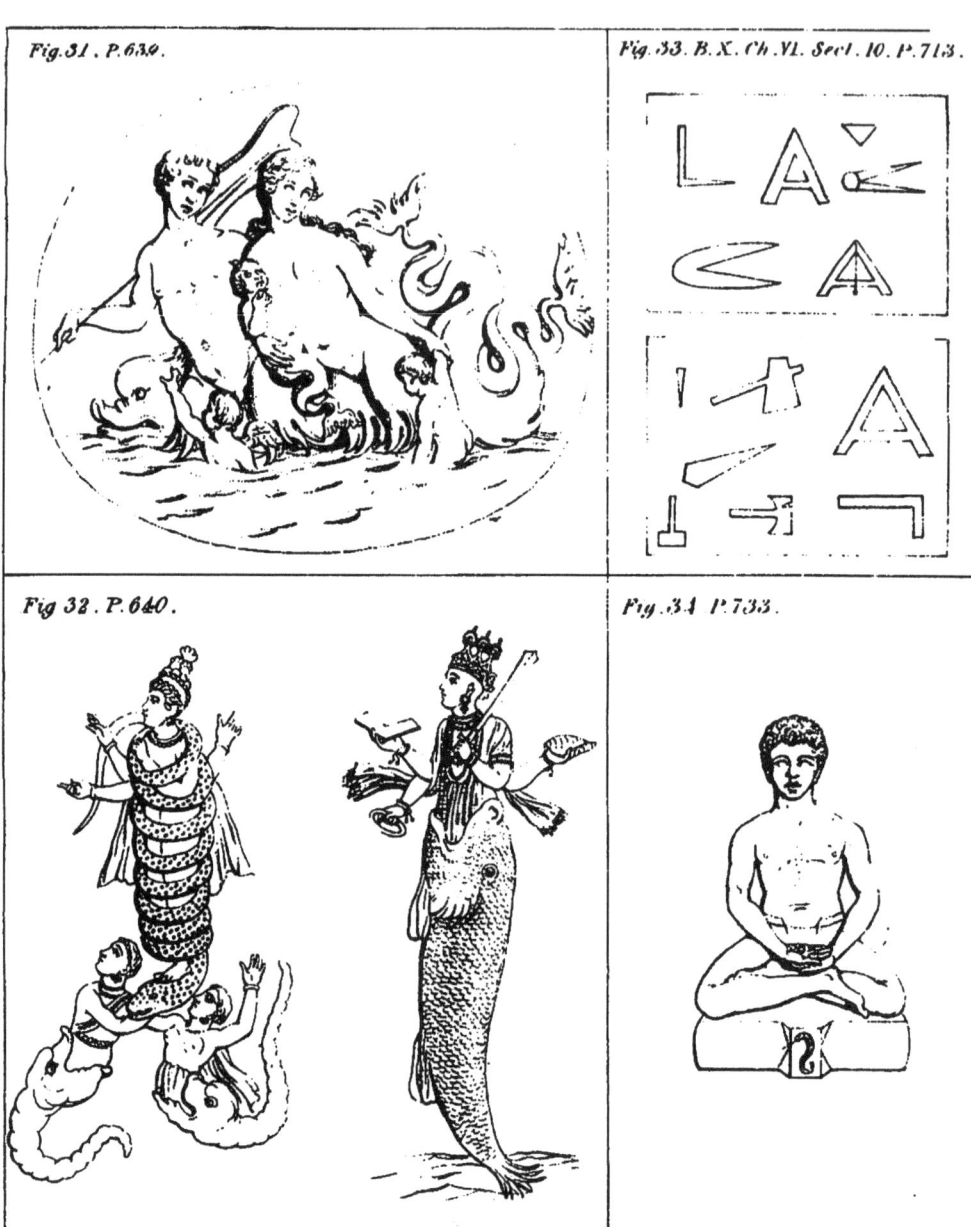

www.ingramcontent.com/pod-product-compliance
Lightning Source LLC
Chambersburg PA
CBHW060311230426
43663CB00009B/1668